THE OVERSTREET®
INDIAN ARROWHEADS
IDENTIFICATION AND PRICE GUIDE

6TH EDITION

BY ROBERT M. OVERSTREET

SPECIAL CONTRIBUTORS TO THIS EDITION:
Chief Jerry L. Faircloth, John Grenawalt, and Duncan Caldwell

SPECIAL ADVISORS TO THIS EDITION:
Tommy Beutell • John Byrd • Nick Cavallini • Jerry Chubbuck
Gary Davis • Tom Davis • Gary Fogelman • Dr. Richard Michael Gramly
Ron L. Harris • Bill Jackson • Glen Kizzia • Mike McCoy
Bob McWilliams • Donald Meador • Charles D. Meyer • Bob Miller
Lyle Nickel • Shawn Novack • Rodney Peck • Michael Redwine
Floyd Ritter • Dwain Rogers • Dick Savidge • Jerry Scott
Charles Shewey • Mike Speer • Ben E. Stermer • Art Tatum
Jim Tatum, PhD • Jeb Taylor • Greg Truesdell • Warner Williams

ABOUT THE FRONT COVER: Folsom points were used in the western United States between 10,000 and 11,000 years ago and represent one of the rarest fluted forms. Folsom man used these points in hunting the extinct bison. The Folsoms on the cover were found in west Texas, New Mexico, Montana and North Dakota. A special thanks is due Dr. Michael Gramly for allowing us to use his photograph of bison antiquus taken at the LaBrae Tar Pits in California. The Folsom point was named from examples found with extinct bison near Folsom, New Mexico in 1926.

Important Notice: All of the information, including valuations, in this book has been compiled from the most reliable sources, and every effort has been made to eliminate errors and questionable data. Nevertheless, the possibility of error always exists in a work of such immense scope. The publisher and the author will not be held responsible for losses which may occur in the purchase, sale, or other transaction of items because of information contained herein. Readers who feel they have discovered errors are invited to *write* and inform us so that the errors may be corrected in subsequent editions. All advertising is accepted in good faith. If any item advertised is not as represented, and enough unsolved complaints are received, Gemstone will discontinue advertising space with that vendor. Gemstone also reserves the right to reject any advertisement without explanation.

THE CONFIDENT COLLECTOR: THE OVERSTREET INDIAN ARROWHEADS IDENTIFICATION AND PRICE GUIDE (6th Edition) is an original publication of Avon Books, Inc. This edition has never before appeared in book form.

AVON BOOKS, INC.
1350 Avenue of the Americas
New York, New York 10019

Published by arrangement with Gemstone Publishing, Inc.
Library of Congress Catalog Card Number: 96-95437
ISBN: 0-380-80781-5

First Avon Books Trade Printing: July 1999
AVON TRADEMARK REG. U.S. PAT. OFF. AND IN OTHER COUNTRIES, MARCA REGISTRADA, HECHO EN U.S.A.
Printed in the U.S.A.
10 9 8 7 6 5 4 3 2 1

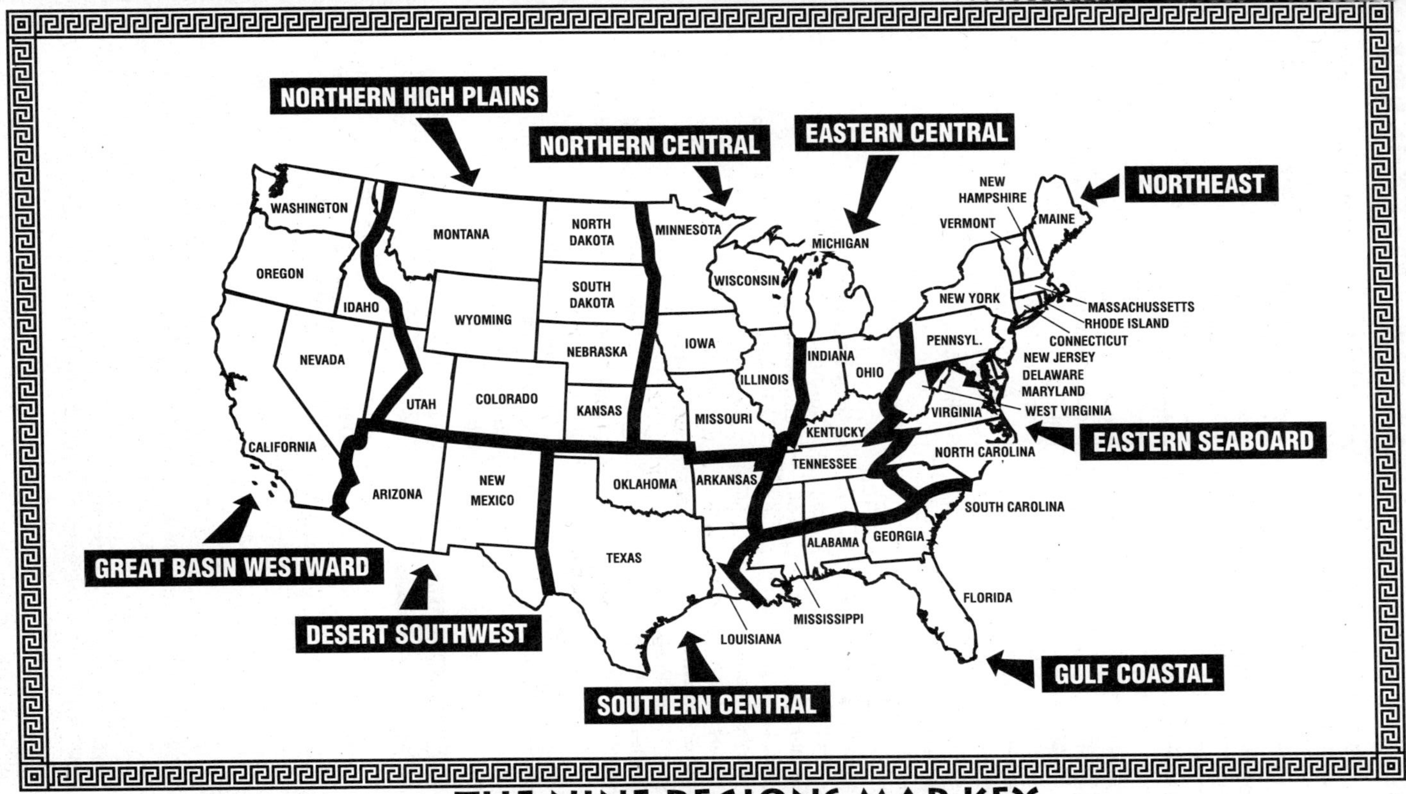

THE NINE REGIONS MAP KEY

This book is divided into nine regions and is set up starting with the Northeast and ending with the Great Basin Westward (east to west, right to left on this map). This is your key to the contents of this book, and versions of the map highlighting each individual section appear at the beginning of each regional section.

TABLE OF CONTENTS

ADVERTISERS

In Bowling Green, KY (Formerly the Owensboro Show)

UNIVERSITY PLAZA HOTEL CONFERENCE CENTER

1021 Wilkinson Trace, Bowling Green, KY 42103

The Indian Artifacts Show is now conveniently located one hour from Nashville, TN and less than two hours from Louisville, KY and Evansville, IN. The Convention Center is connected to the hotel and boasts 19,580 sq. ft. of showroom space in one large room. With over 300 booths, there's plenty to see, buy, sell, or trade!

DATES

August 6th—8th, 1999
August 4th—6th, 2000
August 3rd—5th, 2001
August 2nd—4th, 2002
August 1st—3rd, 2003

*Annually on the first Saturday and Sunday in August with a **Sneak Preview** on Friday afternoon*

ADMISSION IS CHARGED

on Friday, Saturday & Sunday

LODGING

University Plaza Hotel
1-800-801-1777 Ext. 1032
for room reservations.
Much lower rates for show attendance

TABLES

To reserve booth space or for information, contact:

KATHY GERBER
812-547-4881
P.O. Box 7, Tell City, IN 47586
Fax—812-547-2525
E-mail—agerber@psci.net

GERBER SHOWS, INC.
P.O. Box 7, Tell City, IN 47586 (812-547-4881)
E-mail—agerber@psci.net

ACKNOWLEDGMENTS

A very special thanks is due John Grenawalt and Duncan Caldwell for their excellent articles and for their contribution of photographs used in this edition. My gratitude is also due the following people that so generously provided important data and or photographs used in this reference work: Tom Addis, Chuck Andrew, Robert Beasley, Jerry Beaver, Jim Bergstrom, Pete Bostrum, Ken Bovat (photographer, N.Y.), Phillip H. Cain, Nick Cavallini, Jerry Chubbuck, Tony Clinton, Jim & Janice Cunningham, Kevin L. Dowdy, Ted Filli, Tom Fouts, Daniel Fox, Steven Fox, Jeff Galgoci, Dr. Michael Gramly, Frank & Kathy Hindes, Bill Jackson, Mark L. Jewell, Glen Kizzia, Mike Long, Skip Mabe, Edward Mason, J. McCullough, Charles E. Meyer, Ron Miller, Lyle Nickel, Leslie S. Pfeiffer, Alan L. Phelps, Michael Redwine, Jay Roach, George Roberts, Dwain Rogers, David Ross, Bob Roth, Arlene & Lori Rye, Larry Allan Stanley, Art Tatum, Jim Tatum, Jeb Taylor, Brian K. Tilley, Kirk Trivalpiece, Steve Wallman, Lyons D. Woody and John W. Young.

I am also in debt to Dr. Michael Gramly for his valuable advice and loan of some rare photographs. This book also contains photos from the collections of Ray Acra, Dick Agin, Ralph Allen, Tommy Beutell, John Byrd, Roland Callicutt, Charles Shewey, Leo Paul Davis, Tom Evans, Gary Fogelman, William German, Kenneth Hamilton, Scott Hanning, Jim Hill, Glenn Leesman, Charles D. Meyer, Sherri A. Monfee, Buzzy Parker, Floyd Ritter, Richard Savidge, Mike Speer, Scott Tickner, P.K. Veazey, R.S. Walker, Blake Warren and Warner Williams. We want to sincerely thank these people for making their collections available to us.

We also thank Tom Davis, Don Meador and Jeb Taylor for providing hundreds of excellent photographs for this edition; to Art Tatum for his many hours of expert help, photographs and points sent in for photographing.

Very special credit is due my wife Caroline, who not only advises cover and layout designs, but is of trememdous help to me at the artifact shows handing out brochures and talking with collectors and dealers. Thanks also to the staff of Gemstone Publishing--J. C. Vaughn (Executive Editor), Arnold T. Blumberg (Editor), Brenda Busick (Creative Director), and Mark Huesman (Pricing Coordinator)--for their invaluable assistance in the production of this edition.

Our gratitude is given to all of our special advisors for their dedicated advice and input as well as help in typing, grading, and pricing; and to those who wish their names not to be listed and especially to the following people who either provided photographs, points for photographing or additional data:

Tim Addis
Larry Allan
David Amos
Murphy Anderson
Jerry Beaver
Ken Bovat
Leroy Bryson
Terry Burdette
Jim Catoe
Owen Collins
Brad Cooley
Suzan Crowe
Jim Cunningham
Janice Cunningham
Billy Dobbs
Gay Dobbs
Kevin Dowdy
David Edgeland
Forest Fenn
Franklin Fosdick
Blake Garrard
Gene Garrard
Pat Garrard
Dr. Jay Goldberg
Cindy Golden
Thomas A. Grace
Les Grubbe
Newell Harrison
James Hemming
Frank Hindes
Kathy Hindes
Mark L. Jewell
Patrick Keefe
Ray Kilgore
Steve Langly
Ron Larson
Tim Lindenbaum
Grace Lively
Mike Long
Jimmy Mabe
Edward Mason
Sandy McConnell
W. David Myres
Sam Murphy
Frank Nifong
Harlan Olson
Ernest Orem
Buzzy Parker
Joe Payne
Erwin Peake
Howard Peake
Tony Putty
John Retherford
Jamie Richardson
Phillip Richardson
Pat Robinson
Arlene Rye
Lori Rye
Jerry Scott
Hank Senn
George W. Shanks, Jr.
David Shaw
Paul Shilkofski
Andy Sizemore
Allen B. Smith
Larry A. Stanley
Tom Stanton
Dale Strader
Kirk Trivalpiece
Charlotte Thweatt
Marvin Thweatt
Brian K. Tilley
Mark Wagoner
R.S. Walker
Becky Wilkes
Jeff Wilkes
Jimmy Wilkes
Brian Wood
Brian Wrage
John W. Young
Lousie Young

STONE AGE RAW MATERIALS

John Grenawalt*

Today, those who collect, study, and appreciate the stone tools of early man will assign three characteristics to an artifact: its type, its provenance (locality where found), and its material. The type designation, which is covered in detail in this book, is important because it will relate the artifact to a period in prehistoric time (such as Paleo, Archaic, or Woodland), and will usually relate the artifact to a geographic area. Much has been said and written lately about the importance of accurate provenance and documentation of the origins of artifacts. An accurate description of the material can tell much about the relic, as there are a number of unique stone, or lithic types that have known sources. Knowledge of these sources can reveal details about the travels and trade networks of early peoples.

Prehistoric people were quick to learn the sources of the best lithic materials. In cases where the stone occurred in localized areas, there is evidence of large-scale quarrying over long periods of time. Some of these quarry sites are now preserved as "open air museums," such as Flint Ridge State Memorial near Newark, Ohio and Alibates Flint Quarries National Monument, north of Amarillo, Texas. Even today, these sites yield hammerstones and large mauls which were used to quarry the stone. Since the people had often traveled long distances to the quarry site, they could not return to their home regions with large pieces of stone of varying quality. The quarry sites are littered with flakes and pieces of material discarded as the ancient flintknappers reduced the masses of stone to "quarry blades," which were composed of the best quality material in a readily portable form. These blades were usually oval or teardrop in shape and were designed to be a preform from which a variety of tools could subsequently be knapped.

There is often confusion about lithic types and the terminology that applies to them. There is a tendency to call all lithic materials "flint," and, unfortunately, there is not a standard nomenclature for the many lithic types. This article will attempt to describe the most important lithic types and will then list and illustrate some of the prominent types from each of the geographical areas in this book within which the point types are described.

Although many varieties of stone have been used for tools and weapons, early peoples sought out certain types. The stone types that were most desired were those which broke with a conchoidal fracture, that is, a shell-shaped break that could be controlled and would fracture in a predictable, repeatable fashion. This would render a sharp edge, sometimes in combination with flutes or notches to attach the projectile point or knife to a shaft or handle. Modern-day flintknappers have revived the lost art of manufacturing stone tools. The techniques used were percussion flaking (knocking off flakes with a hammerstone or piece of antler), followed by detailed pressure flaking (pressing off small flakes with a pointed tool). Knowledge of flintknapping techniques creates new appreciation for the talents of the ancient artisans. While the stone tools were obviously created for utilitarian ends, some combined material and technique in such a way that they could be considered works of art.

I have chosen to describe the lithic, or stone types which were most often used for chipped artifacts (points, knives, scrapers, drills, and related tools) as members of three primary groups. My way of describing the lithic types is arbitrary. It is only one way of describing these stone types, whose origins are often complex. For those readers who wish to expand on this subject, a list of references is appended.

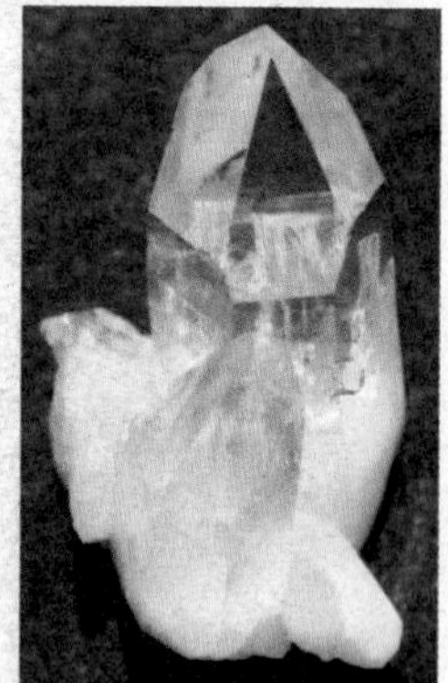

Figure (1) Phenocrystalline quartz, single quartz crystal. Source: Arkansas.

1. Crypto-crystalline quartz is the largest and most varied of the three groups. The common mineral quartz, or silica (SiO_2) is found in nature as pheno-crystalline quartz, with distinct crystal characteristics (Figure 1) and as crypto-crystalline quartz, where the individual crystals are so small as to be microscopic. Many references term this second type of quartz **chalcedony**, and list varieties that differ in texture, color, and degree of transparency. In almost all cases, the stone is precipitated from silica-bearing water solutions. Figure 2 shows the two types of quartz in a single specimen. A piece of Alibates flint, with its characteristic red and white bands, has been found to contain a cavity which is lined with sparkling crystals of phenocrystalline quartz.

Flint in the mineralogical sense is found as nodules, often in limestone. The flint from the White Cliffs of Dover in the UK is well known. The nodules of Georgetown flint from Texas are of similar form. **Chert** is similar by most definitions to flint. Some authorities describe chert as a more granular stone, but others ascribe to it the same qualities as flint, and I choose to use the two terms interchangeably. It is found as nodules and as bedded deposits in limestone or other sedimentary rock. These deposits may cover large areas, as the Edwards Plateau chert of Texas, Flint Ridge and Coshocton cherts of Ohio, and the very widespread Burlington chert of the midwestern US.

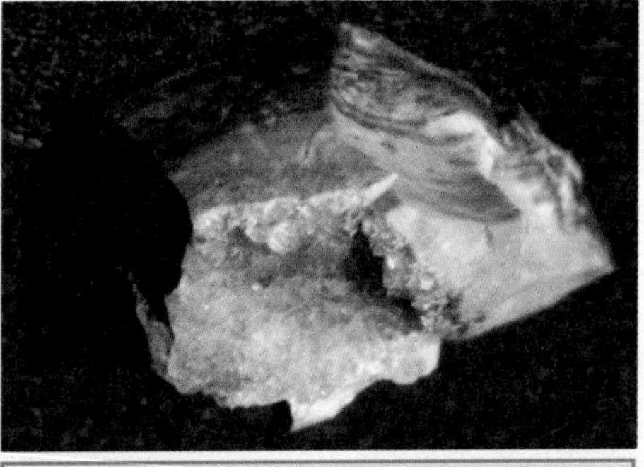

Figure (2) Specimen of Alibates flint (cryptocrystalline quartz) with cluster of crystals (phenocrystalline quartz). Source: Texas Panhandle.

Jasper is a term applied to massive, fine-grained cryptocrystalline quartz which is colored by oxides of iron and other minerals. It is opaque, and is usually found in shades of red, brown, or tan. Nodules of jasper were utilized for stone tools in Colorado, Wyoming, and other western states. Several named varieties of jasper are found in Pennsylvania and adjacent states.

Pseudomorphous chalcedony is an important lithic type for artifacts. A pseudomorph is a replacement, and the silica solutions often replace organic materials. "Petrified", or "agatized", "silicified"....and other names for siliceous wood is found across much of the western and southern US. The silica replaces the wood, and preserves to varying degrees the cell structure, rings, and bark of the original plant. As with other varieties of chalcedony, only dense, fracture-free pieces of petrified wood were suitable for stone tools. Some of the best varieties of petrified wood are colorful and translucent. Others, such as the petrified palm wood of Louisiana and adjacent states, show detailed cell structure of the original wood. A distinctive and very attractive lithic is the silicified coral from Florida. This replacement of ancient coral by silica retains the structure of the coral polyps, and the stone is often translucent and very colorful. Chalcedony can also be a pseudomorph of other rocks and minerals. An important and distinctive lithic of such origin is the Alibates "flint" found in the Texas Panhandle. This material is a silica replacement of the mineral dolomite, a calcium-magnesium carbonate mineral closely related to limestone.

Other types of chalcedony used for artifacts include **carnelian**, a translucent red-to-orange material, and **agate**, which can be found with circular banding or with plant-like manganese dendrites, as the "moss agate" of Montana and Wyoming.

Most forms of crypto-crystalline quartz, or chalcedony, can be found in a variety of forms, or qualities as related to flintknapping. The most desirable forms will display a waxy luster and will be free of internal fractures or inclusions of foreign materials. Some of the varieties could be improved by heat treatment, which altered the structure of the microscopic quartz crystals and rendered the material easier to chip.

2. Igneous Rock is the second group of lithic materials used for stone tools. Igneous rock is formed by the crystallization of lava or magma, which can have a great variety of compositions and conditions of formation. Many of the mountain-forming igneous rocks, such as granite, do not lend themselves to chipped stone tools, as their texture is too granular. They were used widely, however, for tools such as celts and grooved axes, where the stone was pecked to shape, and then rubbed to a polish.

The igneous rocks most used for chipped stone tools were those which cooled rapidly from the melt, so that the crystals were very small. In the case of the most popular lithic from this group, **obsidian**, the cooling was so rapid that crystals did not form at all. Obsidian can be described as a natural glass. It sometimes occurs in massive deposits; Glass Buttes, in eastern Oregon, is a virtual mountain of obsidian. High quality obsidian was sought out by early man, and in some areas, such as the Great Basin of the northwest US, the stone was used almost to the exclusion of all other lithic types. Obsidian is usually a glassy black stone, and it ranges from opaque to nearly transparent. Varieties which are brown or brown banded in black are called "mahogany" obsidian. Some varieties exhibit iridescent sheen and banding. The origins of some obsidians are obvious from their color or other visual features. The origins of obsidians can sometimes be determined by chemical analysis for trace elements. Obsidian was prized and widely traded by early peoples; the spectacular obsidian knives found in some Hopewell mounds in Ohio were found to be made from stone obtained in Wyoming.

Basalt is one of the most common rocks on the earth's surface. It is a fine-grained, dark (usually black) igneous rock rich in silicon and iron. When found with very fine-grained texture and free from internal flaws, it was knapped into artifacts. Artifacts of basalt are found in New Mexico, Arizona, California, and other western states.

Rhyolite is similar in composition to granite, being rich in silicon and aluminum. Being low in iron, rhyolite is found in light colors: white, gray, tan or pink. In its fine-grained varieties, rhyolite could display a conchoidal fracture. It is found in stone tools from the Carolina Piedmont, Virginia, and other states of the eastern and northeastern US. It was often the lithic of choice because those areas did not have the higher quality stone types found elsewhere in the US. **Felsite** is another fine-grained igneous rock that found use for stone tools in the Northeast.

3. Metamorphic rock types comprise the third group of lithics to be described. Metamorphic rocks are those which are transformed by heat and pressure from other rock types, usually the sedimentary rocks which were deposited by water.

Quartzite is a popular lithic which originated as sandstone, a sedimentary rock made up primarily of quartz particles. When sandstone containing sand of 95% quartz, or greater, is metamorphosed, the particles are sintered or fused together. The resultant stone, quartzite, usually displays a sparkly appearance on a freshly-broken surface. A common term is "sugar quartz." Quartzite is widespread across the US, and can be found in large bedded deposits and as alluvial cobbles. The Tallahatta quartzite of Mississippi and nearby states has the appearance of white snowflakes in a translucent matrix. The well known and often spectacular Hixton quartzite of Wisconsin is not a true metamorphic quartzite, but is a sedimentary rock in which grains of sandstone are bonded together by silica. The Hixton lithic appears to be a quartzite, and is usually described as such. In reality, it is a "silicified sandstone," just one of the exceptions to the rules which can make lithic descriptions confusing and difficult.

Novaculite is a metamorphosed chert found primarily in Arkansas. It has a fine, grainy texture, and occurs in a wide range of colors. Its workability is often enhanced by heat treating. In recent times, novaculite has been commercially mined and used for whetstones.

Silicified slate is a distinctive lithic, often green in color, found most often in the states of the Carolina Piedmont and the northeastern US. As mentioned previously, these areas did not offer the variety or quality of lithics that were found in other parts of the country. In some cases, the silicified slate was hard and tough, but did not exhibit a good conchoidal fracture. In such cases, the artifact was ground to shape and sharpened with a fine abrasive stone. This produced very serviceable artifacts, similar to those from other flint-poor areas, such as the High Arctic.

Figure (3) Patina illustrated by obverse and reverse (patinated white) views of blade of Knife river flint. Source: North Dakota.

Patination: A feature of lithic types that is of interest to collectors and professionals is **patina**. Patina is a change of color on the surface of an artifact that occurs over time. In virtually all cases, the patinated surface is lighter in color than the parent stone. In the chalcedony family of lithics, patina can often take the form of an alteration, where water molecules are taken into the silica structure. The patina on obsidian is termed "hydration" and can be used to date some obsidian artifacts where baseline data for the particular obsidian type is available. The tendency for lithics to patinate varies greatly with the different types. Some, such as Knife River flint and Edwards Plateau chert, patinate more readily than others. Soil chemistry and climatic conditions have strong effects on a stone's tendency to patinate. Many artifacts with patina sometimes display the patina on only one face, (Figure 3), which is usually assumed to be the face which lay upward for the centuries and millennia that the artifact lay exposed to the elements. Since patina is usually evidence of age, patinated artifacts are desirable among collectors. The makers and marketers of fraudulent artifacts have used chemical techniques and various coatings to simulate patina. True patina is in, not on, the stone surface. As a collector gains experience in observing the types of true patina, he or she can generally detect these fraudulent attempts to simulate this desirable feature.

MAJOR LITHIC TYPES BY REGIONS

The following section will attempt to describe some of the major lithic types used by prehistoric Americans. The stone types will be described for the nine geographical regions of this book. By no means is it a complete listing--it is an attempt to show exam-

Figure (4) Obsidian, three points exhibiting range of translucency from nearly transparent to opaque (bottom), blade of dual-colored "mahogany" obsidian (top). Source: Western and Southwestern states, especially prominent in the Great Basin.

ples of some of the prominent types. Assigning a lithic to a geographical area done by <u>source</u>, and artifacts made from many lithics would be found in adjacent regions to their source, and even farther away. There were wide trade networks and movements of people. Knife River flint, originating in North Dakota, is represented in artifact collections as far away as Colorado and New York. Some of the Hopewell mounds in Ohio contained artifacts of Knife River flint and of obsidian whose origin was Wyoming.

1. Great Basin Westward

This is one of the areas of the country noted for high quality and colorful lithics. **<u>Obsidian</u>** is widespread and occurs in a variety of forms and colors. Figure 4 shows obsidian artifacts with degrees of translucence ranging from opaque to near transparent, along with the brown and black "mahogany" obsidian.

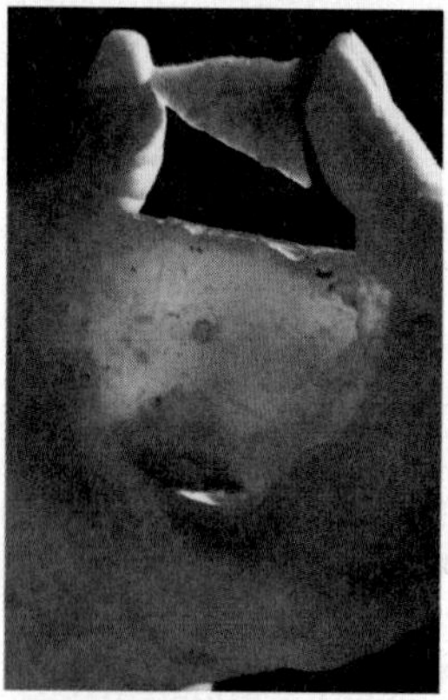

The Great Basin and Pacific Northwest are famous for their "gem points," which are often exquisitely crafted of colorful materials. One of these materials is **<u>carnelian</u>**, a translucent red-to-orange lithic shown in Figure 5 as a point and a piece of rough material.

Figure (5) Carnelian, point and rough sample showing color and translucency. Source: Columbia River, Washington and Oregon.

Figure (6) Pacific Coast jasper, artifacts and rough sample of green phase. Source: Pacific beaches of Washington, Oregon, and California.

A stone often present in frames of NW gem points is **<u>Coastal jasper</u>**, so named because it is found on or near the Pacific beaches of the region. It is found as brick red, brown, and other colors. Figure 6. shows it as a green phase.

Figure (7) Basalt, artifacts (one patinated white) and rough sample. Source: Throughout western states, useable for artifacts when fine grained.

2. Desert Southwest

The desert southwest lithics include obsidian, basalt, and a variety of cryptocrystalline quartz varieties. **<u>Basalt</u>**, when fine grained and crack-free (Figure 7) was often used for stone tools.

<u>Luna agate</u> (Figure 8) is a translucent lithic. Artifacts of the pink-to-red

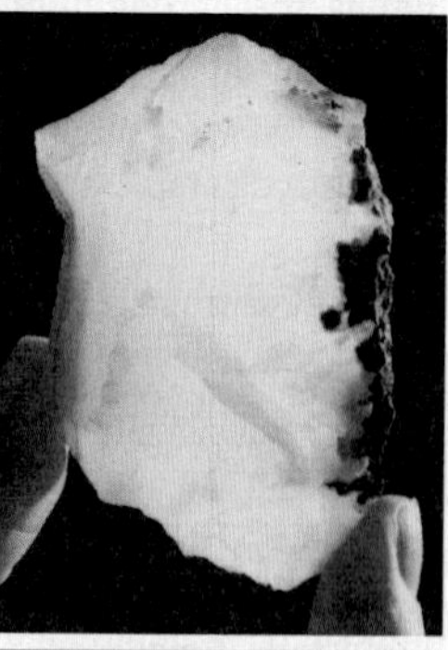

Figure (8) Luna agate, rough sample showing translucence. Source: New Mexico.

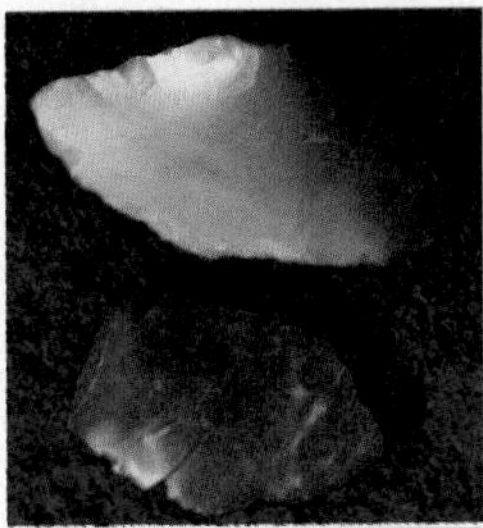

Figure (9) Washington Pass agate, rough samples. Source: New Mexico.

Figure (10) Knife River flint, Pelican Lake point and preform. Source: North Dakota.

Figure (11) Quartzite, Meserve point and uniface knife. Source: Throughout western states, also found in other regions of country.

Washington Pass agate (Figure 9) are attractive.

Figure (12) Brown petrified wood, Paleo points. Source: Much of western US.

3. Northern High Plains

Lithics found on the Northern High Plains are of a variety of types, most of high quality. **Knife River flint**, shown in Figure 10, is a translucent material of root beer color. The primary quarry sites are in Dunn and Mercer Counties in western North Dakota. Knife River flint patinates readily (see Figure 3), and it was prized and traded widely.

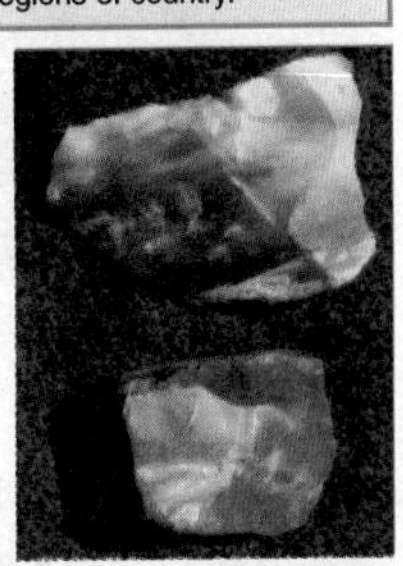

Figure (13} Petrified wood, rough pieces of colorful material. Source: Much of western US.

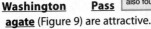

Quartzite (Figure 11) was widely used for artifacts on the Northern High Plains. The stone was found in many areas as alluvial cobbles.

Petrified wood, when found in solid, well-silicified pieces, made very serviceable and often very colorful artifacts. Figure 12 shows two Paleo artifacts of the common brown petrified wood, while Figure 13 illustrates two colorful pieces of rough stone.

Collections from the Northern High Plains often include artifacts of **jasper**, which is usually found as alluvial cobbles. A colorful artifact of jasper is shown in Figure 14.

Figure (16) Burlington chert, white Harahey knife of typical material, knife of heat treated material showing vitreous luster. Source: Illinois, Iowa, and Missouri.

Figure (14) Jasper, Plainview point of red variety. Source: Found across most of US, common in western states.

4. Northern Central

By far the most popular and widespread lithic in the Northern Central area is **Burlington chert.** This material, also known as Crescent chert, occurs primarily in Illinois, Missouri, and Iowa, but is found as artifacts across the entire Midwest. Colors tend to be light in shade, with white, cream, tan, and light pink predominating. Figure 15 shows

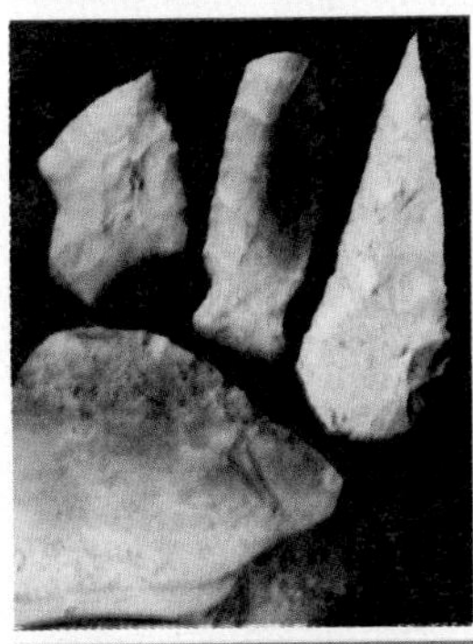

Figure (15) Burlington chert, artifacts and rough sample. Source: Illinois, Iowa and Missouri

a piece of Burlington rough and artifacts of several colors. Burlington chert responded to heat treatment, with the heat transforming dull white or cream varieties to pink, orange, or red, with a waxy, vitreous luster. Figure 16 shows two Burlington chert artifacts, one of which was heat treated.

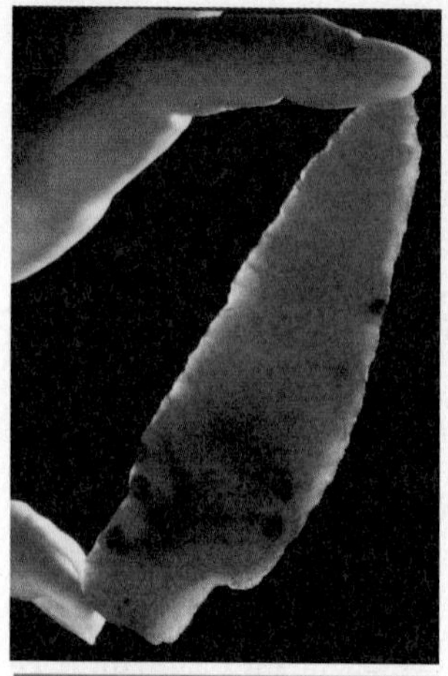

Figure (17) Hixton silicified sandstone, knife showing color and translucence. Source: Wisconsin.

Hixton silicified sandstone, as described earlier, is often called Hixton quartzite, but it was formed from sand grains cemented by chalcedony, not by the metamorphic processes that transform sandstone into true quartzite. This distinctive lithic outcrops on one hill in Jackson County, Wisconsin. It is usually white or pale in color, but can occur as honey or caramel-colored varieties with beautiful translucence (see Figure 17).

Figure (18) Cobden/Dongola chert, rough spherical nodule and rough piece showing banding. Source: Illinois.

Cobden/Dongola is a distinctive chert that occurs as round alluvial nodules in central and southern Illinois. The stone has a banded, often "bullseye" appearance (Figure 18). Another lithic found as nodules in southern Illinois is **Kaolin chert**. Kaolin occurs in a variety of colors, most frequently white, tan, yellow, and orange. The material responds favorably to heat treatment, turning waxy in texture, as shown by the preform in Figure 19.

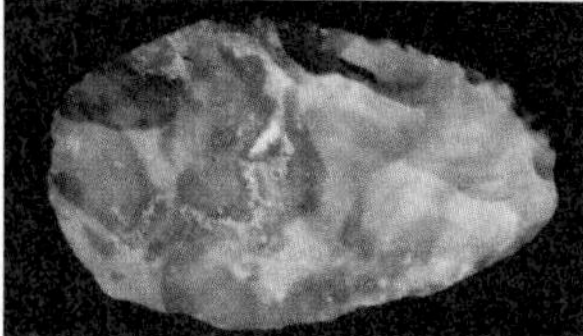

Figure (19) Kaolin chert, biface of heat treated material. Source: Illinois.

Figure (20) Alibates flint, Harahey knife of red-and-white-banded "beefsteak" variety. Source: Texas Panhandle.

5. Southern Central

The Southern Central area contains some unique and widespread lithic types. One of the most distinctive types is **Alibates flint**, which is actually a silica pseudomorph after dolomite, a soft carbonate mineral. The quarries, now a national monument, are north of Amarillo, Texas. Alibates is found in many colors, but most often it can be described as a spectrum of red/purple at one end and white at the other. All types of intermediate combinations are found. One of the most attractive is termed "beefsteak" Alibates. As shown in Figure 20, this material, with its red and white bands, resembles marbled beef.

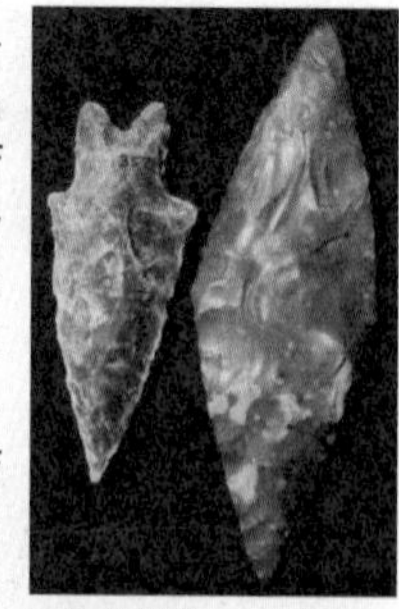

Figure (21) Edwards Plateau Chert, Harahey knife and patinated Pedernales point. Source: Central Texas.

Edwards Plateau chert is found in

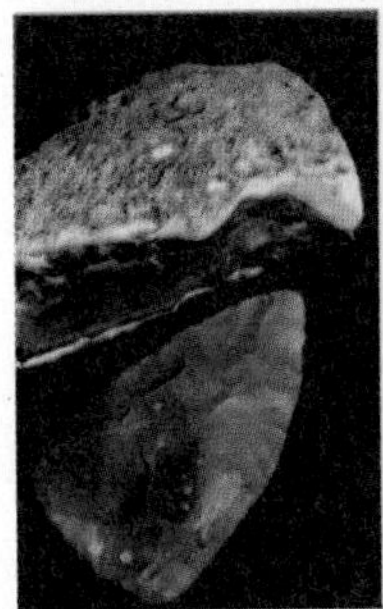

Figure (22) Georgetown chert, biface and rough nodule. Source: Central Texas.

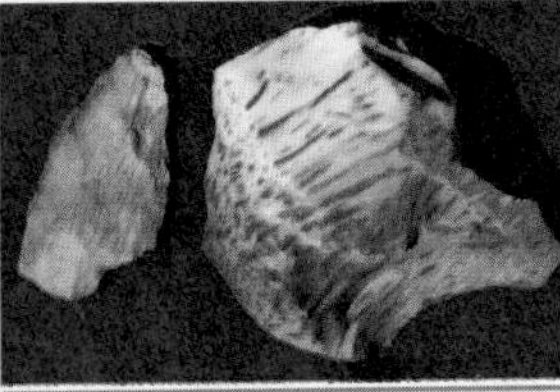

Figure (23) Agatized palm- wood, knife and rough sample showing color and cellular structure. Source: Louisiana and eastern Texas.

many colors and textures in the Cretaceous limestones of central Texas. Often found in shades of tan with white splotches, it patinates readily (Figure 21). A related lithic is **Georgetown chert**, which occurs in root beer and brown shades and is often translucent (Figure 22).

Petrified palmwood is a variety of petrified wood found in eastern Texas and Louisiana that can often be quite colorful (Figure 23), while showing the cell structure of the original wood.

Novaculite (Figure 24), as described earlier, is a metamorphosed chert that benefits from heat treatment. It is found primarily in Arkansas, and comes in many shades, although light colors are most common.

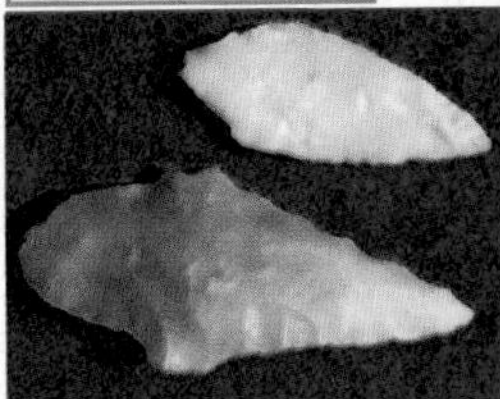

Figure (24) Novaculite, white point and pink point, possibly heat treated. Source: Arkansas.

Figure (25) Flint Ridge chalcedony, blades showing variety of colors. Source: Licking County, Ohio.

6. Eastern Central

The Eastern Central region contains some of the best known and most studied lithic types in the country. Ohio's **Flint Ridge flint** is actually a family of lithics: chert, chalcedony, jasper, and agate. The extensive quarries lie mostly within the boundaries of Flint Ridge State Memorial in Licking County, Ohio. Every color imaginable has been found, and the material was quarried and utilized by early people from Paleo to Late Prehistoric times. Figure 25 shows a variety of hues of this important lithic. Heat treated Flint Ridge material was used by the Hopewell people for their cores and microblades. Figure 26 shows a group of these cores.

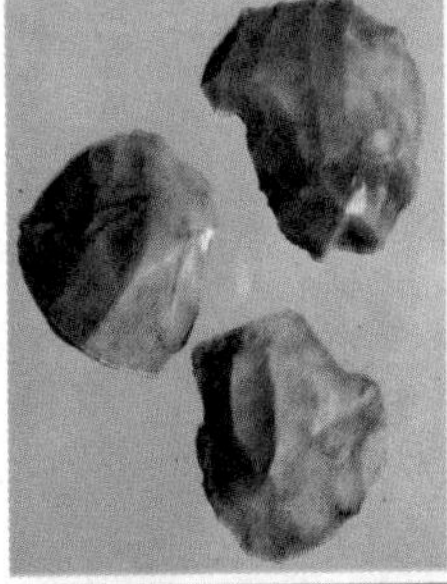

Figure (26) Flint Ridge chalcedony, Hopewell cores of heat treated material. Source: Licking County, Ohio.

Figure (27) Coshocton/ Upper Mercer chert, knives. Source: Ohio.

Another widely used Ohio lithic was **Coshocton/ Upper Mercer chert**. This material occurs across 13 counties and is found in mottled shades of black, blue, and gray (Figure 27). **Carter Cave chert** is an attractive glossy red, yellow or brown chert (Figure 28) occurring in Kentucky but found in adjacent states

Indiana **Harrison County chert/Hornstone** is a gray lithic that is found in nearly spherical nodules. The material often exhibits circular or "bullseye" patterns, as shown in figure 29.

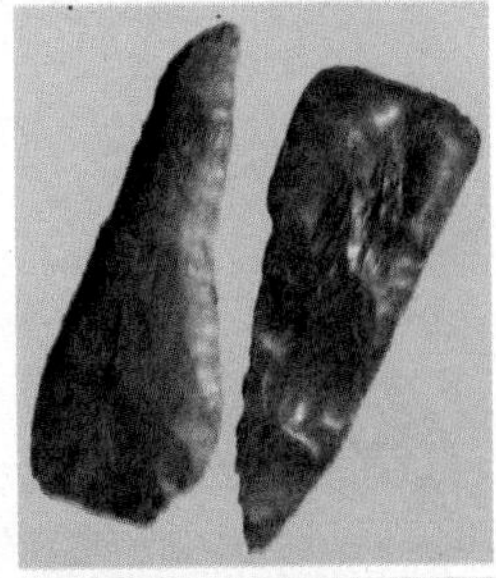

Figure (28) Carter Cave chert, knives. Source: Kentucky.

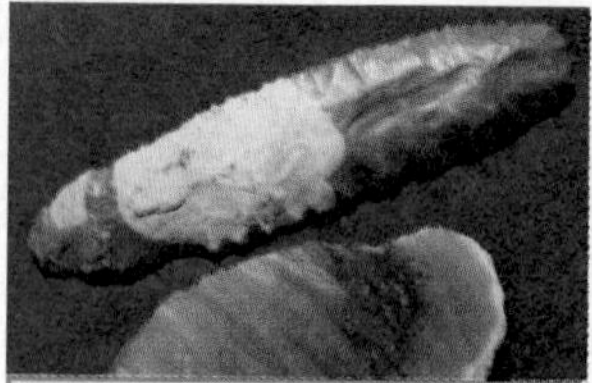

Figure (29) Harrison County chert/ Hornstone, knife with circular pattern, rough piece. Source: Indiana.

Figure (30) Attica chert, ("Indiana Green"), rough sample with Archaic "E Notch" knives. Source: Indiana.

Another Indiana lithic is **Attica chert**, popularly called "Indiana Green." It has green bands in a gray matrix (Figure 30) and outcrops in central Indiana.

Large nodules of **Dover chert** are found near the town of Dover, Tennessee. This lithic, shown in Figure 31, was used by the Mississippian culture for large blades, such as the famous "Duck River Cache," which contained blades up to 28" long. This stone has the unusual characteristic of being easier to chip after it has been soaked in water.

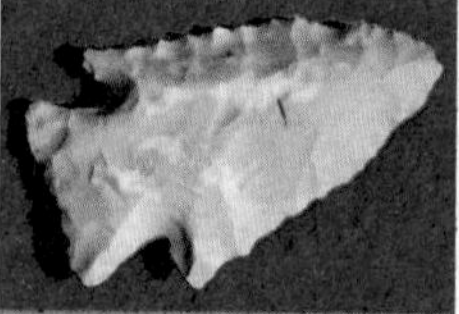

Figure (31) Dover chert, Archaic Bevel point. Source: Tennessee.

7. Gulf Coastal

Many of the lithic types described for the Gulf Coastal region are also prevalent in the southern part of the Eastern Central.

Figure (32) Citronelle/Cata - houla chert, rough piece and blades. Source: Mississippi and adjacent states.

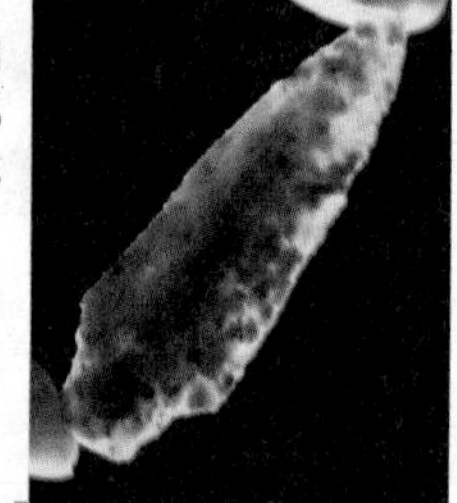

Figure (33) Tallahatta quartzite, point showing translucence and "snow - flake" effect. Source: Mississippi and Alabama.

Citronelle/Catahoula chert is a colorful lithic (Figure 32) found in Mississippi and neighboring states. The geology and terminology of this chert are complex, and undoubtedly local names are also used. **Tallahatta quartzite** is an attractive lithic from Mississippi and Alabama. It is often translucent (Figure 33), with a structure resembling suspended snow- flakes.

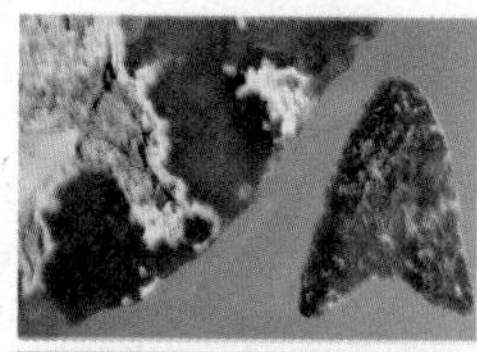

Figure (34) Agatized coral, rough piece and Santa Fe point showing patination on coral polyps. Source: Florida.

Agatized coral (Figure 34) is a silica pseudomorph found in Florida. The polyps of the coral are often visible in the stone, which comes in a variety of colors and is often translucent. Artifacts of agatized coral and **Coastal Plain chert** (Figure 35) are found in the rivers of Florida and Georgia, often in a highly polished condition.

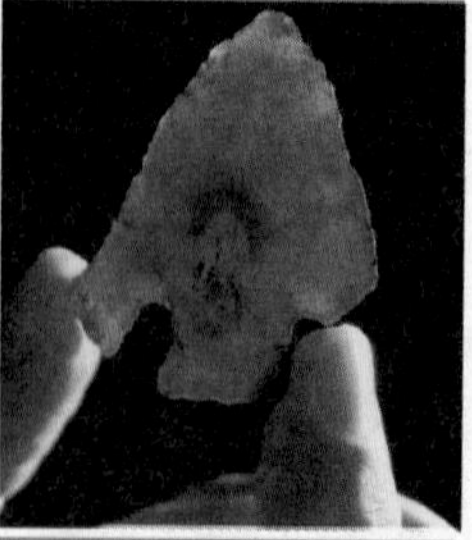

Figure (35) Coastal Plain chert, point showing color and translucence. Source: Florida and Georgia.

8. Eastern Seaboard

The states of the Eastern Seaboard and Northeast were not blessed with the quality or variety of lithics found in other areas of the country. It is a tribute to the skill of the natives of these areas that they made functional, sometimes exotic tools and implements of materials such as milky quartz, which would be passed over in other areas.

The **milky quartz** is actually massive phenocrystalline

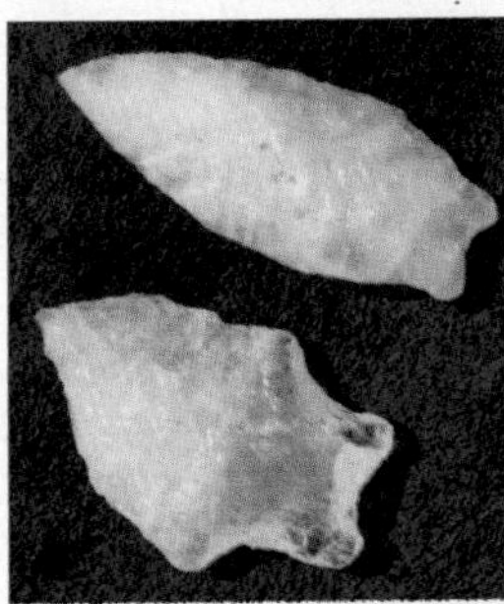

Figure (36) Milky Quartz, points. Source: Virginia, but found across much of US.

Figure (37) Silicified slate, rough piece and Woodland triangular points. Source: Carolina Piedmont, other areas of Eastern Coast.

Figure (38) Rhyolite, Savannah River point. Source: Eastern US and other areas, not generally used when better lithics were available.

quartz (see Figure 1), which was difficult to work because of numerous internal cracks. Some implements of this stone were totally or partially clear quartz crystal, such as shown in Figure 36.

Figure (39) Argillite, drill. Source: Carolina Piedmont and adjacent areas.

Silicified slate (Figure 37) was an important lithic of the Carolina Piedmont and adjacent areas. The igneous rock **rhyolite**, when fine grained and solid, made good artifacts, such as shown in Figure 38. **Argillite** (Figure 39) is a fine-grained sedimentary rock composed of clay minerals which found wide usage in the Carolinas and adjacent areas.

Figure (40) Onondaga chert, Woodland triangles. Source: Western New York State.

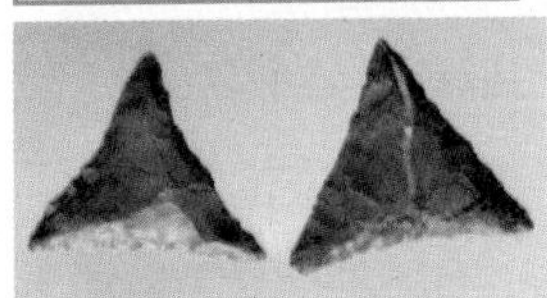

Figure (41) Berks/Lehigh County jasper, Woodland triangles. Source: Pennsylvania.

9. Northeast

Although areas of the Northeast region were lacking high quality lithics, some good types were known. **Onondaga chert** (Figure 40) was a popular material. **Berks/Lehigh County jasper** (Figure 41) was found in a range of colors, from chocolate to red, and its workability was often enhanced by heat treating.

Figure (42) Felsite, knives. Source: New England states. other areas.

In the New England area, **felsite** (Figure 42), a fine-grained igneous rock, served the needs of prehistoric knappers. Rhyolite and argillite, as described in the earlier Eastern Seaboard Region, were also widely used in the Northeast.

**John Grenawalt is a metallurgical engineer with 32 years of service in the steel industry. He grew up in eastern Colorado and graduated from the Colorado School of Mines. He has had a lifelong interest in the earth sciences, and collects artifacts, rocks and minerals, fossils, and meteorites. Artifacts are his primary interest, and he has collected artifacts and lithic specimens from across the US and many foreign countries.*

He enjoys reading, and has accumulated a sizable library on archaeology, anthropology, and his collecting interests. He holds membership in the Indiana Archaeological Society, Archaeological Society of Ohio, American Society for Amateur Archaeology, and Genuine Indian Relic Society, where he is an associate editor of their journal, "Prehistoric American." He as had articles published in this journal, "Indian Artifact Magazine," and other journals.

John enjoys macro photography of his collections and of the collections of friends. He also enjoys written and Internet correspondence with other collectors. He attends as many shows and auctions as possible with his wife Judy, who shares his collecting interests. Judy also collects Indian and Eskimo dolls, baskets, and related art objects.

REFERENCES

1. Bell, Pat & David Wright, "Rocks & Minerals -- Macmillan Field Guides," Macmillan Publishing Company, 1985.

2. Busbey, Arthur B. III, et al, "The Nature Company Guide to Rocks & Fossils," TIME-LIFE Books, 1996.

3. Cipriani, Nicola, "The Encyclopedia of Rocks and Minerals," Barnes & Noble Books, 1996.

4. Collins, Wilkie, Washington, MS - personal communication, 1998.

5. Converse, Robert N., "Ohio Flint Types," Special Publication of the Archaeological Society of Ohio, 1994.

6. DeRegnaucourt, Tony & Jeff Georgiady, "Prehistoric Chert Types of the Midwest," Occasional Monographs Series of the Upper Miami Valley Research Museum, Arcanum. OH, 1998.

7. Dietz, Dewey, Redmond, OR - personal communication, 1998.

8. Fogelman, Gary L., "Lithics Book," Booklet No. 34, The Pennsylvania Artifact Series, Fogelman Publishing Co., 1983.

9. Ford, W.E., "Dana's Textbook of Mineralogy," Fourth Edition, John Wiley & Sons, 1958.

10. Frison, George C., "Prehistoric Hunters of the High Plains," Second Edition, Academic Press, Inc., 1991.

11. Pellant, Chris, & Rogers Phillips, "Rocks, Minerals, & Fossils of the World," Little, Brown & Company, 1990.

12. Pough, Frederick H., "A Field Guide to Rocks and Minerals," Houghton Mifflin Company, 1960.

13. Schick, Kathy D., & Nicholas Toth, "Making Silent Stones Speak," Simon & Schuster, 1993.

14. Waldorf, D.C. & Valerie, "Story in Stone - Flint Types of the Central and Southern U.S.," Mound Builder Books, 1987.

15. Whittaker, John C., "Flintknapping - Making & Understanding Stone Tools," University of Texas Press, 1994.

COLLECTING OLD WORLD PREHISTORIC ARTIFACTS

by Duncan Caldwell

RULES OF THUMB

The European and African artifacts that follow all have some kind of patina, usually a pronounced one that is also different from one side of each artifact to the other. This is due to the fact that most prehistoric tools, being somewhat flat, tended to lie on the surface both before burial and again before discovery, thereby undergoing different changes caused by light, weathering and geological effects on one side from the other. So, as a rule of thumb, do NOT collect Lower and Middle Paleolithic artifacts unless they exhibit some patina, and preferably a different one on each side.

Furthermore, don't expect artifacts that are often a hundred times older than the oldest American ones to be unchipped. After all, they have often undergone Glacial periods, surviving long weathering by frost and high winds on plateaus or rolling in tumultuous thawing rivers before being deposited in gravel-beds. In fact, a collector should be comforted by a little breakage, because depending on whether the posterior chips are ancient or modern, they will show the succession and surprising depths and varieties of patinas, often on the same piece.

Another point to remember is that a famous origin may increase the value of an artifact, but buyers should be circumspect. For example, the consultant has caught several French dealers labeling authentic hand-axes as having come from type sites around St. Acheul, when they were in fact found elsewhere. Consequently, it is essential that the seller be honorable and provide a lifetime guarantee of authenticity.

Finally, collecting artifacts from a time span over 130 times longer than all of American prehistory combined will begin to reveal the vast iceberg of humanity's past, of which American prehistory is just the peak of the tip. As the collector of Paleolithic artifacts explores that vast new domain, he will discover unending nuances and whole zones of mystery, while developing increasing respect for the prowess of ancestors we can *all* truly share. In fact, in their unnatural, geometric, idealized forms, hand-axes contain our species' full potential for artifice and symbolic thought in the bud.

To aid newcomers to this passionate field of study, I recommend both **Tools of the Old and New Stone Age** by Bordaz and the **Handbook of Paleolithic Typology** by Debénath and Dibble (available from Paleoworld.com), as well as my own upcoming book on unpublished prehistoric Old World masterpieces in private collections.

OLD WORLD SECTION

This new section introduces point and tool types from Europe and North Africa from 2.2 million to 3,200 years ago.

Because this is the first time such tools are being presented here, they are arranged in chronological rather than alphabetical order to give the reader an idea of their evolution. Furthermore, many tools are larger than this book, so they can not be presented actual size; dimensions are given instead. Also, only superior specimens have been chosen in many cases, because there is not enough space to show the quality range for each type. Lastly, the multitude of preserved types that arose over a prehistoric period that spanned 2.2 million years as opposed to the Americas' 15,000 is correspondingly bigger, so this section, as opposed to the North American ones, is an overview containing major gaps that the regional consultant hopes to close for laymen in an upcoming book.

Lithics: Some of the materials employed in the manufacture of points and tools from the two representative regions are: **For Europe:** Grand Pressigny flint - Indre et Loire & Vienne regions of France, Jablines flint - Seine et Marne, Thanatian flint - Oise & Somme valleys; jadeite, metahornblendite & dolerite - Brittany; Font-Maure jasper, France; Pelite-quartz - W. Alps; Obsidian - Italy, S. France, Greece; Green slate - W. Russia, Baltic states; etc. **For North Africa:** quartzite, flint, siltstone, jasper, etc. **Important sites:** Because the region and time-frame are so vast, only a few almost random sites are listed. However, an effort has been made to choose tools from famous sites, which are referred to in the captions. **Prices:** Price ranges have been extrapolated from the results of auctions and consultations with dealers from around the world. It should be noted, however, that the highest prices are often paid within the countries of origin by highly competitive local collectors.

EUROPEAN & NORTH AFRICAN POINT AND TOOL TYPES: (Archaeological Periods)

Note: Unlike in the Americas, where "Paleolithic" refers to the period from 15,000 to 8,000 B.P., in the Old World it is split into three sub-sections: the **Lower Paleolithic** from 2.2 million to roughly 250,000 B.P., the **Middle Paleolithic** from 250,000 to approximately 45,000 B.P., and the **Upper Paleolithic** from 45,000 B.P. to 11,000 B.P.

LOWER PALEOLITHIC (CA. 2,200,000 B.P. - 250,000 B.P.)

CHOPPER AND FLAKE TRADITION: Homo habilis & Homo erectus - 2,200,000 - 1,500,000 B.P. with later vestiges in E. Asia, Hungary, etc. **Oldawan I and II industries** - Pebble choppers, Bifacial chopping-tools - Inverse choppers, Clactonian flake tools: notches, denticulates, becs. **Important sites:** Damanisi, Georgia; Longgupo, China (1.8 million); Sangiran, Indonesia; Tatoui, Romania; Orce, Greece; Clacton-on-Sea, U.K., Vértesszöllös, Hungary; Wimereux, France; etc.

ASIAN CHOPPER-CHOPPING TOOL TRADITION:

Important sites: Choukoutien, Patjitan, etc.

ABBEVILLEAN (Early Acheulean):

Homo erectus - 1,500,000 - 780,000 B.P.

Abbevillean hand-axes (Africa & Europe) - **Trihedral picks** (Africa), **Amygdaloid hand-axes, Ficrons. Important sites:** Ubeidiya, Israel; Pingliang, China; Abbeville, France; Konso, Ethiopia; Beni Ikhlef, Algeria; etc.

MID TO LATE ACHEULEAN:

Homo erectus, Homo heidelbergensis, etc. - 780,000 - 250,000 B.P.

HAND-AXE TYPES:

Tihodaine type cleavers (Africa), Chalossian pic, Tabel Balalt type cleaver (Africa), Lanceolate, Kombewa flake cleavers, Backed bifaces, Cordiform hand-axes, Limandes, Ovates, Discoids, Triangular (late transitional form), Elongated triangular, Fusiform hand-axes, Naviforms, Shark's tooth hand-axes, Pélécyformes, Ogivo-triangulaire, Lagéniformes, Micoquekeile, Chalossian pic, Etc.

ASSOCIATED TOOLS: Kombewa flakes (Africa), Centripetal Levallois flakes, Levallois points, Levallois blades, Side-scrapers, Hafted knives (Schöningen), Wooden spears (Schöningen, Germany - ca. 400,000 B.P.).

IMPORTANT SITES (Mid-Acheulean - 780,000 - 500,000 B.P.): St. Acheul, Soleihac & Artenac, France; Petrolona, Greece; Boxgrove, U.K.; Latamne, Syria; Kudaro, Georgia; Beni Ikhlef, Algeria; etc.

IMPORTANT SITES (Late Acheulean - 500,000 - 250,000 B.P.):
Terra Amata & Tantavel, France; Gesher Benot Ya'aqov, Israel (tranchet cleavers); Torralba, Spain; Fontana Ranuccio, Italy; Swanscombe, U.K.; Schöningen & Karlich-Seeufer, Germany; El Ma el Abiod, Algeria; etc.

MIDDLE PALEOLITHIC
(CA. 250,000 B.P. - 40,000 B.P.) - NEANDERTHALS

MTA (Mousterian in the Acheulean Tradition - Europe), **DENTICULATE TOOL TRADITION** (Europe), **QUINA TOOL TRADITION** (Europe, **"MOUSTEROID" FLAKE TOOL INDUSTRY** (North Africa, Middle East), **SANGOAN INDUSTRY** (Africa), **ATERIAN INDUSTRY** (Africa)
Elongated Mousterian points, Levallois points, Mousterian points (wholly retouched), Soyons points, Tayac points, Emireh points, Bifacial leaf-points - Blattspitzen, Aterian points, Raclette side-scrapers (21 types), Limaces, Burins, Cleaver hand-axes, Continuation of Micoquian hand-axes, Levallois points, Small to medium hand-axes (direct soft hammer percussion), Mousterian discs, Convex scrapers, Concave scrapers, Backed knives, first "retouchiors" for pressure flaking, Levallois blade tools, Wooden spears (Lehringen), Borers, Non-Levallois truncated backed blades, Levallois blades.
Important sites: Moustier, La Quina, Combe-Grenal, Laussel, Pech-de-l'Azé, Mauran, Arcy-sur-Cure, Tata, Molodova, High Lodge, Ain Meterchem, etc.

UPPER PALEOLITHIC (40,000 B.P. - 11,000 B.P.)

ULUZZIAN (late Neanderthals - ITALY - Circa 45,000 - 35,000 B.P.):
Crescents, Backed points, Burins, End-scrapers, Flake tools; Bone tools: awls, conical points, biconical points, Etc. **Important site:** Grotta del Cavallo

CHATELPERRONIAN (late Neanderthals - France - ca. 45,000 - 35,000 B.P.)
Châtelperron knives, Châtelperron points, End-scrapers, Truncated pieces, Burins, Incised tooth ornaments, Ivory pendants; Bone tools: awls, ivory pins, digging sticks, tubes, lozenge-shaped points, etc. **Important sites:** Châtelperron, Grotte du Renne, St.-Césaire, Isturitz, Gargas, Caminade Est, Belvis, Quinçay, etc.

AURIGNACIAN (first European Homo Sapiens sapiens - ca. 40,000 - 28,000 B.P.) / LUPEMBIAN (Africa) / SZELETIAN (C. & E. Europe)
Dufour bladelets, Retouched blades, Strangulated blades, Caminade scraper, Carinated (keeled) scraper, Nosed scraper, Plane, Dihedral burins; Bone tools: Split-based atlatl points, etc. **Important sites:** Chauvet, Arcy-sur-Cure, La Ferrassie, Caminade Ouest, Dufour, Baden-Württemberg, Geissenklösterle, Vogelherd, etc.

NOTE: Only widely known Upper Paleolithic cultures are indicated, here. Contemporaneous local forms, such as the various Perigordian levels and their assemblages will be treated elsewhere by the consultant.

GRAVETTIAN & PERIGORDIAN (W. Europe), PAVLOVIAN (C. Europe) & KOSTIENKI (Ukraine & Russia) (Upper Paleolithic, 28,000 - 23,000 B.P.)
Noaille gravers, Kostienki shouldered points, Gravette points, Font Robert points,

Pointed median groove bone points, Micro-gravette points, Obliquely truncated blades, Scrapers on large thin flakes, "Batons de commandment" (wrenches), Dihedral burins, Etc. **Important sites:** La Gravette, Chateau de Corbiac, Cougnac, Peche Merle, La Font-Robert, La Ferrassie, Laugerie Haute, Tursac, Predmosti, Dolni Vestonice, Avdievo, Kostienki, etc.

SOLUTREAN (France & Spain) & EPI-GRAVETTIAN (Italy): Upper Paleolithic, 23,000 - 17,000 B.P.)

Laurel leaf points - bifacial (13 types), Willow leaf points - bifacial, Shouldered points (4 Solutrean types), Bevel based bone points, Tanged bifacial points (Spain), Borers, Bifacial knives, Solutrean unifacial points, End-scrapers, Various dihedral burins, Laugerie Haute micro-scraper, Carinated scraper, Raclettes, Becs. **Important sites:** La Solutré, Volgu, Lascaux, etc.

MAGDALENIAN (Europe), KEBARIAN (Levant), Iberomaursian (N. Africa), etc. (17,000 - 10,500 B.P.)

Teyjat points, dihedral burins, Magdalenian shouldered points, First microliths, Backed blades, End-scrapers, Multiple burin-scraper tools, Parrot-beaked burin, Lacan burin, Harpoons (many types), Eyed needles, Carinated scraper, Thumb-nail scrapers, etc. **Important sites:** Gönnersdorf, Altamira, La Madeleine, Marsoulas, Pincevent, Isturitz, Niaux, Castillo, La Vache, Le Portel, Kesslerloch, etc.

MESOLITHIC (end of glacial period - Europe: ca. 10,500 - 8,000 B.P., Middle East: 13,000 - 10,000 B.P.)

Microliths: small blade fragments retouched into geometric shapes (100s of types): Azilian points, Chaville points, Sauveterre points, Tardenois points, Capsian arrowheads, Trapezes (over 13 types), Rouffignac backed knives, Lunates, Triangles (over 11 types) Microburins, Tranchet chisels, Thumb-nail & other scrapers, Azilian Harpoons, Bone fish hooks, etc. **Important sites:** Tardenois, Mas d'Azil, Sonchamp, Milheeze (Federmesser), Ahrensbourg, Remouchamps, Sauveterre-la-Lémance, Shoukba (Natufian), Horsham, Shippea Hill, Relilai, El Oued, Medjez, etc.

NEOLITHIC (Europe: ca. 8,000 - 5,000 B.P., Middle East: 10,000 - 5,000 B.P.)

Amouq points (I & II), Byblos points, Temassinine points, Labied points, Bifacial leaf points, Tell Mureybet points; Saharan points: At least 9 families consisting of 103 groups encompassing many more types; French flint daggers, Sickle blades, Gouges, Chisels, Antler socket shock absorbers for celts, First polished celts, Antler harpoons, Eyed needles, First ceramic pottery. **Important sites:** ***Europe*** —> Stonehenge, Newgrange, Skara Brae, Barnenez, Carnac, Gavrinis, Michelsberg, Fort-Harrouard, Filatosa, Vinca, Butmir, Cucuteni, Cernavoda; ***W. Asia*** —> Catal Huyuk, Hacilar, Jericho, Dzejtun, Kelteminar, Hissar, Ali Kosh; ***N. Africa*** —> Jaatcha, Tazina, Djerat, Redeyef, Adrar Bous III, etc.

CHALCOLITHIC & BRONZE AGE (W. Europe: 5,000 - 2,800 B.P.)

NOTE: All but the most prestigious tools during these periods still tended to be made of stone.: Egyptian fishtail flint knives, Gerzean flint knives, Armorican flint arrowheads, Scandanavian flint daggers, First Copper, then Bronze tools: Axes, Adzes Chisels, Razors, Bronze arrowheads, Etc. **Important sites:** Cambous & Mont Bego, France; Nagada, Egypt; Hagar Qim & Mnajdra, Malta; Su Nuraxi, Sardinia; etc.

CHOPPERS - Chopper and Flake Tradition, 2,200,000 - depending on region: ca. 1,500,000 to 100,000 B.P.

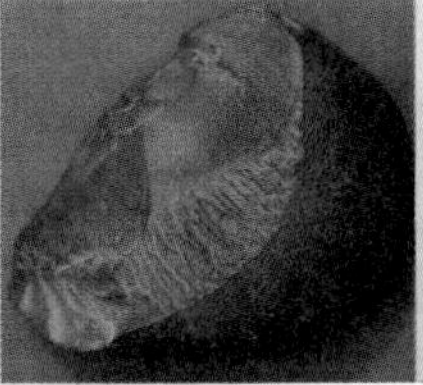

1) 3 1/2" Homo habilis chopper. Taouz, Morocco. 1.9 to 2.2 million B.P. $150 - $200. **NOTES:** Flake scars eroded by wind-blown sand channeling. Large sculptural ones cost more. **2)** 3 1/4" chopper. Central Portugal. Over 800,000 B.P. $180 - $250.

LOCATION: Africa and Europe as far north as Hungary. **DESCRIPTION:** A cobble with 2 or more flakes struck from one side. Although choppers are found throughout the Stone Age, those from early sites which don't produce Acheulean artifacts are sought after as the first lithic vestiges of man's tool-use: **I.D. KEY:** Always patinated.

CHOPPING TOOLS - Chopper and Flake Tradition, 2,200,000 - depending on region: ca. 1,500,000 to 100,000 B.P.

3) 10" chopping tool. Haute Garonne, France. $1,000 - $2,000. **NOTES:** One of the biggest known. Small / crude ones $50 - $200. **LOCATION:** Africa and Southern Europe. **DESCRIPTION:** A cobble with flakes struck bifacially from both sides, usually by alternate flaking forming a sinuous cutting edge. **I.D. KEY:** Always patinated.

PRIMITIVE "ABBEVILLEAN" HAND-AXES - Early Acheulean, 1.9 million B.P. - 600,000 B.P.

The oldest hand-axes are large bifaces and trihedral picks which were made by direct hard-stone percussion. Both forms have been found in Ethiopian sites between levels of volcanic tuff dated at between 1.6 and 1.9 million BP. European specimens are more conservatively dated at over 650,000 BP.

NORTH AFRICAN TYPES:

4) 7 1/8" Homo erectus trihedral pick hand-ax. Quartzite. Beni Ikhlef, Algeria. Dated by comparison with dated series at KGA 10 in Konso, Ethiopia: 1.5 to 2 million years old. $400 - $600. **NOTES:** Stands on base. Wind luster. Burgundy, glossy browns. If plain, 1/4 the price.

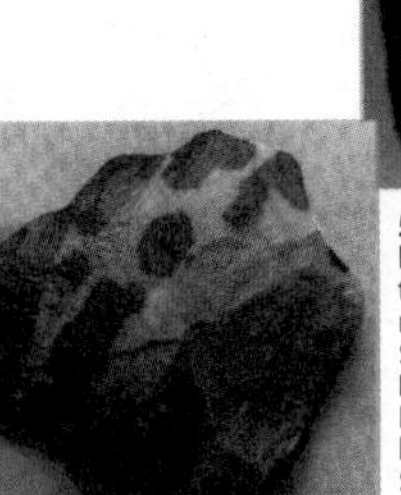

5) 5 1/8" Abbevillean hand-ax. Homo erectus. Quartzite. Algerian Sahara. $800 - $1,000. **NOTES:** Wind gloss. Decorative dark red & beige. If plain: $100 - $200.

EUROPEAN TYPES:

6) 6" Amygdaloid biface. Aisne, France. $600 - $800. **NOTE:** Watertable patina. Black flint turned amber/olive.

7) 6 1/2" Amygdaloid biface. Grey flint turned encrusted orange. Seine Maritime, France. **NOTE:** Without hole $300 - $550. With sculptural feature $1,500 - $2,500. **LOCATION:** Africa and Southern Europe. **DESCRIPTION:** A core tool resulting from the reduction of a large block to a big bifacial or tri-hedral blade flaked by the direct hammerstone technique. The flaking is relatively short and massive, with the percussion bulbs leaving deep scars that produce an inefficient cutting edge, when viewed in hindsight. **I.D. KEY:** Always heavily patinated. Don't confuse with Mesolithic Asturian picks from Iberia which have globular bases.

AFRICAN POINTED HAND-AXES - Lower Paleolithic, mid to late Acheulean, ca. 750,000 - 250,000 B.P. - Homo erectus

8) 4 1/2" discoidal hand-ax with reserved cortex grip. Thebes Egypt. ca. 350,000 B.P. $400 - $700. **NOTE:** Area's glossy yellow ochre through reddish-brown chocolate patinas.

9) 7" "Micoquian" lanceolate hand-ax. Quartzite. Tabel Balalt, Algeria. $900 - $1,500. **NOTES:** Decorative burgundy & beige. Aeolian patina. **DESCRIPTION:** A long slender lanceolate point, often slightly concave sides.

AFRICAN CLEAVER HAND-AXES - Late Acheulean, 500,000 - 250,000 B.P.

10) 10 1/4" Tihodaine cleaver hand-ax. Quartzite. El Beyed, N. Tchigheti, Mauritania. $1,200 - $1,600. **NOTE:** A giant. Small or crude ones as little as $130 - $200.

11) 11" Tihodaine cleaver hand-ax. Quartzite. El Beyed, N. Tchigheti, Mauritania. $2,000 - $3,000. **NOTE:** A giant. Dark wind gloss where exposed. **DESCRIPTION:** A medium to large hand-ax, usually made from a Levallois or Kombewa flake. One side is fully knapped and has an oblique cutting edge formed by a sideways tranchet blow, while the other side is thinned down the sides and around the base, but is otherwise flat. Although rare in the mid to late Acheulean tool-kit of Africa, it is not as rare as cleavers in Europe. The invention of this and other hand-ax types made from large flakes increased tool-making efficiency 3 fold over the Abbevillean method of reducing a block to a single hand-ax - and was crucial to human evolution.

EUROPEAN ACHEULEAN HAND-AXES - Lower Paleolithic, ca. 600,000 (possibly much older) - 250,000 B.P. - Homo erectus

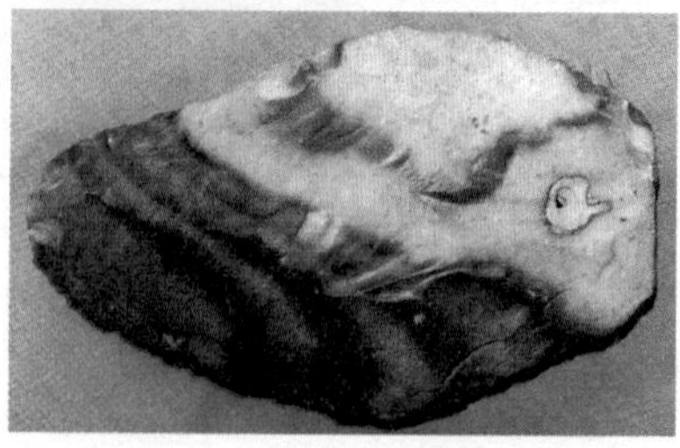

12) 6 3/4" sub-cordiform flint hand-ax. Oise, France. $1,500 - $2,500. **NOTES:** Natural hole through base. Tan & white watertable patina. Modern tip damage. Stripes & hole keep value high.

16) 5 1/2" cordiform hand-ax. Amiens, France. $900 - $1,400. **NOTES:** Blue & white webbed patina on black flint. Super thin & fine.

13) 7 3/4" Micoquian lanceolate hand-ax. 220,000 - 270,000 B.P. Rare. Deep creamy patina on dark flint. Senonais, France. $2,000 -$3,000. **NOTES:** Atypical sculptural grip, thin blade & large size.

17) 4 3/4" triangular hand-ax. Rare. Yonne, France. $800 - $1,200. **DESCRIPTION:** Straight or slightly convex sides, fairly straight base, often sharp, with suggestion of thinning for hafting. Rare because produced only during the transition from the Acheulean to Mousterian.

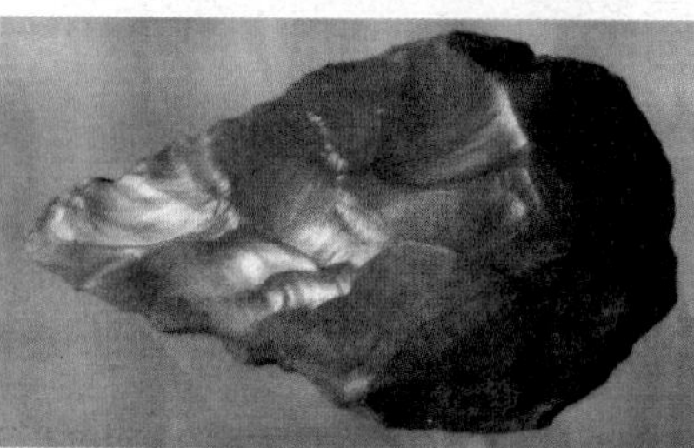

14) 6 1/2" Pélécyforme hand-ax. Indre et Loire, France. Glossy honey patina. $2,000 - $3,000.
DESCRIPTION: Rounded base with slightly concave edges. ca. 220,000 - 300,000 B.P. **NOTE:** Symmetrical & colorful. Smaller rolled ones $250 - $550.

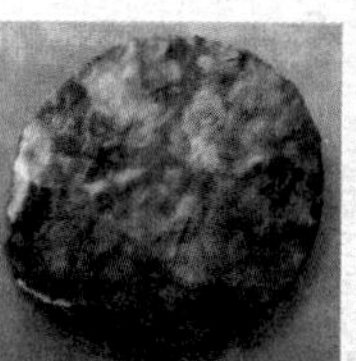

18) 3 1/4" Micoquian typical discoidal hand-ax. Aube, France. $800 - $900. **NOTES:** All round cutting edge. Extremely rare biface.

19) 5 1/2"H x 5 1/4"W discoidal cleaver hand-ax. Early to mid Acheulean Extremely rare. Yonne, France. $1,200 - $1,800. **NOTE:** Orange patina of lower Paleolithic artifacts from region. Originally greyish-brown.

15) 10 1/4" elongated cordiform hand-ax. Indre et Loire, France. $6,000 - $9,000. **DESCRIPTION:** Rounded bases, convex edges, tip pointed or slightly rounded. **NOTE:** One of biggest known.

20) 6" limande cleaver hand-ax. Senonais, France. $1,800 - $2,400. **DESCRIPTION:** Both ends round with fairly straight sides. Elongation index greater than for ovates. Rare. **NOTES:** Grey flint turned lower paleo yellow. Frost cracks from glacial period but no scarring. No residual cortex.

OTHER EUROPEAN ACHEULEAN TOOLS - Lower Paleolithic, ca. 600,000 (possibly much older) - 250,000 B.P. - Homo erectus

SIDE-SCRAPER:

21) 4 1/4" side-scraper. Seine et Marne, France. $80 - $200. **NOTE:** Butterscotch watertable patina.

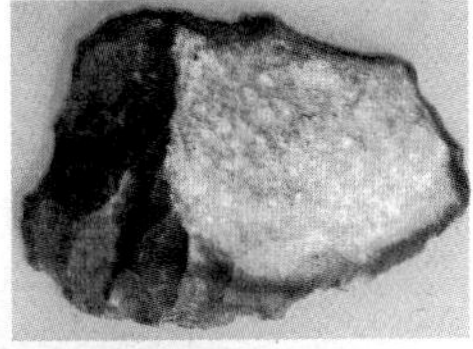

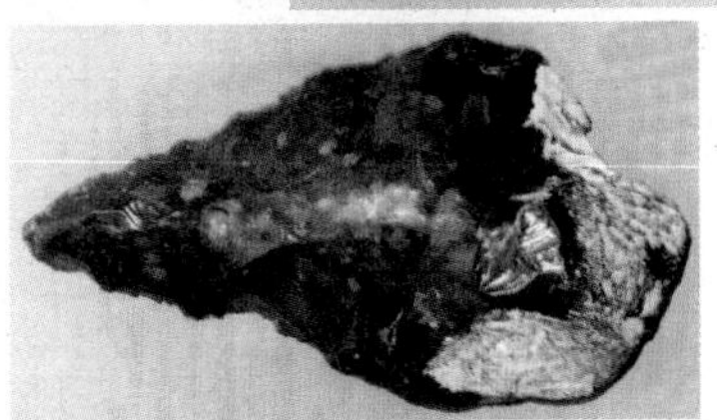

22) 6" convergent unifacial side-scraper. Black flint turned glossy amber to olive green by watertable patina. Oise, France. ca. 300,000 B.P. $900 - $1,100. **NOTES:** Big and colorful: one of the finest. **DESCRIPTION:** Unlike a hand-ax, which fine convergent side-scrapers resemble, most were probably not pointed when first made, but became so with wear and resharpening. Simple side-scrapers are much more common than convergent examples: $100 - $250.

EUROPEAN MOUSTERIAN HAND-AXES - Middle Paleolithic, ca. 250,000 - 45,000 Neanderthal

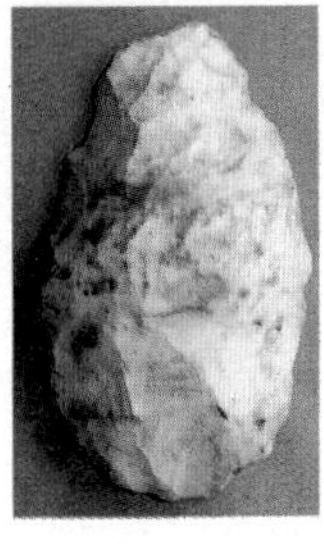

23) 3 3/4" Mousterian hand-ax. Plateau find, Sens, Yonne, France. $150 - $300. **NOTE:** Glossy cream patina of area's mid-paleolithic artifacts. Original flint: dark gray.

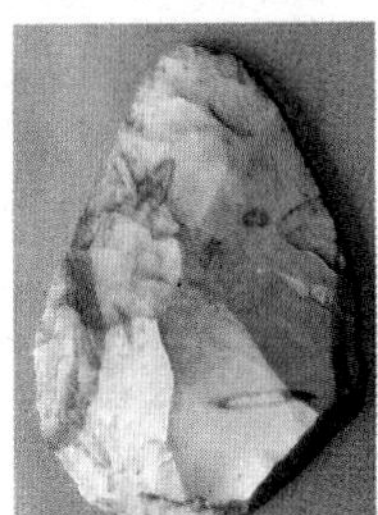

24) 3 1/2" Mousterian hand-ax. Creamy with bluish and orange tints, originally gray. Spiennes, Belgium. $350 - $550. **NOTES:** Famous site, 19th C. label on reverse, typical oblique grip.

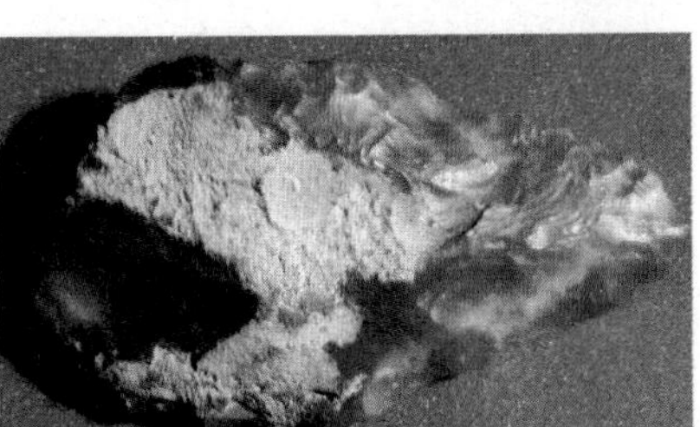

25) 6 1/2" naviform hand-ax. Grand Pressigny, France. $500 - $800. **NOTE:** Lustrous caramel patina on lighter flint. **DESCRIPTION:** Elongated, pointed at both ends.

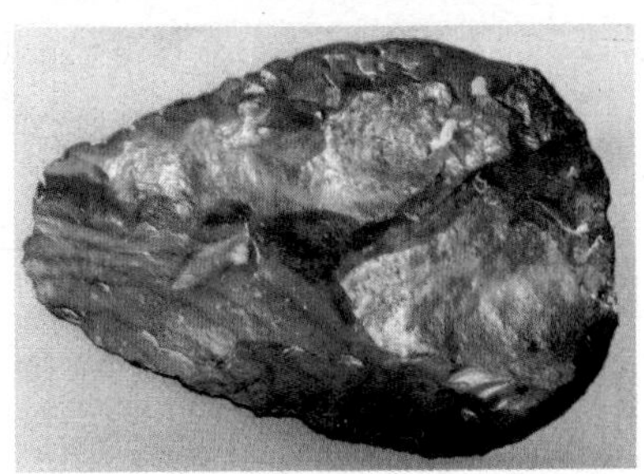

26) 5 3/8" cordiform hand-ax. Black flint turned banded red by watertable. Le Moustier, Dordogne, France. $900 - $1,200 **NOTE:** Type site & color!

27) 4 3/8" MTA cordiform hand-ax. Yonne, France. $850 - $1,100. **NOTES:** Exceptional sharp base, varied cream, beige blue-grey patina. If plain: $250 - $500. **DESCRIPTION:** Flat biface, rounded base, convex edges.

NORTH AFRICAN MID-PALEOLITHIC HAND-AXES - ca. 250,000 - 45,000 B.P.: Neanderthal

28) 5 1/4" elongated cordiform hand-ax. Taouz, Morocco. $500 - $700. **NOTE:** Wind gloss & stippling. Decorative red with band raises value. Others 1/2 price.

29) 4 7/8" limande hand-ax. Quartzite. Beni Ikhlef, Algeria. $800 - $1,000. **NOTE:** Wind gloss other side. Dark red and yellow. If monochrome, 1/4 price.

30) 7" typical cordiform hand-ax. Quartzite. Libyan Desert. $900 - $1,200. **NOTES:** Aeolian gloss. Yellow & orange, quartz inclusions glitter. If plain, 1/4 - 1/2 price.

OTHER NORTH AFRICAN MID-PALEOLITHIC TOOLS - ca. 250,000 - 45,000 B.P.: Neanderthal

31) 6 1/2" backed "saw". Scarlet quartzite. Libyan Desert, Egypt. $750 - $900. **NOTES:** Rare! Overall wind gloss.

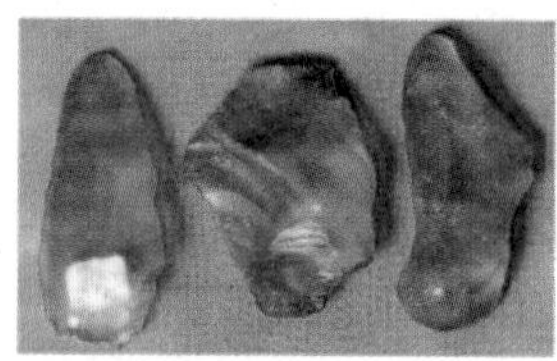

32) Libyan Glass flakes & bladelets. Made from impactite created by a meteor explosion. One on left: 2". Libyan Desert, Egypt. $100 - $200. **NOTE:** Heavy wind erosion. Transparent yellow. Conchoidal fractures.

OTHER EUROPEAN MID-PALEOLITHIC TOOLS - Mousterian, ca. 250,000 - 45,000 B.P.: *MOUSTERIAN POINTS: Neanderthal*

33) 3 1/4" Mousterian Levallois point. Aube, Champagne, France. $100 - $200. **NOTE:** Grey flint patinated white.

34) 2 3/4" Mousterian Levallois point. Senonais, Yonne, France. $200 - $400. **NOTE:** Typical mineral concretions - these often grow from cleavages of frost scars.

35) 3 3/8" classic Mousterian Levallois point. Black flint patinated grey. Plazac, Dordogne. $350 - $650. **NOTE:** Typical facetted striking platform.

36) 3 1/2" unifacial Mousterian point. Grey flint patinated glossy white & blue. Othe, France. $700 - $1,200. **NOTE:** Among the finest known. Super retouch.

37) 3 7/8" Mousterian point turned into a borer. Flint. Senonais, Yonne, France. $80 - $200. **NOTE:** Area's Mousterian fractal web patination.

MOUSTERIAN BIFACIAL KNIVES:

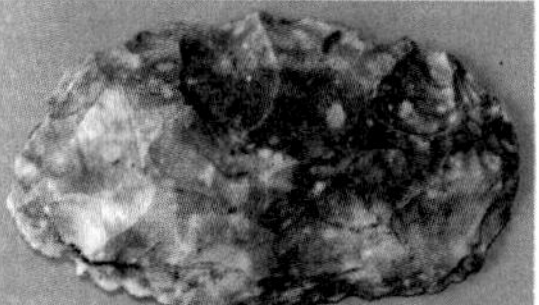

38) 4 3/4" bifacial Mousterian knife. Yonne, France. $350 - $550. **NOTE:** Extremely rare tool type.

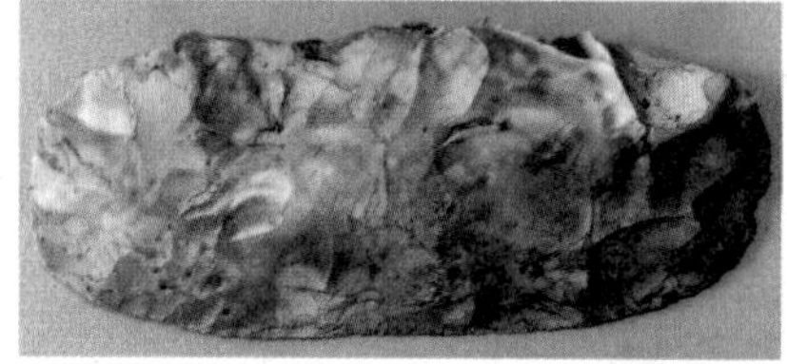

39) 5 5/8" bifacial Mousterian knife. Flint. Yonne, France. $900 - $1,400. **NOTE:** One of the finest. Blue-grey & beige patina. **DESCRIPTION:** One side is finely sharpened, while the other is roughly knapped, suggesting that it was glued into a grooved handle. After the discovery of hafted 400,000 year old Acheulean flints in a coal mine in Schöningen, Germany, Neanderthal creation of complex tools is incontestable. In fact, some "hand-axes" were almost certainly hafted (See Triangular hand-axes).

LATE ACHEULEAN & MOUSTERIAN LEVALLOIS FLAKE & BLADE TOOLS:

40) 4 1/2" Levallois flake tool. Eure, France. $300 - $600. **NOTE:** Facetted striking platform. Irregular examples may be 1/4 the price. **DESCRIPTION:** A large flake of predetermined size and form, often with a facetted striking platform. The invention of the Levallois technique allowed ancient humans to obtain up to 10 times more functional tools from a block than when they had reduced blocks to form hand-axes. As such it was one of humanity's greatest advances.

41) 5 1/8" Levallois blade. Inverse retouch. 1/4" thick. Oise, France. $300 - $500. **NOTE:** Black Thanatian flint turned olive & khaki by watertable. Smaller / plainer pieces: $30 - $150.

LATE ACHEULEAN & MOUSTERIAN LEVALLOIS CORES:

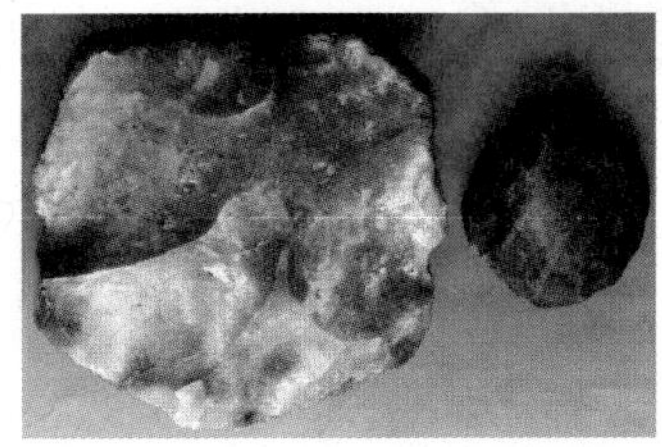

42) a) 10" x 8" Levallois core. Grand Pressigny, France. The side from which flake tools were struck is illustrated. $2,000 - $3,000. **NOTE:** One of largest known. Speckled beige & white patina. **b)** 5 1/2" x 4 1/2" Levallois core. Indre et Loire, France. The back of the core is illustrated to show "tortoise shell" preparation around circumference. $200 - $400. **NOTE:** Amber patina.

VARIOUS UPPER PALEOLITHIC POINTS & TOOLS - Aurignacian, Gravettian, Solutrean, Magdalenian

NOTE: *Despite the fact that Upper Paleolithic tools are often much smaller than the preceding ones, they are also much rarer than them because of the following:*

- *populations were extremely sparse due to glacial conditions*
- *the periods were much shorter and*
- *most sites have been off-limits to collectors for 60 or more years.*

AURIGNACIAN POINTS & OTHER TOOLS ca. 28,000 B.P. - Homo sapiens sapiens

43) 2 1/4" Aurignacian end-scraper. Abri Castanet, Sergeac, Dordogne. $200 - $400. **NOTE:** Famous rock shelter: Bead workshop & earliest art. Normal flake scrapers: $20 - $50.

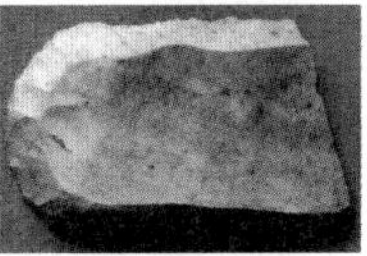

44) 3 3/8" Aurignacian retouched blade / point. Dordogne. $300 - $500. **DESCRIPTION:** The invention of a technique for knapping many standardized blades from prismatic cores in -creased the number of serviceable tool blanks al-most tenfold, giving the masters of the new technology a lethal advantage over Neanderthals, even though Neanderthals appeared to have invented the superficially similar Chatelperronian technique nearly contemporaneously.

GRAVETTE POINTS - ca. 25,000 B.P.

45) a) 3 1/8" Gravette point. Laugerie Haute, Dordogne, France. $800 - $1,500. **NOTE:** Famous & now protected site.
b) 4 5/8" Gravette point. Ancient tip fracture. Corbiac, Dordogne, France. $1,500 and up. **NOTE:** One of the largest known + famous now protected site. **DESCRIPTION:** Backed with a steep retouch along the whole of 1 edge. These upper paleolithic points are far rarer than earlier Mousterian points.

SOLUTREAN SHOULDERED & LAUREL LEAF POINTS - ca. 21,000 B.P.

46) a) 2 1/8" unifacial shouldered point. Parallel pressure flaking. Charente, France. $900 - $1,500. **NOTE:** Broken base, but unbelievably rare.
b) 3 3/4" laurel leaf point. Dordogne, France. Small example of an extremely rare type. $500 - $800.
c) 2 1/2" laurel leaf point. Laugerie Haute, Dordogne. **NOTE:** Famous site, fine but small. $800 - $1,200.
d) 2 9/16" blunted bifacial shouldered point. Placard, Charente, France. **NOTE:** Creamy patina. At least as rare as a Folsom. $900 - $1,500.

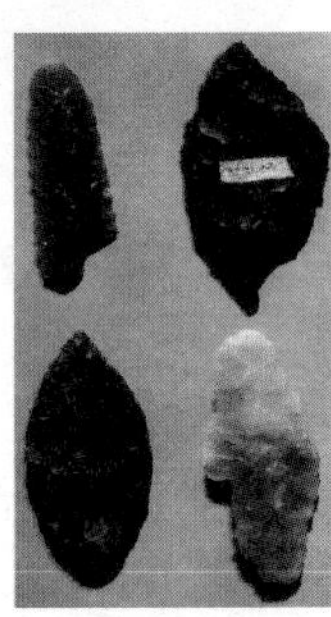

MAGDALENIAN TOOLS - ca. 17,000 - 10,500 B.P.

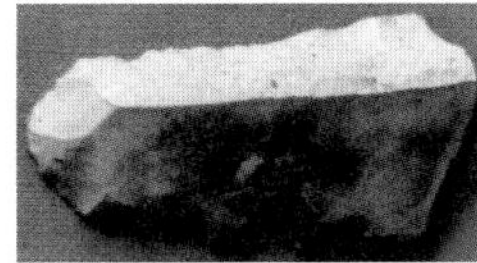

47) 2 1/4" Upper Paleolithic end-scraper. Dordogne, France. $30 - $90.

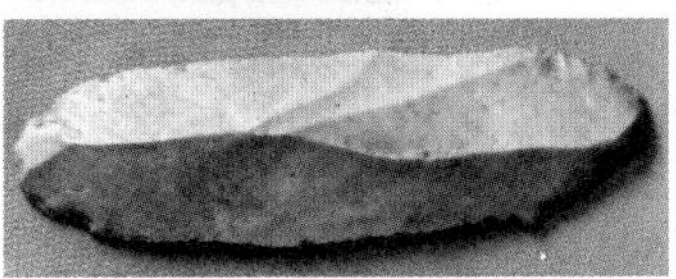

48) 3 1/2" double end-scraper. Magdalenian. Laugerie Basse, Dordogne, France. $350 - $550. **NOTE:** Famous, now protected site.

49) 3" burin (graver). Magdalenian. Dordogne. $100 - $250. **NOTE:** Small ones: 1/4 - 1/2 price. **DESCRIPTION:** There are dozens of burin types, most of which involve truncating a blade and striking one corner of the truncation to remove 1 or more long thin spalls from a length-wise edge, creating a chisel edge where the facets and truncation meet. These tools exist from the end of the Acheulean, but only became common in the Upper Paleolithic. They were used for incising antler, ivory or bone to extract strips for making atlatl points and other tools, as well as for sculpting and engraving images and, finally, for leather-working.

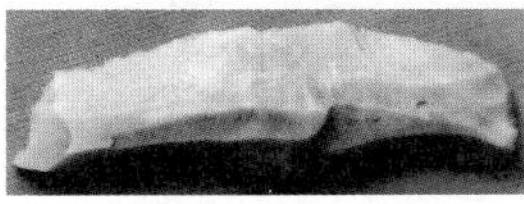

50) 3 backed bladelets. Largest is 1 3/8" long. Magdalenian. Dordogne, France. $60 - $200. **NOTE:** Almost impossible to find. Must be sieved. **DESCRIPTION:** Bladelets backed with steep pressure-flaked retouching up the whole of 1 side were socketed into grooved shafts, to make a wide variety of composite tools which used the same standardized parts. Individual worn blades could be easily popped out and replaced on such tools, leading to a new leap in efficiency. Furthermore, the bladelets were light and easily packed, giving their owners the ability to range much farther from flint sources. The consequence may have been the extinction of many meat-packing animals. Only the bladelets survive.

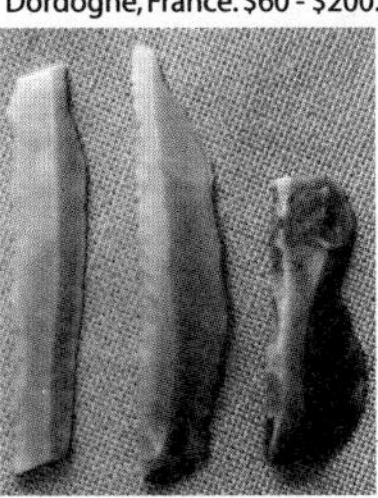

MAGDALENIAN & NEOLITHIC HARPOONS:

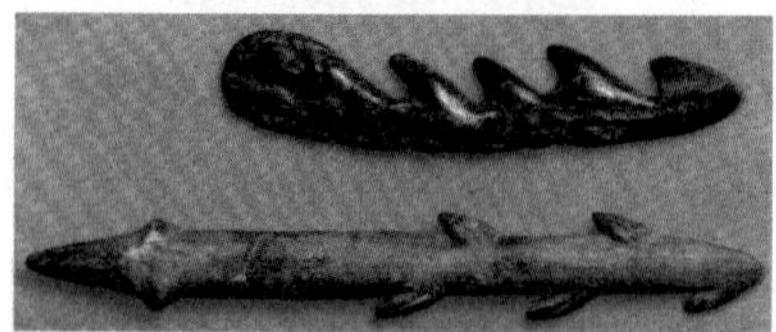

51) a) 4" Neolithic antler harpoon. Single rung of barbs. Submerged lake site, N. Italy. $7,000 - $8,000.
b) 5 5/8" Magdalenian harpoon. Double rungs of engraved barbs. Dordogne, France. $12,000 - $20,000. **NOTE:** Reglued shaft & restored barb tips & base. But one of the best known.
DESCRIPTION: Magdalenian harpoons may have a single or double row of barbs and are often engraved on the barbs or shaft. A few have a hole near the base.
WARNING: It is essential that all bone and antler artifacts be examined microscopically by an academic specialist for signs of forgery. Many forgeries are made using prehistoric materials recovered from caves, peat bogs or lake sites, so neither patination nor carbon dates are sufficient criteria in themselves. The rarity of authentic W. European specimens can not be overstated and is in no way comparable to widely available pre-contact Inuit harpoons preserved in perma-frost.

NEOLITHIC - ca. 8,000 - 5,000 B.P.
EUROPEAN & ASIAN NEOLITHIC PROJECTILE POINTS:

NOTE: Though smaller for the most part, Western European arrowheads are of surpassing rarity by comparison to most American types, being comparable in rarity to scarce Calf Creeks..

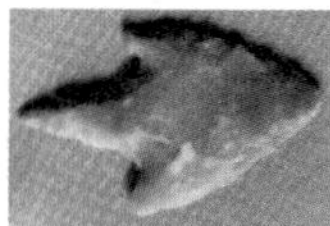

52) 1 11/16" barbed arrowhead with tapering stem. Indre et Loire, France. $180 - $400.

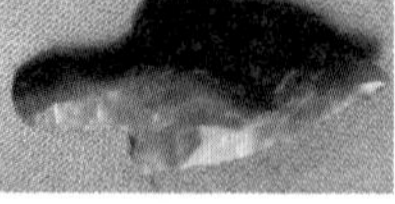

53) 1 1/2" tongue-stemmed arrowhead. Long parallel sided stem and weak barbs. Grand Pressigny, France. $150 - $400.

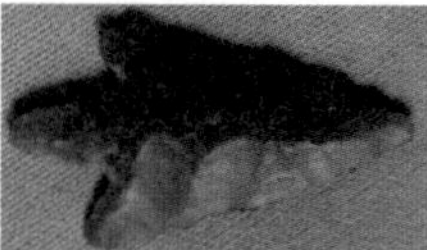

54) 1 1/4" barbed & tanged gem-point. Grand Pressigny, France. $200 - $450.

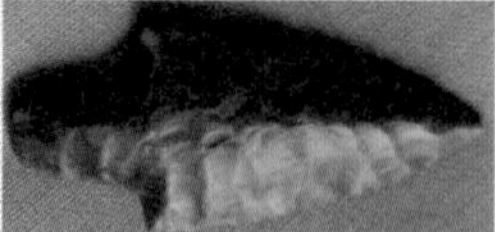

55) 1 7/8" tongue-stemmed arrowhead with slight barbs. Submerged lake site. Lake Chalain, Jura, France. $600 - $900 . **NOTE**: Glossy aquatic patina.

56) 1 1/4" transverse bleeding point. Grand Pressigny, France. $300 - $450. **NOTE:** No equivalent exists in the Americas. Poor specimens $30 - $90. **DESCRIPTION:** Usually a short blade segment truncated at each end and retouched along the truncations to leave a wide razor edge for severing vessels, and a narrower base for hafting. Intact arrows have been found in anaeorbic lake-sites and the Sahara.

57) 1 5/8" long-tanged arrowhead. Calabria, Italy. $250 - $450.

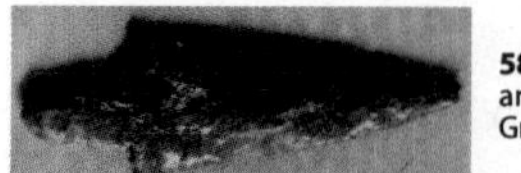

58) 2 7/8" heavy-duty arrowhead. Milos, Greece. $350 - $550.

59) 3 1/8" serrated arrowhead. Southern Sweden. $1,000 - $1,600. **NOTE:** Exceedingly rare.

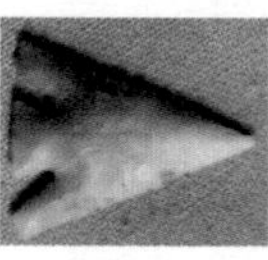

60) 15/16" Dolmenic short barbed gem-point. Brittany, France. $1,500 - $2,000. **NOTE:** Surpassingly rare - 19th C. finds in megalithic graves.

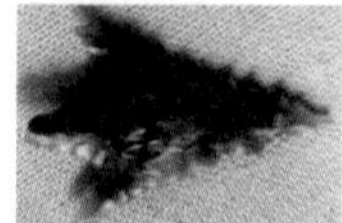

61) 1" serrated arrowhead with fine barbs & tang. India. $200 - $400.

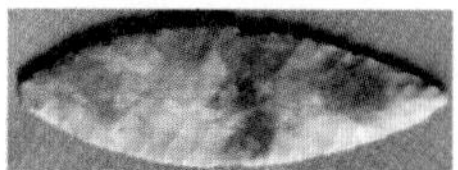

62) 2 3/8" bifacial leaf arrowhead. Afghanistan. Neolithic. $150 - $400. **NOTE:** Parallel oblique flaking. Other side has a creamier patina.

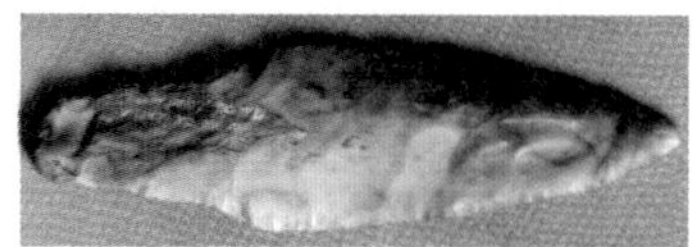

63) 4" spear-point. Denmark. $500 - $750.

64) 5 1/4" spear-point. Denmark. $800 - $1,100. **NOTE:** Parallel oblique flaking.

EUROPEAN FLINT DAGGERS, SICKLES & CHISELS:

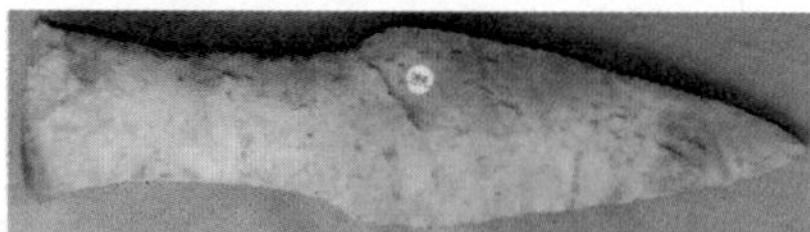

65) 7 7/8" flint dagger based on bronze or copper import. Denmark. $4,000 - $7,000. **NOTE:** "Stitching" along the handle's edges.

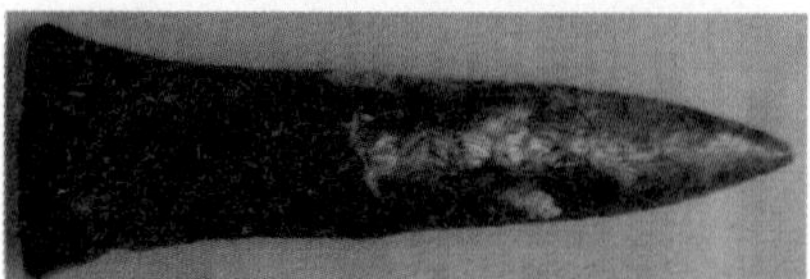

66) 7 1/2" dagger. Denmark. $7,000 - $9,000. **NOTE:** Glossy with "stitching" up sides & centers of the handle. **WARNING:** Increasingly sophisticated fake daggers are being made, making it unwise to buy them at auction unless they have a rich peaty patina. Otherwise, they should be purchased with an unlimited guarantee of authenticity and should be subject to microscopic wear analysis at 400X by an academic specialist.

67) a) 7 1/2" saw-tooth sickle blade. S. Sweden. Beware of large fakes! $1,200 - $2,000 . **NOTE:** Teeth glossy from cutting through cereal stems containing silica particles. Golden peat patina.

b) 5 7/8" polished chisel. S. Sweden. $850 - $1,300. **NOTE:** Amber patina characteristic of peaty soil.

c) 7 1/2" dagger. S. Sweden. $1,500 - $2,800. **NOTE:** Fine blade but no stitching. Shorter daggers as low as $400.

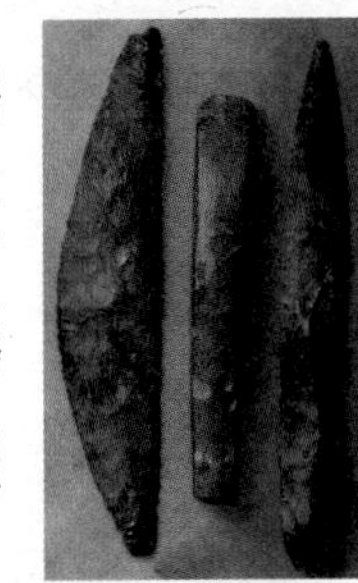

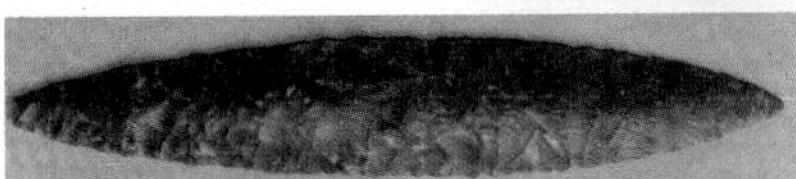

68) 5 3/4" bi-pointed & bifacial dagger. Parallel flaking. Grand Pressigny, France. $5,000 - $8,000. **NOTE:** 1 tip fracture. **DESCRIPTION:** About 370 complete Grand Pressigny daggers, including reglued ones, are known. They may be up to a foot long and are usually made from long thin flakes struck by a leverage system from Neo-Levallois "Pound-of-butter" cores. As most are unifacial, this bifacial example is even rarer. Beware of forgeries.

EUROPEAN NEOLITHIC & COPPER AGE STONE AX TYPES: 8,000 - 4,500 B.P.

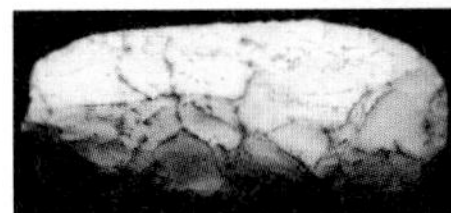

69) 5 1/2" knapped celt. Normandy. ca. 7,000 B.P. $200 - $400. **NOTE:** Dark grey flint turned white.

70) 15 1/4" knapped celt. Dark chocolate flint turned moka. Jablines, Seine et Marne, France. $9,000 - $13,000. **WARNING:** Although Jablines artifacts, which have a deep whitish patina on one side, are rarely faked, counterfeit celts of similar size in accessible Grand Pressigny butterscotch-colored flint are common. They are often soaked in rusty water to give them a deceptive reddish "patina".

71) 3 1/2" polished celt. Green hardstone. Incrustations on other side. Southern France. $350 - $650. **NOTE:** Rare material. Originally inserted into an antler socket.

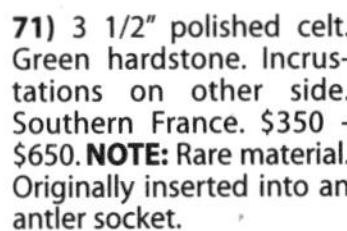

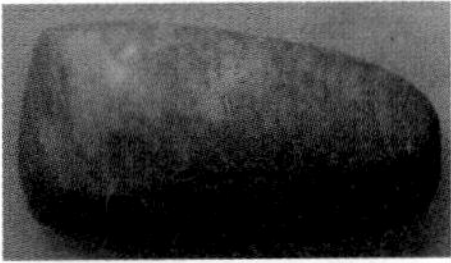

72) 5 3/4" polished celt. Dark flint turned rosy. Aube, France. $600 - $900. **NOTE:** A superior example for a region full of active collectors.

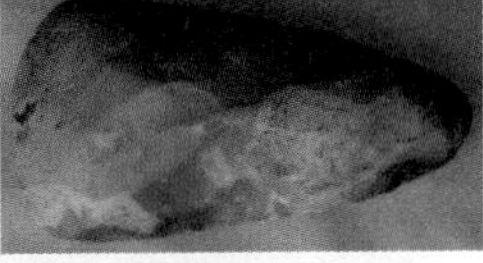

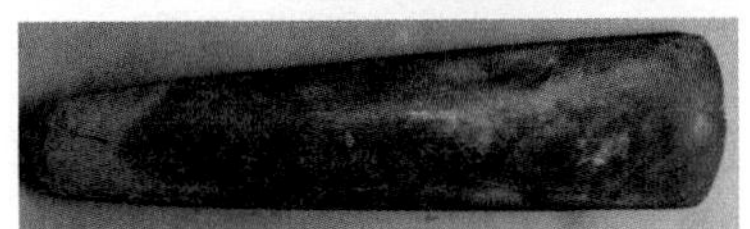

73) 10 1/2" polished Dolmenic celt. Patinated chocolaty flint. Vaucluse, France. $9,000 - $13,000. **NOTES:** 19th C. find in a megalithic dolmen. One of the finest prestige axes.

74) 8" jadeite celt. Dordogne. Traded into the area from Brittany. $7,000 - $9,000. **NOTES:** 19th C. find in a dolmen. Nonexistant in field collections. **WARNING:** Beware of ethnographic celts and machined fakes parading as European Neolithic examples. Consult an expert.

75) 8 1/8" Dolmenic canoe-shaped ceremonial ax. Metahornblendite. Incrustations. Cylindrical reed or bone drilling. Vexin, France. Import from Brittany. $15,000 - $20,000. **DESCRIPTION:** This French type should NOT be confused with the more robust and common battle-axes of Northern Europe. Under 30 complete examples of the former are known from documented sites.

76) 9 1/4" unpolished, square-sided celt. Grey flint turned beige to brown by peat patina. Denmark. $2,000 - $3,200. **NOTE:** Unusually big with slightly flared bit.

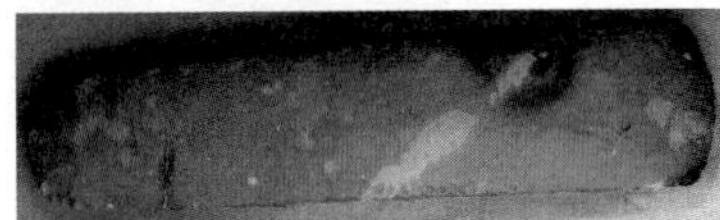

77) 14 1/8" polished square-sided celt. Orange & yellow peat patina. S. Sweden. $9,000 - $14,000. **NOTE:** One of the biggest and most colorful. If only 3" to 4": $200 - $400.

78) 7" boat ax. Hard speckled grey-green stone. Rare type. S. Sweden. $6,000 - $9,000. **NOTE:** Large & finely sculpted. Lesser examples begin at $1,500.

79) 7" knobbed boat ax. Biconical drilling through basalt. S. Sweden. $9,000 - $13,000. **NOTE:** One of the finest.

OTHER EUROPEAN NEOLITHIC TOOLS:

80) 5 5/8" pick. Square cross-section. Yvelines, France. $180 - $250.

81) 7 3/4" pick. Lense cross-section. From the famous flint extraction site at Spiennes, Belgium. $800 - $1,000. **NOTE:** One of the finest.

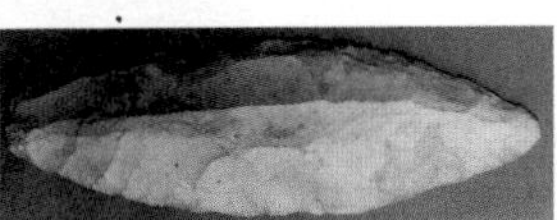

82) 4 3/4" polished tranchet chisel. Foret d'Othe, France. $200 - $400. **NOTE:** Rare polished example. Unpolished ones start at $30.

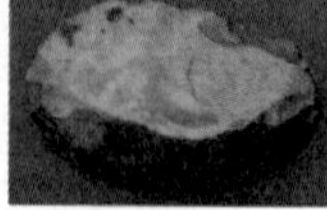

83) 3 3/8" steep carinated scraper. Senonais, Yonne, France. $30 - $80. **NOTE:** Common from the Mousterian on.

84) 2 double end-notch harvesting knives. Aube, France. Neolithic. $140 - $250. **NOTE:** Tool unique to Europe. **DESCRIPTION:** A unifacial or rarely bifacial tool with notches at both ends and a pressure flaked cutting edge along one or both sides. Specimens have been found in anaerobic lake sites with rope looped around the notches to provide a grip. The cutting edges often show cereal gloss. Extremely rare.

EUROPEAN NEOLITHIC BONE & ANTLER TOOLS: NOTE: Bone and antler tools, being organic and perishable are of great rarity. 8,000 - 5,000 B.P.

85) (left to right)
a) 5 1/2" polished bone gouge. Dredged from the Seine in Paris in the 19th Century. $1,800 - $3,000.
b) 6 5/8" bone gouge. Dolmenic find, Alencon, France in 1894. $1,500 - $2,500.
c) 5" antler ax-hoe. Rugen, Germany. $1,000 - $1,700.

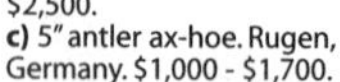

86) a) 6 1/2" polished celt-like blade in forked antler handle. Characteristic glossy tan lake patina. Lake Neufchatel, France. **WARNING:** Untreated bone & antler from lakes crack and warp.
b) 5" polished celt-like blade in original antler grip. Alpine lakesite. $1,800 - $3,500. **NOTE:** Without the grips, the blades might have been identified as talismans.

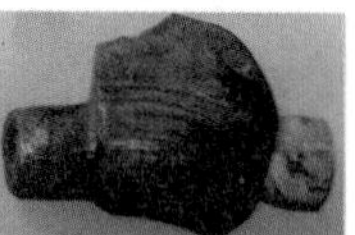

87) 4 1/4" Antler ax buffer - Lake Chalain, Jura, France / rare 2 1/4" fibrolite axlet - Clermont Ferrand, France. $3,200 - $5,500.

NORTH AFRICAN NEOLITHIC TOOLS: 9,000 - 5,000 B.P.

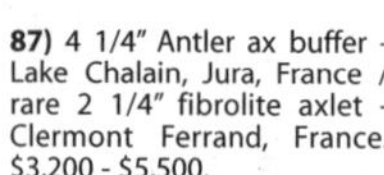

88) 3" serrated sickle blade. Flint. Wind gloss & reddish brown patina. Fayoum, Egypt. $280 - $550.

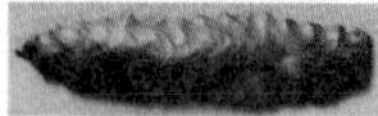

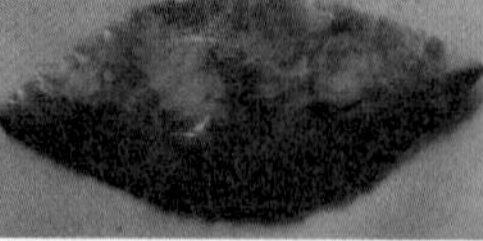

89) 4 5/8" bifacial leaf knife. Wind gloss. Egypt. $600 - $900. **NOTE:** Predynastic artifacts are highly sought after.

90) 4" bifacial leaf knife. Wind gloss. Kem Kem, Morocco. $350 - $600.

SAHARAN NEOLITHIC CELTS - 9,000 - 5,000 B.P.:

91) 5" polished celt. Red, blue & cream flint. Tawny patina on one side. Mali. $150 - $300. **NOTE:** These beautiful celts are fairly common because soil deflation strands artifacts on bedrock.

92) 4 3/4" thin tabular celt. Green siltstone. Brown patina on one side. Kem Kem, Morocco. $150 - $250. **NOTE:** Exceptional overall polish. **DESCRIPTION:** The crudest Saharan celts and chisels are slabs polished at one end. They begin at $20 - $40. Finer celts, chisels and gouges are usually pecked, cylindrical, and polished only at the bit. Well-formed ones over 6 inches are extremely rare. **WARNING:** Beware of specimens with reground bits, plus outright fakes.

93) 5" pecked & polished celt. Rare flaring bit. Hard green stone. Kem Kem, Morocco. $250 - $450.

94) 7" cylindrical pecked & polished celt. Encrusted hardstone. Western Sahara, Morocco. $350 - $550. **NOTE:** Large. Dark wind patina where the celt was exposed.

SAHARAN ARROWHEAD TYPES: NOTE: Here is a random sampling of the 100s of Saharan types. 11,000 - 5,000 B.P.

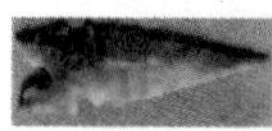

95) 1 1/4" flint arrowhead. Former Spanish Sahara, Morocco. Mesolithic to Neolithic. $50 - $90. **NOTE:** Small or cruder ones begin at $5 - $10.

96) 1 1/8" "Eiffel Tower" gem-point. Rock crystal. Central Sahara, Algeria. Capsian Mesolithic to Early Neolithic culture. $40 - $70. **NOTE:** Translucent.

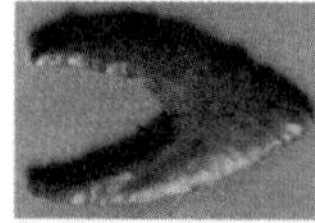

97) 1 9/16" Fayoum arrowhead. Fayoum, Egypt. $500 - $1,000. **NOTE:** Rare & unbroken!

WESTERN EUROPEAN BRONZE AGE AXES - ca. 4,500 - 2,800 B.P.:

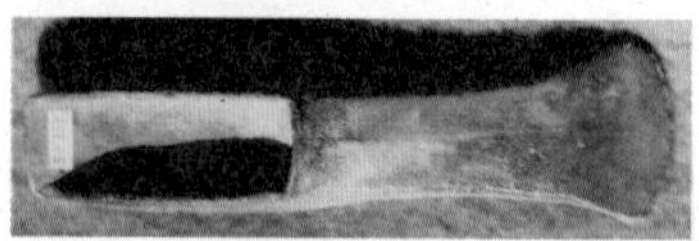

98) 6 1/8" palstave. Mid-Bronze Age, France. $1,200 - $2,000.

99) 4 3/4" decorated bronze ax. Hollow poll & attachment ring. Brittany, Late Bronze Age. $4,000 - $8,000. **NOTE:** Undecorated axes of this format without flared bits were deposited in circular caches with the bits pointing inwards. Being relatively common they range from $590 - $990.

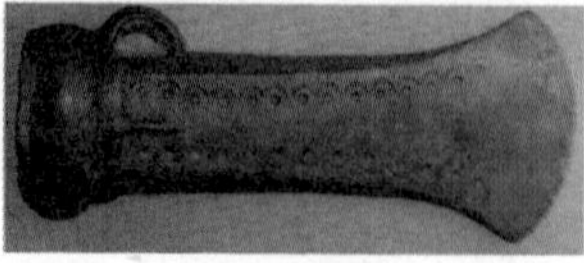

THE LONG JOURNEYS OF SILENT WARRIORS:
THE COREE INDIANS AND THEIR ARROW POINTS

BY J. C. VAUGHN

"The fate of the Chicora Nation is a strange blank place in our history. The Coree lacuna is an abscess that no one wants opened, since we have forgotten its origin and have become accustomed to the pain."

- Al Pate, from his Prologue to **The Coree Are Not Extinct**

They are an ancient, uninterrupted bond with a past that goes back so far as to predate even ancient Rome, Jerusalem and Baghdad, yet they are also a tie to those first Americans who greeted the English explorers who founded the Roanoke Colony in 1585. They are connected to the present as well by age-old methods preserved by generation after generation.

The arrowheads of the Coree Indians of North Carolina tell an amazing, intricate story to those who are willing to listen to the whispered voice of history.

To understand a culture - any culture - one must first understand the time and place in which they live or lived. The Coree, who were related to the Iroquoi people, populated portions of a region now known as North Carolina. Indeed, their descendants may be found in many areas of that state today. According to the Historian of Clay County, North Carolina, the Coree were, along with the Cherokee and others, one of the major Iroquoi-language tribes in the region when early settlers and explorers arrived from England.

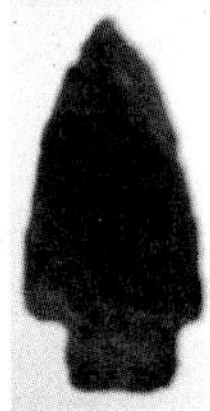

"At the time of the first European contacts, North Carolina was inhabited by a number of native tribes sharing some cultural traits but also distinguished by regional and linguistic variations. Three major language families were represented in North Carolina: Iroquoian, Siouan, and Algonquian. The Iroquoian tribes - the Cherokee, Tuscarora, Meherrin, Coree, and Neuse River (may have been Iroquoian or Algonquian) - were related linguistically and culturally to the Iroquois tribes to the north." [1]

The Coree may very well have been the first to greet the English settlers at the ill-fated Roanoke Colony.

Chief J.L. "Turtle" Faircloth, Sr., chief of the remaining associated members of the Coree Tribe, is among those who have theorized that Roanoke might very well be known today as Cedar Island, located south of the Hatteras Inlet.

In the early period of English exploration, the Indians and explorers intermingled, Chief Turtle points out, because later expeditions were surprised to find blue-eyed Coree who spoke broken English.

According to regional histories, things between the settlers and the Indians went well at first. Then, in 1711, the Tuscarora war broke out. It left many dead on both sides, Chief

SPEARS, ARROWHEADS, DRILL POINTS & KNIVES

Chief J.L. "Turtle" Faircloth's Personal Account

Points having a shank of three-eighths inch width were for regular arrows even if they were two or four inches long, but points having a shank width of half an inch being two inches long were used for spears. There is no doubt about it. Arrows are not any larger at the largest end than three-eighths inch. So we can safely say without argument that points two inches long, in general, were the largest arrow points. All other points longer were either for spears or drill points.

I have drill points from two inches long to four inches long. It all depends on the width of the point and how the shank is made. A drill point is not made like an arrow or spear point.

Some points that look like arrow points, being two to four inches long, are knife points. Knife points are very sharp along the edges, some being an inch or so wide, and always having a flat shank, making it easy to put a knife handle on.

I have used larger arrow points on

Turtle said, and for the most this permanently scattered the Coree Tribe.

Why then are there still Coree today?

They were a strong, adaptable people. They were not fearful of intermingling with the white man. They were characterized by their ability to interact with others, both white and Indian, and they were known for their ability to fight.

As writer Al Pate put it in his familial-historical investigation, **The Coree Are Not Extinct**, "In fact, the Tuscaroras found the coastal Coree resistance so formidable, they willingly entered into a treaty and alliance with the colonial government to restrict their territorial claims to the area between the Pamlico River and the Neuse River."

Tellingly he added, "That is, after the English-authorized colonists had claimed all the territory northeast of the mouth of the Pamlico, as indicated in Colonial Records of North Carolina 1713-1728, Vol. 2, p. 140."[2]

Through assimilating into other tribes, being taken as slaves or living in small groups, the Coree bloodlines survived through good times and bad. Now the tribe and its descendants are actively seeking Federal approval as an official recognized tribe.

Part of the process of seeking recognition, of course, is to lay claim to their own history. This history, like other Native American chronicles, is rich with characters, actions and relics. While much is left to document and some elements are lost to the murky mists of time, the Coree Tribe has left a definite record in the form of its relics. Highly documented among these relics are their arrowheads.

"The Coree Indians living here in Carteret County, North Carolina found themselves lacking for material from which to fashion good points for their weapons," wrote Chief "Turtle" in his 1995 book, Silent Warriors – The Coree Indians. "All they had was bone, a few shells, and once and a while a piece of coral. So they walked all the way to the mountains of North Carolina, Virginia and sometimes to Ohio just to gather raw materials such as flint, quartz, obsidian, jasper and agates."[3]

This was no casual journey. The materials that the Coree sought were meant to make arrowheads to hunt game with, and if necessary to hunt other tribes

"All they had was bone, a few shells, and once and a while a piece of coral. So they walked all the way to the mountains of North Carolina, Virginia and sometimes to Ohio just to gather raw materials such as flint, quartz, obsidian, jasper and agates."

with (and later, of course, the white man). In their way of living, points meant life.

Chief Turtle takes up the story again: "These raw materials were broken into chips where they were found. Chips, also known as 'Blanks,' were usually one inch to eight inches long. About ninety-five percent of the blank chips were small, no longer than four inches. The blanks were carried back to the Coree towns in animal skin bags. Some bags could hold as many as a thousand stone blanks."

Additionally, those who went in search of the materials would often bring entire large pieces of fine quartz back whole. "The old men of the towns were the point makers," the Chief continued. "They used a piece of deer antler to chip off unwanted pieces of rock, being careful to save every piece of the chips for other projects."

Then, when the points were finished, they were three-quarter inch to eight inches in length. A few half-inch points have been found, and some even smaller. Points less than three-quarter inches long to two inches long were generally used for arrow points, for hunting large game and man.

"I know most experts say that arrow points were up to four inches long, but it isn't the case with Coree points," he said. "Stones were scarce here and we had to make the points [we had] do the best job possible."

By the enormous store of history they left us and through the efforts of historians like Chief Turtle, we have already learned much about the Coree Tribe that was previously thought lost. Their legacy at one time looked to be, like so many others, lost following the arrival of the white man. Now, perhaps, that may no longer be true.

Strangely enough, it is a new technology that may offer the best chance for developing, distributing and evaluating what remains of Coree antiquity. Sites on the World Wide Web feature personal histories and offer a means of wide distribution without the problematic process of getting a publisher for one's work. In other words, it's an end-run around the selective historians who have previously placed little importance on understanding the Coree, their place in history, or their future.

Time, though, is not a friend. There is a sense of urgency in documenting the Coree Tribe before too many more memories are forgotten and their voices are lost forever.

reeds and round dowels to make hunting arrows that will bring down a bear or a man using a thirty-five pound draw bow. I have restored spears that have points an inch wide and two inches long up to two and one half inches wide and very long points.

I have knives that I have restored with two inch blades and they work very well...Many of the archeological experts say that arrows were not used by the North American Indians earlier than one thousand years ago. It is not so. I have points and many other weapons, bones and parts of an eight foot long Coree Indian in the museum at Chapel Hill, North Carolina, that have been confirmed and dated to 2500 B.C. Arrows were used by the Coree Indians for at least forty-five hundred years. The points I found in a grave were in such fine condition that they looked like they had just been chipped.

- From **Silent Warriors – The Coree Indians**, ©1999 J.L. Faircloth, Sr.

Chief J.L. "Turtle" Faircloth, Sr. is chief of the remaining associated members of the Coree Tribe. For information about his book, ***Silent Warriors – The Coree Indians****, write to Coree Indian Tribe, Inc., 137 Neal Drive, Atlantic, North Carolina 28511.*

"I know most experts say that arrow points were up to four inches long, but it isn't the case with Coree points. Stones were scarce here and we had to make the points [we had] do the best job possible."

Historians are hungry for information, confirmation and insights both historical and contemporary, but the time for this documentation is now.

"...but I still have curiosity that is not satisfied about the Coree Nation. Please share copies of this material with anyone who is interested. Maybe they can contribute to the growing appreciation of the Native American's role in our nation's development.

"The Faircloths are an old Coharie (Coree) Indian family, well represented in Wayne and Sampson Counties, North Carolina. Details regarding the Indian Faircloths of Sampson County, are in Sketch of the CLASSIFIED INDIANS of Sampson County North Carolina, by Enoch Emanuel. The Pates are not among the families listed, but the Ammonses are. If you can contribute anything to expansion of material relating to the Indians of eastern Virginia, North Carolina and South Carolina, with reference to explicit family relationships, please share it with me." [1]

Sources

1 **The Historian of Clay County** North Carolina website, text published on the World Wide Web at www.main.nc.us/clay/history.html.

2 **The Coree Are Not Extinct**, ©1999 Al Pate, published on the World Wide Web at www.dickshovel.com/cgi-bin/FormMail.pl.

3 **Silent Warriors – The Coree Indians**, ©1999 Chief J.L. "Turtle" Faircloth, Sr.

*J.C. Vaughn is the Executive Editor of Gemstone Publishing where he has contributed to **The Overstreet Comic Book Price Guide, Hake's Price Guide To Character Toys** and other publications. In addition to writing about the history of collectibles, he has authored numerous articles, short stories and screenplays.*

ELEMENTS OF COREE LIFE

AXES were made from stones gathered in the hilly and mountainous areas of western North Carolina. Quartz was the most favored stone.

SHELL WEAPONS: Some arrowheads and spear points were made from seashells when it was difficult to obtain the proper stones to cut.

POTTERY AND DISHES: Large scallop shells were used as bowls. They also made pots from the blue clay found in the region.

JEWELRY: Shells were not only used to make weapons. They were made into necklaces. Pearls were also used, as were small scraps of copper, gold and other materials found by those who traveled to collect materials for points.

FOOD: The Coree have farmed Carteret County for thousands of years. Among their documented animals and crops are hogs, goats, chickens, turkeys, squash, corn and cucumbers. They were also expert fishermen.

HOUSES were built, some up to 20' x 30', with pointed roofs. They were up on poles, off the ground.

RELATIONS WITH OTHER TRIBES: The Coree always fought on the side of their nearest cousins, the Machapurga. They fought on the side of the Tuscarora against the English.

CEREMONIAL SMOKING: They smoked tobacco and grapevine leaves on a regular basis. Smoking was an important part of their lives and was often done with ceremonial pipes. Sometimes smoking included willow leaves and marijuana.

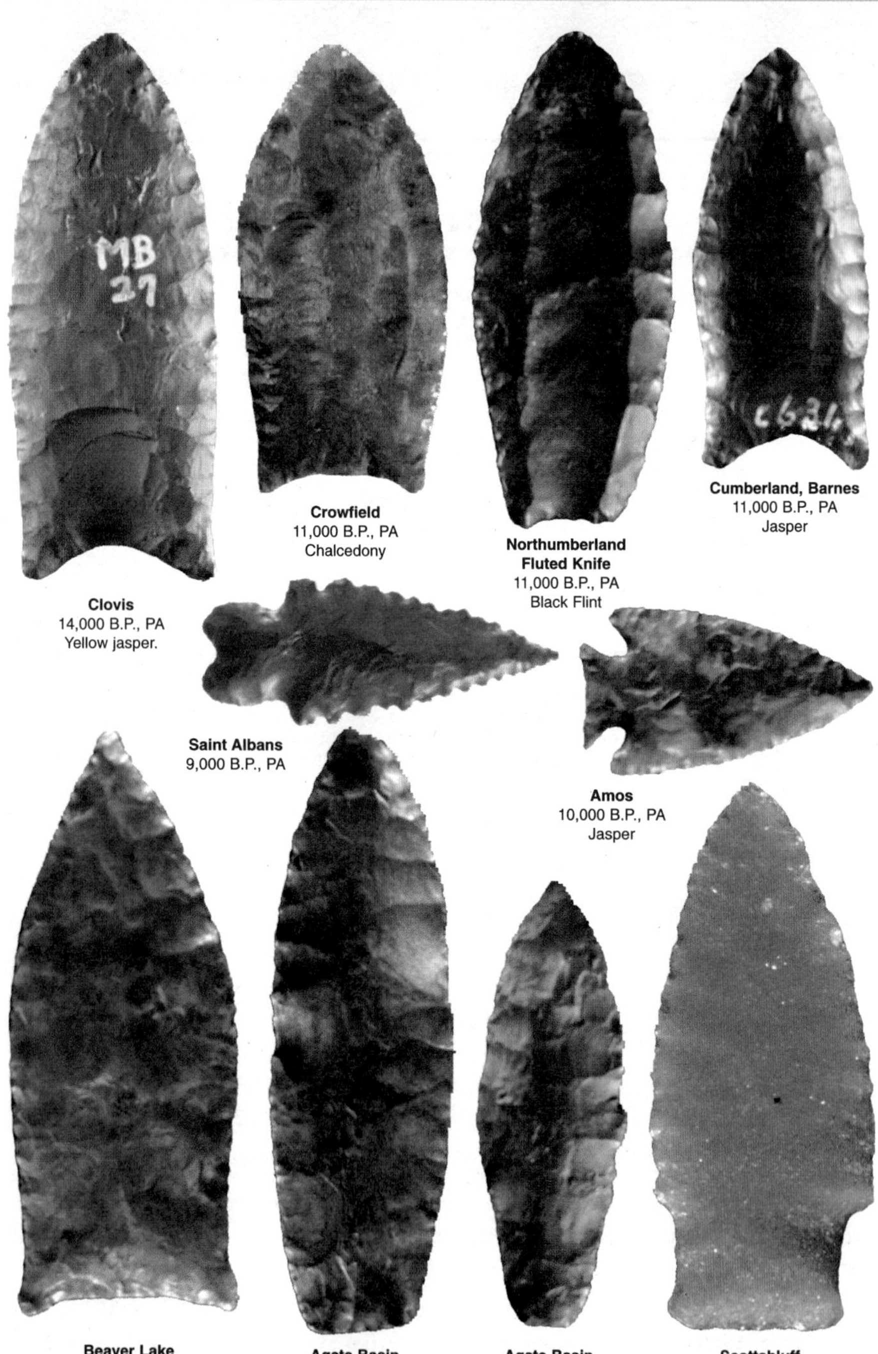

Clovis
14,000 B.P., PA
Yellow jasper.

Crowfield
11,000 B.P., PA
Chalcedony

Northumberland Fluted Knife
11,000 B.P., PA
Black Flint

Cumberland, Barnes
11,000 B.P., PA
Jasper

Saint Albans
9,000 B.P., PA

Amos
10,000 B.P., PA
Jasper

Beaver Lake
11,000 B.P., PA
Onondaga chert

Agate Basin
10,500 B.P., PA
Onondaga Chert

Agate Basin
10,500 B.P., PA
Jasper

Scottsbluff
9,500 B.P., PA
Quartzite

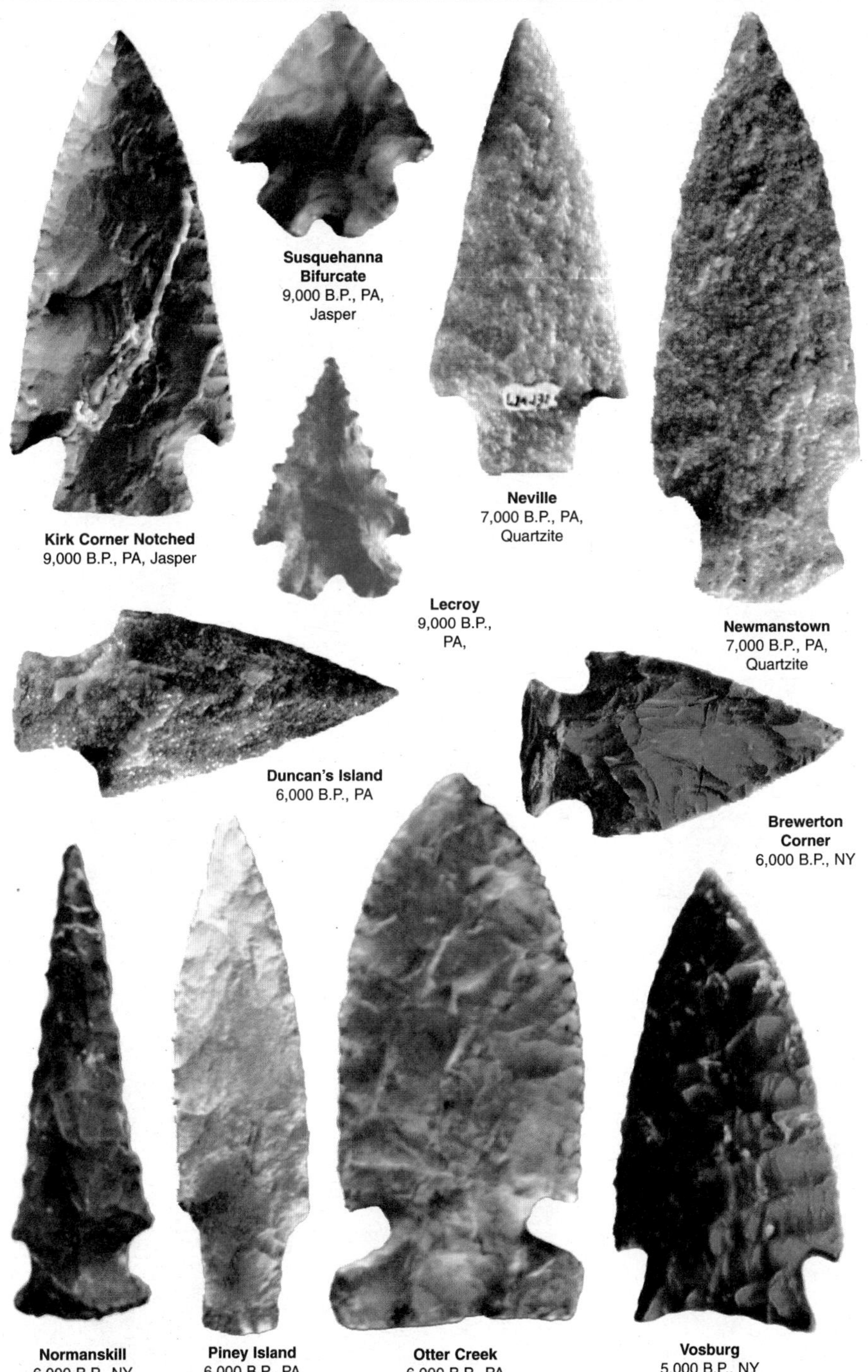

Kirk Corner Notched
9,000 B.P., PA, Jasper

Susquehanna Bifurcate
9,000 B.P., PA, Jasper

Lecroy
9,000 B.P., PA,

Neville
7,000 B.P., PA, Quartzite

Newmanstown
7,000 B.P., PA, Quartzite

Duncan's Island
6,000 B.P., PA

Brewerton Corner
6,000 B.P., NY

Normanskill
6,000 B.P., NY

Piney Island
6,000 B.P., PA

Otter Creek
6,000 B.P., PA

Vosburg
5,000 B.P., NY

Eshbach
5,500 B.P., PA, Vein quartz

Lamoka
5,000 B.P., NY

Schuylkill
4,000 B.P., PA,

Orient
4,000 B.P., PA,
Jasper

Poplar Island
5,000 B.P., PA,
Argillite

Virginsville
5,000 B.P., PA

Bare Island
4,500 B.P., PA, Quartzite

Koens Crispin
4,000 B.P., PA

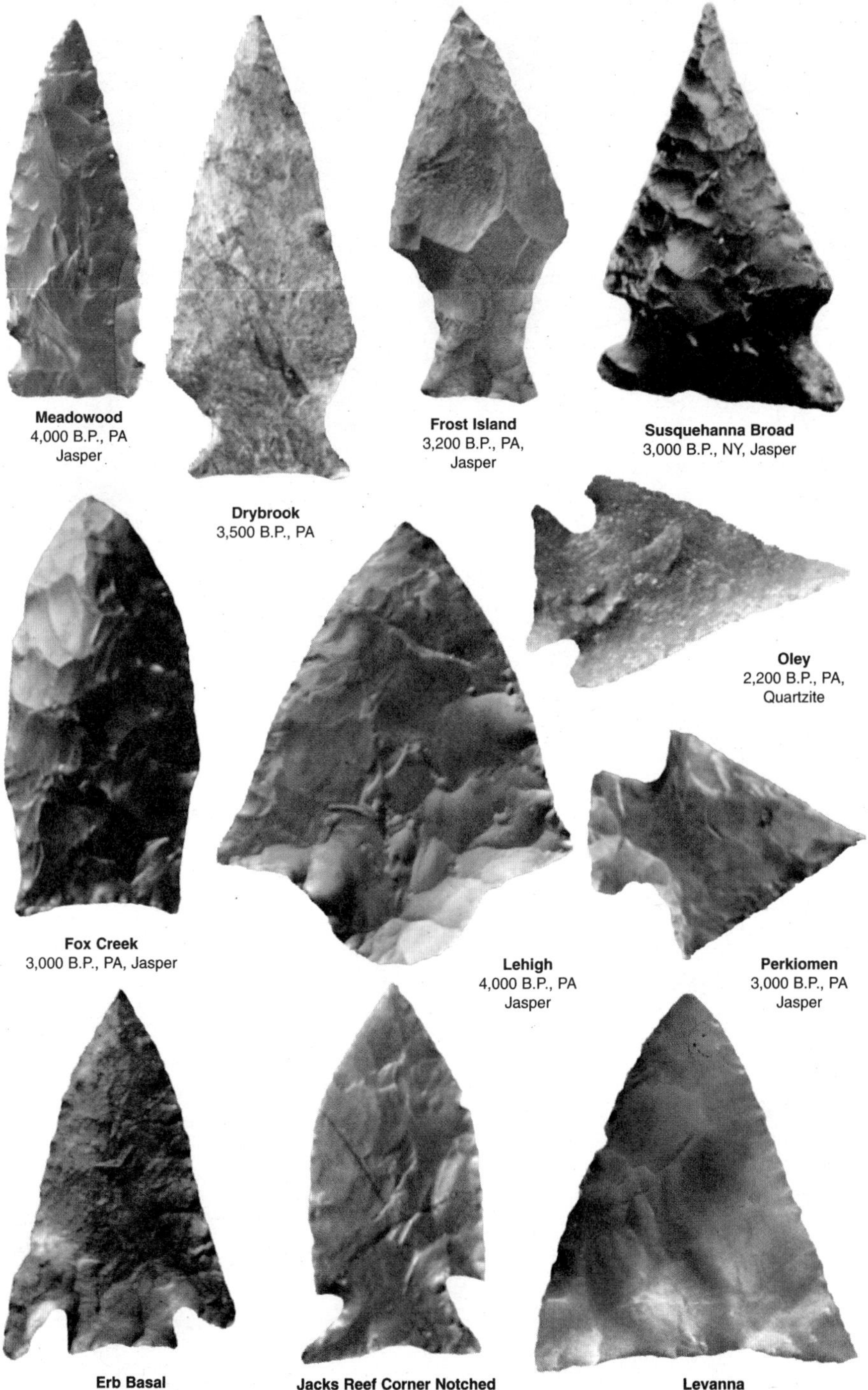

Meadowood
4,000 B.P., PA
Jasper

Drybrook
3,500 B.P., PA

Frost Island
3,200 B.P., PA,
Jasper

Susquehanna Broad
3,000 B.P., NY, Jasper

Oley
2,200 B.P., PA,
Quartzite

Fox Creek
3,000 B.P., PA, Jasper

Lehigh
4,000 B.P., PA
Jasper

Perkiomen
3,000 B.P., PA
Jasper

Erb Basal
2,000 B.P., PA

Jacks Reef Corner Notched
1,500 B.P., PA, Jasper

Levanna
1,300 B.P., PA, Jasper

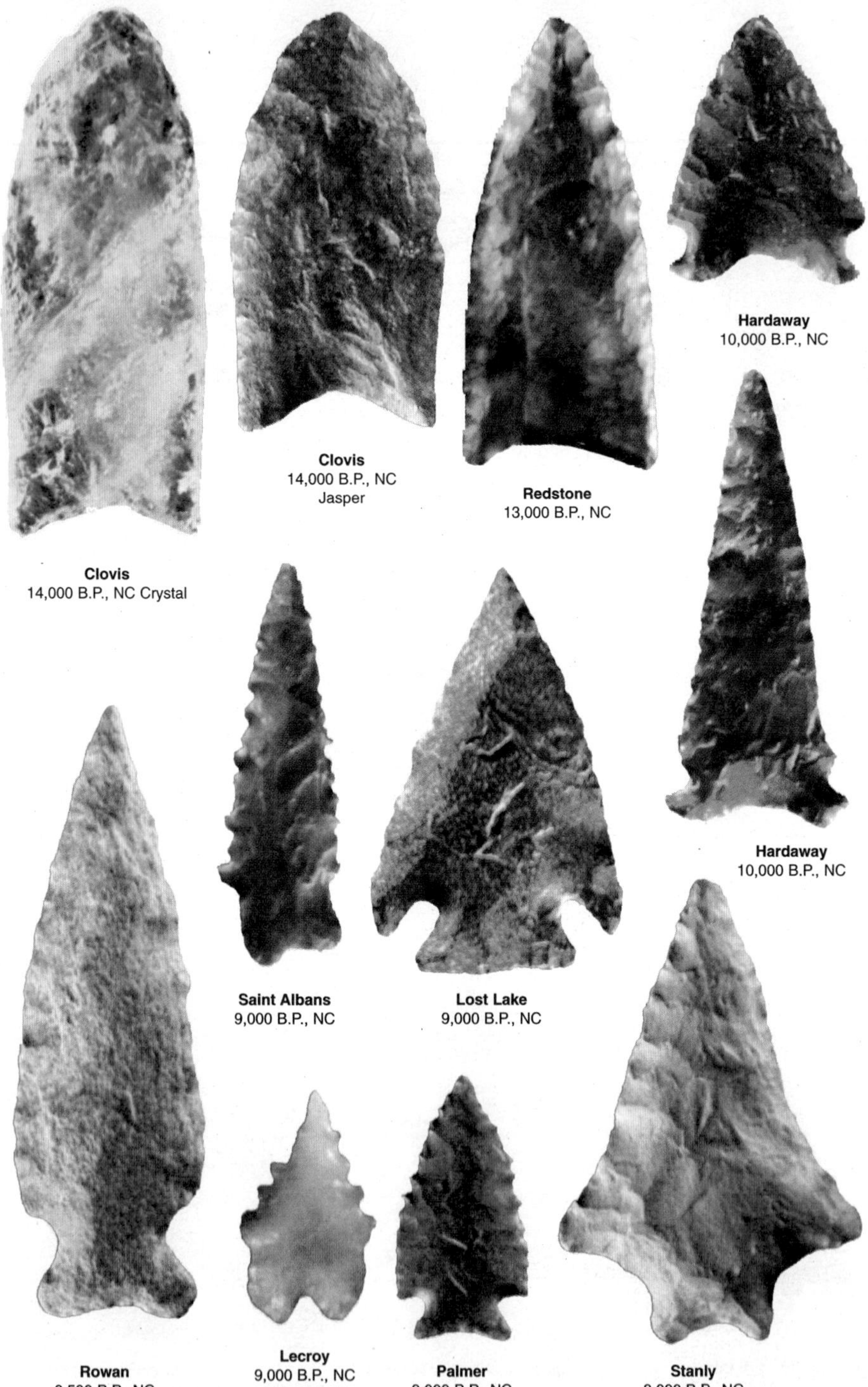

Clovis
14,000 B.P., NC Crystal

Clovis
14,000 B.P., NC
Jasper

Redstone
13,000 B.P., NC

Hardaway
10,000 B.P., NC

Hardaway
10,000 B.P., NC

Saint Albans
9,000 B.P., NC

Lost Lake
9,000 B.P., NC

Rowan
9,500 B.P., NC

Lecroy
9,000 B.P., NC
Milky quartz

Palmer
9,000 B.P., NC

Stanly
8,000 B.P., NC

Stanly Narrow Stem
8,000 B.P., NC

Pine Tree Corner Notched
8,000 B.P.,NC

Guilford Yuma
7,500 B.P., NC Quartzite

Morrow Mountain
7,000 B.P., NC

Yadkin
2,500 B.P., NC

Uwharrie
1,600 B.P., NC

Savannah River
5,000 B.P., NC

Yadkin Eared
2,500 B.P., NC

Randolph
2,000 B.P., NC

Uwharrie
1,600 B.P., NC

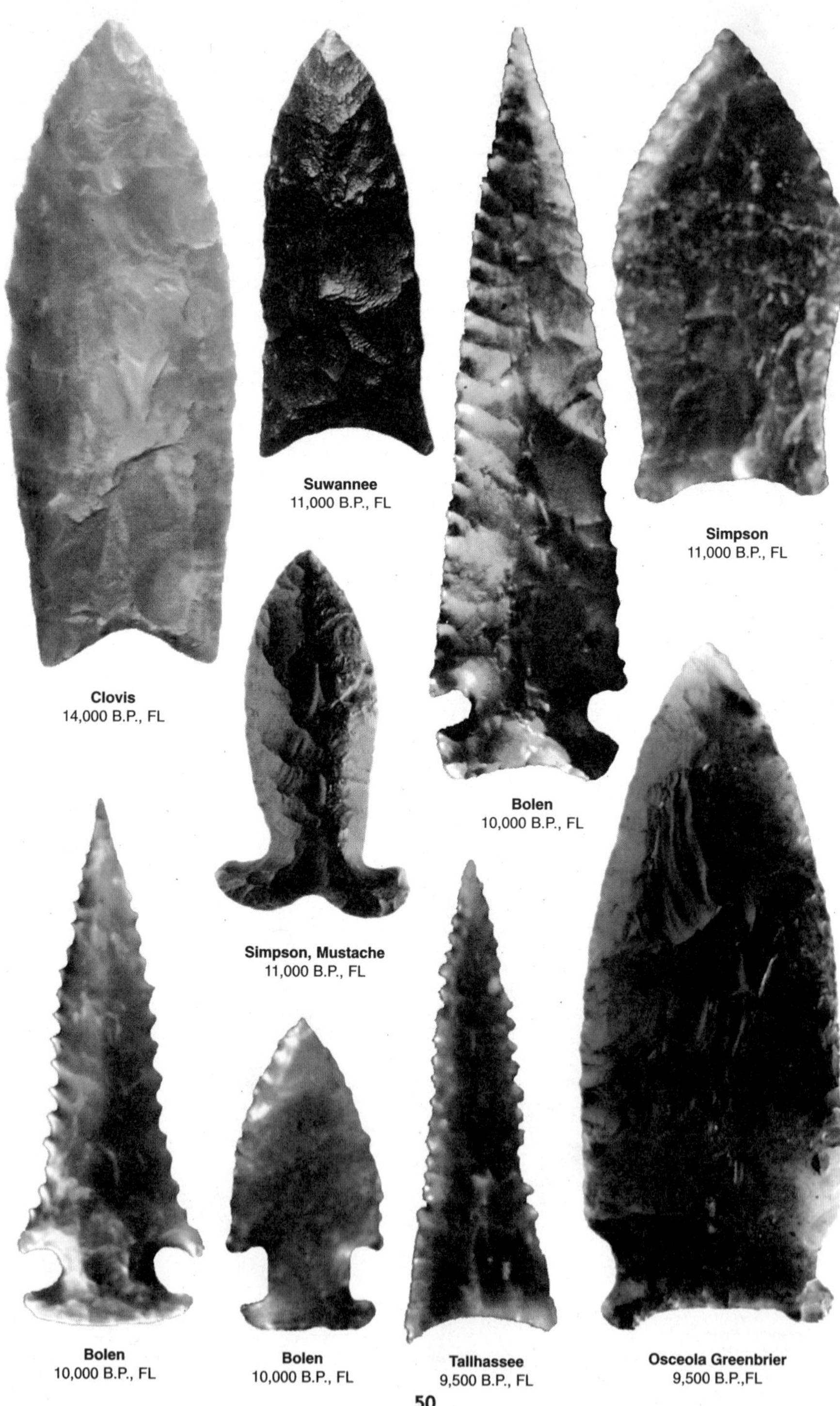

Clovis
14,000 B.P., FL

Suwannee
11,000 B.P., FL

Bolen
10,000 B.P., FL

Simpson
11,000 B.P., FL

Simpson, Mustache
11,000 B.P., FL

Bolen
10,000 B.P., FL

Bolen
10,000 B.P., FL

Tallhassee
9,500 B.P., FL

Osceola Greenbrier
9,500 B.P.,FL

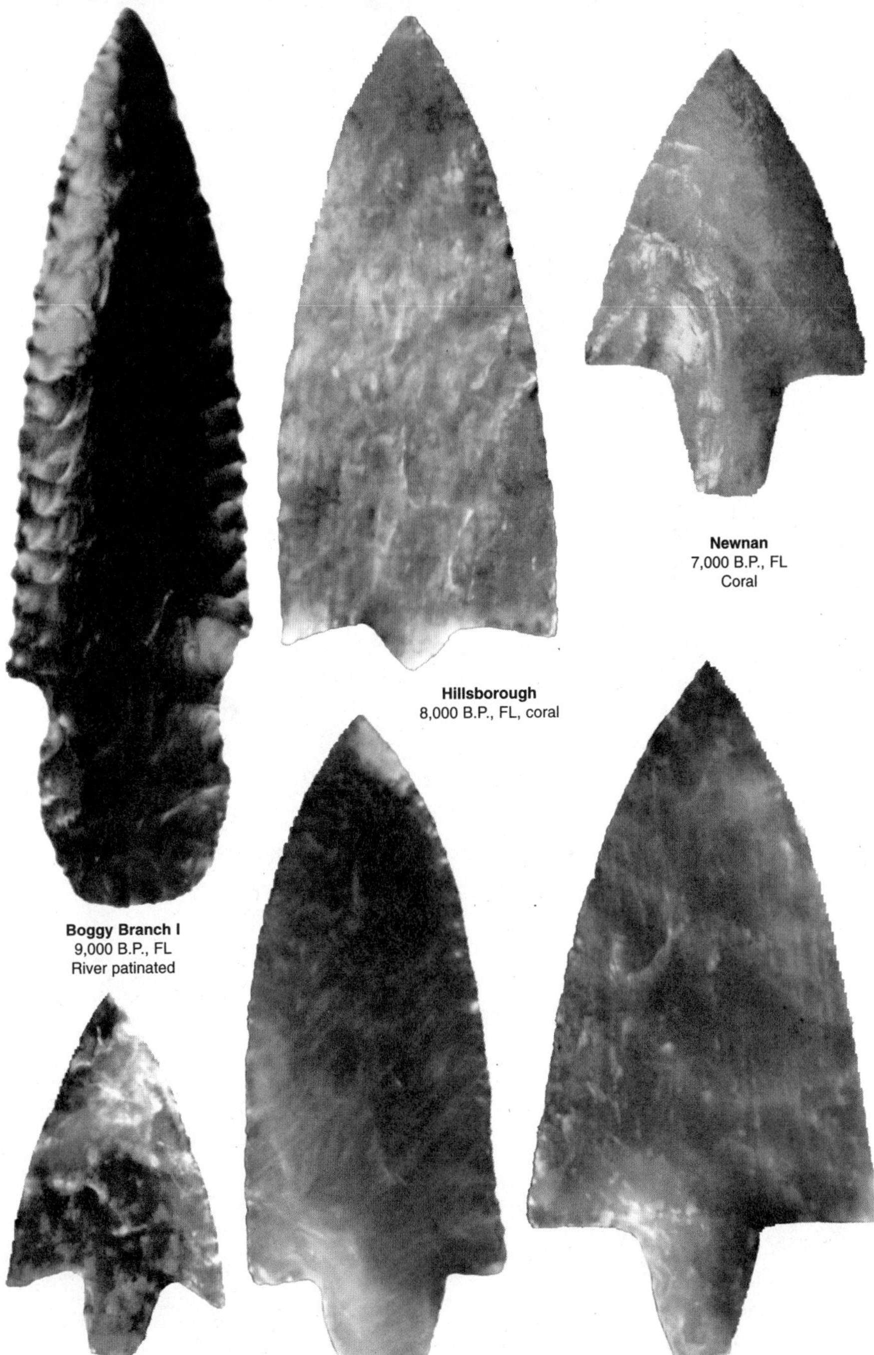

Newnan
7,000 B.P., FL
Coral

Hillsborough
8,000 B.P., FL, coral

Boggy Branch I
9,000 B.P., FL
River patinated

Newnan
7,000 B.P., FL
Coral

Marion
7,000 B.P., FL, coral

Newnan
7,000 B.P., FL, Coral

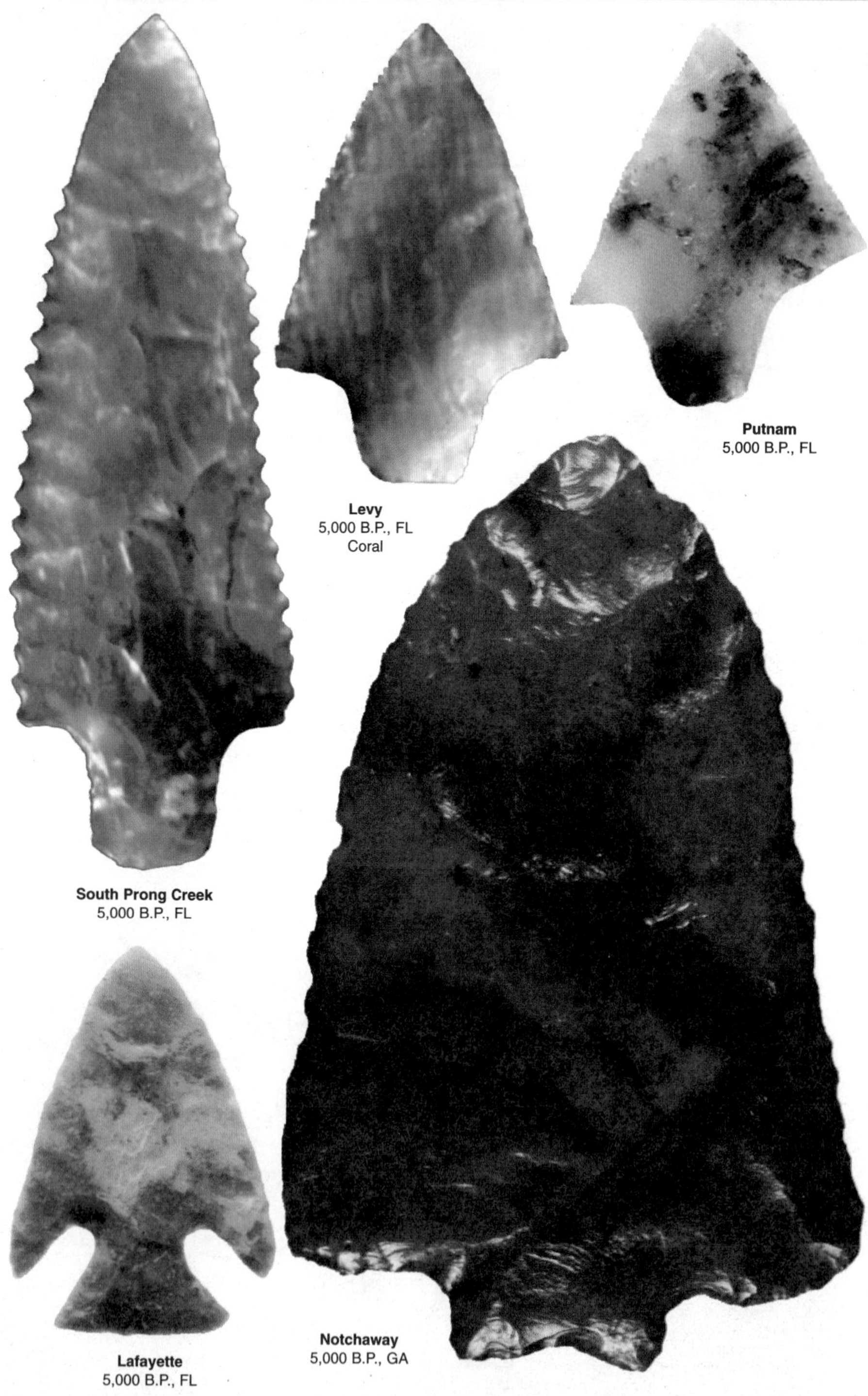

Levy
5,000 B.P., FL
Coral

Putnam
5,000 B.P., FL

South Prong Creek
5,000 B.P., FL

Notchaway
5,000 B.P., GA

Lafayette
5,000 B.P., FL

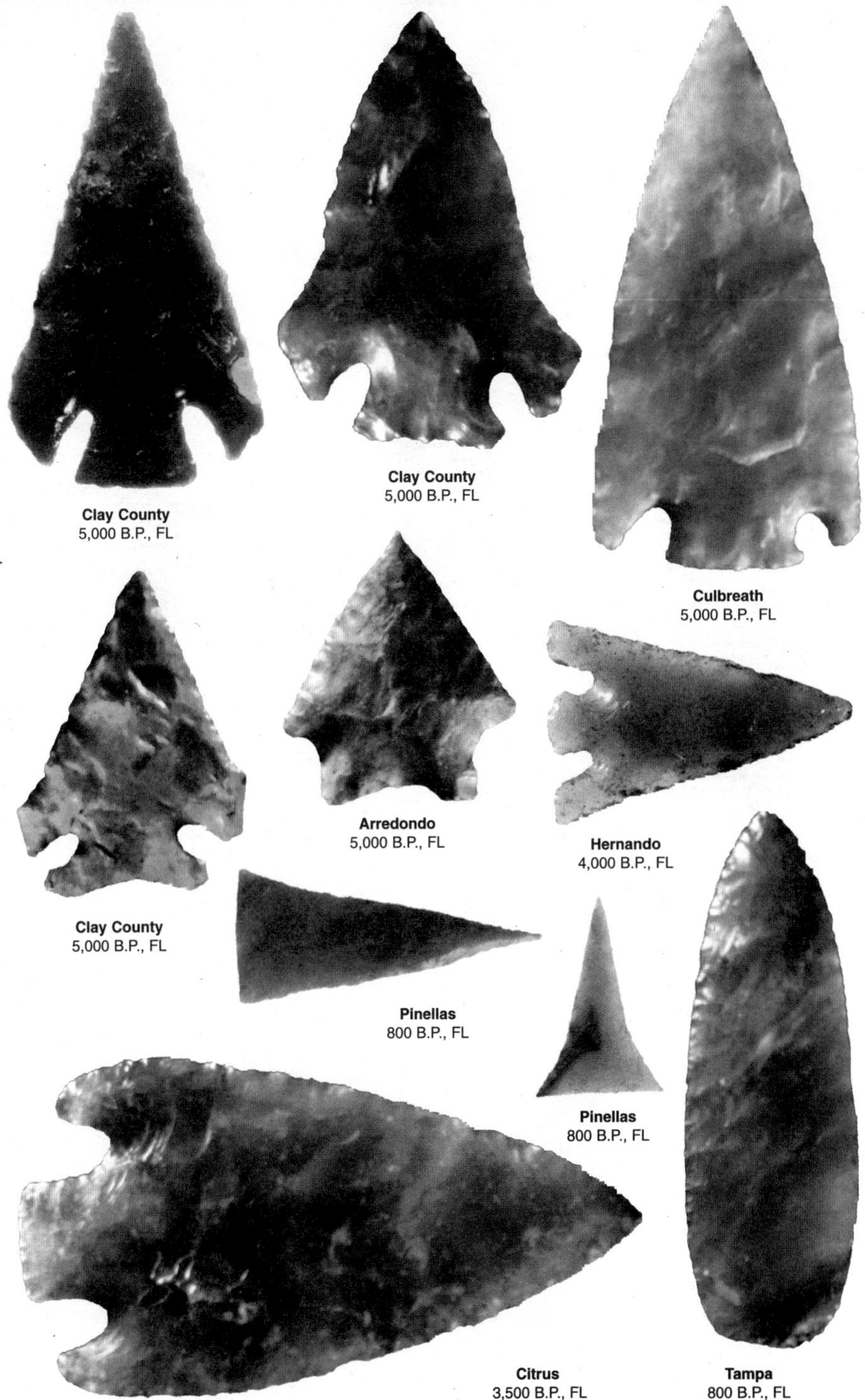

Clay County
5,000 B.P., FL

Clay County
5,000 B.P., FL

Culbreath
5,000 B.P., FL

Clay County
5,000 B.P., FL

Arredondo
5,000 B.P., FL

Hernando
4,000 B.P., FL

Pinellas
800 B.P., FL

Pinellas
800 B.P., FL

Citrus
3,500 B.P., FL

Tampa
800 B.P., FL

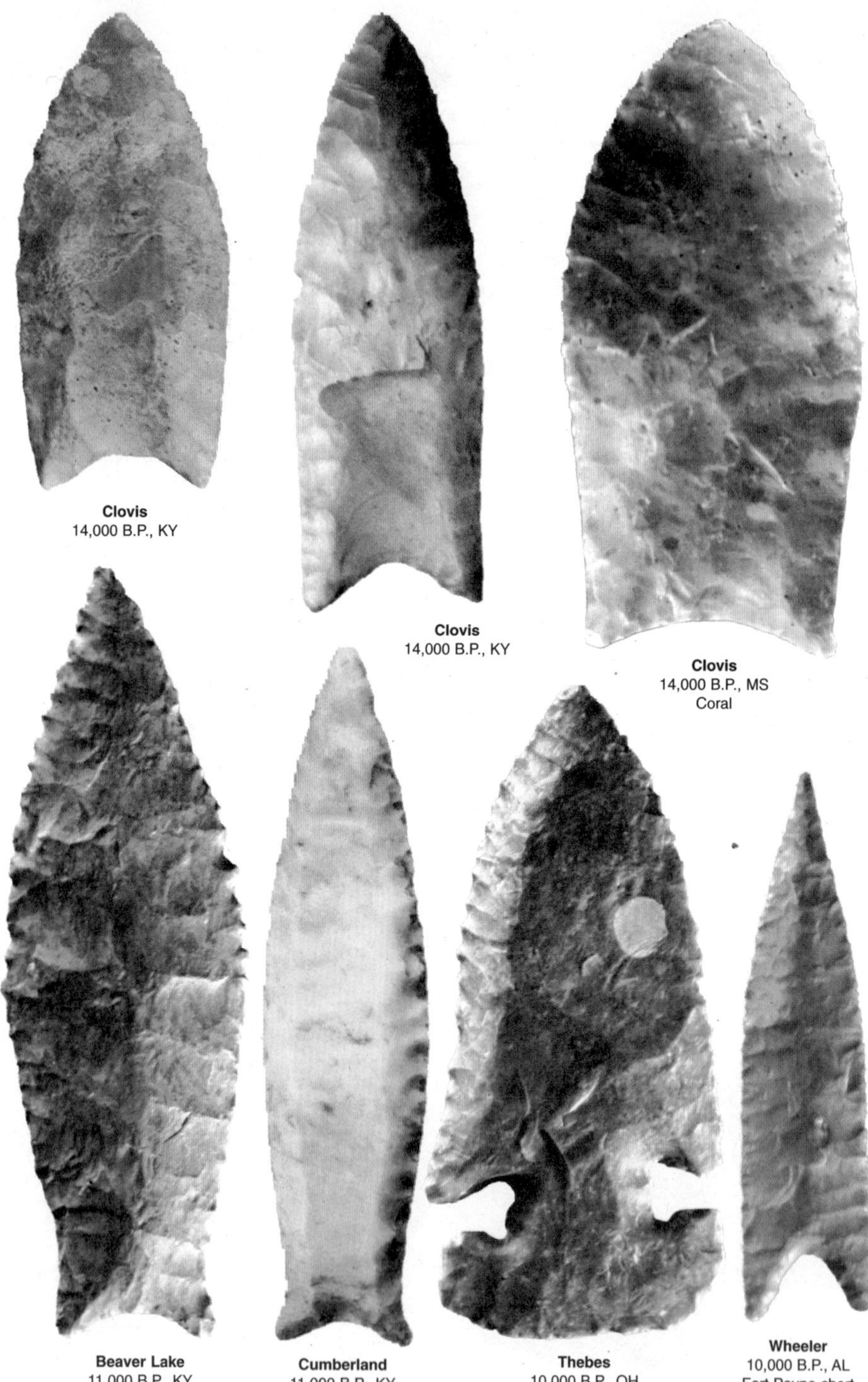

Clovis
14,000 B.P., KY

Clovis
14,000 B.P., KY

Clovis
14,000 B.P., MS
Coral

Beaver Lake
11,000 B.P., KY

Cumberland
11,000 B.P., KY

Thebes
10,000 B.P., OH

Wheeler
10,000 B.P., AL
Fort Payne chert

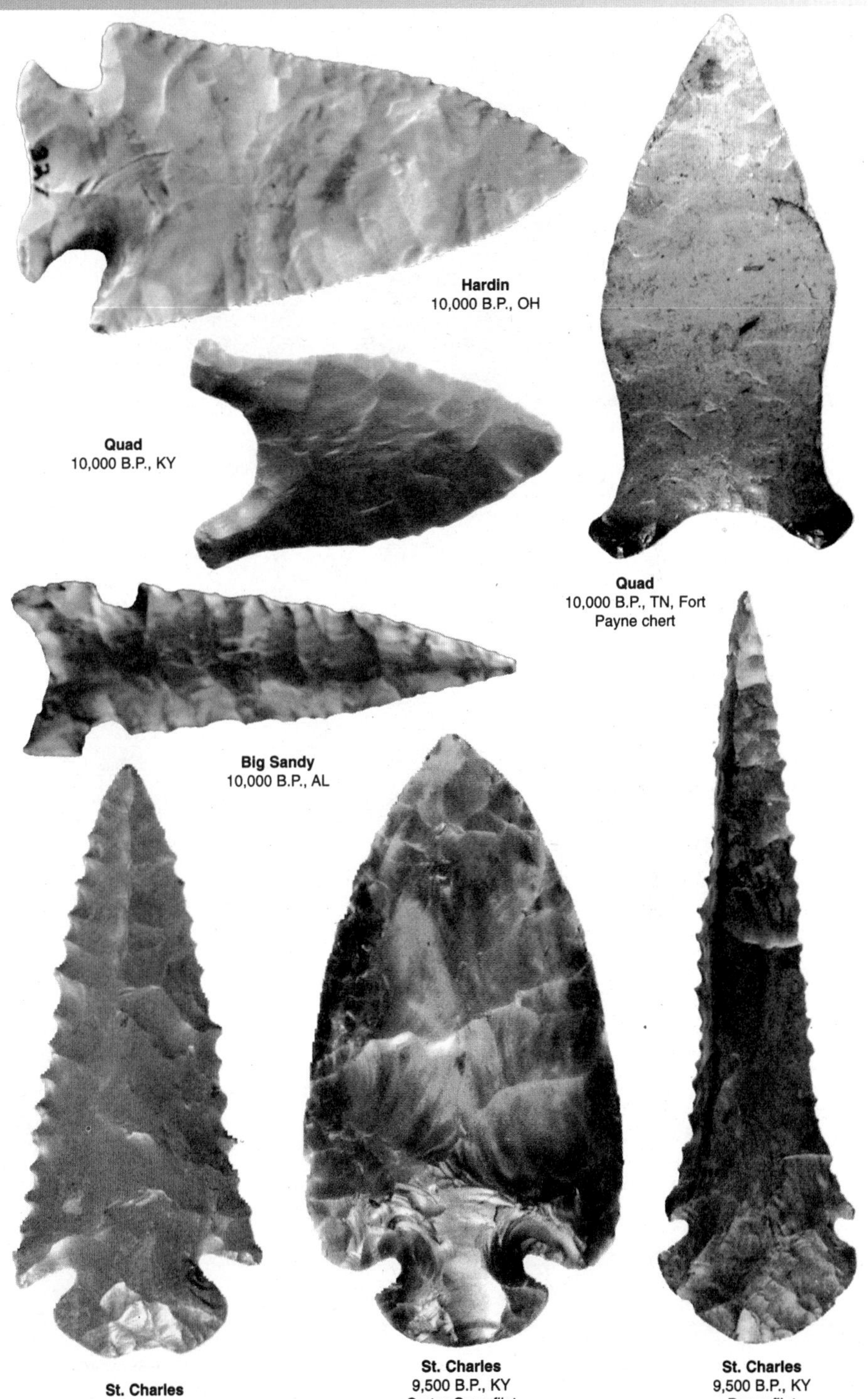

Hardin
10,000 B.P., OH

Quad
10,000 B.P., KY

Quad
10,000 B.P., TN, Fort
Payne chert

Big Sandy
10,000 B.P., AL

St. Charles
9,500 B.P., KY

St. Charles
9,500 B.P., KY
Carter Cave flint

St. Charles
9,500 B.P., KY
Dover flint

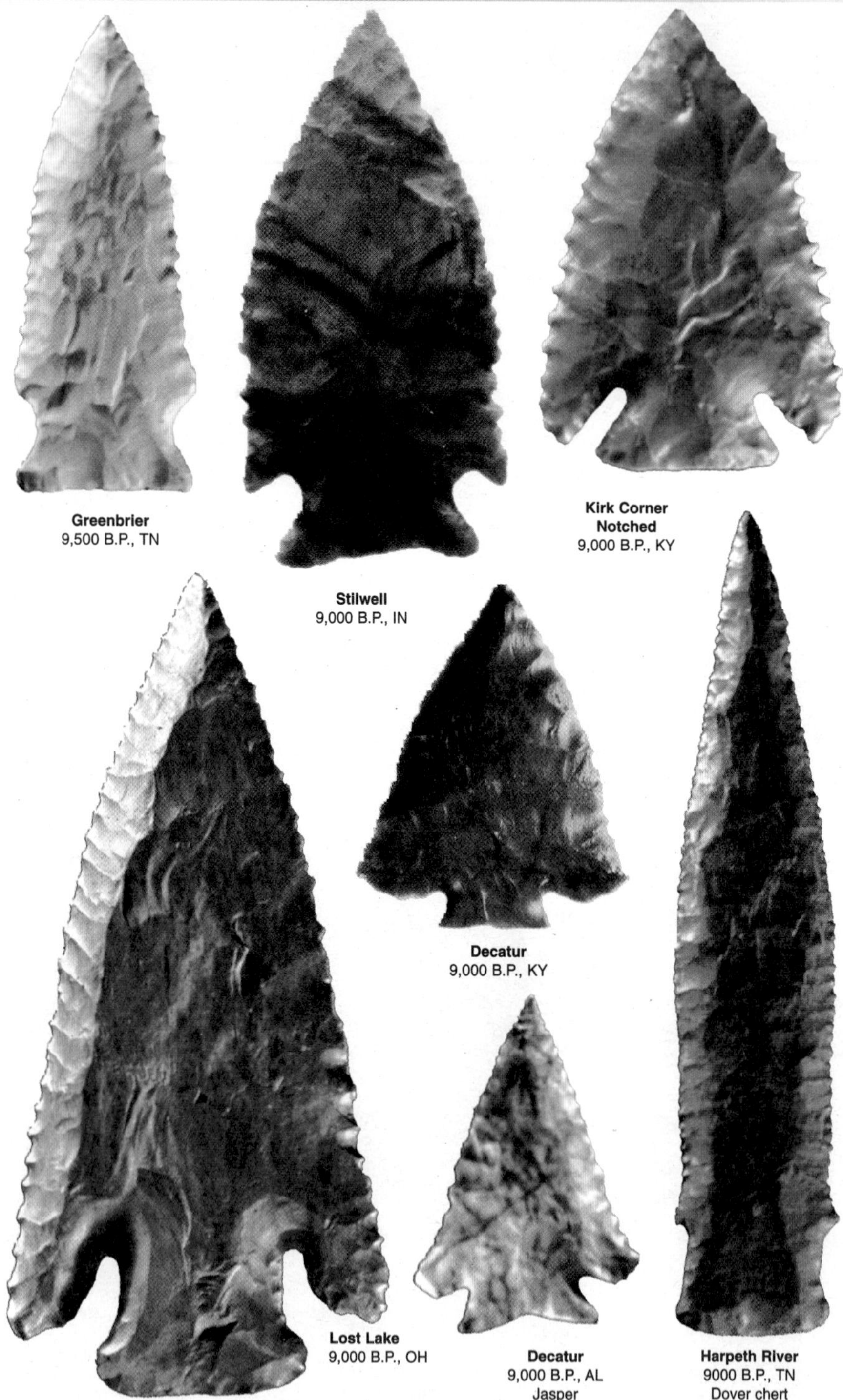

Greenbrier
9,500 B.P., TN

Stilwell
9,000 B.P., IN

Kirk Corner Notched
9,000 B.P., KY

Decatur
9,000 B.P., KY

Lost Lake
9,000 B.P., OH

Decatur
9,000 B.P., AL
Jasper

Harpeth River
9000 B.P., TN
Dover chert

Palmer
9,000 B.P., OH

Lake Erie
9,000 B.P., OH

Pine Tree
8,000 B.P., AL

Warrick
9,000 B.P., IN

Kirk Serrated
9,000 B.P., KY

Pine Tree
8,000 B.P., KY

Buck Creek
6,000 B.P., TN
Horse Creek chert

Pine Tree
8,000 B.P., TN
Fort Payne chert

Heavy Duty
7,000 B.P., IN

Buck Creek
6,000 B.P., KY

Afton
5,000 B.P., OH

Elora
6,000 B.P., GA

Ashtabula
4,000 B.P., OH

Motley
4,500 B.P., KY

Copena Classic
4,000 B.P., KY

INTRODUCTION

Hunting arrowheads has been a popular pastime for many Americans over the past one hundred years. Even the Indians themselves cherished and collected rock crystals, gem stones, and points. In the past, large collections were put together with very little effort, since few people hunted and the supply of good artifacts was plentiful. Plowed fields along creeks and rivers, as well as river banks and dry lake beds, are the most popular places for hunting relics, as the early Indians' built their villages and hunted game in such locations. The Indians' food supply, such as fish, game, mussels, etc. lived in or along rivers, creeks, springs, ponds, swamps and lakes. Early man preyed on this abundant food supply, migrating along these water routes, moving from place to place in search of better hunting grounds, as the game became depleted.

Fields are plowed in the Fall or Spring of each year. The most likely sites for hunting, of course, would be the large flat areas close to the original river or creek banks. Hunting in areas that may be large enough to support a small village and are on high ground, protected from a flooding river, are especially productive places. Village sites were usually built where a creek converged with a large river. Field hunting should be attempted after a hard rain. Heavy rains will create deep gullies and washed-out areas exposing the relics.

Here is where you can get lucky, especially if you are the first person in the field. All a collector has to do is walk along and pick up pieces of history. Be sure to ask permission before entering private property. Most farmers will give permission to enter their land if approached in a friendly manner.

Plowed fields next to springs and cave openings have also produced relics. Such a place is Castillian Springs, just above Nashville, Tennessee. Here, next to the spring, there are salt licks for animals. The Indians occupied and lived in this area for thousands of years from the Paleo to Woodland periods and later. The herd animals would always migrate here for salt and watering, providing the Indians with plentiful meat and nourishment right in their own backyard. Erosion around the spring has in the past produced many excellent artifacts. From fluted points to Doves, to Lost Lakes, to stemmed types, this area has been rich with many types of points.

Another similar site is Nickajack Cave and its surrounding fields, just below Chattanooga, Tennessee. Overhangs and rock shelters along rivers and creeks where early man lived, as well as river lands, have produced fine artifacts as well.

In the 1930s, the blow-outs, or dust storms, in the plains states produced many fine projectile points. The top layer of soil blew away, exposing relics left centuries ago by the Indians.

Sand bar hunting along the Tennessee River became possible after the Tennessee Valley Authority built their dams and began controlling the river level in the 1930's. During the development of the TVA system, hunting was excellent. Lake levels were dropped during the winter months, exposing the sand bars which were originally high areas in the now inundated fields along the river channel areas where the early Indians built their villages and camp sites. As winter storms raged through the Tennessee Valley, the lake lev-

Most points illustrated in this book are shown actual size and are believed to be genuine prehistoric artifacts. We have gone to great lengths to insure that only authentic points are included. Any errors discovered will be deleted in future editions. This is not a "for Sale" list of points. The illustrated examples are for identification and value purposes only.

els would rise and fall and the racing river would cut into the sand bars, exposing relics for anyone to merely come along and pick up.

Today most of the sand bars and plowed fields in many states have been "hunted out." But the energetic hunter can still find new relic-producing sites if he gathers his facts, follows all leads, studies maps of likely areas and hunts whenever he can. Sooner or later he will get lucky.

However, most collectors are neither energetic nor imaginative, and build their collections by systematically purchasing specimens one at a time. **Genuine** points can be found for sale at relic shows, and sometimes in local collections that come up for sale. **Warning:** fake relics (all recently made and aged) are being offered to the public everywhere as genuine prehistoric artifacts. Knowing the history or pedigree of a point is very important in the process of determining whether or not it is a genuine pre-Columbian piece. Before purchasing a relic from anyone, be sure the dealer will guarantee it to be a genuine, pre-Columbian piece, and will give you your money back should you later discover otherwise. Many reputable dealers will give you a money back guarantee. Whenever possible, you should have an expert examine any and every piece for its authenticity before you buy.

HOW TO USE THIS BOOK

This book is set up by regions of the country to make it easy for you to classify your collection. All points in each region are arranged in alphabetical order. First turn to the region that applies to you. The book is set up beginning with the Northeast section, continuing westward to the Great Basin-Westward section. The nine regions are: Northeastern, Eastern Seaboard, Gulf Coastal, Eastern Central, Southern Central, Northern Central, Desert Southwest, Northern High Plains and Great Basin Westward.

CLASSIFICATION: Projectile points come in many shapes, colors and sizes. Their quality varies from thick, crude forms to very thin, beautifully flaked, symmetrical specimens. Over the past fifty years, hundreds of points have been classified and given names. The names of people, rivers, creeks, lakes, mountains, towns, etc. have been used in naming point types. Many of the types come from sites that were excavated from undisturbed stratigraphic layers where carbon dating was made. These forms of data are important in placing each type in time and showing the relationship of one type to another. You will soon see that most of the early types evolved into the later forms.

This book includes as many point types as possible with the idea of expanding to more types in future updated editions as the information becomes available to us. The point types are arranged in alphabetical order by section of the country. The archeological period and approximate dates of popular use are given for each point type. A general distribution area is given, along with a brief description of each type. There are several factors that determine a given type: **1**-Shape or form. **2**-Size. **3**-Style or flaking. **4**-Thickness or thinness. **5**-Kind of material

NEW ARROWHEADS LISTED

The field of Archaeology is an on-going science where sites are constantly being found and excavated. Occassionally, new types are discovered, named and reported in their published literature. As a result, the interrelationship of types, their age, as well as geographical dispersion is always changing. Due to this, the region boundaries may change in future editions. We are constantly on the outlook for photographs as well as the documentation of these types so they can be added to future volumes of this book. The author would appreciate receiving any photos and reports of this nature.

ARROWHEAD VALUES LISTED

Values listed in this book are for your information only. None of the points shown are for sale. Under each type, we have attempted to show a photographic spread of size, quality and variation of form (where available), from low to high grade, with corresponding prices. All values listed in this book are in U.S. currency and are wholesale/retail prices based on (but not limited to) reports from our extensive network of experienced advisors which include convention sales, mail order, auctions and unpublished personal sales. Overstreet, with several decades of market experience, has developed a unique and comprehensive system for gathering, documenting, averaging and pricing data on arrowheads. The end result is a true fair market value for your use. We have earned the reputation for our cautious, conservative approach to pricing arrowheads. You, the collector, can be assured that the prices listed in this volume are the most accurate and useful in print.

The low price is the wholesale price (the price dealers may pay for that point). **The high price** is the retail price (the price a collector may pay for that point). Each illustration also gives a brief description pointing out special features when applicable. The prices listed have been averaged from the highest and lowest prices we have seen, just prior to publication. We feel that this will give you a fair, realistic price value for each piece illustrated. If your point matches the illustrated example in both size, color, and quality, the listed value would then apply. **Warning:** The slightest dings or nicks can dramatically drop the grade and value of a point. Please see Grade vs. Value following this section.

HIGH PRICE- RETAIL PRICE
LOW PRICE - WHOLESALE PRICE

IMPORTANT NOTE: This book is not a dealer's price list, although some dealers may base their prices on the values listed. The true value of any arrowhead is what you are willing to pay. The top price listed is an indication of what collectors would pay while the lower price is what dealers would possibly pay. For one reason or another, these collectors might want a certain piece badly and will pay over the list price for comparable quality. This commonly occurs on many high grade, rare points.

DEALER'S POSITION

Dealers are not in a position to pay the full prices listed, but work on a percentage depending largely on the amount of investment required and the quality of material offered. What a dealer will pay depends on how long it will take him to sell the individual piece or collection after making the investment; the higher the demand and better the grade, the more the percentage. Most dealers are faced with expenses such as advertising, travel, telephone and mailing, rent, employee salaries, plus convention costs. These costs all go in before the relics are sold.

The high demand relics usually sell right away but the lower grades are difficult to sell due to their commonality and low demand. Sometimes a dealer will have cost tied up for several years before finally selling everything. Remember, his position is that of handling, demand, and overhead. Most dealers are victims of these economics.

GRADE AND ITS EFFECT ON VALUE

Presented below are examples of the same point type in grades 10 through 3 and the effect on value. All are equal size and quality, except for the defects. These examples illustrate how value drops with grade. True number 10s are rare and the slightest dings or nicks can easily cause the value to drop dramatically.

When the novice grades points to determine value, it is a common mistake to grade his #5s and #6s as #9s and 10s. True 9s and 10s must be superb. They have to be perfect for 10s and near perfect for 9s, thin, symmetrical, and of high quality to reach this grade. Color, translucency and high quality material enhance value.

When dealers look at a collection to buy, they are faced with the economics of having to buy the whole collection to get the few points that they really want. For example, a virgin collection of 1000 complete points, all found by the owner, that is still intact and not picked over, would break down as follows: 92% (920 points) would be low grade, worth below $20 each with the remaining 8% worth $20 or more each. As you can see, most collections are loaded with low grade points making it very difficult for anyone to pay a large price just to get the few choice pieces.

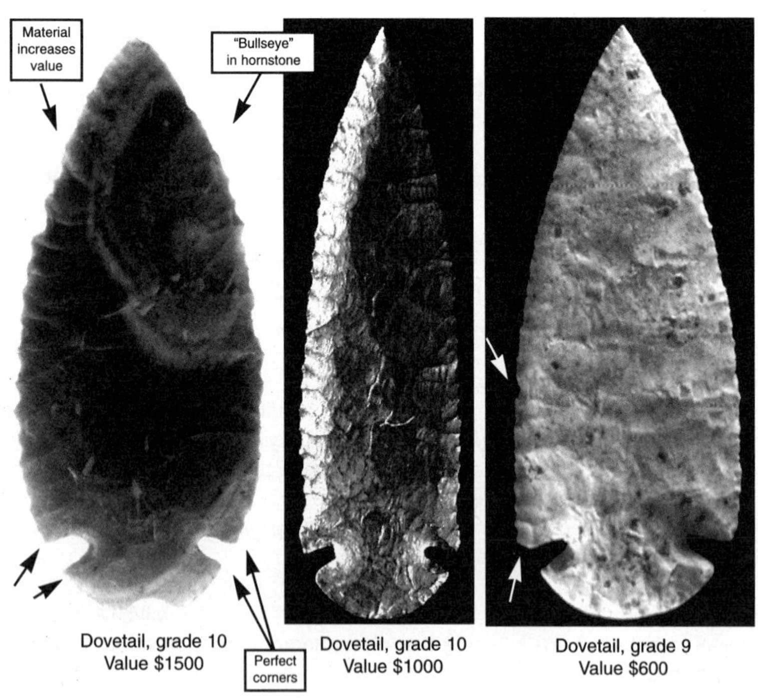

Dovetail, grade 10
Value $1500

Dovetail, grade 10
Value $1000

Dovetail, grade 9
Value $600

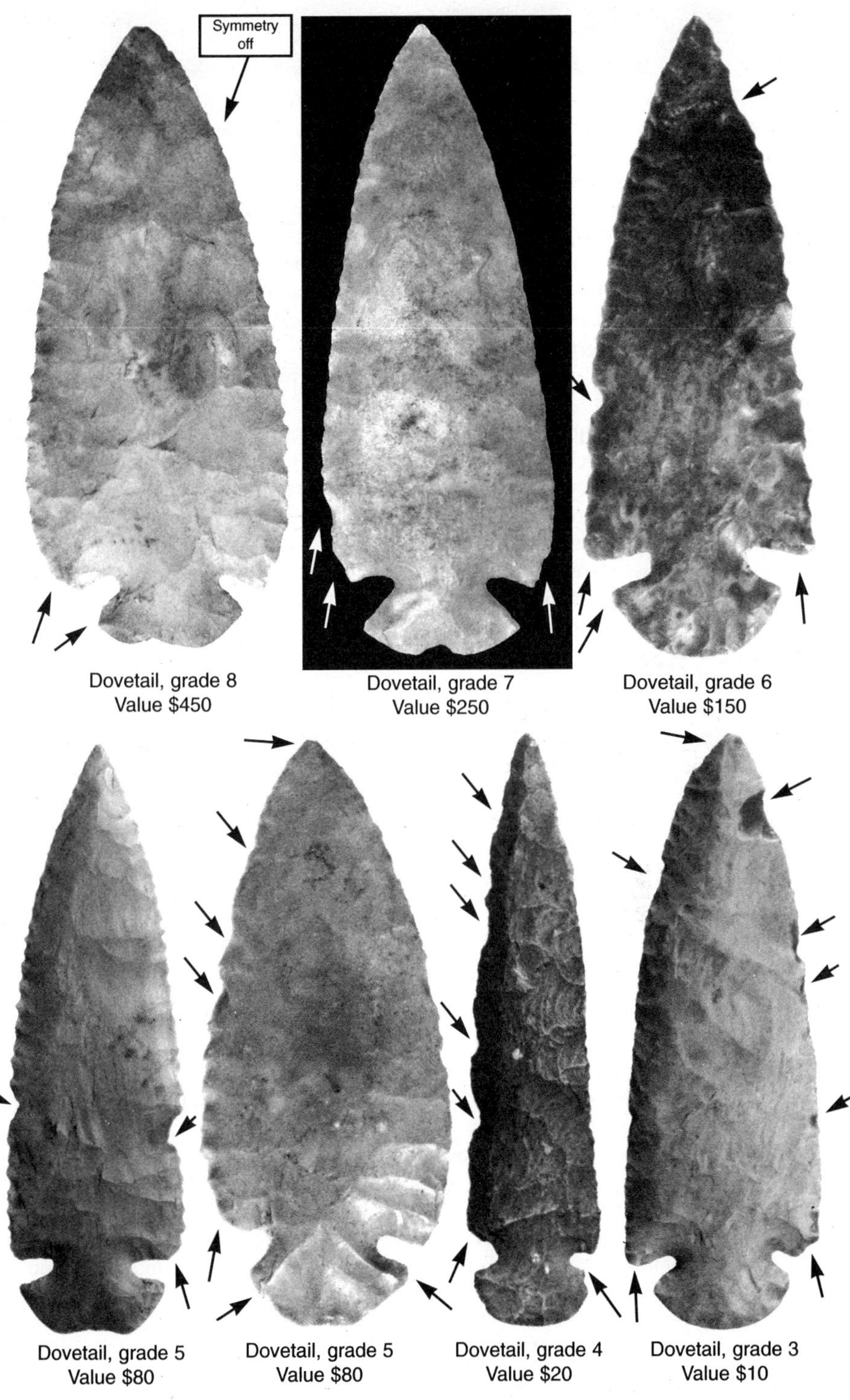

Dovetail, grade 8
Value $450

Dovetail, grade 7
Value $250

Dovetail, grade 6
Value $150

Dovetail, grade 5
Value $80

Dovetail, grade 5
Value $80

Dovetail, grade 4
Value $20

Dovetail, grade 3
Value $10

HOW TO GRADE POINTS

Before a point's true value can be assessed, its condition or state of preservation as well as quality must be determined. The better the quality and condition, and the larger the size, the more valuable the point. Perfect points that are classic for the type, thin, made of high quality materials with perfect symmetry and flaking are worth several times the price of common, but complete, low grade field points.

FACTORS THAT INFLUENCE THE GRADE AND VALUE OF POINTS:

Condition: Perfection is the rule. Nicks, chips, and breakage reduce value.

Size: Everything else being equal, a larger point will grade higher than a smaller point and larger points are worth more.

Form: The closer a point comes to being a classic for the type, the higher the grade and value.

Symmetry: Points with good balance and design are higher grade and worth more.

Flaking: Points with precision percussion and secondary flaking, a minimum of hinge fractures and problem areas are higher grade and worth more. Points with unusual flaking patterns, such as collateral or oblique transverse, enhance grade and value.

Thinness: The thinner the better.

After all the above steps have been considered, then the reader can begin to assign a grade to his point. Points are graded on a scale of 1 to10+, where a 10+ is the best and a 1 is the lowest grade for a complete point.

GRADING DEFINITIONS

Grade 10+: The exceptional perfect point. One of the few half dozen best known to exist. Perfect in every way, including thinness, flaking, material, symmetry and form. The best example you would ever expect to see of any given type. This grade is extremely rare, and applies to medium to large size points that normally occur in a given type.

Grade 10: A perfect point, including thinness, flaking, symmetry and form. This grade is extremely rare, and applies to <u>all</u> <u>sizes</u> of points that normally occur in a given type. A point does not have to be the largest known to qualify for this grade.

Grade 8 or 9: Near perfect but lacking just a little in size or material or thinness. It may have a small defect to keep it out of a 10 category. Still very rare, most high grade points would fall into this category.

Grade 6 or 7: Better than the average grade but not quite nice enough to get a high ranking. Flaking, size, and symmetry are just a little above the average. Points in this grade are still very hard to find in most states. A very collectible grade.

Grade 4 or 5: The average quality that is found. The flaking, thickness, and symmetry is average. 2 or 3 very minute nicks may be seen but none that would be considered serious.

Grade 1-3: Field grade points that have below average overall quality. Better points with more serious faults or dings would fall into this grade. The most common grade found and correspondingly, the least valuable.

Broken points: Usually little to no value. However, good high grade broken backs of popular type points have fetched good prices. Examples would be Paleo points and many of the rare Archaic beveled and notched types.

PRICING POINTS

After a point has been graded and assigned a grade number, it should be compared with similar points in the alphabetical listings. The prices listed will give the reader a guide as to the probable value of his point, but be careful, compare grade with grade. If your point has a little ear or tip broken, the value is affected drastically. Of course, state of perfection, thinness, rarity of type, quality of material and flaking, and size all enter into determining a value. Usually with everything being equal, the larger the size the higher the price.

Many factors affect value and should be considered when determining a price for your point. Besides those listed under Grading Points, the following should be considered:

FACTORS THAT INFLUENCE VALUE:

Provenance: When a point has been properly documented as to where and when it was found and by whom, the value increases. Points from key sites such as the Clovis site in New Mexico, the Quad site in Alabama, the Nuckolls site in Tennessee, the Hardaway site in North Carolina, etc. increases value. Well documented points from famous collections show increased value. Points that have been published show an increase in demand and makes them easier to sell (the wise investor should have all points checked before purchase, whether published or not, because many fakes have been published as genuine). Local points usually bring higher prices than imports from other states.

Material & Color: Most points are made of common local gray to brown cherts, but the type of material can enhance value. Points made from colorful or high quality material such as agate, petrified wood, agatized coral, quartz, crystal, flint, jasper, Horse Creek chert, Buffalo River chert, Flint Ridge chert, Carter Cave chert, Dover chert, etc. will increase value. Some materials became glassier and more colorful when heat treated by the Indians and would enhance the appearance. Certain local materials are more collectible in various states, such as rhyolite in North and South Carolina, Dover in Tennessee, Carter Cave chert or Kentucky hornstone in Kentucky, Flint Ridge chert in Ohio, Knife River flint in North and South Dakota, jasper in Pennsylvania, agatized coral in Florida or petrified wood in Arizona and New Mexico. Usually, points that are transparent or have pretty colors alone will sell for higher prices.

Symmetry: The left and right sides of points must be balanced to receive the highest grades. Value decreases as symmetry is lost.

Rarity: Obviously, some point types are scarcer and much harder to find than others. For instance,Clovis, which is found in most of North America, is more common than Folsom, which is rarely found in just a few western states. Paleo points are much more rare out west than in the east.

Popularity of Type: Market demand for certain point types can greatly influence the supply and value. The value of these points can vary with changing market demands and available supplies. Points with slight damage, such as a nick off the tip or wing, suffer a cut in value of about 60 percent. Medium damage, such as a missing wing, will cut the value about 90 percent. Field grade pieces and halves are usually sold at five dollars per gallon. The very best points have no top retail price and are always in very high demand. Local points are usually worth more in the area where they are found.

HOW TO CLASSIFY ARROWHEADS

It's as easy as **one, two, three** (well, seven actually) if you take the following steps. All arrowheads, according to their shape, have been divided into eight different forms listed below.

1. The country is divided into nine sections.

2. Decide which of the categories #1-8 listed below that your point belongs.

3. Go to the Thumbnail Guide at the beginning of the section that applies to your locale.

4. Match your arrowhead to one of the photos in that section.

5. Look up the name under the photo that matches your point in the alphabetical section.

6. Look at the numerous examples, actual size, and make a more detailed comparison.

7. If your point still does not match exactly, go back to the **Thumbnail Guide Section** and look for another match and start over with step four.

THE 8 FORMS OF ARROWHEADS

1. **Auriculate.** These points have **ears** and a concave base.
   A. Auriculate Fluted. A fluted point is one that has a **channel flake** struck off one or both faces from the base.
   B. Auriculate Unfluted. All other eared forms are shown here.

2. **Lanceolate.** Points without notches or **shoulders** fall into this group. Bases are round, straight, concave or convex.

3. **Corner Notched.** The base-end has corner notches for **hafting**.

4. **Side Notched.** The base-end has side notches for **hafting**.

5. **Stemmed.** These points have a **stem** that is short or long, expanding or contracting. All stemmed points have **shoulders**.

6. **Stemmed-Bifurcated.** Since a number of stemmed points occur that have the base split into two **lobes**, they have been grouped together.

7. **Basal Notched.** This form has notches applied at the **base**.

8. **Arrow Points.** These points are generally small, thin triangle and other forms grouped for easy identification.

*See glossary for underlined words.

IDENTIFICATION/CLASSIFICATION

The following drawings illustrate point nomenclature used by collectors and professionals everywhere for point shapes and features.

AURICULATE FORMS

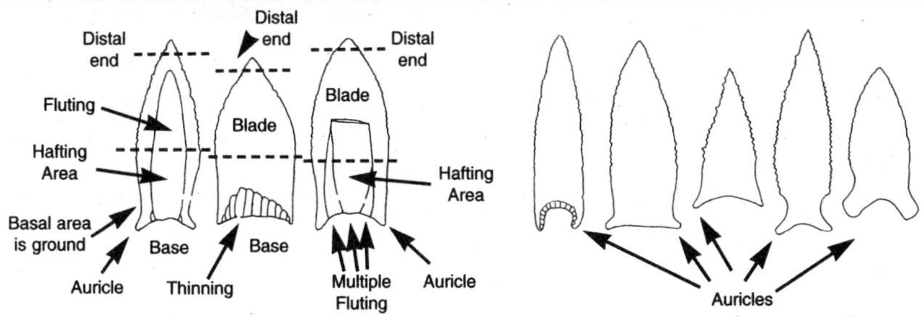

This is the basic form of the Paleo Period. Flaking tends to be parallel and the entire hafting area is usually ground.

LANCEOLATE FORMS

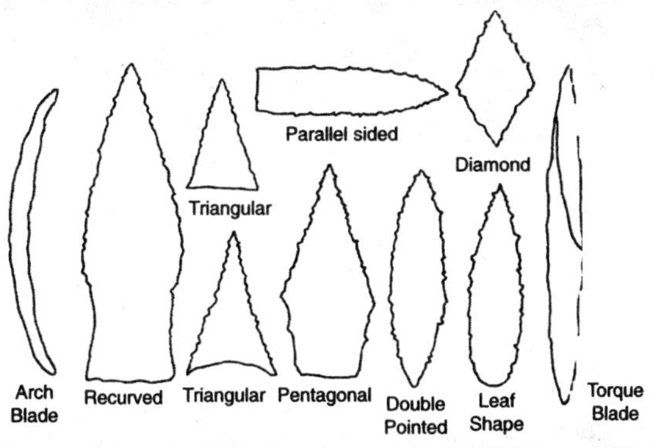

STEMMED FORMS
(THESE DRAWINGS APPLY TO POINTS OF ALL SIZES)
BASAL EDGE TYPES / SHOULDER TYPES

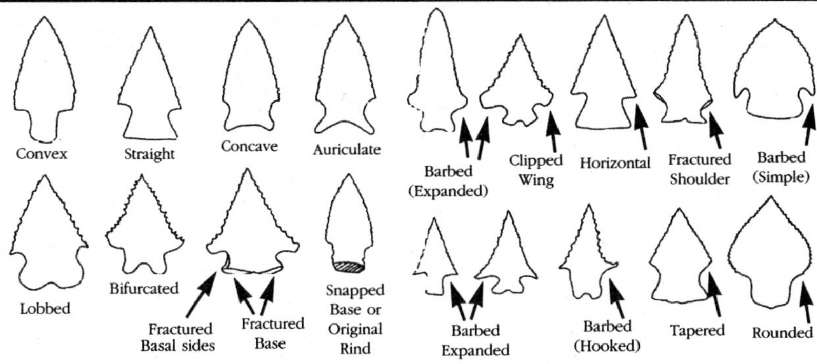

Note: The Basal Edge begins the hafting area of a point.

Note: The shoulder divides the blade from the hafting area.

BASAL, CORNER & SIDE NOTCHED FORMS

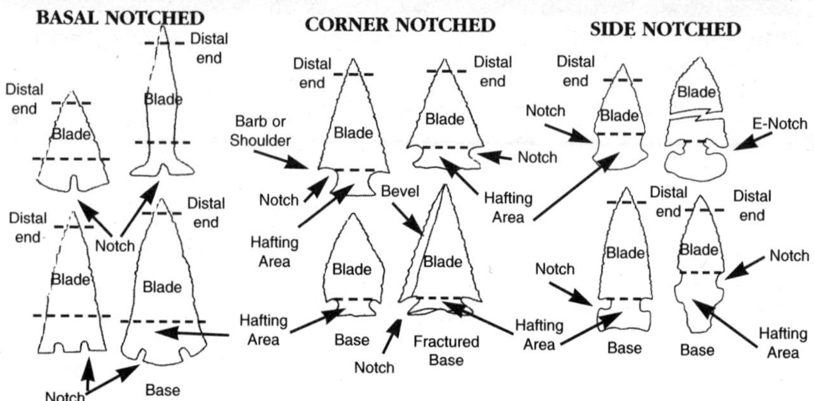

Basal notched forms appeared in the early Archaic Period and reappeared in the Woodland Period. Not a popular form of hafting since only a few types are known.

Corner notched forms appeared in the early Archaic Period and reappeared again in the Woodland Period and lasted to Historic times.

Side notched forms began in Transitional Paleo times and persisted through the Archaic Period, reappearing in Woodland times lasting into the Historic Period.

STEMMED FORMS
(HAFTING AREA TYPES)
(THESE DRAWINGS APPLY TO POINTS OF ALL SIZES)

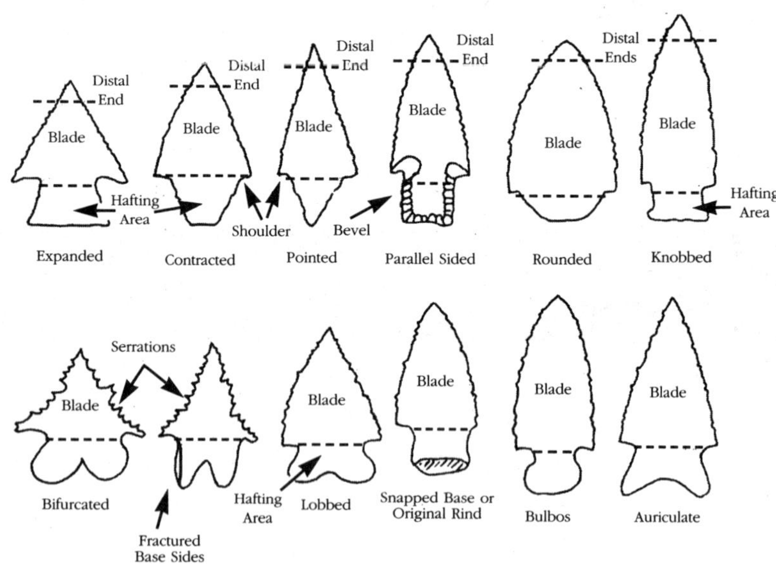

Note: Stemmed types began as early as the Paleo Period, but didn't really become popular until the Woodland Period. Consequently, this form has the most types and is the most difficult to classify.

BLADE BEVELING TYPES / BLADE EDGE TYPES

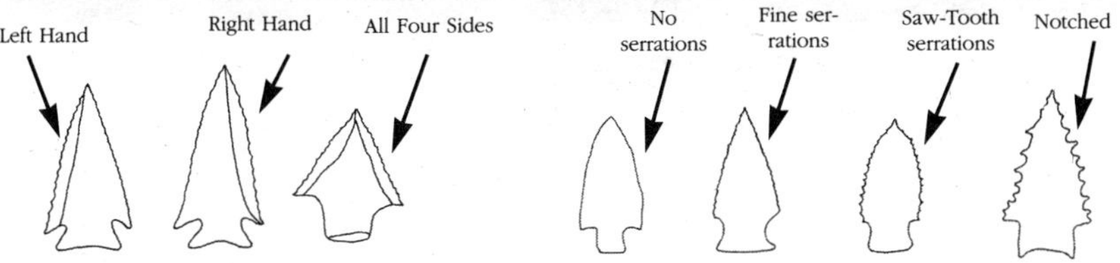

Note: Alternate blade beveling began in the early Archaic Period and continued into the Woodland Period. Beveled points are very popular among collectors.

DISTAL ENDS

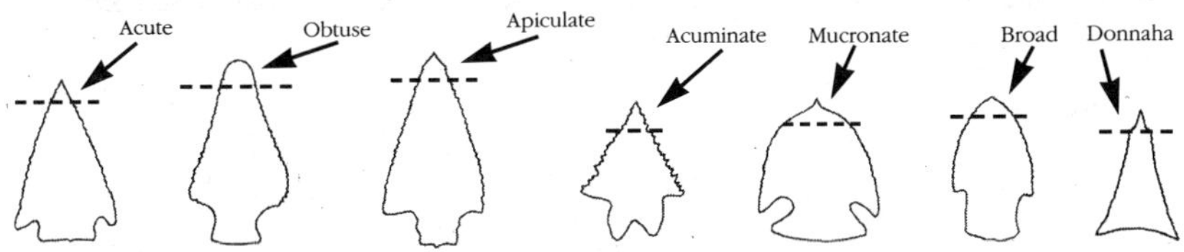

Note: The distal end of a point is located at the very tip and describes the shape of the penetrating part of the knife or projectile point.

POINT CROSS-SECTIONS
(THESE DRAWINGS APPLY TO POINTS OF ALL SIZES)

Elliptical

Round

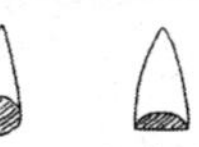
Uniface or Plano-convex

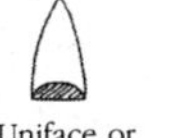
Rhomboid

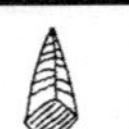
Median Ridged

Flattened

Fluted

Note: The cross-section of a point represents its form if broken at mid-section.

FLAKING TYPES
(THESE DRAWINGS APPLY TO POINTS OF ALL SIZES)

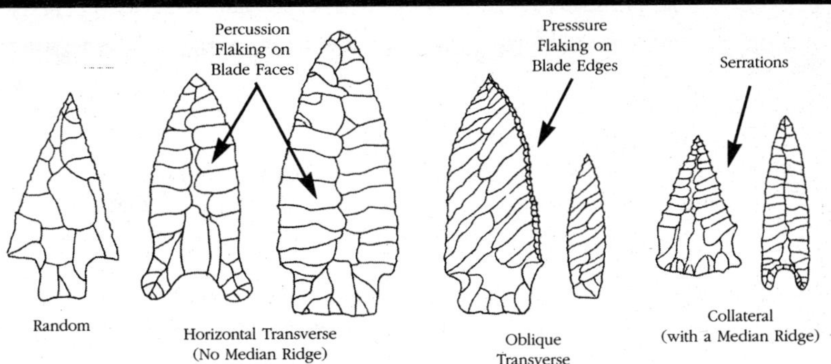

Note: Points are rough shaped with an elk antler billet or hammer stone. Then fine pressure flaking is applied to the blade and stem edges with a sharp pointed antler. Billet and deer antler are alternated until the point is finally finished. During the flaking process, edges are lightly ground to prevent hinge fracturing on the blade edges.

CULTURAL PERIODS

The American Indian Middle to Eastern U.S.

(Includes sections: Northeast, Eastern Seaboard, Gulf Coastal, Eastern Central, Southern Central and Northern Central)

Paleo .... c. 14,000 - 11,000 B.P.
Late Paleo .... c. 12,000 - 10,000 B.P.
Transitional Paleo .... c. 11,000 - 9,000 B.P.
Early Archaic .... c. 10,000 - 7,000 B.P.
Middle Archaic .... c. 7,000 - 4,000 B.P.
Late Archaic .... c. 4,000 - 3,000 B.P.
Woodland .... c. 3,000 - 1,300 B.P.
Mississippian .... c. 1,300 - 400 B.P.
Historic .... c. 450 - 170 B.P.

Note: The dates given above are only approximations and should be used in a general context only. This data is constantly being revised as new information becomes available. **B.P. means "before present."** In 1998 new data was released to correct previously published dates acquired through carbon dating. All points are now older than first realized.

The American Indian West

(Includes sections: Desert Southwest, Northern High Plains and Great Basin-Westward)

Paleo .... c. 14,000 - 8,000 B.P.
Early Archaic .... c. 8,000 - 5,500 B.P.
Middle Archaic .... c. 5,500 - 3,300 B.P.
Late Archaic .... c. 3,500 - 2,300 B.P.

Desert Traditions:

Transitional .... c. 2,300 - 1,600 B.P.
Developmental .... c. 1,600 - 700 B.P.
Classic .... 700 - 400 B.P.
Historic .... c. 400 - 170 B.P.

Note: The dates given above are only approximations and should be used in a general context only. This data is constantly being revised as new information becomes available. **B.P. means "before present."**

COLLECTING POINTS

WHY COLLECT PROJECTILE POINTS?

Whether you collect ancient Chinese cloisonné, Egyptian tomb pieces, or projectile points, there is a particular satisfaction in possessing a piece of history from the distant past--to hold in your hand an object that was made by someone thousands of years ago.

Projectile points may very well be the earliest evidence of man's ability to create, style, and manufacture objects of symmetry and beauty. If you ever have the privilege of seeing an exceptional piece, made of the finest material, and flaked to perfection, take a close look. You will soon realize that these early tools of man were made for two reasons: function and beauty. They represent a unique art form crafted by the world's earliest artists. Unique, because, like snowflakes, each specimen is an original and no two are exactly alike.

Many different materials were utilized in crafting these points. From crude slate, conglomerate or quartzite, to high quality flint, agate, jasper, chalcedony, petrified wood or volcanic obsidian, the list is endless. The Indians went to great lengths to obtain high quality material from the popular flint and chert quarries known to them, such as Dover in Northwest Tennessee, Flint Ridge in Ohio, and the many obsidian sources of the west. It is believed that extensive trade networks for flint and other objects were established in the earliest times and extended over vast areas from coast to coast.

The variations in shape and flaking style are clues to dating and identifying point types. The novice should study points from the different periods illustrated in this book and become familiar with the various styles produced. Generally speaking, the older Paleo and Archaic types are better made, exhibiting the finest flaking, thinness, edge work, and symmetry ever produced by man. The earliest points are mostly auriculate or eared. Some are grooved in the center or fluted. Later, these forms basically became side-notched, corner-notched, basal-notched or stemmed. With the introduction of the bow, most points became smaller and lighter with stemmed bases. However, during the Woodland period, Paleo auriculate and Archaic notched forms reappeared for a short period of time.

Some collectors specialize in a particular type, while others try to assemble a collection of many shapes and types. Most collectors are only interested in points from their immediate locale, and only if found by them. However, this author has learned after many years of hunting, that the only way to put together a quality collection is through intelligent buying. It's a rare occurrence today to find an outstanding piece for your collection by hunting in thefield.

FIRE DAMAGED POINTS

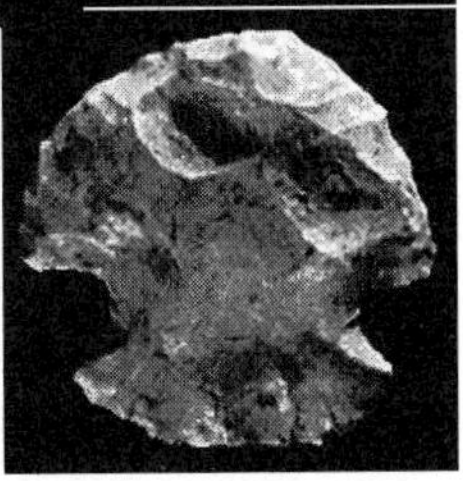

Points made of flint, chert, chalcedony, and other materials are susceptible to damage when in close contact with fire and heat. This can occur when points shot at an animal are left in the butchered meat that is cooked over a fire. Fire damaged flint reflects a rather unique appearance, usually a circular pitted, or pock-marked look not unlike miniature moon craters.

(Examples of fire damaged points) Note typical pitting damage to the surfaces.

There have been theories that the intense heat of fire actually brings about a molecular change or rearrangement of molecules. This undue stress or tension causes a change in the material which induces the pock-marks to form. This has been questioned and criticized by some geologists who flatly state that no such action takes place.

The acceptable and more logical explanation is that the change is purely physical. That is, the heat from the fire is applied and transferred in such a random and uneven manner that the coefficients of contraction and expansion cause the damage or pitting.

The resultant conflict of expansion and non-expansion coefficients flake off the flint material due to tensions within itself. The resultant flake is quite different from a pressure or percussion flake in that it is circular and, of course, non-controllable. The examples illustrated show points with the typical pitting associated with fire damage:

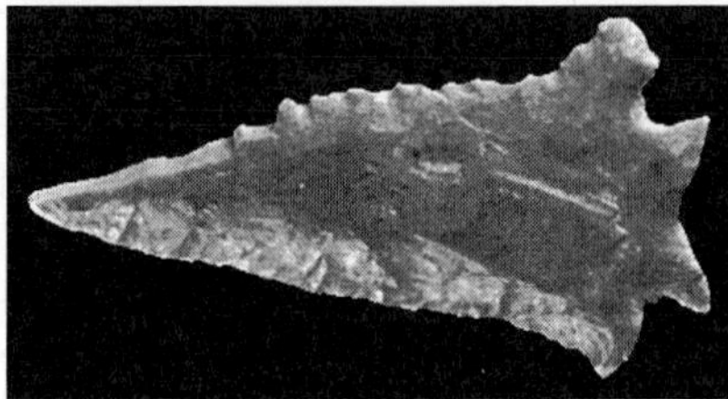

Decatur points typically are fractured at the base, shoulders and rarely, the tip. This example shows a long tip fracture which could be caused from impact.

IMPACT FRACTURES

When spear and arrow points are thrown or shot, they sometimes collide with hard objects such as bone in animals or rock or wood when the target is missed. If the angle at the point of impact is just right, the resulting blow will fracture the point, forming a flute or channel that runs from the tip toward the base. In other examples the fracturing will run up the side, or the tip of the point will simply snap off. Occasionally, these broken points with impact fluting are remade into new points with the flute channel still visible (see illustration). These should not be confused with real fluted Paleo points that were found by later Indians and rechipped into a more recent point, also with the fluting still present. Points with well defined impact fractures are interesting additions to any collection and should not be overlooked when going through the junk boxes.

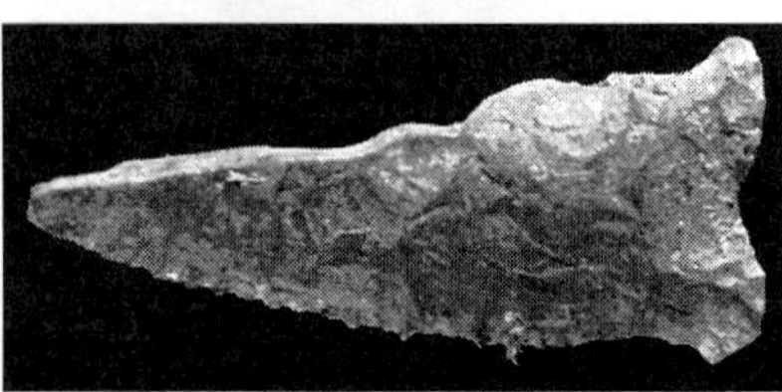

Typical impact fractures on above greenbrier points. The top point was salvaged with the tip repaired after the impact.

HAFTING

All finished arrow points and most knives were made to be inserted or tied onto a shaft or handle. To prevent movement, sinew, gut, and rawhide were used to tie the stone blades onto the shafts or handles. Fibers from hair and plants (grasses, tree bark, yucca, vines, etc.) were also employed for lashing.

Pitch, asphalt and resin were used as adhesives (when available) to glue the lashings to the stone and shaft. In some of the western states where climates are very dry, complete specimens of arrows and knives have been found preserved in caves. On rare occasions complete arrows and knives have been found with hafting completely intact. Of course, during the Indian wars out west in the 1800s, perfect hafted specimens were collected and saved from the battlefields as well. Cane and many types of wood were employed for arrow shaft usage while bone, ivory and wooden handles were crafted for holding the knives.

Above: A rare example of a hafted arrow-point on a wooden shaft. This arrow was found in New Mexico or Nevada. The binding is fashioned of fibres from a local plant.

DATING AND NAMING POINT TYPES

For decades, professional archaeologists and collectors have been interested in the age and classification of projectile points. Of course the best information has come from archaeologically controlled scientific excavations where exact locations, cultural association, and carbon dating of associated matter with point types was made.

The carbon deposits from animal and vegetable remains are taken from these stratigraphic layers and dated through the carbon-14 process and other techniques. This gives an age for each layer and its associated artifacts. In 1997 it was reported that all previously published carbon-14 dates are now slightly older than realized. Adjustments should be made on a logarithmic scale with age. **Clovis** is now believed to be about 2,000 years earlier.

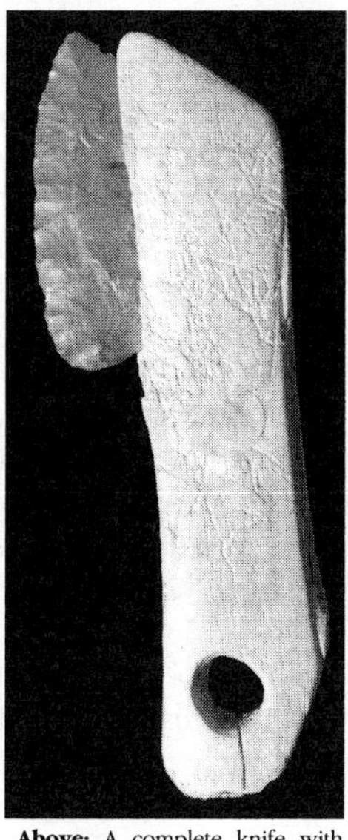

Above: A complete knife with bone handle and flint blade recovered in eastern Colorado. Note drilled hole in handle

Above: A complete knife with bone handle and flint blade recovered 4 feet below the floor of a dry cave in Fort Rock desert in south central Oregon. Note the tally marks at the rear of the handle and the gut hafting and gum or asphaltum adhesive cementing the blade to the handle.

Many of these sites were occupied for thousands of years by various peoples who left projectile points around their campfires, buried for future discovery with thousands more lost through usage and breakage. The face of the land next to rivers where many of these sites are, is always changing due to flooding. Indian villages and campsites were either being eroded away or buried under silt deposited by the flooding river. Later, the sites that were destroyed would become occupied again, waiting for the next inundation. Over a period of thousands of years, these sites accumulated many stratified layers of silt, some of which contain evidence of human occupation. The most recent culture would be near the top with the oldest at the deepest levels.

Some of these excavated areas produce important point types which were named after the site from which they were found. Sometimes popular "type styles" such as **Clovis** are found all across the country while others are very localized and found only in a few counties. Some of the more famous type sites are **Cahokia** at St. Clair and Madison counties in Illinois, **Eva** and **Nuckolls** in northwest Tennessee, **Quad** and **Pine Tree** in northwest Alabama, **Clovis** near Clovis, New Mexico, **Folsom** near Folsom, New Mexico, **Graham Cave** in Montgomery Co., Missouri, **Midland** near Midland, Texas and **Sandia** from the Sandia Cave near Albuquerque, New Mexico. There are many more sites too numerous to list here.

These excavations have provided valuable information about point types and their cultural relationships. Papers published (by the archaeologists who worked the sites) about these excavations were the first attempt at typing or classifying projectile points. These papers and books are still important reference sources today and belong in every reference library.

WHY ANOTHER ARROWHEAD BOOK?

The author of this book has felt the need for a more comprehensive book on arrowheads; a book that would not only show more detail in each illustration, but a spread of variations for each type as well. Many of the existing type books give only one example of each type, usually a pen and ink drawing. Since most point types have many variations, it is difficult and frustrating to classify a collection from only one example of each type. There is also a problem classifying points from artwork because we are at the mercy of the artist to accurately portray the subtleties of each type illustrated.

We believe, as well as other collectors, that only photographs can properly show the flaking technique, patination, and other factors that are important in cultural period classification. Also, the texture of the material, beveling, serrations, etc. are shown in much more detail with photographs. In this volume, where we felt there was a need, several specimens of a type are shown. We have also included additional supportive information to ensure that this book is the most helpful and comprehensive of its kind to collectors.

All mistakes are our own. We have gone to great lengths to ensure that only genuine pre-Columbian artifacts are used for illustrations. Where there was any question of a point's authenticity we did not include it. There were also problems in classifying some of the variants and placing the photographs under their proper types. Again, errors in this area, as they occur, will be remedied in future editions.

This reference work is not inclusive of all known types, although hundreds are named and listed. These will be added in future editions as good examples become available for us to photograph. We solicit your comments, critique and type suggestions for future editions of this work.

HOW POINTS WERE MADE

Decades ago this author was spending his weekends hunting rivers, fields and streams for the elusive #9s and 10s but usually coming home with the average 3s and 4s. His hunting territory covered several states including dozens of private farms, rivers, creeks and lakes. The usual procedure when hunting on private land was always to ask permission. This required a short visit with the owner who would be sizing you up before allowing access to his land. Some of the farmers were very suspicious of strangers because of their hidden whisky stills.

During these interesting visits, I would hear stories of how the farmers thought the Indians made arrowheads. A common tale was that the Indians would heat up a container of water. After getting it as hot as they could, they would take an eagle feather, dipping it in the scoulding water, then carefully releasing drops onto the flint causing an immediate fracturing to occur. Eventually they would end up with a finished arrowhead. Although this story was pretty common, I don't think any of the farmers ever tried it to see if it would really work.

Actually flint tools are made by the art of knapping flint. Hundreds of thousands of years ago, far away from this country, early homo erectines learned how to knap flint. The earliest forms from Africa have been dated to 2.2 million years ago. Secrets of the knappers art came with the first peoples to inhabit the Americas. Beginning with Paleo Man the best sources for quarrying flint and chert were soon found. The technique of exposing flint to heat to change its molecular structure making it more "glassy" and easier to flake was learned prior to Paleo times. Heat treating changes the color as well, sometimes making it difficult to match the altered stone with local sources.

(examples of a group of spent cores made from spalls)

Although small points were crafted from local materials such as small nodules that can be found along rivers and streams, the larger points were made from a large nodule. The flintknapper takes the nodule and knocks off a chunk forming a spall. He then strikes off long slivers that can be crafted into points. As the slivers are struck off, a circular core is formed. Eventually the core is discarded and the process starts over. Flint flakes can be removed easily in the direction of the force applied. Indians used hammer stones, elk billits, and other tools in rough shaping the stone through percussion blows. After a suitable form was achieved with the proper thickness, the final shaping was accomplished using tools such as the fine tips of antlers. This procedure is called "pressure flaking" and was carefully applied to all edges and was used to create the notches on side and corner notched points.

BUYING POINTS

FINDING VERSUS BUYING POINTS

Why would a collector want to buy points instead of just finding his own? The answer to this question is very simple. Many people who collect just don't have the time to spend hunting in the field. In most cases, you can buy points cheaper than you can find them, when you consider travel, lodging, food, and the money you could be earning if you were at home. But the best reason for buying is to acquire quality pieces that are not available or found in your immediate area of hunting. Not all collectors are fortunate enough to live in an area that produces high quality material. Many collectors hunt in plowed fields that do sometimes produce high quality points, but unfortunately most are broken or chipped by the plow and cutting harrow.

One collector lived and hunted in central Alabama and Mississippi for ten years, keeping every piece that was found. Later, when he took a realistic look at his collection, it was only worth about $1,000.00 and the points in the collection looked very common. He began selling everything but the most perfect pieces. He used the money to finance hunting trips to other areas that were strong with quality points, and also began to buy nice pieces as they became available. His previous collection was basically all the same color. He soon found that points from other areas were more colorful, and within three years he had built a large collection that anyone would be proud to own. He kept up this style of collecting for several years and has owned many super quality pieces worth a substantial amount of money. If he had not ventured out into other hunting areas his collection today would still be worth little and of low quality. Try acquiring a quality item, whether it be stone, bone, pottery, or flint. After all, isn't this what collecting is all about?

HOW TO BUY AUTHENTIC RELICS

The best way to recognize an old point is by knowing how both river and field patination affects the type of flint from which the point is made. Each point type also has its own style of chipping that you should study and understand. A Paleo point never has random flaking, while Archaic and Woodland points do. You should understand that changes in patination along the edges or near the tip of an arrowhead are signs of rechipping. Hinge fractures are good indicators to the authenticity of a point. An old point will patinate underneath the hinge fractures while recently applied patina will only be on the surface. Hold the point up to a light source and look along the edges for restoration. You can also lightly tap the surface of a point with a steel knife blade to find a restored area. The restored spot will have a dull sound. Restored areas will also look different under a black light.

If you go to a show, flea market, or someone's house to buy relics, you should first size up the collection or inventory that is for sale. Look for any questionable pieces. If the relics past the test, then you must determine if the person selling the relics is trustworthy. If he looks untrustworthy, you should probably not take the risk.

But if you are convinced the person is of good character and the piece you want really looks good and authentic, you could use the following guidelines to protect yourself. First, ask for a money back guarantee in writing. Some dealers will comply but may put a time limit on it. Also ask if the point has been restored or rechipped. Second, you could ask for a satisfaction guarantee. This means that if you do get a piece that becomes questionable later, you would be able to trade it for another item of equal value that you feel is a good authentic piece. This arrangement would help you feel more secure about what you are buying. Third, especially if a lot of money is at risk, you should tell the person that you want to send the relic to someone for authentication before the sale is final. If a lot of money is at risk, you may want to get more than one opinion. Ask around to find out who the best authenticators are for your area.

There is a lot of competition in the Indian relic market. Some people will condemn a competitor's piece to persuade you to buy from them. They will also try to buy a good item from you at a cheap price. Others may say a relic is bad just to convince you that they are experts. To be truly knowledgeable in Indian relics, this book will help, but you need to learn as much as you can. Study the flint types of your collecting area and how they look with natural patination. Learn to match flaking styles with types. Simply look at as many good authentic points as you can. Remember, the people who think they know more than everyone else are usually the ones who get burned.

MARKET REPORTS

The arrowhead market has continued to enjoy significant growth over the past two years. This book is reaching more collectors than ever before and artifact show attendance has been good. While at the shows, we have noticed an increase in people who are authenticating relics, which is a true sign of increased interest. Collectors should know that relic authentication is very difficult and requires experts who have many years of experience. Since anyone can paper (authenticate) a relic, the wise collector should still check expensive relics (although papered) with experts they trust before spending large sums of money.

Many collectors are still having good luck hunting and finding choice relics in their areas. Some recent finds reported to us include such rare types as **Allen, Clovis, Eden, Folsom, Midland**, etc.

Of course high grade examples of all Paleo types have been setting record prices across the country. A group of three Knife River **Folsom** points from North Dakota sold for $20,000. Another nice agate **Folsom** from New Mexico brought $8500. A 6" high grade Texas **Clovis** had a turned down offer of $15,000! A 4" **Eden** from Wyoming with a broken base sold for $2200. **Cody Complex** knives from North Dakota were getting from $600 to over $3000 each.

Many high grade Archaic points were in high demand from **Dovetails** in Ohio to **Lost Lakes** in Kentucky and Tennessee. Mississippian to Historic arrow points, when in top grade were getting high prices. Extremely high grade Caddo **Agee** points from Arkansas have been selling recently for $800 to $3000 each.

There is no question about it, this market is on the move with record sales occuring every day not only on the Internet but from auctions, dealers lists and at shows. The following market reports were prepared by some of our advisors from around the country and are included here for your information.

TOM DAVIS - STANTON, KY

The artifact marketplace has been very healthy over the past two years; from excellent auction sales to convention sales to mail order. In March of last year we auctioned off the famous Ken Partain collection. Many collectors and dealers participated in this auction which was a real opportunity for everyone to acquire a few choice pieces for their collections. In fact, all the auctions we were involved in last year were very healthy with record prices being paid for choice pieces.

Paleo points have been very popular and continue to command high prices when they grade in the 9 to 10 range. Since we are a National dealer and sell artifacts from all over the country, we can say that interest in high grade relics of most types is on the increase. All of our lists were virtual sell-outs and it is becoming more difficult to replace the choice pieces that we sell.

We have seen a pick-up in interest for top quality points with minor expert restoration, or rechipped points, if reasonably priced. What use to be $1.00 points a few years ago are now bringing $2-$3 each now. Northwest gem points, Texas bird points and Southeastern arrow points in high grade are in demand. Authentic points made out of colorful material from southern Georgia, southern Alabama and Florida continue to bring top dollar. We have difficulty stocking points from the Northeast, but when we do offer them for sell, they sell very fast.

Pottery of all grades is making a strong comeback. From Caddo to Quapaw red and white to greyware, all are doing well. Slate relics and pipes are very strong. Single pipes have sold for up to $33,000 at auction last year. Overall, the entire market is very strong and healthy. We would like to report a few more record auction sales: A 3" **Adena** – $2,700; a 4" **Adena** – $5,500, a 6" **Adena** – $10,700; a 3-3/4" **Buck Creek** – $1050; a 3-1/2" **Clovis** – $4,700; a 4-5/8" **Dovetail** – $4,500; a 5-1/2" **Mehlville** – $3,600.

BILL AND DONNA JACKSON - OXNARD, CA

We would like to thank Gemstone Publishing for allowing us to provide our input on the ever growing artifact collecting industry. Because of this publication, there are new collectors everywhere who are able to make educated judgements on purchases, and sellers everywhere who use this guide to help them price their pieces wisely. Because our clientele consists of thousands of collectors and dealers from all 50 states and many foreign countries, we feel we have a good idea what the current market is like, not just in our area, but across the nation and around the world.

The following impressions are true of our business, but we also believe them to be universal in this market. Paleo pieces continue to be the most highly sought after, followed by Archaic era **Dovetails** and **Lost Lakes**. But to say any Paleo or Early Archaic piece is always preferred over any later piece is not accurate. While we have sold several **Clovis** and **Cumberland** points in excess of $10,000 apiece, indeed, the highest price we have ever received for an artifact was paid for a wonderful relic from the Hopewell Culture.

It has been our experience that the number one criterion of an artifact's desirability is its condition (symmetry and shape). Number two is its color (material). Number three is its size (all things else equal, larger can bring multiples more), and lastly, but not foremost, as often assumed, is type. Therefore a huge perfect **Clovis** made of colorful Flint Ridge is highly collectable, and is worth whatever it takes to acquire it . We have learned the indisputable fact is that *perfection is priceless, and everything else is negotiable!*

The growing popularity of internet relic offerings has produced a number of new "dealers," "authenticators," and self proclaimed "experts." The best advice we can give to those looking to build a collection is that if something is too good to be true, it always is! Trust only those who offer a money back guarantee, and who allow time for you to obtain opinions from known authenticators.

With that in mind, we feel that investing in artifacts is wiser than any other investing arena, and is certainly more fun.

Our market trends indicate that western gem points, Florida agatized coral points, and perfect Texas pieces are becoming more and more sought after, and represent super investments at this time. Slate and hardstone remain undervalued and represent great buys as well. But don't rule out anything if it is perfect, colorful, and authentic.

Basically, we see an onslaught of interest and the resultant exponential explosion in the number of collectors entering the hobby at the same time as the really good artifacts are appearing less and less often. Our attitude is simply, if it is perfect or colorful, guaranteed authentic, and you like it... buy it! Whatever you pay today will likely look cheap in a couple of years.

GARY L. FOGELMAN - TURBOTVILLE, PA

The following information has been garnered from attendance at auctions, flea markets, and shows, and receipt of dealer price lists and after-auction prices-realized lists, and personal involvement in selling artifacts.

Not a lot has changed in the past year, except for the high-end values of the better artifacts, which keeps going up and up. There were several auctions throughout the year, one of note, while collectors continue to haunt yard sales and household auctions and occasionally come up with something nice in that way. Flea markets and shows continue to be popular places to sell, and secure relics, and several planned events throughout the year help the collectors that buy with their endeavors.

There was one really good auction this year, that of the F.J. Hesse collection in New York State. This collection was full of superior items from the Northeast and elsewhere, and prices realized here can act as a barometer of the way things are.

Several flint types eagerly sought by collectors here in the Northeast were present, in good size and quantity. These included **Susquehanna Broadpoints**, **Perkiomen Broadpoints**, **Genesee** points, **Atlantic Phase Blades**, **Orient Fishtails**, and others. These excite interest because they can be large in size, with the better ones made of good grade flints from the area. There were numerous examples of all of these, most in range, and most sold in the $200-$500 range. A couple of exceptions: a 4-3/4" **Perkiomen Broadpoint** made of brown jasper sold for $5800, the highest price paid for a piece of flint, perhaps the highest lot in the entire auction. A 4-1/4" **Susquehanna** of jasper sold for $1700. Two nice **Dovetails**, 3-5" in length and made of translucent quartzite, both from Illinois, sold for $500 each.

Fluted points always sell well, the dozen in this collection being no exception. Average price was $350-$450 for points in the 2-3" range. The range was $240 for a 1" chalcedony point to $950 for a 2" jasper fluted point from New Jersey.

A wide array of nice stone tools was contained in the Hesse collection. Let's begin with gouges. These always sell well providing they have nice form and aren't too banged up. Those in this collection would have to be classed as better examples, most in the 5-8" range. Prices spread from $170-$525. I've seen larger specimens sell for much more, and naturally this holds true for everything.

Axes, full grooved and 3/4 grooved, in the 4-9" range, sold for $230-$500. Celts, which have to be nice to bring much of anything, sold for $100-$260. Some of these were of hardstone, the top one being made of Ohio Puddingstone.

There were some large, and unique, pestles involved in the collection, and they sold at good prices. The pestles were nicely formed and symmetrical, 18-20" long, and sold for $250-$375. One human-face effigy pestle sold for $1500, while a bear head effigy pestle sold for $950.

Ground slate points, knives and ulus are also avidly sought, and there were some nice examples of all. The ulu's were 4-6" in length, one of them was tallied, and they sold for $375-$775. The points/knives, 2-4" in length, went for $160-$240.

Beveled adzes are another artifact form mostly found in the Northeast, and some nice ones were sold off. At 4-6" in length, the prices varied from $140-$300.

Oh, the bannerstones! There were several top-drawer bannerstones, of elegant style, unique material, and pictured in the bannerstone book. One sold for $3500, another for $1700. Others, still nice, sold for $1000 down to $375.

Among the same general category, boatstones sold for $240-$775, bar amulets about the same except for the beauty of a large, exquisite one, which sold for $3100. (These prices, by the way, do not include the 10% buyers premium or applicable state taxes!)

Also in the slate line, pendents and gorgets sold for $150 all the way to $1600, while another brought $1300. And let's not forget birdstones. A nice bar type brought a value of $2800, while others of smaller and various forms brought anywhere from $675 (the only one below a thousand), to $1850. An average would probably be $1500-$1700.

Many nice pipes, plain, fancy and effigy, were knocked down. The plain pipes went for $525-$900. These were mainly perfect, nice specimens. Among the effigy pipes, the prices were generally over $1000, like $1300, $1800, $2000 and $2500. The effigies consisted of human face effigies and animal and bird forms common among the Iroquois. And, a unique 3piece set of Ohio Pipestone tube pipes in 3 stages of development, sold for $2600.

Some nice bone combs, awls, fish hooks and harpoons brought good prices, as such items usually do, being much more rare than stone items. Bone combs also usually have effigies involved and some of these did, the combs ranged from $1220 to $1750, and usually these were not even complete items, but rather portions of combs. Bone fish hooks went for what I thought were very good prices, but the hooks were unique, and large, bringing from $160-$525. Harpoons too, some nicely serrated ones, sold for $270-$450. Little catlinite maskettes went from $400 to $1450.

Clay pots, another scarce item in general, were amply represented in the Hesse collection. These ranged from those 6" to those 9" or so in height. Some had considerable restoration, some minimal, but it didn't seem to matter, especially if there was ample decoration or effigies involved on the vessels. Clay pots, a hard-to-come-by item in the Northeast, are finally beginning to realize what they should. For too long they've been under-valued, and I feel they still are, for the number that are available. The dozen or more in this sale went from $600 to $1800.

Besides restoration on the pottery, restoration was affected to some of the better quality flint, and I've noticed, the better the quality or rarity, the less and less it matters anymore. As always, restored items are providing a way to obtain rare, unique and better quality pieces that are prohibitively expensive.

Overall, the trend from the past continues. The better quality, rare and well documented items will continue to command high prices, as they should. The influx of fakes each year assures this. The Northeast is not immune to fakes, and they show up at many auctions and household sales. Someone continues to make **Susquehanna Broadpoints** and **Perkiomen Broadpoints** out of jasper and rhyolite, while some collectors continue to purchase un-documented nice pieces through the mail from unreliable sources.

RON HARRIS - HICKORY, NC

Collectors in this region are eagerly seeking Paleo points such as Eastern Fluted **Clovis, Hardaway, Hardaway Daltons** and **Alamance** types.

Also in great demand are well made archaic corner notched types such as **Kirk** and **Palmer**. Well made stemmed points in demand include large **Savannah River, Kirk Serrated** and **Morrow Mountain** types.

Bifurcated points in demand in the region include **Lecroy, Stanley** and **Kirks**. The larger **Yadkins**, well made **Caraway** and **Uwharrie** woodland points are of much interest to area collectors.

The artifact market in this region as a whole is growing considerably with more and more people becoming interested in artifact collecting and attending artifact related shows and sales. Well made, thin, colorful material points are very popular and prices at various shows in the area reflect this. However, some sellers have greatly overpriced their specimens and those items won't move until prices have been adjusted to accomodate the market.

Some older collections throughout the territory have recently been sold mostly as a whole rather than individually. The new buyers generally keep select artifacts for their personal collection and sell the rest on an individual basis in an effort to recoup their outlay or the best part of it.

Buyers have to beware of purchases due to a great many fakes being on the market from out of the area. However, typically, lithic material from this region characteristicly is difficult to artificially patinate and is usually easily detected.

With more and more "No-Till" type farming, more and more construction and road work and less and less general farming, it is increasingly more difficult to find sites to surface hunt in most of the areas. This is resulting in more and more interest in artifact shows, swaps and sales rather than depending in the find-your-own approach.

Field Points in the region tend to hold at $3.00 to $5.00 in bulk. Quality point prices and points that are not plentiful will continue to command higher prices as dictated by the market and demand.

In general, the market for the region is good and the outlook for 1999 is even better.

JIM AND CARLOS TATUM - TAMPA, FL

The artifact market in the Gulf Coastal Region during the last two years has been healthy. Interest has never been higher nor activity more intense. Attendance at shows has been high and consistent, trading has been brisk and collecting activity in the field has been frequent and productive.

Some regions of the south have experienced recent extensive flooding which eroded fields and moved sand on the river bottoms. This resulted in a flurry of activity by artifact hunters, and a great many new additions have appeared in collections, some of which must naturally become available on the market. Likewise, activity generates activity and many new faces are appearing at the shows as new collectors are attracted to the hobby, in spite of (or because off) more and more restrictions on acquisition and possession of artifacts.

As is to be expected, the market continues to be very strong for top quality rock, especially fine Paleos, **Hillsboroughs** and **Hernandos**. Likewise, high grade stone and especially coral continues to be in demand. Perhaps gaining in strength during the past two years is in an interest in small, true arrowheads --**Pinellas, Tampas, Yadkins, Ichetucknees, Copenas** -- and in good bone work (known as Florida Black Bone in other regions). **Waller knives** have taken a recent jump in popularity and point restorations are gaining in acceptance and are moving more and more as an increasing number of collectors are seeking high quality points which have higher and higher prices. This demand for quality restoration work is being met by an increasing number of new artisans who are offering their services on the market.

Pottery continues to be scarce and will probably become more so; compared to the Midwest, slate and ground stone is over-priced in Florida but will probably hold or increase in value due to its extreme scarcity. Interest in Contact Period material continues to be strong. Interest in Historic beads is probably at an all time high, due in part to the material recently produced by the "Trading Post" site in southwest Florida, the largest bead find in North America. Low-end material is very weak: A point worth $20 five years ago is still worth about $20 and thus has lost value due to inflation. Fossils, especially those possibly associated with early man, such as Pleistocene mastodon and mammoth teeth, are seen with increasing frequency at the shows and seem to be moving briskly.

Regrettably, fakes on the market are more abundant than ever and this is a black mark on the entire hobby. In spite of laudable efforts to curtail their circulation at shows, they continue to flourish, and I don't know the answer to this problem. Knap-ins are increasing in frequency and I like to see this, but we must continue to put pressure on knappers to sign their work. It is of some significance that five years ago there were perhaps a handful of authenticators and now there are dozens.

All in all, the Southeast has enjoyed a recent period of productive activity and a few high dollar transactions have been reported. A cache of four or five large spears was said to have exchanged hands for a five-figure sum this past year, and there have been reports of several Archaic and Paleo points selling for between five and 10 thousand each.

M. K. McCOY - MOUNT JULIET, TN

Not much has changed since the last book was published. Museum quality points of all types are bringing a premium-in most cases more than the top dollar as shown in #5. Prices on lower grade points seem to be stagnant, and in most cases are not bringing book prices. **Paleos** (fluted) points, **Dovetails**, and **Lost Lake** points are still the best desired points in this area with **Lost Lake** points showing the most significant increase in the past two years. **Bentons** are off a bit as are **Harpeth Rivers**. The demand for Mississippian artifacts seems to be limited to a smaller number of advanced collectors. (I'm refering to Ceremonial artifacts such as Duck River swords, etc.). **Knight Island** and **Jacks Reef** points have really increased in value if they are top quality. As always, early archaic points (**Pine Trees**, **Greenbriars** etc.) are much more in demand than woodland points (**Copena**, **Adena** etc.) although super examples of these types are bringing top dollar.

Attendance at local shows has been good this year. Earlier in the year buying was a bit soft but picked up later in the year.

Important sales that I'm aware of include a number of **Lost Lake** points in the $4-$8,000 range, a 6" **Copena** at $3,300, a 9" **Pickwick** at $6,000, a colorful **Adena Blade** (5-1/2") at $4,000 and a 6 point **Benton cache** at $4,500.

DONALD F. MEADOR - DALLAS, TX

The Texas market in 1998 has been better than ever. Certain types such as **Clovis**, **Folsom**, **Midland**, **Milnesand**, large **Plainviews**, **Andice**, **Eden**, **Firstview** and **Scottsbluff** have more than doubled in price this year. Museum quality pieces are bringing high dollar and are much sought after. I see many new faces here and a lot of type collections starting.

As a whole, artifacts are the best investment I know of. A nice G9 **Midland** sold for $900 and a broken **Folsom** brought $500.

LYLE G. NICKEL - ENID, OK

The artifact market in the South Central United States appears to be strong and growing. The trend will probably continue, as more collectors become active in the buying and selling of artifacts. This market is controlled, as are most other markets, by supply and demand. Looking at that aspect, in itself, says that high grading artifacts are going to be subject to higher price fluctuations.

As always, the earliest flint (**Clovis, Folsom, Scottsbluff, Eden, Plainview** and **Allen**) receives the most attention. However, other point types (**Bell, Andice, Calf Creek, Dalton, Montell, Tang Knives**) in the G7 - G10 range are in demand. Mississippian period points (**Hayes, Agee**, in particular) are also going up in value. High grading artifacts of most any time period are now very collectible.

With arrowhead collecting being what it is today, there are very important things for the collector to consider. First and foremost, "Is this a genuine prehistoric artifact?" You don't need to grade it if it's not old! Modern knappers are schooled and very good at their craft. Know what you're doing or get help. There are genuine artifacts for sale.

Also, be honest with yourself in grading a piece. Grade 9 and 10 points are very rare, and the grading of points will vary with each collector's individual preferences (perfection, quality of chipping, color and material).

A market that I believe will have future promise is restored flint of high quality. Pottery has also shown increased interest at sales and auctions of late.

A few prices that we have seen recently include a 5" **Clovis** selling for $6,000.00+ and a restored (one complete barb) **Calf Creek** for $500.00+. It is very common to see **Scottsbluffs** and other forms of similar age and high quality with an asking price of $1,000.00+.

JOHN BYRD - PIEDMONT, SC

In the brief span of two years, since the last price guide was published, some astounding changes have occurred. More states have attempted to restrict or outlaw artifact collecting while the prices of some scarce types have reached amounts unimaginable several years ago. Despite this, the hobby continues to flourish.

It is distressing to see so many state legislatures caving in to radical special interest groups. A number have already made it illegal to even dig for Indian relics on private property. To me this is a direct encroachment upon our basic constitutional rights. As if these new laws are not bad enough, government agencies are prosecuting honest people by taking existing legislation far beyond its original intent. But, does this discourage the collecting of Indian artifacts? Not at all. The only thing it has done is create an inflated market value for these relics.

Particularly scarce or high quality artifacts have increased many fold in value. Paleo-Indian items in particular have risen dramatically in cost with many fine authentic examples reaching five figure prices. This trend is great if you are selling but it is getting to the place where most average collectors cannot afford good representative specimens. This causes me some concern for the young collectors just starting out. We will probably see a lot fewer people collecting artifacts in the future for strictly economic reasons.

I commented in the fifth edition on the fast growing popularity of nice quality broken artifacts. This area of interest has proven to be even hotter than expected. The supply of quality damaged relics has started to rapidly decrease now. I have even seen broken reproductions turning up for sale at the shows.

When you look at it in terms of supply and demand, this hobby will continue to be a good investment for the foreseeable future. But, be prepared to pay more for quality genuine artifacts.

BEN STERMER - PHOENIX, AZ

Native American projectile points of the western United States have long been highly regarded by collectors for their great variety, excellent workmanship and quality of material. Included are the famed "gem points" of the Columbia River, the serrated **Calapooya** points of Oregon's Willamette Valley, the unique Great Basin forms, and some equally beautiful points from California. Values for top quality pieces have increased during the past few years, and demand remains very strong. Points of fine material, with good workmanship and symmetry, as well as excellent provenance, will nearly always bring a higher price. Less common points, such as the **Klickitat**, the **Calapooya**, and the **Stockton** are much sought after simply for the fact that they are found in very limited numbers, and their areas of distribution are quite small in comparision to other types of the same period. Several forms from the Great Basin are still available at very reasonable prices. Early forms, many of which have not been "officially" named yet, such as the "early leaf" and "early stemmed" points should prove to be very good investments.

Many of the "early stemmed" points bear a strong resemblance to points of the Cody Complex, yet have much smaller price tags. Other "sleepers" are the **Cascade**, **Humboldt**, **Crescents**, and the early eared forms. Knives from the west are becoming increasingly popular. Large obsidian blades from Oregon and northern California are quite valuable. Smaller hafted knives can be found at reasonable prices; i.e., **Columbia Mule Ear**, **Plateau Pentagonal**, etc.

The future of collecting projectile points from the American west remains bright. For years, typology in this region was somewhat lacking in comparision with the east, but in recent years has become more complete.

GREGORY J. TRUESDELL (LENDS HIS HORSES GALLERY)

As the prices for mid-western and southern relics, particularly early Archaic and Paleo pieces, continue to rise to some lofty heights, northwest gempoints and obsidian point prices are really starting to escalate. High demand for really high quality pieces is driving the price of even lower grade, colorful pieces up continually. The market for other items seems to be all over the board with quality baskets and beadwork far outdistancing other areas of the Amerind market. Pottery and jewelry seem to be at the bottom of the market as are Navajo blankets.

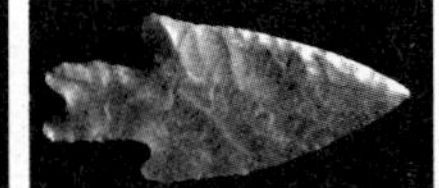

BUSINESS CARD DIRECTORY

You can have your business listed here for very reasonable rates. Send for details and deadline information for the next Guide. The following companies have paid to be included. We can not assume any responsibility in your dealings with these businesses. This list is provided for your information only. Remember, to be included in the next edition, call, fax or write for rates. **Arrowhead Guide**, Gemstone Publishing, Inc. 1966 Greenspring Drive, Suite LL3, Timonium, MD 21093. Call (888) 375-9800 Ext. 249, or fax (410) 560-7143, or e-mail **ads@gemstonepub.com**.

COLORADO - BUY - WYOMING
SELL

PALEO
WANTED
Collections Marbles

Bob Roth
25540 HWY 392
Greeley, CO 80631
(970) 352-5259

Jeb Taylor

P.O. Box 882
Buffalo, WY 82834

Indian Artifacts
Buy • Sell • Trade
Birch Bark Canoes
(307) 684-7042
Cell Phone: (509) 990-0235

FLINT/STONE/SLATE/POTTERY, ETC.

QUALITY RESTORATION

Buy • Sell • Appraisals • Consignments
DENNIS BUSHEY
113 Pine Forest Drive
Selma, AL 36701 • (334) 875-5299

LONNIE HARTLINE

5000 S.E. 48th
Oklahoma City, OK 73135
(405) 677-7745

Collector of Indian Relics
Buy, Sell or Trade

ARROWHEADS POTTERY

PREHISTORIC ARTIFACTS
BUY SELL TRADE
Ron Smith
(502) 395-0202
335 Princess Jennifer Dr.
Calvert City, Ky 42029

BACK TO EARTH®

ROCKS AND RELICS
Larry Garvin
Dept. 06
17 North LaSalle Drive
South Zanesville, OH 43701

EAGLE EYE GALLERY
146 Jay Street · Schenectady, NY 12305
(518) 346-3845

Native American Artifacts and Arts ·
Prehistoric Artifacts · Erthnographic Arts ·
Fossils · Minerals · Books · Antiques · Collectibles

GALLERY
- PRE COLUMBIAN ART -
JACK BOND
(813) 988-2132 · 11301 N. 56TH ST · TEMPLE TERRACE, FL 33617

CLASSIFIED ADS/DIRECTORY

You can have your business listed here for very reasonable rates. Send for details and deadline information for the next Guide. The following companies have paid to be included. We can not assume any responsibility in your dealings with these businesses. This list is provided for your information only. When planning your trips, it would be advisable to make appointments in advance. Remember, to be included in the next edition, call, fax or write for rates. **Arrowhead Guide**, Gemstone Publishing, Inc. 1966 Greenspring Drive, Suite LL3, Timonium, MD 21093. Call (888) 375-9800 Ext. 249, or fax (410) 560-7143, or e-mail **ads@gemstonepub.com**.

NEW YORK

Eagle Eye Gallery
146 Jay Street
Schenectady, NY 12305
Tel: (518) 346-3845

NORTH CAROLINA

The Coree Tribe, Inc.
137 Neal Drive
Atlantic, North Carolina 28511
Booklet available – Silent Warriors – The Coree Indians, by Chief J.L. "Turtle" Faircloth, Sr. Send $6.00 (postage paid). Referenced in the article in this book!

Advertise!

NORTHEASTERN SECTION:

This section includes point types from the following states: Conneticut, Delaware, Maine, Maryland, Massachusetts, New Hampshire, New Jersey, New York, Pennsylvania, Vermont.

The points in this section are arranged in alphabetical order and are shown **actual size**. All types are listed that were available for photographing. Any missing types will be added to future editions as photographs become available. We are always interested in receiving sharp, black and white or color glossy photos or color slides of your collection. Be sure and include a ruler in the photograph so that proper scale can be determined.

Lithics: Materials employed in the manufacture of projectile points from this region are: argillite, Coshocton chert, Coxsackie chert, crystal quartz, dolomite, felsite, Helderberg cherts, jasper, Ledge Ridge chert, Onondaga chert, quartzite, rhyolite, shale, slate, siltstone, vein quartz.

Important sites: Bull Brook (Paleo, Ipswich, Mass.), Burwell-Karako (Conn.), John's Bridge (Early Archaic, Conn.), Neville (Early Archaic, Manchester, NH), Plenge (Paleo, NJ), Shoop (Paleo, Dauphin Co., PA), Vail (Paleo, Maine).

Regional Consultant:
Gary Fogelman

Special Advisors:
Dr. Richard Michael Gramly
Richard Savidge

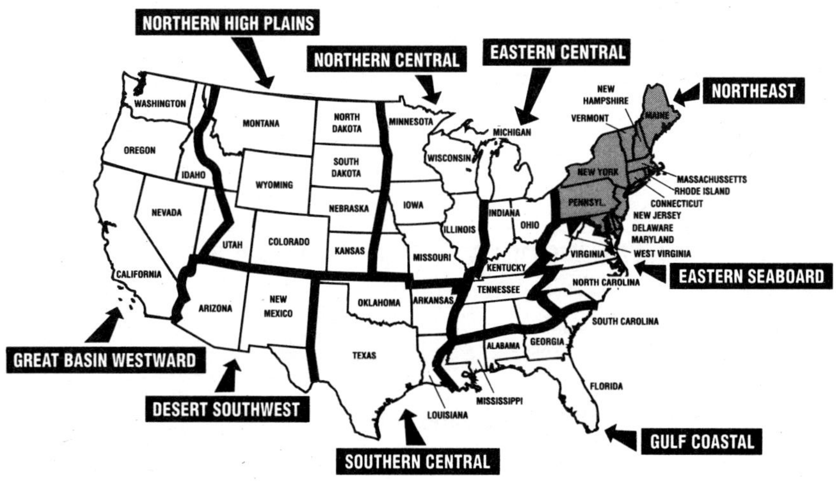

NORTHEASTERN POINT TYPES
(Archaeological Periods)

PALEO (14,000 B.P - 8,000 B.P.)

Agate Basin
Amos
Angostura
Arden
Beaver Lake
Charleston Pine Tree
Clovis
Crowfield
Cumberland (Barnes)
Dalton Classic
Dalton Nuckolls
Debert
Decatur
Eden
Graver
Hardaway
Haw River
Holcomb
Kanawha
Kessel
Northumberland Fluted Knife
Ohio Lanceolate
Palmer
Redstone
Scottsbluff
Scraper
Taunton Riv. Bif.

EARLY ARCHAIC (8,000 B.P - 6,500 B.P.)

Brodhead Side-Notched
Crooked Creek
Dovetail
Kirk Corner Notched
Kirk Serrated
Kirk Serrated Bifurcated
Kline
Lake Eerie
LeCroy
MacCorkle
Muncy Bifurcate
Neville
Penn's Creek Series
Penn's Creek Bifurcate

MID-LATE ARCHAIC (6,000 B.P - 4,000 B.P.)

Bare Island
Brewerton Auriculate
Brewerton Corner Notched
Brewerton Side Notched
Burwell
Chillesquaque
Crooked Creek
Dewart Stemmed
Drill
Duncan's Island
Genesee
Ground Slate
Guilford
Kanawha
Kittatiny
Lacawaxan
Lake Eerie Bifurcate
Lamoka
Lost Lake
Lycoming County
MacCorklen
Milford/Eshback
Morrow Mountain
Newmanstown
Otter Creek
Patuxent
Penn's Creek
Penn's Creek Bifurcate
Piedmont, Northern
Piney Island
Poplar Island
St. Albans
Savannah River
Snook Kill
Stanly
Strike-A-Lite I
Susquehanna Bifurcate
Taconic Stemmed
Vernon
Vestal Notched
Virginsville
Vosburg
Wapanucket

TERMINAL ARCHAIC (3,800 B.P - 3,000 B.P.)

Ashtabula
Conodoquinet/Canfield
Drill
Drybrook Fishtail
Frost Island
Koens Crispin
Lehigh
Mansion Inn
Meadowood
Normanskill
Nyack Side Notched
Orient Fishtail
Perkiomen Broadpoint
Schuylkill
Snook Kill
Susquehanna Broadpoint

EARLY-MIDDLE WOODLAND (2,800 B.P - 1,500 B.P.)

Adena
Adena Blade
Adena (Robbins)
Bennington Quail Tail
Erb Basal Notched
Forest Notched
Fox Creek
Garver's Ferry Corner Notched
Hellgramite
Kiski Notched
Meadowood
Oley
Ovates
Piscataway
Port Maitland
Sand Hill Stemmed
Tocks Island
Waratan

LATE WOODLAND (1,500 B.P - 500 B.P.)

Erie Triangle
Goddard
Jacks Reef Corner Notched
Jacks Reef Pentagonal
Levanna
Madison
Raccoon Notched
Randolph
Susquehannock
Vincent
Web Complex Blades

HISTORIC (350 B.P - 200 B.P.)

Trade Points

NE

NORTHEASTERN UNITED STATES
THUMBNAIL GUIDE SECTION

The following references are provided to aid the collector in easier and quicker identification of point types. All photos are exactly 30% of acutal size and are proportional to each other. Each point pictured in this section represents a classic form for the type. When a match is found, go to the alphabetical location of that type for more examples in true actual size.

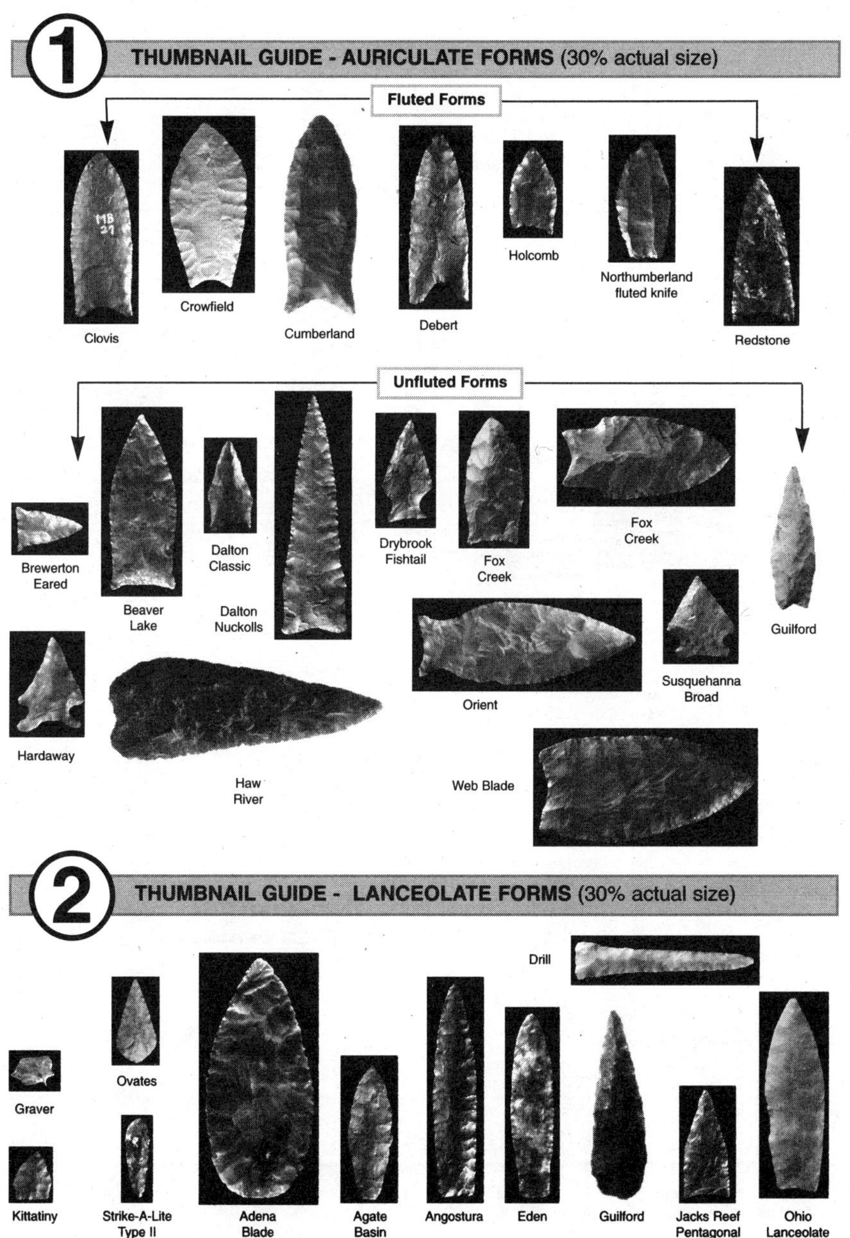

THUMBNAIL GUIDE - CORNER NOTCHED FORMS (30% actual size)

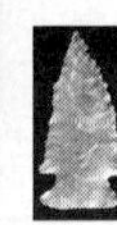

Amos · Arden · Brewerton · Crooked Creek · Decatur · Jacks Reef · Kiski Notched · Kline · Lycoming County · Oley · Palmer

Scraper · Susquehanna Broad · Vestal Notched · Charleston Pine Tree · Dovetail · Kirk · Lost Lake · Vosburg · Perkiomen

THUMBNAIL GUIDE - SIDE NOTCHED FORMS (30% actual size)

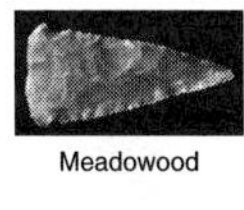

Brewerton · Brodhead · Goddard · Hellgramite · Kessel · Meadowood · Otter Creek

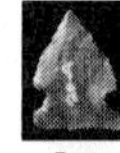

Port Maitland · Raccoon Notched · Strike-A-Lite Type I · Susquehanna Broad · Wapanucket

THUMBNAIL GUIDE - STEMMED FORMS (30% actual size)

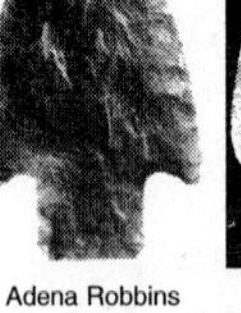
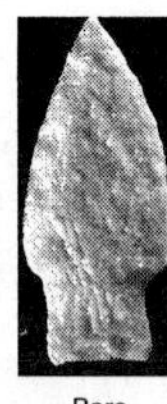

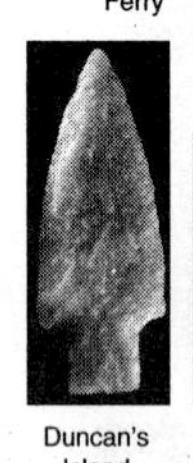

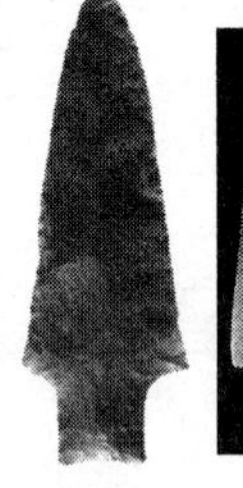

Adena Robbins · Bare Island · Burwell · Chillesquaque · Dewart Stemmed · Drill · Duncan's Island · Garver's Ferry · Fox Creek · Genesee · Ground Slate

Penn's Creek · Randolph · Hoover's Island · Kirk Serrated · Lamoka · Neville · Newmanstown · Piedmont Northern · Piney Island · Sandhill Stemmed · Savannah River · Scottsbluff

THUMBNAIL GUIDE - Stemmed Forms (continued)

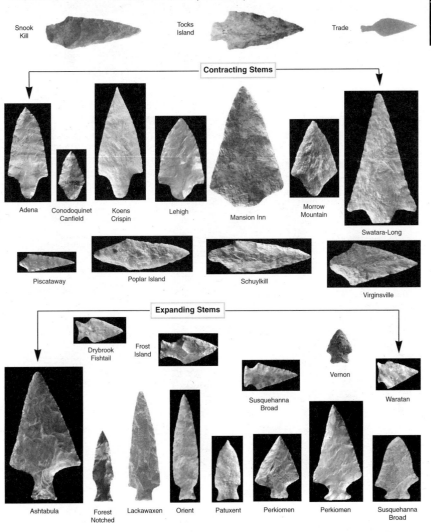

Snook Kill

Tocks Island

Trade

Contracting Stems

Adena

Conodoquinet Canfield

Koens Crispin

Lehigh

Mansion Inn

Morrow Mountain

Swatara-Long

Piscataway

Poplar Island

Schuylkill

Virginsville

Expanding Stems

Drybrook Fishtail

Frost Island

Vernon

Waratan

Susquehanna Broad

Ashtabula

Forest Notched

Lackawaxen

Orient

Patuxent

Perkiomen

Perkiomen

Susquehanna Broad

6 THUMBNAIL GUIDE - STEMMED-BIFURCATED FORMS (30% actual size)

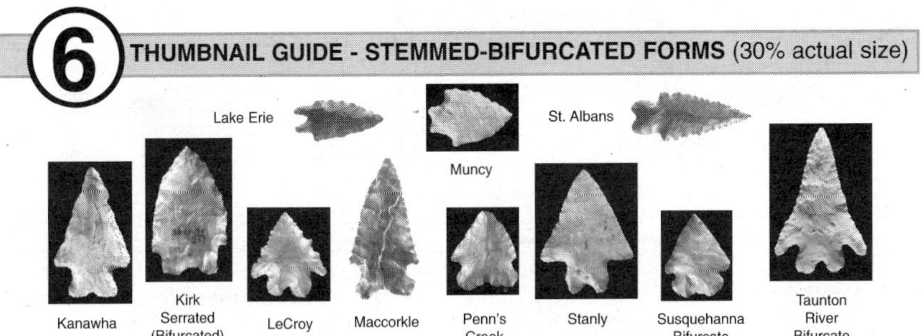

Lake Erie

Muncy

St. Albans

Kanawha

Kirk Serrated (Bifurcated)

LeCroy

Maccorkle

Penn's Creek

Stanly

Susquehanna Bifurcate

Taunton River Bifurcate

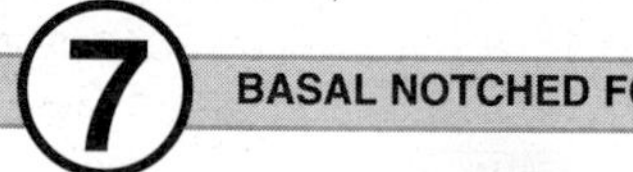

TRIANGLES

Erb Basal

Eshback

Erie Triangle

Levanna

Madison

Susquehannock Triangle

ADENA - Late Archaic to late Woodland, 3000 - 1200 B.P.

(Also see Adena Blade, Koens Crispin, Lehigh, Neville, Piney Island, Turkeytail)

G6, $20-$40
PA.

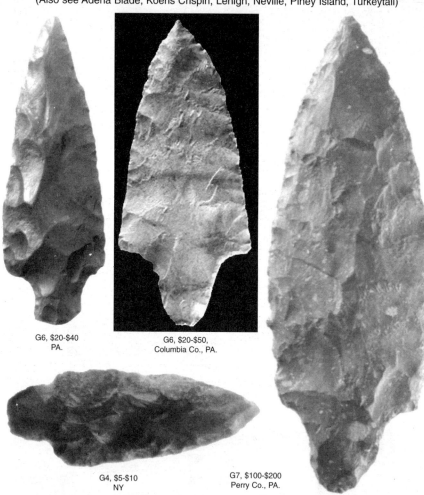

G6, $20-$50,
Columbia Co., PA.

G4, $5-$10
NY

G7, $100-$200
Perry Co., PA.

LOCATION: Northeastern to Southeastern states. **DESCRIPTION:** A medium to large, thin, narrow, triangular blade with a medium to long, narrow to broad rounded "beaver tail" stem. Most examples are from average to excellent quality. Bases can be ground. Has been found with *Nolichucky, Camp Creek, Candy Creek, Ebenezer* and *Greenville* points (Rankin site, Cocke Co., TN). **I.D. KEY:** Rounded base, woodland flaking.

ADENA BLADE - Late Archaic to Woodland, 3000 - 1200 B.P.

(Also see Adena, Turkeytail)

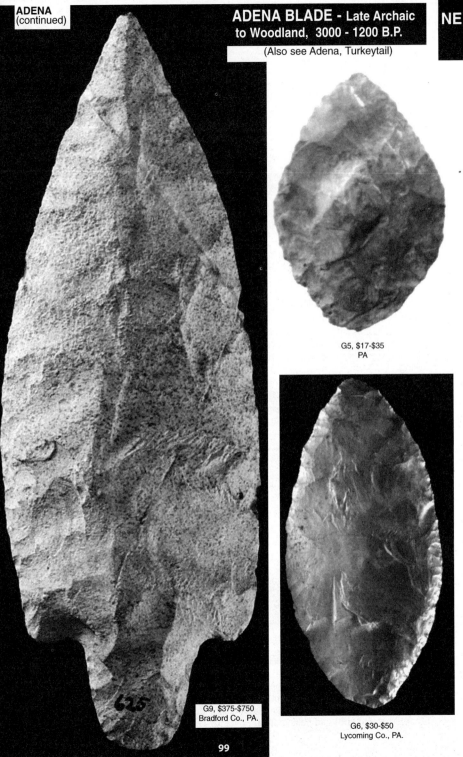

G9, $375-$750
Bradford Co., PA.

G5, $17-$35
PA

G6, $30-$50
Lycoming Co., PA.

ADENA BLADE (continued)

LOCATION: Southeastern to Northeastern states.**DESCRIPTION:** A large size, thin, broad, ovate blade with a rounded base and is usually found in caches. **I.D. KEY:** Woodland Flaking, large direct strikes.

ADENA - ROBBINS - Late Archaic to Woodland, 3000 - 1800 B.P.

(Also see Duncan's Island, Genesee, Neville and Piedmont)

G8, $75-$150
Western NY

LOCATION: Eastern to Southeastern states. **DESCRIPTION:** A large, broad, triangular point that is thin and well made with a long, wide, rounded to square stem that is parallel sided. The blade has convex sides and square to slightly barbed shoulders. Many examples show excellent secondary flaking on blade edges. **I.D. KEY:** Square base, heavy secondary flaking.

AGATE BASIN - Transitional Paleo to early Archaic, 10,500 - 8000 B.P.

(Also see Angostura and Eden)

G6, $200-$400
Montgomery Co., PA.

G5, $75-$150
Berks Co., PA.

G7, $250-$450
Lycoming Co., PA.

LOCATION: Midwestern to Northeastern states. **DESCRIPTION:** A medium to large size lanceolate blade, usually of high quality. Bases are either convex, concave or straight, and are usually ground. Some examples are median ridged and have random to parallel flaking. **I.D. KEY:** Basal form and flaking style.

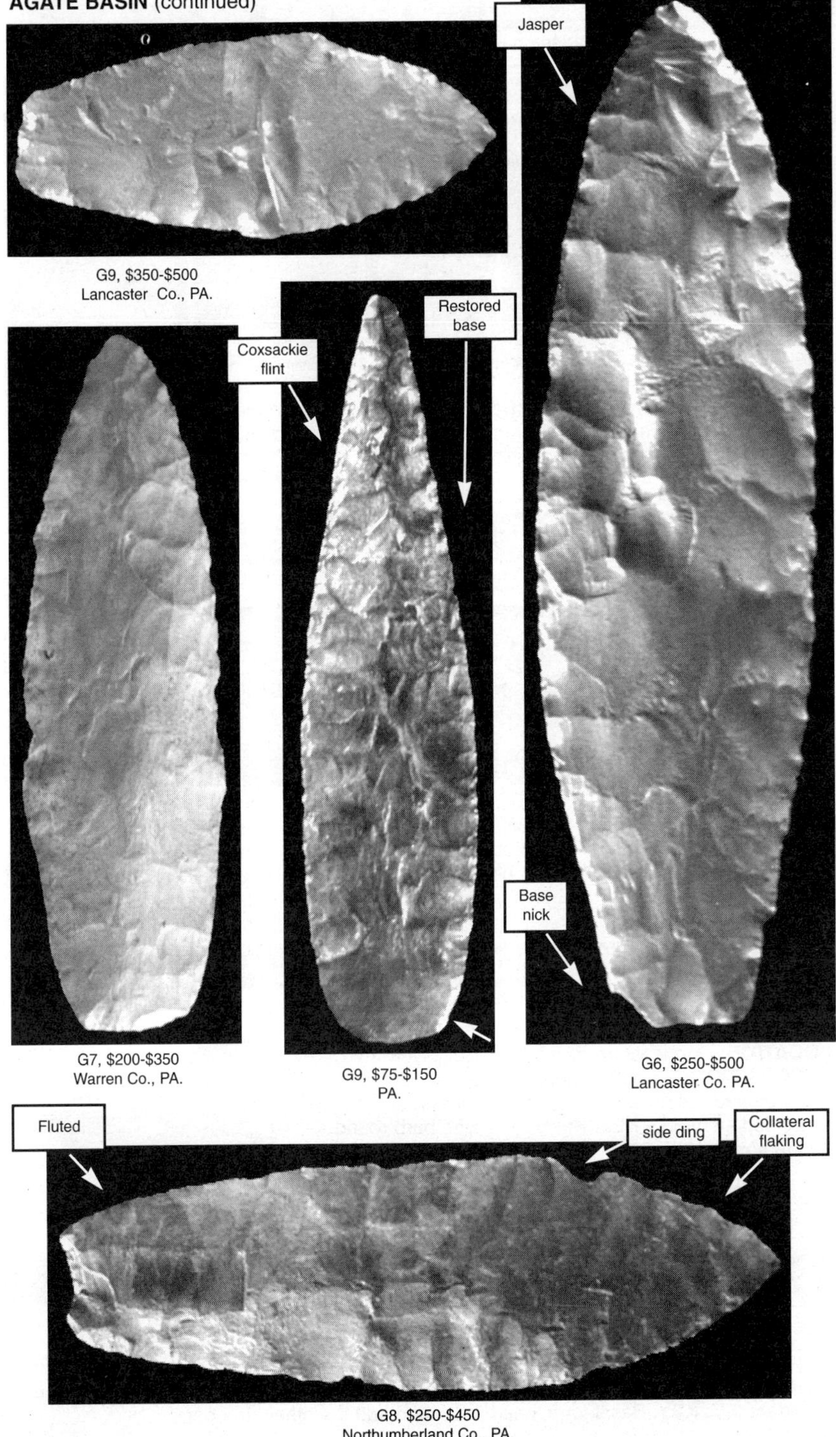

G9, $350-$500
Lancaster Co., PA.

G7, $200-$350
Warren Co., PA.

G9, $75-$150
PA.

G6, $250-$500
Lancaster Co. PA.

G8, $250-$450
Northumberland Co., PA.

AMOS - Early Archaic, 10,000 - 9000 B.P.

(Also see Charleston Pine Tree, Kirk Corner Notched, Palmer)

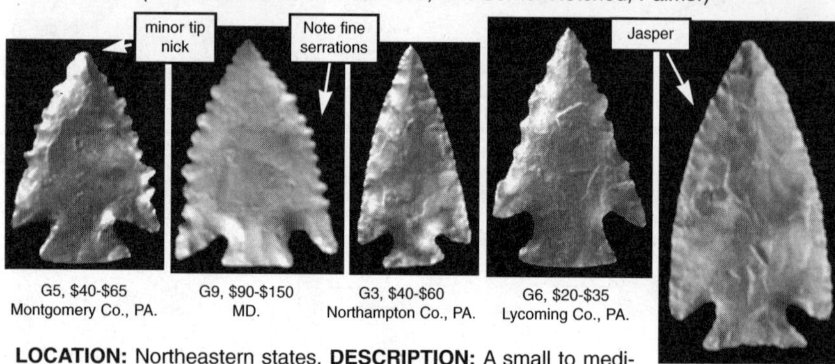

G5, $40-$65 Montgomery Co., PA.

G9, $90-$150 MD.

G3, $40-$60 Northampton Co., PA.

G6, $20-$35 Lycoming Co., PA.

G8, $75-$150 Luzerne Co., PA.

LOCATION: Northeastern states. **DESCRIPTION:** A small to medium size corner notched point with serrated edges and barbed shoulders. The base is straight to convex. **I.D. KEY:** Edgework.

ANGOSTURA - Transitional Paleo to mid-Archaic, 10,000 - 8000 B.P.

(Also see Agate Basin, Browns Valley, Clovis-unfluted, Eden, Guilford and Plainview)

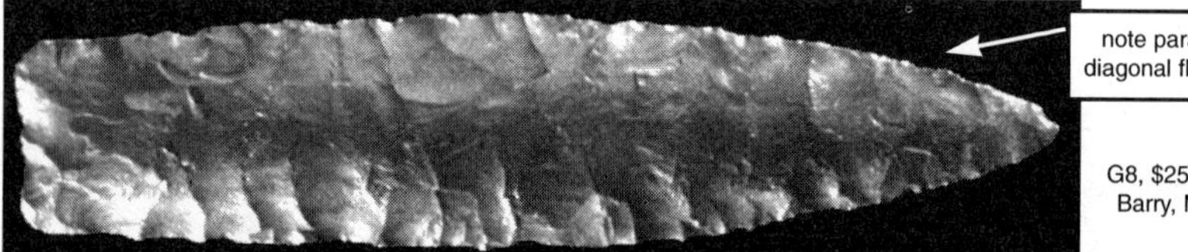

G8, $250-400 Barry, Mass.

LOCATION: Eastern states. **DESCRIPTION**: A medium to large size lanceolate blade with a contracting, concave base. Both broad and narrow forms occur. Flaking can be parallel oblique to random. Bases are not usually ground but are thinned. **I.D. KEY:** Basal form, early flaking on blade.

ARDEN - Early Archaic, 9000 - 8000 B.P.

(Also see Charleston Pine Tree)

LOCATION: Northeastern states, especially New York. **DESCRIPTION:** A small to medium size, serrated, corner notched point with barbed shoulders and an expanded stem. **I.D. KEY:** Basal form, one barb round and the other stronger.

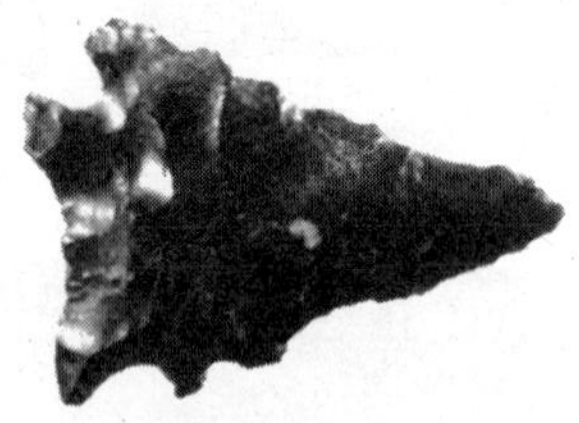

G4, $5-$10 NY

ASHTABULA - Late Archaic to Woodland, 4000 - 2500 B.P.

(Also see Koens Crispin, Lehigh, Perkiomen and Susquehanna Broad)

LOCATION: Northeastern states, especially Northeastern Ohio and Western Penn. **DESCRIPTION:** A medium to large size, broad, thick, expanded stem point with tapered shoulders. **I.D. KEY:** Basal form, one barb round and the other stronger.

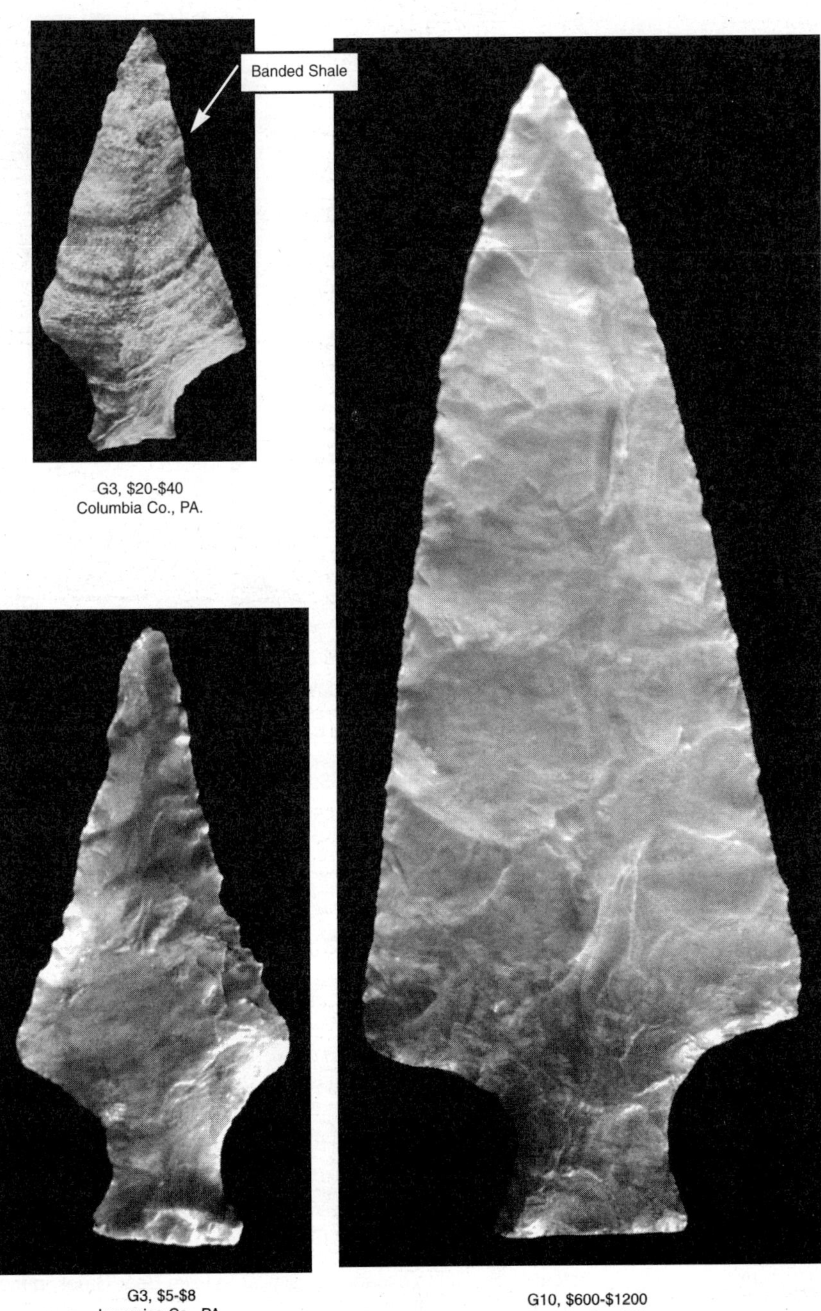

G3, $20-$40
Columbia Co., PA.

G3, $5-$8
Lycoming Co., PA.

G10, $600-$1200
Broome Co., NY.

BARE ISLAND - Late Archaic, 4500 - 1500 B.P.

(Also see Duncan's Island, Lackawaxen, Lamoka, Neville, Newmanstown, Piedmont, Piney Island, Poplar Island, Snook Kill)

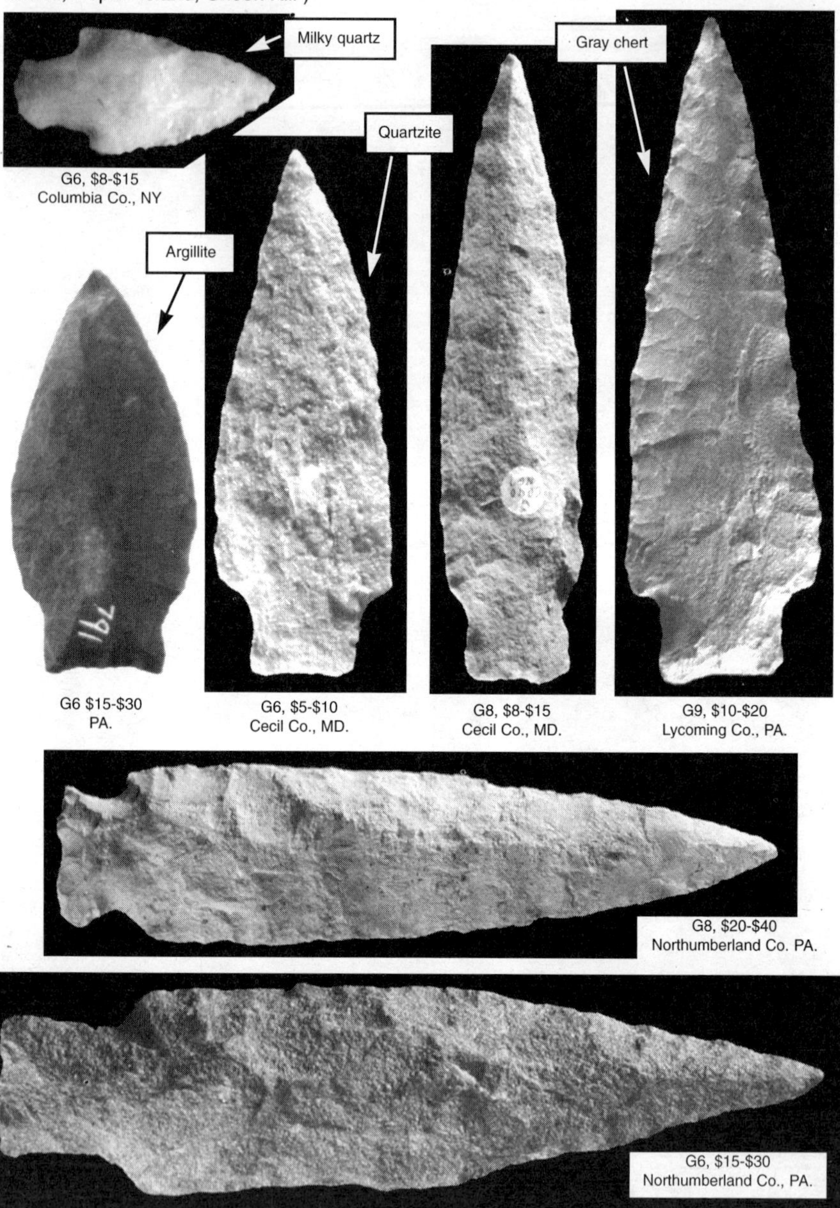

G6, $8-$15
Columbia Co., NY

G6 $15-$30
PA.

G6, $5-$10
Cecil Co., MD.

G8, $8-$15
Cecil Co., MD.

G9, $10-$20
Lycoming Co., PA.

G8, $20-$40
Northumberland Co. PA.

G6, $15-$30
Northumberland Co., PA.

LOCATION: Northeastern states. **DESCRIPTION:** A medium to large size, narrow, thick stemmed point with tapered shoulders. One shoulder is higher than the other and the blade is convex to straight. The stem is parallel to expanding. Similar to Little Bear Creek in the Southeast. **I.D. KEY:** Narrow stemmed point.

BARNES

(See Cumberland-Barnes)

BEAVER LAKE - Paleo, 12,000 - 8000 B.P.

(Also see Clovis Unfluted, Cumberland and Orient)

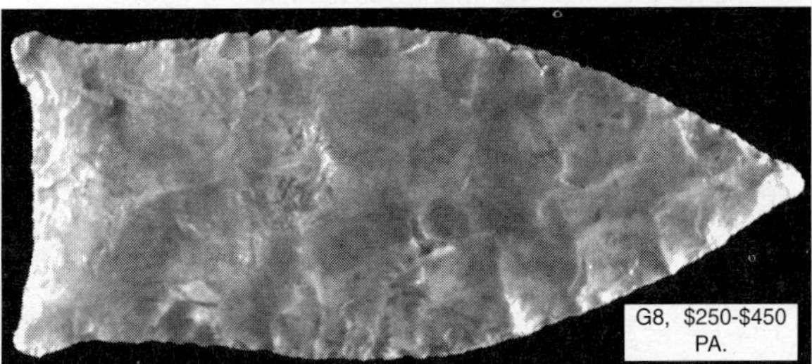
G8, $250-$450
PA.

LOCATION: Southeastern to Northeastern states. **DESCRIPTION:** A medium to large size lanceolate blade with flaring ears. Associated with *Cumberland*, but thinner than unfluted *Cumberlands*. Bases are ground and blade edges are recurved. **I.D. KEY:** Paleo flaking, shoulder area.

BREWERTON CORNER NOTCHED - Middle to Late Archaic, 6000 - 4000 B.P.

(Also see Crooked Creek, Jacks Reef, Kirk, Kiski, Lycoming County, Palmer)

G6, $5-$10
Lycoming Co., PA.

G5, $10-$20
Columbia Co., NY.

G10, $20-$40
Columbia Co., NY.

G7, $12-$25
Columbia Co., NY.

LOCATION: Eastern to midwestern states. **DESCRIPTION:** A small size, thick, triangular point with faint corner notches and a concave, straight or convex base. Called *Freeheley* in Michigan. **I.D. KEY:** Width, thickness.

BREWERTON EARED-TRIANGULAR - Middle to Late Archaic, 6000 - 4000 B.P.

(Also see Fox Creek, Steubenville & Yadkin)

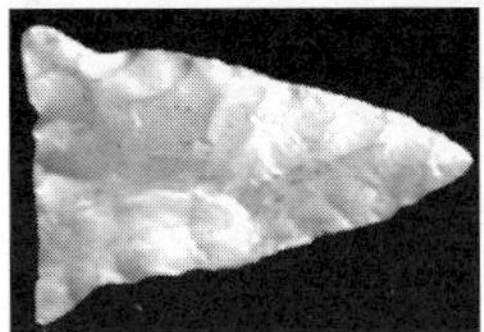
G7, $4-$8
Chester Co., PA.

G7, $4-$8
Cent., PA.

G7, $4-$8
Northampton Co., PA. Yellow Jasper.

LOCATION: Eastern to midwestern states. **DESCRIPTION:** A small size, triangular, eared point with a concave base. **I.D. KEY:** Tiny basal ears.

BREWERTON SIDE-NOTCHED - Late Archaic, 6000 - 4000 B.P.

(Also see Meadowood, Otter Creek, Perkiomen, Susquehanna Broad)

G4, $3-$6
Lycoming Co., PA.

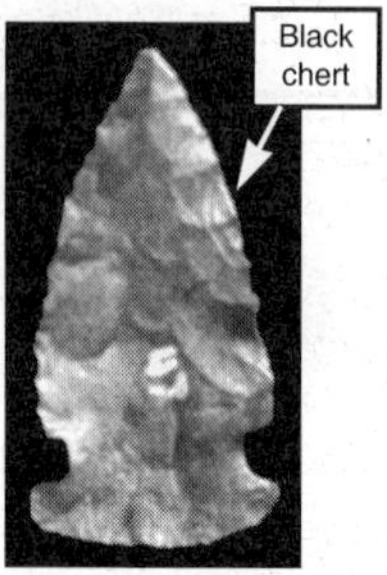

Black chert

G5, $5-$10
Union Co., PA. Chert.

G5, $4-$10
Luzerne Co., PA.

G5, $4-$8
Lycoming Co., PA.

G5, $4-$10
Lycoming Co., PA.

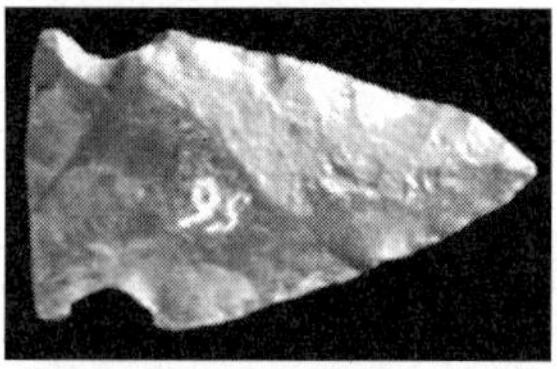

G5, $4-$8
Monroe
Co., PA.

G5 $4-$8
Lycoming Co., PA.

LOCATION: Eastern to midwestern states. **DESCRIPTION:** A small size, thick, triangular point with shallow side notches and a concave to straight base. **I.D. KEY**. Small side notched point.

BRODHEAD SIDE-NOTCHED - Early Archaic , 9000 - 7000 B.P.

(Also see Bennington Quail Tail, Brewerton, Crooked Creek, Dovetail, Kiski, Lycoming Co.)

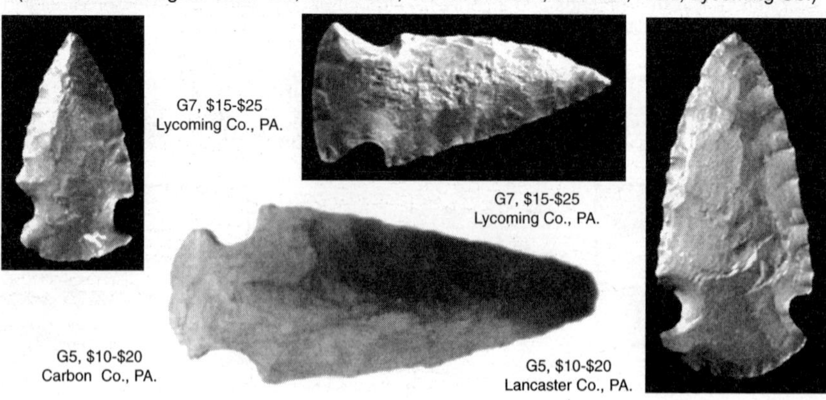

G7, $15-$25
Lycoming Co., PA.

G7, $15-$25
Lycoming Co., PA.

G5, $10-$20
Carbon Co., PA.

G5, $10-$20
Lancaster Co., PA.

LOCATION: Northeastern states. **DESCRIPTION:** A medium size, side to corner notched point with an expanded, convex base. The notching occurs near the base and are wide. **I.D. KEY:** Wide notches, convex base.

BURWELL - Late Archaic, 5000 - 4000 B.P.

LOCATION: Northeastern states. **DESCRIPTION:** A small size, parallel stemmed point with weak, tapered shoulders and a short blade. The base is concave. **I.D. KEY:** Broad, parallel stem, tapered shouders.

G6, $4-$8
Washingtonboro, PA.

CHARLESTON PINE TREE - Early Archaic, 10,000 - 7000 B.P.

(Also see Arden, Kirk Corner Notched, Lycoming Co., Oley, Palmer, Vestal Notched, Vosburg)

G3, $5-$20 Lycoming Co., PA. · G9, $35-$65 NY. · G6, $25-$75 Lycoming Co., PA. · G5, $25-$75 Lycoming Co., PA.

LOCATION: Eastern to Southeastern states. The St. Albans site is in West Virginia. Points here were dated to 9,900 B.P. **DESCRIPTION:** A medium to large size, corner notched, usually serrated point with parallel flaking to the center of the blade forming a median ridge. The bases are ground and can be concave, convex, straight, bifurcated or auriculate. Called *Pine Tree* in the Southeast. **I.D. KEY:** Archaic flaking with long flakes to the center of the blade.

CHILLESQUAQUE SERIES - Mid Archaic, 6,000 - 5,000 B.P.

(Also see Lycoming County Series and Penn's Creek Series)

LOCATION: Northeastern states. **DESCRIPTION:** A small size, corner to side notched to expanded stem point. Shoulders can be strong to tapered. **I.D. KEY**. Wide side to corner notches.

G5, $5-$10
Lancaster Co., PA.

CLOVIS - Early Paleo, 14,000 - 11,000 B.P.

(Also see Crowfield, Cumberland, Debert, Holcomb & Redstone)

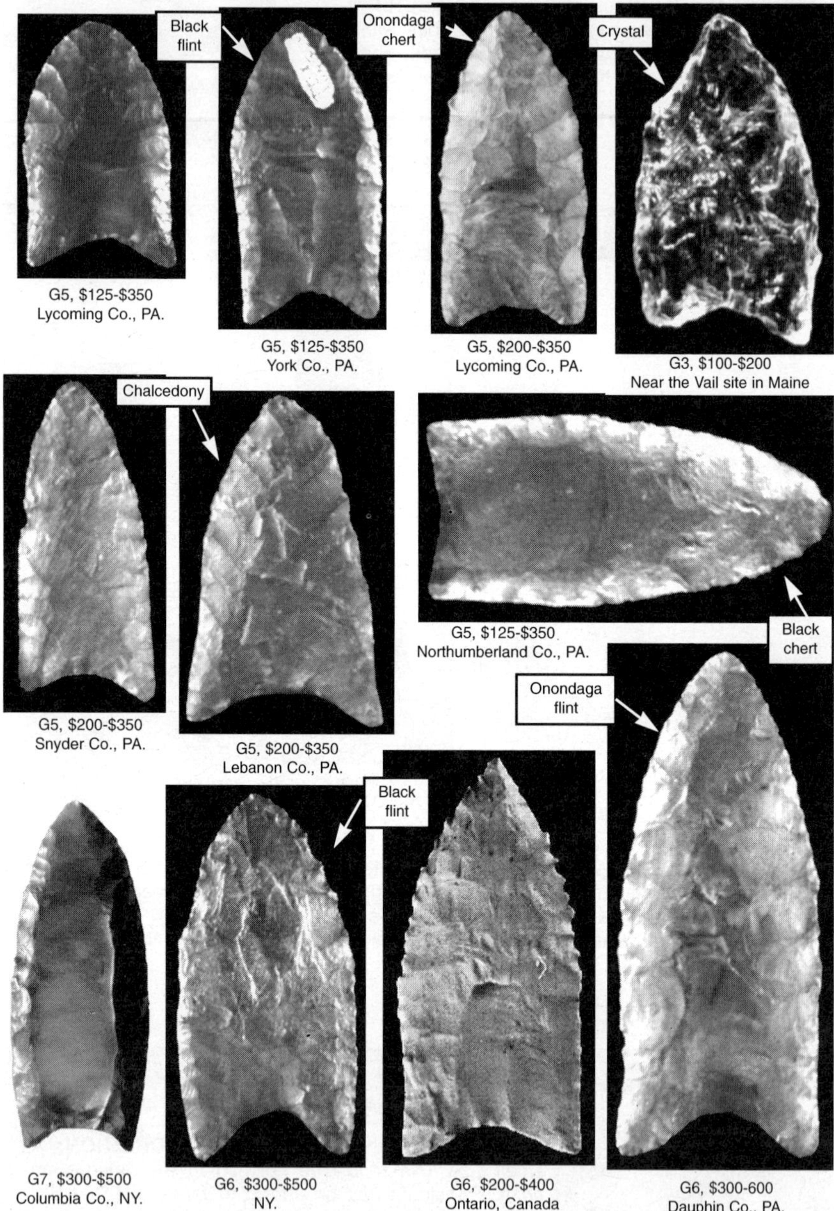

G5, \$125-\$350
Lycoming Co., PA.

G5, \$125-\$350
York Co., PA.

G5, \$200-\$350
Lycoming Co., PA.

G3, \$100-\$200
Near the Vail site in Maine

G5, \$125-\$350
Northumberland Co., PA.

G5, \$200-\$350
Snyder Co., PA.

G5, \$200-\$350
Lebanon Co., PA.

G7, \$300-\$500
Columbia Co., NY.

G6, \$300-\$500
NY.

G6, \$200-\$400
Ontario, Canada

G6, \$300-600
Dauphin Co., PA.

LOCATION: All of North America. **DESCRIPTION:** A medium to large size, auriculate, fluted, lanceolate point with convex sides and a concave base that is ground. Most examples are fluted on both sides about 1/3 the way up from the base. The flaking can be random to parallel. The oldest point type in the hemisphere. Materials used in this area are: Argillite, black flint, chalcedony, conglomerate, coshocton, coxsackie, jasper, Onondaga, quartz crystal, quartzite, rhyolite, shale & upper Mercer black chert. **I.D. KEY:** Auricles and fluting.

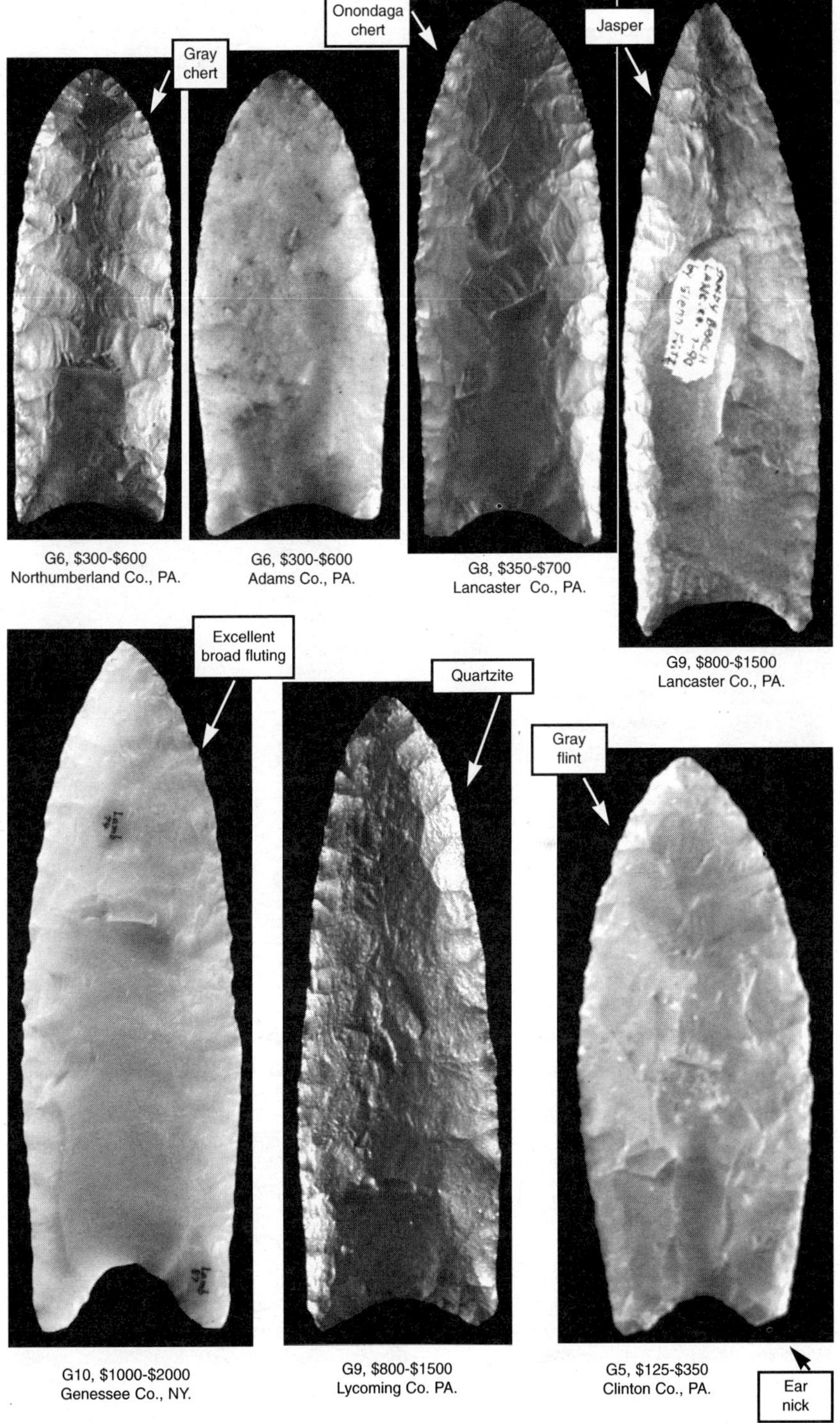

G6, $300-$600
Northumberland Co., PA.

G6, $300-$600
Adams Co., PA.

G8, $350-$700
Lancaster Co., PA.

G9, $800-$1500
Lancaster Co., PA.

G10, $1000-$2000
Genessee Co., NY.

G9, $800-$1500
Lycoming Co. PA.

G5, $125-$350
Clinton Co., PA.

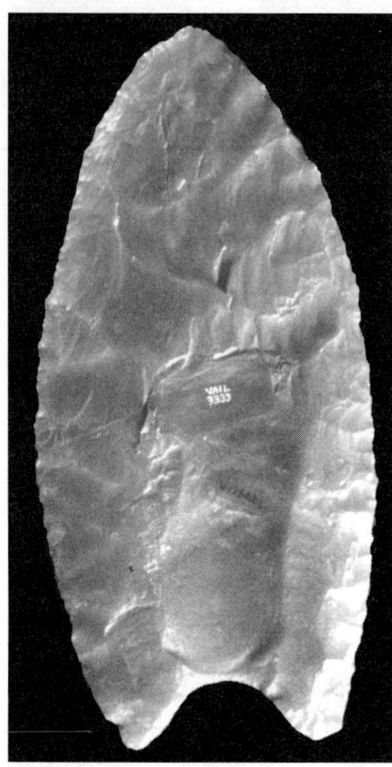

G10, $2000-$4,000
Oxford Co., ME.

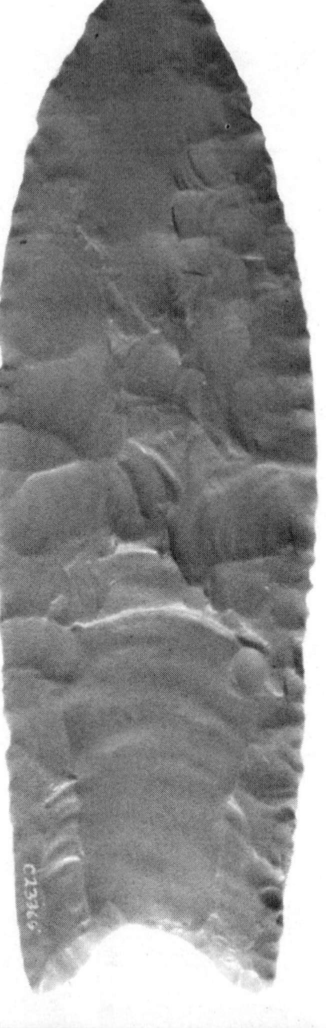

G10, $7,000-$15,000
NY, Lamb site.

CONODOQUINET/CANFIELD - Late Archaic, 4000 - 3500 B.P.

(Also see Dewart Stemmed, Duncan's Island, Lehigh, Lamoka, Morrow Mountain, Neville, Piscataway, Sandhill Stemmed)

G5, $4-$8
Lycoming Co., PA.

G3 $4-$8
Lycoming Co., PA.

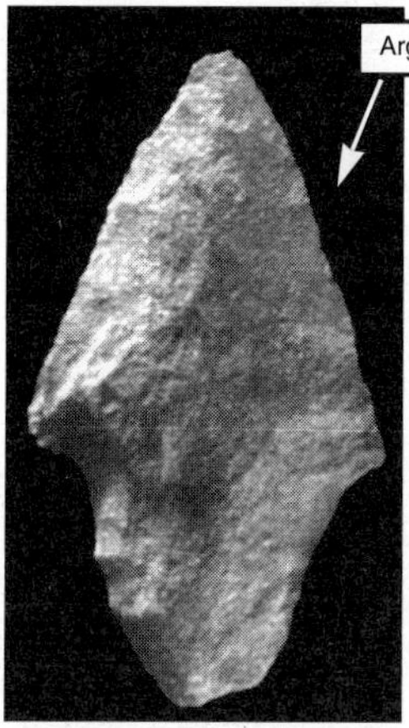

CONODOQUINET/CANFIELD (continued)

Argilitte

G3, $4-$8
Lycoming Co., PA.

Siltstone

G5, $4-$8
Union Co., PA.

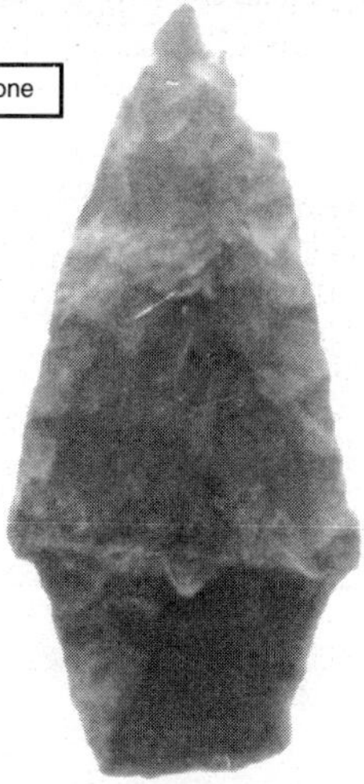

G5, $4-$9
NY.

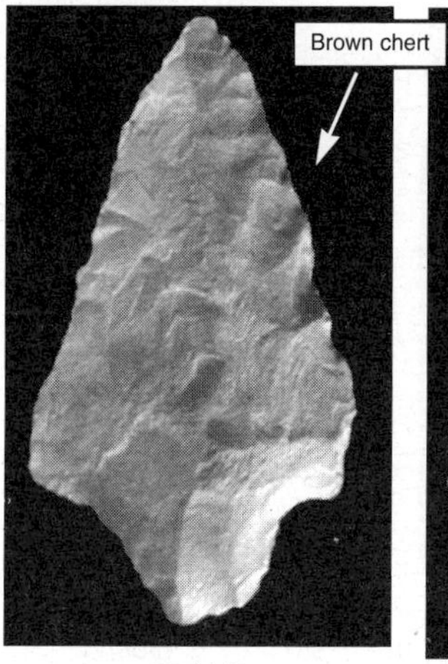

Brown chert

G3, $4-$8
Lycoming Co., PA.

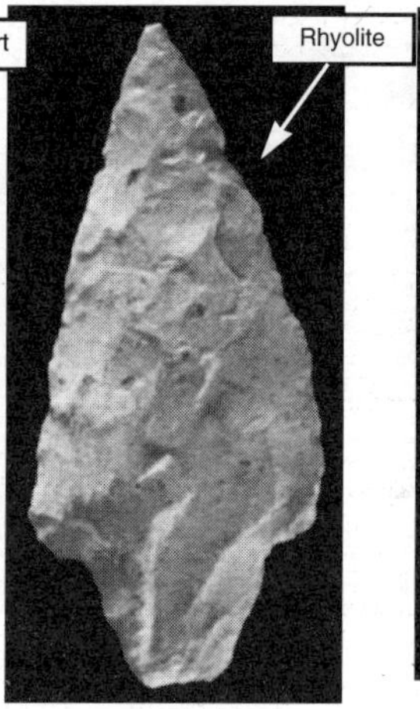

Rhyolite

G3, $4-$8
Lycoming Co., PA.

Gray flint

G3, $4-$8
Lycoming Co., PA.

LOCATION: Northeastern states. **DESCRIPTION:** A medium size, narrow, contracted stem point with sloping shoulders. Base is rounded to pointed. **I.D. KEY:** Base form.

CROOKED CREEK SERIES - Early Archaic, 9000 - 5000 B.P.

(Also see Brewerton, Decatur, Dovetail, Kiski, Lycoming County and Palmer)

LOCATION: Northeastern states. **DESCRIPTION:** A small to medium size, short, corner to side notched point with a broad base that has rounded to squared corners. Shoulders are barbed to rounded. **I.D. KEY:** Short, notched point with a large base.

G5, $5-$15
Lycoming Co., PA.

CROWFIELD - Late Paleo, 11,000 - 10,000 B.P.

(Also see Clovis, Cumberland, Debert, Holcomb, Plainview)

Restored Ear

Note multiple fluting

Broken and glued with piece missing.

G7, $250-$500
Dauphin Co., PA.

Onondaga chert

G10, $450-$700
Lancaster/York Co., PA.

Very thin cross section

G2, $200-$400
Ontario, Canada, type site.

G10, $800-$1500
Chautauqua Co., NY.

LOCATION: Northeastern states. **DESCRIPTION:** A medium size, thin, auriculate, fluted point with a concave base. Commonly multiple fluted and the basal area is ground. This point is widest near the tip. Believed to be later than *Clovis*. **I.D. KEY:** Multiple flutes, blade form.

CUMBERLAND (Barnes) - Paleo, 11,000 - 10,000 B.P.

(Also see Beaver Lake, Clovis, Crowfield, Debert, Holcomb, Plainview, Redstone)

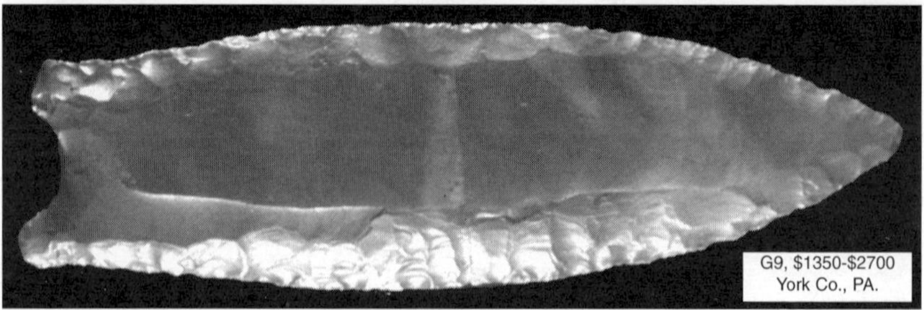
G9, $1350-$2700
York Co., PA.

CUMBERLAND (Barnes) (continued)

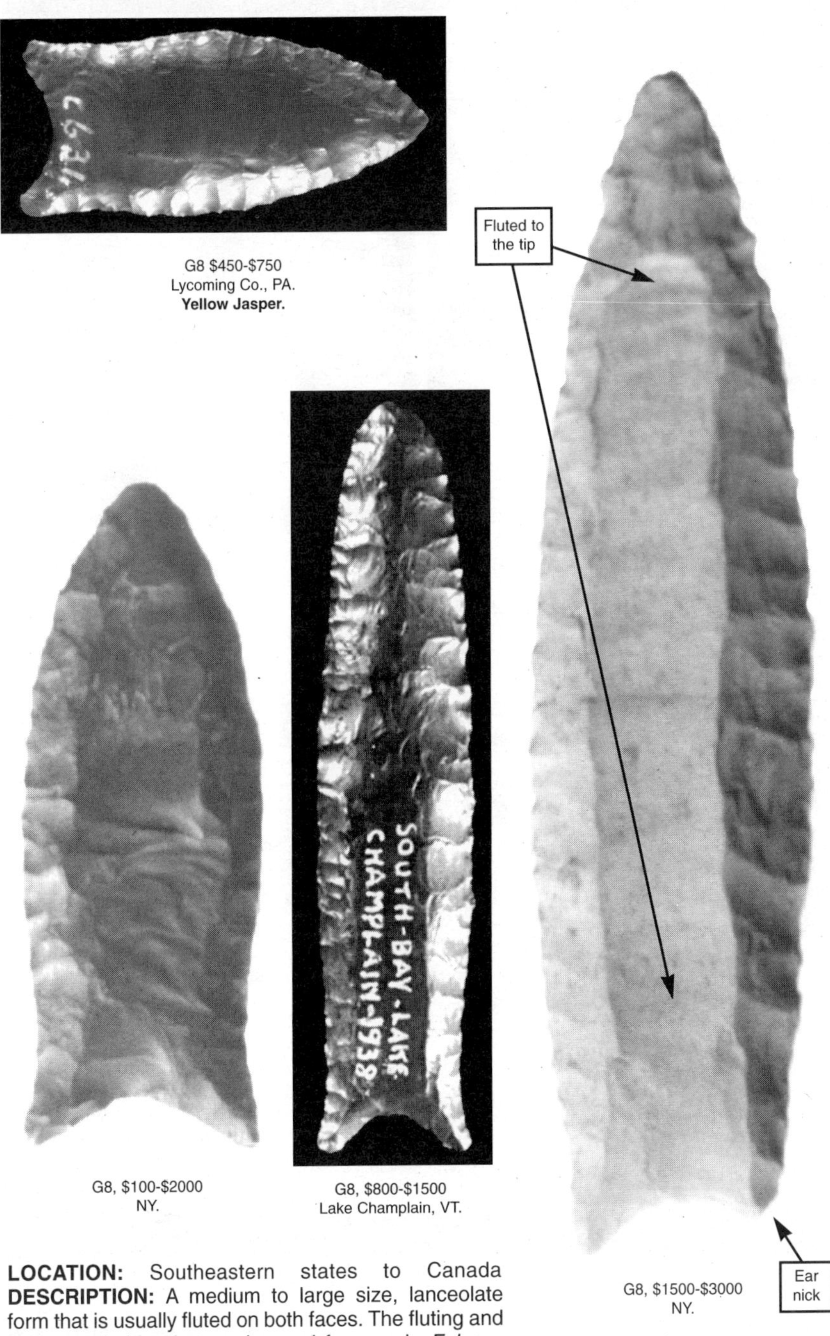

G8 $450-$750
Lycoming Co., PA.
Yellow Jasper.

G8, $100-$2000
NY.

G8, $800-$1500
Lake Champlain, VT.

G8, $1500-$3000
NY.

LOCATION: Southeastern states to Canada **DESCRIPTION:** A medium to large size, lanceolate form that is usually fluted on both faces. The fluting and flaking technique is an advanced form as in *Folsom*, with the flutes usually extending the entire length of the blade. Bases are ground on all examples. **I.D. KEY:** Paleo flaking, indirect pressure fluted.

DALTON CLASSIC - Early Archaic, 9500 - 8000 B.P.

(Also see Clovis, Crowfield, Debert, Hardaway, Holcomb, Plainview)

G4, $40-$75
Berks Co., PA.

G4, $40-$75
Berks Co., PA.

G6, $75-$150
Lebanon Co., PA.

G6, $50-$150
PA.

LOCATION: Midwestern to Eastern states. **DESCRIPTION:** A medium to large size, thin, auriculate, fishtailed point. Usually finely serrated and sometimes fluted. Beveling may occur on one side of each face but is usually on the right side. All bases are ground. **I.D. KEY:** Basal form and flaking style.

DALTON-NUCKOLLS - Early Archaic, 9500 - 5000 B.P.

(Also see Angostura, Dalton Classic, Plainview)

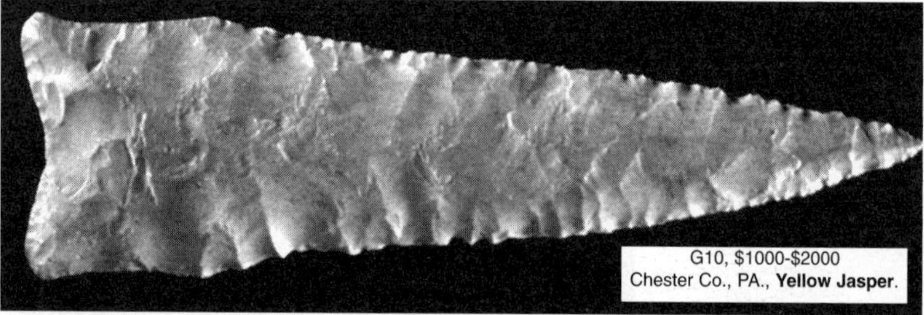

G10, $1000-$2000
Chester Co., PA., **Yellow Jasper**.

LOCATION: Midwestern to Northeastern states. Type site is in Humphreys Co., TN. **DESCRIPTION:** A medium to large size variant form, probably occuring from resharpening the *Greenbrier Dalton*. Bases are squared to lobbed to eared, and have a shallow concavity. Bases are gound and some examples are fluted. **I.D. KEY:** Broad base and shoulders, flaking on blade.

DEBERT - Paleo, 11,000 - 9500 B. P.

(Also see Clovis, Crowfield, Cumberland, Dalton, Holcomb)

LOCATION: Northeastern states. Type site is the Vail site in Maine. **DESCRIPTION:** A medium to large size, thin, auriculate point that evolved from *Clovis*. Most examples are fluted twice on each face resulting in a deep basal concavity. The second flute usually removed traces of the first fluting. A very rare form of late *Clovis*. **I.D. KEY:** Deep basal notch.

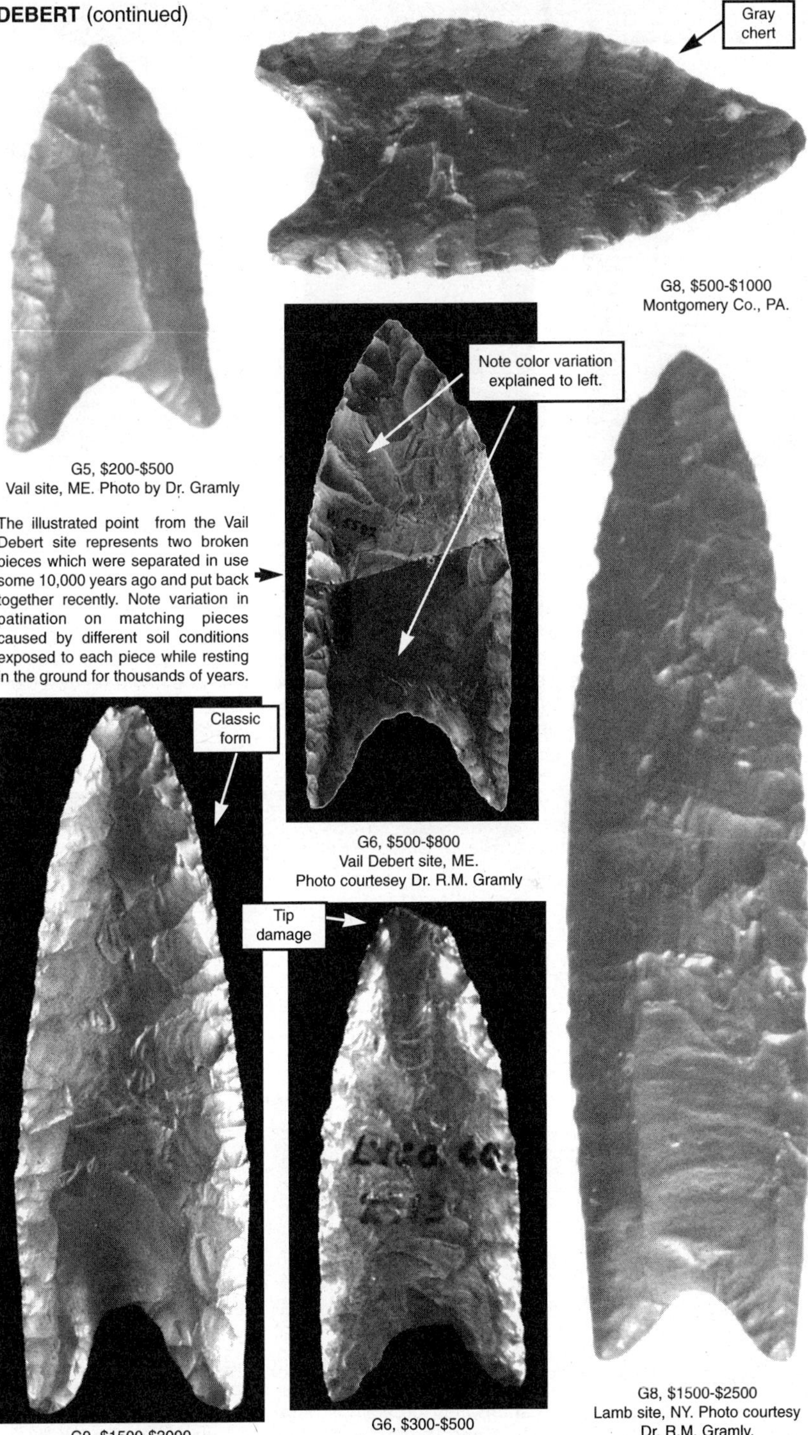

G5, $200-$500
Vail site, ME. Photo by Dr. Gramly

G8, $500-$1000
Montgomery Co., PA.

The illustrated point from the Vail Debert site represents two broken pieces which were separated in use some 10,000 years ago and put back together recently. Note variation in patination on matching pieces caused by different soil conditions exposed to each piece while resting in the ground for thousands of years.

G6, $500-$800
Vail Debert site, ME.
Photo courtesey Dr. R.M. Gramly

G9, $1500-$3000
Snyder Co., PA. **Yellow Jasper**.

G6, $300-$500
Lycoming Co., PA.

G8, $1500-$2500
Lamb site, NY. Photo courtesy
Dr. R.M. Gramly.

DECATUR - Early Archaic, 9000 - 3000 B.P.

(Also see Charleston Pine Tree, Dovetail, Kirk, Kiski, Lost Lake, Palmer)

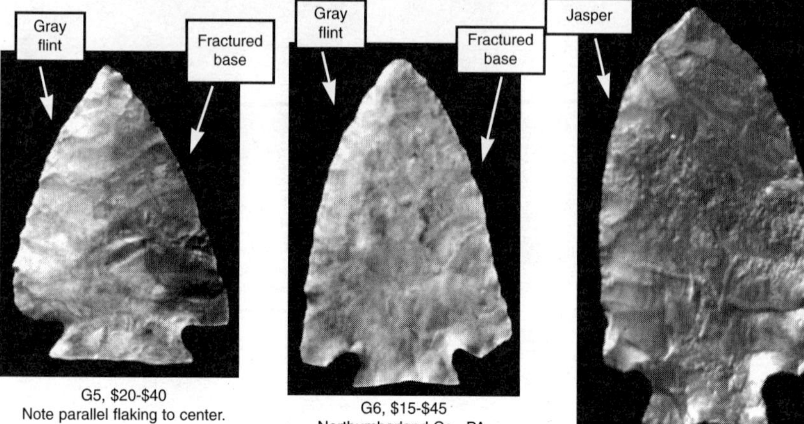

G5, $20-$40
Note parallel flaking to center.

G6, $15-$45
Northumberland Co., PA.

G2, $5-$10
Lycoming Co., PA.

LOCATION: Eastern states. **DESCRIPTION:** A small to medium size, thin, serrated, corner notched point that is usually beveled on one side of each face. The base is usually broken off (fractured) by a blow inward from each corner of the stem. Sometimes the sides of the stem and backs of the tangs are also fractured, and rarely the tip may be fractured by a blow on each side directed towards the base. Bases are usually ground and flaking is of high quality. **I.D. KEY:** Squared base, one barb shoulder.

DEWART STEMMED - Late Archaic, 5000 - 2500 B.P.

(Also see Bare Island, Duncan's Island, Garver's Ferry, Lamoka, Neville, Piney Island)

G4 $4-$8
Peach Bottom, PA.

G4 $4-$8
Northumberland Co., PA.

G6 $5-$10
Lycoming Co., PA.

LOCATION: Northeastern states. **DESCRIPTION:** A medium size, narrow, stemmed point with strong shoulders. Tips are sharp and the stem is parallel to contracting. The base is normally unfinished. **I.D. KEY:** Unfinished base.

DOVETAIL - Early Archaic, 9500 - 8000 B.P.

(Also see Brodhead side notched, Decatur, Kirk, Kline, Lost Lake, St. Charles & Thebes)

G2, $12-$25
Lancaster Co., PA.
Yellow Jasper.

G4, $20-$35
NJ.

G2, $12-$25
Lancaster Co., PA.

G4, $20-$35
PA. Coshocton chert.

G4, $50-$100
Lycoming Co., PA.

G8, $250-$500, Monmouth Co., NJ.

G6, $125-$250
Lancaster Co., PA.

LOCATION: Midwest to Eastern states. **DESCRIPTION:** Also known as *St. Charles*. A medium to large size, corner notched, dovetailed base point. The blade is beveled on one side of each face when resharpened. Bases are straight, convex or bifurcated and are ground and can be fractured from both corners of the base. **I.D. KEY:** Dovetailed base.

DRILL - Paleo to Historic, 14,000 - 200 B.P.

(Also see Graver, Randolph and Scraper)

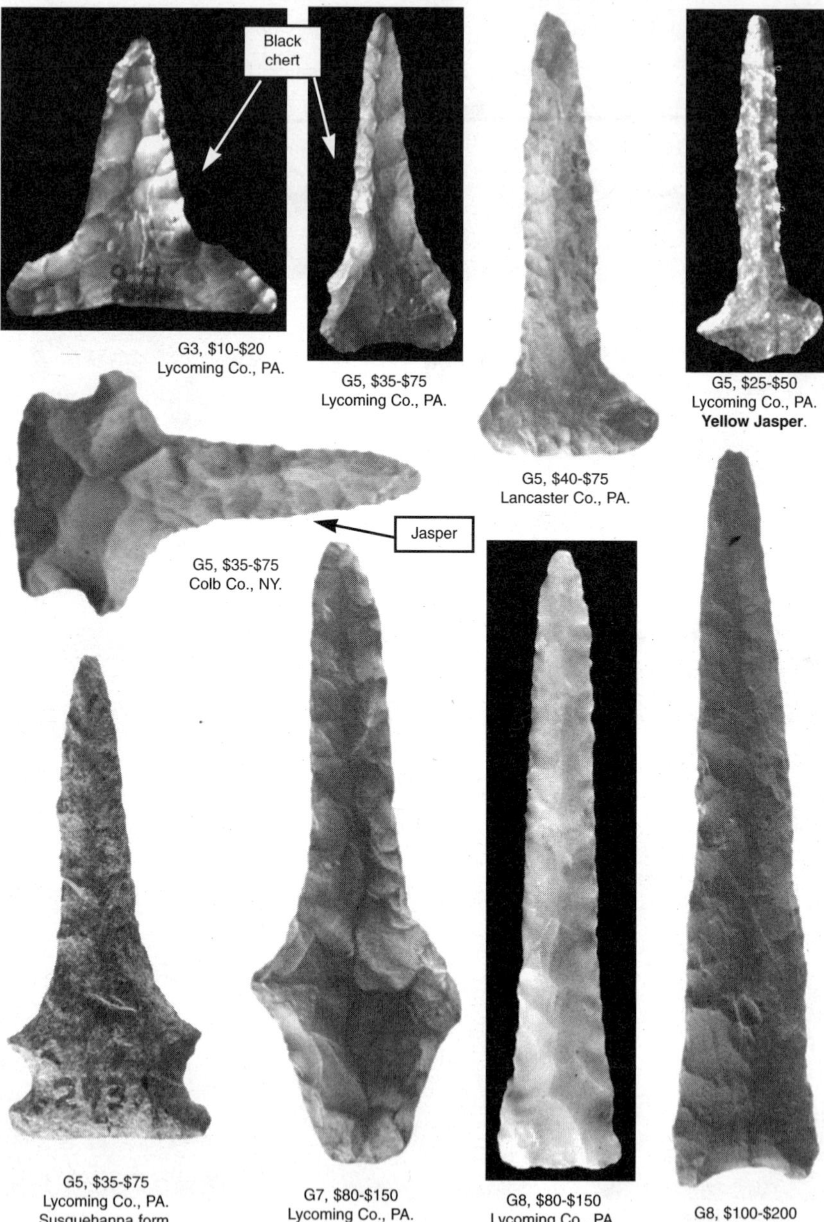

G3, $10-$20
Lycoming Co., PA.

G5, $35-$75
Lycoming Co., PA.

G5, $40-$75
Lancaster Co., PA.

G5, $25-$50
Lycoming Co., PA.
Yellow Jasper.

G5, $35-$75
Colb Co., NY.

G5, $35-$75
Lycoming Co., PA.
Susquehanna form.

G7, $80-$150
Lycoming Co., PA.

G8, $80-$150
Lycoming Co., PA.

G8, $100-$200
Dauphin Co., PA.

LOCATION: Everywhere. **DESCRIPTION:** Although many drills were made from scratch, all point types ended up in the drill form. Usually, heavily resharpened and broken points were salvaged and rechipped into drills. These objects were certainly used as drills (evidence of extreme edge wear), but there is speculation that some of these forms may have been used as pins for clothing, ornaments, ear plugs and other uses. **I.D. KEY:** Very narrow blade form.

DRYBROOK FISHTAIL - Late Archaic to Woodland, 3500 - 2500 B.P.

(Also see Forest Notched, Frost Island, Orient, Patuxent, Perkiomen, Susquehanna Broad)

G4, $10-$20
Luzerne Co., PA.

G4, $5-$10
Washingtonboro, PA.

G6, $15-$25
Lycoming Co., PA.

G5, $10-$20
Centre Co., PA.

G7, $10-$45
Luzerne Co., PA.

G7, $15-$30
Lycoming Co., PA.

G8, $10-$45
Lancaster Co., PA.

G8, $10-$45
Lycoming Co., PA.

G8, $25-$55
Columbia Co., PA.

G8, $25-$55
Monroe Co., PA.

LOCATION: Northeastern states. **DESCRIPTION**: A medium size, narrow, triangular point that expands towards the base. Shoulders are rounded and taper into an expanded base. The base is straight to concave. Some examples have basal ears that are rounded to pointed. **I.D. KEY:** Basal form, rounded shoulders.

DUNCAN'S ISLAND - Mid to Late Archaic, 6000 - 4000 B. P.

(Also see Bare Island, Dewart Stemmed, Neville, Newmanstown, Piney Island, Piedmont)

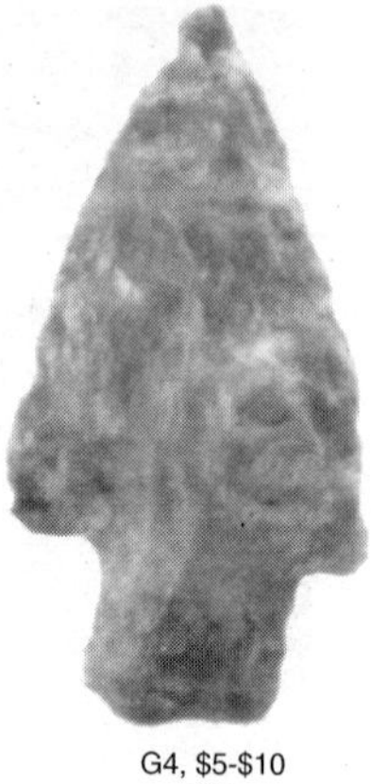

G4, $5-$10
NY.

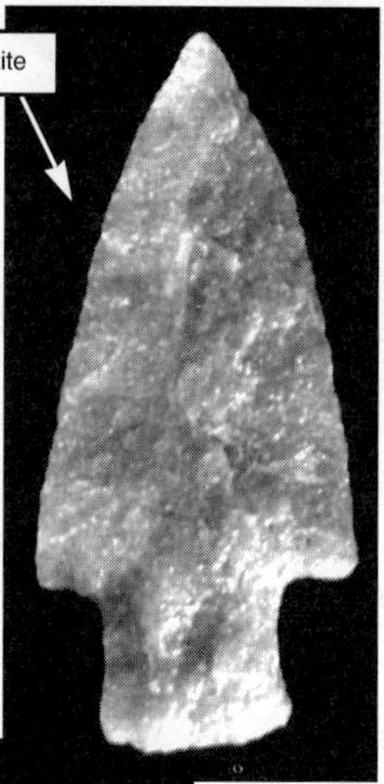

Quartzite

G7 $15-$30
Montgomery Co., PA.

Quartzite

G8, $25-$50
PA.

Quartzite

G5, $15-$30
Lancaster Co., PA.

Argillite

G6, $30-$60
PA.

LOCATION: Northeastern states. **DESCRIPTION:** A medium to large size stemmed point with convex sides and a medium length square stem. The base is usually straight to slightly convex. Shoulders are straight to tapered. **I.D. KEY:** Square stem.

EDEN - Transitional Paleo to Early Archaic, 9500 - 7500 B.P.

(Also see Agate Basin, Angostura, Plainview, Scottsbluff)

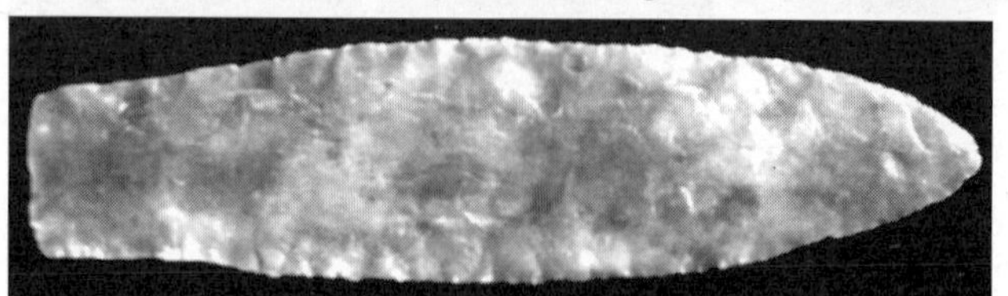

G7, $200-$400
Lebanon Co., PA.

EDEN (continued)

LOCATION: Midwestern to Northeastern states. **DESCRIPTION:** A medium to large size, narrow, lanceolate point with very weak shoulders. The base is rectangular shaped and is ground. Many examples have a median ridge and collateral to oblique parallel flaking. **I.D. KEY:** Small shoulders, lanceolate form.

ERB BASAL NOTCHED - Mid-Woodland, 2000 - 1200 B.P.

(Also see Eshback, Oley)

G4, $5-$10
NJ/PA.

G8, $15-$30
Montgomery
Co., PA.

G6, $5-$15
NJ/PA.

G4, $5-$10
PA.

G7, $25-$50
Union Co., PA.

G7, $25-$40
Union Co., PA.

G7, $25-$40
Centre Co., PA.

G8, $30-$50
Columbia Co., PA.

LOCATION: Northeastern states. **DESCRIPTION:** A small to medium size, broad, basal notched point. Tangs can drop even with or below the base. **I.D. KEY:** Basal form.

ERIE TRIANGLE - Late Woodland, 1500 - 200 B.P.

(Also see Levanna, Madison, Susquehannock Triangle, Yadkin)

LOCATION: Northeastern states. **DESCRIPTION:** A small size, thin, triangular point with sharp basal corners and a straight to concave base. **I.D. KEY:** Triangular form.

G5, $3-$8
Lycoming Co., PA.

ESHBACK - Late Archaic, 5500 - 3500 B.P.

(Also see Erb Basal Notched, Oley)

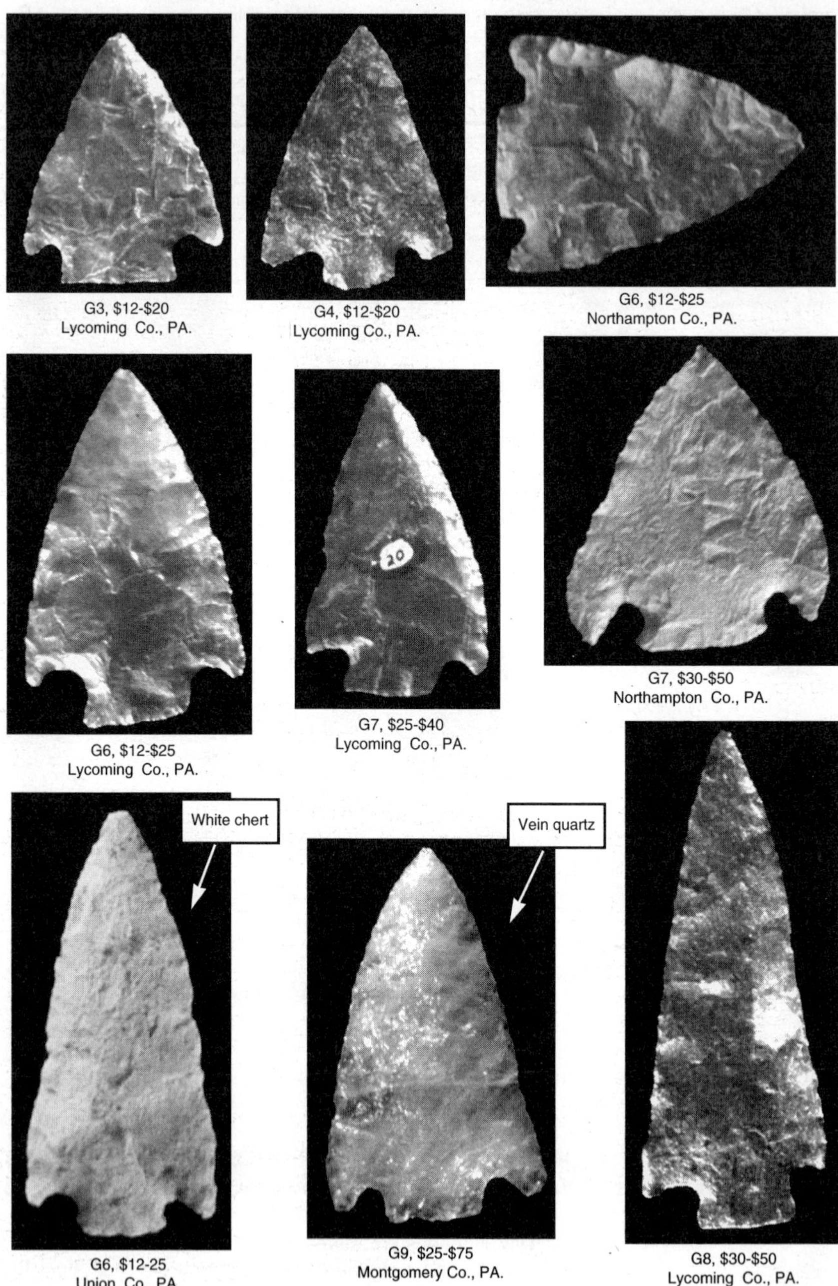

G3, $12-$20
Lycoming Co., PA.

G4, $12-$20
Lycoming Co., PA.

G6, $12-$25
Northampton Co., PA.

G7, $30-$50
Northampton Co., PA.

G7, $25-$40
Lycoming Co., PA.

G6, $12-$25
Lycoming Co., PA.

G6, $12-25
Union Co., PA.

G9, $25-$75
Montgomery Co., PA.

G8, $30-$50
Lycoming Co., PA.

LOCATION: Northeastern states. **DESCRIPTION:** A small to medium size, broad, basal notched point. Tangs can extend beyond the base. Bases are straight, concave or convex. Similar to *Eva* points found in the Southeast. **I.D. KEY:** Basal form.

FOREST NOTCHED - Early Woodland, 3000 - 2000 B.P.

(Also see Drybrook, Frost Island, Orient, Patuxent, Perkiomen and Susquehanna Broad, Table Rock)

LOCATION: Northeastern. **DESCRIPTION:** A medium size, narrow point with very wide side notches. The basal area is relatively long and expands. The base is straight. Shoulders are rounded. **I.D. KEY:** Base form and rounded shoulders.

G6, $5-$15
Clinton Co., PA.

FOX CREEK - Woodland, 2500 - 1200 B.P.

(Also see Dalton and Savannah River)

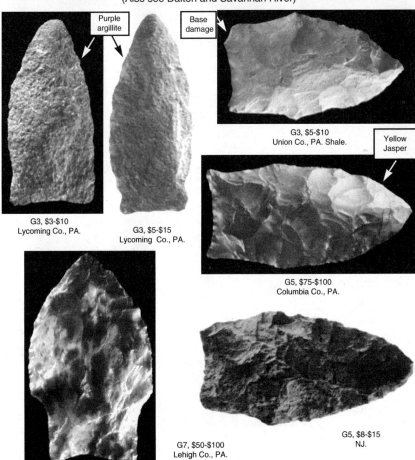

Purple argillite

Base damage

G3, $3-$10
Lycoming Co., PA.

G3, $5-$15
Lycoming Co., PA.

G3, $5-$10
Union Co., PA. Shale.

Yellow Jasper

G5, $75-$100
Columbia Co., PA.

G7, $50-$100
Lehigh Co., PA.

G5, $8-$15
NJ.

LOCATION: Northeastern. **DESCRIPTION:** A medium size blade with a squared to tapered hafting area and a straight to concave base. Shoulders, when present are very weak and tapered. **I.D. KEY:** Basal form.

FOX CREEK (continued)

Gray chert

Yellow Jasper

Jasper

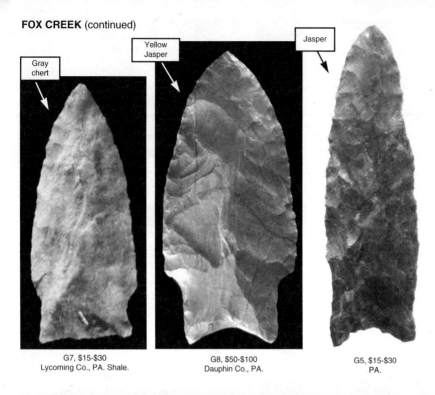

G7, $15-$30
Lycoming Co., PA. Shale.

G8, $50-$100
Dauphin Co., PA.

G5, $15-$30
PA.

FROST ISLAND - Late Archaic -Early Woodland, 3200 - 2500 B.P.

(Also see Drybrook, Forest Notched, Orient, Patuxent, Perkiomen, Susquehanna Broad)

G6, $12-$25
Lycoming Co., PA.

G6, $25-$40
Lycoming Co., PA.

G6, $25-$40
Centre Co., PA.

G7, $30-$50
Clinton Co., PA.

LOCATION: Northeastern states. **DESCRIPTION:** A medium to large size expanded stem point with rounded shoulders. Side notches are broader than the *Forest Notched* type. **I.D. KEY:** Long expanded base, rounded shoulders.

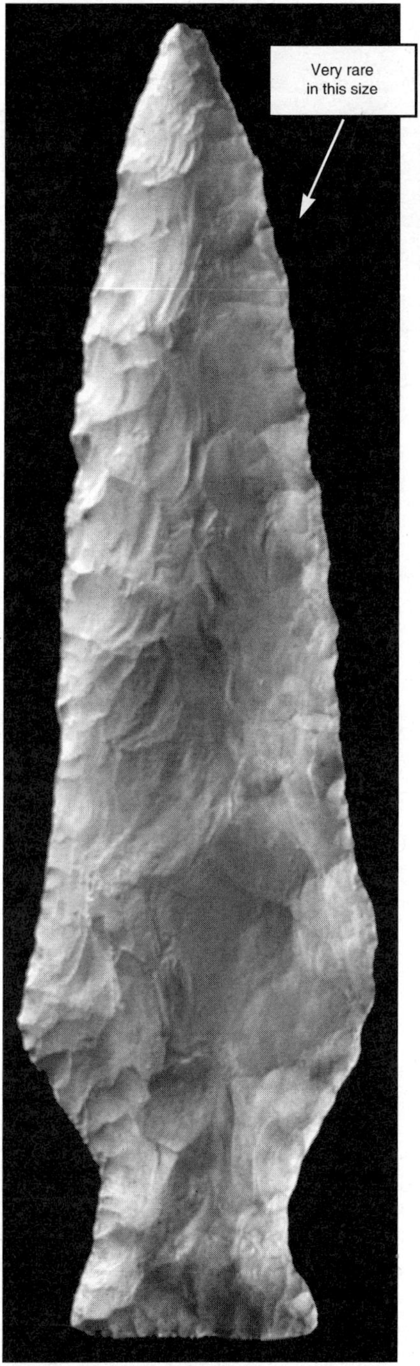

Very rare in this size

G10, $400-$700
Broome Co., NY.

GARVER'S FERRY - Late Woodland, 1800 - 1300 B.P.

(Also see Cave Spring, Crooked Creek, Dewart Stemmed, Lamoka, Neville)

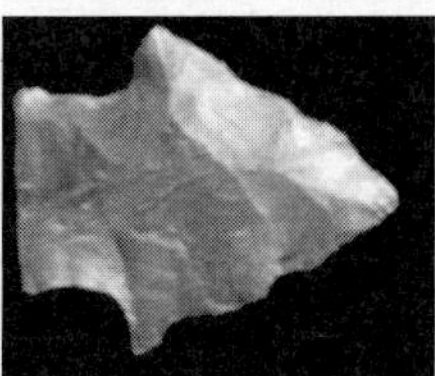

G6, $5-$10
Lycoming Co., PA.
Yellow Jasper.

LOCATION: Northeastern states. **DESCRIPTION:** A small size dart point with a short stem that is slightly expanding. The base is straight. Some examples are corner notched. **I.D. KEY:** Basal form, early flaking. **I.D. KEY:** Expanded stem, small size.

GENESEE - Late Archaic, 5000 - 4000 B.P.

(Also see Bare Island, Newmanstown, and Piedmont)

G4, $10-$20
PA.

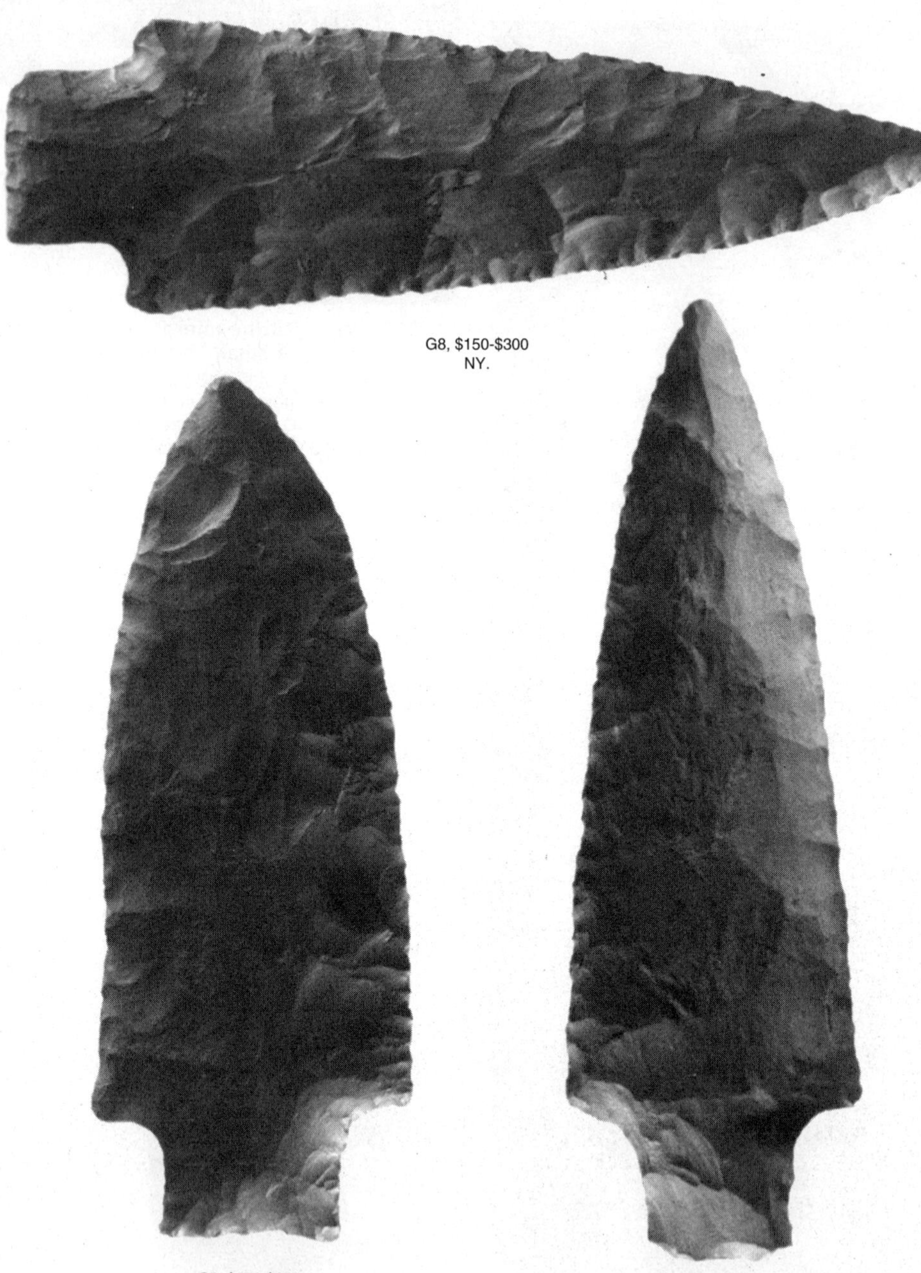

G8, $150-$300
NY.

G9, $150-$200
NY.

G9, $150-$300
Dauphin Co., PA.

LOCATION: Northeastern states. Named for the Genesee Valley located in New York state. **DESCRIPTION:** A medium to large size point with prominent shoulders, a thick cross section and a squarish base. Shoulders can be straight to tapered to slightly barbed. Basal area can be ground. **I.D. KEY:** Expanded base, usually thin.

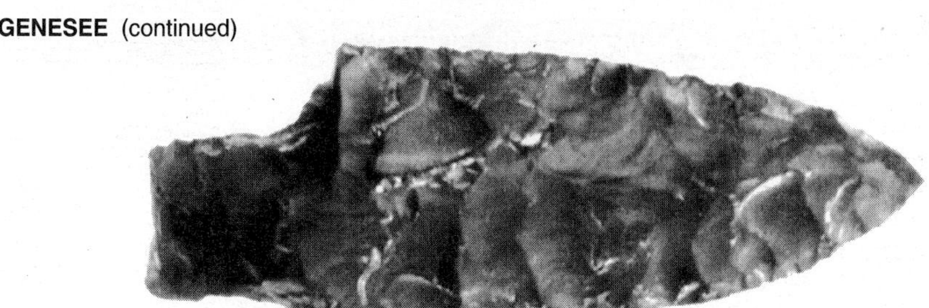

G6, $50-$100
Columbia Co., NY.

G10, $200-$350
Lancaster Co., PA.

G10, $250-$400
NY.

GODDARD - Mississippian, 1000 - 800 B.P.

(Also see Jacks Reef & Raccoon Notched)

G6, $2-$5
N. ME.

G7, $2-$5
N. ME.

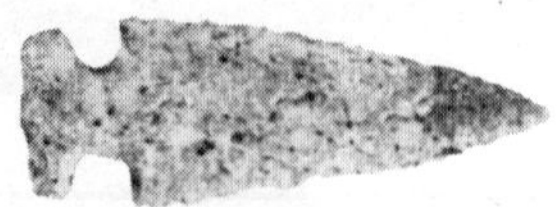

G5, $2-$5
N. ME.

LOCATION: Northeastern states. Type site is located at Penobscot Bay, Maine. **DESCRIPTION:** A small to medium side, thin, narrow, side to corner notched point with a straight to convex base. Similar in style to Jacks Reef Corner Notched and Raccoon Creek points. Also similar to Knight Island points of the Southeast. A late Ceramic Period point. Some examples in the type area are made of high grade, colorful material that would be worth more. **I.D. KEY:** Thin, side notched point.

GRAVER - Paleo to Archaic, 14,000 - 4000 B.P.

(Also see Drill & Scraper)

G8, $20-$40
Dauphin Co., PA.
Shoop site.
Onondaga chert

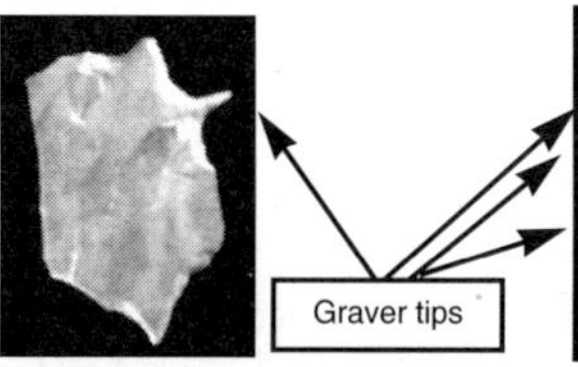

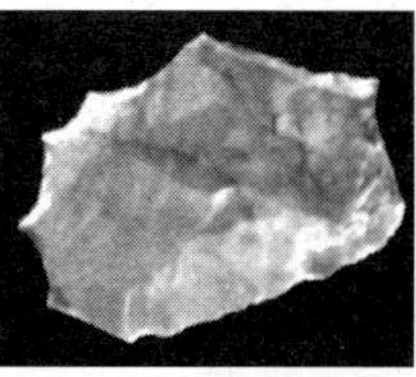

G8, $20-$40
Dauphin Co., PA.
Shoop site.
Onondaga chert

LOCATION: Paleo and Archaic sites everywhere **DESCRIPTION:** An irregular shaped uniface tool with sharp, pointed projections used for puncturing, incising, tattooing, etc. Some examples served a dual purpose for scraping as well. In later times, *Perforators* took the place of *Gravers.*

GROUND SLATE - Archaic, 6000 - 4500 B.P.

(Also see Bare Island)

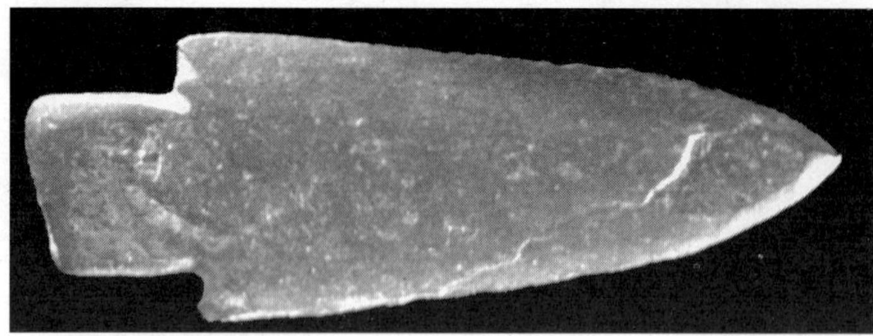

G6, $50-$100
Eastern PA.

LOCATION: Northeastern states. **DESCRIPTION:** A large size stemmed point completely ground from slate. Bases vary from expanding to contracting. Examples of facial grinding of flaked Paleo and Archaic points have been found in the Eastern U.S.

GUILFORD - Middle Archaic, 6500 - 5000 B.P.

(Also see Agate Basin)

G6, $8-$15
NY.

G7, $8-$15
NY.

Guilford Yuma form

G6, $15-$25
MD.

LOCATION: Eastern seaboard to Northeastern states. **DESCRIPTION:** A medium to large size, thick, narrow lanceolate point. The base varies from round to straight to eared. Another variation has weak shoulders defining a stemmed area. **I.D. KEY:** Thickness, early parallel flaking.

HARDAWAY - Late Paleo, 9500 - 8000 B.P.

(Also see Dalton-Greenbrier and Palmer)

LOCATION: Eastern states. Type site is in Stanly Co., NC, Yadkin River. Very rare in Northeast. **DESCRIPTION:** A small to medium size point with shallow side notches and expanded auricles forming a wide, deeply concave base. Ears and base are usually ground. This type evolved from the Dalton point. **I.D. KEY:** Eared form, heavy grinding in shoulders, paleo parallel flaking.

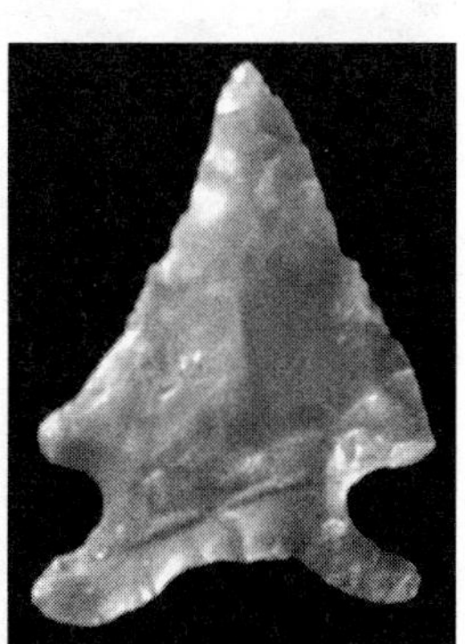

G5, $20-$40
Lycoming Co., PA.
Yellow Jasper.

HAW RIVER - Transitional Paleo, 11,000 - 8000 B.P.

G8, $40-$75
NY.

IMPORTANT: Shown 85% of actual size

LOCATION: Eastern seaboard to Northeastern states. **DESCRIPTION:** A medium to large size, broad, elliptical blade with a basal notch and usually rounded tangs that turn inward. **I.D. KEY:** Notched base.

HELLGRAMITE - Early Woodland, 3000 - 2500 B.P.

(Also see Brewerton, Kessel, Kirk, Meadowood)

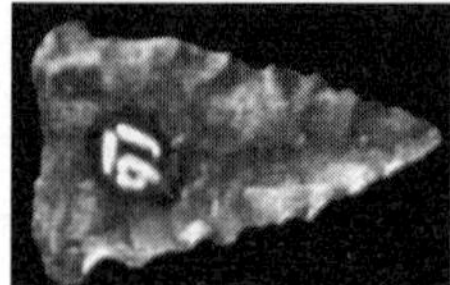

G3, $3-$10
Lycoming Co., PA.
Chert.

G3, $3-$10
Lancaster
Co., PA.

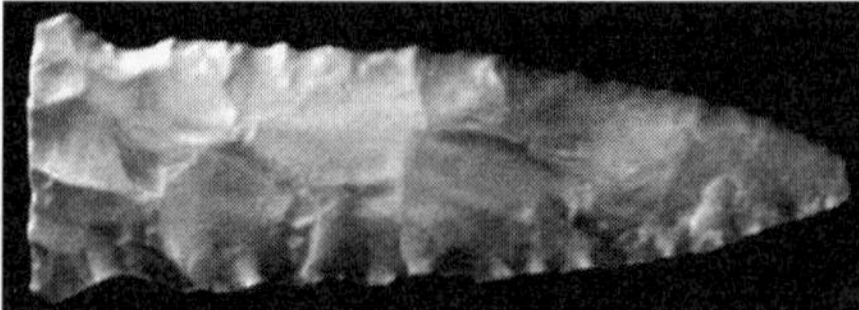

LOCATION: Northeastern states. **DESCRIPTION:** A small to medium size triangular point with very weak side notches. The blade edges are finely serrated and the base is straight to convex. **I.D. KEY:** Weak notches, serrated edges.

HOLCOMB- Paleo, 11,000 - 10,000 B.P.

(Also see Clovis, Crowfield, Cumberland, Dalton, Debert, Plainview)

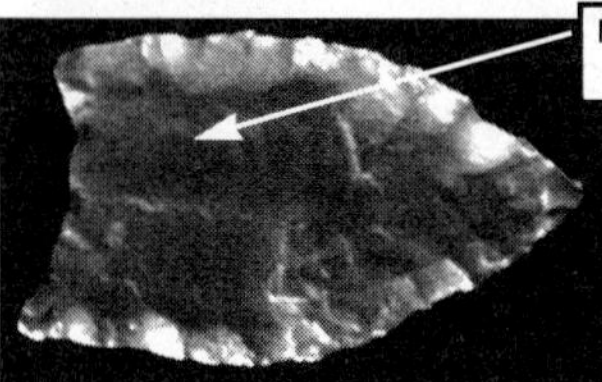

Note multiple flutes

G6, $75-$150
Tioga Co., PA.

LOCATION: Northeastern states. **DESCRIPTION:** A small to medium size, thin, fluted point with a concave base. Basal area is ground. More than one fluting strike is common. **I.D. KEY:** Small fluted point.

HOOVER'S ISLAND- Archaic, 6000 - 4000 B.P.

(Also see Bare Island, Duncan's Island, Genesee, Lackawaxen, Newmanstown, Patuxent, Piedmont, Piney Island)

G6, $15-$25
Northumberland Co., PA.

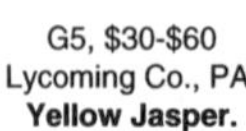

G5, $30-$60
Lycoming Co., PA.
Yellow Jasper.

G7, $75-$150
Lycoming Co., PA. **Yellow Jasper.**

LOCATION: Pennsylvania to northern Maryland. **DESCRIPTION:** A medium to large size, broad, expanded to parallel stemmed point. Bases are straight to concave. Basal corners are sharp. Shoulders are tapered to rounded. **I.D. KEY:** Sharp basal corners, tapered shoulders. Belongs to the Piedmont series and is also known as Southern Piedmont.

JACKS REEF CORNER NOTCHED - Late Woodland to Mississippian, 1500 - 1000 B.P.

(Also see Kiski, Lycoming Co., Oley, Palmer, Raccoon Notched, Vosburg)

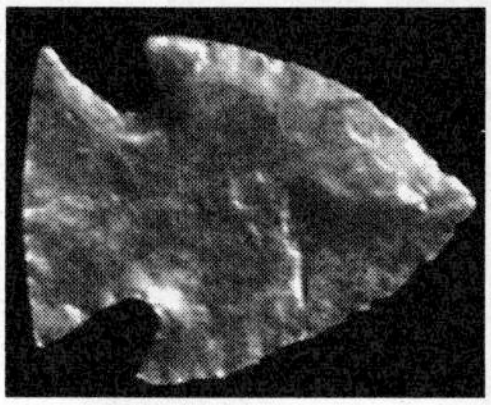

G7, $20-$40
Eastern Shore, MD.

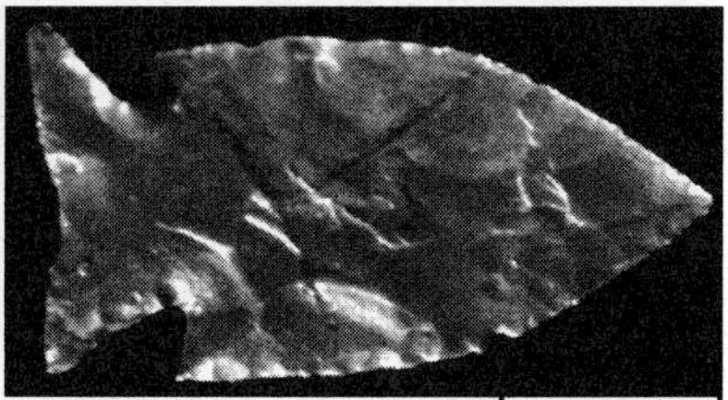

G6, $20-$40
Lehigh Co., PA.

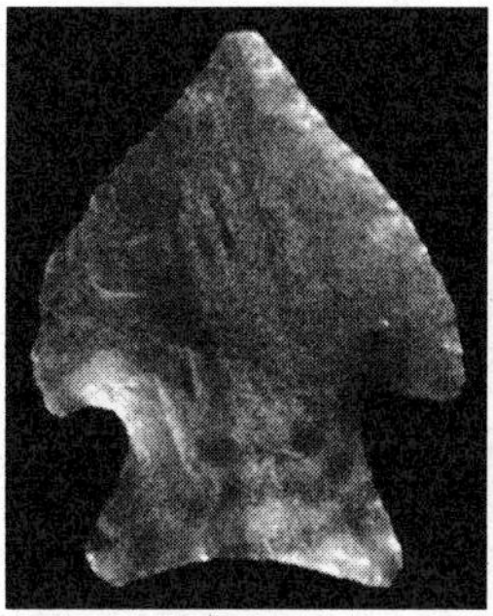

A classic perfect example

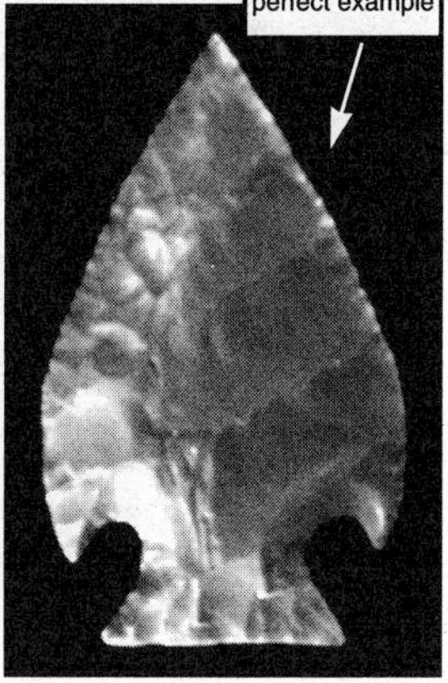

G7, $20-$35
NY

G6, $20-$40
Dauphin Co., PA.

G7, $30-$50, NJ.

G10, $100-$200
Dauphin Co., PA. **Yellow Jasper.**
Classic form. Excellent quality.

LOCATION: Southeastern to Northeastern states. **DESCRIPTION:** A small to medium size, very thin, corner notched point that is well made. The blade is convex to pentagonal. Some examples are widely corner notched and appear to be expanded stem points with barbed shoulders. **I.D. KEY:** Thinness, sharp corners.

JACKS REEF CORNER NOTCHED (continued)

Slight side damage

Slight tip damage

G9, $80-$150
Ripley, NY.

G6, $20-$40
Lancaster Co., PA. **Yellow Jasper.**

G9, $75-$150
Lycoming Co., PA. **Yellow Jasper.**
Perfect base and tangs.

JACKS REEF PENTAGONAL - Late Woodland to Mississippian, 1500 - 1000 B.P.

(Also see Erie Triangle, Levanna, Madison, Susquehannock Triangle)

G4, $4-$8
Lycoming Co., PA.
Onondaga chert.

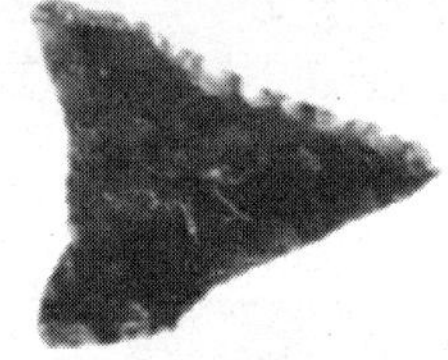

G5, $3-$5
Lycoming Co., PA.

G5, $3-$5
PA. Jasper.

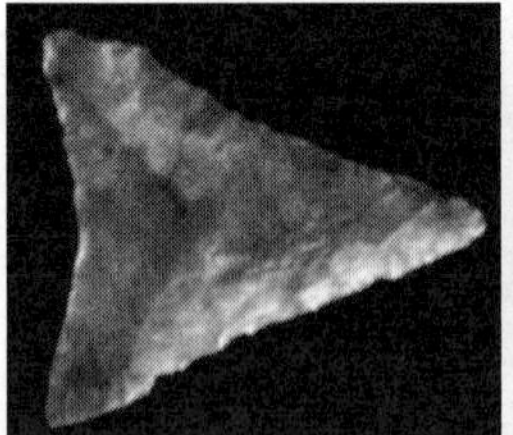

G6, $8-$15
Monroe Co., PA.
Onondaga chert.

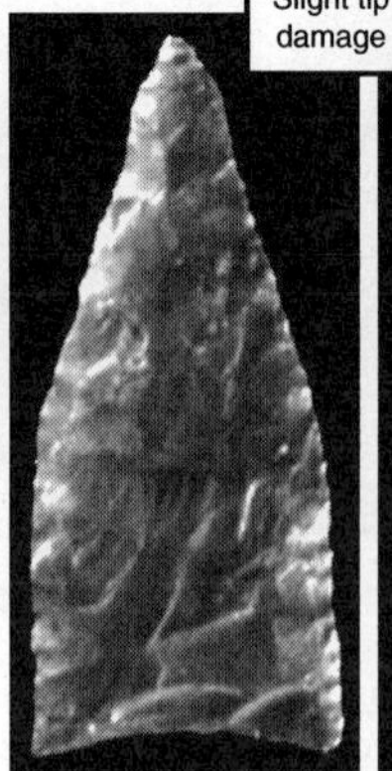

G8, $25-$40
Lycoming Co., PA.

Slight tip damage

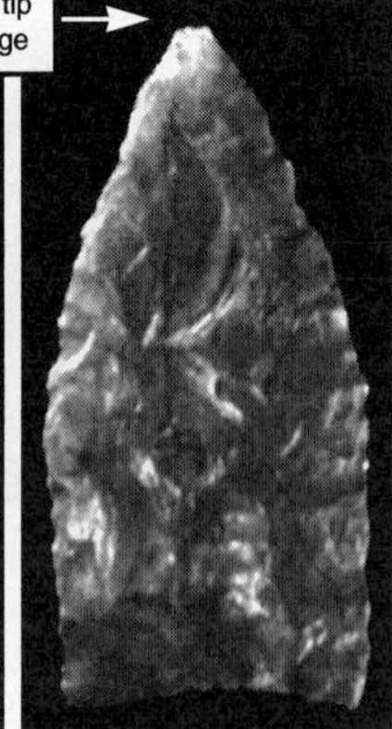

G6, $20-$40
Centre Co., PA.

LOCATION: Southeastern to Northeastern states. **DESCRIPTION:** A small to large size , very thin, five sided point with a sharp tip. The hafting area is usually contracted with a slightly concave to straight base. This type is called *Pee Dee* in North and South Carolina. **I.D. KEY:** Pentagonal form.

KANAWHA - Early Archaic, 9000 - 5000 B.P.

(Also see Kirk Serrated, Lake Erie, LeCroy, MacCorkle, Penn's Creek, St. Albans, Stanly, Susquehanna Birfurcate)

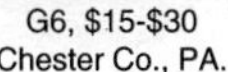

G6, $15-$30
Chester Co., PA.

G5, $10-$20
Union Co., PA.

LOCATION: Southeastern to Northeastern states. Type site is in Kanawha Co., WVA. **DESCRIPTION:** A small to medium size, fairly thick, shallowly bifurcated stemmed point. The basal lobes are usually rounded and the shoulders are tapered. Believed to be the ancestor to the *Stanly* type. **I.D. KEY:** Archaic flaking, weak basal lobes.

KESSEL- Early Archaic, 10,000 - 8000 B.P.

(Also see Cache River, Goddard, Hellgramite, Meadowood, Raccoon Notched)

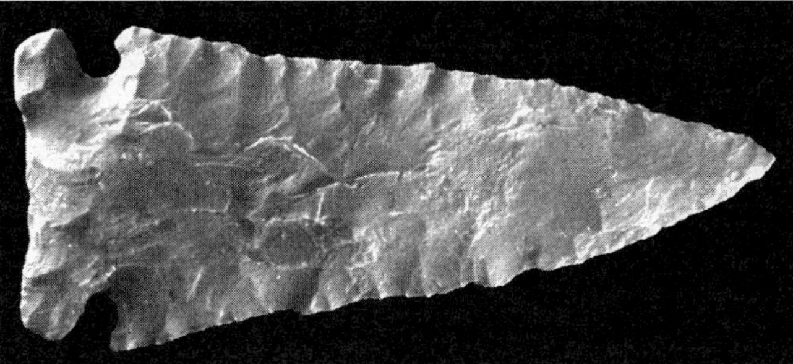

G7, $25-$50
Burlington Co., NJ.

LOCATION: Northeastern states. **DESCRIPTION:** A medium to large size, thin, triangular side notched point. Notches are close to the base, are very narrow and angle in from the sides. The base is concave. Almost identical in form and age to the *Cache River* type from Arkansas.**I.D. KEY:** Basal notches, thinness.

Black chert

G8, $20-$40
W. PA.

KIRK CORNER NOTCHED - Early to Mid-Archaic, 9000 - 6000 B.P.

(Also see Amos, Brewerton, Charleston Pine Tree, Crooked Creek, Palmer)

LOCATION: Southeastern to Northeastern states. **DESCRIPTION:** A medium to large size, corner notched point. Blade edges can be convex to recurved and are finely serrated on many examples. The base can be convex, concave, straight, bifurcated or auriculate. Points that are beveled on one side of each face would fall under the *Lost Lake* or *Hardin* type. **I.D. KEY:** Secondary edgework.

G2, $3-$5
Lycoming Co., PA.

G3, $5-$15
Northampton Co., PA.

G3, $5-$15
Lycoming Co., PA.

G3, $8-$15
Lehigh Co., PA.

G8, $50-$125
Montgomery Co., PA.

G8, $100-$200
Snyder Co., PA.

G3, $8-$15
Northumberland Co., PA.

KIRK Serrated - Early to Mid-Archaic, 9000 - 6000 B.P.

(Also see Bare Island, Duncan's Island, Fountain Creek, Genesee, Heavy Duty, Lackawaxen, Neville, Newmanstown)

G5 $5-$20
Lycoming Co., PA.

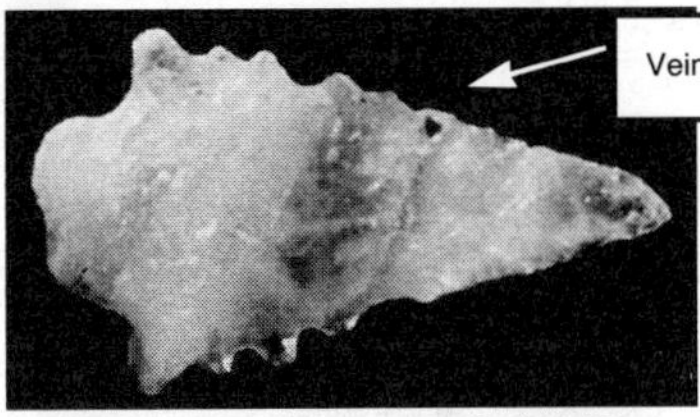

Vein quartz

G5 $15-$25
MD.

Gray flint

G7 $15-$35
NY.

Quartzite

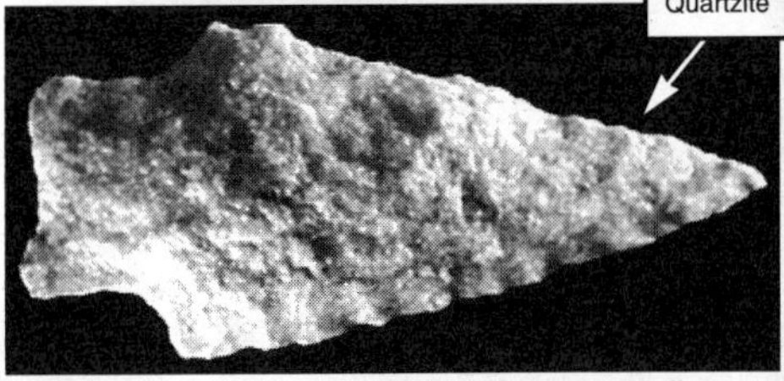

G5, $10-$20
Cent. PA.

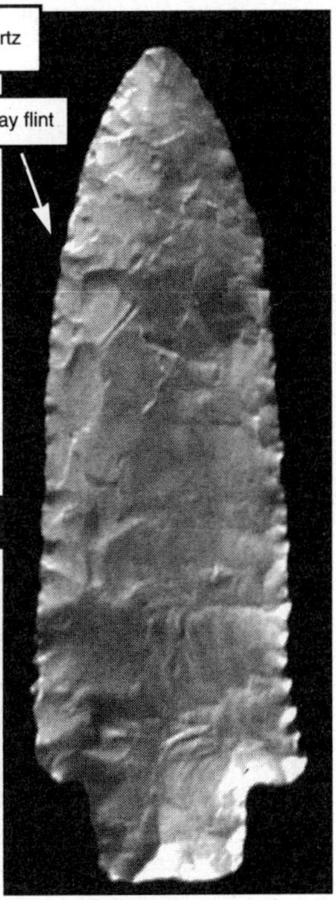

G6, $40-$75
Lycoming Co., PA.

LOCATION: Eastern states. **DESCRIPTION:** A medium to large size, barbed, stemmed point with deep notches or fine serrations along the blade edges. The stem is parallel, contracting or expanding. The stem sides may be steeply beveled on opposite faces. The base can be concave, convex or straight, and can be very short. The shoulders are usually strongly barbed. This form is believed to have evolved into *Stanly* and other types. **I.D. KEY:** Serrations.

KISKI NOTCHED - LATE WOODLAND, 2000 - 1400 B.P.

(Also see Brewerton, Crooked Creek, Jacks Reef, Lycoming Co., Palmer)

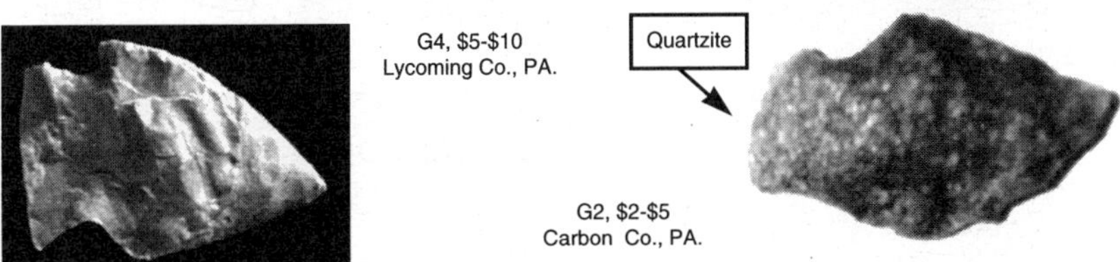

G4, $5-$10
Lycoming Co., PA.

G2, $2-$5
Carbon Co., PA.

LOCATION: Northeastern states. **DESCRIPTION:** A small size side or corner notched point. **I.D. KEY:** Notching and size.

KITTATINY - Middle Archaic, 6000 - 5000 B.P.

(Also see Brewerton Eared, Jacks Reef Pentagonal, Levanna)

KITTATINY (continued)

LOCATION: Northeastern states. **DESCRIPTION:** A small size lanceolate blade with recurved side edges. The base is straight, with the corners forming tiny ears. The stem is square to expanding. The *Nolichucky* type found in the Southeast is similar in outline. **I.D. KEY:** Triangular and basal form.

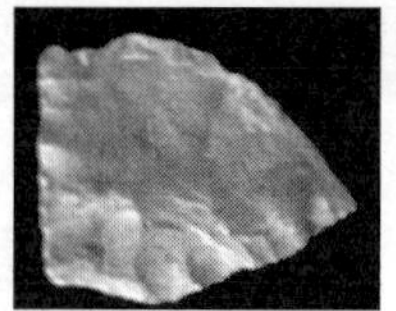

G5, $5-$10
Lycoming Co., PA. **Yellow Jasper.**

KLINE - Early Archaic, 9000 - 7000 B.P.

(Also see Brodhead Side Notched, Dovetail, Kirk, Lycoming Co., Susquehanna Broad)

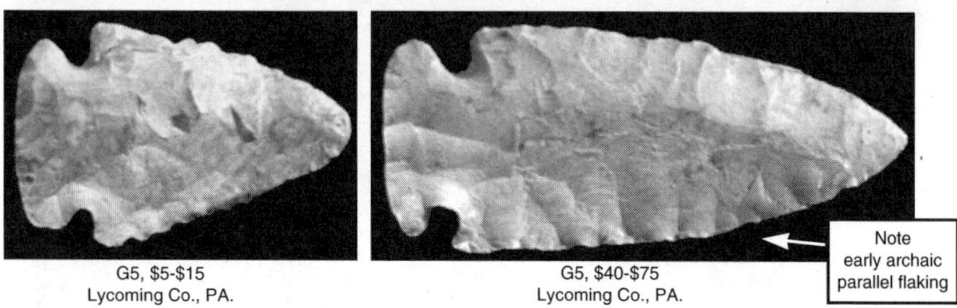

G5, $5-$15
Lycoming Co., PA.

G5, $40-$75
Lycoming Co., PA.

LOCATION: Northeastern states. **DESCRIPTION:** A medium to large size corner notched point with a convex base that is ground. Shoulders are strong and are horizontal to slightly barbed. Basal corners are rounded. **I.D. KEY:** Corner notching, early flaking.

KOENS CRISPIN - Late Archaic, 4000 - 3000 B.P.

(Also see Adena, Lehigh, Morrow Mountain, Poplar Island, Schuylkill, Virginsville,)

G9, $250-$500
Carbon Co., PA.

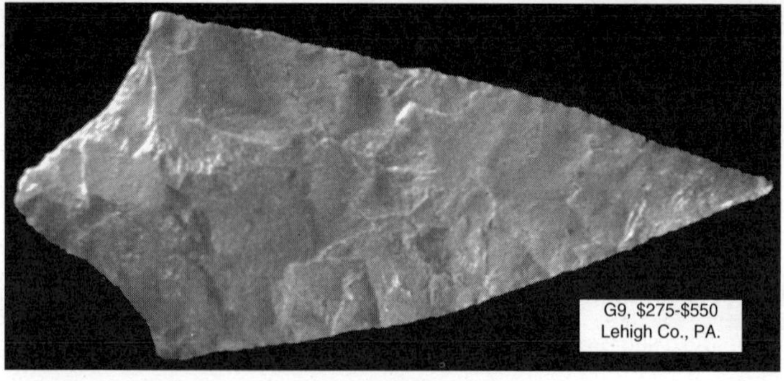

G9, $275-$550
Lehigh Co., PA.

KOENS CRISPIN (continued)

G6, $40-$75
Lancaster Co., PA.

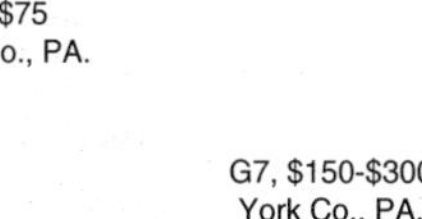

G7, $150-$300
York Co., PA.

LOCATION: Northeastern states. **DESCRIPTION:** A medium to large size, broad, contracted stem point with a rounded base. Shoulders are tapered to straight. Generally poorer quality than the *Lehigh* type. **I.D. KEY:** Contracted stem, strong shoulders.

LACKAWAXEN - Archaic, 6000 - 4000 B.P.

(Also see Bare Island, Duncan's Island, Neville, Piedmont, Tocks Island)

G5, $5-$15
Northampton Co., PA.

LOCATION: Northeastern states. **DESCRIPTION:** A medium to large size, narrow, expanded to contracting to parallel stemmed point with strong, tapered shoulders. **I.D. KEY:** Long, narrow stemmed point.

G6, $10-$25
Northampton Co., PA.

LAKE ERIE - Early to Mid-Archaic, 9000 - 5000 B.P.

(Also see Erie Triangle, Fox Valley, Kirk-Bifurcated, LeCroy, MacCorkle, Penn's Creek, St. Albans, Stanly, Susquehanna Bifurcate)

G5, $8-$15
Northumberland Co., PA.

G3, $2-$5
Cent. PA.

G5, $8-$15
Cent. PA.

LOCATION: Norheastern states. **DESCRIPTION:** A small to medium size, thin, deeply notched or bifurcated stemmed point. The basal lobes are parallel with a tendency to turn inward and are pointed. The outward sides of the basal lobes are usually fractured from the base towards the tip and can be fround. **I.D. KEY:** Pointed basal lobes.

LAMOKA - Middle Archaic, 5500 - 4500 B.P.

(Also see Deward Stemmed, Duncan's Island, Garver's Ferry, Neville, Piney Island, Randolph)

G2, $1-$2
Lycoming Co., PA.

G3, $1-$2
Lycoming Co., PA.

G3, $1-$2
Lycoming Co., PA.

G3, $1-$2
Monroe Co., PA.

G6, $6-$12
Columbia Co. NY.

G5, $6-$12
Columbia Co. NY.

LOCATION: Northeastern states. **DESCRIPTION:** A small to medium size, narrow, thick, spike point. The shoulders are tapered and the stem is square to contracting to expanding. The base on some examples shows the natural rind of the native material used. Called *Bradley Spike* in the Southeast. **I.D. KEY:** Thick, spike point.

LAMOKA (continued)

G5, $4-$8 Lycoming Co., PA. | G6, $6-$12 Columbia Co., NY. | G6, $7-$15 Lycoming Co., PA. | G5, $7-$15 Monroe Co., PA. | G5, $7-$15 Lycoming Co., PA.

LECROY - Early to Mid-Archaic, 9000 - 5000 B.P.

(Also see Decatur, Kanawha, Kirk Serrated, Lake Erie, MacCorkle, Charleston Pine Tree, St. Albans, Stanly, Susquehanna Bifurcate & Taunton River Bifurcate)

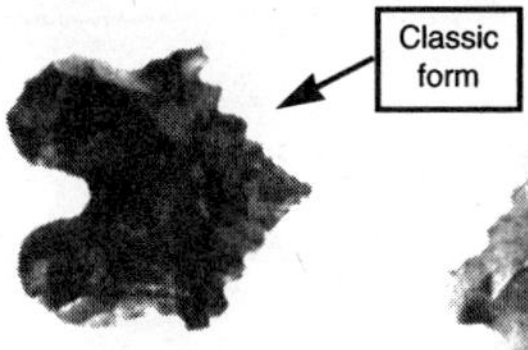

Classic form

G5, $10-$20 Union Co., PA.

G3, $10-$20 Union Co., PA.

G3, $4-$8 Northumberland Co., PA.

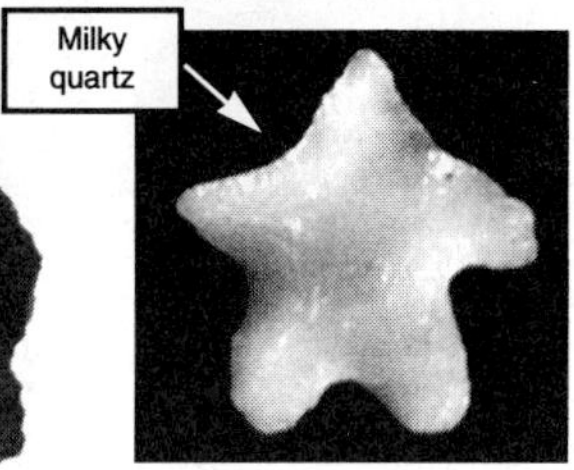

Milky quartz

G3 $4-$8 Montgomery Co., PA.

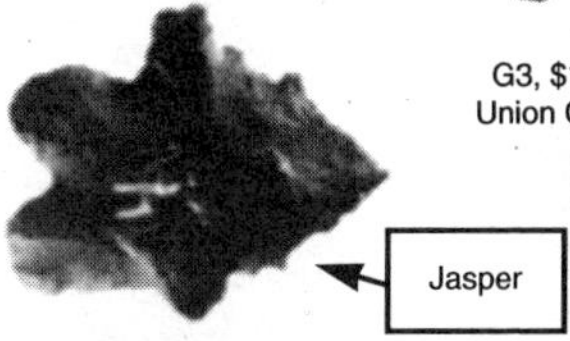

Jasper

G3, $10-$20 Lycoming Co., PA.

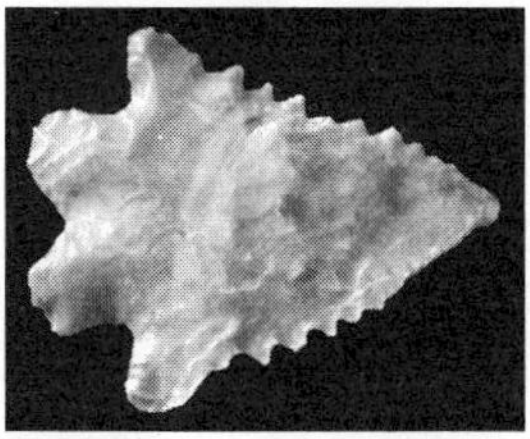

G7, $15-$25 Lancaster Co., PA.

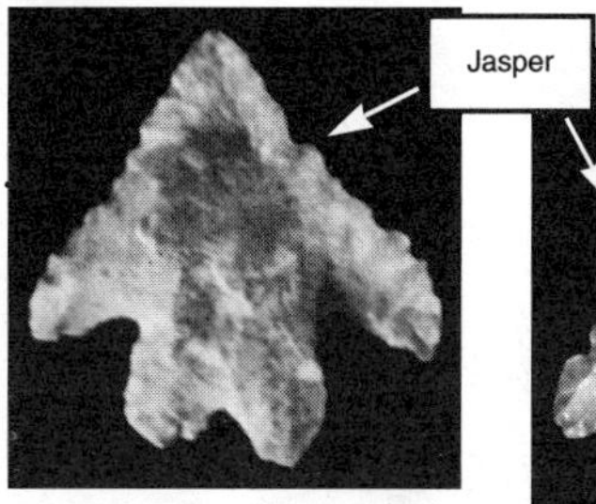

Jasper

G6, $10-$20 Monmouth Co., NJ.

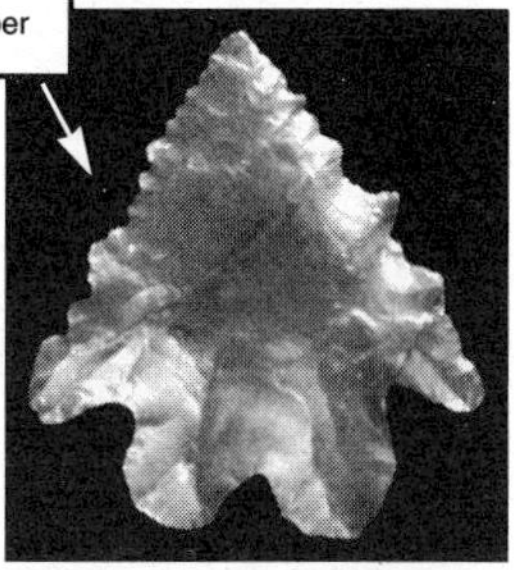

G8, $12-$25 MD. **Yellow Jasper**.

LOCATION: Eastern states. **DESCRIPTION:** A small to medium size, thin, bifurcated point with deeply notched or serrated blade edges. Basal ears can either droop or expand out. The base is usually large in comparison to the blade size. Bases can be ground. **I.D. KEY:** Basal form, thinness.

LECROY (continued)

G5, $5-$10
Union Co., PA.

G9, $25-$50
Union Co., PA.

G9, $25-$50
Lycoming Co., PA.

G7, $10-$20
Lycoming Co., PA.

LEHIGH - Late Archaic, 4000 - 3000 B.P.

(Also see Adena, Koens Crispin, Morrow Mountain, Poplar Island, Schuylkill, Virginsville)

Jasper

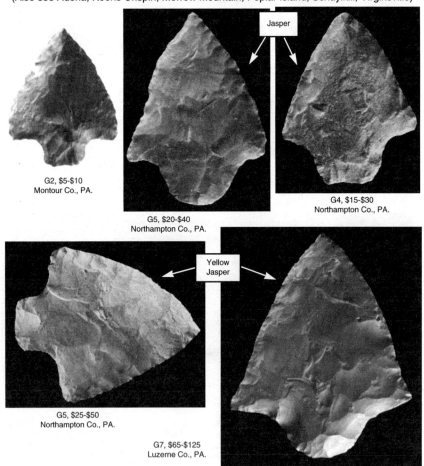

G2, $5-$10
Montour Co., PA.

G5, $20-$40
Northampton Co., PA.

G4, $15-$30
Northampton Co., PA.

Yellow
Jasper

G5, $25-$50
Northampton Co., PA.

G7, $65-$125
Luzerne Co., PA.

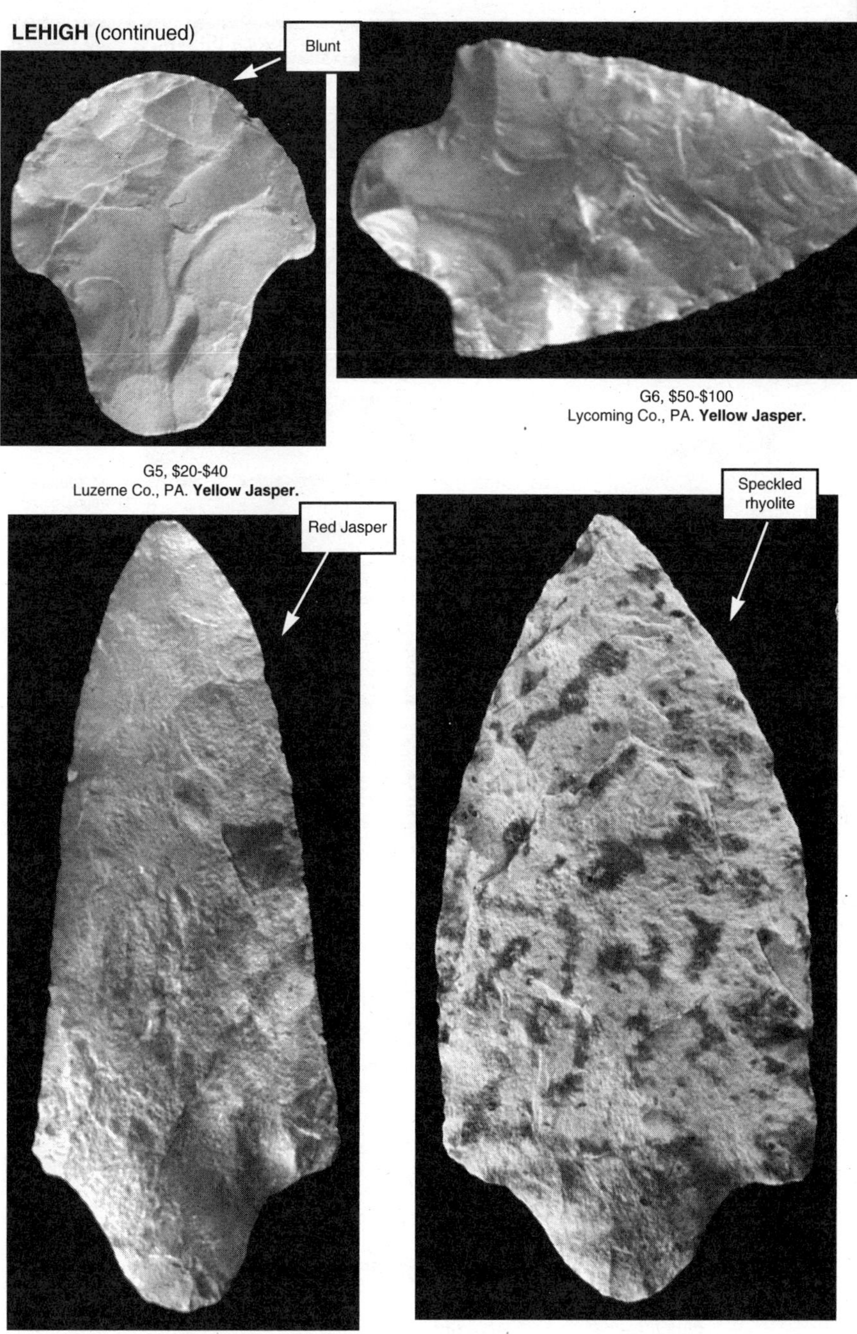

G5, $20-$40
Luzerne Co., PA. **Yellow Jasper.**

G6, $50-$100
Lycoming Co., PA. **Yellow Jasper.**

G9, $75-$150
York Co., PA.

G8, $100-$200
Lancaster Co., PA.

LOCATION: Northeastern states. **DESCRIPTION:** A medium to large size, broad, contracted to square stemmed point. Shoulders are horizontal to contracting. The base is straight to rounded. **I.D. KEY:** Broad, contracting stem .

LEVANNA - Late Woodland to Mississippian, 1300 - 600 B.P.

(Also see Madison, Susquehannock Triangle)

G3, $5-$10
Northumberland Co., PA.

G6, $10-$20
Union Co., PA.

G6, $10-$20
PA.

G6, $10-$20
NJ.

G6, $8-$15
Columbia Co., NY.

G7, $20-$30
Oswego Co., NY.

G7, $25-$35
PA.

G8, $20-$35
Oswego Co., NY.

G6, $15-$25
PA.

G8, $12-$25
PA.

G7, $25-$35
MD.

G7, $15-$35
Montgomery Co., PA.

LOCATION: Northeastern states. **DESCRIPTION:** A small to medium size, thin, triangular point with a concave to straight base. Believed to be replaced by *Madison* points in later times. Some examples have the basal corners fractured. Called *Yadkin* in North Carolina. **I.D. KEY:** Medium thick cross section triangle.

LEVANNA (continued)

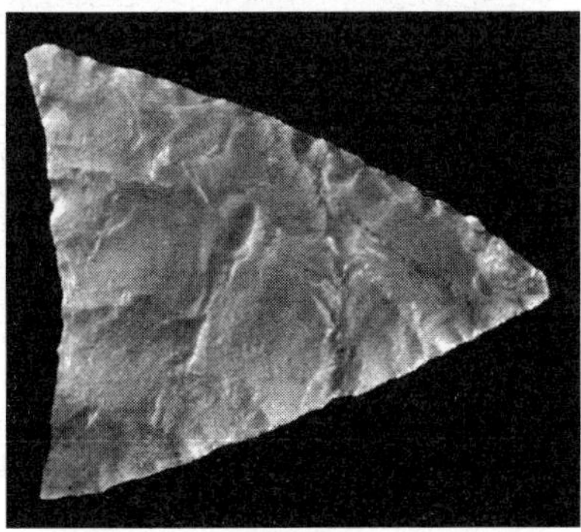

G8, $20-$35
Burlington Co. NJ.

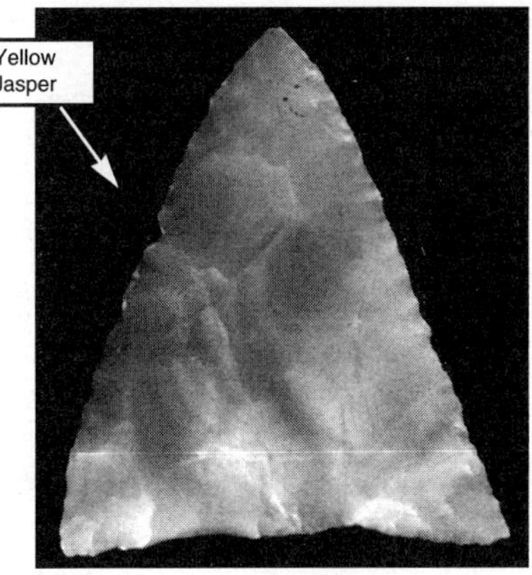

G8, $50-$100
Burlington Co., NJ.

LOST LAKE - Early Archaic, 9000 - 6000 B.P.

(Also see Charleston Pine Tree, Decatur, Dovetail, Kirk)

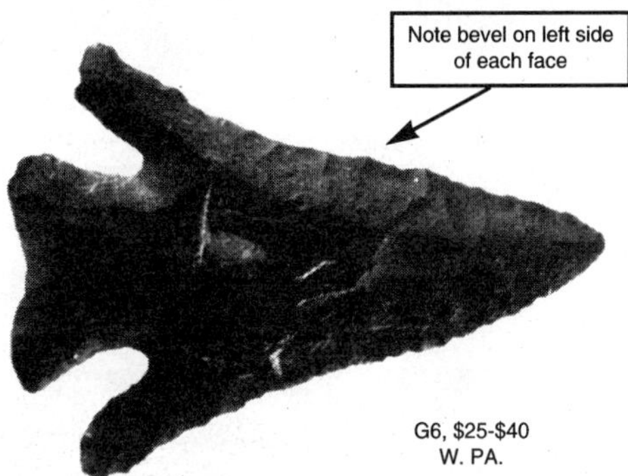

G6, $25-$40
W. PA.

LOCATION: Southeastern, Midwestern to Northeastern states. **DESCRIPTION:** A medium to large size, broad, corner notched point that is beveled on one side of each face. Some examples are finely serrated. Bases are ground. Unbeveled examples would fall into the *Kirk Corner Notched* type. **I.D. KEY:** Notching and opposite beveled blade edge.

LYCOMING COUNTY SERIES - Middle Archaic, 6000 - 4000 B.P.

(Also see Brewerton, Crooked Creek, Garver's Ferry, Otter Creek, Penn's Creek)

LOCATION: Pennsylvania. **DESCRIPTION:** A local variation of the Brewerton type. A small to medium size point with strong shoulders. The series occurs as side notched, corner notched and stemmed forms.

G2, $4-$7
Lycoming Co., PA., jasper

MACCORKLE - Early Archaic, 8000 - 6000 B.P.

(Also see Kanawha, Kirk Serrated, Lake Erie, LeCroy, Penn's Creek, St. Albans, Stanly, Susquehanna Bifurcate)

G4, $8-$15
Union Co., PA.

MACCORKLE (continued)

LOCATION: Midwestern to Eastern states. **DESCRIPTION:** A medium to large size, thin, usually serrated, widely corner notched point with large round ears and a deep notch in the center of the base. Bases are usually ground. Called *Nottoway River Bifurcate* in Virginia. **I.D. KEY:** Basal notching, early Archaic flaking.

G6, $25-$45
Union Co., PA.

MADISON - Mississippian, 1100 - 200 B.P.

(Also see Jacks Reef, Levanna, Susquehannock triangle)

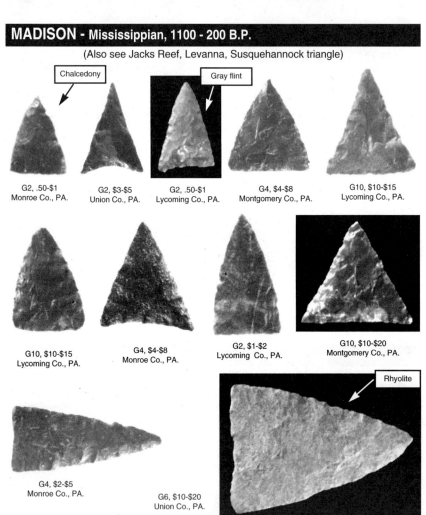

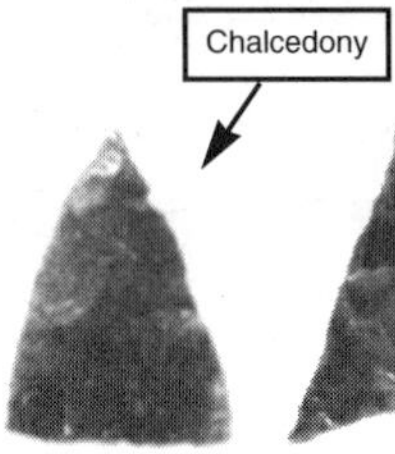

Chalcedony

G2, .50-$1
Monroe Co., PA.

G2, $3-$5
Union Co., PA.

Gray flint

G2, .50-$1
Lycoming Co., PA.

G4, $4-$8
Montgomery Co., PA.

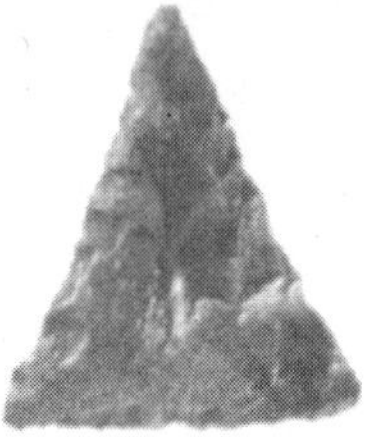

G10, $10-$15
Lycoming Co., PA.

G10, $10-$15
Lycoming Co., PA.

G4, $4-$8
Monroe Co., PA.

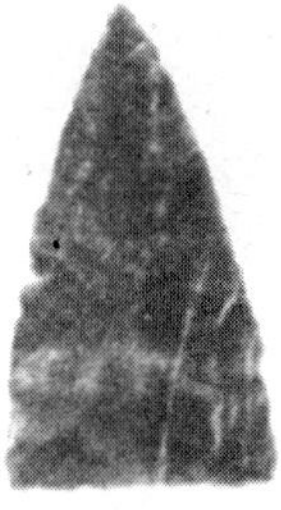

G2, $1-$2
Lycoming Co., PA.

G10, $10-$20
Montgomery Co., PA.

G4, $2-$5
Monroe Co., PA.

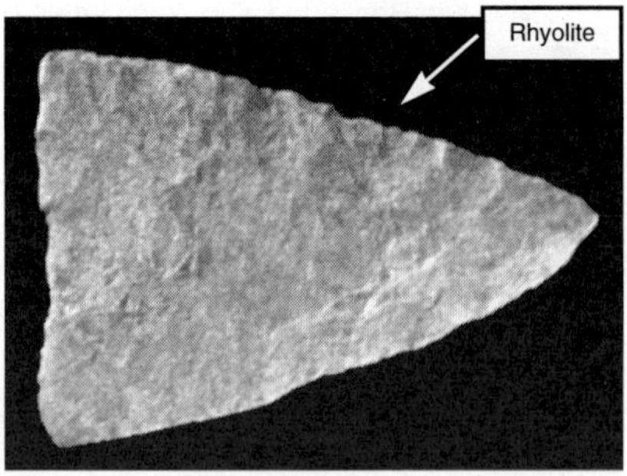

Rhyolite

G6, $10-$20
Union Co., PA.

LOCATION: Midwestern to Eastern states. Type site is in Madison Co., IL. Found at Cahokia Mounds (un-notched Cahokias). Used by the Kaskaskia tribe into the 1700s. **DESCRIPTION:** A small to medium size, thin, triangular point with usually straight sides and base. Some examples are notched on two to three sides. Many are of high quality and some are finely serrated. **I.D. KEY:** Thin triangle.

MANSION INN - Late Archaic, 4000 - 3500 B.P.

(Also see Koens Crispin, Lehigh, Morrow Mountain, Schuylkill, Virginsville, Web Blade)

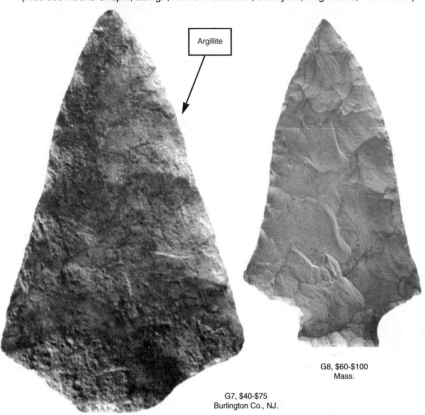

Argillite

G8, $60-$100
Mass.

G7, $40-$75
Burlington Co., NJ.

LOCATION: Northeastern states, Maryland to Mass. **DESCRIPTION:** A large size, broad, blade with a short, contracting stem. Believed to be preforms related to the Perkiomen and Susquehanna types. **I.D. KEY:** Size and base form.

MEADOWOOD - Late Archaic to early Woodland, 4000 - 2500 B.P.

(Also see Kessel, Otter Creek, Wapanucket)

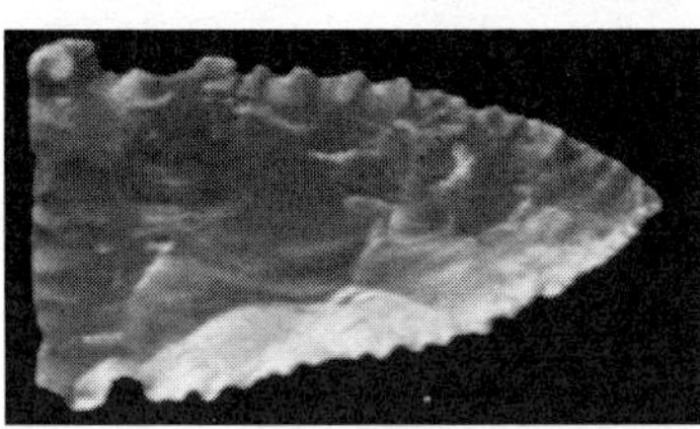

G6, $25-$50
Luzerne Co., PA.

G5, $20-$40
NJ.

LOCATION: Northeastern states. **DESCRIPTION:** A medium to large size point with shallow side notches near the base. The base can be straight to slightly convex. Blade edges can be straight to slightly convex to recurved. Some specimens show a lot of reworking and may be used up and asymmetrical.

MEADOWOOD (continued)

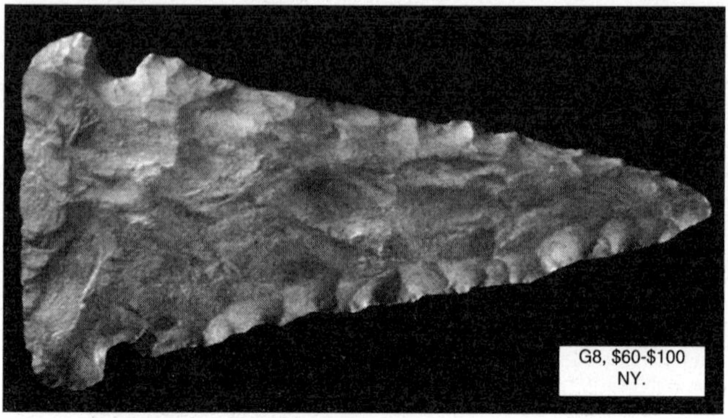

G8, $60-$100
NY.

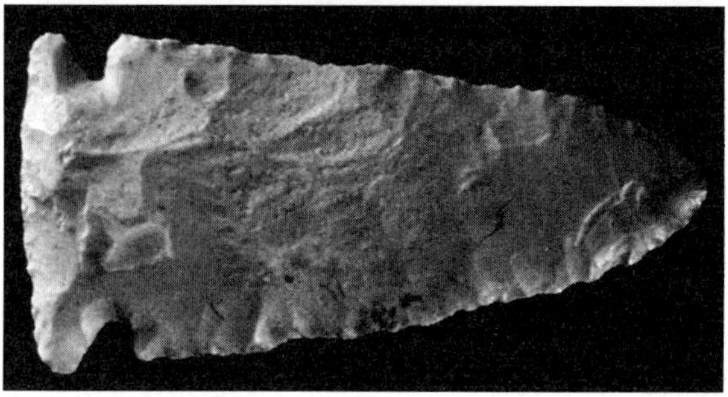

G6, $25-$50
Luzerne Co., PA.

G8, $45-$80
NY.

MORROW MOUNTAIN - Mid-Archaic, 7000 - 5000 B.P.

(Also see Koens Crispin, Lehigh, Poplar Island, Swatara/Long, Virginsville)

G5, $12-$25
PA.

G4, $10-$20
Lancaster Co., PA.

LOCATION: Northeastern states. **DESCRIPTION:** A medium to large size, broad, triangular point with a very short, contracting to rounded stem. Shoulders are usually weak but can be barbed. The blade edges on some examples are serrated with needle points. **I.D. KEY:** Contracted base and Archaic parallel flaking.

MUNCY BIFURCATE - Archaic, 8500 - 7000 B.P.

(Also see Cave Spring, Fox Valley, Kanawha, Stanly)

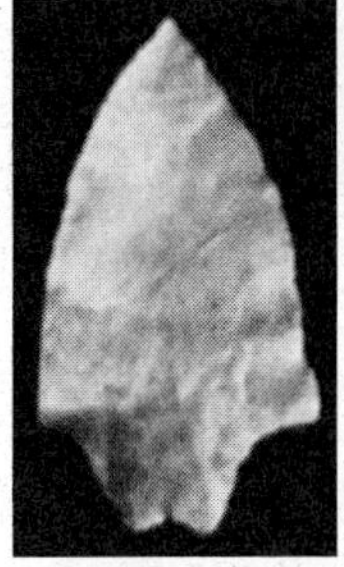
G6, $5-$10
Lycoming Co., PA.

G4, $3-$6
Lycoming Co., PA.

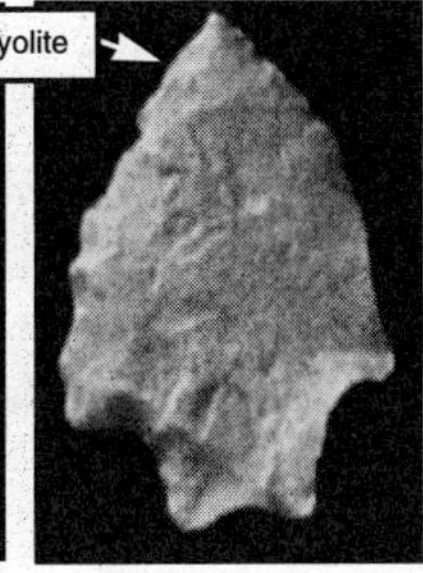
G5, $4-$8
Union Co., PA.

LOCATION: Northeastern states. **DESCRIPTION:** A small to medium point with prominent shoulders and a contracting to parallel sided stem. The Base has a shallow notch. **I.D. KEY:** Base form.

NEVILLE - Archaic, 7000 - 6000 B.P.

(Also see Adena Robbins, Bare Island, Duncan's Island, Newmanstown, Snook Kill)

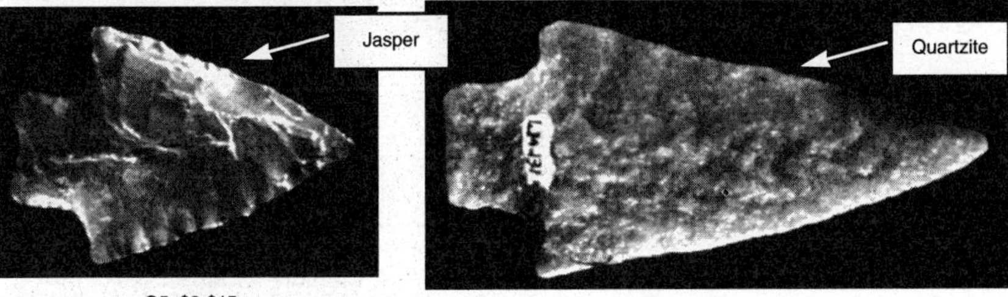

G5, $8-$15
Chester Co., PA.

G7, $15-$25
Montgomery Co., PA.

NEVILLE (continued)

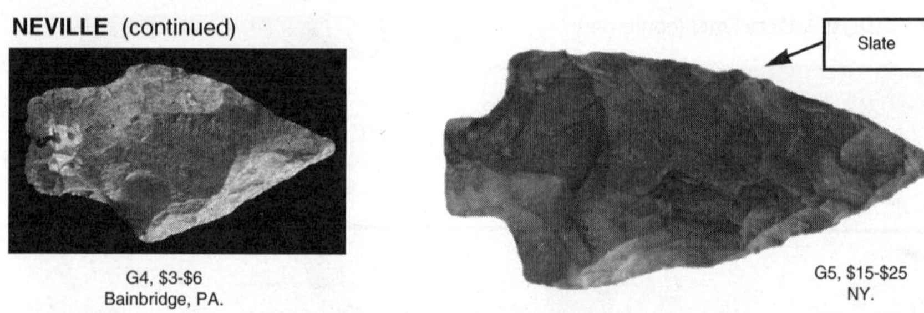

G4, $3-$6
Bainbridge, PA.

G5, $15-$25
NY.

LOCATION: Northeastern states. **DESCRIPTION:** A medium size, triangular point with barbed to horizontal shoulders and a short, square to contracting stem. **I.D. KEY:** Stem form.

NEWMANSTOWN - Archaic, 7000 - 5000 B.P.

(Also see Bare Island, Duncan's Island, Lackawaxen, Neville, Piedmont, Tocks Island)

G4, $4-$8
Washingtonboro, PA.

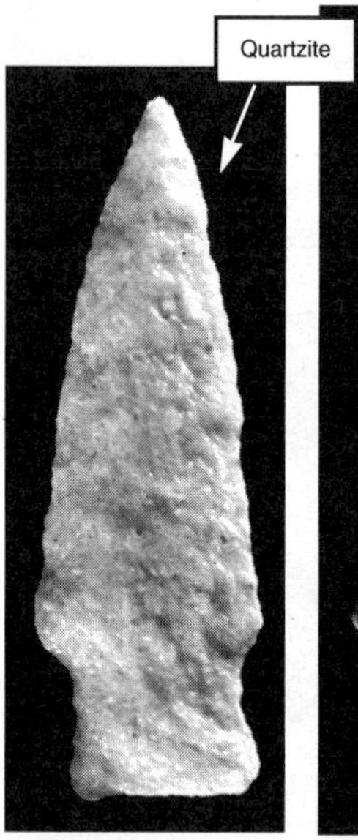

G5, $8-$15
Cecil Co., MD.

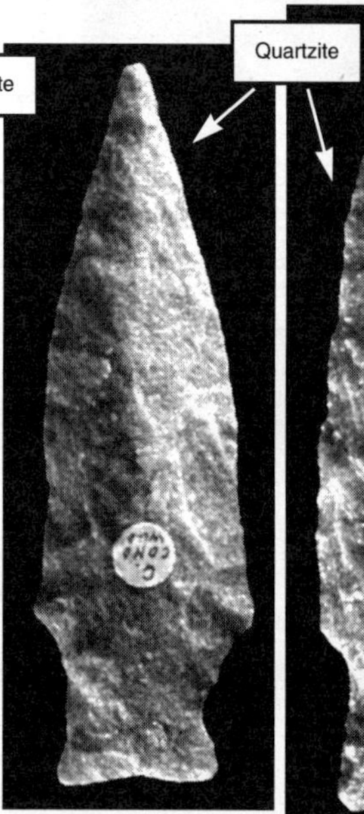

G6, $10-$20
Cecil Co., MD.

G6, $10-$20
Cecil Co., MD.

G4, $4-$8
Long Level, PA.

G7, $15-$25
Cecil Co., MD.

LOCATION: Northeastern states. **DESCRIPTION:** A medium to large size, narrow, stemmed point with a sharp tip and a short, expanding base.

NEWMANSTOWN (continued)

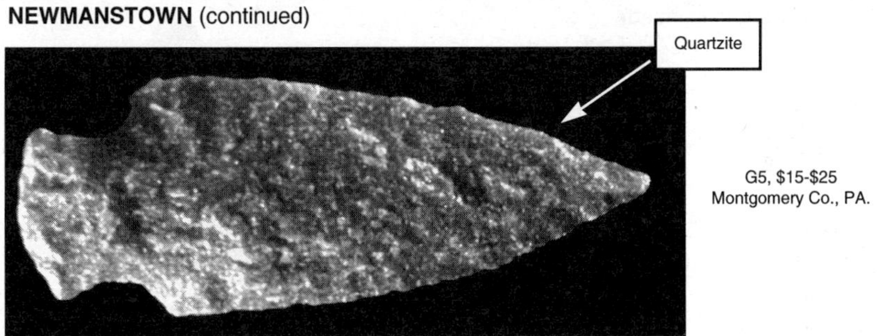

G5, $15-$25
Montgomery Co., PA.

NORMANSKILL- Late Archaic to early Woodland, 4000 - 2500 B.P.

(Also see Drybrook, Meadowood, Orient, Susquehanna Broad, Tocks Island)

G5, $8-$15
Carbon Co., PA.

Slate

G6, $15-$25
NY.

G7, $30-$60
Columbia Co., NY.

G6, $25-$45
Columbia Co., NY.

Tip damage

G2, $5-$10
Columbia Co., NY.

G5, $15-$30
Columbia Co., NY.

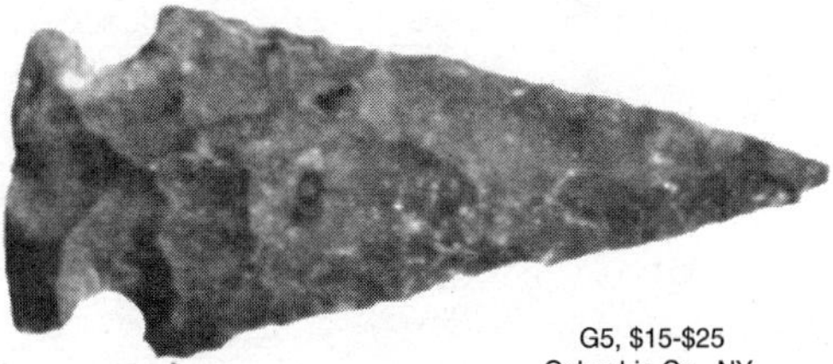

G5, $15-$25
Columbia Co., NY.

LOCATION: Northeastern states. **DESCRIPTION:** A medium size, narrow, expanded stemmed to widely corner notched point with strong shoulders that are generally at right angles. High and low shoulders are common. **I.D. KEY:** Base notching.

G6, $20-$35
Columbia Co., PA.

G5, $15-$25
Columbia Co., PA.

G5, $15-$30
NY.

NORTHUMBERLAND FLUTED KNIFE - Paleo, 12,000 - 10,000 B. P.

(Also see Clovis, Crowfield, Cumberland, Debert, Holcomb, Plainview, Redstone)

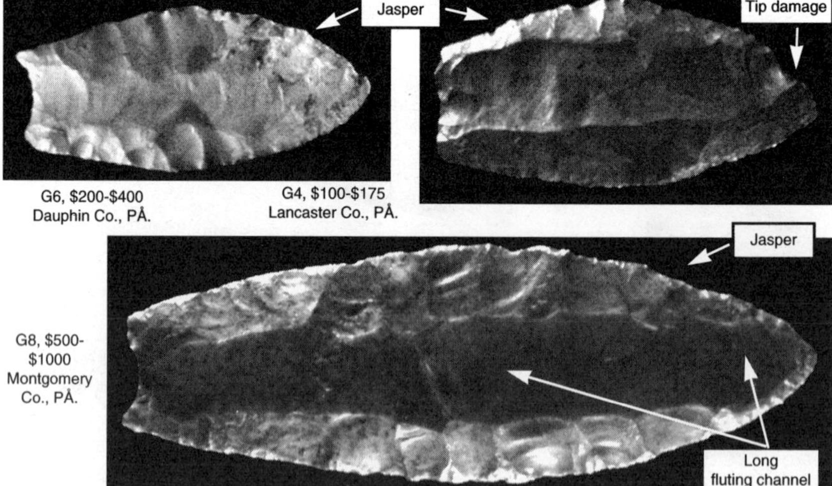

G6, $200-$400
Dauphin Co., PÅ.

G4, $100-$175
Lancaster Co., PÅ.

G8, $500-$1000
Montgomery Co., PÅ.

LOCATION: Northeastern states. **DESCRIPTION:** A medium to large size, lanceolate form that is usually fluted on both sides. Fluting can extend to the tip. A variant form of the *Barnes Cumberland*, but the base form is different. **I.D. KEY:** Paleo flaking, indirect pressure fluted.

NORTHUMBERLAND FLUTED KNIFE (continued)

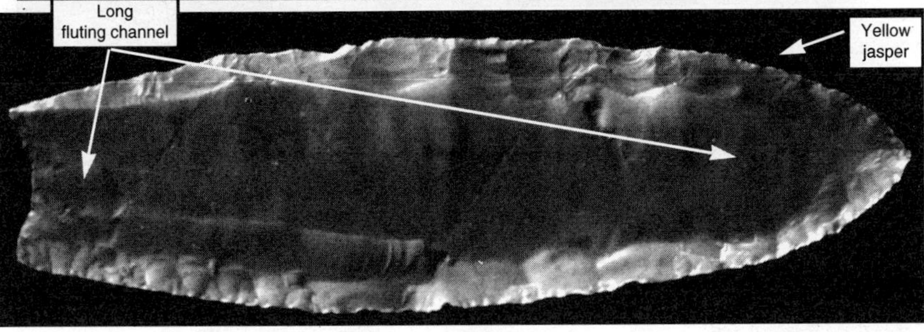

G5, $175-$350
Schuylkill Co., PA.

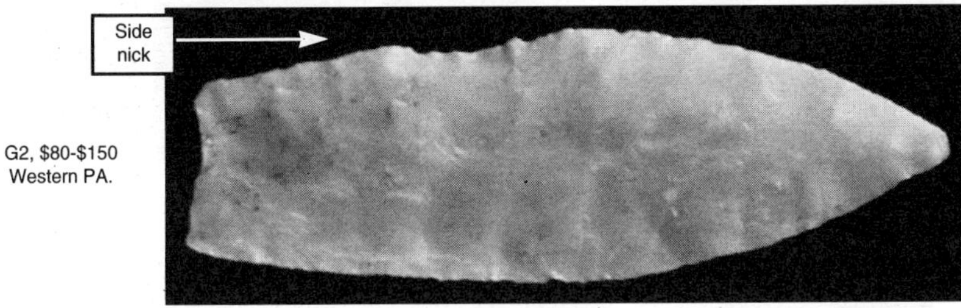

G9, $1500-$2500
PA.

OHIO LANCEOLATE - Late Paleo, 10,500 - 7000 B.P.

(Also see Beaver Lake, Clovis, Dalton, Cumberland)

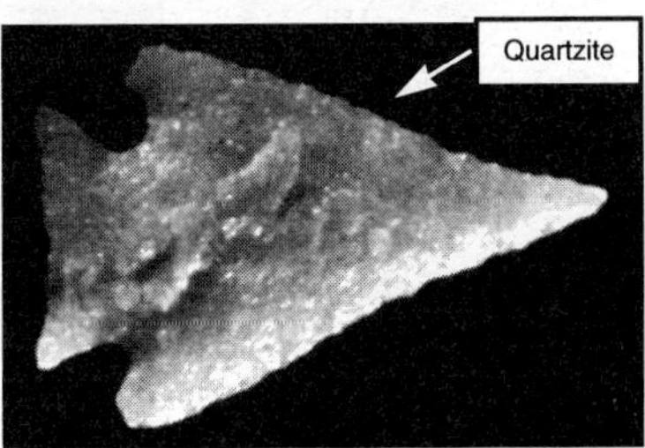

G2, $80-$150
Western PA.

LOCATION: Ohio into W. Pennsylvania. **DESCRIPTION:** A medium to large size lanceolate point with parallel to convex sides and a concave base that is ground. Flaking is early collateral to oblique transverse. Bases can be thinned or fluted. **I.D. KEY:** Base form parallel flaking.

OLEY - Woodland, 2200 - 1500 B. P.

(Also see Charleston Pine Tree, Erb Basal Notched, Eshbach, Vestal Notched)

LOCATION: Southeast Pennsylvania. **DESCRIPTION:** A small to medium size corner notched barbed point with an expanding base. Blade edges are concave to recurved. Base is concave. **I.D. KEY:** Base form and barbs.

G8, $35-$50
Montgomery
Co., PA.

OLEY (continued)

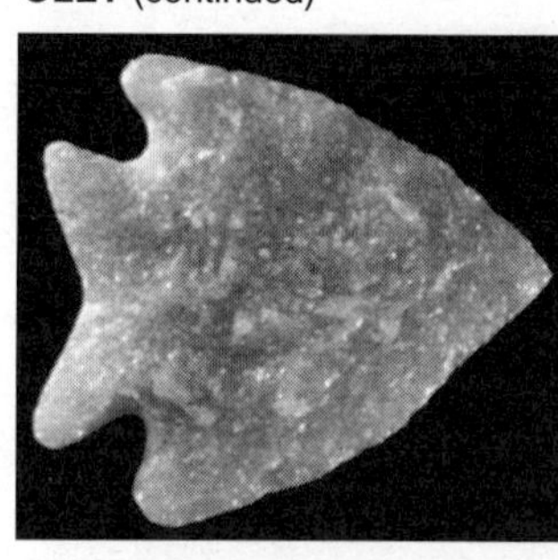

G8, $25-$40
Union
Co., PA.

G8, $25-$45
Lancaster Co., PA.

ORIENT - Late Archaic to Woodland, 4000 - 2500 B. P.

(Also see Drybrook, Forest Notched, Frost Island, Susquehanna Broad, Perkiomen)

G4, $10-$15
Bainbridge, PA.

G5, $15-$25
Northampton Co., PA.

G6, $20-$35
Northampton Co., PA.

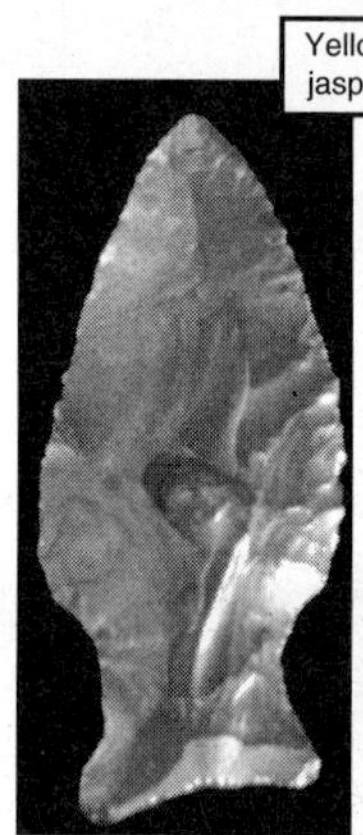

G5, $15-$25
Clinton Co., PA.

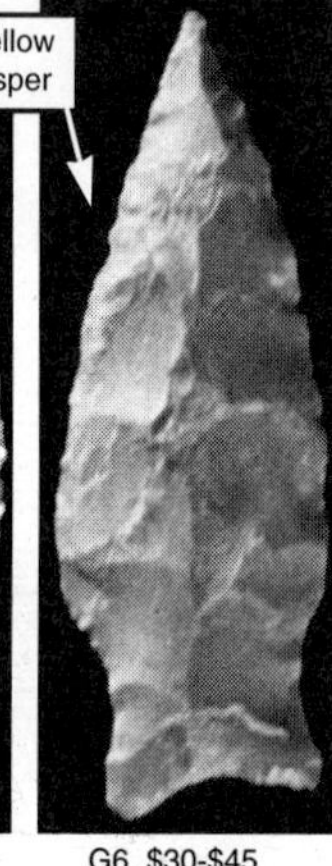

G6, $30-$45
Lancaster Co., PA.
Yellow Jasper

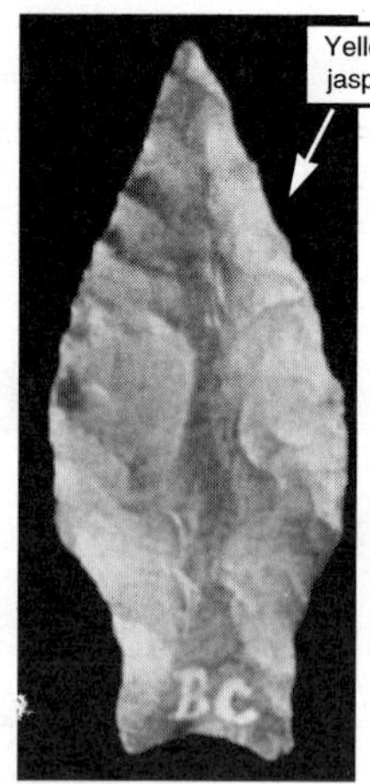

G6, $35-$50
Lancaster Co., PA.

Base
nick

G3, $10-$20
Northumberton Co., PA.

Out of
symmetry

G5, $100-$200
Northampton Co., PA.

ORIENT (continued)

Yellow jasper

G10, $200-$400
Lancaster Co., PA.

LOCATION: Northeastern states. **DESCRIPTION:** A small to medium size point with broad side notches, rounded shoulders and an expanding base. The base on some examples form auricles. **I.D. KEY:** Base form and rounded shoulders.

OTTER CREEK - Mid to Late Archaic, 5000 - 3500 B.P.

(Also see Brewerton Side Notched, Goddard, Perkiomen, Raccoon Notched, Susquehan - na Broad)

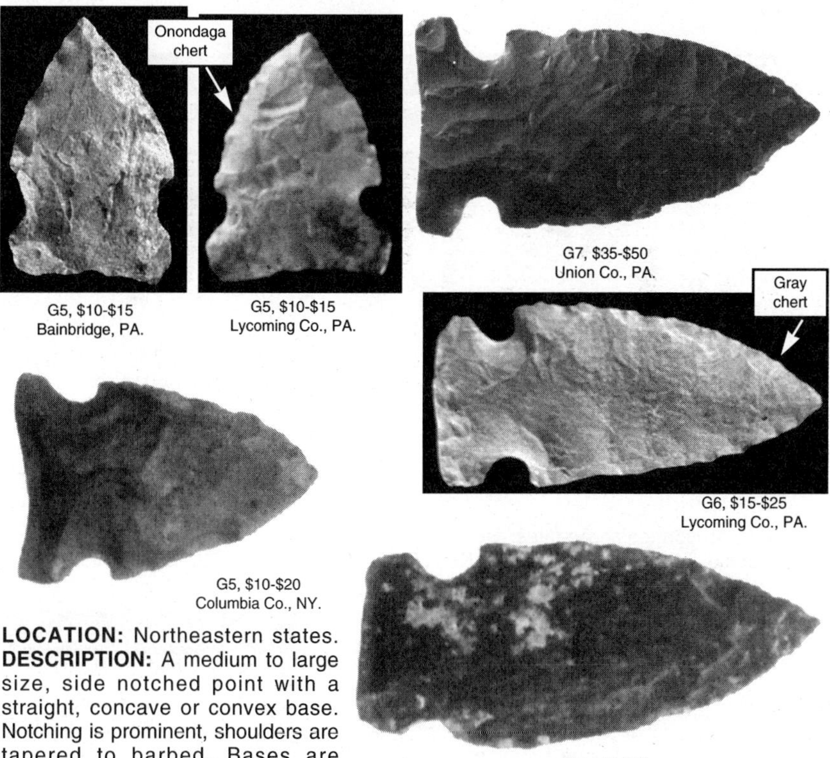

G5, $10-$15
Bainbridge, PA.

G5, $10-$15
Lycoming Co., PA.

G7, $35-$50
Union Co., PA.

G6, $15-$25
Lycoming Co., PA.

G5, $10-$20
Columbia Co., NY.

G7, $30-$50
Columbia Co., NY.

LOCATION: Northeastern states. **DESCRIPTION:** A medium to large size, side notched point with a straight, concave or convex base. Notching is prominent, shoulders are tapered to barbed. Bases are ground. **I.D. KEY:** Side notching.

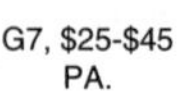

G7, $25-$45
PA.

G6, $30-$60
PA.

G7, $30-$60
Wayne Co., PA.

OVATES - Woodland, 3000 - 2000 B.P.

(Also see Nodena (Arkansas), Strike-A-Lite Type II)

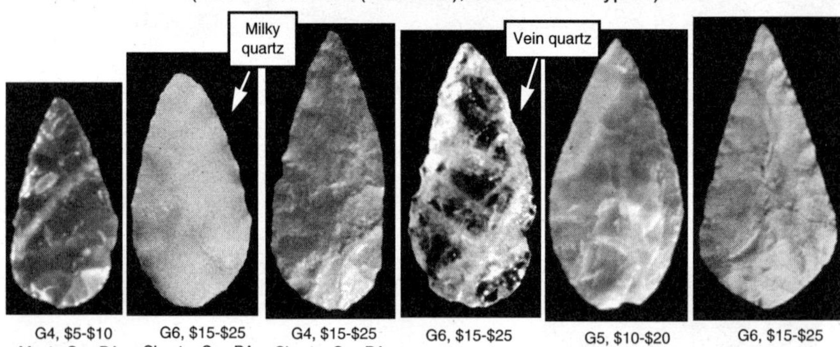

G4, $5-$10 Montg.Co., PA. | G6, $15-$25 Chester Co., PA. | G4, $15-$25 Chester Co., PA. | G6, $15-$25 Lycoming Co., PA. | G5, $10-$20 Montgomery Co., PA. | G6, $15-$25 Berks Co., PA.

LOCATION: Northeastern states. **DESCRIPTION:** A small size tear-drop shaped point with rounded shoulders and base. **I.D. KEY:** Ovoid form.

PALMER - Early Archaic, 9000 - 8000 B.P.

(Also see Amos, Brewerton, Charleston Pine Tree, Kirk Corner Notched, Kiski, Kline)

LOCATION: Eastern states. **DESCRIPTION:** A small to medium size, corner-notched point with a ground concave, convex, or straight base. Shoulders are barbed to contracting. Many are serrated and large examples would fall under the *Charleston Pine Tree* or *Kirk* Type. **I.D. KEY:** Basal form and notching.

PALMER (Continued)

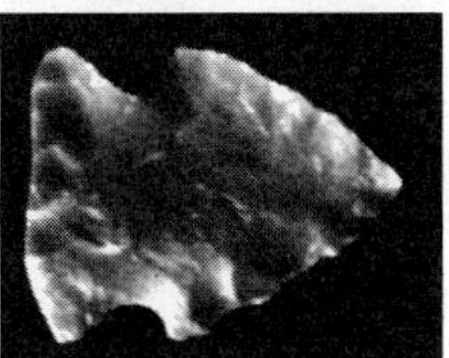

G4, $10-$20
Union Co., PA.

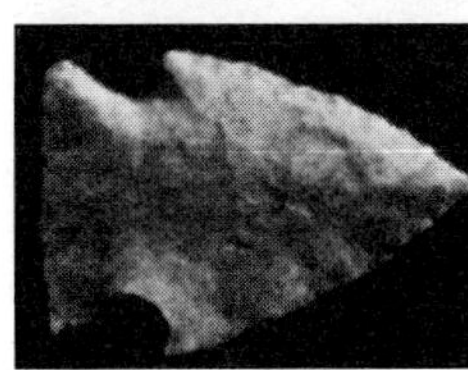

G6, $20-$35
Union Co., PA.

G6, $20-$35
Monroe Co., PA.
Yellow Jasper.

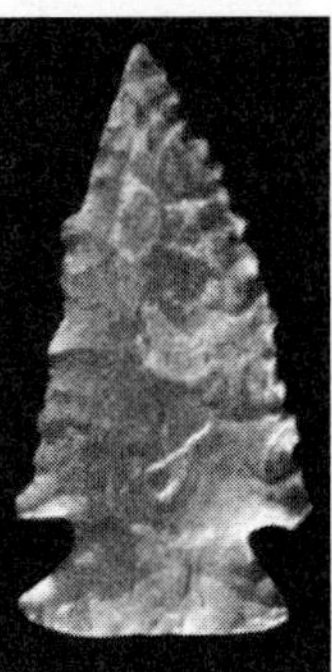

G6, $20-$35
luzerne Co., PA.

G8, $20-$35
NY.

PATUXENT - Late Archaic, 4000 - 3000 B.P.

(Also see Bare Island, Duncan's Island, Frost Island, Orient, Piedmont)

LOCATION: Southeastern PA., MD., VA. **DESCRIPTION:** A small to medium size point with weak, tapered shoulders and an expanding base. The base is concave forming ears. **I.D. KEY:** Basal form and weak shoulders.

G5, $15-$25
Montgomery Co., PA.

PENN'S CREEK SERIES - Early Archaic, 9000 - 7000 B.P.

(Also see Lycoming County Series)

G4, $4-$8
Peach Bottom, PA.

LOCATION: Central Pennsylvania. **DESCRIPTION:** A small size point that is stemmed, corner or side notched.

PENN'S CREEK BIFURCATE- Early Archaic, 9000 - 7000 B.P.

(Also see, Culpepper, Kirk Serrated Bifurcated, LeCroy, MacCorkle, St. Albans, Susquehanna Bifurcate)

LOCATION: Pennsylvania. **DESCRIPTION:** A small size bifurcated point with Archaic flaking. Shoulders are weakly barbed and the base expands to ears. **I.D. KEY:** Basal form and early flaking.

G4, $10-$20
Northumberton Co., PA.

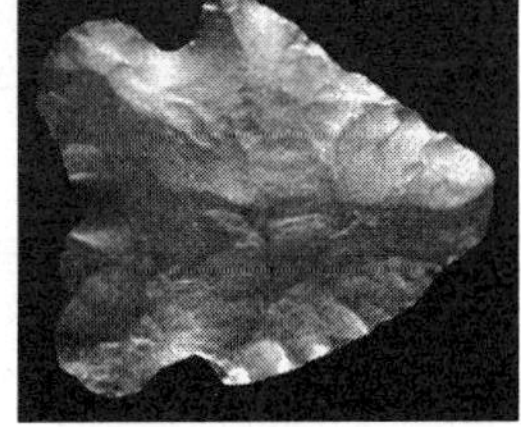

PERKIOMEN- Late Archaic to early Woodland, 4000 - 2500 B.P.

(Also see Ashtabula, Frost Island, Manson Inn, Susquehanna Broad, Waratan)

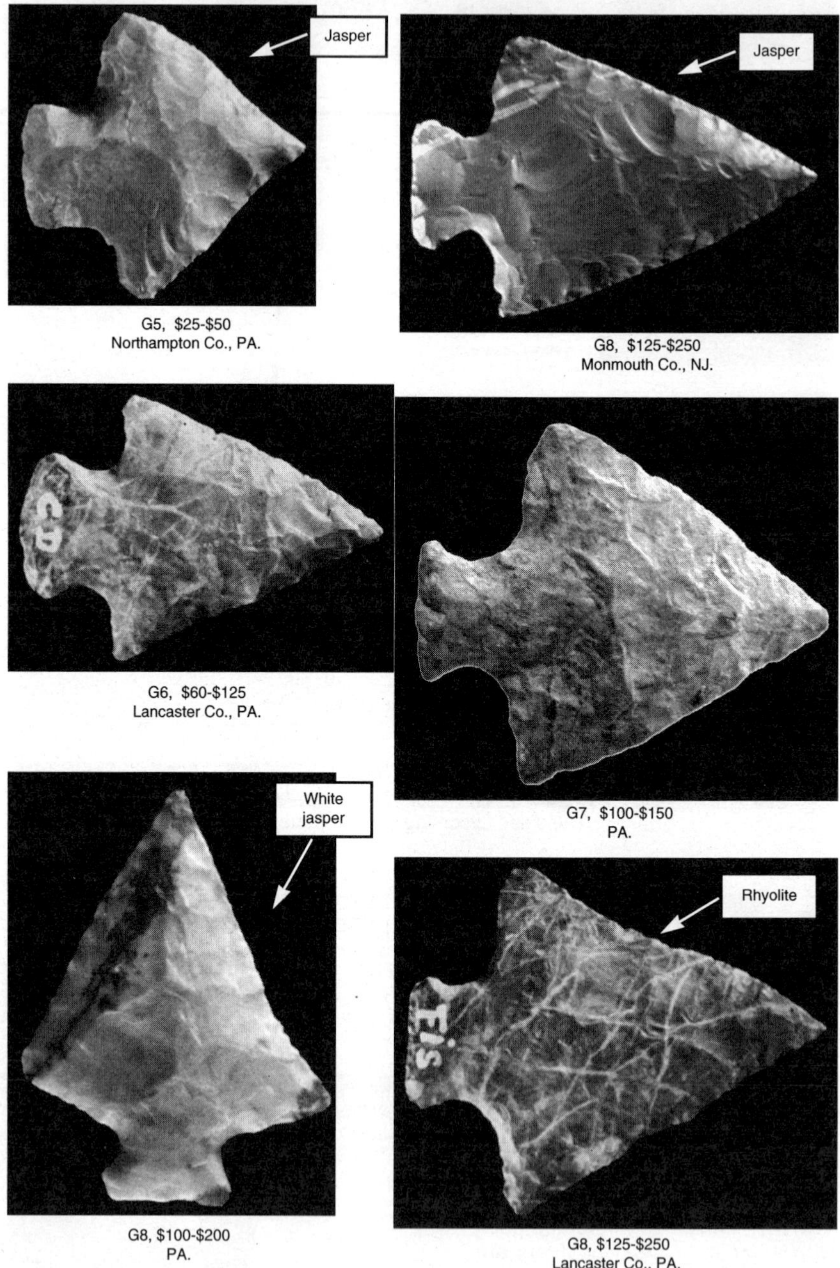

G5, $25-$50
Northampton Co., PA.

G8, $125-$250
Monmouth Co., NJ.

G6, $60-$125
Lancaster Co., PA.

G7, $100-$150
PA.

G8, $100-$200
PA.

G8, $125-$250
Lancaster Co., PA.

LOCATION: Northeastern states. **DESCRIPTION:** A medium to large size broad point with strong shoulders and a small, expanding base that is usually bulbous. Blades can be asymmetrical. **I.D. KEY:** Broad shoulders and small base.

G8, $125-$250
Centre Co., PA.

G8, $100-$200
Berks Co., PA.

G9, $250-$500
Montgomery Co., PA.

G9, $300-$600
Monmouth Co., NJ.

PIEDMONT-NORTHERN VARIETY - Archaic, 6000 - 4000 B.P.

(Also see Bare Island, Duncan's Island, Genesee, Hoover's Island, Neville, Lackawaxen, Newmanstown, Patuxent, Piney Island, Tocks Island)

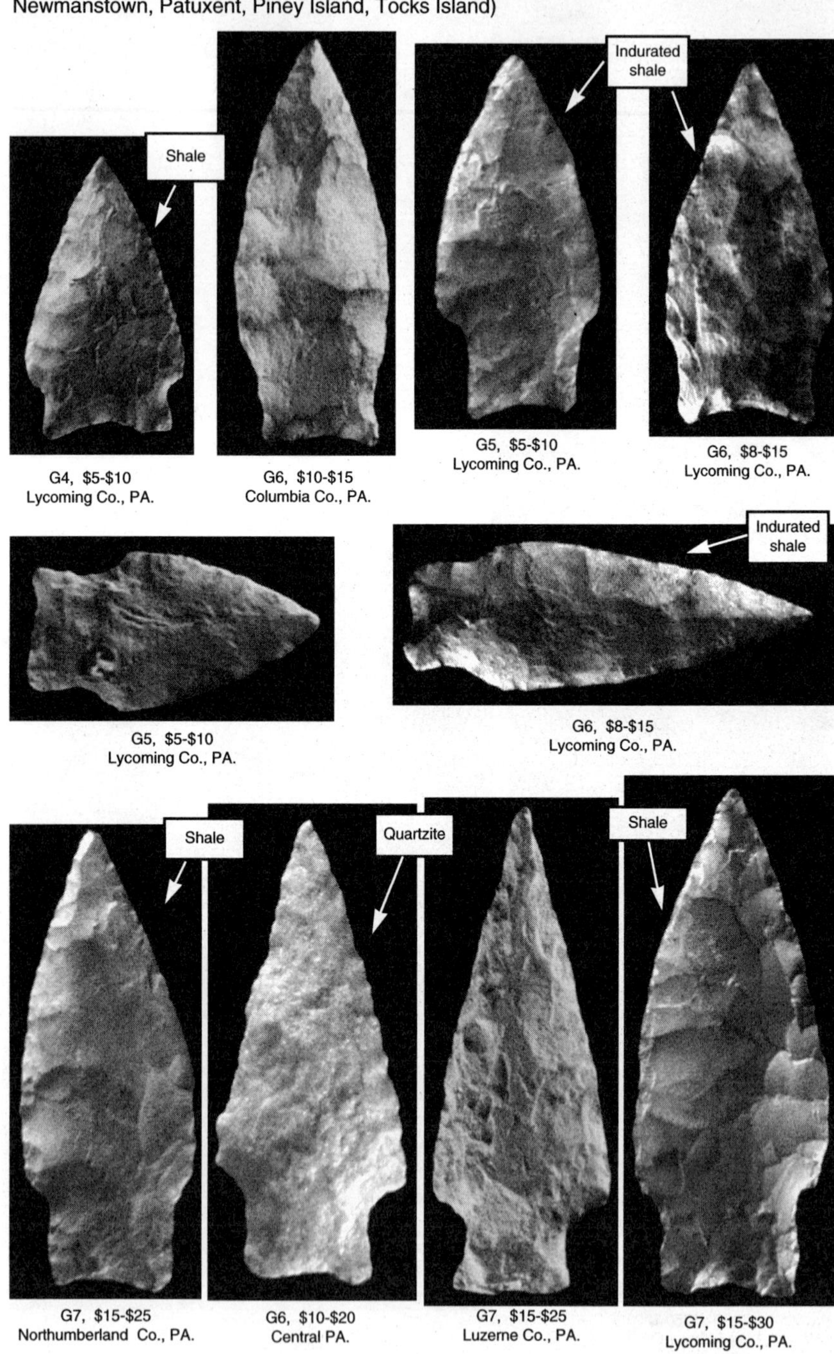

G4, $5-$10
Lycoming Co., PA.

G6, $10-$15
Columbia Co., PA.

G5, $5-$10
Lycoming Co., PA.

G6, $8-$15
Lycoming Co., PA.

G5, $5-$10
Lycoming Co., PA.

G6, $8-$15
Lycoming Co., PA.

G7, $15-$25
Northumberland Co., PA.

G6, $10-$20
Central PA.

G7, $15-$25
Luzerne Co., PA.

G7, $15-$30
Lycoming Co., PA.

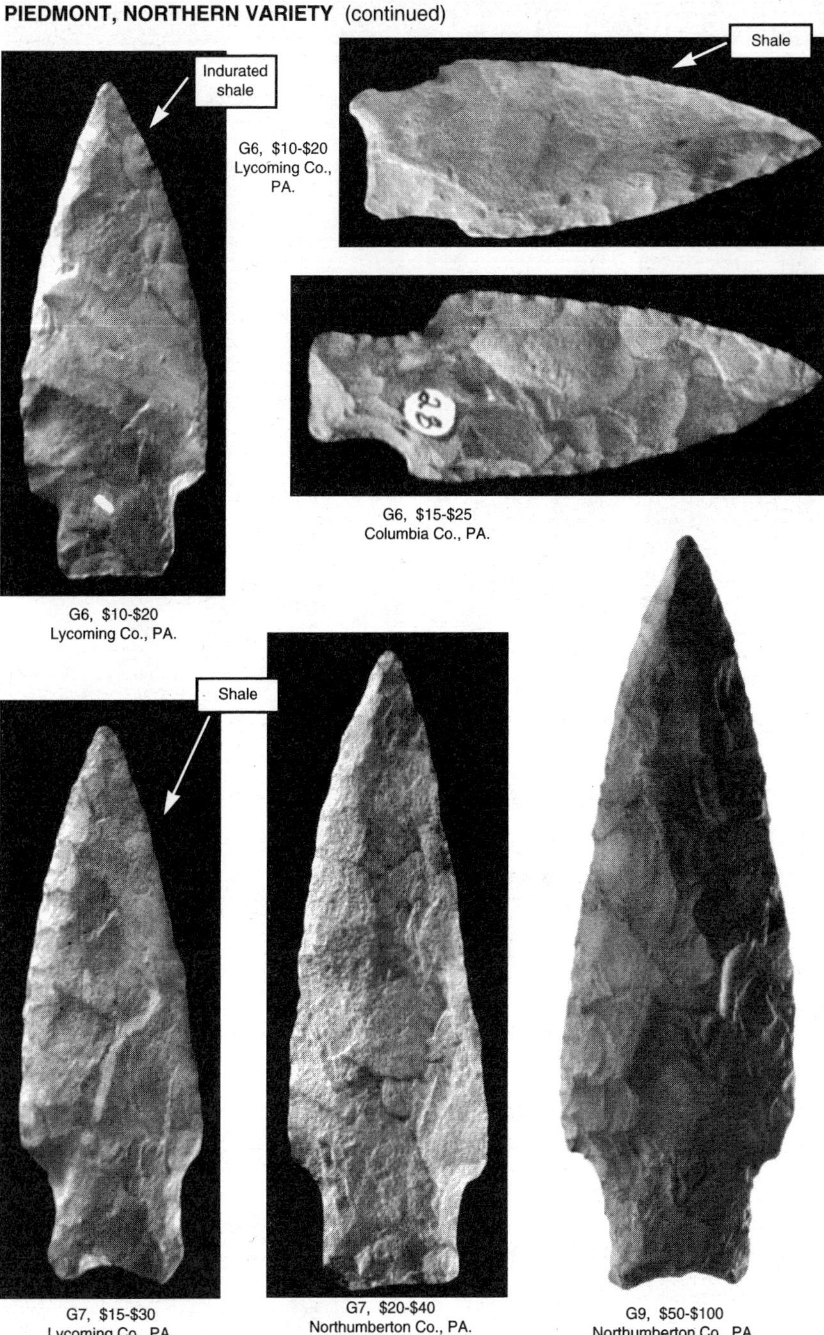

G6, $10-$20
Lycoming Co., PA.

G6, $10-$20
Lycoming Co., PA.

G6, $15-$25
Columbia Co., PA.

G7, $15-$30
Lycoming Co., PA.

G7, $20-$40
Northumberton Co., PA.

G9, $50-$100
Northumberton Co., PA.

LOCATION: Central Pennsylvania northward. **DESCRIPTION:** A medium to large size, narrow stemmed point. Base varies from straight to convex, from square to expanding or contracting. Shoulders are usually tapered. Named by Fogelman. Usually made of siltstone and indurated shale. **I.D. KEY:** Base form and narrow width.

PINEY ISLAND - Late Archaic, 6000 - 2000 B.P.

(Also see Bare Island, Duncan's Island, Lamoka, Patuxent, Piedmont)

Indurated shale

Broken & glued

G6, $20-$35
Northampton Co., PA.

G5, $15-$25
Columbia Co., PA.

G5, $15-$25
Northumberland Co., PA.

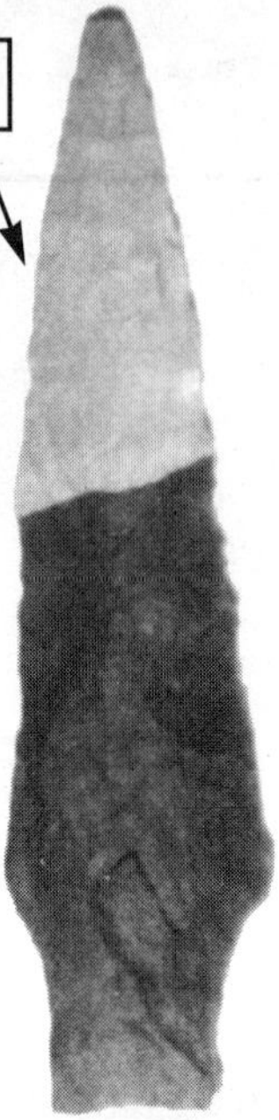

G3, $5-$10
Carbon Co., PA.
Color variation caused by diff. in patination.

G8, $25-$50
Carbon Co., PA.

LOCATION: Northeastern states. **DESCRIPTION:** A medium size, narrow, long stemmed point with tapered shoulders. **I.D. KEY:** Basal form and narrow width.

PISCATAWAY - Mid to late Woodland, 2500 - 500 B.P.

(Also see Morrow Mountain, Poplar Island, Schuylkill, Virginsville)

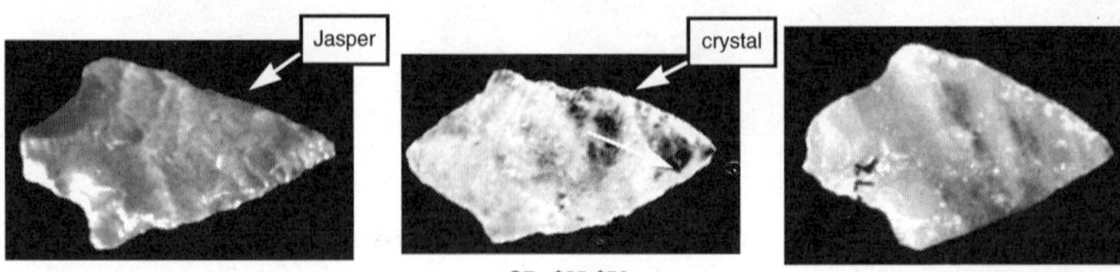

G4, $5-$10
Lancaster Co., PA.

G7, $35-$50
Lycoming Co., PA. Crystal.

G8, $25-$50
Chester Co., PA.
Orange/white quartz.

PISCATAWAY (continued)

Quartzite
Milky quartz
Quartzite
Argillite
Jasper

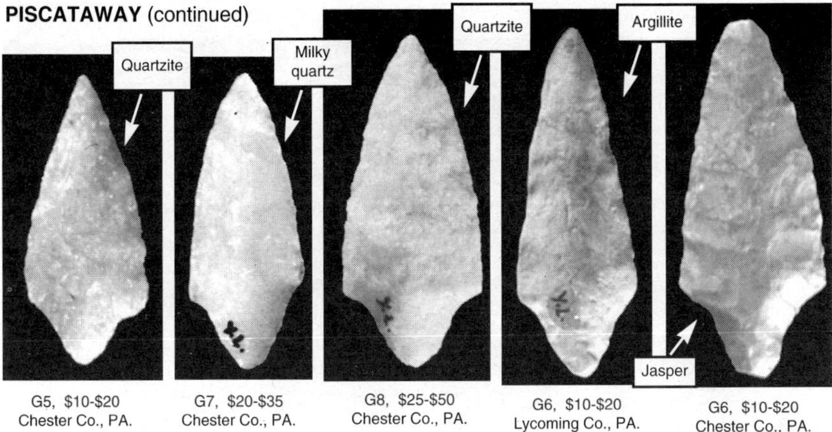

G5, $10-$20
Chester Co., PA.

G7, $20-$35
Chester Co., PA.

G8, $25-$50
Chester Co., PA.

G6, $10-$20
Lycoming Co., PA.

G6, $10-$20
Chester Co., PA.

LOCATION: Eastern to Northeastern states. **DESCRIPTION:** A small to medium size, very narrow triangular point with tapered shoulders and a short tapered stem. The base is pointed to rounded. **I.D. KEY:** Basal form and narrow width.

POPLAR ISLAND - Mid-Archaic, 6000 - 4000 B.P.

(Also see Koens Crispin, Morrow Mountain, Piscataway, Schuylkill, Virginsville)

G7, $35-$50
Carbon Co., PA.

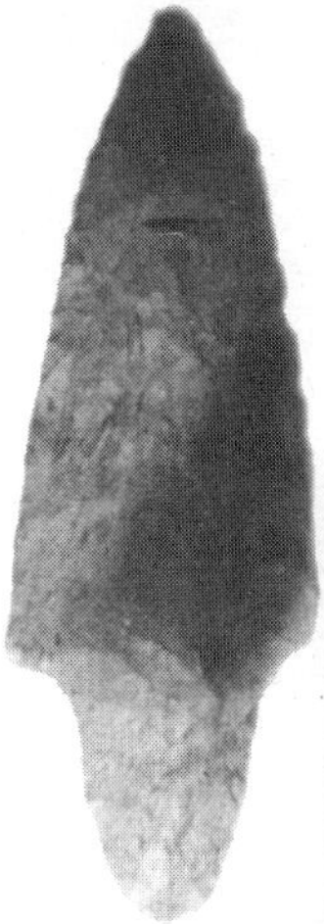

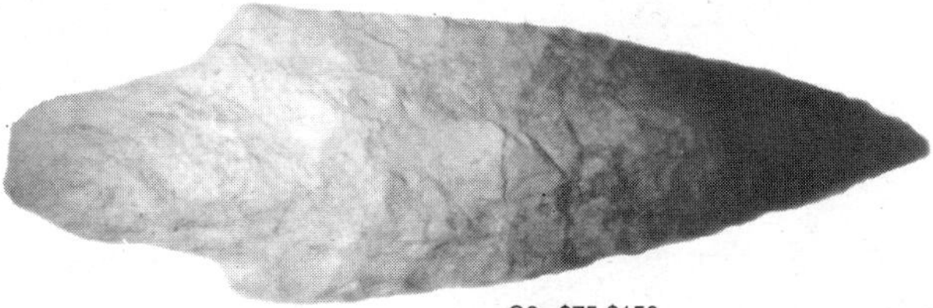

G8, $75-$150
Carbon Co., PA.

Argillite

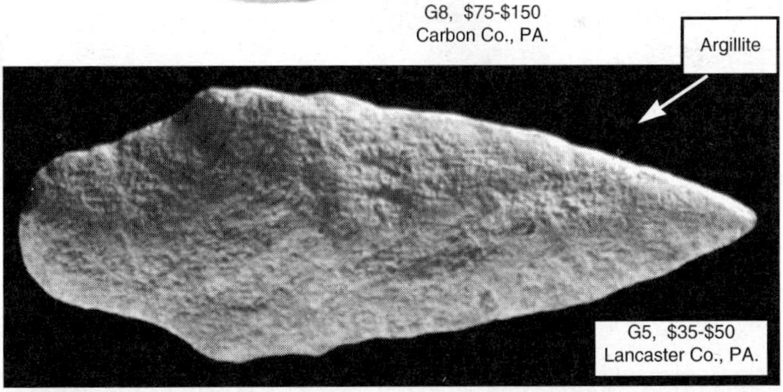

G5, $35-$50
Lancaster Co., PA.

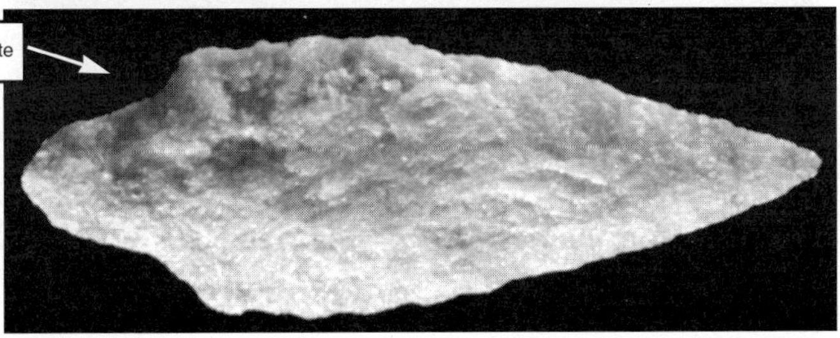

Quartzite

G6, $75-$150
York Co., PA.

POPLAR ISLAND (continued)

G6, $75-$150
Lancaster Co., PA.

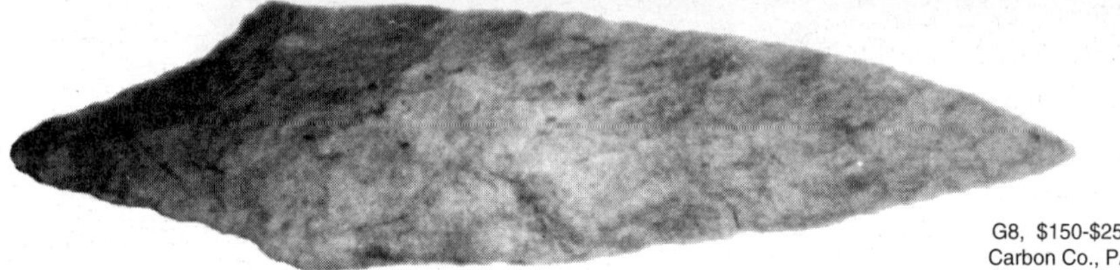

G8, $150-$250
Carbon Co., PA.

LOCATION: Northeastern states. **DESCRIPTION:** A medium to large size, narrow, triangular point with tapered shoulders and a long contracting base. The base can be pointed to rounded. **I.D. KEY:** Basal form and narrow width.

PORT MAITLAND - Mid Woodland, 2500 - 1400 B.P.

(Also see Brewerton, Goddard, Raccoon Notched)

G3, $4-$8
Union Co., PA.
Onandaga chert.

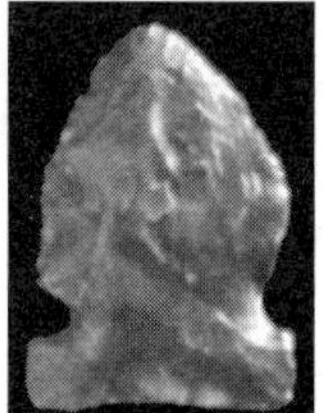

G3, $4-$8
Lycoming Co., PA.
Onandaga chert.

G2, $3-$5
Lycoming Co., PA.
Onandaga chert.

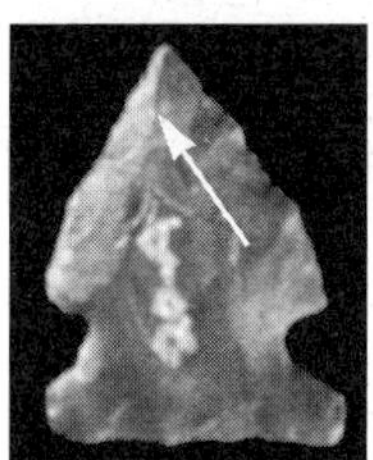

G4, $4-$8
Lycoming Co., PA.
Gray chert.

LOCATION: Northeastern states. **DESCRIPTION:** A small size side notched point with a straight to slightly concave base. Side notches form square corners at the base. **I.D. KEY:** Notching form and small size.

RACCOON NOTCHED - Late Woodland, 1500 - 1000 B.P.

(Also see Brewerton, Goddard, Jacks Reef, Port Maitland)

LOCATION: Northeastern states. **DESCRIPTION:** A small to medium size, thin, side notched point. Blade edges are convex to pentagonal shape. Known as *Knight Island* in Southeast. **I.D. KEY:** Side notching and thinness.

G5, $15-$25
Union Co., PA.

RANDOLPH - Woodland to Historic, 2000 - 200 B.P.

(Also see Dewart Stemmed, Lamoka)

G7, $5-$10
Union Co., PA.

G5, $3-$7
Union Co., PA.

LOCATION: Eastern to Northeastern states. **DESCRIPTION:** A medium size, narrow, thick, spike point with tapered shoulders and a short to medium, contracted, rounded stem. Many examples have exaggerated spikes along the blade edges. **I.D. KEY:** Blade form and spikes.

REDSTONE - Paleo, 13,000 - 9000 B.P.

(Also see Clovis, Crowfield, Cumberland, Debert, Holcomb)

LOCATION: Southeastern to Northeastern states. **DESCRIPTION:** A small to large size, thin, auriculate, fluted point with convex sides expanding to a wide, deeply concave base. Fluting can extend most of the way down each face. Multiple flutes are usual. A very rare type. **I.D. KEY:** Batan fluted, edgework on the hafting area.

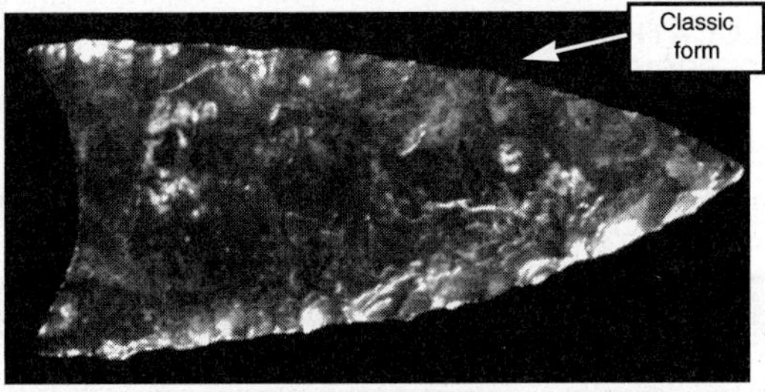

G7, $300-$500
Lycoming Co., PA. Coshocton chert.

ST. ALBANS - Early to Mid-Archaic, 9000 - 5000 B.P.

(Also see Charleston Pine Tree, Decatur, Fox Valley, Kanawha, Kirk Serrated, Lake Erie, LeCroy, MacCorkle, Stanly & Susquehanna Bifurcate)

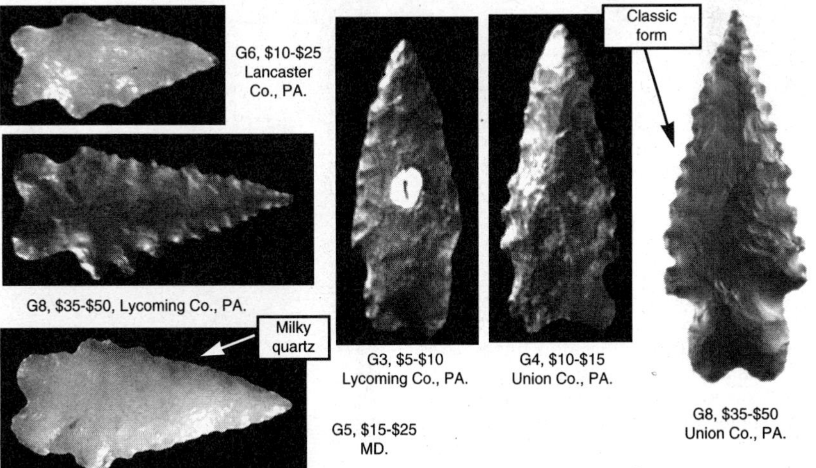

G6, $10-$25 Lancaster Co., PA.

G8, $35-$50, Lycoming Co., PA.

G5, $15-$25 MD.

G3, $5-$10 Lycoming Co., PA.

G4, $10-$15 Union Co., PA.

G8, $35-$50 Union Co., PA.

LOCATION: Eastern to Northeastern states. **DESCRIPTION:** A small to medium size, usually serrated, bifurcated point. Basal lobes usually flare outward, and are weakly bifurcated. **I.D. KEY:** Weak bifurcation, base more narrow than shoulders.

SANDHILL STEMMED - Mid-Woodland, 2200 - 1700 B.P.

(Also see Dewart Stemmed, Garver's Ferry, Lamoka, Morrow Mountain)

G9, $5-$15
Lycoming Co., PA.

G4, $4-$8
Lycoming Co., PA.

G5, $5-$10
Lycoming Co., PA.

G7, $10-$15
Lycoming Co., PA.

G3, $4-$8
Lycoming Co., PA.

LOCATION: Northeastern states. **DESCRIPTION:** A small point with a straight to contracting base. Shoulders are tapered to slightly barbed.

SAVANNAH RIVER - Mid Archaic to Woodland, 5000 - 2000 B.P.

(Also see Fox Creek, Genesee, Piedmont)

Quartzite

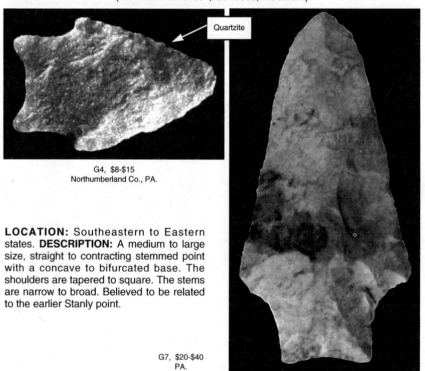

G4, $8-$15
Northumberland Co., PA.

LOCATION: Southeastern to Eastern states. **DESCRIPTION:** A medium to large size, straight to contracting stemmed point with a concave to bifurcated base. The shoulders are tapered to square. The stems are narrow to broad. Believed to be related to the earlier Stanly point.

G7, $20-$40
PA.

SCHUYLKILL - Late Archaic, 4000 - 2000 B.P.

(Also see Adena, Condoquinet Canfield, Koens Crispin, Lehigh, Morrow Mountain, Piscataway, Poplar Island, Virginsville)

G6, $60-$100
PA.

G5, $20-$40
Columbia Co., PA.

G7, $50-$75
York Co., PA.

G4, $10-$20
York Co., PA.

G6, $25-$50
Carbon Co., PA.

LOCATION: Northeastern states. **DESCRIPTION:** A medium to large size, narrow point with a long, tapered, rounded stem. Shoulders are usually at a sharper angle than Poplar Island. **I.E. KEY:** Sharp corners, narrow blade, long tapering stem.

SCOTTSBLUFF - Transitional Paleo, 9500 - 7000 B.P.

(Also see Fox Creek, Hardin, Holland and Steubenville)

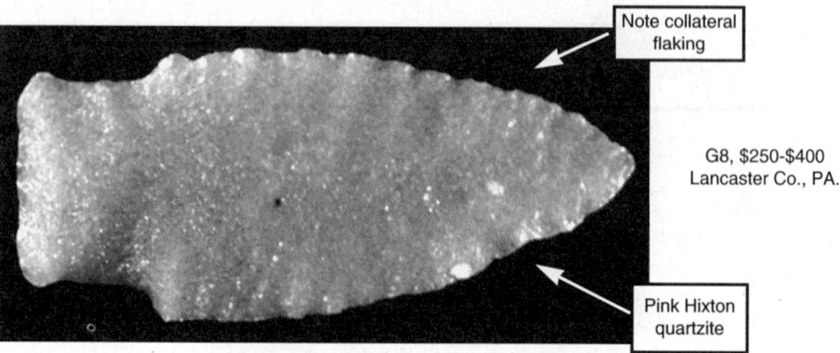

G8, $250-$400
Lancaster Co., PA.

LOCATION: Midwestern to Northeastern states. **DESCRIPTION:** A medium to large size, lanceolate point with convex to parallel sides, weak shoulders, and a broad parallel to expanding stem. The hafting area is ground. Most examples have horizontal to oblique parallel flaking and are of high quality and thinness.

SCRAPER - Paleo to Archaic, 14,000 - 5000 B.P.

(Also see Drill, Graver, Strike-A-Lite)

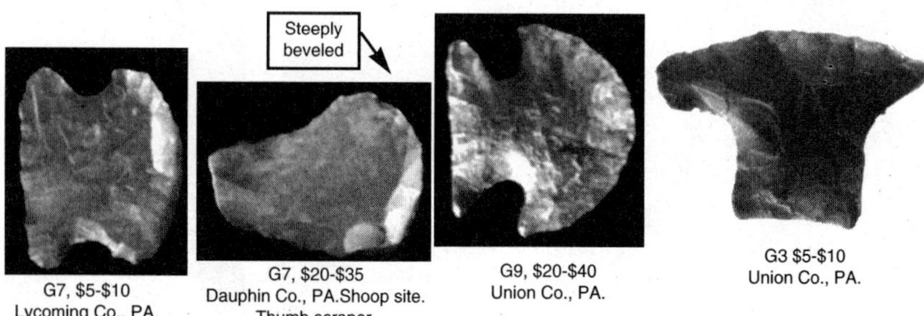

G7, $5-$10
Lycoming Co., PA.

G7, $20-$35
Dauphin Co., PA.Shoop site.
Thumb scraper.

G9, $20-$40
Union Co., PA.

G3 $5-$10
Union Co., PA.

LOCATION: Paleo to early Archaic sites everywhere. **DESCRIPTION:** Thumb, Duckbill, and Turtleback forms are small to medium size, thick, ovoid shaped, uniface, scraping tools that are steeply beveled, especially at the broadest end. Side scrapers are long hand-held uniface flakes with beveling on all blade edges of one face. Broken points are also utilized as scrapers.

SNOOK KILL - Late Archaic, 4000 - 2000 B.P.

(Also see Dewart Stemmed, Koens Crispin, Lehigh, Sandhill Stemmed)

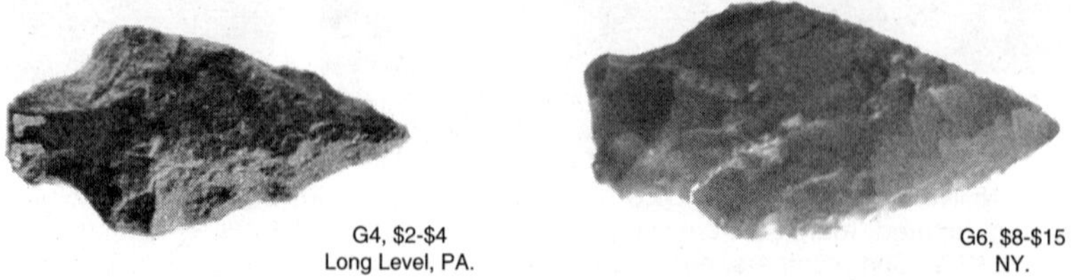

G4, $2-$4
Long Level, PA.

G6, $8-$15
NY.

SNOOK KILL (continued)

G5, $15-$30
NY.

Impact fracture

LOCATION: New York and adjoining states. **DESCRIPTION:** A small to medium size point with tapered shoulders and a short, contracting to parallel sided base. Base can be straight to convex. **I.D. KEY:** Short stem, tapered tangs.

STANLY - Early Archaic, 8000 - 5000 B.P.

(Also see Fox Valley, Kanawha, Kirk-Bifurcated, LeCroy, Muncy, Savannah River)

G3, $3-$6
Lycoming Co., PA.

G4, $20-$35
Union Co., PA.

G2, $2-$4
Union Co., PA.

G6, $20-$35
Union Co., PA.

G7, $25-$50
Lancaster Co., PA.

G8, $25-$50
Lancaster Co., PA.
Classic form.

LOCATION: Southeastern to Northeastern states. **DESCRIPTION:** A small to medium size, broad shoulder point with a small birfurcated stem. Some examples are serrated and show high quality flaking. The shoulders are very prominent and can be tapered, horizontal or barbed. **I.D. KEY:** Tiny bifurcated base.

STRIKE-A-LITE, type I - Early to late Archaic, 9000 - 4000 B.P.

(Also see Drill, Scraper)

LOCATION: Northeastern states. **DESCRIPTION:** A small to medium size friction tool made either from scratch or from broken points. The blunt-end of these objects are beveled from both sides, to create an edge for striking a hard object to emit sparks for igniting combustible material for the creation of fire. These are unlike blunts or scrapers of similar form that are only beveled on one side of the face. The striking edge usually shows extreme wear.

STRIKE-A-LITE, type I (Continued)

G4, $5-$10
Lycoming Co., PA.

G4, $5-$10
Lycoming Co., PA.

G4, $4-$8
Northumberland Co., PA.
Rhyolite

G5, $5-$10
Lycoming Co., PA.
Rhyolite.

STRIKE-A-LITE, type II - Woodland, 3000 - 1000 B.P.

(Also see Drill, Ovates)

LOCATION: Northeastern states. **DESCRIPTION:** A small size, narrow, tear drop form created for striking a hard object to emit sparks for egniting combustible material for the creation of fire. The striking edge usually shows extreme wear.

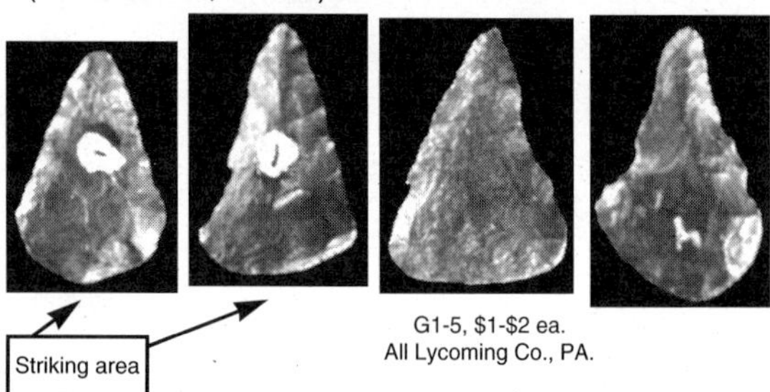

G1-5, $1-$2 ea.
All Lycoming Co., PA.

SUSQUEHANNA BIFURCATE - Early Archaic, 9000 - 6000 B.P.

(Also see Kanawha, Kirk Serrated, Lake Erie, LeCroy, MacCorkle, Muncy, Penn's Creek, St. Albans, Stanly, and Taunton River Bifurcate)

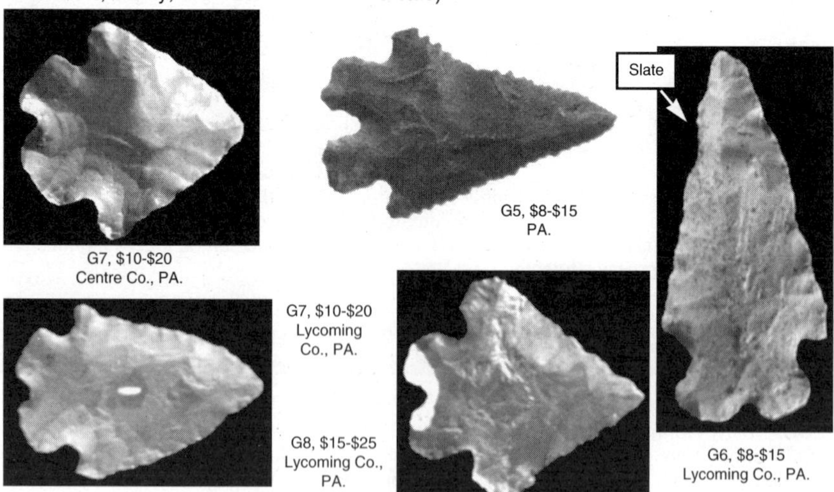

G7, $10-$20
Centre Co., PA.

G5, $8-$15
PA.

G7, $10-$20
Lycoming
Co., PA.

G8, $15-$25
Lycoming Co.,
PA.

G6, $8-$15
Lycoming Co., PA.

LOCATION: Northeastern states. **DESCRIPTION:** A small to medium size bifurcated point with barbed shoulders and squared basal ears. **I.D. KEY:** Square basal ears.

SUSQUEHANNA BIFURCATE (Continued)

Tip damage

G8, $15-$25
Dauphin Co., PA.

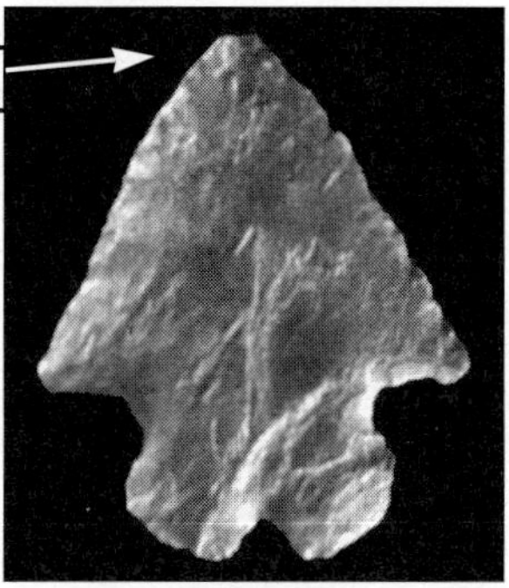

G6, $10-$20
Lycoming Co., PA.

G7, $20-$35
Lycoming Co., PA.

Yellow jasper

G7, $25-$50
Columbia Co., NY

G8, $40-$70
Central PA.

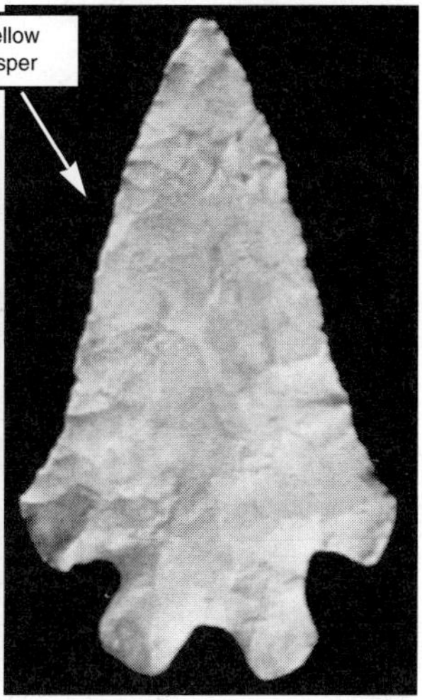

G9, $60-$100
Columbia Co., PA.

SUSQUEHANNA BROAD - Early Woodland, 3500 - 2700 B.P.

(Also see Ashtabula, Drybrook, Frost Island, Orient, Patuxent, Perkiomen and Waratan)

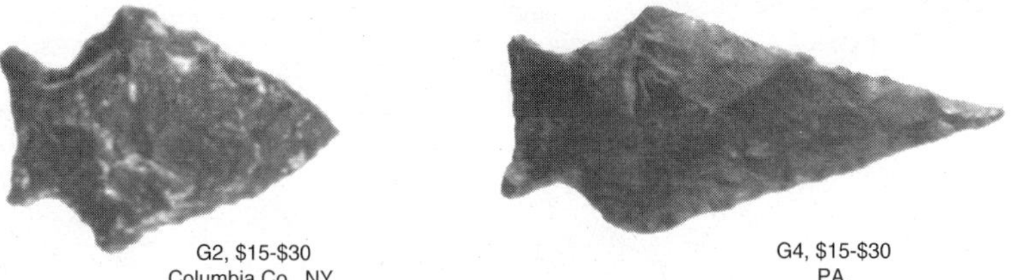

G2, $15-$30
Columbia Co., NY.

G4, $15-$30
PA.

LOCATION: Northeastern states. **DESCRIPTION:** A medium to large size, broad, expanded stem point with tapered to clipped wing shoulders. The blade width varies from narrow to broad. Many examples are asymmetrical. Early forms have ground bases. An extremely popular type in the collecting area.

G4, $20-$35
Lycoming Co., PA.

G4, $15-$25
Columbia Co., NY.

G5, $25-$50
Columbia Co., NY.

G5, $15-$25
Luzerne Co., PA.

G4, $10-$15
Northumberland Co., PA.

G5, $20-$35
Lycoming Co., PA.

G5, $15-$25
Dauphin Co., PA.

G7, $35-$75
Lycoming Co., PA.

G7 $80-$150
Monroe Co., PA.

G9, $180-$300
W. PA.

G7, $40-$80
NY.

G6, $80-$150
Columbia Co., NY.

G8, $200-$400
Lycoming Co., PA.

SUSQUEHANNOCK TRIANGLE - Late Woodland, 1500 - 400 B.P.

(Also see Erie Triangle, Levanna, Madison, Yadkin)

G6, $15-$25
Lycoming Co., PA.
Yellow Jasper.

LOCATION: Pennsylvania. **DESCRIPTION:** A small to medium size triangle. Some examples can be serrated. **I.D. KEY:** Triangle.

G7, $25-$40
NJ. **Yellow Jasper.**

SWATARA-LONG - Archaic, 5000 - 4000 B.P.

(Also see Koens Crispin, Lehigh, Morrow Mountain, Poplar Island & Virginsville))

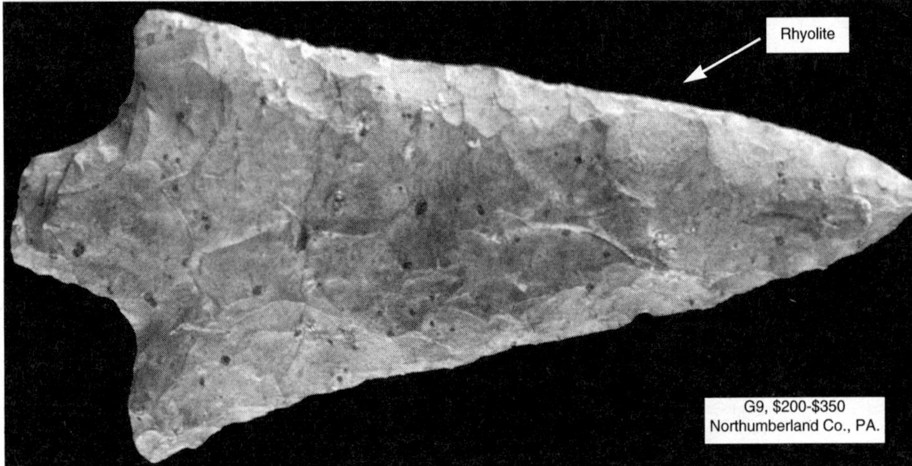

G9, $200-$350
Northumberland Co., PA.

LOCATION: Northeastern states. **DESCRIPTION:** A medium to large, broad, stemmed point with a straight to contracting stem. Shoulders are rounded, tapered or barbed.

TAUNTON RIVER BIFURCATE - Early Archaic, 9000 - 8000 B.P.

(Also see LeCroy, MacCorkle, Susquehanna Bifurcate)

LOCATION: New England states. **DESCRIPTION:** A medium size barbed point with an expanding bifurcated base. Lobes are parallel sided and rounded. **I.D. KEY:** Barbs, bifurcated base.

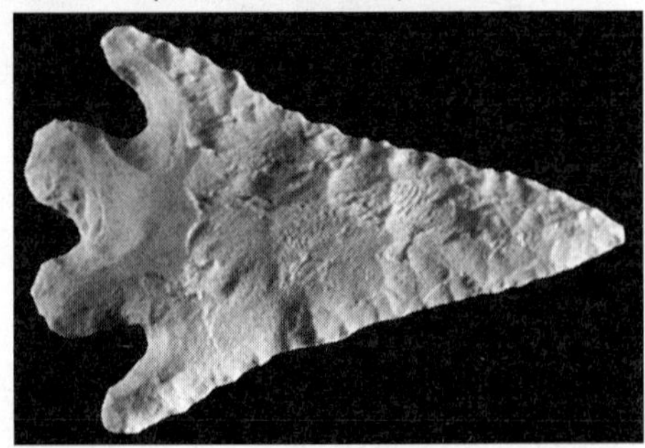

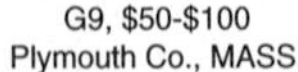

G9, $50-$100
Plymouth Co., MASS.

TOCKS ISLAND - Early to mid-Woodland, 1700 - 1500 B.P.

(Also see Bare Island, Duncan's Island, Lackawaxen, Susquehanna Broad)

LOCATION: Lower Hudson river area. **DESCRIPTION:** A small to medium size stemmed point with a small, expanding base. Shoulders are barbed. **I.D. KEY:** Short expand ing stem.

G5, $40-$80
Monmouth Co., NJ.

TRADE POINTS - Historic, 400 - 170 B.P.

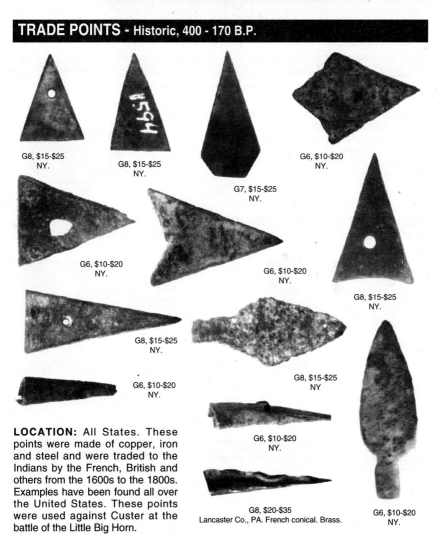

G8, $15-$25
NY.

G8, $15-$25
NY.

G7, $15-$25
NY.

G6, $10-$20
NY.

G6, $10-$20
NY.

G6, $10-$20
NY.

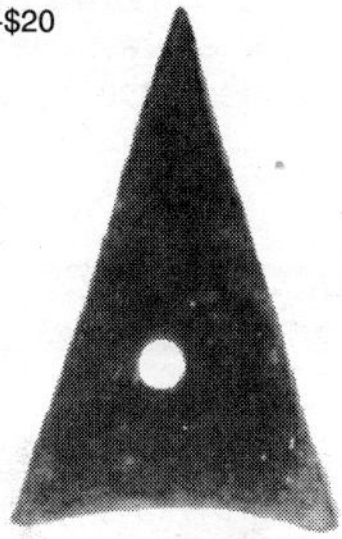

G8, $15-$25
NY.

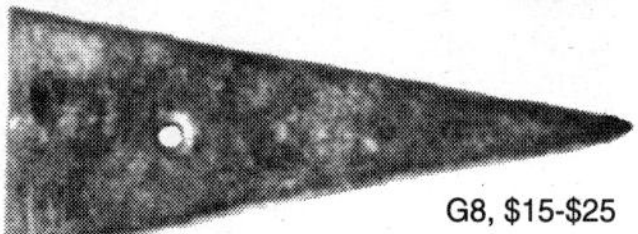

G8, $15-$25
NY.

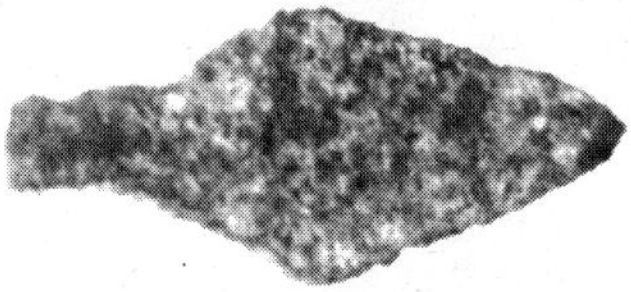

G8, $15-$25
NY

G6, $10-$20
NY.

G6, $10-$20
NY.

G8, $20-$35
Lancaster Co., PA. French conical. Brass.

G6, $10-$20
NY.

LOCATION: All States. These points were made of copper, iron and steel and were traded to the Indians by the French, British and others from the 1600s to the 1800s. Examples have been found all over the United States. These points were used against Custer at the battle of the Little Big Horn.

TRADE POINTS (Continued)

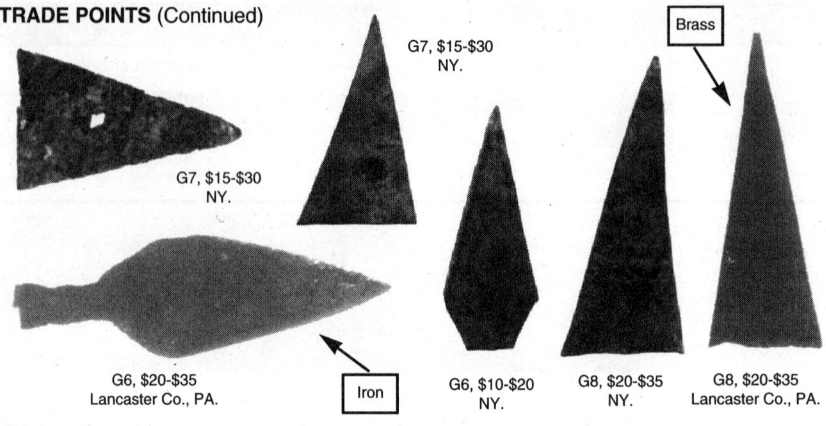

G7, $15-$30 NY.

G7, $15-$30 NY.

G6, $20-$35 Lancaster Co., PA.

G6, $10-$20 NY.

G8, $20-$35 NY.

G8, $20-$35 Lancaster Co., PA.

VERNON - Early Woodland, 2800 - 2500 B.P.

(Also see Brewerton, Kiski, Kline, Lycoming Co.)

LOCATION: Northeastern states. **DESCRIPTION:** A small to medium size triangular point with a short, expanding stem. The base has rounded corners and the shoulders are usually barbed. **I.D. KEY:** Expanded base, barbed shoulders.

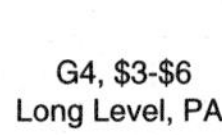

G4, $3-$6
Long Level, PA.

VESTAL NOTCHED - Late Archaic, 4500 - 4 000 B.P.

(Also see Brewerton, Kiski, Kline, Lycoming Co.)

G6, $5-$15
Columbia Co., PA.

G6, $5-$15
Columbia Co., PA.

LOCATION: Northeastern states. **DESCRIPTION:** A small to medium size triangular point with a short, expanding stem. The base has rounded corners and the shoulders are usually barbed. **I.D. KEY:** Expanded base, barbed shoulders.

VIRGINSVILLE - Mid-Archaic, 5000 - 3000 B.P.

(Also see Adena, Conodoquinet Canfield, Lehigh, Koens-Crispin, Morrow Mountain, Piscataway, Poplar Island, Schuylkill)

LOCATION: Northeastern states. **DESCRIPTION:** A medium to large size triangular point with contracting shoulders and base that is usually rounded. **I.D. KEY:** Diamond shape.

G7, \$20-\$35
Berks Co., PA. Rhyolite.

G5, \$10-\$20
PA.

G6, \$15-\$25
PA.

G7, \$20-\$35
Lancaster Co., PA.

G7, \$25-\$50
Lancaster Co., PA.

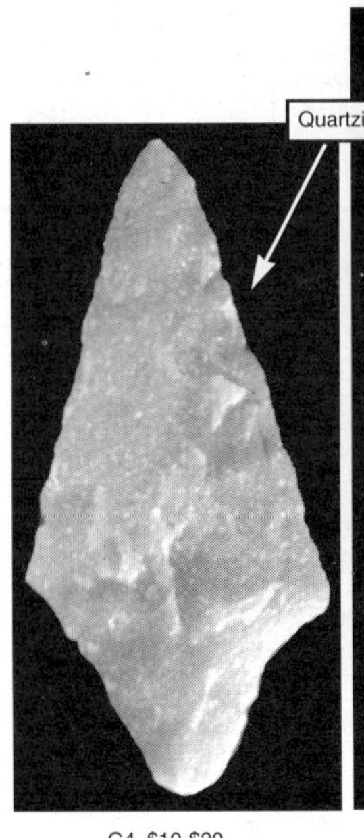

G4, $10-$20
Montgomery Co., PA.

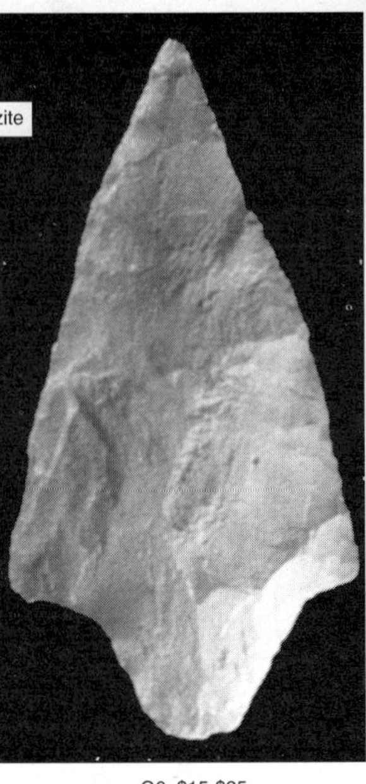

G6, $15-$25
Lancaster Co., PA.

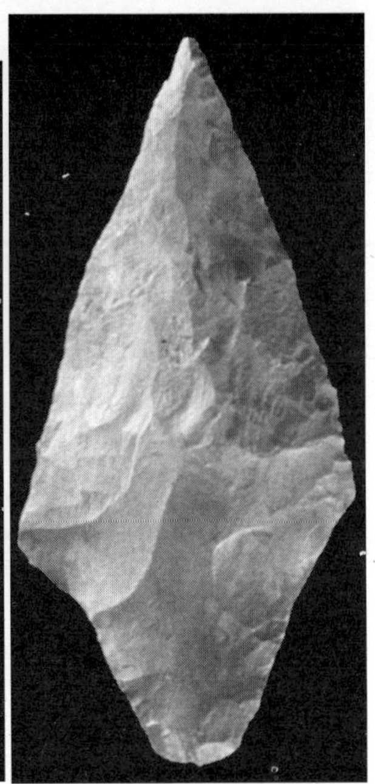

G7, $20-$35
Lancaster Co., PA.

VOSBURG - Archaic, 5000 - 4000 B.P.

(Also see Brewerton, Crooked Creek, Goddard, Jacks Reef, Kiski)

G8, $20-$35
Lycoming Co., PA.

G5, $10-$20
Lycoming Co., PA.

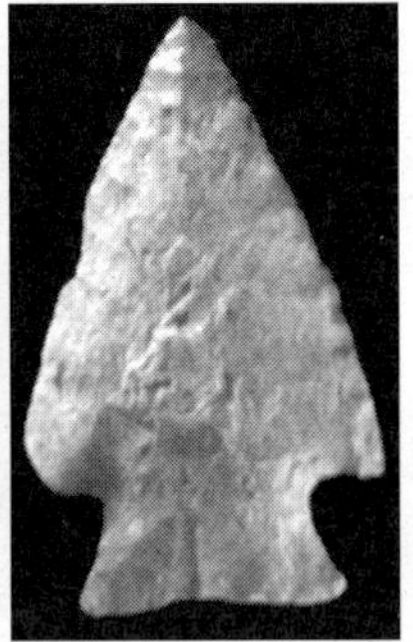

G6, $15-$25
Lycoming Co., PA.

G7, $20-$35
Lycoming Co., PA.

G5, $10-$20
Lycoming Co., PA.

LOCATION: Northeastern states. **DESCRIPTION:** A small to medium size corner notched point with a short, expanding base that is sometimes eared. **I.D. KEY:** Broad expanding base.

G6, $15-$25
Union Co., PA.

VOSBURG (Continued)

G7, $20-$35
Northampton Co., PA.

G5, $20-$35
Bainbridge, PA.

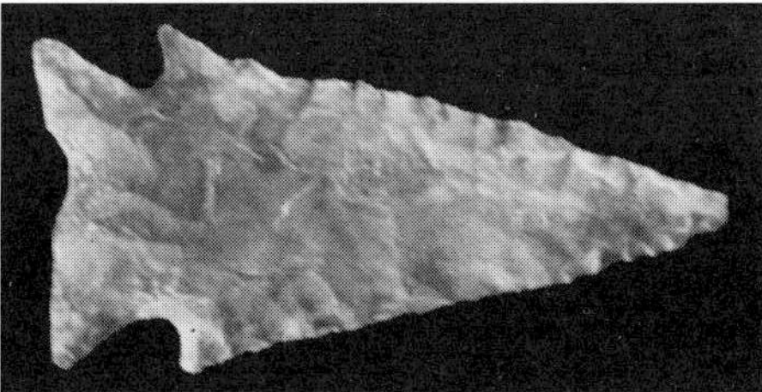

G7, $20-$35
Union Co., PA.

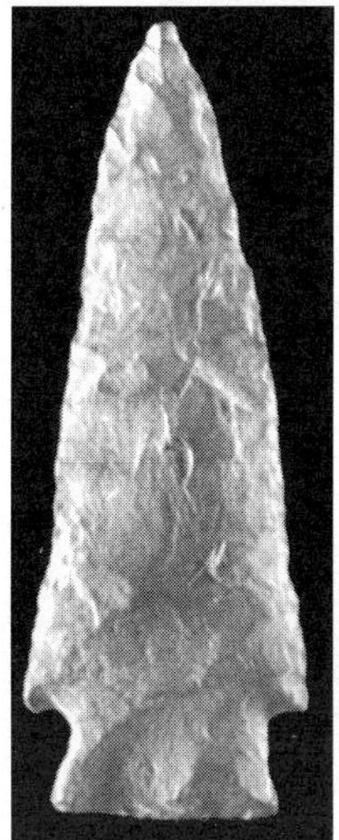

G7, $20-$35
Centre Co., PA.

G10, $150-$250
Columbia Co., NY.

WAPANUCKET - Mid-Archaic, 6000 - 4000 B.P.

(Also see Bare Island, Benton (Central East), Genesee, Lackawaxen, Meadowood, Newmanstown, Piedmont, Tocks Island)

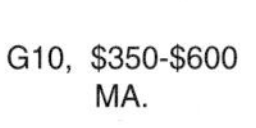

G10, $350-$600
MA.

LOCATION: Northeastern states. **DESCRIPTION:** A medium to very large size short stemmed point. Bases can be corner or side notched, knobbed, bifurcated or expanded. Found in caches and closely resembles the Benton point found further south. **I.D. KEY:** Large size, notched blade.

WARATAN Woodland, 3000 - 1000 B.P.

(Also see Drybrook, Frost Island, Perkiomen, Susquehanna Broad)

LOCATION: Eastern states. **DESCRIPTION:** A small to medium size point with usually broad, tapered shoulders, weak corner notches and a very short, broad, concave base. The base expands on some examples giving the appearance of ears or auricles. **I.D. KEY:** Short, broad, eared base.

G6, $20-$35
Montgomery Co., PA.

WEB BLADE - Woodland, 1500 - 500 B.P.

(Also see Adena Blade)

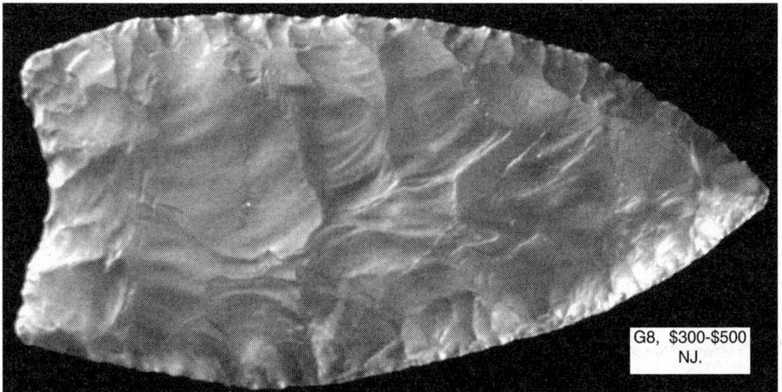

G8, $300-$500
NJ.

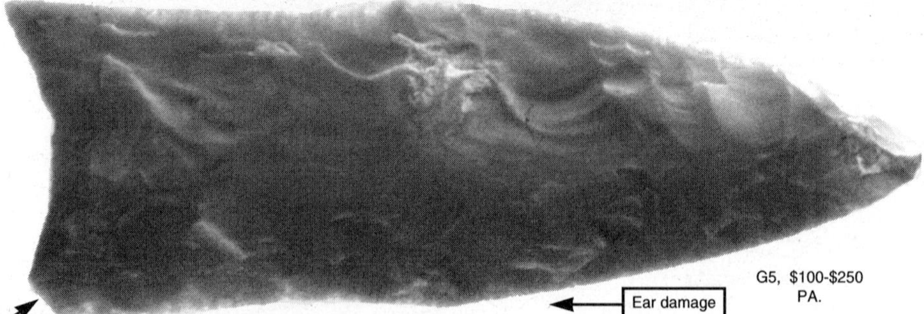

G5, $100-$250
PA.

LOCATION: Northeastern states. **DESCRIPTION:** A large size, lanceolate blade with a thin cross section. Bases can be concave to straight. Believed to be related to the Adena culture. **I.D. KEY:** Large, thin blade.

EASTERN SEABOARD SECTION:

This section includes point types from the following states:
North Carolina, South Carolina, Virginia and West Virginia

The points in this section are arranged in alphabetical order and are shown **actual size**. All types are listed that were available for photographing. Any missing types will be added to future editions as photographs become available. We are always interested in receiving sharp, black and white or color glossy photos or color slides of your collection. Be sure to include a ruler in the photograph so that proper scale can be determined.

Lithics: Argillite, crystal, chalcedony, chert, flint, jasper, limestone, quartz, quartzite, rhyolite, shale, siltstone, slate, vein quartz.

Important sites: Baucom site, Union Co. N.C., Hardaway site in Stanly Co., NC. St. Albans site, Kanawha Co. WVA., Williamson site, Dinwiddie Co., VA.

Regional Consultants:
David Abbott
Ron L. Harris
Rodney Peck
Warner Williams

Special Advisors:
Tommy Beutell
Tom Davis

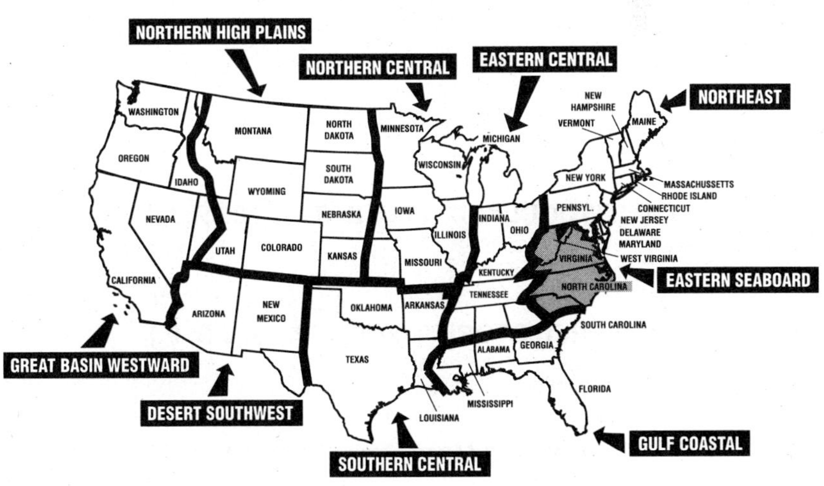

EASTERN SEABOARD POINT TYPES
(Archaeological Periods)

PALEO (14,000 B. P. - 10,000 B. P.)

Clovis
Clovis Unfluted
Drill
Redstone

LATE PALEO (12,000 B. P. - 10,000 B. P.)

Alamance
Quad
Simpson

TRANSITIONAL PALEO (11,000 B. P. - 9,000 B. P.)

Big Sandy
Bolen Bevel
Bolen Plain
Hardaway
Hardaway Blade
Hardaway Dalton
Hardaway Palmer

EARLY ARCHAIC (10,000 B. P. - 7,000 B. P.)

Decatur
Dovetail
Ecusta
Edgefield Scraper
Fishspear
Fountain Creek
Fox Valley
Garth Slough
Guilford Yuma
Jude
Kanawha
Kirk Corner Notched
Kirk Serrated
Kirk Serrated-Bifurcated
Kirk Side Notched
Lecroy
Lost Lake
Palmer
Patrick Henry
Rowan
St. Albans
Southampton
Stanly
Stanly Narrow Stem
Taylor
Thebes
Waller Knife

MIDDLE ARCHAIC (7,000 B. P. - 5,000 B. P.)

Appalachian
Brewerton Eared
Brewerton Side Notched
Buffalo Stemmed
Guilford Round Base
Guilford Stemmed
Guilford Staright Base
Halifax
Heavy Duty
Morrow Mountain
Morrow Mountain Straight Base
Otter Creek

LATE ARCHAIC (5,000 B. P. - 3,000 B. P.)

Dismal Swamp
Exotic Forms
Holmes
Savannah River

EARLY WOODLAND (3,000 B. P. - 2,100 B. P.)

Adena
Adena Robbins
Armstrong
Fox Creek
Greeneville
Gypsy
Potts
Waratan
Wateree
Will's Cove
Yadkin
Yadkin Eared

MIDDLE WOODLAND (2,100 B. P. - 1,500 B. P.)

Randolph

LATE WOODLAND (1,500 B. P. - 1,000 B. P.)

Jack's Reef Corner Notched
Pee Dee
Uwharrie

LATE PREHISTORIC (1,000 B. P. - 500 B. P.)

Badin
Caraway
Clarksville
Occaneechee

HISTORIC (450 B. P. - 170 B. P.)

Hillsboro
Trade Points

EASTERN SEABOARD
THUMBNAIL GUIDE SECTION

ES

The following references are provided to aid the collector in easier and quicker identification of point types. All photos are exactly 30% of actual size and are proportional to each other. Each point pictured in this section represents a classic form for the type. When a match is found, go to the alphabetical location of that type for more examples in actual size.

1 THUMBNAIL GUIDE - AURICULATE FORMS (30% actual size)

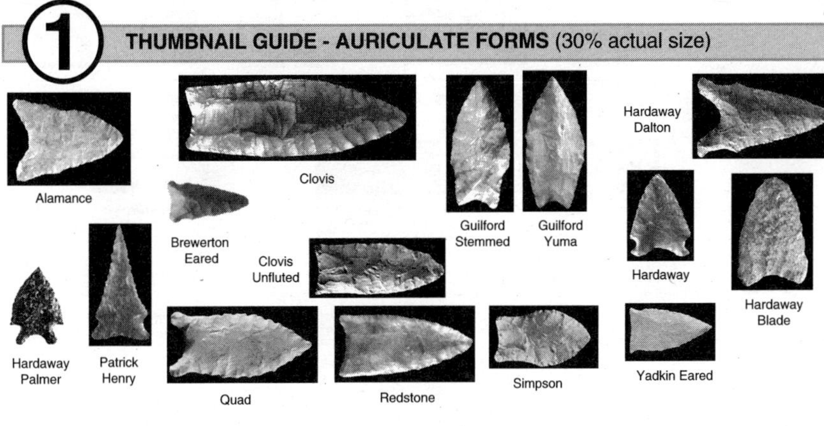

THUMBNAIL GUIDE - LANCEOLATE FORMS (30% actual size)

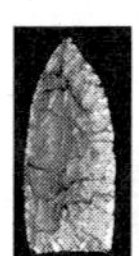
Greeneville

Guilford Round

Guilford Straight

Pee Dee

THUMBNAIL GUIDE - CORNER NOTCHED FORMS (30% actual size)

Decatur

Dovetail

Drill

Fountain Creek

Jacks Reef Corner Northced

Kirk Corner Notched

Lost Lake

Palmer

Patrick Henry

Potts

Thebes

Waratan

THUMBNAIL GUIDE - SIDE NOTCHED FORMS (30% actual size)

Big Sandy

Bolen Bevel

Bolen Plain

Brewerton Side Notched

Ecusta

Edgefield Scraper

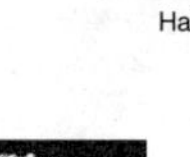

Halifax

Kirk Side Notched

Otter Creek

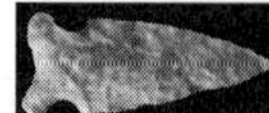

Rowan

Taylor

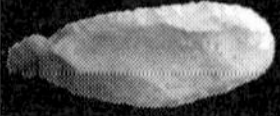

Waller Knife

THUMBNAIL GUIDE - STEMMED FORMS (30% of actual size)

Expanded Stems

Fishspear

Garth Slough

Halifax

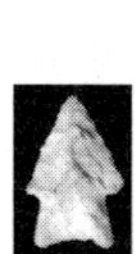

Jude

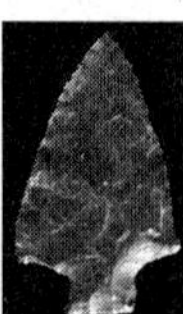

Dismal Swamp

Contracting Stems

Adena

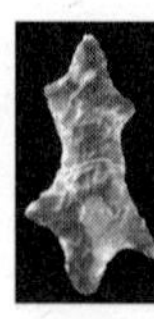

Exotic Lizard?

Holmes

Kirk Serrated

Morrow Mountain

Randolph

Morrow Mountain Straight Base

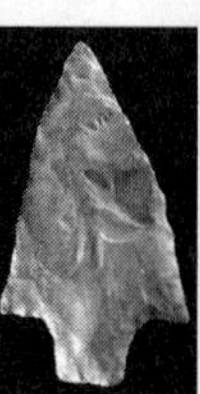

Savannah River

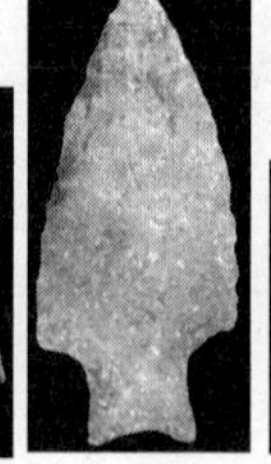

Savannah River

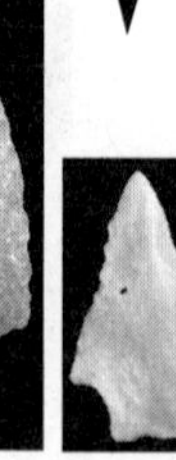

Savannah River

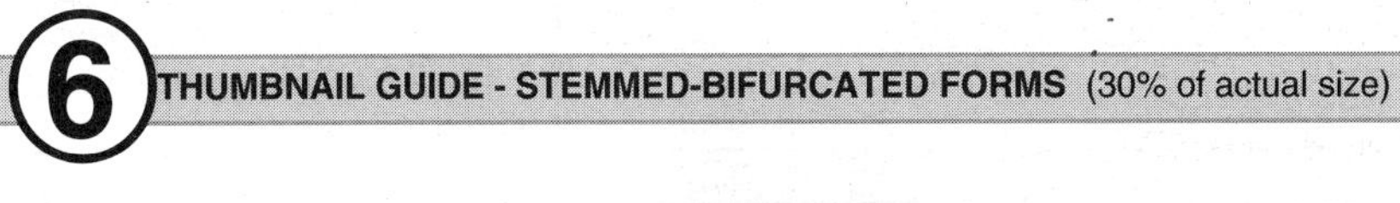

6 THUMBNAIL GUIDE - STEMMED-BIFURCATED FORMS (30% of actual size)

7 THUMBNAIL GUIDE - TRIANGLES (30% of actual size)

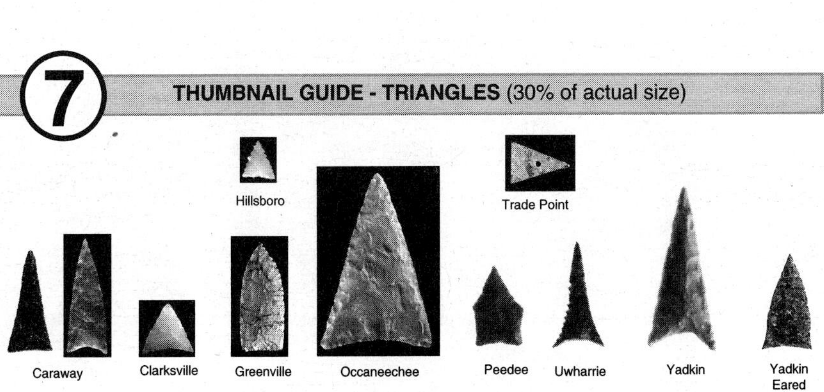

ADENA - Late Archaic to early Woodland, 3000 - 1200 B. P.

(Also see Savannah River)

LOCATION: Eastern to Southeastern states. **DESCRIPTION:** A medium to large, thin, narrow, triangular blade that is sometimes serrated, and with a medium to long, narrow to broad rounded "beaver tail" stem. Most examples are from average to excellent quality. Bases can be ground. **I.D. KEY:** Rounded base, woodland flaking.

G4, $3-$6
Kanawha Co., WVA.

ADENA ROBBINS - Late Archaic to early Woodland, 3000 - 1200 B. P.

(Also see Savannah River)

G3, $2-$4
Putnam Co., WVA.

LOCATION: Eastern to Southeastern states. **DESCRIPTION:** A medium to large, thin, narrow, triangular blade that is sometimes serrated, and with a medium to long, narrow to broad rounded "beaver tail" stem. Most examples are from average to excellent quality. Bases can be ground. **I.D. KEY:** Rounded base, woodland flaking.

ALAMANCE - Late Paleo, 10,000 - 8000 B. P.

(Also see Hardaway)

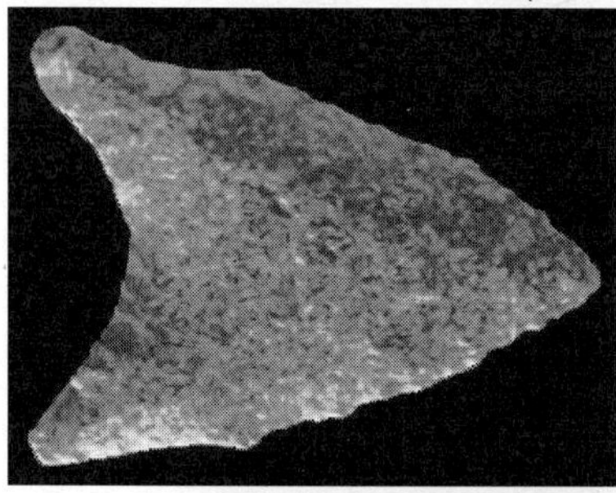

G7, $115-$225
Durham Co., NC.

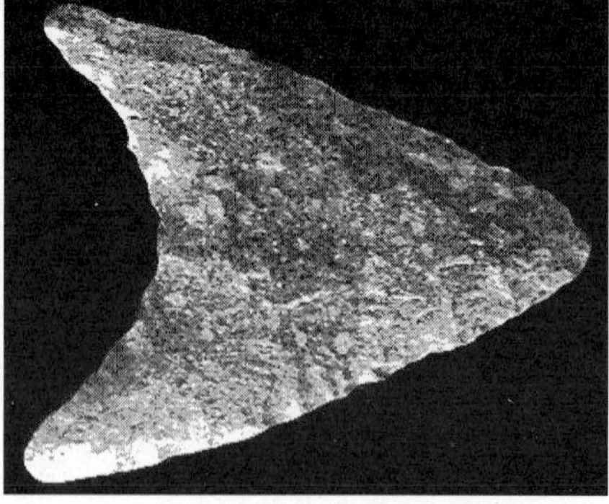

G7, $75-$150
Guilford Co., NC.

G9, $200-$400, Moore Co., NC.

ALAMANCE (continued)

LOCATION: Coastal states from Virginia to Florida. **DESCRIPTION:** A broad, short, auriculate point with a deeply concave base. The broad basal area is usually ground and can be expanding to parallel sided. A variant form of the *Dalton-Greenbrier* evolving later into the *Hardaway* type. **I.D. KEY:** Width of base and strong shoulder form.

ANGELICO CORNER-NOTCHED (See Decatur)

APPALACHIAN - Middle Archaic, 6000 - 3000 B. P.

(Also see Rowan, Savannah River and Southampton)

G8, $65-$125
McDowell Co., NC.

G7, $50-$100
Randolph Co., NC.

LOCATION: East Tennessee and Georgia into the Carolinas. **DESCRIPTION:** A medium to large size, rather crudely made stemmed point with a concave, straight or convex base. Most examples are made of quartzite. Shoulders are tapered and the base is usually ground. Related to *Savannah River* points. **I.D. KEY:** Basal form.

ARMSTRONG - Woodland, 2450 - 1600 B. P.

(Also see Brewerton, Ecusta, Palmer, Patrick Henry and Potts)

LOCATION: West Virginia and neighboring states. **DESCRIPTION:** A small, short, corner notched point with barbed shoulders. Base is straight to convex and expands. **I.D. KEY:** Tangs and broad notches.

G4, $3-$5
Kanawha Co., WVA.

BADIN - Late Prehistoric, 1000 - 800 B. P.

(Also see Caraway, Fox Creek, Guildord and Hillsboro)

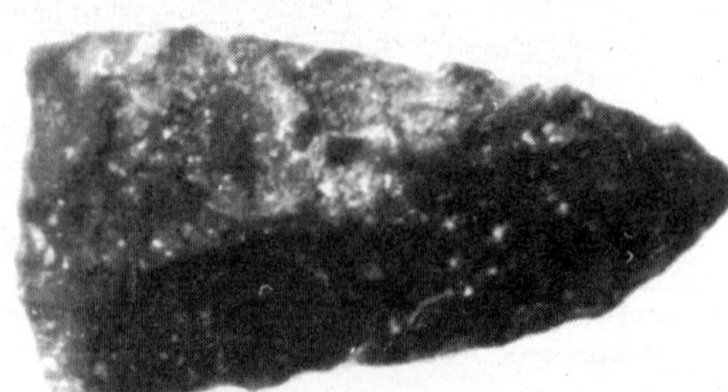

LOCATION: Carolinas to Virginia. **DESCRIPTION:** A medium size triangular point that is larger and thicker than Hillsboro. Sides are concave with straight to slightly convex or concave bases. **I.D. KEY:** Thickness and crudeness.

G5, $4-$8
Montgomery Co., NC.

BIG SANDY - Transitional Paleo to Late Archaic, 10,000 - 3000 B. P.

(Also see Autauga, Bolen, Godar, Pine Tree and Rowan)

Broad base

G2, $3-$6
Mason Co., WVA.

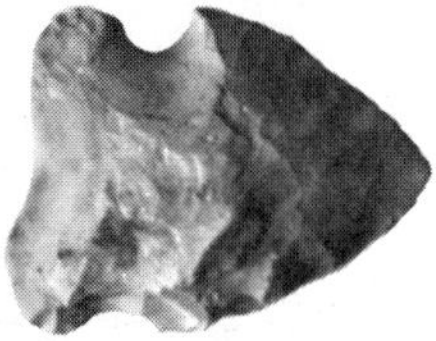

G3, $4-$8
Kanawha Co., NC.

Milky quartz

G2, $4-$7
Moore Co., NC.

G6, $35-$70
Randolph Co., NC.

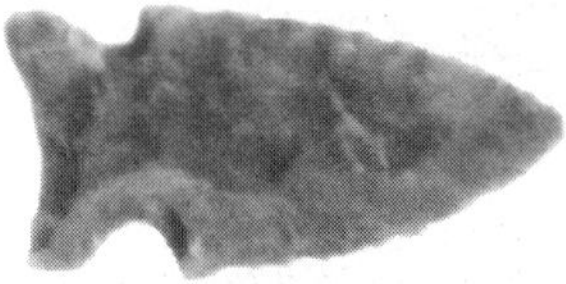

G4, $16-$12
VA.

Contracted base form

G4, $6-$12
Southampton Co., VA.

LOCATION: Southeastern states. **DESCRIPTION:** A small to medium size, side notched point with early forms showing heavy basal grinding, serrations, and horizontal flaking. **I.D. KEY:** Basal form and blade flaking.

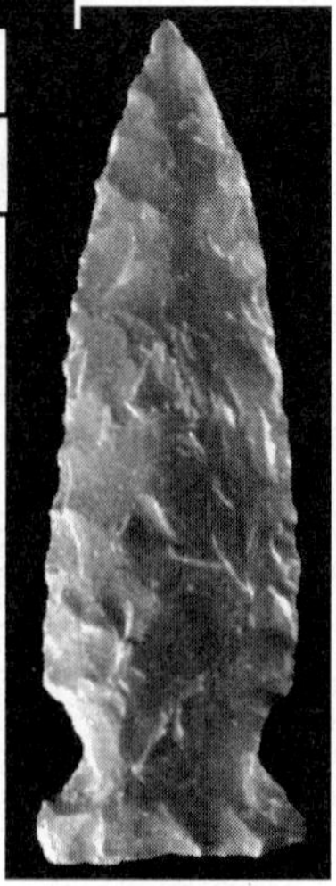

G6, $35-$70
Randolph Co., NC.

G8, $50-$100
Randolph Co., NC.

BOLEN BEVEL - Early Archaic, 10,000 - 7000 B. P.

(Also see Big Sandy and Patrick Henry)

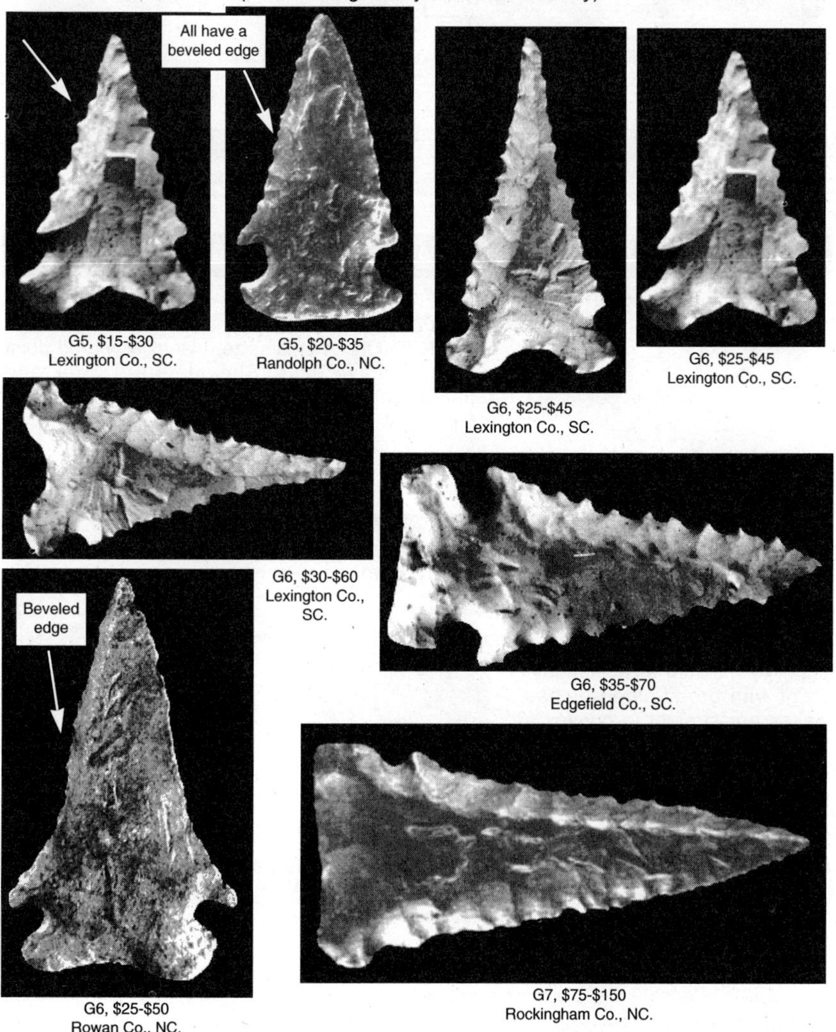

G5, $15-$30
Lexington Co., SC.

G5, $20-$35
Randolph Co., NC.

G6, $25-$45
Lexington Co., SC.

G6, $25-$45
Lexington Co., SC.

G6, $30-$60
Lexington Co., SC.

G6, $35-$70
Edgefield Co., SC.

G6, $25-$50
Rowan Co., NC.

G7, $75-$150
Rockingham Co., NC.

LOCATION: Eastern states. **DESCRIPTION:** A small to medium size, side-notched point with early forms showing basal grinding, beveling on one side of each face, and serrations. Bases can be straight, concave or convex. The side notch is usually broader than in *Big Sandy* points. E-notched or expanded notching also occurs on early forms. **I.D. KEY:** Basal form and notching.

BOLEN PLAIN - Early Archaic, 9000 - 7000 B. P.

(Also see Big Sandy and Taylor))

LOCATION: Eastern states. **DESCRIPTION:** A small to medium size, side-notched point with early forms showing basal grinding and serrations. Bases are straight, concave or convex. The side notches are usually broader than in the *Big Sandy* type, and can be expanded to E-notched on some examples. **I.D. KEY:** Basal form and flaking on blade.

BOLEN PLAIN (continued)

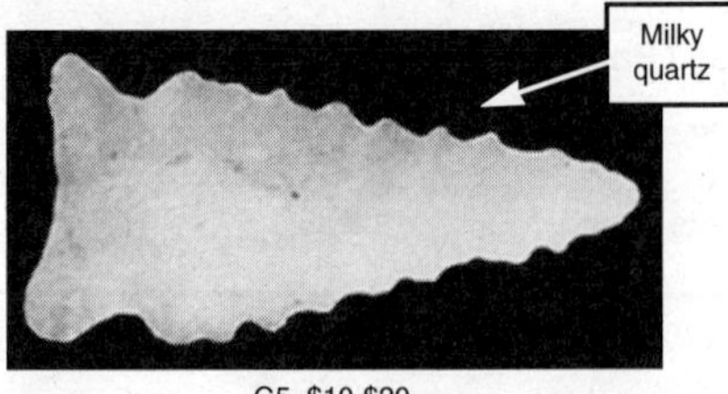

G5, $10-$20
Anderson Co., SC.

Milky quartz

G5, $10-$20
Anderson Co., SC.

BREWERTON EARED - Middle Archaic, 6000 - 4000 B. P.

(Also see Hardaway, Yadkin Eared)

G4, $3-$5
Kanawha Co., WV.

LOCATION: Eastern to midwestern states. **DESCRIPTION:** A small size, triangular, eared point with a concave base. Shoulders are weak and tapered. Ears are the widest part of the point. **I.D. KEY:** Small ears, weak shoulders.

BREWERTON SIDE NOTCHED - Middle Archaic, 6000 - 4000 B. P.

(Also see Big Sandy, Hardaway, Palmer)

LOCATION: Eastern to midwestern states. **DESCRIPTION:** A small to medium size triangular point with broad side notches. Bases are straight to convex to concave. **I.D. KEY:** Thickness and width.

G5, $6-$10
Mason Co., WV.

G6, $8-$15
Mason Co., WV.

BUFFALO STEMMED - Middle Archaic, 6000 - 4000 B. P.

(Also see Holmes, Savannah River)

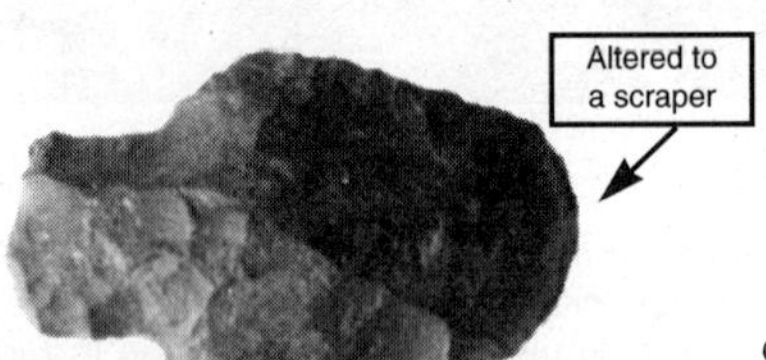

Altered to a scraper

G5, $6-$10
Putnam Co., WV.

LOCATION: West Virginia. **DESCRIPTION:** A medium size, broad, parallel stemmed point with tapered shoulders. **I.D. KEY:** Width, squared stem.

CARAWAY - Late Prehistoric, 1000 - 200 B. P.

(Also see Clarksville, Hillsboro, Uwharrie and Yadkin)

LOCATION: Coincides with the Mississippian culture in the Eastern states. **DESCRIPTION:** A small to medium size, thin, triangular point with usually straight sides and base, although concave bases are common. Some examples are notched on two to three sides. Many are of high quality and some are finely serrated. Similar to *Madison* found elsewhere.

CARAWAY (continued)

Serrated edge

Serrated edge

G2, $3-$6
Randolph Co., NC.

G3, $5-$10
Randolph Co., NC.

G3, $3-$6
Randolph Co., NC.

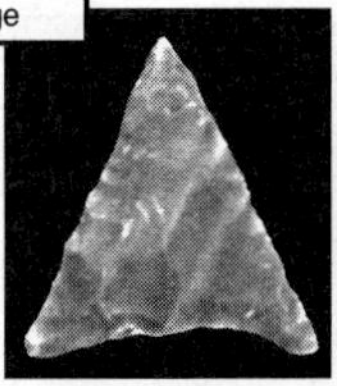

G5, $5-$10
Randolph Co., NC.

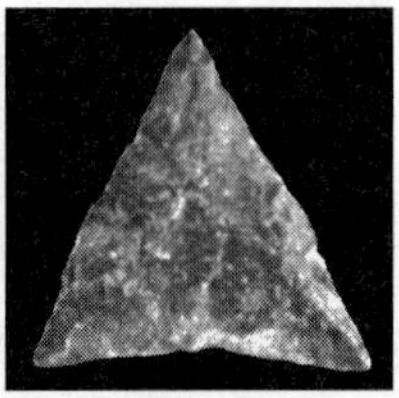

G6, $5-$10
Randolph Co., NC.

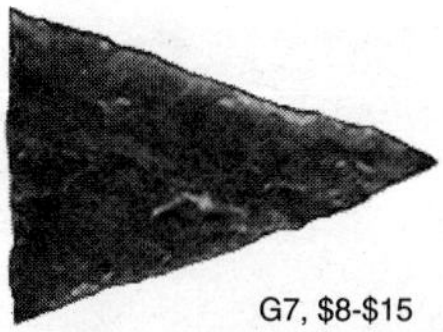

ES

G7, $8-$15
Randolph Co., NC.

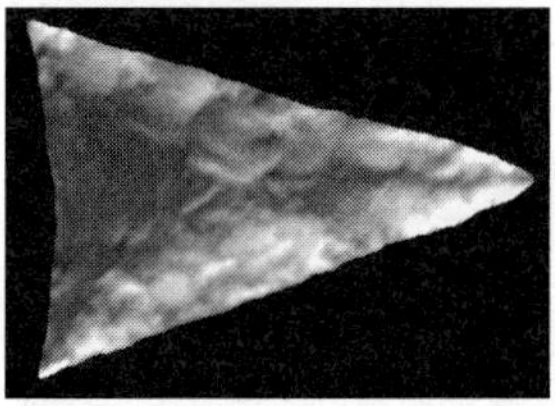

G8, $15-$25
Randolph Co., NC.

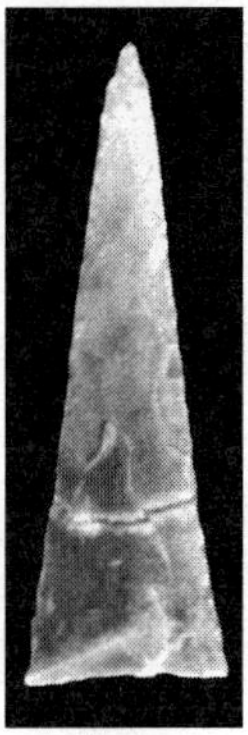

G7, $10-$20
Randolph Co., NC.

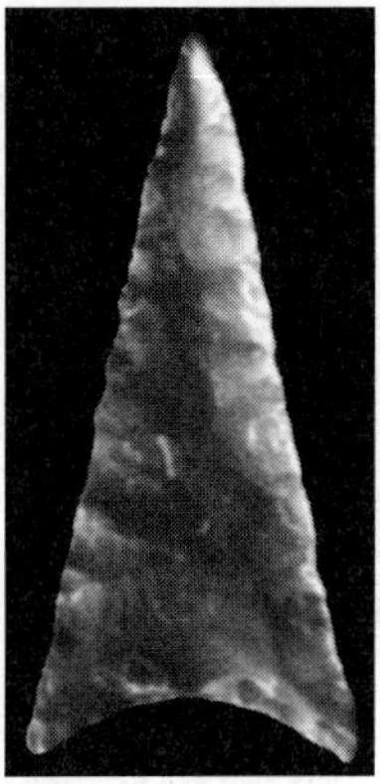

G8, $15-$25
Randolph Co., NC.

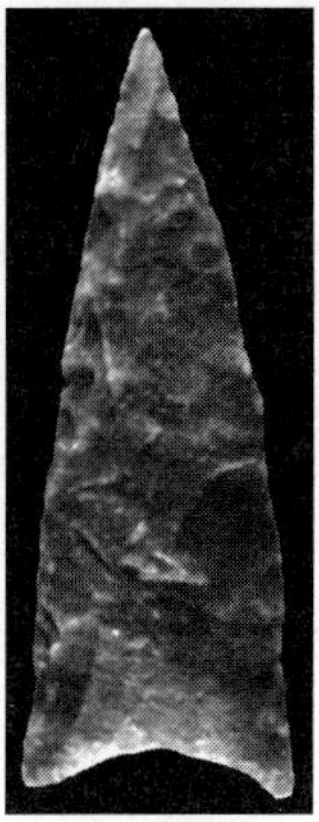

G6, $20-$35
Randolph Co., NC.

CHARLESTON (See Pine Tree)

CLARKSVILLE - Late Prehistoric, 1000 - 500 A. D.

(Also see Caraway, Hillsboro, Uwharrie and Yadkin)

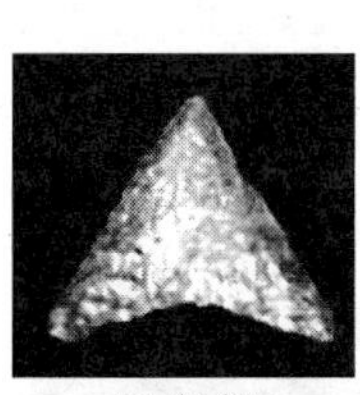
G3, $3-$5
Union Co., SC.

G3, $3-$5
Newberry Co., SC.

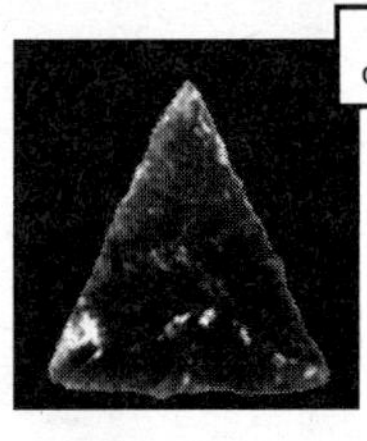
G3, $3-$5
Randolph Co., NC.

Milky quartz

G6, $4-$8
Randolph Co., NC.

LOCATION: Far Eastern states. **DESCRIPTION:** A small size triangular point with all three sides approximately the same width. The base is straight to slightly concave. Examples made from quartzite and quartz tend to be thick in cross section.

CLOVIS - Early Paleo, 14,000 - 9000 B. P.

(Also see Redstone, Quad and Simpson)

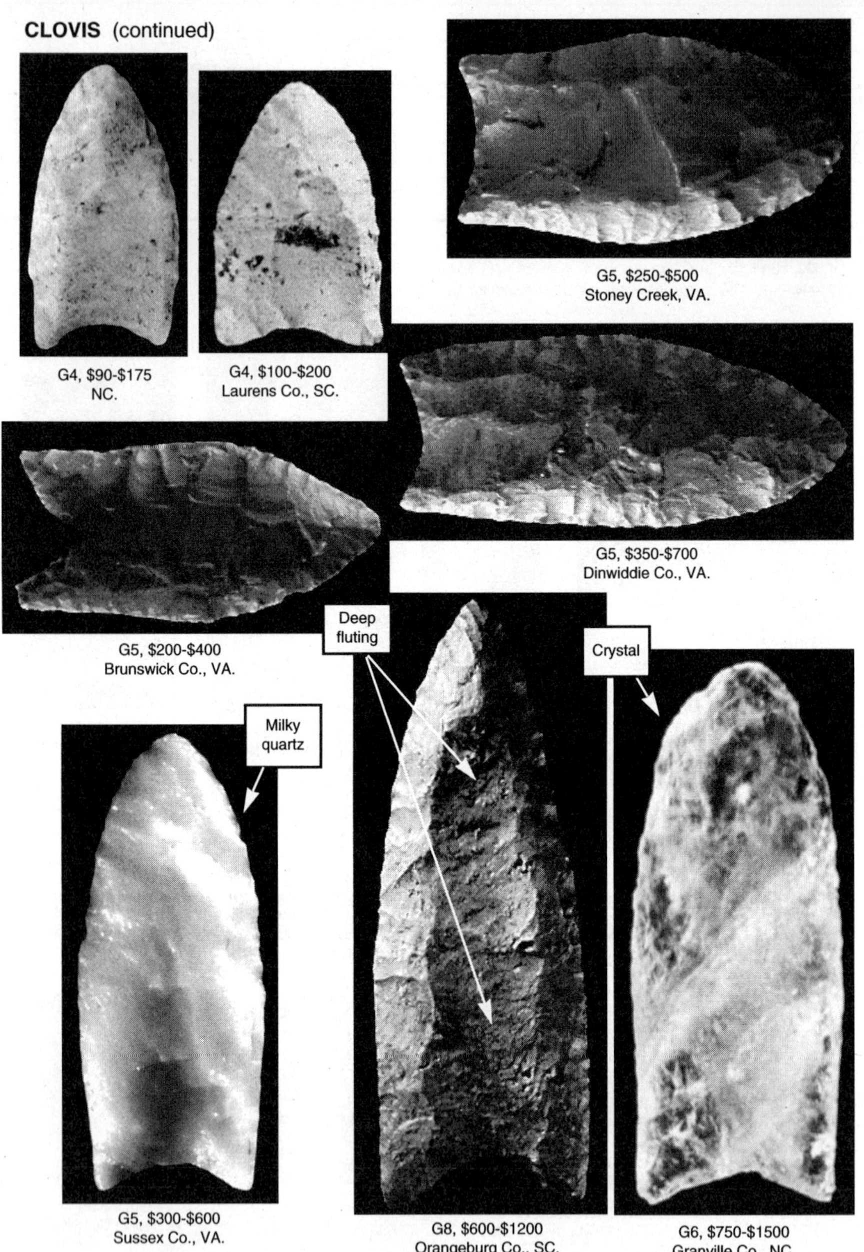

G4, $90-$175
NC.

G4, $100-$200
Laurens Co., SC.

G5, $250-$500
Stoney Creek, VA.

G5, $350-$700
Dinwiddie Co., VA.

G5, $200-$400
Brunswick Co., VA.

G5, $300-$600
Sussex Co., VA.

G8, $600-$1200
Orangeburg Co., SC.

G6, $750-$1500
Granville Co., NC.

LOCATION: All of North America. **DESCRIPTION:** A medium to large size, auriculate, fluted, lanceolate point with convex sides and a concave base that is ground. Most examples are fluted on both sides about 1/3 the way up from the base. The flaking can be random to parallel. *Clovis* is the earliest point type in the hemisphere. It is believed that this form was developed here after early man crossed the Bering Straits to reach this continent about 50,000 years ago. Current theories place the origin of *Clovis* in the Southeastern U.S. since more examples are found in Florida, Alabama and Tennessee than anywhere else. **I.D. Key:** Paleo flaking, shoulders, batan fluting instead of indirect style.

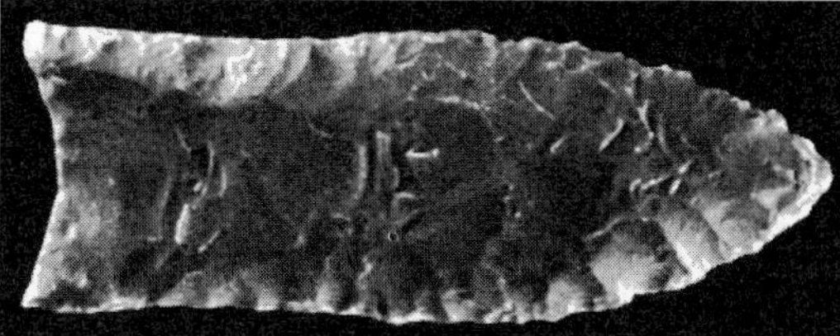

G6, $400-$800
Brunswick Co., VA.

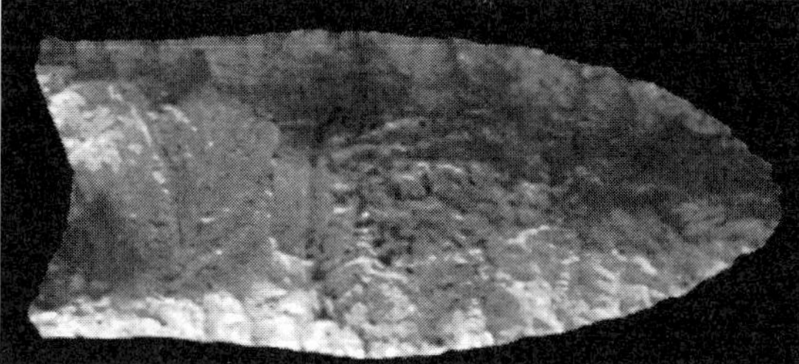

G6, $500-$1000
Coeburn, VA.

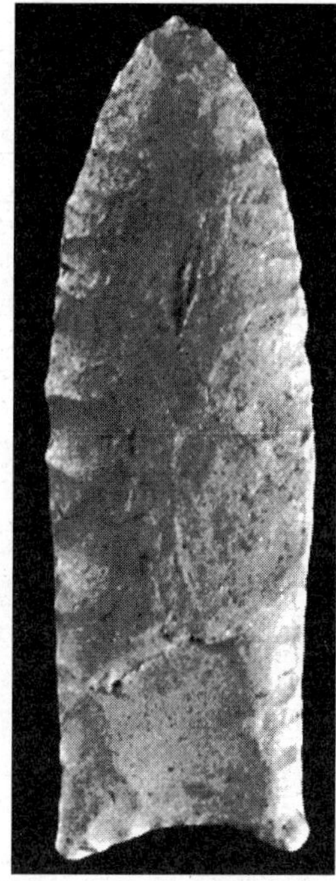

G9, $1000-$2000
Nottaway Co., VA.

G9, $900-$1800
Mason Co., WVA.

CLOVIS-UNFLUTED - Paleo, 14,000 - 9000 B. P.

(Also see Simpson)

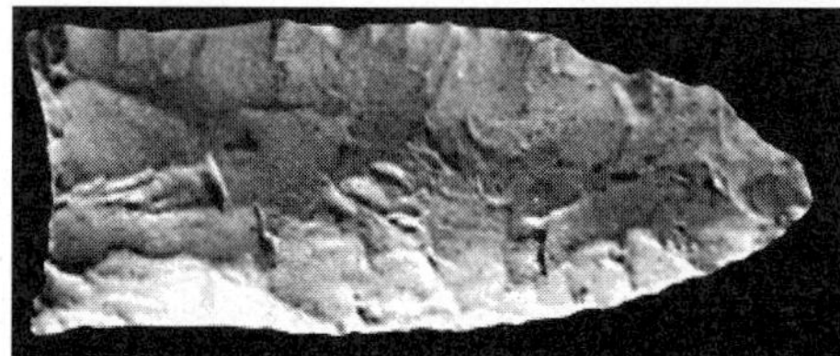

LOCATION: All of North America. **DESCRIPTION:** A medium to large size, auriculate point identical to fluted *Clovis,* but not fluted. A very rare type.

G5, $100-$200
Sussex Co., VA. Basal thinning.

DECATUR - Early Archaic, 9000 - 3000 B. P.

(Also see Dovetail, Ecusta and Palmer)

LOCATION: Eastern states. **DESCRIPTION:** A small to medium size, serrated, corner notched point that is usually beveled on one side of each face. The base is usually broken off (fractured) by a blow inward from each corner of the stem. Sometimes the side of the stem and backs of the tangs are also fractured, and rarely the tip may be fractured by a blow on each side directed towards the base. Bases are usually ground and flaking is high quality. Basal and shoulder fracturing also occurs in Abbey, *Dovetail*, *Eva*, *Kirk*, *Motley* and *Snyders*. Unfractured forms are called *Angelico Corner-Notched* in Virginia.

DECATUR (continued)

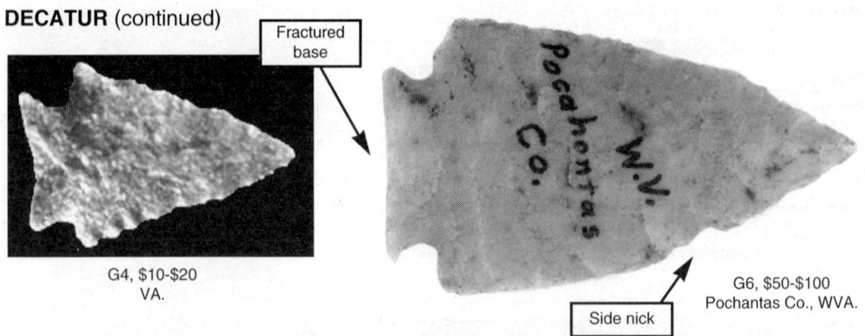

G4, $10-$20
VA.

G6, $50-$100
Pochantas Co., WVA.

DISMAL SWAMP - Late Archaic to early Woodland, 3500 - 2000 B. P.

(Also see Garth Slough, Savannah River and Waratan)

LOCATION: North Carolina to Virginia. Similar to *Perkiomen* found in Pennsylvania. **DESCRIPTION:** A medium to large size, broad point with strong shoulders and a small, expanding base that is usually bulbous, blades can be asymmetrical. **I.D. KEY:** Broad shoulders and small base.

G6, $20-$35
Bethany, WV.

DOVETAIL - Early Archaic, 9500 - 8000 B. P.

(Also see Bolen Beveled and Decatur)

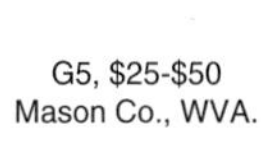

G5, $25-$50
Mason Co., WVA.

LOCATION: Midwest into the southeast. **DESCRIPTION:** Also known as *St. Charles*. A medium to large size, corner notched, dovetailed base point. The blade is beveled on one side of each face (usually the left side) on resharpened examples. Bases are always convex. Straight bases would place a point into the *Lost Lake* type. Bases are ground and can be fractured on both sides or center notched on some examples. **I.D. KEY:** Dovetailed base.

DRILL - Paleo to Historic, 14,000 - 200 B. P.

LOCATION: All of North America. **DESCRIPTION:** Although many drills were made from scratch, all point types were made into the drill form. Usually, heavily resharpened and broken points were salvaged and rechipped into drills. These objects were certainly used as drills (evidence of extreme edge wear), but there is speculation that some of these forms may have been used as pins for clothing, ornaments, ear plugs and other uses.

DRILL (continued)

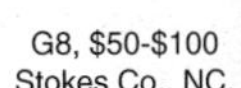

G8, $50-$100
Stokes Co., NC.

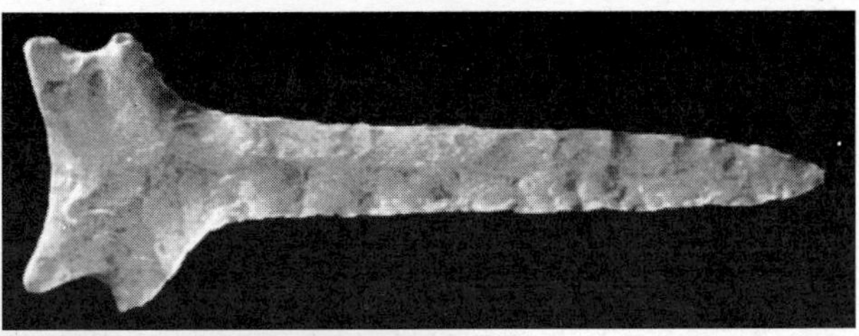

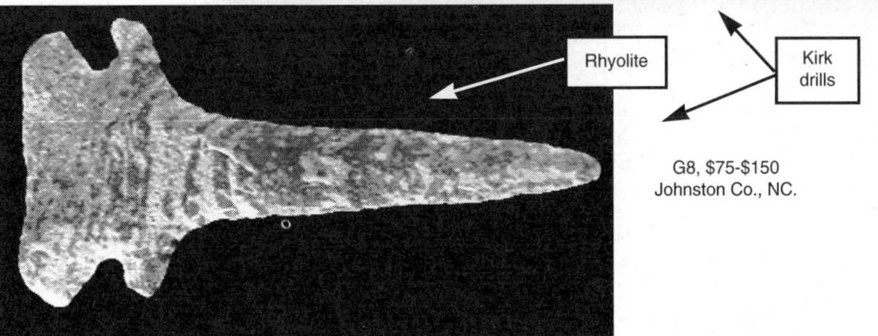

G8, $75-$150
Johnston Co., NC.

ECUSTA - Early Archaic, 8000 - 5000 B. P.

(Also see Bolen Plain, Palmer and Potts)

G5, $10-$20
Bethany, WVA.

G7, $10-$20
Bethany, WVA.

G7, $10-$20
Bethany, WVA.

LOCATION: Southeastern states. **DESCRIPTION:** A small size, serrated, side-notched point with usually one side of each face steeply beveled, although examples exist with all four sides beveled and flaked to a median ridge. The base and notches are ground. Very similar to *Autauga*, with the latter being corner-notched.

EDGEFIELD SCRAPER - Early Archaic, 9000 - 6000 B. P.

LOCATION: Southern Atlantic coast states. **DESCRIPTION:** A medium to large size corner notched point that is asymmetrical. Many are uniface and usually steeply beveled along the diagonal side. The blade on all examples leans heavily to one side. Used as a hafted scraper.

G8, $40-$60
Edgefield Co., SC.

EXOTIC FORMS - Woodland to Mississippian, 5000 - 1000 B. P.

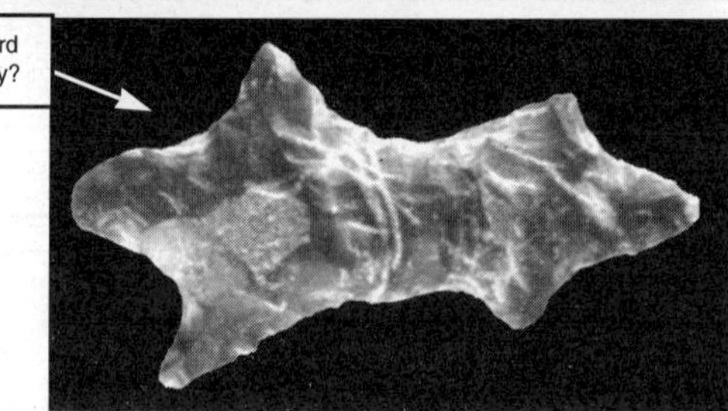

G8, $40-$75
Granville Co., NC.

G8, $30-$55
Randolph Co., NC.

LOCATION: Everywhere. **DESCRIPTION:** The forms illustrated here are very rare. Some are definitely effigy forms while others may be no more than unfinished and unintentional doodles.

FISHSPEAR - Early to Mid-Archaic, 9000 - 6000 B.P.

(Also see Randolph)

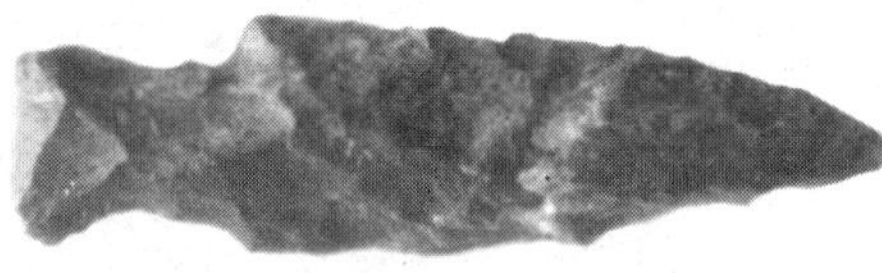

G5, $10-$20
Kanawha Co., WVA.

LOCATION: Northeastern states. **DESCRIPTION:** A medium to large size, narrow, thick, stemmed point with broad side notches to an expanding stem. Bases are usually ground and blade edges can be serrated. Named due to its appearance that resembles a fish. **I.D. KEY:** Narrowness, thickness and long stem.

FOUNTAIN CREEK - Early Archaic, 9000 - 7000 B. P.

(Also see Kirk Serrated)

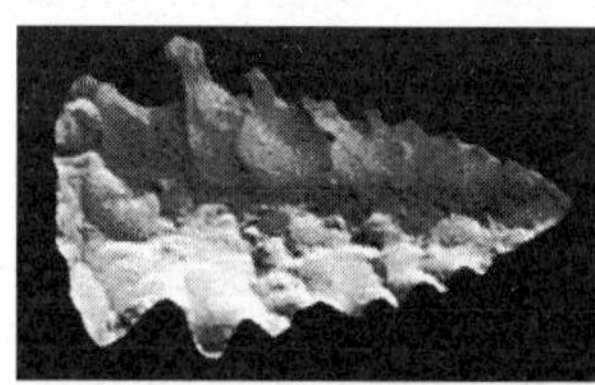

G6, $15-$30
Wayne Co., NC.

G7, $20-$40
Chatham Co., NC.

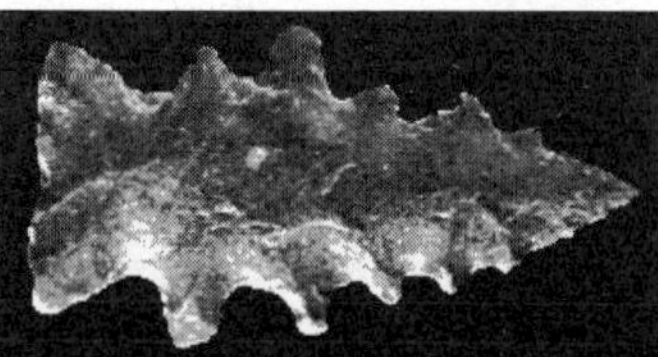

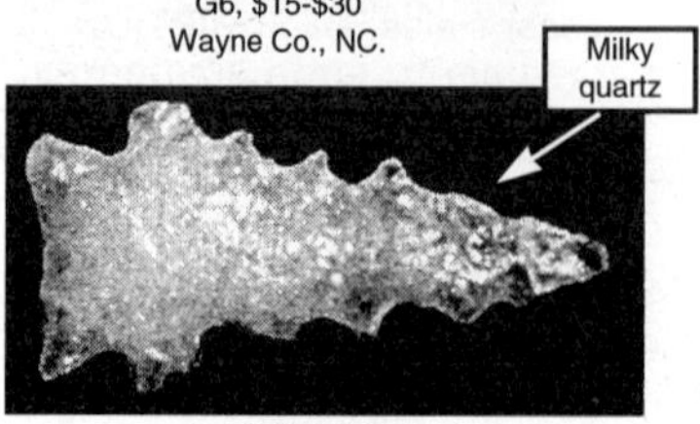

G4, $10-$20
Fairfield Co., SC.

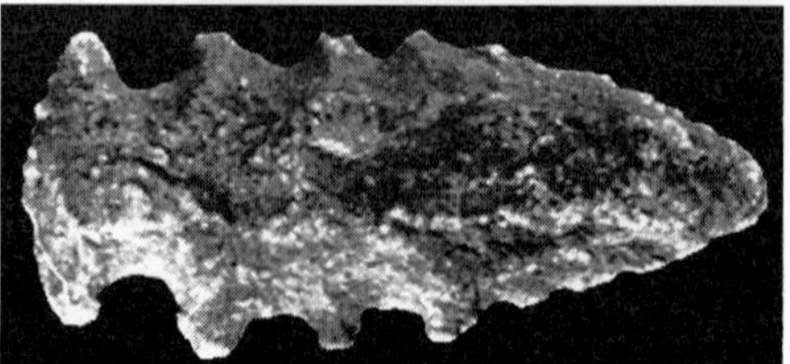

G4, $15-$30
Davidson Co., NC.

FOUNTAIN CREEK (continued)

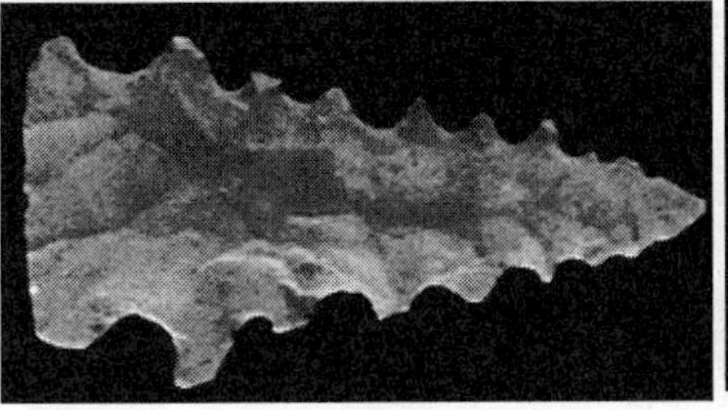

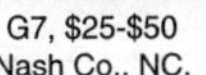

G7, $25-$50
Nash Co., NC.

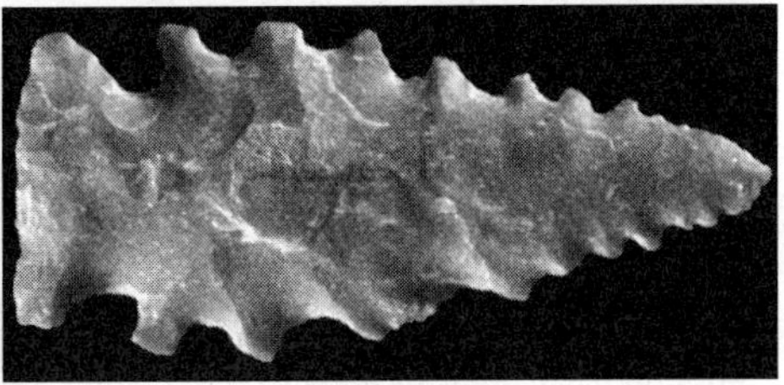

G9, $35-$70
Randolph Co., NC.

ES

LOCATION: Eastern states. **DESCRIPTION:** A medium size, narrow corner notched to expanded stemmed point with notched blade edges and a short, rounded base which is ground. **I.D. KEY:** Edgework. **I.D. KEY:** Exaggerated barbs.

FOX CREEK - Woodland, 2500 - 1200 B. P.

(Also see Badin, Guilford Stemmed)

LOCATION: Northeastern states. **DESCRIPTION:** A medium size blade with a squared to tapered hafting area and a straight to slightly concave base. Shoulders, when present are very weak and tapered.

G6, $8-$15
Bethany, WV.

FOX VALLEY - Early to Middle Archaic, 9000 - 4000 B. P.

(Also see Garth Slough, Jude, Kanawha, Kirk, Lake Erie, LeCroy and Stanly)

LOCATION: Eastern states. **DESCRIPTION:** A small size, triangular point with flaring shoulders and a short bifurcated stem. Shoulders are sometimes clipped winged and have a tendency to turn towards the tip. Blades exhibit early parallel flaking and the edges are usually serrated. **I.D. KEY:** Bifurcated base and barbs.

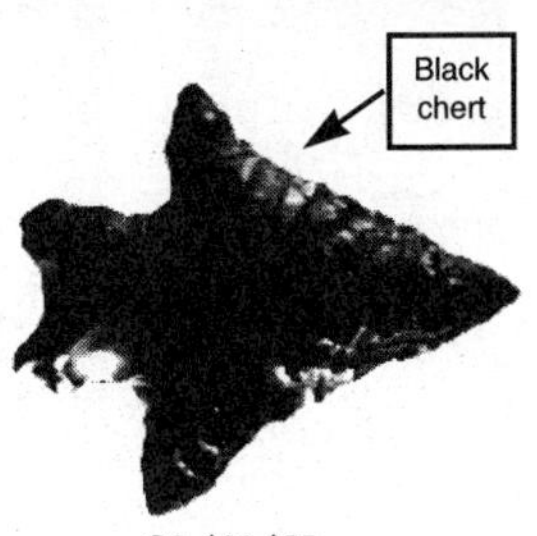

G6, $30-$55
Mecklenburg Co., VA.

GARTH SLOUGH - Early Archaic, 9000 - 4000 B. P.

(Also see Fox Valley and Stanly)

G6, $25-$50
Pearson Co., NC.

LOCATION: Southeastern states. **DESCRIPTION:** A small size point with wide, expanded barbs and a small squared base. Rare examples have the tangs clipped (called clipped wing). The blade edges are concave with fine serrations. A similar type of a later time period, called *Catahoula*, is found in the Midwestern states. A bifurcated base would place it into the *Fox Valley* type. **I.D. KEY:** Expanded barbs, early flaking.

GREENEVILLE - Woodland, 3000 - 1500 B.P.

(Also see Caraway, Clarksville, Madison)

LOCATION: Southeast to eastern states. **DESCRIPTION:** A small to medium size lanceolate point with convex sides becoming contracting to parallel at the base. The basal edge is slightly concave, convex or straight. This point is usually wider and thicker than *Guntersville*, and is believed to be related to *Camp Creek*, *Ebenezer* and *Nolichucky* points.

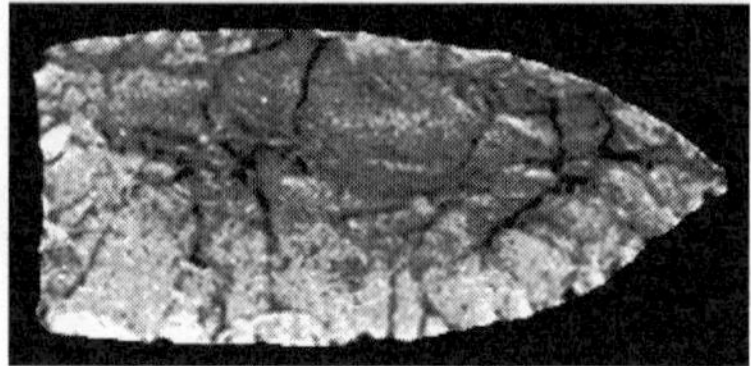

G8, $15-$30
Davidson Co., NC.

GUILFORD-ROUND BASE - Middle Archaic, 6500 - 5000 B. P.

(Also see Cobbs)

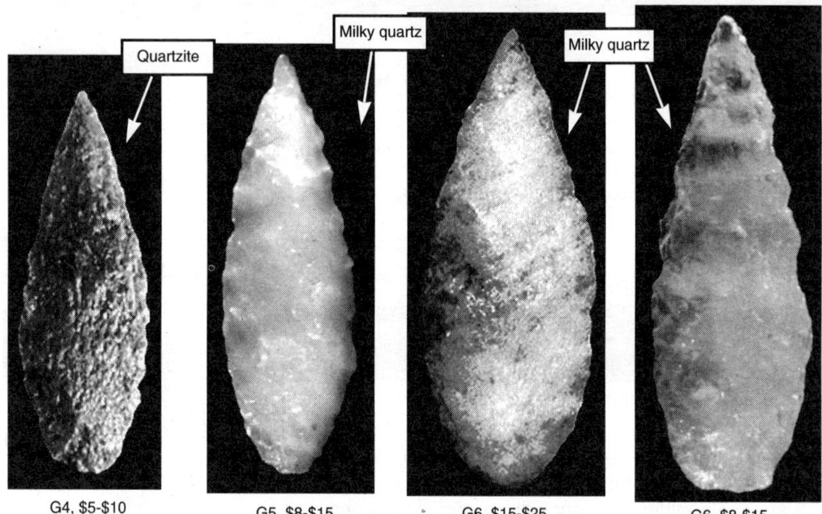

G4, $5-$10
Sussex Co., VA.

G5, $8-$15
Randolph Co., NC.

G6, $15-$25
Fairfield Co., SC.

G6, $8-$15
Randolph Co., NC.

LOCATION: North Carolina and surrounding areas. **DESCRIPTION:** A medium to large size, thick, narrow, lanceolate point with a convex, contracting base. This type is usually made of Quartzite or other poor quality flaking material which results in a more crudely chipped form than *Lerma* (its ancestor). **I.D. KEY:** Thickness, archaic blade flaking.

G6, $20-$40
Chester Co., SC.

G8, $20-$40
Randolph Co., NC.

GUILFORD-STEMMED - Middle Archaic, 6500 - 5000 B. P.

(Also see Stanly Narrow Stem, Waratan and Yadkin Eared)

ES

G5, $6-$12
Dinwiddie Co., VA.

G4, $5-$10
Sussex Co., VA.

G5, $15-$30
Daw Island, SC.

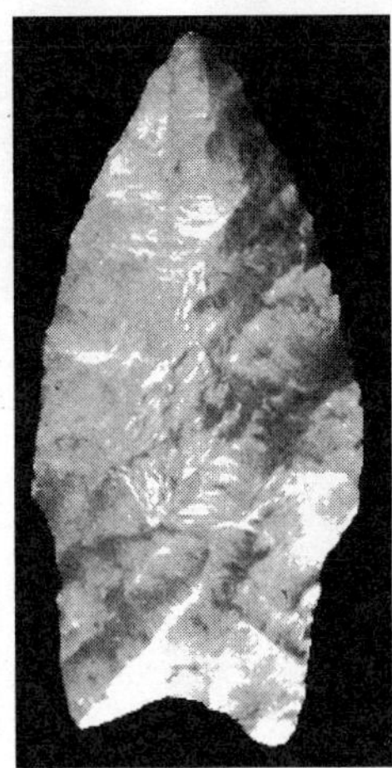

G6, $20-$40
Orangeburg Co., SC.

G6, $25-$50
Daw Island, SC.

LOCATION: Far Eastern states. **DESCRIPTION:** A medium size, thick, narrow, lanceolate point with a straight to concave, contracting base. All examples have weak, tapered shoulders. Some bases are ground. Called *Briar Creek* in Georgia.

GUILFORD-STRAIGHT BASE - Middle Archaic, 6500 - 5000 B. P.

(Also see Fox Creek)

G4, $5-$10
Rowan Co., NC.

LOCATION: Far Eastern states. **DESCRIPTION:** A medium size, thick, narrow, lanceolate point with a contracting stem and a straight base. This point is similar to *Greene* points, a later period New York Woodland type.

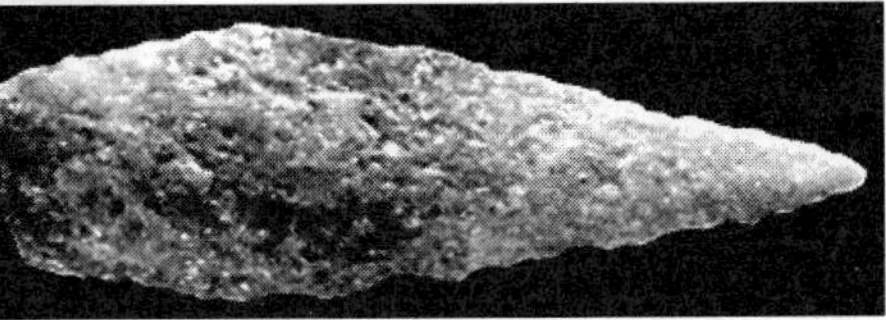

G4, $5-$10
Dinwiddie Co., VA.

GUILFORD-STRAIGHT BASE (continued)

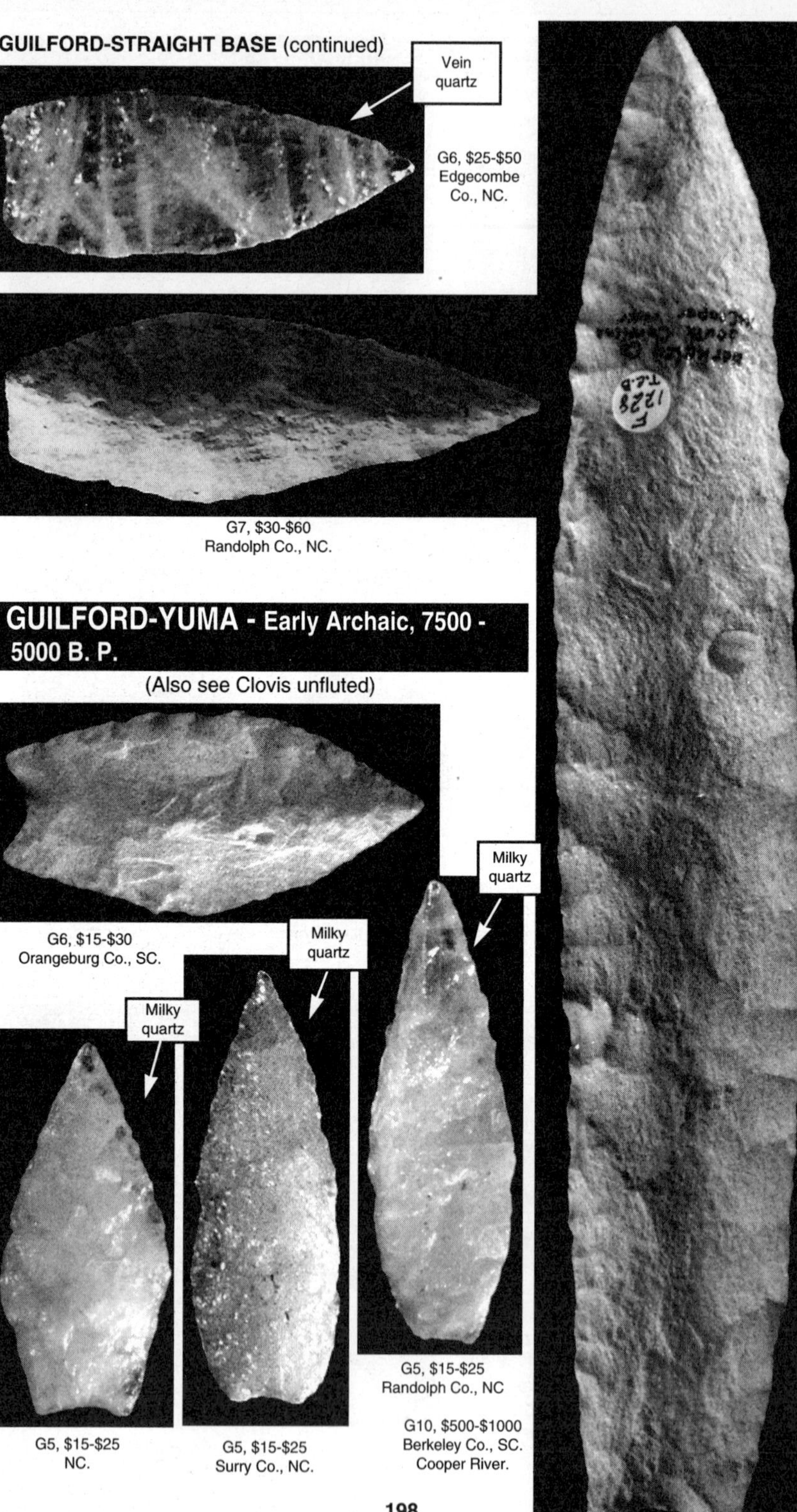

G6, $25-$50
Edgecombe Co., NC.

G7, $30-$60
Randolph Co., NC.

GUILFORD-YUMA - Early Archaic, 7500 - 5000 B. P.

(Also see Clovis unfluted)

G6, $15-$30
Orangeburg Co., SC.

G5, $15-$25
Randolph Co., NC

G10, $500-$1000
Berkeley Co., SC.
Cooper River.

G5, $15-$25
NC.

G5, $15-$25
Surry Co., NC.

GUILFORD YUMA (continued)

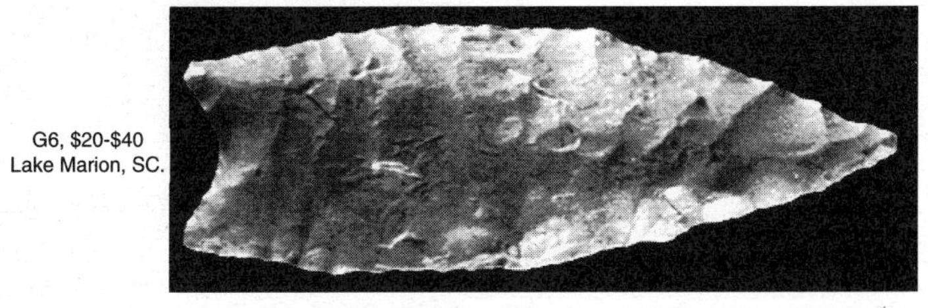

G6, $20-$40
Lake Marion, SC.

LOCATION: Far Eastern states. **DESCRIPTION:** A medium to slightly large size, thick, narrow, lanceolate point witth a contracting stem and a concave base. Quality of flaking is governed by the type of material, usually quartzite, slate, rhyolite and shale. Bases can be ground. Believed to be an early form for the type and may be related to the *Conerly* type.

GYPSY - Woodland, 2500 - 1500 B. P.

(Also see Dovetail)

LOCATION: North Carolina. **DESCRIPTION:** A small to medium size triangular point with a bulbous stem. Shoulders are usually well defined and can be barbed. **I.D. KEY:** Bulbous base.

G8, $15-$30
Surry Co., NC.

HALIFAX - Middle to Late Archaic, 6000 - 3000 B. P.

(Also see Holmes and Rowan)

Tip nick

G1, .50-$1
Mason Co., WVA.

Milky quartz

G2, $2-$4
Southampton Co., VA.

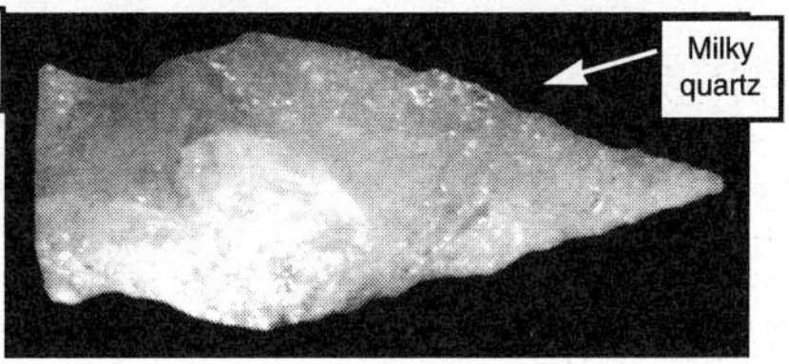

Milky quartz

G3, $3-$6
Sussex Co., VA.

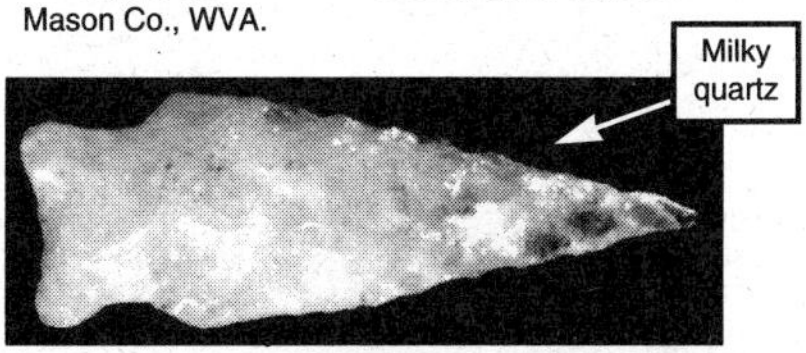

Milky quartz

G7, $4-$8
Sussex Co., VA.

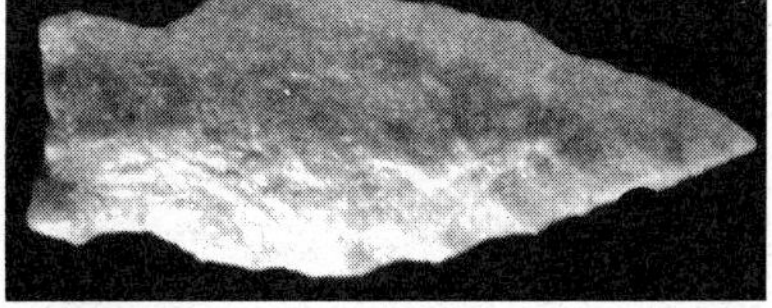

G5, $5-$10
Sussex Co., VA.

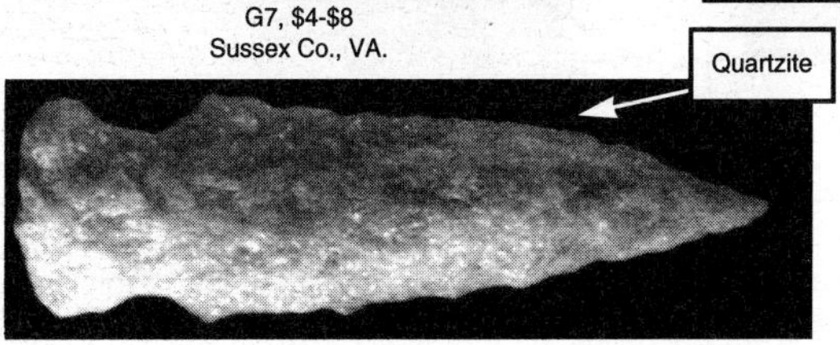

Quartzite

G6, $15-$25
Dinwiddie Co., VA.

HALIFAX (continued)

G6, $15-$25
Dinwiddie Co., VA.

LOCATION: Southeastern states. **DESCRIPTION:** A small to medium size, narrow, side notched to expanded stemmed point. Shoulders can be weak to strongly tapered. Typically one shoulder is higher than the other. North Carolina examples are made of quartz, rhyolite and shale.

HARDAWAY - Late Paleo, 9500 - 8000 B. P.

(Also see Alamance, Hardaway-Dalton, Patrick Henry and Taylor)

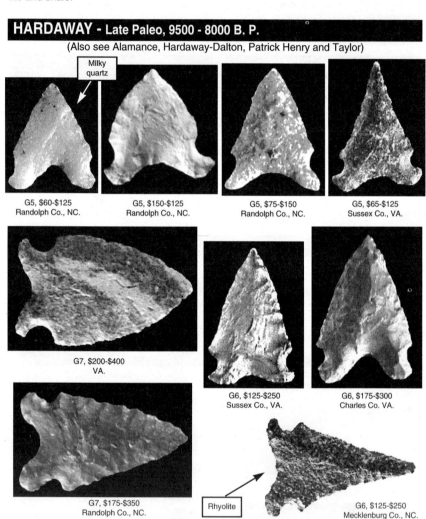

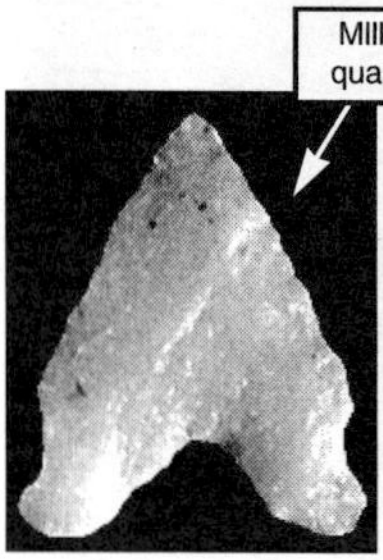

Milky quartz

G5, $60-$125
Randolph Co., NC.

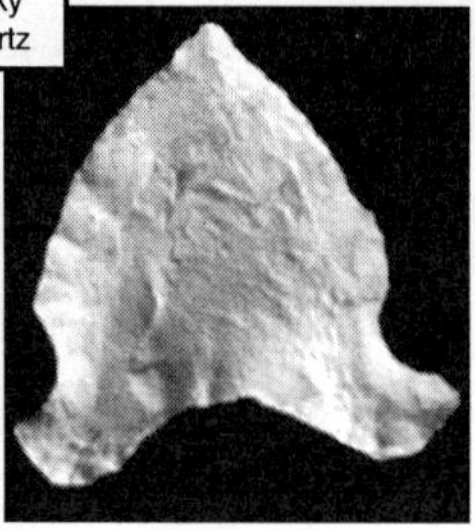

G5, $150-$125
Randolph Co., NC.

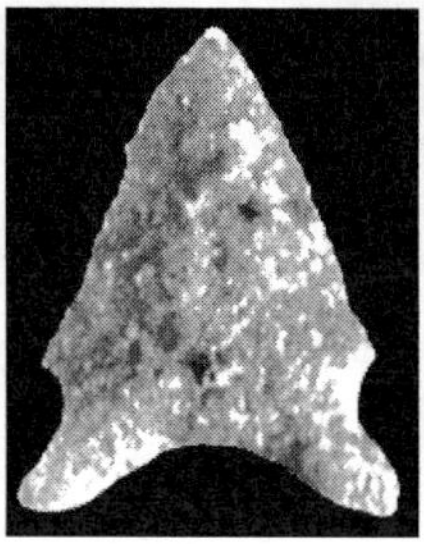

G5, $75-$150
Randolph Co., NC.

G5, $65-$125
Sussex Co., VA.

G7, $200-$400
VA.

G6, $125-$250
Sussex Co., VA.

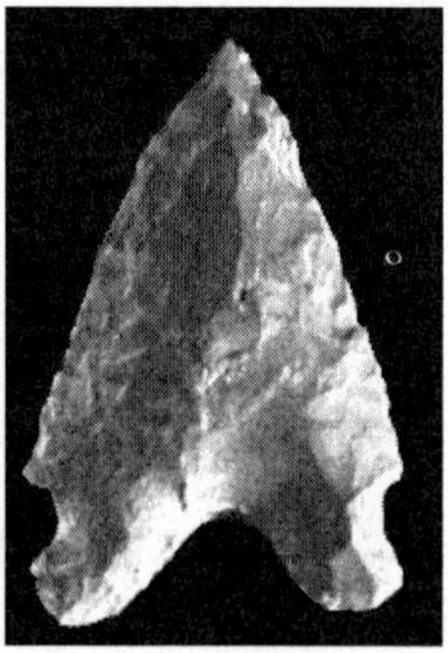

G6, $175-$300
Charles Co. VA.

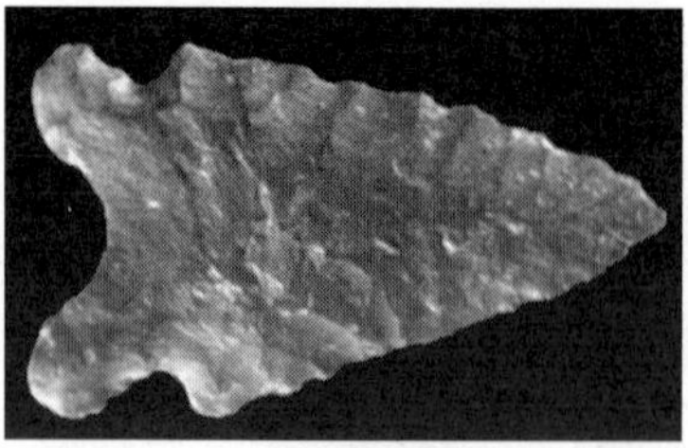

G7, $175-$350
Randolph Co., NC.

Rhyolite

G6, $125-$250
Mecklenburg Co., NC.

LOCATION: Southeastern states, especially North Carolina. Type site is Stanly Co. NC, Yadkin River. **DESCRIPTION:** A small to medium size point with shallow side notches and expanded auricles forming a wide, deeply concave base. Wide specimens are called *Cow Head Hardaways* in North Carolina. Ears and base are usually heavily ground. This type evolved from the *Dalton* point. **I.D. KEY:** Heavy grinding in shoulders, paleo flaking.

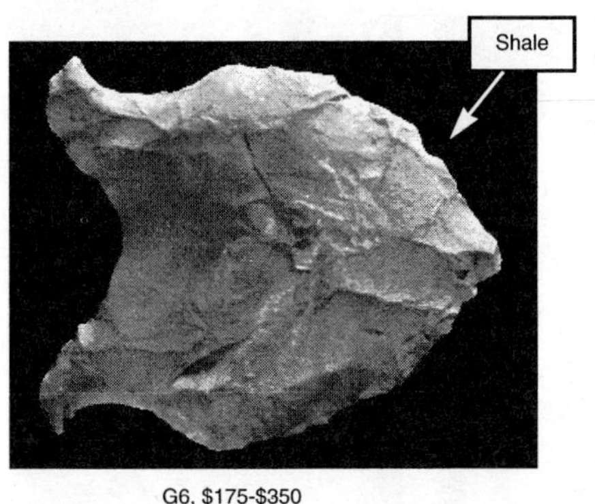

G6, $175-$350
Cent. NC.

G8, $300-$550
Cent. NC.

G6, $150-$300
Moore Co., NC.

G6, $100-$200
Moore Co., NC.

G7, $225-$450
Montgomery Co., NC.

HARDAWAY BLADE - Late Paleo, 9500 - 9000 B. P.

(Also see Alamance)

LOCATION: North Carolina. **DESCRIPTION:** A small to medium size, thin, broad, blade with a concave base. The base usually is ground and has thinning strikes. A preform for the *Hardaway* point.

G4, $20-$40
Cent. NC.

HARDAWAY-DALTON - Late Paleo, 9500 - 8000 B. P.

(Also see Alamance and Hardaway)

LOCATION: Southeastern states. **DESCRIPTION:** A small to medium size, serrated, auriculate point with a concave base. Basal fluting or thinning is common. Bases are ground. Ears turn outward or have parallel sides. A cross between *Hardaway* and *Dalton*. **I.D. KEY:** Width of base, location found.

G5, $75-$150
Randolph Co., NC.

G5, $90-$175
Cent. NC.

G7, $250-$500
Randolph Co., NC.

G5, $100-$200
Harnet Co., NC.

G8 $400-$800
Randolph Co., NC.

G7, $300-$550
Davidson Co., NC.

G8, $225-$450
Montgomery Co., NC.

G9, $450-$900
Randolph Co., NC.

HARDAWAY PALMER - Transitional Paleo, 9500 - 8000 B. P.

(Also see Hardaway and Palmer)

G9, $65-$125
Montgomery Co., NC.

LOCATION: Southeastern states. **DESCRIPTION:** A cross between *Hardaway* and *Palmer* with expanded auricles and a concave base that is ground.

HEAVY DUTY - Early to Middle Archaic, 7000 - 5000 B. P.

(Also see Appalachian, Kirk Serrated and Southampton)

LOCATION: Eastern states. **DESCRIPTION:** A medium to large size, thick, serrated point with a parallel stem and straight to slightly concave base. A variant of *Kirk Serrated* found in the Southeast. **I.D. KEY:** Base, thickness, flaking.

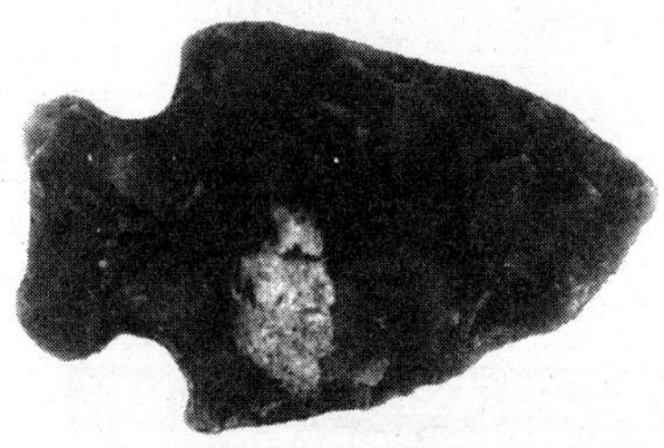

G4, $10-$20
Putnam Co., WVA.

HILLSBORO - Historic, 300 - 200 B. P.

(Also see Caraway and Clarksville)

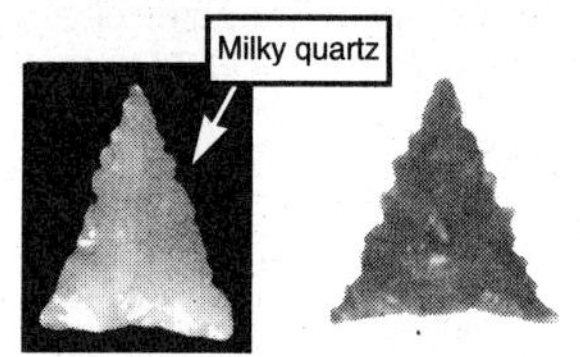

G3, $3-$7
Randolph Co., NC.

G4, $8-$15
Randolph Co., NC.

G4, $8-$15
Randolph Co., NC.

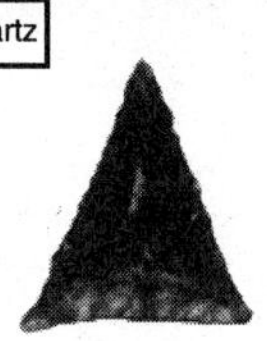

G4, $8-$15
Randolph Co., NC.

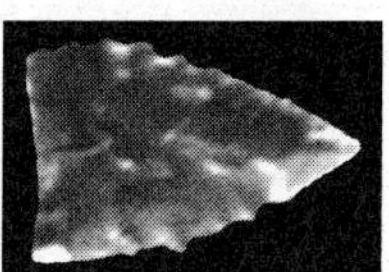

G6, $8-$15
Randolph Co., NC.

LOCATION: North Carolina. **DESCRIPTION:** A small size, thin, triangular, arrow point with a straight to concave base. Blade edges can be serrated. Smaller than Badin to very small size.

HOLMES - Late Archaic, 4000 - 3000 B. P.

(Also see Savannah River, Southampton and Stanly Narrow Blade)

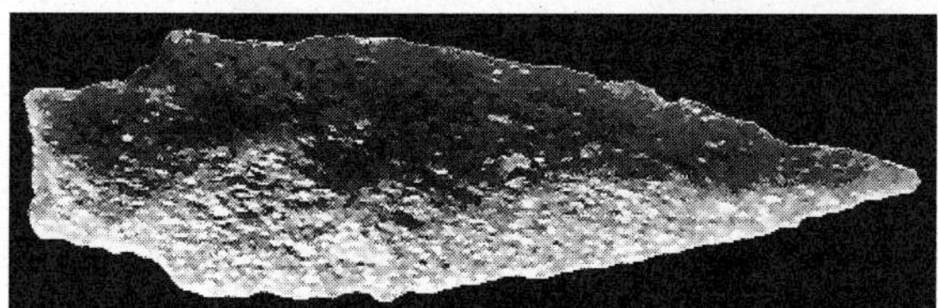

LOCATION: Far Eastern states. **DESCRIPTION:** A medium size, narrow point with weak, tapered shoulders and a slight concave base.

G5, $10-$20
Sussex Co., VA.

JACKS REEF CORNER NOTCHED - Late Woodland to Mississippian, 1500 - 1000 B. P.

(Also see Kirk Corner Notched)

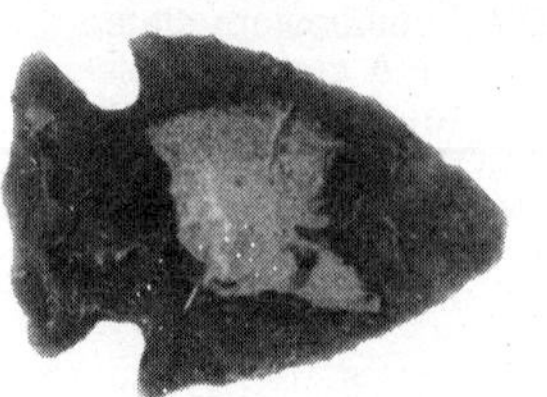

G4, $10-$20
Mason Co., WV.

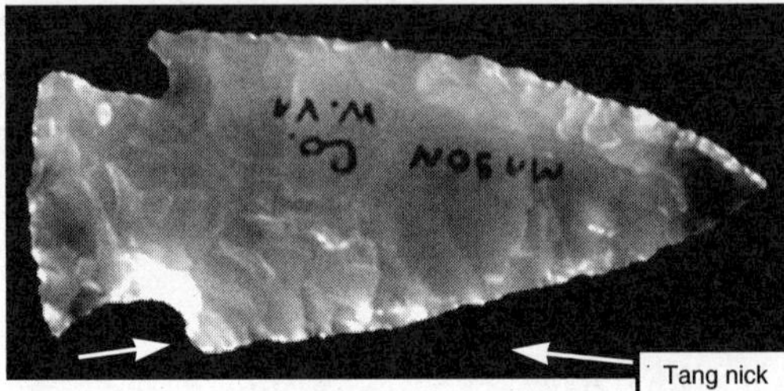

G6, $20-$40
Mason Co., WV.

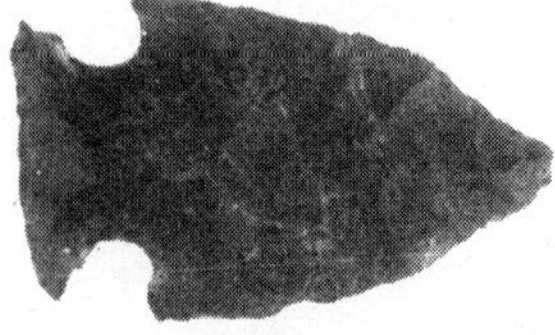

G4, $10-$20
Mason Co., WV.

LOCATION: Southeastern states. **DESCRIPTION:** A small to medium size, very thin, cornoer notched point that is well made. The blade is convex to pentagonal. Some examples are widely corner notched and appear to be expanded stem points with barbed shoulders. Rarely, they are basal notched. **I.D. KEY:** Thinness, made by the birdpoint people.

JACKS REEF PENTAGONAL

(See Peedee)

JUDE - Early Archaic, 9000 - 6000 B. P.

(Also see Fox Valley, Garth Slough, Halifax and LeCroy)

G3, $3-$5
Montgomery Co., NC.

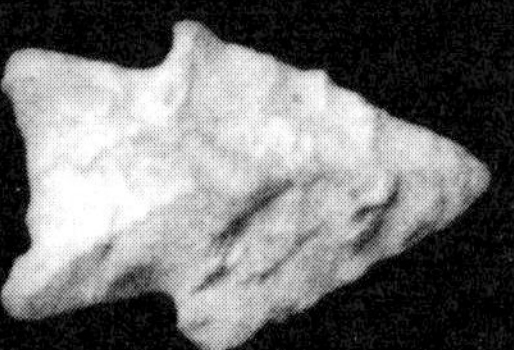

LOCATION: Southeastern states. **DESCRIPTION:** A small size, short, barbed, expanded to parallel stemmed point. Stems can be as large as the blade. Rare in this area. **I.D. Key:** Basal form and flaking.

G5, $8-$15
Montgomery Co., NC.

KANAWHA - Early Archaic, 9000 - 5000 B. P.

(Also see Fox Valley, Kirk Serrated-Bifurcated, LeCroy, St. Albans, Southampton, Stanly)

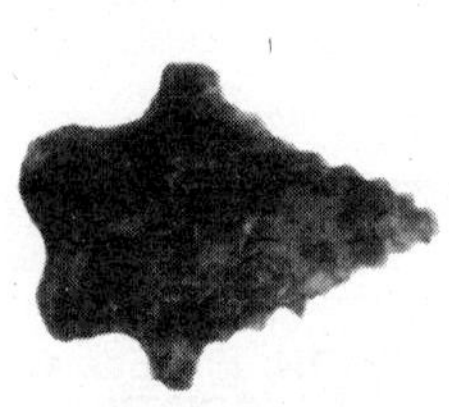

G3, $5-$10
Kanawha Co., WVA.

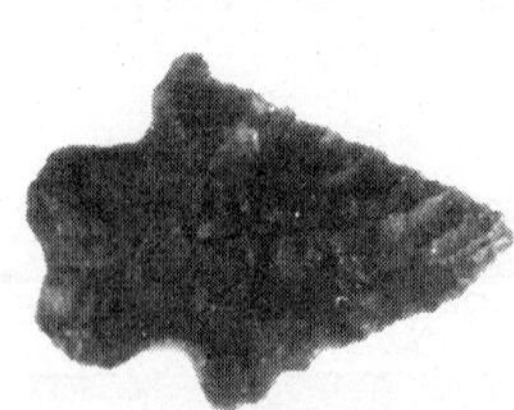

G5, $10-$20
Kanawha Co., WVA.

G8, $20-$40
Roch Branch, WVA.

LOCATION: Type site is in Kanawha Co., WVA. Eastern to Southeastern states. **DESCRIPTION:** A small to medium size, fairly thick, shallowly bifurcated stemmed point. The basal lobes are usually rounded and the shoulders tapered. Believed to be the ancestor to the *Stanly* type. The St. Albans site dated Kanawha to 8,200 B.P.

KIRK CORNER NOTCHED - Early to Middle Archaic, 9000 - 6000 B. P.

(Also see Bolen, Dovetail, Jacks Reef Corner Notched Lost Lake, Taylor and Thebes)

G2, $4-$8
St. Albans, WVA.

G7, $20-$40
Richmond Co., NC.

G5, $25-$50
Richmond Co., NC.

G6, $30-$60
Randolph Co., NC.

G8, $60-$120
Central NC.

G7, $100-$200
Mason Co., WVA.

G7, $150-$300
Stokes Co., NC.

LOCATION: Eastern states. **DESCRIPTION:** A medium to large size, corner notched point. Blade edges can be convex to recurved and are finely serrated on many examples. The base can be convex, concave, straight or auriculate. Points that are beveled on one side of each face would fall under the *Lost Lake* type. **I.D. KEY:** Secondary edgework.

G8, $75-$150
Randolph Co., NC.

G6, $35-$70
Randolph Co., NC.

G5, $25-$50
Mason Co., WVA.

G8, $75-$150
Stokes Co., NC.

G10, $1500-$3000
Surry Co., NC.

KIRK SERRATED - Early to Middle Archaic, 9000 - 6000 B. P.

(Also see Bolen, Fountain Creek, Heavy Duty, and Stanly)

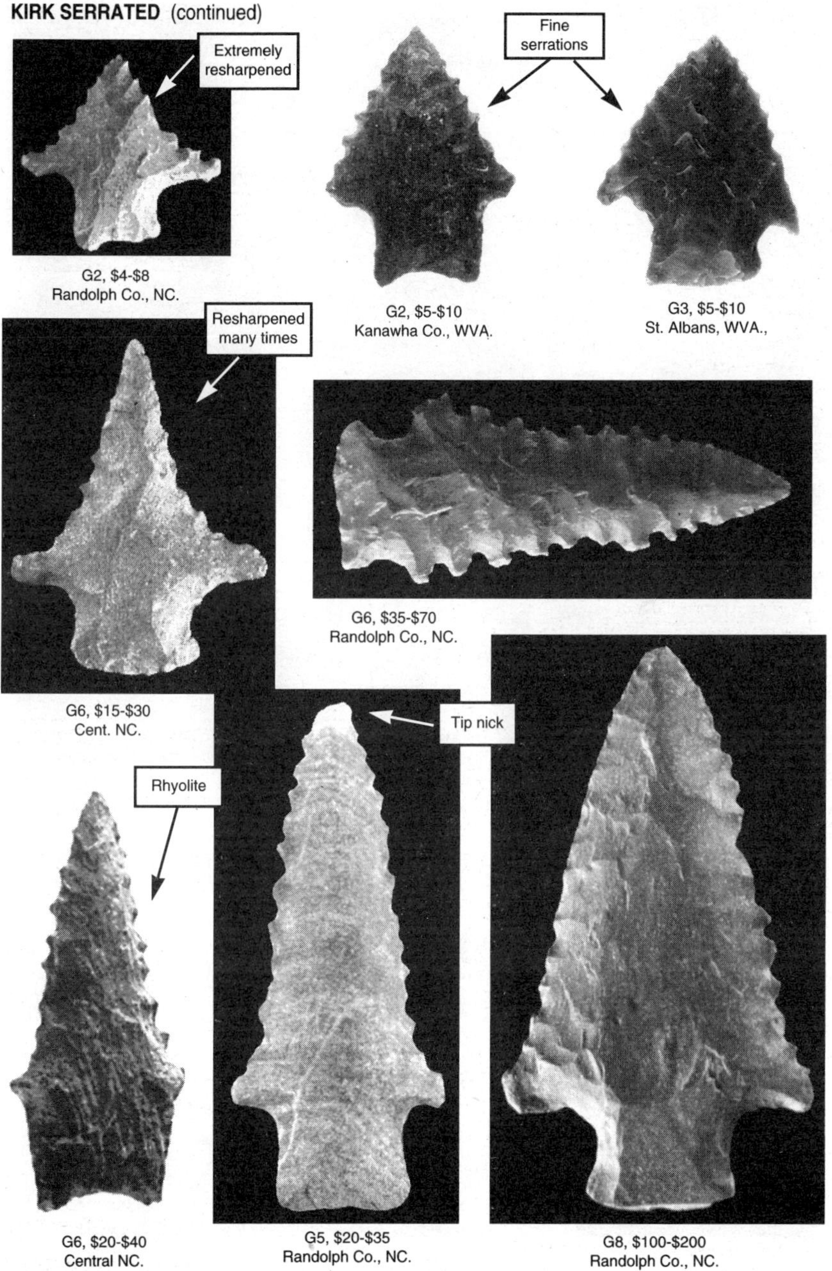

G2, $4-$8
Randolph Co., NC.

G2, $5-$10
Kanawha Co., WVA.

G3, $5-$10
St. Albans, WVA.,

G6, $35-$70
Randolph Co., NC.

G6, $15-$30
Cent. NC.

G6, $20-$40
Central NC.

G5, $20-$35
Randolph Co., NC.

G8, $100-$200
Randolph Co., NC.

LOCATION: Southeastern to Eastern states. **DESCRIPTION:** A medium to large size, barbed, stemmed point with deep notches or fine serrations along the blade edges. The stem is parallel to expanding. The stem sides may be steeply beveled on opposite faces. Some examples also have a distinct bevel on the right side of each blade edge. The base can be concave, convex or straight, and can be very short. The shoulders are usually strongly barbed. Believed to have evolved into *Stanly* and other types. The St. Albans site dated this type from 8,850 to 8,980 B.P. **I.D. KEY:** Serrations.

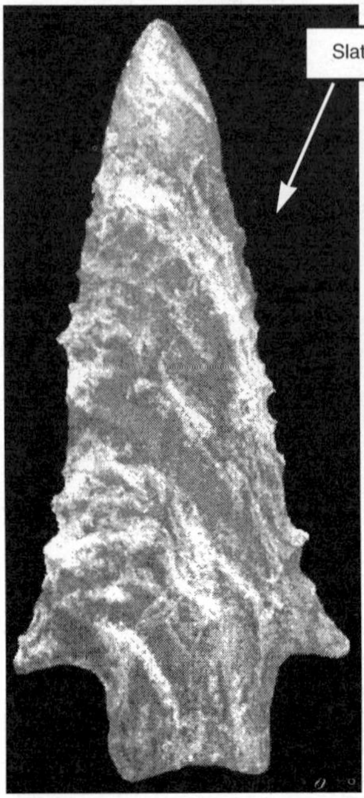

Slate

G8, $115-$225
Newberry Co., SC.

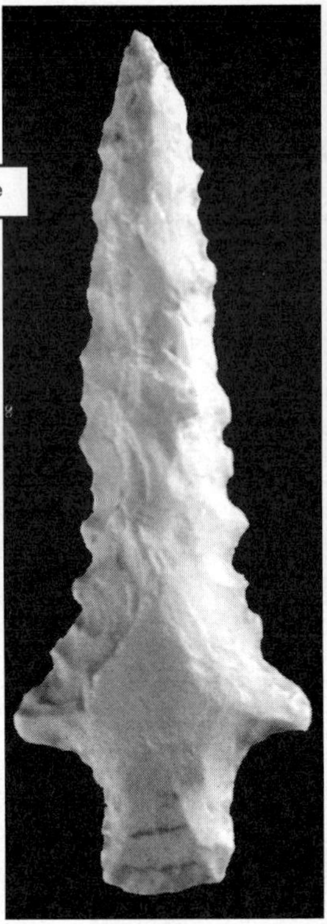

G9, $100-$200
Randolph Co., NC.

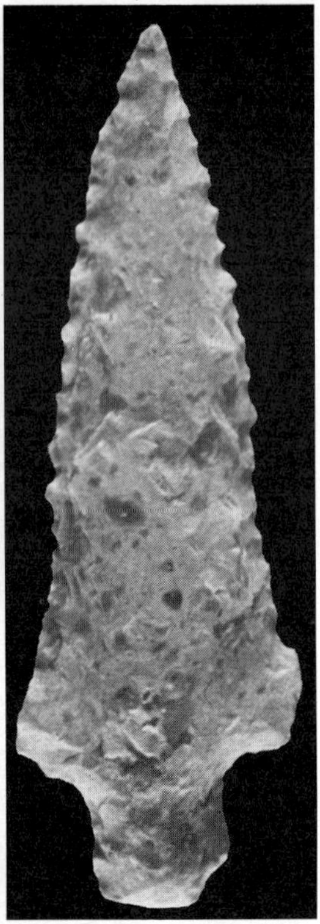

G8, $35-$70
Randolph Co., NC.

KIRK SERRATED-BIFURCATED - Early Archaic, 9000 - 7000 B. P.

(Also see Cave Spring, Fox Valley, LeCroy, St. Albans, Southhampton & Stanly)

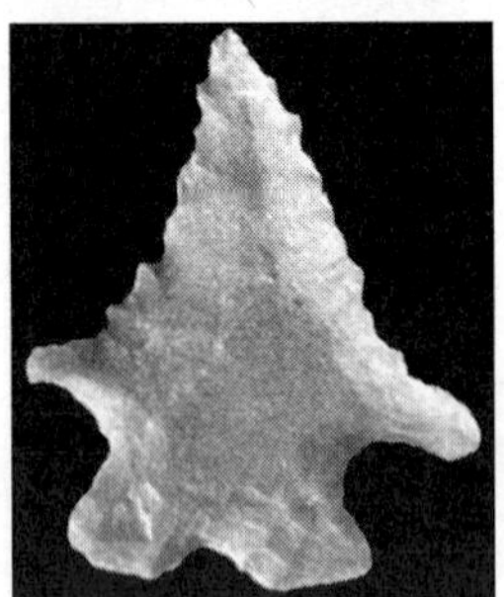

G7, $20-$35
Randolph Co., NC.

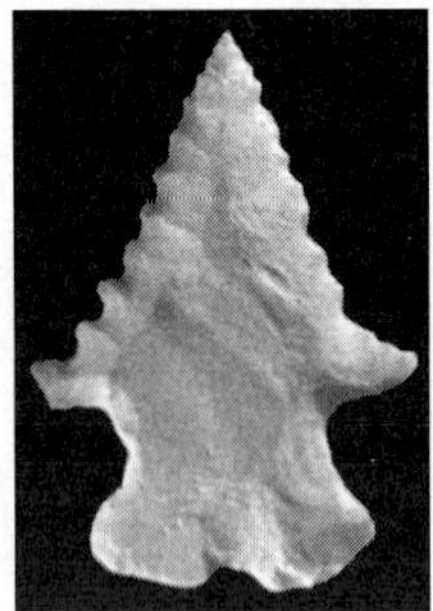

G6, $20-$35
Randolph Co., NC.

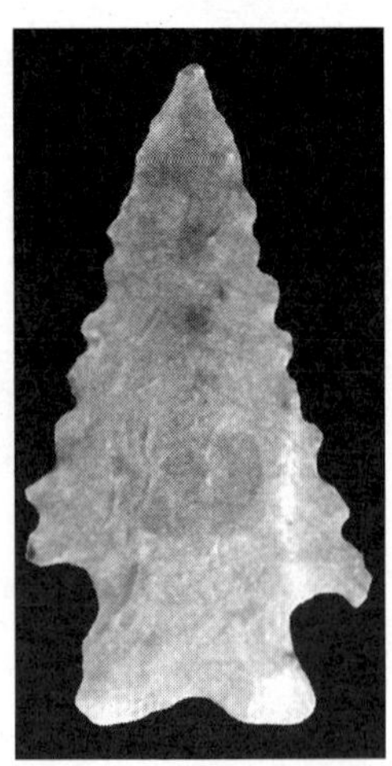

G6, $25-$45
Randolph Co., NC.

LOCATION: Southeastern to Eastern states. **DESCRIPTION:** A medium to large point with deep notches or fine serrations along the blade edges. The stem is parallel sided to expanded and is bifurcated. Believed to be an early form for the type which later developed into *Stanly* and others. Some examples have a steep bevel on the right side of each blade edge.

G7, $65-$125
Cabell Co., WVA.

G8, $40-$80
Randolph Co., NC.

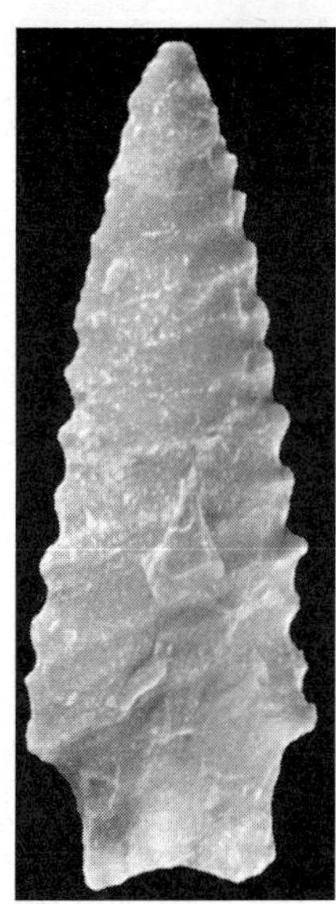
G6, $15-$30
Randolph Co., NC.

KIRK SIDE NOTCHED - Early to Middle Archaic, 9000 - 6000 B. P.

(Also see Big Sandy, Otter Creek)

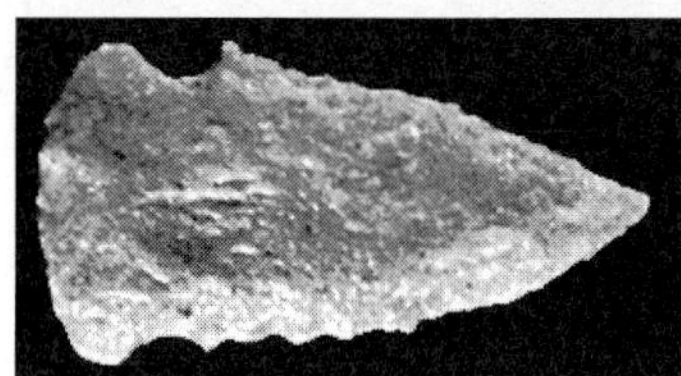
G6, $5-$10
Sussex Co., VA.

G6, $20-$40
Randolph Co., NC.

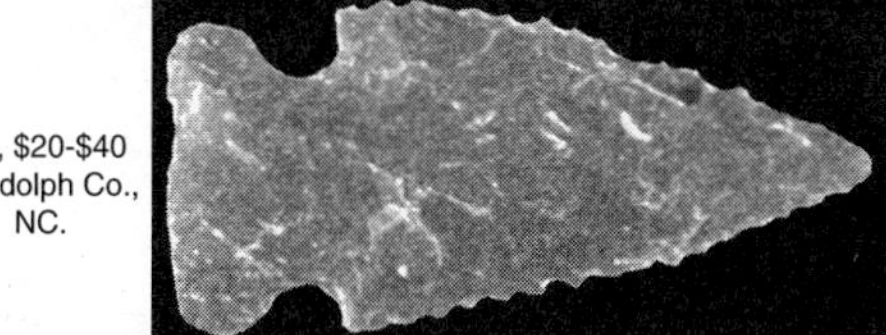

LOCATION: Eastern states. **DESCRIPTION:** A medium to large size, side notched point with basically horizontal shoulders. Edges can be serrated. **I.D. KEY:** Base form, Kirk edgework.

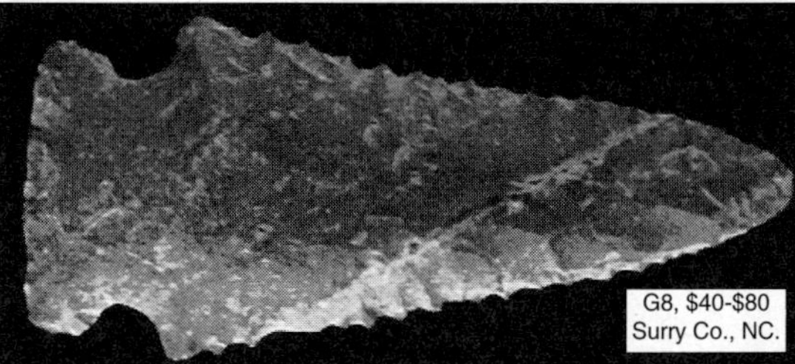
G8, $40-$80
Surry Co., NC.

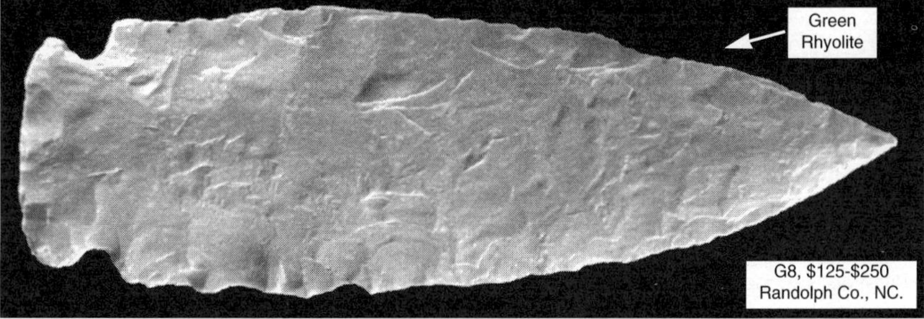

G8, $125-$250
Randolph Co., NC.

LECROY - Early to Middle Archaic, 9000 - 5000 B. P.

(Also see Decatur, Fox Valley, Kanawha, Kirk Serrated-Bifurcated, St. Albans, Southampton and Stanly)

G4, $10-$20
Wilkes Co., NC.

G4, $10-$20
Emporia Co., VA.

G5, $15-$30
Stokes Co., NC.

G5, $15-$25
Randolph Co., NC.

G8, $20-$35
Guilford Co., NC.

G5, $15-$30
GuilfordCo., NC.

G7, $20-$35
Randolph Co., NC.

G7, $15-$30
Rockingham Co., NC.

G6, $15-$30
Rockingham Co., NC.

G7, $25-$45
Randolph Co., NC.

G8, $20-$40
Randolph Co., NC.

LOCATION: Southeastern states. Type site-Hamilton Co., TN. **DESCRIPTION:** A small to medium size, thin, usually broad point with deeply notched or serrated blade edges and a deeply bifurcated base. Basal ears can either droop or expand out. The stem is usually large in comparison to the blade size. Some stem sides are fractured in Northern examples *(Lake Erie)*. Bases are usually ground. St. Albans site dated *LeCroy* to 8,300 B.P. **I.D. KEY:** Basal form.

LOST LAKE - Early Archaic, 9000 - 6000 B. P.

(Also see Bolen, Decatur, Dovetail, Kirk Corner Notched, Palmer and Taylor)

LOCATION: Southeastern states. **DESCRIPTION:** A medium to large size, broad, corner notched point that is beveled on one side of each face. The beveling continues when resharpened and creates a flat rhomboid cross section. Most examples are finely serrated and exhibit high quality flaking and symmetry. Also known as *Deep Notch.* **I.D. KEY:** Notching, secondary edgework is always opposite creating at least slight beveling.

LOST LAKE (continued)

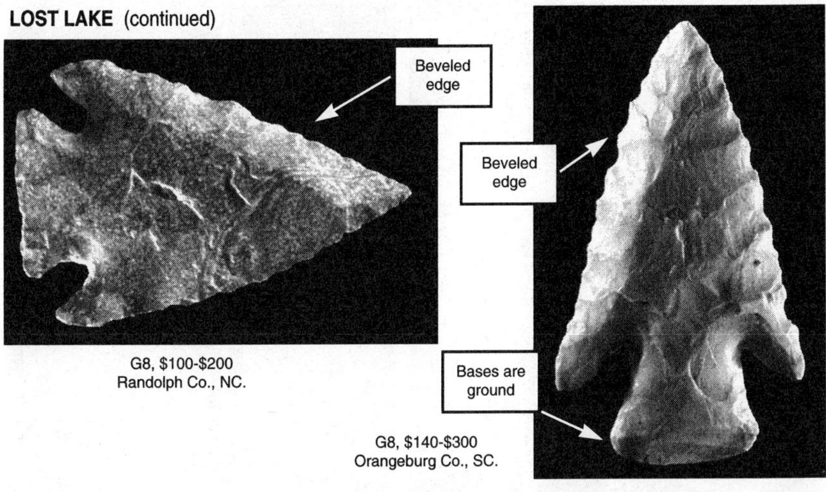

G8, $100-$200
Randolph Co., NC.

G8, $140-$300
Orangeburg Co., SC.

MORROW MOUNTAIN - Middle Archaic, 7000 - 5000 B. P.

(Also see Adena and Randolph)

G6, $8-$15
Randolph Co., NC.
Type II.

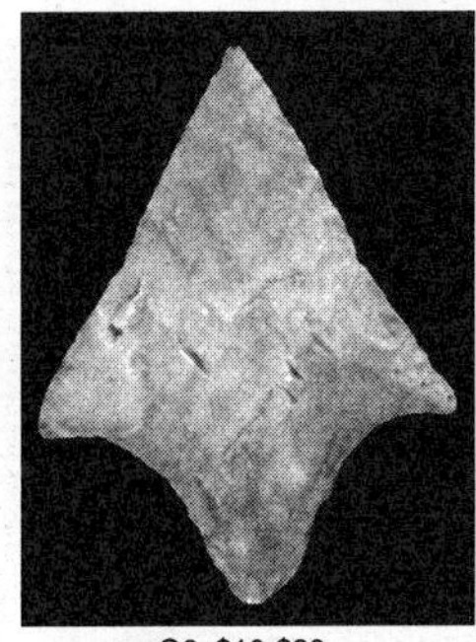

G6, $10-$20
Randolph Co., NC.
Type I.

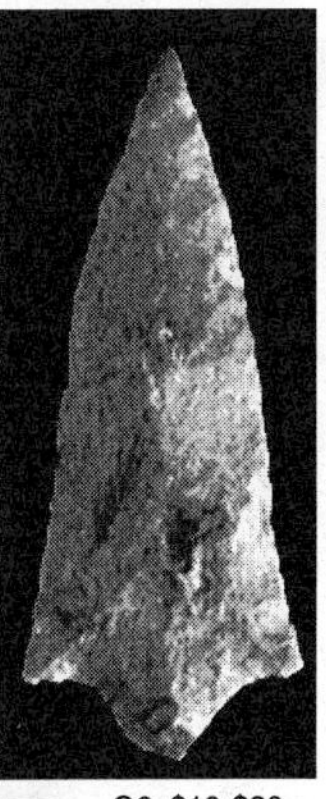

G6, $10-$20
Moore Co., NC.
Type II.

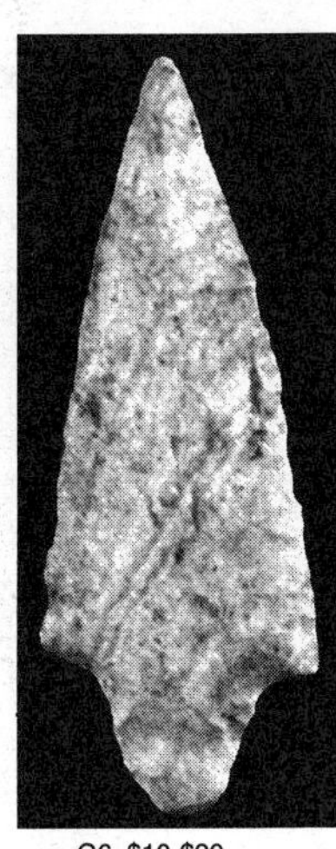

G6, $10-$20
Randolph Co., NC. Type II

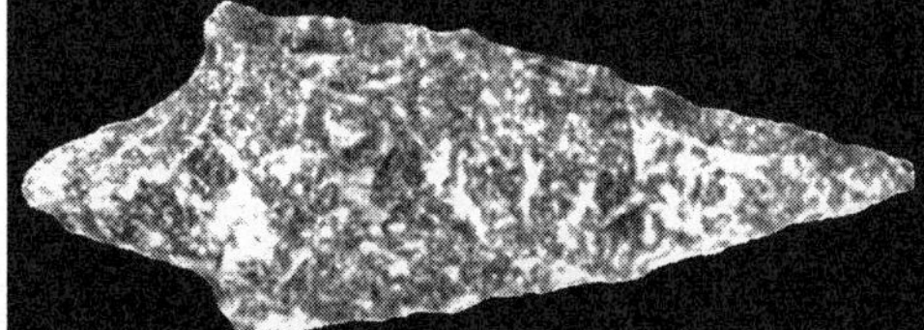

G6, $15-$25
Randolph Co., NC. Type II.

LOCATION: Midwestern to Southeastern states. **DESCRIPTION:** A medium to large size, triangular point with a very short contracting to rounded stem. Shoulders are usually weak but can be barbed. The blade edges on some examples are serrated with needle points. **I.D. KEY:** Contracted base and Archaic parallel flaking.

G7, $15-$25
Randolph Co., NC. Type I

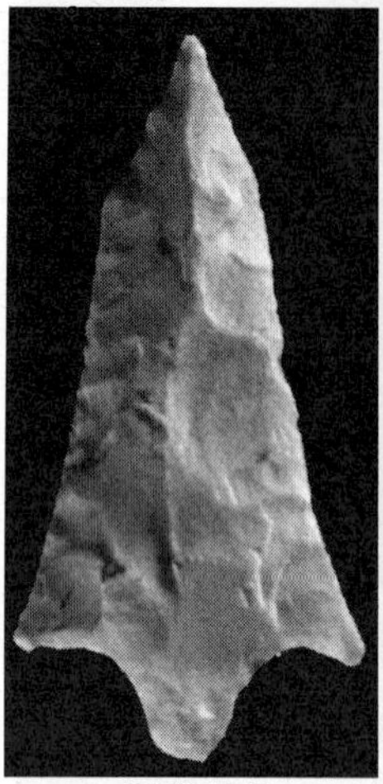

G7, $25-$45
Randolph Co., NC.

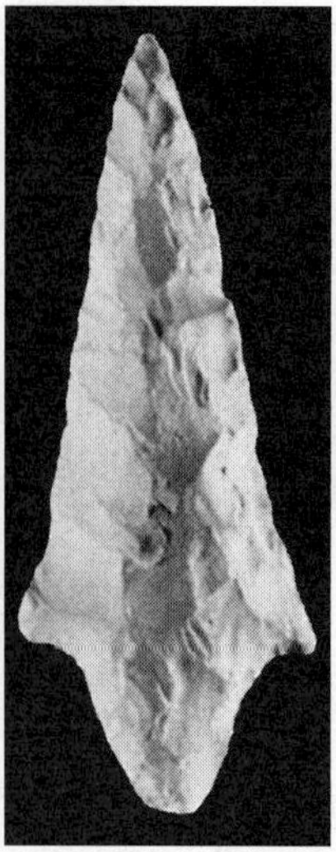

G7, $25-$45
Randolph Co., NC. Type II

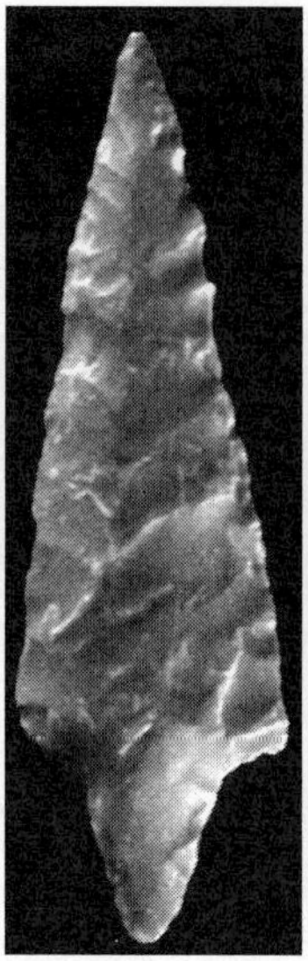

G7, $25-$45
Randolph Co., NC. Type II

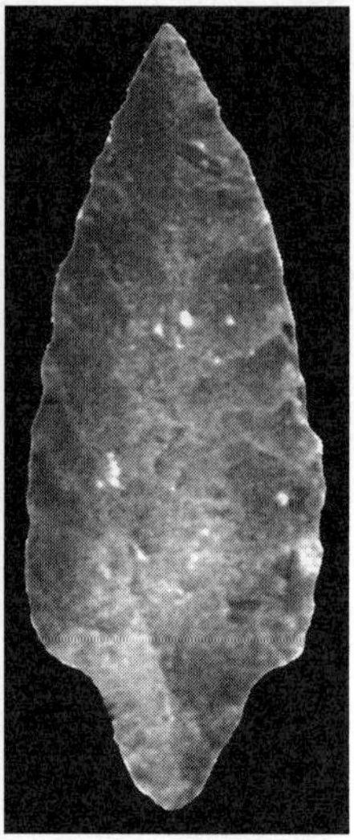

G7, $25-$45
Randolph Co., NC. Type I

Quartzite

Milky quartz

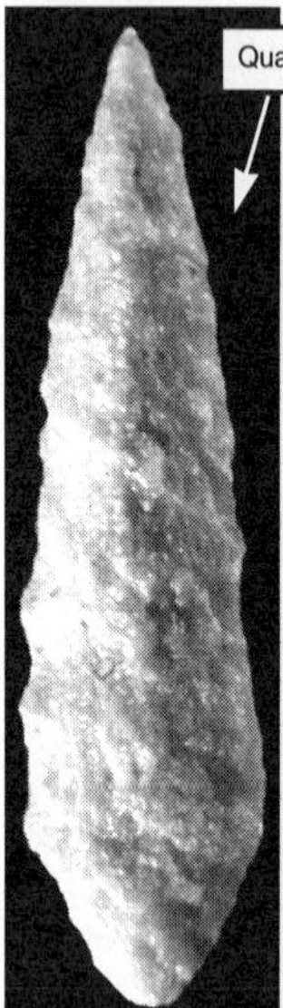

G7, $15-$25
Randolph Co., NC..,
Type II

G9, $25-$50
Randolph Co., NC.
Type II

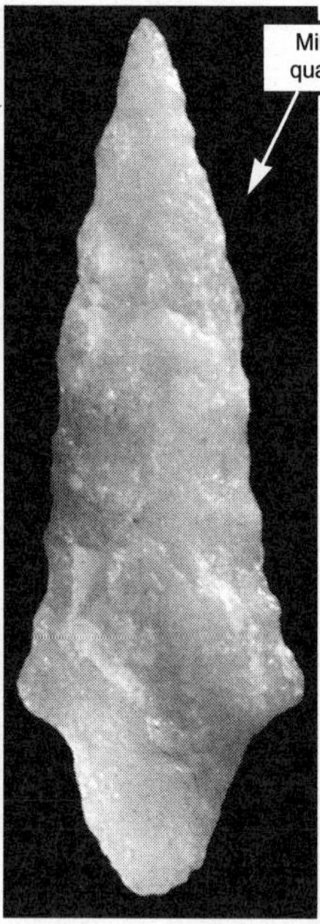

G9, $35-$70
Randolph Co., NC.
Type II

G9, $45-$90
Randolph Co., NC.
Type I

G8, $25-$50
Montgomery Co., NC.
Type II

ES

MORROW MOUNTAIN STRAIGHT BASE - Middle Archaic, 7000 - 5000 B. P.

(Also see Adena and Savannah River)

LOCATION: Southeastern states. **DESCRIPTION:** A medium size, thin, strongly barbed point with a contracting stem and a straight base. Some examples are serrated and have a needle tip. Look for Archaic parallel flaking.

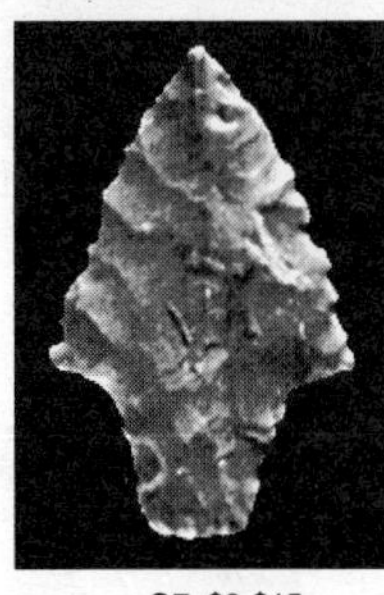

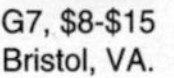

G7, $8-$15
Bristol, VA.

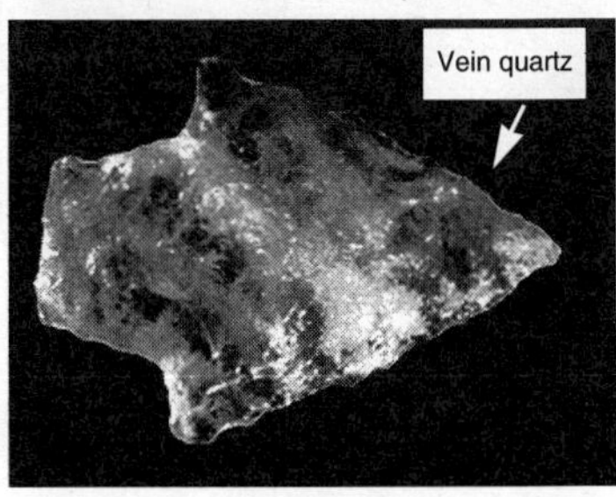

G7, $10-$20
Johnson Co., NC.

OCCANEECHEE - Mississippian to Historic, 600 - 400 B. P.

(Also seeYadkin)

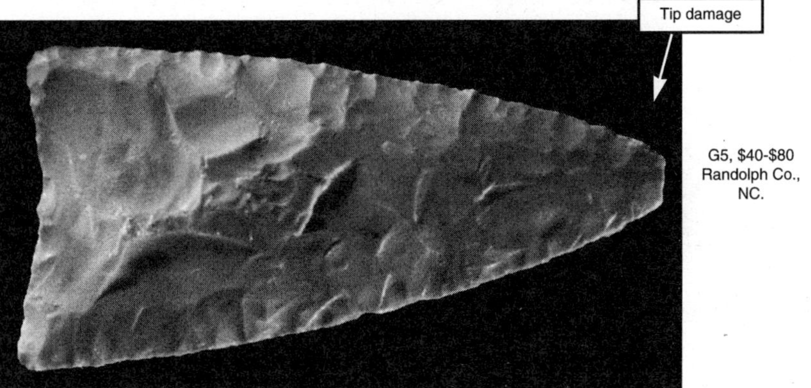

G5, $40-$80
Randolph Co., NC.

LOCATION: North Carolina. **DESCRIPTION:** A large size triangular point with a concave base. Base corners can be sharp to rounded.

OTTER CREEK - Middle to Late Archaic, 6000 - 3500 B. P.

(Also see Big Sandy and Rowan)

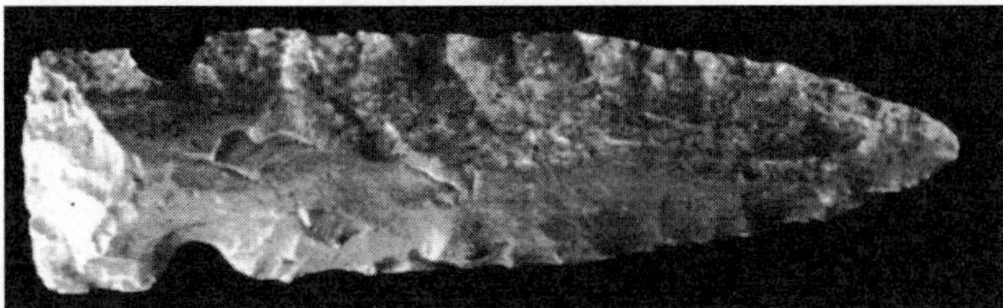

G6, $15-$30
Bethany, WVA.

LOCATION: Northeastern states. **DESCRIPTION:** A medium to large size, narrow side-notched point with a straight, concave or convex base. Notching is prominent, shoulders are tapered to barbed. Bases are ground. **I.D. KEY:** Side notching.

PALMER - Early Archaic, 9000 - 6000 B. P.

(Also see Ecusta, Hardaway-Palmer, Kirk Corner Notched and Taylor)

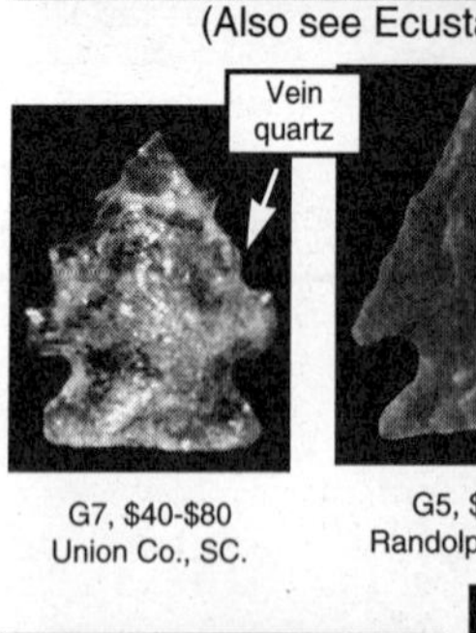

G7, $40-$80
Union Co., SC.

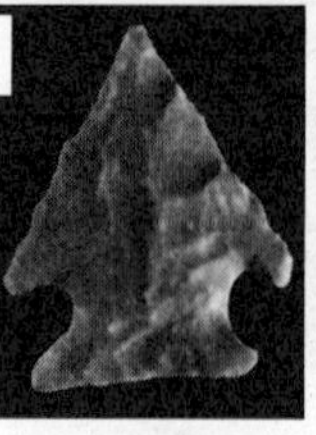

G5, $15-$30
Randolph Co., NC.

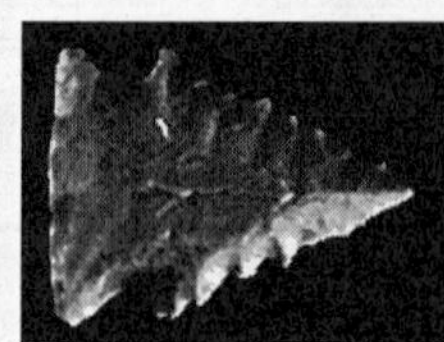

G6, $25-$50
Wayne Co., NC.

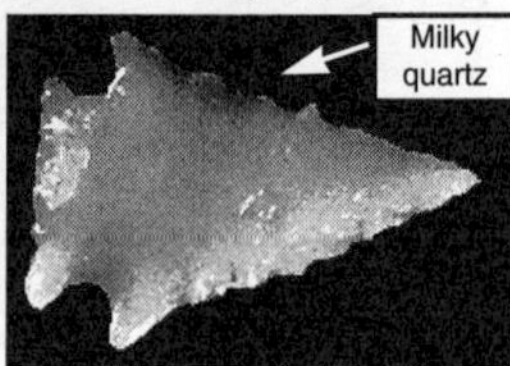

G7, $25-$50
Surry Co., NC.

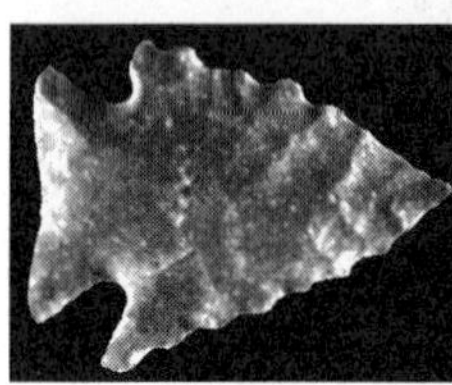

G6, $20-$35
Randolph Co., NC.

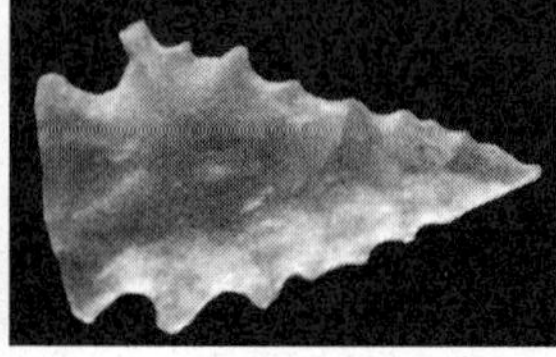

G7, $25-$45
Randolph Co., NC.

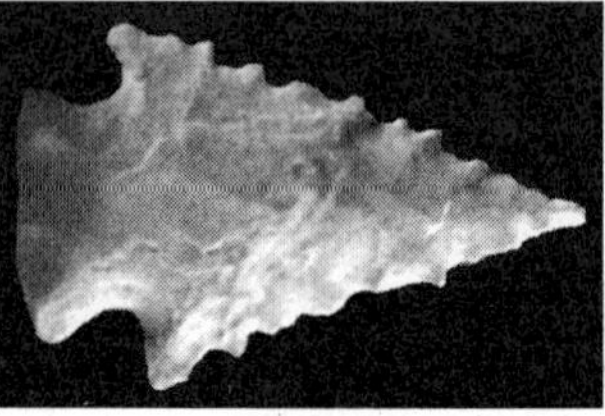

G8, $50-$100
Randolph Co., NC.

G8, $50-$100
Rockingham Co., NC.

G6, $25-45
Putnam Co., WVA.

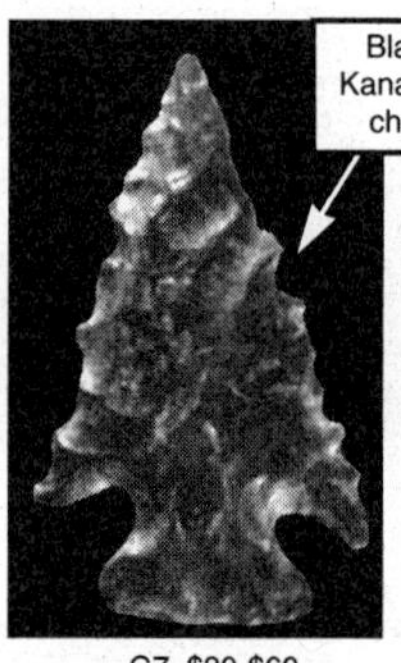

G7, $30-$60
Putnam Co., WVA.

G10, $100-$200
Randolph Co., NC.

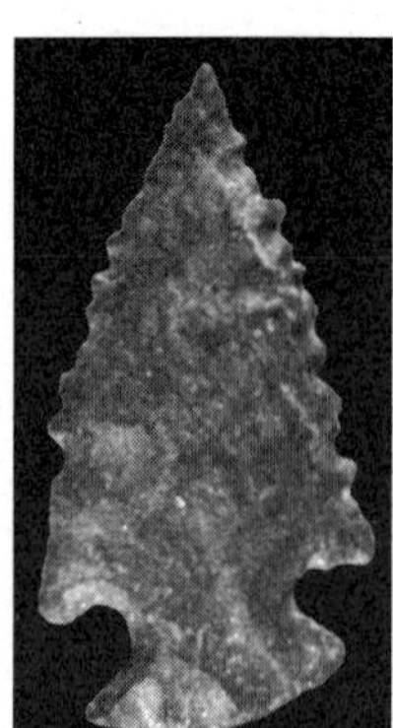

G7, $90-$175
Putnam Co., WV.

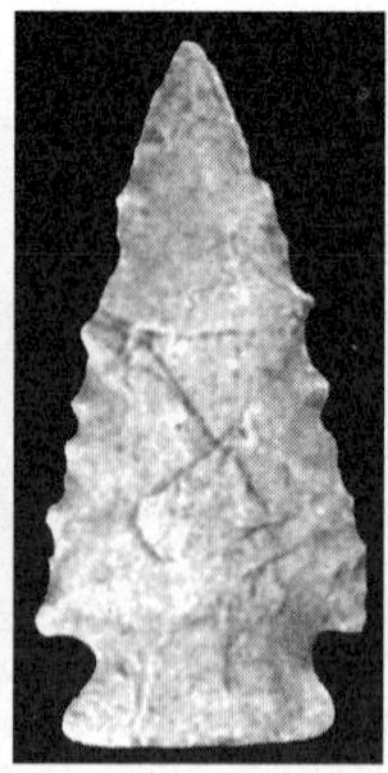

G3, $5-$10
Randolph Co., NC.

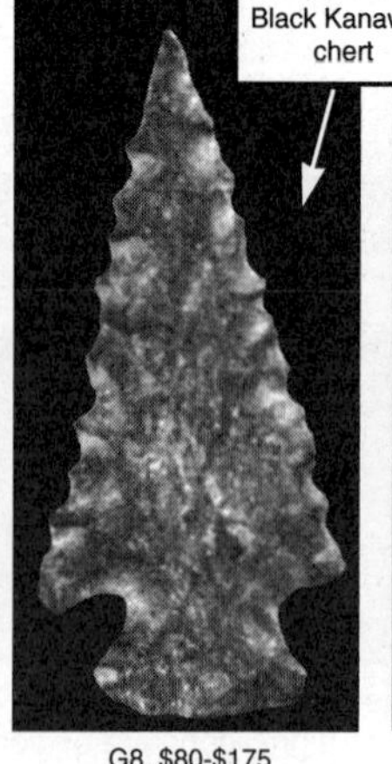

G8, $80-$175
Putnam Co., WVA.

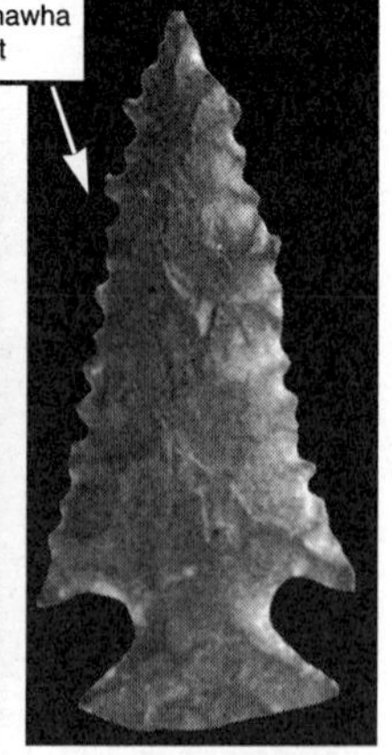

G9, $120-$225
Putnam Co., WV.

LOCATION: Southeastern to Eastern states. **DESCRIPTION:** A small size, corner notched, triangular point with a ground concave, convex or straight base. Many are serrated and large examples would fall under the *Pine Tree* or *Kirk* type. This type developed from *Hardaway* in North Carolina where cross types are found.

PATRICK HENRY - Early Archaic, 9500 - 8500 B. P.

(Also see Bolen, Decatur, Palmer and Taylor)

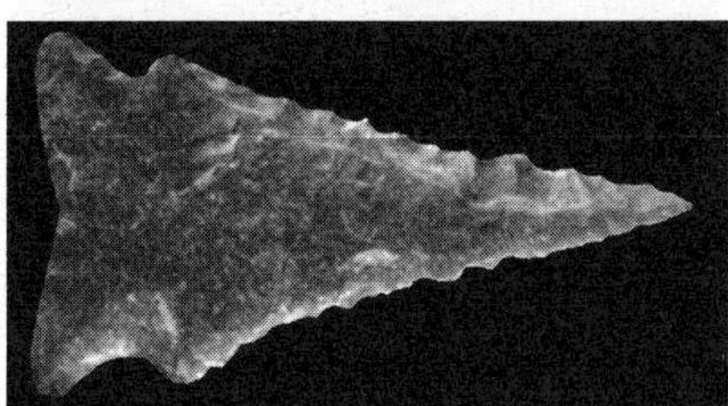

LOCATION: Eastern seaboard states. **DESCRIPTION:** A medium size corner notched point with a fish-tailed base. Blade edges can be serrated and the basal area is ground.

G8, $50-$100
Randolph Co., NC.

PEE DEE - Late Woodland to Mississippian, 1500 - 1000 B. P.

(Also see Caraway and Jacks Reef)

G3, $5-$10
Smyth Co., VA.

G2, $5-$8
Wilkes Co., NC.

G4, $10-$25
Yadkin Co., NC.

G7, $15-$30
Randolph Co., NC.

G2, $5-$8
Randolph Co., NC.

G5, $15-$30
Wilkes Co., NC.

G7, $20-$40
Randolph Co., NC.

LOCATION: Eastern seaboard states. **DESCRIPTION:** A small to large size, very thin, five sided point with a sharp tip. The hafting area is usually contracted with a slightly concave to straight base. Called *Jacks Reef* elsewhere.

POTTS - Woodland, 3000 - 1000 B. P.

(Also see Ecusta and Waratan)

LOCATION: Far Eastern states. **DESCRIPTION:** A medium size triangular point with a short, straight base that has shallow corner notches.

G5, $8-$15
Rockingham Co., NC.

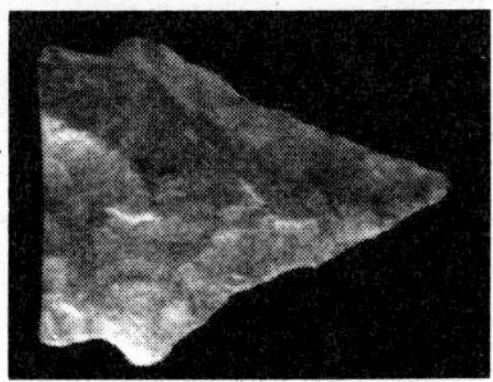

QUAD - Late Paleo, 10,000 - 6000 B. P.

(Also see Simpson and Waratan)

G5, $100-$225
Myrtle Beach, SC.

G7, $225-$450
Orangeburg Co., SC.

LOCATION: Southeastern states. **DESCRIPTION:** A medium to large size lanceolate point with flaring "squared" auricles and a concave base which is ground. Most examples show basal thinning and some are fluted. **I.D. KEY:** Paleo flaking, squarish auricles.

RANDOLPH - Woodland to Historic, 2000 - 200 B. P.

(Also see Morrow Mountain)

G2, $2-$5
Guilford Co., NC.

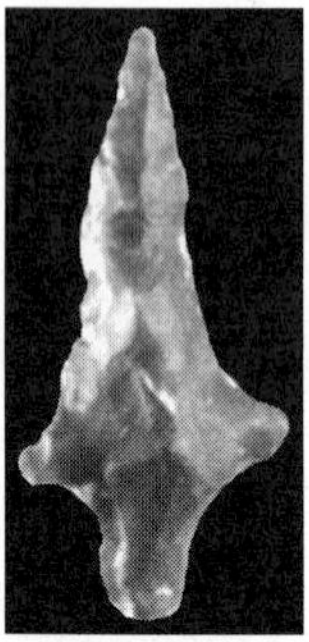

G4, $5-$10
Randolph Co., NC.

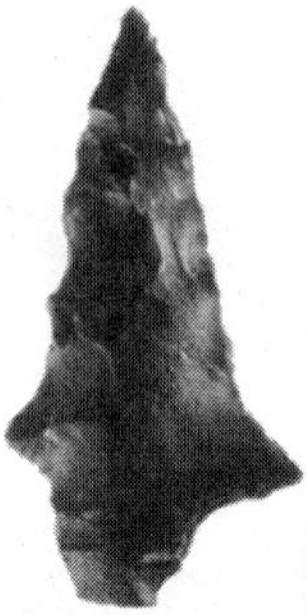

G5, $10-$20
Randolph Co., NC.

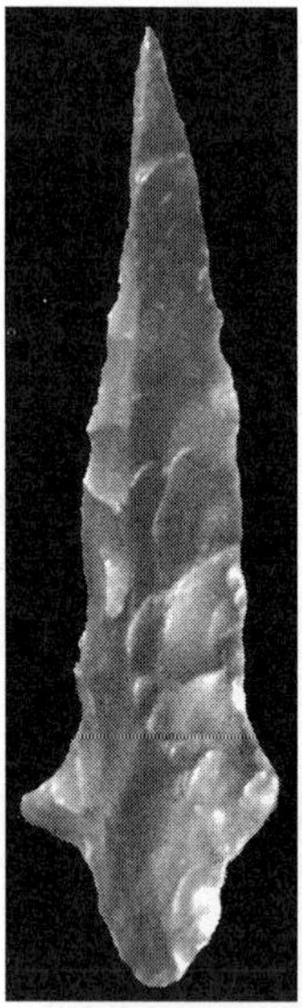

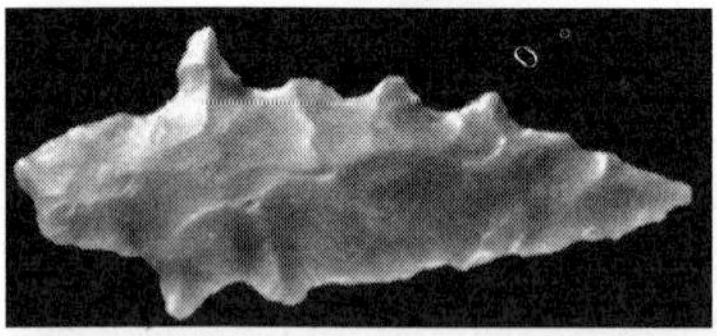

G8, $20-$35
Randolph Co., NC.

G8, $25-$50
Randolph Co., NC.

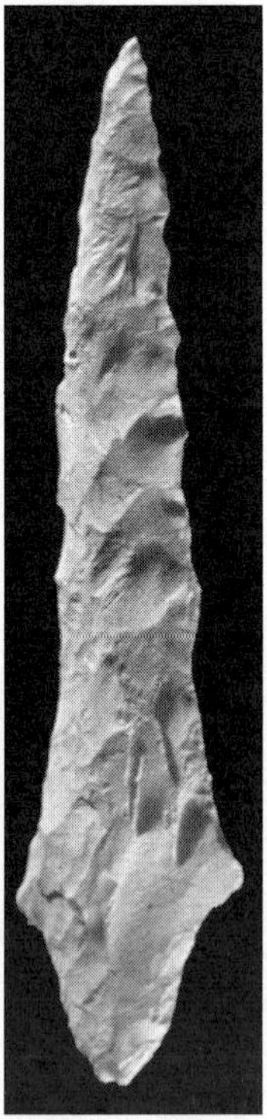

G9, $35-$65
Randolph Co., NC.

G8, $15-$30
Randolph Co., NC.

LOCATION: Far Eastern states. Type site is Randolph Co. NC. **DESCRIPTION:** A medium size, narrow, thick, spike point with tapered shoulders and a short to medium contracted, rounded stem. Many examples from North Carolina have exaggerated spikes along the blade edges.

REDSTONE - Paleo, 13,000 - 9000 B. P.

(Also see Clovis)

LOCATION: Southeastern states. **DESCRIPTION:** A medium to large size, thin, auriculate, fluted point with convex sides expanding to a wide, deeply concave base. The hafting area is ground. This point is widest at the base. Fluting can extend most of the way down each face. Multiple flutes are usual. (**Warning:** The most common resharpened *Clovis* point is often sold as this type. *Redstones* are extrememly rare and are almost never offered for sale.) **I.D. KEY:** Batan fluted, edgework on the hafting area.

G7, $600-$1,200
Randolph Co., NC.

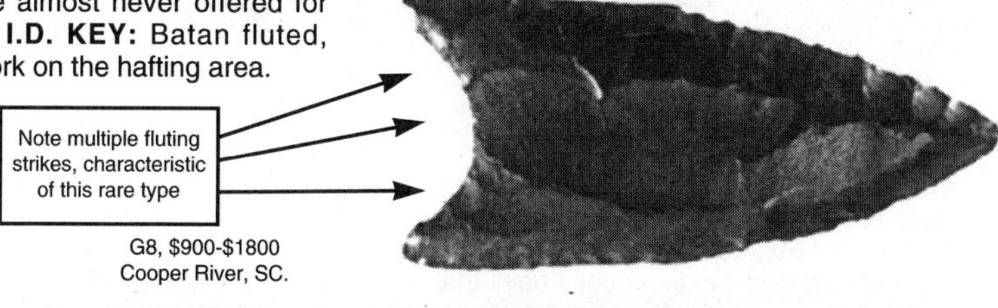

G8, $900-$1800
Cooper River, SC.

ROWAN - Transitional Paleo, 9500 - 8000 B. P.

(Also see Big Sandy and Bolen)

G5, $8-$15
Moore Co., NC.

G6, $15-$25
Randolph Co., NC.

G6, $15-$30
Randolph Co., NC.

G6, $15-$30
Randolph Co., NC.

G6, $20-$40
Randolph Co., NC.

G6, $25-$50
Randolph Co., NC.

ROWAN (continued)

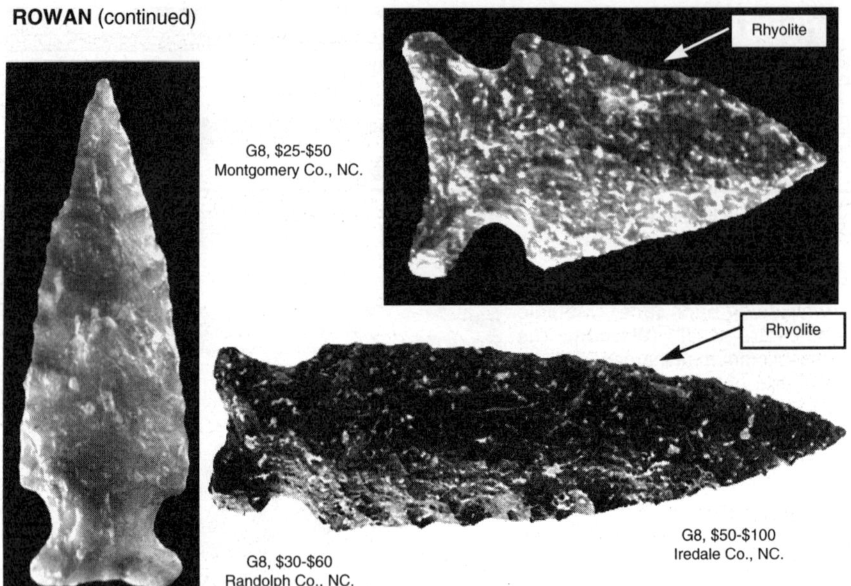

G8, $25-$50
Montgomery Co., NC.

G8, $30-$60
Randolph Co., NC.

G8, $50-$100
Iredale Co., NC.

LOCATION: Far Eastern states. Type site is Rowan Co., North Carolina. **DESCRIPTION:** A medium to large size, side-notched point that can be easily confused with the *Big Sandy* type. The basal area is usually wider than the blade. Some examples have expanded ears, and grinding commonly occurs around the basal area. Believed to be an intermediate form developing from *Dalton, Quad, Greenbrier* or *Hardaway* and changing into *Big Sandy* and other later side notched forms.

ST. ALBANS - Early to Middle Archaic, 9000 - 5000 B. P.

(Also see Decatur, Fox Valley, Kanawha, Kirk Serrated-Bifurcated, LeCroy, Southampton and Stanly)

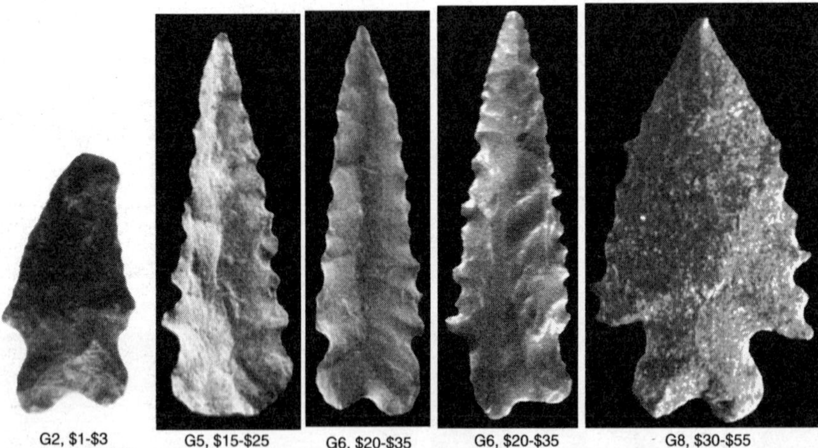

G2, $1-$3
Kanawha Co., WVA.

G5, $15-$25
Randolph Co., NC.

G6, $20-$35
Randolph Co., NC.

G6, $20-$35
Randolph Co., NC.

G8, $30-$55
Montgomery Co., NC.

LOCATION: Eastern states. **DESCRIPTION:** A small to medium size, usually serrated, bifurcated point. Basal lobes usually flare outward and most examples are sharply barbed. The basal lobes are more shallow than in the *LeCroy* type, otherwise they are easily confused. St. Albans site dated this type to 8,870 B.P. **I.D. KEY:** Shallow basal lobes.

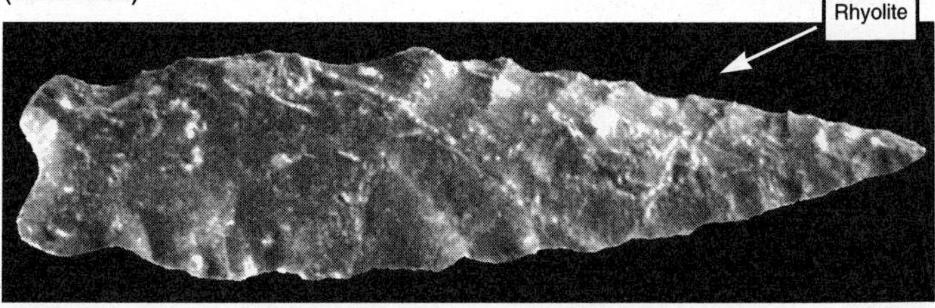

G7, $30-$60
Randolph Co., NC.

SAVANNAH RIVER - Middle Archaic to Woodland, 5000 - 2000 B. P.

(Also see Appalachian, Kirk and Stanly)

G5, $15-25
Raleigh, NC.

G5, $15-$25
Cent. NC.

Classic form

G4, $10-$20
Randolph Co., NC.

G7, $50-$100
Randolph Co., NC.

G7, $60-$120
Randolph Co., NC.

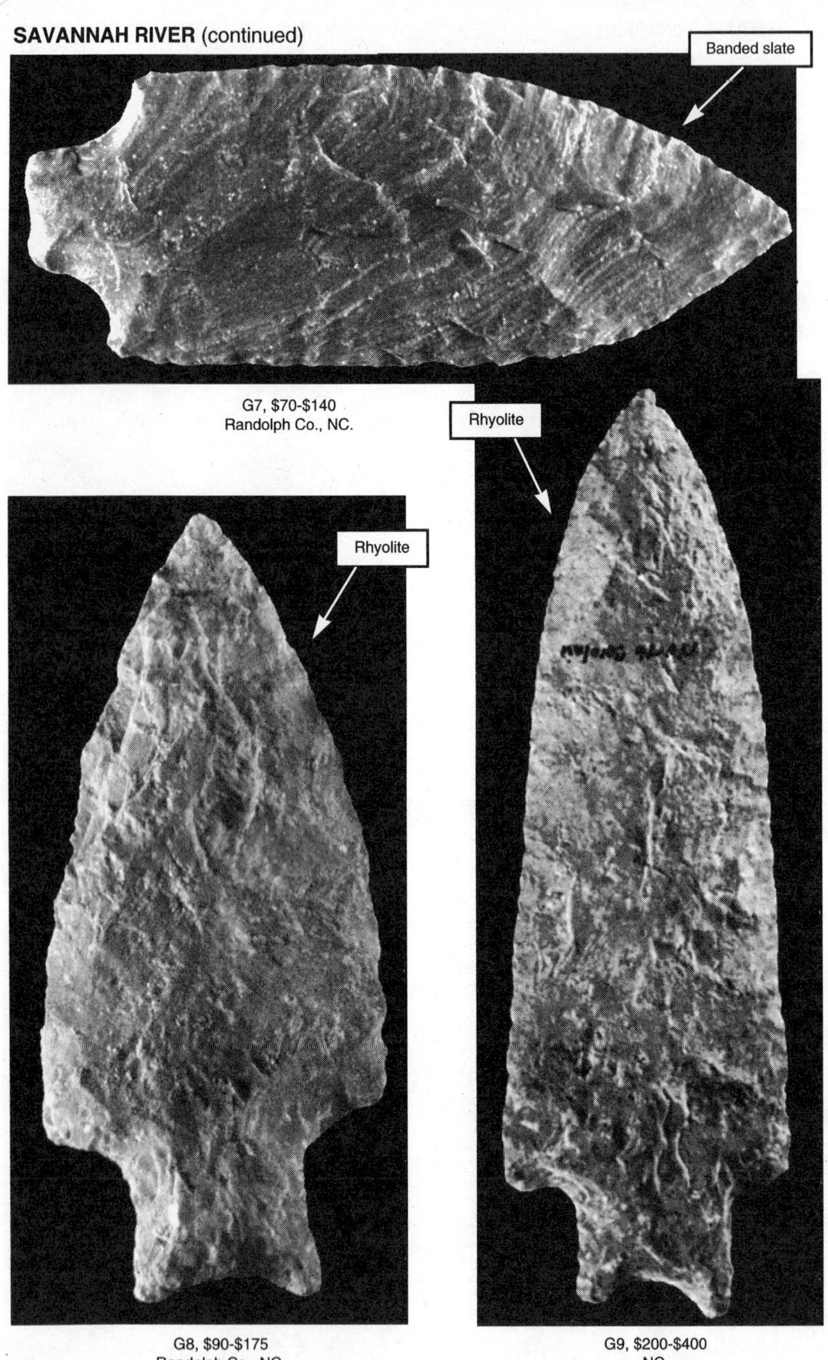

G7, $70-$140
Randolph Co., NC.

G8, $90-$175
Randolph Co., NC.

G9, $200-$400
NC.

LOCATION: Southeastern to Eastern states. **DESCRIPTION:** A medium to large size, straight to contracting stemmed point with a concave to bifurcated base. The shoulders are tapered to square. The stems are narrow to broad. Believed to be related to the earlier *Stanly* point.

SIMPSON - Late Paleo, 12,000 - 8000 B. P.

(Also see Clovis-unfluted and Quad)

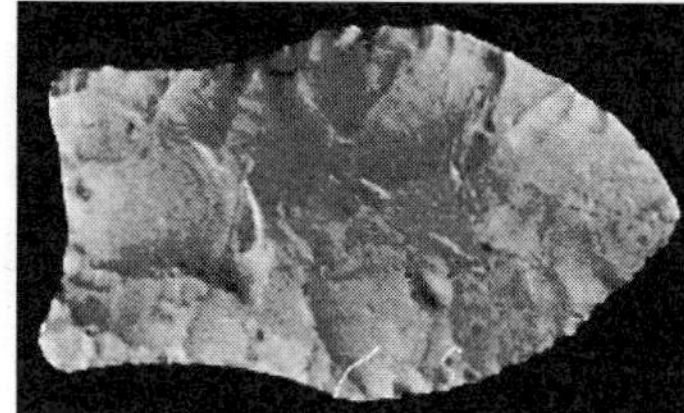

G4, $125-$250
Edgefield Co., SC.

LOCATION: Southern Southeastern states. **DESCRIPTION:** A medium to large size lanceolate, auriculate blade with recurved sides, outward flaring ears and a concave base. The hafting area constriction is more narrow than in the *Suwannee* type. Fluting is absent.

G10, $3000 -$6000 Lake Marion, SC.

SOUTHAMPTON - Early Archaic, 8000 - 6000 B. P.

(Also see Kanawha, St. Albans and Stanly)

G3, $3-$6
Sussex Co., VA.

G4, $5-$10
Southampton Co., VA.

Milky quartz

G5, $5-$10
Sussex Co., VA.

G5, $5-$10
Cent. NC.

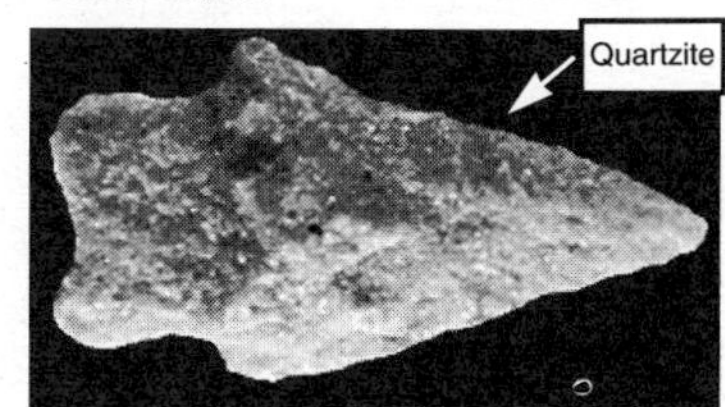

G5, $5-$10, Dinwiddie Co., VA.

LOCATION: Far Eastern states. **DESCRIPTION:** A medium to large size, narrow, thick, bifurcated stemmed point. The basal lobes can expand and the center notch is shallow. Bases are usually ground.

STANLY - Early Archaic, 8000 - 5000 B. P.

(Also see Fox Valley, Garth Slough, Kirk Serrated-Bifurcated, Savannah River and Southampton)

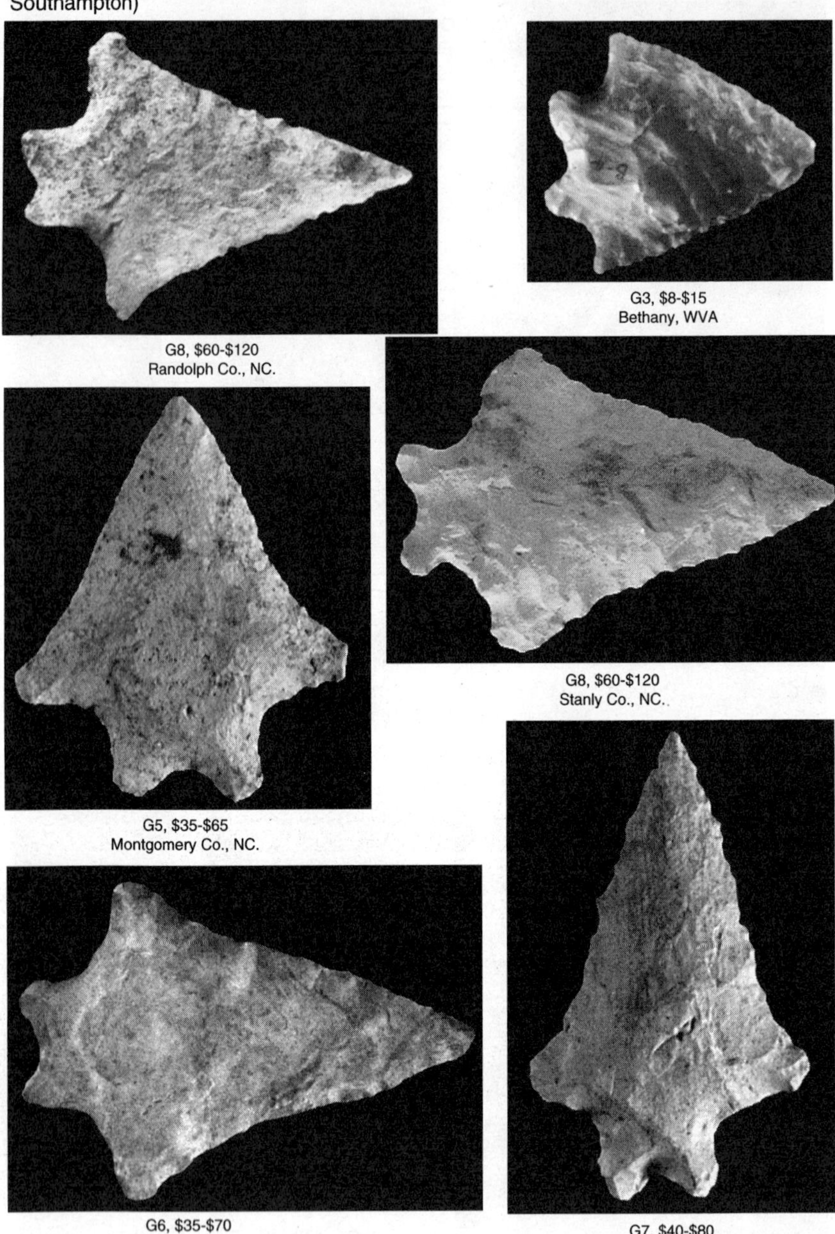

G8, $60-$120
Randolph Co., NC.

G3, $8-$15
Bethany, WVA

G8, $60-$120
Stanly Co., NC.

G5, $35-$65
Montgomery Co., NC.

G6, $35-$70
Randolph Co., NC.

G7, $40-$80
Rockingham Co., NC.

LOCATION: Southeastern to Eastern states. Type site is Stanly Co., N.C. **DESCRIPTION:** A small to medium size, broad shoulder point with a small bifurcated stem. Some examples are serrated and show high quality flaking. The shoulders are very prominent and can be tapered, horizontal or barbed. **I.D. KEY:** Tiny bifurcated base.

STANLY NARROW STEM - Early Archaic, 8000 - 5000 B. P.

(Also see Kirk Serrated-Bifurcated, St. Albans, Savannah River & Southampton)

G4, $10-$20
Stokes Co., NC.

G5, $8-$15
Moore Co., NC.

G3, $5-$10
Alleghany Co., NC.

G5, $20-$35
Randolph Co., NC.

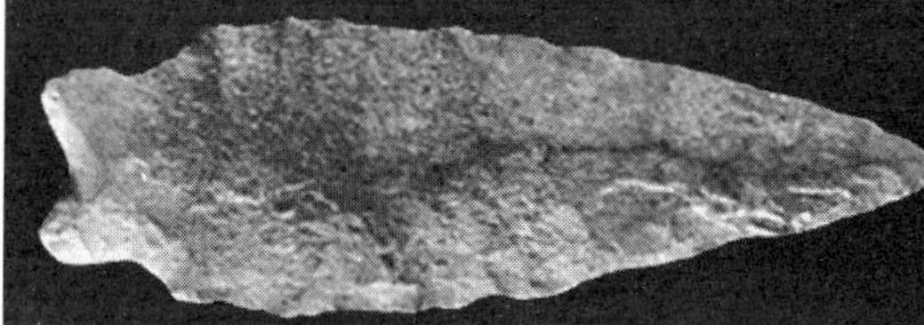

G5, $20-$35
Randolph Co., NC.

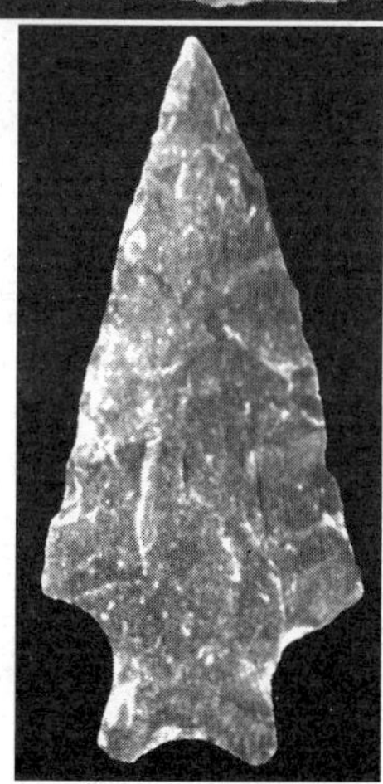

G6, $20-$40
Randolph Co., NC.

LOCATION: Far Eastern states. **DESCRIPTION:** A medium size, narrow shoulder point with a parallel sided stem and a concave base. Believed to have evolved from *Kirk* points and later evolved into *Savanna River* points. Similar to *Northern Piedmont* in in Penn.

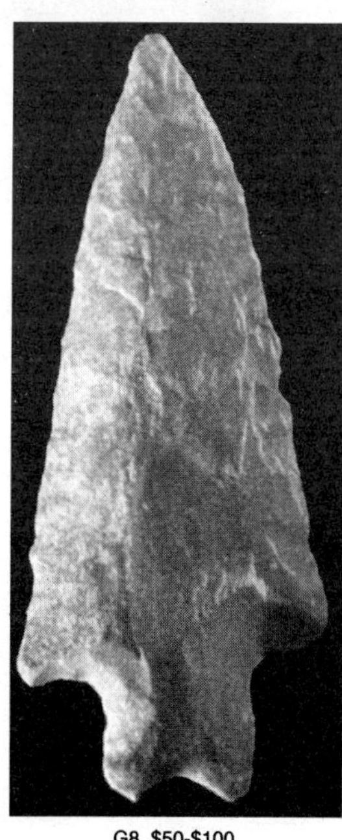

G8, $50-$100
Randolph Co., NC.

G7, $35-$65
Davidson Co., NC.

STANLY NARROW STEM (continued)

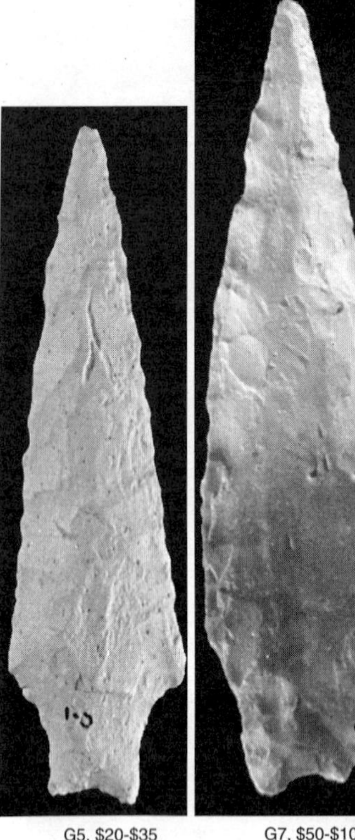

G5, $20-$35
Chatnam Co., NC.

G7, $50-$100
Randolph Co., NC.

G8, $90-$175
Moore Co., NC.

G10, $150-$300
Montgomery Co., NC.

TAYLOR - Early Archaic, 9000 - 6000 B. P.

(Also see Ecusta, Hardaway, Kirk and Palmer)

G7, $20-$40
Moore Co., NC.

G5, $25-$50
Randolph Co., NC.

G3, $15-$30
Moore Co., NC.

G5, $25-$50
Durham Co., NC.

G7, $35-$70
Randolph Co., NC.

G9, $75-$150
Kershaw Co., SC.

TAYLOR (continued)

LOCATION: Far Eastern states. **DESCRIPTION:** A medium to large size, side notched to auriculate point with a concave base. Basal areas are ground. Blade edges can be serrated. A cross between *Hardaway* and *Palmer*. Called *Van Lott* in South Carolina.

THEBES - Early Archaic, 10,000 - 8000 B. P.

(Also see Big Sandy, Bolen, Dovetail, Kirk Corner Notched and Lost Lake)

LOCATION: Midwestern to Eastern states. **DESCRIPTION:** A medium to large size, wide, blade with deep, angled side notches that are parallel sided and squared. Resharpened examples have beveling on one side of each face. The bases of this type have broad proportions and are concave, straight or convex and are ground. Some examples have unusual side notches called Key Notches. This type of notch is angled into the blade to produce a high point in the center, forming the letter E.

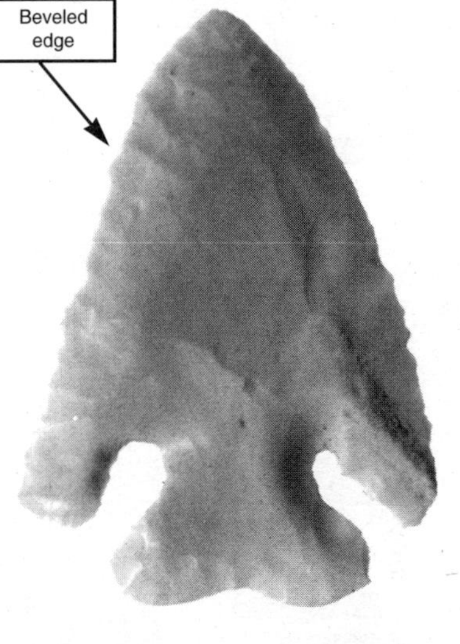

G8, $100-$200
WV.

TRADE POINTS - Historic, 400 - 170 B. P.

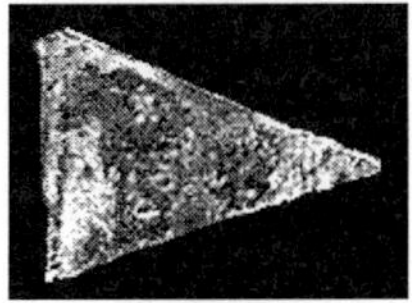

$10-$20
NC. Copper.

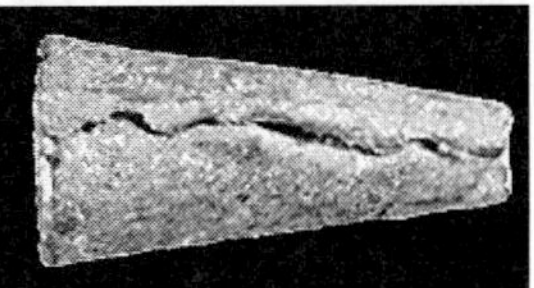

$10-$20
NC. French conical trade point. Ca. 1700-1763.

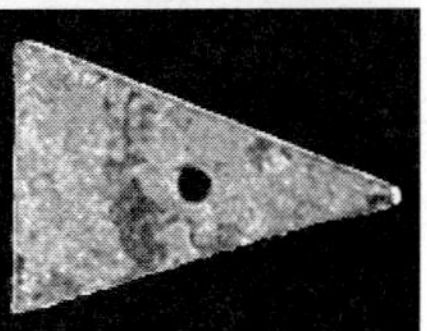

$20-$35
NC. Copper, Ca. 1800.

These points were made of copper, iron, and steel and were traded to the Indians by the French, British and others from the 1600s to the 1800s. Examples have been found all over the United States.

UWHARRIE - Late Woodland, 1600 - 1000 B. P.

(Also see Caraway, Clarksville, Hillsboro, Pee Dee and Yadkin)

G4, $3-$6
Randolph Co., NC.

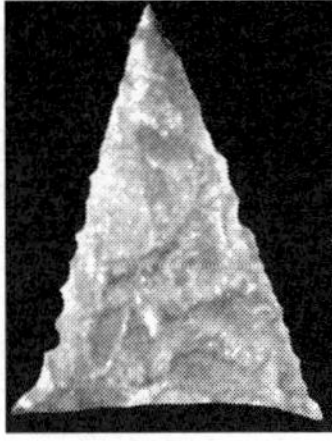

G4, $5-$10
Randolph Co., NC.

G5, $15-$25
Randolph Co., NC.

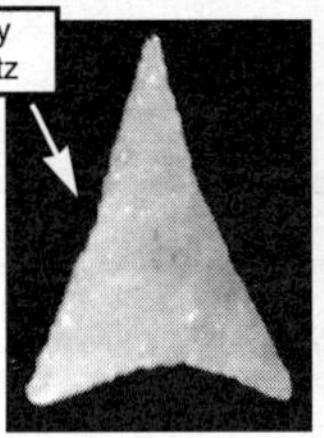

G5, $10-$20
Randolph Co., NC.

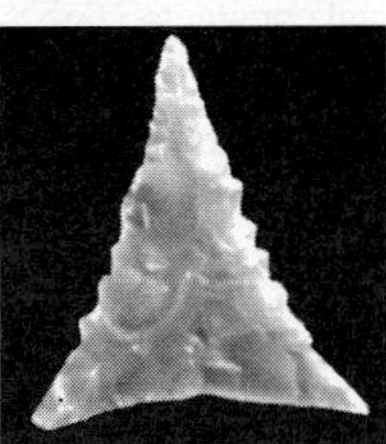

G6, $20-$35
Randolph Co., NC.

UWHARRIE (continued)

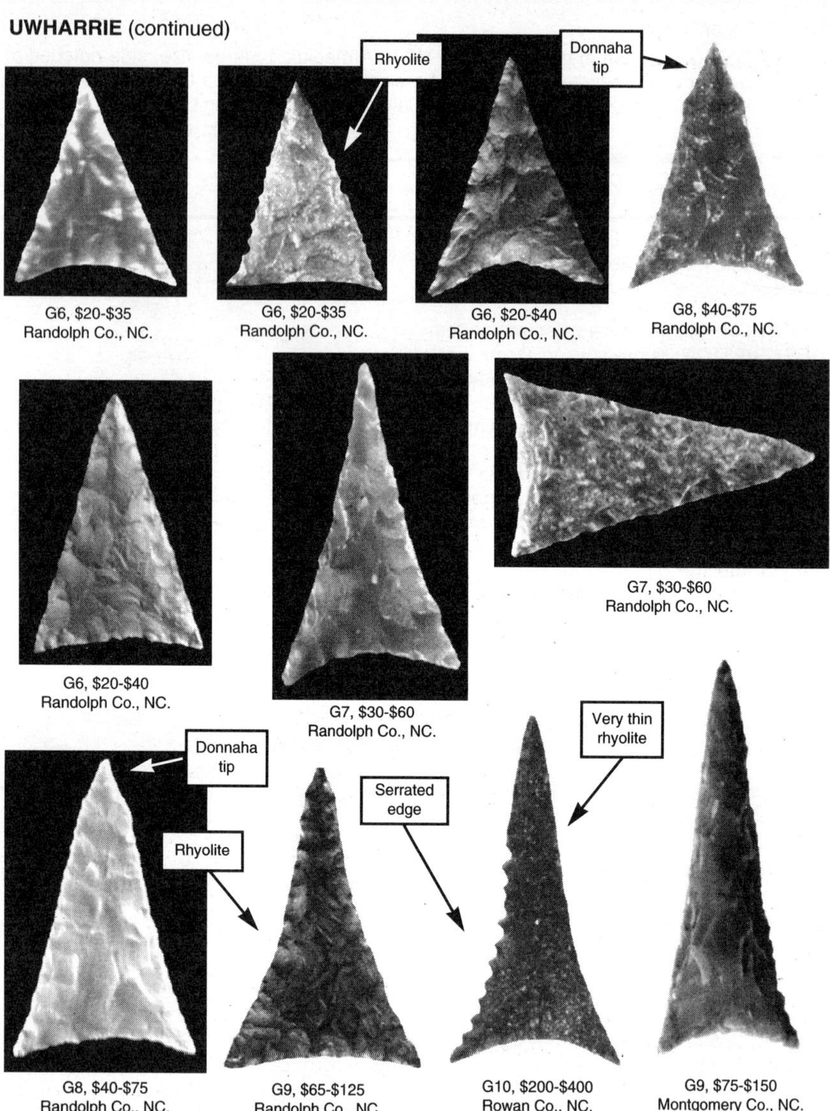

G6, $20-$35
Randolph Co., NC.

G6, $20-$35
Randolph Co., NC.

G6, $20-$40
Randolph Co., NC.

G8, $40-$75
Randolph Co., NC.

G6, $20-$40
Randolph Co., NC.

G7, $30-$60
Randolph Co., NC.

G7, $30-$60
Randolph Co., NC.

G8, $40-$75
Randolph Co., NC.

G9, $65-$125
Randolph Co., NC.

G10, $200-$400
Rowan Co., NC.

G9, $75-$150
Montgomery Co., NC.

LOCATION: North and South Carolina. **DESCRIPTION:** A small to medium size, thin, triangular point with concave sides and base. Tips and corners can be very sharp. Side edges are straight to concave. Called *Hamilton* in Tennessee. Some examples have special constricted tips called *Donnaha Tips.* Smaller than *Yadkin.*

WALLER KNIFE - Early Archaic, 9000 - 5000 B. P.

(Also see Edgefield Scraper)

LOCATION: Southern Southeastern states. **DESCRIPTION:** A medium size double uniface knife with a short, notched base, made from a flake. Only the cutting edges have been pressure flaked.

WALLER KNIFE (continued)

G7, $20-$35
SC.

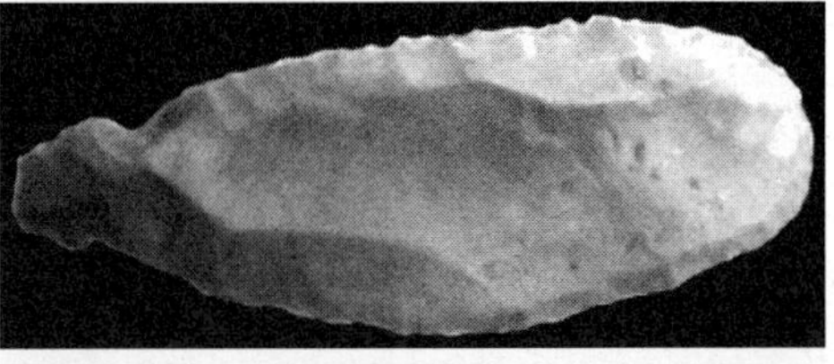

ES

WARATAN - Woodland, 3000 - 1000 B. P.

(Also see Potts and Yadkin)

G7, $8-$15
Southampton Co., VA.

G6, $6-$12
Sussex Co., VA.

G7, $10-$20
Davidson Co., NC.

LOCATION: Far Eastern states. **DESCRIPTION:** A medium to large size point with usually broad, tapered shoulders, weak corner notches and a very short, broad, concave base. The base expands on some examples giving the appearance of ears or auricles.

WATEREE - Woodland, 3000 - 1500 B. P.

(Also see Will's Cove)

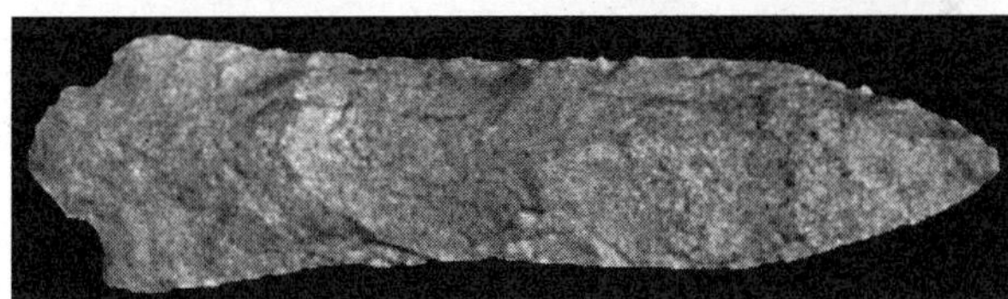

G6, $20-$35
Fairfield Co., SC.

LOCATION: Far Eastern states. **DESCRIPTION:** A medium size, narrow point with a recurvate blade, horizontal shoulders and a very short stem. Similar to North Carolina's *Will's Cove*.

WILL'S COVE - Woodland, 3000 - 1000 B. P.

(Also see Wateree)

LOCATION: Far Eastern states. **DESCRIPTION:** A medium size, very narrow point with horizontal shoulders and a short, narrow stem with parallel sides and a straight base.

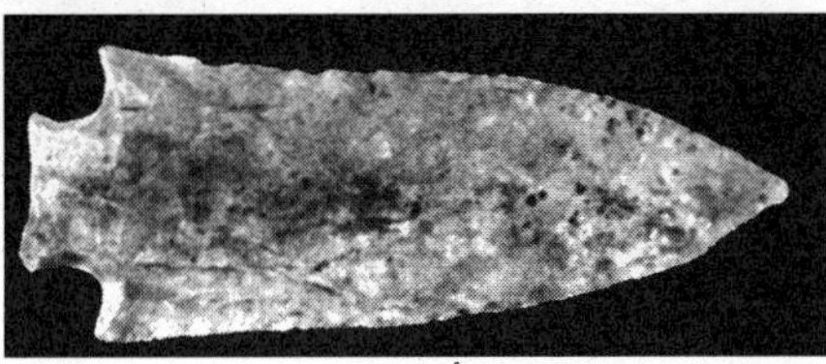

G6, $20-$40
Randolph Co., NC.

WILL'S COVE (continued)

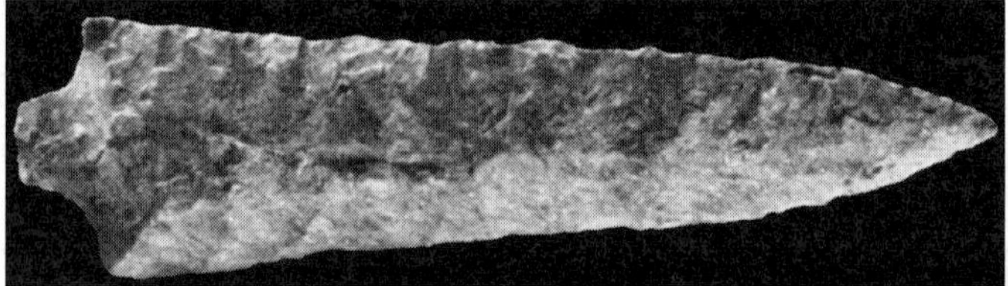

G6, $50-$80
Randolph Co., NC.

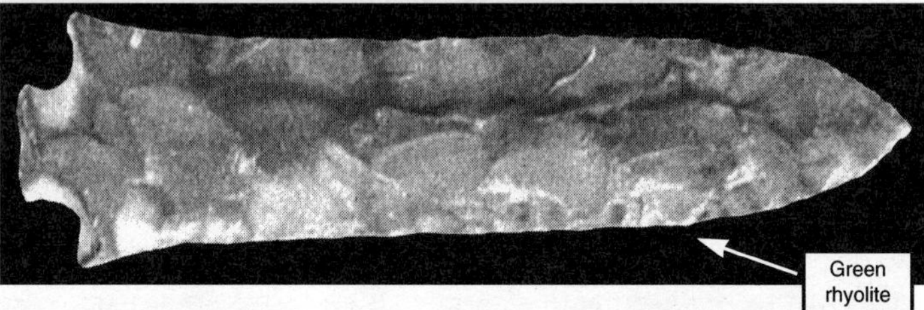

G10, $150-$300
Randolph Co., NC. The best known example.

Green
rhyolite

YADKIN - Woodland to Mississippian, 2500 - 500 B. P.

(Also see Caraway, Nolichucky, Occaneechee and Uwharrie)

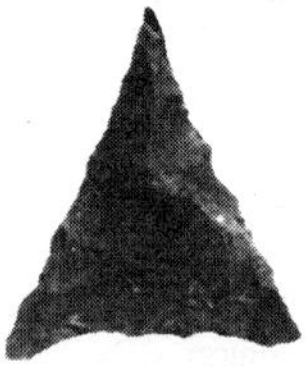

G4, $8-$15
Randolph Co., NC.

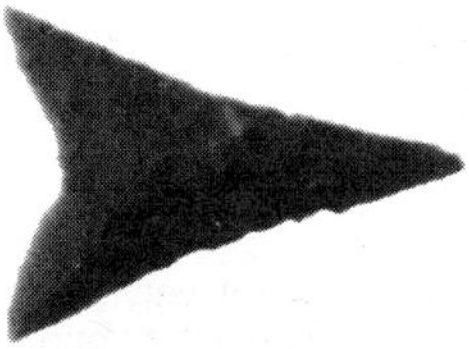

G5, $15-$30
Montgomery Co., NC.

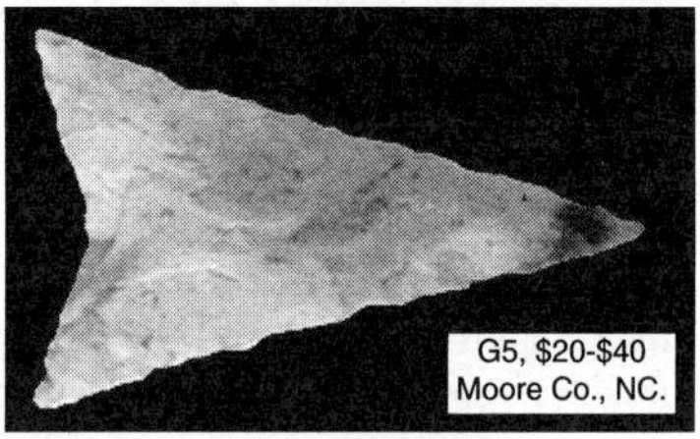

G5, $20-$40
Moore Co., NC.

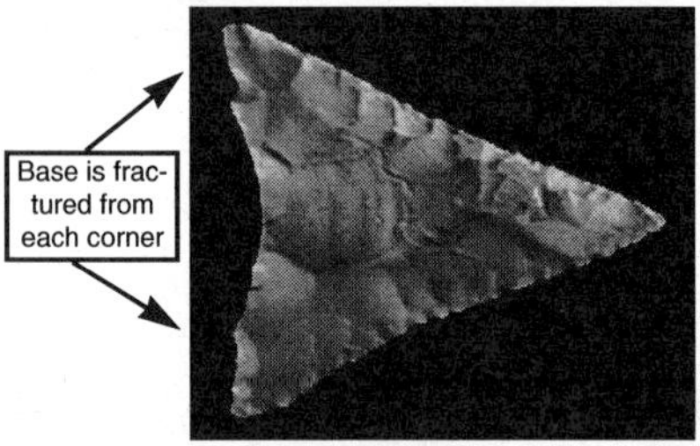

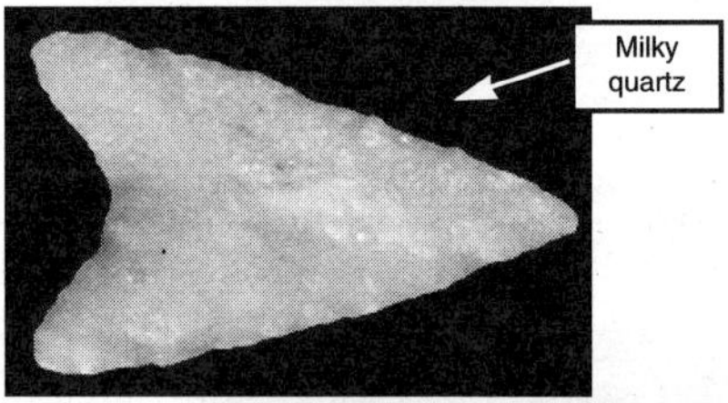

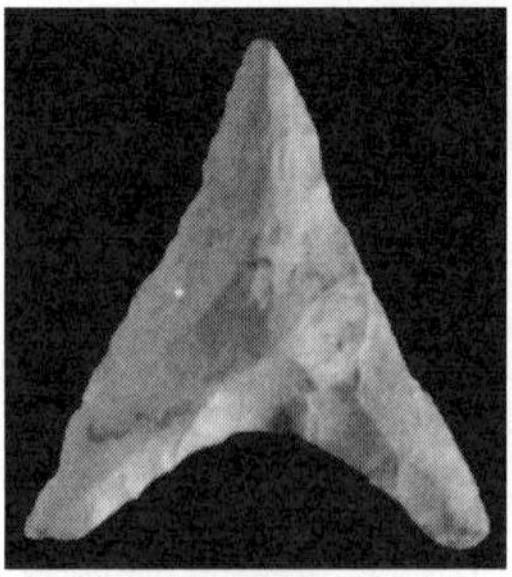

Base is fractured from each corner

G9, $20-$40
Bethany, WVA.

Milky
quartz

G5, $20-$40
Iredell Co., NC.

G4, $8-$15
Surry Co., NC.

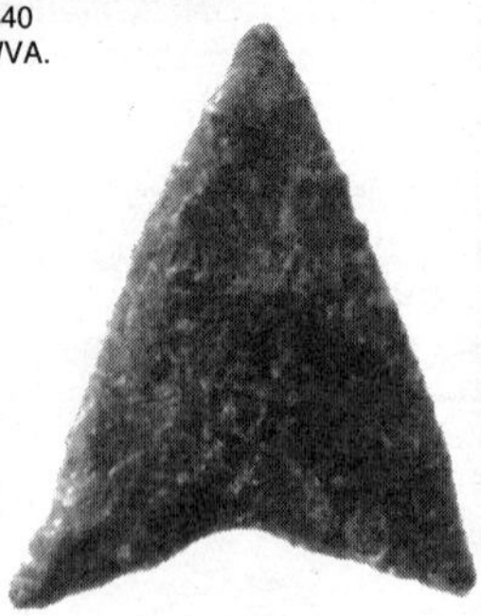

G5, $20-$40
VA.

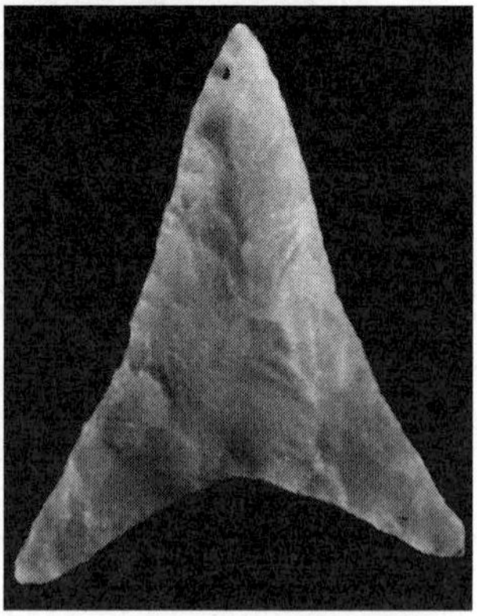

G7, $40-$80
Randolph Co., NC.

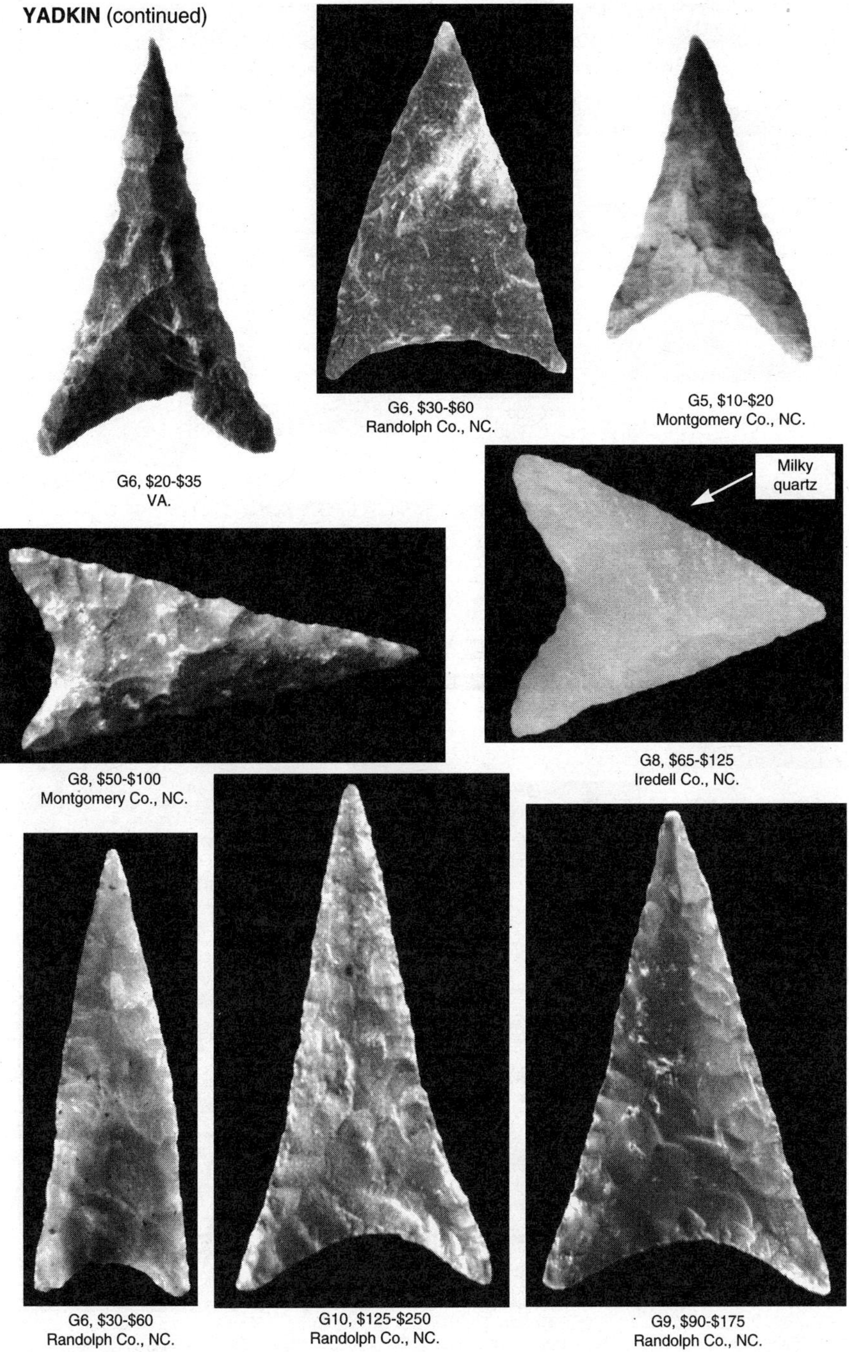

G6, $20-$35
VA.

G6, $30-$60
Randolph Co., NC.

G5, $10-$20
Montgomery Co., NC.

G8, $50-$100
Montgomery Co., NC.

G8, $65-$125
Iredell Co., NC.

G6, $30-$60
Randolph Co., NC.

G10, $125-$250
Randolph Co., NC.

G9, $90-$175
Randolph Co., NC.

LOCATION: Southeastern and Eastern states. Type site is Yadkin River in central North Carolina. **DESCRIPTION:** A small to medium size, broad based, fairly thick, triangular point with a broad, concave base and straight to convex to recurved side edges. Called *Levanna* in New York.

YADKIN-EARED - Woodland to Mississippian, 2500 - 500 B. P.

(Also see Guilford-Yuma, Hardaway, Potts, and Waratan)

G4, $5-$10
Davidson Co., NC.

G6, $15-$30
Johnson Co., NC.

G6, $20-$40
Rowan Co., NC.

G6, $20-$40
Randolph Co., NC.

G6, $15-$25
Randolph Co., NC.

G8, $40-$75
Randolph Co., NC.

G5, $15-$25
Sussex Co., VA.

G6, $20-$40
Randolph Co., NC.

G6, $20-$40
Randolph Co., NC.

G7, $45-$90
Randolph Co., NC.

LOCATION: Eastern seaboard states, esp. North Carolina. **DESCRIPTION:** A small to medium size triangular, auriculate point with a concave base. The ears are produced by a shallow constriction or notching near the base. The notches are steeply beveled on one edge of each face on some examples.

GULF COASTAL SECTION:

This section includes point types from the following states:
Florida, S. Alabama, S. Georgia, S. Mississippi, S. South Carolina and S.E. Louisiana.

The points in this section are arranged in alphabetical order and are shown **actual size**. All types are listed that were available for photographing. Any missing types will be added to future editions as photographs become available. We are always interested in receiving sharp, black and white, color glossy photos or color slides of your collection. Be sure to include a ruler in the photograph so that proper scale can be determined.

GC

Lithics: Agate, agatized coral, agite, chalcedony, chert, conglomerate, flint, Coastal Plains chert, crystal quartz, hematite, petrified palmwood, quartzite, Tallahatta quartzite and vein quartz.

Special note: Points that are clear, colorful, made of coral, fossilized palmwood or other exotic material will bring a premium price when offered for sale. Exotic materials are pointed out where known.

Regional Consultants:
Tommy Beutell
Gary Davis
Shawn Novak
Jerry Scott
Jim Tatum
Red Knight

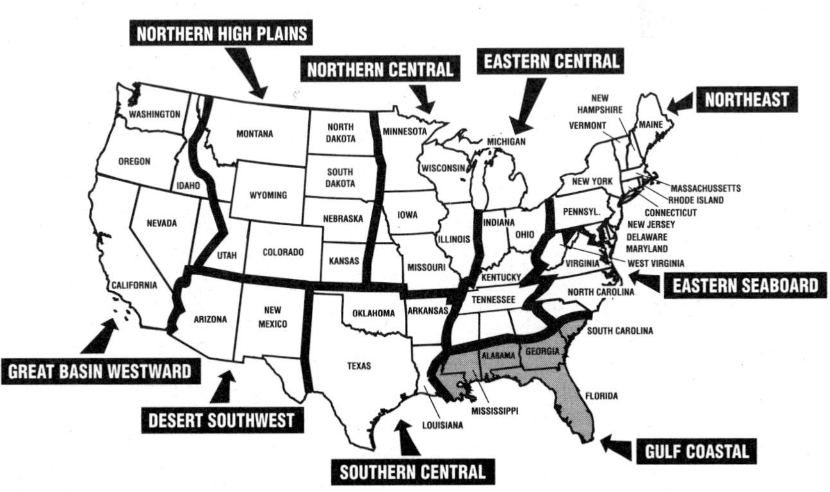

GULF COASTAL
(Archaeological Periods)

PALEO (14,000 B. P. - 11,000 B. P.)

Bone Pin
Clovis
Drill
Redstone

LATE PALEO (12,000 B. P. - 10,000 B. P.)

Beaver Lake
Simpson
Simpson-Mustache
Suwannee

TRANSITIONAL PALEO (11,000 B. P. - 9,000 B. P.)

Bolen Bevel
Bolen Plain
Chipola
Cowhouse Slough
Gilchrist
Hardin
Marianna
Santa Fe
Stanfield
Tallahassee
Waller Knife
Wheeler

EARLY ARCHAIC (10,000 B. P. - 7,000 B. P.)

Boggy Branch
Conerly
Edgefield
Hamilton
Hardee Beveled
Hillsborough
Kirk Corner Notched
Kirk Serrated
Osceola Greenbrier
Six Mile Creek
Taylor Stemmed
Thonotosassa
Union Side Notched
Wacissa
Westo

MIDDLE ARCHAIC (7,000 B. P. - 4,000 B. P.)

Abbey
Alachua
Arredondo
Bascom
Clay County
Cottonbridge
Culbreath
Cypress Creek
Elora
Lafayette
Ledbetter
Levy
Marion
Morrow Mountain
Newnan
Notchaway
Pickwick
Putnam
Savannah River
Seminole
South Prong Creek
Sumter

LATE ARCHAIC (4,000 B. P. - 3,000 B. P.)

Citrus
Flint River
Hernando
Santa Fe
Tallahassee

WOODLAND (3,000 B. P. - 1,300 B. P.)

Adena
Bradford
Broad River
Broward
Columbia
Duval
Jackson
Oauchita
Ocala
O'leno
Sarasota
Sting Ray Barb
Taylor
Weeden Island

MISSISSIPPIAN (1300 B. P. - 400 B. P.)

Itcheetucknee
Pinellas
Safety Harbor
Tampa

GULF COASTAL
THUMBNAIL GUIDE SECTION

The following references are provided to aid the collector in easier and quicker identification of point types. All photos are exactly 30% of actual size and are proportional to each other. Each point pictured in this section represents a classic form for the type. When a match is found, go to the alphabetical location of that type for more examples in actual size.

GC

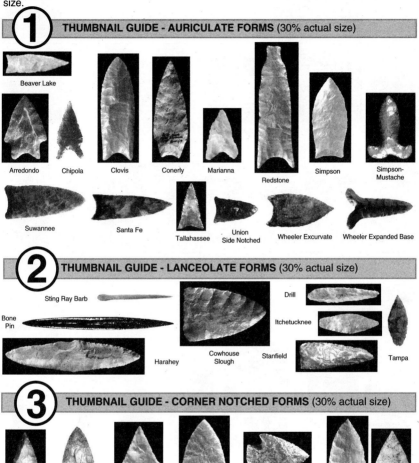

1 THUMBNAIL GUIDE - AURICULATE FORMS (30% actual size)

Beaver Lake

Arredondo

Chipola

Clovis

Conerly

Marianna

Redstone

Simpson

Simpson-Mustache

Suwannee

Santa Fe

Tallahassee

Union Side Notched

Wheeler Excurvate

Wheeler Expanded Base

2 THUMBNAIL GUIDE - LANCEOLATE FORMS (30% actual size)

Sting Ray Barb

Bone Pin

Harahey

Cowhouse Slough

Drill

Itchetucknee

Stanfield

Tampa

3 THUMBNAIL GUIDE - CORNER NOTCHED FORMS (30% actual size)

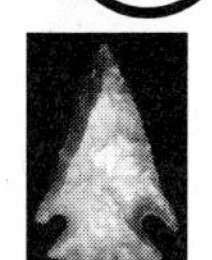

Bolen Beveled

Bolen Plain

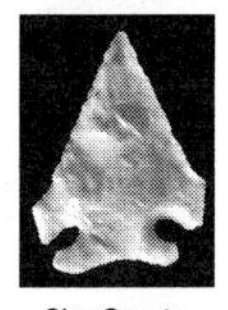

Clay County

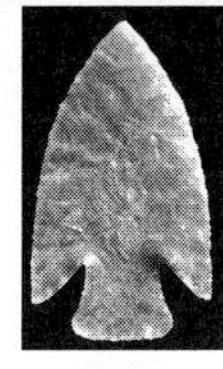

Hardin

Kirk Corner Notched

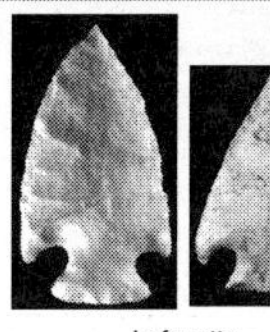

Lafayette

4 THUMBNAILGUIDE - SIDE NOTCHED FORMS (30% actual size)

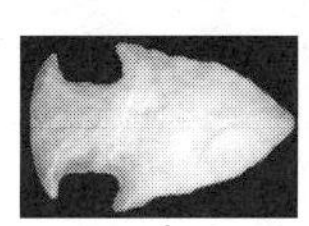

Bolen Plain

Bolen Beveled

Edgefield Scraper

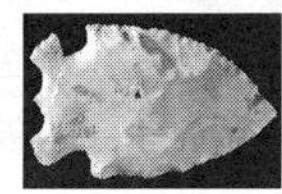

Osceola Greenbrier Type I

Osceola Greenbrier Type II

Waller Knife

5 THUMBNAIL GUIDE - STEMMED FORMS (30% of actual size)

Jackson

Columbia

Duval

Gilchrist

Hamilton

Kirk Serrated

Notchaway

Seminole

Taylor Stemmed

Savannah River

Six Mile Creek

Savannah River

Pickwick

Sarasota

Savannah River

South Prong Creek

Wacissa

THUMBNAIL GUIDE - BASAL NOTCHED FORMS (30% of actual size)

Citrus

Culbreath

Clay County

Hernando

Lafayette

THUMBNAIL GUIDE - ARROW POINTS (30% of actual size)

O'leno

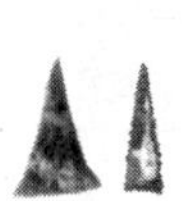
Pinellas

Safety Harbor

ABBEY - Early to Middle Archaic, 6000 - 4000 B. P.

(Also see Alachua, Cottonbridge, Elora, Levy, Notchaway, Pickwick, Savannah River, Six Mile Creek, South Prong Creek and Wacissa)

G4, $15-$25
Escambia Co., AL.

G4, $15-$25
Decatur Co., GA.

G6, $20-$35
Decatur Co., GA.

G3, $8-$15
Decatur Co., GA.

G6, $20-$35
Decatur Co., GA.

G6, $20-$35
Decatur Co., GA.

ABBEY (continued)

LOCATION: GA, AL, FL. **DESCRIPTION:** A medium sized, broad, stemmed point that is fairly thick and is steeply beveled on all four sides of each face. Blade edges are concave to straight. Shoulders are broad and tapered. A relationship to *Elora, Maples* and *Pickwick* has been suggested. **I.D. KEY:** Expanded barbs & fine edgework.

ADENA - Late Archaic to late Woodland, 3000 - 1200 B. P.

(Also see Alachua, Cypress Creek, Elora, Levy, Pickwick, Putnam, Sumter and Thonotosassa)

LOCATION: Eastern to Southeastern states. **DESCRIPTION:** A medium to large, thin, narrow, triangular blade that is sometimes serrated, and with a medium to long, narrow to broad rounded "beaver tail" stem. Most examples are from average to excellent quality. **I.D. KEY:** Rounded base, woodland flaking.

G6, $15-$30
Dale Co., AL.

GC

ALACHUA - Middle Archaic, 6000 - 5000 B. P.

(Also see Abbey, Cypress Creek, Hardee Beveled, Levy, Marion, Morrow Mountain, Newnan, Putnam, Six Mile Creek)

G6, $15-$30
Marion Co., FL.

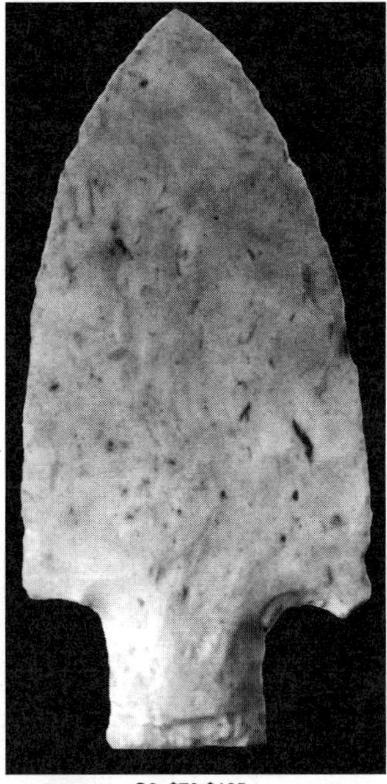

G8, $70-$125
FL.

G6, $20-$35
Burke Co., GA.

LOCATION: Gulf Coastal states. **DESCRIPTION:** *Newnans* with horizontal shoulders and straight stems that don't contract as much. **I.D. KEY:** Squared base, one barb shoulder.

ALACHUA (continued)

G6, $30-$60
Miller Co., GA.

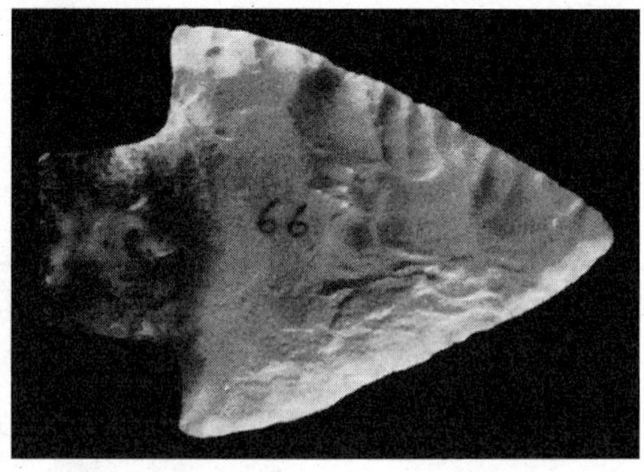

G6, $30-$60
Alachua Co., FL.

Clear

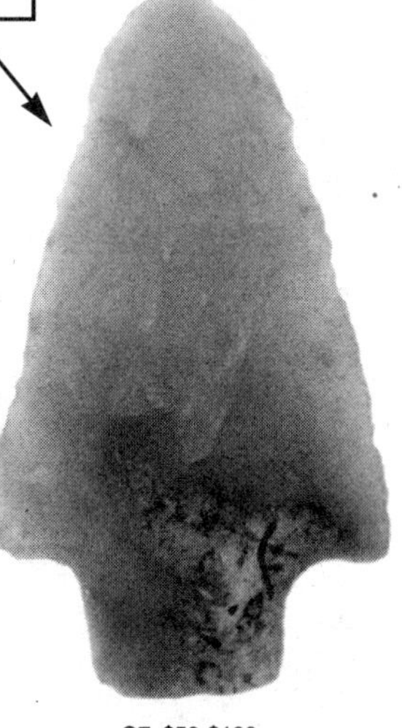

G7, $50-$100
FL.

G6, $40-$70
Burke Co., GA.

ARREDONDO - Middle to Late Archaic, 5000 - 3000 B. P.

(Also see Buzzard Roost Creek, Kirk Serrated, Savannah River, Seminole and Wacissa)

G6, $20-$35
Marion Co., FL.

G9, $50-$100
FL.

ARREDONDO
(continued)

LOCATION: AL, GA, FL. **DESCRIPTION:** A thick, small to medium size point with a short, broad blade and a wide, bifurcated base which can be thinned. Could be related to *Savannah River* points. **I.D. KEY:** Basal form and thickness.

G9, $140-$275
FL.

GC

BASCOM - Middle to Late Archaic, 4500 - 3500 B. P.

(Also see Morrow Mountain and Savannah River)

G10, $100-$200
Savannah, GA. Briar
Creek. Excellent quality

G6, $40-$75
Burke Co., GA. Cache.

BASCOM (continued)

LOCATION: AL, GA. **DESCRIPTION:** A large size, broad point with shoulders tapering to the base which is usually straight. Possibly a variant form of the *Maples* point. **I.D.KEY:** Basal form.

BEAVER LAKE - Paleo, 11,000 - 8000 B. P.

(Also see Simpson, Suwannee and Tallahassee)

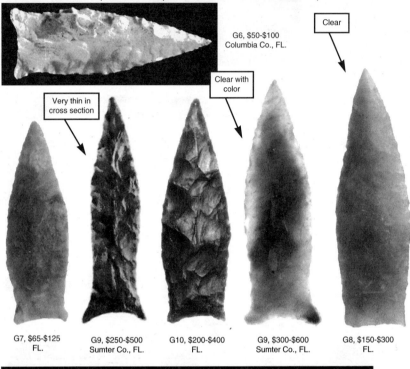

G6, $50-$100
Columbia Co., FL.

Clear

Clear with color

Very thin in cross section

G7, $65-$125
FL.

G9, $250-$500
Sumter Co., FL.

G10, $200-$400
FL.

G9, $300-$600
Sumter Co., FL.

G8, $150-$300
FL.

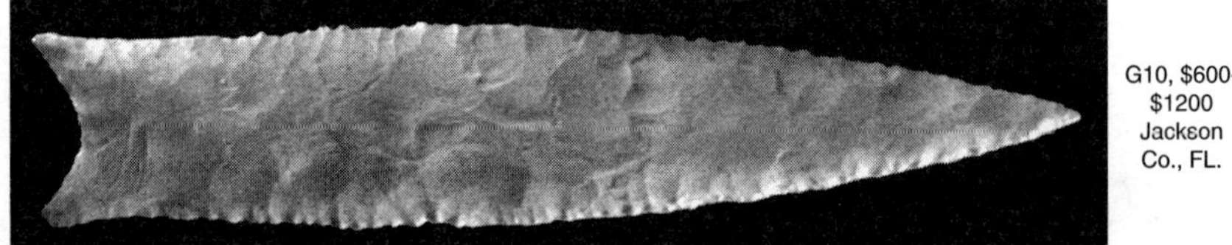

G10, $600-$1200
Jackson Co., FL.

LOCATION: Southeastern states. **DESCRIPTION:** A medium to large size lanceolate blade with flaring ears. Contemporaneous and associated with *Cumberland*, but thinner than unfluted *Cumberlands*. Bases are ground and blade edges are recurved. **I.D. KEY:** Paleo flaking, shoulder area.

BOGGY BRANCH-TYPE I - Early to Middle Archaic, 9000 - 6000 B. P.

(Also see Kirk Serrated and South Prong Creek)

LOCATION: Small area in SE AL & SW GA. **DESCRIPTION:** A medium to large size serrated point with weak shoulders and a large bulbous base which is usually ground. Blade flaking is similar to *Kirk Serrated.* Most examples are made of coastal plains chert. Very rare in the small type area. **I.D. KEY:** Basal form and edgework.

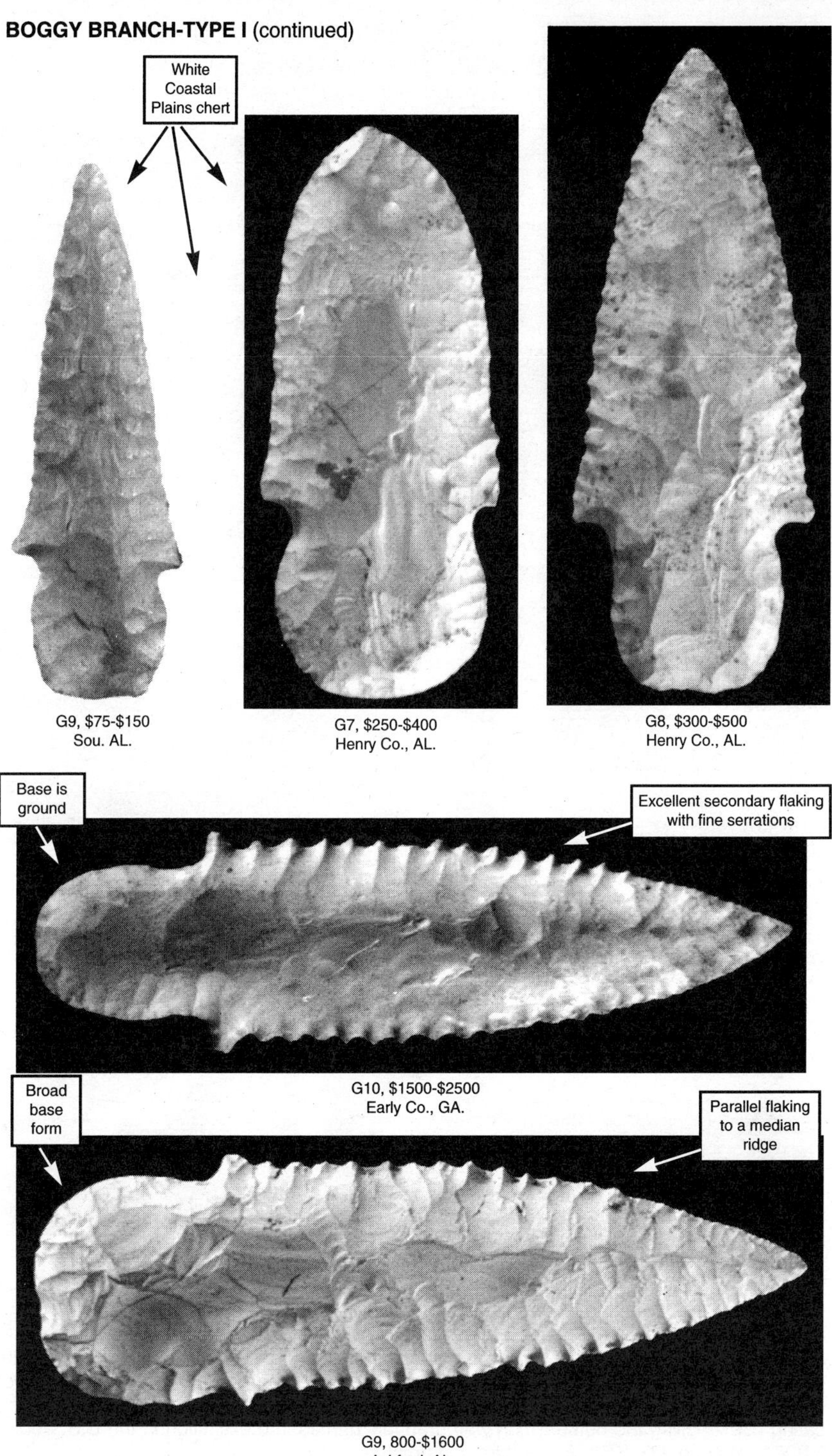

G9, $75-$150
Sou. AL.

G7, $250-$400
Henry Co., AL.

G8, $300-$500
Henry Co., AL.

G10, $1500-$2500
Early Co., GA.

G9, 800-$1600
Ashford, AL.

BOGGY BRANCH-TYPE II - Early to Middle Archaic, 9000 - 600 B. P.

(Also see Kirk Serrated and South Prong Creek)

G3, $8-$12
Henry Co., AL.

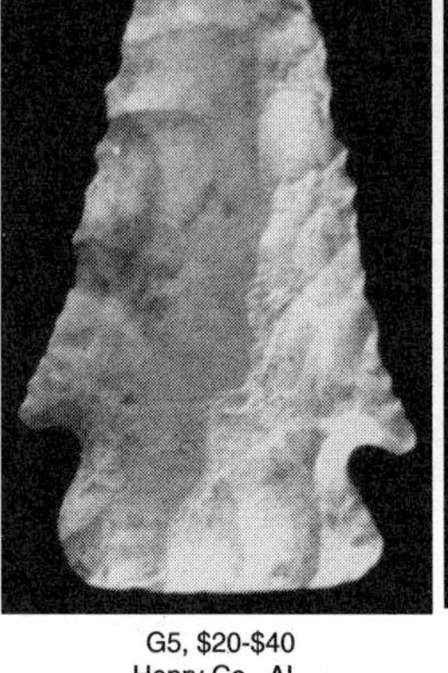

G5, $20-$40
Henry Co., AL.

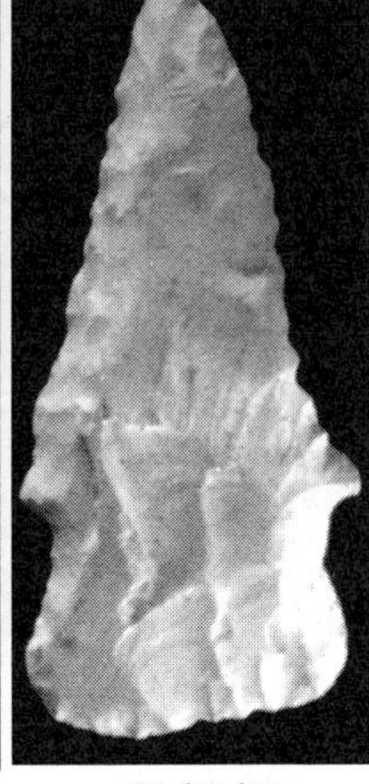

G4, $10-$20
Henry Co., AL.

LOCATION: Southern, Southeastern states. **DESCRIPTION:** A small to medium size serrated point with weak shoulders and a bulbous base which is usually ground. The base is shorter and smaller than in type I. **I.D. KEY:** Basal form and early flaking.

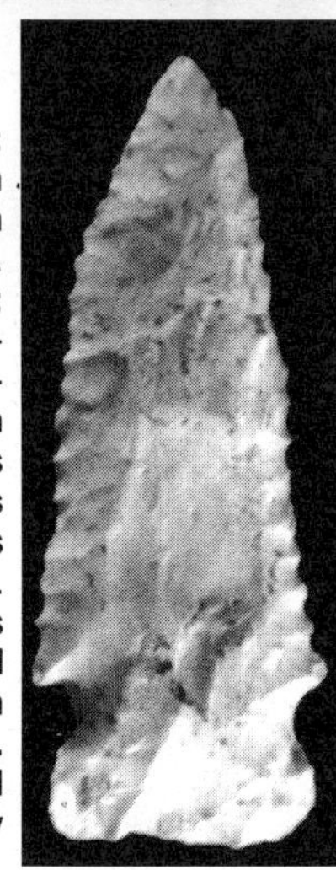

G4, $10-$20
Henry Co., AL.

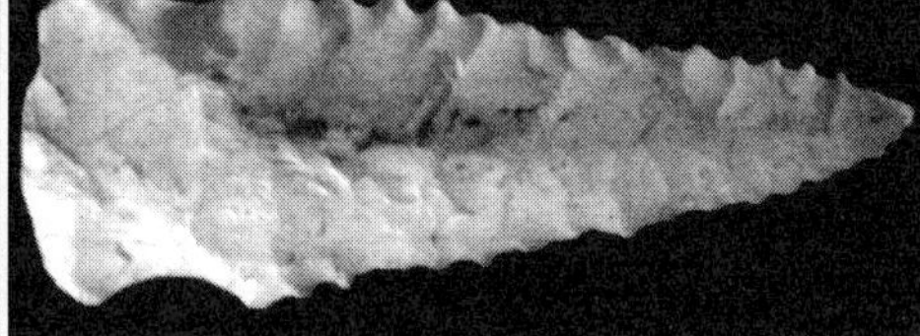

G5, $20-$30
Henry Co., AL.

BOLEN BEVEL - Early Archaic, 10,000 - 7000 B. P.

(Also Clay County, Lafayette, Lost Lake and Osceola Greenbrier)

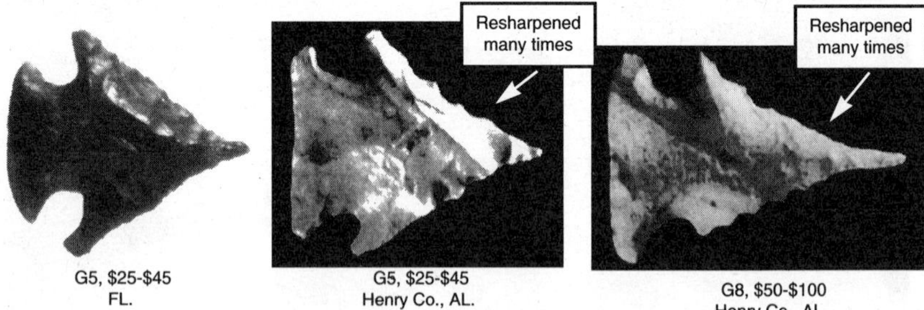

G5, $25-$45
FL.

G5, $25-$45
Henry Co., AL.

G8, $50-$100
Henry Co., AL.

LOCATION: Southeastern states including Florida. **DESCRIPTION:** A small to medium size, side to corner notched point with early forms showing basal grinding, beveling on one side of each face, and serrations. Bases can be straight, concave or convex. The side notch is usually broader than in *Big Sandy* points. E-notched or expanded notching also occurs on early forms. **Note:** *Bolens* have been found with horse remains in Florida indicating use in killing the horse which was probably hunted into extinction in the U.S. about 7,000 years ago. **I.D. KEY:** Basal form and notching.

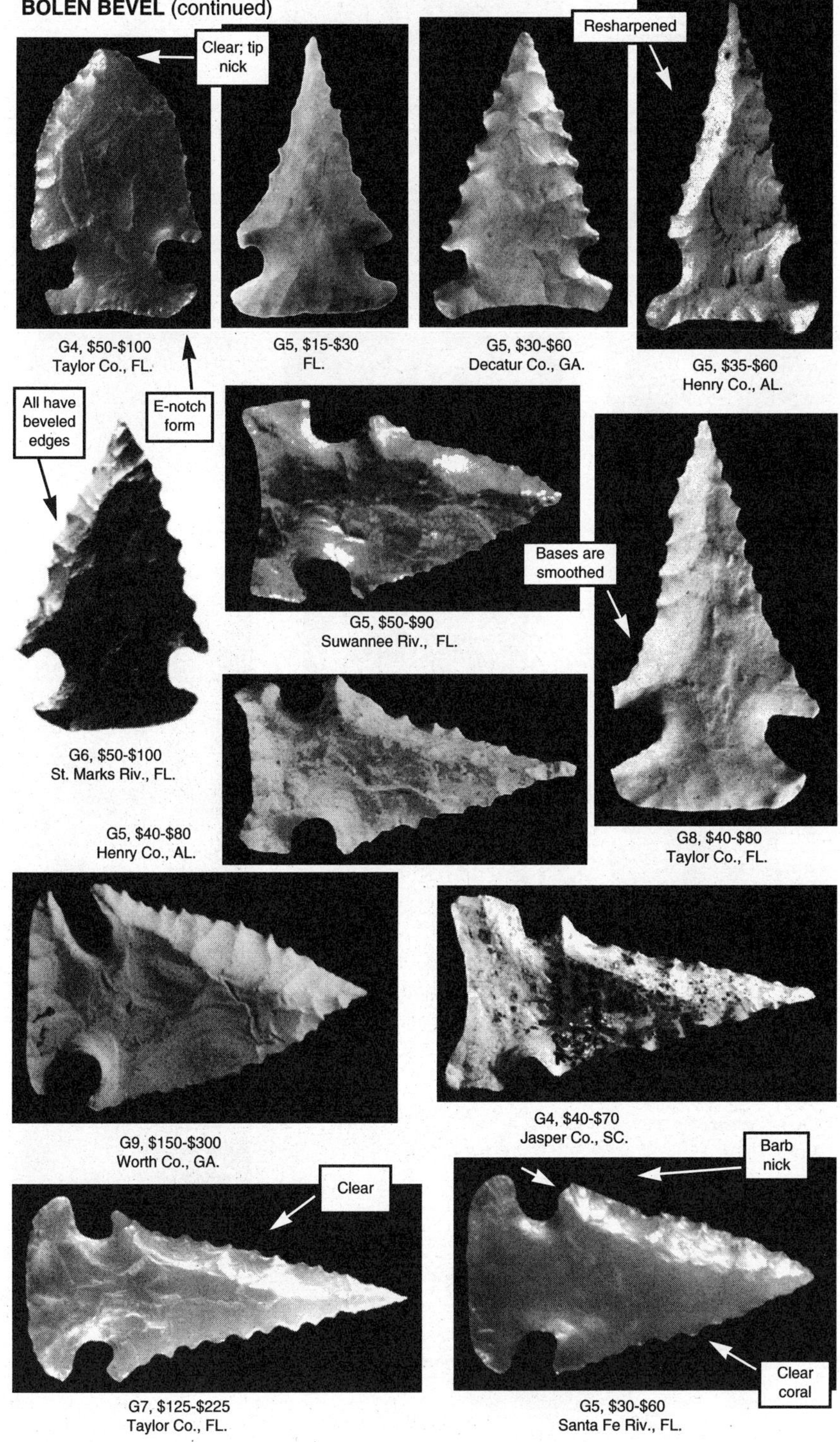

G4, $50-$100
Taylor Co., FL.

G5, $15-$30
FL.

G5, $30-$60
Decatur Co., GA.

G5, $35-$60
Henry Co., AL.

G6, $50-$100
St. Marks Riv., FL.

G5, $50-$90
Suwannee Riv., FL.

G5, $40-$80
Henry Co., AL.

G8, $40-$80
Taylor Co., FL.

G9, $150-$300
Worth Co., GA.

G4, $40-$70
Jasper Co., SC.

G7, $125-$225
Taylor Co., FL.

G5, $30-$60
Santa Fe Riv., FL.

BOLEN BEVEL (continued)

G8, $150-$300
Hillsborough Co., FL.

G8, $300-$500
NW cent. FL.

G9, $300-$550
Columbia Co., FL.

G8, $250-$500
Jefferson Co., FL.

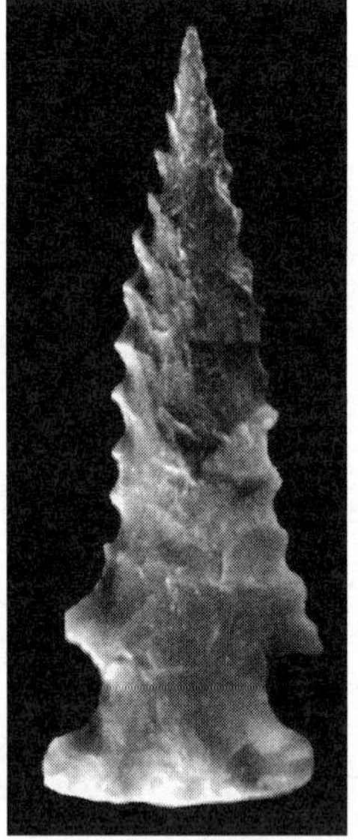

G8, $200-$350
Taylor Co., FL.

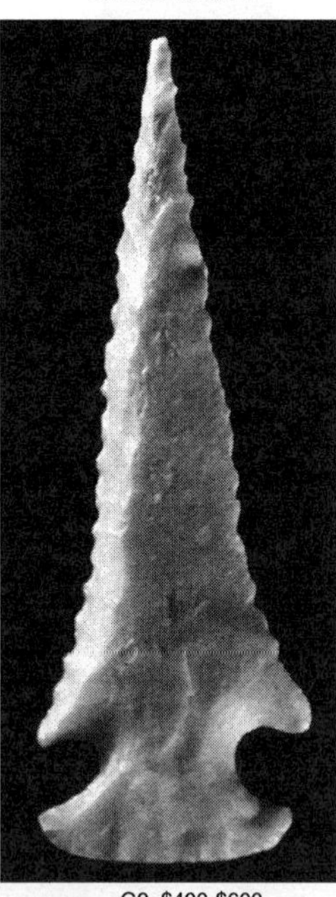

G9, $400-$600
Lafayette Co., FL.

G10, $600-$1000
Columbia Co., FL.

BOLEN PLAIN - Early Archaic, 9000 - 7000 B. P.

(Also see Chipola, Kirk Corner Notched, Osceola Greenbrier and Taylor)

G5, $100-$165
Santa Fe River, FL.

G10, $80-$150
Suwannee Co., FL.

G6, $50-$75
Decatur Co., GA.

G9, $60-$125
FL.

G10, $80-$150
FL.

G10, $175-$350
FL.

G7, $100-$200
Aucilla Riv., FL.

GC

LOCATION: Eastern states. **DESCRIPTION:** A small to medium size, side to corner notched point with early forms showing basal grinding and serrations. Bases are straight, concave or convex. The side notches are usually broader than in the *Big Sandy* type, and can be expanded to E-notched on some examples. **I.D. KEY:** Basal form and flaking on blade.

Needle tip

Clear

G9, $250-$500
FL.

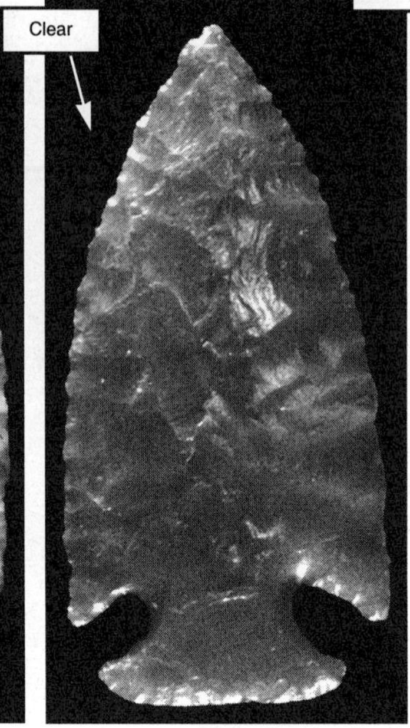

G9, $500-$700
Dougherty Co., GA.

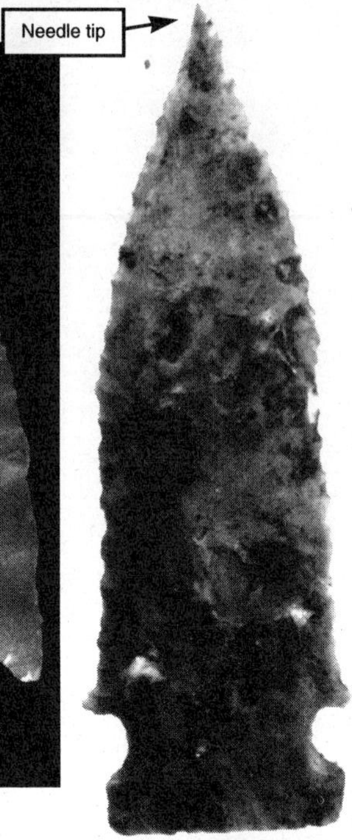

G10, $250-$450
FL.

BONE PIN - Transitional Paleo to Historic, 12,000 - 200 B. P.

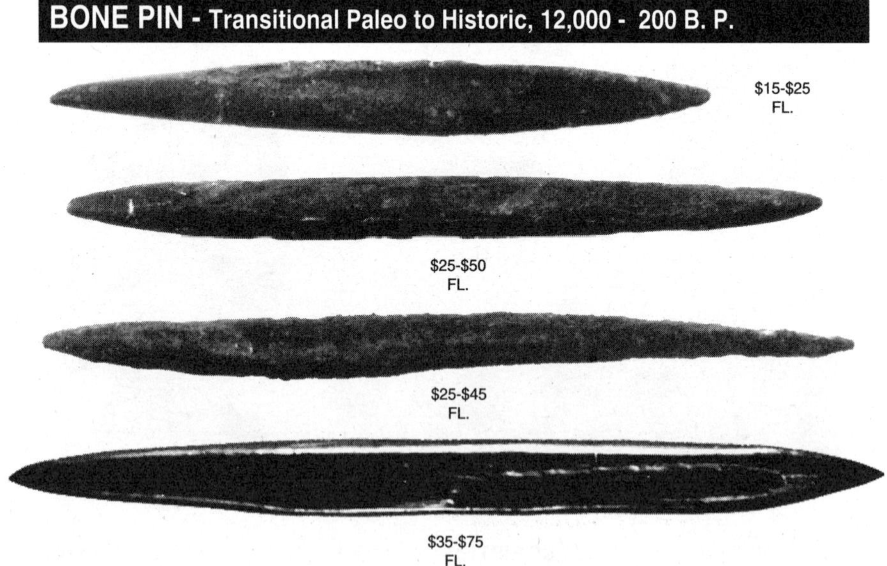

$15-$25
FL.

$25-$50
FL.

$25-$45
FL.

$35-$75
FL.

LOCATION: Florida. **DESCRIPTION:** Medium to large size, slender, double pointed spear pins made from deer leg bone, some camel and rarely mammoth. Less than 1% are mammoth ivory. The bone is usually blackened with age.

BRADFORD - Woodland to Mississippian, 2000 - 800 B. P.

(Also see Duval)

LOCATION: Southern Southeastern states. **DESCRIPTION:** A medium size, narrow, expanded stem point with tapered to rounded shoulders.

G3, $3-$6
Hillsborough Co., FL.

BROAD RIVER - Woodland, 3000 - 1500 B. P.

(Also see Broward, Savannah River and Wacissa)

G5, $8-$12
Beaufort Co., SC.

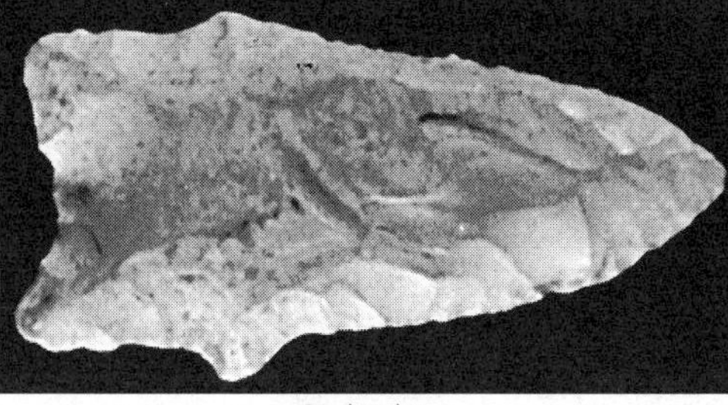

G6, $10-$15
Henry Co., AL.

LOCATION: Southern Southeastern states. **DESCRIPTION:** A small size, thick point with small shoulder barbs, a parallel sided stem and a straight to concave base.

BROWARD - Woodland to Mississippian, 2000 - 800 B. P.

(Also see Bradford and Broad River)

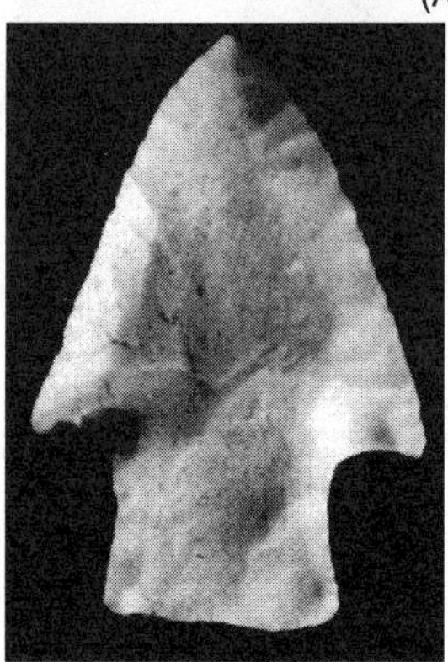

G6, $20-$35
Pasco Co., FL.

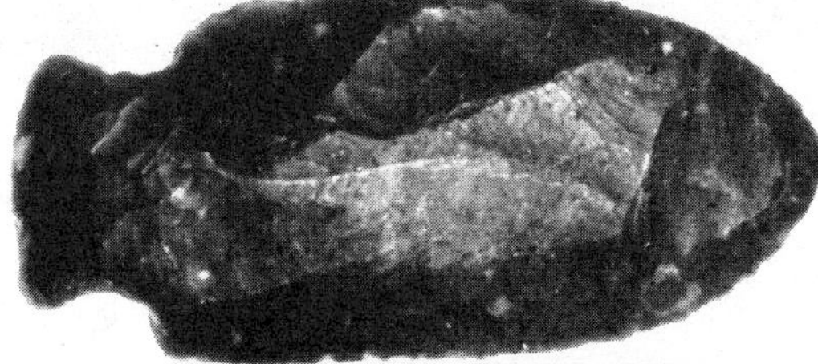

G6, $20-$40
FL.

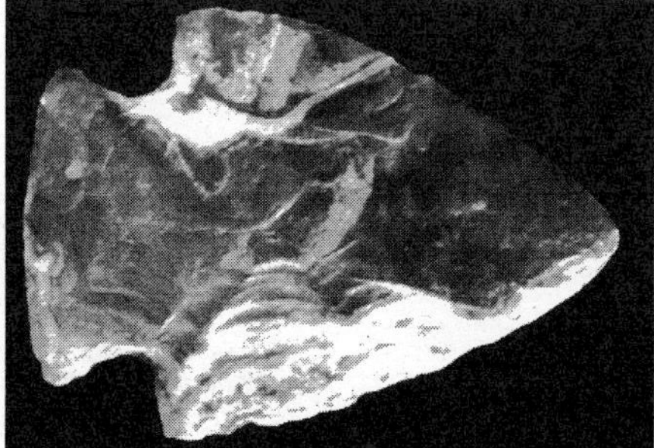

G5, $15-$30
Choctaw Co., AL.

LOCATION: Southern Southeastern states. **DESCRIPTION:** A medium to large size triangular point with tapered to square shoulders and a short expanding base. The base can be straight, concave or convex. Basal corners can be sharp to rounded. **I.D. KEY:** High and low barbs.

CHIPOLA - Early Archaic, 10,000 - 8000 B. P.

G8, $125-$200
Chipola River, FL.

G9, $300-$550
Hamilton Co., FL.

LOCATION: Southern Southeastern states. **DESCRIPTION:** A small to medium size triangular point with long, expanding auricles and a tapered shoulder. Bases are deeply concave and are thinned. Rare in type area.

CITRUS - Late Archaic to Woodland, 3500 - 2000 B. P.

(Also see Culbreath and Hernando)

LOCATION: Southern Southeastern states including Florida. **DESCRIPTION:** A medium to large size basal-notched point. The stem is wider than *Hernando.* **I.D. Key:** Notches and later flaking on blade.

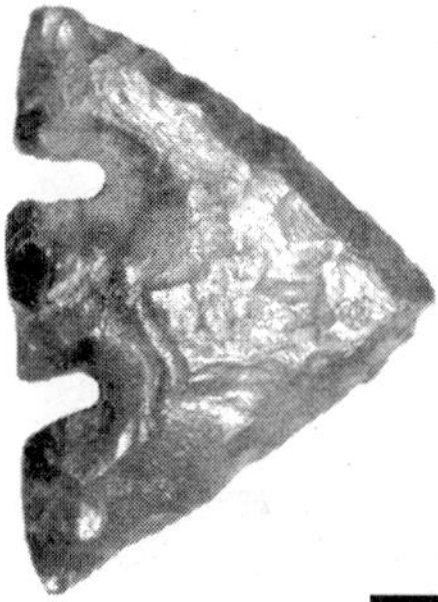

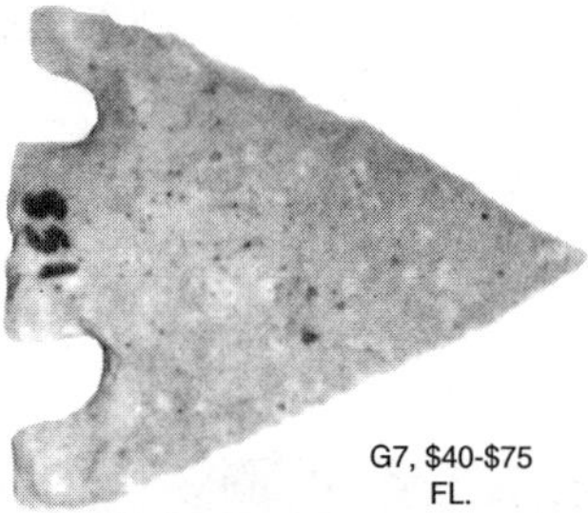

G7, $40-$75
FL.

G6, $30-$60
FL.

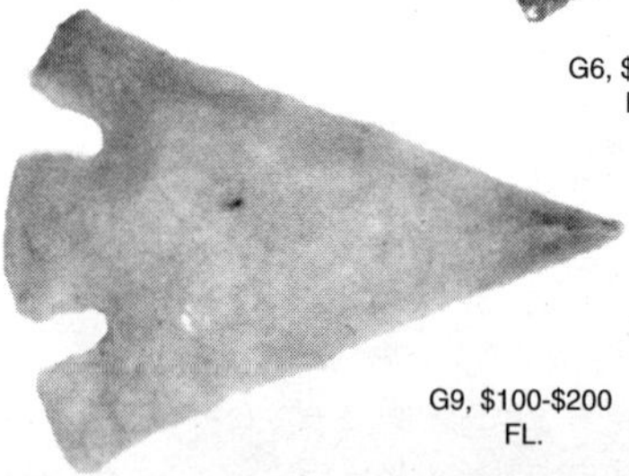

G9, $100-$200
FL.

G7, $100-$175
NW Cent. FL.

G8, $200-$400
Hillsborough Co., FL.

G9, $125-$250
FL.

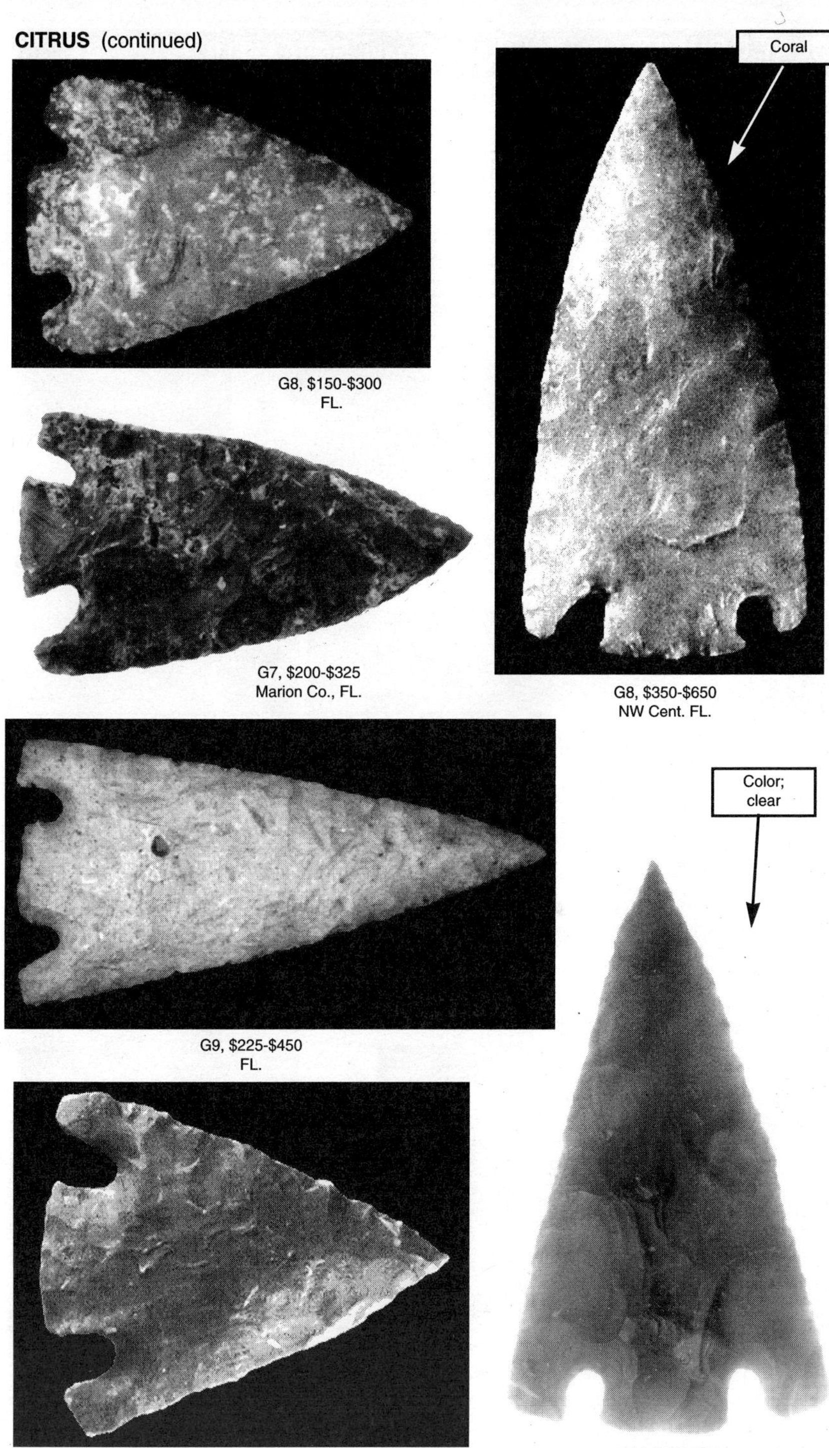

G8, $150-$300
FL.

G7, $200-$325
Marion Co., FL.

G8, $350-$650
NW Cent. FL.

G9, $225-$450
FL.

G6, $80-$150
Pasco Co., FL.

G10, $400-$800
FL.

CLAY COUNTY - Middle to Late Archaic, 5000 - 3500 B. P.

((Also see Kirk Corner Notched and Lafayette)

G8, $75-$150
Central FL.

G8, $75-$150
Burke Co., GA.

G6, $30-$60
Burke Co., GA.

G6, $150-$250
Dodge Co., GA.

G8, $250-$450
GA.

G6, $250-$400
Taylor Co., FL.

G8, $200-$300
Suwannee Co., FL.

LOCATION: Southern Southeastern states including Florida. **DESCRIPTION:** A medium to large size basal-notched point with outward-flaring, squared shoulders (clipped wing). Blades are recurvate. **I.D. Key:** Deep notches and squared barbs.

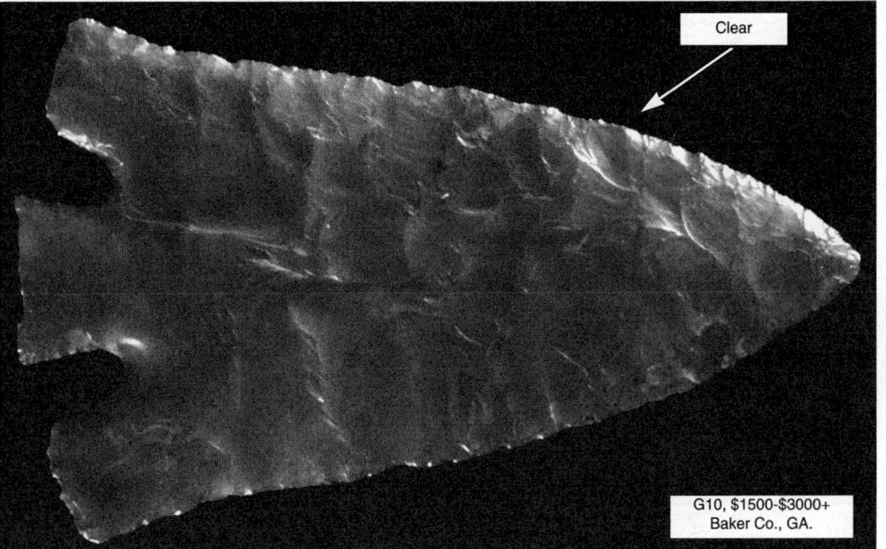

G10, $1500-$3000+
Baker Co., GA.

CLOVIS - Early Paleo, 14,000 - 9000 B. P.

(Also see Chipola, Redstone, Simpson and Suwanee)

G8, $300-$600
FL.

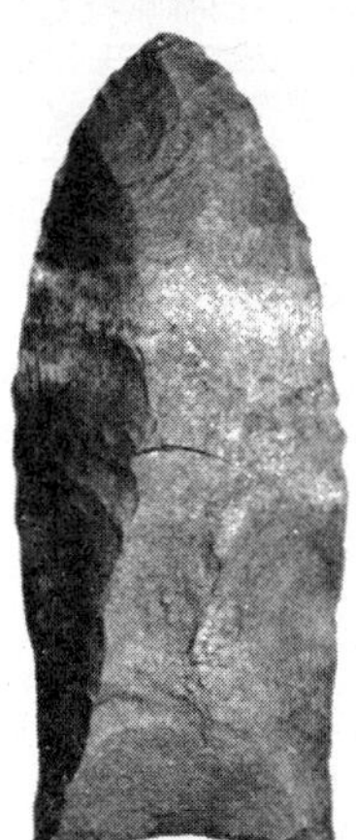

G9, $400-$800
Aucilla River, FL.

G6, $475-$950
Aucilla River, FL.

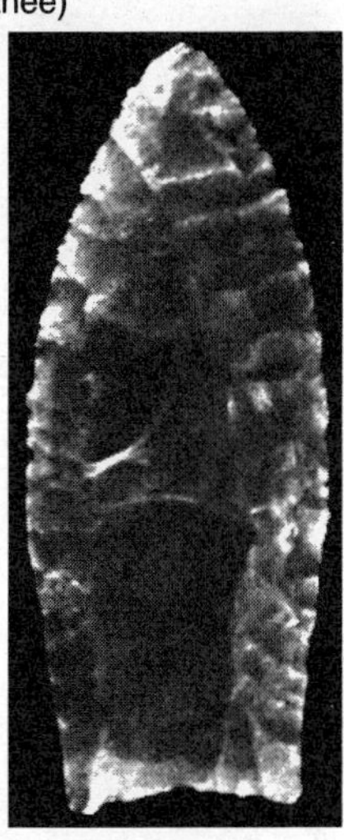

G8, $900-$1800
Suwannee River, FL.

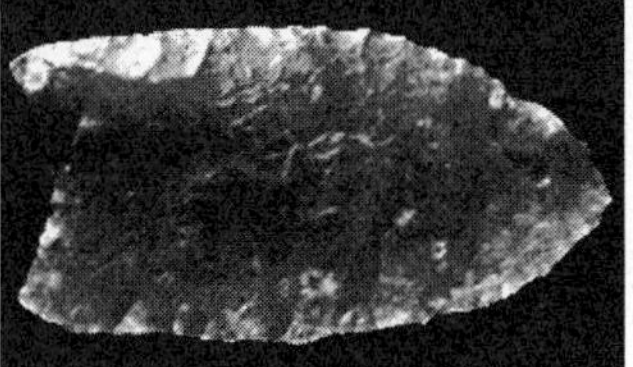

G4, $125-$250
Suwannee River, FL.

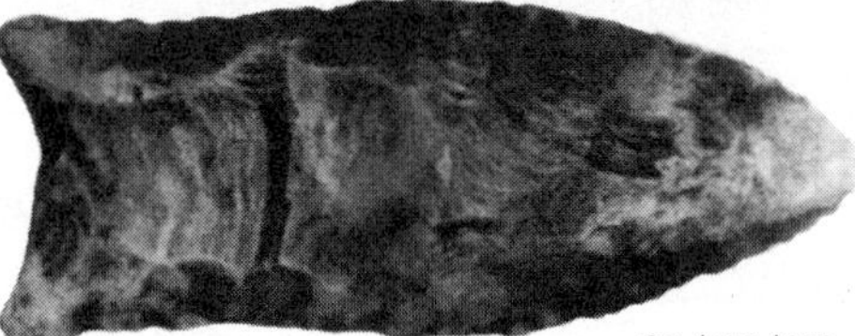

G8, $475-$950
FL.

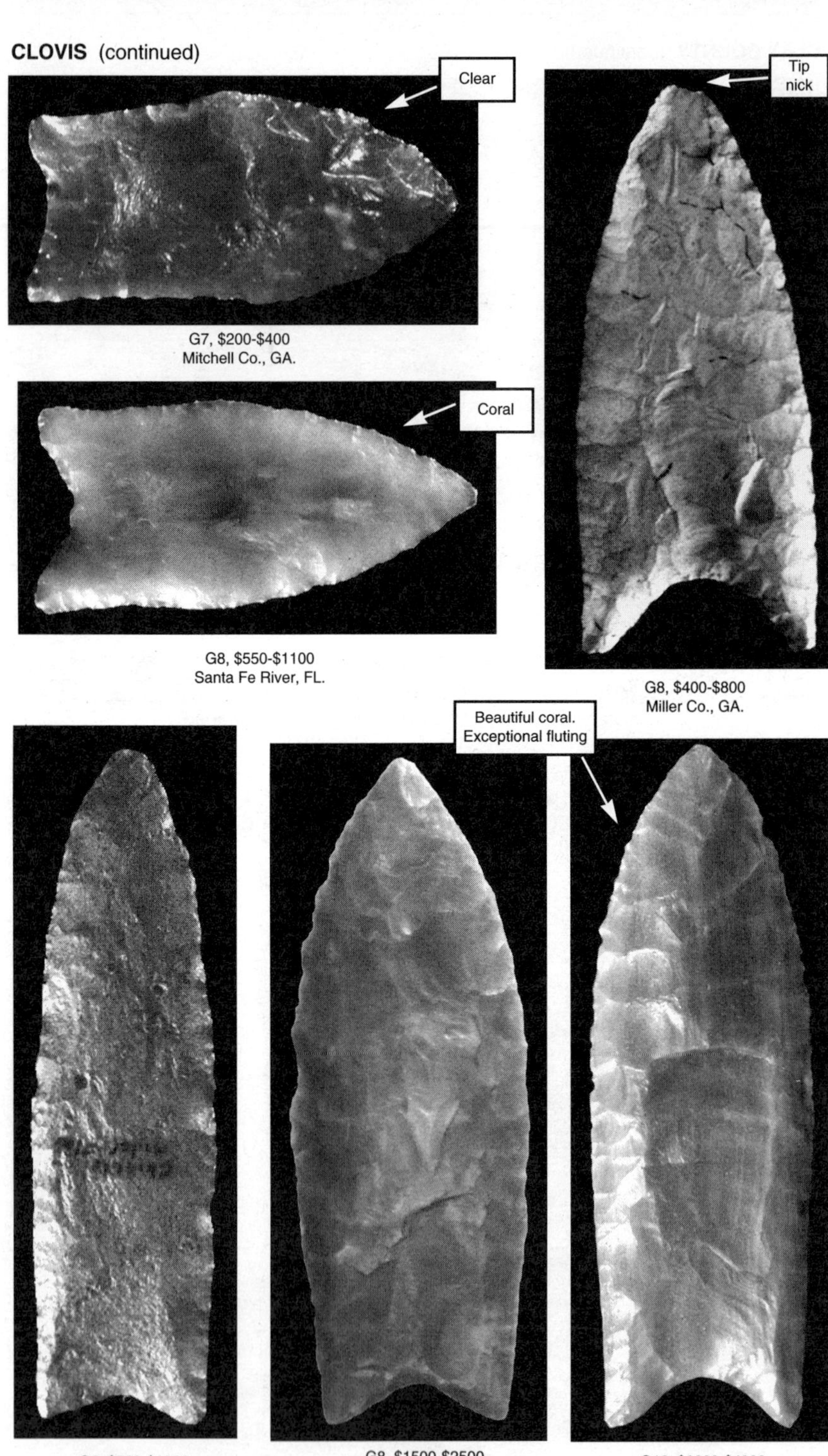

G7, $200-$400
Mitchell Co., GA.

G8, $550-$1100
Santa Fe River, FL.

G8, $400-$800
Miller Co., GA.

G6, $500-$1000
Chipola River, FL.

G8, $1500-$2500
FL.

G10, $2000-$4000
FL.

CLOVIS (continued)

LOCATION: All of North America. **DESCRIPTION:** A medium to large size, auriculate, fluted, lanceolate point with convex sides and a concave base that is ground. Most examples are fluted on both sides about 1/3 the way up from the base. The flaking can be random to parallel. *Clovis* is the earliest point type in the hemisphere. It is believed that this form was developed here after early man crossed the Bering Straits to reach this continent about 50,000 years ago. Current theories place the origin of *Clovis* in the Southeastern U.S. since more examples are found in Florida, Alabama and Tennessee than anywhere else. **I.D. Key:** Paleo flaking, shoulders, batan fluting instead of indirect style.

COLUMBIA - Woodland, 2000 - 1000 B. P.

(Also see Hamilton, Ledbetter and Thonotosassa)

G4, $10-$20
FL.

LOCATION: Southern Southeastern states. **DESCRIPTION:** A medium to large size stemmed point. Shoulders are tapered to horizontal and are weak. Stem is short and slightly expanding. Base is straight.

G5, $20-$40
FL.

G9, $75-$150
FL.

G10, $100-$200
FL.

G10, $125-$250
FL.

CONERLY - Middle Archaic, 7500 - 4500 B. P.

(Also see Beaver Lake, Simpson and Suwanee)

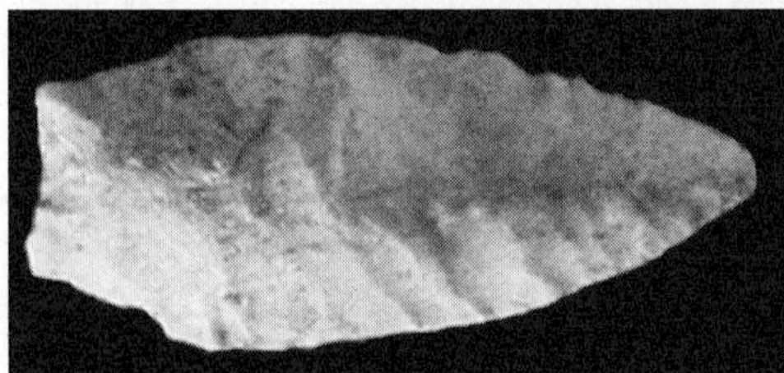

G5, $25-$50
Burke Co., GA.

G8, $50-$100
Briar Creek
Burke Co., GA.

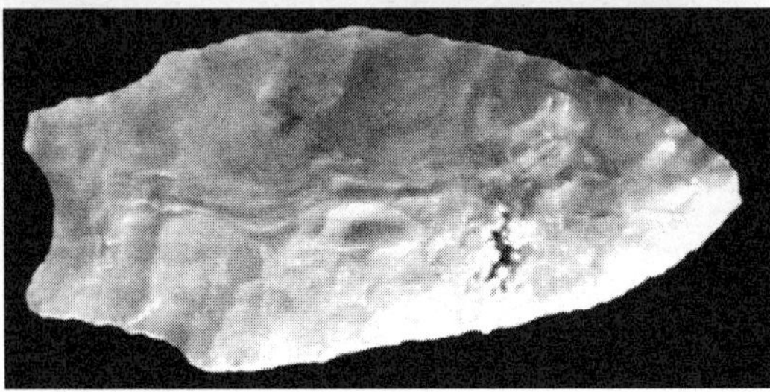

G6, $30-$60
Burke Co., GA.

G8, $35-$70
Screven Co., GA.

G8, $150-$250
Briar Creek
Burke Co., GA.

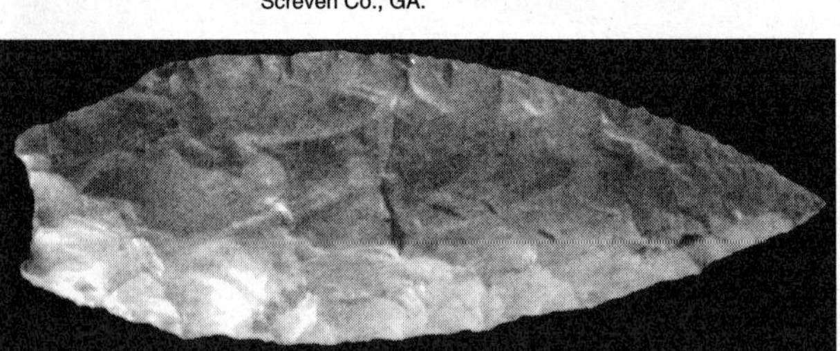

G8, $100-$200
Burke Co., GA.

G8, $200-$350
Briar Creek
Savannah River, GA.

CONERLY (continued)

LOCATION: Southern Southeastern states, especially Tennessee, Georgia and Florida. **DESCRIPTION:** A medium to large auriculate point with a contracting, concave base which can be ground. On some examples, the hafting area can be seen with the presence of very weak shoulders. The base is usually thinned. Believed to be related to the *Guilford* type. **I.D. Key:** Base concave, thickness, flaking.

COTTONBRIDGE - Middle Archaic, 6000 - 4000 B. P.

(Also see Abbey and Elora)

LOCATION: Southern Gulf states. **DESCRIPTION:** A medium size, broad, stemmed point that is fairly thick and beveled on all four sides. Shoulders are tapered and blade edges are straight. Base is small and rounded with contracting sides.

G7, $35-$60
Henry Co., AL.

GC

COWHOUSE SLOUGH - Transitional Paleo, 10,000 - 6000 B. P.

(Also see Suwannee)

G6, $90-$180
FL.

G5, $65-$125
Lawrence Co., AL.

LOCATION: Southeastern states. **DESCRIPTION:** A medium to large size, broad, lanceolate blade with a contracting, straight to concave base which may be ground as well as fluted or thinned. I.D. Key: Paleo flaking.

CULBREATH - Late Archaic to Woodland, 5000 - 3000 B. P.

(Also see Citrus, Clay County, Hernando, Kirk Corner Notched and Lafayette)

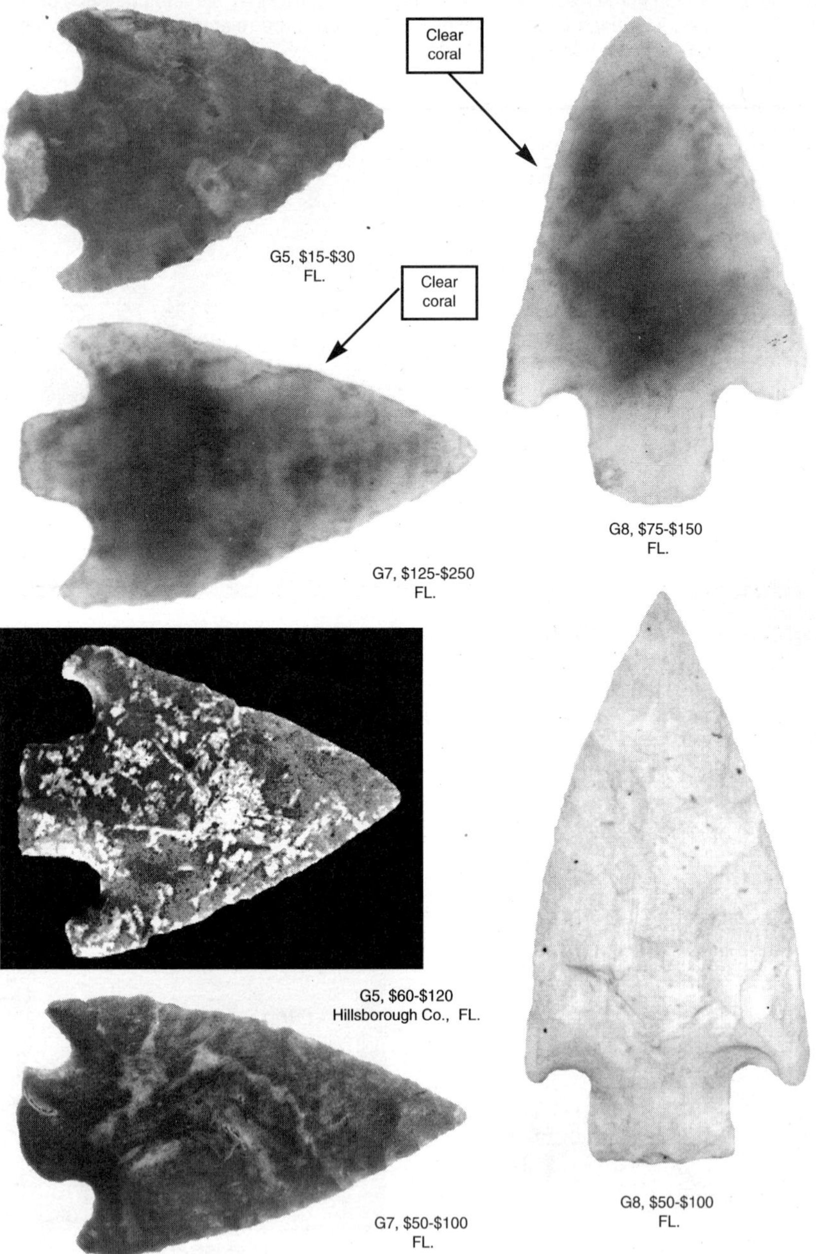

G5, $15-$30
FL.

G8, $75-$150
FL.

G7, $125-$250
FL.

G5, $60-$120
Hillsborough Co., FL.

G8, $50-$100
FL.

G7, $50-$100
FL.

LOCATION: Southern Gulf states. **DESCRIPTION:** A medium to large size, broad, basal notched point, Tangs are rounded and blade edges are convex. On some examples the tangs do not reach the base. The earlier *Eva* point found in Kentucky and Tennessee could be a Northern cousin. **I.D. Key:** Notching.

G6, $40-$80
Marion Co., FL.

G8, $350-$700
Polk Co., FL.

G9, $125-$250
FL.

G10, $450-$900
Hillsborough Co., FL.

CYPRESS CREEK - Middle Archaic, 7000 - 3000 B. P.

(Also see Alachua, Hillsborough, Levy, Morrow Mountain, Putnam and Sumter)

G4, $15-$25
FL.

G8, $50-$100
Pasco Co., FL., St. Joe.

G7, $30-$60
Pasco Co., FL.

G5, $25-$50
FL.

LOCATION: Southern Southeastern states. **DESCRIPTION:** A medium size point with a short, pointed to rounded contracting base. Shoulders have short barbs and can be asymmetrical with one barbed and the other tapered.

DRILL - Paleo to Historic, 14,000 - 200 B. P.

(Also see Edgefield Scraper)

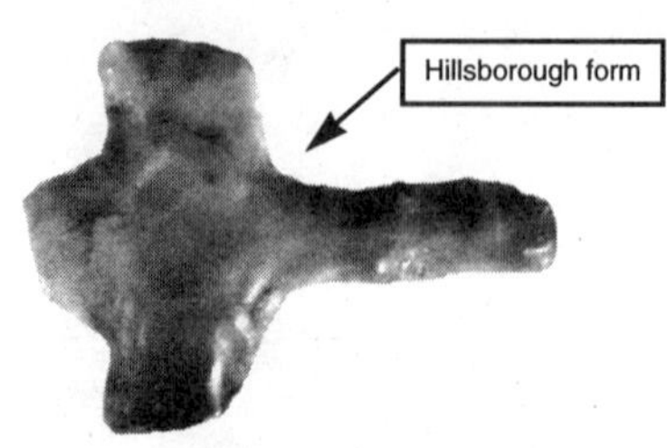

G5, $15-$25
Hillsborough Co., FL.

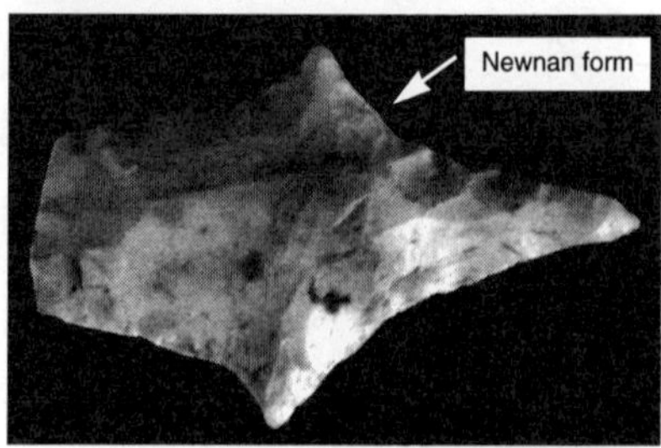

G9, $25-$45
Marion Co., FL.

DRILL (continued)

LOCATION: Everywhere. **DESCRIPTION:** Although many drills were made from scratch, all point types were made into the drill form. Usually, heavily resharpened and broken points were salvaged and rechipped into drills. These objects were certainly used as drills (evidence of extreme edge wear), but there is speculation that some of these forms may have been used as pins for clothing, ornaments, ear plugs and other uses.

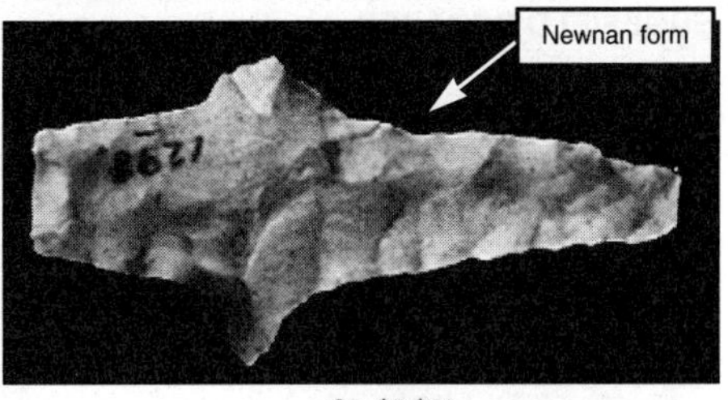

G5, $8-$15
Marion Co., FL.
Newnan

DUVAL - Late Woodland, 2000 - 1000 B. P.

(Also see Bradford)

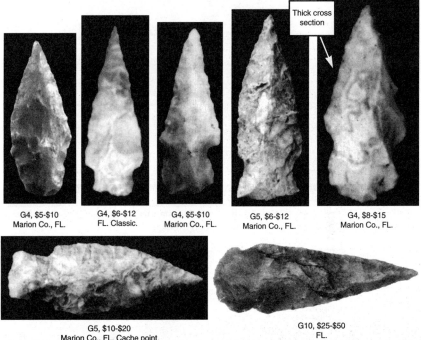

Thick cross section

G4, $5-$10
Marion Co., FL.

G4, $6-$12
FL. Classic.

G4, $5-$10
Marion Co., FL.

G5, $6-$12
Marion Co., FL.

G4, $8-$15
Marion Co., FL.

G5, $10-$20
Marion Co., FL. Cache point

G10, $25-$50
FL.

LOCATION: Gulf states. **DESCRIPTION:** A small to medium size, narrow, spike point with shallow side notches, an expanding stem and a straight to concave base. The base can be slight to moderate.

EDGEFIELD SCRAPER - Early Archaic, 9000 - 6000 B. P.

LOCATION: Southern Atlantic coast states, especially South Carolina, Georgia, Alabama and Florida. **DESCRIPTION:** A medium to large size corner notched point that is asymmetrical. Many are uniface and usually steeply beveled along the diagonal side. The blade on all examples leans heavily to one side. Used as a hafted scraper.

EDGEFIELD SCRAPER (continued)

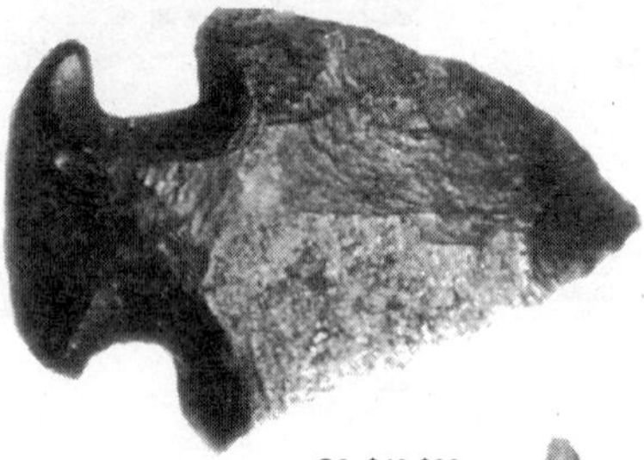

G8, $40-$80
FL.

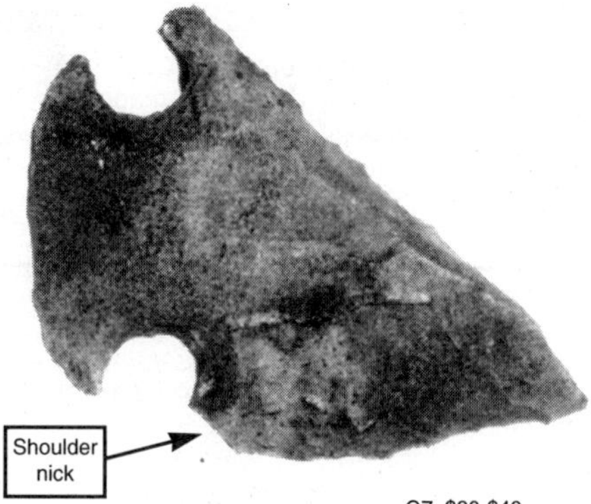

Shoulder nick

G7, $20-$40
FL.

G10, $65-$125
FL.

G10, $65-$125
FL.

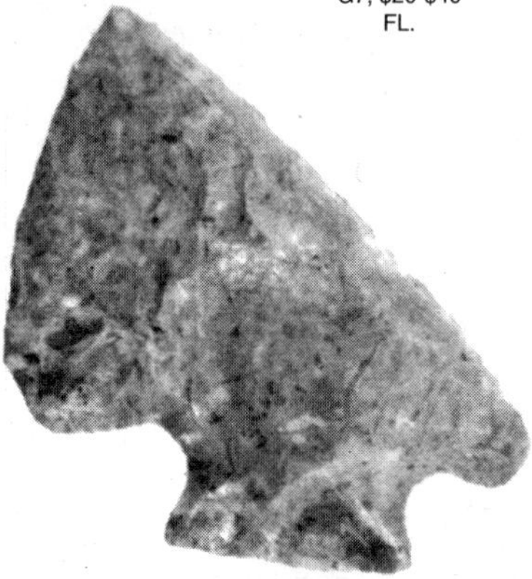

G10, $65-$125
FL.

ELORA - Middle to Late Archaic, 6000 - 3000 B. P.

(Also see Abbey, Alachua, Cottonbridge, Levy, Newnan, Notchaway, Pickwick, Putnam, Savannah River, Six Mile Creek and South Prong Creek)

G3, $8-$15
Decatur Co., GA.

G3, $8-$15
Decatur Co., GA.

G6, $20-$35
FL.

ELORA (continued)

Thick cross section

G7, $15-$30
Hillsborough Co., FL.

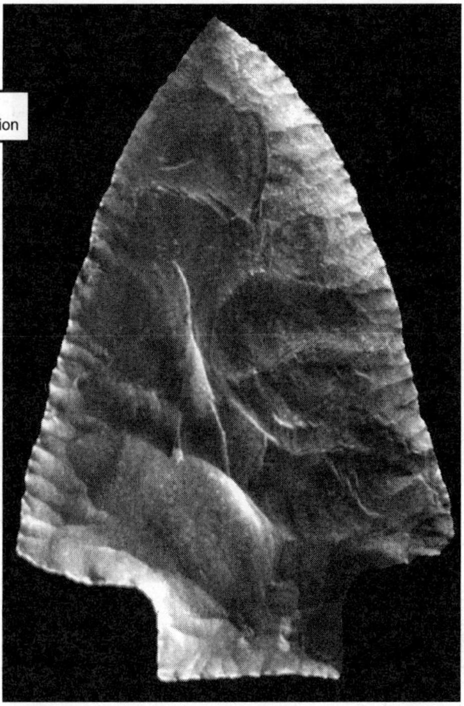

G8, $100-$150
Taylor Co., FL.

LOCATION: Southeastern states. **DESCRIPTION:** A medium size, broad, thick point with tapered shoulders and a short, contracting stem that is sometimes fractured or snapped off. However, some examples have finished bases. Early examples are serrated. **I.D. KEY:** One barb sharper, edgework.

FLINT RIVER - Late Archaic, 4000 - 3000 B. P.

(Also see Elora and Pickwick)

G6, $100-$175
Flint River, GA.

LOCATION: Southern GA, AL & northern FL. **DESCRIPTION:** A medium to large size, expanded shoulder, contracted stem point. A southern cousin to the *Pickwick* type.

GILCHRIST - Early Archaic, 10,000 - 7000 B. P.

(Also see Duval, Beaver Lake and Taylor)

G6, $20-$40
Marion Co., FL.

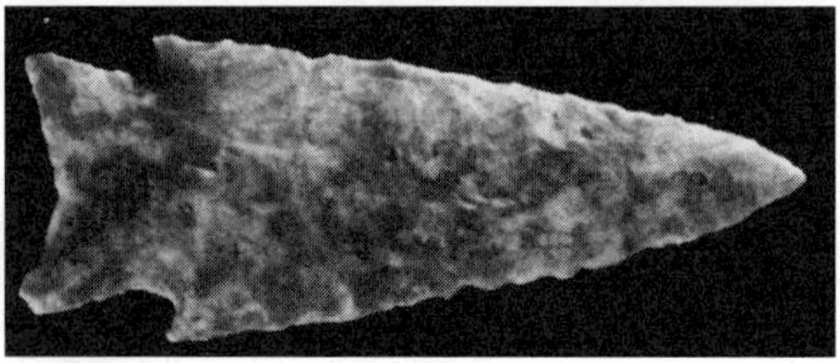

G8, $125-$250
Marion Co., FL.

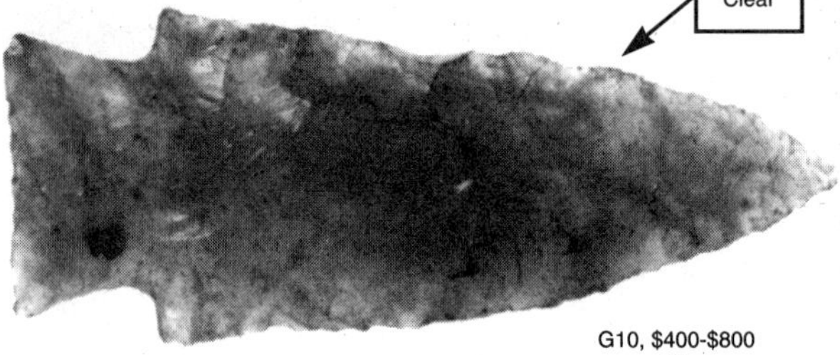

Clear

G10, $400-$800
FL.

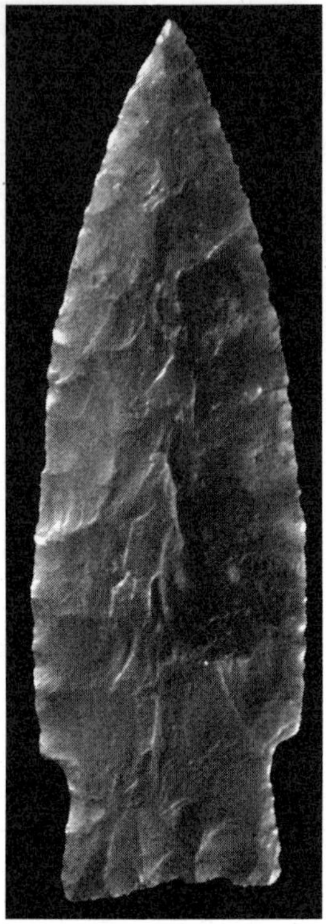

G9, $400-$600
Levy Co., FL.

LOCATION: Southern Southeastern states. **DESCRIPTION:** A small to medium size, broad point with a short stem that is square, bifurcated or auriculate. Shoulders are weak and can be tapered, horizontal or slightly barbed. The blade can be straight or concave and could be ground. Early forms may be related to *Suwannee.*

GREENBRIER

(See Osceola Greenbrier)

HAMILTON - Early Archaic, 8000 - 5000 B. P.

(Also see Columbia, Kirk, Savannah River, Seminole and Thonotosassa)

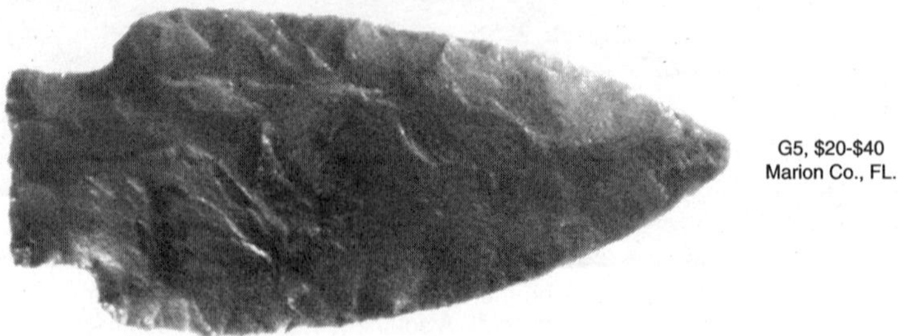

G5, $20-$40
Marion Co., FL.

G6, $40-$80
Suwannee Riv., FL.

G7, $50-$100
Hillsborough Co., FL.

G7, $75-$150
FL.

G8, $125-$250
FL.

LOCATION: Southern Southeastern states. **DESCRIPTION:** A large size, thick, broad stemmed point with a convex to straight squarish base. Shoulders are horizontal to slightly tapered. Base is straight to incurvate. **I.D. KEY:** Small shoulders, basal form.

HARAHEY - Mississippian, 700 - 350 B. P.

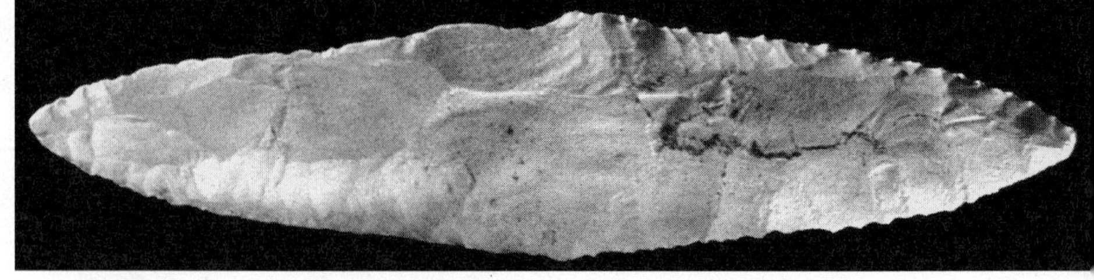

G8, $150-$300
Early Co., GA.

LOCATION: Midwestern to Eastern states. **DESCRIPTION:** A large, double pointed knife that is usually beveled on one or all four sides of each face. The cross section is rhomboid. The true buffalo skinning knife. **I.D. Key:** Two and four beveled double pointed form.

HARDEE BEVELED - Early to Middle Archaic, 8000 - 5000 B. P.

(Also see Alachua, Levy, Marion and Putnam)

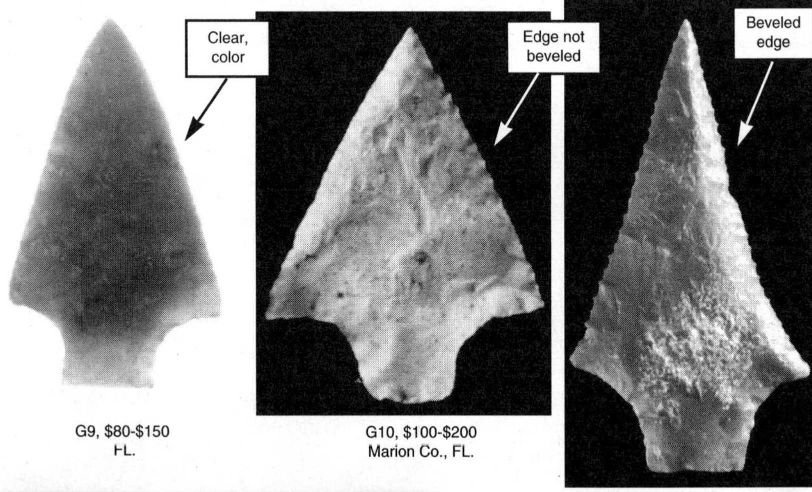

G9, $80-$150
FL.

G10, $100-$200
Marion Co., FL.

G8, $100-$250
Hillsborough Co., FL.

G6, $40-$75
Marion Co., FL.

LOCATION: Southern Southeastern states. **DESCRIPTION:** A medium to large size stemmed point that occurs in two forms. One has a distinct bevel on one side of each face. The other has the typical bifacial beveling. Shoulders are tapered to horizontal and are sharp. This type resembles the other Florida Archaic stemmed points (see above) except for the bevel and may be their ancestor. **I.D. KEY:** Beveling and sharp shoulders.

G8, $150-$250
Pasco Co., FL., Land O' Lakes.

G7, $75-$150
Marion Co., FL.

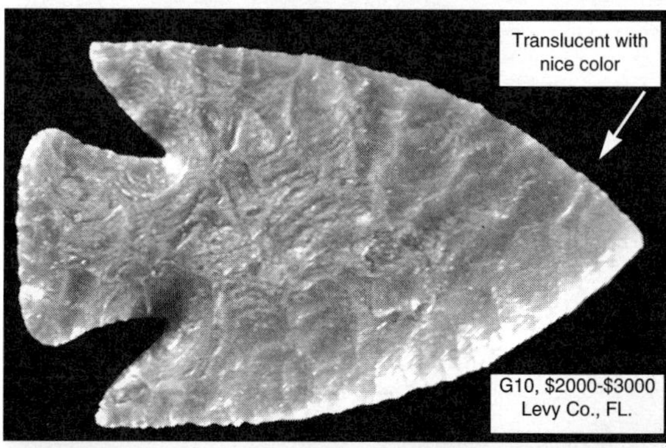

G9, $150-$300
Citrus Co., FL.

HARDIN - Early Archaic, 9000 - 6000 B. P.

(Also see Cypress Creek, Kirk Corner Notched, Lafayette and Ocala)

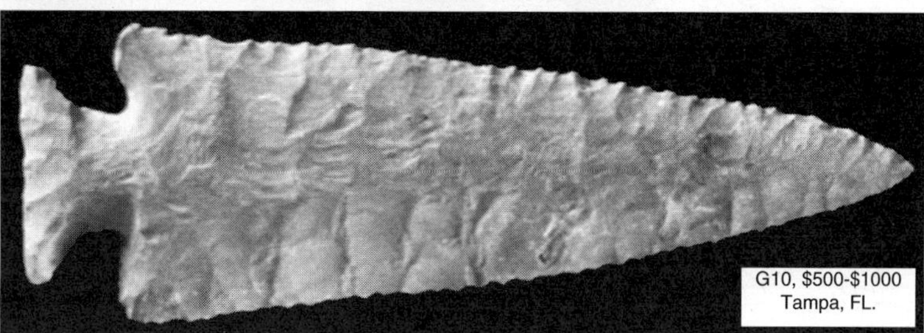

G10, $2000-$3000
Levy Co., FL.

LOCATION: Midwestern to Eastern states. **DESCRIPTION:** A large, well made triangular barbed point with an expanded base that is usually ground. Resharpened examples have one beveled edge on each face. This type is believed to have evolved from the *Scottsbluff* type. **I.D. Key:** Notches and stem form.

G10, $500-$1000
Tampa, FL.

HERNANDO - Late Archaic, 4000 - 2500 B. P.

(Also see Citrus and Culbreath)

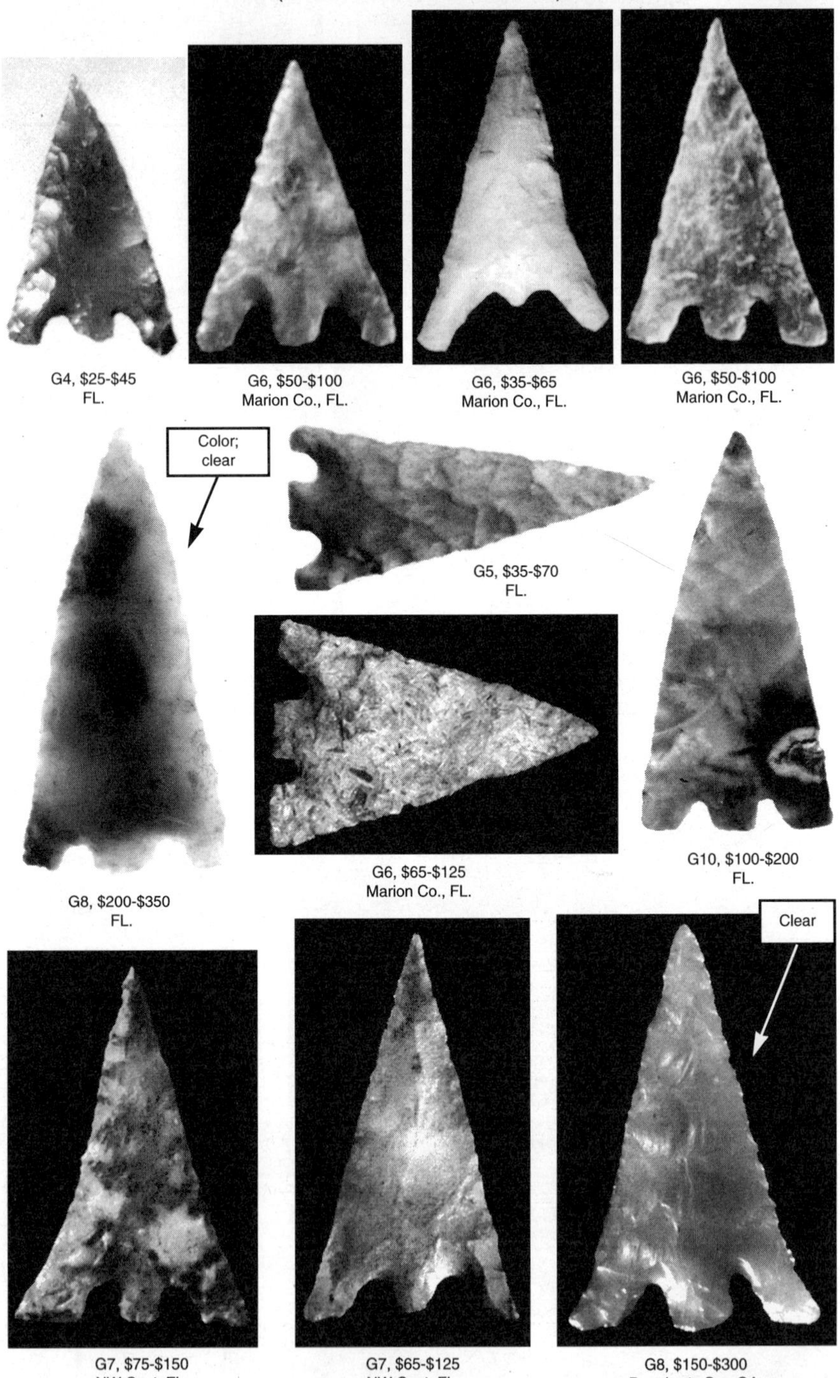

G4, $25-$45
FL.

G6, $50-$100
Marion Co., FL.

G6, $35-$65
Marion Co., FL.

G6, $50-$100
Marion Co., FL.

G5, $35-$70
FL.

G8, $200-$350
FL.

G6, $65-$125
Marion Co., FL.

G10, $100-$200
FL.

G7, $75-$150
NW Cent. FL.

G7, $65-$125
NW Cent. FL.

G8, $150-$300
Dougherty Co., GA.

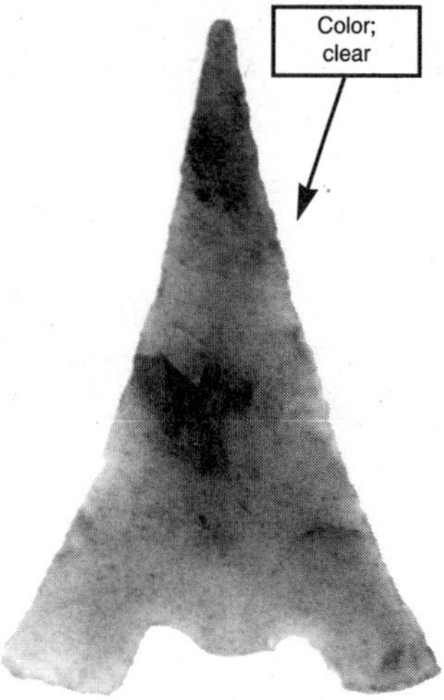

G9, $225-$450
FL.

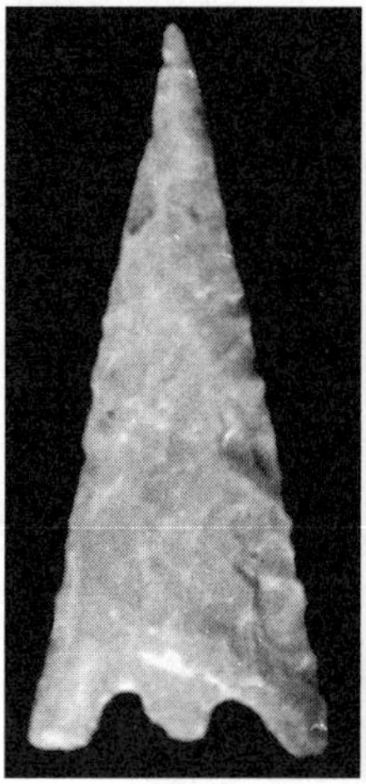

G8, $90-$175
Marion Co., FL.

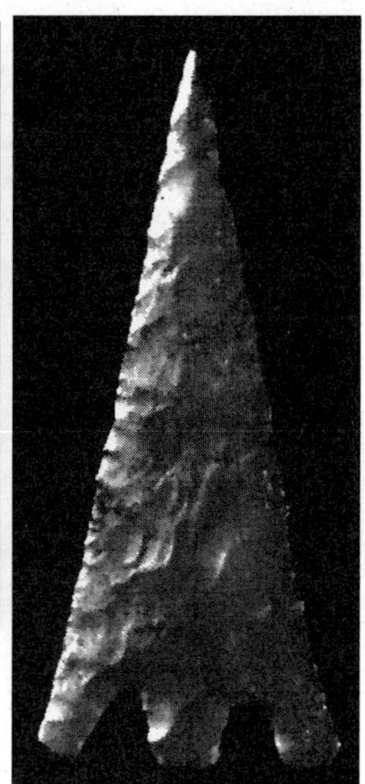

G10, $250-$600
NW Cent. FL.

G9, $125-$250
FL

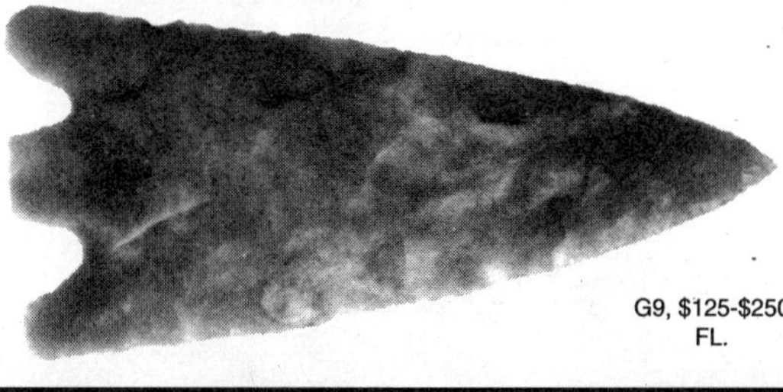

G9, $125-$250
FL.

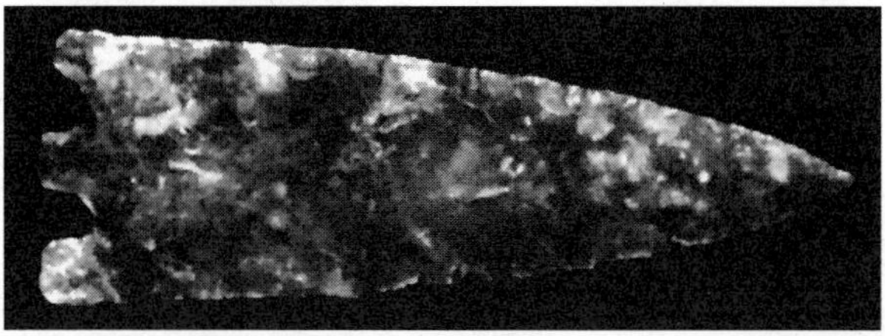

G9, $250-$400
NW Cent. FL.

LOCATION: Georgia, Alabama and Flordia. **DESCRIPTION:** A medium to large size, basal notched, triangular point with wide flaring tangs that may extend beyond the base. Side edges are straight to concave. Similar in outline only to the much earlier *Eva* type. Has been found in same layer with a form (Copena?) resembling Tallhassee, but not as old. **I.D. KEY:** Early flaking and narrow stem.

HILLSBOROUGH - Middle Archaic, 7000 - 5000 B. P.

(Also see Marion and Newman)

LOCATION: Florida only. **DESCRIPTION:** A medium to large size, broad, triangular point with a small contracting base. Shoulders are barbed and can expand beyond the base.

G5, $50-$80
Alachua Co., FL.

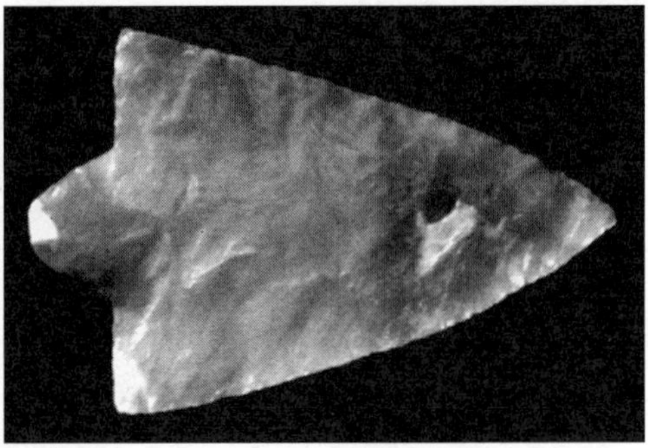

G8, $150-$300
Pasco Co., FL.

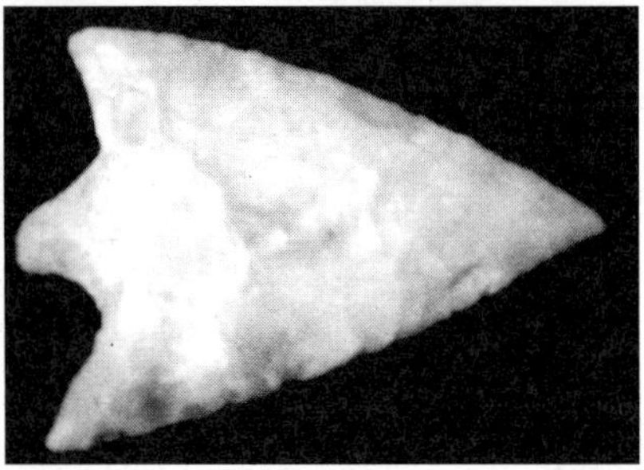

G8, $125-$200
Marion Co., FL.

G7, $50-$100
FL.

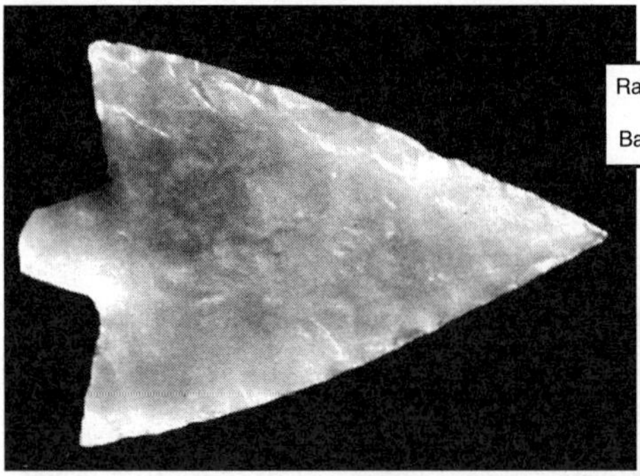

G8; $175-$350
Pasco Co., FL.

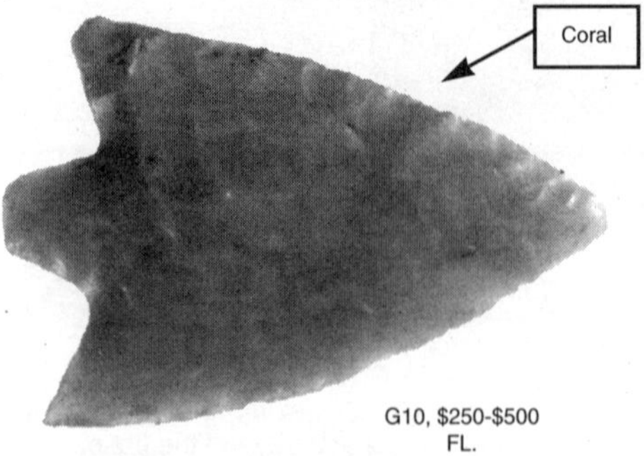

G10, $250-$500
FL.

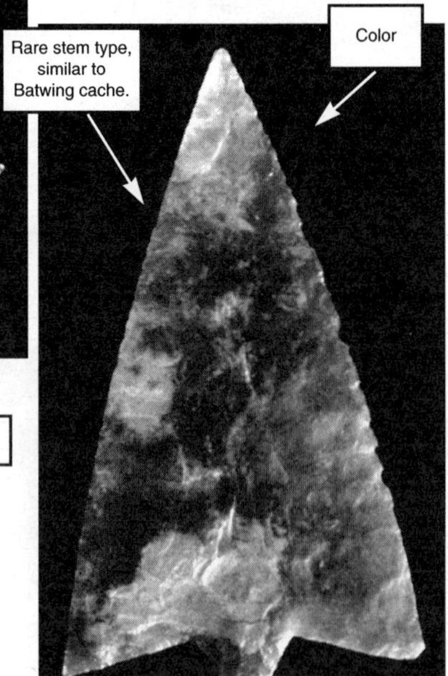

G9, $500-$1000
Polk Co., FL.

Thin cross section

Patenated white

G9, $400-$800
FL.

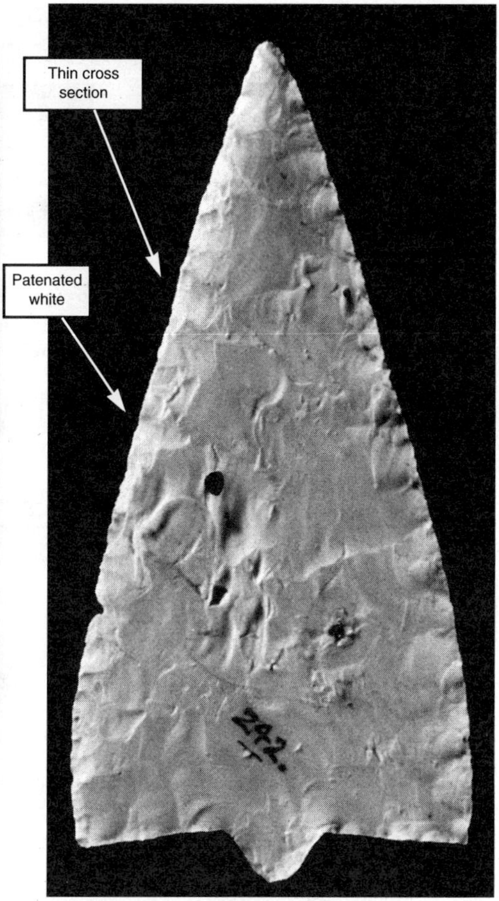

G9, $500-$1000
Marion Co., FL.

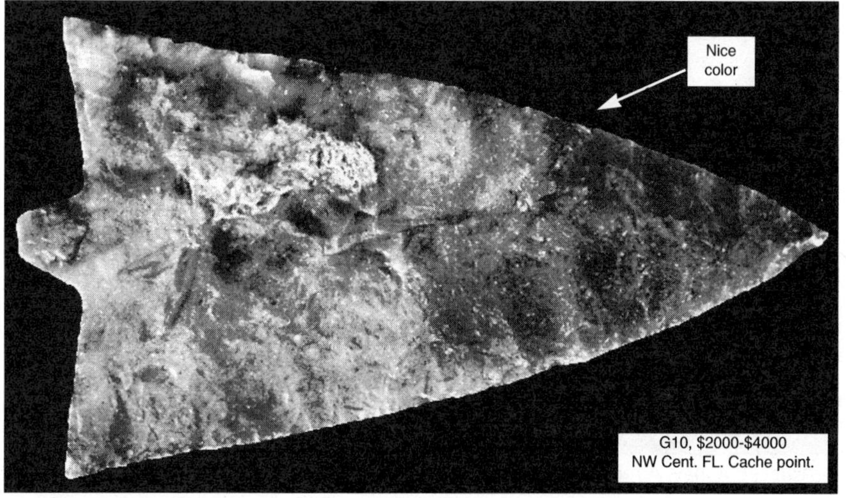

G10, $2000-$4000
NW Cent. FL. Cache point.

ITCHETUCKNEE - Mississippian to Historic, 700 - 200 B. P.

(Also see Pinellas)

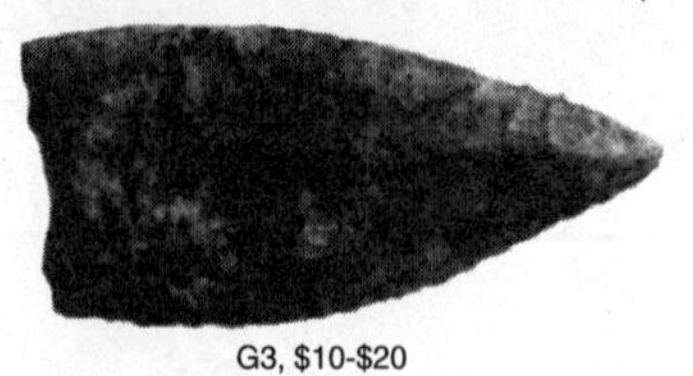

G3, $10-$20
FL.

G7, $50-$75
Marion Co., FL.

LOCATION: Southeastern states. **DESCRIPTION:** A small to medium size, thin, narrow, lanceolate point with usually a straight base. Flaking quality is excellent. This point is called *Guntersville* to the north. **I.D. KEY:** Narrowness and blade expansion

JACKSON - Late Woodland to Mississippian, 2000 - 700 B. P.

(Also see Duval)

LOCATION: Coastal states. **DESCRIPTION:** A small size, thick, triangular point with wide, shallow side notches. Some examples have an unfinished rind or base. Called *Swan Lake* in upper Southeastern states

G10, $20-$35
FL.

G5, $8-$15
FL.

KIRK CORNER NOTCHED - Early to Middle Archaic, 9000 - 6000 B. P.

(Also see Bolen, Hardin and Lafayette)

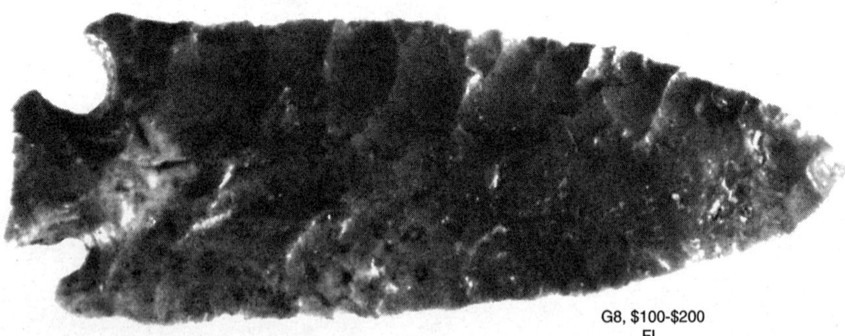

G8, $100-$200
FL.

LOCATION: Southeastern states. **DESCRIPTION:** A medium to large size, corner notched point. Blade edges can be convex to recurved and are finely serrated on many examples. The base can be concave, convex, straight or auriculate. **I.D. KEY**: Secondary edgework.

KIRK SERRATED - Early to Middle Archaic, 9000 - 6000 B. P.

(Also see Abbey, Arredondo, Boggy Branch, Bolen, Elora, Hamilton and Six Mile Creek)

G6, $10-$20
Pasco Co., FL.

G6, $8-$15
Pasco Co., FL.

G6, $8-$15
Pasco Co., FL.

G7, $15-$30
FL.

G8, $30-$60
FL.

G10, $120-$250
FL.

G5, $8-$15
Pasco Co., FL.

G7, $20-$40
FL.

LOCATION: Eastern to Gulf Coastal states. **DESCRIPTION:** A medium to large size, barbed, stemmed point with deep notches or fine serrations along the blade edges. The stem is parallel, contracting or expanding. The stem sides may be steeply beveled on opposite faces. Some examples also have a distinct bevel on the right side of each blade edge. The base can be concave, convex or straight, and can be very short. The shoulders are usually strongly barbed. **I.D. KEY:** Serrations.

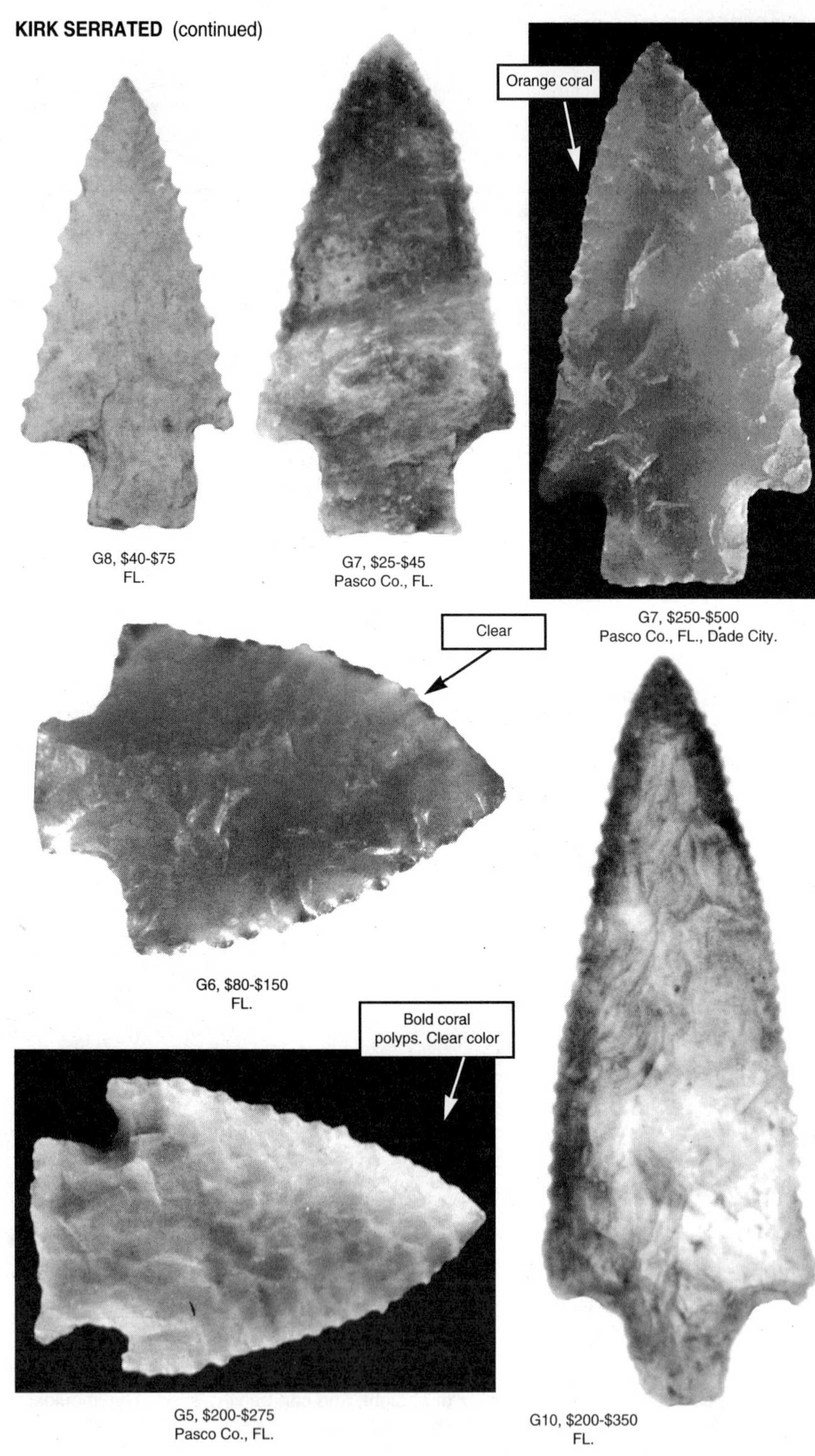

G8, $40-$75
FL.

G7, $25-$45
Pasco Co., FL.

G7, $250-$500
Pasco Co., FL., Dade City.

G6, $80-$150
FL.

G5, $200-$275
Pasco Co., FL.

G10, $200-$350
FL.

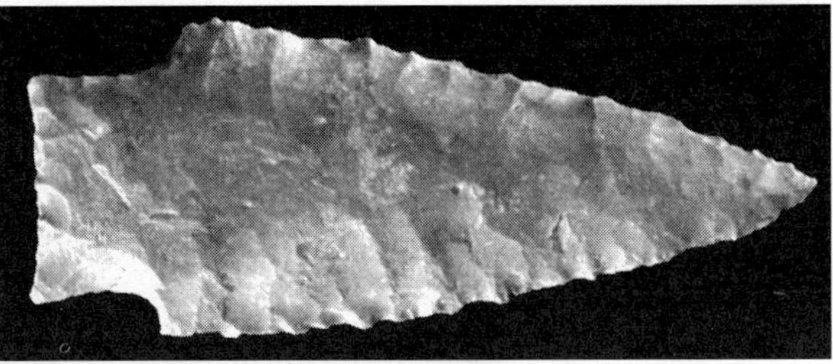

G8, $40-$80
Marion Co., FL.

G8, $150-$300
Marion Co., FL.

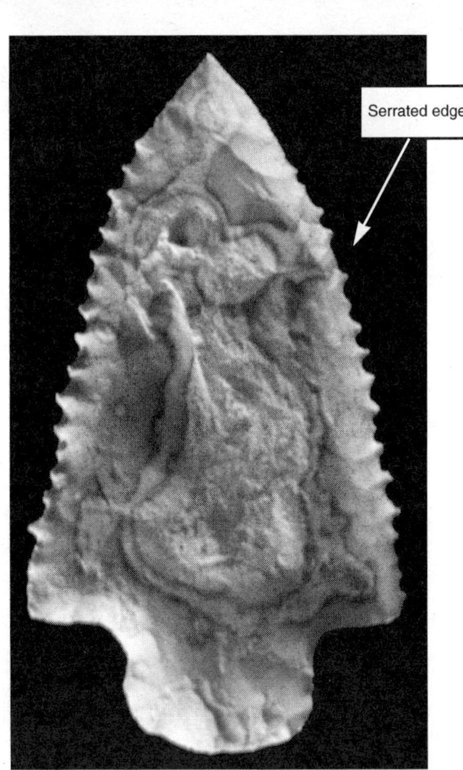

G9, $400-$650
Hillsborough Co., FL.

G7, $75-$150
Pasco Co., FL.

LAFAYETTE - Late Archaic, 5000 - 3500 B. P.

(Also see Bolen, Clay, Culbreath and Kirk Corner Notched)

G6, $30-$60
Marion Co., FL.

G7, $40-$80
Pinellas Co., FL.

G8, $90-$175
Marion Co., FL.

G7, $35-$70
Marion Co., FL.

G8, $75-$150
FL.

G9, $250-$500
FL.

LOCATION: Southern to Southeastern states. **DESCRIPTION:** A medium size, broad, corner-notched point with a straight to concave base. Tangs and basal corners are more rounded than pointed. Related to *Clay* points. Previously shown (in error) as *Ocala* points.

G5, $20-$30
FL.

G8, $65-$125
FL.

G9, $400-$800
Marion Co., FL.

LEON - Woodland - Mississippian, 1500 - 1000 B. P.

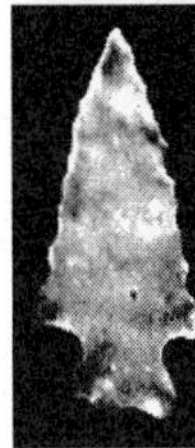

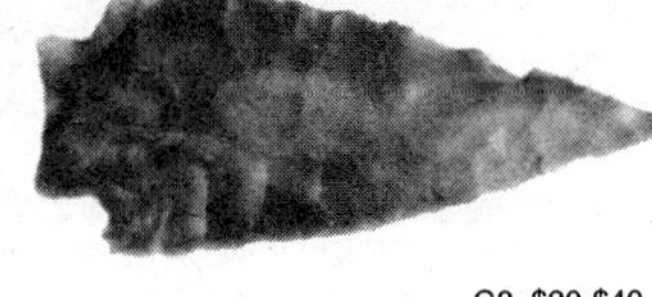

G7, $10-$20
Hillsborough Co., FL.

G8, $20-$40
FL.

LOCATION: Southern to Southeastern states. **DESCRIPTION:** A medium size, broad, contracted stemmed point with wide, tapered to slightly barbed shoulders. May have evolved from the earlier *Newnan* form. **I.D. KEY:** Edgework and one ear is stronger.

LEVY - Late Archaic, 5000 - 3000 B. P.

(Also see Abbey, Alachua, Cypress Creek, Elora, Hardee Beveled, Marion, Newnan, Oauchita, Putnam, Savannah River and Sumter)

G7, $75-$150
Marion Co., FL.

G7, $20-$50
FL.

G9 $100-$200
FL.

G8, $50-$100
FL.

G6, $100-$200
Hillsborough Co., FL.

G10, $200-$350
Decatur Co., GA.

LOCATION: Southern to Southeastern states. **DESCRIPTION:** A medium size, broad, contracted stemmed point with wide, tapered to slightly barbed shoulders. May have evolved from the earlier *Newnan* form. **I.D. KEY:** Edgework and one ear is stronger.

MARIANNA - Transitional Paleo, 10,000 - 8500 B. P.

(Also see Conerly)

LOCATION: Southern to Southeastern states. **DESCRIPTION:** A medium size lanceolate point with a constricted, concave base. Look for parallel to oblique flaking.

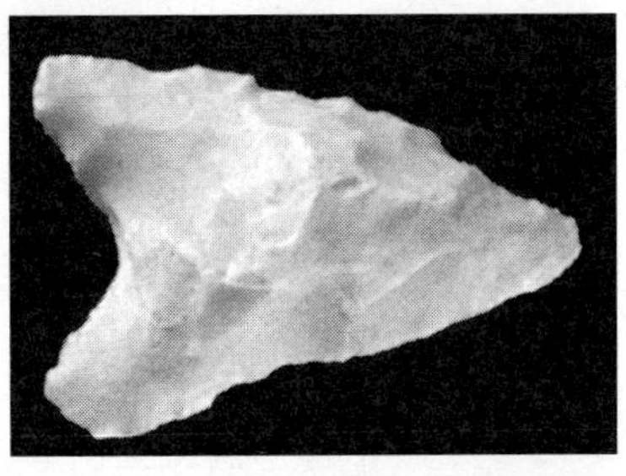

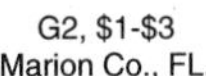

G2, $1-$3
Marion Co., FL.

MARION - Middle Archaic, 7000 - 3000 B. P.

(Also see Adena, Alachua, Cottonbridge, Cypress Creek, Hardee Beveled, Levy, Morrow Mountain, Newnan, Pickwick and Putnam)

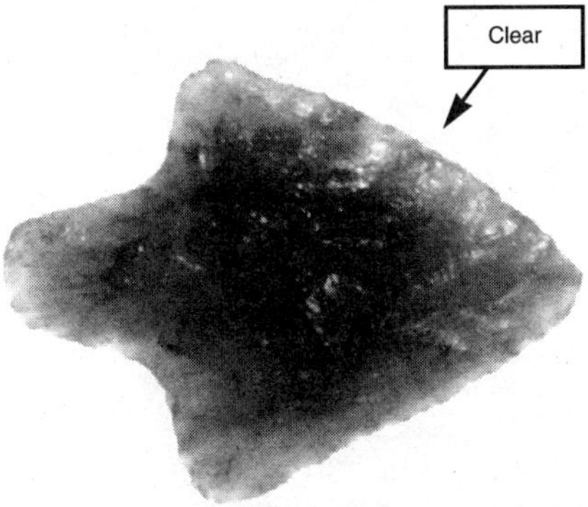

Clear

G8, $100-$200
FL.

G8, $50-$100
FL.

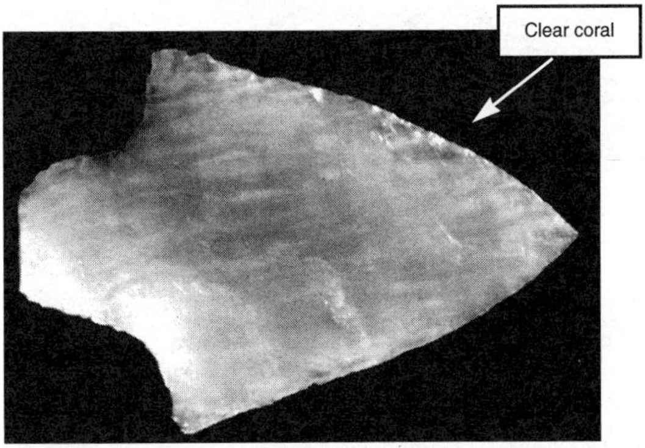

Clear coral

G8, $250-$300
St. Joe, Pasco Co., FL.

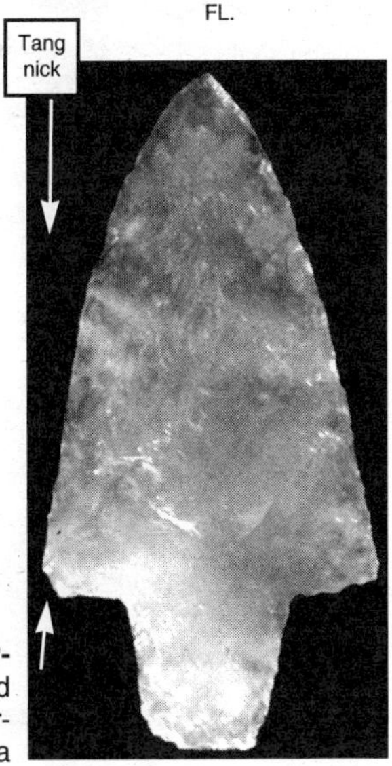

Tang nick

G8, $50-$100
Polk Co., FL.

LOCATION: Southern to Southeastern states. **DESCRIPTION:** A medium to large size, broad, contracted stemmed point with slightly tapered shoulders and rounded basal corners. *Marions* with *Newnan* type squarish bases represent a *Marion/Newnan* cross type. **I.D. KEY:** Tapered shoulders, rounded stem.

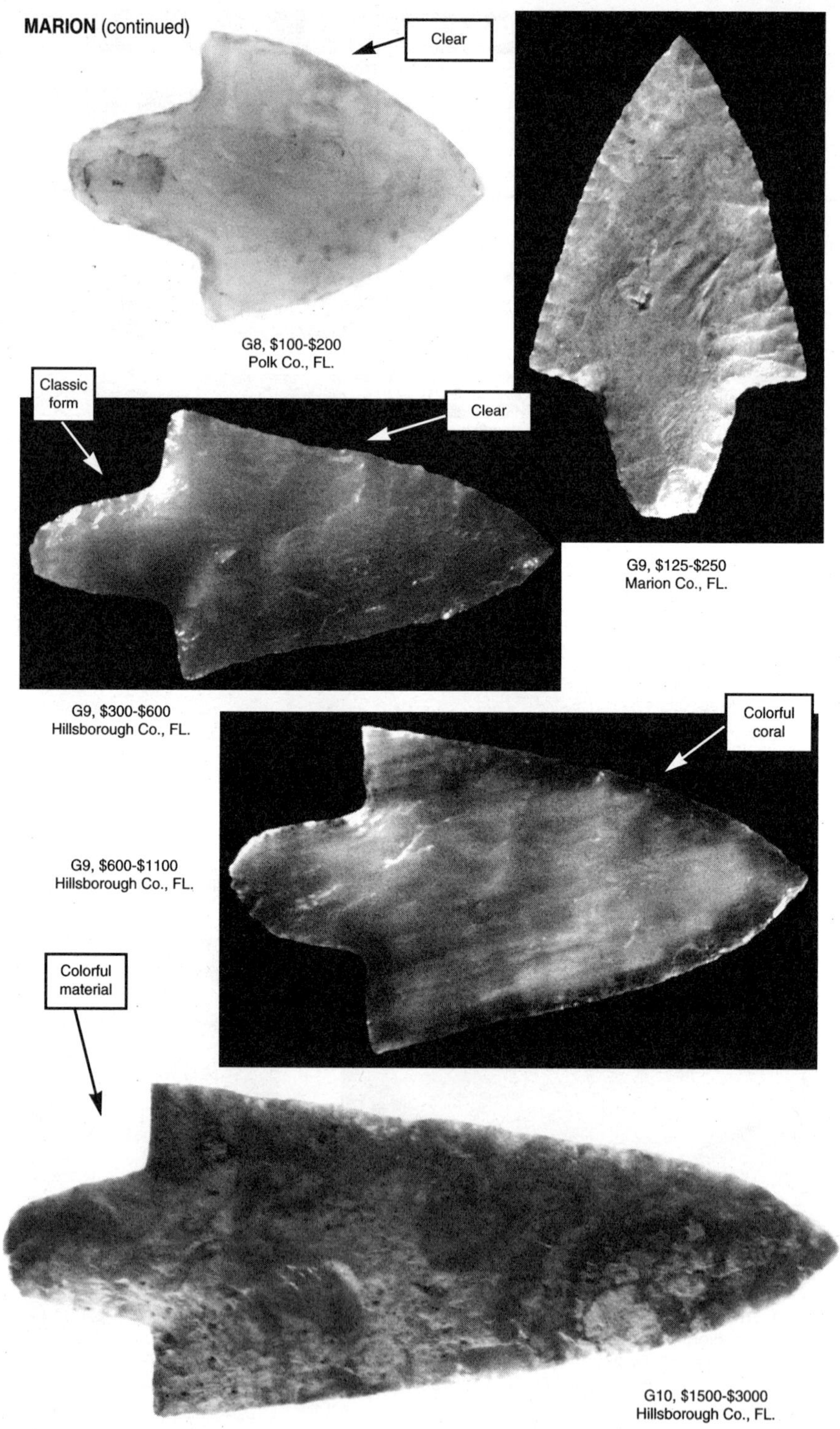

G8, $100-$200
Polk Co., FL.

G9, $125-$250
Marion Co., FL.

G9, $300-$600
Hillsborough Co., FL.

G9, $600-$1100
Hillsborough Co., FL.

G10, $1500-$3000
Hillsborough Co., FL.

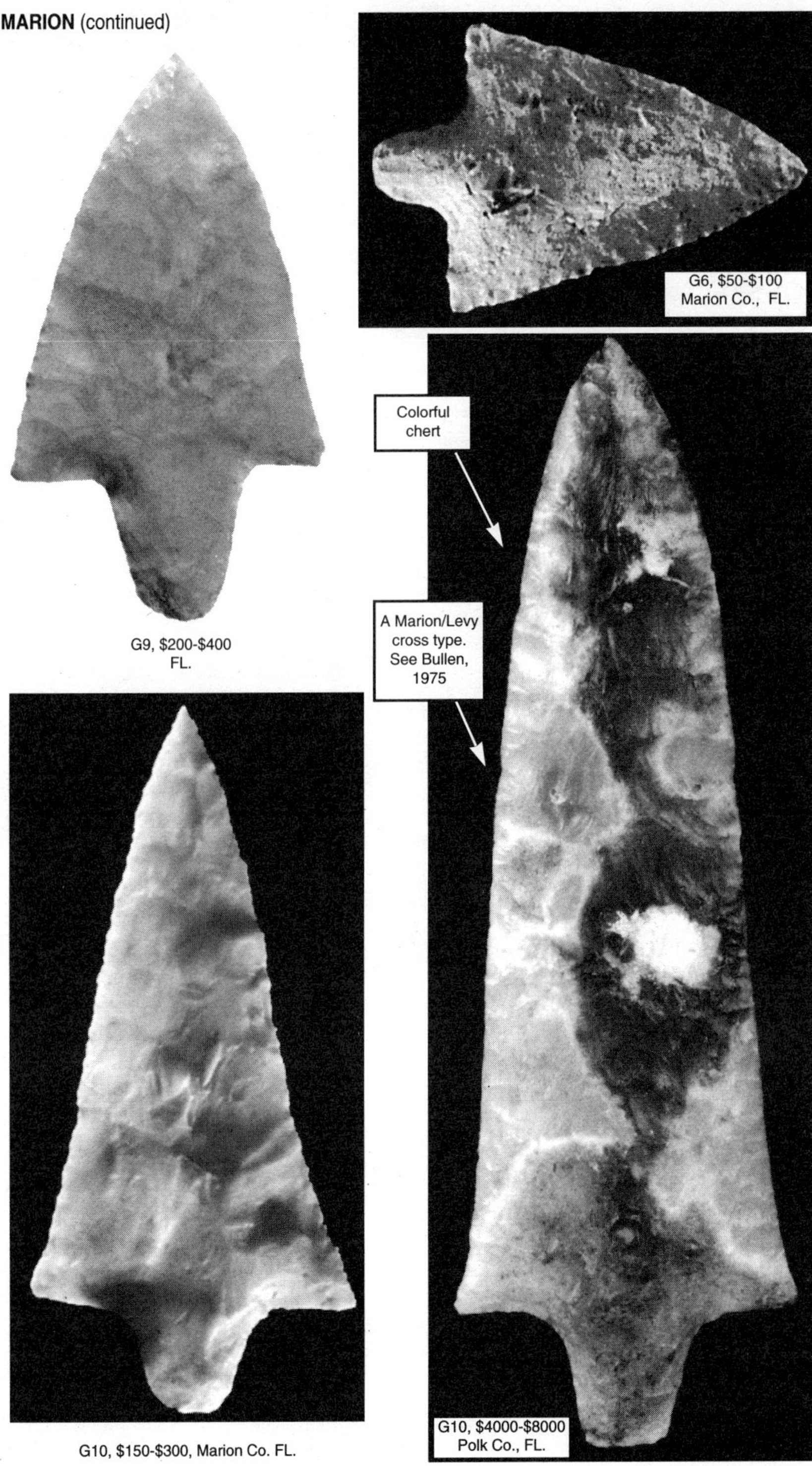

G6, $50-$100
Marion Co., FL.

G9, $200-$400
FL.

G10, $150-$300, Marion Co. FL.

G10, $4000-$8000
Polk Co., FL.

MORROW MOUNTAIN - Middle Archaic, 7000 - 5000 B. P.

(Also see Bascom, Cypress Creek, Eva, Marion, Putnam and Thonotosassa)

G4, $50-$100
Marion Co., FL.

LOCATION: Midwestern to Southeastern states. **DESCRIPTION:** A medium to large size, triangular point with a very short contracting to rounded stem. Shoulders are usually weak, but can be barbed. The blade edges on some examples are serrated with needle points. **I.D. KEY:** Contracted base and Archaic parallel flaking.

NEWNAN - Middle Archaic, 7000 - 3000 B. P.

(Also see Adena, Alachua, Cypress Creek, Hardee Beveled, Hillsborough, Levy, Marion, Morrow Mountain, Oauchita and Putnam)

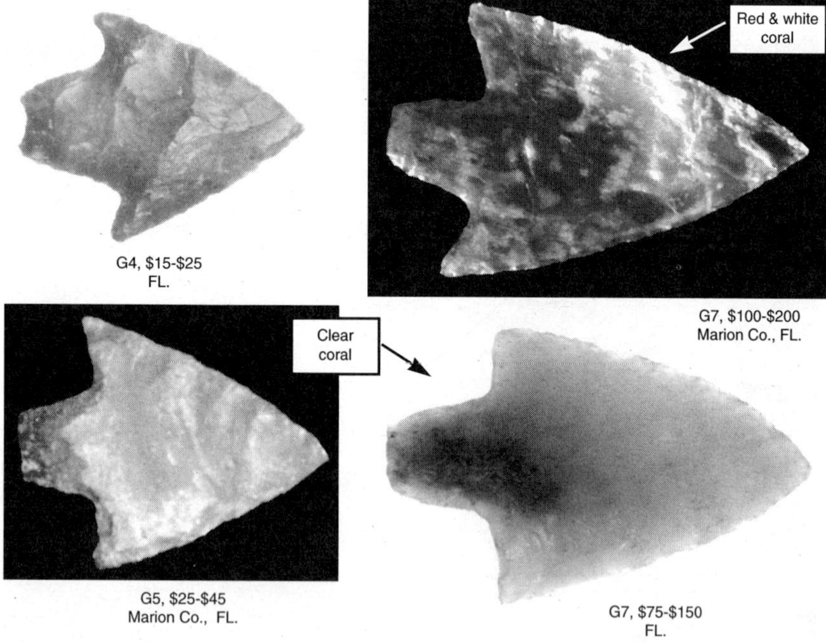

G4, $15-$25
FL.

G7, $100-$200
Marion Co., FL.

G5, $25-$45
Marion Co., FL.

G7, $75-$150
FL.

LOCATION: Southern Southeastern states. **DESCRIPTION:** A medium to large size, broad, stemmed point with a short to long contracting base. Shoulders form a straight line and are horizontal to downward and outward sloping. Stems have contracted, straight sides and a straight to rounded base. *Newnans* with *Marion*-type rounded bases represent a *Newnan/Marion* cross type and would fall under *Marion* if the shoulders slope up.

G9, $150-$300
FL.

G8, $175-$350
FL.

GC

G6, $90-$175
FL.

G8, $175-$350
Pasco Co., FL.

G6, $100-$200
Alachua Co., FL.

G9, $200-$400
Polk Co., FL.

G9, $300-$600
FL.

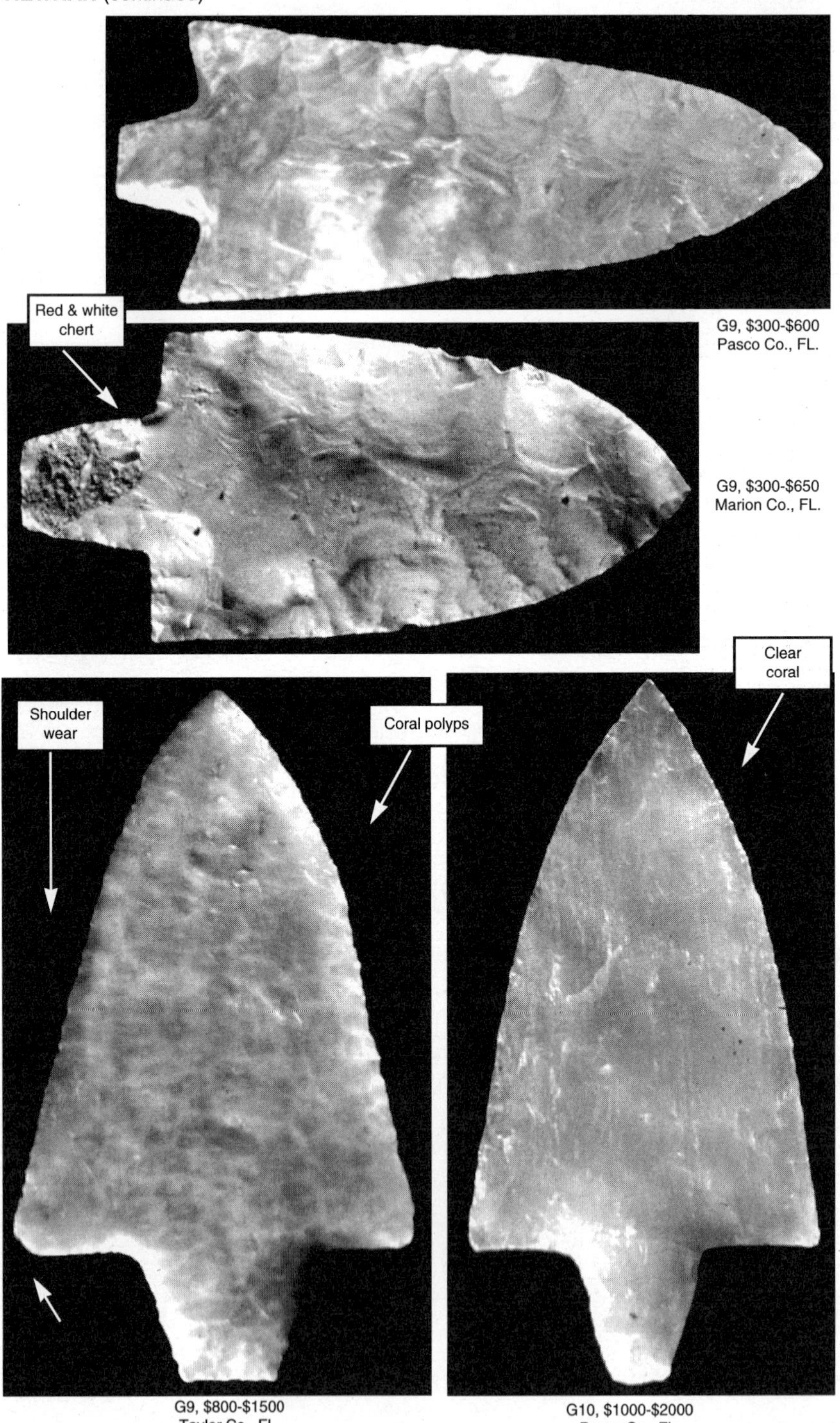

G9, $300-$600
Pasco Co., FL.

G9, $300-$650
Marion Co., FL.

G9, $800-$1500
Taylor Co., FL.

G10, $1000-$2000
Pasco Co., FL.

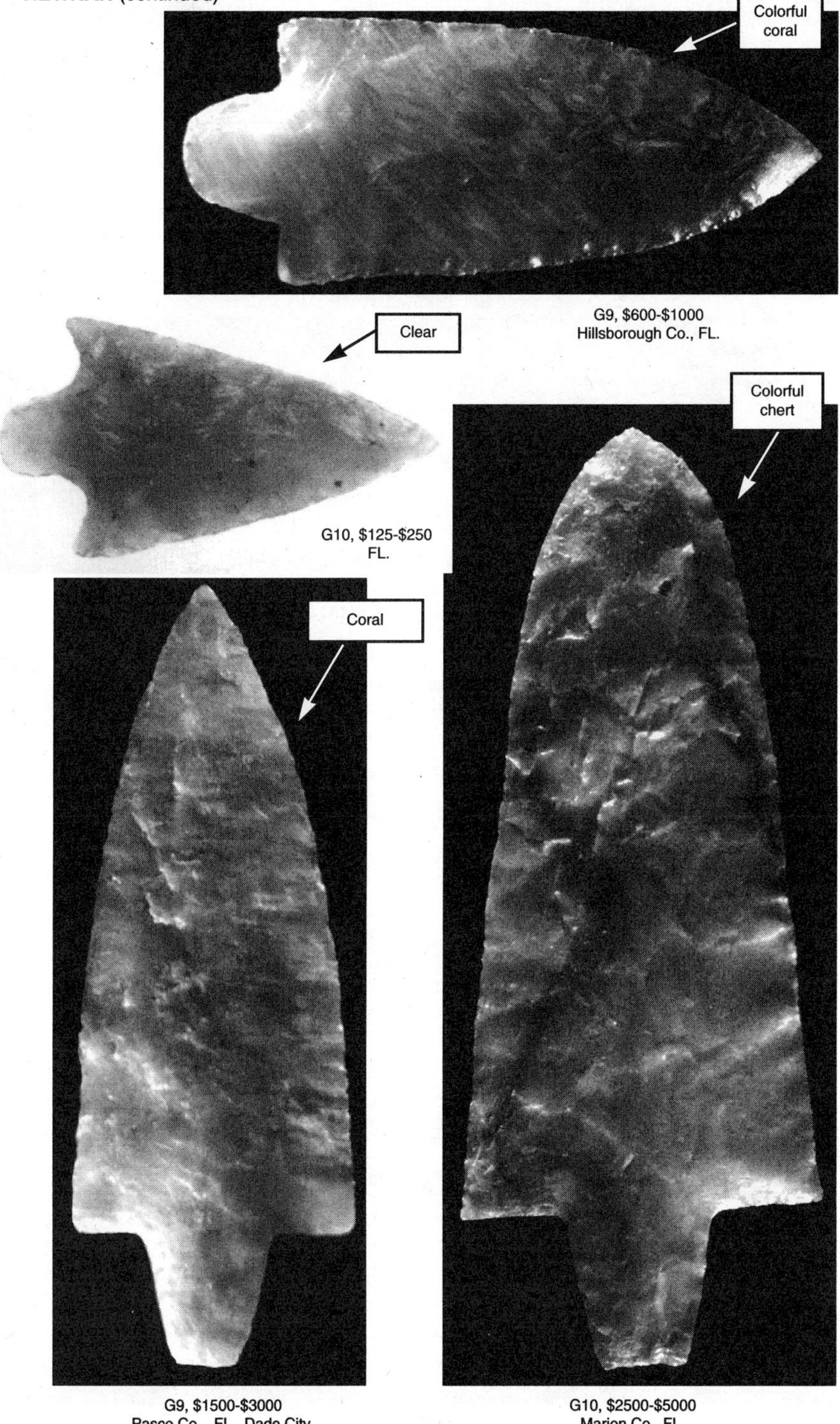

G9, $600-$1000
Hillsborough Co., FL.

G10, $125-$250
FL.

G9, $1500-$3000
Pasco Co., FL., Dade City.

G10, $2500-$5000
Marion Co., FL.

NOTCHAWAY - Mid Archaic-Woodland, 5000 - 2000 B. P.

(Also see Abbey, Elora, Savannah River)

G9, $250-$500
Decatur Co., GA.

LOCATION: Southern Southeastern states. **DESCRIPTION:** A medium to large size, very broad blade with tapered to rounded shoulders and a very short, concave base.Basal stem and shoulders usually occur with sharp corners. **I.D.KEY:** Large size and base form.

OAUCHITA - Woodland, 3000 - 1500 B. P.

(Also see Levy and Newnan)

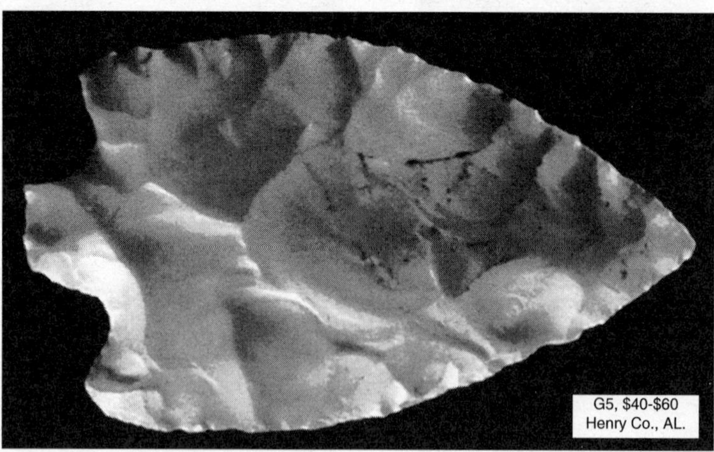

G5, $40-$60
Henry Co., AL.

LOCATION: Southern Southeastern states. **DESCRIPTION:** A medium to large size, broad, point with a short contracted stem and drooping shoulders.

OCALA (Does not exist; all are Lafayette points; see Lafayette)

O'LENO - Woodland, 2000 - 800 B. P.

(Also see Yadkin)

O'LENO (continued)

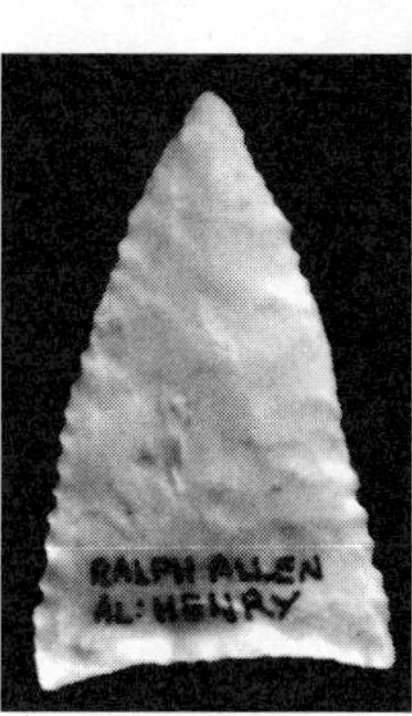

G7, $20-$35
Henry Co., AL.

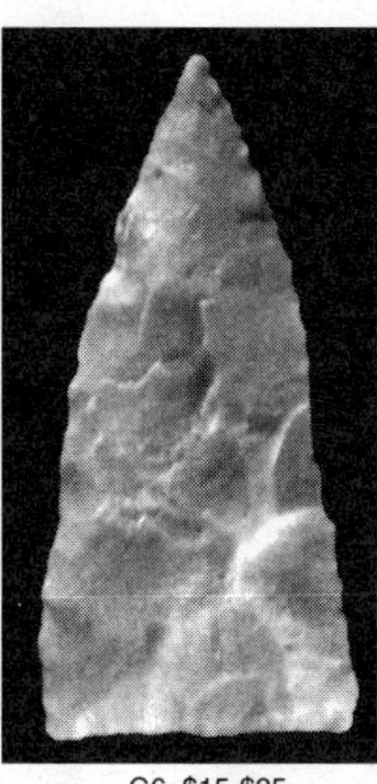

G6, $15-$25
Silver River, FL.

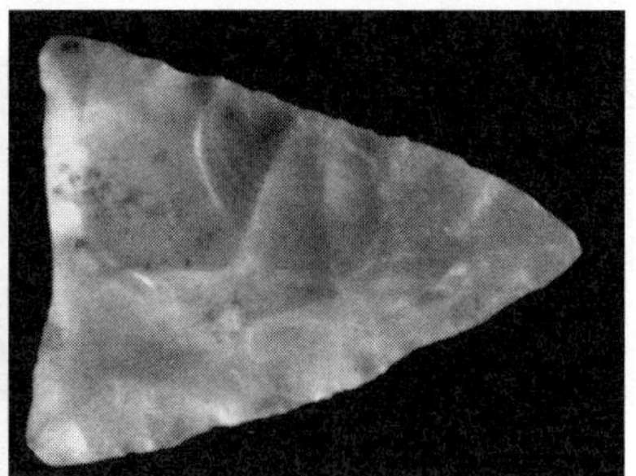

G5, $8-$15
Henry Co., AL.

LOCATION: Southern Southeastern states. **DESCRIPTION:** A medium size, broad, triangle point with a straight to slightly concave base.

GC

OSCEOLA-GREENBRIER - Transitional Paleo, 9500 - 6000 B. P.

(Also see Bolen)

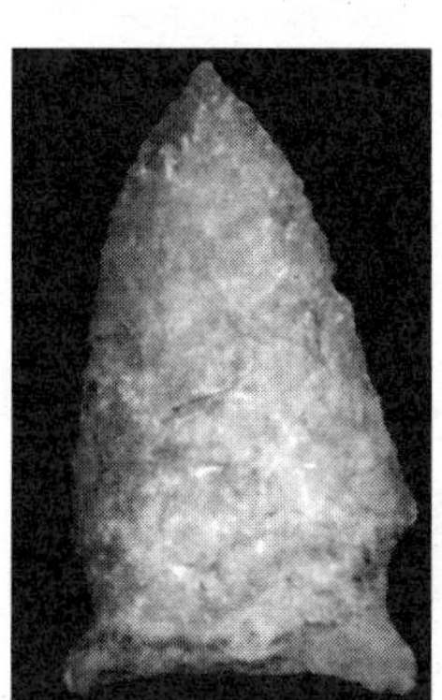

G4, $50-$100, Type I
FL.

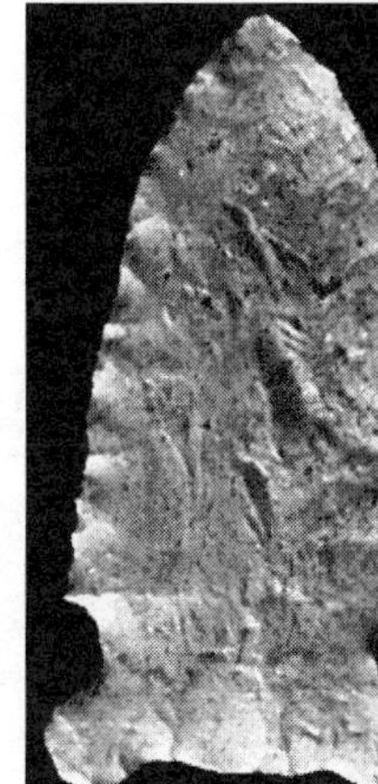

G5, $100-$200 Type I
Santa Fe Riv., FL.

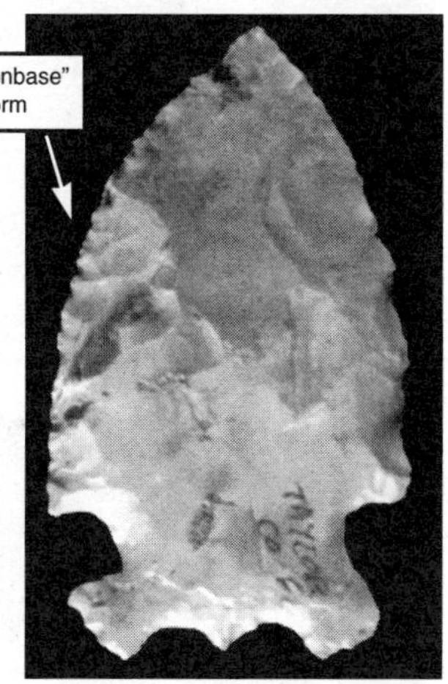

G6, $150-$250, Type I
Taylor Co., FL.

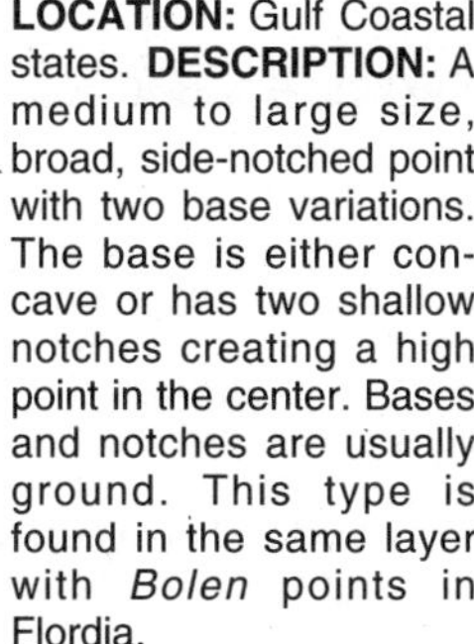

LOCATION: Gulf Coastal states. **DESCRIPTION:** A medium to large size, broad, side-notched point with two base variations. The base is either concave or has two shallow notches creating a high point in the center. Bases and notches are usually ground. This type is found in the same layer with *Bolen* points in Flordia.

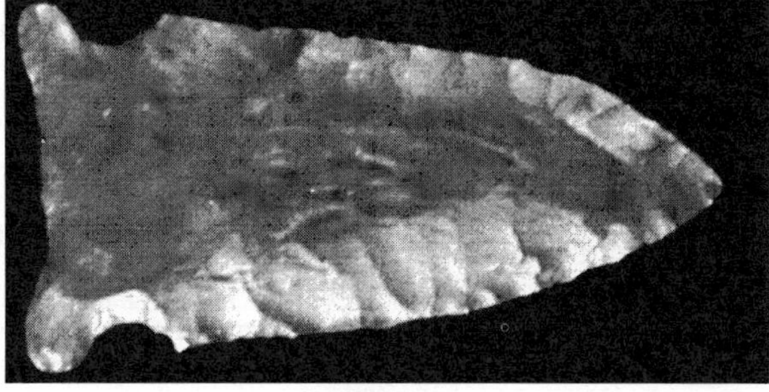

G8, $200-$350, Type II
NW Cent. FL.

OSCEOLA GREENBRIER (continued)

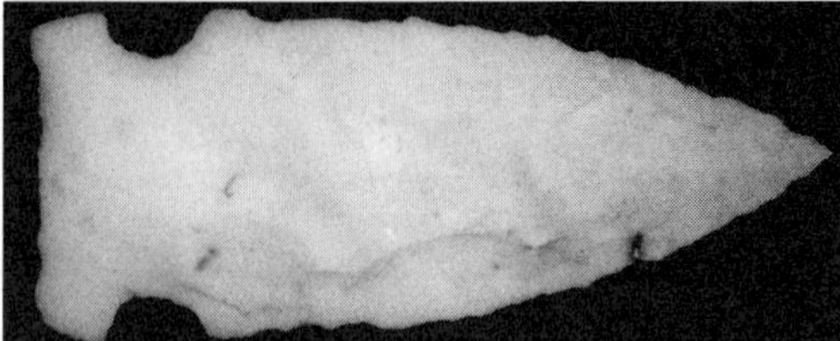

G9, $65-$125, Type II, FL.

G9, $150-$300, Type II, FL.

G8, $250-$500, Type I
Santa Fe River, FL.

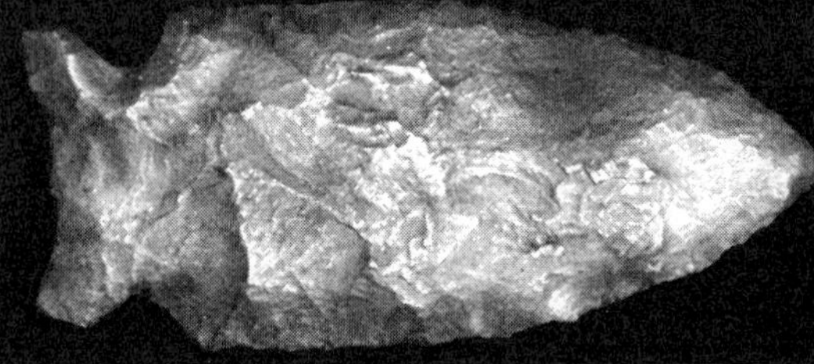

G8, $65-$125, Type II
FL.

PICKWICK - Middle to Late Archaic, 6000 - 3500 B. P.

(Also see Elora, Flint River and Savannah River)

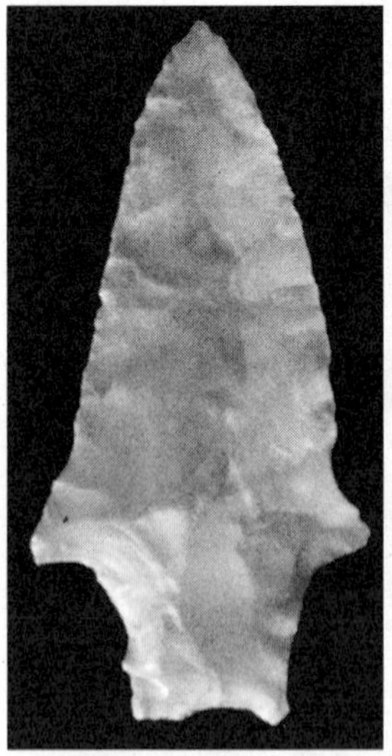

G5, $20-$35
Marion Co., FL.

G5, $20-$40
Marion Co., FL.

LOCATION: Found North of the Suwanee River into Georgia and Alabama. **DESCRIPTION:** A medium to large size, expanded shoulder, contracted to expanded stem point. Blade edges are recurved, and many examples show fine secondary flaking with serrations. Some are beveled on one side of each face. The bevel is steep and shallow. Shoulders are horizontal, tapered or barbed and form sharp angles. Some stems are snapped off or may show original rind.

PICKWICK (continued)

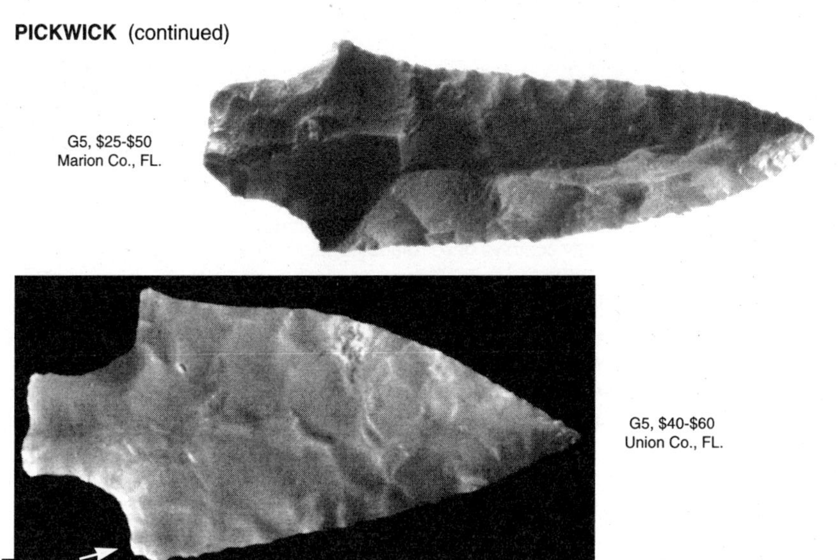

G5, $25-$50
Marion Co., FL.

Damage

G5, $40-$60
Union Co., FL.

GC

PINELLAS - Mississippian, 800 - 400 B. P.

(Also see O'Leno, Talahassee and Yadkin)

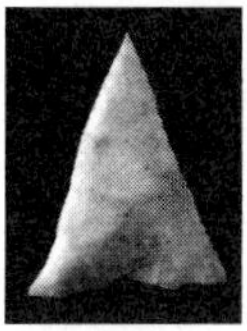

G3, $4-$7
FL.

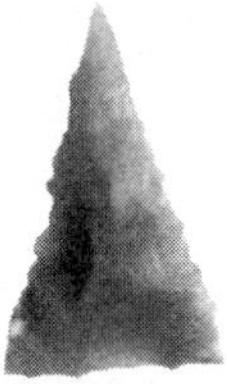

G5, $10-$20
FL.

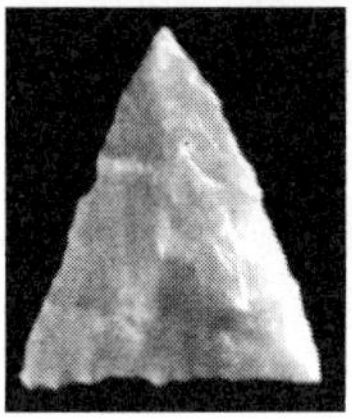

G8, $12-$25
Burke Co., GA.

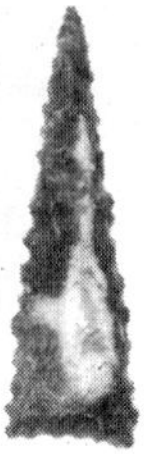

G9, $12-$35
FL.

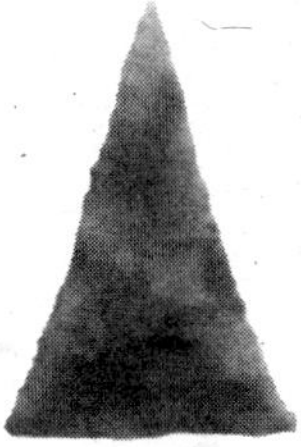

G7, $20-$35
FL.

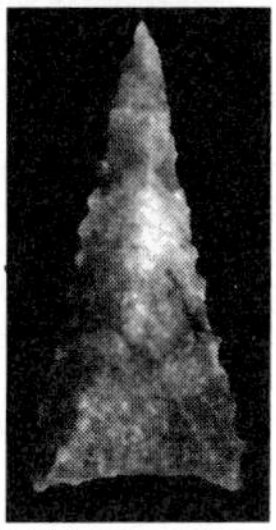

G7, $12-$25
FL.

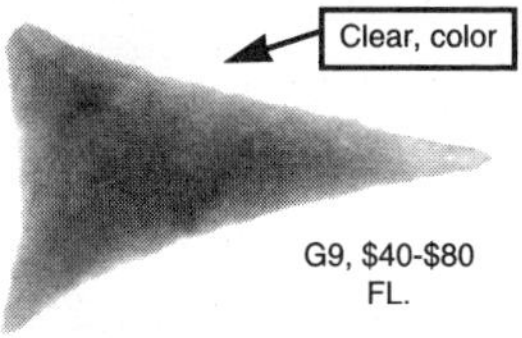

Clear, color

G9, $40-$80
FL.

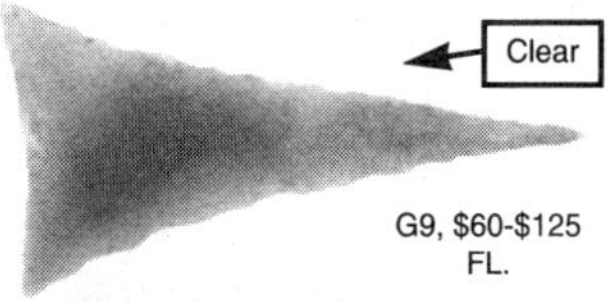

Clear

G9, $60-$125
FL.

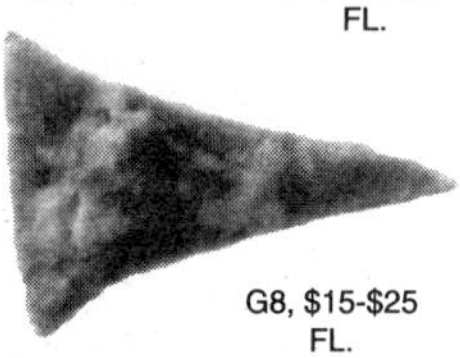

G8, $15-$25
FL.

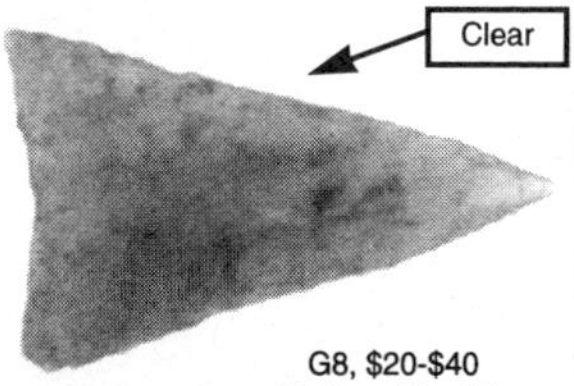

Clear

G8, $20-$40
Madison Co., FL.

G10, $40-$75
Marion Co., FL.

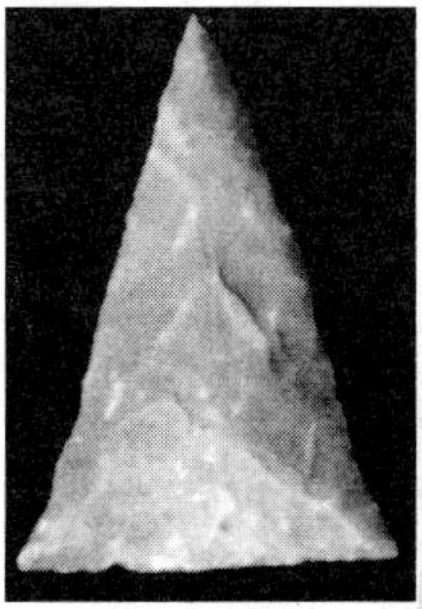

Clear, color

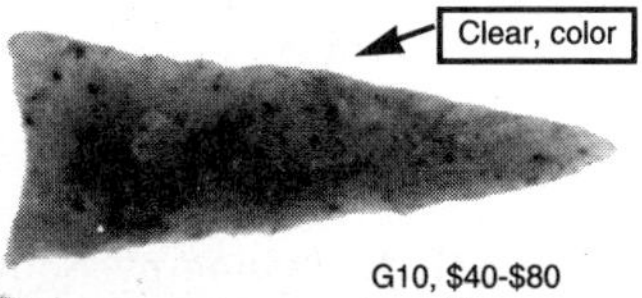

G10, $40-$80
FL.

G9, $20-$40
FL.

G10, $45-$90
FL.

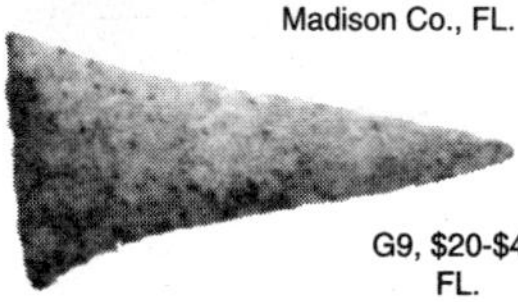

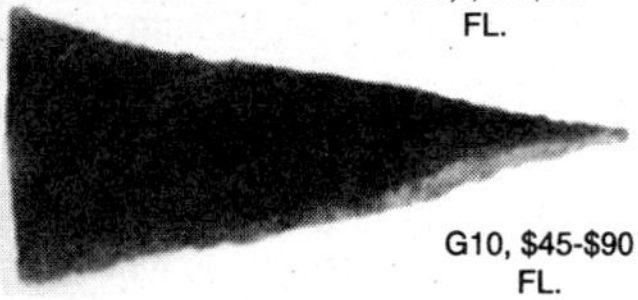

PINELLAS (continued)

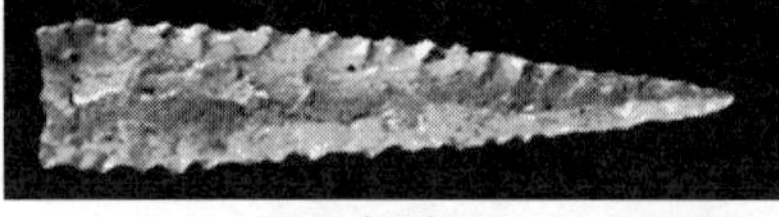

G10, $65-$125
Gilchrist Co., FL.

G8, $65-$125
Madison Co., FL.

LOCATION: Gulf Coastal states. **DESCRIPTION:** A small, narrow, thick to thin, triangular point with a straight to slightly concave base. Blade edges can be serrated.

PUTNAM - Late Archaic, 5000 - 3000 B. P.

(Also see Cypress Creek, Hardee Beveled, Levy, Marion, Morrow Mountain, Newnan, Sumter and Thonotosassa)

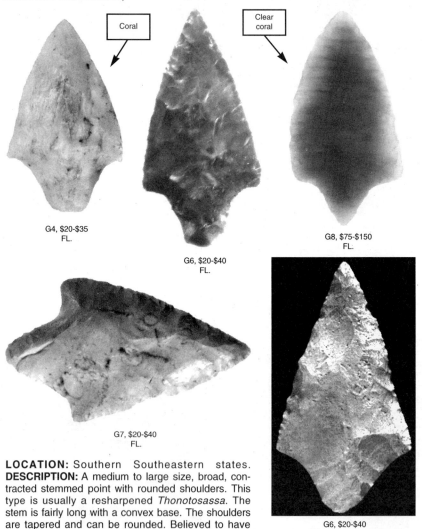

Coral

Clear coral

G4, $20-$35
FL.

G6, $20-$40
FL.

G8, $75-$150
FL.

G7, $20-$40
FL.

LOCATION: Southern Southeastern states. **DESCRIPTION:** A medium to large size, broad, contracted stemmed point with rounded shoulders. This type is usually a resharpened *Thonotosassa*. The stem is fairly long with a convex base. The shoulders are tapered and can be rounded. Believed to have evolved from the Marion type.

G6, $20-$40
Hillsborough Co., FL.

G9, $125-$250
Marion Co., FL.

G7, $25-$50
FL.

G9, $100-$200
FL.

G10, $250-$500
FL.

REDSTONE - Paleo, 13,000 - 10000 B. P.

(Also see Clovis, Simpson and Suwannee)

G10, $3000-$4000
Jackson Co., FL, Chipola River.

LOCATION: Southern Southeastern to gulf states. **DESCRIPTION:** A medium to large size, thin auriculate fluted point with convex sides expanding to a wide, deeply concave base. The hafting area is ground. This point is widest at the base. Fluting can extend most of the way down each face. Multiple flutes are usual. A very rare type. **I.D. KEY:** Batan fluted, edgework on the hafting area.

SAFETY HARBOR - Mississippian, 800 - 600 B. P.

(Also see O'Leno, Talahassee and Pinellas)

G5, $15-$25
Sumter Co., FL.

G9, $75-$150
Sumter Co., FL.

LOCATION: Gulf Coastal states. **DESCRIPTION:** A medium size, narrow, thin, triangular point with a concave base. Basal corners are sharp. Blade edges can be serrated.

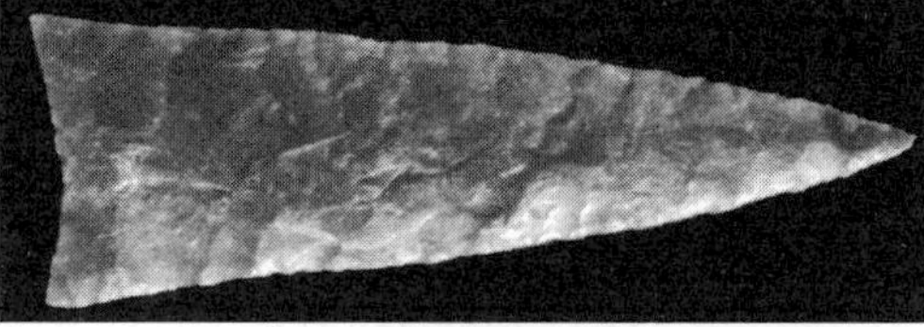

G10, $125-$250
Sumter Co., FL.

SANTA FE - Trans. Paleo and Late Archaic to Woodland, 9500 - 8000 B.P. and 3500 - 2500 B. P.

(Also see Beaver Lake and Tallahassee)

G2, $12-$25
Hillsborough Co., FL.

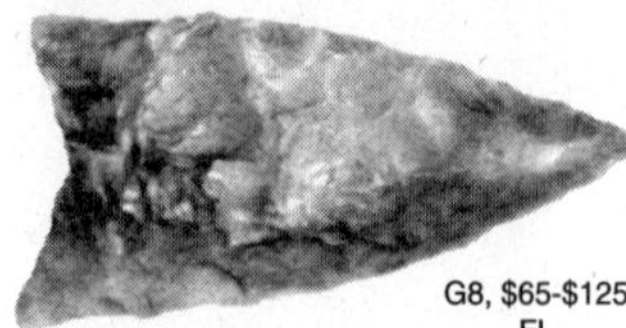

G8, $65-$125
FL.

LOCATION: Gulf Coastal states. **DESCRIPTION:** A medium to large size auriculate point with expanding auricules and a concave base. Hafting area is not well defined. Blade edges are not serrated as in *Tallahassee.* Believed to have been made in Dalton times, 9500-8000 B.P. and again in late Archaic times (Copena?), 4000-2500 B.P. Has also been found with the late Archaic *Hernando* points. **I.D. KEY:** One sharper tang, symmetry.

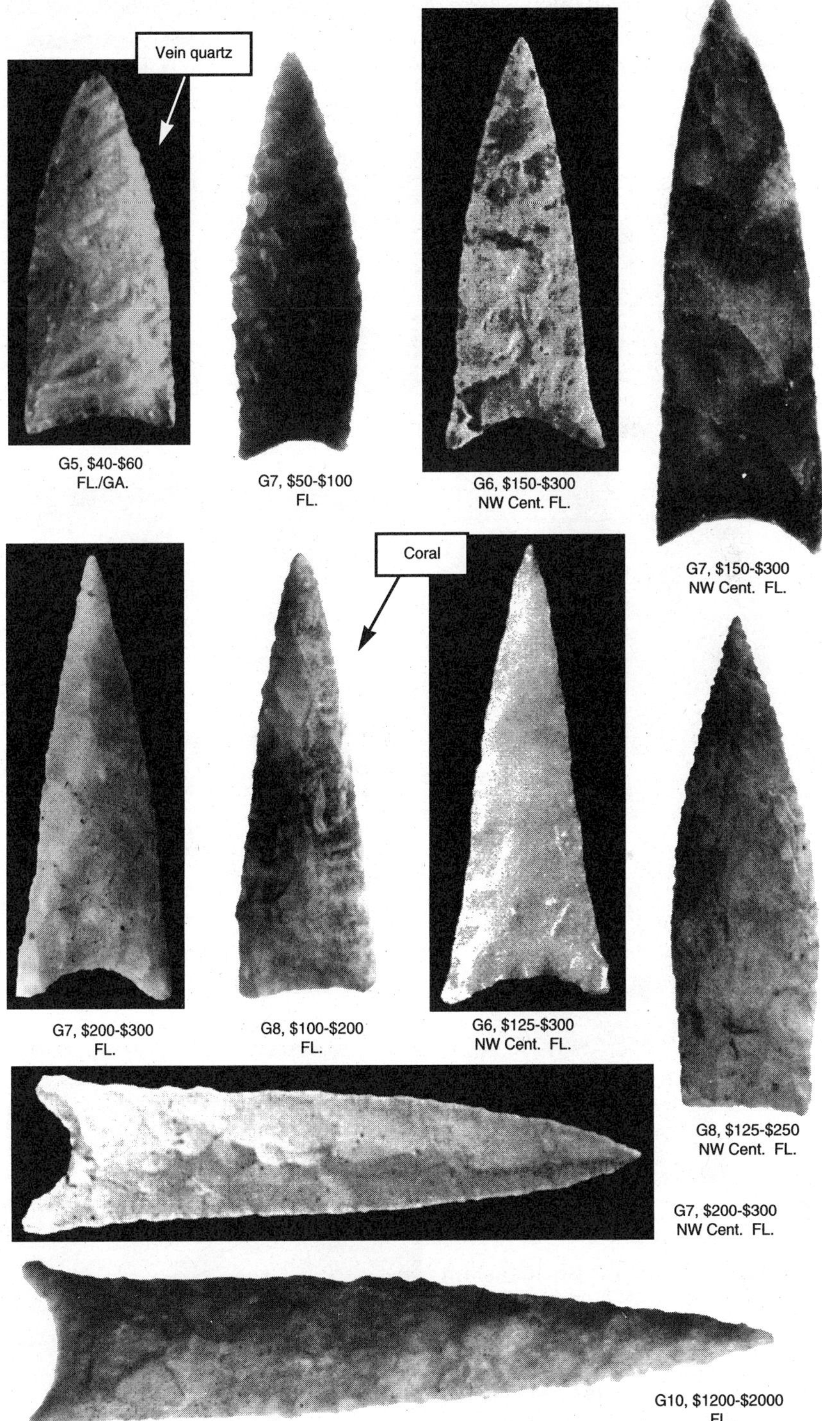

G5, $40-$60
FL./GA.

G7, $50-$100
FL.

G6, $150-$300
NW Cent. FL.

G7, $150-$300
NW Cent. FL.

G7, $200-$300
FL.

G8, $100-$200
FL.

G6, $125-$300
NW Cent. FL.

G8, $125-$250
NW Cent. FL.

G7, $200-$300
NW Cent. FL.

G10, $1200-$2000
FL.

GC

SARASOTA - Woodland, 3000 - 1500 B. P.

(Also see Ledbetter and Pickwick)

G6, $100-$200
Santa Fe River, FL.

LOCATION: Southern Southeastern states. **DESCRIPTION:** A medium to large size stemmed point with horizontal shoulders. The base can be parallel sided to slightly expanding or contracting. Blade edges are slightly convex to recurved. Similar to the northern *Pickwick* type.

SAVANNAH RIVER - Middle Archaic to Woodland, 5000 - 2000 B. P.

(Also see Abbey, Arredondo, Bascom, Elora, Hamilton, Kirk, Levy, Seminole, Thonotosassa and Wacissa)

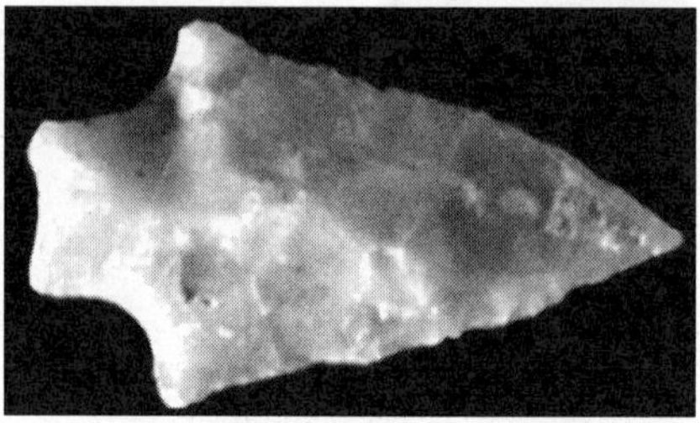

G5, $15-$30
Burke Co., GA.

Made into scraper

G4, $8-$15
Burke Co., GA.

G4, $8-$15
Burke Co., GA.

G5, $50-$75
Burke Co., GA.

G4, $15-$30
Burke Co., FL.

G5, $25-$45
Burke Co., FL.

G8, $150-$300
Lee Co., GA.

G4, $15-$25
Burke Co., GA.

G6, $65-$125
Dodge Co., GA.

LOCATION: Southeastern to Eastern states. **DESCRIPTION:** A medium to large size, straight to contracting stemmed point with a concave to bifurcated base. The shoulders are tapered to square. The stems are narrow to broad. Believed to be related to the earlier *Stanly* point.

G5, $30-$60
Decatur Co., GA.

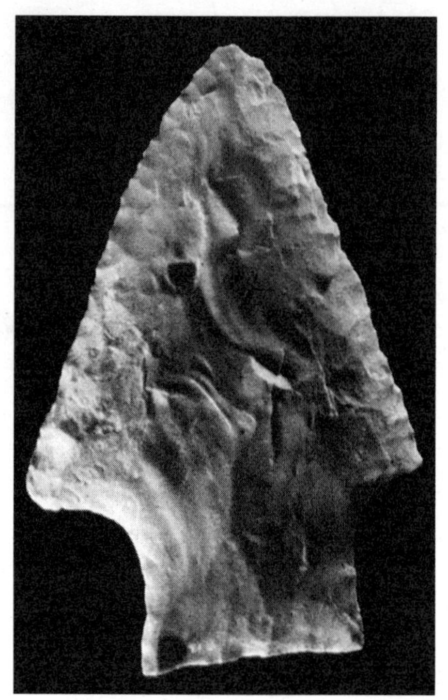

G5, $30-$60
Taylor Co., FL.

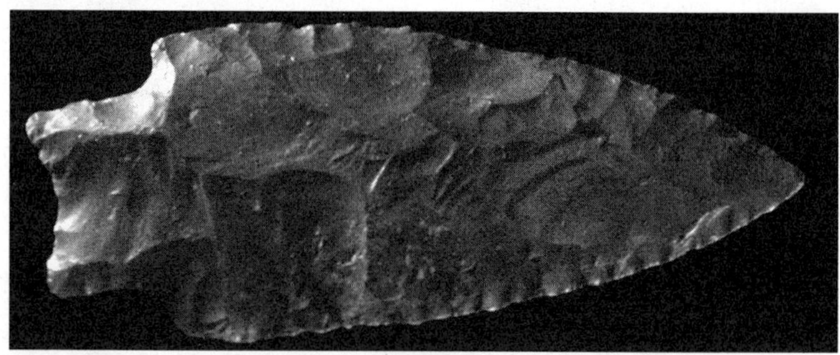

G9, $175-$350
FL.

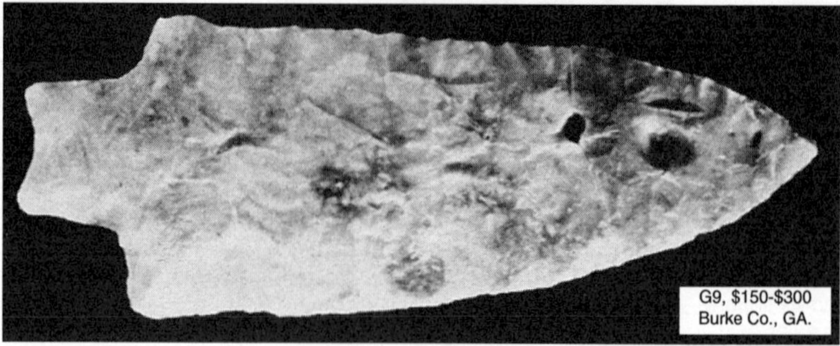

G9, $150-$300
Burke Co., GA.

G9, $200-$350
Burke Co., GA.

G9, $125-$250
Burke Co., GA.

SEMINOLE - Late Archaic, 5000 - 3500 B. P.

(Also see Abbey, Elora, Hamilton, Levy, Savannah River and Wacissa)

G7, $40-$75
Decatur Co., GA.

G8, $75-$150
Burke Co., GA.

LOCATION: Gulf Coastal states. **DESCRIPTION:** A medium to large size, broad point with barbed shoulders and a concave base.

(Also see Beaver Lake, Clovis, Conerly, Simpson-Mustache and Suwannee)

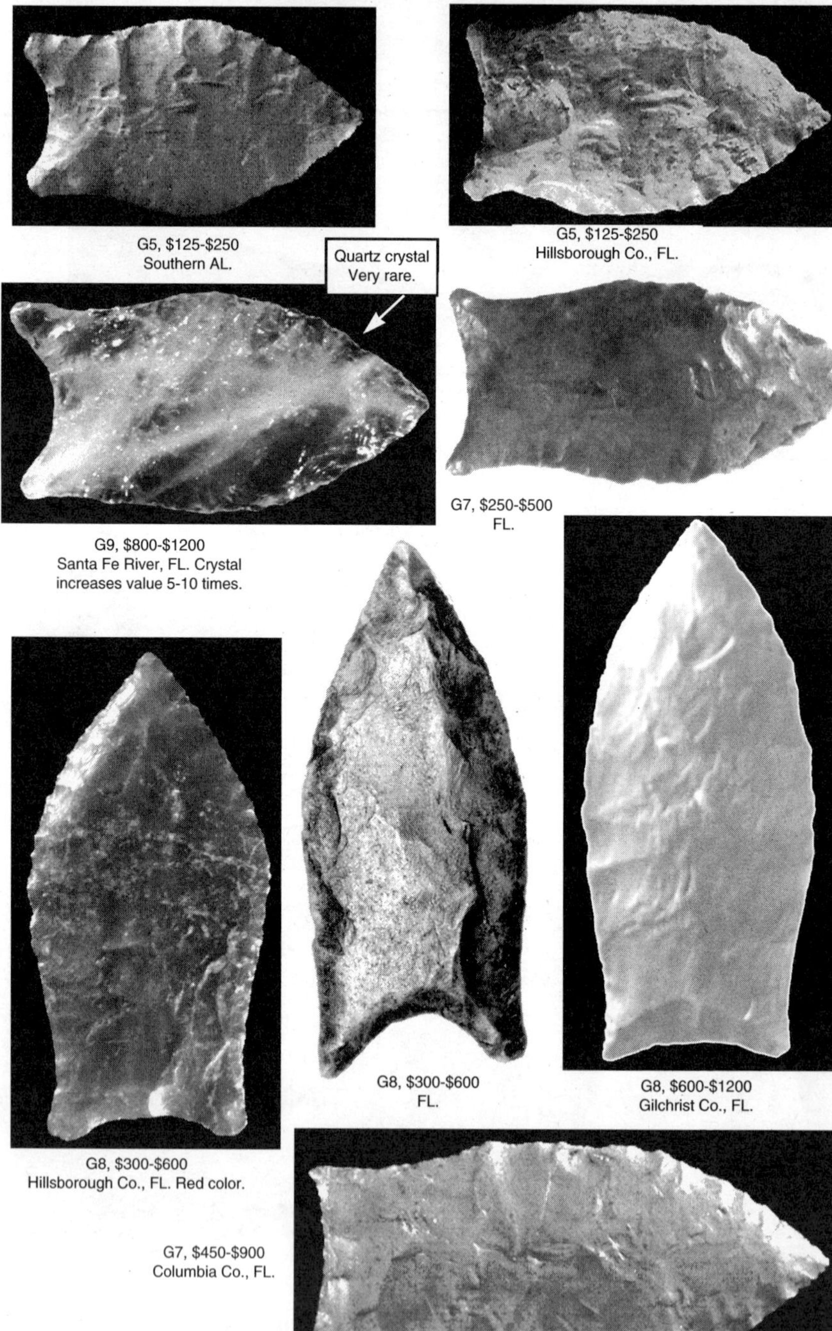

G5, $125-$250
Southern AL.

G5, $125-$250
Hillsborough Co., FL.

G9, $800-$1200
Santa Fe River, FL. Crystal increases value 5-10 times.

G7, $250-$500
FL.

G8, $300-$600
Hillsborough Co., FL. Red color.

G8, $300-$600
FL.

G8, $600-$1200
Gilchrist Co., FL.

G7, $450-$900
Columbia Co., FL.

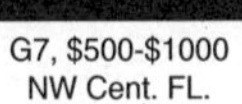

G7, $500-$1000
NW Cent. FL.

G6, $400-$800
NW Cent. FL.

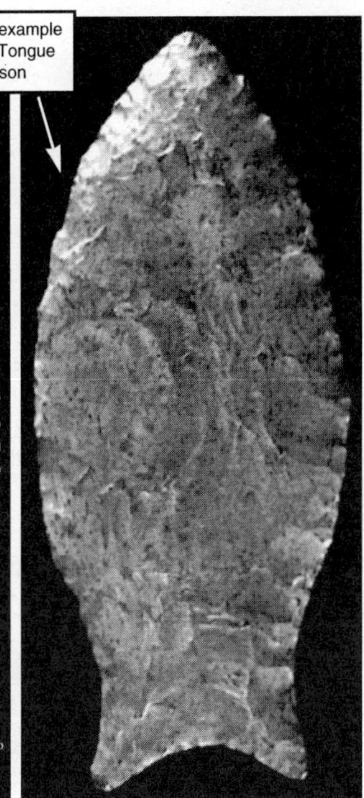

G10, $1500-$2800
Santa Fe Riv., FL.

G7, $600-$1000
Steinhatchee Riv., FL.

G10, $1500-$3000
Santa Fe Riv., FL.

G9, $1600-$3200
Jackson Co., FL.

LOCATION: Gulf Coastal states. **DESCRIPTION:** A medium to large size lanceolate, auriculate blade with recurved sides, outward flaring ears and a concave base. The hafting area constriction is more narrow than in the *Suwannee* type. Fluting is absent or weak.

SIMPSON-MUSTACHE - Late Paleo, 12,000 - 8000 B. P.

(Also see Beaver Lake, Conerly, Suwannee and Wheeler Expanded Base)

LOCATION: Florida. **DESCRIPTION:** A small to medium size, narrow point with large up-turning ears and a convex base. Very rare in the type area. Fluting is absent. Only about a dozen including broken ones are known. A very rare type.

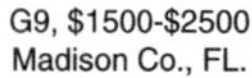

G9, $1500-$2500
Madison Co., FL.

G10, $3000-$6000
Suwannee Co., FL.

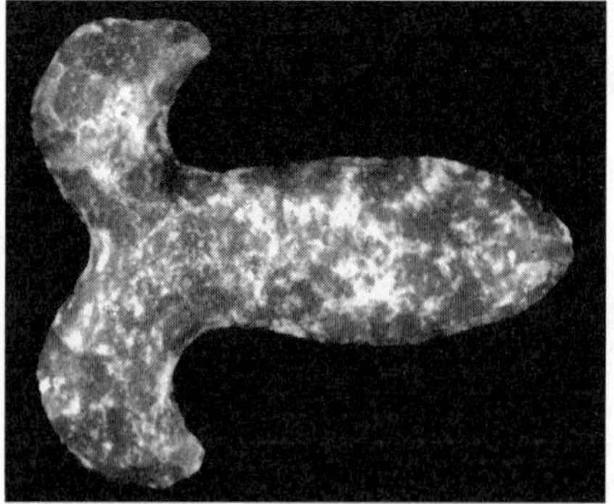

G9, $2000-$4000
Suwannee Co., FL.

SIX MILE CREEK - Middle Archaic, 7500 - 5000 B. P.

(Also see Cottonbridge, Elora, Kirk Serrated and South Prong Creek)

SIX MILE CREEK
(continued)

LOCATION: Gulf Coastal states. **DESCRIPTION:** A medium to large size, broad, stemmed, serrated point. The serrations are uniquely formed by careful pressure flaking applied from the side of only one face. Normal *Kirk* serrations are pressure flaked alternately from both faces. Believed to be a later *Kirk* variant.

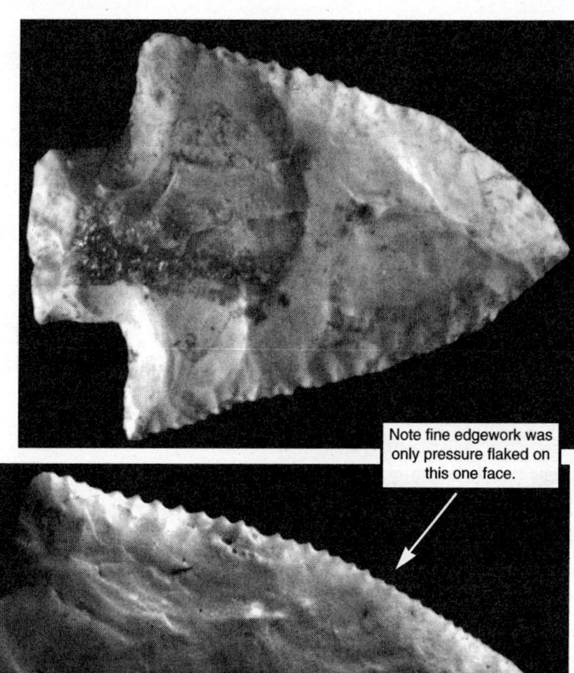

G7, $70-$140
Decatur Co., GA.

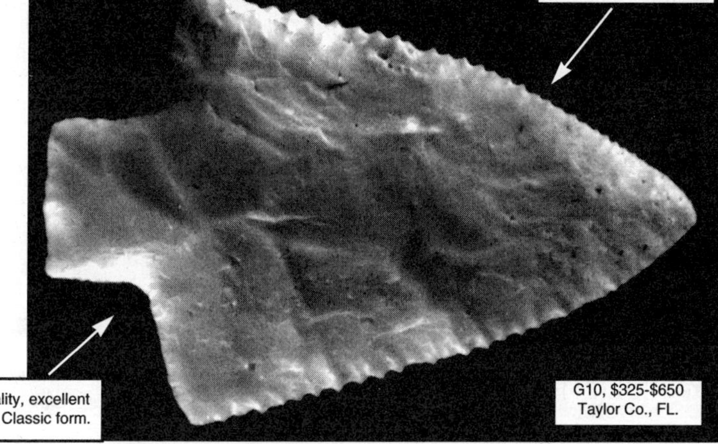
Note fine edgework was only pressure flaked on this one face.
Hjigh quality, excellent example. Classic form.

G10, $325-$650
Taylor Co., FL.

SOUTH PRONG CREEK - Late Archaic, 5000 - 3000 B. P.

(Also see Abbey, Cottonbridge, Elora, Savannah River and Six Mile Creek)

LOCATION: Southern Southeastern states. **DESCRIPTION:** A large size, broad shouldered point with a small rectangular stem. Blade edges are usually bifacially serrated beginning at each shoulder and terminating about 1/3 the way from the tip.

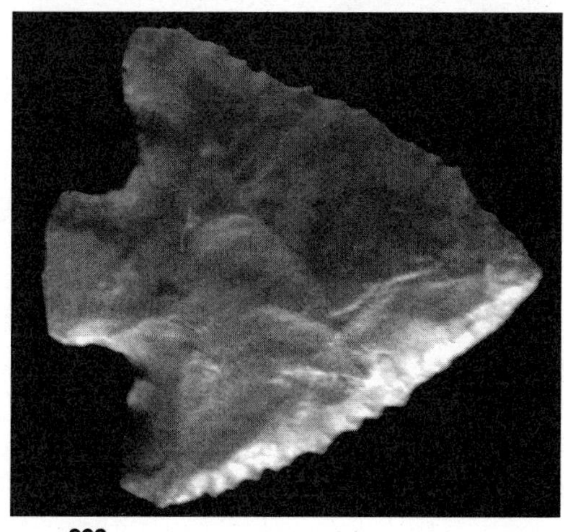

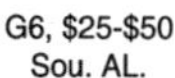

G6, $25-$50
Sou. AL.

SOUTH PRONG CREEK
(continued)

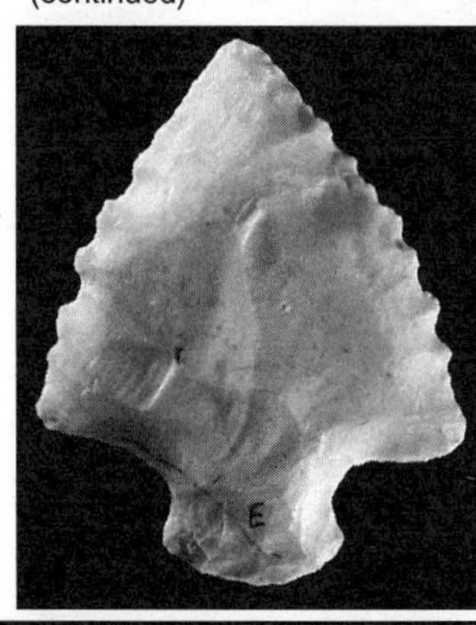

G5, $25-$35
Decatur Co., GA.

G6, $30-$50
Henry Co., AL.

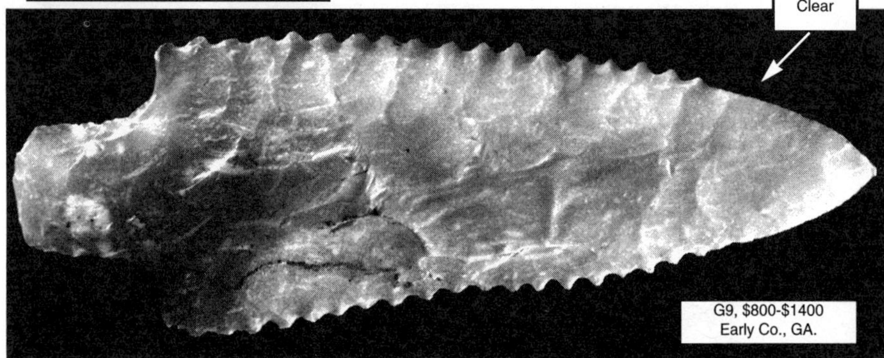

G9, $800-$1400
Early Co., GA.

STANFIELD - Transitional Paleo, 10,000 - 8000 B. P.

G4, $10-$20
Hillsborough Co., FL.

LOCATION: Southeastern states. **DESCRIPTION:** A medium to large size, narrow, lanceolate point with parallel sides and a straight base. Some rare examples are fluted. Bases can be ground.

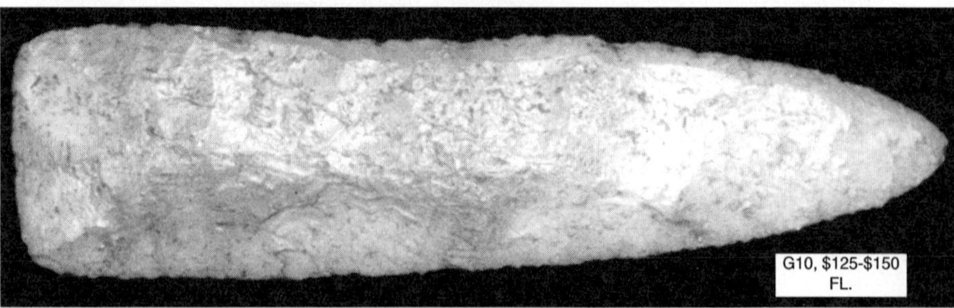

G10, $125-$150
FL.

STANFIELD (continued)

G3, $5-$10
Marion Co., FL.

STING RAY BARB - Woodland-Historic, 2500 - 400 B. P.

G5, $10-$20
FL.

LOCATION: Florida. **DESCRIPTION:** Not only bone and wood were utilized as arrow points. These barbs taken from Rays were hafted to shafts as well. Found on coastal occupation sites.

GC

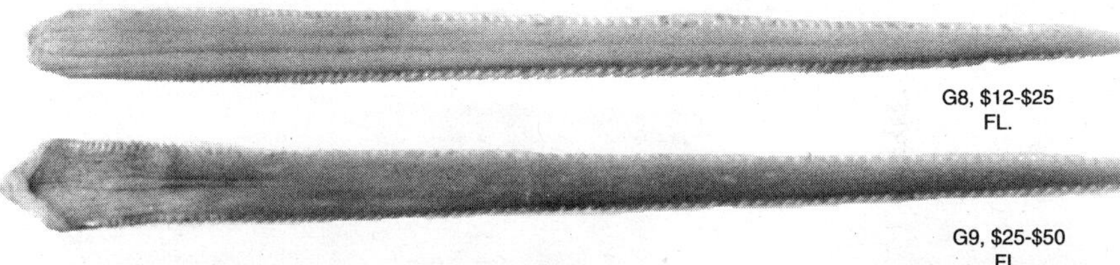

G8, $12-$25
FL.

G9, $25-$50
FL.

SUMTER - Middle Archaic, 7000 - 5000 B. P.

(Also see Adena, Elora, Kirk, Levy, Putnam and Thonotosassa)

LOCATION: Southern Southeastern states. **DESCRIPTION:** A medium to large size, broad, thick point with weak, tapered shoulders and a contracting stem. These may be small versions of the *Thonotosassa* type and are believed to be related. **I.D. KEY:** Asymmetrical shoulders.

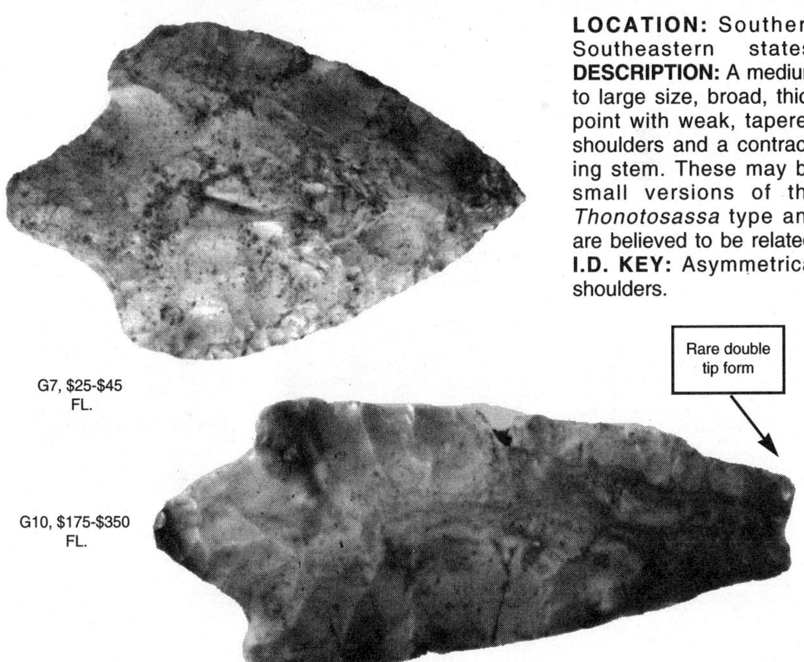

G7, $25-$45
FL.

G10, $175-$350
FL.

SUMTER (continued)

G5, $12-$25
Hillsborough Co., FL.

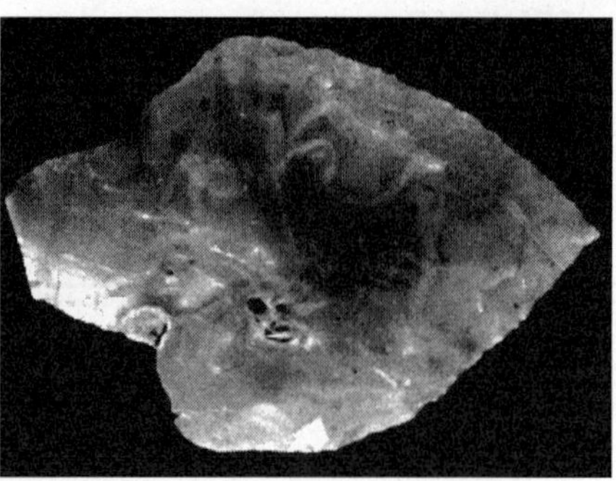

G5, $15-$30
Hillsborough Co., FL.

SUWANNEE - Late Paleo, 12,000 - 9000 B. P.

(Also see Beaver Lake, Clovis, Conerly, Simpson and Union Side Notched)

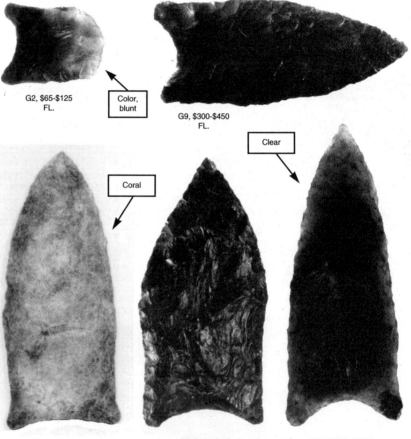

G2, $65-$125
FL.

Color, blunt

G9, $300-$450
FL.

Clear

Coral

G8, $600-$1200
FL.

G7, $450-$900
Santa Fe Riv., FL.

G10, $1500-$2500
FL.

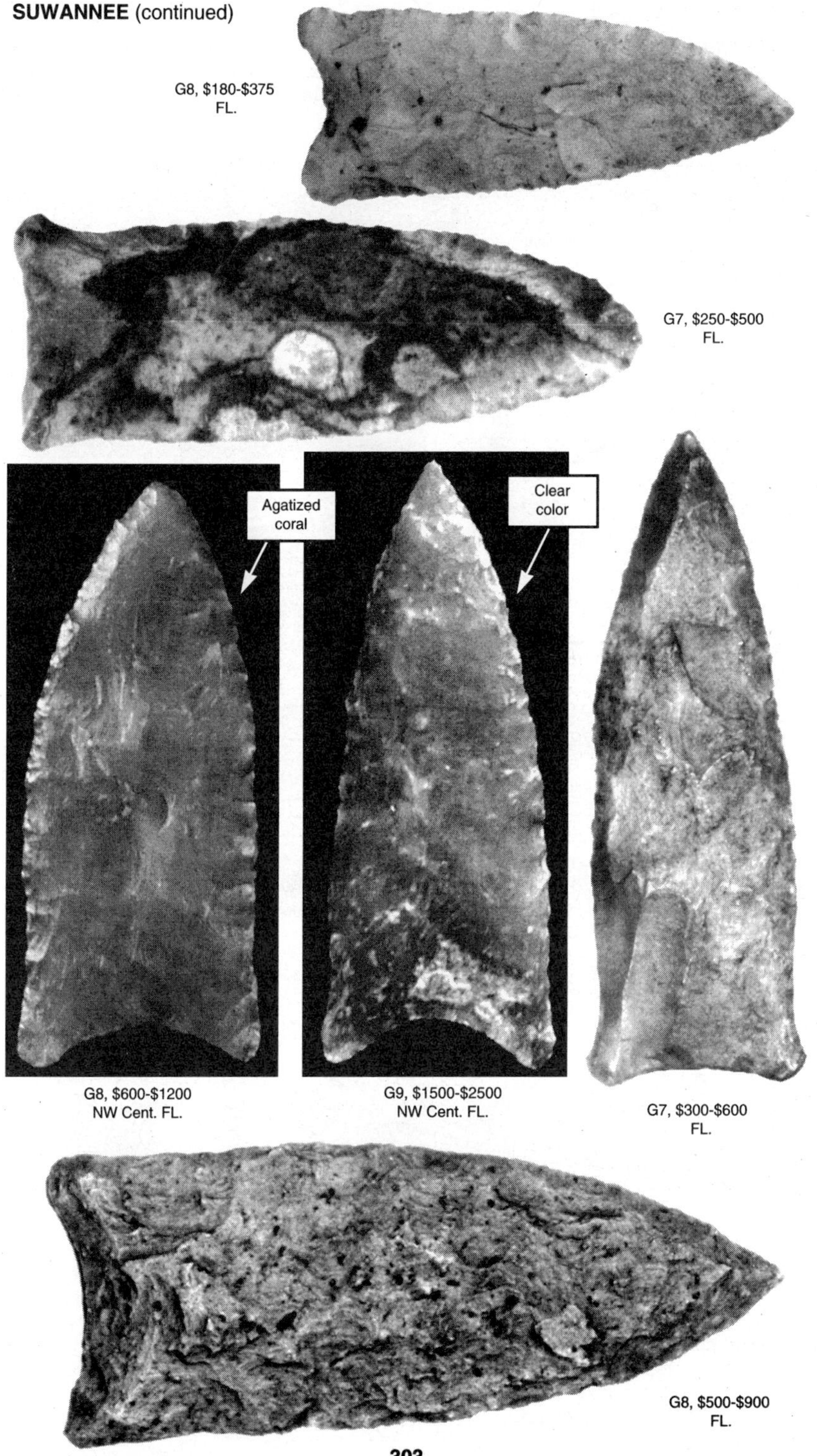

G8, $180-$375
FL.

G7, $250-$500
FL.

G8, $600-$1200
NW Cent. FL.

G9, $1500-$2500
NW Cent. FL.

G7, $300-$600
FL.

G8, $500-$900
FL.

SUWANNEE (continued)

LOCATION: Southern Southeastern states. **DESCRIPTION:** A medium to large size, fairly thick, broad, auriculate point. The basal constriction is not as narrow as in *Simpson* points. Most examples have ground bases and are usually unfluted. **I.D. KEY:** Thickness and broad hafting area.

TALLAHASSEE - Trans. Paleo and Late Archaic to Woodland, 9500 - 8000 B.P. and 3500 - 2500 B. P.

(Also see Beaver Lake, Pinellas, Sante Fe and Yadkin)

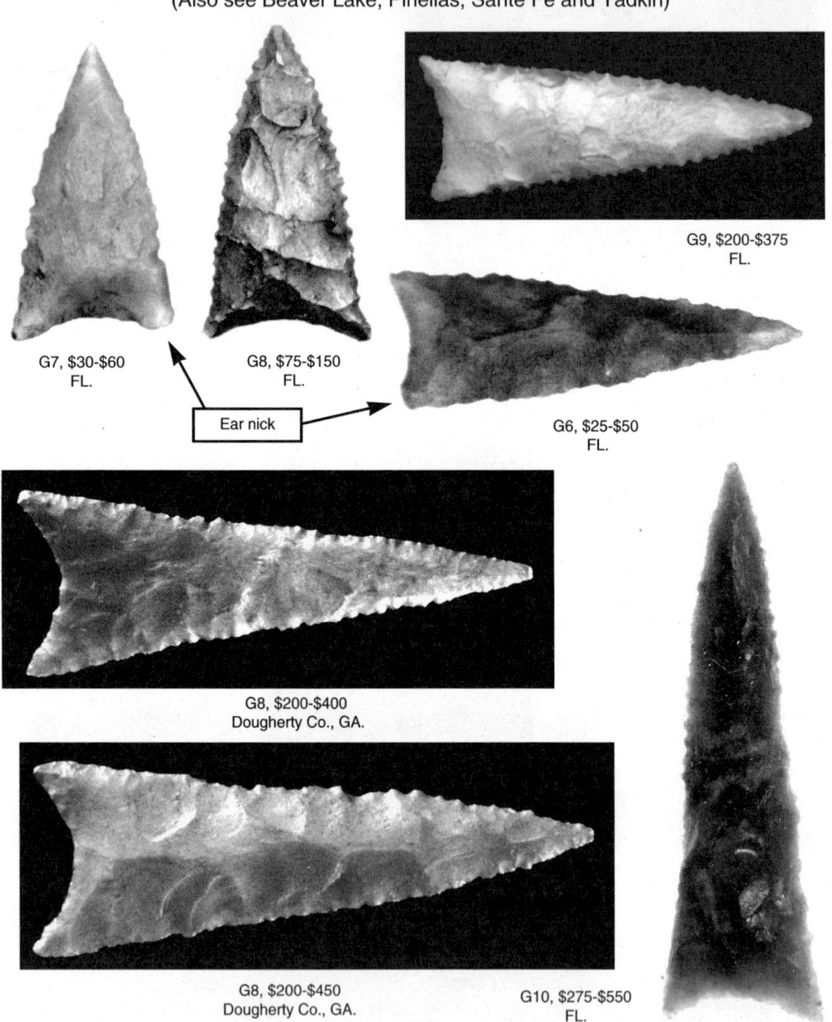

G7, $30-$60
FL.

G8, $75-$150
FL.

G9, $200-$375
FL.

G6, $25-$50
FL.

G8, $200-$400
Dougherty Co., GA.

G8, $200-$450
Dougherty Co., GA.

G10, $275-$550
FL.

LOCATION: Gulf Coastal states. **DESCRIPTION:** A medium to large size, thin, triangular, serrated auriculate point with a concave base. The shoulders usually expand and are an extension of the blade itself. The blade edges are resharpened on each face rather than the usual *Dalton* procedure of beveling on opposite faces. Believed to have been made in Dalton times, 9500-8000 B.P. and again in late Archaic times, 4000-2500 B.P. Has also been found with the late Archaic *Hernando* points. **I.D. KEY:** One sharper tang, edge-work. **I.D. KEY:** Serrated edges.

G10, $1200-$2500
Levy Co., FL.

TAMPA - Mississippian, 800 - 400 B. P.

(Also see O'Leno and Pinellas)

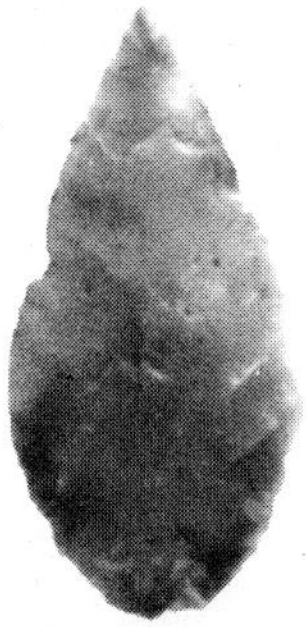

Clear

Clear red coral

G7, $10-$20
FL.

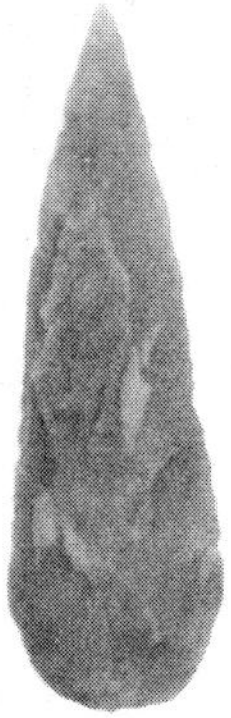

G9, $40-$80
FL.

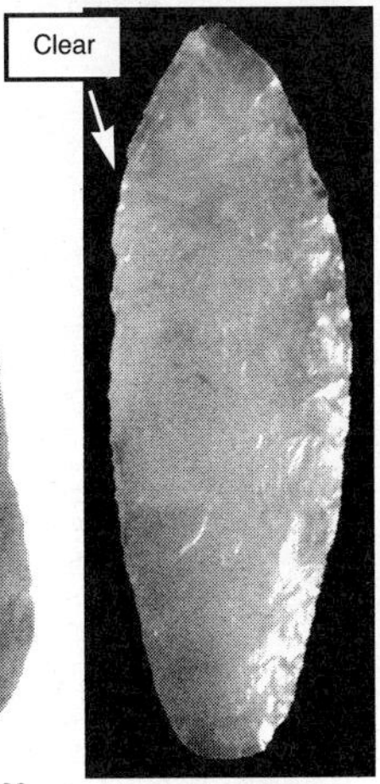

G5, $75-$150
Alachua Co., FL.

G10, $90-$175
FL.

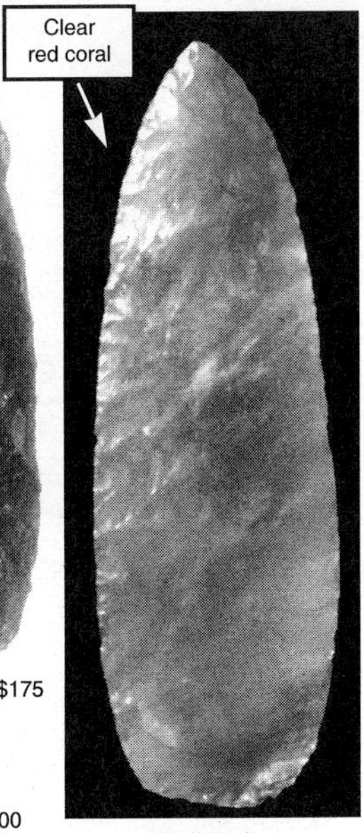

G10, $100-$200
FL.

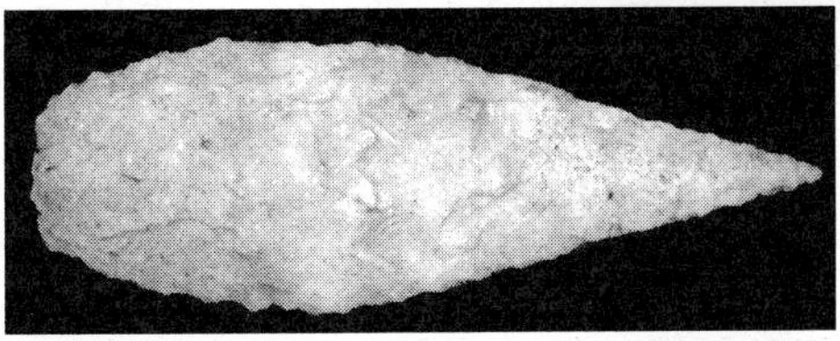

G9, $175-$300
Pasco Co., FL.

LOCATION: Gulf Coastal states. **DESCRIPTION:** A small size, narrow to broad, tear drop shaped point with a rounded base. Similar to the *Nodena* type found further north. A rare point.

TAYLOR STEMMED - Woodland, 3000 - 1300 B. P.

(Also see Kirk)

LOCATION: Far Eastern States. **DESCRIPTION:** A medium to large size, side notched to auriculate point with a concave base. Basal areas are ground. Blade edges can be serrated. Called *Van Lott* in South Carolina.

G5, $15-$25
FL.

THONOTOSASSA - Early Archaic, 8000 - 5000 B. P.

(Also see Hamilton, Morrow Mountain, Putnam, Savannah River and Sumter)

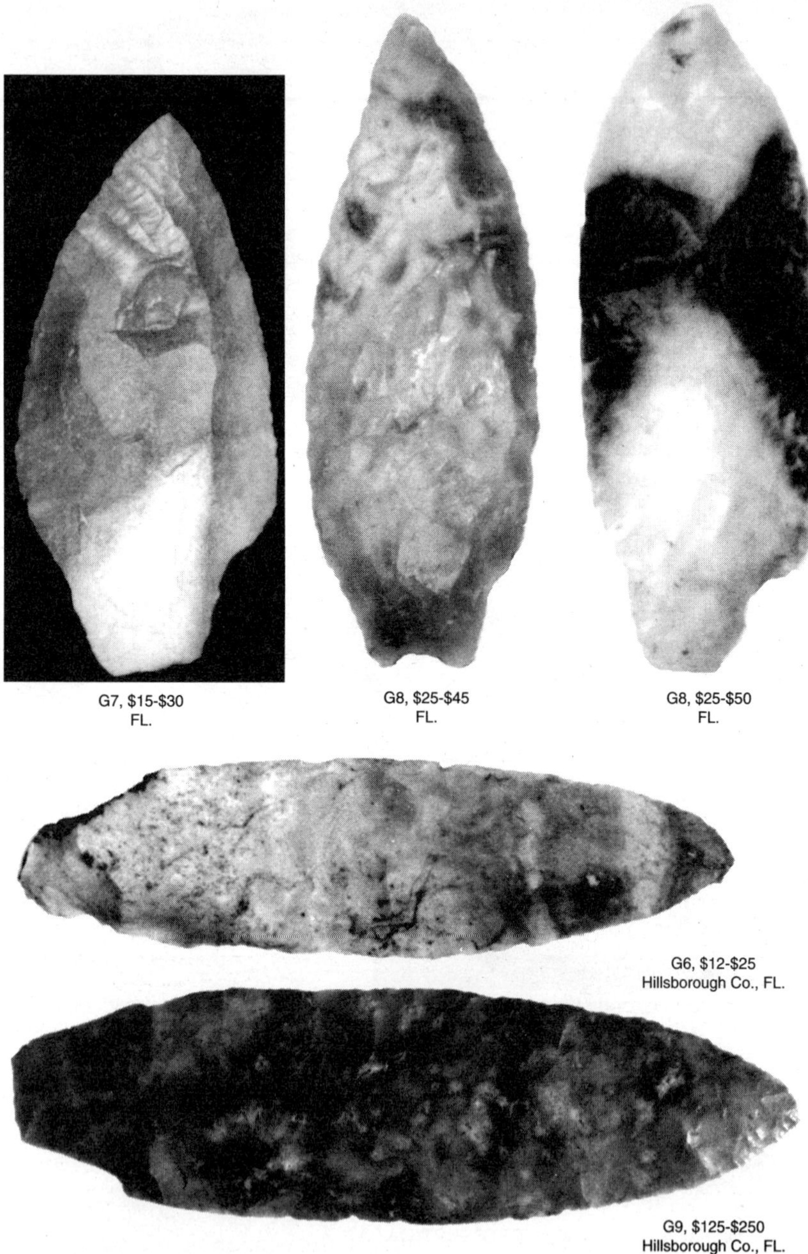

G7, $15-$30
FL.

G8, $25-$45
FL.

G8, $25-$50
FL.

G6, $12-$25
Hillsborough Co., FL.

G9, $125-$250
Hillsborough Co., FL.

LOCATION: Florida only. **DESCRIPTION:** A large size, narrow, usually heavy, crudely made blade with weak shoulders and a stem that can be parallel sided to contracting. The base can be straight to rounded. Believed to be related to the smaller *Sumter* type. Also believed to be the first Florida point with heated stone.

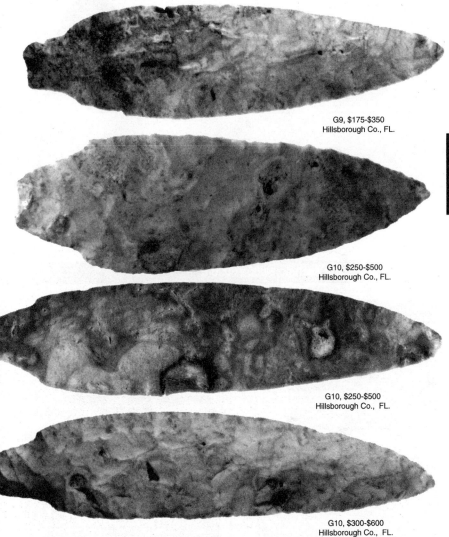

G9, $175-$350
Hillsborough Co., FL.

G10, $250-$500
Hillsborough Co., FL.

G10, $250-$500
Hillsborough Co., FL.

G10, $300-$600
Hillsborough Co., FL.

UNION SIDE NOTCHED - Late Paleo, 10,000 - 8000 B. P.

(Also see Beaver Lake, Osceola Greenbrier and Suwannee)

G8, $75-$150
FL.

G7, $40-$85
FL.

UNION SIDE NOTCHED (continued)

LOCATION: Gulf Coastal states. **DESCRIPTION:** A medium to large size, broad blade with weak side notches expanding into auricles. Base can be straight to slightly concave or convex and is usually heavily ground all around the basal area.

G10, $250-$500
FL.

G9, $150-300
FL.

WACISSA - Early Archaic, 9000 - 6000 B. P.

(Also see Abbey, Arredondo, Bolen, Kirk Serrated and Seminole)

G4, $6-$12
FL.

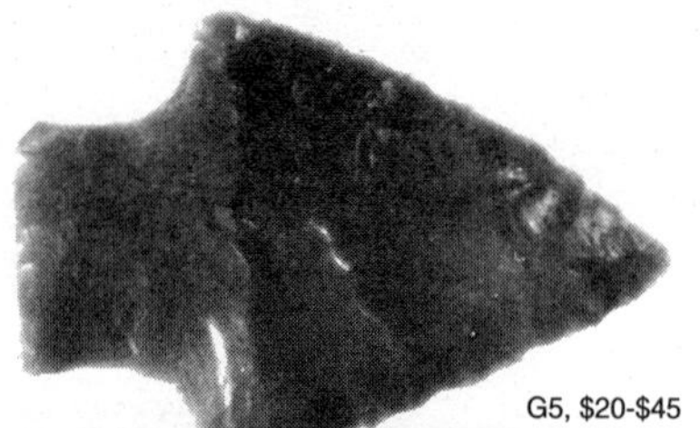

G5, $20-$45
FL.

G3, $20-$40
Madison Co., FL.

G4, $25-$50
Houston Co., AL.

LOCATION: Gulf Coastal states. **DESCRIPTION:** A small to medium size, thick, short, broad stemmed point that is beveled on all four sides. Shoulders are moderate to weak and horizontal to slightly barbed. Some examples are serrated.

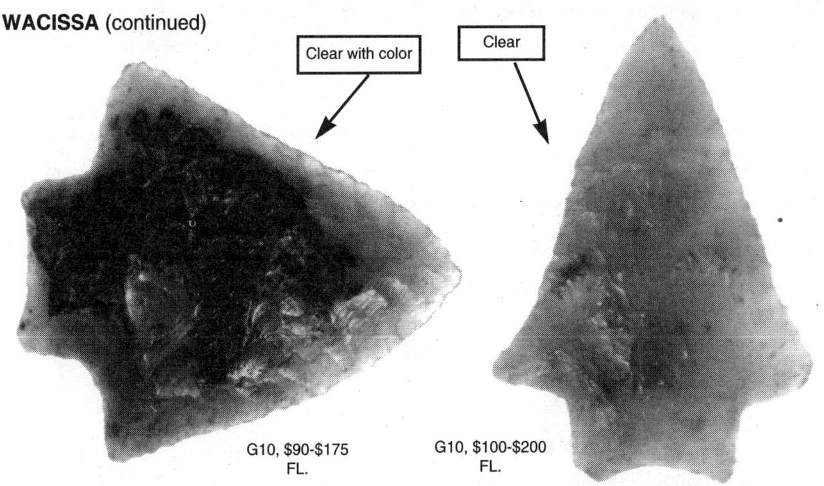

WACISSA (continued)

Clear with color

G10, $90-$175
FL.

Clear

G10, $100-$200
FL.

WALLER KNIFE - Early Archaic, 9000 - 5000 B. P.

(Also see Edgefield Scraper)

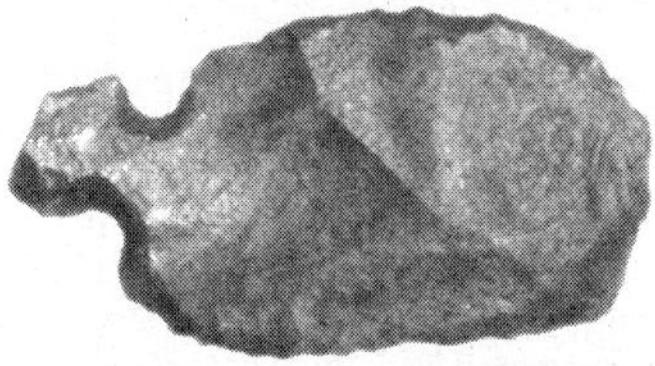

G4, $20-$40
FL.

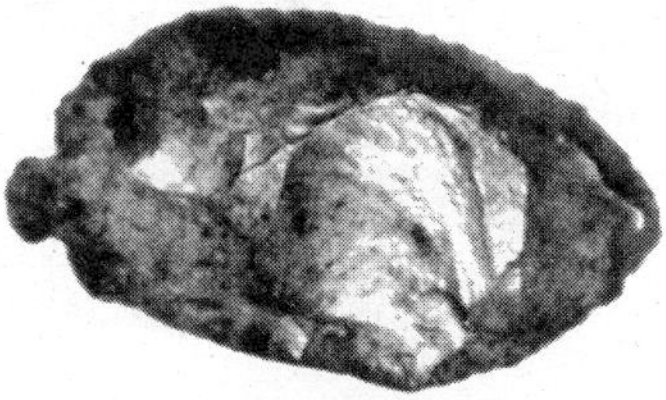

G4, $15-$30
FL.

Crafted from flakes, all are uniface, with edgework only on face showing

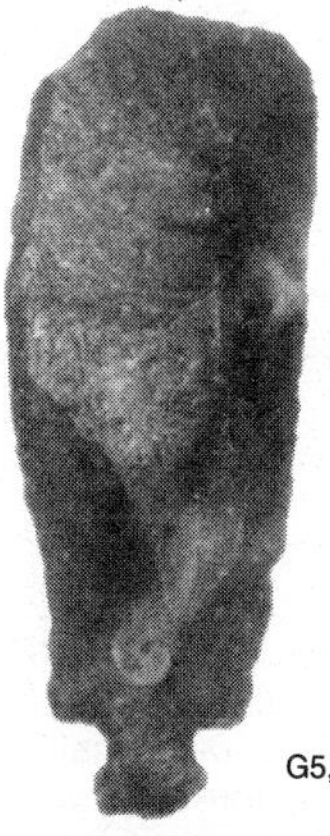

G5, $20-$40
FL.

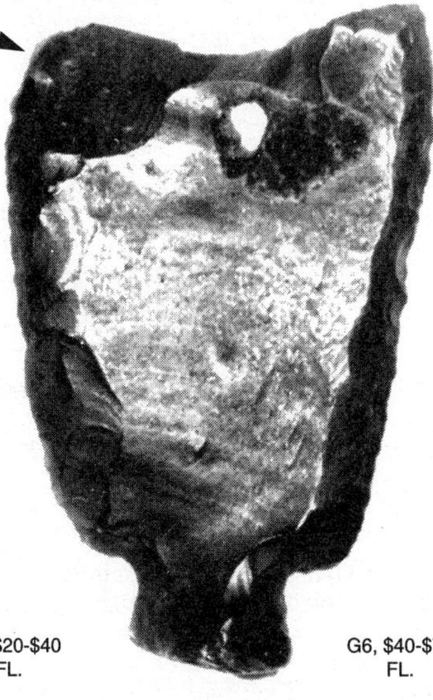

G6, $40-$75
FL.

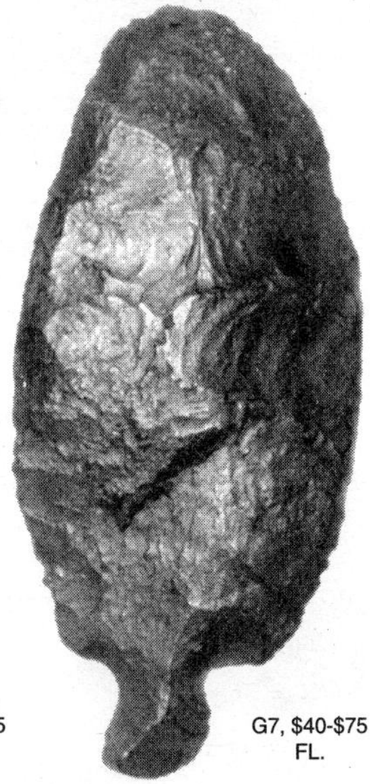

G7, $40-$75
FL.

LOCATION: Gulf Coastal states. **DESCRIPTION:** A medium size double uniface knife with a short, notched base, made from a flake. Only the cutting edges have been pressure flaked.

WEEDEN ISLAND - Woodland, 2500 - 1000 B. P.

(Also see Jackson)

Impact fracture

G5, $5-$9 FL.

G7, $5-$9 FL.

G6, $2-$5 FL.

G8, $12-$25 FL.

G8, $12-$25 FL.

LOCATION: Guld Coastal states. **DESCRIPTION:** A small size triangular point with a contracting stem. Shoulders can be tapered to barbed. Bases are straight to rounded.

WESTO - Middle Archaic, 7500 - 5000 B. P.

(Also see Morrow Mountain)

G6, $15-$25
FL.

LOCATION: Florida. **DESCRIPTION:** A medium size, triangular point with a very short contracting to rounded stem. Shoulders are usually weak but can be barbed. Blade edges can be serrated. **I.D. KEY:** Contracted base and early flaking.

WHEELER - Transitional Paleo, 10,000 - 8000 B. P.

(Also see Beaver Lake and Simpson-Mustache)

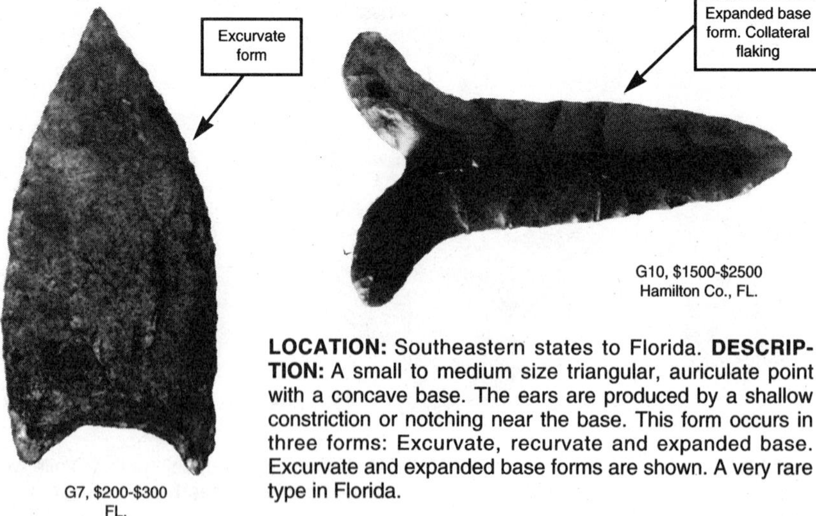

G10, $1500-$2500
Hamilton Co., FL.

G7, $200-$300
FL.

LOCATION: Southeastern states to Florida. **DESCRIPTION:** A small to medium size triangular, auriculate point with a concave base. The ears are produced by a shallow constriction or notching near the base. This form occurs in three forms: Excurvate, recurvate and expanded base. Excurvate and expanded base forms are shown. A very rare type in Florida.

EASTERN CENTRAL SECTION:

This section includes point types from the following states:
Alabama, Georgia, Indiana, Kentucky, Michigan, Mississippi, Ohio and Tennessee.

The points in this section are arranged in alphabetical order and are shown **actual size**. All types are listed that were available for photographing. Any missing types will be added to future editions as photographs become available. We are always interested in receiving sharp, black and white or color glossy photos or color slides of your collection. Be sure to include a ruler in the photograph so that proper scale can be determined.

Lithics: Materials employed in the manufacture of projectile points from this region include: agate, chalcedony, chert, crystal, flint, limestone, quartz and quartzite.

EC

Important Sites: Nuckolls, Humphreys Co., TN.; Cotaco, Cotaco Creek, Morgan Co., AL.; Cumberland, Cumberland River Valley, TN.; Damron, Lincoln Co., TN.; Elk River, Limestone Co., AL.; Eva, Benton Co., TN.; Quad, Limestone Col, AL.; Pine Tree, Limestone Co., AL.; Dover Flint, Humphreys Co., TN.; Redstone, Madison Co., AL.; Plevna (Dovetail), Madison Co., AL.; Stone Pipe, Wheeler Reservoir, Limestone Co., AL. for Wheeler and Decatur points.

Regional Consultants:
Tom Davis
Mike K. McCoy

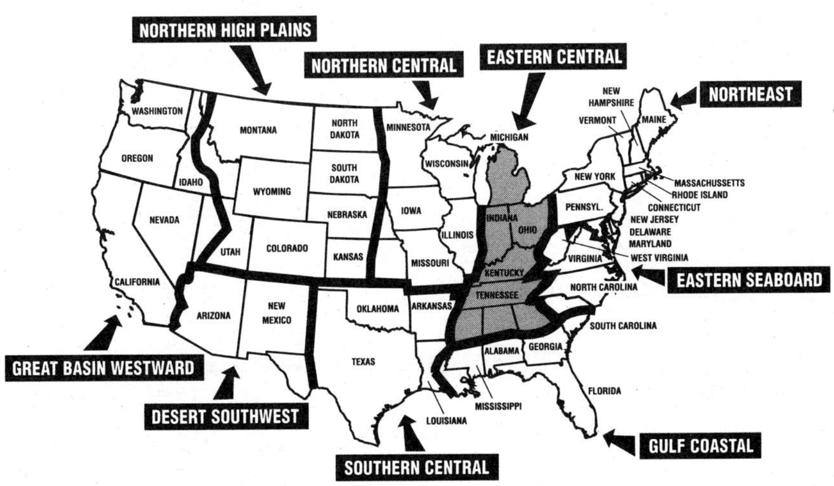

EASTERN CENTRAL
(Archaeological Periods)

PALEO (14,000 B. P. - 11,000 B. P.)

Beaver Lake
Clovis
Clovis Unfluted
Cumberland
Debert
Folsom
Graver
Lancet
Redstone
Scraper

TRANSITIONAL PALEO (11,000 B. P. - 9,000 B. P.)

Agate Basin
Alamance
Alberta
Big Sandy
Big Sandy Broad Base
Big Sandt Contracted Base
Big Sandy E-Notched
Big Sandy Leighton Base
Browns Valley
Cache River
Cave Spring
Dalton Classic
Dalton Colbert
Dalton Greenbrier
Dalton Hemphill
Dalton Nuckolls
Golondrina
Greenbrier
Hardaway
Hardaway Dalton
Haw River
Hi-Lo
Hinds
Holland
Jeff
Lerma Rounded Base
Marianna
Meserve
Ohio Lanceolate
Paint Rock Valley
Plainview
Quad
Square Knife
Stanfield
Thebes
Wheeler Excurvate
Wheeler Expanded
Wheeler Recurvate
Wheeler Triangular

EARLY ARCHAIC (10,000 B. P. - 7,000 B. P.)

Angostura
Autauga
Cobbs Triangular
Coldwater
Conerly
Crawford Creek
Damron
Decatur
Decatur Blade
Ecusta
Elk River
Eva
Fishspear
Fountain Creek
Fox Valley
Frederick
Garth Slough
Hardin
Harpeth River
Heavy Duty
Johnson
Jude
Kanawha
Kirk Corner Notched
Kird Serrated
Kirk Serrated-Bifurcated
Kirk Snapped Base
Lake Erie
Lecroy
Leighton
Limeton Bifurcate
Lost Lake
MacCorkle
Neuberger
Newton Falls
Palmer
Perforator
Pine Tree
Pine Tree Corner Notched
Rice Lobbed
Russel Cave
St. Albans
St. Charles
Stanly
Steubenville
Stilwell
Tennessee River
Warrick
White Springs

MIDDLE ARCHAIC (7,000 B. P. - 4,000 B. P.)

Afton
Appalachian
Benton
Benton Blade
Benton Bottle Neck
Benton Double Notched
Benton Narrow Blade
Big Slough
Brewerton Corner Notched
Brewerton Eared Triangular
Brewerton Side Notched
Buck Creek
Buggs Island
Buzzard Roost Creek
Copena Auriculate
Cypress Creek
Elora
Exotic Forms
Frazier
Halifax
Kays
Ledbetter
Limestone
Maples
McIntire
Morrow Mountain
Morrow Mountain Round Base
Morrow Mountain Straight Base
Motley
Mountain Fork
Mulberry Creek
Patrick
Pickwick
Ramey Knife
Savage Cave
Savannah River
Searcy
Sedalia
Smith
Tortugas
Wade

LATE ARCHAIC (4,000 B. P. - 3,000 B. P.)

Ashtabula
Bakers Creek
Beacon Island
Bradley Spike
Copena Classic
Copena Round Base
Copena Triangular
Corner Tang Knife
Dagger
Etley
Evans
Flint Creek
Flint River Spike
Little Bear Creek
Meadowood
Merom
Mud Creek
Orient
Pontchartrain Type I & II
Rankin
Rheems Creek
Shoals Creek
Smithsonia
Snake Creek
Sublet Ferry
Swan Lake
Table Rock
Turkeytail-Fulton
Turkeytail-Harrison
Turkeytail-Hebron

WOODLAND (3,000 B. P. - 1,300 B. P.)

Addison Micro-Drill
Adena
Adena Blade
Adena-Dickson
Adena-Narrow Stem
Adena-Notched Base
Adena Robbins
Adena-Waubesa
Benjamin
Camp Creek
Candy Creek
Coosa
Cotaco Creek
Cotaco Creek Blade
Cotaco-Wright
Cupp
Durant's Bend
Durst
Duval
Ebenezer
Fairland
Gibson
Greeneville
Hamilton
Hamilton Stemmed
Hopewell
Jacks Reef Corner Notched
Jacks Reef Pentagonal
Knight Island
Montgomery
Morse Knife
Mouse Creek
New Market
Nolichucky
North
Nova
Ohio Double Notched
Red Ochre
Ross
Sand Mountain
Schild Spike
Snyders
Tear Drop
Vallina
Washington
Yadkin

MISSISSIPPIAN (1300 B. P. - 400 B. P.)

Duck River Sword
Fort Ancient
Fort Ancient Blade
Guntersville
Harahey
Keota
Levanna
Lozenge
Madison
Nodena

HISTORIC (450 B. P. - 170 B. P.)

Trade Points

EASTERN CENTRAL
THUMBNAIL GUIDE SECTION

The following references are provided to aid the collector in easier and quicker identification of point types. All photos are exactly 30% of actual size and are proportional to each other. Each point pictured in this section represents a classic form for the type. When a match is found, go to the alphabetical location of that type for more examples in actual size.

EC

1 THUMBNAIL GUIDE - AURICULATE FORMS (30% actual size)

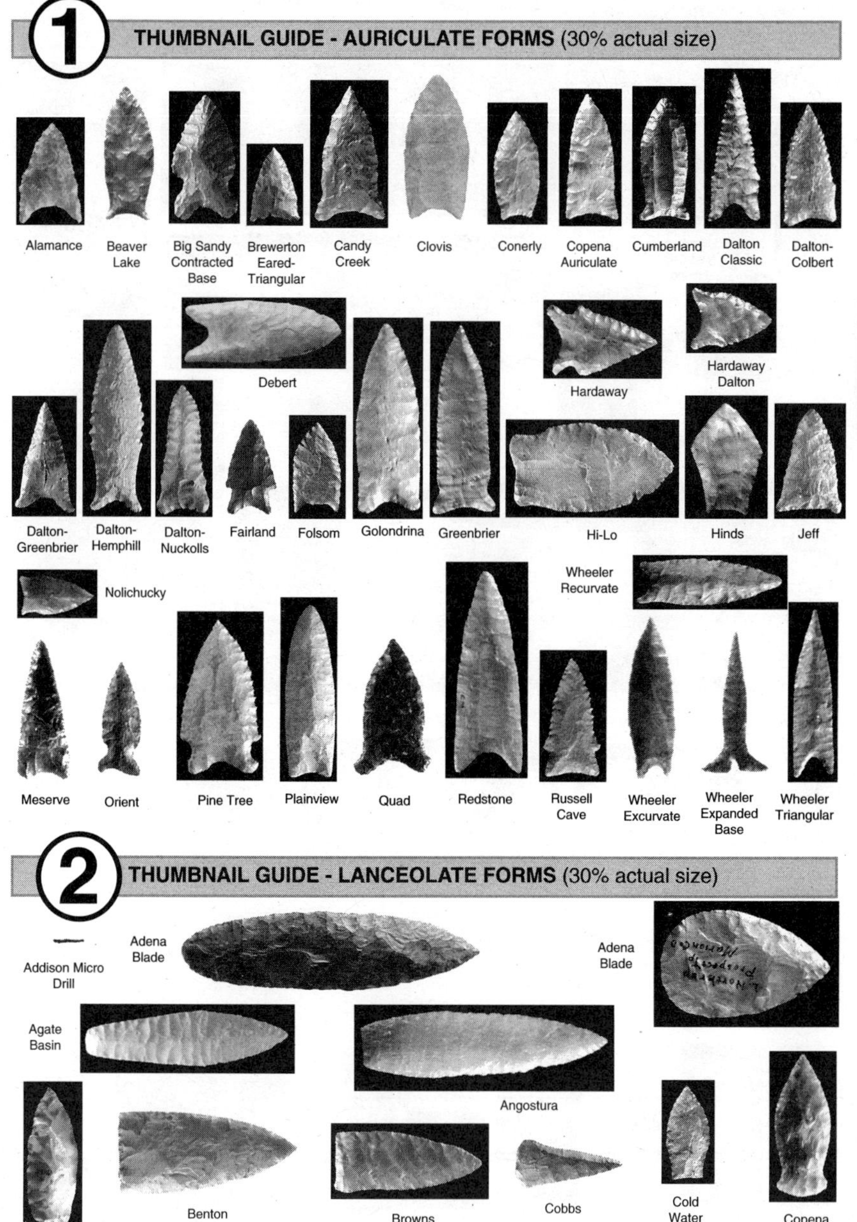

Alamance, Beaver Lake, Big Sandy Contracted Base, Brewerton Eared-Triangular, Candy Creek, Clovis, Conerly, Copena Auriculate, Cumberland, Dalton Classic, Dalton-Colbert

Debert, Hardaway, Hardaway Dalton

Dalton-Greenbrier, Dalton-Hemphill, Dalton-Nuckolls, Fairland, Folsom, Golondrina, Greenbrier, Hi-Lo, Hinds, Jeff

Nolichucky, Wheeler Recurvate

Meserve, Orient, Pine Tree, Plainview, Quad, Redstone, Russell Cave, Wheeler Excurvate, Wheeler Expanded Base, Wheeler Triangular

2 THUMBNAIL GUIDE - LANCEOLATE FORMS (30% actual size)

Addison Micro Drill, Adena Blade, Adena Blade

Agate Basin, Angostura

Benjamin, Benton Blade, Browns Valley, Cobbs, Cold Water, Copena Classic

THUMBNAIL GUIDE - Lanceolate Forms (continued)

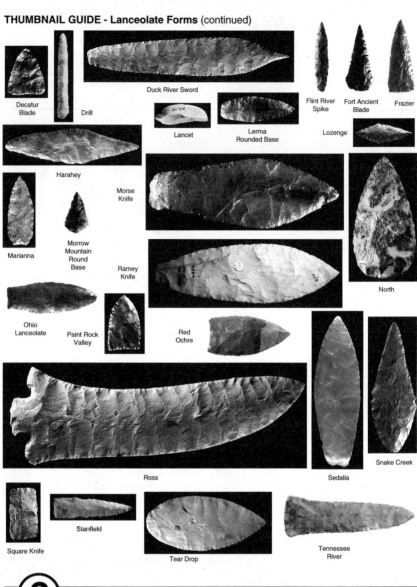

Decatur Blade

Drill

Duck River Sword

Flint River Spike

Fort Ancient Blade

Frazier

Lancet

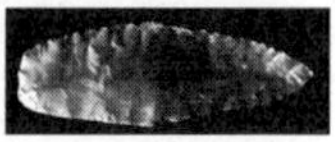

Lerma Rounded Base

Lozenge

Harahey

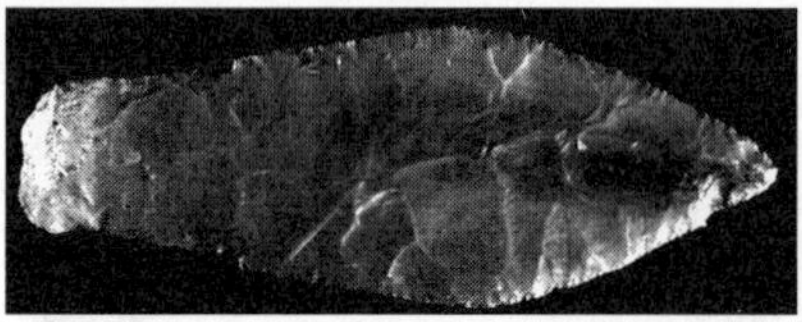

Morse Knife

North

Marianna

Morrow Mountain Round Base

Ramey Knife

Ohio Lanceolate

Paint Rock Valley

Red Ochre

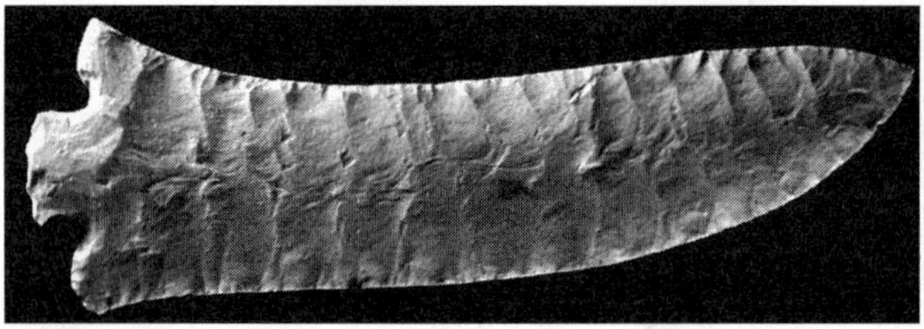

Ross

Sedalia

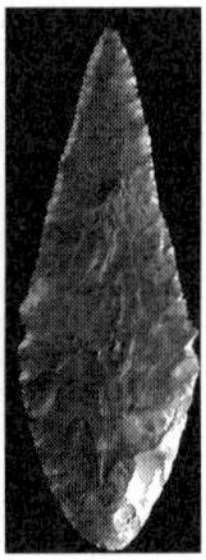

Snake Creek

Square Knife

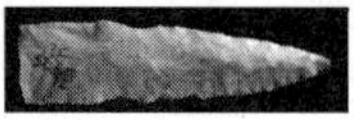

Stanfield

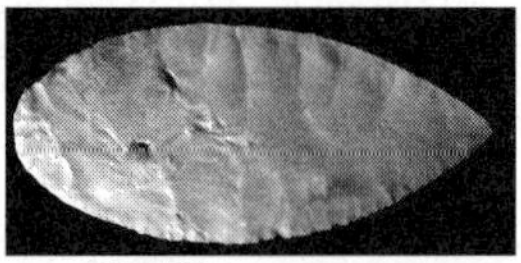

Tear Drop

Tennessee River

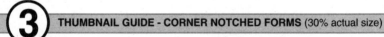

3 THUMBNAIL GUIDE - CORNER NOTCHED FORMS (30% actual size)

Autauga

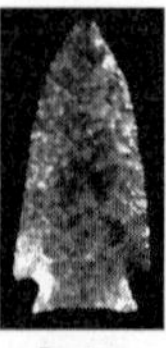

Benton

Brewerton Corner Notched

Corner Tang

Decatur

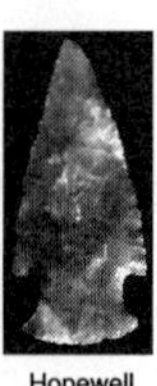

Hopewell

Jacks Reef Corner Notched

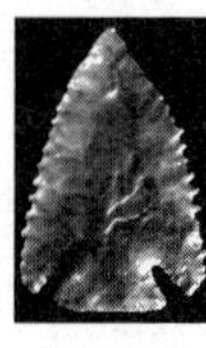

Kirk Corner Notched

Limestone

THUMBNAIL GUIDE - Corner Notched Forms (continued)

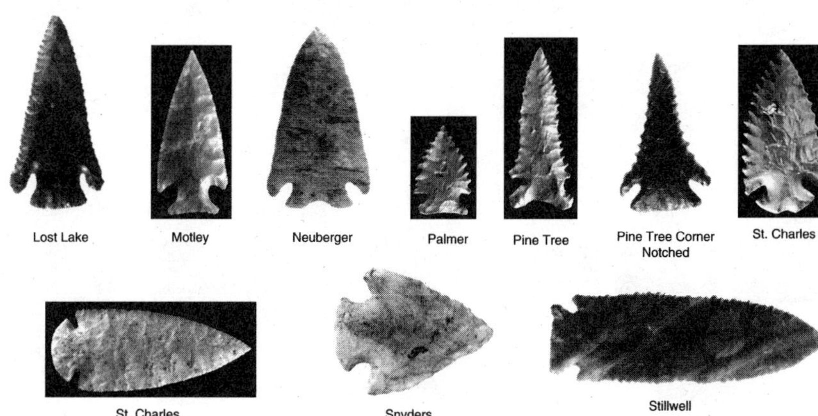

Lost Lake | Motley | Neuberger | Palmer | Pine Tree | Pine Tree Corner Notched | St. Charles

St. Charles | Snyders | Stillwell

4 THUMBNAILGUIDE - SIDE NOTCHED FORMS (30% actual size)

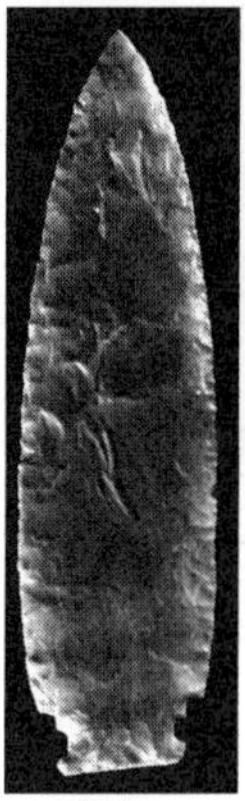

Benton Double Notch

Benton Side Notched

Big Sandy

Big Sandy Broad Base

Big Sandy E-Notched

Big Sandy Leighton Base

Brewerton Side Notched

Cache River

Damron

Durst

Ecusta

Evans

Exotic

Fishspear

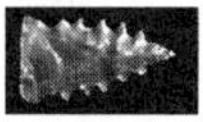

Fountain Creek

Halifax

Knight Island

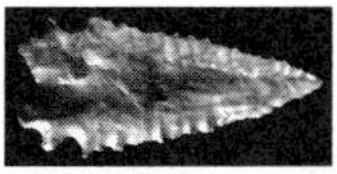

Leighton

Meadowood

Merom

Newton Falls

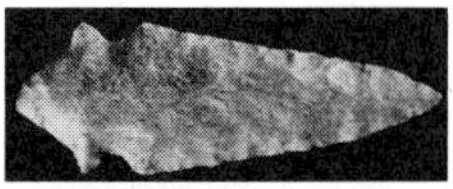

Ohio Double Notch

Savage Cave

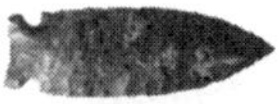

Sublet Ferry

Swan Lake

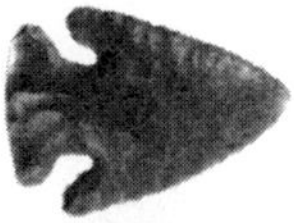

Thebes

Turkey Tail Fulton

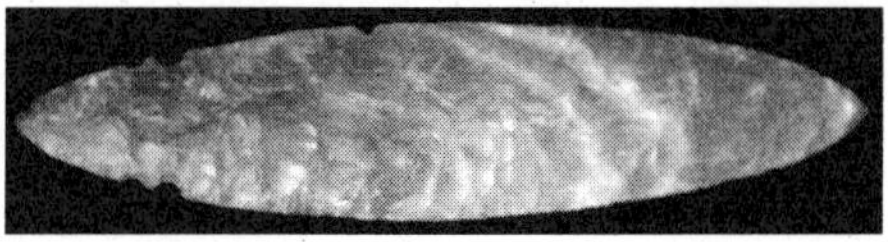

Turkeytail (Harrison)

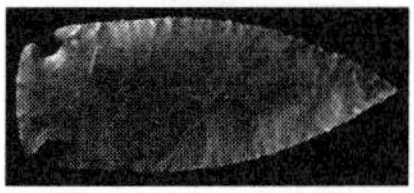

Warrick

5 THUMBNAIL GUIDE - STEMMED FORMS (30% of actual size)

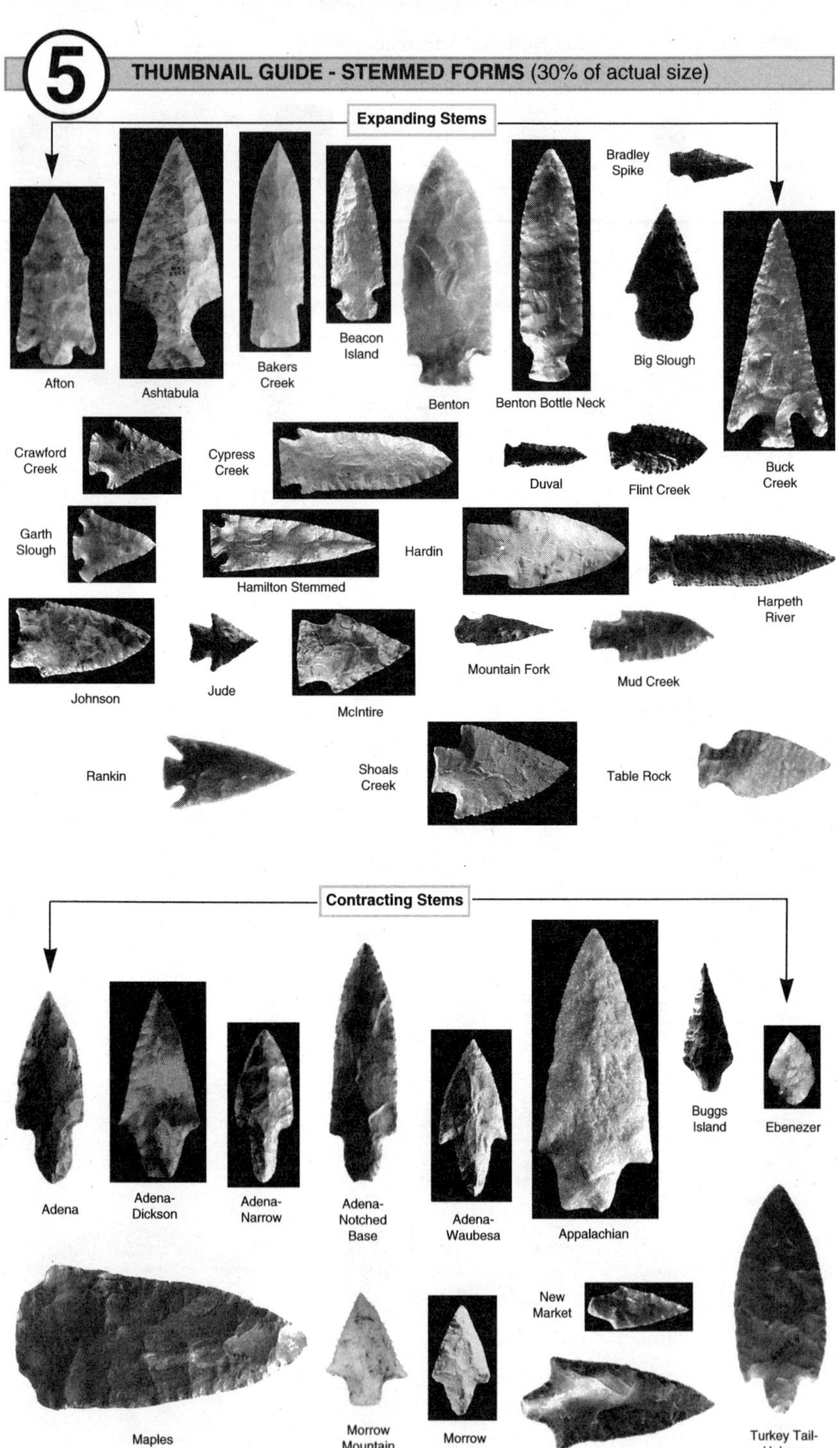

Expanding Stems
Afton
Ashtabula
Bakers Creek
Beacon Island
Benton
Benton Bottle Neck
Bradley Spike
Big Slough
Buck Creek
Crawford Creek
Cypress Creek
Duval
Flint Creek
Garth Slough
Hamilton Stemmed
Hardin
Harpeth River
Johnson
Jude
McIntire
Mountain Fork
Mud Creek
Rankin
Shoals Creek
Table Rock
Contracting Stems
Adena
Adena-Dickson
Adena-Narrow
Adena-Notched Base
Adena-Waubesa
Appalachian
Buggs Island
Ebenezer
Maples
Morrow Mountain Straight Base
Morrow Mountain
New Market
Pickwick
Turkey Tail-Hebron

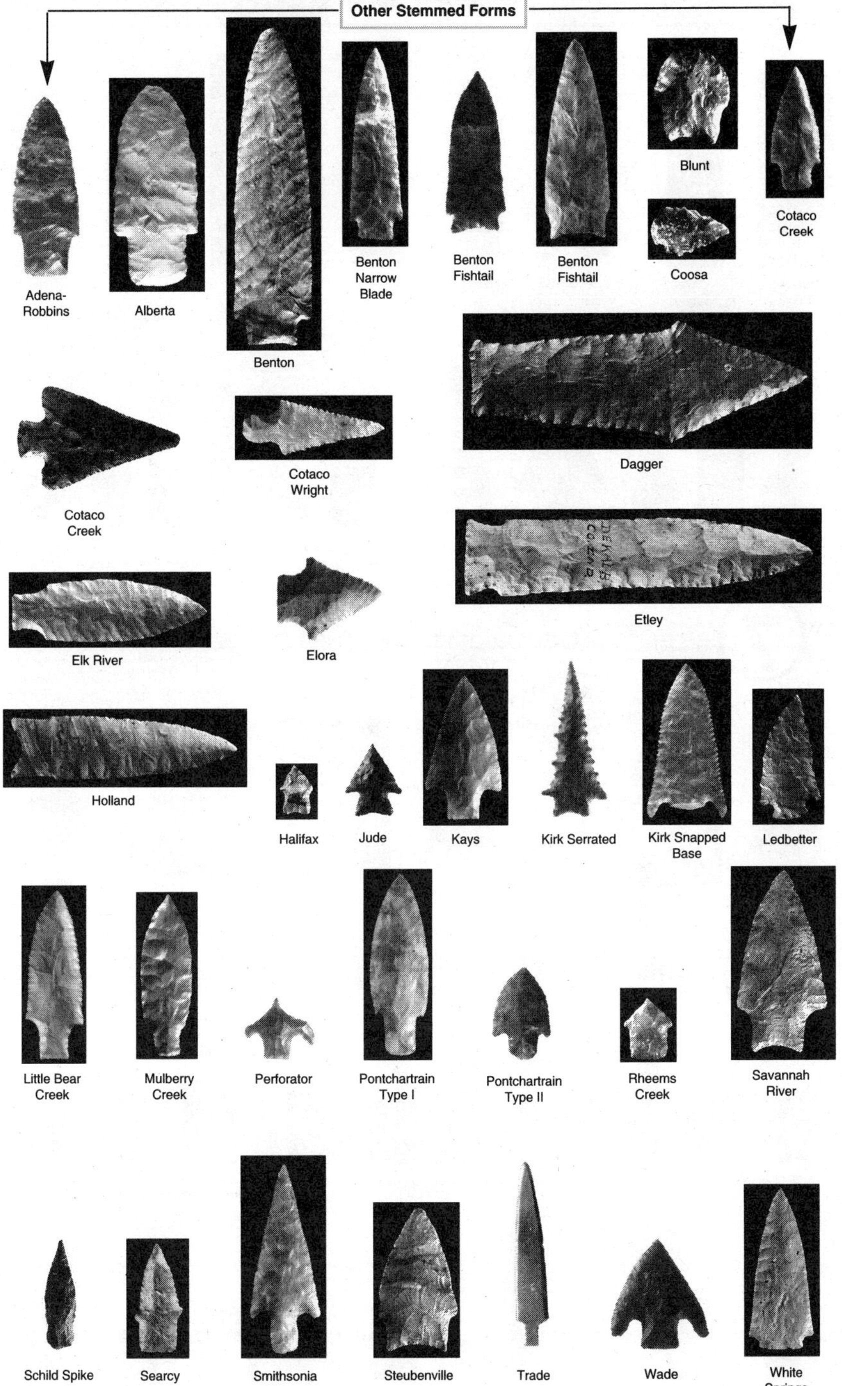
Other Stemmed Forms
Adena-Robbins
Alberta
Benton
Benton Narrow Blade
Benton Fishtail
Benton Fishtail
Blunt
Coosa
Cotaco Creek
Cotaco Creek
Cotaco Wright
Dagger
Etley
Elk River
Elora
Holland
Halifax
Jude
Kays
Kirk Serrated
Kirk Snapped Base
Ledbetter
Little Bear Creek
Mulberry Creek
Perforator
Pontchartrain Type I
Pontchartrain Type II
Rheems Creek
Savannah River
Schild Spike
Searcy
Smithsonia
Steubenville
Trade
Wade
White Springs

THUMBNAIL GUIDE - STEMMED-BIFURCATED FORMS (30% of actual size)

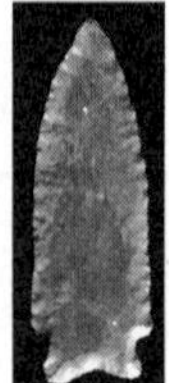

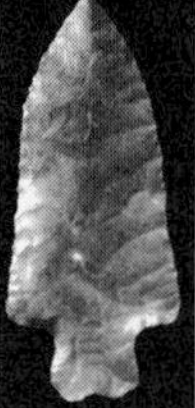
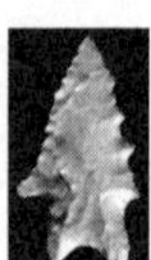

Buzzard Roost Creek | Cave Spring | Fox Valley | Frederick | Haw River | Heavy Duty | Kirk Serrated-Bifurcated | Kanawha

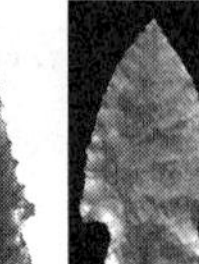

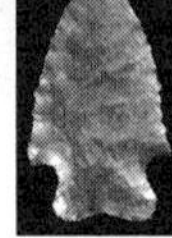

LeCroy | Lake Erie | Limeton | MacCorkle | Neuberger | Patrick | Pine Tree | Rice Lobbed | St. Albans | Stanly

THUMBNAIL GUIDE - BASAL NOTCHED FORMS (30% of actual size)

Eva

Garth Slough
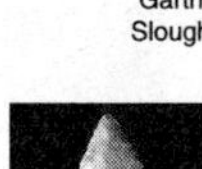

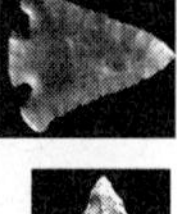
Buck Creek

Hamilton Stemmed

Rankin

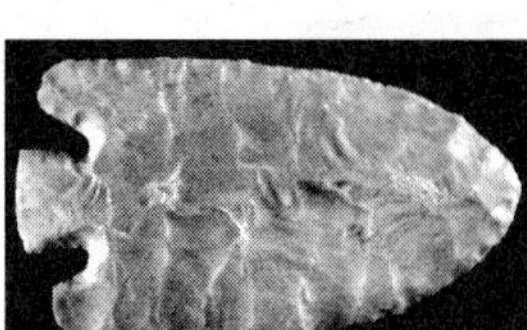
Smith

Wade

THUMBNAIL GUIDE - ARROW POINTS (30% of actual size)

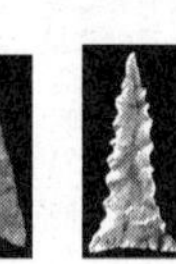

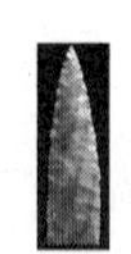

Keota
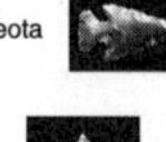

Durant's Bend | Camp Creek | Fort Ancient | Greeneville | Guntersville | Hamilton | Jacks Reef Pentagonal | Jacks Reef Corner Notched | Knight Island | Levanna

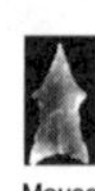

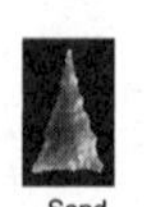

Madison | Montgomery | Mouse Creek | Nodena | Nova | Sand Mountain | Tortugas | Valina | Washington | Yadkin

ADDISON MICRO-DRILL - Late Woodland to Mississippian, 2000 - 1000 B. P.

(Also see Drill, Flint River Spike and Schild Spike)

$3-$5 each
Shown actual size. All found in Bradley & Hamilton Co., TN.

LOCATION: Examples have been found in Alabama, Kentucky, Illinois, North Carolina, North Georgia and Tennessee. **DESCRIPTION:** Very small to medium size, narrow, slivers, flattened to rectangular in cross section. Theory is that this is the final form of a drilling process. The original form were flint slivers with sharp edges that were used as drills. As the sliver was turned in the drilling process, the opposite edges in the direction of movement began to flake off. As the drilling operation proceeded, the edges became steeper as more and more of each side was flaked. Eventually a thin, steeply flaked, rectangular drill form was left and discarded. Unique in that these micro artifacts are not made and then used, but are created by use, and discarded as the edges became eroded away by extremely fine flaking, thus reducing their effectiveness as a cutting edge.

EC

ADENA - Late Archaic to Late Woodland, 3000- 1200 B. P.

(Also see Adena Blade, Bakers Creek, Kays, Little Bear Creek and Turkeytail)

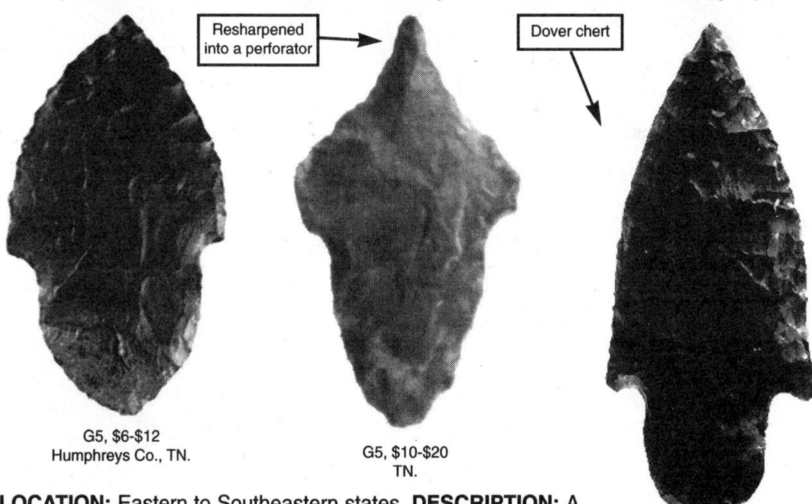

G5, $6-$12
Humphreys Co., TN.

G5, $10-$20
TN.

G5, $25-$45
Parsons, TN.

LOCATION: Eastern to Southeastern states. **DESCRIPTION:** A medium to large, thin, narrow, triangular blade that is sometimes serrated, and with a medium to long, narrow to broad rounded "beaver tail" stem. Most examples are from average to excellent quality. Bases can be ground. Has been found with *Nolichucky, Camp Creek, Candy Creek, Ebenezer* and *Greeneville* points (Rankin site, Cocke Co., TN). **I.D. KEY:** Rounded base, woodland flaking.

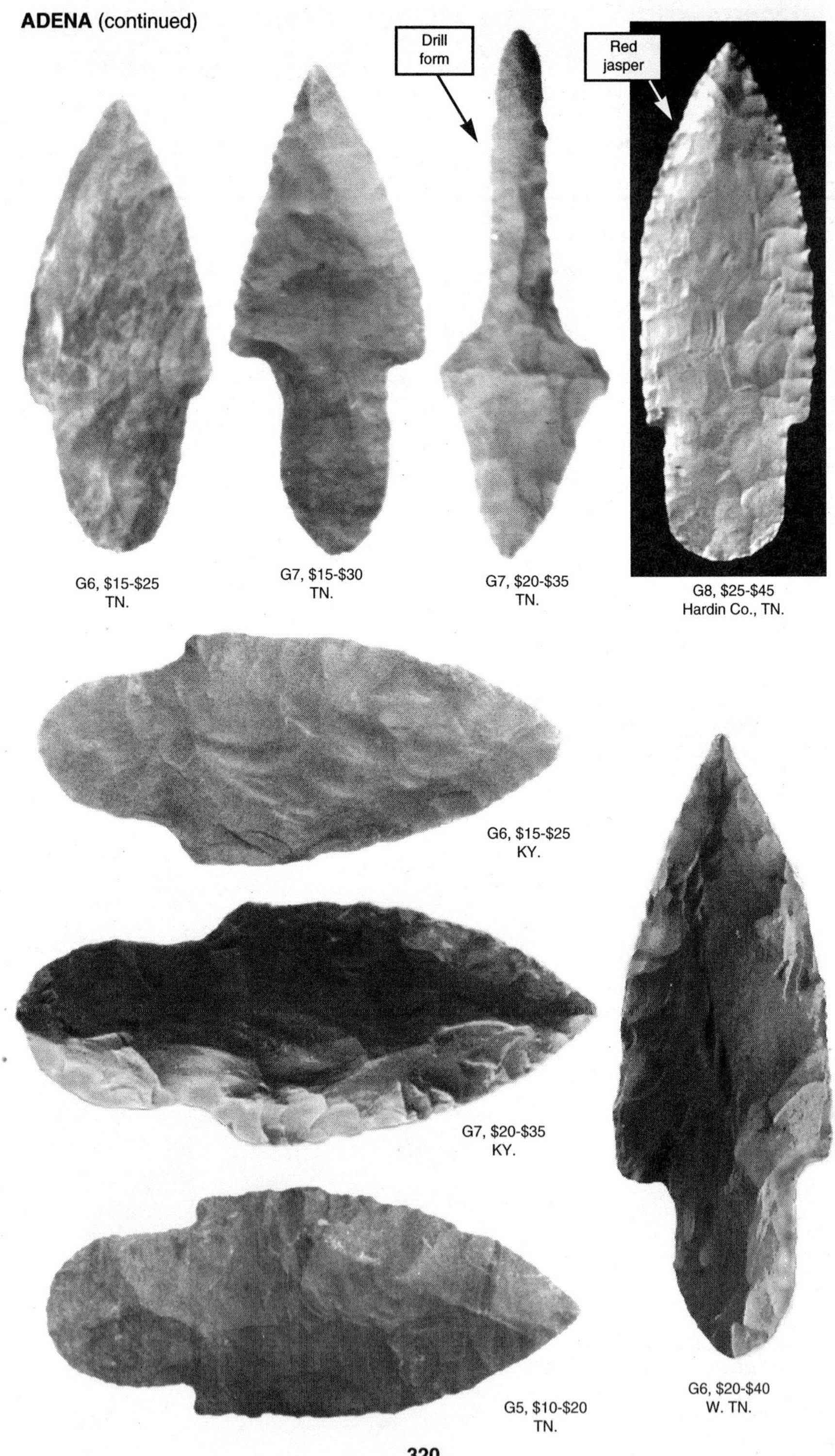

G6, $15-$25
TN.

G7, $15-$30
TN.

G7, $20-$35
TN.

G8, $25-$45
Hardin Co., TN.

G6, $15-$25
KY.

G7, $20-$35
KY.

G6, $20-$40
W. TN.

G5, $10-$20
TN.

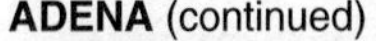

G5, $15-$25
Humphreys Co., TN.

G7, $25-$45
KY.

G6, $15-$30
KY.

EC

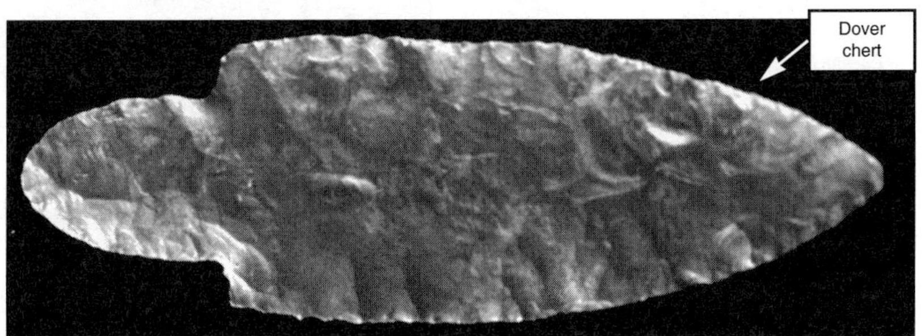

G7, $35-$65
Middle TN.

G9, $100-$200
OH.

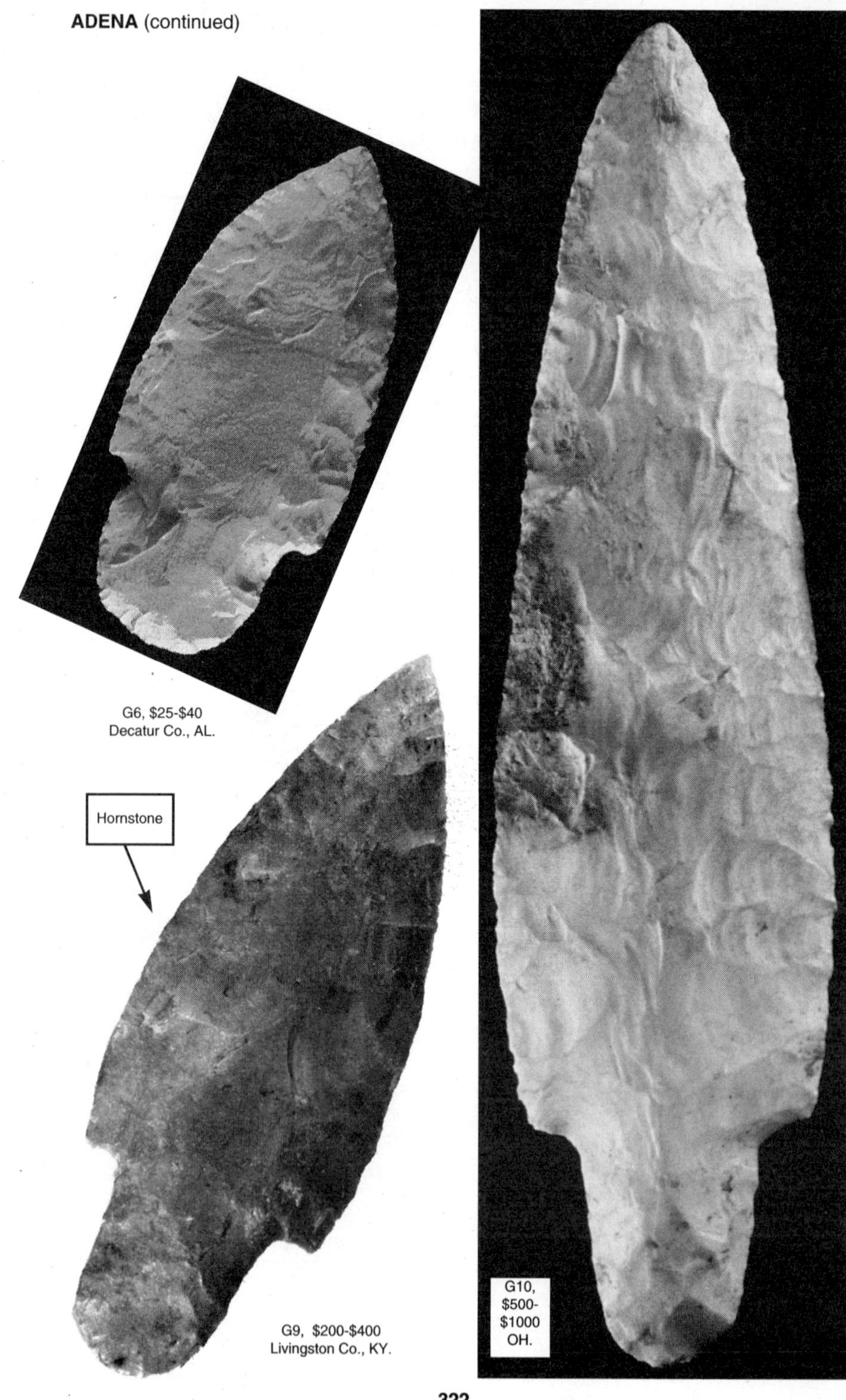

G6, $25-$40
Decatur Co., AL.

G9, $200-$400
Livingston Co., KY.

G10,
$500-
$1000
OH.

ADENA BLADE - Late Archaic to Woodland, 3000-1200 B. P.

(Also see Copena, North, Tear Drop and Tennessee River)

G5, $15-$25
KY.

G5, $25-$45
Marion Co., OH.

G8, $40-$75
TN.

G5, $15-$30
Marion Co., OH.

EC

LOCATION: Midwestern to Eastern states. **DESCRIPTION:** A large size, thin, broad, ovate blade with a rounded base. Usually found in caches. **I.D. KEY:** Woodland Flaking, large direct strikes.

ADENA-DICKSON - Woodland, 2500 - 1600 B. P.

(Also see Gary and Morrow Mountain)

G5, $5-$10
Meigs Co., TN.

G4, $10-$20
Allen Co., KY.

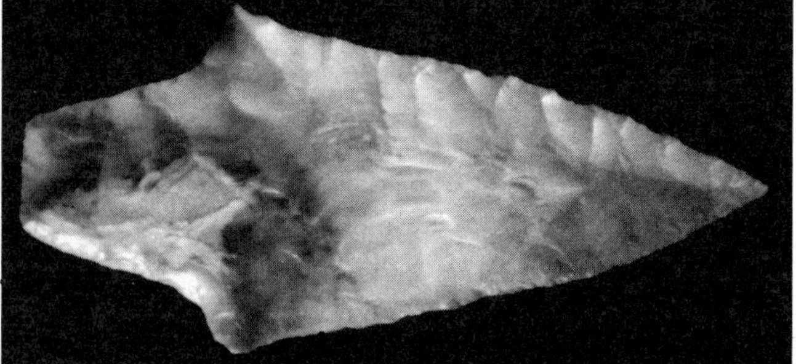

G8, $75-$150
OH.

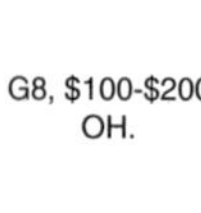

G8, $100-$200
OH.

LOCATION: Midwestern states. Type site: Fulton Co., MO., Dickson mounds, Don F. Dickson, 1927. **DESCRIPTION:** A medium to large size point with tapered shoulders and a contracting stem. High quality flaking and thinness is evident on most examples. **I.D. KEY:** Basal form.

ADENA-NARROW STEM - Late Archaic-Woodland, 3000 - 1200 B. P.

(Also see Little Bear Creek)

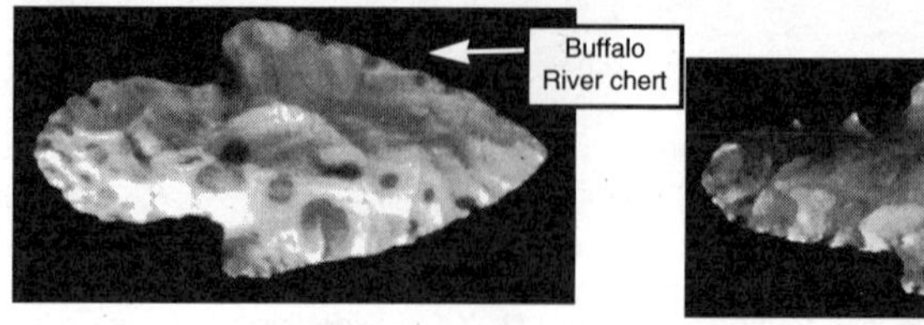

G7, $15-$30
W. TN.

G7, $10-$20
Humphreys Co., TN.

G4, $5-$10
S.E. TN.

G8, $15-$25
KY.

G7, $20-$40
W. TN.

G8, $20-$40
Humphreys Co., TN.

G9, $150-$200
Humphreys Co., TN.

G9, $150-$250
Clifton, TN.

LOCATION: Eastern to Southeastern states. **DESCRIPTION:** A medium to large, thin, narrow triangular blade that is sometimes serrated, with a medium to long, narrow, rounded stem. Most examples are well made. **I.D. KEY:** Narrow rounded base with more secondary work than ordinary *Adena.*

ADENA-NOTCHED BASE - Late Archaic-Woodland, 3000 - 1200 B. P.

(Also see Adena and Little Bear Creek)

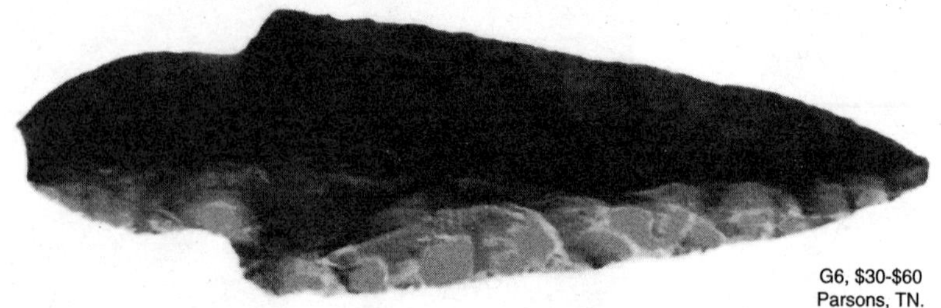

G6, $30-$60
Parsons, TN.

LOCATION: Southeastern states. **DESCRIPTION:** Identical to *Adena*, but with a notched or snapped-off concave base. **I.D. KEY:** Basal form different.

ADENA-ROBBINS - Late Archaic to Woodland, 3000 - 1800 B. P.

(Also see Alberta, Kays, Little Bear Creek, Mulberry Creek and Pontchartrain)

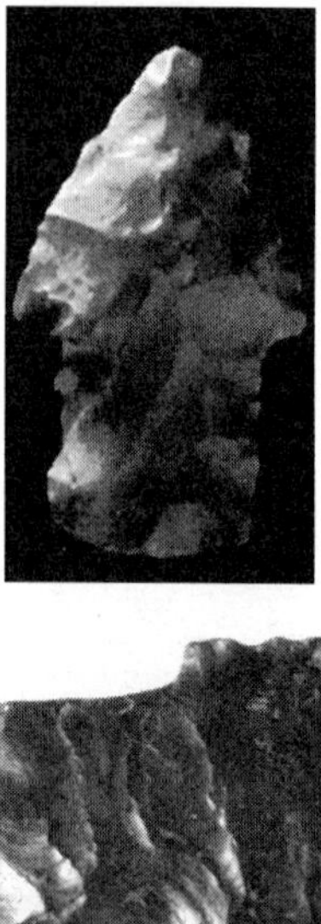

Used as a knife

G6, $15-$25
Geauga Co., OH.

G5, $5-$10
Madison, IN.

Red jasper

G9, $50-$100
KY.

G7, $20-$35
TN.

LOCATION: Eastern to Southeastern states. **DESCRIPTION:** A large, broad, triangular point that is thin and well made with a long, wide, rounded stem that is parallel sided. The blade has convex sides and square shoulders. Many examples show excellent secondary flaking on blade edges. **I.D. KEY:** Squared base, heavy secondary flaking.

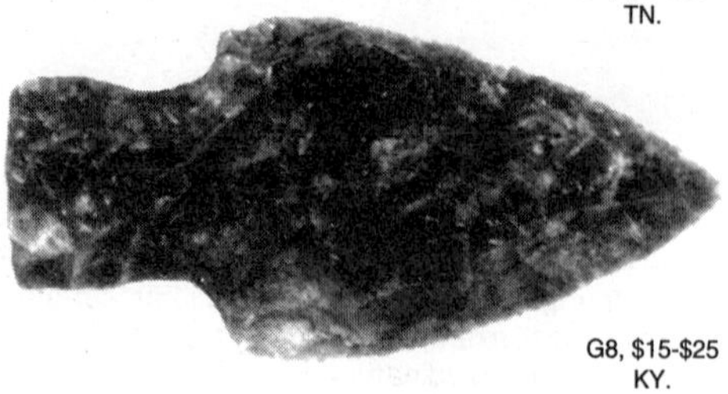

G8, $15-$25
KY.

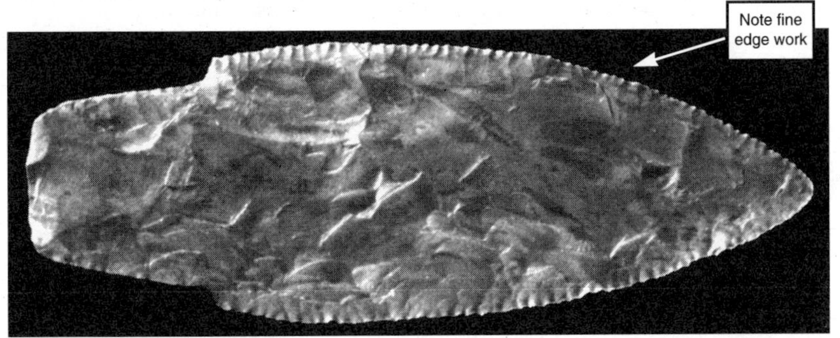

G10, $250-$500
Trigg Co., KY.

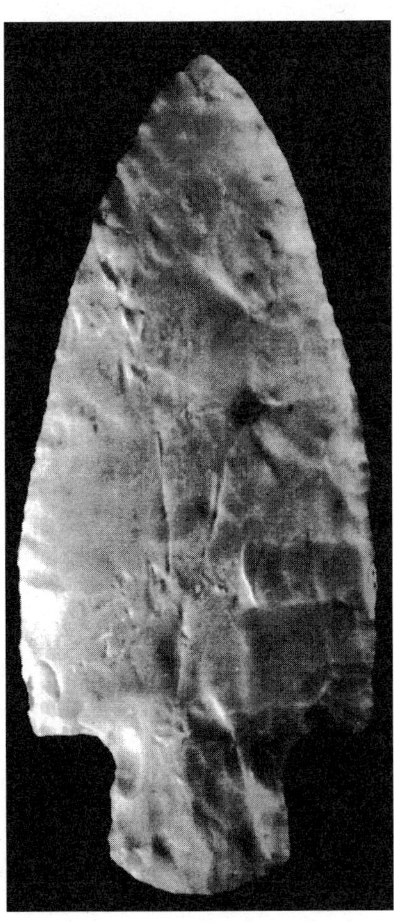

G8, $150-$250
OH.

G8, $100-$200
Richland Co., OH.

ADENA-WAUBESA - Woodland, 2500 - 1500 B. P.

(Also see Adena, Little Bear Creek and Turkeytail-Hebron)

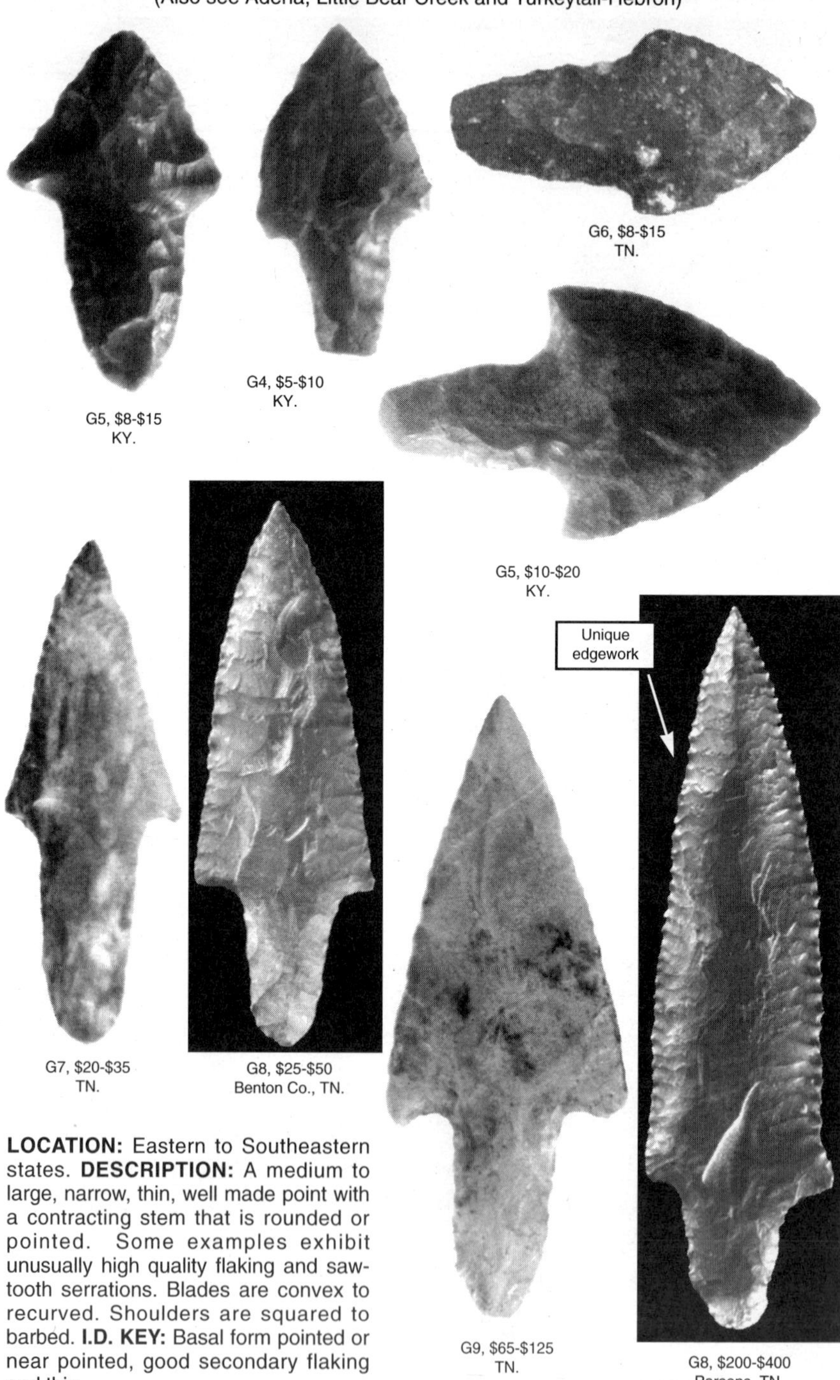

G5, $8-$15
KY.

G4, $5-$10
KY.

G6, $8-$15
TN.

G5, $10-$20
KY.

G7, $20-$35
TN.

G8, $25-$50
Benton Co., TN.

G9, $65-$125
TN.

G8, $200-$400
Parsons, TN.

LOCATION: Eastern to Southeastern states. **DESCRIPTION:** A medium to large, narrow, thin, well made point with a contracting stem that is rounded or pointed. Some examples exhibit unusually high quality flaking and saw-tooth serrations. Blades are convex to recurved. Shoulders are squared to barbed. **I.D. KEY:** Basal form pointed or near pointed, good secondary flaking and thin.

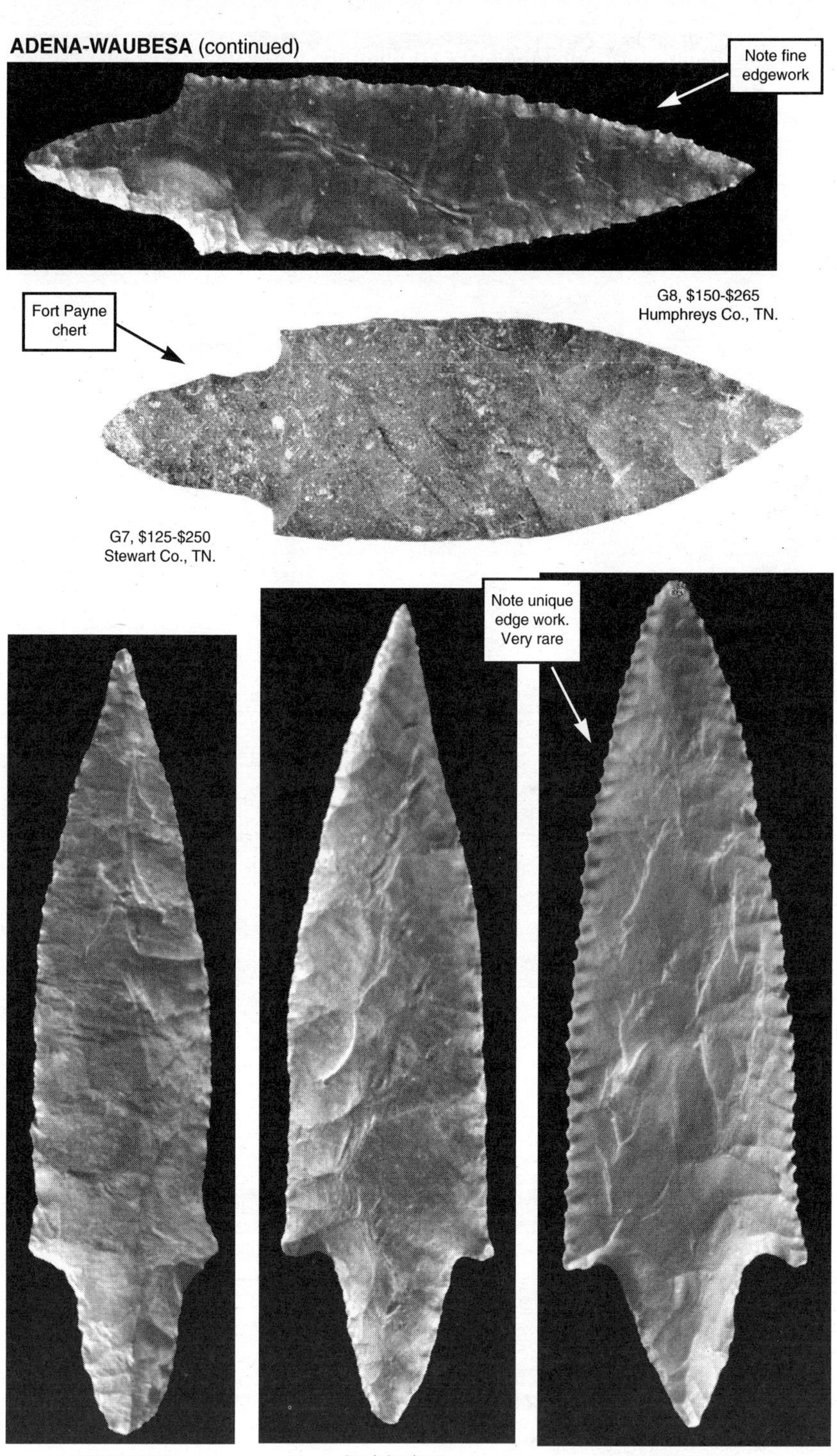

G8, $150-$265
Humphreys Co., TN.

G7, $125-$250
Stewart Co., TN.

G7, $80-$150
Humphreys Co., TN.

G9, $125-$250
Humphreys Co., TN.

G10, $200-$400
Humphreys Co., TN.

AFTON - Middle Archaic to early Woodland, 5000 - 2000 B. P.

(Also see Jacks Reef Corner Notched)

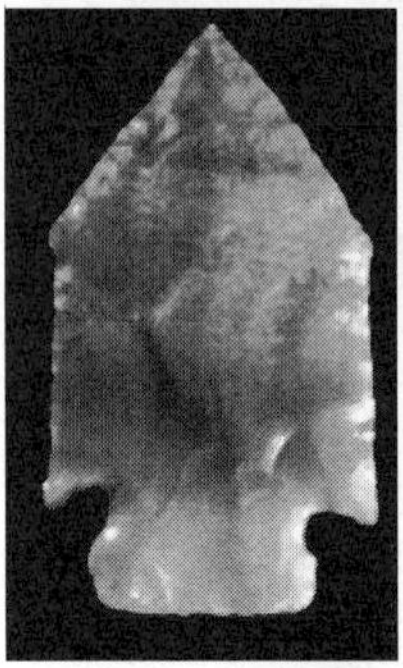

G6, $40-$60
OH.

G5, $20-$35
Pulaski Co., KY.

G4, $10-$20
Limestone Co., AL.

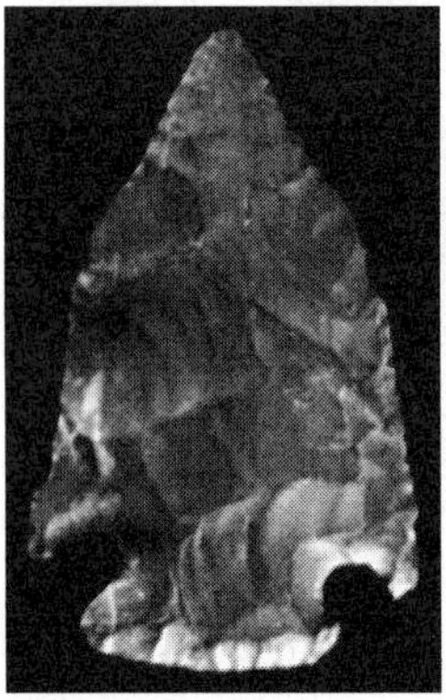

Unusual "knobbed" corners

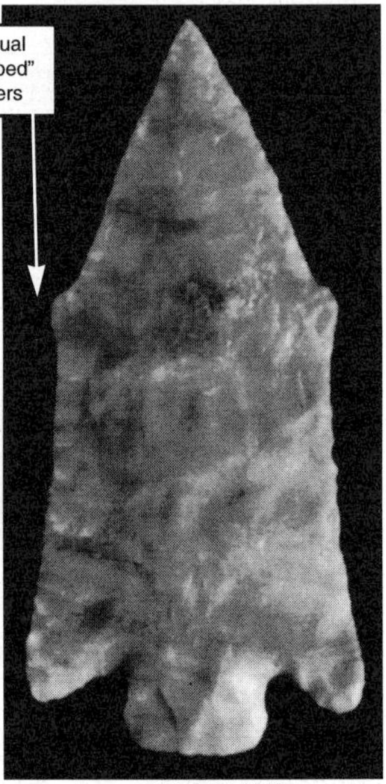

G5, $20-$35
OH.

G5, $20-$35
Knox Co., OH.

G10, $400-$750
Seneca Co., OH.

LOCATION: Southeastern to Midwestern states. **DESCRIPTION:** A medium to large size pentagonal shaped point with a flaring or corner notched stem. Some examples are base notched. **I.D. KEY:** Blade form.

AGATE BASIN - Transitional Paleo to Early Archaic, 10,500 - 8000 B. P.

(Also see Angostura, Lerma and Sedalia)

G5, $35-$65
Geauga Co., OH.

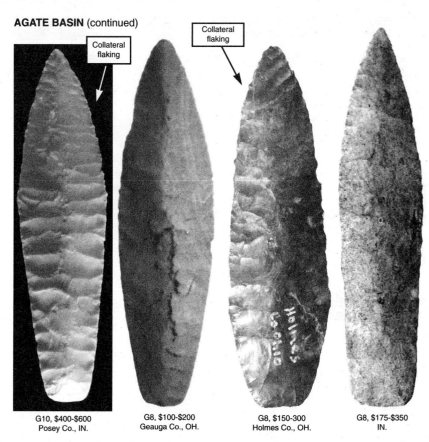

Collateral flaking

Collateral flaking

G10, $400-$600
Posey Co., IN.

G8, $100-$200
Geauga Co., OH.

G8, $150-300
Holmes Co., OH.

G8, $175-$350
IN.

LOCATION: Pennsylvania to Texas to Montana. **DESCRIPTION:** A medium to large size lanceolate blade of high quality. Bases are either convex, concave or straight and are usually ground. Some examples are median ridged and have random to parallel collateral flaking. **I.D. KEY:** Basal form and flaking style.

ALAMANCE - Late Paleo, 10,000 - 8000 B. P.

(Also see Dalton, Hardaway and Haw River)

G5, $10-$15
Southeast, TN.

G7, $25-$35
Autauga Co., AL.

LOCATION: Coastal states from Virginia to Florida. **DESCRIPTION:** A broad, short, auriculate point with a deeply concave base. The broad basal area is usually ground and can be expanding to parallel sided. A variant form of the *Dalton-Greenbrier* evolving later into the *Hardaway* type. **ID. KEY:** Width of base and strong shoulder form.

ALBERTA - Transitional Paleo to Early Archaic, 9500 - 8000 B. P.

(Also see Holland and Scottsbluff)

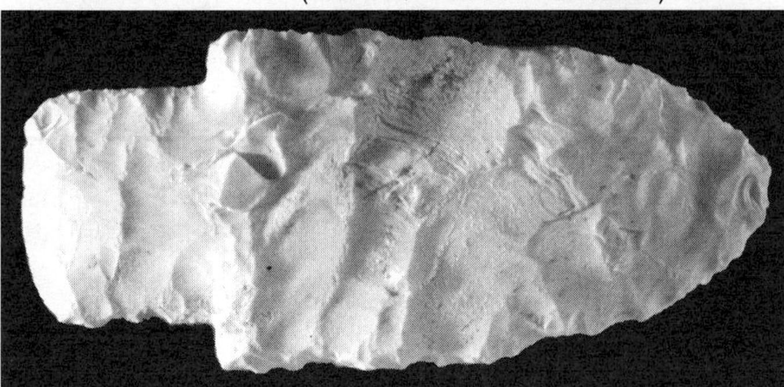

G5, $175-$350
MI.

LOCATION: Northern states and Canada from Pennsylvania, Michigan to Montana. **DESCRIPTION:** A medium to large size point with a broad, long, parallel stem and weak shoulders. Believed to belong to the *Cody Complex* and is related to the *Scottsbluff* type. **I.D.. KEY:** Long stem, short blade.

ANGOSTURA - Early Archaic, 10,000 - 8000 B. P.

(Also see Browns Valley, Clovis-Unfluted, Paint Rock Valley, Plainview and Wheeler)

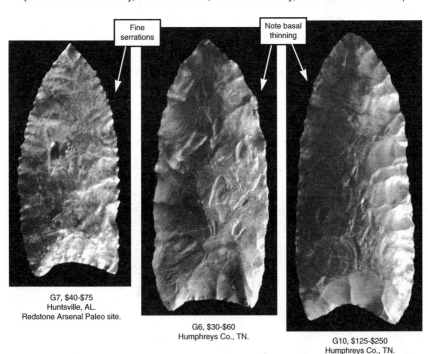

Fine serrations

Note basal thinning

G7, $40-$75
Huntsville, AL.
Redstone Arsenal Paleo site.

G6, $30-$60
Humphreys Co., TN.

G10, $125-$250
Humphreys Co., TN.

LOCATION: Eastern to Southeastern states. **DESCRIPTION**: A medium to large size lanceolate blade with a contracting, concave base. Both broad and narrow forms occur. Flaking can be parallel oblique to random. Bases are not usually ground but are thinned. **I.D. KEY:** Basal form, early flaking on blade.

ANGOSTURA (continued)

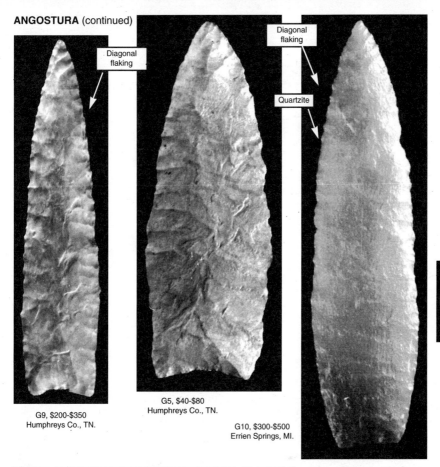

Diagonal flaking

G9, $200-$350
Humphreys Co., TN.

G5, $40-$80
Humphreys Co., TN.

Diagonal flaking

Quartzite

G10, $300-$500
Errien Springs, MI.

APPALACHIAN - Mid-Archaic, 6000 - 3000 B. P.

(Also see Hamilton and Savannah River)

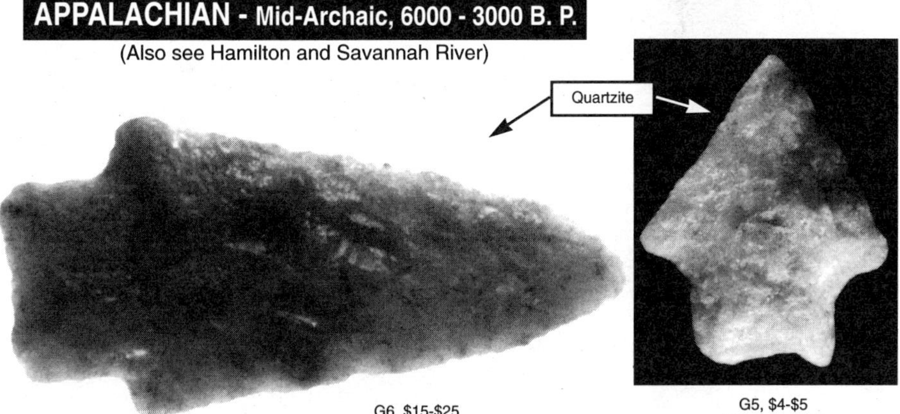

G6, $15-$25
Florence, AL.

G5, $4-$5
Blount Co., TN.

LOCATION: Southeastern states. **DESCRIPTION:** A medium to large size, rather crudely made stemmed point with a concave base. Most examples are made of quartzite. Shoulders are tapered and the base is usually ground. **I.D. KEY:** Basal form.

G7, $50-$100
Paulding Co., GA.

Quartzite

G5, $30-$55
Hamilton Co., TN.

G8, $90-$175
Norris Lake, TN.

ASHTABULA - Late Archaic, 4000 - 1500 B. P.

(Also see Table Rock)

G7, $150-$300
Carroll Co., OH.

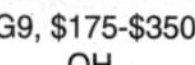

G9, $175-$350
OH.

G8, $125-$250
Shelby Co., OH.

LOCATION: Northeastern states, especially Northeastern Ohio and Western Penn. **DESCRIPTION:** A medium to large size, broad, thick, expanded stem point with tapered shoulders. **I.D. KEY:** Basal form, one barb round and the other stronger.

G6, $125-$250
OH.

G8, $250-$500
OH.

G9, $350-$700
OH.

AUTAUGA - Early Archaic, 9000 - 7000 B. P.

(Also see Brewerton, Ecusta and Palmer)

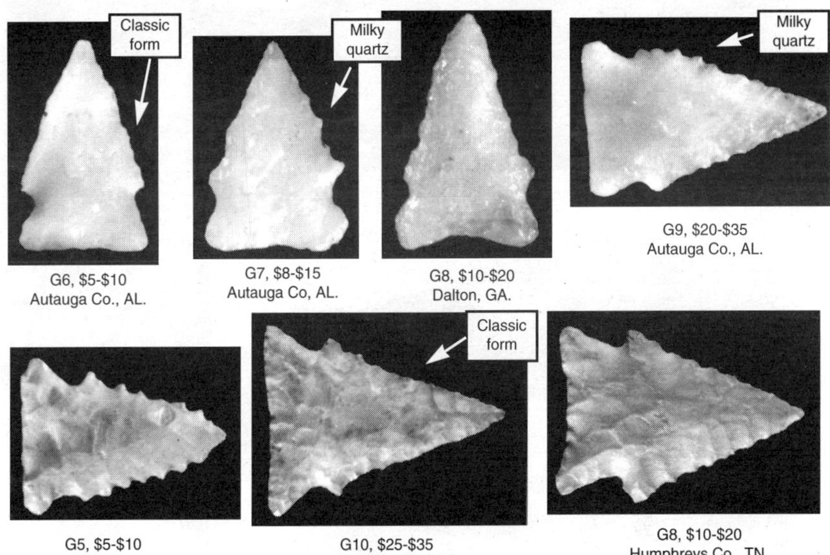

G6, $5-$10
Autauga Co., AL.

G7, $8-$15
Autauga Co, AL.

G8, $10-$20
Dalton, GA.

G9, $20-$35
Autauga Co., AL.

G5, $5-$10
Autauga Co., AL.

G10, $25-$35
Tishimingo Co., MS.

G8, $10-$20
Humphreys Co., TN.

EC

LOCATION: Southeastern states. **DESCRIPTION:** A small weakly corner notched point with a straight base, that is usually ground, and straight blade edges that are serrated. Blades can be beveled on one side of each face. **I.D. KEY:** Archaic flaking on blade.

BAKERS CREEK - Late Archaic to Woodland, 4000 - 1300 B. P.

(Also see Copena, Harpeth River, Mud Creek and Swan Lake)

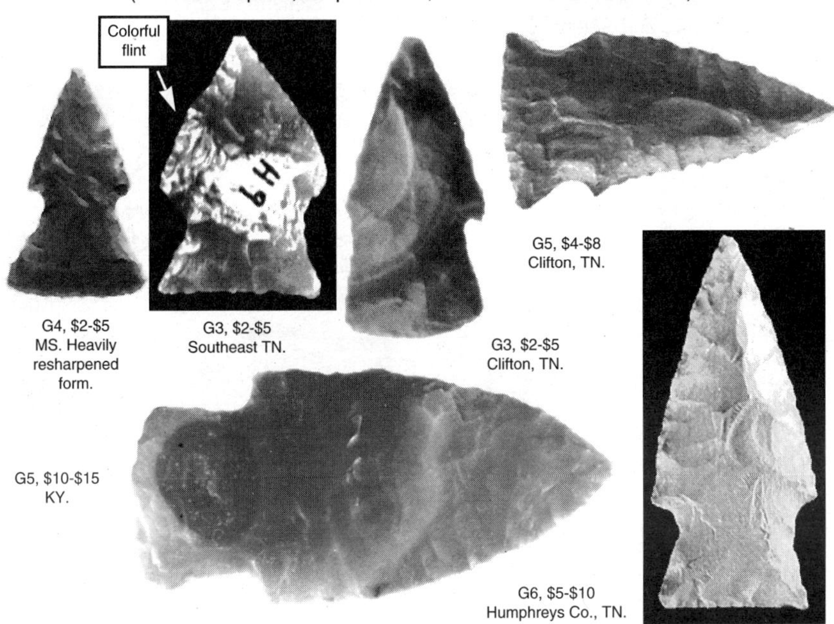

G4, $2-$5
MS. Heavily resharpened form.

G3, $2-$5
Southeast TN.

G3, $2-$5
Clifton, TN.

G5, $4-$8
Clifton, TN.

G5, $10-$15
KY.

G6, $5-$10
Humphreys Co., TN.

BAKERS CREEK (continued)

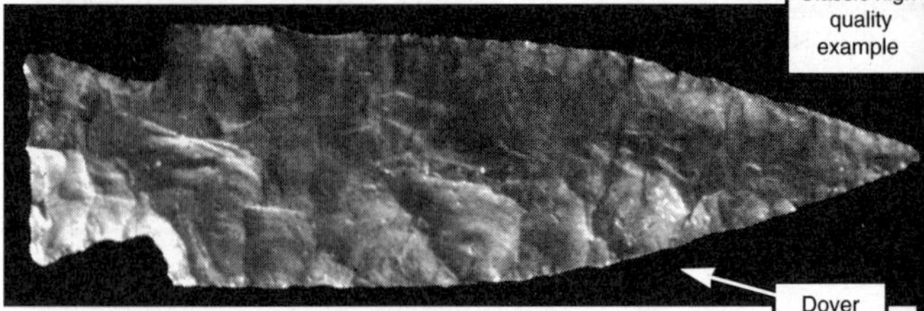

Classic high quality example

Dover chert

G8, $60-$100
Humphreys Co., TN.

G8, $20-$40
Humphreys Co., TN.

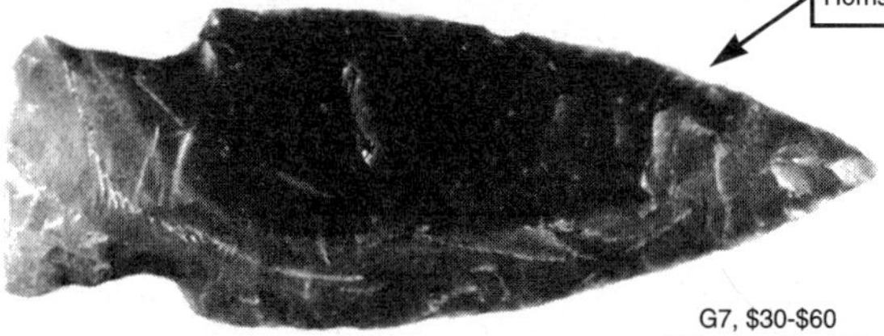

Hornstone

G7, $30-$60
Livingston Co., KY.

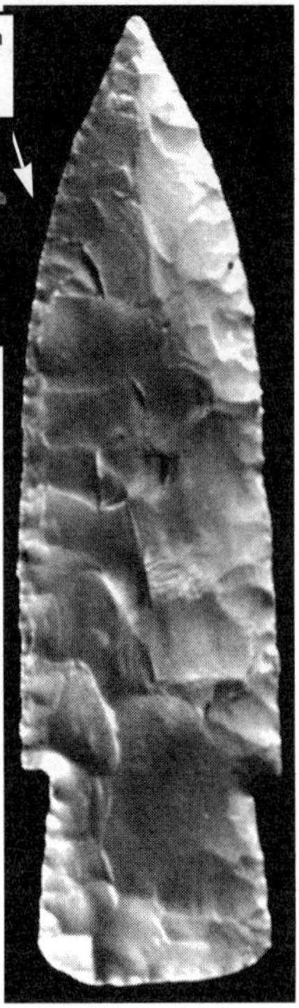

G10, $80-$160
Lauderdale Co., AL.

LOCATION: Southeastern states. **DESCRIPTION:** A small to large size expanded stem point with tapered or barbed shoulders. Bases are concave to convex to straight. related to *Copena* (found with them in caches) and are called Stemmed *Copenas* by some collectors. Called *Lowe* and *Steuben* in Illinois. **I.D. KEY:** Expanded base, usually thin.

BEACON ISLAND - Late Archaic, 4000 - 3000 B. P.

(Also see Big Slough and Flint Creek)

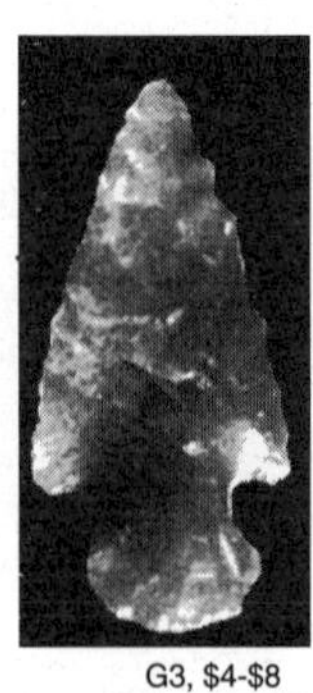

G3, $4-$8
Meigs Co., TN.

G3, $3-$6
Florence, AL.

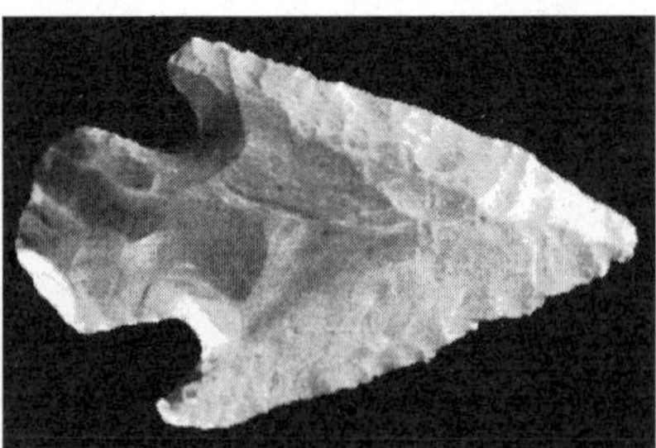

G4, $8-$12
Lauderdale Co., AL.

LOCATION: Southeastern states. **DESCRIPTION:** A small to large size triangular point with a bulbous stem. Shoulders are usually well defined and can be barbed. Similar to *Palmillas* in Texas. **I.D. KEY:** Bulbous base.

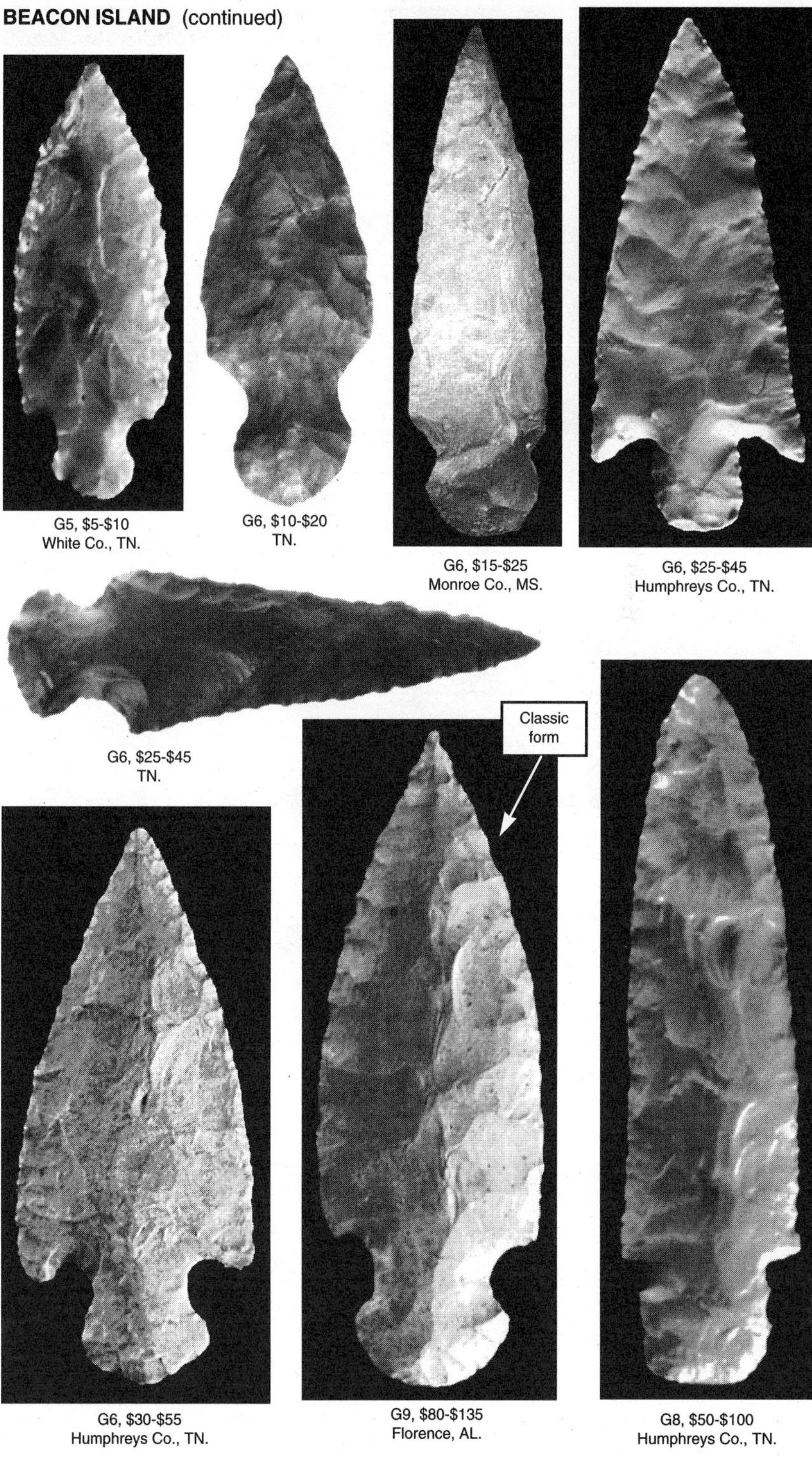

G5, $5-$10
White Co., TN.

G6, $10-$20
TN.

G6, $15-$25
Monroe Co., MS.

G6, $25-$45
Humphreys Co., TN.

G6, $25-$45
TN.

G6, $30-$55
Humphreys Co., TN.

G9, $80-$135
Florence, AL.

G8, $50-$100
Humphreys Co., TN.

BEAVER LAKE - Paleo, 12,000 - 8000 B. P.

(Also see Candy Creek, Cumberland, Golondrina and Quad)

G4, $45-$75
KY.

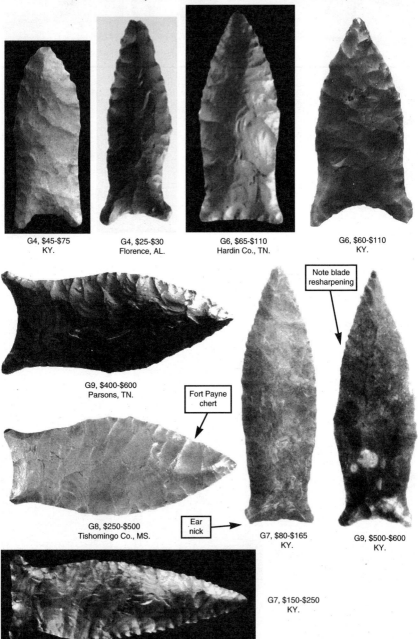

G4, $25-$30
Florence, AL.

G6, $65-$110
Hardin Co., TN.

G6, $60-$110
KY.

Note blade resharpening

G9, $400-$600
Parsons, TN.

Fort Payne chert

G8, $250-$500
Tishomingo Co., MS.

Ear nick

G7, $80-$165
KY.

G9, $500-$600
KY.

G7, $150-$250
KY.

LOCATION: Southeastern states. **DESCRIPTION:** A medium to large size lanceolate blade with flaring ears. Contemporaneous and associated with *Cumberland*, but thinner than unfluted *Cumberlands*. Bases are ground and blade edges are recurved. **I.D. KEY:** Paleo flaking, shoulder area.

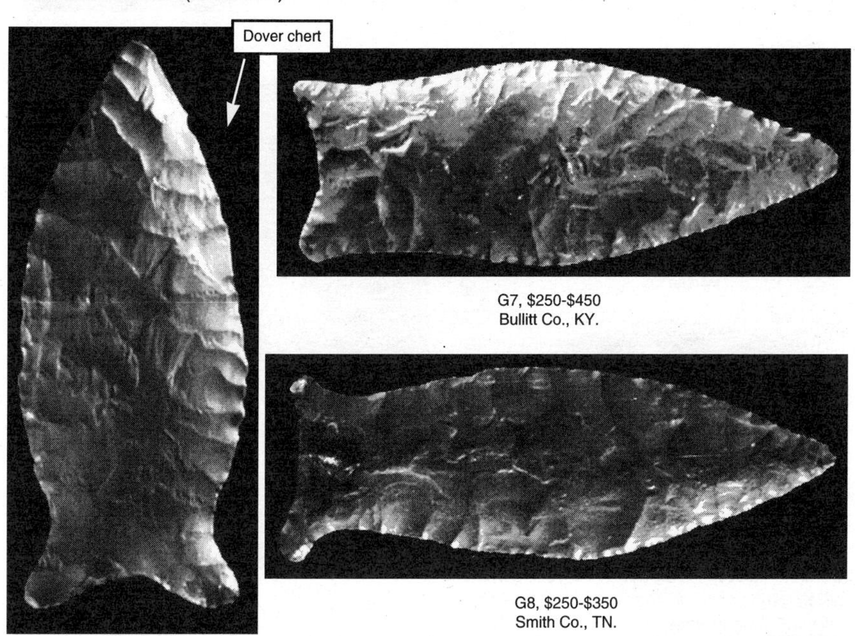

G7, $250-$450
Bullitt Co., KY.

G8, $250-$350
Smith Co., TN.

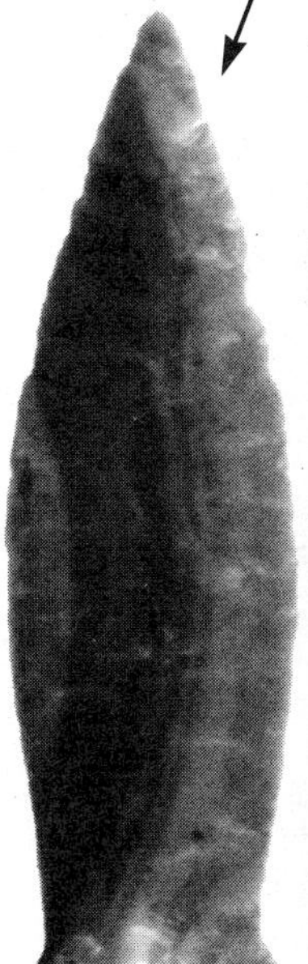

G9, $250-$500
Humphreys Co., TN.

Hornstone

Excellent form

Fort Payne chert

G10, $1000-$2000
KY.

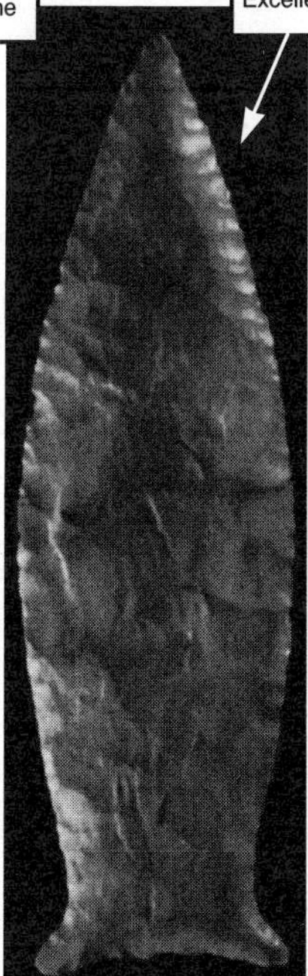

G10, $1000-$2000
Smith Co., TN.

G10, $900-$1800
KY.

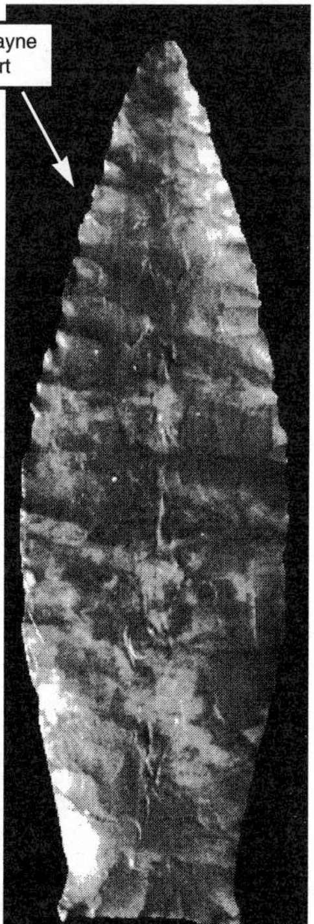

G8, $275-$550
KY.

BENJAMIN - Woodland, 3000 - 1600 B. P.

(Also see Copena Round Base and Montgomery)

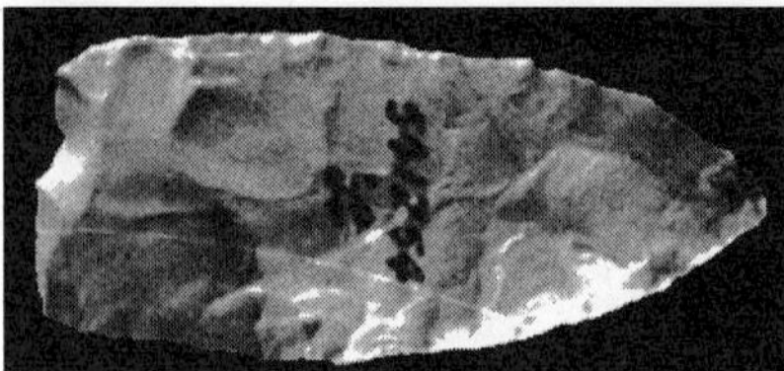

G4, $2-$3
Morgan Co., AL.

G5, $2-$5
Morgan Co., AL.

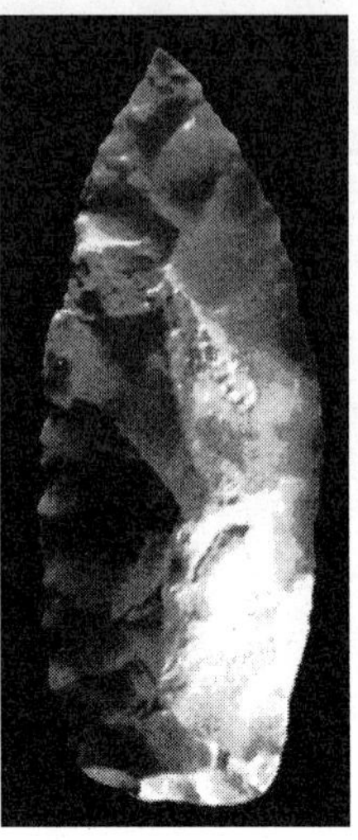

G5, $2-$5
Limestone Co., AL.

G4, $2-$4
Limestone Co., AL.

LOCATION: Southeastern states. **DESCRIPTION:** A medium to large size, thin, narrow, lanceolate point with random flaking and a rounded base. This point has been found in association with *Copena.*

BENTON - Middle Archaic, 6000 - 4000 B. P.

(Also see Buzzard Roost Creek, Elk River and Turkeytail)

G3, $3-$6
TN.

G6, $10-$20
TN.

G5, $8-$15
TN.

LOCATION: Southeastern to Midwestern states. **DESCRIPTION:** A medium to very large size, broad, stemmed point with straight to convex sides. Bases can be corner or side notched, double notched, knobbed, bifurcated or expanded. Some examples show parallel oblique flaking. All four sides are beveled and basal corners usually have tangs. Examples have been found in Arkansas with a steeply beveled edge on one side of each face.(Transition form?). Found in caches with *Turkeytail* points in Mississippi on *Benton* sites. *Bentons* and *Turkeytails* as long as 16-3/4 inches were found together on this site and dated to about 4000 B.P. **I.D. KEY:** Wide squared, eared or notched base.

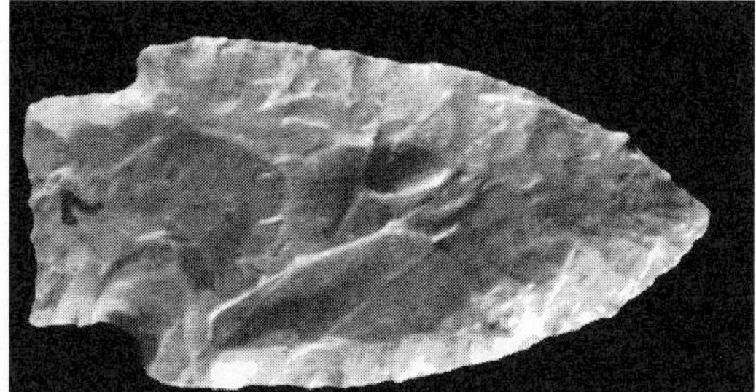

G5, $10-$20
Florence, AL.

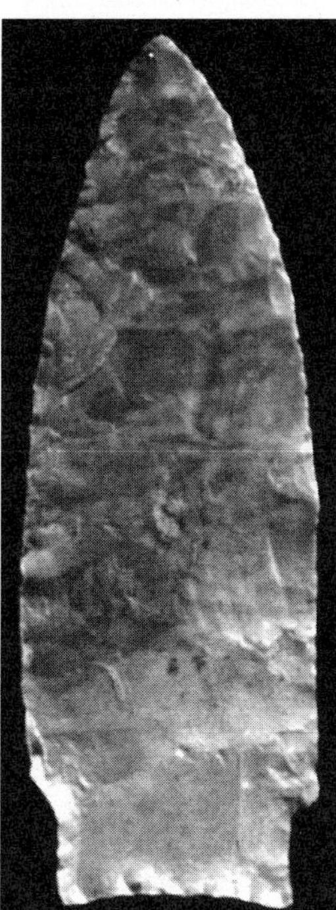

G7, $50-$100
Lee Co., MS.

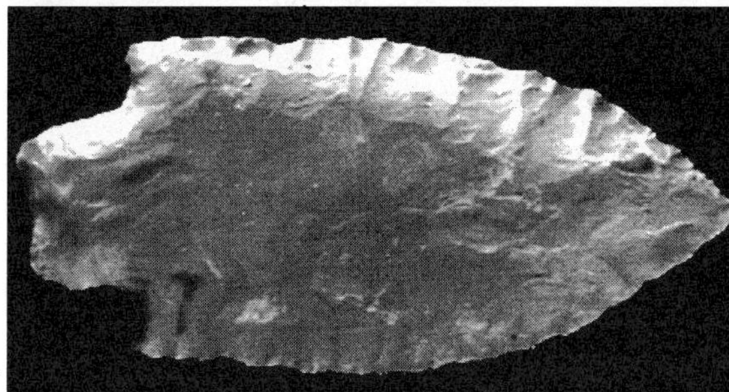

G6, $20-$40
Florence, AL.

G8, $100-$200
KY.

Part of a cache

G8, $200-$350
Monroe Co., MS.

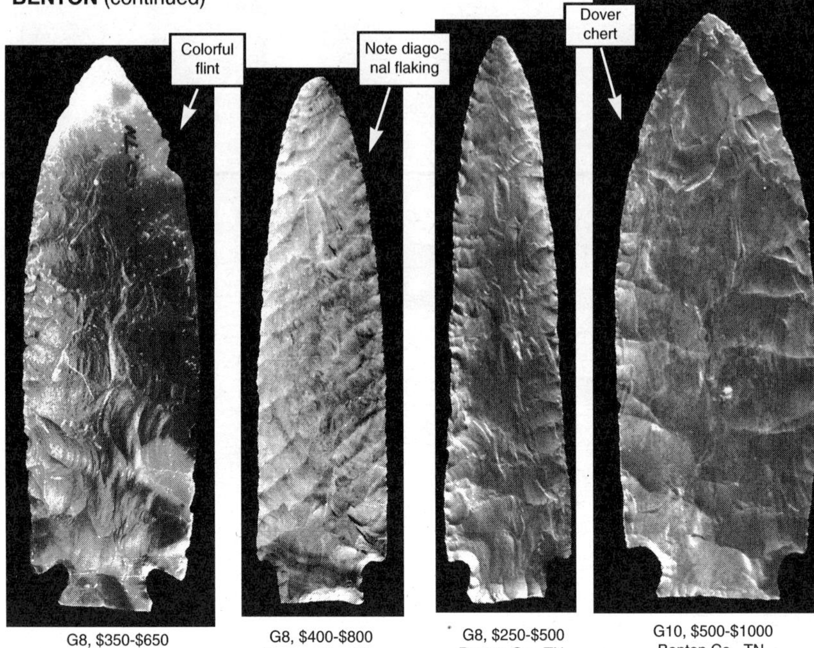

G8, $350-$650
Sumner Co., TN.

G8, $400-$800
Sumner Co., TN.

G8, $250-$500
Benton Co., TN.

G10, $500-$1000
Benton Co., TN.

IMPORTANT:
All points on this page shown 50% of actual size.

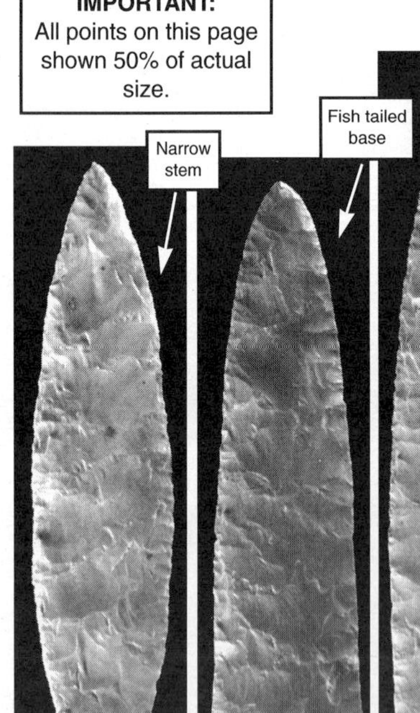

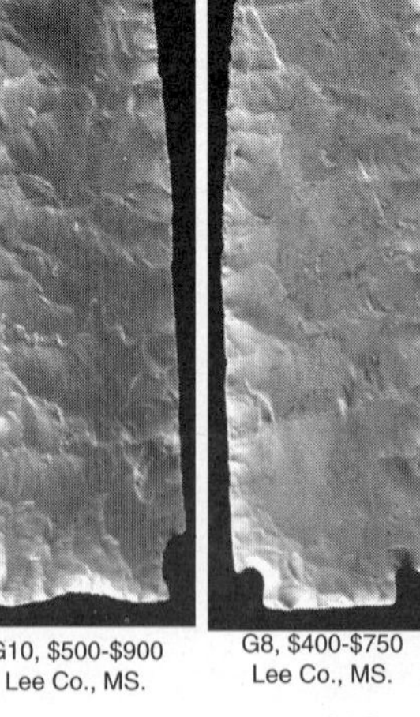

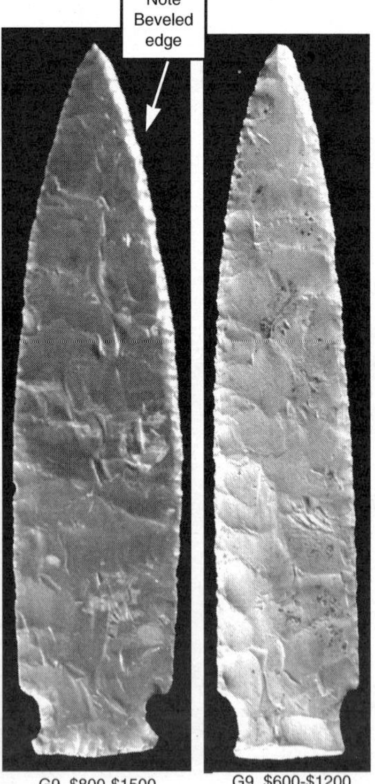

G10, $500-$900
Lee Co., MS.

G10, $500-$900
Lee Co., MS.

G8, $400-$750
Lee Co., MS.

G9, $800-$1500
Monroe Co., MS.

G9, $600-$1200
Lee Co., MS.

BENTON (continued)

Extremely rare (Polished Green Stone)

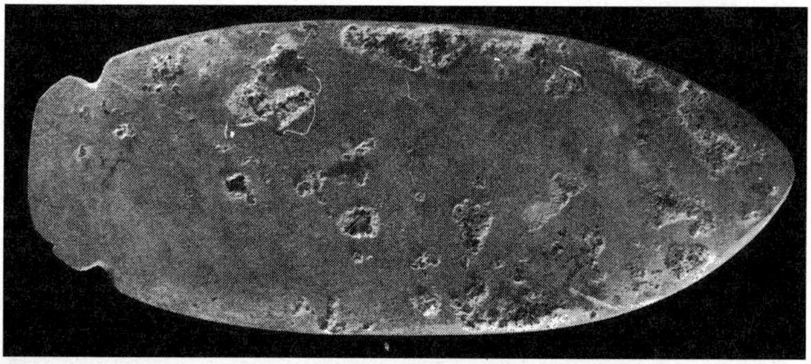

G10, $1000-$2000
Lee Co., MS.

Fort Payne chert

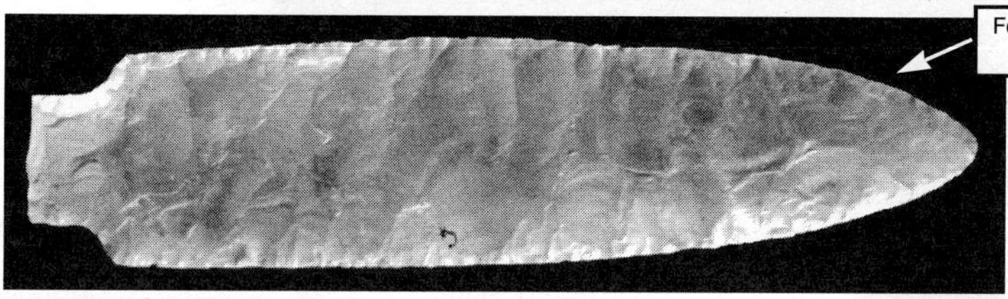

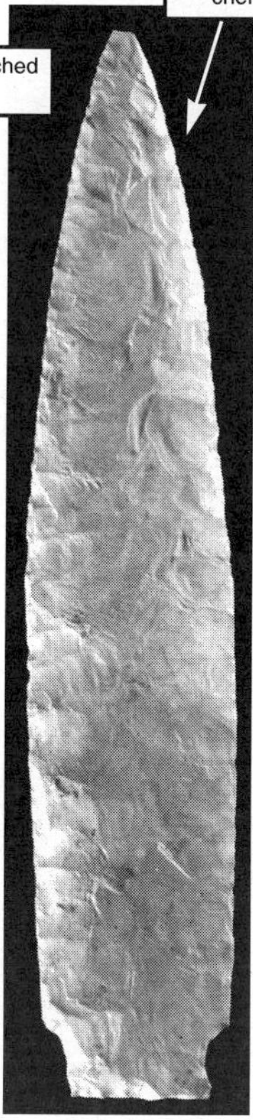

G10, $1000-$2000
Lee Co., MS.

IMPORTANT: All points on this page shown 50% of actual size.

Side notched form

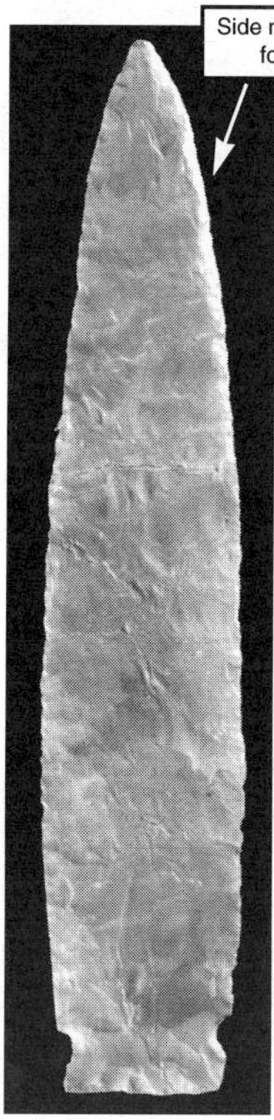

Fort Payne chert

Un-notched form

G9, $800-$1500
Lee Co., MS.

G9, $800-$1500
Lee Co., MS.

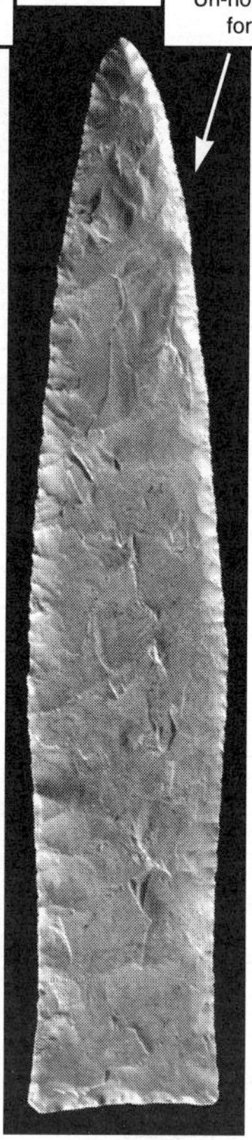

G10, $800-$1500
Lee Co., MS.

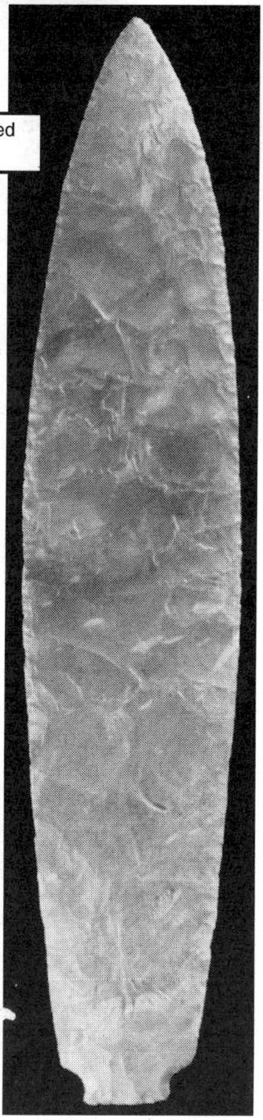

G10, $2000-$4000
Lee Co., MS.

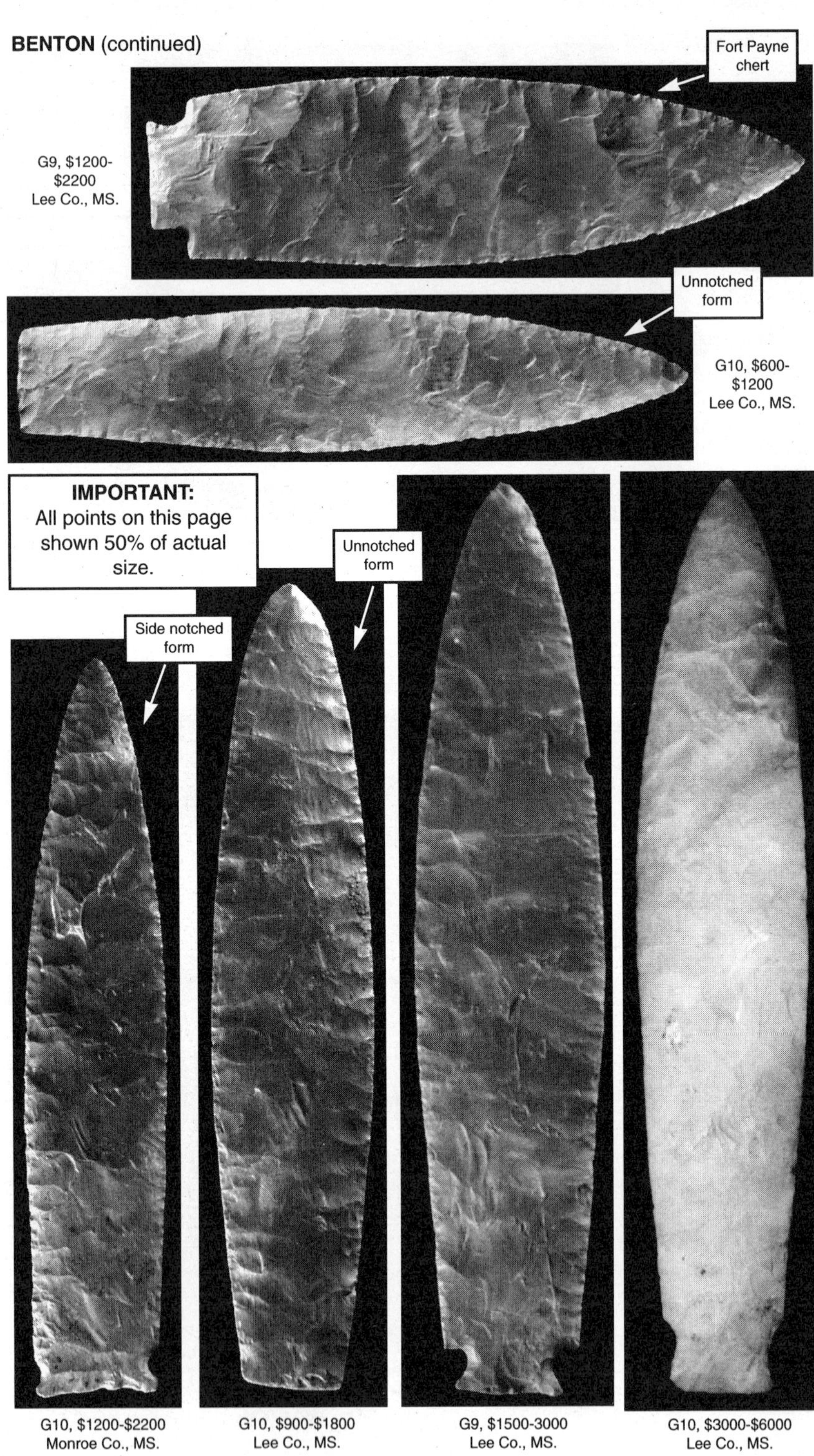

G9, $1200-$2200
Lee Co., MS.

G10, $600-$1200
Lee Co., MS.

G10, $1200-$2200
Monroe Co., MS.

G10, $900-$1800
Lee Co., MS.

G9, $1500-3000
Lee Co., MS.

G10, $3000-$6000
Lee Co., MS.

BENTON BLADE - Middle Archaic, 6000 - 4000 B. P.

(Also see Benton and Copena)

G8, $45-$70
Marion Co., AL. Cache point.

LOCATION: Southeastern to Midwestern states. **DESCRIPTION:** A medium to very large size, broad, finished blade used either as a knife or as a preform for later knapping into a *Benton* point. Usually found in caches. **I.D. KEY:** Archaic flaking similar to the *Benton* type.

BENTON-BOTTLE NECK - Middle Archaic, 6000 - 4000 B. P.

(Also see Benton, Copena and Table Rock)

G7, $100-$125
KY.

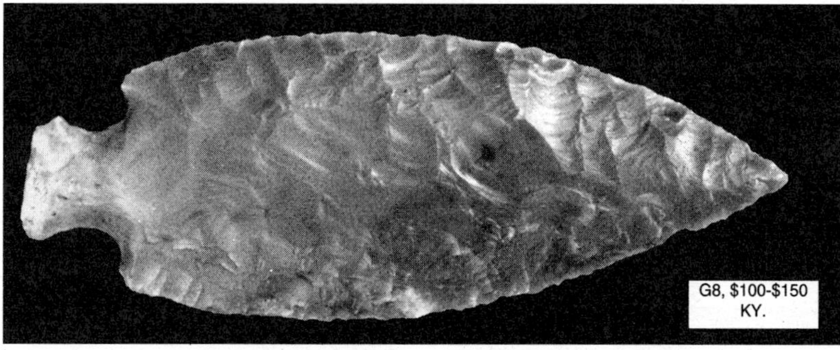

G8, $100-$150
KY.

EC

LOCATION: Southeastern to Midwestern states. **DESCRIPTION:** A medium to large size, narrow blade with tapered shoulders and an expanding stem that is usually convex. A variant form of the Benton cluster. **I.D. KEY:** Tapered shoulders, expanding stem.

BENTON DOUBLE-NOTCHED - Middle Archaic, 6000 - 4000 B. P.

(Also see Benton, Copena and Turkeytail)

IMPORTANT:
All double notched Bentons shown 50% of actual size

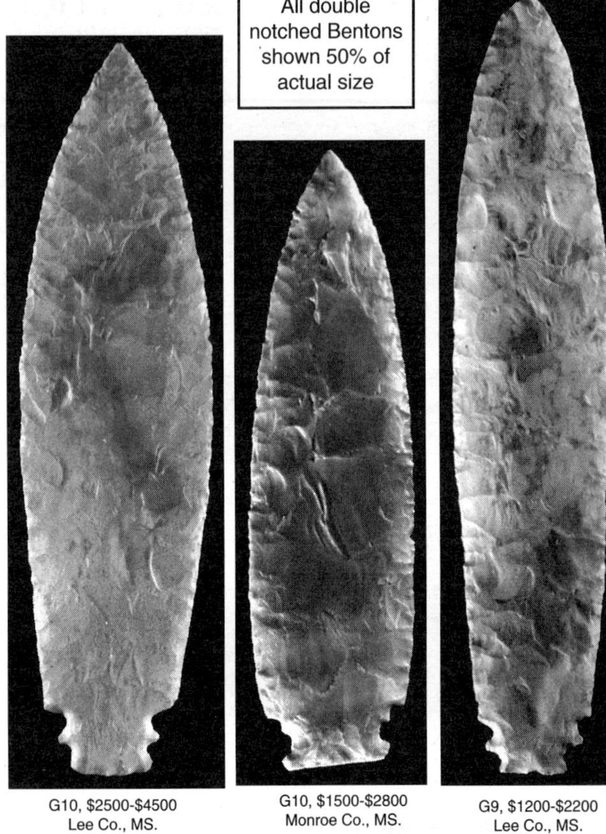

G10, $2500-$4500
Lee Co., MS.

G10, $1500-$2800
Monroe Co., MS.

G9, $1200-$2200
Lee Co., MS.

G10, $1500-$3000
Lee Co., MS.

LOCATION: Southeastern to Midwestern states. **DESCRIPTION:** A medium to very large size, broad, finished blade with double notches on each side of the blade at the base. Used as a knife and usually found in caches. Has been found associated with un-notched and double to triple notched *Turkeytail* blades in Mississippi. Unique and rare. **I.D. KEY:** Multiple notching at base.

BENTON-NARROW BLADE - Middle Archaic, 6000 - 4000 B. P.

(Also see Elk River, Kays and Little Bear Creek)

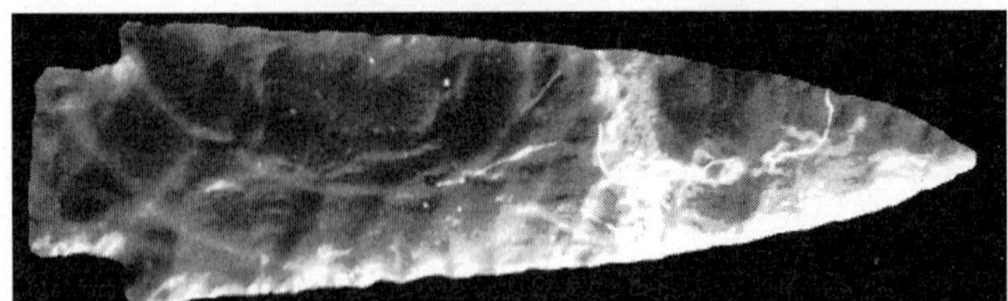

G8, $40-$75
Hamilton Co. TN.

LOCATION: Southeastern to Midwestern states. **DESCRIPTION:** A medium to large size, narrow, stemmed variant of the *Benton* form.

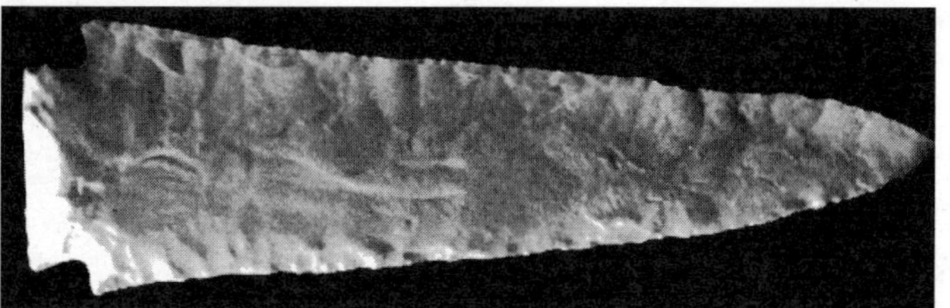

G9, $50-$100
Morgan Co., AL.

BIG SANDY - Transitional Paleo to Late Archaic, 10,000 - 3000 B. P.

(Also see Cache River, Pine Tree and Savage Cave)

Heavily resharpened

G5, $4-$8
Jackson Co., AL.

G3, $4-$8
IN.

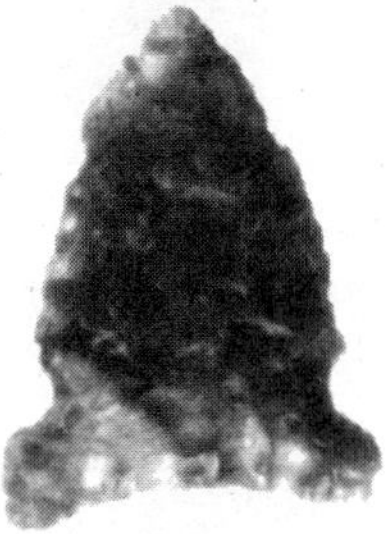

G6, $8-$15
KY.

G6, $15-$25
TN.

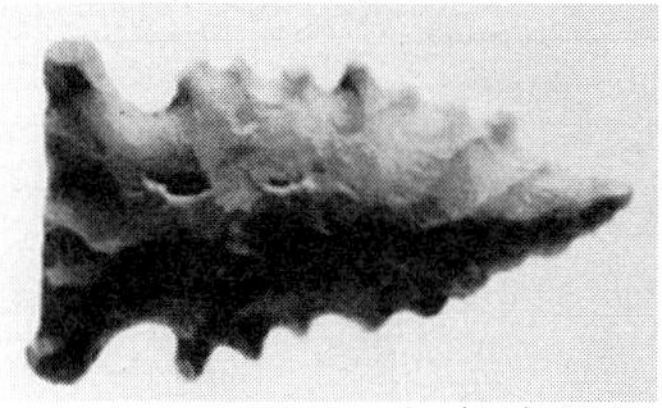

Tang nick

G7, $20-$40
N. AL.

G4, $10-$20
N. AL.

G6, $15-$30
TN.

G8, $50-$100
KY.

G5, $15-$30
N. AL.

G9, $40-$80
KY.

LOCATION: Southeastern states. **DESCRIPTION:** A small to medium size, side-notched point with early forms showing heavy basal grinding, serrations, and horizontal flaking. This type may be associated with the *Frazier* point, being an unnotched form. Some examples have been carbon dated to 10,000 B.P., but most are associated with Mid-Archaic times. **I.D. KEY:** Basal form and blade flaking.

G7, $35-$65
GA.

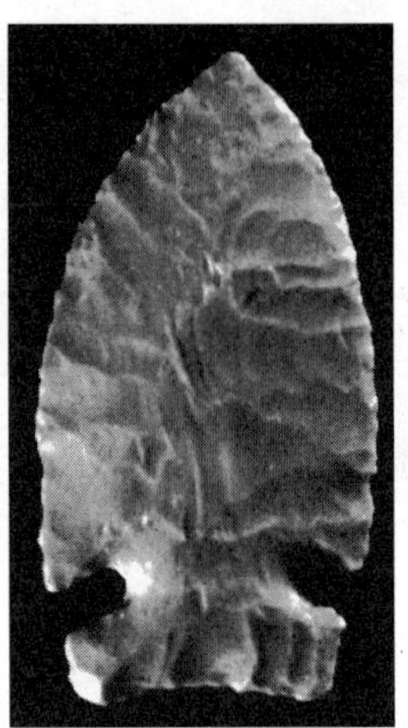

G8, $35-$65
Jessamine Co., KY.

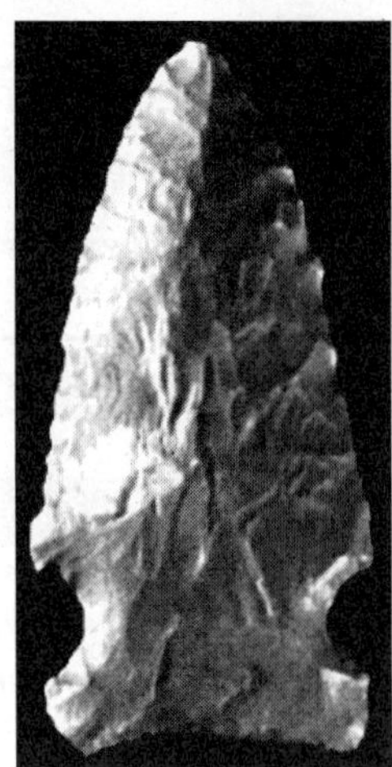

G7, $40-$75
Humphreys Co., TN.

G7, $125-$250
Trimble Co., KY.

G8, $90-$185
TN.

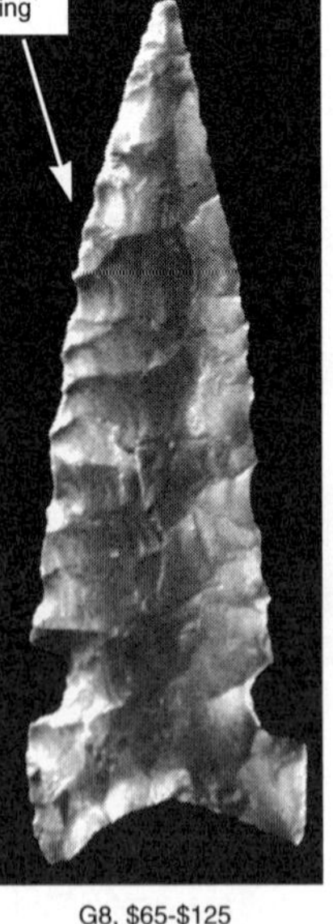

G8, $65-$125
Florence, AL.

G8, $65-$125
TN.

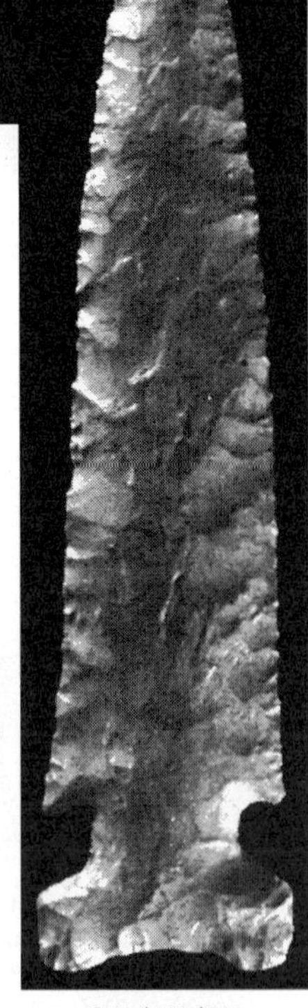

G10, $400-$800
Decatur Co., TN.

BIG SANDY-BROAD BASE - Transitional Paleo to Early Archaic, 10,000 - 7000 B. P.

(Also see Cache River and Savage Cave)

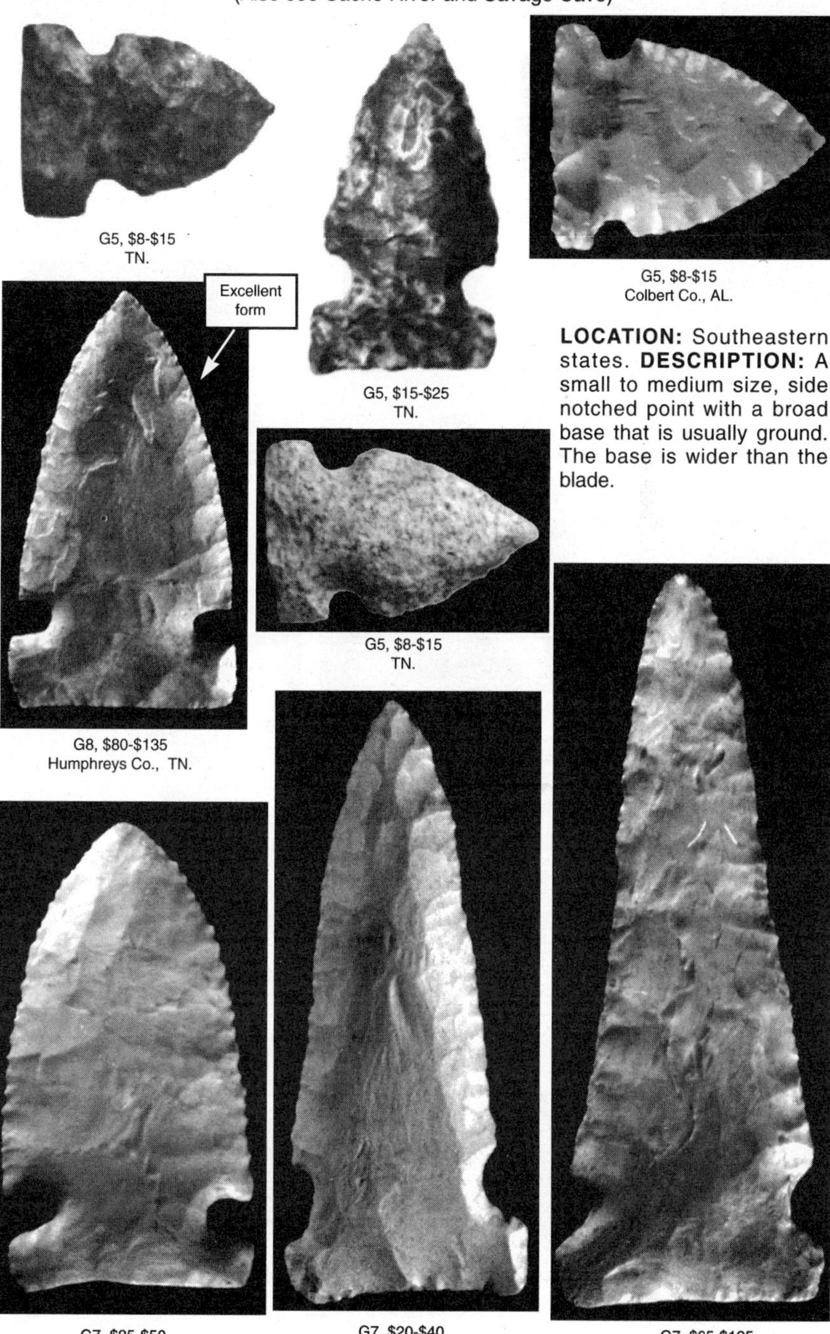

G5, $8-$15
TN.

G5, $15-$25
TN.

G5, $8-$15
Colbert Co., AL.

LOCATION: Southeastern states. **DESCRIPTION:** A small to medium size, side notched point with a broad base that is usually ground. The base is wider than the blade.

EC

G8, $80-$135
Humphreys Co., TN.

G5, $8-$15
TN.

G7, $25-$50
S.W. KY.

G7, $20-$40
Humphreys Co., TN.

G7, $65-$125
Mt. Sterling, KY.

BIG SANDY-CONTRACTED BASE - Transitional Paleo to Early Archaic, 10,000 - 7000 B. P.

(Also see Pine Tree and Quad)

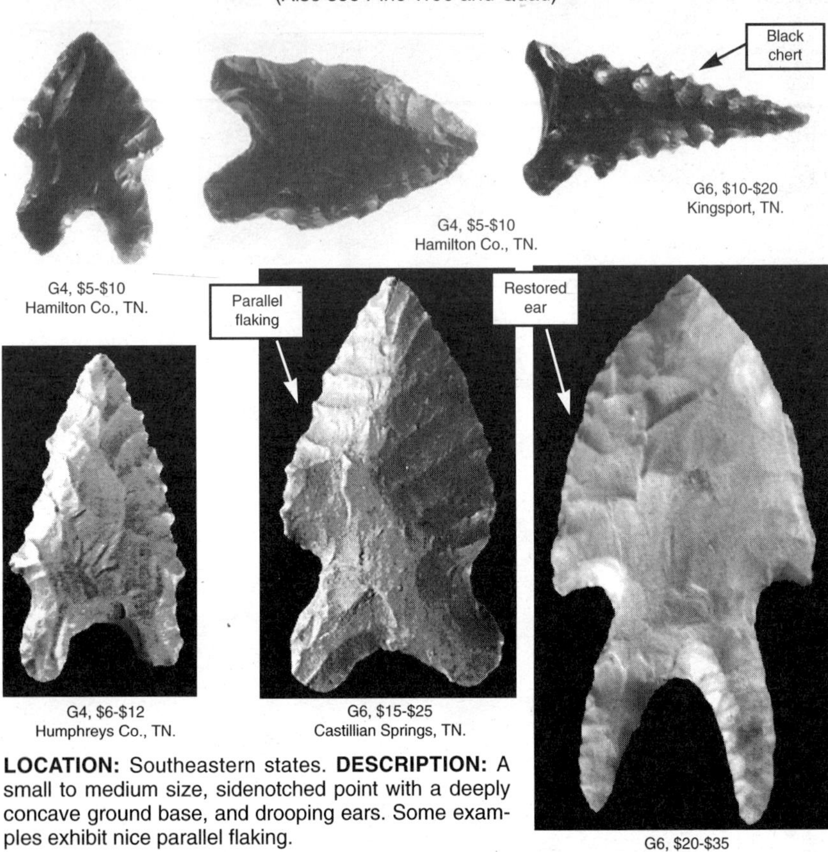

G4, $5-$10
Hamilton Co., TN.

G4, $5-$10
Hamilton Co., TN.

G6, $10-$20
Kingsport, TN.

G4, $6-$12
Humphreys Co., TN.

G6, $15-$25
Castillian Springs, TN.

G6, $20-$35
Humphreys Co., TN.

LOCATION: Southeastern states. **DESCRIPTION:** A small to medium size, sidenotched point with a deeply concave ground base, and drooping ears. Some examples exhibit nice parallel flaking.

BIG SANDY E-NOTCHED - Transitional Paleo to Early Archaic, 10,000 - 7000 B. P.

(Also see Leighton & Thebes)

Heavy white patination

E-notched base and sides

Tip nick

G2, $3-$6
Humphreys Co., TN.

G7, $20-$40
Jackson Co., AL.

G4, $8-$15
TN.

BIG SANDY (continued)

G7, $40-$75
Humphreys Co., TN.

G8, $50-$100
Coffee Lake, AL.

G10, $150-$300
Humphreys Co., TN.

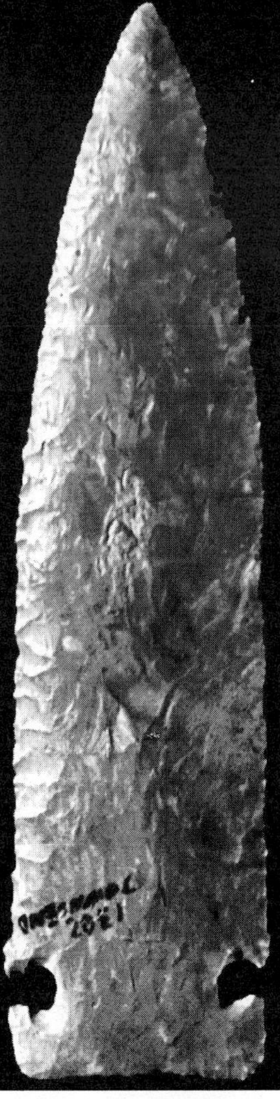

G10, $900-$1700
Clarksville, TN.

LOCATION: Southeastern states. **DESCRIPTION:** A small to medium size expanded side-notched point. The notching is unique and quite rare for the type. This type of notch is angled into the blade to produce a high point or nipple in the center, forming the letter E. Also called key-notched. Rarely, the base is also E-notched. The same notching occurs in the *Bolen* and *Thebes* types. **I.D. KEY:** Two flake notching system.

EC

BIG SANDY-LEIGHTON BASE - Transitional Paleo to Early Archaic, 10,000 - 7000 B. P.

(Also see Leighton and Thebes)

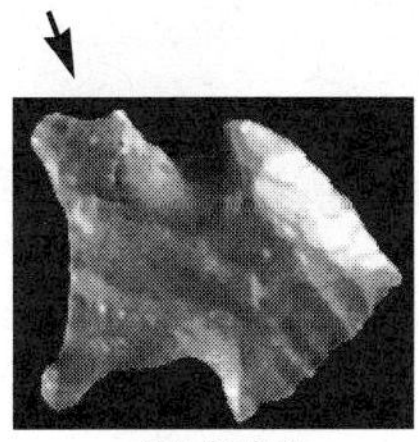

G4, $5-$10
Decatur, AL.

G4, $6-$12
Jackson Co., AL.

G4, $8-$15
Warren Co., TN.

BIG SANDY-LEIGHTON (continued)

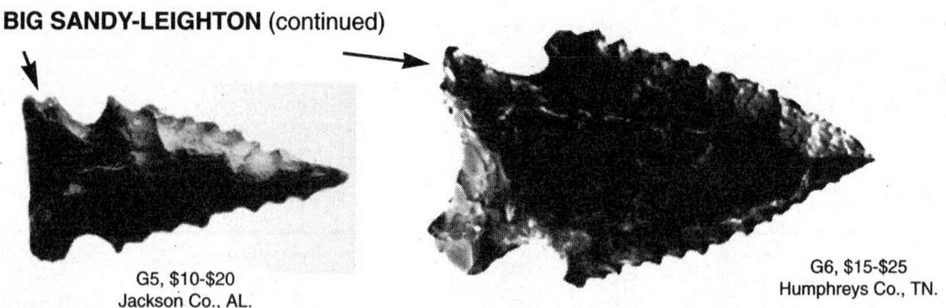

G5, $10-$20
Jackson Co., AL.

G6, $15-$25
Humphreys Co., TN.

LOCATION: Southeastern states. **DESCRIPTION:** A small to medium size side notched point with a small notch in one or both sides of the base (see *Leighton* points). The notch or notches were used to facilitate hafting. **I.D. KEY:** Basal side notching.

BIG SLOUGH - Middle Archaic, 7000 - 4000 B. P.

(Also see Beacon Island and Elk River)

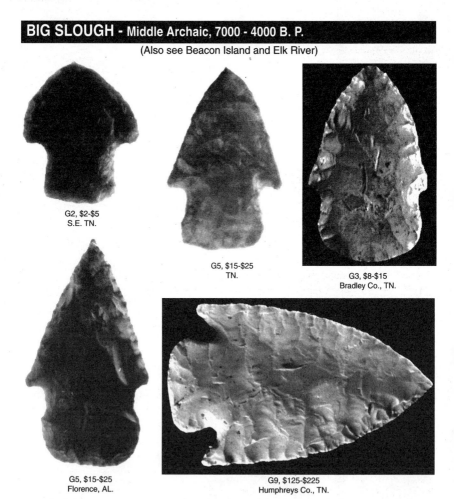

G2, $2-$5
S.E. TN.

G5, $15-$25
TN.

G3, $8-$15
Bradley Co., TN.

G5, $15-$25
Florence, AL.

G9, $125-$225
Humphreys Co., TN.

LOCATION: Southeastern states. **DESCRIPTION:** A medium to large size, broad, stemmed point with a bulbous base. The blade is convex to recurved. The shoulders may show a weak to medium tang. **I.D. KEY:** Basal form and barbs.

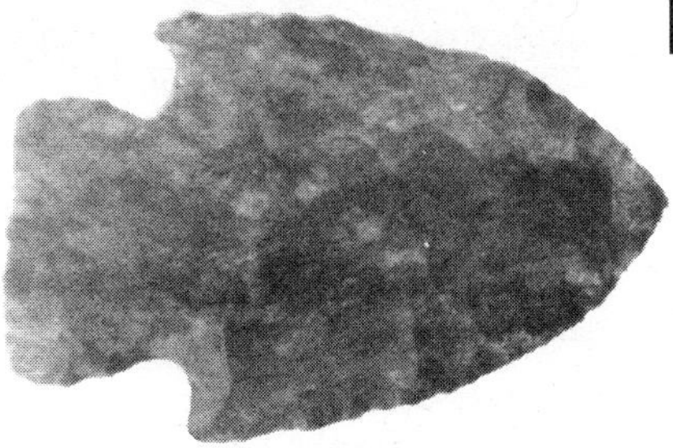

BIG SLOUGH (continued)

Dover chert

G6, $15-$30
TN.

G6, $25-$50
Jackson Co., AL.

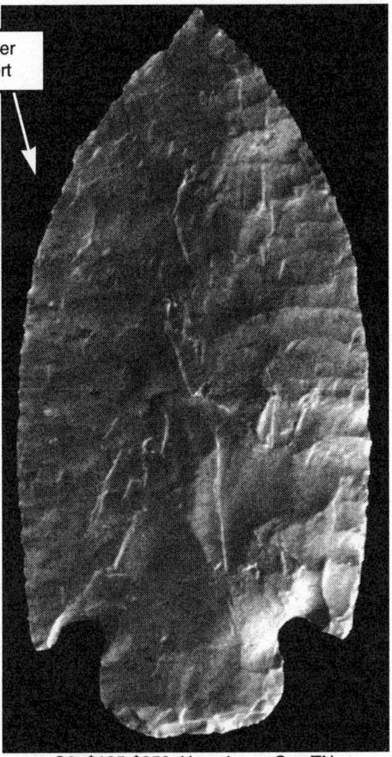

G9, $125-$250, Humphreys Co., TN.

EC

BLUNT - Paleo to Woodland, 12,000 - 1000 B. P.

(Also see Drill, Perforator and Scraper)

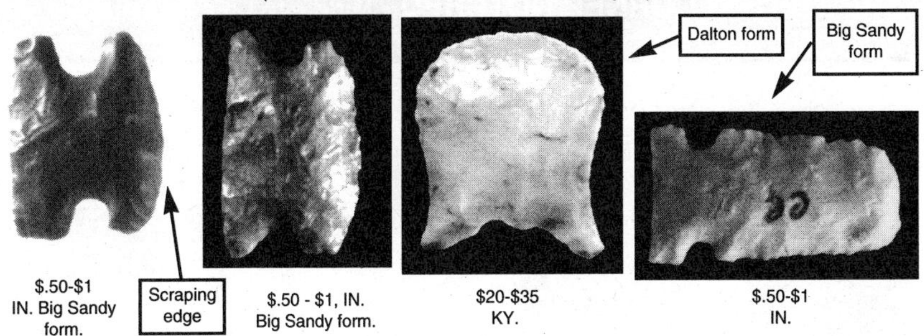

$.50-$1
IN. Big Sandy
form.

$.50 - $1, IN.
Big Sandy form.

$20-$35
KY.

$.50-$1
IN.

LOCATION: Throughout North America. **DESCRIPTION:** Blunts are usually made from broken points that are rechipped into this form, but can be made from scratch. All point types can occur as blunts. Some collectors call this form Stunners believing they were made to stun animals, not to kill. However, most archaeologists think they were used as knives and for scraping hides.

BRADLEY SPIKE - Late Archaic to Woodland, 4000 - 1800 B. P.

(Also see Flint River Spike, Mountain Fork, New Market and Schild Spike)

G3, $2-$4
S.E. TN.

G4, $3-$6
Limestone
Co., AL.

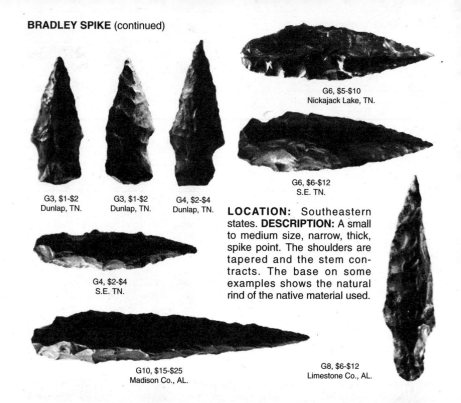

G6, $5-$10
Nickajack Lake, TN.

G6, $6-$12
S.E. TN.

G3, $1-$2
Dunlap, TN.

G3, $1-$2
Dunlap, TN.

G4, $2-$4
Dunlap, TN.

LOCATION: Southeastern states. **DESCRIPTION:** A small to medium size, narrow, thick, spike point. The shoulders are tapered and the stem contracts. The base on some examples shows the natural rind of the native material used.

G4, $2-$4
S.E. TN.

G10, $15-$25
Madison Co., AL.

G8, $6-$12
Limestone Co., AL.

BREWERTON CORNER NOTCHED - Middle to Late Archaic, 6000 - 4000 B. P.

(Also see Autauga)

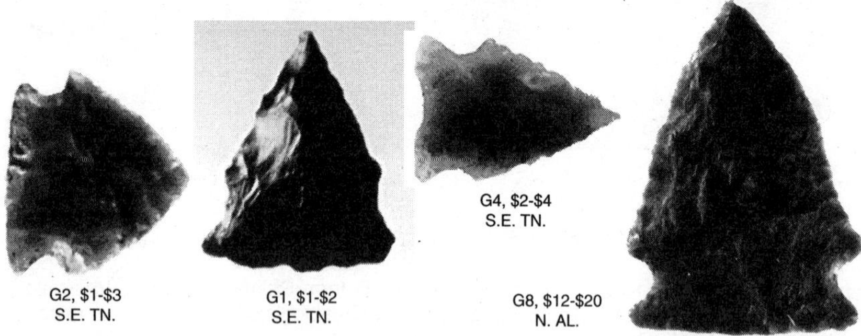

G4, $2-$4
S.E. TN.

G2, $1-$3
S.E. TN.

G1, $1-$2
S.E. TN.

G8, $12-$20
N. AL.

LOCATION: Eastern to Midwestern states. **DESCRIPTION:** A small size, triangular point with faint corner notches and a concave base. Called *Freeheley* in Michigan. **I.D. KEY:** Width, thickness.

BREWERTON EARED-TRIANGULAR - Mid-Archaic, 6000 - 4000 B. P.

(Also see Autauga, Nolichucky and Yadkin)

LOCATION: Eastern to Midwestern states. **DESCRIPTION:** A small size, triangular, eared point with a concave base. Shoulders are weak and tapered. Ears are widest part of point.

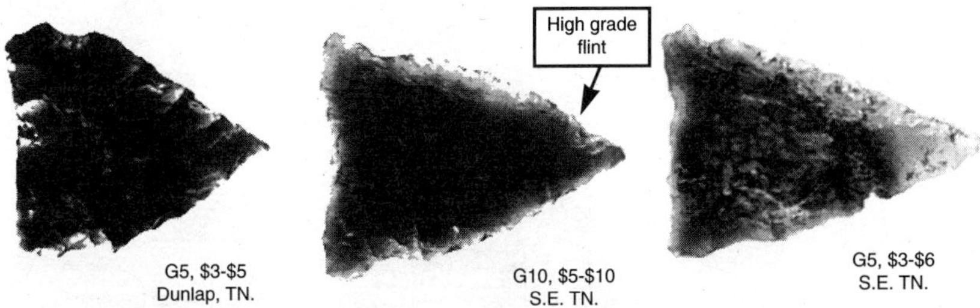

G5, $3-$5 Dunlap, TN.

G10, $5-$10 S.E. TN.

G5, $3-$6 S.E. TN.

BREWERTON SIDE NOTCHED - Mid-Archaic, 6000 - 4000 B. P.

(Also see Big Sandy and Hardaway)

G2, $1-$2 Trimble Co., KY.

G4, $2-$4 Harrison Co., IN.

G3, $2-$4 Walker Co., GA.

G4, $2-$5 Harrison Co., IN.

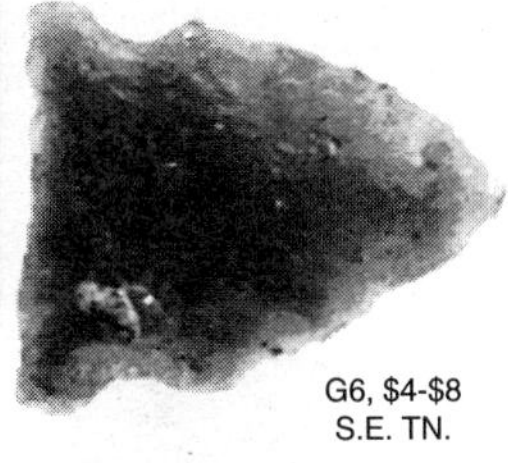

G6, $4-$8 S.E. TN.

LOCATION: Eastern to Midwestern states. **DESCRIPTION:** A small to medium size, triangular point with shallow side notches and a concave base.

BROWNS VALLEY - Transitional Paleo, 10,000 - 8000 B. P.

(Also see Angostura and Clovis)

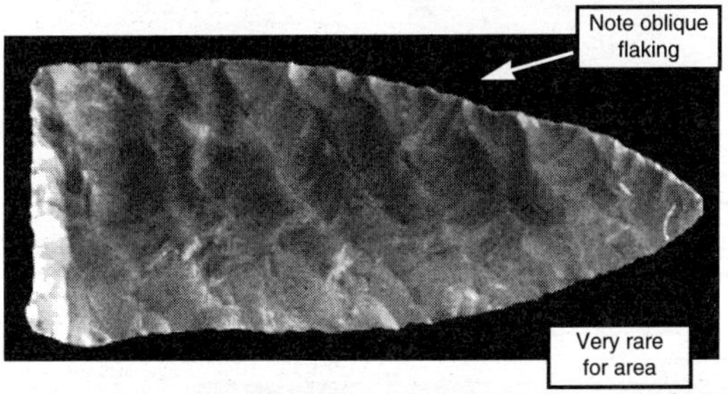

LOCATION: Upper Midwestern states. **DESCRIPTION:** A medium to large, thin, lanceolate blade with usually oblique to horizontal transverse flaking and a concave to straight base which can be ground. **I.D. KEY:** Paleo transverse flaking.

G7, $150-$250 Morgan Co., AL. Note oblique flaking & steeply beveled base.

BUCK CREEK - Middle to Late Archaic, 6000 - 3500 B. P.

(Also see Hamilton, Motley, Rankin, Smithsonia, Table Rock and Wade)

G5, $15-$25 KY.

G6, $25-$45 IN.

G5, $8-$15
KY.

G7, $35-$70
Dickson Co., TN.

G7, $65-$125
IN.

G10, $600-$1200, IN.

G6, $25-$50
KY.

G8, $80-$150
IN.

G8, $175-$350
Humphreys Co.,
TN.

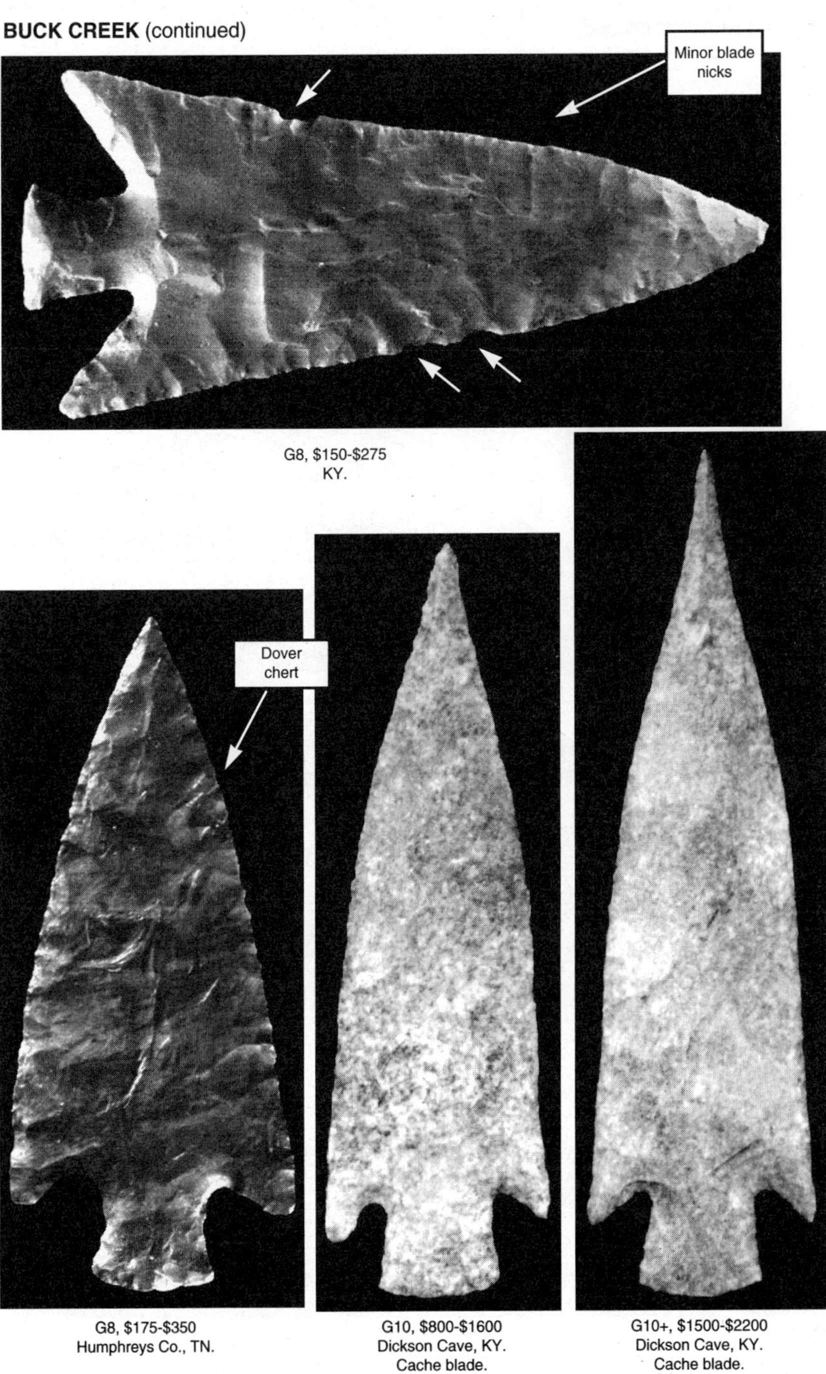

G8, $150-$275
KY.

G8, $175-$350
Humphreys Co., TN.

G10, $800-$1600
Dickson Cave, KY.
Cache blade.

G10+, $1500-$2200
Dickson Cave, KY.
Cache blade.

LOCATION: Kentucky and surrounding states. **DESCRIPTION:** A large, thin, broad, stemmed point with strong barbs and high quality flaking. Some have needle tips, blade edges are convex to recurved. Blade width can be narrow to broad. **I.D. KEY:** Barb expansion and notching.

BUCK CREEK (continued)

G10, $800-$1500
KY.

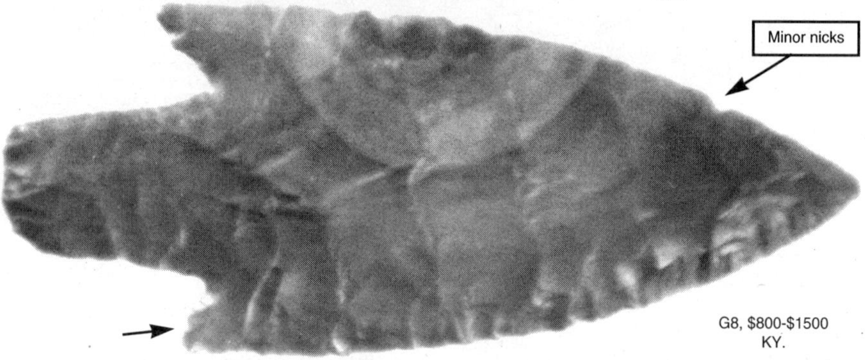

Minor nicks

G8, $800-$1500
KY.

BUGGS ISLAND - Mid to Late Archaic, 5500 - 3500 B. P.

(Also see Ebenezer)

G2, $1-$2
S.E. TN.

G3, $1-$3
Dunlap, TN.

G5, $3-$6
S.E. TN.

LOCATION: Eastern states. **DESCRIPTION:** A small to medium size point with a contracting stem and tapered shoulders. The base is usually straight.

BUZZARD ROOST CREEK - Middle Archaic, 6000 - 4000 B. P.

(Also see Benton and Kirk Serrated)

LOCATION: Southeastern states.**DESCRIPTION:** A medium to large size, stemmed point with a bifurcated base. Believed to be related to the *Benton* point. Found in Arkansas with the blade steeply beveled on one side of each face (transition form?). **I.D. KEY:** Bifurcated base and basal width. Found with *Benton* points. A notched base *Benton.*

G2, $1-$3
S.E. TN.

G4, $2-$4
Marion Co., TN.

G4, $5-$10
N. AL.

G5, $5-$10
KY.

G5, $10-$20
Decatur, AL.

G4, $8-$15
Humphreys Co., TN.

G5, $10-$20
Florence, AL.

G8, $150-$250
Meigs Co., TN.

CACHE RIVER - Trans. Paleo to Middle Archaic, 10,000 - 5000 B. P.

(Also see Big Sandy and Knight Island)

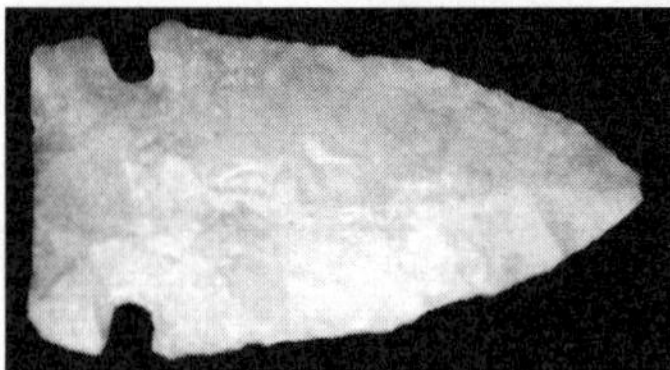

LOCATION: Arkansas into Oklahoma. **DESCRIPTION:** A small to medium size, fairly thin, side-notched, triangular point with a concave base. Could be related to *Big Sandy* points. **I.D. KEY:** Base form, narrow notched and flaking of blade.

G5, $25-$50
Chickasaw Co., MS.

Not typical for area

CAMP CREEK - Woodland, 3000 - 1500 B. P.

(Also see Greeneville, Hamilton, Madison, Nolichucky and Yadkin)

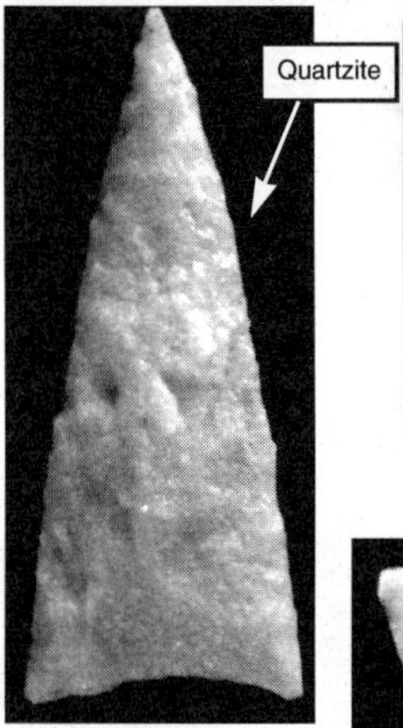

Quartzite

G7, $20-$35
Johnson City, TN.

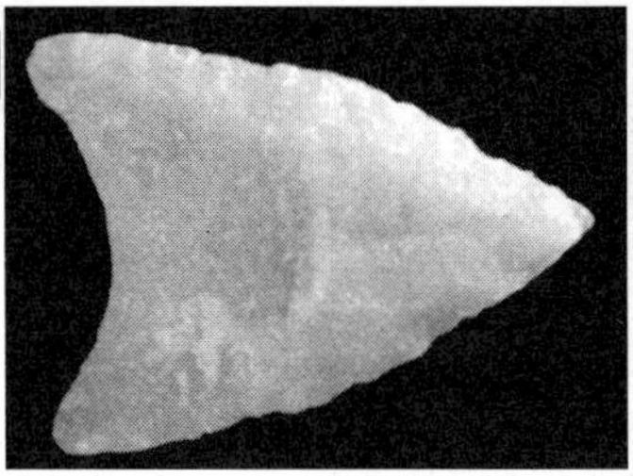

G6, $8-$15
Cocke Co., TN.

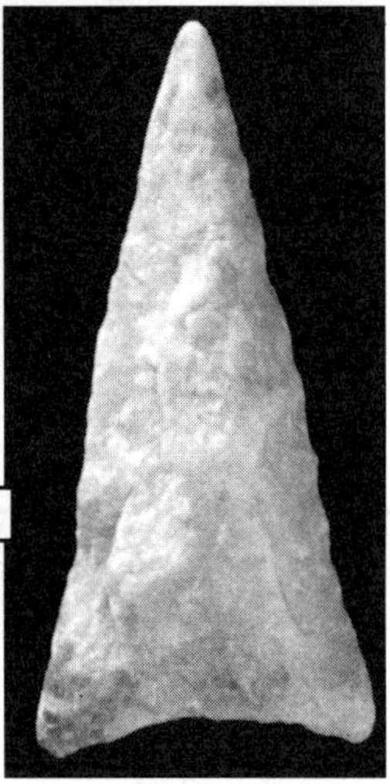

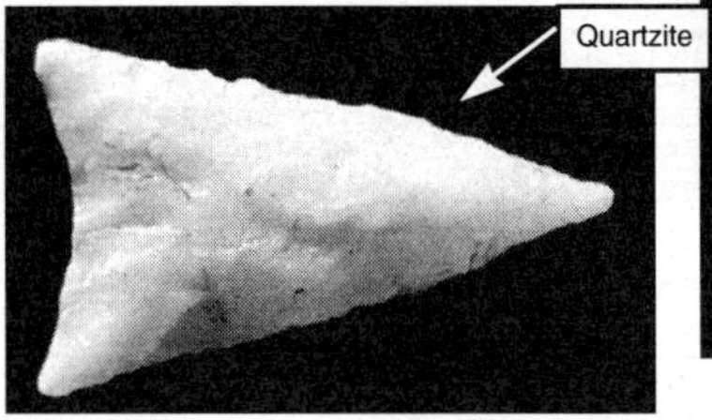

Quartzite

G6, $10-$20
Cocke Co., TN.

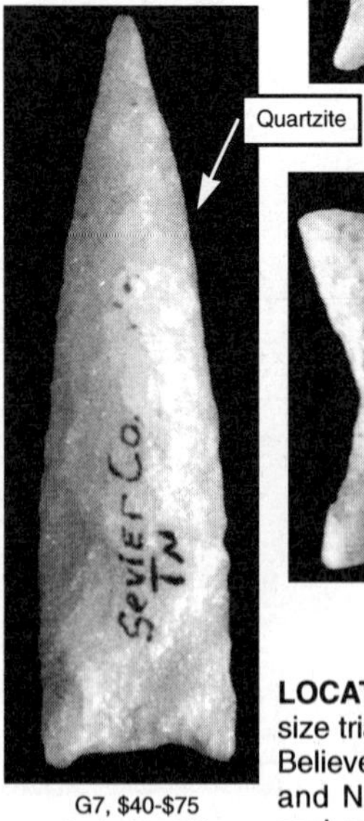

G7, $20-$40
Cocke Co., TN.

Quartzite

G7, $40-$75
Sevier Co., TN.

Quartzite

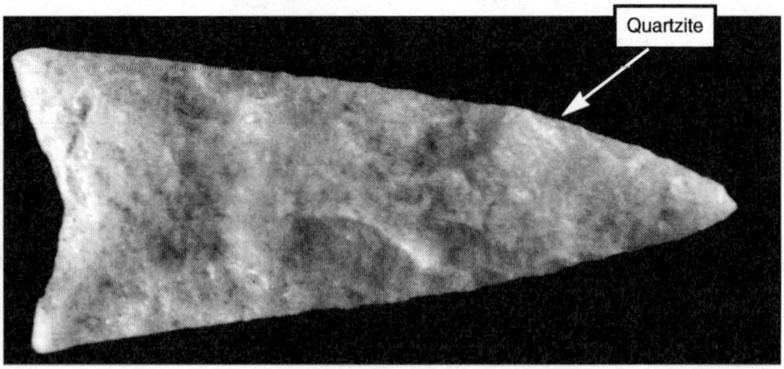

G9, $70-$140
Dayton, TN.

LOCATION: Southeastern states. **DESCRIPTION:** A small to medium size triangular point with straight to convex sides and a concave base. Believed to have evolved into Hamilton points; related to Greeneville and Nolichucky points. Has been found with Adena stemmed in caches (Rankin site, Cocke Co.,TN).

G6, $25-$55
Bristol, TN.

CANDY CREEK - Early Woodland, 3000 - 1500 B. P.

(Also see Beaver Lake, Camp Creek, Copena, Dalton, Nolichucky and Quad)

G2, $2-$5
Putnam Co., TN.

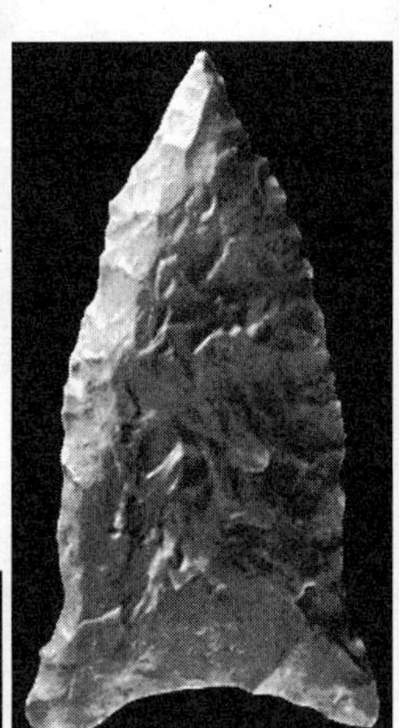

G7, $15-$30
Morgan Co., AL.

G9, $25-$50
Bradley Co., TN.

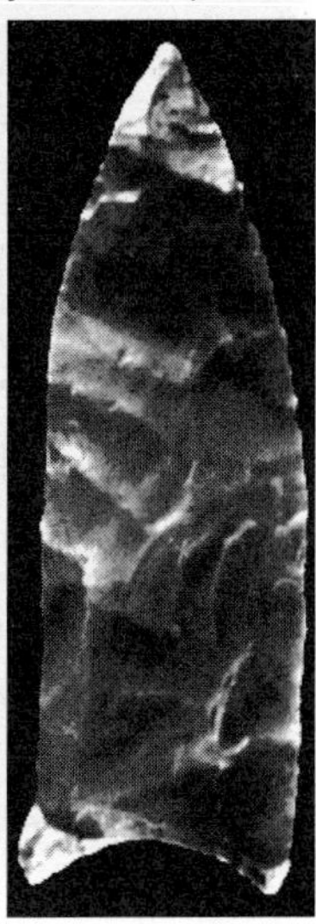

G5, $10-$20
Dayton, TN.

G7, $10-$20
Nickajack Lake, TN.

LOCATION: Southeastern states. **DESCRIPTION:** A medium size, lanceolate, eared point with a concave base and recurved blade edges. Bases may be thinned or fluted and lightly ground. Flaking is of the random Woodland type and should not be confused with the earlier auriculate forms that have the parallel flaking. These points are similar to *Cumberland*, *Beaver Lake*, *Dalton* and *Quad*, but are shorter and of poorer quality. It is believed that Paleo people survived in East Tennessee to 3,000 B.P., and influenced the style of the *Candy Creek* point. Believed to be related to *Copena, Camp Creek, Ebenezer, Greenville* and *Nolichucky* points. **I.D. KEY:** Ears, thickness and Woodland flaking.

CAVE SPRING - Transitional Paleo to Early Archaic, 9000 - 8000 B. P.

(Also see Dalton-Hemphill, Jude and Patrick)

LOCATION: Southeastern states. **DESCRIPTION**: A small to medium size, stemmed point with a shallow bifurcated base. Blade edges are usually straight; shoulders are either tapered or barbed, and the stem usually expands with a tendency to turn inward at the base which is usually ground. **ID. KEY:** Early Archaic flaking.

CAVE SPRING (continued)

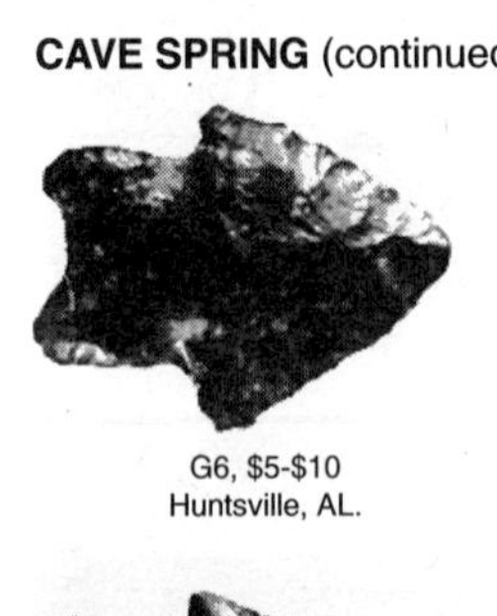

G6, $5-$10
Huntsville, AL.

G7, $10-$15
Humphreys Co., TN.

G7, $10-$15
Morgan Co., AL.

G7, $15-$25
Colbert Co., AL.

G10, $25-$50
Marion Co., AL.

CLOVIS - Early Paleo, 14,000 - 9000 B. P.

(Also see Angostura, Browns Valley, Cumberland, Dalton and Redstone)

G5, $100-$200
KY.

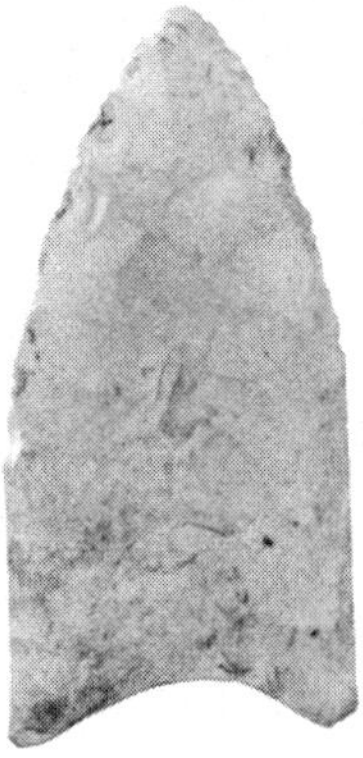

G6, $150-$300
IN.

G5, $120-$200
KY.

G5, $150-$275
Castillian Springs, TN.

Dover chert

G7, $350-$700
Humphreys Co., TN.

G6, $200-$400
IN.

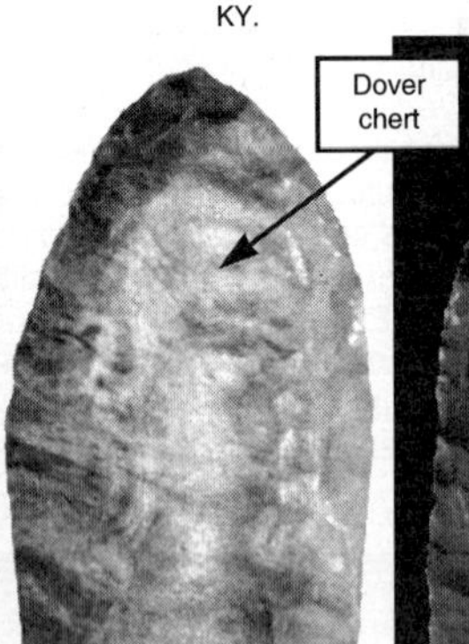

G7, $300-$600
Lee Co., MS.

G6, $175-$350
Lauderdale Co., AL.

G7, \$500-\$1000
OH.

G6, \$400-\$800
Pickett Co., TN.

G8, \$450-\$900
Lewis Co., KY.

EC

G6, \$300-\$600
E. TN.

G4, \$150-\$300
KY.

G8, \$800-\$1500
OH.

G10, \$1000-\$2000
AL.

G5, \$125-\$250
TN.

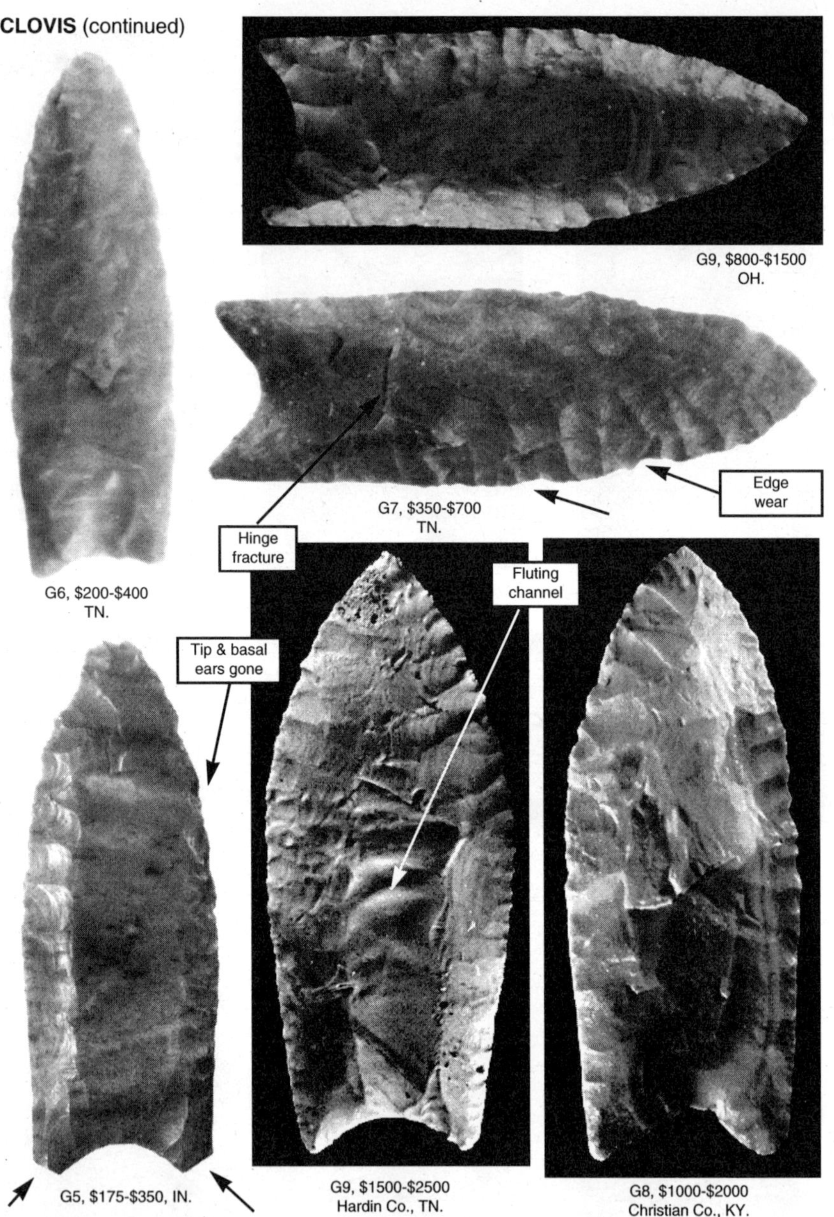

G9, $800-$1500
OH.

G6, $200-$400
TN.

G7, $350-$700
TN.

G5, $175-$350, IN.

G9, $1500-$2500
Hardin Co., TN.

G8, $1000-$2000
Christian Co., KY.

LOCATION: All of North America. **DESCRIPTION:** A medium to large size, auriculate, fluted, lanceolate point with convex sides and a concave base that is ground. Most examples are fluted on both sides about 1/3 the way up from the base. The flaking can be random to parallel. *Clovis* is the earliest point type in the hemisphere. It is believed that this form was brought here when early man crossed the Bering Straits to reach this continent between 50,000 and 12,000 years ago. *Clovis* probably developed in Siberia or China. There is no pre-*Clovis* evidence here (crude forms that would pre-date *Clovis).* The first *Clovis* find associated with Mastodons was in 1979 at Mastodon State Park, Jefferson Co., MO. in the Kimmswick bone bed dated to 12,000 B.P. **I.D. Key:** Paleo flaking, shoulders, batan fluting instead of indirect style.

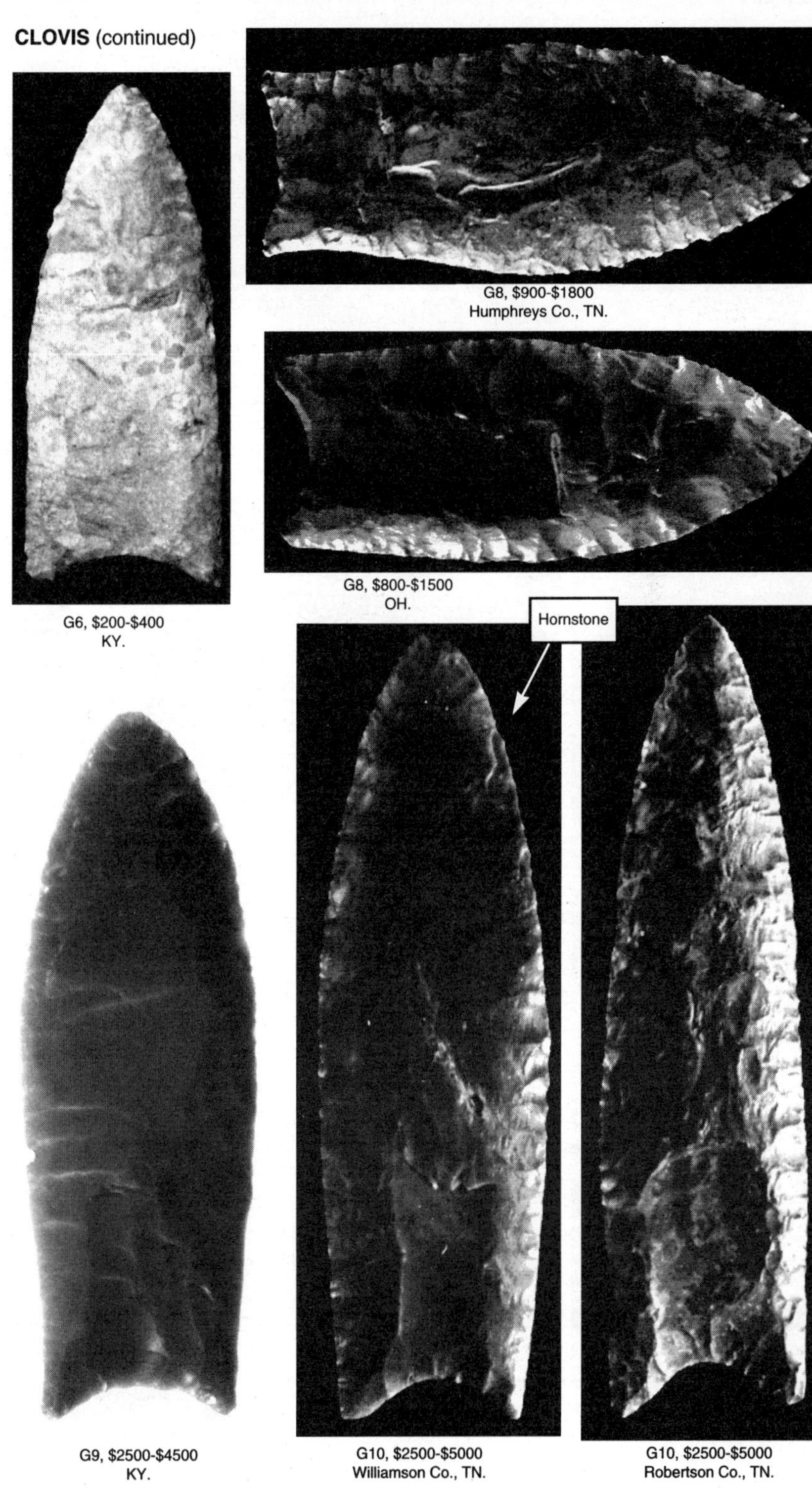

G8, $900-$1800
Humphreys Co., TN.

G8, $800-$1500
OH.

G6, $200-$400
KY.

G9, $2500-$4500
KY.

G10, $2500-$5000
Williamson Co., TN.

G10, $2500-$5000
Robertson Co., TN.

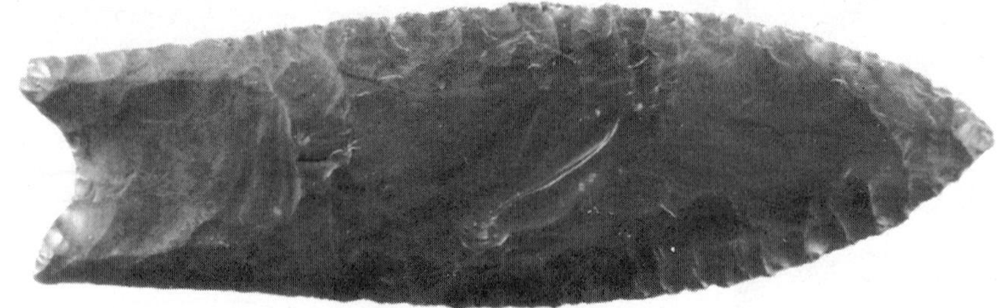

G10, $2500-$5000
OH.

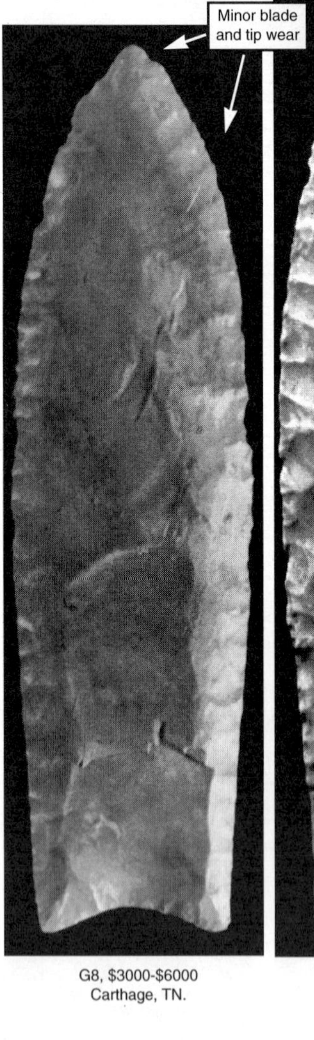

Minor blade and tip wear

Patinated Buffalo River chert

G8, $3000-$6000
Carthage, TN.

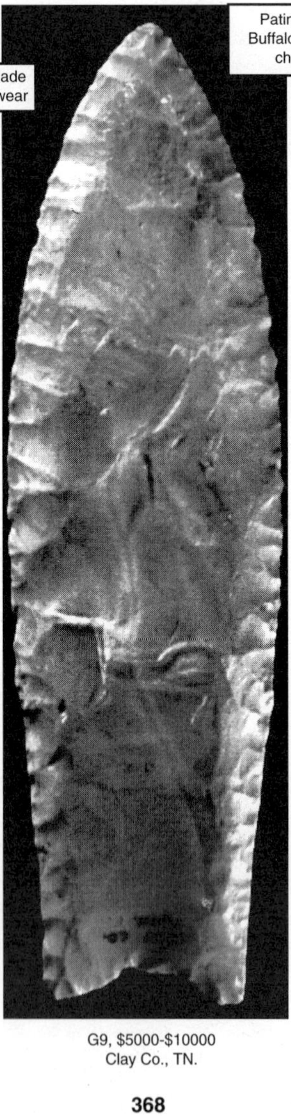

G9, $5000-$10000
Clay Co., TN.

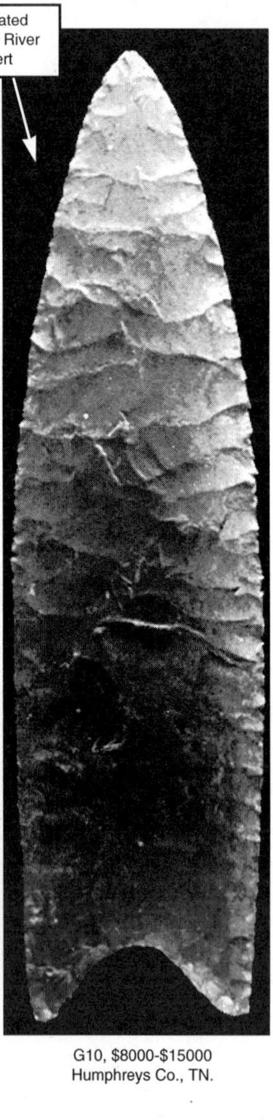

G10, $8000-$15000
Humphreys Co., TN.

CLOVIS-UNFLUTED - Paleo, 14,000 - 9000 B. P.

(Also see Angostura, Beaver Lake, Candy Creek, Golondrina and Plainview)

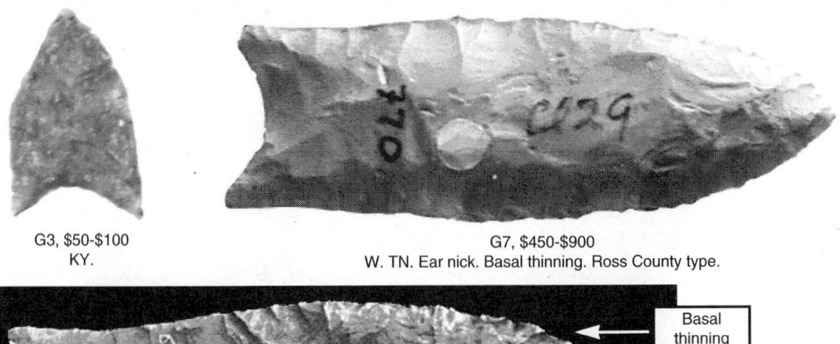

G3, $50-$100
KY.

G7, $450-$900
W. TN. Ear nick. Basal thinning. Ross County type.

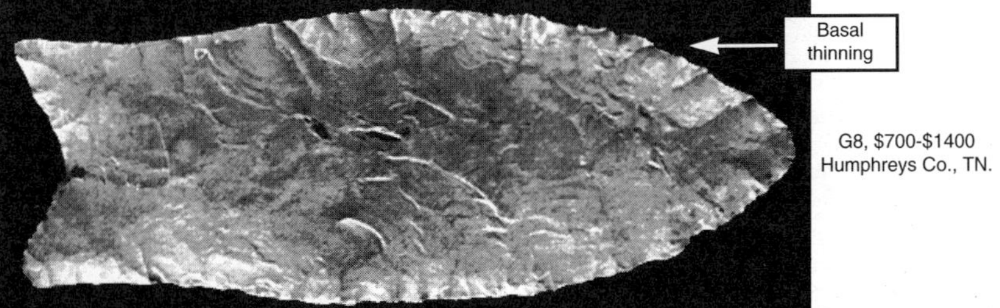

G8, $700-$1400
Humphreys Co., TN.

LOCATION: All of North America. **DESCRIPTION:** A medium to large size, auriculate point identical to fluted *Clovis,* but not fluted. A very rare type.

COBBS TRIANGULAR - Early Archaic, 8000 - 5000 B. P.

(Also see Abasolo, Decatur, Lerma, Lost Lake and St. Charles)

G8, $75-$150
Tishomingo Co., MS.

LOCATION: Southeastern states. **DESCRIPTION:** A medium to large size, thin, lanceolate blade with a broad, rounded to square base. One side of each face is usually steeply beveled. These are un-notched preforms for early Archaic beveled types such as *Decatur, Dovetail, Lost Lake,* etc.

G7, $30-$60
Crittenden Co., KY.

G9, $175-$350
AL.

G8, $45-$90
KY.

COLDWATER - Early Archaic, 10,000 - 9000 B. P.

(Also see Conerly and Hi-Lo)

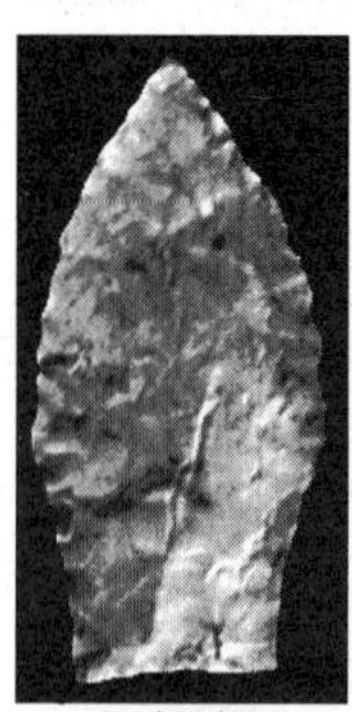

G5, $45-$90
Marion Co., AL.

G6, $100-$200
Franklin Co., MS.

LOCATION: E. Texas into W. Tenn. and Alabama. **DESCRIPTION:** A medium size lanceolate point with weak tapered shoulders, a short stem and a straight base. **I.D. KEY:** One high shoulder.

CONERLY - Middle Archaic, 7500 - 4500 B. P.

(Also see Beaver Lake, Browns Valley and Coldwater)

CONERLY (continued)

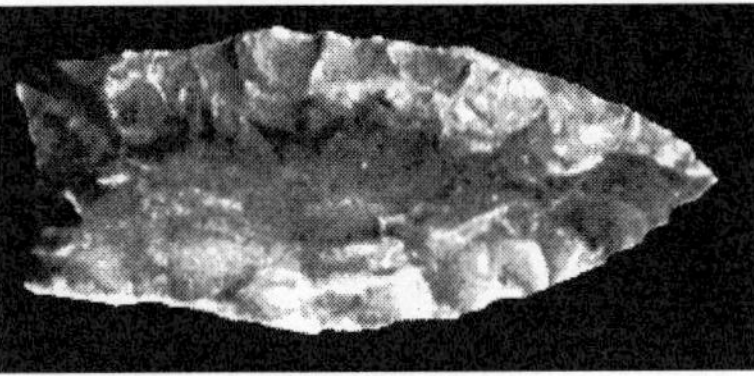

G7, $25-$50
Putnam Co., TN.

G8, $45-$90
Bradley Co., TN.

LOCATION: Southern Southeastern states, especially Tennessee, Georgia and Florida. **DESCRIPTION:** A medium to large auriculate point with a contracting, concave base which can be ground. On some examples, the hafting area can be seen with the presence of very weak shoulders. The base is usually thinned. Believed to be related to the *Guilford* type. **I.D. Key:** Base concave, thickness, flaking.

COOSA - Woodland, 2000 - 1500 B. P.

(Also see Crawford Creek)

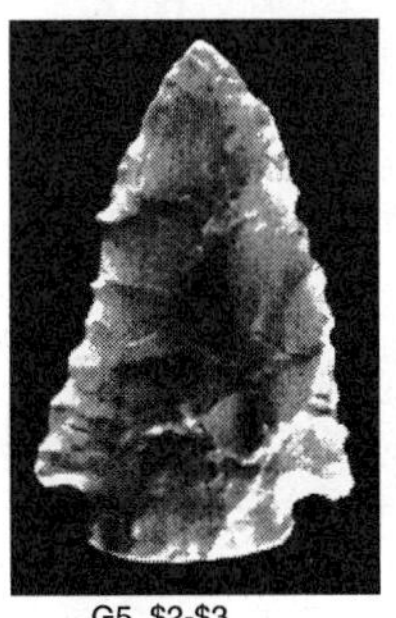

G5, $2-$3
Meigs Co., TN.

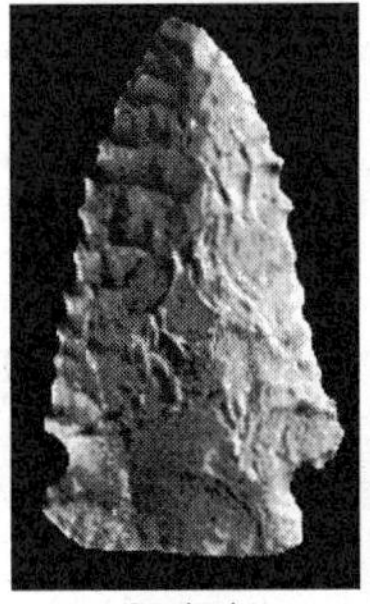

G5, $2-$4
Meigs Co., TN.

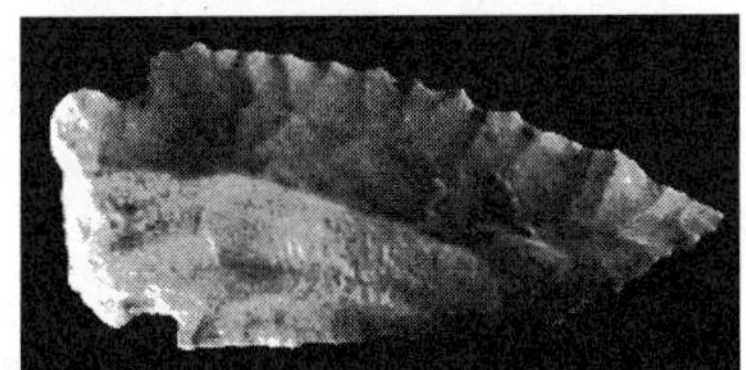

G5, $2-$3
Jackson Co., AL.

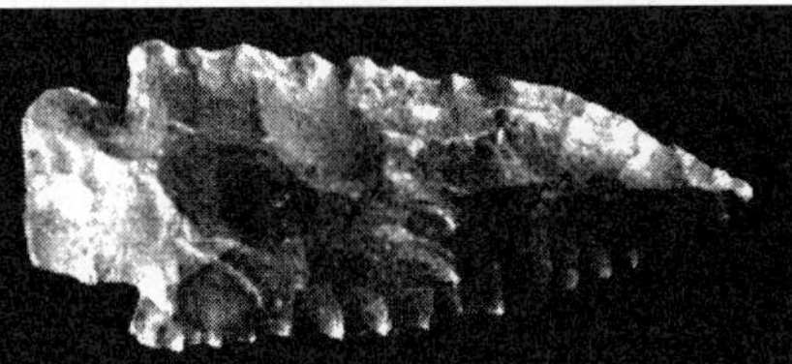

G5, $2-$4
Jackson Co., AL.

LOCATION: Southeastern states. **DESCRIPTION:** A medium size, usually serrated medium grade point with a short stem. Some examples are shallowly side-notched. Shoulders are roughly horizontal. **I.D. Key:** Serrated blade edges, bulbous stem.

COPENA-AURICULATE - Middle Archaic-Woodland, 5000 - 2500 B. P.

(Also see Candy Creek, Beaver Lake, Clovis, Quad and Yadkin)

G8, $12-$20
Nickajack Lake, TN.

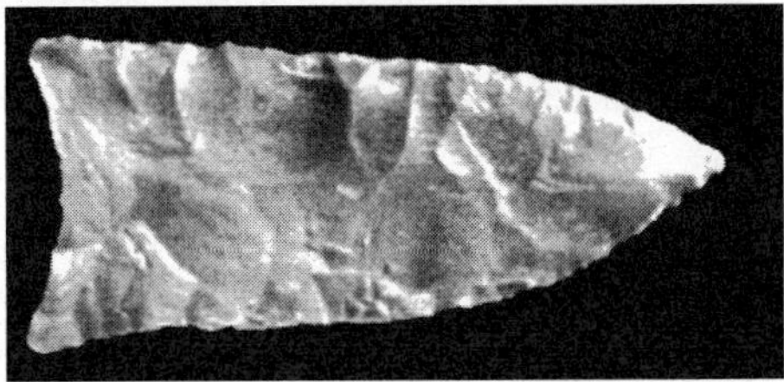

G7, $15-$30
Decatur, AL.

G9, $70-$140
Humphreys Co., TN.

G7, $10-$20
KY.

G8, $50-$95
Meigs Co., TN.

LOCATION: Southeastern states. **DESCRIPTION:** A medium to large size, lanceolate point with straight to recurved blade edges and a concave, auriculate base. Could be confused with *Beaver Lake, Candy Creek, Clovis, Cumberland* or other auriculate forms. Look for the random Woodland flaking on this type. **I.D. Key:** Concave base.

COPENA-CLASSIC (Shield form) - Late Archaic to Woodland, 4000 - 1200 B. P.

(Also see Bakers Creek & Nolichucky)

G6, $15-$30
TN.

G8, $30-$60
TN.

G7, $25-$45
TN.

LOCATION: Southeastern states. **DESCRIPTION:** A medium to large size, lanceolate point with recurved blade edges and a straight to slightly convex base. This point usually occurs in Woodland burial mounds, but is also found in late Archaic sites in Tennessee. The Alabama, Tennessee forms are usually very thin with high quality primary and secondary flaking.

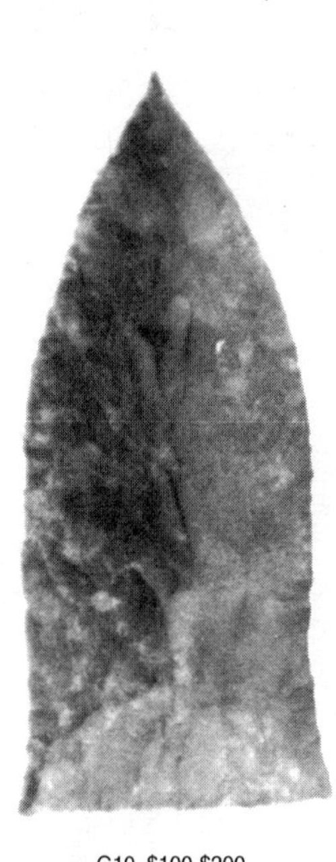

G10, $100-$200
TN.

G7, $40-$75
TN.

G8, $50-$100
TN.

G9, $65-$125
TN.

G10, $300-$600
TN. Cache point

EC

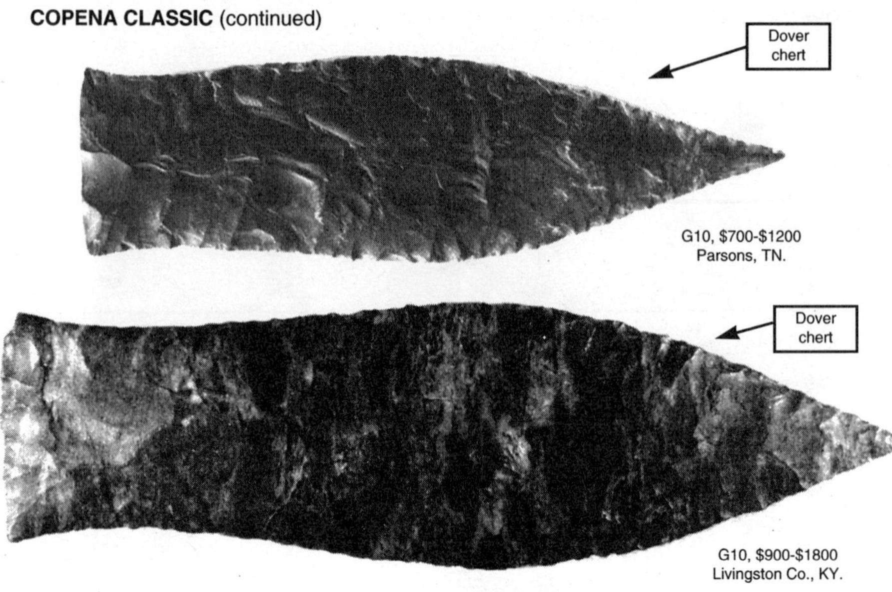

G10, $700-$1200
Parsons, TN.

G10, $900-$1800
Livingston Co., KY.

COPENA-ROUND BASE - Late Archaic to Woodland, 4000 - 1200 B. P.

(Also see Frazier & Tennessee River)

G5, $5-$10
Florence, AL.

G5, $5-$10
Florence, AL.

LOCATION: Southeastern states. **DESCRIPTION:** A medium to large size lanceolate blade with a rounded base. Blade edges become parallel towards the base on some examples.

G6, $15-$25
Davidson Co., TN.

G5, $12-$20
Parsons., TN.

COPENA-TRIANGULAR - Late Archaic to Woodland, 4000 - 1800 B. P.

(See Benton Blade & Frazier)

G3, $5-$10
Walker Co., AL.

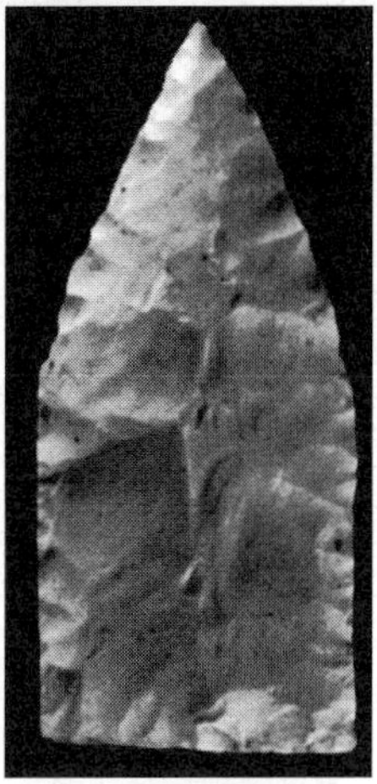

G4, $10-$15
Parsons, TN.

G5, $10-$20
New Era, TN.

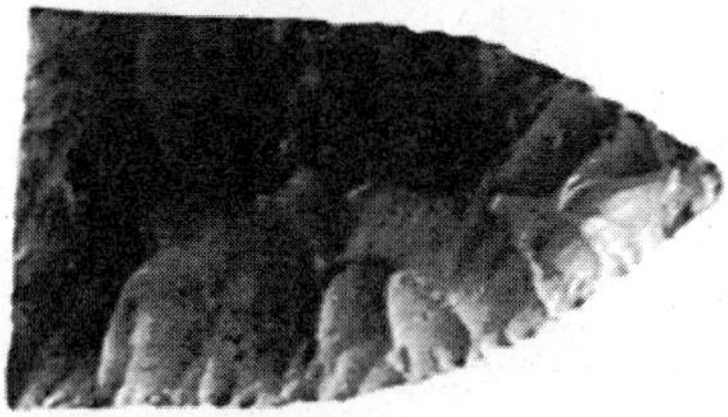

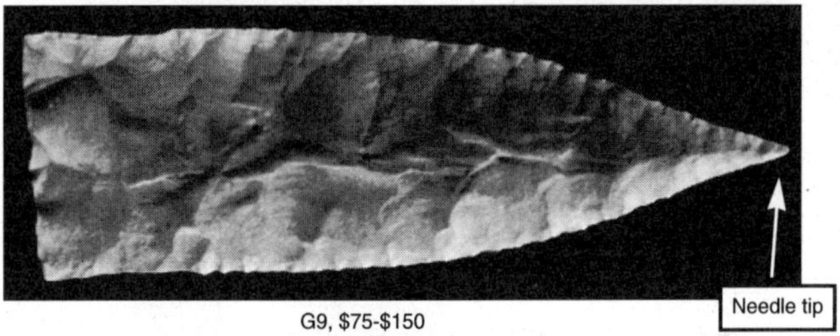

Needle tip

G9, $75-$150
Decatur Co., TN.

G8, $30-$60
TN.

EC

LOCATION: Southeastern states. **DESCRIPTION:** A medium to large size lanceolate blade with a straight base. Blade edges become parallel towards the base. Some examples show a distinct hafting area near the base where the blade edges form a very weak shoulder and become slightly concave.

CORNER TANG KNIFE - Late Archaic to Woodland, 4000 - 2000 B. P.

G4, $1-$2
Portland Lake, TN.

G4, $1-$2
W. TN.

LOCATION: Western to Southeastern states. **DESCRIPTION:** The eastern form is a medium size blade with only one of the basal corners notched for hafting. On some examples, the opposite basal corner expands. The Western form is notched producing a tang at a corner for hafting. The Western form has been reproduced in recent years.

COTACO CREEK - Woodland, 2500 - 2000 B. P.

(Also see Flint Creek and Little Bear Creek)

G5, $8-$15
TN.

G5, $10-$20
Florence, AL.

G3, $6-$12
Walker Co., AL.

G8, $75-$150
Cliffton, TN.

G5, $15-$25
Coffee Lake, AL.

G6, $20-$40
Walker Co., AL.

G9, $200-$375
Florence, AL. Classic.

LOCATION: Southeastern states. **DESCRIPTION:** A small to medium size, well made, broad, triangular stemmed point with wide rounded to square shoulders. Blade edges are usually finely serrated and some examples have blunt tips. I.D. Key: Edgework and rounded shoulders.

COTACO CREEK BLADE - Woodland, 2500 - 2000 B. P.

IMPORTANT: Shown 50% of actual size.

G9, $250-$425
Florence, AL.

G10, $550-$1000
Parsons, TN.

LOCATION: Southeastern states. **DESCRIPTION:** A medium to large size lanceolate blade with a rounded base. Blade edges expand past mid-section. Some examples are side notched for hafting.

EC

COTACO-WRIGHT - Woodland, 2500 - 1800 B. P.

(Also see Flint Creek and Little Bear Creek)

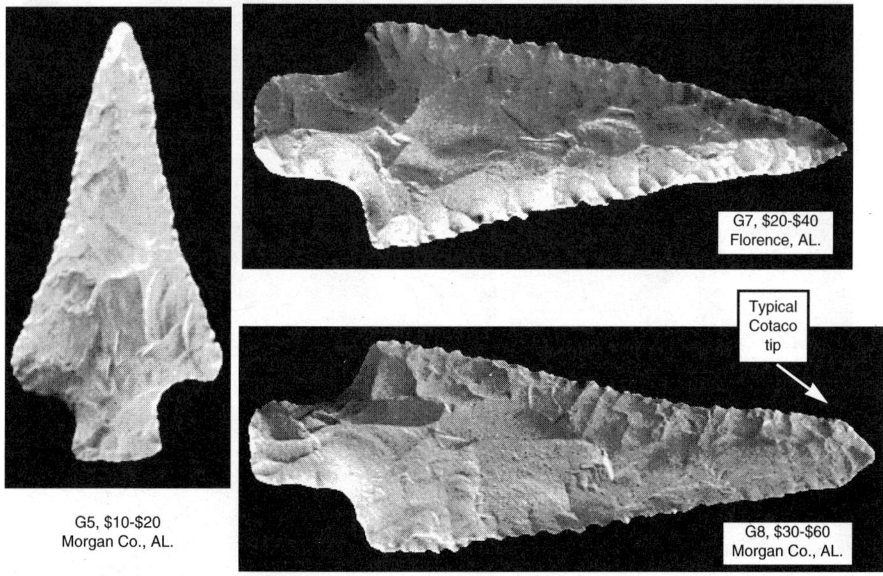

G7, $20-$40
Florence, AL.

G5, $10-$20
Morgan Co., AL.

G8, $30-$60
Morgan Co., AL.

LOCATION: Southeastern states. **DESCRIPTION:** A small to medium size, well made, narrow, triangular stemmed point with rounded to square shoulders. Blade edges are usually finely serrated and some have blunt tips.

CRAWFORD CREEK - Early Archaic, 8000 - 5000 B. P.

(Also see Coosa, Mud Creek and White Springs)

CRAWFORD CREEK (continued)

G8, $15-$30
Limestone Co., AL.

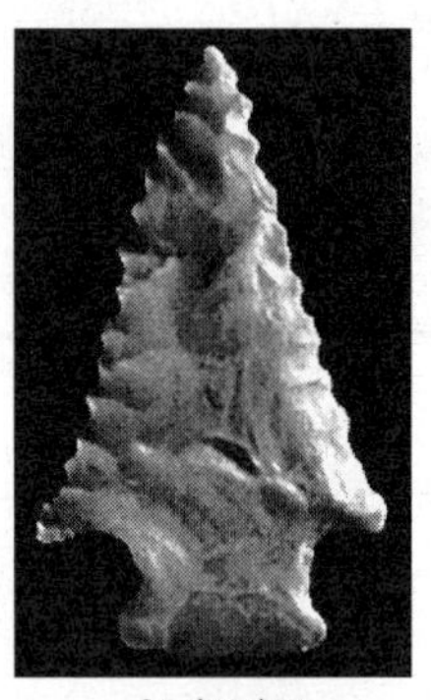

G6, $10-$20
Morgan Co., AL.

G7, $10-$20
Limestone Co., AL.

LOCATION: Southeastern states. **DESCRIPTION:** A small to medium size point that is usually serrated with a short, straight to expanding stem. Shoulders are square to tapered. Blade edges are straight to convex. **I.D. Key:** Early edgework.

CUMBERLAND - Paleo, 12,000 - 8000 B. P.

(Also see Beaver Lake, Clovis, Copena Auriculate and Quad)

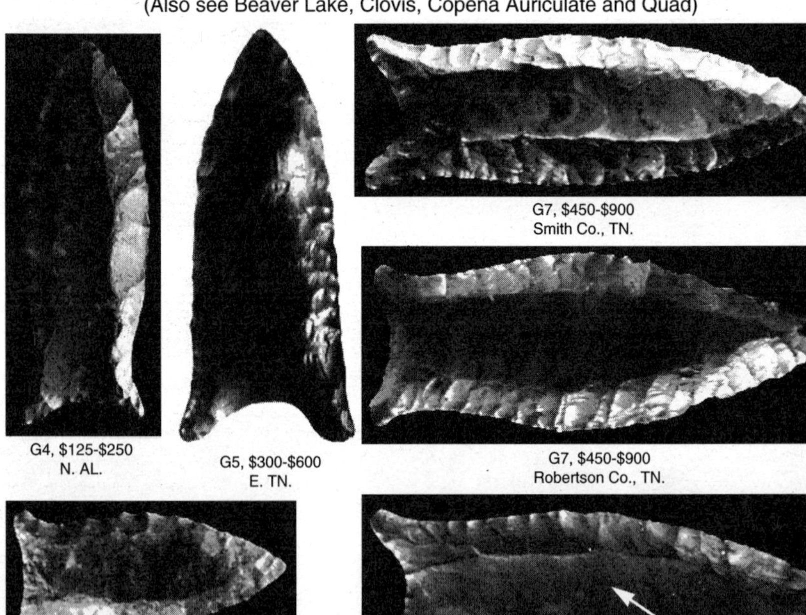

G7, $450-$900
Smith Co., TN.

G4, $125-$250
N. AL.

G5, $300-$600
E. TN.

G7, $450-$900
Robertson Co., TN.

G3, $100-$200
Limestone Co., AL.

G8, $800-$1500
Lauderdale Co., AL.

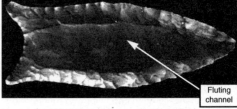

LOCATION: Southeastern states to Canada. **DESCRIPTION:** A medium to large size, lanceolate, eared form that is usually fluted on both faces. The fluting and flaking technique is an advanced form as in *Folsom*, with the flutes usually extending the entire length of the blade. Bases are ground on all examples. An unfluted variant which is thicker than *Beaver Lake* has been found. This point is scarce everywhere and has been reproduced in large numbers. **I.D. Key:** Paleo flaking, indirect pressure fluting.

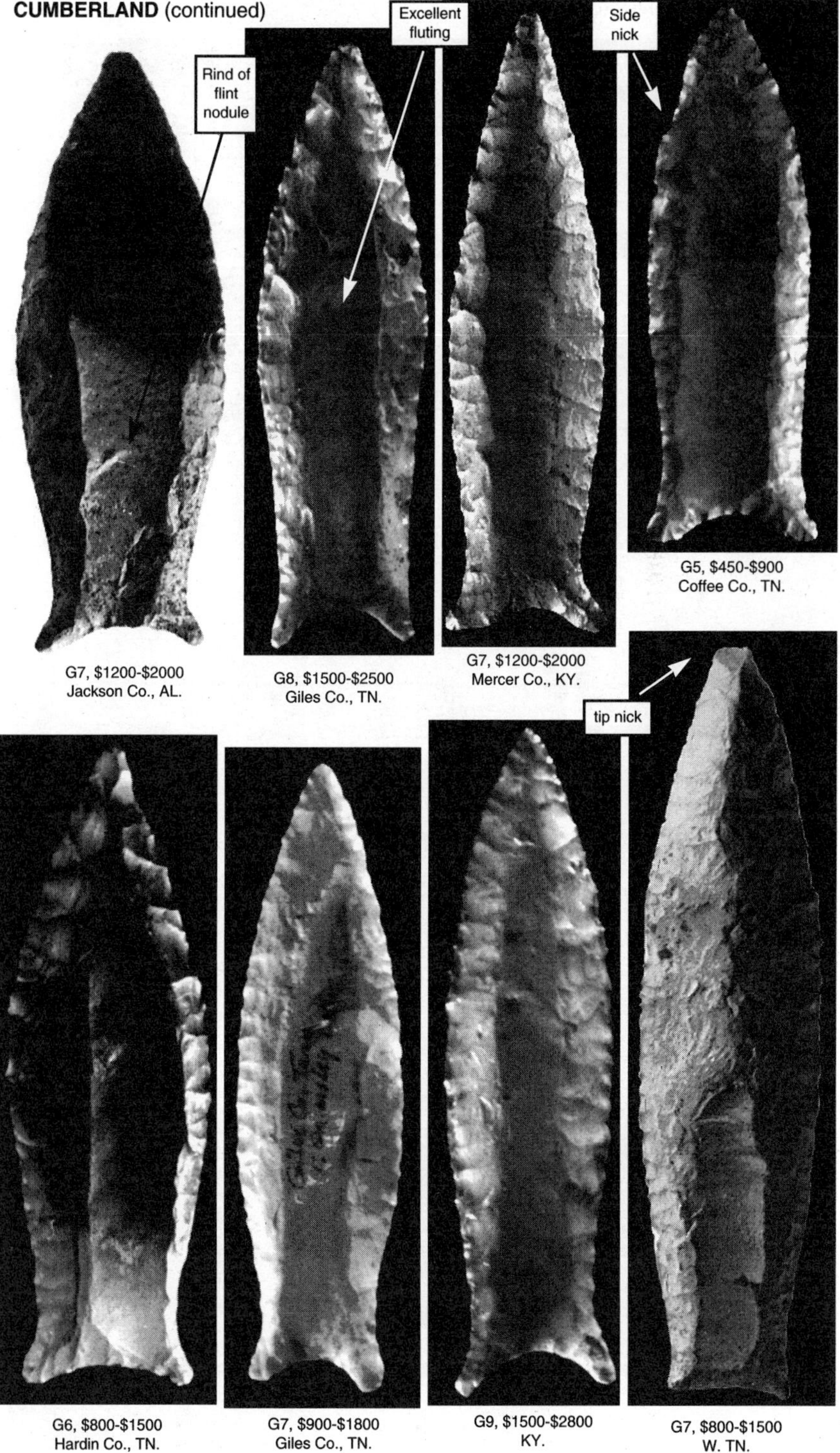

G7, $1200-$2000
Jackson Co., AL.

G8, $1500-$2500
Giles Co., TN.

G7, $1200-$2000
Mercer Co., KY.

G5, $450-$900
Coffee Co., TN.

G6, $800-$1500
Hardin Co., TN.

G7, $900-$1800
Giles Co., TN.

G9, $1500-$2800
KY.

G7, $800-$1500
W. TN.

EC

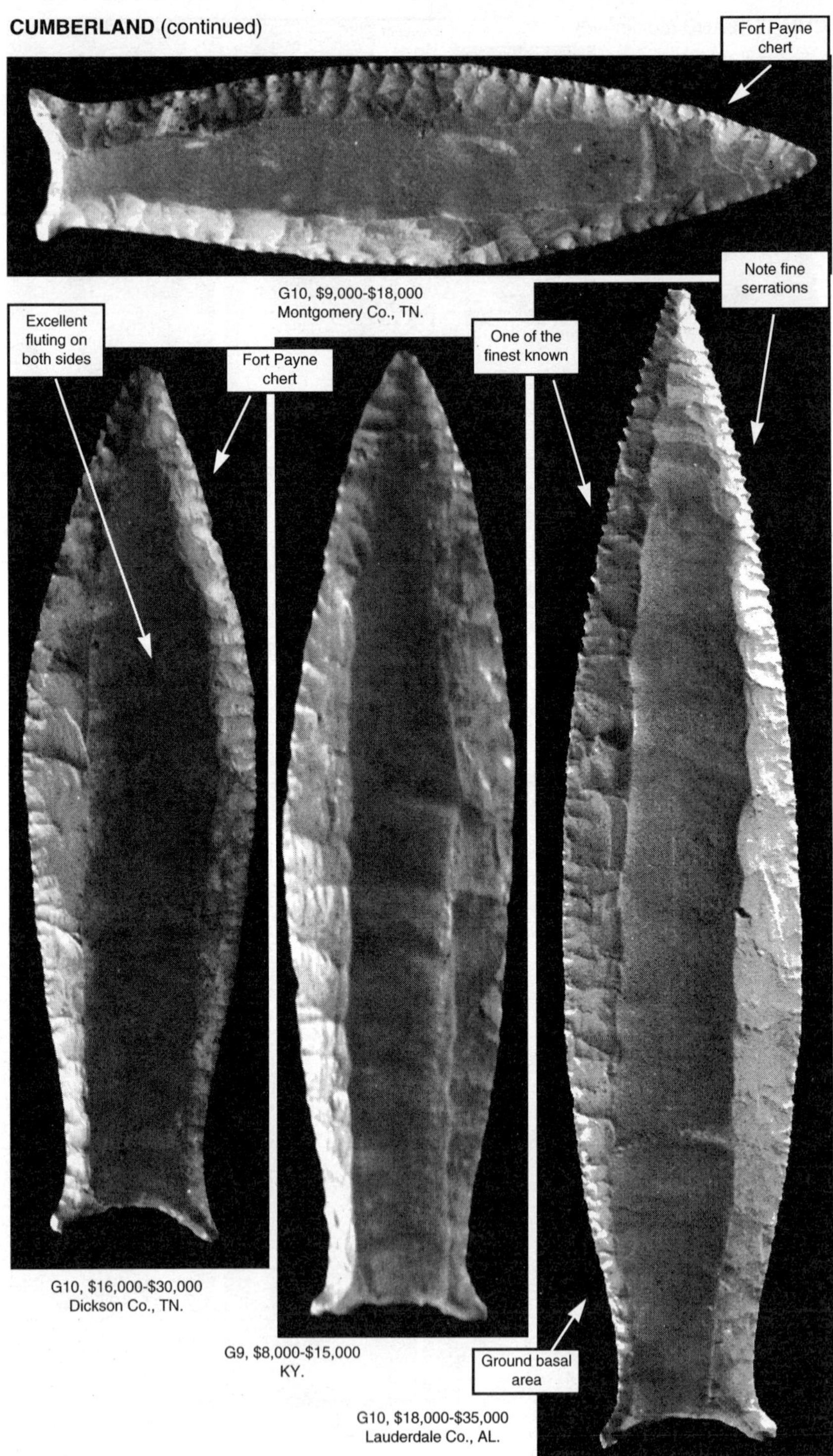

G10, $9,000-$18,000
Montgomery Co., TN.

G10, $16,000-$30,000
Dickson Co., TN.

G9, $8,000-$15,000
KY.

G10, $18,000-$35,000
Lauderdale Co., AL.

CUPP - Late Woodland to Mississippian, 1500 - 600 B. P.

(Also see Buck Creek, Hamilton, Motley, Smithsonia and Snyders)

LOCATION: Eastern states. **DESCRIPTION:** A medium to large size, narrow point with wide corner notches, shoulder barbs and a convex base. Similar to *Motley*, but the base stem is shorter and broader.

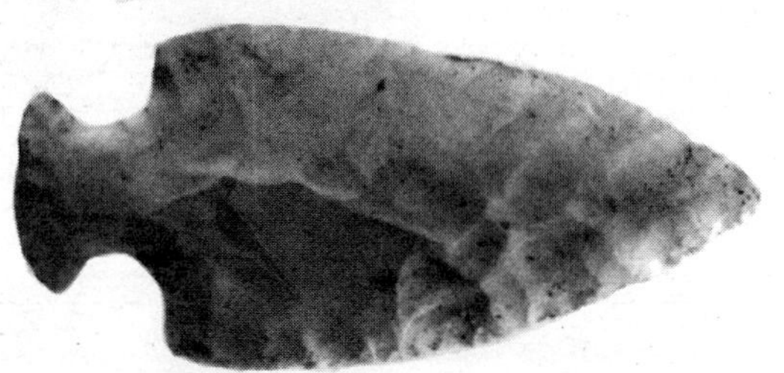

G7, $25-$45
MI.

CYPRESS CREEK - Middle to Late Archaic, 5000 - 3000 B. P.

(Also see Hardin, Kirk Corner Notched and Lost Lake)

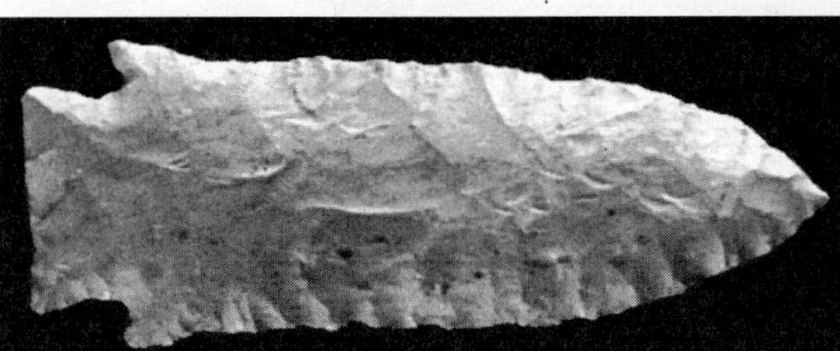

G6, $45-$70
Giles Co., TN.

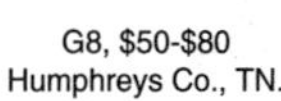

G8, $50-$80
Humphreys Co., TN.

LOCATION: Southeastern states. **DESCRIPTION:** A medium to large size, broad stemmed point with an expanded base and drooping "umbrella" shoulder tangs. A cross between Lost Lake and Kirk Corner Notched. The blade is beveled on all four sides. **I.D. KEY:** Archaic flaking, shoulders droop.

DAGGER - Late Archaic to Woodland, 4000 - 1500 B. P.

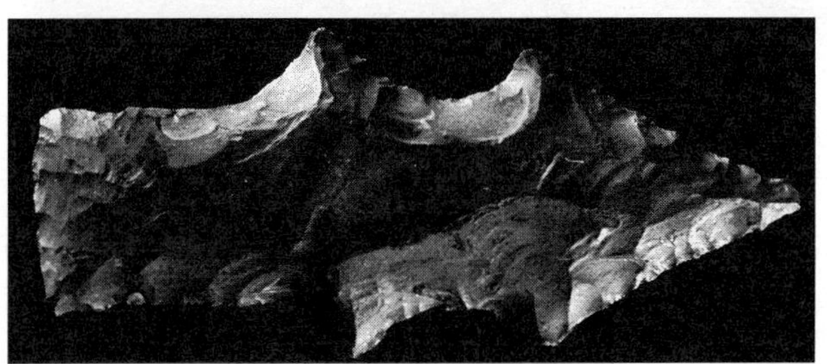

IMPORTANT: SHOWN 50% OF ORIGINAL SIZE

G8, $800-$1500
Montgomery Co., TN.

DAGGER (continued)

LOCATION: Southeastern states. **DESCRIPTION:** A large size knife with a handle fashioned for holding or for hafting. Most examples have a very thick cross section and are rare everywhere. Beware of counterfeits.

G9, $800-$1500
Humphreys Co., TN.

G10, $1600-$2500
Stewart Co., TN.

IMPORTANT: DAGGERS SHOWN 50% OF ORIGINAL SIZE

DALTON-CLASSIC - Early Archaic, 9500 - 8000 B. P.

(Also see Clovis, Debert and Hardaway)

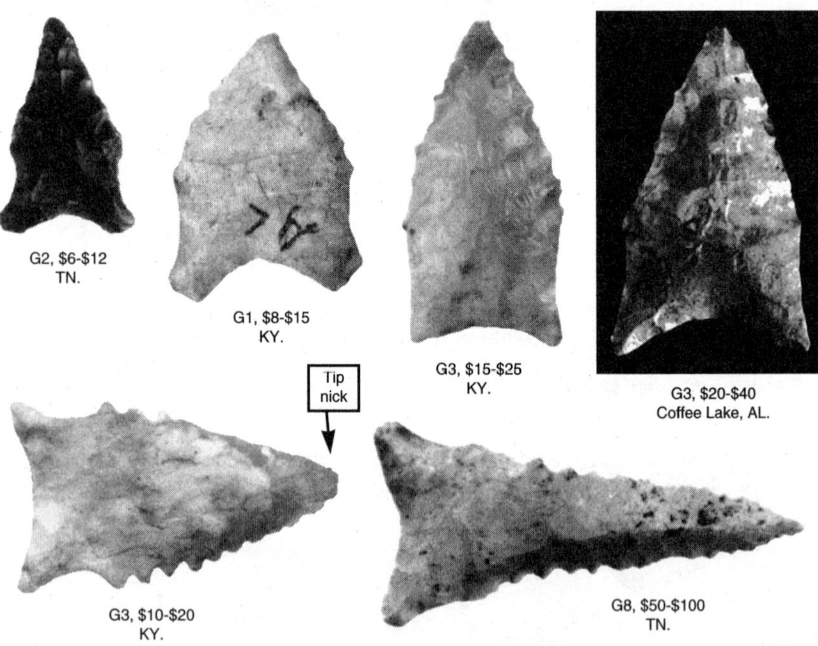

G2, $6-$12
TN.

G1, $8-$15
KY.

G3, $15-$25
KY.

G3, $20-$40
Coffee Lake, AL.

G3, $10-$20
KY.

G8, $50-$100
TN.

LOCATION: Midwestern to Southeastern states. **DESCRIPTION:** A medium to large size, thin, auriculate, fishtailed point. Many examples are finely serrated and exhibit excellent flaking. Beveling may occur on one side of each face but is usually on the right side. All have basal grinding. This early type spread over most of the Eastern and Midwestern U.S. and strongly influenced many other types to follow.

DALTON CLASSIC (continued)

G8, $80-$150
KY.

G8, $65-$125
TN.

G8, $65-$125
AL.

G9, $150-$200
Humphreys Co., TN.

DALTON-COLBERT - Early Archaic, 9500 - 5000 B. P.

(Also see Dalton-Nuckolls, Plainview and Searcy)

G4, $20-$35
Hamilton Co., TN.

G4, $20-$35
Florence, AL.

G4, $20-$35
Franklin Co., TN.

G7, $20-$45
TN.

G5, $30-$60
Hamilton Co., TN.

G10, $200-$350
Stewart Co., TN.

LOCATION: Midwestern to Southeastern states. **DESCRIPTION:** A medium to large size, auriculate form with a squared base and a weakly defined hafting area which is ground. Some examples are serrated and exhibit parallel flaking of the highest quality. **I.D. KEY:** Large shoulders.

DALTON-GREENBRIER - Early Archaic, 9500 - 6000 B. P.

(Also see Greenbrier, Hardaway and Haw River)

G6, $20-$40
Jackson Co., AL.

G4, $15-$30
S.E. TN.

G4, $15-$30
Huntsville, AL.

G5, $15-$30
Lowndes Co., MS.

G6, $40-$70
Walker Co., AL.

G6, $30-$60
Jackson Co., AL.

G5, $35-$55
N. AL.

G7, $60-$120
Humphreys Co., TN.

LOCATION: Midwestern to Eastern states and Florida. **DESCRIPTION:** A medium to large size, auriculate form with a concave base and drooping to expanding auricles. Many examples are serrated, some are fluted on both sides, and all have basal grinding. Resharpened examples are usually beveled on the right side of each face although left side beveling does occur. Thinness and high quality flaking is evident on many examples. This early type spread over most the U.S. and strongly influenced many other types to follow. **I.D. KEY:** Expanded auricles.

DALTON-HEMPHILL - Early Archaic, 9500 - 6000 B. P.

(Also see Cave Spring, Hardaway and Holland)

LOCATION: Midwestern to Eastern states. **DESCRIPTION:** A medium to large size point with expanded auricles and horizontal, tapered to weak shoulders. Blade edges are usually serrated and bases are ground. In later times, this variant developed into the *Hemphill* point. **I.D. KEY:** Straightened extended shoulders.

DALTON-HEMPHILL (continued)

G8, $100-$200
KY.

G8, $200-$350
Henry Co., TN.

G8, $300-$550
Obion Co., TN.

EC

DALTON-NUCKOLLS - Early Archaic, 9500 - 5000 B. P.

(Also see Dalton-Colbert and Hardaway)

G5, $20-$40
Humphreys Co., TN.

G6, $25-$50
Humphreys Co., TN.

G5, $20-$40
Humphreys Co., TN.

G7, $50-$100
Trigg Co., KY.

LOCATION: Midwestern to Southeastern states. Type site is in Humphreys Co., TN. **DESCRIPTION:** A medium to large size variant form, probably occuring from resharpening the Greenbrier Dalton. Bases are squared to lobbed to eared, and have a shallow concavity. **I.D. KEY:** Broad base and shoulders, flaking on blade.

DALTON-NUCKOLLS (continued)

G8, $100-$200
Livingston Co., KY.

G4, $20-$40
Humphreys Co., TN.

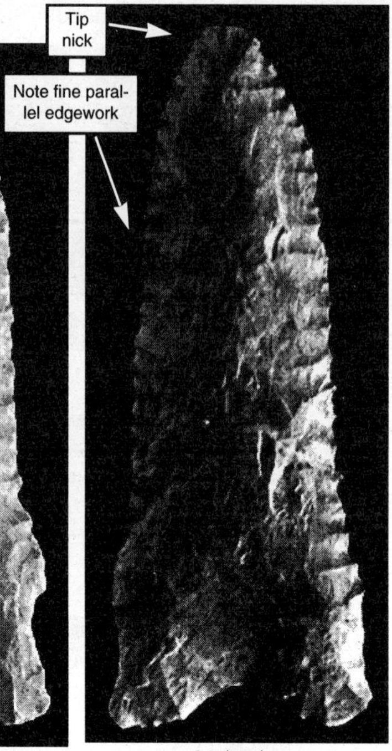

G5, $30-$60
Humphreys Co., TN.

DAMRON - Early to Middle Archaic, 8000 - 4000 B. P.

(Also see Autauga, Ecusta, Gibson, Palmer and St. Charles)

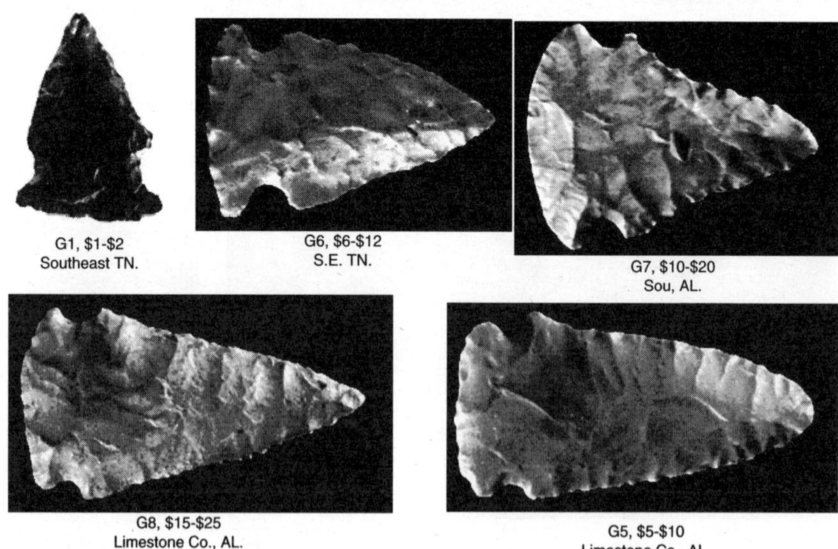

G1, $1-$2
Southeast TN.

G6, $6-$12
S.E. TN.

G7, $10-$20
Sou, AL.

G8, $15-$25
Limestone Co., AL.

G5, $5-$10
Limestone Co., AL.

LOCATION: Southeastern states. **DESCRIPTION:** A small to medium size, triangular, side-notched point with a wide, prominent, convex to straight base. **I.D. KEY:** Basal form.

DEBERT- Paleo, 11,000 - 9500 B. P.

(Also see Clovis and Dalton)

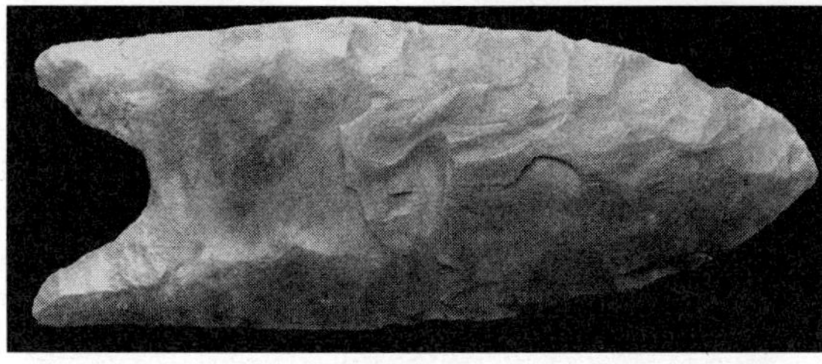

G8, $800-$1500
KY.

LOCATION: Northeastern to Eastern states. **DESCRIPTION:** A medium to large size, thin, auriculate point that evolved from *Clovis*. Most examples are fluted twice on each face resulting in a deep basal concavity. The second flute usually removed traces of the first fluting. A very rare form of late *Clovis* **I.D. KEY:** Deep basal notch.

DECATUR - Early Archaic, 9000 - 3000 B. P.

(Also see Cobbs Triangular, Dovetail, Hardin, Kirk and Lost Lake)

EC

G7, $60-$80
Hamilton Co., TN.

Actual size photos of an excellent example found in Hamilton Co., TN. These oblique photos illustrate the fractured tangs, stem sides and base that occur on this type. In rare cases the tip is also fractured on both sides. Shoulder and base fracturing also occurs in Abbey, Dovetail, Kirk and other Archaic forms.

G3, $4-$8
Walker Co., AL.

G4, $10-$20
Huntsville, AL.

G3, $4-$8
KY.

G3, $4-$8
S.E. TN.

LOCATION: Eastern states. **DESCRIPTION:** A small to medium size, serrated, corner notched point that is usually beveled on one side of each face. The base is usually broken off (fractured) by a blow inward from each corner of the stem. Sometimes the sides of the stem and backs of the tangs are also fractured, and rarely the tip may be fractured by a blow on each side directed towards the base. Bases are usually ground and flaking is of high quality. Basal/shoulder fracturing also occurs in *Dovetail, Eva, Kirk, Motley* and *Snyders*. Unfractured forms are called *Angelico Corner-Notched* in Virginia.

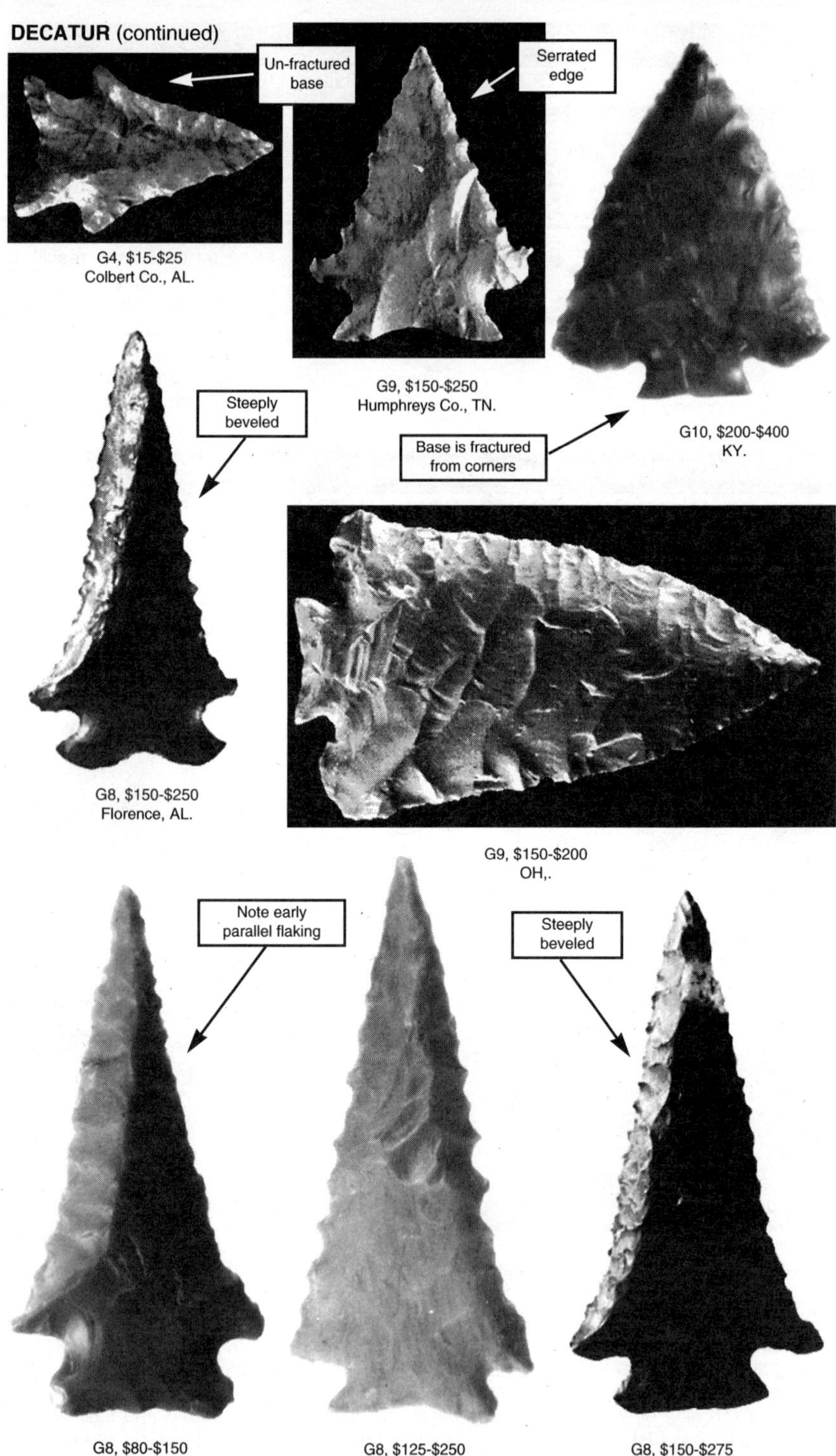

G4, $15-$25
Colbert Co., AL.

G9, $150-$250
Humphreys Co., TN.

G10, $200-$400
KY.

G8, $150-$250
Florence, AL.

G9, $150-$200
OH,.

G8, $80-$150
TN.

G8, $125-$250
IN.

G8, $150-$275
Coffee Lake, AL.

G10, $300-$600
TN.

G10, $350-$650
Herlan, KY.

G8, $180-$300
Coffee Lake, AL. Unusual base form. Base is fractured. found on a Decatur site.

DECATUR BLADE - Early Archaic, 9000 - 3000 B. P.

(Also see Hardaway Blade)

LOCATION: Eastern states. **DESCRIPTION:** A medium to large size, broad triangular blade with rounded corners and a straight base. A preform for *Decatur* points found on Decatur chipping sites.

G7, $5-$10
Morgan Co., AL. Found on a Decatur chipping site along with dozens of Decatur points.

DOVETAIL

(See St. Charles)

DRILL - Paleo to Historic, 14,000 - 200 B. P.

(Also see Addison Micro-Drill and Scraper)

LOCATION: Everywhere. **DESCRIPTION:** Although many drills were made from scratch, all point types were made into the drill form. Usually, heavily resharpened and broken points were salvaged and rechipped into drills. These objects were certainly used as drills (evidence of extreme edge wear), but there is speculation that some of these forms may have been used as pins for clothing, ornaments, ear plugs and other uses.

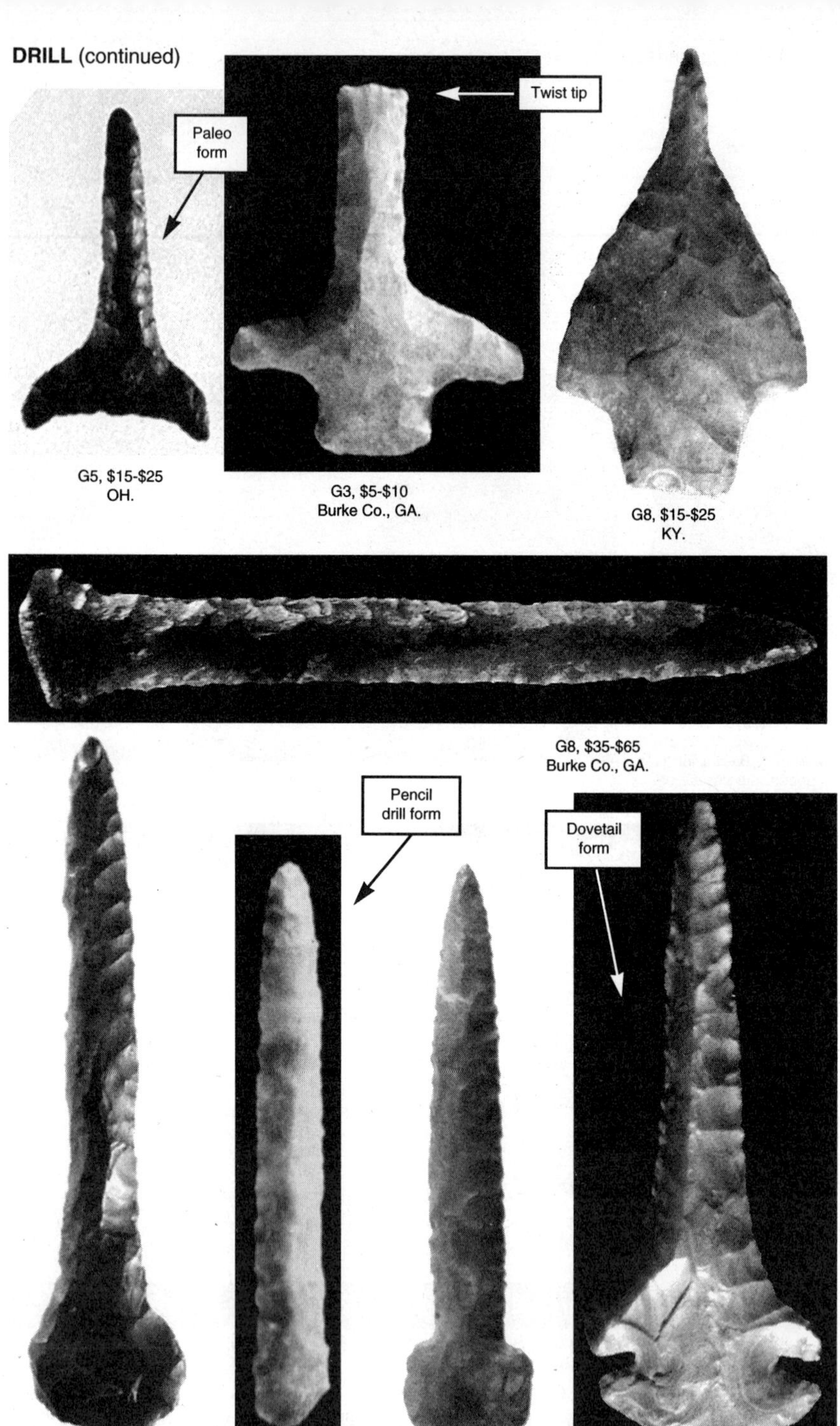

G5, $15-$25
OH.

G3, $5-$10
Burke Co., GA.

G8, $15-$25
KY.

G8, $35-$65
Burke Co., GA.

G8, $25-$45
OH.

G4, $10-$20
Burke Co., GA.

G6, $25-$45
KY.

G7, $90-$175
Lowndes Co., MS.

DUCK RIVER SWORD - Mississippian, 1100 - 600 B. P.

(Also see Adena Blade, Morse Knife and Tear Drop)

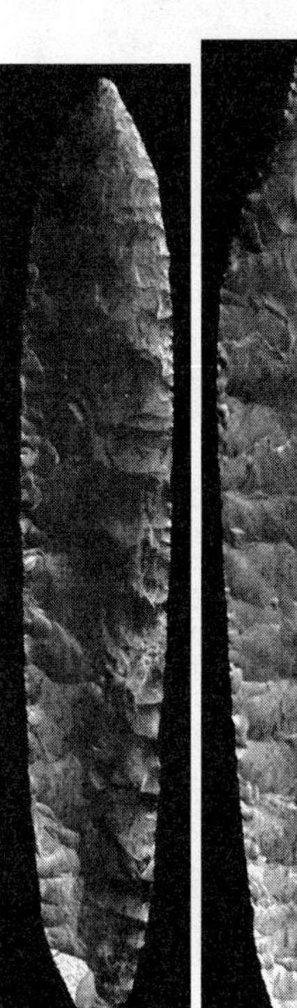

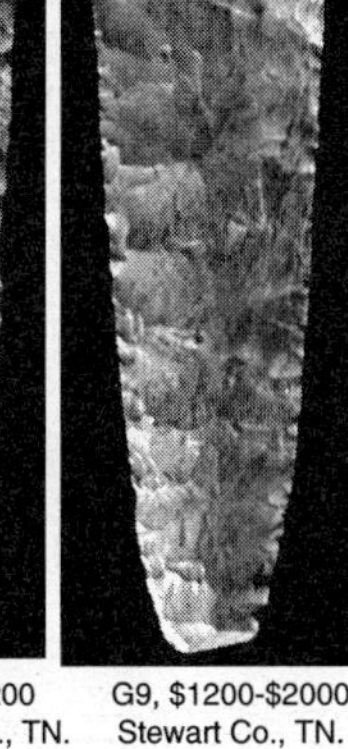

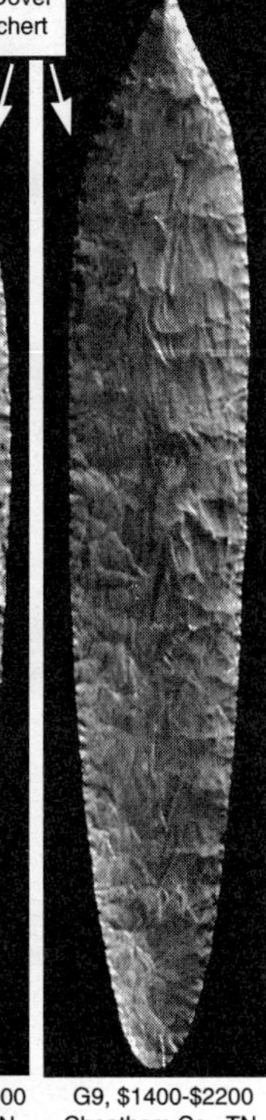

G8, $600-$1200
Montgomery Co., TN.

G9, $1200-$2000
Stewart Co., TN.

G9, $1400-$2200
Cheatham Co., TN.

G9, $2000-$2800
Stewart Co., TN.

G10, $3000-$4800
TN.

IMPORTANT
All points above are shown 1/2 size.

LOCATION: Southeastern states. **DESCRIPTION:** A very large, narrow, double pointed ceremonial blade with a rounded base and a mucronate tip. Made by the Mississippians and used in their Eagle dances, as depicted on their shell gorgets, particularly at the Great Busk festival in the Fall. The famous Duck River cache of this type was found in the 1940s on the Duck River in Tennessee with lengths up to 30 inches. All are made of dover flint. Beware of reproductions.

DURANT'S BEND - Woodland to Mississippian, 1600 - 1000 B. P.

(Also see Nova and Washington)

G5, $2-$3 ea., All Dallas Co., AL.

LOCATION: Alabama. **DESCRIPTION:** A small size, narrow, triangular point with flaring ears and a serrated blade. Made from nodular black chert or milky quartz.

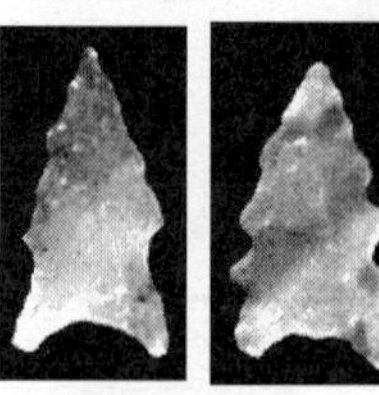

G7, \$5-\$10 ea.
All Dallas Co., AL.

G7, \$8-\$15
Dallas Co., AL.

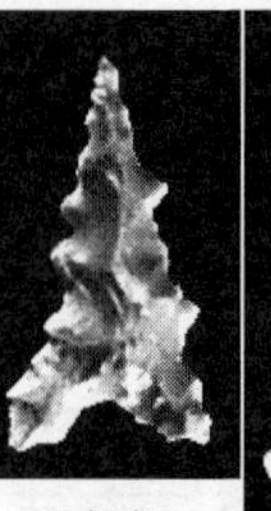

G10, \$25-\$45
Dallas Co., AL.

DURST - Woodland, 3000 - 2500 B. P.

(Also see Mud Creek and Swan Lake)

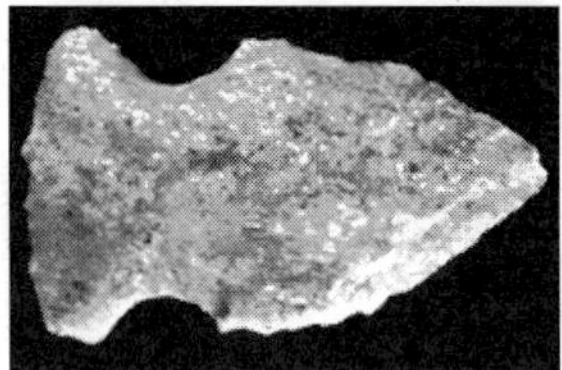

G5, \$2-\$4
Walker Co., AL.

G3, \$1-\$3
Sequatchie River, TN.

LOCATION: Midwestern to Southeastern states. **DESCRIPTION:** A small, thick, wide side-notched point with a large flaring and rounded base. Called *Holston Side-Notched* in Virginia.

DUVAL - Late Woodland, 2000 - 1000 B. P.

(Also see Bradley, Flint River & Schild Spike and Fishspear)

G6, \$2-\$4
Bristol, TN.

G6, \$2-\$4
Catoosa Co.,
GA.

LOCATION: Southeastern states. **DESCRIPTION:** A small to medium size, narrow, spike point with shallow side notches and a straight to concave base. The base can be slight to moderate.

EBENEZER - Woodland, 2000 - 1500 B. P.

(Also see Buggs Island, Gary, Montgomery and Morrow Mountain)

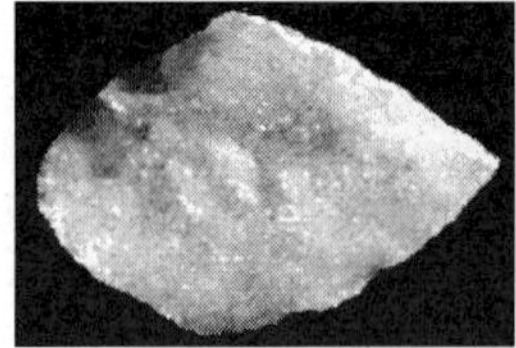

G8, \$2-\$4
Dallas Co., AL.

G5, \$1-\$2
Lawrence Co., AL.

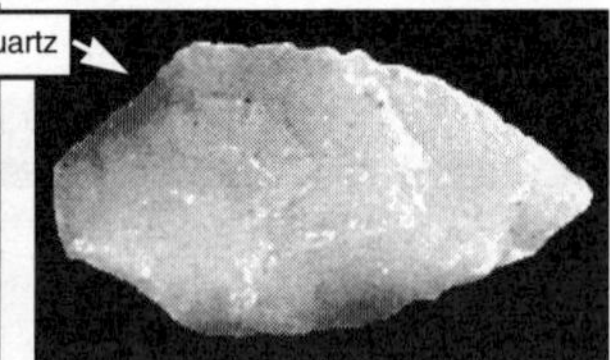

G8, \$3-\$6
Dallas Co., AL.

LOCATION: Southeastern states. **DESCRIPTION:** A small size, broad, triangular point with a short, rounded stem. Some are round base triangles with no stem. Shoulders are tapered to square. Very similar to the earlier *Morrow Mountain Round Base* but with random Woodland chipping. Related to *Candy Creek, Camp Creek* and *Nolichucky.*

ECUSTA - Early Archaic, 8000 - 5000 B. P.

(Also see Autauga, Brewerton, Damron and Palmer)

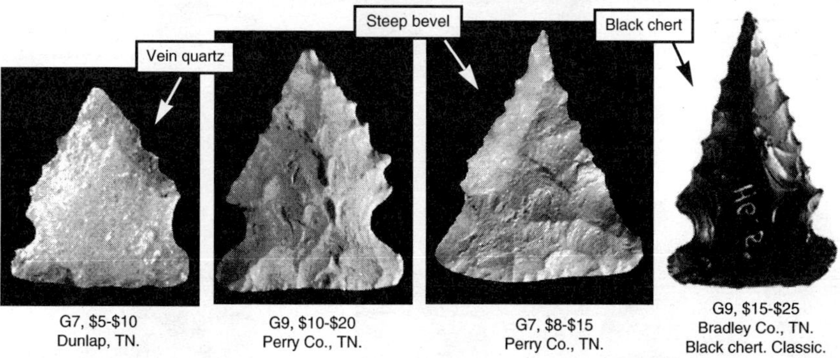

G7, $5-$10
Dunlap, TN.

G9, $10-$20
Perry Co., TN.

G7, $8-$15
Perry Co., TN.

G9, $15-$25
Bradley Co., TN.
Black chert. Classic.

LOCATION: Southeastern states. **DESCRIPTION:** A small size, serrated, side-notched point with usually one side of each face steeply beveled. Although examples exist with all four sides beveled and flaked to a median ridge. The base and notches are ground. Very similar to *Autauga*, with the latter being corner-notched.

EC

ELK RIVER - Early Archaic, 8000 - 5000 B. P.

(Also see Benton and Buzzard Roost Creek)

Note diagonal flaking

G6, $20-$40
Limestone Co., AL.

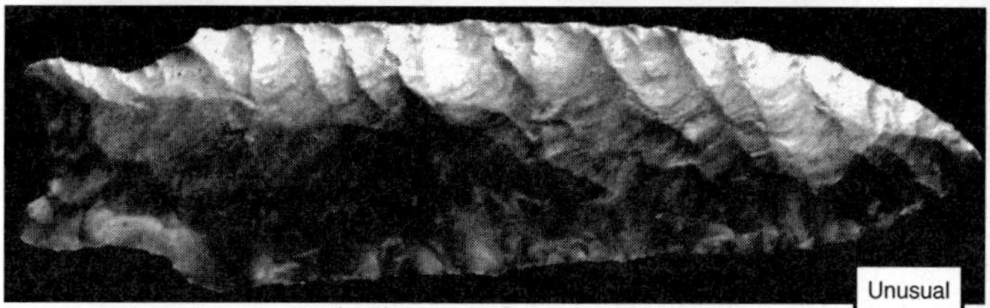

G7, $40-$95, Humphreys Co., TN.

Unusual bulbous base

G6, $35-$60, Humphreys Co., TN.

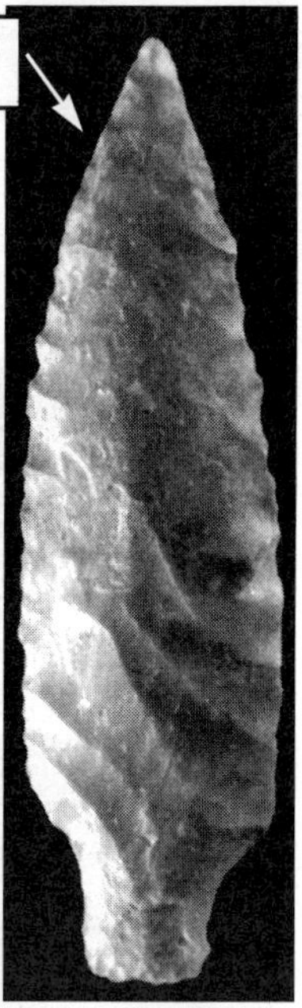

G6, $25-45
Humphreys Co., TN.

LOCATION: Southeastern states. **DESCRIPTION:** A medium to large size, narrow, stemmed blade with oblique parallel flaking. Shoulders are tapered, straight or barbed. Stems are parallel, contracting, expanding, bulbous or bifurcated. Believed to be related to *Benton* points. **I.D. KEY:** Squared base, diagonal parallel flaking.

ELK RIVER (continued)

Note diagonal flaking

G9, $100-$200
Walker Co., AL.

G8, $100-$200
KY.

G10, $250-$450
TN.

ELORA - Middle to Late Archaic, 6000 - 3000 B. P.

(Also see Maples, Pickwick and Savannah River)

G5, $8-$15
GA.

LOCATION: Southeastern states. **DESCRIPTION:** A medium size, broad, thick point with tapered shoulders and a short, contracting stem that is sometimes fractured or snapped off. However, some examples have finished bases. Early examples are serrated. **I.D. KEY:** One barb sharper, edgework.

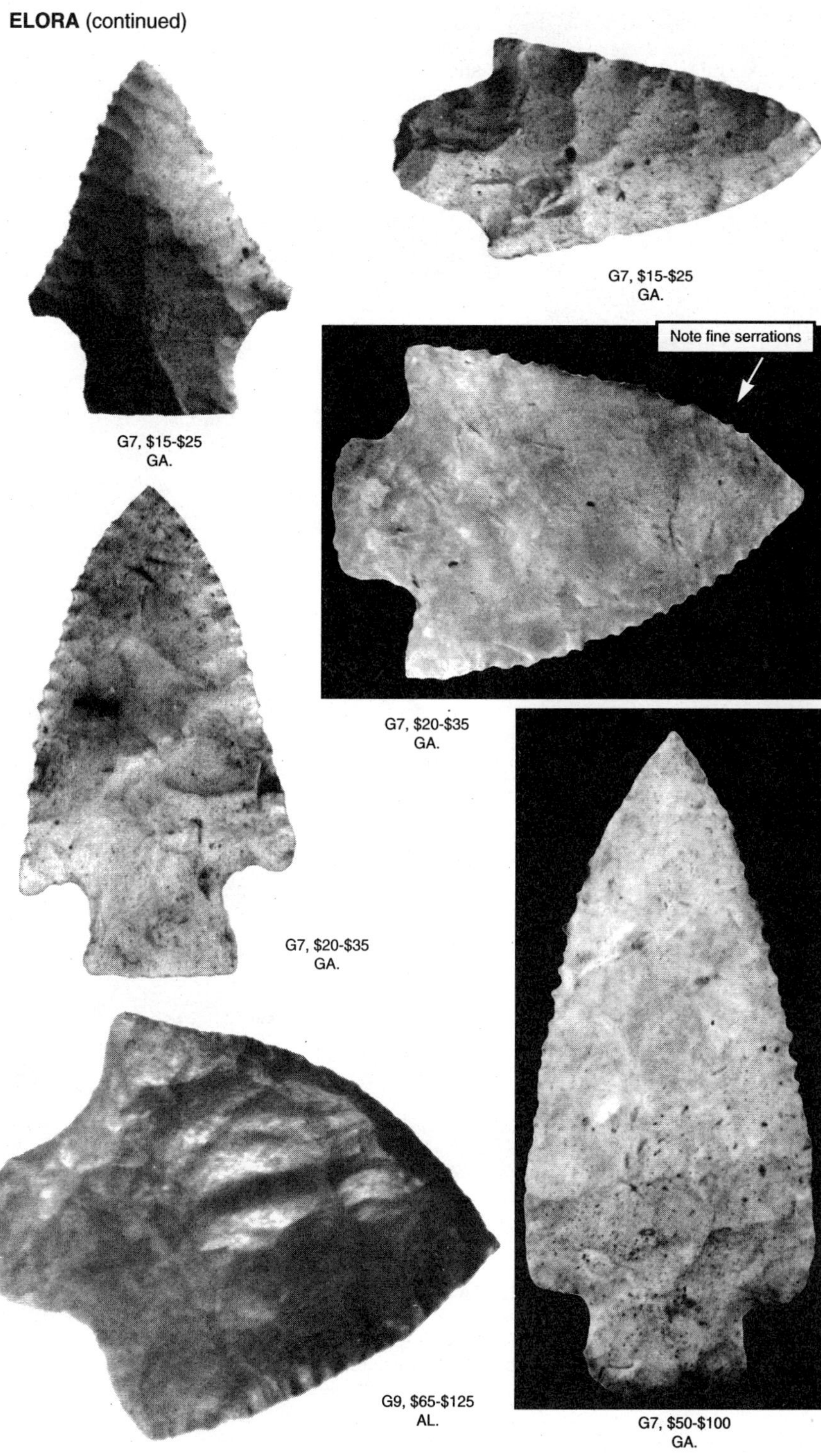

G7, $15-$25
GA.

G7, $15-$25
GA.

G7, $20-$35
GA.

G7, $20-$35
GA.

G9, $65-$125
AL.

G7, $50-$100
GA.

ETLEY - Late Archaic, 4000 - 2500 B. P.

(Also see Hardin, Mehlville, Pickwick and Stilwell)

LOCATION: Southeastern states. **DESCRIPTION:** A medium size, broad, thick point with tapered shoulders and a short, contracting stem that is sometimes fractured or snapped off. However, some examples have finished bases. Early examples are serrated. **I.D. KEY:** One barb sharper, edgework.

G8, $200-$350
Dekalb Co., IN.

EVA - Early to Middle Archaic, 8000 - 5000 B. P.

(Also see Hamilton Stemmed and Wade)

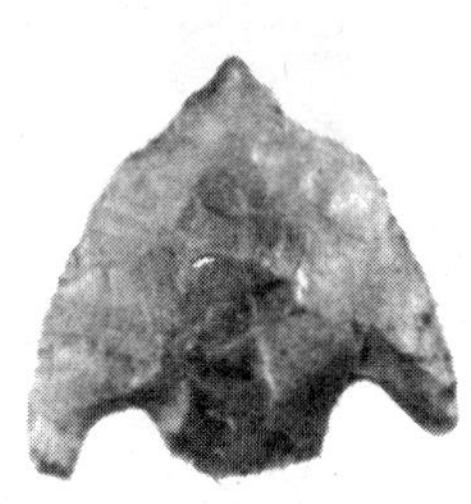

G4, $8-$15
New Era, TN.

G5, $15-$25
Humphreys Co., TN.

Note early collateral flaking

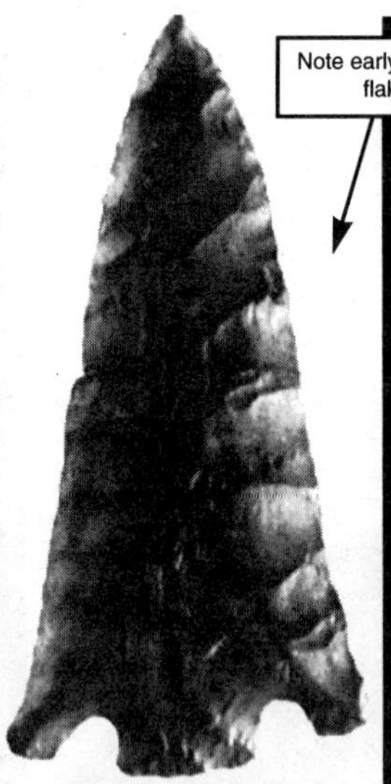

G8, $60-$100
KY.

G6, $50-$100
Parsons, TN.

LOCATION: West Tennessee to SW Kentucky. Type site, Eva island in Humphreys Co., TN. **DESCRIPTION:** A medium to large size, triangular point with shallow basal notches, recurved sides and sometimes flaring tangs. Early examples show parallel flaking. **I.D. KEY:** Basal notches, Archaic flaking. A large Eva cache was found that included a Pickwick point.

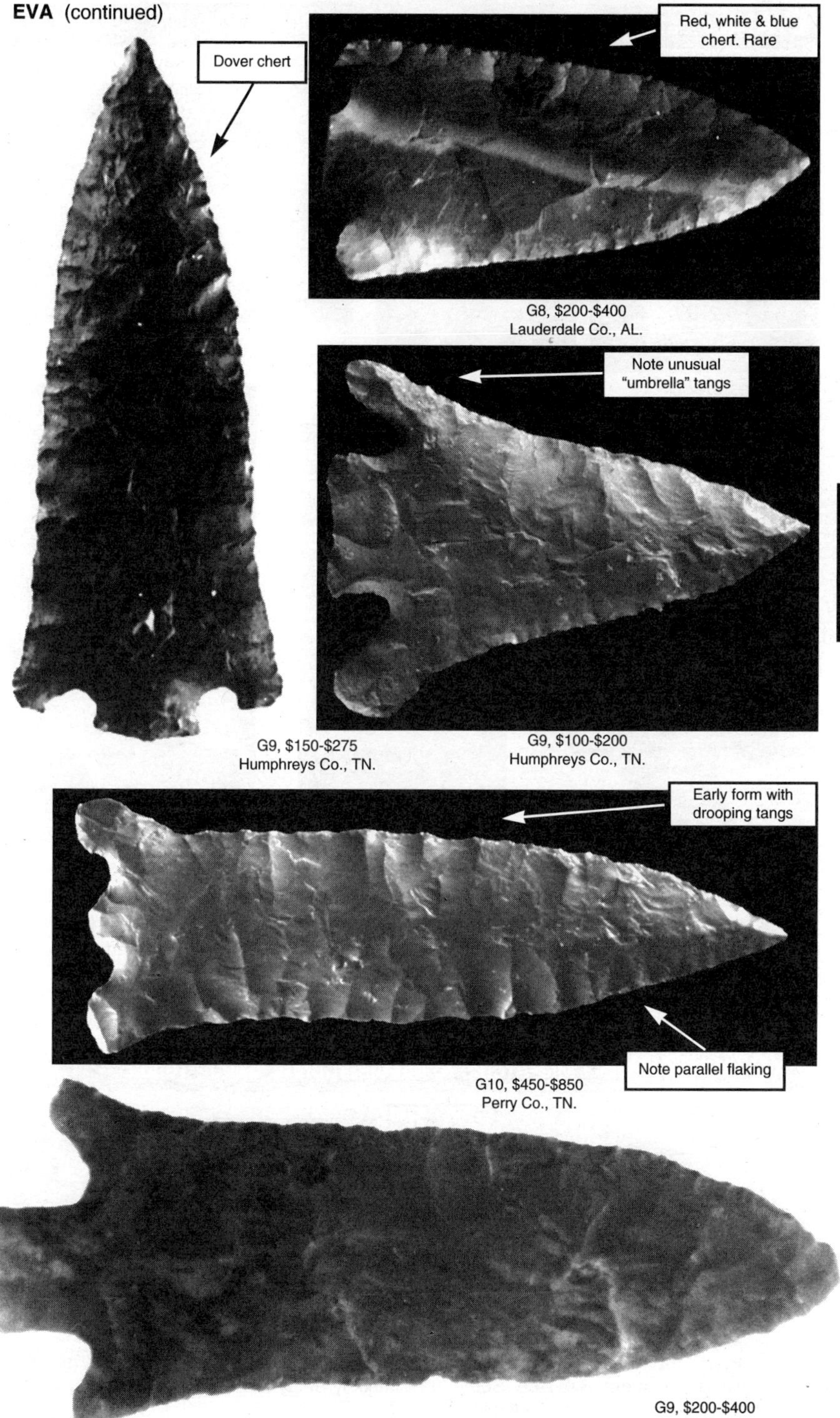

G8, $200-$400
Lauderdale Co., AL.

G9, $150-$275
Humphreys Co., TN.

G9, $100-$200
Humphreys Co., TN.

G10, $450-$850
Perry Co., TN.

G9, $200-$400
TN.

EVANS - Late Archaic to Woodland, 4000 - 2000 B. P.

(Also see Benton, Leighton, Ohio Double-Notched and Turkeytail)

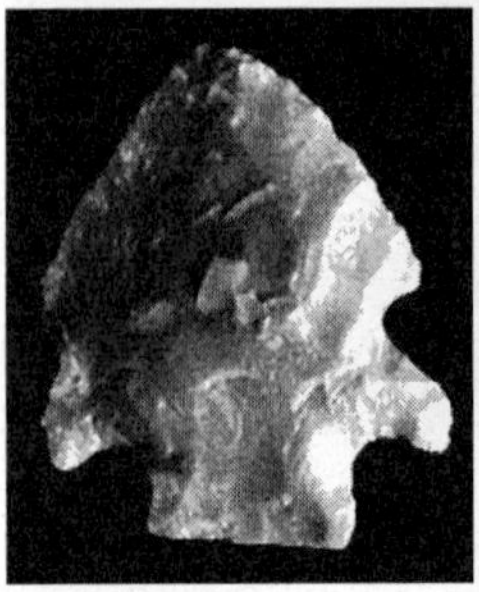

G5, $10-$20
Hamilton Co., TN.

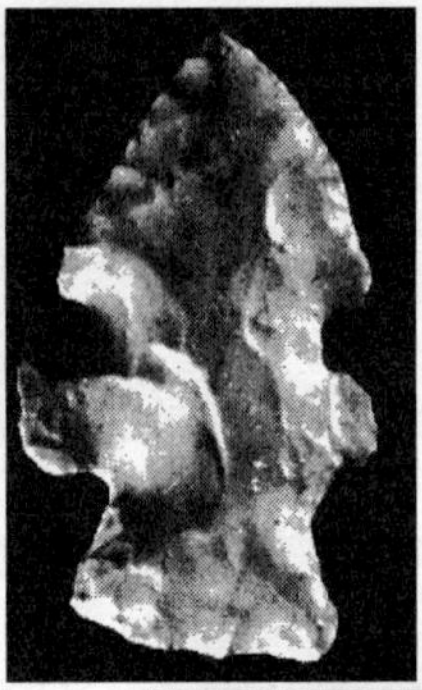

G6, $20-$35
Natchez, MS.

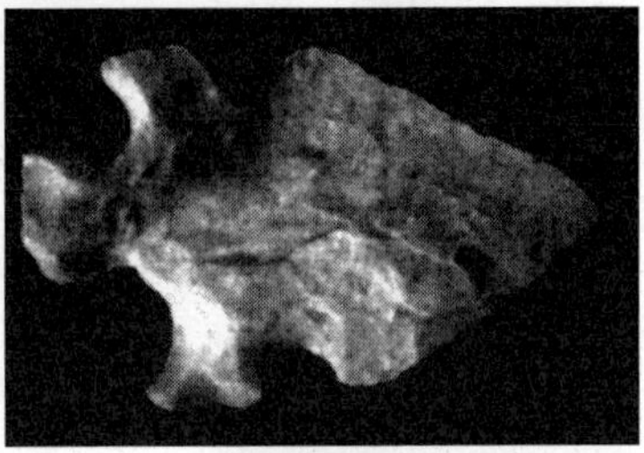

G6, $20-$40
Natchez, MS.

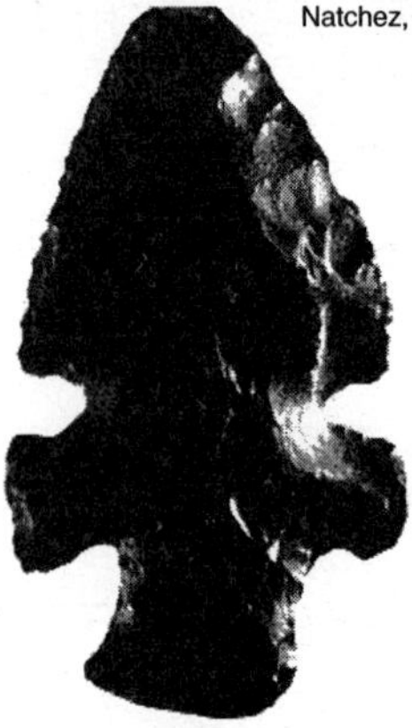

G4, $15-$25
Natchez, MS.

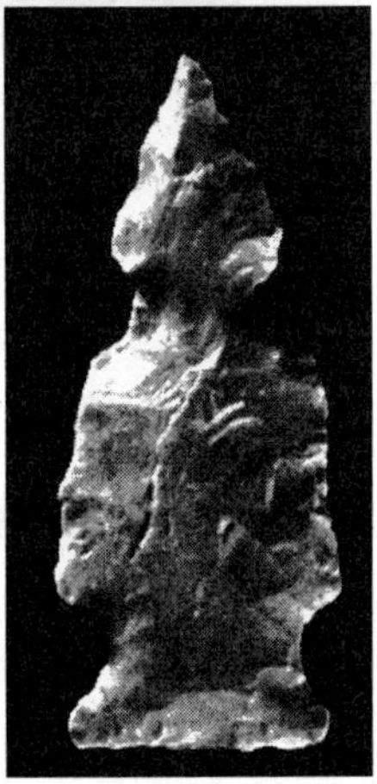

G5, $15-$25
KY.

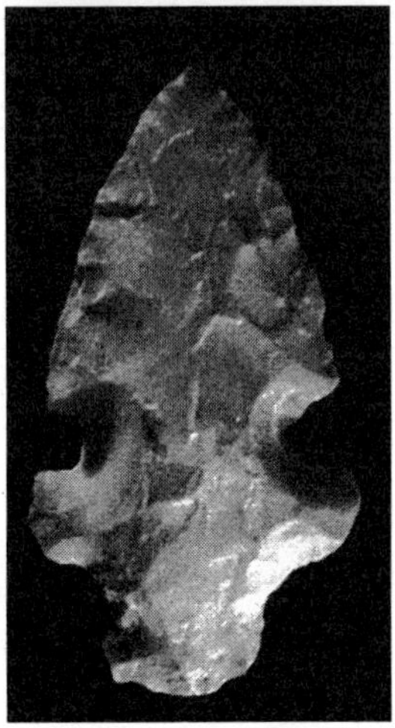

G8, $25-$50
Natxhez, MS.

LOCATION: Midwestern to Southeastern states. **DESCRIPTION:** A medium to large size stemmed point that is notched on each side somewhere between the point and shoulders. A similar form is found in Ohio and called *Ohio Double-Notched.*

EXOTIC FORMS - Mid-Archic to Mississippian, 5000 - 1000 B. P.

Made from
Adena Waubesa

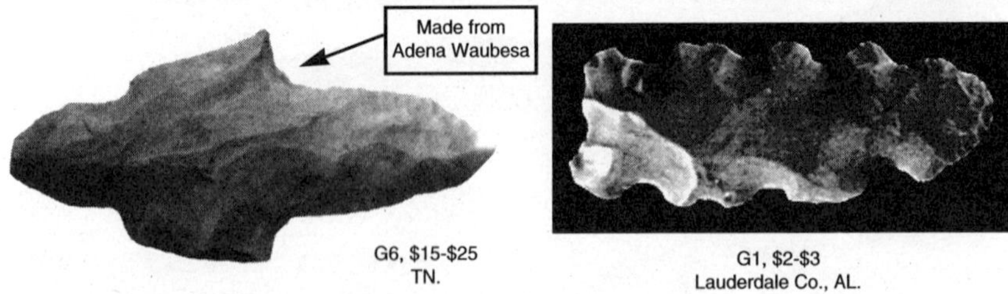

G6, $15-$25
TN.

G1, $2-$3
Lauderdale Co., AL.

LOCATION: Throughout North America. **DESCRIPTION:** The forms illustrated on this and the following pages are very rare. Some are definitely effigy forms while others may be no more than unfinished and unintentional doodles.

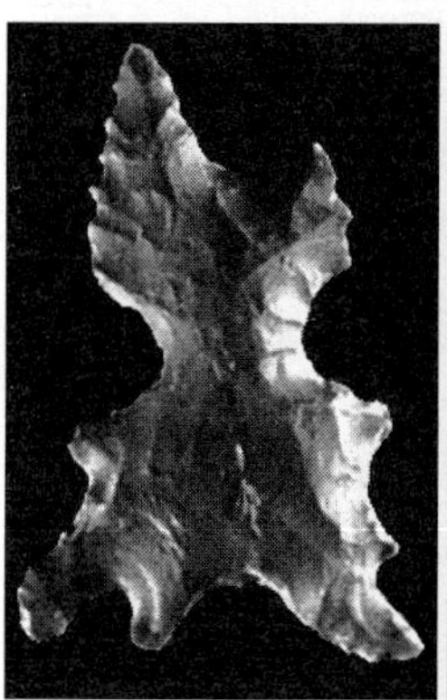
G7, $40-$80
Humphreys Co., TN.

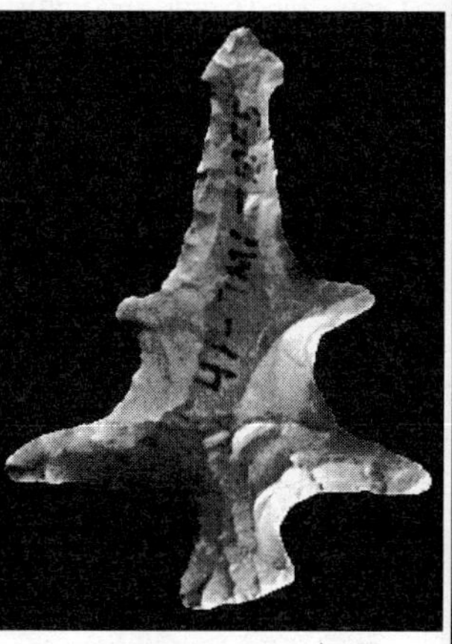
G7, $60-$100
Lauderdale Co., AL.

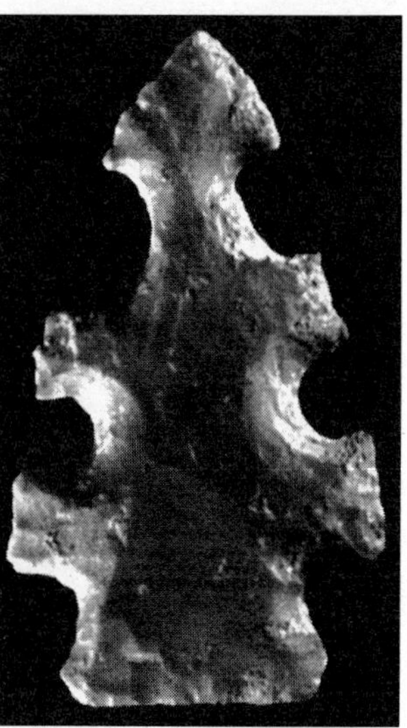
G10, $100-$200
TN.

FAIRLAND - Woodland, 3000 - 1500 B. P.

(Also see Hardaway, Johnson, Limestone and Steubenville)

G6, $10-$20
MS.

G6, $5-$25
Perry Co., TN.

LOCATION: Texas, Arkansas, and Mississippi. **DESCRIPTION:** A small to medium size, thin, expanded stem point with a concave base that is usually thinned. Shoulders can be weak and tapered to sightly barbed. **I.D. KEY:** Basal form, systematic form of flaking.

FISHSPEAR - Early to Middle Archaic, 9000 - 4000 B. P.

(Also see Duval and Table Rock)

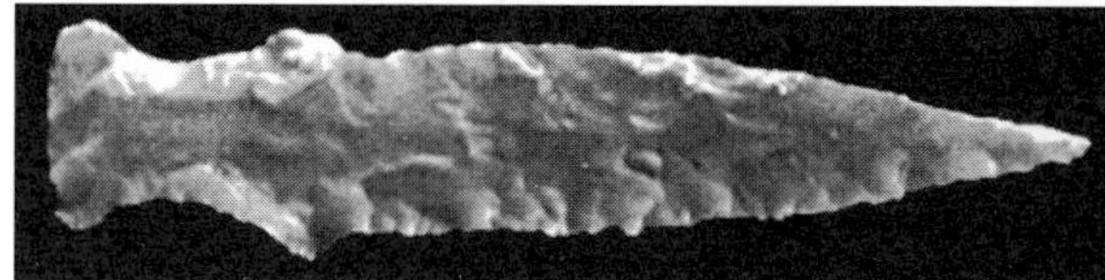
G8, $35-$65
Parsons, TN.

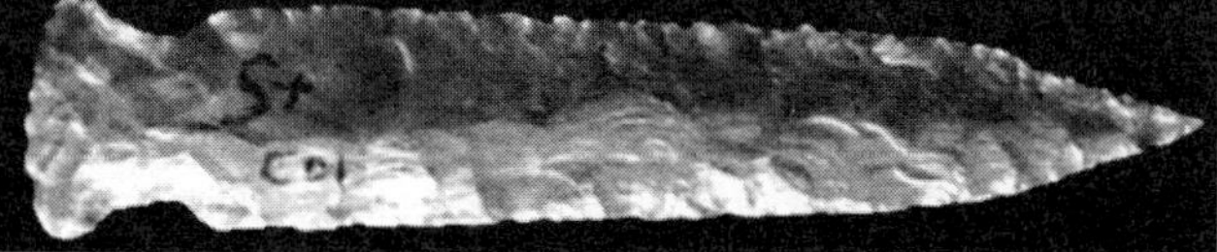
G9, $60-$100
West TN.

LOCATION: Eastern states. **DESCRIPTION:** A medium to large size, narrow, thick, point with wide side notches. Bases are usually ground and blade edges can be serrated. Named due to its appearance that resembles a fish.

FLINT CREEK - Late Archaic to Woodland, 3500 - 1000 B. P.

(Also see Cotaco Creek, Mud Creek and Pontchartrain)

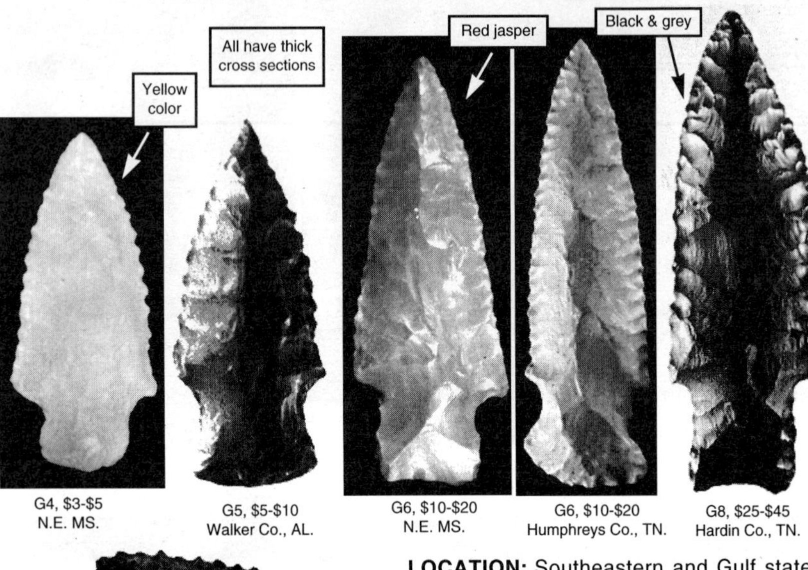

G4, $3-$5 N.E. MS.

G5, $5-$10 Walker Co., AL.

G6, $10-$20 N.E. MS.

G6, $10-$20 Humphreys Co., TN.

G8, $25-$45 Hardin Co., TN.

G5, $5-$10 Walker Co., AL.

LOCATION: Southeastern and Gulf states. **DESCRIPTION:** A medium to large size, narrow, thick, serrated, expanded stem point. Shoulders can be horizontal, tapered or barbed. Base can be expanded, parallel sided or rounded. **I.D. KEY:** Thickness and flaking near point.

FLINT RIVER SPIKE - Late Archaic to Woodland, 4000 - 1800 B. P.

(Also see Bradley Spike and Schild Spike)

G7, $8-$15 West TN.

LOCATION: Southeastern states. **DESCRIPTION:** A small to medium size, narrow, spike point with no stem or shoulders. Blade sides are usually convex and the base can be either straight or rounded. **I.D. KEY:** Thickness and narrow blade.

FOLSOM - Paleo, 11,000 - 9000 B. P.

(Also see Clovis, Cumberland, Redstone and Wheeler)

LOCATION: Midwestern to Western states. **DESCRIPTION:** A small to medium size, thin, high quality, fluted point with contracted, pointed auricles and a concave base. Fluting usually extends the entire length of each face. A very rare type, even in area of highest incidence. Usually found in association with extinct bison fossil remains. **I.D.KEY:** Flaking style (Excessive secondary flaking)

G8, $900-$1500 Huntsville, AL., Redstone Arsenal Paleo site.

FORT ANCIENT - Mississippian to Historic, 800 - 400 B. P.

(Also see Hamilton, Madison and Sand Mountain)

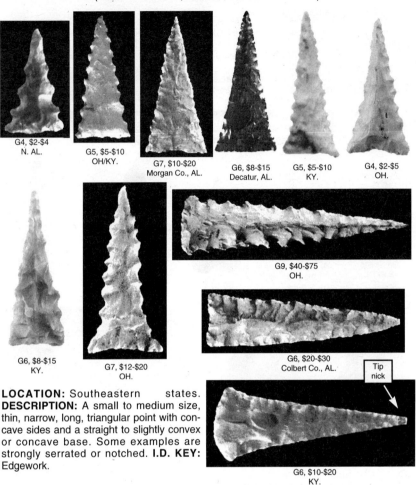

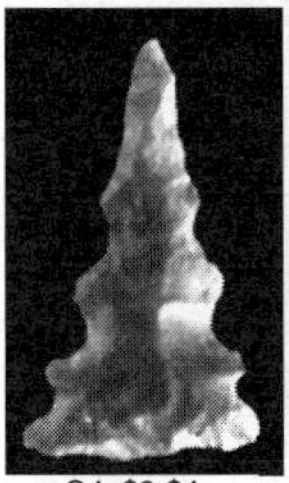

G4, $2-$4
N. AL.

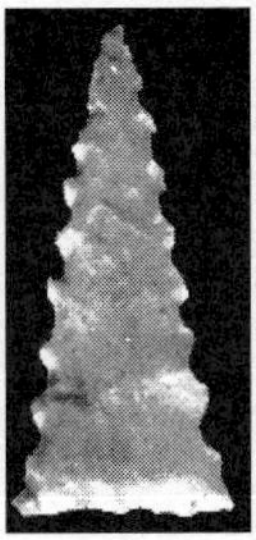

G5, $5-$10
OH/KY.

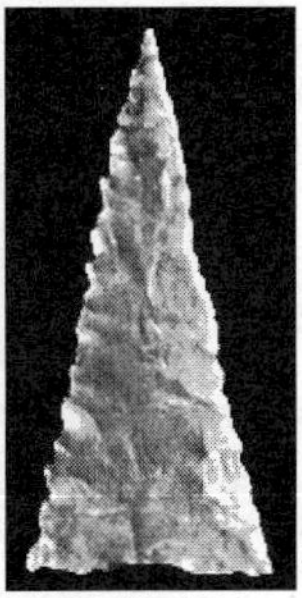

G7, $10-$20
Morgan Co., AL.

G6, $8-$15
Decatur, AL.

G5, $5-$10
KY.

G4, $2-$5
OH.

G6, $8-$15
KY.

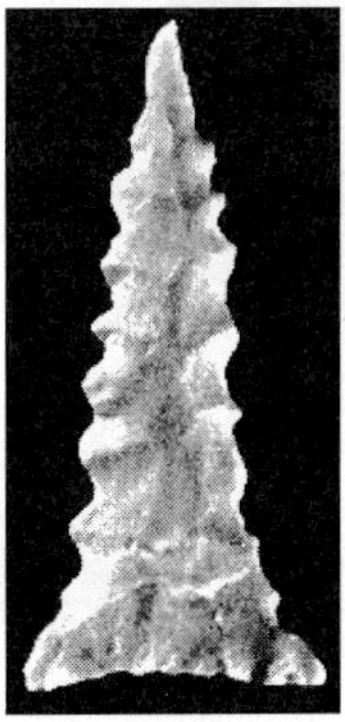

G7, $12-$20
OH.

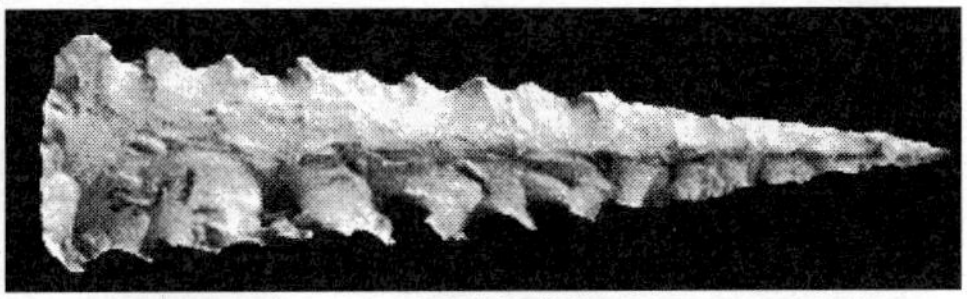

G9, $40-$75
OH.

G6, $20-$30
Colbert Co., AL.

Tip nick

G6, $10-$20
KY.

LOCATION: Southeastern states. **DESCRIPTION:** A small to medium size, thin, narrow, long, triangular point with concave sides and a straight to slightly convex or concave base. Some examples are strongly serrated or notched. **I.D. KEY:** Edgework.

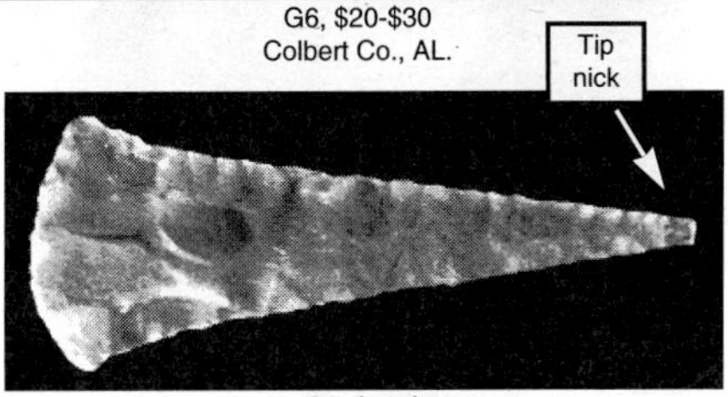

EC

FORT ANCIENT BLADE - Mississippian to Historic, 800 - 400 B. P.

(Also see Copena)

G8, $10-$20
KY.

G8, $15-$30
Mason Co., KY.

LOCATION: Eastern to Southeastern states. **DESCRIPTION:** A medium size triangular blade with a squared base. Blade edges expand to meet the base **I.D. KEY:** Basal form.

FOUNTAIN CREEK - Early Archaic, 9000 - 7000 B. P.

(Also see Kirk Serrated)

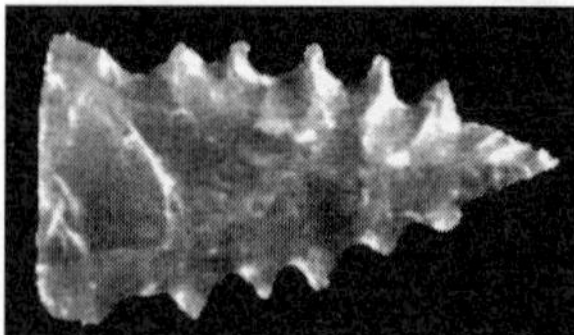

LOCATION: North Carolina into east Tennessee. **DESCRIPTION:** A medium size, narrow point with notched blade edges and a short, rounded base which is ground. **I.D. KEY:** Edgework.

G10, $20-$35
Dayton, TN.

FOX VALLEY - Early to Middle Archaic, 9000 - 4000 B. P.

(Also see Frederick, Jude, Kanawha, Kirk, LeCroy and Stanly)

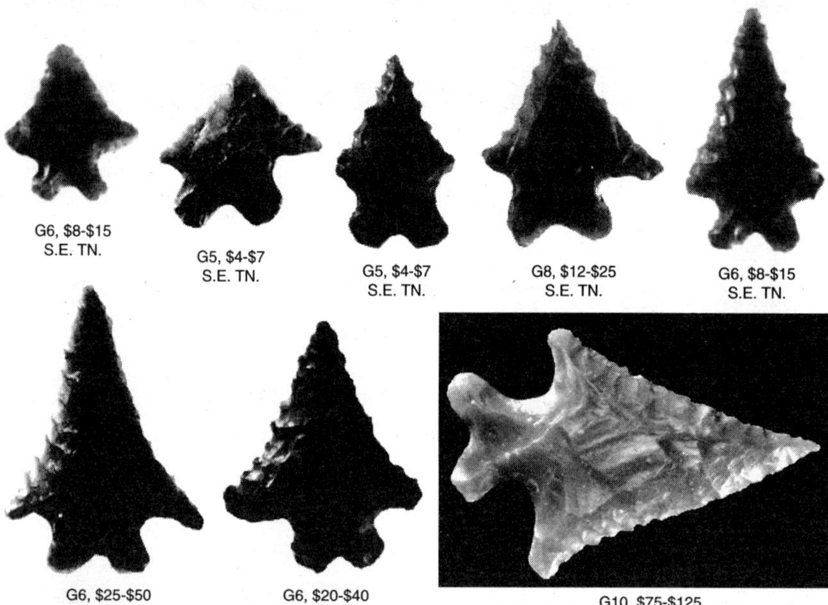

G6, $8-$15
S.E. TN.

G5, $4-$7
S.E. TN.

G5, $4-$7
S.E. TN.

G8, $12-$25
S.E. TN.

G6, $8-$15
S.E. TN.

G6, $25-$50
Monteray, TN.

G6, $20-$40
Watts Bar, TN.

G10, $75-$125
Wayne Co., KY.

LOCATION: Eastern states. **DESCRIPTION:** A small size, triangular point with flaring shoulders and a short bifurcated stem. Shoulders are sometimes clipped winged and have a tendency to turn towards the tip. Blades exhibit early parallel flaking and the edges are usually serrated. **I.D. KEY:** Bifurcated base and barbs.

FRAZIER - Middle to Late Archaic, 7000 - 3000 B. P.

(Also see Big Sandy and Copena)

G9, $15-$30
Smith Co., TN.

LOCATION: Southeastern states. **DESCRIPTION:** A generally narrow, medium to large size lanceolate blade with a slightly concave to straight base. Flaking technique and shape is identical to that of *Big Sandy* points (minus the notches) and is found on *Big Sandy* sites. Could this type be unnotched *Big Sandy's*? **I.D. KEY:** Archaic flaking.

G9, $25-$35
West TN.

FREDERICK - Early to Middle Archaic, 9000 - 4000 B. P.

(Also see Fox Valley, Garth Slough, Jude, Kirk, LeCroy, Rice Lobbed and Stanly)

G4, $6-$12
TN.

G6, $15-$30
CookevilleTN.
Classic form.

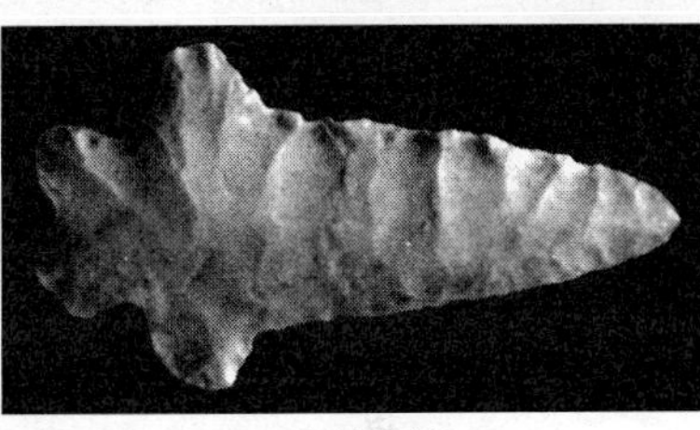

G7, $20-$40
S.E. TN. Classic form.

LOCATION: Southeastern states. **DESCRIPTION:** A small to medium size point with flaring shoulders and an extended narrow bifurcated base. A variation of the Fox Valley type. In the classic form, shoulders are almost bulbous and exaggerated.

GARTH SLOUGH - Early Archaic, 9000 - 4000 B. P.

(Also see Fox Valley, Frederick, Jude and Stanly)

G5, $8-$15
Chattanooga, TN.

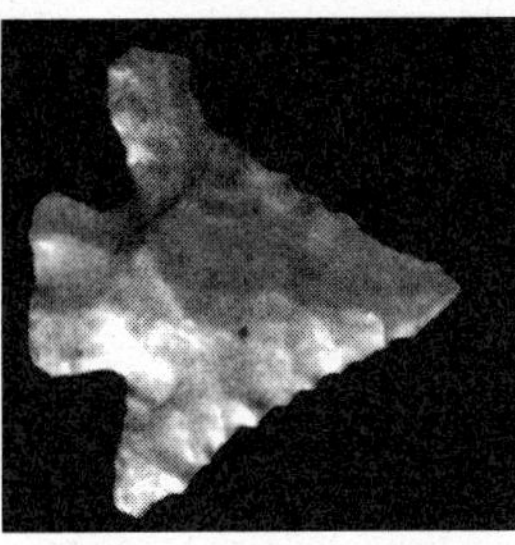

G6, $15-$30
W. TN.

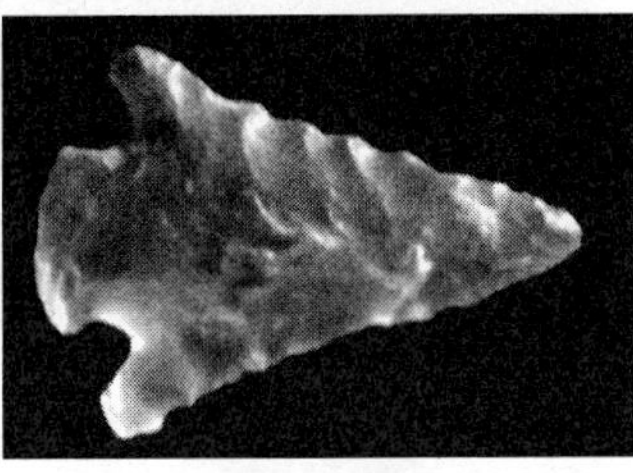

G5, $15-$25
Morgan Co., AL.

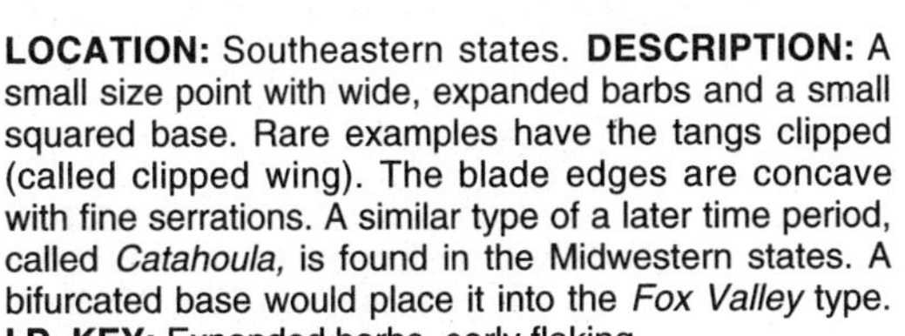

LOCATION: Southeastern states. **DESCRIPTION:** A small size point with wide, expanded barbs and a small squared base. Rare examples have the tangs clipped (called clipped wing). The blade edges are concave with fine serrations. A similar type of a later time period, called *Catahoula,* is found in the Midwestern states. A bifurcated base would place it into the *Fox Valley* type. **I.D. KEY:** Expanded barbs, early flaking.

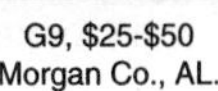

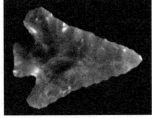

G9, $25-$50
Morgan Co., AL.

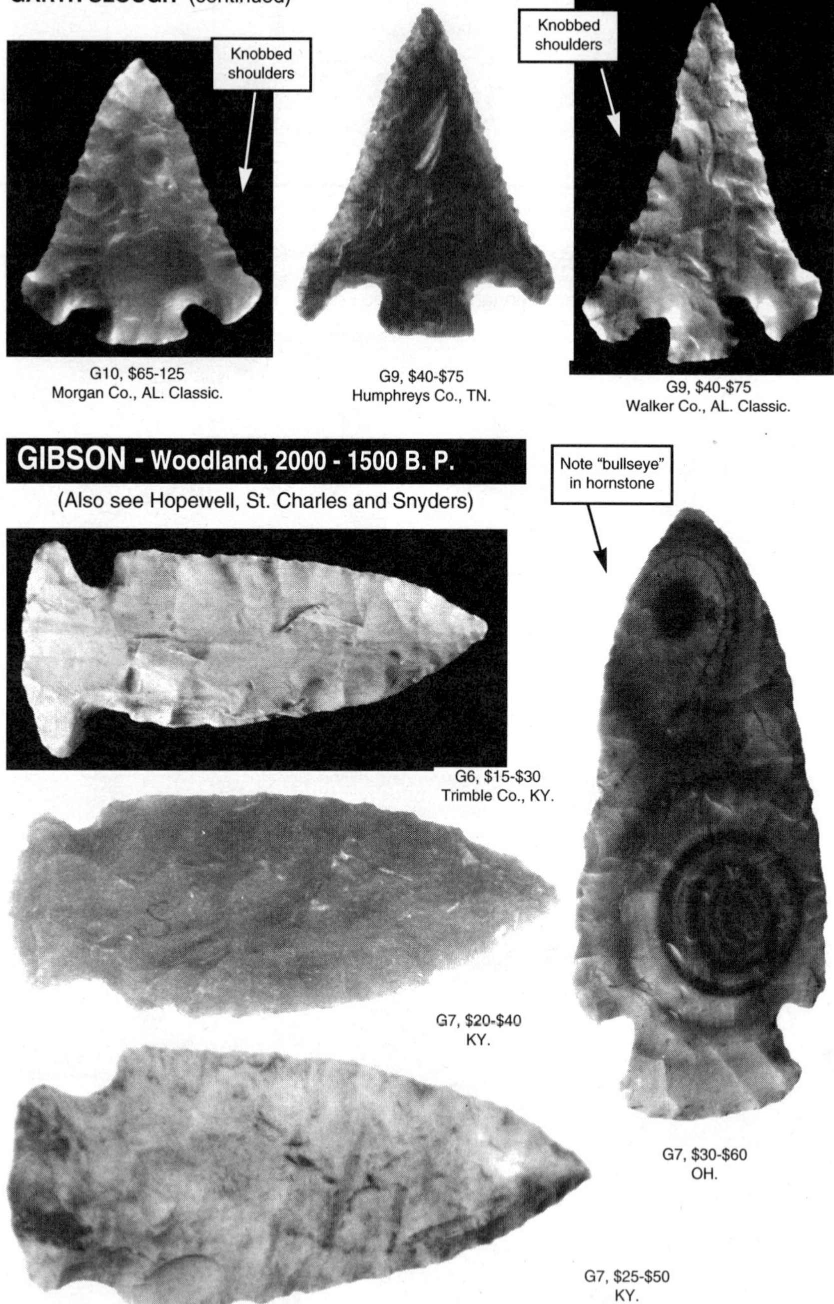

G10, $65-125
Morgan Co., AL. Classic.

G9, $40-$75
Humphreys Co., TN.

G9, $40-$75
Walker Co., AL. Classic.

GIBSON - Woodland, 2000 - 1500 B. P.

(Also see Hopewell, St. Charles and Snyders)

G6, $15-$30
Trimble Co., KY.

G7, $20-$40
KY.

G7, $30-$60
OH.

G7, $25-$50
KY.

LOCATION: Midwestern to Eastern states. Type site is in Calhoun Co., Illinois. **DESCRIPTION:** A medium to large size side to corner notched point with a large, convex base. The base is typically broader than the blade. Made by the *Snyders* people. **I.D. KEY:** Short, broad base.

GOLONDRINA - Transitional Paleo, 9000 - 7000 B. P.

(Also see Angostura, Beaver Lake, Clovis Unfluted, Dalton, Jeff and Quad)

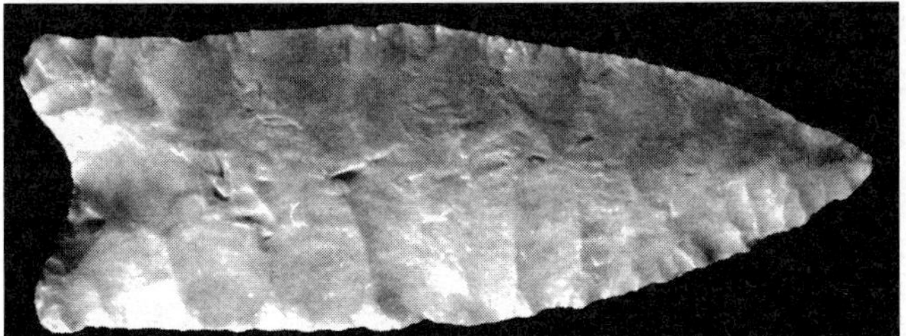

G8, $200-$400
Dyersburg, TN.

LOCATION: Texas into Arkansas and W. Tennessee. **DESCRIPTION:** A medium to large size auriculate point with rounded ears and a deeply concave base. Believed to be related to Dalton. **I.D. Key:** Expanded ears, paleo flaking.

GRAVER - Paleo to Archaic, 14,000 - 4000 B. P.

(Also see Perforator and Scraper)

G6, $10-$15
Humphreys Co., TN.

G6, $25-$40
Humphreys Co., TN.

LOCATION: Found on Paleo and Archaic sites throughout North America. **DESCRIPTION:** An irregular shaped uniface tool with sharp, pointed projections used for puncturing, incising, tattooing, etc. Some examples served a dual purpose for scraping as well. In later times, *Perforators* took the place of *Gravers*.

GREENBRIER - Transitional Paleo, 9500 - 6000 B. P.

(Also see Dalton-Greenbrier, Hardaway and Pine Tree)

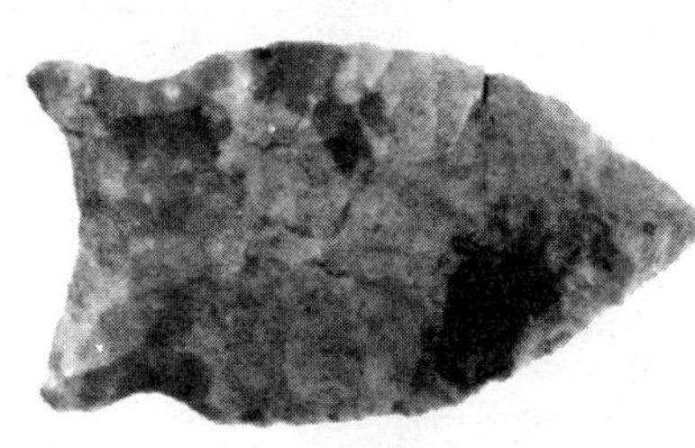

G6, $45-$90
KY.

LOCATION: Southeastern states. **DESCRIPTION:** A medium to large size, auriculate point with tapered shoulders and broad, weak side notches. Blade edges are usually finely serrated. The base can be concave, lobbed, eared, straight or bifurcated and is ground. Early examples can be fluted. This type developed from the *Dalton* point as well as directly from the *Clovis* point, and later evolved into other types such as the *Pine Tree* point. **I.D. KEY:** Heavy grinding in shoulders, good secondary edgework.

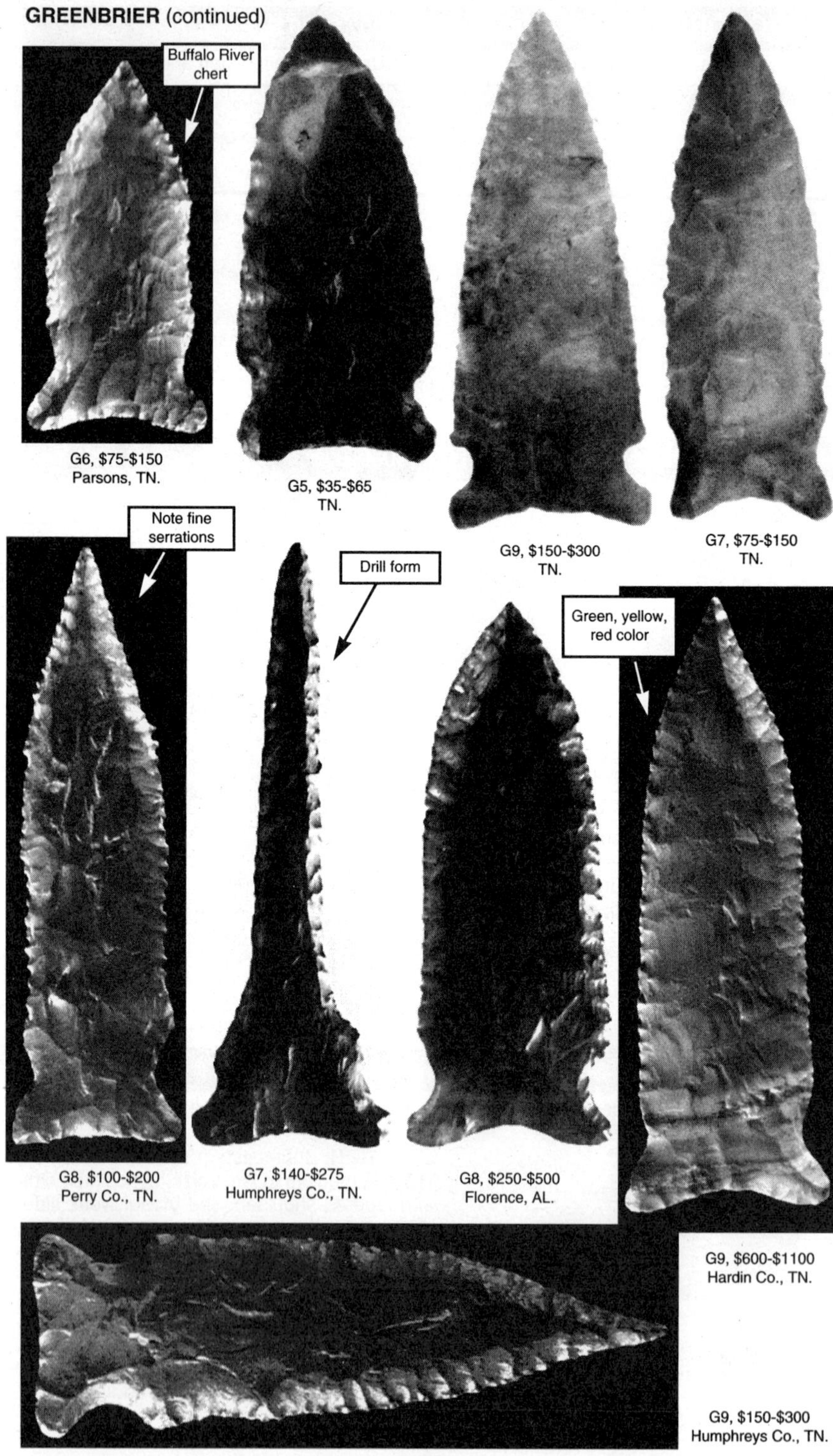

G6, $75-$150
Parsons, TN.

G5, $35-$65
TN.

G9, $150-$300
TN.

G7, $75-$150
TN.

G8, $100-$200
Perry Co., TN.

G7, $140-$275
Humphreys Co., TN.

G8, $250-$500
Florence, AL.

G9, $600-$1100
Hardin Co., TN.

G9, $150-$300
Humphreys Co., TN.

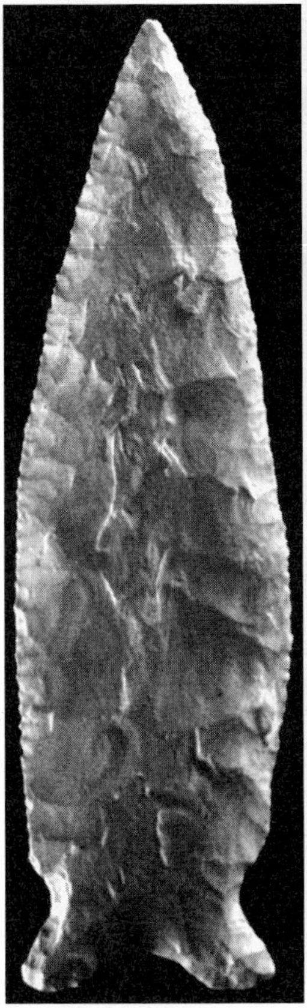

Red jasper

G10, $800-$1600
Hardin Co., TN.

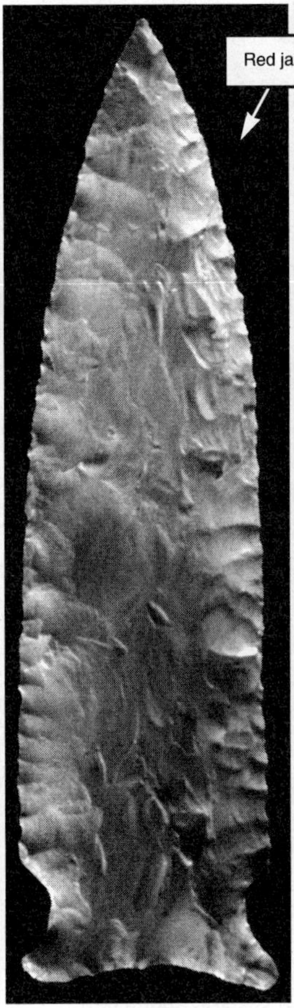

G9, $900-$1800
Parsons, TN.

G10, $1500-$2500
Hardin Co., TN. Classic.

EC

GREENEVILLE - Woodland, 3000 - 1500 B. P.

(Also see Camp Creek, Guntersville, Madison and Nolichucky)

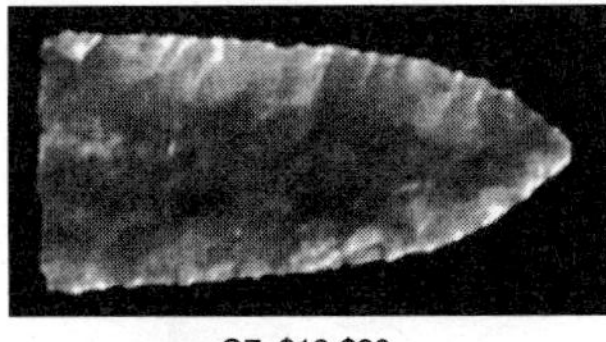

G7, $12-$20
E. KY.

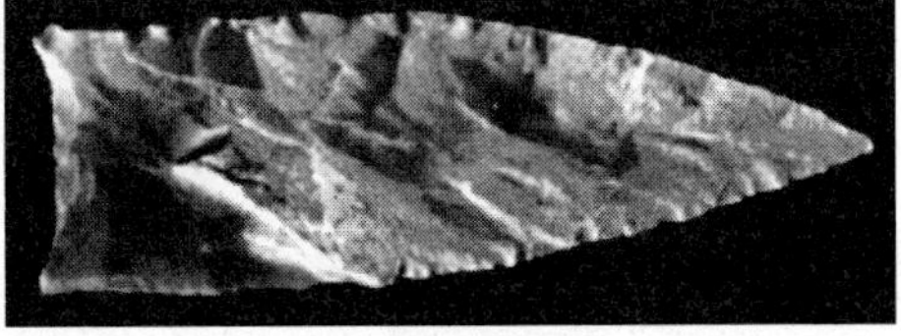

G10, $25-$45
Coffee Lake, AL.

LOCATION: Southeastern states. **DESCRIPTION:** A small to medium size lanceolate point with convex sides becoming contracting to parallel at the base. The basal edge is slightly concave, convex, or straight. This point is usually wider and thicker than *Guntersville*, and is believed to be related to *Camp Creek, Ebenezer* and *Nolichucky* points.

GREENEVILLE (continued)

G8, $20-$35
Florence, AL.

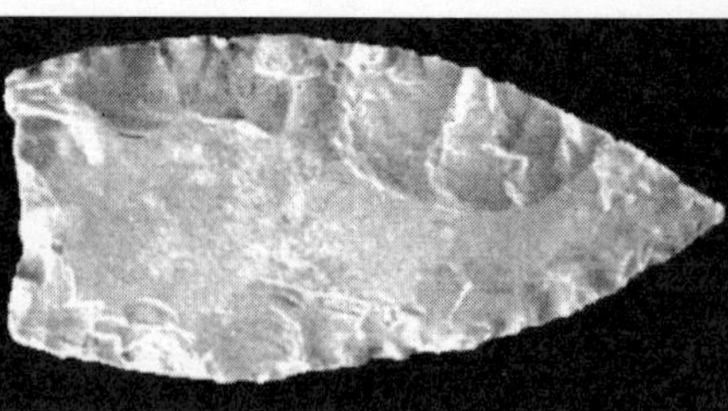

G10, $10-$15
Dayton, TN.

GUNTERSVILLE - Mississippian to Historic, 700 - 200 B. P.

(Also see Camp Creek, Greeneville, Madison and Nodena)

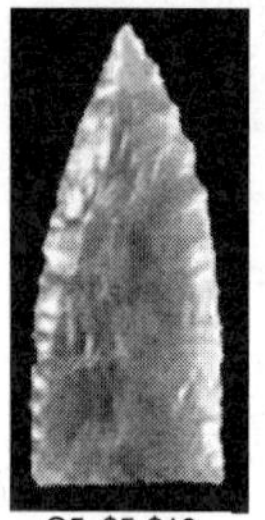

G5, $5-$10
Meigs Co., TN.

G9, $25-$50
Hamilton Co., TN.

G9, $20-$25
Cherokee Co., AL.

G7, $10-$20
Meigs Co., TN.

G9, $15-$30
Henry Co., AL.

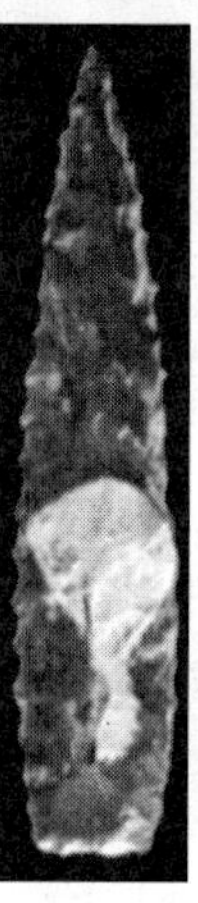

G9, $25-$50
Dayton, TN.

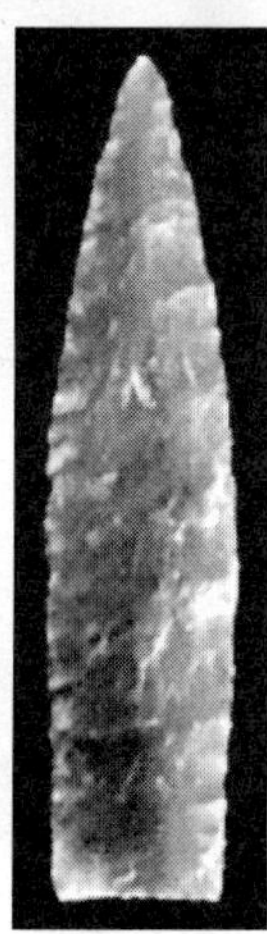

G10, $40-$75
Cherokee Co., AL.

LOCATION: Southeastern states. **DESCRIPTION:** A small to medium size, thin, narrow, lanceolate point with usually a straight base. Flaking quality is excellent. Formerly called *Dallas* points. **I.D. KEY:** Narrowness & blade expansion.

HALIFAX - Middle to Late Archaic, 6000 - 3000 B. P.

(Also see Bakers Creek, Jude, Rheems Creek and Swan Lake)

G5, $2-$3
Bradley Co., TN.

G4, $2-$3
Hinds Co., MS.

G5, $2-$3
Hinds Co., MS.

G5, $2-$3
Leflore Co., MS.

G5, $2-$4
S.E. TN.

G6, $5-$10
Walker Co., AL.

LOCATION: Southeastern states. **DESCRIPTION:** A small to medium size, narrow, side notched to expanded stemmed point. Shoulders can be weak to strongly tapered. Typically one shoulder is higher than the other. North Carolina examples are made of quartz, ryolite and shale.

HAMILTON - Woodland to Mississippian, 1600 - 1000 B. P.

(Also see Camp Creek, Fort Ancient, Madison and Sand Mountain)

G4, $6-$10
Bradley Co., TN.

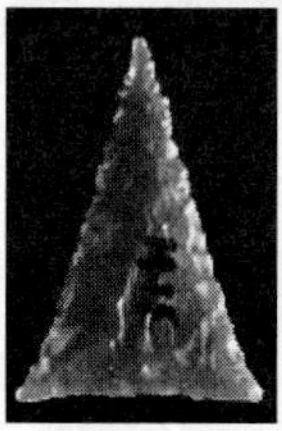

G6, $8-$15
Bradley Co., TN.

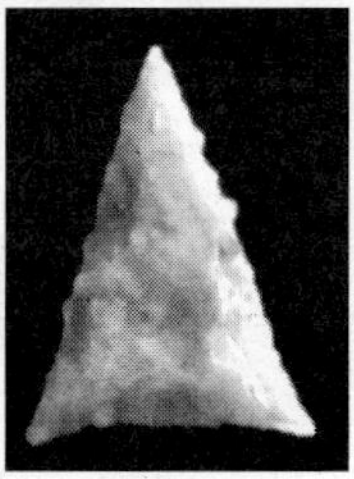

G7, $12-$20
Burke Co., GA.

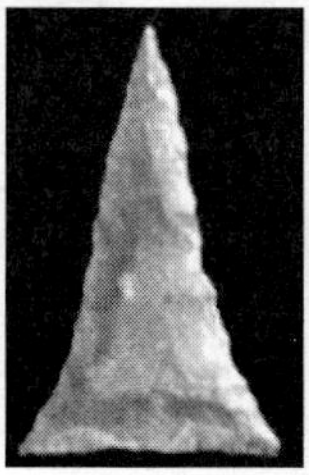

G7, $10-$20
Burke Co., GA.

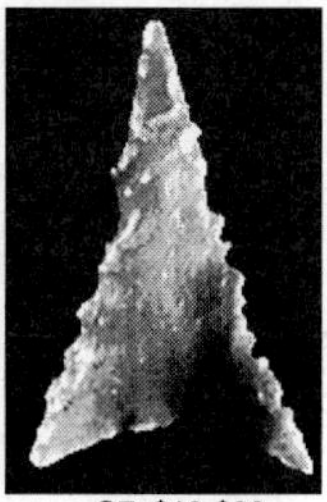

G7, $10-$20
Hamilton Co., TN.

Milky quartz

G7, $15-$25
Bristol, TN.

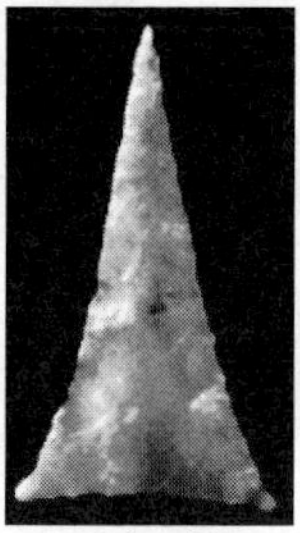

G8, $15-$25
Bristol, TN.

G9, $25-$40
Bradley Co., TN.

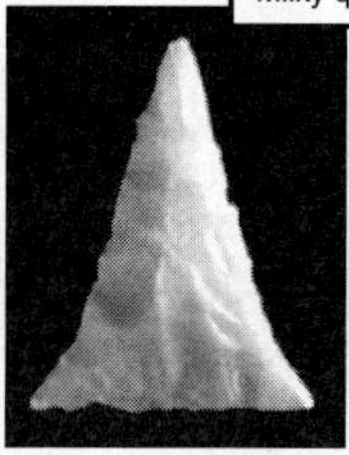

G5, $6-$12
Burke Co., GA.

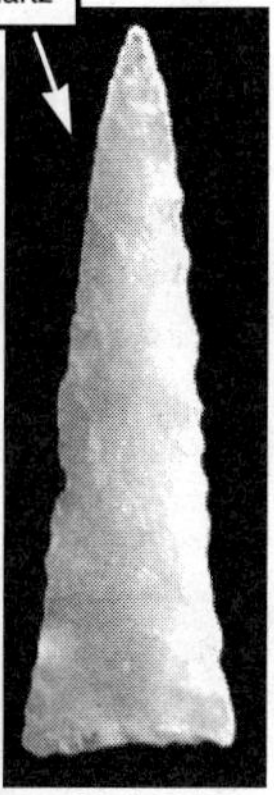

G6, $15-$25
Burke Co., GA.

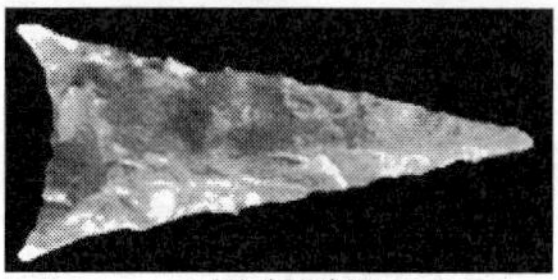

G7, $15-$25
Hamilton Co., TN.

G6, $15-$25
Burke Co.,
GA.

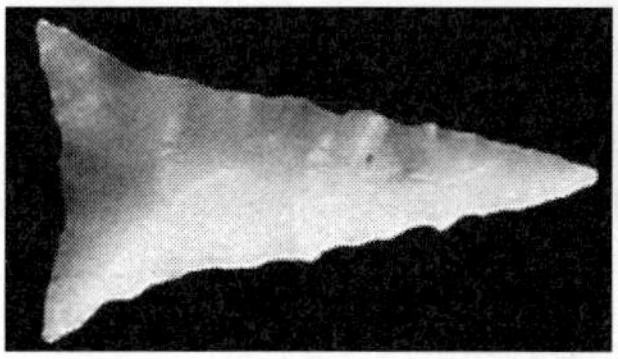

EC

LOCATION: Southeastern states. **DESCRIPTION:** A small to medium size triangular point with concave sides and base. Many examples are very thin, of the highest quality, and with serrated edges. Side edges can also be straight. This type is believed to have evolved from *Camp Creek* points. Called *Uwharrie* in North Carolina. Some North Carolina and Tennessee examples have special constricted tips called *Donnaha Tips.*

HAMILTON-STEMMED - Late Woodland to Mississippian, 3000 - 1000 B. P.

(Also see Buck Creek, Motley, Rankin, Smithsonia and Wade)

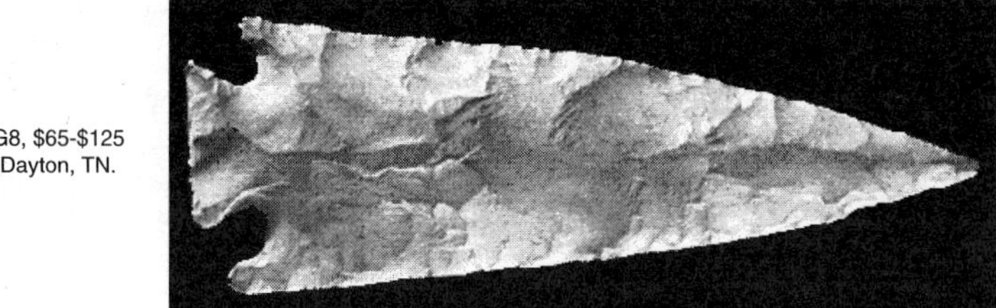

G8, $65-$125
Dayton, TN.

LOCATION: Southeastern states. **DESCRIPTION:** A medium to large size, barbed, expanded stem point. Most examples have a sharp needle like point, and the blade edges are convex to recurved. Called *Rankin* in Northeast Tenn.

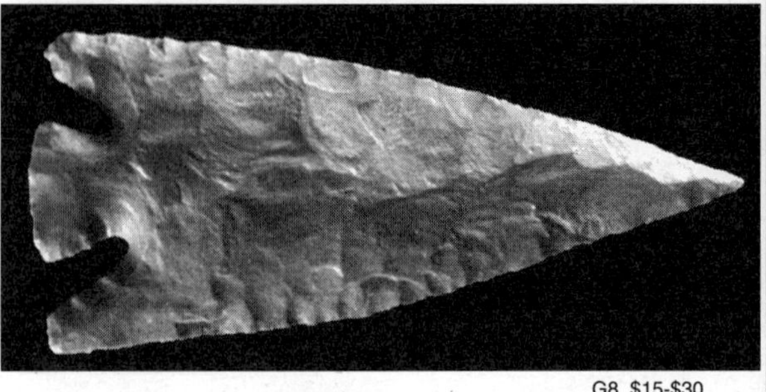

G10, $200-$350
Meigs Co., TN.

G8, $15-$30
Meigs Co., TN.
Classic.

HARAHEY - Mississippian, 700 - 350 B. P.

(Also see Lerma, Ramey Knife and Snake Creek)

G6, $90-$150
KY.

LOCATION: Kentucky to Texas, Arkansas and Missouri. **DESCRIPTION:** A large size, double pointed knife that is usually beveled on one side of each face. The cross section is rhomboid.

HARDAWAY - Late Paleo, 9500 - 8000 B. P.

(Also see Alamance, Dalton-Greenbrier, Haw River, Russel Cave, San Patrice and Wheeler)

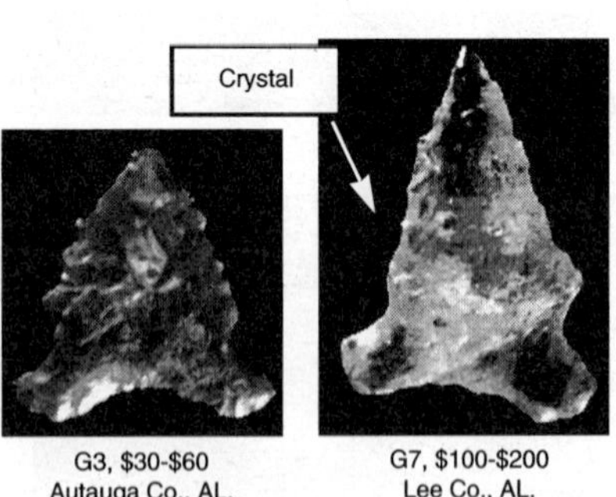

Crystal

G3, $30-$60
Autauga Co., AL.

G7, $100-$200
Lee Co., AL.

G5, $30-$60
Nickajack Lake, TN.

G6, $100-$200
Lake Seminole, GA.

LOCATION: Southeastern states. **DESCRIPTION:** A small to medium size point with shallow side notches and expanded auricles forming a wide, deeply concave base. Wide specimens are called *Cow Head Hardaways* in North Carolina. Ears and base are usually heavily ground. This type evolved from the *Dalton* point. **I.D. KEY:** Heavy grinding in shoulders, paleo flaking.

HARDAWAY (continued)

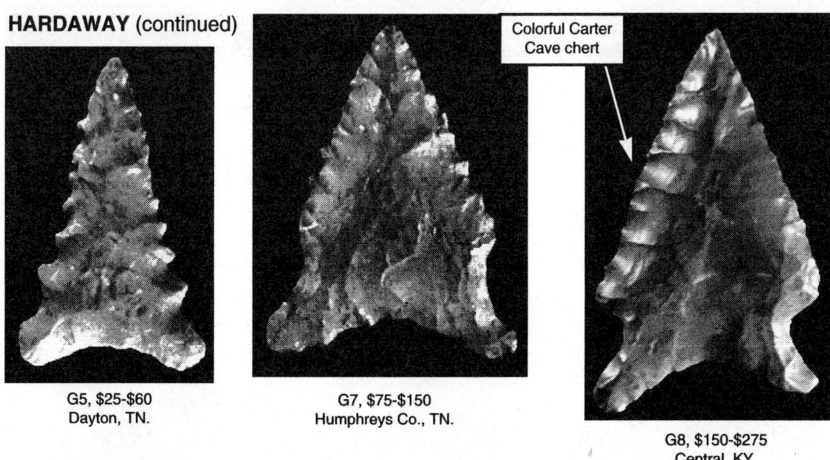

G5, $25-$60
Dayton, TN.

G7, $75-$150
Humphreys Co., TN.

G8, $150-$275
Central KY.

HARDAWAY-DALTON - Late Paleo, 9500 - 8000 B. P.

(Also see Alamance and Dalton)

EC

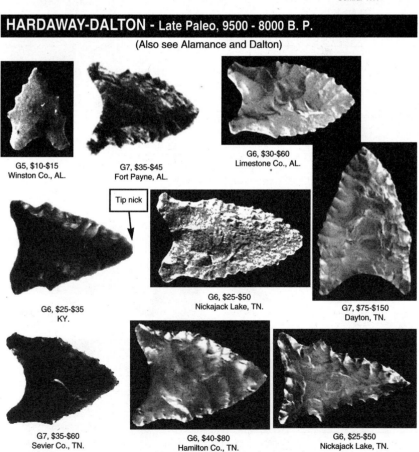

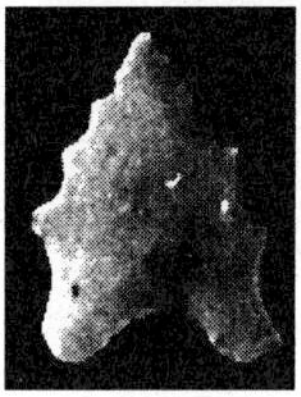

G5, $10-$15
Winston Co., AL.

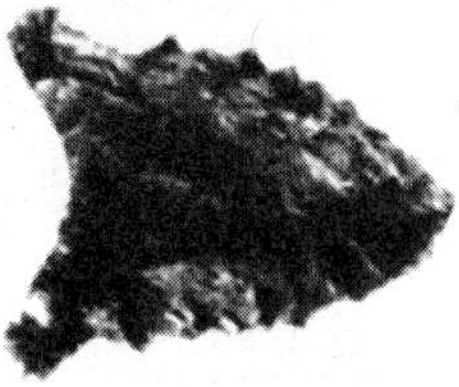

G7, $35-$45
Fort Payne, AL.

G6, $30-$60
Limestone Co., AL.

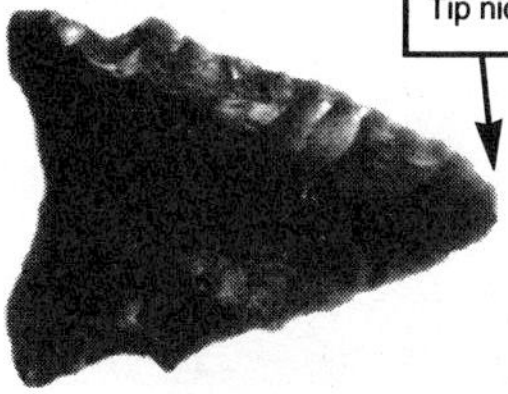

Tip nick

G6, $25-$35
KY.

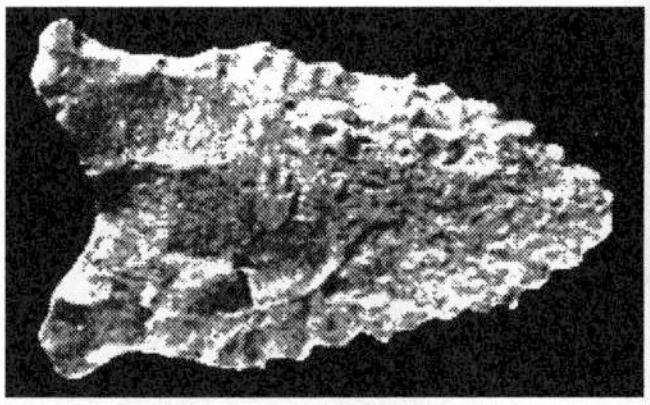

G6, $25-$50
Nickajack Lake, TN.

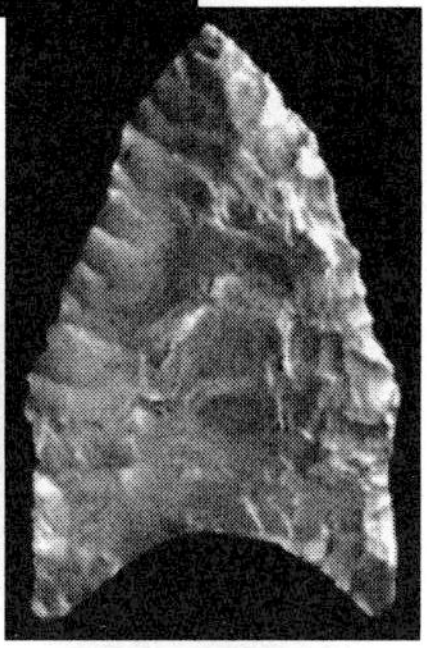

G7, $75-$150
Dayton, TN.

G7, $35-$60
Sevier Co., TN.

G6, $40-$80
Hamilton Co., TN.

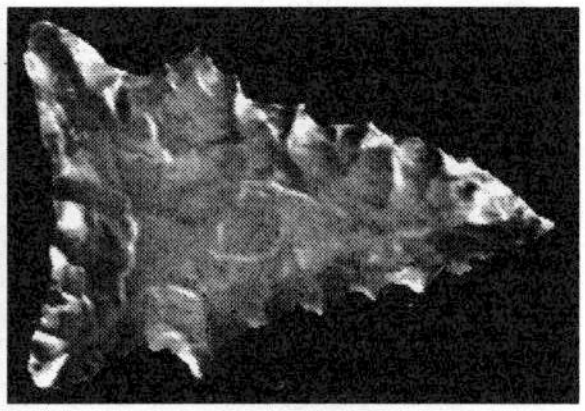

G6, $25-$50
Nickajack Lake, TN.

LOCATION: Southeastern states. **DESCRIPTION:** A small to medium size, serrated, auriculate point with a concave base. Basal fluting or thinning is common. Bases are ground. Ears turn outward or have parallel sides. A cross between *Hardaway* and *Dalton*. **I.D. KEY:** Width of base, location found.

HARDIN - Early Archaic, 9000 - 6000 B. P.

(Also see Buck Creek, Cypress Creek, Kirk, Lost Lake, Scottsbluff, St. Charles & Stilwell)

G3, $15-$30
OH.

G5, $35-$70
Tishomingo Co., MS.

LOCATION: Midwestern to Eastern states. **DESCRIPTION:** A large size, well made triangular barbed point with an expanded base that is usually ground. Resharpened examples have one beveled edge on each face. This type is believed to have evolved from the *Scottsbluff* type. **I.D. Key:** Notches and stem form.

G9, $200-$400
KY.

G7, $65-$125
KY.

G5, $30-$60
IN.

G7, $450-$900
KY.

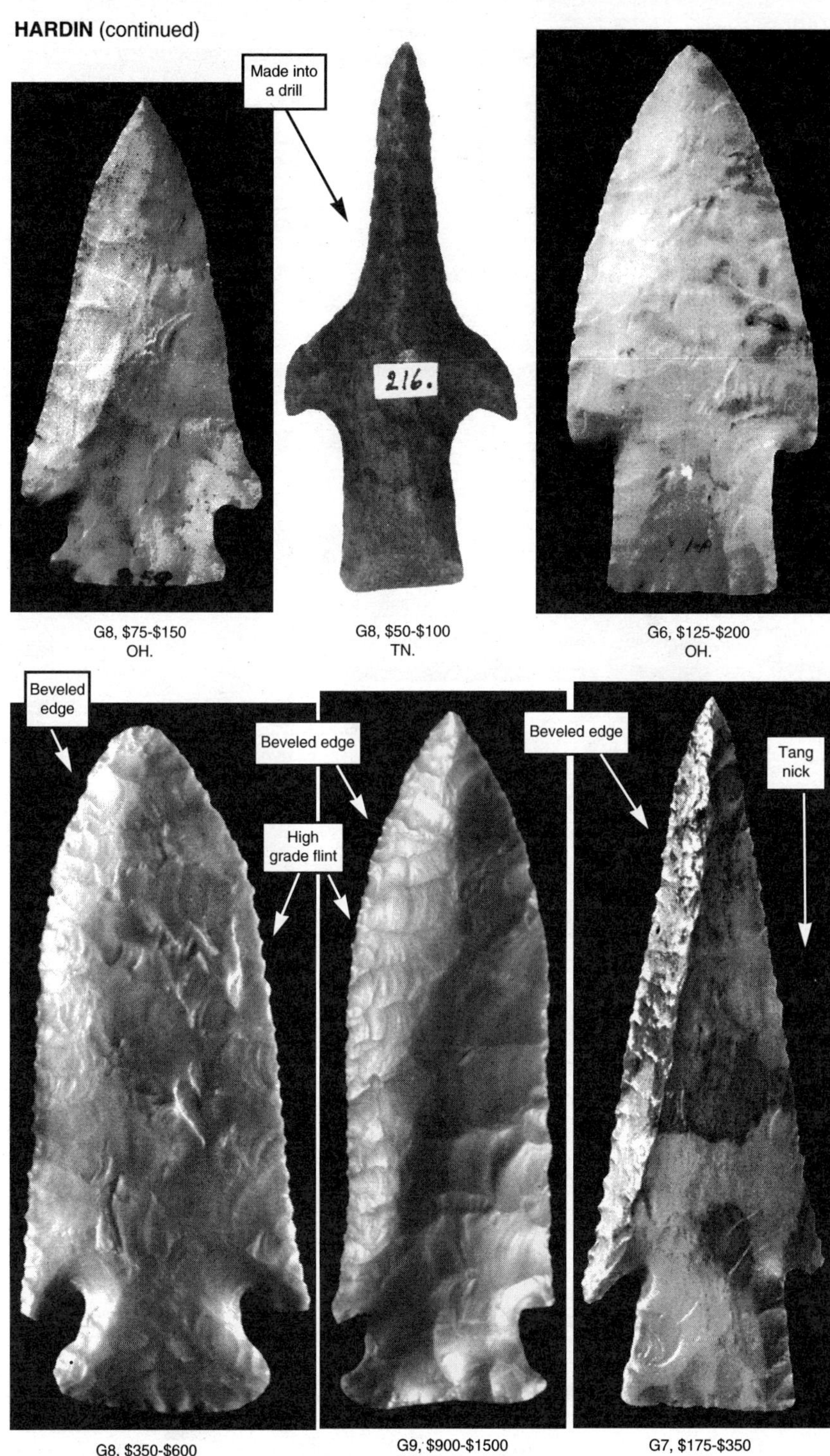

G8, $75-$150
OH.

G8, $50-$100
TN.

G6, $125-$200
OH.

G8, $350-$600
Trimble Co., KY.

G9, $900-$1500
Trimble Co., KY.

G7, $175-$350
KY.

G7, $250-$500
Portsmouth, OH.

G6, $150-$300
Lee Co., MS.

G9, $750-$1500
KY.

G8, $800-$1500
OH.

HARPETH RIVER - Early Archaic, 9000 - 8000 B. P.

(Also see Bakers Creek, Dalton-Nuckolls, Mud Creek, Russell Cave and Searcy)

G6, $25-$50
TN.

G7, $90-$175
Trigg Co., KY.

G7, $75-$100
Humphreys Co., TN.

G6, $35-$70
TN.

G9, $225-$450
Humphreys Co., TN.

G9, $125-$250
Davidson Co., TN.

G9, $250-$500
Humphreys Co., TN.

EC

LOCAT ION: Southwestern Kentucky into the Southeastern states. **DESCRIPTION:** A medium to large size, narrow, thick, serrated stemmed point that is steeply beveled on all four sides. The hafting area either has shallow side notches or an expanding stem. The base is usually thinned and ground. Rarely, the base is bifurcated. **I.D. KEY:** Weak notches, edgework.

G10, $1500-$2600
Humphreys Co., TN.

HAW RIVER - Transitional Paleo, 11,000 - 8000 B. P.

(Also see Golondrina and Hardaway)

LOCATION: Southeastern states, especially North Carolina. **DESCRIPTION:** A medium to large size, thin, broad, elliptical blade with a basal notch and usually, rounded tangs that turn inward. Believed to be ancestor to the *Alamance* point. **I.D. Key:** Notched base.

G5, $15-$30
Southeast, TN.

HEAVY DUTY - Early to Middle Archaic, 7000 - 5000 B. P.

(Also see Harpeth River and Kirk Serrated)

All have thick cross sections

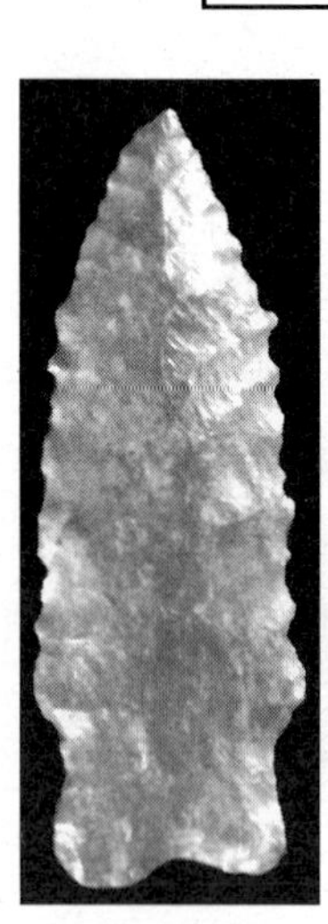

G5, $20-$35
Fayette Co., KY.

G5, $15-$30
KY.

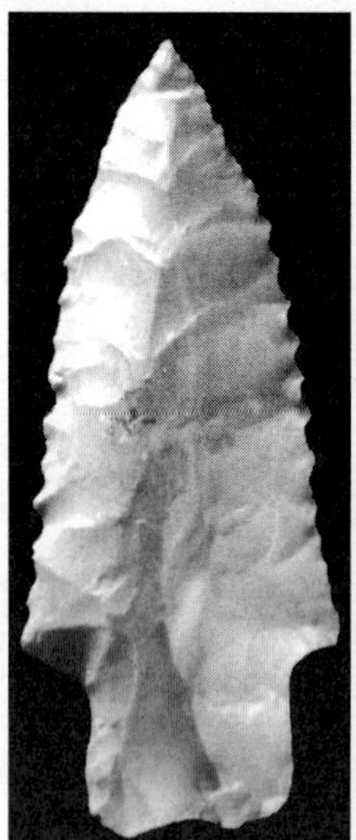

G6, $30-$55
Harrison Co., KY.

G6, $35-$65
Russell Co., KY.

LOCATION: Eastern states. **DESCRIPTION:** A medium to large size, thick, serrated point with a parallel stem and a straight to slightly concave base. A variant of Kirk Serrated found in the Southeast. **I.D. KEY:** Base, thickness, flaking.

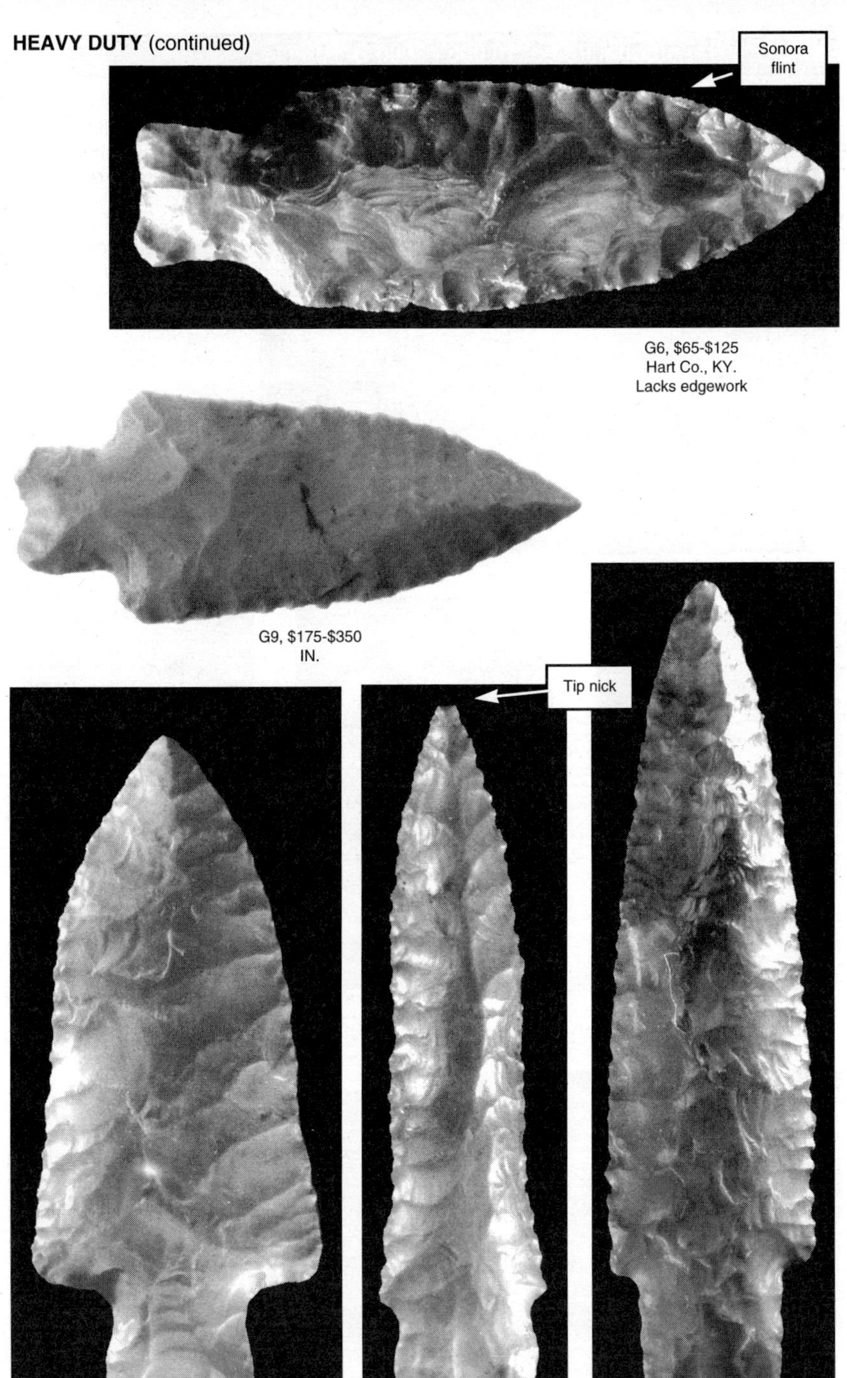

G6, $65-$125
Hart Co., KY.
Lacks edgework

G9, $175-$350
IN.

G9, $300-$550
OH.

G6, $40-$80
Stewart Co., TN.

G8, $150-$300
OH.

HI-LO - Transitional Paleo, 10,000 - 8000 B. P.

(Also see Angostura, Golondrina, Jeff and Paint Rock Valley)

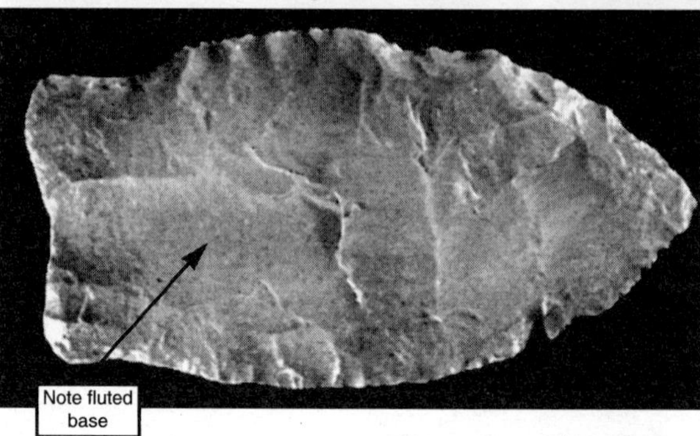

LOCATION: Midwestern states. **DESCRIPTION:** A medium to large size, broad, eared, lanceolate point with a concave base. Believed to be related to *Plainview* and *Dalton* points.

G5, $50-$100
Barren Co., KY.

HINDS - Transitional Paleo, 10,000 - 6000 B. P.

(Also see Quad)

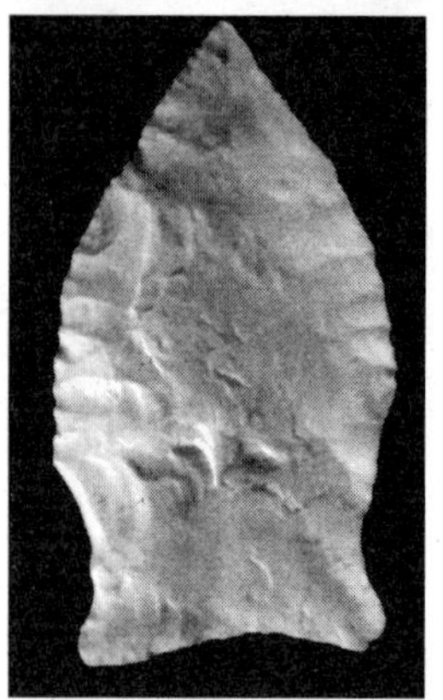

G6, $75-$150
Lee Co., MS.

G5, $65-$125
Dyersburg, TN.

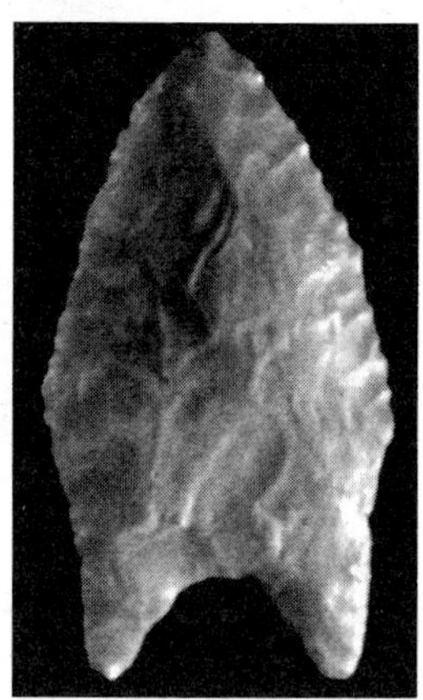

G7, $125-$250
Hardin Co., TN.

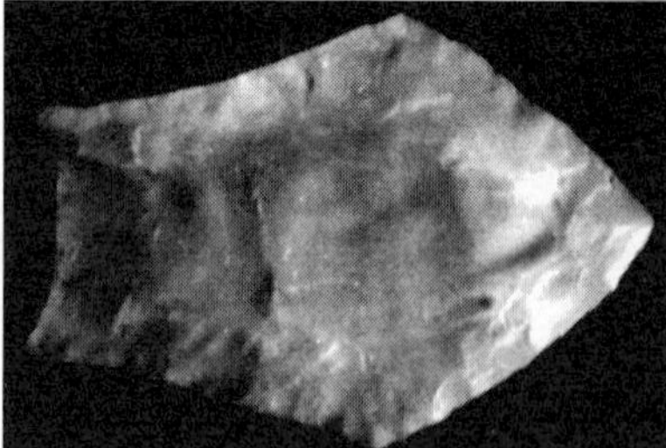

G7, $150-$300
Sou. MS.

G9, $200-$400
Florence, AL.

LOCATION: Tennessee, N. Alabama, Mississippi, Louisiana and Arkansas. **DESCRIPTION:** A short, broad, usually auriculate point with basal grinding. Shoulders taper into a long contracting stem. Some examples are basally thinned or fluted. Similar to *Pelican* points found in Texas.

Fluting channel

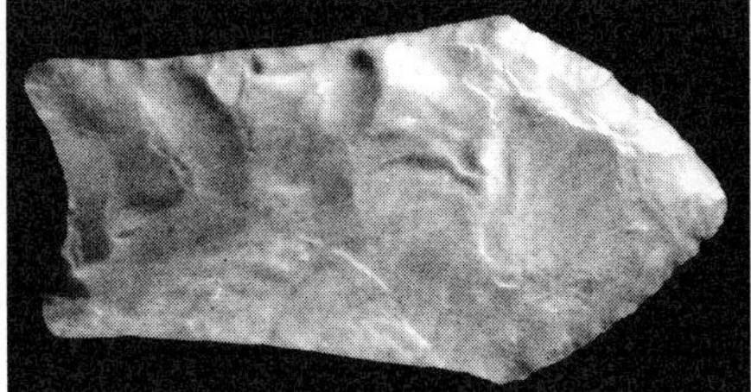

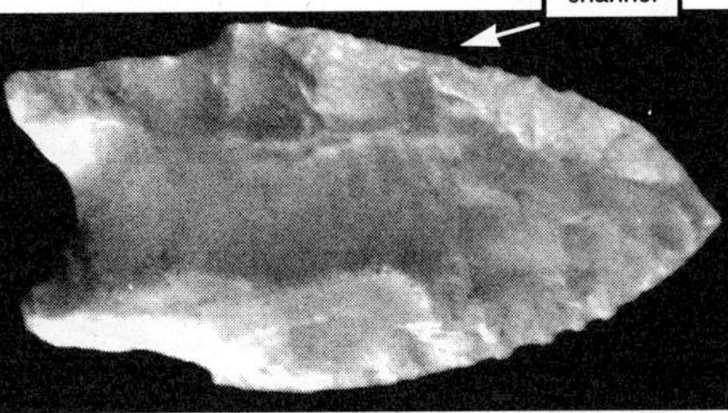

G8, $200-$400
Sou. MS.

G7, $150-$275
NW, TN.

HOLLAND - Transitional Paleo, 9500 - 7500 B. P.

(Also see Dalton, Hardin and Scottsbluff)

G8, $100-$200
West Memphis, TN.

Note early diagonal flaking

LOCATION: Midwestern states. **DESCRIPTION:** A medium to large size lanceolate blade that is very well made. Shouldes are weak to nonexistant. Bases can be knobbed to auriculate and are usually ground. Some examples have horizontal to oblique transverse flaking. **I.D. KEY:** Weak shoulders, early flaking.

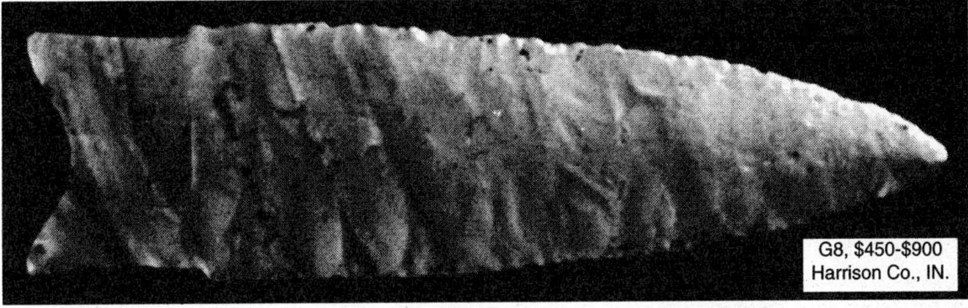

G8, $450-$900
Harrison Co., IN.

HOPEWELL - Woodland, 2500 - 1500 B. P.

(Also see Gibson, North, St. Charles and Snyders)

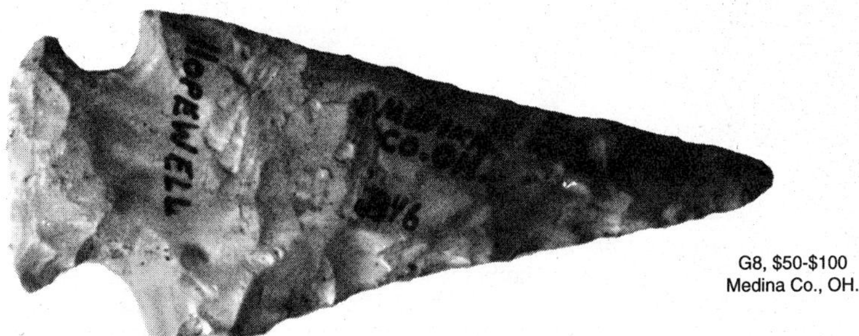

G8, $50-$100
Medina Co., OH.

G6, $30-$60
Carroll Co., OH.

G5, $20-$35
OH.

G9, $75-$125
KY.

LOCATION: Midwestern to Eastern states. **DESCRIPTION:** A large size, broad, corner notched point that is similar to *Snyders.* Made by the Hopewell culture.

JACKS REEF CORNER NOTCHED - Late Woodland to Mississippian, 1500 - 1000 B. P.

(Also see Afton and Knight Island)

G5, $20-$35
KY.

G4, $8-$15
KY.

G7, $65-$125
KY.

G7, $15-$30
KY.

G5, $15-$30
Morgan Co., AL.

G6, $25-$45
Florence, AL.

LOCATION: Southeastern states. **DESCRIPTION:** A small to medium size, very thin, corner notched point that is well made. The blade is convex to pentagonal. Some examples are widely corner notched and appear to be expanded stem points with barbed shoulders. Rarely, they are basal notched. **I.D. KEY:** Thinness, made by the birdpoint people.

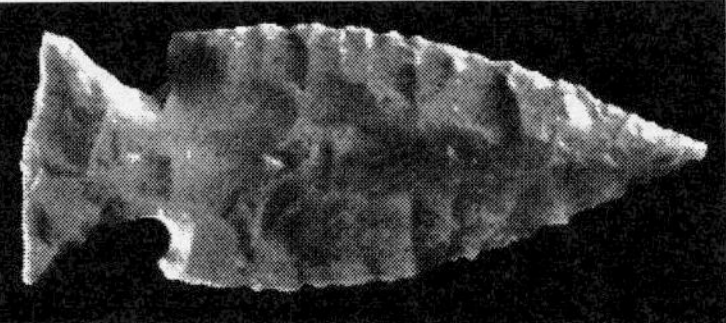

G7, $30-$60
Morgan Co., AL.

G4, $8-$15
Fulton, KY.

G8, $85-$165
Florence, AL.

G9, $150-$300
Hardin Co., TN.

G10, $300-$600
Hardin Co., TN.

G10, $200-$400
Hardin Co., TN.

JACKS REEF PENTAGONAL - Late Woodland to Mississippian, 1500 - 1000 B. P.

(Also see Madison and Mouse Creek)

G5, $8-$15
KY.

G4, $3-$5
Morgan Co., AL.

G9, $25-$35
Dayton, TN.

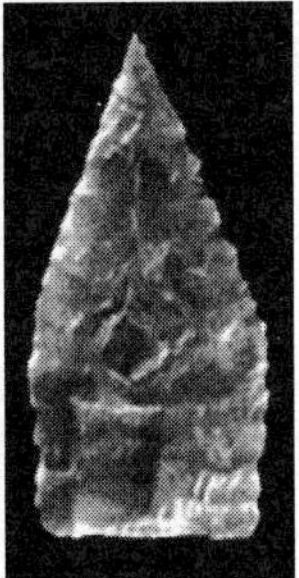

G8, $15-$25
Morgan Co., AL.

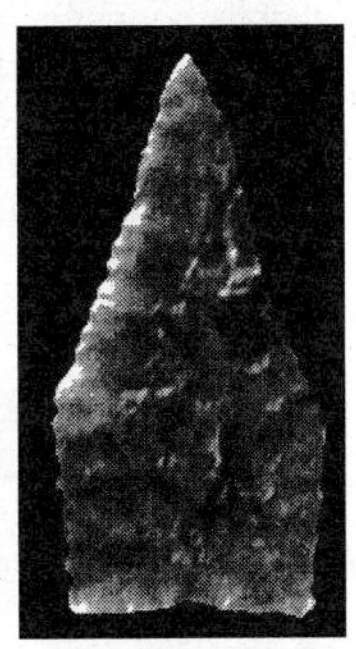

G8, $15-$25
Huntsville, AL.

G7, $25-$45
Morgan Co., AL.

LOCATION: Southeastern states. **DESCRIPTION:** A small to large size, very thin, five sided point with a sharp tip. The hafting area is usually contracted with a slightly concave to straight base. This type is called *Pee Dee* in North and South Carolina.

G8, $40-$75
Humphreys Co., TN.

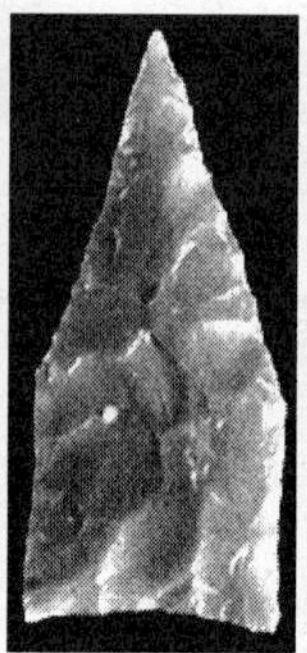

G8, $45-$75
OH.

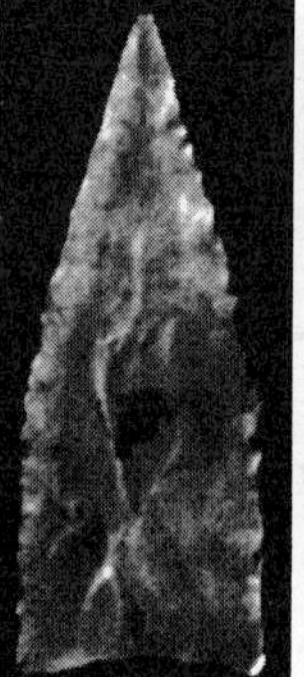

G8, $35-$65
Florence, AL.

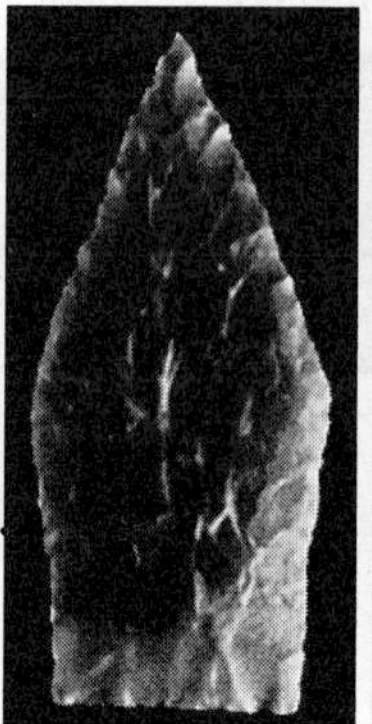

G8, $45-$75
Morgan Co., AL.

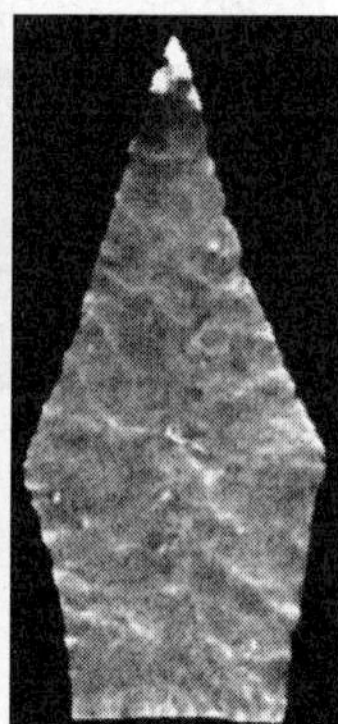

G10, $100-$200
Warren Co., TN.

JEFF - Late Paleo, 10,000 - 8000 B. P.

(Also see Angostura, Browns Valley, Golondrina, Hi-Lo, Paint Rock Valley and Quad)

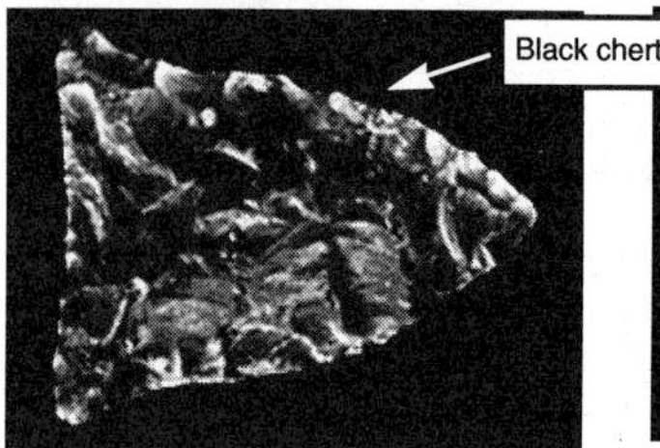

G7, $65-$125
Jackson Co., AL.

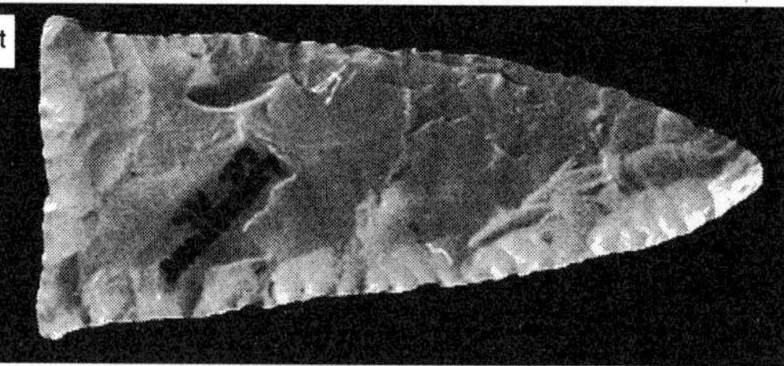

G9, $125-$225
Limestone Co., AL.

LOCATION: Southeastern states. **DESCRIPTION:** A medium sized, wide, lanceolate point with expanded auricles. The base is straight to slightly concave, is usually beveled or thinned, and may be ground. Auricles can either extend downward or out to the side. Some examples show fine pressure flaking on the blade edges. **I.D. KEY:** One shoulder stronger.

G7, $75-$150
Huntsville, AL.

JOHNSON - Early to Middle Archaic, 9000 - 5000 B. P.

(Also see Fairland, McIntire and Savannah River)

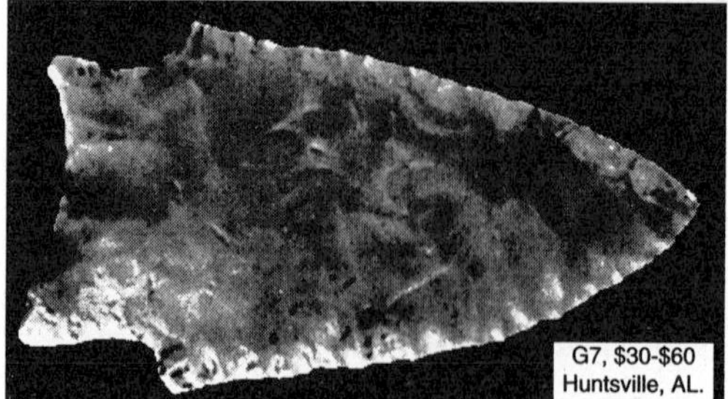

G7, $30-$60
Huntsville, AL.

LOCATION: Midwestern to Southeastern states. **DESCRIPTION:** A medium size, thick, well made, expanded stem point with a broad, concave base. Shoulders can be slightly barbed, straight or tapered. Basal corners are rounded to pointed to auriculate. Bases are thinned and ground. **I.D. KEY:** Pointed ears and thickness.

JOHNSON (continued)

G5, $15-$25
Natchez, MS.

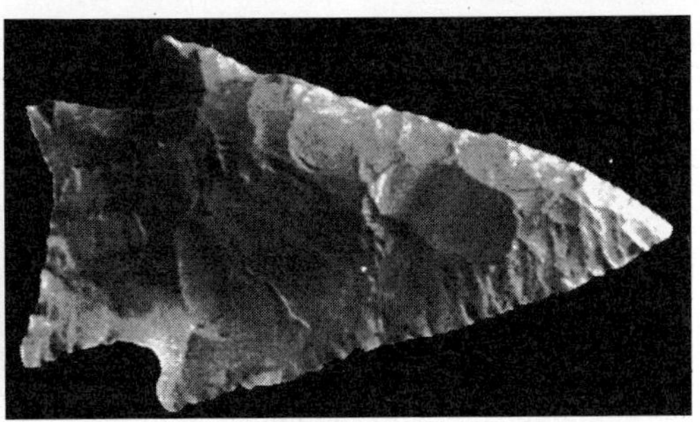

G8, $45-$75
Coffee Lake, AL.

JUDE - Early Archaic, 9000 - 6000 B. P.

(Also see Cave Spring, Fox Valley, Garth Slough, Halifax, LeCroy, McIntire and Rheems Creek)

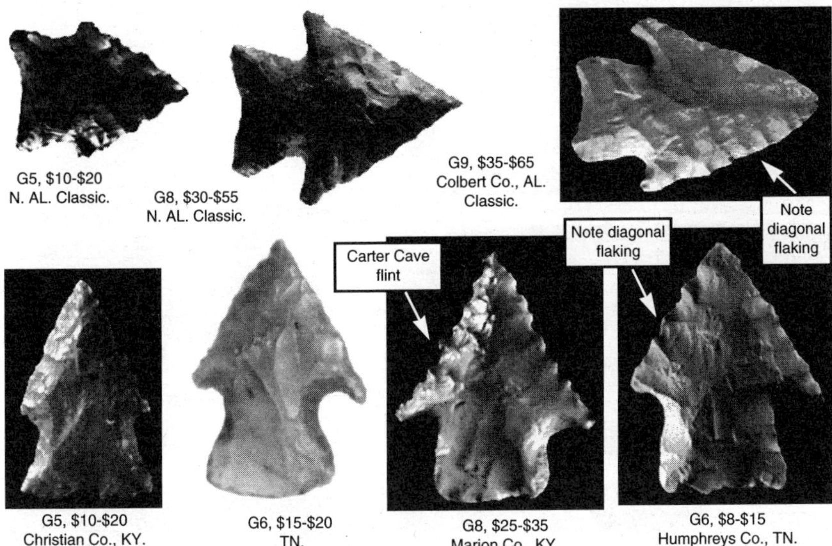

G5, $10-$20
N. AL. Classic.

G8, $30-$55
N. AL. Classic.

G9, $35-$65
Colbert Co., AL.
Classic.

G5, $10-$20
Christian Co., KY.

G6, $15-$20
TN.

G8, $25-$35
Marion Co., KY.

G6, $8-$15
Humphreys Co., TN.

EC

LOCATION: Southeastern states. **DESCRIPTION:** A small size, short, barbed, expanded to parallel stemmed point with straight to convex blade edges. Stems are usually as large or larger than the blade. Bases are straight, concave, convex or bifurcated. Shoulders are either square, tapered or barbed. This is one of the earliest stemmed points along with *Pelican*. Some examples have serrated blade edges that may be beveled on one side of each face. **I.D. KEY:** Basal form and flaking.

KANAWHA - Early Archaic, 9000 - 5000 B. P.

(Also see Fox Valley, Jude, Kirk Serrated-Bifurcated, LeCroy, St. Albans and Stanly)

G6, $4-$7
S.E. TN.

G3, $1-$2
Catoosa Co., GA.

KANAWHA (continued)

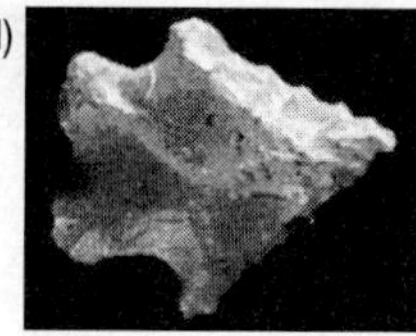

G5, $3-$5
Chattanooga, TN.

LOCATION: Eastern to Southeastern states. **DESCRIPTION:** A small to medium size, fairly thick, shallowly-bifurcated stemmed point. The basal lobes are usually rounded and the shoulders tapered. Believed to be the ancestor to the *Stanly* type.

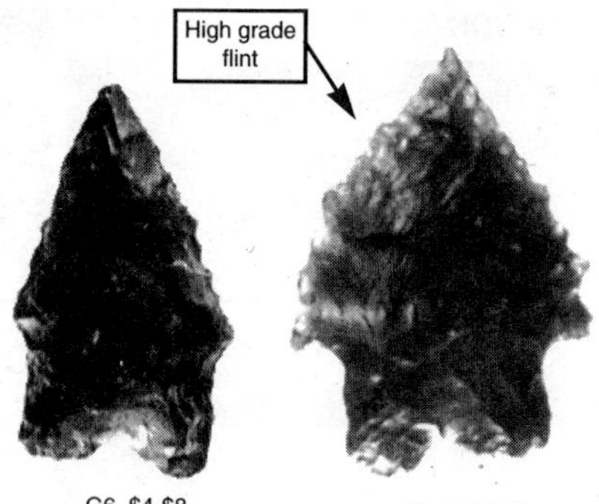

G6, $4-$8
Christian Co., KY.

G9, $20-$35
Logan, KY.

KAYS - Middle Archaic to Woodland, 5000 - 2000 B. P.

(Also see Little Bear Creek and McIntire)

G5, $4-$8
Morgan Co., AL.

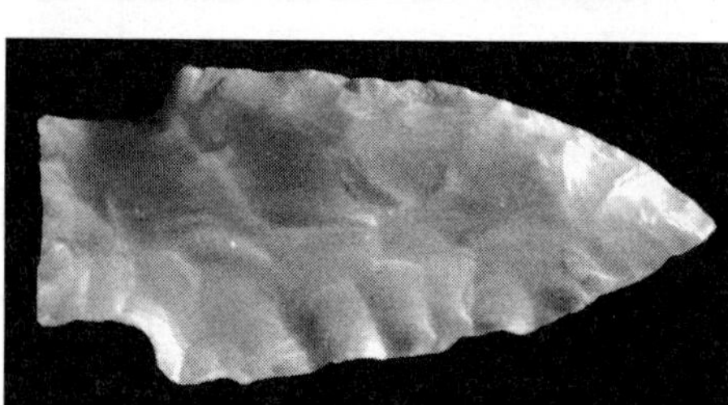

G5, $5-$10
Morgan Co., AL.

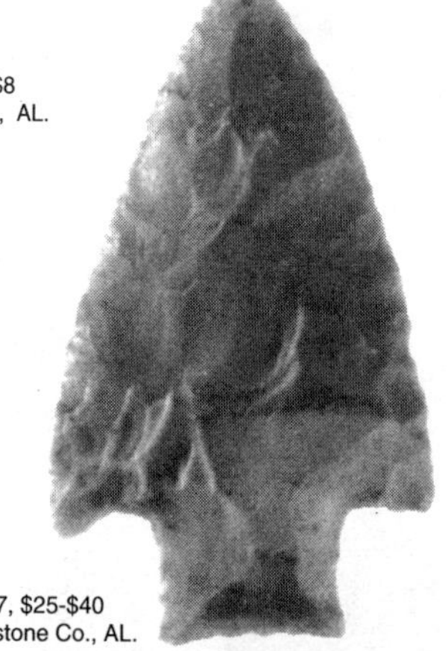

G7, $25-$40
Limestone Co., AL.

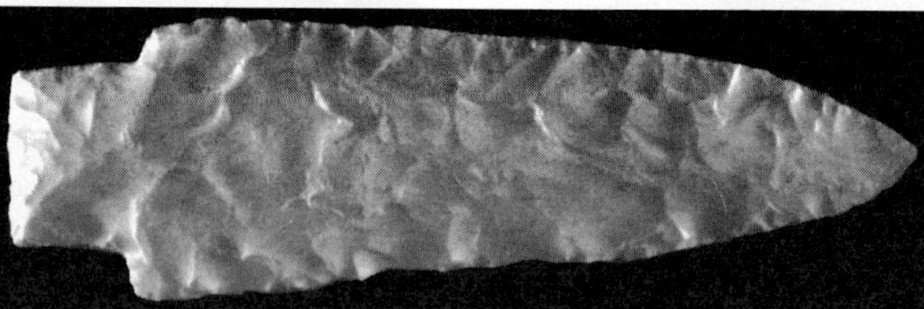

G9, $55-$100
Meigs Co., TN.

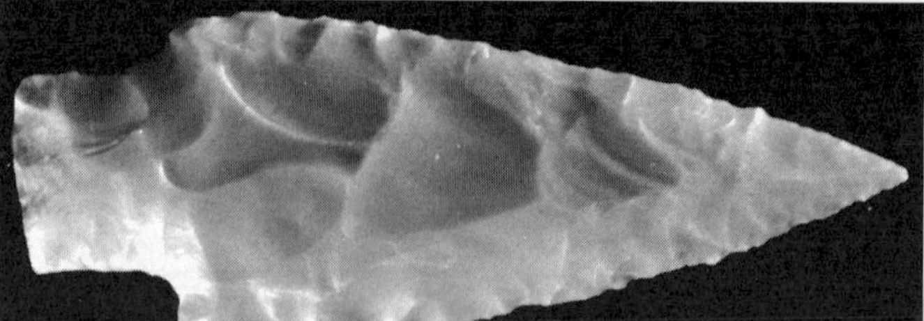

G7, $30-$60
Decatur Co., AL.

KAYS (continued)

LOCATION: Southeastern states. **DESCRIPTION:** A medium to large size, narrow, parallel sided stemmed point with a straight base. Shoulders are tapered to square. The blade is straight to convex. **I.D. KEY:** One barb is higher.

G7, $25-$40
Decatur, AL.

KEOTA - Mississippian, 800 - 600 B. P.

(Also see Merom)

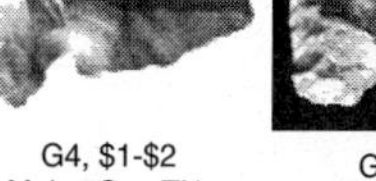

G4, $1-$2
Meigs Co., TN.

G4, $1-$2
Meigs Co., TN.

G5, $5-$10
Wash. Co., AL.

LOCATION: Okla, Ark, S.E. TN. & N. AL. **DESCRIPTION:** A small size, thin, triangular, side to corner-notched point with a rounded base.

KIRK CORNER NOTCHED - Early to Middle Archaic, 9000 - 6000 B. P.

(Also see Cypress Creek, Lost Lake, Pine Tree and St. Charles)

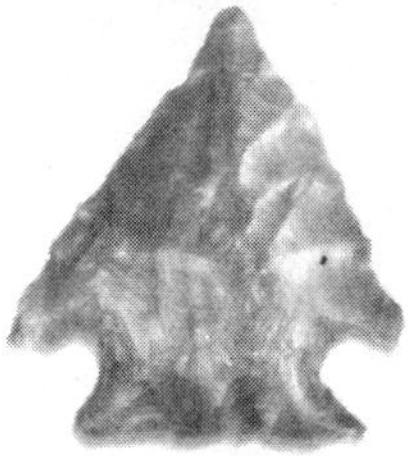

G4, $3-$5
KY.

G5, $5-$10
KY.

Banded chert

G7, $40-$80
Dunlap, TN.

G7, $100-$200
KY.

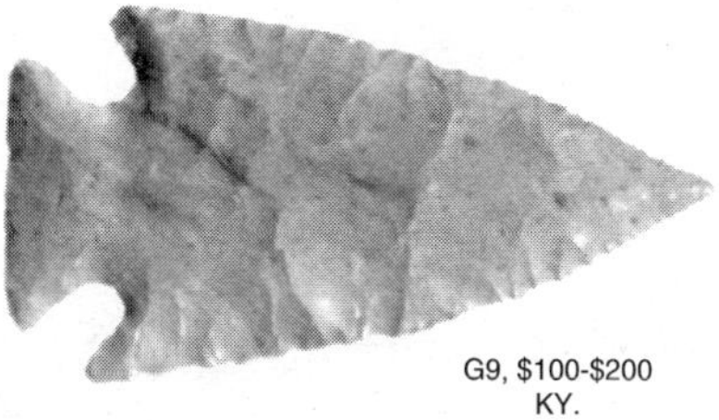

G9, $100-$200
KY.

LOCATION: Southeastern states. **DESCRIPTION:** A medium to large size, corner notched point. Blade edges can be convex to recurved and are finely serrated on many examples. The base can be convex, concave, straight or auriculate. Points that are beveled on one side of each face would fall under the *Lost Lake* type. **I.D. KEY:** Secondary edgework.

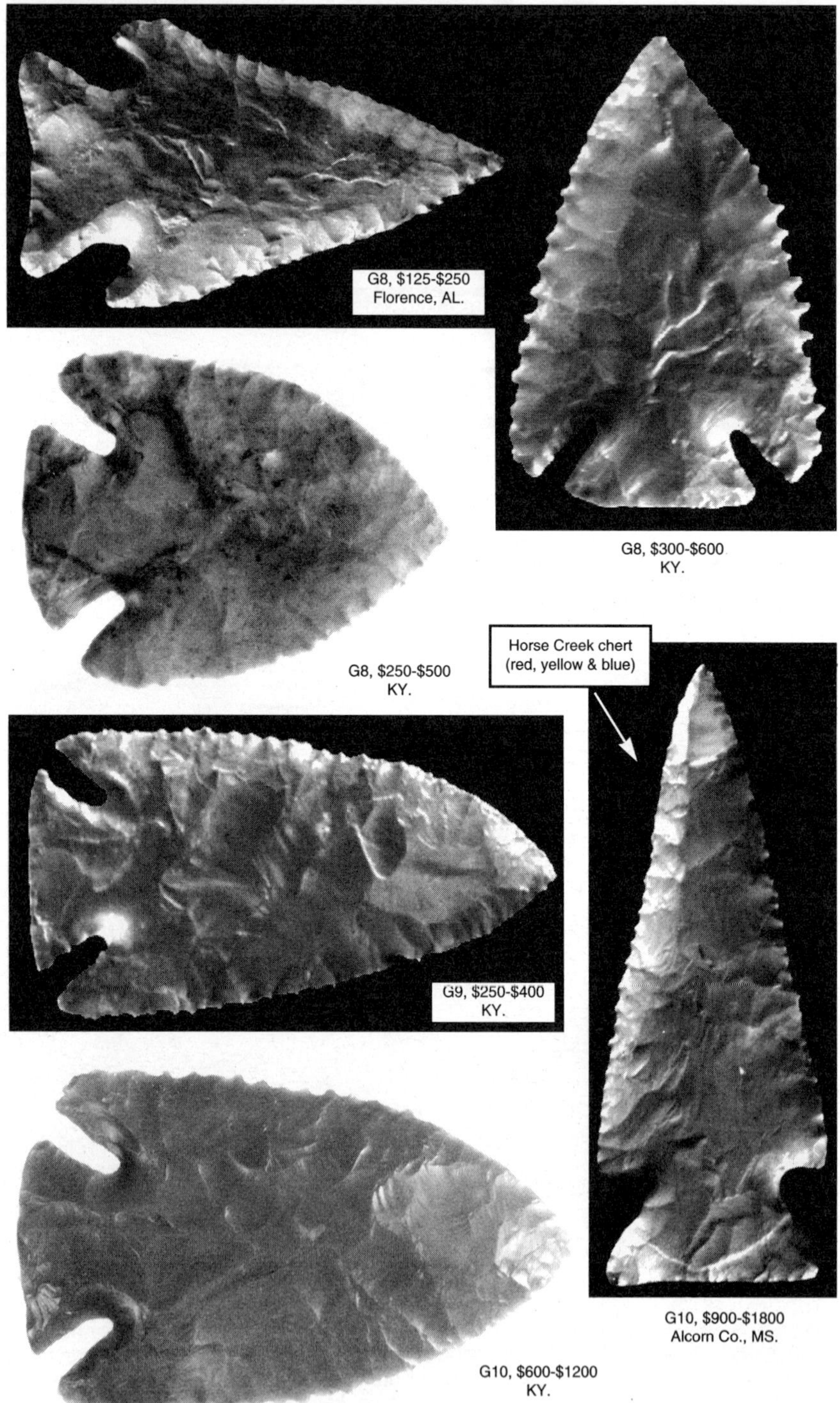

G8, $125-$250
Florence, AL.

G8, $300-$600
KY.

G8, $250-$500
KY.

G9, $250-$400
KY.

G10, $900-$1800
Alcorn Co., MS.

G10, $600-$1200
KY.

KIRK CORNER NOTCHED (continued)

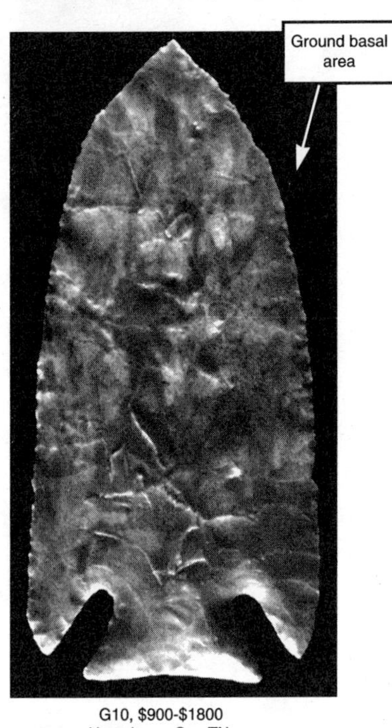

G10, $900-$1800
Humphreys Co., TN.

G9, $600-$1200
KY.

KIRK SERRATED - Early to Middle Archaic, 9000 - 6000 B. P.

(Also see Hamilton, Heavy Duty and Stanly)

G3, $15-$30
KY.

G3, $15-$30
Florence, AL.

G5, $20-$40
OH.

G8, $45-$75
OH.

G5, $20-$40
TN.

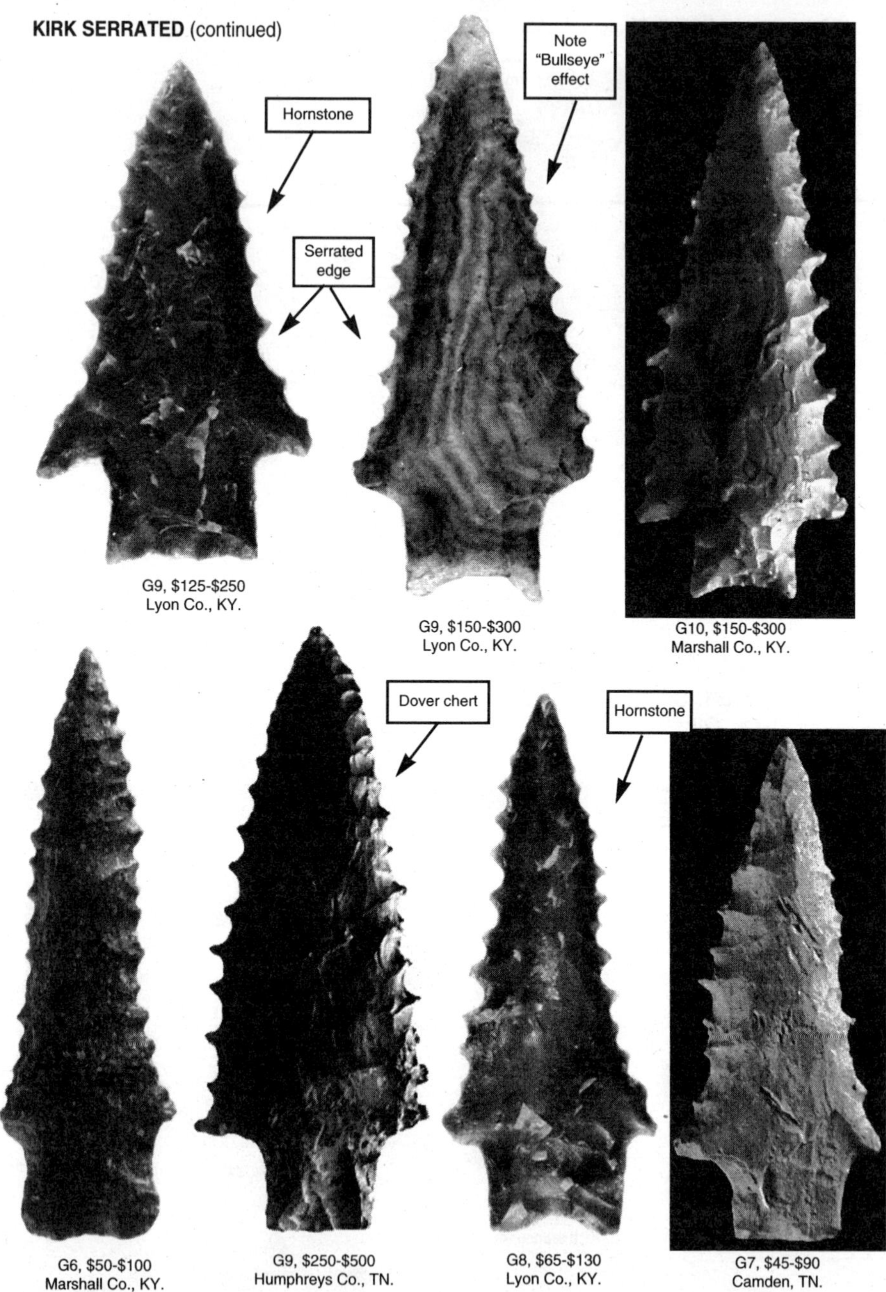

G9, $125-$250
Lyon Co., KY.

G9, $150-$300
Lyon Co., KY.

G10, $150-$300
Marshall Co., KY.

G6, $50-$100
Marshall Co., KY.

G9, $250-$500
Humphreys Co., TN.

G8, $65-$130
Lyon Co., KY.

G7, $45-$90
Camden, TN.

LOCATION: Southeastern to Eastern states. **DESCRIPTION:** A medium to large size, barbed, stemmed point with deep notches or fine serrations along the blade edges. The stem is parallel to expanding. The stem sides may be steeply beveled on opposite faces. Some examples also have a distinct bevel on the right side of each blade edge. The base can be concave, convex or straight, and can be very short. The shoulders are usually strongly barbed. Believed to have evolved into *Stanly* and other types. **I.D. KEY:** Serrations.

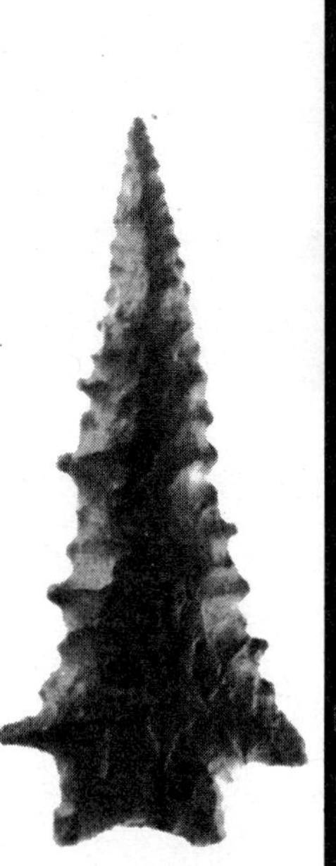

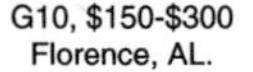

G10, $150-$300
Florence, AL.

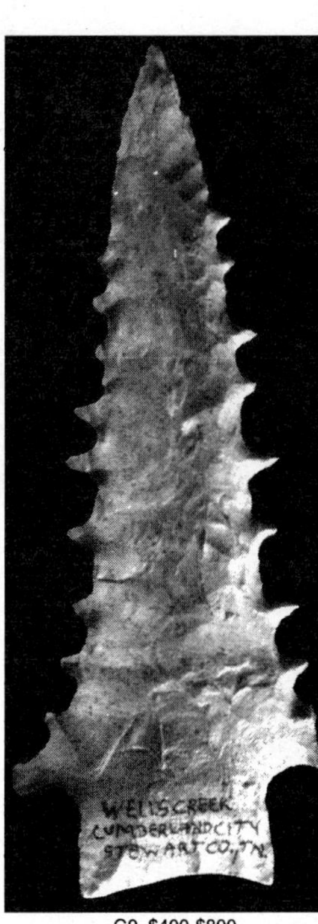

G9, $400-$800
Stewart Co., TN.

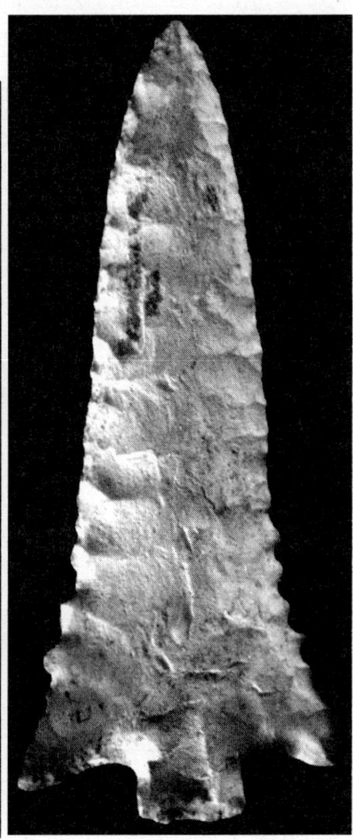

G9, $200-$400
Franklin Co., AL.

KIRK SERRATED-BIFURCATED - Early Archaic, 9000 - 7000 B. P.

(Also see Cave Spring, Fox Valley, LeCroy, St. Albans and Stanly)

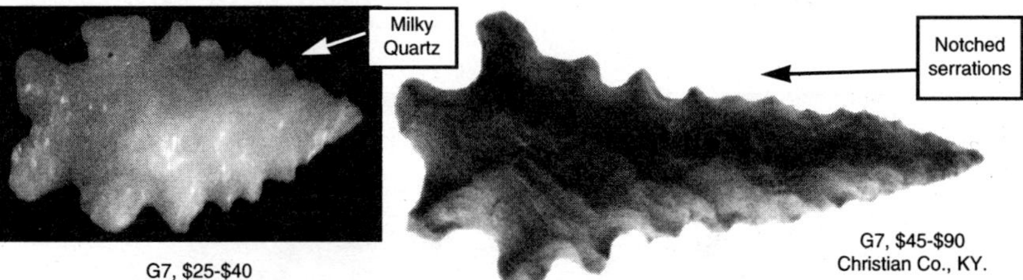

G7, $25-$40
N.E. TN.

G7, $45-$90
Christian Co., KY.

LOCATION: Southeastern to Eastern states. **DESCRIPTION:** A medium to large size point with deep notches or fine serrations along the blade edges. The stem is parallel sided to expanded and is bifurcated. Believed to be an early form for the type which later developed into *Stanly* and other types. Some examples have a steep bevel on the right side of each blade edge.

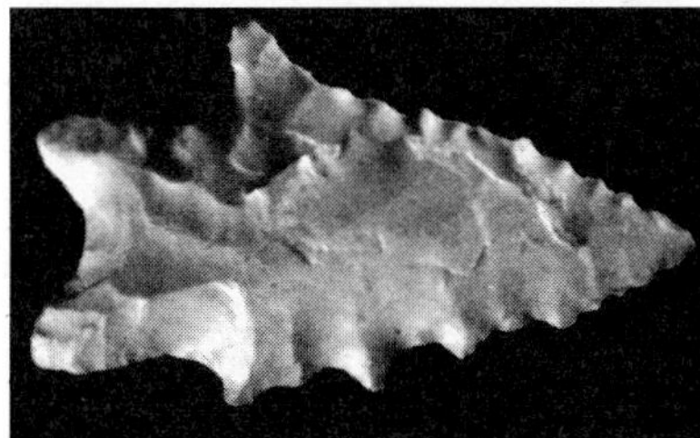

G6, $25-$50
Cleveland, OH.

KIRK SERRATED-BIFURCATED (continued)

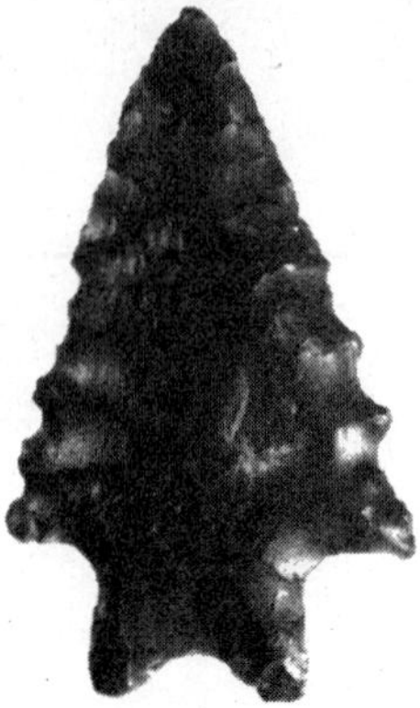

G6, $20-$40
OH.

G6, $20-$40
GA.

G7, $25-$45
Walker Co., GA.

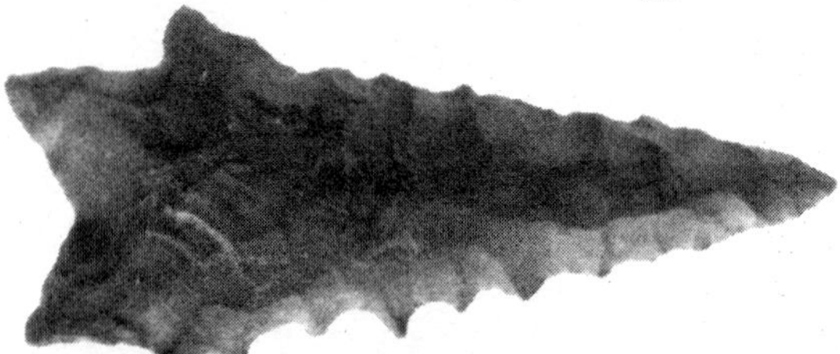

G6, $45-$90
Marshall Co., KY.

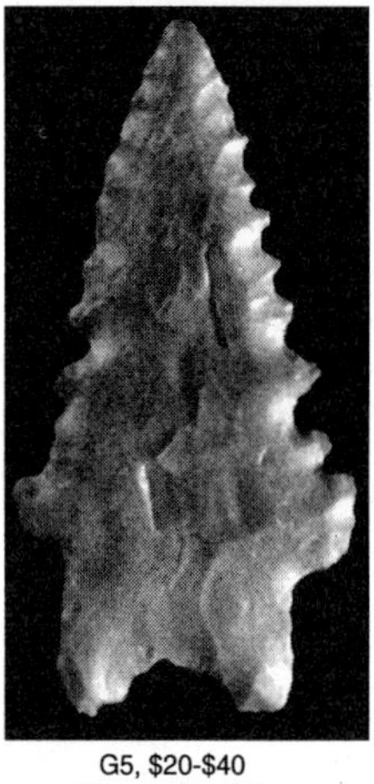

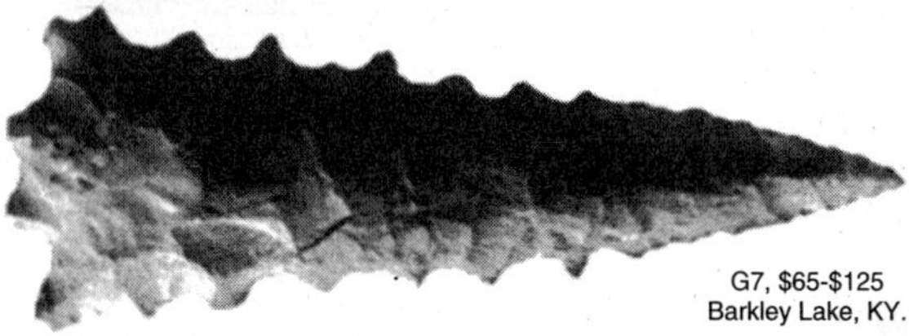

G7, $65-$125
Barkley Lake, KY.

G5, $20-$40
Stewart Co., TN.

KIRK SNAPPED BASE - Early to Middle Archaic, 9000 - 6000 B. P.

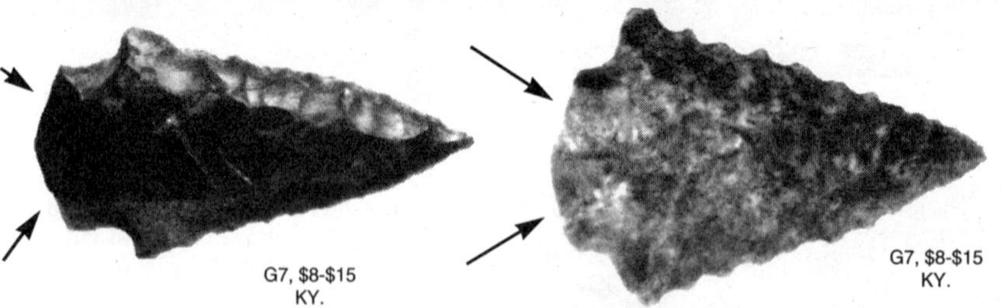

G7, $8-$15
KY.

G7, $8-$15
KY.

LOCATION: Southeastern to Eastern states. **DESCRIPTION:** A medium to large size, usually serrated, blade with long tangs and a base that has been snapped or fractured off. The shoulders are also fractured on some examples. This proves that the fracturing was intentional as in *Decatur* and other types.

KIRK SNAPPED BASE (continued)

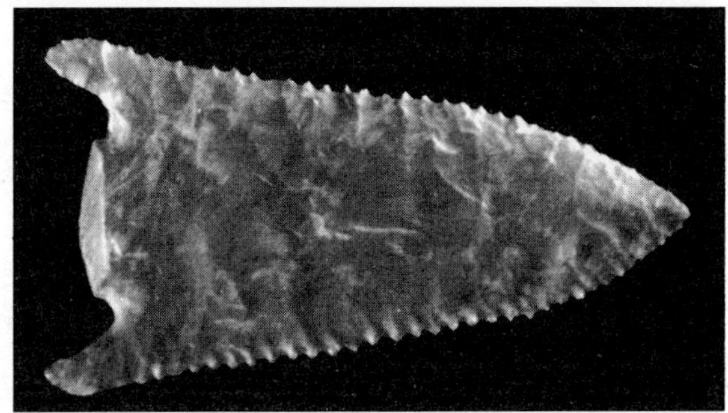

Note where base was snapped off

G10, $35-$70
Humphreys Co., TN.
Excellent quality.

KNIGHT ISLAND - Late Woodland, 1500 - 1000 B. P.

(Also see Cache River and Jacks Reef)

G5, $10-$15
S.E. TN.

G5, $25-$45
Humphreys Co., TN.

G9, $75-$150
W. TN.

G9, $75-$125
Savannah, TN.

G7, $40-$80
KY.

G10, $125-$250
Humphreys Co., TN.

LOCATION: Southeastern states. **DESCRIPTION:** A small to medium size, very thin, narrow, side-notched point with a straight base. Longer examples can have a pentagonal apperarance. Called *Racoon Creek* in Ohio. A side-notched Jacks Reef. **I.D. KEY:** Thinness, basal form. Made by the bird point people.

LAKE ERIE - Early to Middle Archaic, 9000 - 5000 B. P.

(Also see Fox Valley, Jude, Kirk Serrated-Bifurcated, LeCroy, MacCorkle, St. Albans and Stanly)

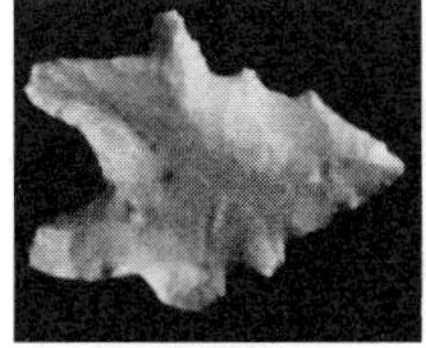

G5, $4-$8
Caroll, Co., OH.

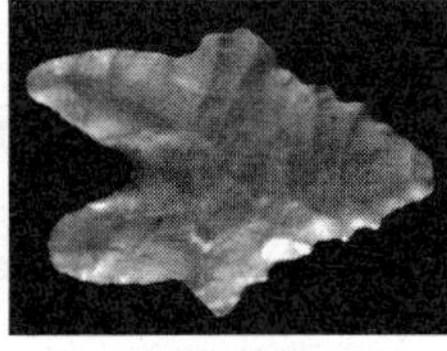

G5, $4-$8
OH.

LOCATION: Northeastern states. **DESCRIPTION:** A small to medium size, thin, deeply notched or serrated, bifurcated stemmed point. The basal lobes are parallel with a tendency to turn inward and are pointed. The outward sides of the basal lobes are usually fractured from the base towards the tip and can be ground.

EC

G9, $15-$25
Ross Co., OH. Classic

G8, $25-$50
OH.

G8, $35-$65
Carroll Co., OH.

G9, $45-$90
Cleveland, OH.

G9, $65-$125
Cleveland, OH.

LANCET - Paleo to Archaic, 14,000 - 5000 B. P.

(Also see Drill and Scraper)

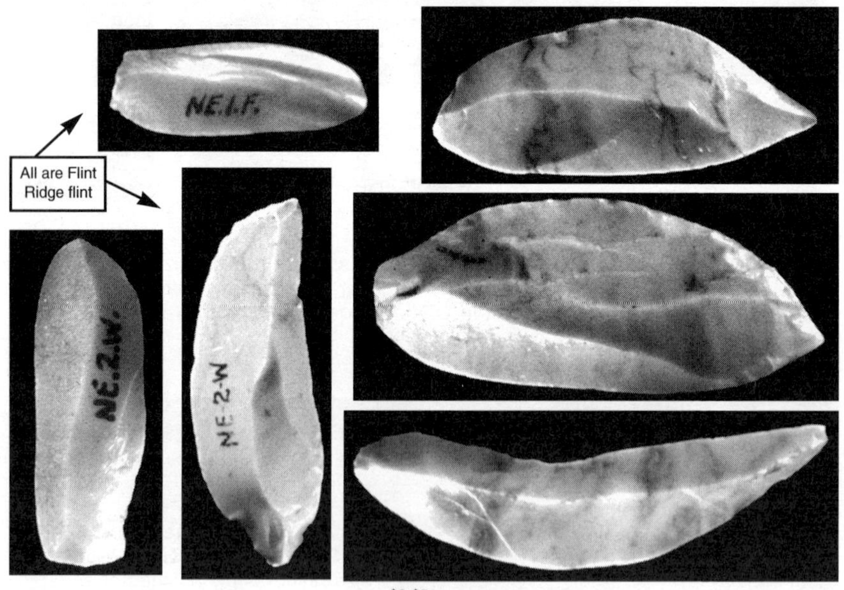

$3-$5 ea.
All from Flint Ridge, OH.

LOCATION: Found on all early man sites. **DESCRIPTION:** A medium to large size sliver used as a knife for cutting. Recent experiments proved that these knives were sharper than a surgeon's scalpel. Similar to *Burins* which are fractured at one end to produce a sharp point.

LECROY - Early to Middle Archaic, 9000 - 5000 B. P.

(Also see Decatur, Fox Valley, Jude, Kanawha, Kirk Serrated-Bifurcated, Lake Erie, MacCorkle, Pine Tree, Rice Lobbed, St. Albans and Stanly)

G3, $3-$5
TN.

G4, $4-$8
S.E. TN.

G4, $10-$20
Monteray, TN.

G4, $6-$12
S.E. TN.

G3, $6-$12
S.E. TN.

G4, $8-$15
S.E. TN.

G6, $10-$20
Hamilton Co., TN.

G8, $40-$75
S.E. TN.

G4, $4-$8
GA.

G10, $30-$60
Dayton, TN.

G7, $10-$15
S.E. TN.

G7, $15-$25
TN.

G6, $20-$40
Bradley Co., TN.

G9, $50-$100
Livingston Co., KY.

G7, $20-$40
Lauderdale Co., AL.

LOCATION: Southeastern states. Type site-Hamilton Co., TN. **DESCRIPTION:** A small to medium size, thin, usually broad point with deeply notched or serrated blade edges and a deeply bifurcated base. Basal ears can either droop or expand out. The stem is usually large in comparison to the blade size. Some stem sides are fractured in Northern examples *(Lake Eerie).* Bases are usually ground. **I.D. KEY:** Basal form.

LEDBETTER - Middle to Late Archaic, 6000 - 3500 B. P.

(Also see Little Bear Creek, Mulberry Creek and Pickwick)

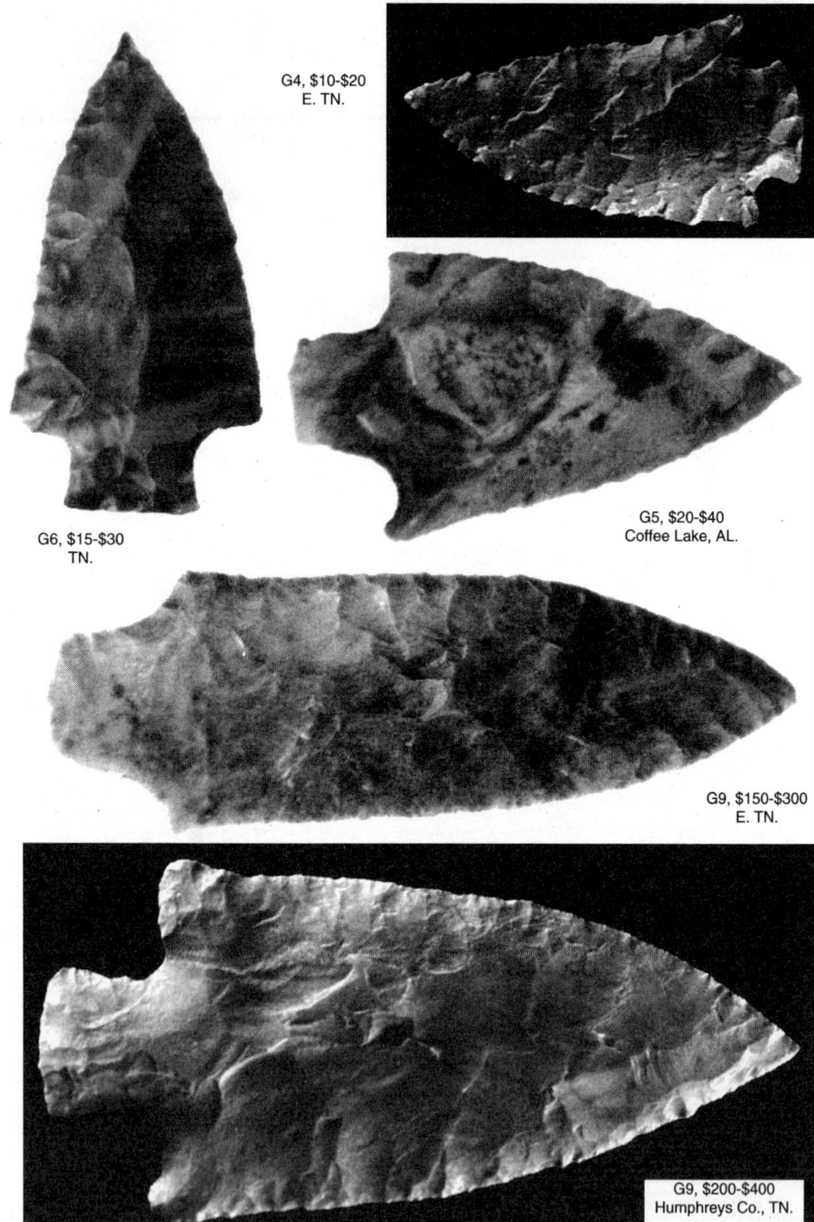

G4, $10-$20
E. TN.

G6, $15-$30
TN.

G5, $20-$40
Coffee Lake, AL.

G9, $150-$300
E. TN.

G9, $200-$400
Humphreys Co., TN.

LOCATION: Southeastern states. **DESCRIPTION:** A medium to large size asymmetrical point with a short, usually fractured or snapped base. One blade edge is curved more than the other. Shoulders are tapered, squared or slightly barbed. Some examples show fine pressure flaking along the blade edges. Believed to be *Pickwick* knives. **I.D. KEY:** Blade form.

LEIGHTON - Early Archaic, 8000 - 5000 B. P.

(Also see Benton, Big Sandy, Evans and Ohio Double Notched)

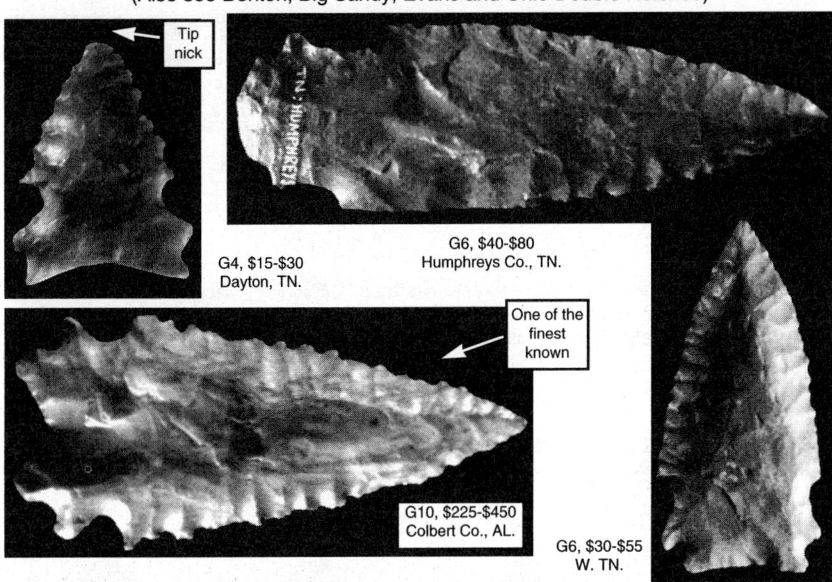

G4, $15-$30
Dayton, TN.

G6, $40-$80
Humphreys Co., TN.

G10, $225-$450
Colbert Co., AL.

G6, $30-$55
W. TN.

EC

LOCATION: Southeastern states. **DESCRIPTION:** A medium to large size, double side-notched point that is usually serrated and has a concave base that is ground. **I.D. kEY:** Basal notching, archaic flaking.

LERMA ROUNDED BASE - Trans. Paleo-Mid-Archaic, 10,000 - 5000 B. P.

(Also see Adena Blade, Harahey, North, Paleo Knife, Snake Creek and Tear Drop)

LOCATION: Siberia to Alaska, Canada, Mexico, South America, and across the U.S. **DESCRIPTION:** A large size, narrow, thick, lanceolate blade with a rounded base. Some Western examples are beveled on one side of each face. Flaking tends to be collateral and finer examples are thin in cross section.

IMPORTANT:
Lermas are shown 50% of actual size

G10, $250-$400
Carthage, TN.

G10, $200-$400
Parsons, TN.

G10, $400-$800
Humphreys Co., TN.

LEVANNA - Late Woodland to Mississippian, 1300 - 600 B. P.

(Also see Hamilton, Madison and Yadkin)

G9, $8-$15
Bristol, TN.

G8, $8-$15
Pulaski Co., KY.

G8, $8-$15
Pulaski Co., KY.

G8, $10-$20
Trimble Co., KY.

LOCATION: Southeastern to Northeastern states. **DESCRIPTION:** A small to medium size, thin, triangular point with a concave to straight base. Believed to be replaced by Madison points in later times. Called *Yadkin* in North Carolina. **I.D. KEY:** Medium thick cross section.

LIMESTONE - Late Archaic to Early Woodland, 5000 - 2000 B. P.

(Also see Fairland, Johnson, McIntire)

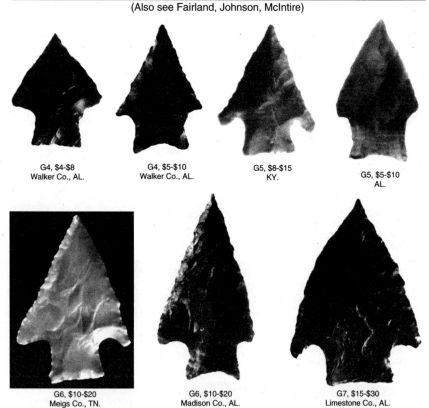

G4, $4-$8
Walker Co., AL.

G4, $5-$10
Walker Co., AL.

G5, $8-$15
KY.

G5, $5-$10
AL.

G6, $10-$20
Meigs Co., TN.

G6, $10-$20
Madison Co., AL.

G7, $15-$30
Limestone Co., AL.

LOCATION: Southeastern states. **DESCRIPTION:** A small to medium size, triangular stemmed point with an expanded, concave base and barbed to tapered shoulders. Blade edges are concave, convex or straight. **I.D. KEY:** Concave base, one barb is higher.

LIMETON BIFURCATE - Early Archaic, 9000 - 6000 B. P.

(Also see Haw River)

LOCATION: Eastern states. **DESCRIPTION:** A medium size, crudely made, broad, lanceolate blade with a central notch in the base.

G6, $5-$10
Southeast, TN.

LITTLE BEAR CREEK - Late Archaic to late Woodland, 4000 - 1500 B. P.

(Also see Adena, Kays, Mulberry Creek, Pickwick and Ponchartrain)

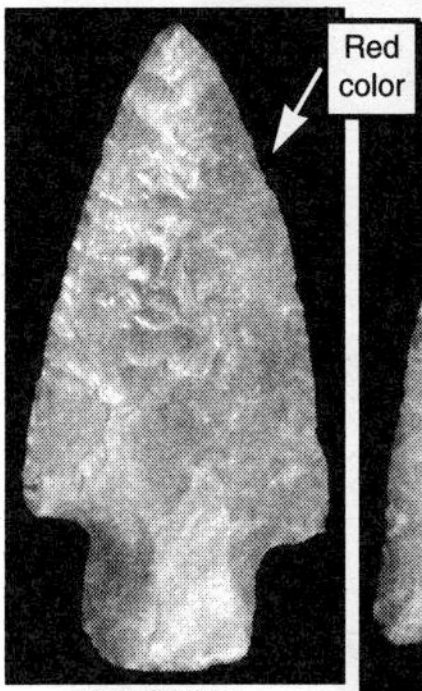

Red color

G6, $5-$10
N.E. MS.

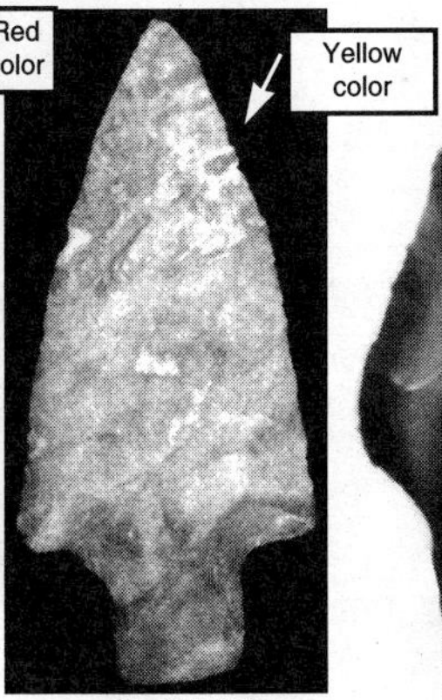

Yellow color

G6, $10-$20
N.E. MS.

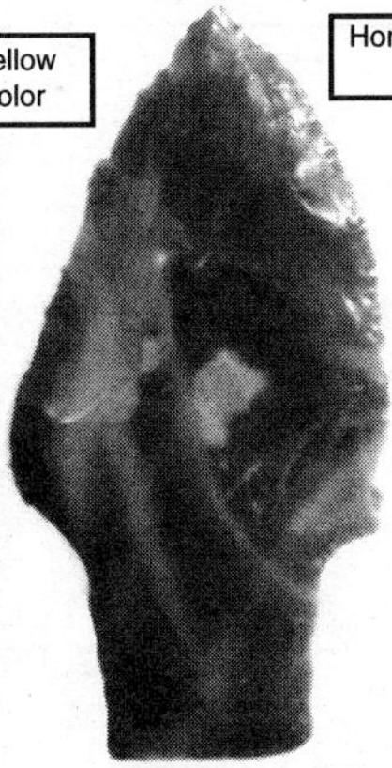

G6, $10-$20
TN.

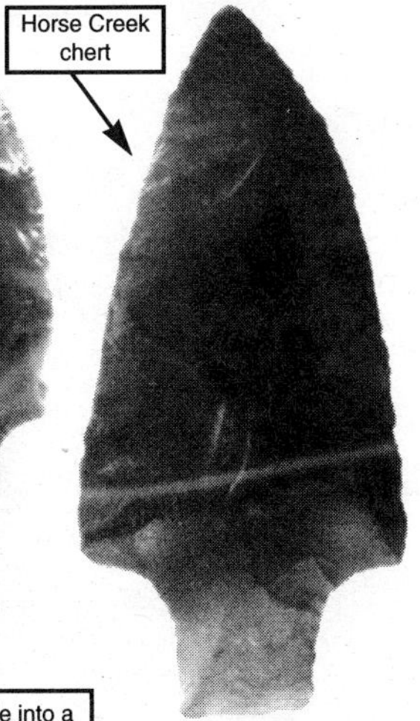

Horse Creek chert

G8, $50-$100
TN.

G10, $125-$225
Florence, AL.

G7, $20-$35
Florence, AL.

G5, $20-$40
Florence, AL.

Made into a perforator

G8, $25-$50
TN.

G10, $200-$400
Hardin Co., TN.

G10, $500-$1000
Lauderdale Co., AL.

G10, $200-$400
Livingston Co., KY.

G9, $200-$400
TN.

LOCATION: Southeastern states. **DESCRIPTION:** A medium to large size, narrow point with a long parallel stem that may contract or expand slightly. Blade edges are slightly convex. Shoulders are usually squared, tapered or slightly barbed. The base can be fractured or snapped off. Blade edges can be beveled on one side of each face and finely serrated. Called *Sarasota* in Florida. **I.D. KEY:** Straight base, woodland flaking.

(Also see Cobbs, Cypress Creek, Hardin, Kirk Corner Notched, St. Charles and Thebes)

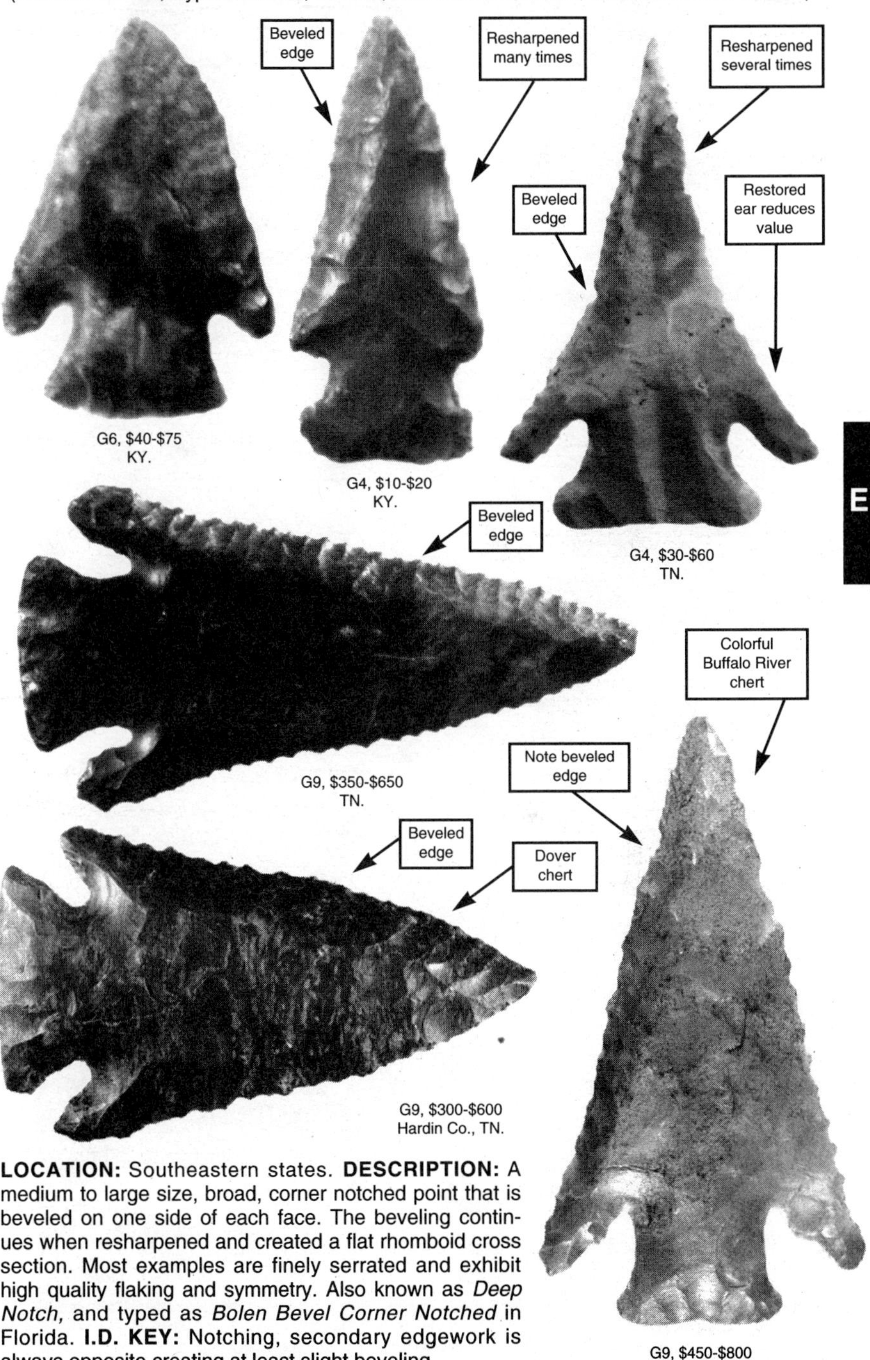

G6, $40-$75
KY.

G4, $10-$20
KY.

G4, $30-$60
TN.

G9, $350-$650
TN.

G9, $300-$600
Hardin Co., TN.

G9, $450-$800
Hardin Co., TN.

LOCATION: Southeastern states. **DESCRIPTION:** A medium to large size, broad, corner notched point that is beveled on one side of each face. The beveling continues when resharpened and created a flat rhomboid cross section. Most examples are finely serrated and exhibit high quality flaking and symmetry. Also known as *Deep Notch,* and typed as *Bolen Bevel Corner Notched* in Florida. **I.D. KEY:** Notching, secondary edgework is always opposite creating at least slight beveling.

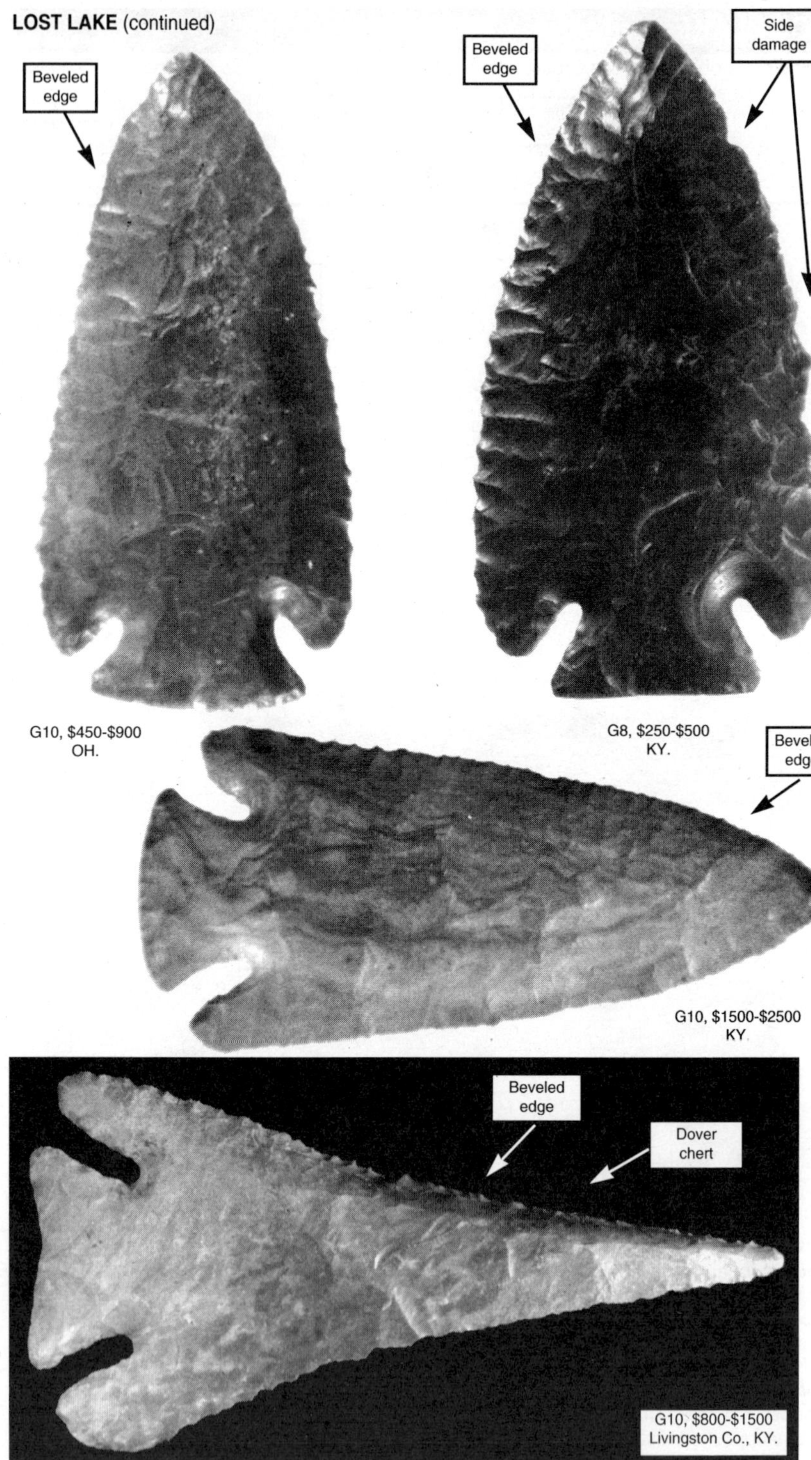

G10, $450-$900
OH.

G8, $250-$500
KY.

G10, $1500-$2500
KY.

G10, $800-$1500
Livingston Co., KY.

LOZENGE - Mississippian, 1000 - 400 B. P.

(Also see Nodena)

LOCATION: Midwestern to Southeastern states. **DESCRIPTION:** A small size, narrow, thin, double pointed arrow point.

G8, $8-$15
KY.

MACCORKLE - Early Archaic, 8000 - 6000 B. P.

(Also see Kirk Serrated-Bifurcated, LeCroy, Rice Lobbed and St. Albans)

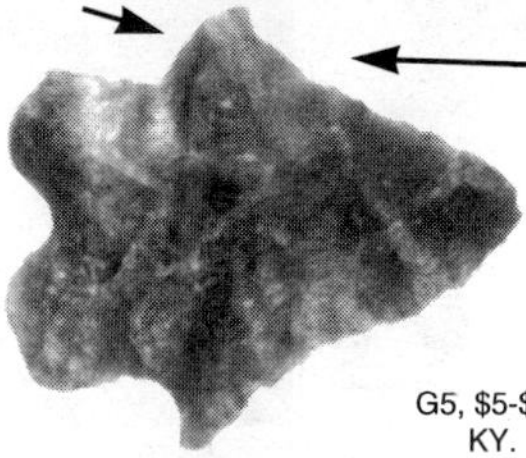

Tang damage

G5, $5-$10
KY.

G8, $35-$65
Stark Co., OH.

Coshocton chert

G6, $15-$30
S.E. TN.

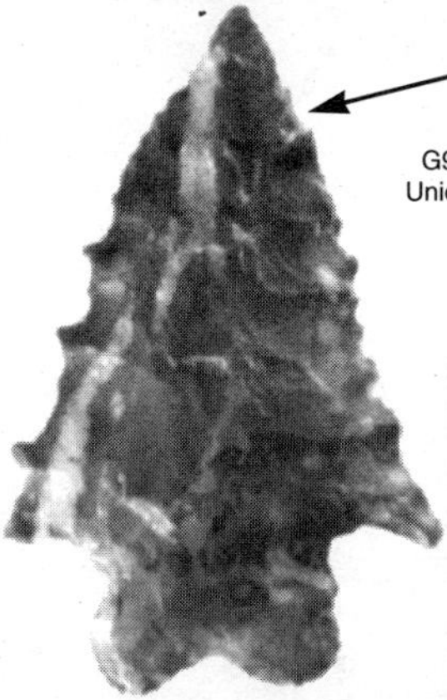

Coshocton chert

G9, $35-$65
Union Co., OH.

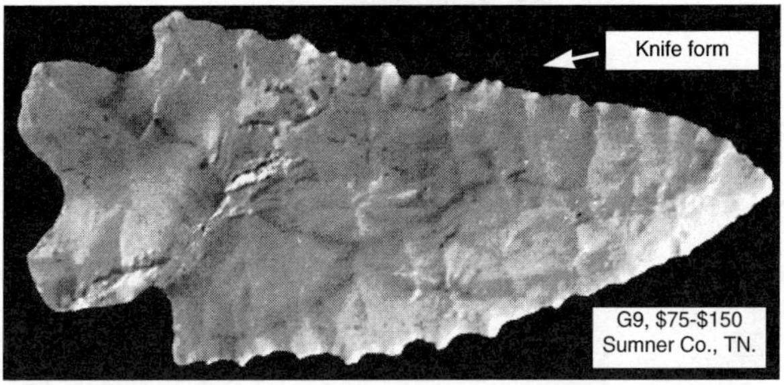

G8, $40-$75
IN.

Knife form

G9, $75-$150
Sumner Co., TN.

LOCATION: Midwestern to Southeastern states. **DESCRIPTION:** A medium to large size, thin, usually serrated, widely corner notched point with large round ears and a deep notch in the center of the base. Bases are usually ground. The smaller examples can be easily confused with the *LeCroy* point. Shoulders and blade expand more towards the base than *LeCroy*, but only in some cases. Called *Nottoway River Bifurcate* in Virginia. **I.D. KEY:** Basal notching, early Archaic flaking.

MADISON - Mississippian, 1100 - 200 B. P.

(Also see Camp Creek, Guntersville, Hamilton, Levanna, Maud and Valina)

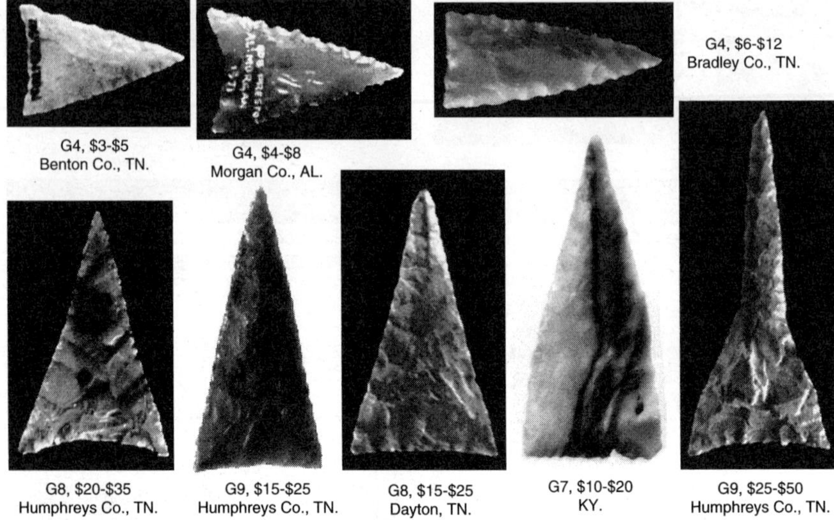

G4, $3-$5
Benton Co., TN.

G4, $4-$8
Morgan Co., AL.

G4, $6-$12
Bradley Co., TN.

G8, $20-$35
Humphreys Co., TN.

G9, $15-$25
Humphreys Co., TN.

G8, $15-$25
Dayton, TN.

G7, $10-$20
KY.

G9, $25-$50
Humphreys Co., TN.

LOCATION: Coincides with the Mississippian culture in the Eastern states. **DESCRIPTION:** A small to medium size, thin, triangular point with usually straight sides and base. Some examples are notched on two to three sides. Many are of high quality and some are finely serrated.

MAPLES - Middle Archaic, 4500 - 3500 B. P.

(Also see Elora, Morrow Mountain and Savannah River)

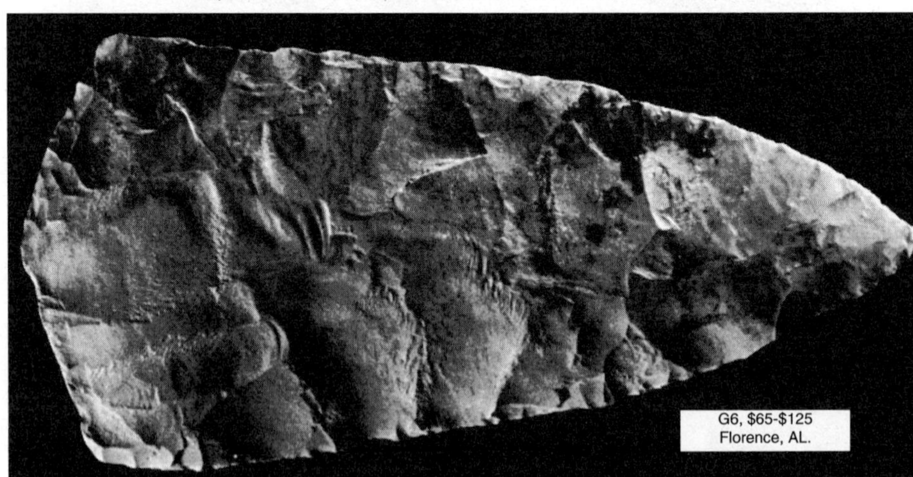

G6, $65-$125
Florence, AL.

LOCATION: Southeastern states. **DESCRIPTION:** A very large, broad, thick, short stemmed blade. Shoulders are tapered and the stem is contracting with a concave to straight base. Usually thick and crudely made, but fine quality examples have been found. Flaking is random and this type should not be confused with *Morrow Mountain* which has Archaic parallel flaking. **I.D. KEY:** Thickness, notching, flaking.

MARIANNA - Transitional Paleo, 10,000 - 8500 B. P.

(Also see Angostura, Browns Valley and Conerly)

LOCATION: Southern to Southeasterm states. **DESCRIPTION:** A medium size lanceolate point with a constricted, concave base. Look for parallel to oblique flaking.

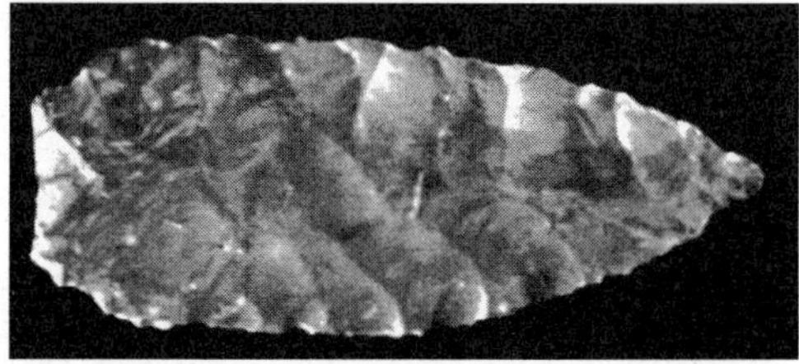

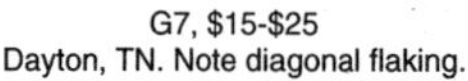

G7, $15-$25
Dayton, TN. Note diagonal flaking.

MCINTIRE - Middle to Late Archaic, 6000 - 4000 B. P.

(Also see Kays, Limestone, Mud Creek and Smithsonia)

G5, $8-$15
New Era, TN.

G6, $10-$20
Morgan Co., AL.

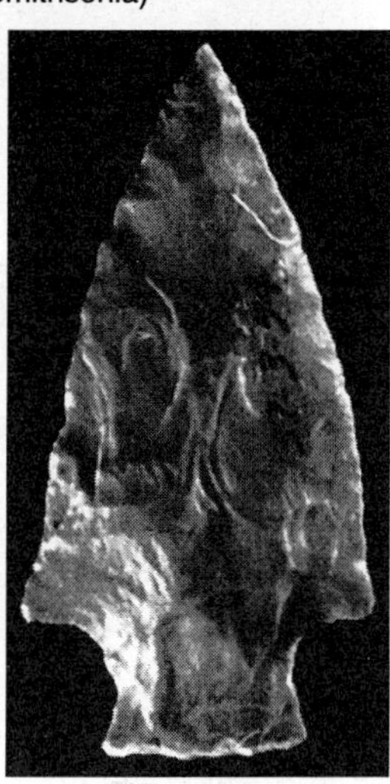

G6, $15-$25
Limestone Co., AL.

LOCATION: Southeastern states. **DESCRIPTION:** A medium to large point with straight to convex blade edges and a broad parallel to expanding stem. Shoulders are square to slightly barbed and the base is usually straight.

MEADOWOOD - Late Archaic to Woodland, 4000 - 2000 B. P.

(Also see Big Sandy and Newton Falls)

G7, $30-$65
OH.

LOCATION: Northeastern to Eastern states. **DESCRIPTION:** Medium to large size, thick, broad side notched point. Notches occur close to the base. This point is found from Indiana to New York.

MEROM - Late Archaic, 4000 - 3000 B. P.

(Also see Keota)

LOCATION: Midwestern to Southeastern states. **DESCRIPTION:** A small size, triangular, point with wide side notches and a convex base.

G5, $1-$3
Meigs Co., TN.

G7, $3-$5
TN.

MESERVE - Transitional Paleo to Middle Archaic, 9500 - 4000 B. P.

(Also see Dalton)

G8, $50-100
OH.

LOCATION: Midwestern states, rarely into Ohio. **DESCRIPTION:** A medium size, auriculate form with a blade that is beveled on one side of each face. Beveling extends into the basal area. This type is related to *Dalton* points.

MONTGOMERY - Woodland, 2500 - 1000 B. P.

(Also see Benjamin, Ebenezer and Morrow Mountain)

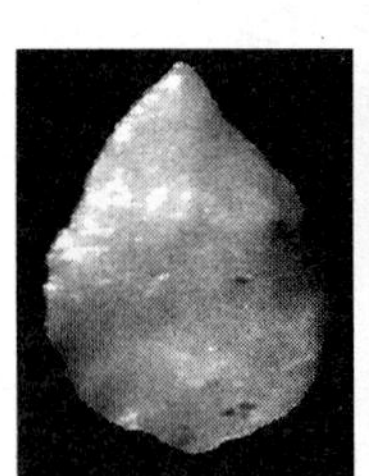

G5, $1-$2
Montgomery Co., AL.

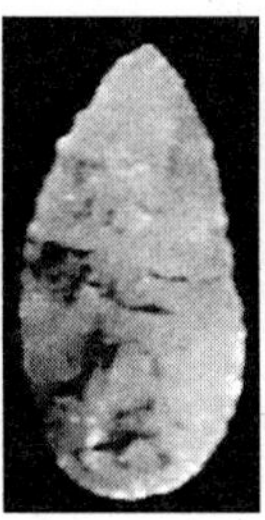

G4, $1-$2
Montgomery Co., AL.

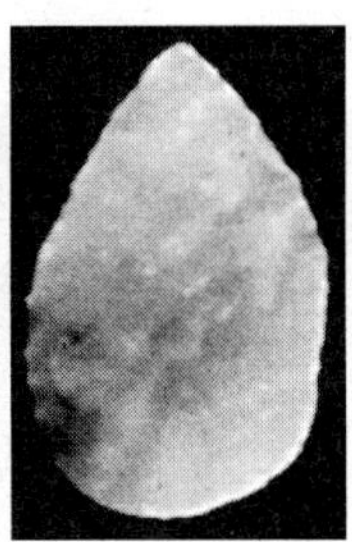

G5, $1-$2
Montgomery Co., AL.

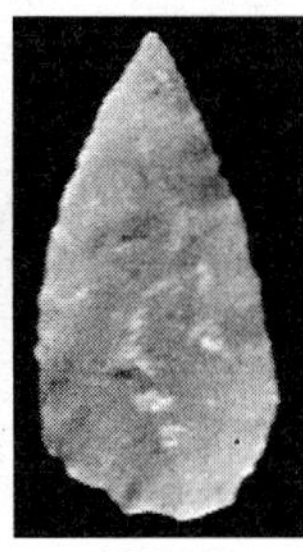

G5, $1-$2
Autauga Co., AL.

G5, $1-$2
Dallas Co., AL.

LOCATION: Southeastern states. **DESCRIPTION:** A small, broad, tear-drop shaped point with a rounded base. Flaking is random. This type is similar to Catan found in Texas.

MORROW MOUNTAIN - Middle Archaic, 7000 - 5000 B. P.

(Also see Buggs Island, Cypress Creek, Ebenezer, Eva and Maples)

G5, $5-$10
Walker Co., AL.

G5, $5-$10
Burke Co., GA.

G6, $15-$30
Burke Co., GA.

G5, $1-$2
Burke Co., GA.

G7, $25-$45
Barboar Co., AL.

G9, $40-$75
AL.

G9, $100-$200
N. AL.

LOCATION: Midwestern to Southeastern states. **DESCRIPTION:** A medium to large size, triangular point with a very short contracting to rounded stem. Shoulders are usually weak but can be barbed. The blade edges on some examples are serrated with needle points. **I.D. KEY:** Contracted base and Archaic parallel flaking.

MORROW MOUNTAIN ROUNDED BASE -
Middle Archaic, 7000 - 5000 B. P.

(Also see Ebenezer and Montgomery)

LOCATION: Midwestern to Southeastern states. **DESCRIPTION:** A small to medium size tear-drop point with a pronounced, short, rounded base and no shoulders. Some examples have a straight to slightly convex base. This type has similarities to Gypsum Cave points found in the Western states.

MORROW MTN. ROUND BASE (continued)

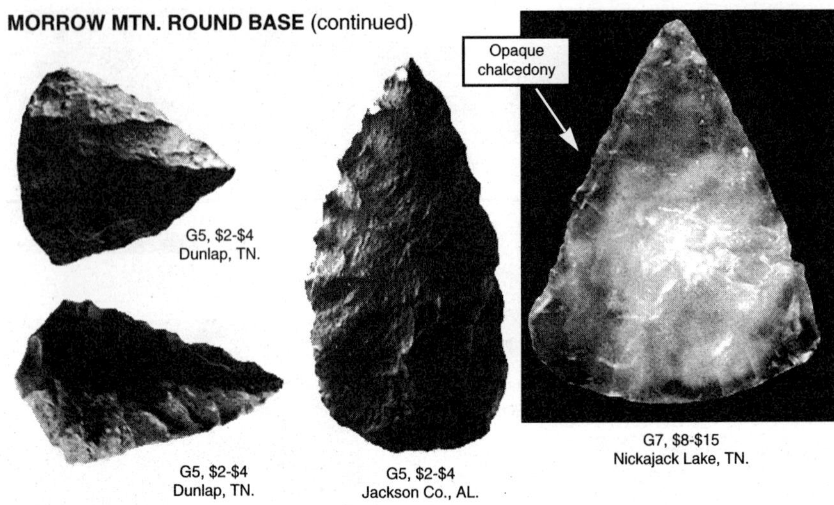

G5, \$2-\$4
Dunlap, TN.

G5, \$2-\$4
Dunlap, TN.

G5, \$2-\$4
Jackson Co., AL.

G7, \$8-\$15
Nickajack Lake, TN.

MORROW MOUNTAIN STRAIGHT BASE - Middle Archaic, 7000 - 5000 B. P.

(Also see Mud Creek)

G6, \$5-\$10
Bristol, TN.

G6, \$10-\$20
Autauga Co., AL.

G6, \$8-\$15
Decatur, AL.

G8, \$20-\$40
S.E. TN.

LOCATION: Southeastern states. **DESCRIPTION:** A medium size, thin, strongly barbed point with a contracting stem and a straight base. Some examples are serrated and have a needle tip. Look for Archaic parallel flaking.

MORSE KNIFE - Woodland, 3000 - 1500 B. P.

(Also see Cotaco Creek, Duck River Sword, Ramey Knife and Snake Creek)

LOCATION: Midwestern to Southeastern states. **DESCRIPTION:** A large lanceolate blade with a long contracting stem and a rounded base. The widest part of the blade is towards the tip.

IMPORTANT:
These are shown 50% of actual size

G10, $600-$1000
TN.

Glued

G7, $150-300
IN.

MOTLEY - Late Archaic to Woodland, 4500 - 2500 B. P.

(Also see Buck Creek, Hamilton, Smithsonia, Snyders and Wade)

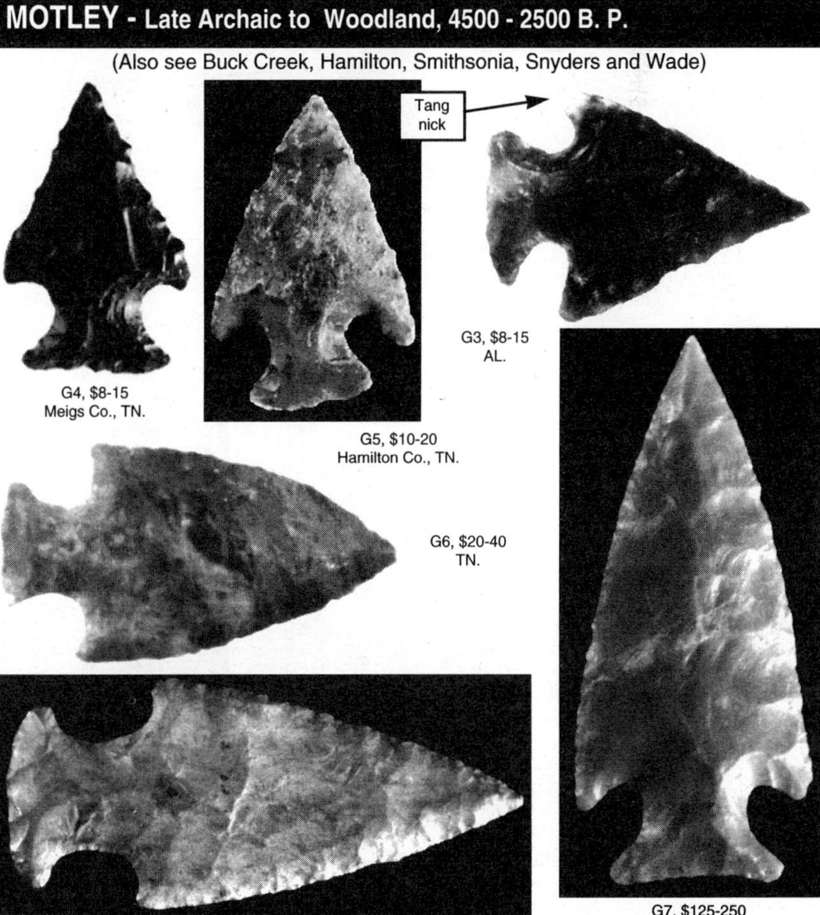

G4, $8-15
Meigs Co., TN.

G5, $10-20
Hamilton Co., TN.

G3, $8-15
AL.

G6, $20-40
TN.

G7, $75-150, Dickson Cave, KY.

G7, $125-250
Meigs Co., TN.

MOTLEY (continued)

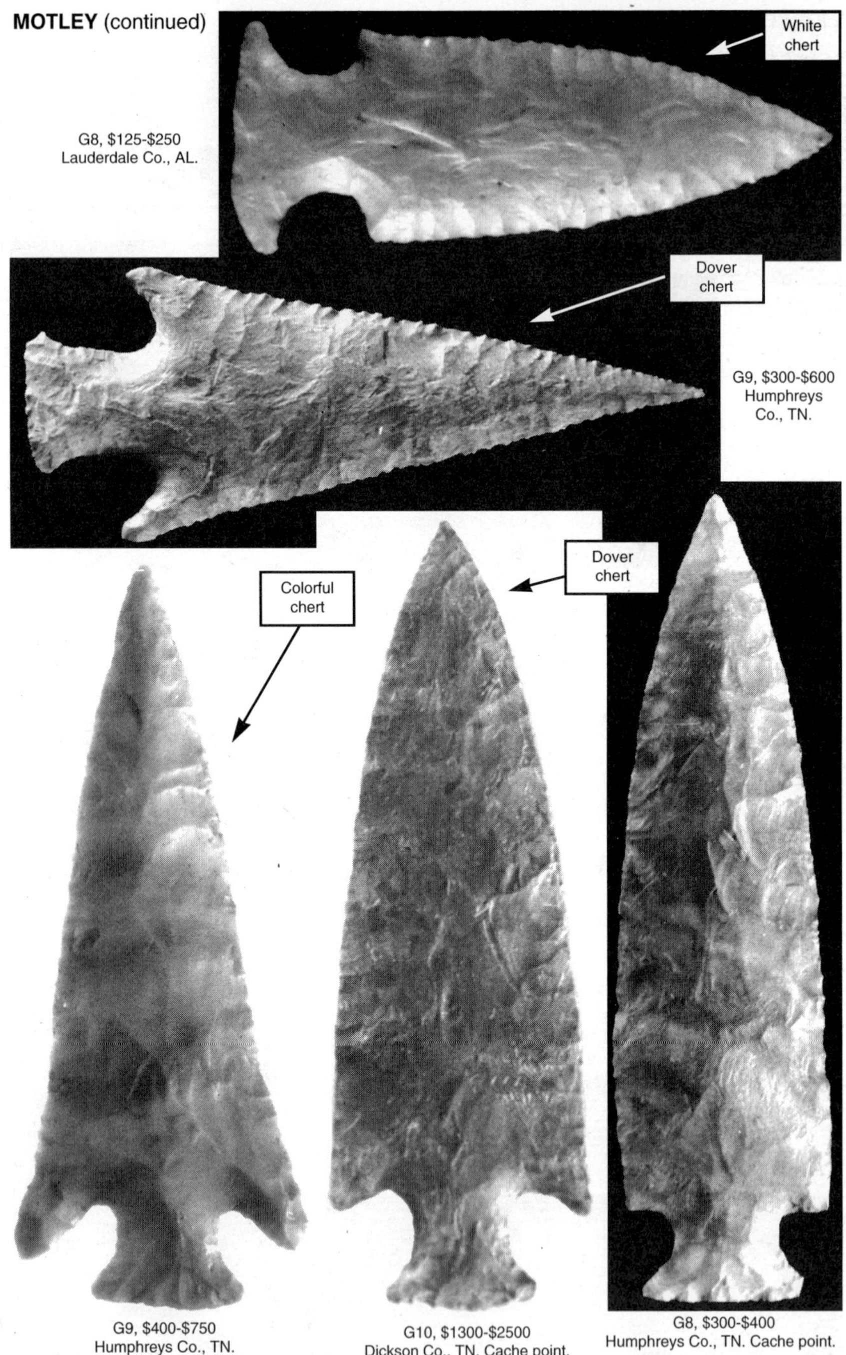

G8, $125-$250
Lauderdale Co., AL.

G9, $300-$600
Humphreys
Co., TN.

G9, $400-$750
Humphreys Co., TN.

G10, $1300-$2500
Dickson Co., TN. Cache point.

G8, $300-$400
Humphreys Co., TN. Cache point.

LOCATION: Southeastern states. **DESCRIPTION:** A medium to large size, expanded stemmed to widely corner notched point with strong barbs. The blade edges and the base are convex to straight. Has been found associated with *Wade* points in caches. Called *Epps* in Louisiana.

MOUNTAIN FORK - Middle Archaic to Woodland, 6000 - 2000 B. P.

(Also see Bradley, Flint River and Schild Spike, Duval and New Market)

G6, $2-$4
Decatur, AL.

G6, $2-$4
Limestone Co., AL.

LOCATION: Southeastern states. **DESCRIPTION:** A small to medium size, narrow, thick, stemmed point with tapered shoulders.

MOUSE CREEK - Woodland, 1500 - 1000 B. P.

(Also see Jacks Reef Pentagonal)

G6, $15-$25
TN.

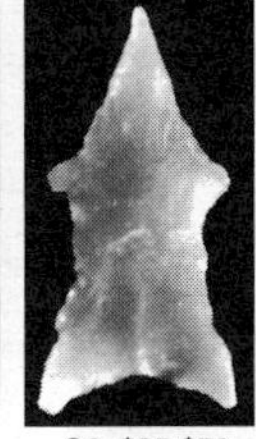

G7, $20-$35
Madison Co., AL.

G9, $35-$70
Bradley Co., TN.

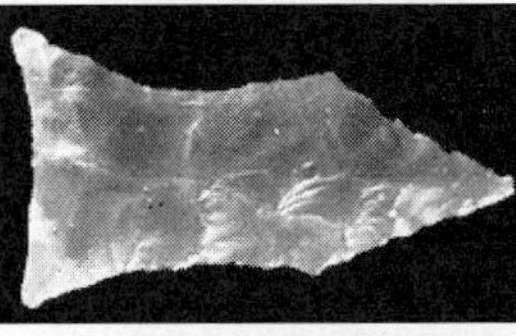

G8, $30-$60
Morgan Co., TN.

LOCATION: Southeastern states. **DESCRIPTION:** A small to medium size, thin, pentagonal point with prominent shoulders, a short pointed blade and a long, expanding stem. The base is concave with pointed ears. The hafting area is over half the length of the point. This type is **very rare** and could be related to Jacks Reef.

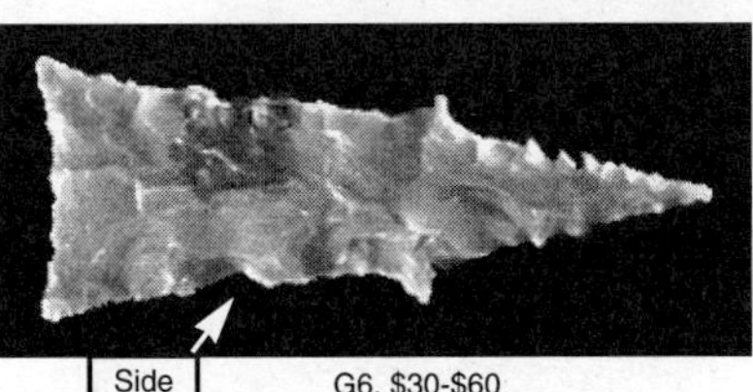

Side nick

G6, $30-$60
Dayton, TN.
Side nick

MUD CREEK - Late Archaic to Woodland, 4000 - 2000 B. P.

(Also see Bakers Creek, Beacon Island, Flint Creek, Little Bear Creek, McIntire and Mulberry Creek)

G5, $2-$4
S.E. TN.

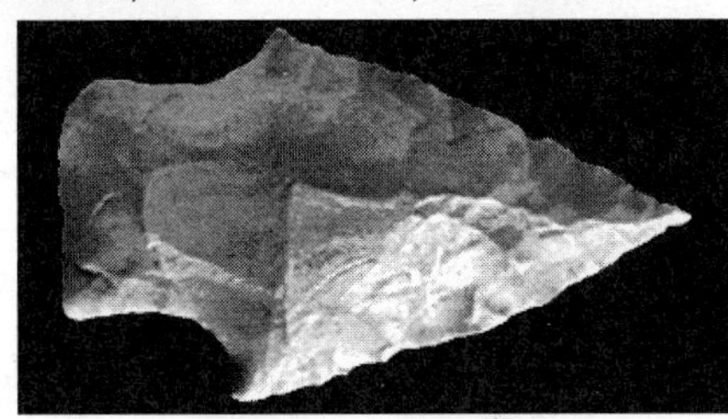

G5, $5-$8
Walker Co., AL.

LOCATION: Southeastern states. **DESCRIPTION:** A medium size point with slightly recurved blade edges, a narrow, needle like tip, square to tapered shoulders and an expanded stem. Called *Patuxent* in Virginia. **I.D. KEY:** Thickness, point form, high barb.

G8, $5-$10
S.E. TN.

MUD CREEK (continued)

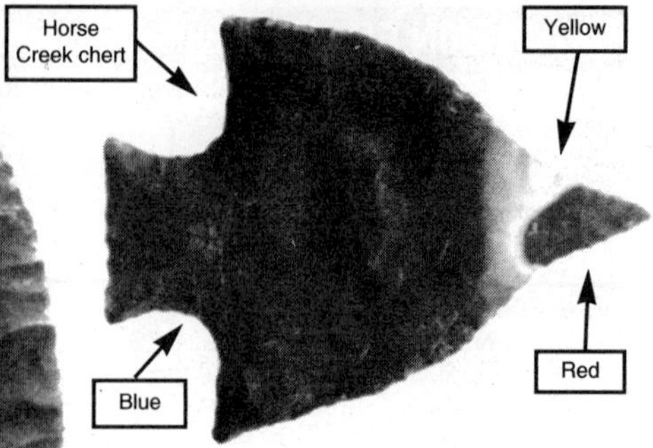

Horse Creek chert

Yellow

Blue

Red

G10, $100-$200
AL.

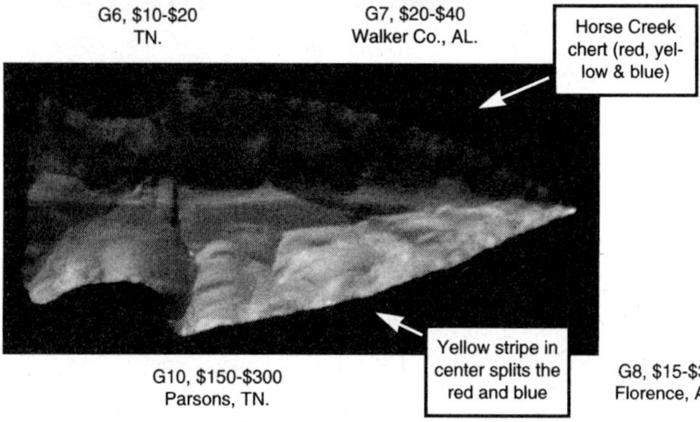

G6, $10-$20
TN.

G7, $20-$40
Walker Co., AL.

Horse Creek chert (red, yellow & blue)

Yellow stripe in center splits the red and blue

G10, $150-$300
Parsons, TN.

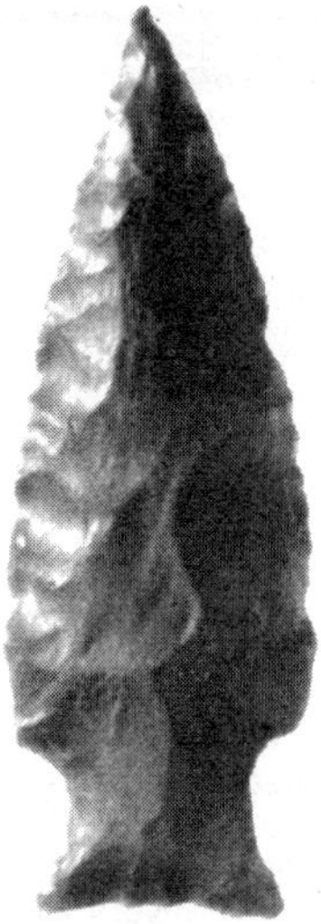

G8, $15-$30
Florence, AL.

MULBERRY CREEK - Mid-Archaic to Woodland, 5000 - 3000 B. P.

(Also see Little Bear Creek and Pickwick)

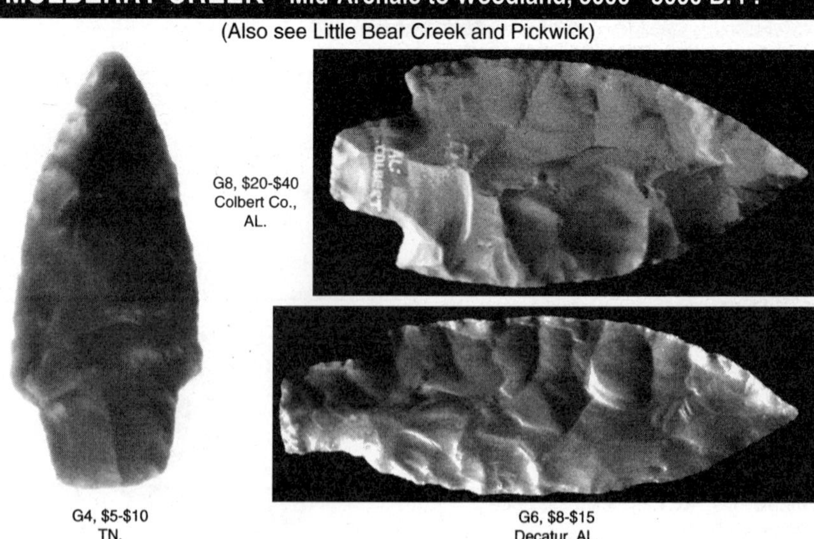

G8, $20-$40
Colbert Co.,
AL.

G4, $5-$10
TN.

G6, $8-$15
Decatur, AL.

G8, $30-$60
Benton Co., TN.

G6, $15-$25
Decatur, AL.

G8, $30-$60
Florence, AL.

G10, $175-$350
Colbert Co., AL.

G9, $300-$600
Colbert Co., AL.

LOCATION: Southeastern states. **DESCRIPTION:** A medium to large size, thick, stemmed point with recurved blade edges. Shoulders are usually tapered, but can be barbed. The blade is widest near the center of the point. Stems can be expanding, parallel or contracting.

NEUBERGER - Early-Mid Archaic, 9000 - 6000 B. P.

(Also see Kirk Corner Notched and Pine Tree)

LOCATION: Southeastern states. **DESCRIPTION:** A medium to large size, broad, corner notched point with a short, auriculated base. Blade edges are recurved and the base is indented. Shoulders curve in towards the base.

G10, $250-$500
TN.

NEWTON FALLS- Early to Mid-Archaic, 7000 - 5000 B. P.

(Also see Big Sandy and Meadowood)

G8, $20-$35
OH.

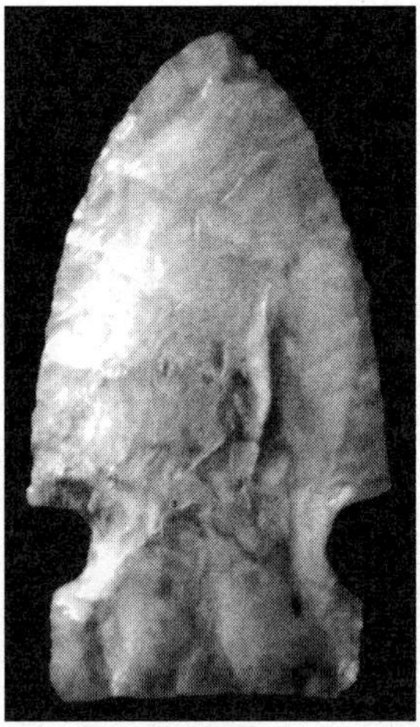

G9, $25-$50
OH.

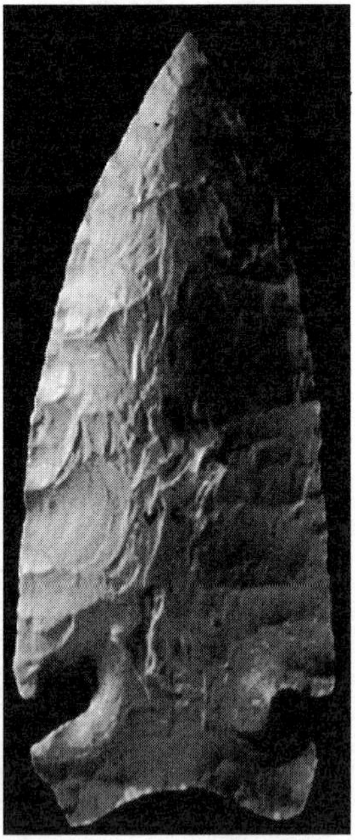

G9, $250-$500
OH.

G9, $300-$600
Alexander, OH.

NEWTON FALLS (continued)

LOCATION: Ohio and surrounding states. **DESCRIPTION:** A medium to large size, narrow, side notched point with paralled sides on longer examples and a straight to concave base which could be ground. Similar to *Big Sandy, Godar, Hemphill* and *Osceola* found in other areas. **I.D. KEY:** Size and narrowness.

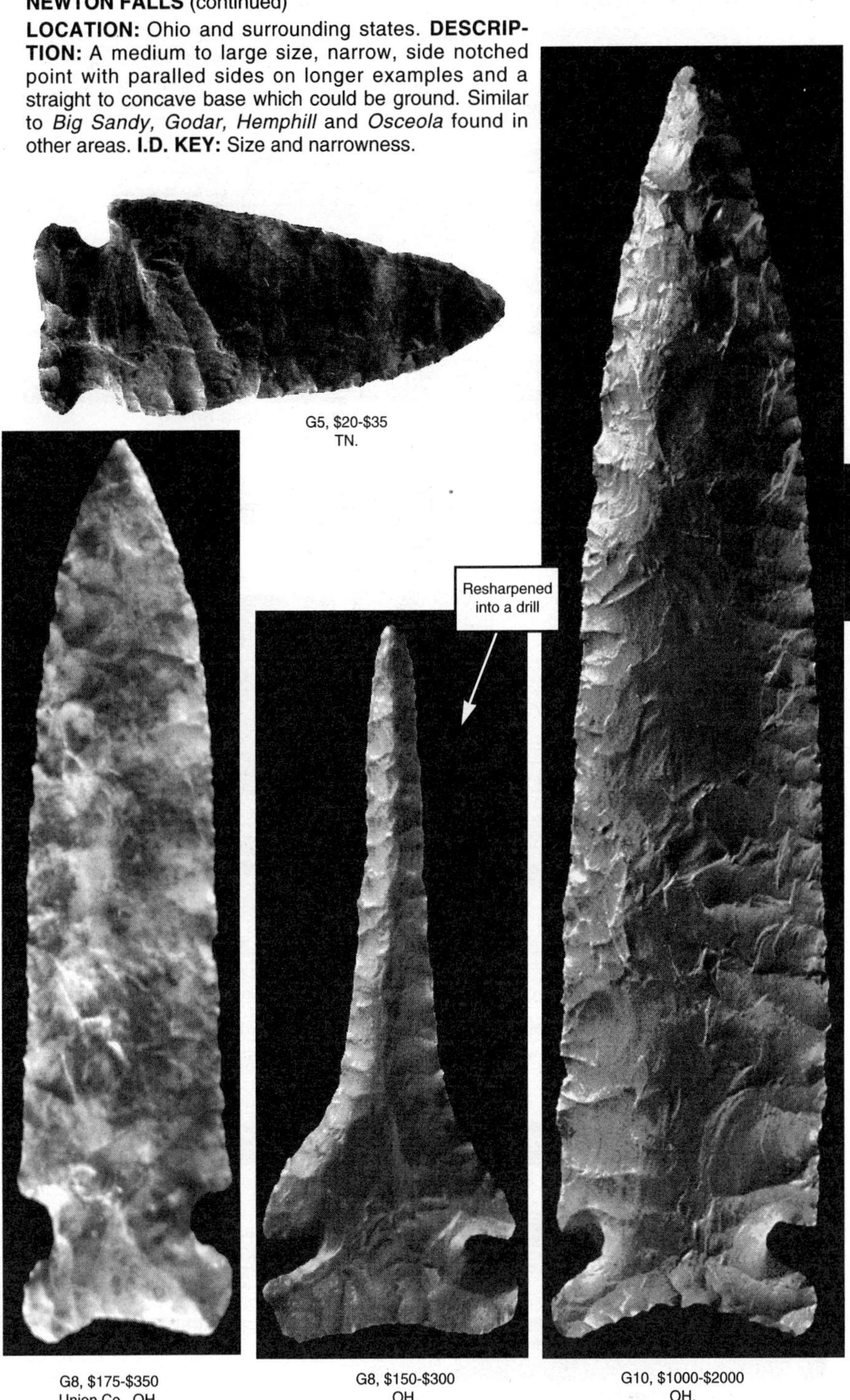

G5, $20-$35
TN.

G8, $175-$350
Union Co., OH.

G8, $150-$300
OH.

G10, $1000-$2000
OH.

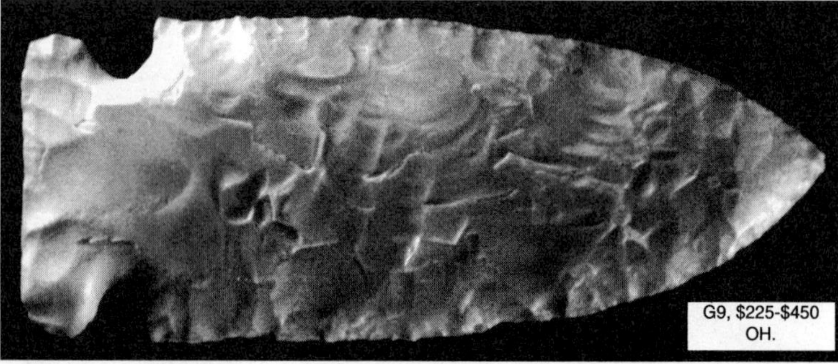
G9, $225-$450
OH.

NEW MARKET - Woodland, 3000 - 1000 B. P.

(Also see Bradley Spike, Duval, Flint River and Schild Spike)

G4, $3-$6
Limestone Co., AL.

G5, $8-$15
N. AL.

G6, $5-$10
Humphreys Co., TN.

G5, $8-$15
Limestone Co., AL.

G5, $8-$15
Limestone Co., AL.

G7, $15-$25
Morgan Co., AL.

G7, $20-$35
Decatur, AL.

LOCATION: Southeastern states. **DESCRIPTION:** A small to medium size point with tapered shoulders and an extended, rounded base. Shoulders are usually asymmetrical with one higher than the other.

NODENA - Mississippian to Historic, 600 - 400 B. P.

(Also see Guntersville and Lozenge)

G8, $10-$20, Polk Co., TN.

LOCATION: Midwestern to Southeastern states. **DESCRIPTION:** A small to medium size, narrow, thin elliptical shaped arrow point with a pointed to rounded base. Some examples have oblique, parallel flaking. Called *Tampa* in Flordia. Used by the Quapaw Indians.

G9, $50-$100
Florence, AL.

G10, $120-$200
Hamilton Co., TN.

G9, $20-$40
Polk Co., TN.

NOLICHUCKY - Woodland, 3000 - 1500 B. P.

(Also see Camp Creek, Candy Creek, Copena Auriculate, Greeneville and Yadkin)

G7, $8-$15
Meigs Co., TN.

G5, $2-$4
Meigs Co., TN.

G5, $2-$4
Bristol, TN.

G6, $5-$10
Bristol, TN.

G9, $15-$25
Clarksville, TN.

G8, $10-$20
Dayton, TN.

G9, $25-$50
Dayton, TN.

LOCATION: Southeastern states. **DESCRIPTION:** A small to medium size, triangular point with recurved blade edges and a straight to concave base. Most examples have small pointed ears at the basal corners. Bases could be ground. Believed to have evolved from *Candy Creek* points and later developed into *Camp Creek*, *Greeneville* and *Guntersville* points. Found with *Ebenezer*, *Camp Creek*, *Candy Creek* and *Greeneville* in caches (Rankin site, Cocke Co. TN.) **I.D. KEY:** Thickness and hafting area.

NORTH - Woodland, 2200 - 1600 B. P.

(Also see Adena Blade, Hopewell, Snyders and Tear Drop)

NORTH (continued)

G8, $175-$325
Sidney, OH.

LOCATION: Midwestern to Eastern states. **DESCRIPTION:** A large, thin, elliptical, broad, well made blade with a concave blade. This type is usually found in caches and is related to the Snyders point of the Hopewell culture. Believed to be unnotched Snyders points.

NOVA - Woodland to Mississippian, 1600 - 1000 B. P.

(Also see Durant's Bend and Washington)

G8, $3-$5
Dallas Co., AL.

G5, $1-$2
Dallas Co., AL.

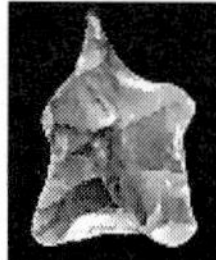

G6, $1-$3
Dallas Co., AL.

G2, $1-$2
Dallas Co., AL.

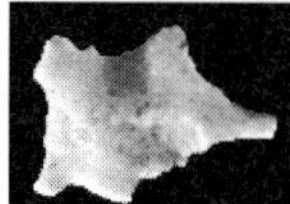

LOCATION: Southeastern states. **DESCRIPTION:** A small point shaped like a five pointed star.

OHIO DOUBLE NOTCHED - Woodland, 3000 - 2000 B. P.

(Also see Benton, Evans and Leighton)

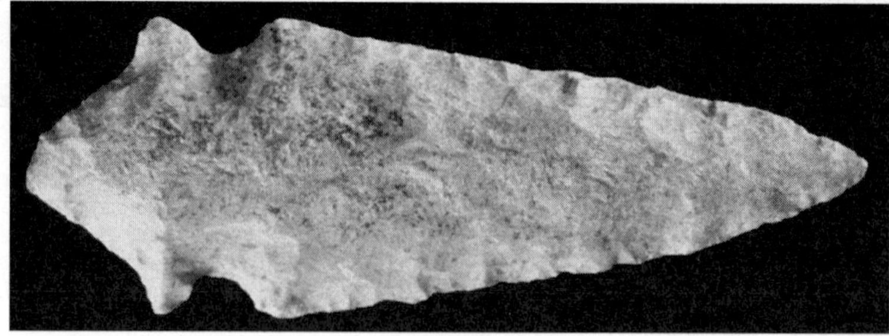

G8, $100-$200
Trimble Co., KY.

LOCATION: Ohio and surrounding states. **DESCRIPTION:** A medium to large size, narrow, rather crude, point with side notches on both sides and a short base that is usually notched.

OHIO LANCEOLATE -Transitional Paleo-Early Archaic, 10,500 - 8000 B. P.

(Also see Agate Basin)

LOCATION: Ohio and surrounding states. **DESCRIPTION:** A medium to large size lanceolate point with a straight base. Blade edges are slightly recurved becoming constricted at the basal hafting area.

G7, $100-$200
Geauga Co., OH.

ORIENT - Late Archaic to Woodland, 4000 - 2500 B. P.

(Also see Big Sandy Auriculate)

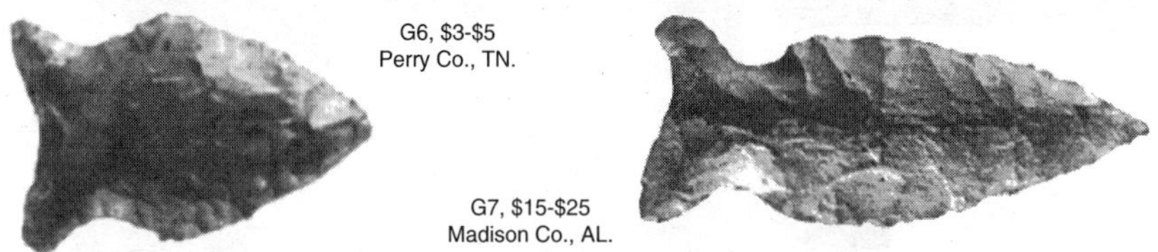

G6, $3-$5
Perry Co., TN.

G7, $15-$25
Madison Co., AL.

LOCATION: Midwestern to Eastern states. **DESCRIPTION:** A small to medium size point with broad side notches, rounded shoulders and an expanging base. The base on some examples form auricles. **I.D. KEY:** Base form and rounded shoulders.

EC

PAINT ROCK VALLEY - Transitional Paleo, 10,000 - 6000 B. P.

(Also see Angostura, Frazier, Hardaway Blade, Jeff and Tortugas)

G3, $2-$5
Madison Co., AL.

G6, $12-$20
Fort Payne, AL.

G7, $15-$25
Colbert Co., AL.

G8, $20-$40
Walker Co., AL.

LOCATION: Southeastern states. **DESCRIPTION:** A medium size, wide, lanceolate point with a concave base. Flaking is usually parallel with fine secondary work on the blade edges. The bases may be multiple fluted, thinned or beveled.

PALMER - Early Archaic, 9000 - 6000 B. P.

(Also see Autauga, Ecusta, Kirk Corner Notched and Pine Tree)

PALMER (continued)

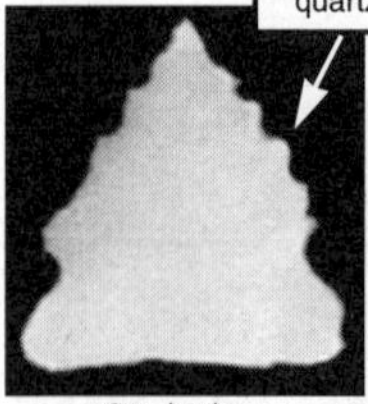

Milky quartz

G3, $4-$8
Burke Co., GA.

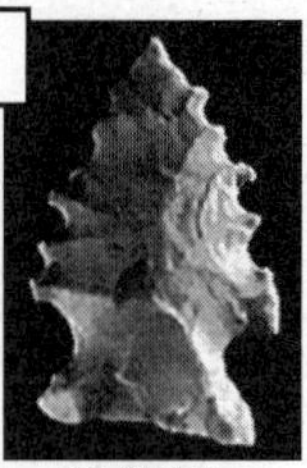

G4, $5-$10
Dayton, TN.

G6, $8-$15
Jefferson Co., TN.

G6, $8-$15
Dayton, TN.

G5, $5-$10
Newport, TN.

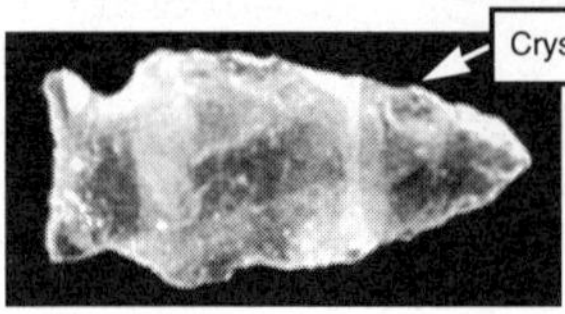

Crystal

G4, $10-$15
Burke Co.,GA.

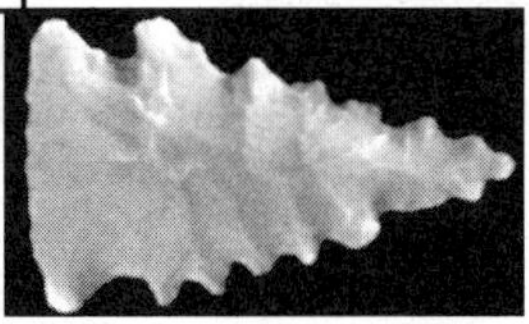

G7, $10-$15
Jefferson Co., TN.

G6, $8-$15
Dayton, TN.

Serrated edge

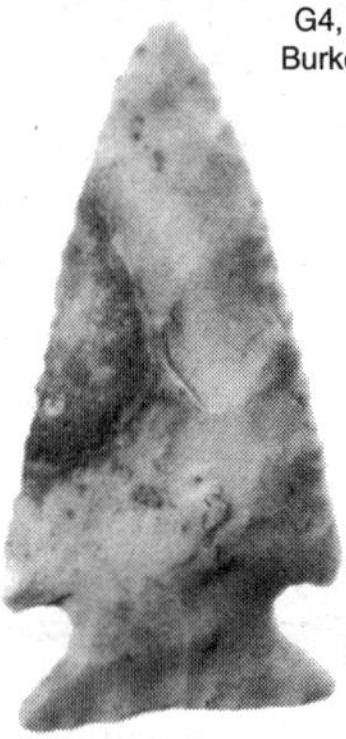

G8, $15-$25
IN.

G6, $10-$20
Smith Lake, AL.

G9, $30-$60
Dayton, TN.

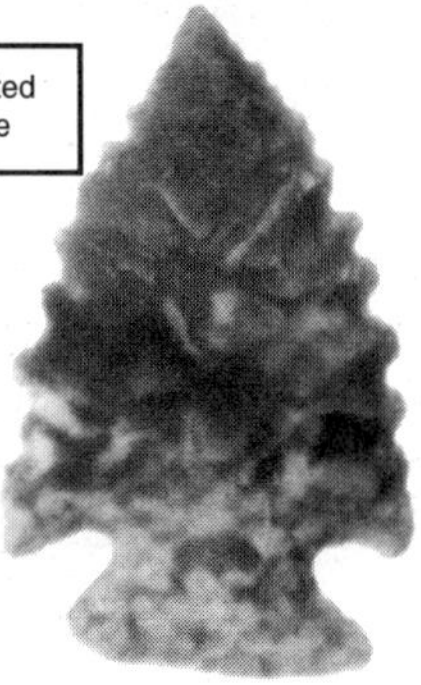

G9, $20-$40
KY.

LOCATION: Southeastern to Eastern states. **DESCRIPTION:** A small size, corner notched, triangular point with a ground concave, convex or straight base. Many are serrated and large examples would fall under the *Pine Tree* or *Kirk* type. This type developed from *Hardaway* in North Carolina where cross types are found.

PATRICK - Mid-Archaic, 5000 - 3000 B. P.

(Also see Cave Spring, Stanly and Wheeler)

G5, $3-$6
Southeastern TN.

G5, $5-$10
KY.

G7, $8-$15
Dunlap., TN.

LOCATION: Eastern states. **DESCRIPTION:** A small to medium size, narrow point with very weak shoulders and a long, parallel sided, bifurcated base.

PELICAN

(See Hinds)

PERFORATOR - Archaic to Mississippian, 9000 - 400 B. P.

(Also see Drill, Graver and Lancet)

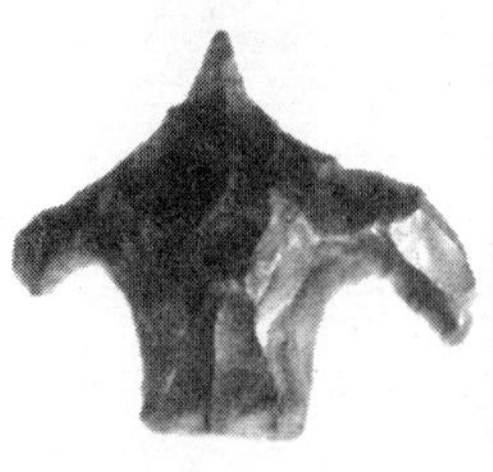

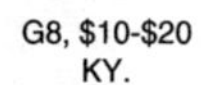

G8, $10-$20
KY.

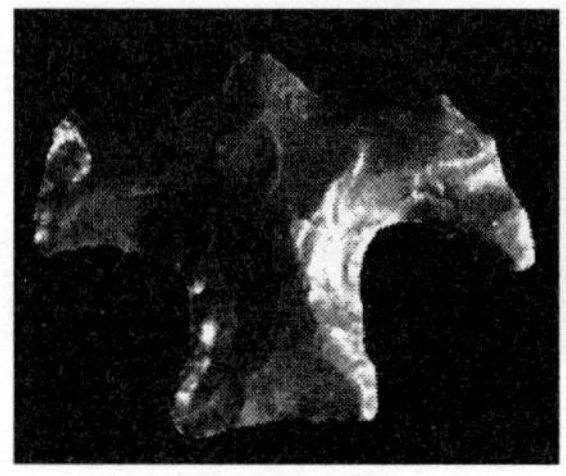

G2, $2-$5
Walker Co., GA.

G7, $10-$20
Barren Co., KY.

LOCATION: Archaic and Woodland sites everywhere. **DESCRIPTION:** A jabbing projection at the tip would qualify for the type. It is believed that *perforators* were used for tattooing, incising or to punch holes in leather or other materials or objects. Paleo peoples used *Gravers* for the same purpose. All Archaic and Woodland cultures converted their points into this type. Therefore, most point types could occur in this form.

PICKWICK - Middle to Late Archaic, 6000 - 3500 B. P.

(Also see Elora, Ledbetter, Little Bear Creek, Mulberry Creek and Shoals Creek)

G6, $25-$50
AL.

G5, $20-$35
TN.

G7, $40-$75
TN.

LOCATION: Southeastern states. **DESCRIPTION:** A medium to large size, expanded shoulder, contracted to expanded stem point. Blade edges are recurved, and many examples show fine secondary flaking with serrations. Some are beveled on one side of each face. The bevel is steep and shallow. Shoulders are horizontal, tapered or barbed and form sharp angles. Some stems are snapped off or may show original rind.

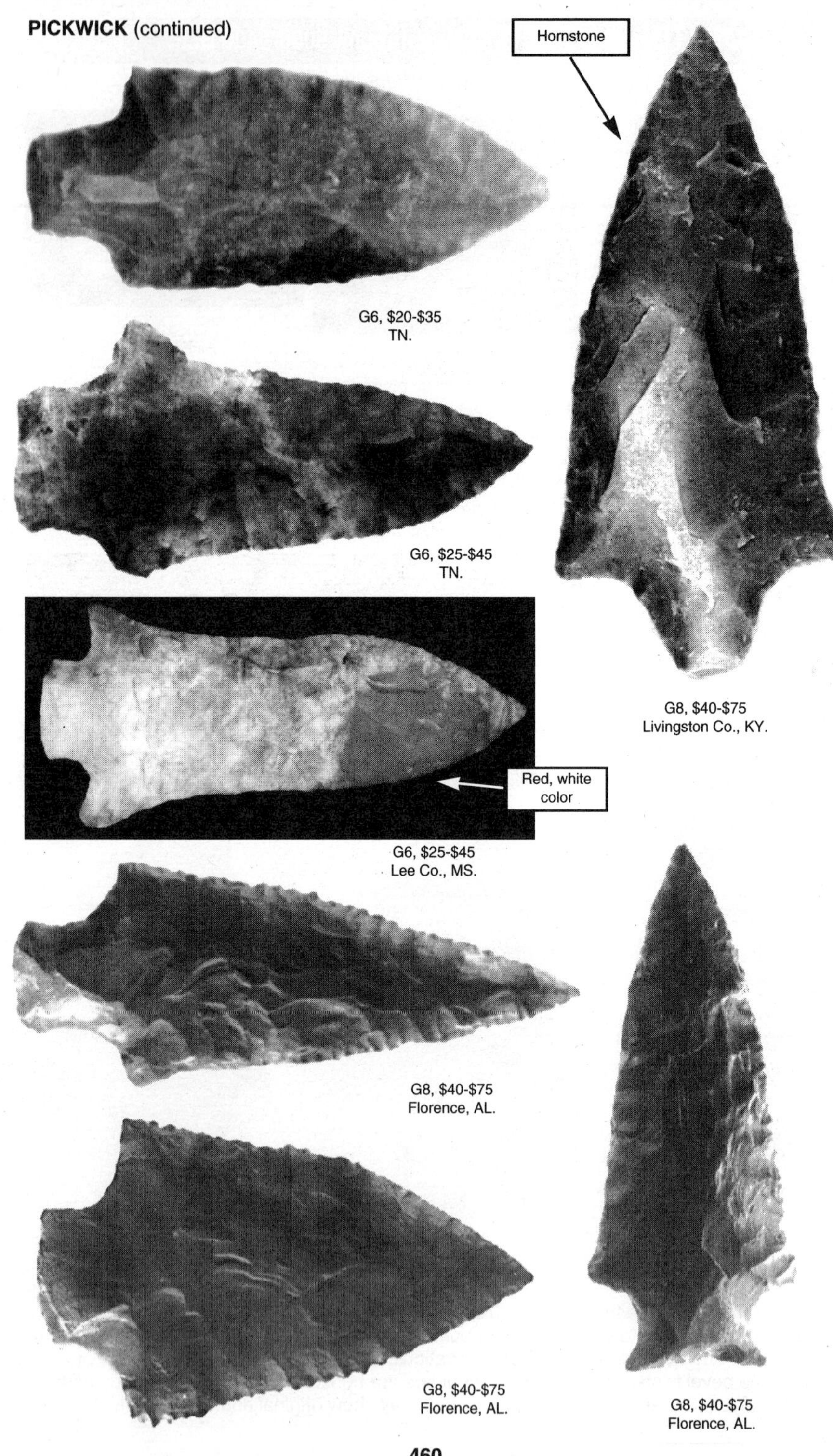

G6, $20-$35
TN.

G6, $25-$45
TN.

G8, $40-$75
Livingston Co., KY.

G6, $25-$45
Lee Co., MS.

G8, $40-$75
Florence, AL.

G8, $40-$75
Florence, AL.

G8, $40-$75
Florence, AL.

G9, $150-$300
TN.

G10, $250-$500
TN.

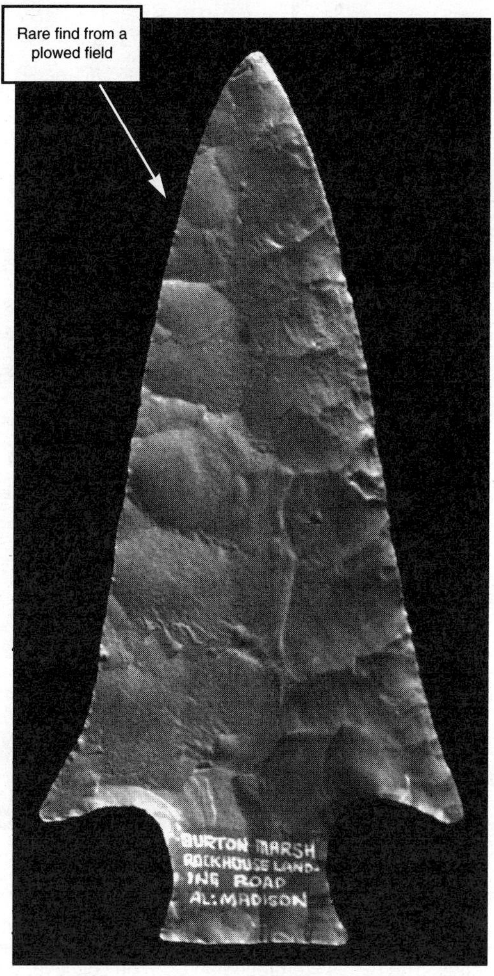

G10, $900-$1700
Madison Co., AL.

PINE TREE - Early Archaic, 8000 - 5000 B. P.

(Also see Big Sandy, Greenbrier, Kirk and Palmer)

G5, $15-$30
N.E. MS.

G7, $20-$40
Livingston Co., KY.

G7, $15-$30
KY.

G6, $20-$40
KY.

G5, $15-$30
OH.

G9, $150-$300
Florence, AL.

G9, $200-$400
Lauderdale Co,. AL.

LOCATION: Southeastern states. **DESCRIPTION:** A medium to large size, side notched, usually serrated point with parallel flaking to the center of the blade forming a median ridge. The bases are ground and can be concave, convex, straight, or auriculate. This type developed from the earlier *Greenbrier* point. Small examples would fall into the *Palmer* type. **I.D. KEY:** Archaic flaking with long flakes to the center of the blade.

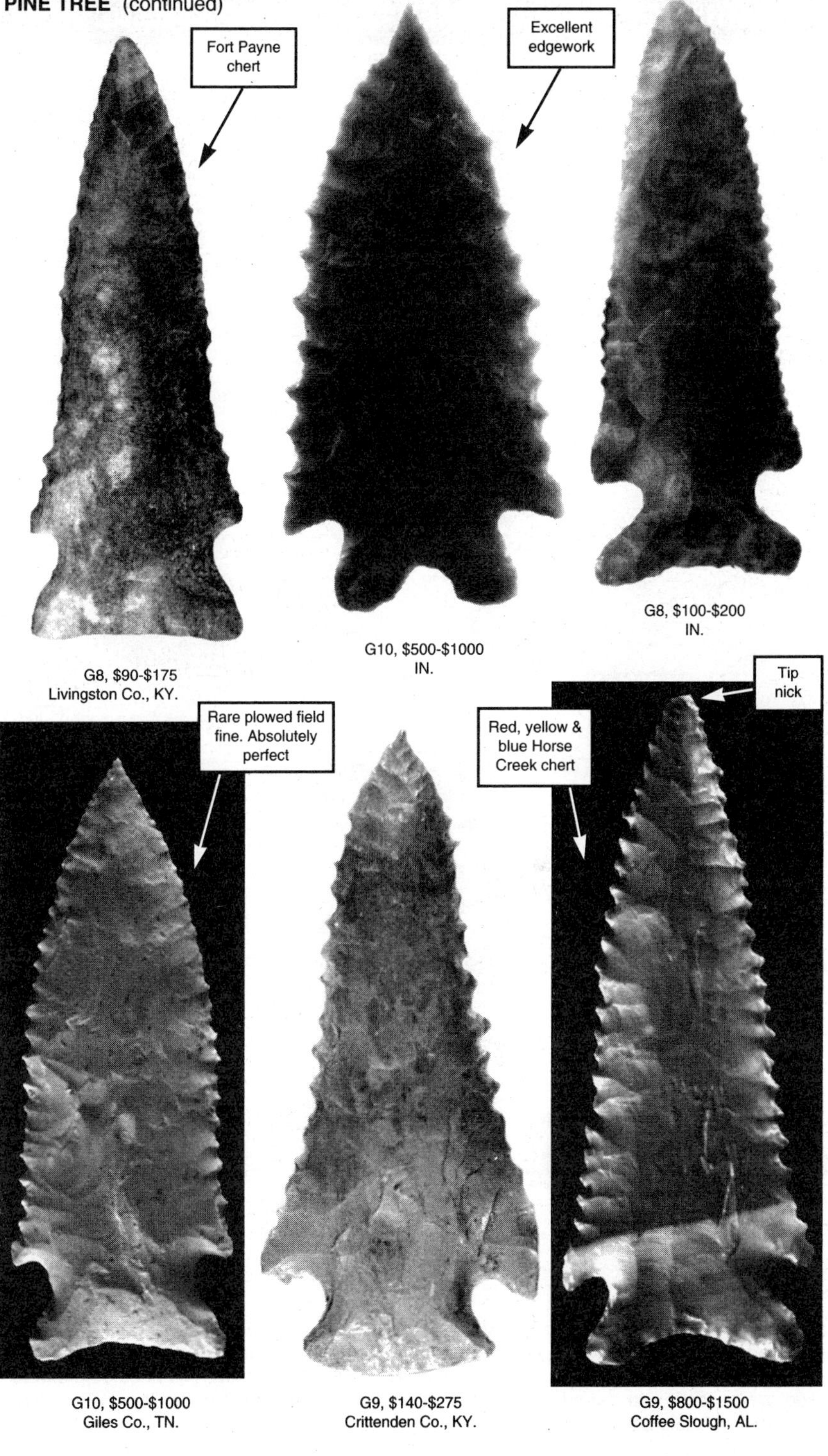

G8, $90-$175
Livingston Co., KY.

G10, $500-$1000
IN.

G8, $100-$200
IN.

G10, $500-$1000
Giles Co., TN.

G9, $140-$275
Crittenden Co., KY.

G9, $800-$1500
Coffee Slough, AL.

PINE TREE CORNER NOTCHED - Early Archaic, 8000 - 5000 B. P.

(Also see Kirk and Palmer)

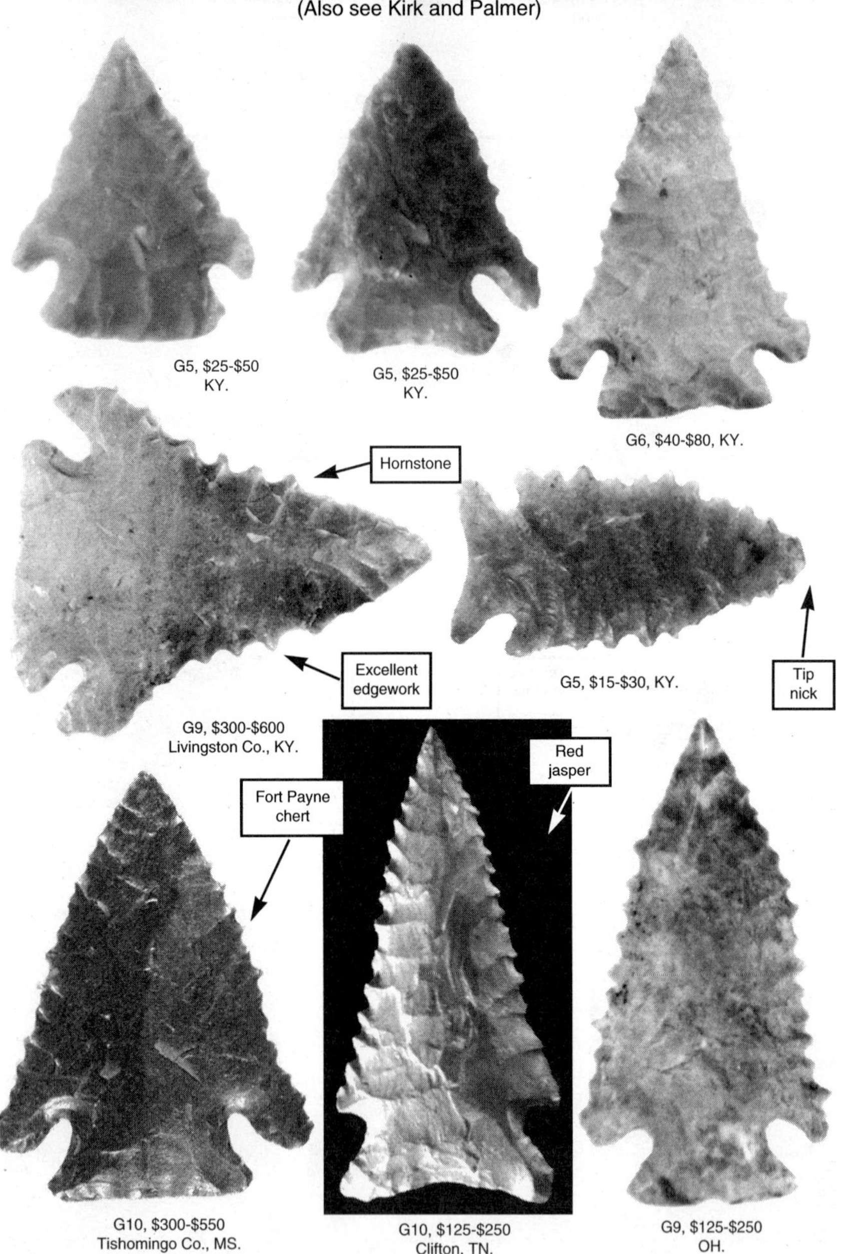

G5, $25-$50 KY.

G5, $25-$50 KY.

G6, $40-$80, KY.

G9, $300-$600 Livingston Co., KY.

G5, $15-$30, KY.

G10, $300-$550 Tishomingo Co., MS.

G10, $125-$250 Clifton, TN.

G9, $125-$250 OH.

LOCATION: Southeastern States**. DESCRIPTION:** A small to medium size, thin, corner notched point with a concave, convex, straight, bifurcated or auriculate base. Blade edges are usually serrated and flaking is parallel to the center of the blade. The shoulders expand and are barbed. The base is ground. Small examples would fall under the *Palmer* type**. I.D. KEY:** Archaic flaking to the center of each blade.

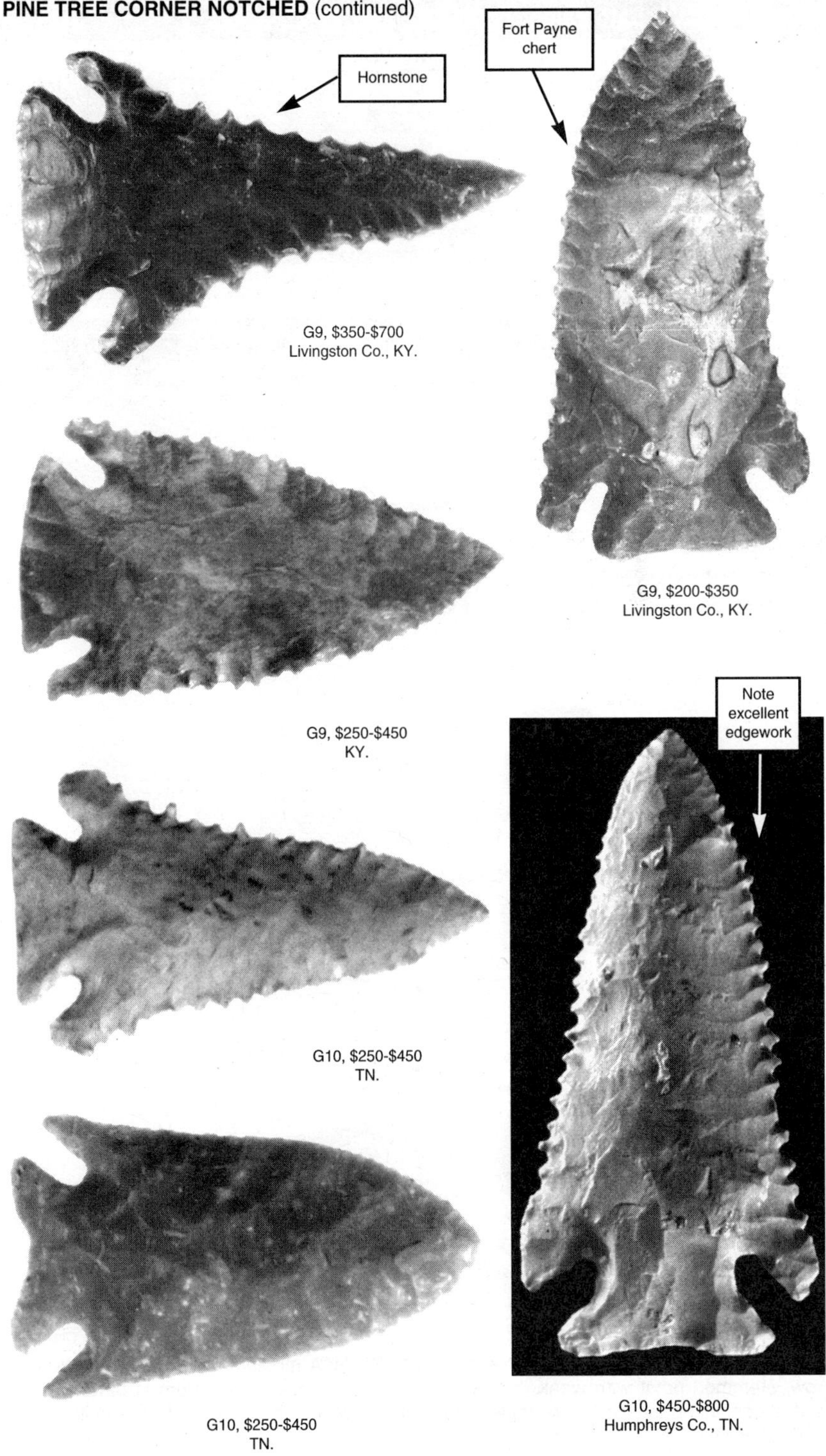

G9, $350-$700
Livingston Co., KY.

G9, $200-$350
Livingston Co., KY.

G9, $250-$450
KY.

G10, $250-$450
TN.

G10, $450-$800
Humphreys Co., TN.

G10, $250-$450
TN.

PLAINVIEW- Late Paleo, 10,000 - 7000 B. P.

(Also see Angostura, Browns Valley, Clovis and Dalton)

LOCATION: DESCRIPTION: A medium size, thin, lanceolate point with usually parallel sides and a concave base that is ground. Some examples are thinned or fluted and are believed to be related to the earlier *Clovis* and contemporary *Dalton* type. Flaking is of high quality and can be collateral to oblique transverse.

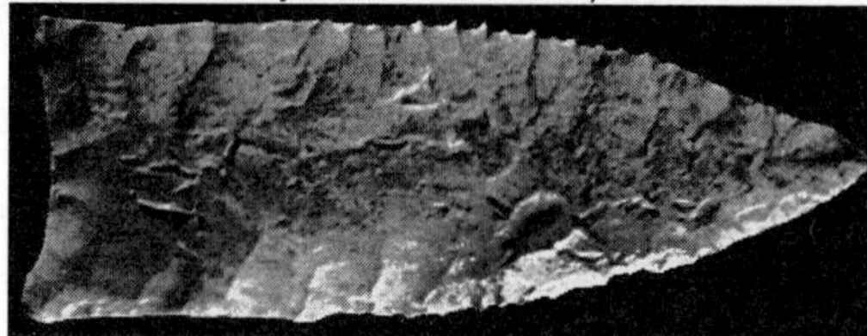

G6, $75-$150
W. Memphis, TN.

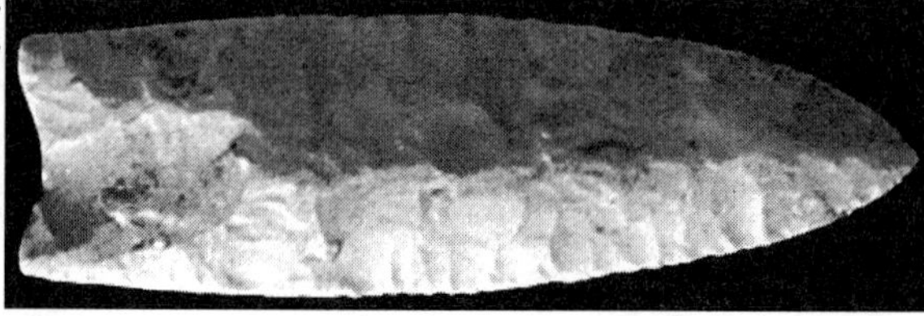

G9, $300-$600
Central OH.

PLEVNA

(See St. Charles)

PONTCHARTRAIN (Type I) - Late Archaic-Woodland, 4000 - 2000 B. P.

(Also see Little Bear Creek and Mulberry Creek)

G6, $20-$40
TN.

G8, $80-$160
TN. Classic.

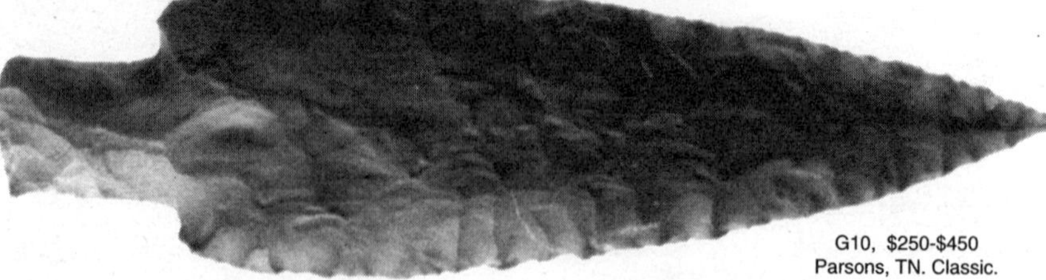

G10, $250-$450
Parsons, TN. Classic.

LOCATION: Mid-southeastern states. **DESCRIPTION:** A medium to large size, thick, narrow, stemmed point with weak, tapered or barbed shoulders. The stem is parallel sided with a concave base. Some examples are finely serrated and are related and similar to the *Flint Creek* type.

PONTCHARTRAIN (Type II) - Woodland, 3400 - 2000 B. P.

(Also see Buck Creek, Hardin and Hamilton Stemmed)

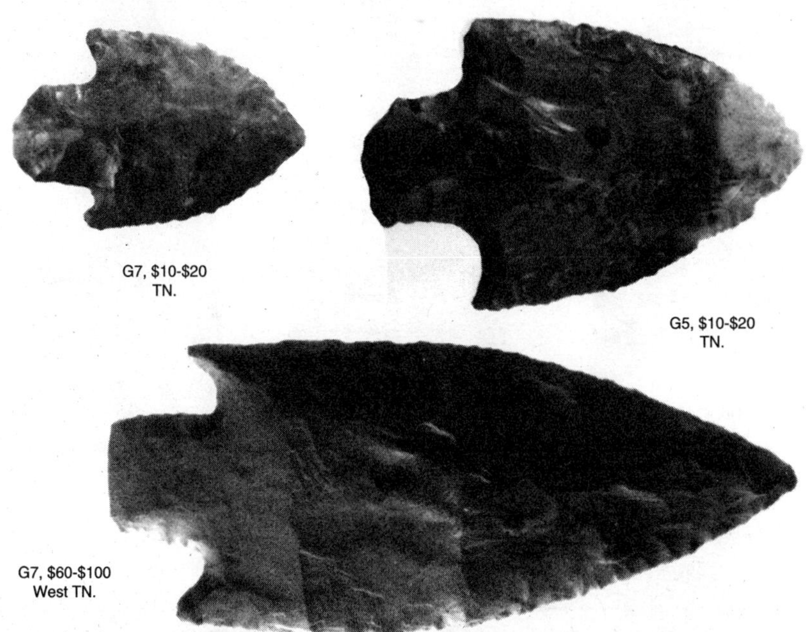

G7, $10-$20
TN.

G5, $10-$20
TN.

G7, $60-$100
West TN.

LOCATION: Mid-southeastern states. **DESCRIPTION:** A medium to large size, broad, stemmed point with barbed shoulders. The stem is parallel to slightly contracting and the base is straight to convex.

QUAD - Late Paleo, 10,000 - 6000 B. P.

(Also see Beaver Lake, Candy Creek, Cumberland, Golondrina and Hinds)

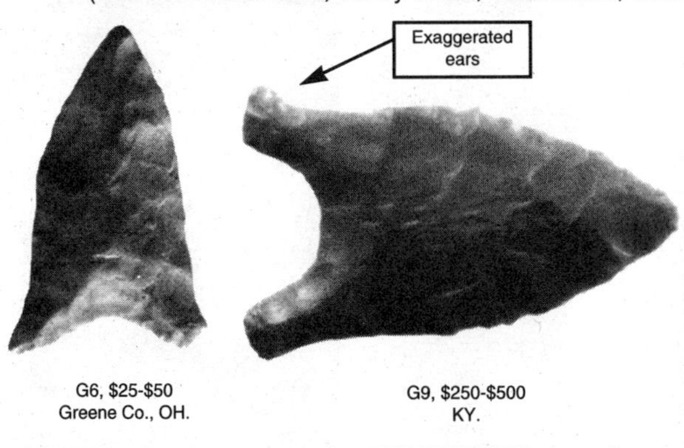

G6, $25-$50
Greene Co., OH.

G9, $250-$500
KY.

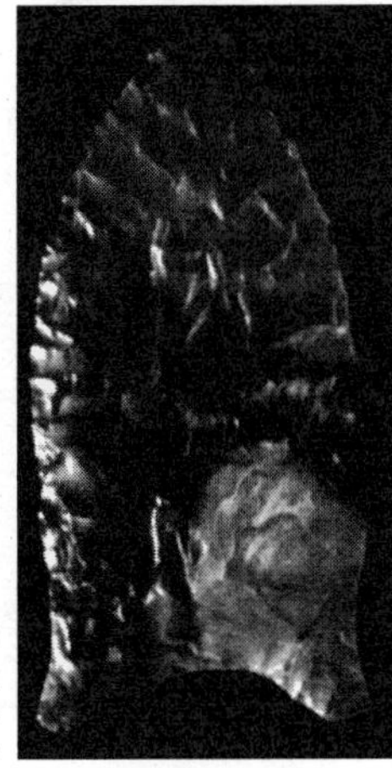

G8, $125-$250
Stewart Co., TN.

LOCATION: Southeastern states. **DESCRIPTION:** A medium to large size lanceolate point with flaring "squared" auricles and a concave base which is ground. Most examples show basal thinning and some are fluted. Believed to be related to the earlier Cumberland point. **I.D. KEY:** Paleo flaking, squarish auricles.

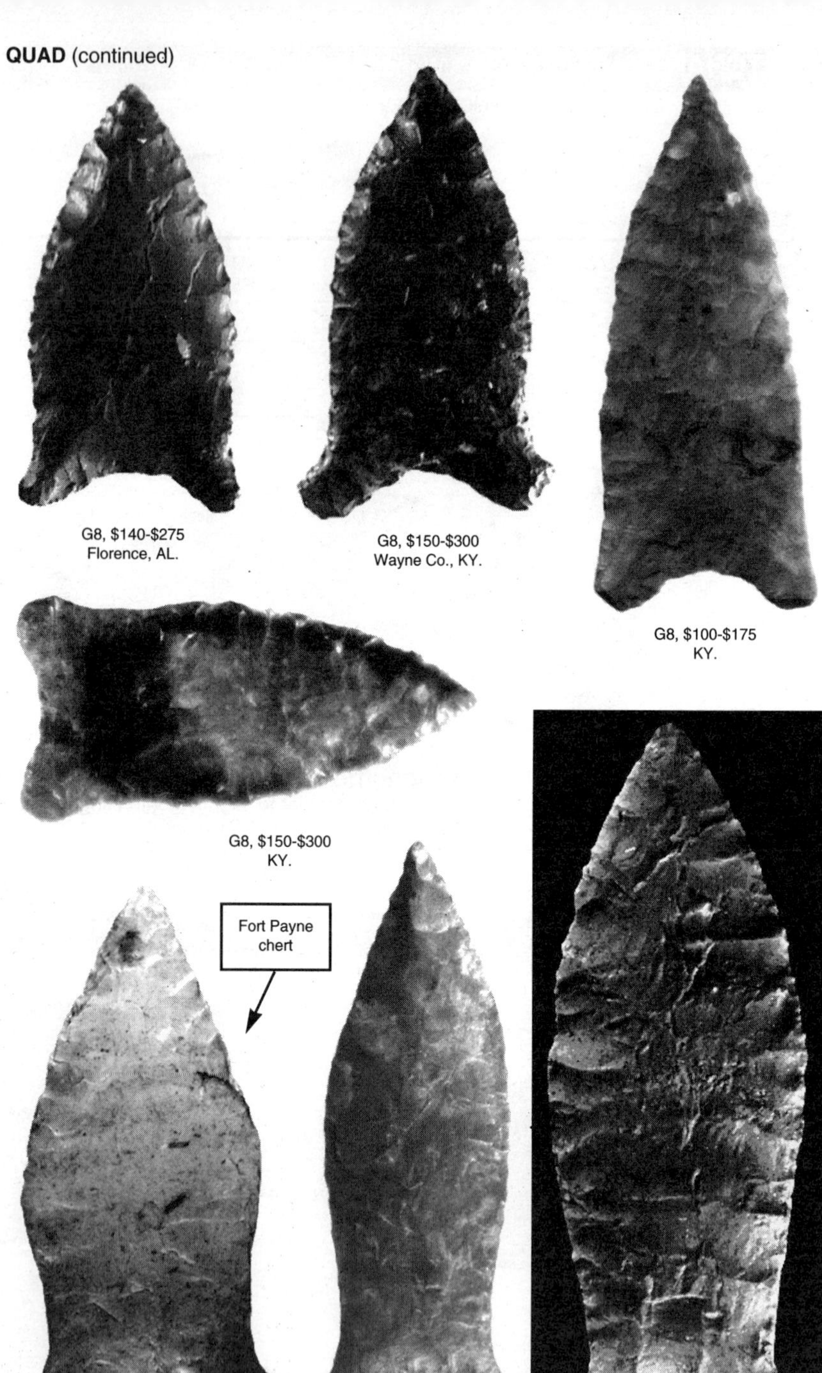

G8, $140-$275
Florence, AL.

G8, $150-$300
Wayne Co., KY.

G8, $100-$175
KY.

G8, $150-$300
KY.

G9, $400-$800
Benton Co., TN.

G10, $300-$600
Bullitt Co., KY.

G10, $800-$1500
Trimble Co., KY.

RAMEY KNIFE - Middle Archaic, 5000 - 4000 B. P.

(Also see Cotaco Creek and Morse Knife)

IMPORTANT:
Shown 50%
actual size.

G8, $450-$900
Rhea Co., TN.

LOCATION: Type site is at the Cahokia Mounds in IL. **DESCRIPTION:** A large size broad, lanceolate blade with a rounded base and high quality flaking. The Tenn. form is similar to the Illinois form.

RANKIN - Late Archaic-Woodland, 4000 - 2500 B. P.

(Also see Buck Creek, Hamilton Stemmed and Wade)

Smoky quartz

G8, $80-$140
Wayne Co., KY.

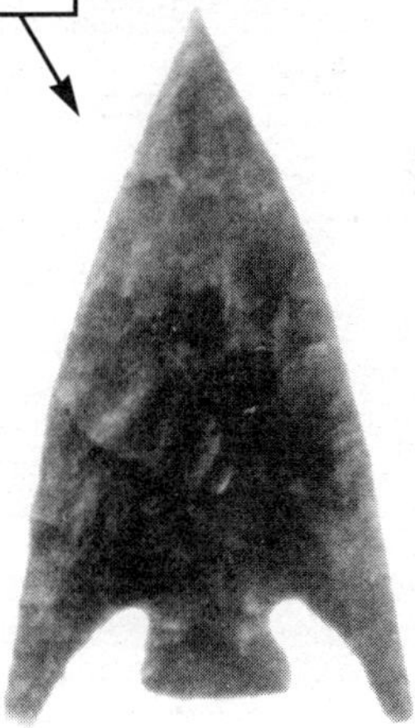

G10, $90-$175
Wayne Co., KY.

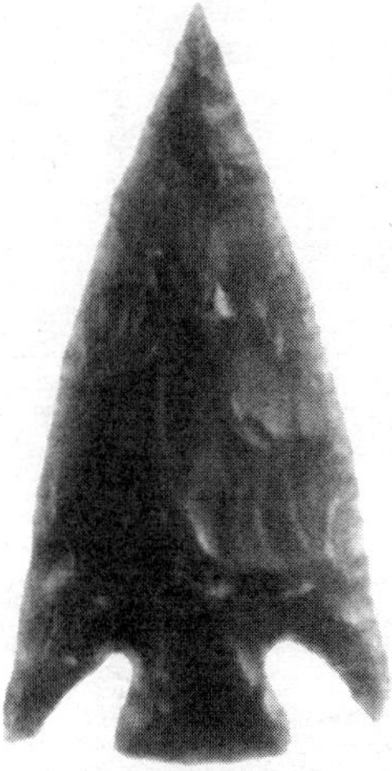

G10, $90-$175
Wayne Co., KY.

All are from a cache made from a local flint called Smoky quartz

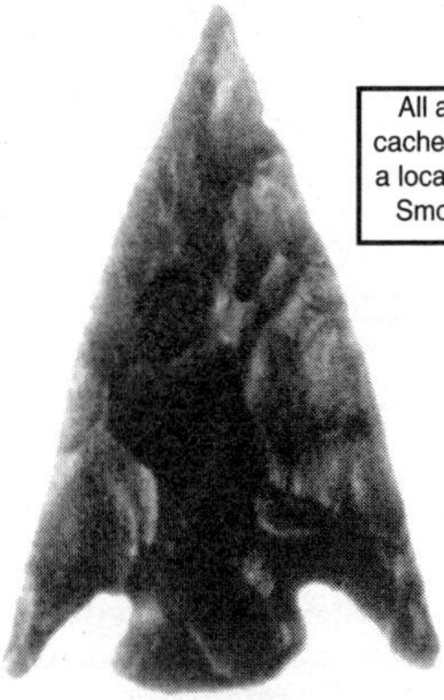

G8, $50-$100
Wayne Co., KY.

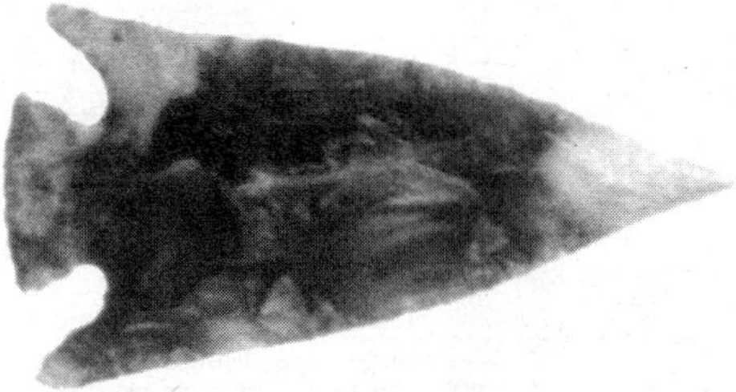

G10, $100-$200
Wayne Co., KY.

LOCATION: Tennessee into Kentucky. **DESCRIPTION:** A medium size, thin, well made barbed point with a short, expanding stem. Barbs are pointed and can extend beyond the base. Blade is recurved with a needle tip. **I.D. KEY:** Drooping barbs, short base.

RED OCHRE - Woodland, 3000 - 1500 B. P.

(Also see Adena Blade, Copena Round Base and Tennessee River)

LOCATION: Midwestern to South eastern states. **DESCRIPTION:** A large, thin, broad blade with a contracting basal area. The base is convex to straight. Very similar to *Wadlow* which has the parallel sides. Possibly related to the *Turkeytail* type.

G8, $45-$90
KY.

G8, $70-$140
Humphreys Co., TN.

REDSTONE - Paleo, 13,000 - 9000 B. P.

(Also see Clovis and Cumberland)

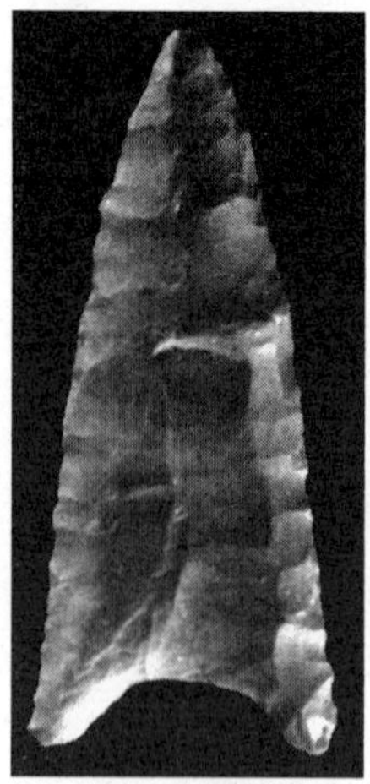

G6, $200-$350
Stewart Co., TN.

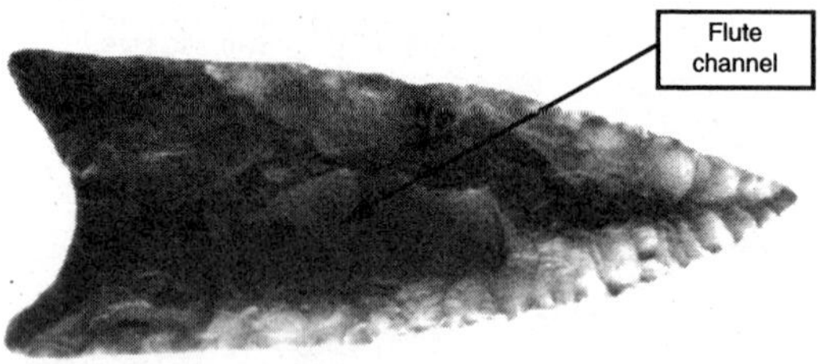

G9, $900-$1800
Limestone Co., AL.

LOCATION: Southeastern states. **DESCRIPTION:** A medium to large size, thin, auriculate, fluted point with convex sides expanding to a wide, deeply concave base. The hafting area is ground. This point is widest at the base. Fluting can extend most of the way down each face. Multiple flutes are usual. (**Warning:** The more common resharpened Clovis point is often sold as this type. Redstones are extremely rare and are almost never offered for sale.) **I.D. KEY:** Batan fluted, edgework on the hafting area.

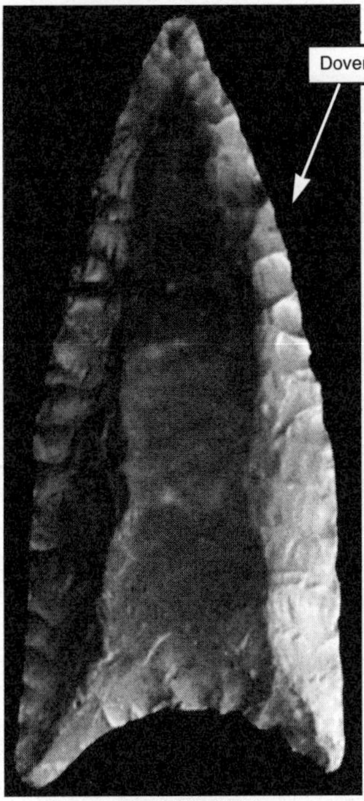

REDSTONE (continued)

Dover chert

Black chert

G9, $1500-$2500
Humphreys Co., TN.

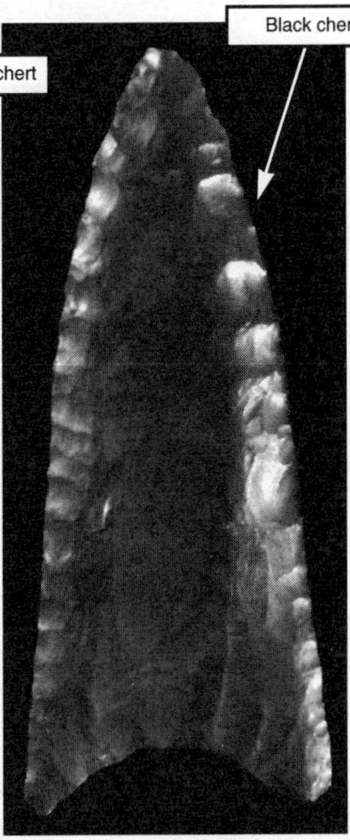

G9, $1800-$3000
Florence, AL.

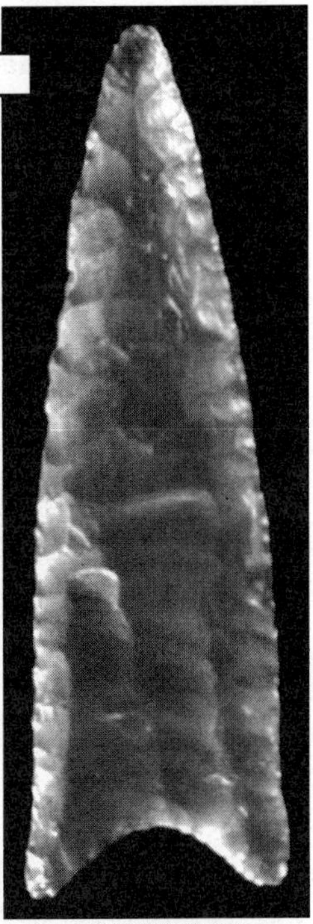

G9, $1800-$3000
N. AL.

G9, $3000-$6000
Humphreys Co., TN.
Found in a cache of three.

RHEEMS CREEK - Late Archaic to Woodland, 4000 - 2000 B. P.

(Also see Halifax and Jude)

G2, $1-$2
Northern AL.

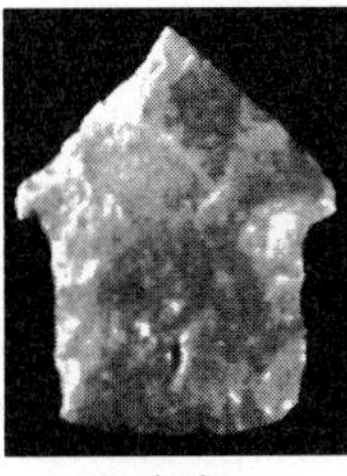
G3, $2-$4
Huntsville, AL.

G6, $3-$6
Northern AL.

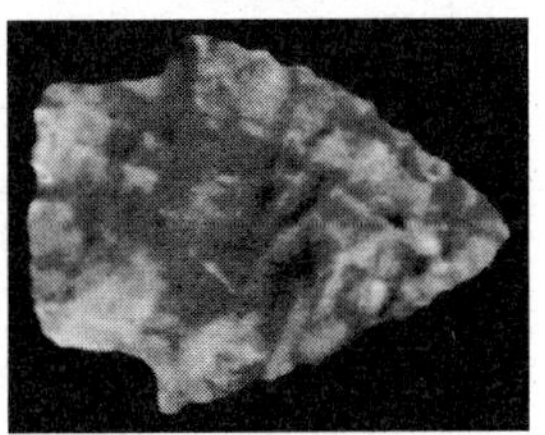
G6, $3-$6
Walker Co., AL.

RHEEMS CREEK (continued)

LOCATION: Southeastern states. **DESCRIPTION:** A small size, stubby, parallel sided, stemmed point with straight shoulders. Similar to Halifax which expands at the base.

RICE LOBBED - Early Archaic, 9000 - 5000 B. P.

(Also see Fox Valley, LeCroy, MacCorkle and Pine Tree)

G8, $50-$100
OH.

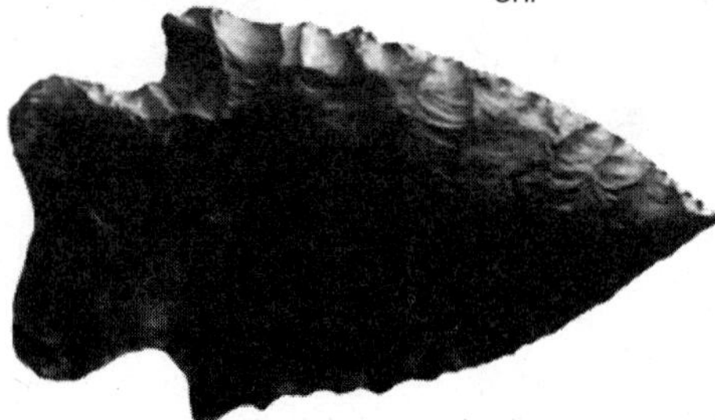

G8, $50-$100
OH.

G8, $80-$150
Salt Lick, KY.

LOCATION: Midwestern to Northeastern states. **DESCRIPTION:** A medium to large size bifurcated to lobbed base point with serrated blade edges. The base has a shallow indentation compared to the other bifurcated types. Shoulders are sharp and prominent. Called *Culpepper Bifurcate* in Virginia.

ROSS - Woodland, 2500 - 1500 B. P.

(Also see Hopewell, North & Snyders)

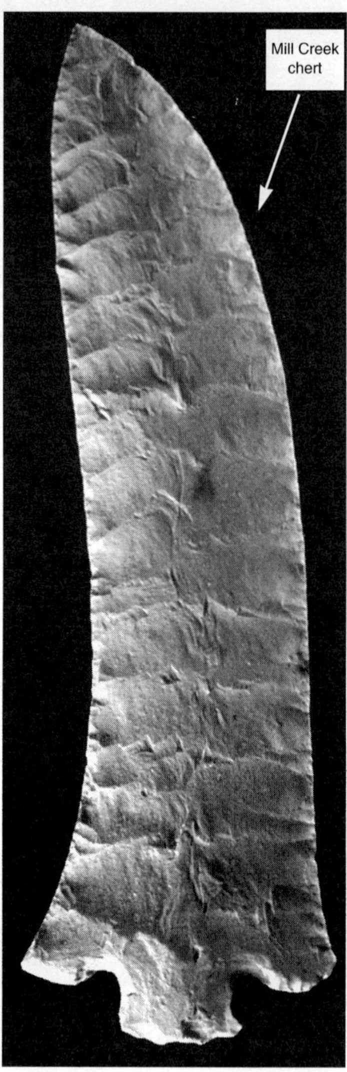

G10, $2500-$4500
Tell City, IN.

IMPORTANT: Shown 50% of actual size.

LOCATION: Midwestern to Eastern states. **DESCRIPTION:** A very large size ceremonial blade with an expanded, rounded base. Some examples have a contracting "V" shaped base. **I.D. KEY:** Size, base form.

RUSSELL CAVE - Early Archaic, 9000 - 7000 B. P.

(Also see Hardaway, Harpeth River, Pine Tree and Searcy)

G6, $15-$25
Davidson Co., TN.

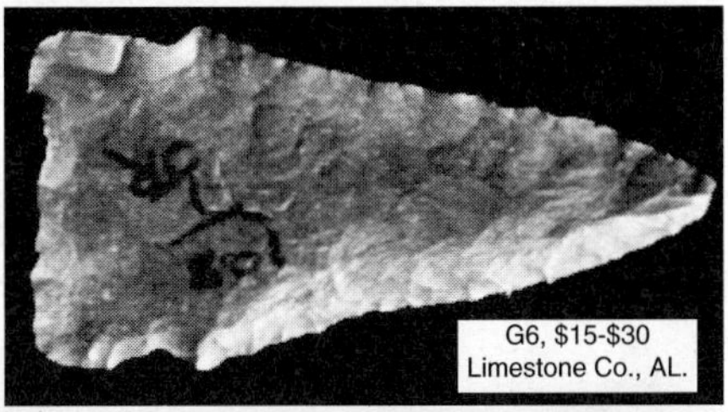

G6, $15-$30
Limestone Co., AL.

G6, $15-$25
TN.

G9, $40-$80
Humphreys Co., TN.

G9, $45-$90
Huntsville,AL.

G9, $70-$135
Camden, TN.

LOCATION: Southeastern states. **DESCRIPTION:** A medium size, triangular point with weak shoulders and an expanding to auriculate base. The stem appears to be an extension of the blade edges, expanding to the base. Most examples are serrated and beveled on one side of each face, although some examples are beveled on all four sides. The base is straight, concave, bifurcated or auriculate. **I.D. KEY:** Notched base and edgework.

ST. ALBANS - Early to Middle Archaic, 9000 - 5000 B. P.

(Also see Decatur, Fox Valley, Jude, Kanawha, Kirk Serrated-Bifurcated, Lake Erie, LeCroy, MacCorkle, Pine Tree, Rice Lobbed and Stanly)

G8, $15-$25
Cumberland Co., KY.

G7, $15-$25
OH.

ST. ALBANS (continued)

LOCATION: Eastern states. **DESCRIPTION:** A small to medium size, usually serrated, bifurcated point. Basal lobes usually flare outward and most examples are sharply barbed. The basal lobes are more shallow than in the *LeCroy* type, otherwise they are easily confused. **I.D. KEY:** Shallow basal lobes.

ST. CHARLES - Early Archaic, 9500 - 8000 B. P.

(Also see Gibson, Kirk Corner Notched, Thebes and Warrick)

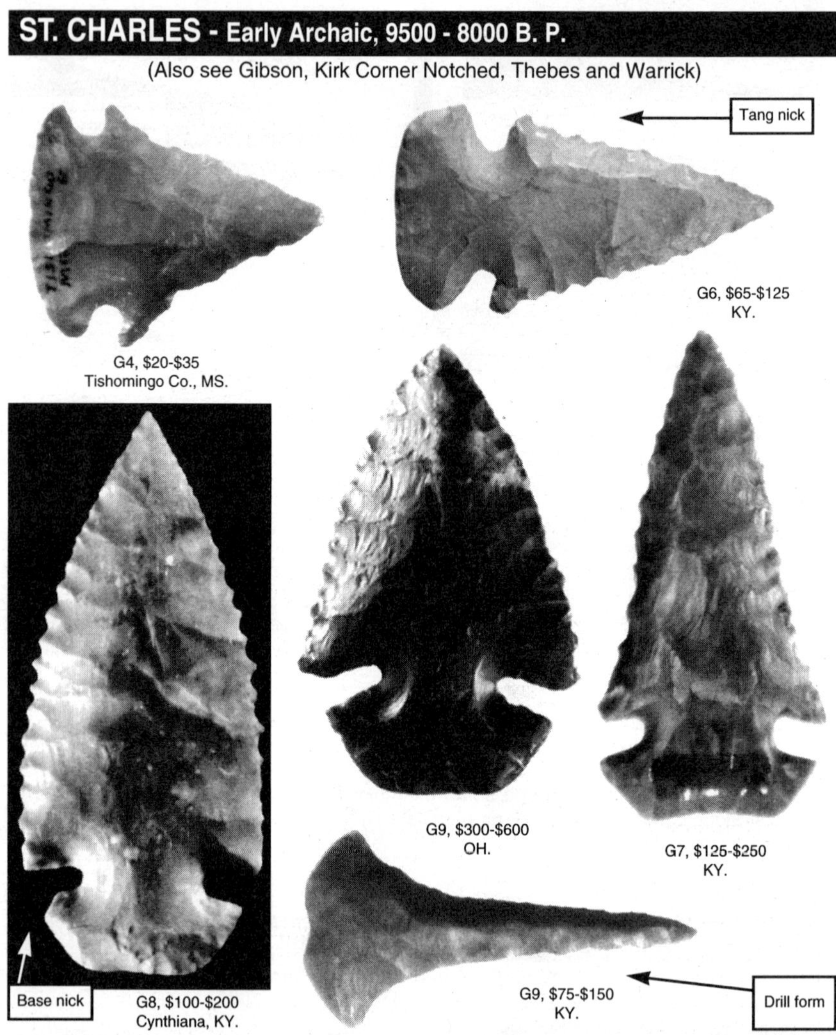

G4, $20-$35
Tishomingo Co., MS.

G6, $65-$125
KY.

G8, $100-$200
Cynthiana, KY.

G9, $300-$600
OH.

G7, $125-$250
KY.

G9, $75-$150
KY.

LOCATION: Midwestern to Eastern states. **DESCRIPTION:** A medium to large size, broad, thin, elliptical, corner notched point with a dovetail base. First stage forms are not beveled. Beveling on opposite sides of each face occurs during the resharpening process. The base is convex and most examples exhibit high quality flaking. There is a rare variant that has the barbs clipped (clipped wing) as in the *Decatur* type. There are many variations on base style from bifurcated to eared, rounded or squared. Base size varies from small to very large. Contemporary with the ***Hardin*** and ***Decatur*** points. Formally called ***Dovedail*** and ***Plevna*** which were the resharpened (beveled) forms. It was previously reported in error that the unbeveled forms were from the late Archaic when actually all are the same type from the early Archaic period. **I.D. KEY:** Dovetail base.

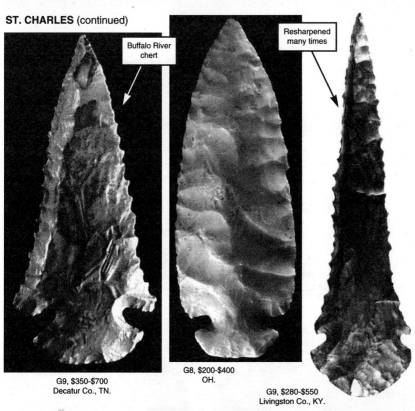

Buffalo River chert

G9, $350-$700
Decatur Co., TN.

G8, $200-$400
OH.

Resharpened many times

G9, $280-$550
Livingston Co., KY.

G7, $200-$400
KY.

G8, $250-$500
KY.

G7, $100-$200
Clermont Co., OH.

G8, $600-$1000
OH.

G10, $700-$1200
KY.

G10, $1500-$2500
Humphreys Co., TN.

G7, $250-$450
OH.

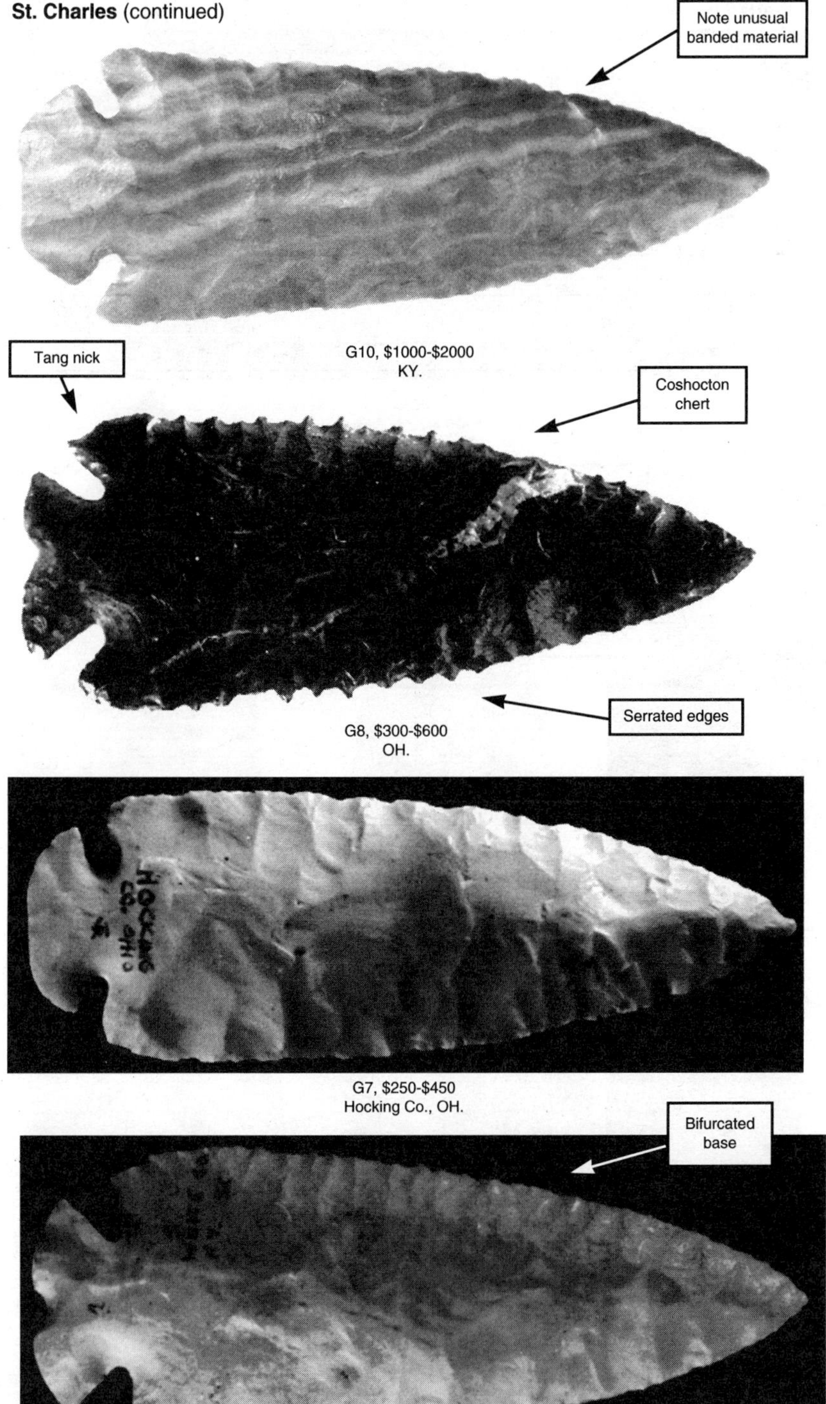

G10, $1000-$2000
KY.

G8, $300-$600
OH.

G7, $250-$450
Hocking Co., OH.

G8, $250-$500
White Co., KY.

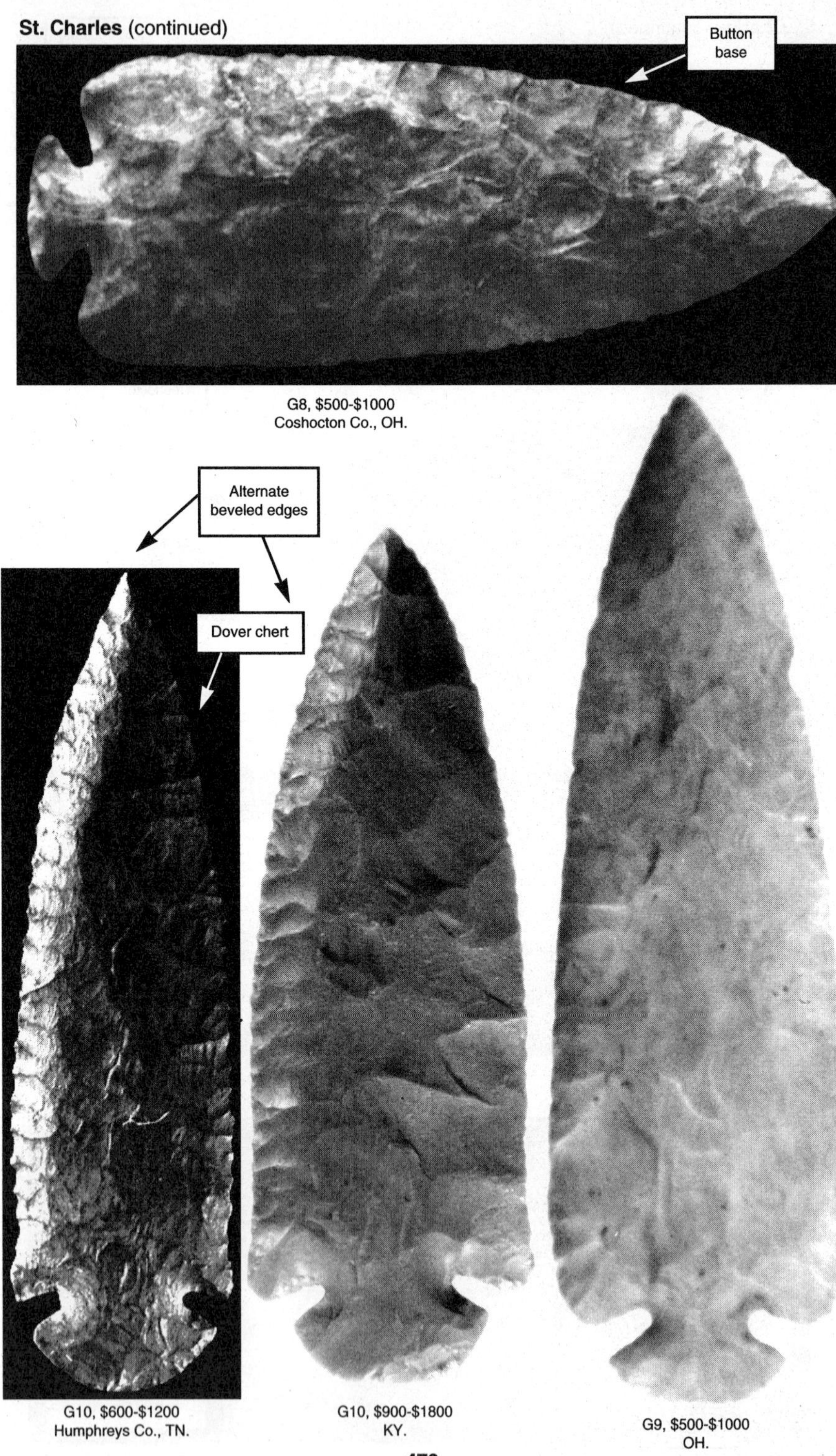

G8, $500-$1000
Coshocton Co., OH.

G10, $600-$1200
Humphreys Co., TN.

G10, $900-$1800
KY.

G9, $500-$1000
OH.

SAND MOUNTAIN - Late Woodland to Mississippian, 1500 - 400 B. P.

(Also see Durant's Bend, Fort Ancient and Madison)

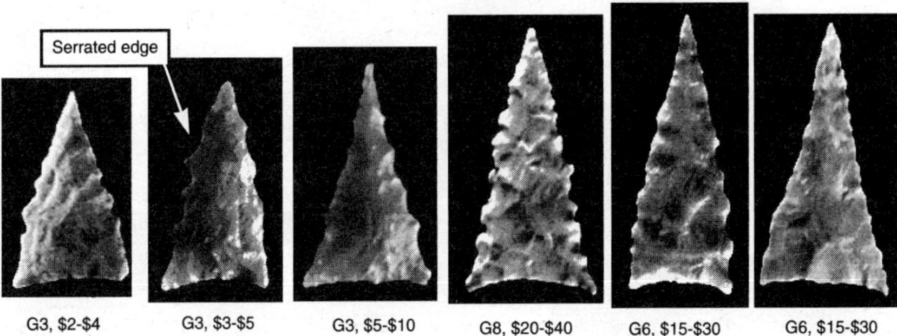

G3, $2-$4 Middle TN. | G3, $3-$5 Dunlap, TN. | G3, $5-$10 Decatur, AL. | G8, $20-$40 Morgan Co., AL. | G6, $15-$30 Limestone Co., AL. | G6, $15-$30 Limestone Co., AL.

LOCATION: Southeastern states. **DESCRIPTION:** A small size, triangular point with serrated blade edges and a concave base. A straight base would place it in the *Fort Ancient* type. **I.D. KEY:** Basal corners are not symmetrical.

EC

SAVAGE CAVE - Early to Middle Archaic, 7000 - 4000 B. P.

(Also see Big Sandy and Newton Falls)

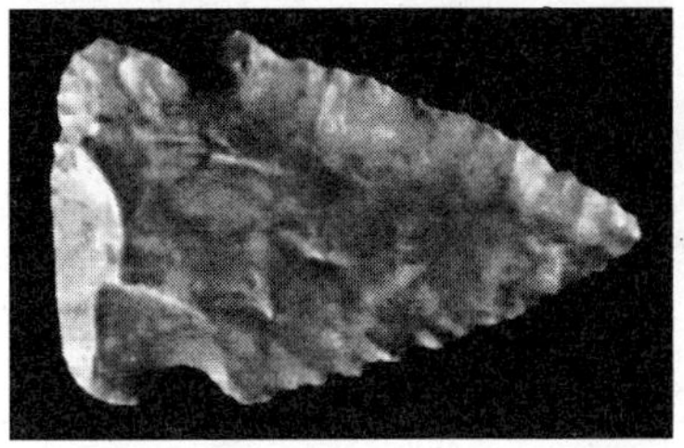

G5, $8-$15
Meigs Co., TN.

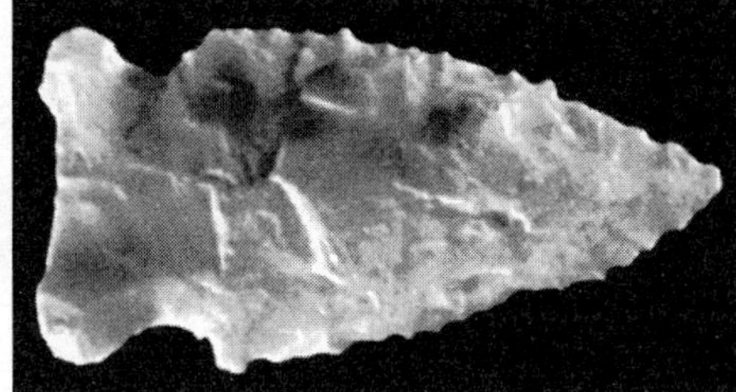

G5, $8-$15
Henry Co., AL.

LOCATION: Kentucky surrounding states. **DESCRIPTION:** A medium to large size, broad, side notched point that is usually serrated. Bases are generally straight but can be slightly concave or convex.

SAVANNAH RIVER - Middle Archaic to Woodland, 5000 - 2000 B. P.

(Also see Appalachian, Elora, Hamilton, Johnson, Kirk, Maples and Stanly)

LOCATION: Southeastern to Eastern states. **DESCRIPTION:** A medium to large size, straight to contracting stemmed point with a concave to bifurcated base. The shoulders are tapered to square. The stems are narrow to broad. Believed to be related to the earlier *Stanly* point.

G5, $4-$8
Dayton, TN.

G6, $20-$40
Andersonville, GA.

G6, $35-$70
Dodge Co., GA.

Tang
wear

G8, $75-$150
Crisp Co., GA.

SCHILD SPIKE - Woodland, 1500 - 1000 B. P.

(Also see Bradle Spike, Flint River Spike and New Market)

G4, $5-$10
S.E. TN.

LOCATION: Northeastern states. **DESCRIPTION:** A small to medium size, narrow, thick, spike point with shallow side notches.

SCRAPER - Paleo to Archaic, 14,000 - 5000 B. P.

(Also see Drill, Graver and Lancet)

LOCATION: Paleo to early Archaic sites throughout North America. **DESCRIPTION:** Thumb, Duckbill and Turtleback forms are small to medium size, thick, ovoid shaped, uniface, scraping tools that are steeply beveled, especially at the broadest end. Side scrapers are long hand - held uniface flakes with beveling on all blade edges of one face. Scraping was done primarily from the sides of these blades.

SCRAPER (continued)

Side nicks

G4, \$2-\$5
Humphreys Co., TN.

G4, \$2-\$5
Humphreys Co., TN. Duckbill form.

G3, \$3-\$5
Humphreys Co., TN. Dover chert.

G7, \$5-\$10
Humphreys Co., TN.

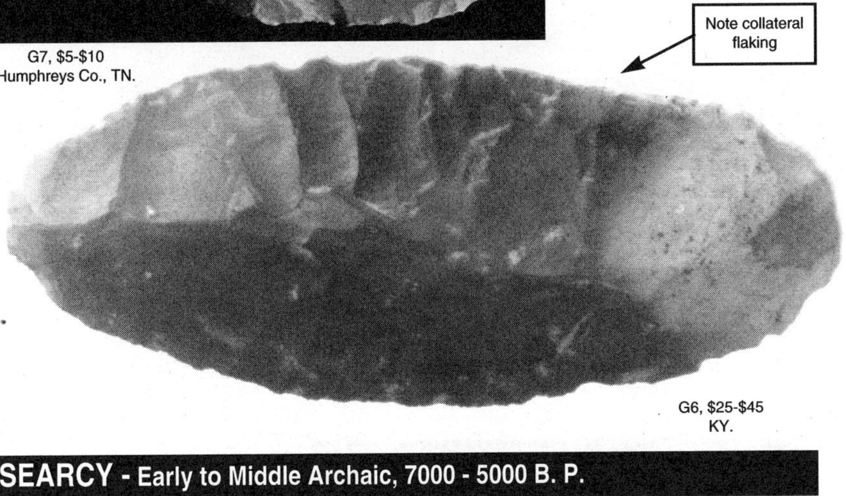

Note collateral flaking

G6, \$25-\$45
KY.

EC

SEARCY - Early to Middle Archaic, 7000 - 5000 B. P.

(Also see Dalton-Colbert, Harpeth River, Kirk Serrated and Russell Cave)

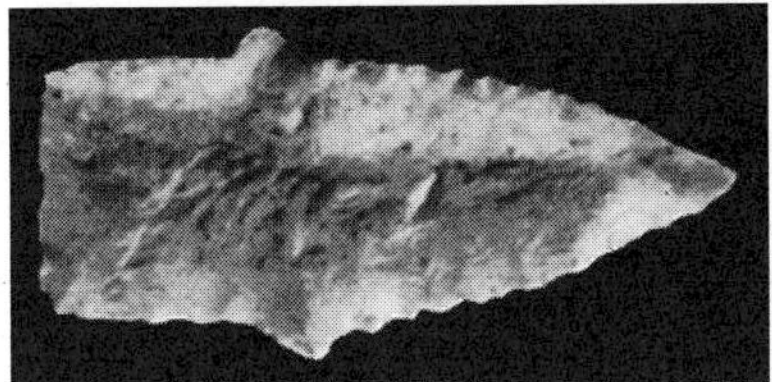

G5, \$15-\$25
Meigs Co., TN.

G6, \$15-\$25
W. TN.

SEARCY (continued)

LOCATION: Midwestern states. **DESCRIPTION:** A small to medium size, thin, lanceolate point with a squared hafting area that (usually) has concave sides and base which is ground. Many examples are serrated.

SEDALIA - Mid to Late Archaic, 5000 - 3000 B. P.

(Also see Agate Basin, Lerma and Ohio Lanceolate)

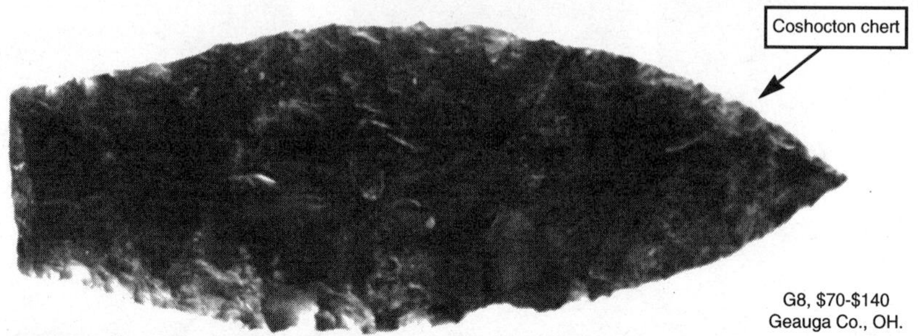

Coshocton chert

G8, $70-$140
Geauga Co., OH.

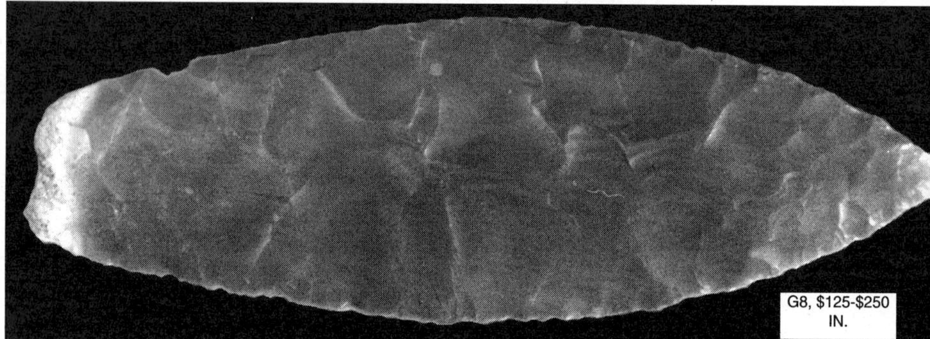

G8, $125-$250
IN.

LOCATION: Midwestern states. **DESCRIPTION:** A medium to large size, narrow, lanceolate blade with straight to convex sides and base. Flaking is usually cruder than in *Agate Basin.* Developed from the *Nebo Hill* type.

SHOALS CREEK - Late Archaic to Woodland, 4000 - 2000 B. P.

(Also see Elora, Ledbetter, Little Bear Creek and Pickwick)

LOCATION: Southeastern states. **DESCRIPTION:** A medium to large size point with serrated edges, an expanded base and sharp barbs.

G6, $15-$30
Lawrence Co., AL.

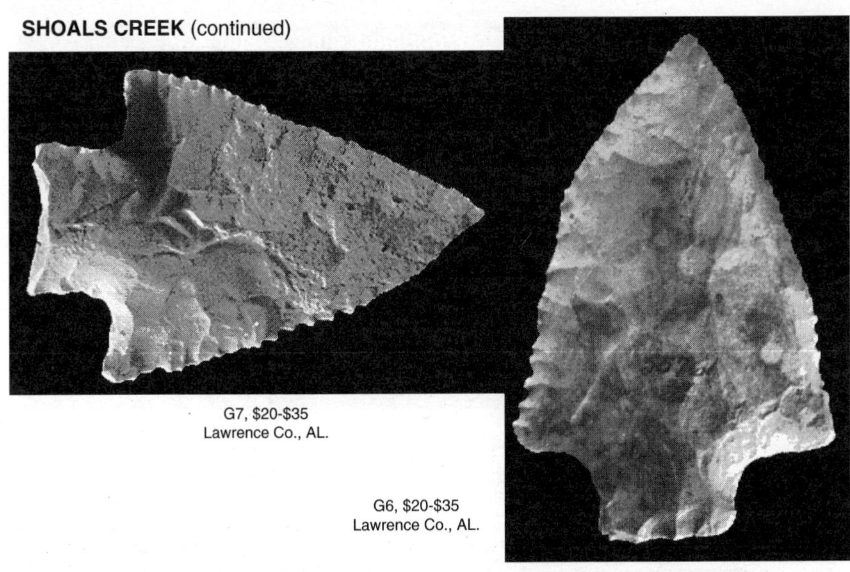

G7, $20-$35
Lawrence Co., AL.

G6, $20-$35
Lawrence Co., AL.

SMITH - Middle Archaic, 7000 - 4000 B. P.

(Also see Eva and Wade)

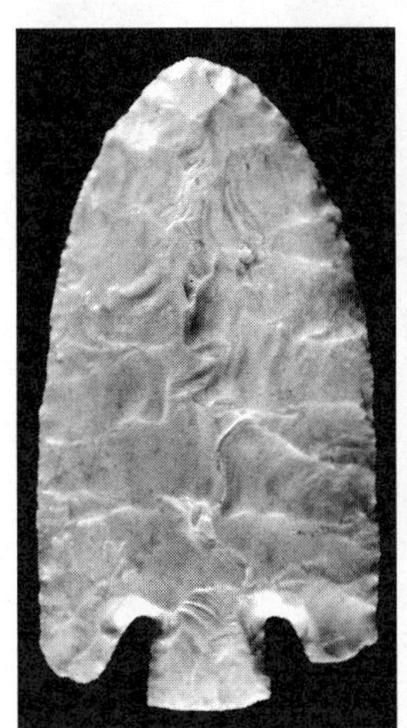

G7, $175-$350
OH.

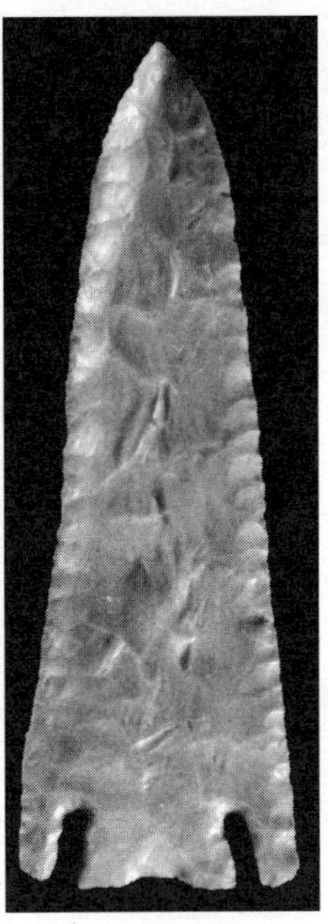

G9, $600-$1200
OH.

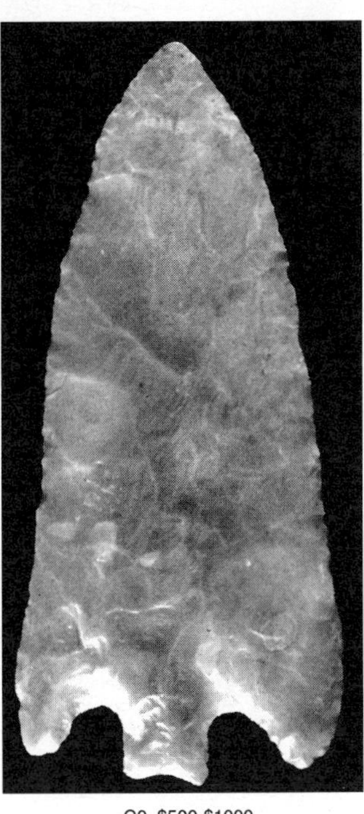

G9, $500-$1000
IN.

IMPORTANT:
Shown 50%
actual size.

LOCATION: Midwestern states into Ohio. **DESCRIPTION:** A very large size, broad, point with long parallel shoulders and a squared to slightly expanding base. Some examples may appear to be basally notched due to the long barbs.

SMITHSONIA - Late Archaic to Woodland, 4000 - 1500 B. P.

(Also see Buck Creek, Hamilton, Motley, Table Rock and Wade)

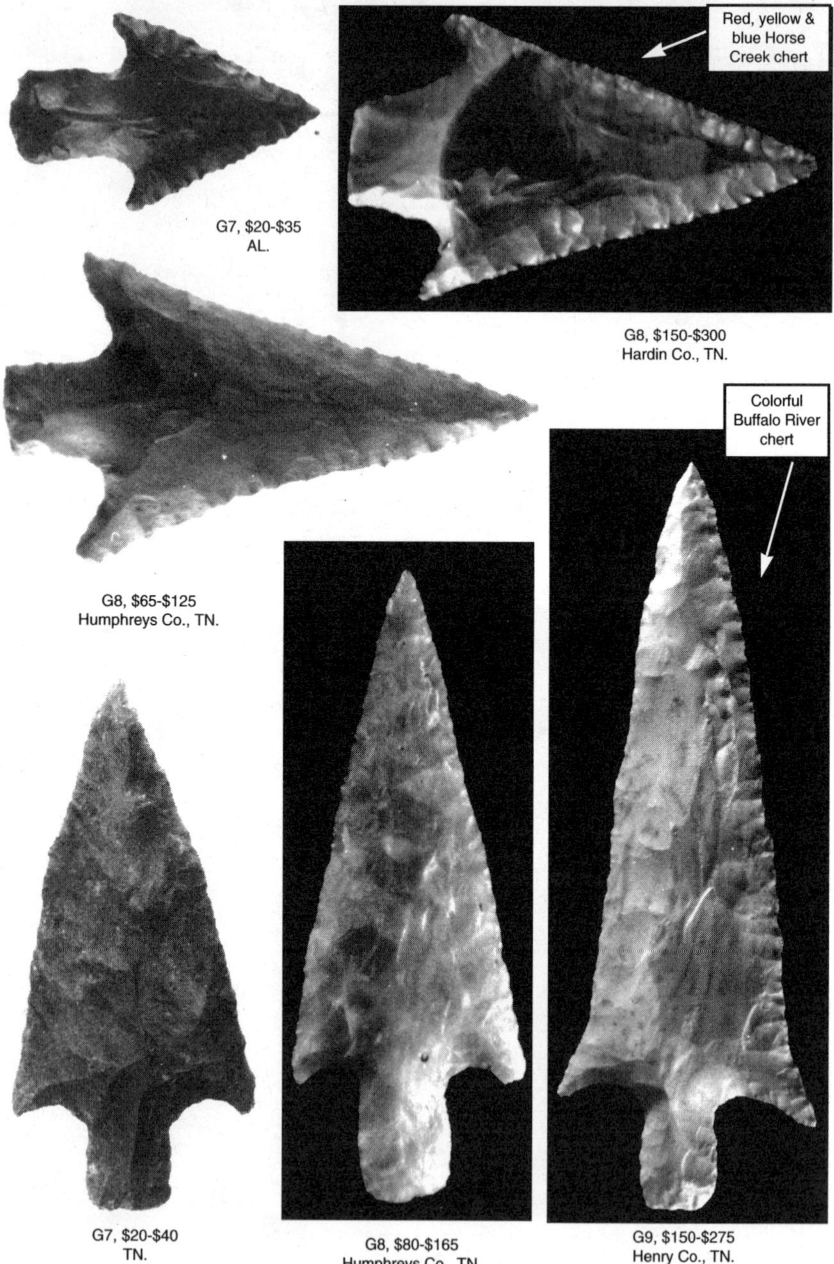

G7, $20-$35
AL.

G8, $150-$300
Hardin Co., TN.

G8, $65-$125
Humphreys Co., TN.

G7, $20-$40
TN.

G8, $80-$165
Humphreys Co., TN.

G9, $150-$275
Henry Co., TN.

LOCATION: Southeastern states. **DESCRIPTION:** A medium size, triangular point with tapered to barbed shoulders and a parallel sided stem with a straight base. Many examples have finely serrated blade edges which are usually straight. **I.D. KEY:** High barb on one side and fine edgework.

SNAKE CREEK - Late Archaic, 4000 - 3000 B. P.

(Also see Morse and Ramey Knife)

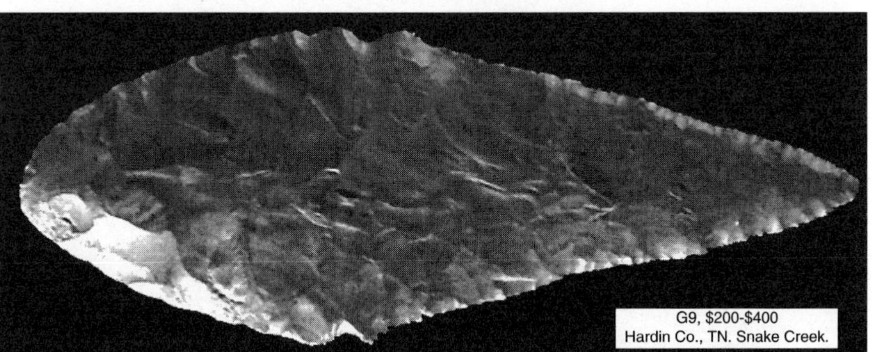

G9, $200-$400
Hardin Co., TN. Snake Creek.

LOCATION: Southeastern states **DESCRIPTION:** A large size, broad, ovoid blade with shallow side notches about half way between the base and tip. Double side notches are common. the stem contracts to a rounded base.

EC

SNYDERS (Hopewell) - Woodland, 2500 - 1500 B. P.

(Also see Buck Creek, Hopewell, Motley and North)

G5, $20-$40
MI.

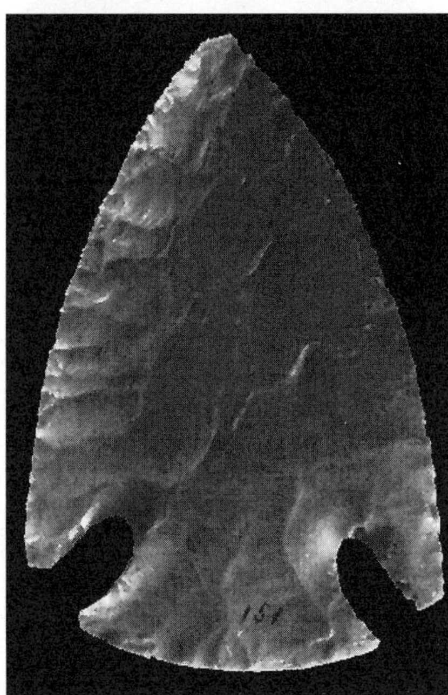

G8, $150-$350
IN.

LOCATION: Midwestern to Eastern states. **DESCRIPTION:** A medium to large size, broad, thin, wide corner notched point of high quality. Blade edges and base are convex. Many examples have intentional fractured bases. This point has been reproduced in recent years. **I.D. KEY:** Size and broad corner notches.

G10, $200-$400
OH.

G9, $200-$350
OH.

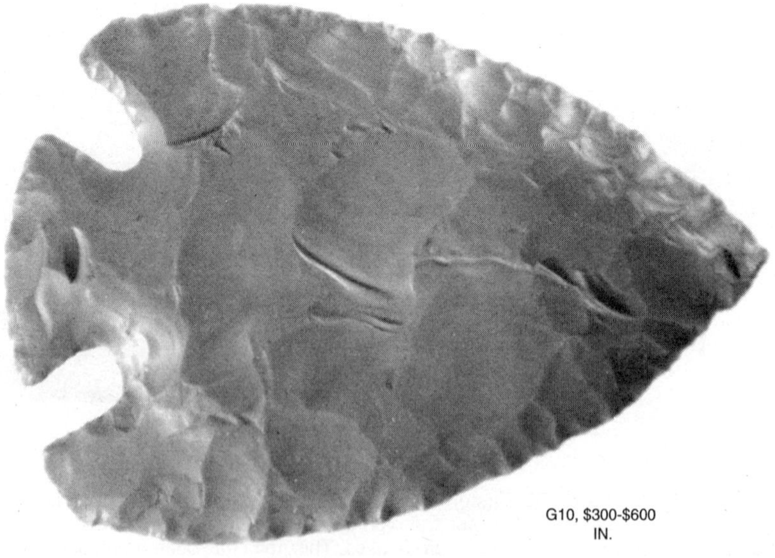

G10, $300-$600
IN.

SQUARE KNIFE - Late Paleo to Early Archaic, 10,000 - 8000 B. P.

(Also see Angostura, Fort Ancient Blade and Frazier)

G2, $5-$10
Humphreys Co., TN.

G8, $35-$45
TN.

G7, $20-$40
OH.

LOCATION: Midwestern states. **DESCRIPTION:** A medium to large size squared blade that is sometimes fluted from either or both ends on Paleo examples.

STANFIELD - Transitional Paleo, 10,000 - 8000 B. P.

(Also see Angostura, Fort Ancient Blade, Frazier and Tennessee River)

G3, $10-$20
Humphreys Co., TN.

G6, $15-$25
Colbert Co., AL.

LOCATION: Southeastern states. **DESCRIPTION:** A medium to large size, narrow, lanceolate point with parallel sides and a straight base. Some rare examples are fluted. Bases can be ground.

G8, $20-$35
Colbert Co., AL.

STANLY - Early Archaic, 8000 - 5000 B. P.

(Also see Fox Valley, Frederick, Garth Slough, Kirk Serr.-Bifurcated and Savannah River)

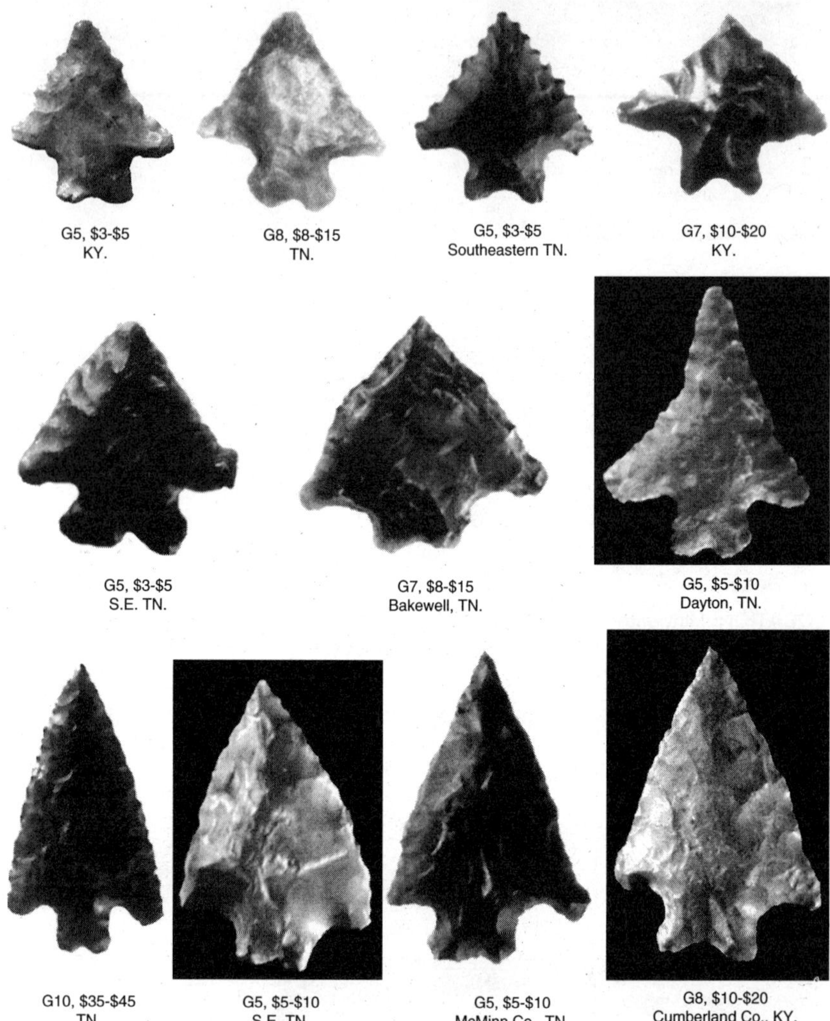

G5, $3-$5 KY.

G8, $8-$15 TN.

G5, $3-$5 Southeastern TN.

G7, $10-$20 KY.

G5, $3-$5 S.E. TN.

G7, $8-$15 Bakewell, TN.

G5, $5-$10 Dayton, TN.

G10, $35-$45 TN.

G5, $5-$10 S.E. TN.

G5, $5-$10 McMinn Co., TN.

G8, $10-$20 Cumberland Co., KY.

LOCATION: Southeastern to Eastern states. Type site is Stanly Co., N.C. **DESCRIPTION:** A small to medium size, broad shoulder point with a small bifurcated stem. Some examples are serrated and show high quality flaking. The shoulders are very prominent and can be tapered, horizontal or barbed. **I.D. KEY:** Tiny bifurcated base.

STEUBENVILLE - Early Archaic, 9000 - 6000 B. P.

(Also see Holland)

LOCATION: Ohio into the Northeast. **DESCRIPTION:** A medium to large size, Broad, triangular point with weak tapered shoulders, a wide parallel sided stem and a concave base. The basal area is ground. Believed to be developed from the *Scottsbluff* type.

G9, $25-$40
OH.

G7, $20-$30
OH.

STILWELL - Early Archaic, 9000 - 7000 B. P.

(Also see Kirk Corner Notched and Pine Tree)

LOCATION: Midwestern to Eastern states. **DESCRIPTION:** A medium to large size, corner notched point with usually serrated blade edges. The shoulders are barbed. The base is concave and ground. The blade edges are convex, parallel or recurved. This type may be related to *Kirk.*

G6, $50-$100
OH.

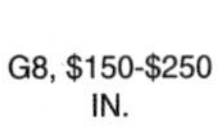

G8, $150-$250
IN.

Dover chert

Found by a diver at the bottom of the Tennessee River

G10, $900-$1800
Benton Co., TN.

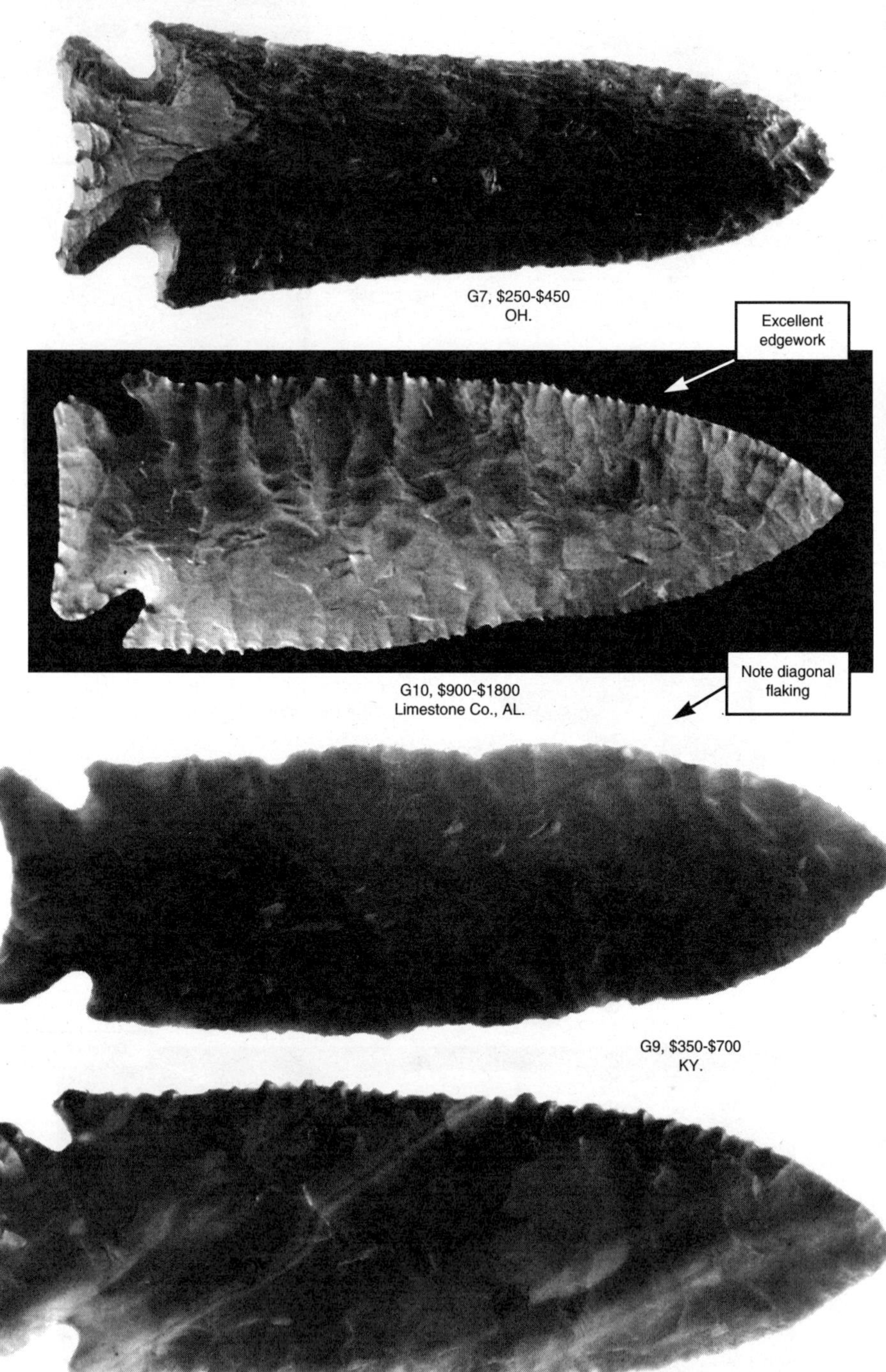

G7, $250-$450
OH.

G10, $900-$1800
Limestone Co., AL.

G9, $350-$700
KY.

G9, $500-$1000
IN.

SUBLET FERRY - Late Archaic to Woodland, 4000 - 2000 B. P.

(Also see Big Sandy, Brewerton Side Notched, Coosa and Meadowood)

G6, $8-$15
Putnam Co., TN.

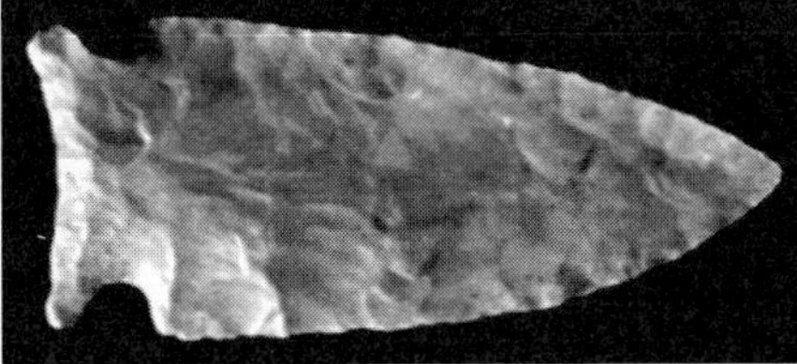

G8, $15-$30
Humphreys Co., TN.

LOCATION: Southeastern states. **DESCRIPTION:** A small to medium size point with side notches that are very close to the base. The base is straight to slightly convex. Blade edges are straight to convex and may be serrated.

G10, $35-$70
TN.

G10, $45-$80
Humphreys Co., TN.

EC

SWAN LAKE - Late Archaic to Woodland, 3500 - 2000 B. P.

(Also see Bakers Creek, Durst and Halifax)

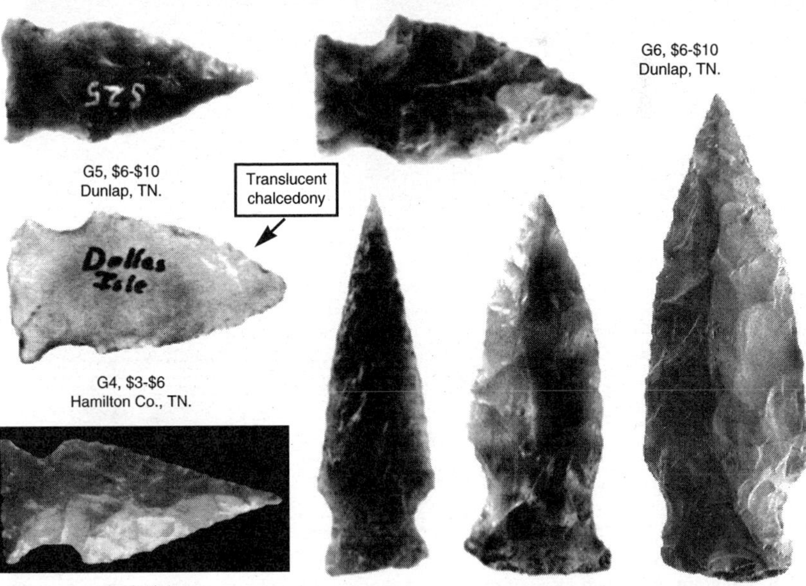

G5, $6-$10
Dunlap, TN.

G6, $6-$10
Dunlap, TN.

G4, $3-$6
Hamilton Co., TN.

G7, $6-$12
Walker Co., AL.

G7, $8-$15
Dunlap, TN.

G9, $10-$20
Dunlap, TN.

G9, $10-$20
Northern AL.

SWAN LAKE (continued)

LOCATION: Southeasten to Eastern states. **DESCRIPTION:** A small size, thick, triangular point with wide, shallow side notches. Some examples have and unfinished rind or base. Similar to the side-notched *Lamoka* in New York. Called *Jackson* in Florida.

TABLE ROCK - Late Archaic, 4000 - 3000 B. P.

(Also see Buck Creek, Fishspear, Motley and Smithsonia)

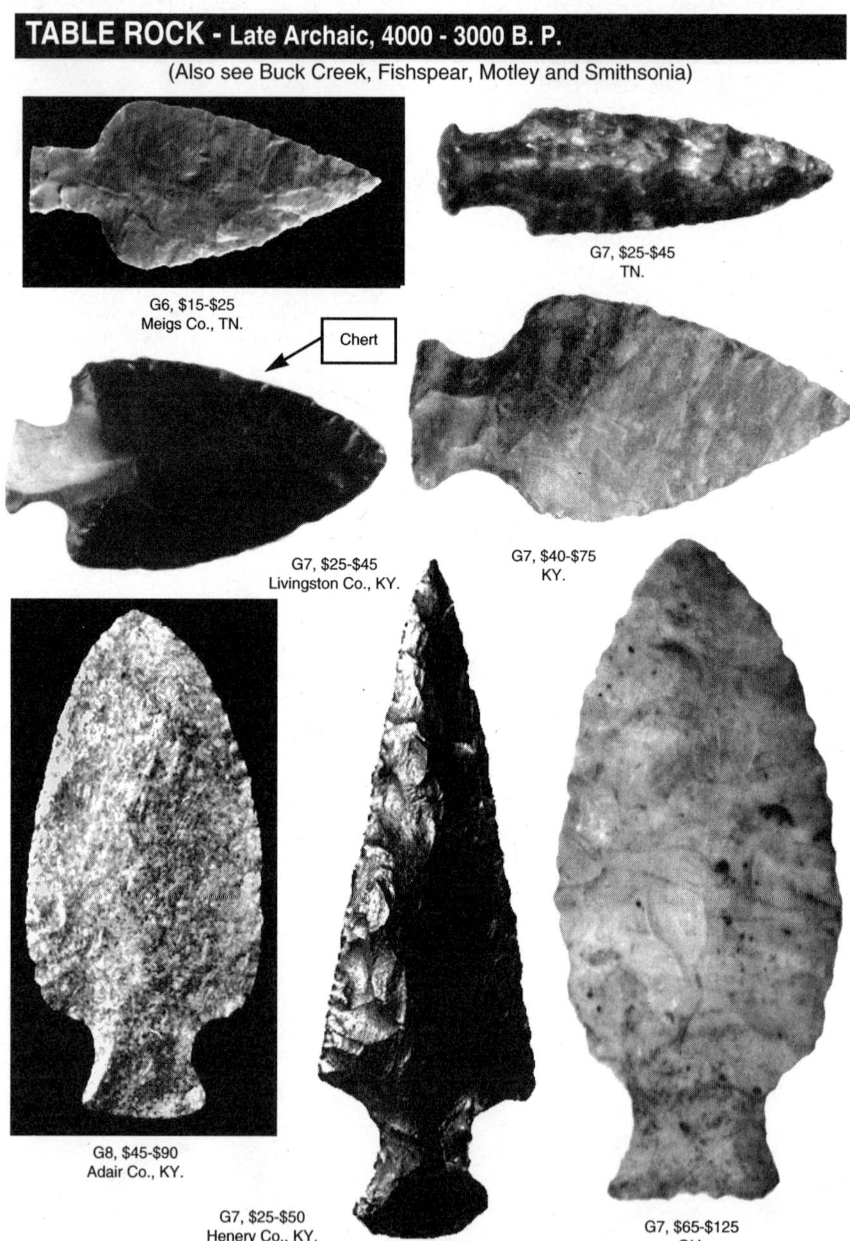

G6, $15-$25
Meigs Co., TN.

G7, $25-$45
TN.

G7, $25-$45
Livingston Co., KY.

G7, $40-$75
KY.

G8, $45-$90
Adair Co., KY.

G7, $25-$50
Henery Co., KY.

G7, $65-$125
OH.

LOCATION: Midwestern to Northeastern states. **DESCRIPTION:** A medium to large size, expanded stem point with straight to tapered shoulders. Shoulders can be sharp or rounded. This point type is also know as "Bottleneck".

G6, $25-$45
OH.

TEAR DROP - Woodland, 2000 - 1000 B. P.

(Also see Adena Blade and Red Ochre)

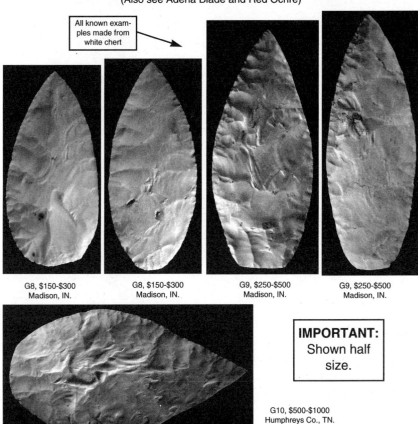

All known examples made from white chert

G8, $150-$300
Madison, IN.

G8, $150-$300
Madison, IN.

G9, $250-$500
Madison, IN.

G9, $250-$500
Madison, IN.

IMPORTANT: Shown half size.

G10, $500-$1000
Humphreys Co., TN.
Cache blade.

LOCATION: Southeastern states. **DESCRIPTION:** A large size, broad, thin, ellipitcal blade with a rounded to straight base. Usually found in caches and are believed to be a little later than the *Adena* blades. Usually made from a special white chert. Some examples have been found stained with red ochre.

TENNESSEE RIVER - Early Archaic, 9000 - 6000 B. P.

(Also see Adena Blade, Cobbs Triangular, Kirk and Red Ochre)

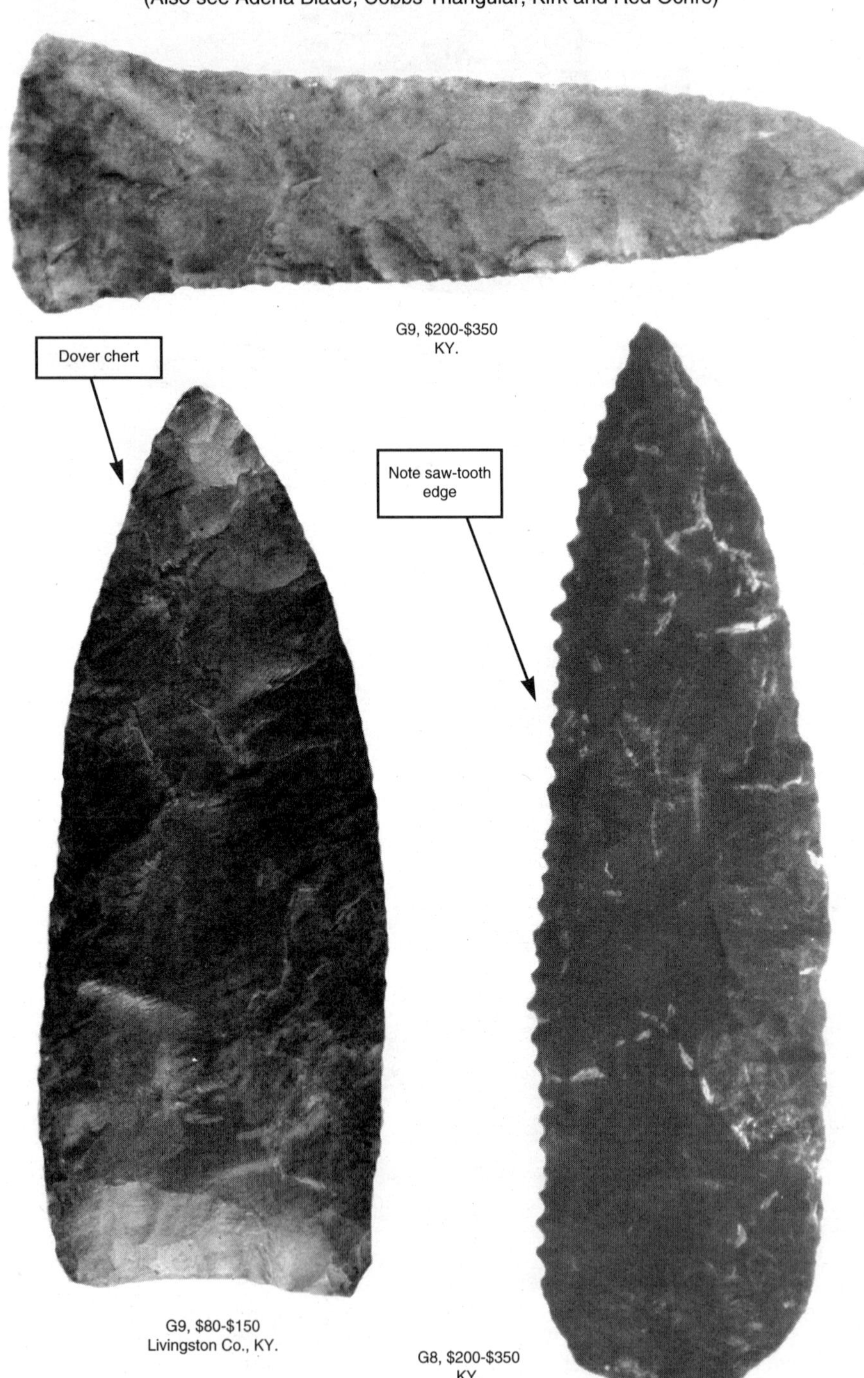

G9, $200-$350
KY.

G9, $80-$150
Livingston Co., KY.

G8, $200-$350
KY.

TENNESSEE RIVER (continued)

LOCATION: Southeastern states. **DESCRIPTION:** These are unnotched preforms for early Archaic types such as *Kirk, Eva*, etc. and would have the same description as that type without the notches. Bases can be straight, concave or convex. **I.D. KEY:** Archaic style edgework.

TENNESSEE SWORD

(See Duck River Sword)

THEBES - Early Archaic, 10,000 - 8000 B. P.

(Also see Big Sandy E-Notched, Lost Lake and St. Charles)

G6, $75-$150
KY.

G4, $25-$50
OH.

G8, $115-$225
Fairfield Co., OH.

G10, $150-$300
OH.

G7, $125-$250, IN.

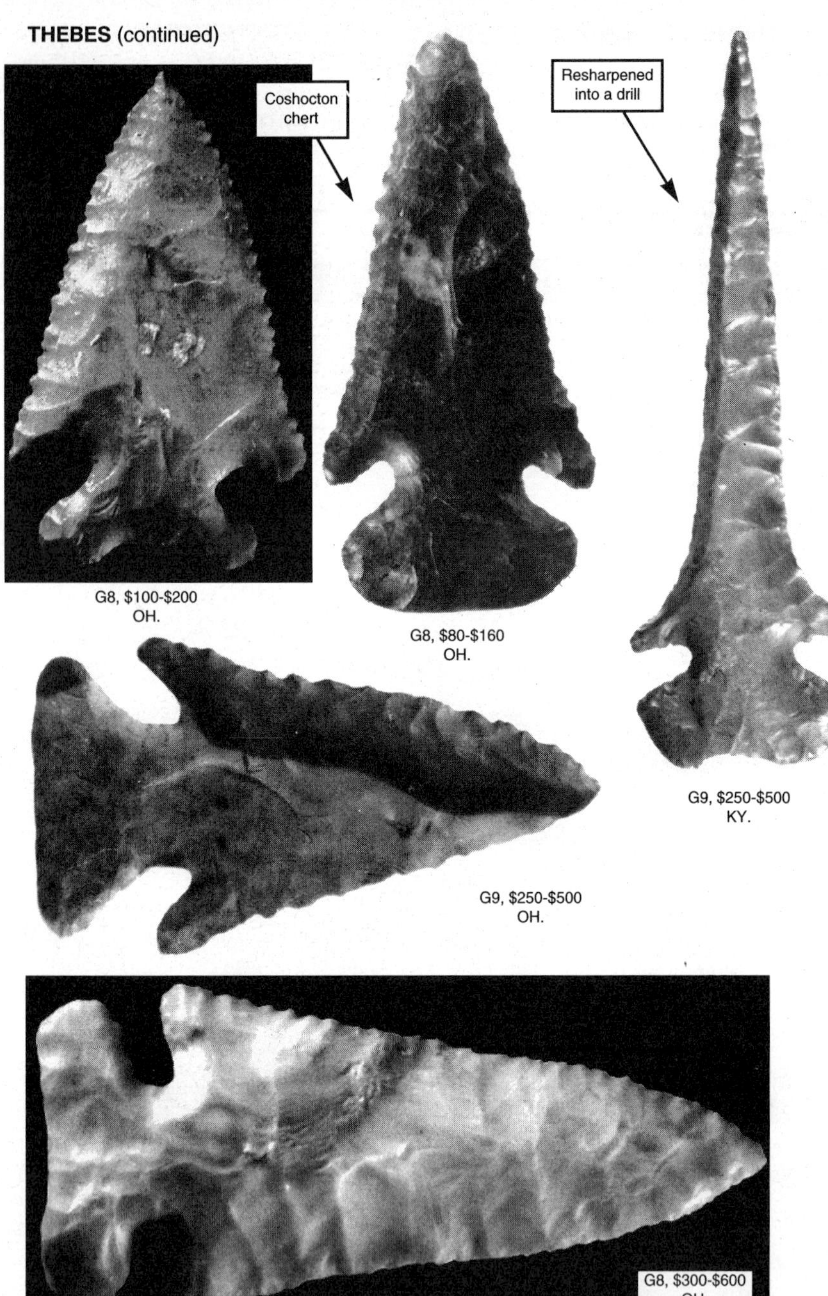

G8, $100-$200
OH.

G8, $80-$160
OH.

G9, $250-$500
KY.

G9, $250-$500
OH.

G8, $300-$600
OH.

LOCATION: Midwestern states. **DESCRIPTION:** A medium to large size, wide, blade with deep, angled side notches that are parallel sided and squared. Resharpened examples have beveling on one side of each face. The bases of this type have broad proportions and are concave, straight or convex and are ground. Some examples have unusual side notches called Key notch. This type of notch is angled into the blade to produce a high point in the center, forming the letter E. See *Big Sandy E-Notched*..

TORTUGAS - Middle Archaic to Woodland, 6000 - 1000 B. P.

(Also see Frazier and Levanna)

G5, $2-$4
Tishomingo
Co., MS.

G7, $10-$20
W. TN.

G8, $15-$25
Parsons, TN.

LOCATION: Midwestern to Southeastern states. **DESCRIPTION:**A medium size, fairly thick, triangular point with straight to convex sides and base. Some examples are beveled on one side of each face. Bases are usually thinned. This type is much thicker than *Madison* points. Smaller examples would fall in the *Matamoros* type.

EC

TRADE POINTS - Historic, 400 - 170 B. P.

These points were made of copper, iron, and steel and were traded to the Indians by the French, British and others from the 1600s to the 1800s. Examples have been found all over the United States.

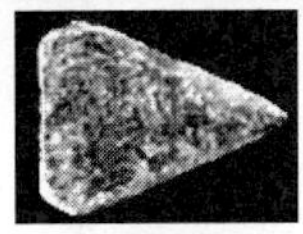

$10-$20
Tellico Plains, TN.

$20-$40, French conical
Elmore Co., AL. Circa 1700-1763

$75-$150
Eastern U.S.

TURKEYTAIL-FULTON - Late Archaic to Woodland, 4000 - 2500 B. P.

(Also see Adena)

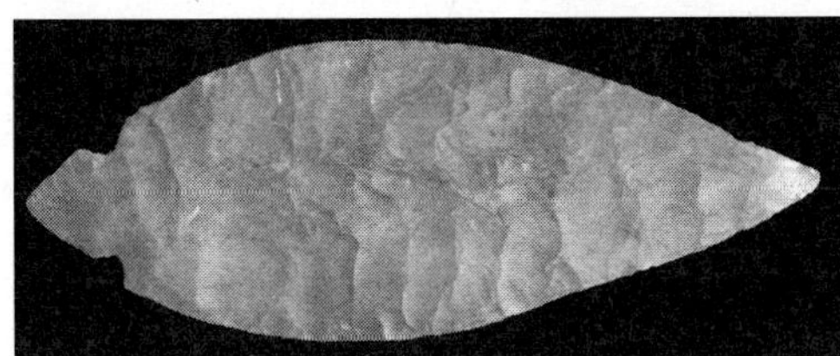

IMPORTANT:
This point is
shown 1/2 size

G7, $400-$600
KY.

LOCATION: Midwestern to Eastern states. **DESCRIPTION:** A medium to large size, wide, thin, elliptical blade with shallow notches very close to the base. This type is usually found in caches and has been reproduced in recent years. Made by the Adena culture. Found in late *Benton* caches in Mississippi, carbon dated to about 4000 B.P.

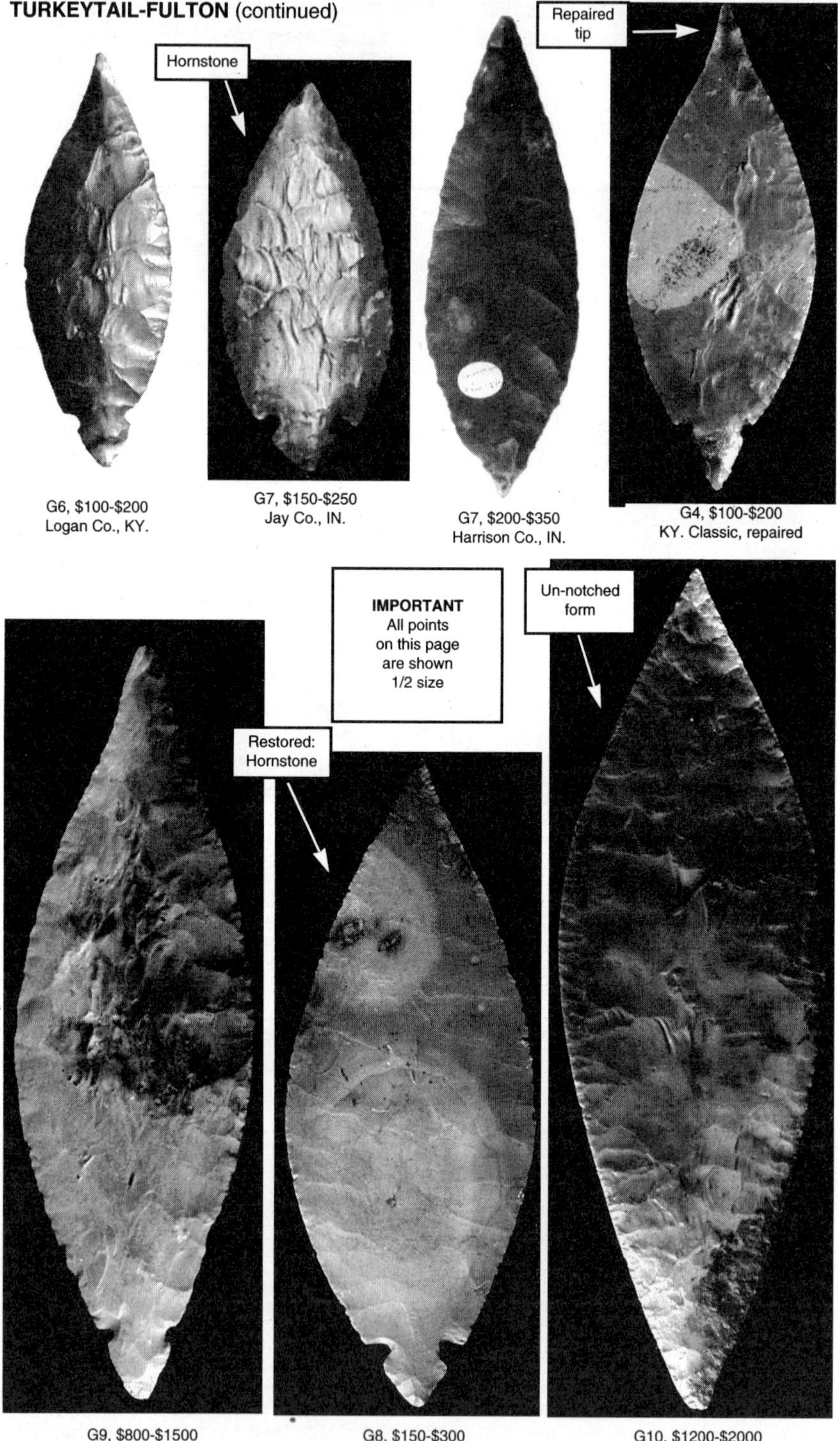

G6, $100-$200
Logan Co., KY.

G7, $150-$250
Jay Co., IN.

G7, $200-$350
Harrison Co., IN.

G4, $100-$200
KY. Classic, repaired

G9, $800-$1500
KY.

G8, $150-$300
KY. Classic form, restored

G10, $1200-$2000
Paris, TN.

TURKEYTAIL-HARRISON - Late Archaic to Woodland, 4000 - 2500 B. P.

(Alse see Adena)

G6, $15-$25
KY.

G6, $25-$45
IN.

LOCATION: Midwestern to Eastern states. **DESCRIPTION:** A medium to very large size, narrow, elliptical blade with tapered, horizontal or barbed shoulders, and an elongated, diamond-shaped stem in the form of a turkey's tail. Large examples may have fine pressure flaking on one edge of each face. Made by the Adena culture. Found in late *Benton* caches in Mississippi. Carbon dated to about 4000 B.P. Lengths up to 20 inches known.

IMPORTANT:
All points on this page are shown actural size

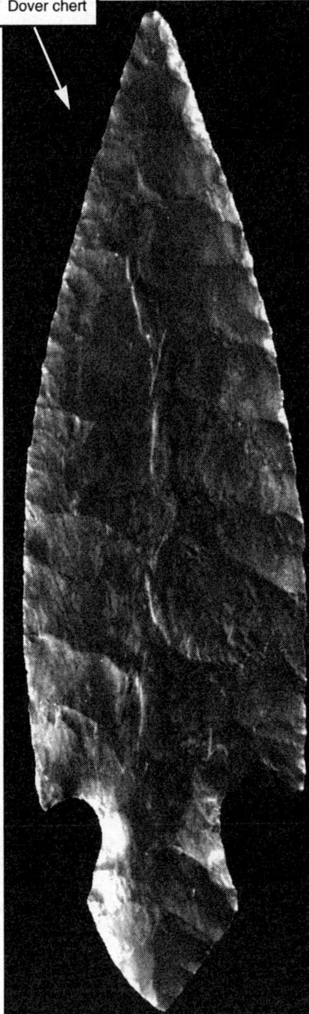

G7, $25-$50
IN.

G10, $450-$900
TN.

G10, $800-$1600
Humphreys Co., TN.

TURKEYTAIL-HEBRON - Late Archaic to Woodland, 4000 - 2500 B. P.

LOCATION: Midwestern states.
(Also see Adena Waubesa)

DESCRIPTION: A medium to large size blade with rounded, barbed shoulders, and a narrow, small, rounded base.

TURKEYTAIL-TUPELO - Mid-Archaic, 4750 - 3900 B. P.

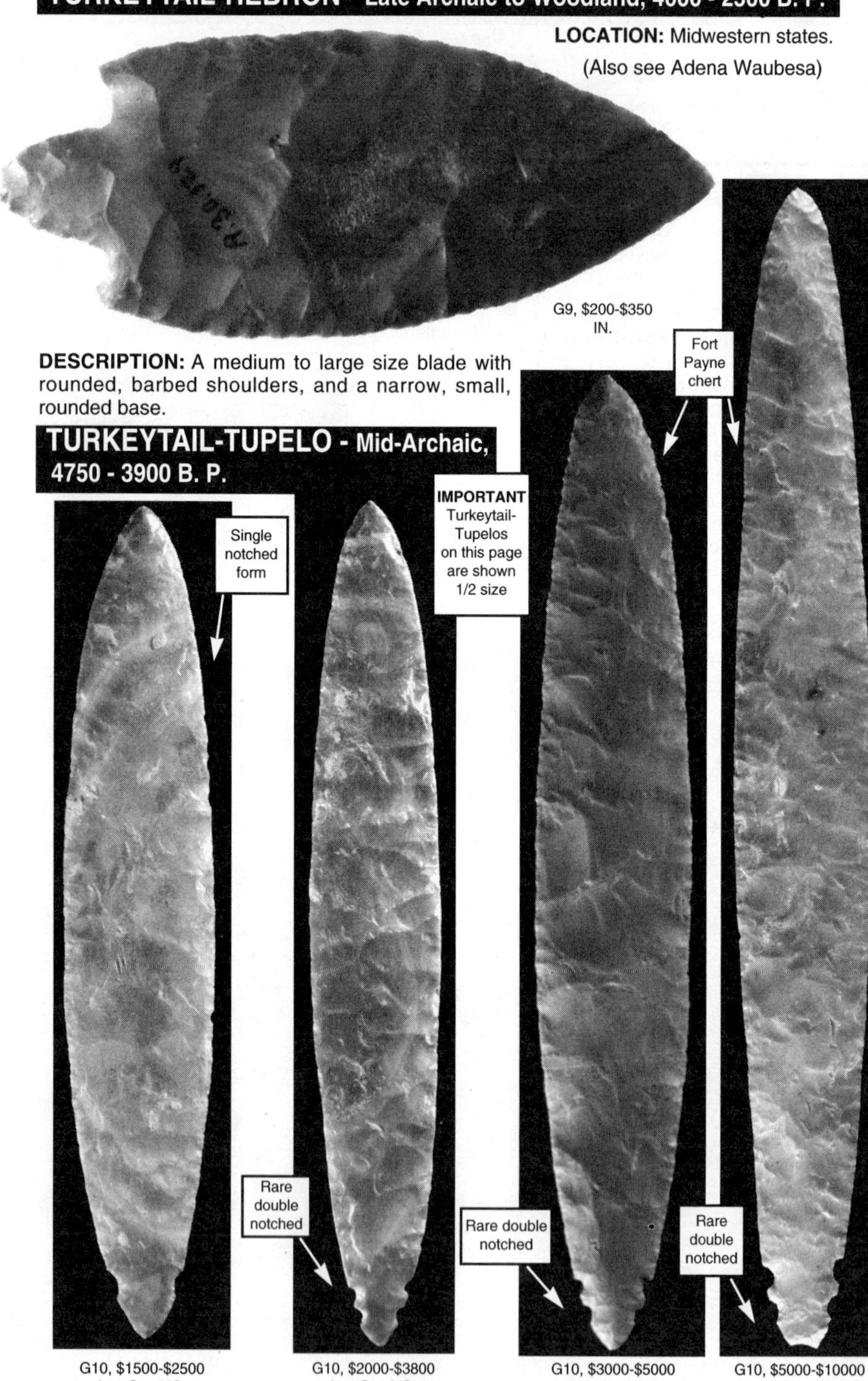

G9, $200-$350
IN.

G10, $1500-$2500
Lee Co., MS.

G10, $2000-$3800
Lee Co., MS.

G10, $3000-$5000
Lee Co., MS.

G10, $5000-$10000
Lee Co., MS.

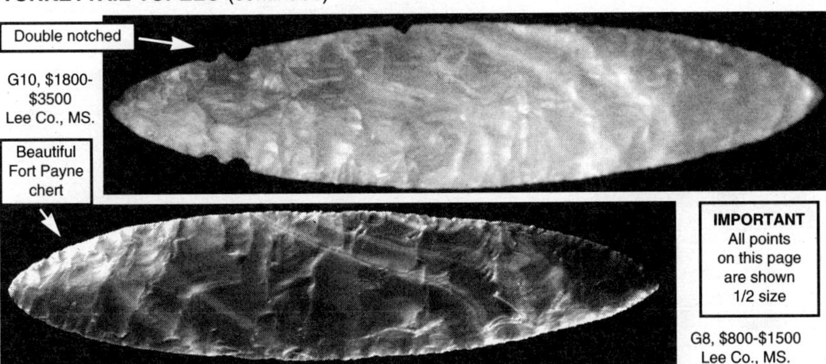

G10, $1800-$3500
Lee Co., MS.

IMPORTANT
All points on this page are shown 1/2 size

G8, $800-$1500
Lee Co., MS.

LOCATION: Mississippi, Alabama & Tennessee. **DESCRIPTION:** A large size, thin, well-made blade that is found in caches with large Benton points. Some are not notched, but most have single, double or triple notches. Polishing occurs on the edges and surfaces of a few examples. These are unique and 1000 years older than the northern type.

VALINA - Woodland, 2500 - 1000 B. P.

(Also see Madison and Morrow Mountain)

G5, $.50-$.75
Sequatchie Valley, TN.

G5, $.25-$.50
Meigs Co., TN.

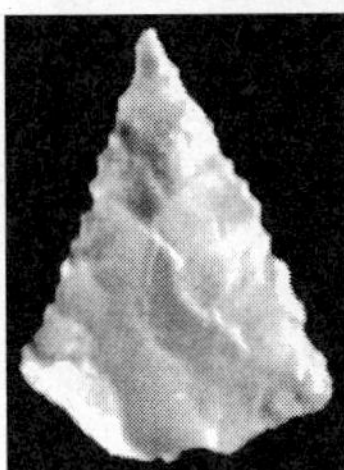

G7, $1-$2
Meigs Co., TN.

LOCATION: Eastern states. **DESCRIPTION:** A small size, broad triangle with rounded basal corners and a convex base.

WADE - Late Archaic to Woodland, 4500 - 2500 B. P.

(Also see Buck Creek, Eva, Hamilton Stemmed, Motley, Rankin and Smithsonia)

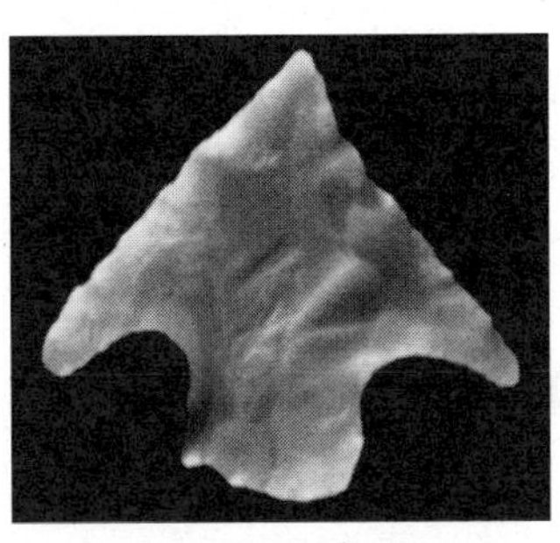

G2, $12-$20
Dayton, TN.

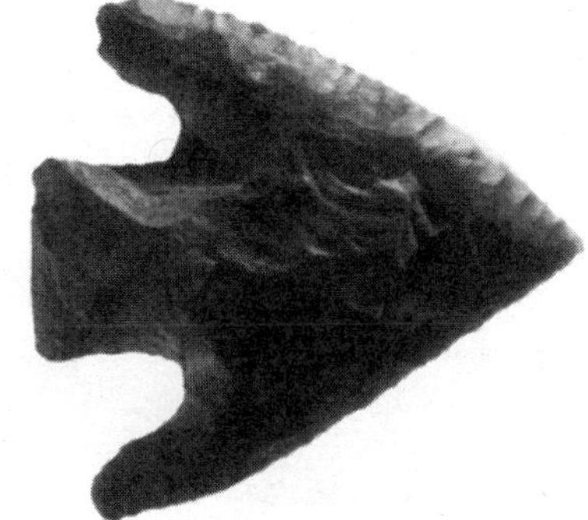

G7, $45-$80
Coffee Lake, AL.

LOCATION: Southern states. **DESCRIPTION:** A medium to large size, broad, well barbed, stemmed point. The blade is straight to convex. The stem is straight to expanding. On some examples, the barbs almost reach the base. Has been found with *Motley* points in caches.

G6, $20-$40
KY.

G7, $40-$80
KY.

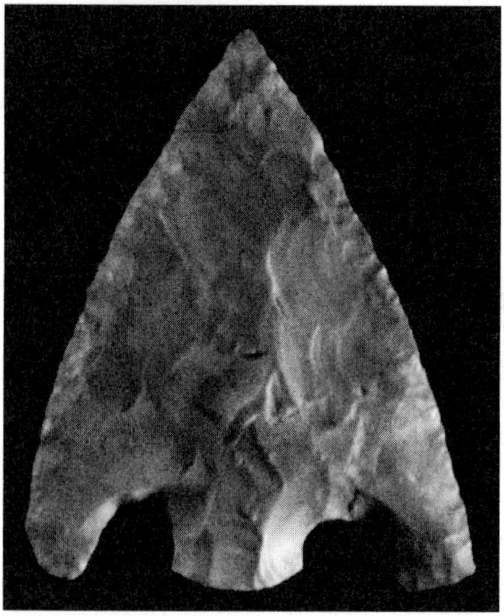

G7, $80-$150
Dayton, TN.

G6, $40-$80
Clarksville, TN.

WARRICK - Early Archaic, 9000 - 5000 B. P.

(Also see Hardin and St. Charles)

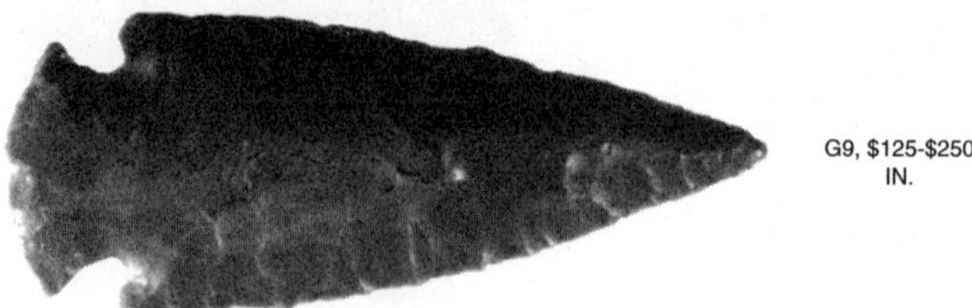

G9, $125-$250
IN.

LOCATION: Ohio and adjacent states. **DESCRIPTION:** A medium to large size, side-notched point. Notching is very close to the base. Bases are ground and flaking is of high quality.

WARRICK (continued)

G9, $125-$250
IN.

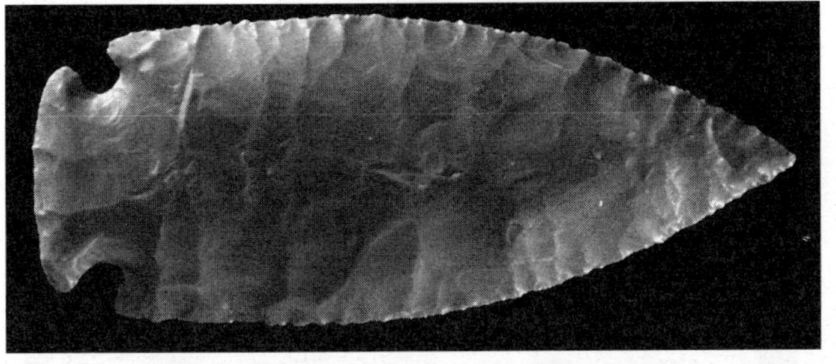

G10, $400-$600
Harrison Co.,IN.

EC

WASHINGTON - Woodland, 3000 - 1500 B. P.

(Also see Durant's Bend and Nova)

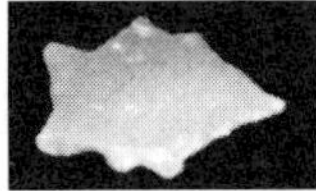

G2, $.25-$.50
Dallas Co., AL. Classic.

LOCATION: Southeastern states. **DESCRIPTION:** A small size, serrated, corner to side notched point with a concave, expanded base.

WHEELER EXCURVATE - Transitional Paleo, 10,000 - 8000 B. P.

(Also see Angostura)

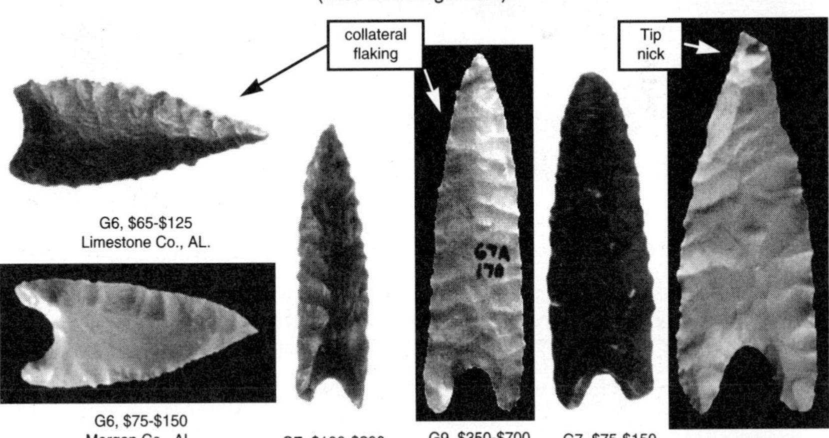

G6, $65-$125
Limestone Co., AL.

G6, $75-$150
Morgan Co., AL.

G7, $100-$200
Limestone Co., AL.

G9, $350-$700
Limestone Co., AL.

G7, $75-$150
OH.

G4, $30-$60
Limestone Co., AL.

LOCATION: Southeastern states. **DESCRIPTION:** A small to medium size, lanceolate point with a deep concave base that is steeply beveled. Some examples are fluted, others are finely serrated and show excellent quality collateral flaking. Most bases are deeply notched but some examples have a more shallow concavity. Basal grinding is absent. The ears on some examples turn inward. Blade edges are excurvate. **I.D. KEY:** Base form and flaking style.

WHEELER EXCURVATE (continued)

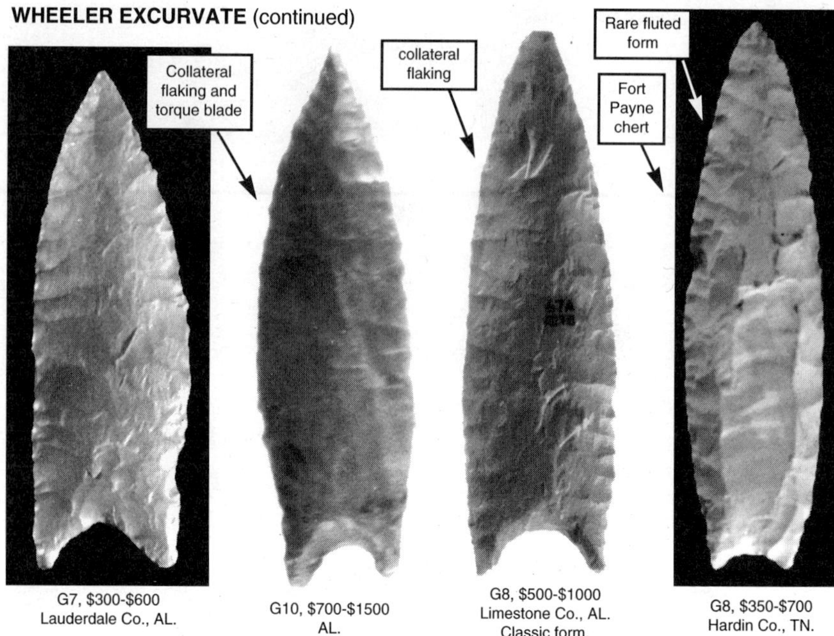

G7, $300-$600
Lauderdale Co., AL.

G10, $700-$1500
AL.

G8, $500-$1000
Limestone Co., AL.
Classic form.

G8, $350-$700
Hardin Co., TN.

WHEELER EXPANDED BASE - Transitional Paleo, 10,000 - 8000 B. P.

G4, $20-$40
W. TN.

G2, $8-$15
Coffee Lake, AL.
Broken back.

G10, $1500-$2500
Hardin Co., TN. The finest example known.

G5, $30-$60
Savannah, TN.

LOCATION: Northwest Alabama and southern Tennessee. **DESCRIPTION:** A small to medium size, very narrow, thin, lanceolate point with expanding, squared ears forming a "Y" at the base which is "V" notched. Most examples have high quality collateral flaking. This very rare type has been found on *Wheeler* sites in the type area. Scarcity of this type suggests that it was not in use but for a short period of time. **I.D. KEY:** Notch and ears.

WHEELER RECURVATE - Transitional Paleo 10,000 - 8000 B. P.

(Also see Patrick)

LOCATION: Southeastern states. **DESCRIPTION:** A small to medium size, lanceolate point with recurved blade edges and a deep concave base that is steeply beveled. The blade edges taper towards the base, forming the hafting area. Basal grinding is absent. Rare examples are fluted.

G5, $45-$90
Southeastern TN.

G9, $450-$900
Trigg Co., KY.

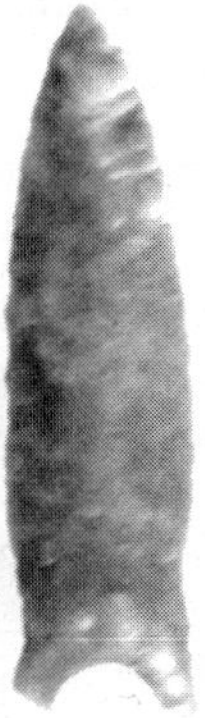

G9, $150-$250
AL.

G9, $350-$600
Smith Co., TN.

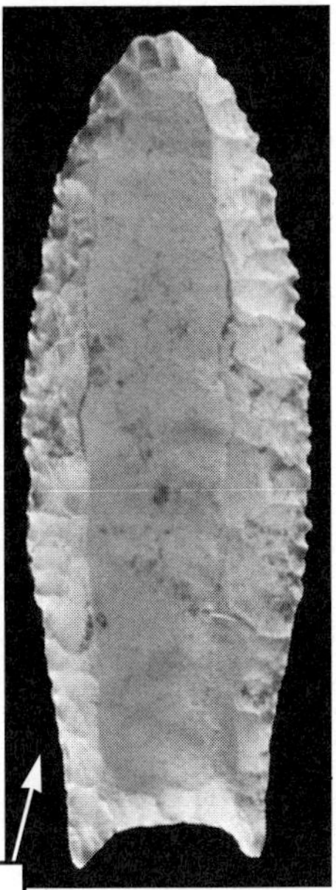

Very rare fluted form

G9, $1500-$2500
Colbert Co., AL.

WHEELER TRIANGULAR - Transitional Paleo 10,000 - 8000 B. P.

(Also see Camp Creek, Copena, Madison and Sand Mountain)

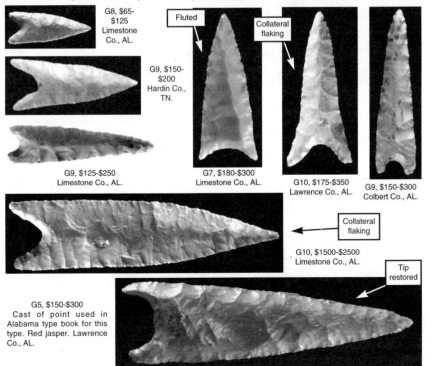

G8, $65-$125
Limestone Co., AL.

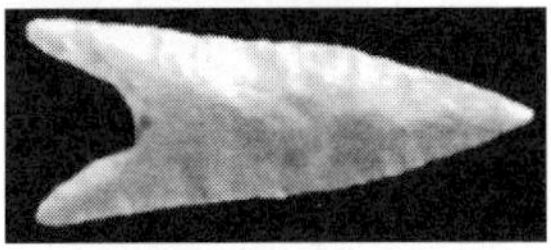

G9, $150-$200
Hardin Co., TN.

Fluted

Collateral flaking

G9, $125-$250
Limestone Co., AL.

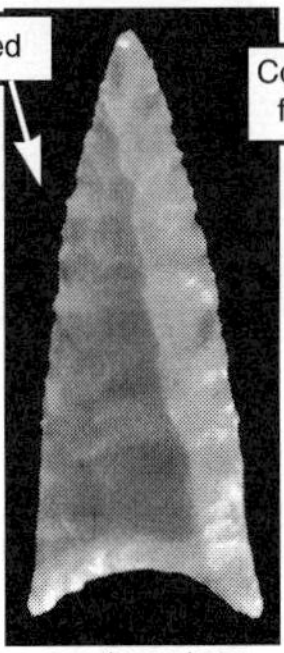

G7, $180-$300
Limestone Co., AL.

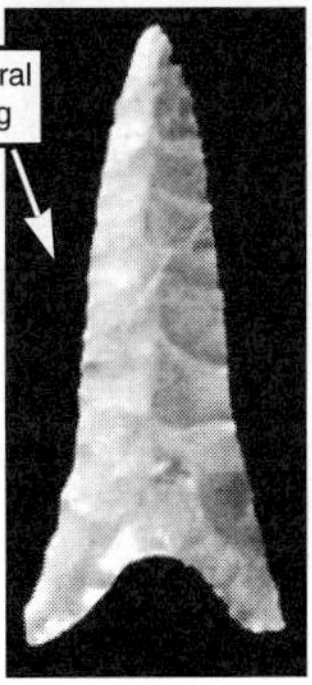

G10, $175-$350
Lawrence Co., AL.

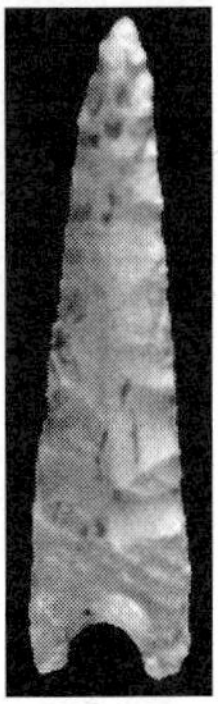

G9, $150-$300
Colbert Co., AL.

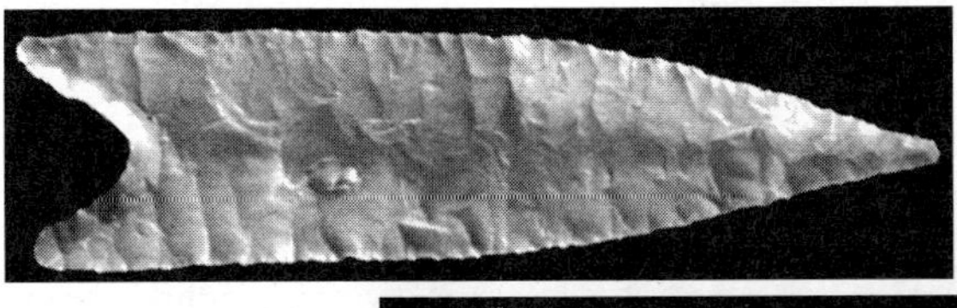

Collateral flaking

G10, $1500-$2500
Limestone Co., AL.

Tip restored

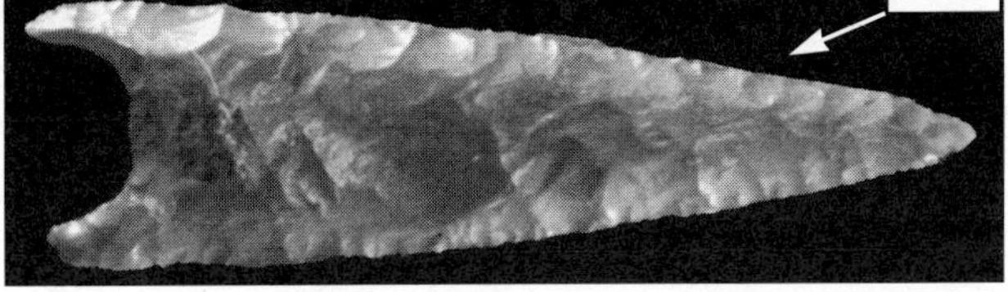

G5, $150-$300
Cast of point used in Alabama type book for this type. Red jasper. Lawrence Co., AL.

LOCATION: Southeastern states. **DESCRIPTION:** A small to medium size, lanceolate point with straight sides and a deep concave base that is steeply beveled. On some examples, the ears point inward toward the base. This is a rare form and few examples exist. **I.D. KEY:** Beveled base and Paleo flaking.

WHITE SPRINGS - Early to Middle Archaic, 8000 - 6000 B. P.

(Also see Benton)

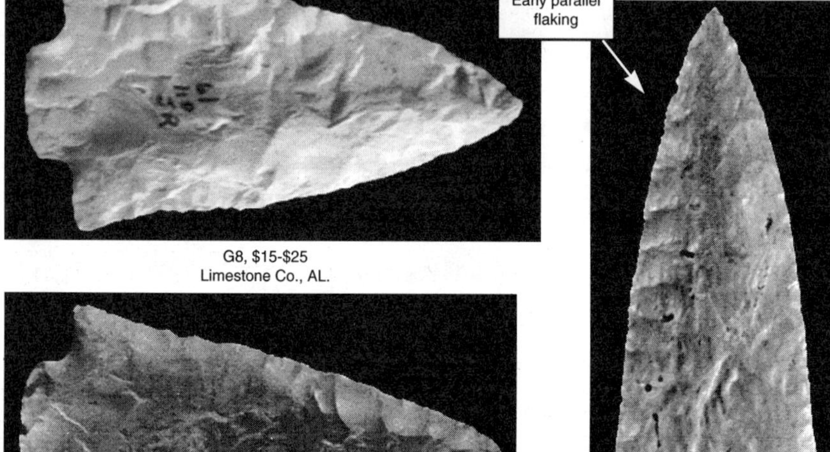

G8, $15-$25
Limestone Co., AL.

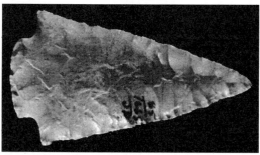

G8, $20-$30
Limestone Co., AL.

G10, $45-$80
Colbert Co., AL.

LOCATION: Southeastern states. **DESCRIPTION:** A medium size, broad, triangular point with a medium to wide very short straight stem. Shoulders are usually square and the base is straight, slightly convex or concave. **I.D. KEY:** Short base and early flaking.

YADKIN - Woodland to Mississippian, 2500 - 500 B. P.

(Also see Camp Creek, Hamilton, Levanna and Nolichucky)

G9, $15-$20
Bristol, TN.

G6, $5-$10
Bristol, TN.

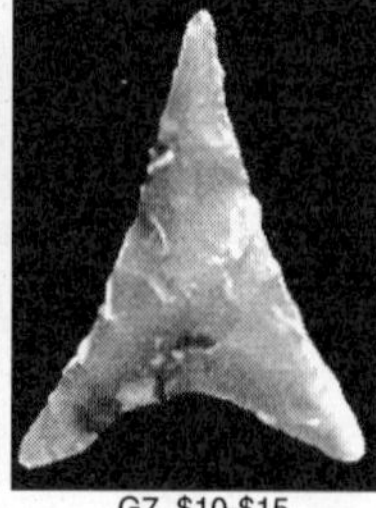

G7, $10-$15
Bristol, TN.

LOCATION: Southeastern and Eastern states. **DESCRIPTION:** A small to medium size, broad based, fairly thick, triangular point with a broad, concave base and straight to convex to recurved side edges.

SOUTHERN CENTRAL SECTION:

This section includes point types from the following states:
Arkansas, Louisiana, Oklahoma, Texas

The points in this section are arranged in alphabetical order and are shown **actual size**. All types are listed that were available for photographing. Any missing types will be added to future editions as photographs become available. We are always interested in receiving sharp, black and white or color glossy photos or color slides of your collection. Be sure and include a ruler in the photograph so that proper scale can be determined.

Lithics: Materials employed in the manufacture of projectile points from this region are: basalt, chalcedony, chert, conglomerate, crystal, flint, novaculite, obsidian, quartz, quartzite with lesser amounts of agate, jasper, and petrified wood.

Regional Consultant:
Dwain Rogers

Special Advisors:
Nick Cavallini, Tom Davis, Glen Kizzia, Bob McWilliams, Donald Meador, Bob Miller, Jack Myers, Lyle Nickel, Michael Redwine, Michael Speer, Art Tatum

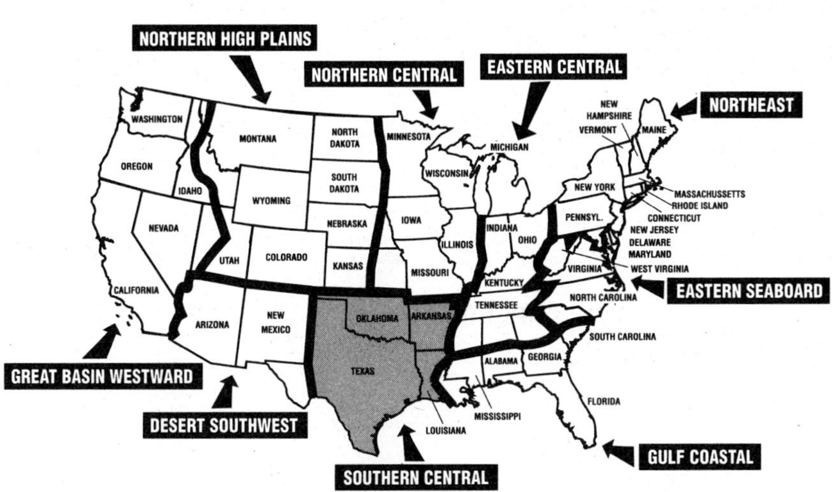

SOUTHERN CENTRAL

(Archaeological Periods)

PALEO (14,000 B.P. - 11,000 B.P.)

Chopper
Clovis
Goshen
Graver
Midland
Scraper

LATE PALEO (12,000 B.P. - 10,000 B.P.)

Agate Basin
Folsom
Hell Gap
Rodgers Side Hollowed
Square Knife

TRANSITIONAL PALEO (11,000 B.P. - 9,000 B.P.)

Alberta
Allen
Angostura
Arkabutla
Barber
Big Sandy
Browns Valley
Cache River
Golondrina
Mahaffey
Midland
Milnesand
Paleo Knife
Pelican
Plainview
Red River Knife
San Patrice-Hope Var.
San Patrice-Keithville Var.
San Patrice-St. Johns Var.
Scottsbluff I & II

EARLY ARCHAIC (10,000 B.P. - 7,000 B.P.)

Andice
Baker
Bandy
Bassett
Calf Creek
Dalton Breckenridge
Dalton Classic
Dalton Greenbrier
Dalton Hemphill
Darl Stemmed
Dovetail
Early Stemmed
Early Stemmed Lanceolate
Early Triangular
Firstview
Gower
Graham Cave
Hardin
Hidden Valley
Holland
Hoxie
Jetta
Johnson
Martindale
Meserve
Perforator
Pike County
Rice Lobbed
Rice Shallow Side Notched
Rio Grande
Savage Cave
Searcy
Victoria
Wells
Zella
Zephyr

MIDDLE ARCHAIC (7,000 B.P. - 4,000 B.P.)

Abasolo
Almagre
Bell
Brewerton Eared
Brewerton Side Notched
Bulverde
Carrizo
Carrolton
Dawson
Exotic
Frio
Godar
Hemphill
Hickory Ridge
Hidden Valley
Kerrville Knife
Kinney
La Jita
Lange
Langtry
Langtry-Arenosa
Lerma Pointed Base
Lerma Rounded BaseMarshall
Matanzas
Montell
Motley
Nolan
Palmillas
Pandale
Pedernales
Raddatz
Refugio
Savannah River
Tortugas
Travis
Uvalde
Val Verde
White River
Williams
Zorra

LATE ARCHAIC (4,000 B.P. - 3,000 B.P.)

Base Tang Knife
Big Creek
Castroville
Catan
Coahuila
Conejo
Corner Tang Knife
Covington
Dallas
Delhi
Elam
Ellis
Ensor
Ensor Split-Base
Epps
Evans
Friday
Gahagan
Gary
Hale
Marcos
Matamoros
Mid-Back Tang
Morhiss
Pandora
Pontchartrain
Sabine
Table Rock
Trinity
Turkeytail-Harrison
Zella

WOODLAND (3,000 B.P. - 1,300 B.P.)

Adena Blade
Adena Dickson
Adena-Robbins
Alba
Charcos
Cupp
Darl
Darl Blade
Duran
Edgewood
Edwards
Fairland
Figueroa
Friley
Gibson
Godley
Hare Biface
Knight Island
Morill
Oauchita
Paisano
Peisker Diamond
Pogo
Reed
Rockwall
San Gabriel
San Saba
Shumla
Sinner
Steuben
Yarbrough

MISSISSIPPIAN (1300 B.P. - 400 B.P.)

Agee
Bassett
Blevins
Bonham
Caddoan Blade
Caracara
Catahoula
Cliffton
Dardanelle
Fresno
Garza
Harahey
Harrell
Haskell
Hayes
Homan
Howard
Huffaker
Keota
Livermore
Lott
Maud
Mineral Springs
Moran
Morris
Nodena
Perdiz
Sabinal
Sallisaw
Scallorn
Sequoyah
Starr
Steiner
Talco
Toyah
Washita
Young

HISTORIC (450 B.P. - 170 B.P.)

Cuney
Guerrero
Trade Points

SOUTHERN CENTRAL
THUMBNAIL GUIDE SECTION

The following references are provided to aid the collector in easier and quicker identification of point types. All photos are exactly 30% of acutal size and are proportional to each other. Each point pictured in this section represents a classic form for the type. When a match is found, go to the alphabetical location of that type for more examples in true actual size.

① THUMBNAIL GUIDE - AURICULATE FORMS (30% actual size)

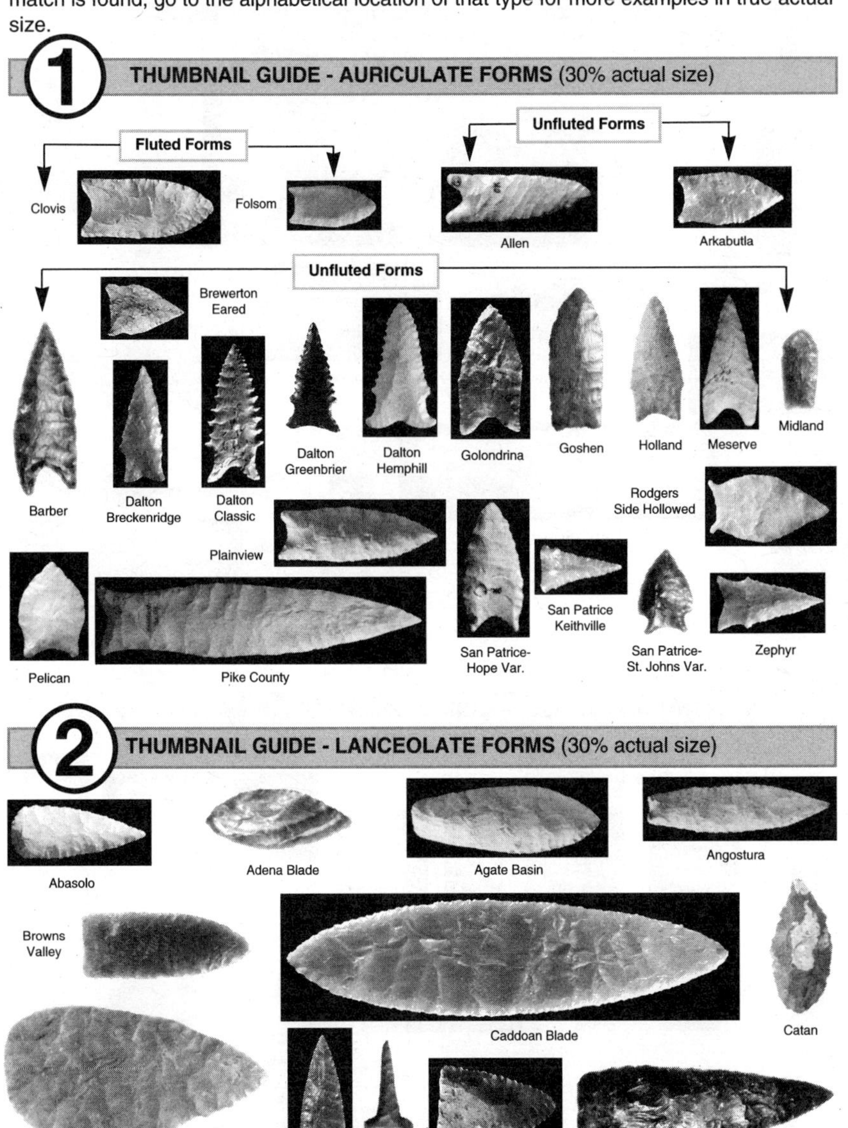

Gahagan

Graver

Kinney

SC

THUMBNAIL GUIDE - Lanceolate Forms (continued)

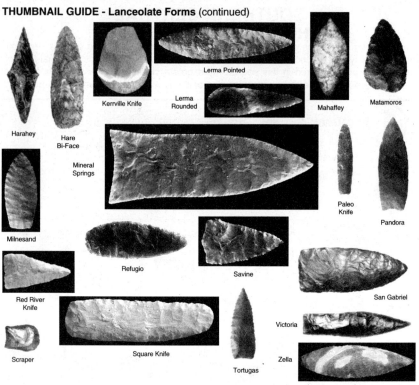

Harahey

Hare Bi-Face

Kerrville Knife

Lerma Pointed

Lerma Rounded

Mahaffey

Matamoros

Mineral Springs

Milnesand

Paleo Knife

Pandora

Refugio

Savine

Red River Knife

San Gabriel

Victoria

Scraper

Square Knife

Tortugas

Zella

3 THUMBNAIL GUIDE - CORNER NOTCHED FORMS (30% actual size)

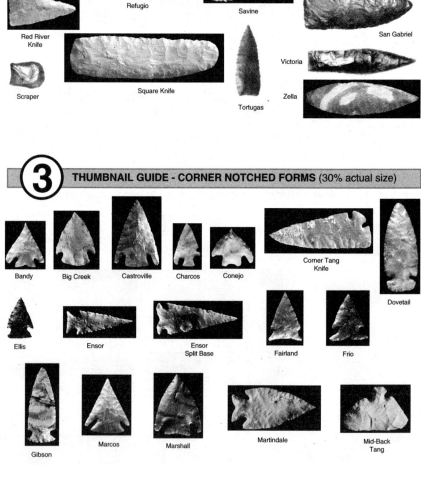

Bandy

Big Creek

Castroville

Charcos

Conejo

Corner Tang Knife

Dovetail

Ellis

Ensor

Ensor Split Base

Fairland

Frio

Gibson

Marcos

Marshall

Martindale

Mid-Back Tang

THUMBNAIL GUIDE - SIDE NOTCHED FORMS (30% actual size)

Big Sandy

Brewerton Side Notched

Cache River

Evans

Figueroa

Godar

Graham Cave

Godley

Hemphill

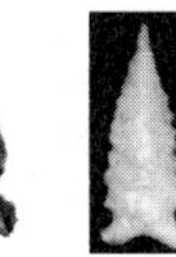

Hickory Ridge

Paisano

Raddatz

Rice Shallow Side Notched

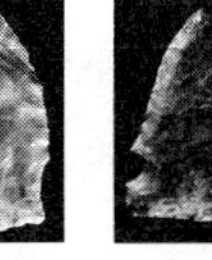

Savage Cave

White River

5 THUMBNAIL GUIDE - STEMMED FORMS (30% of actual size)

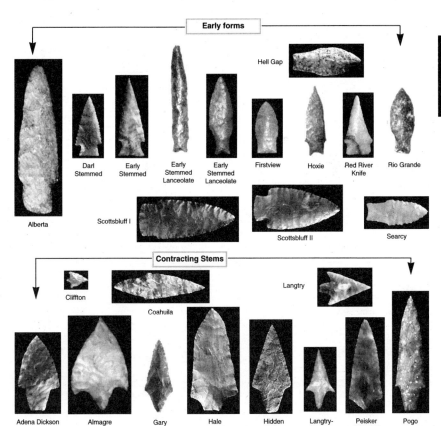

Early forms

Hell Gap

Alberta

Darl Stemmed

Early Stemmed

Early Stemmed Lanceolate

Early Stemmed Lanceolate

Firstview

Hoxie

Red River Knife

Rio Grande

Scottsbluff I

Scottsbluff II

Searcy

Contracting Stems

Cliffton

Coahuila

Langtry

Adena Dickson

Almagre

Gary

Hale

Hidden Valley

Langtry-Arenosa

Peisker Diamond

Pogo

SC

THUMBNAIL GUIDE - Stemmed Forms (continued)

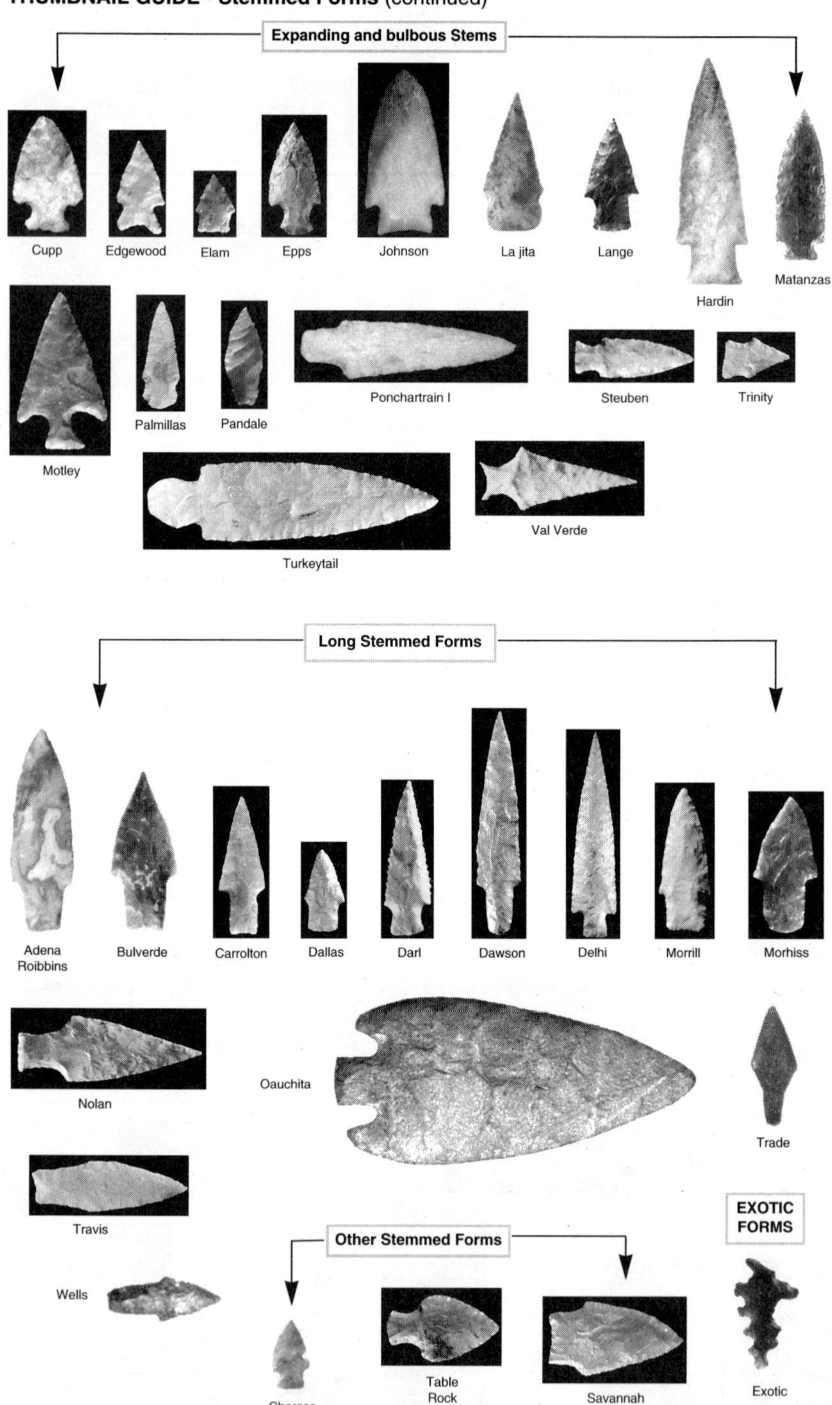
Expanding and bulbous Stems
Cupp
Edgewood
Elam
Epps
Johnson
La jita
Lange
Hardin
Matanzas
Motley
Palmillas
Pandale
Ponchartrain I
Steuben
Trinity
Turkeytail
Val Verde
Long Stemmed Forms
Adena Roibbins
Bulverde
Carrolton
Dallas
Darl
Dawson
Delhi
Morrill
Morhiss
Nolan
Oauchita
Trade
Travis
Wells
Other Stemmed Forms
Charcos
Table Rock
Savannah River
EXOTIC FORMS
Exotic

6 THUMBNAIL GUIDE - STEMMED-BIFURCATED FORMS (30% of actual size)

Baker

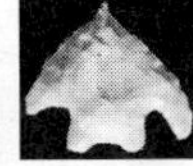

Conejo

Ensor Split Base

Jetta

Uvalde

Pedernalis

Frio

Gower

Montell

7 THUMBNAIL GUIDE - BASAL NOTCHED FORMS (30% of actual size)

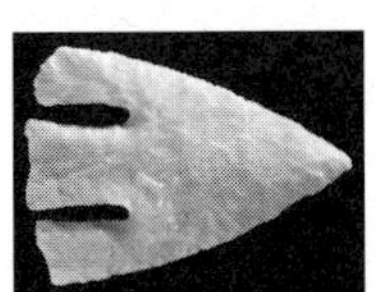
Andice

Base Tang

Base Tang

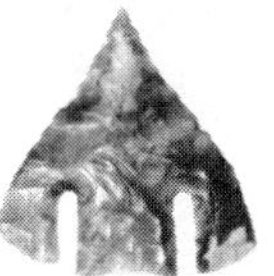
Bell

Calf Creek

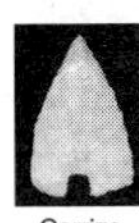
Carrizo

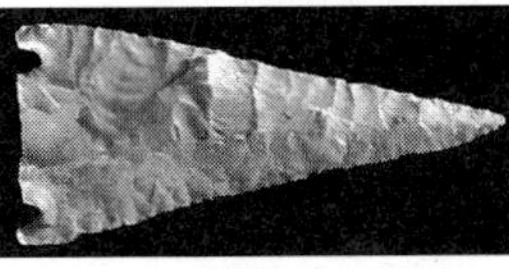
San Saba

Shumla

8 THUMBNAIL GUIDE - ARROW POINTS (30% of actual size)

Agee

Alba

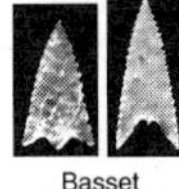
Basset

Blevins

Bonham

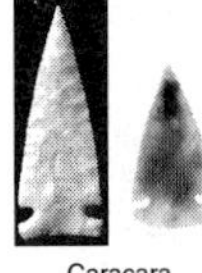
Caracara

Catahoula

Cuney

Dardanelle

Duran

Edwards

Friley

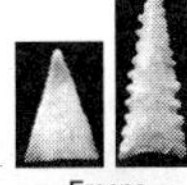
Fresno

Garza

Guerro

Harrell

Haskell

Hayes

Homan

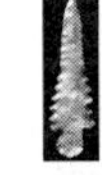
Howard

Huffaker

Keota

Knight Island

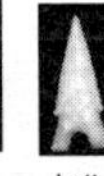
Livermore

Lott

Maud

Moran

Morris

Nodena

Perdiz

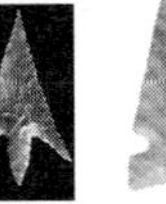
Reed

Rockwall

Sabinal

Sallisaw

Scallorn

Sequoyah

Sinner

Steiner

Talco

Toyah

Washita

ABASOLO - Early to Middle Archaic, 7000 - 5000 B. P.

(Also see Catan and Matamoros)

G3, $4-$6
Travis Co., TX.

G3, $3-$5
TX.

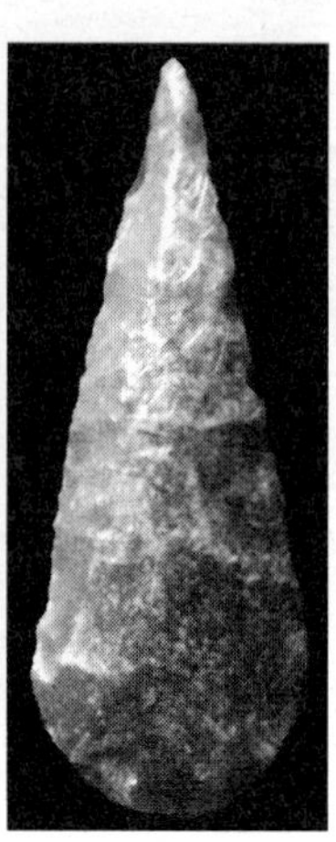
G6, $8-$15
TX.

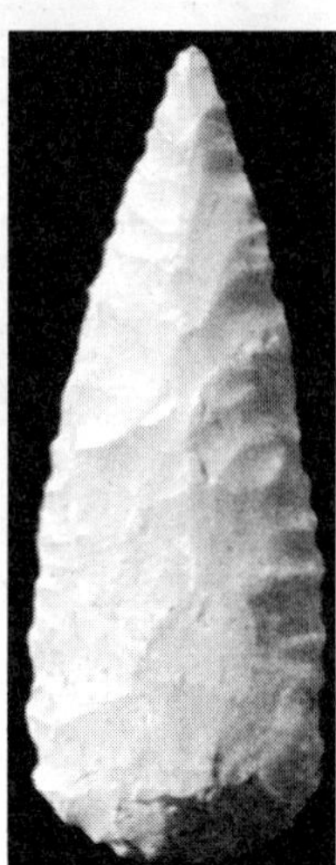
G6, $10-$20
McMullin Co., TX.

LOCATION: Southern Midwestern states and Mexico. **DESCRIPTION:** A medium to large size, broad, lanceolate point with a rounded base. The blade can be beveled on one side of each face and the base can be thinned. **I.D. KEY:** Early form of flaking on blade with good secondary edgework and rounded base.

ADENA BLADE - Late Archaic to Late Woodland, 3000 - 1200 B. P.

(Also see Harahey, Lerma, Pandora)

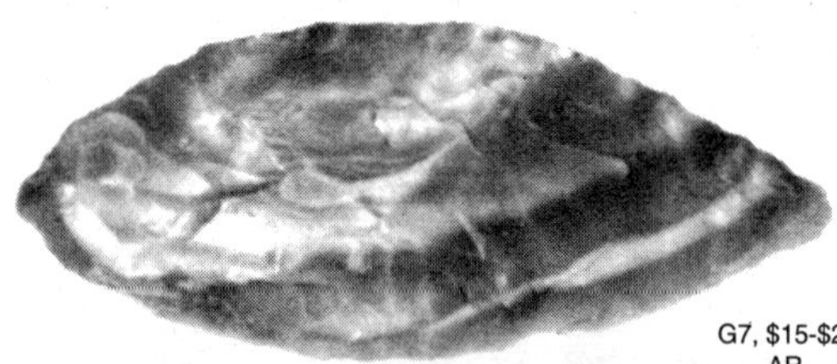
G7, $15-$25
AR.

LOCATION: Midwestern states and Mexico. **DESCRIPTION:** A large size, thin, broad, ovate blade with a rounded to pointed base and is usually found in caches. **I.E. KEY:** Woodland flaking, large direct strikes.

ADENA-DICKSON - Late Archaic to Woodland, 2500 - 1600 B. P.

(Also see Gary, Hidden Valley and Morrow Mountain)

G8, $30-$60
Clay Co., AR.

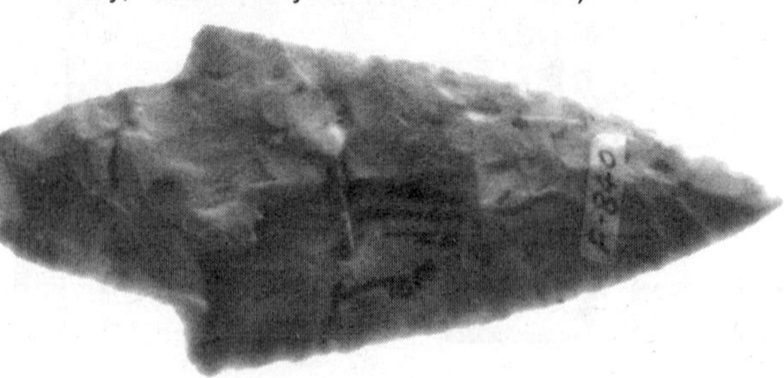

LOCATION: Midwestern states. **DESCRIPTION:** A medium to large size point with tapered shoulders and a contracting stem. High quality flaking and thinness is evident on most examples. **I.D. KEY:** Basal form.

G5, $15-$25
AR.

G5, $20-$40
AR.

SC

ADENA-ROBBINS - Late Archaic to Woodland, 3000 - 1800 B. P.

(Also see Bulverde, Carrolton and Wells)

LOCATION: Midwestern states. **DESCRIPTION:** A large, broad, triangular point that is thin and well made with a long, wide, rounded stem that is parallel sided. The blade has convex sides and square shoulders. Many examples show excellent secondary flaking on blade edges. **I.D. KEY:** Squared base, heavy secondary flaking.

G5, $15-$25
AR.

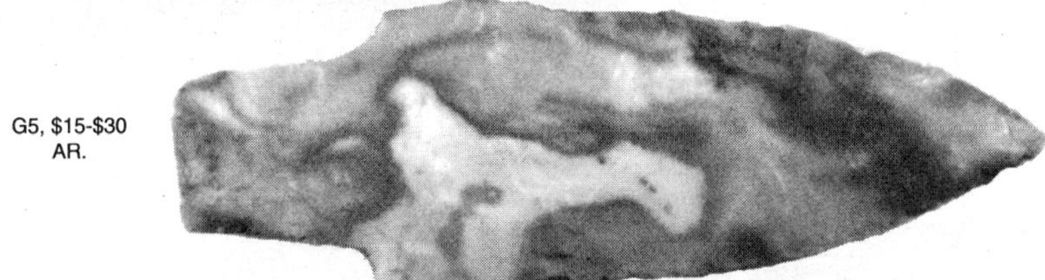

G5, $15-$30
AR.

AGATE BASIN - Transitional Paleo to Early Archaic, 10,500 - 8000 B. P.

(Also see Allen, Angostura, Eden, Hell Gap, Lerma, Mahaffey and Sedalia)

AGATE BASIN (continued)

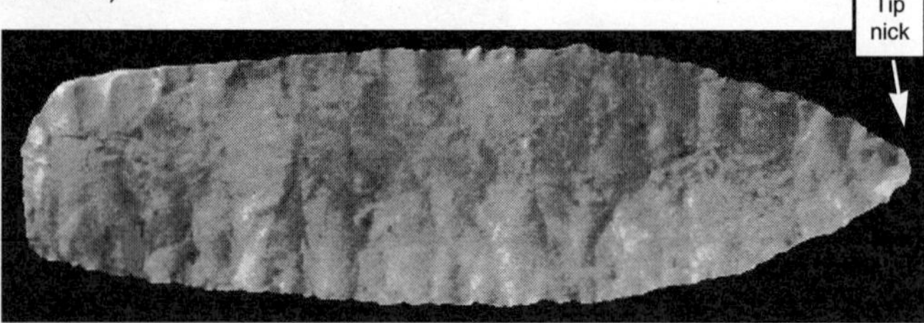

G7, $125-$250
Union Parrish, LA.

G4, $100-$200
Osage Co., OK.

LOCATION: New Mexico to Montana eastward to Pennsylvania. **DESCRIPTION:** A medium to large size lanceolate blade of usually high quality. Bases are either convex, concave or straight, and are normally ground. Some examples are median ridged and have random to parallel flaking. **I.D. KEY:** Basal form and flaking style.

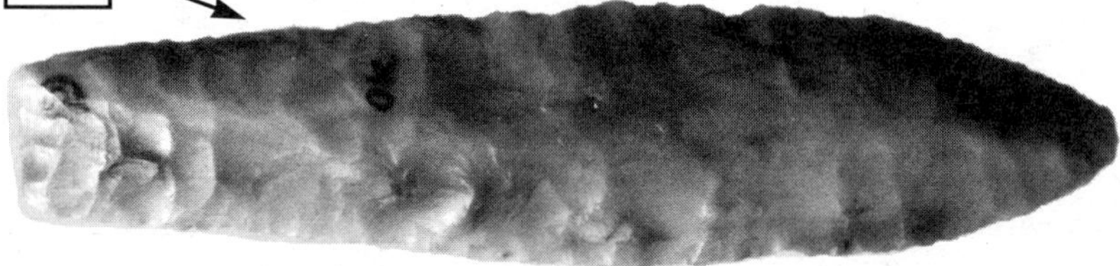

G6, $175-$350
Osage Co., OK.

AGEE - Mississippian, 1200 - 700 B. P.

(Also see Alba, Dardanelle, Hayes, Homan and Keota)

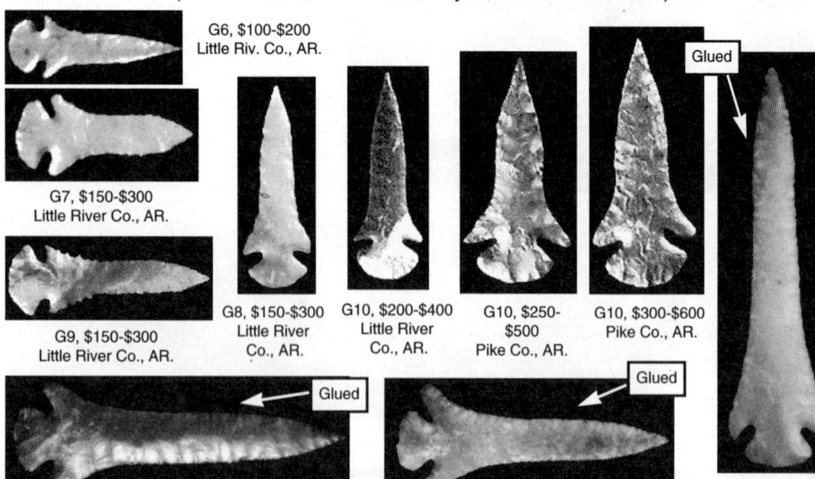

G6, $100-$200
Little Riv. Co., AR.

G7, $150-$300
Little River Co., AR.

G9, $150-$300
Little River Co., AR.

G8, $150-$300
Little River
Co., AR.

G10, $200-$400
Little River
Co., AR.

G10, $250-
$500
Pike Co., AR.

G10, $300-$600
Pike Co., AR.

G9, $400-$800
Pike Co., AR.

G9, $400-$800
Pike Co., AR.

G9, $200-$400
Pike Co., AR.

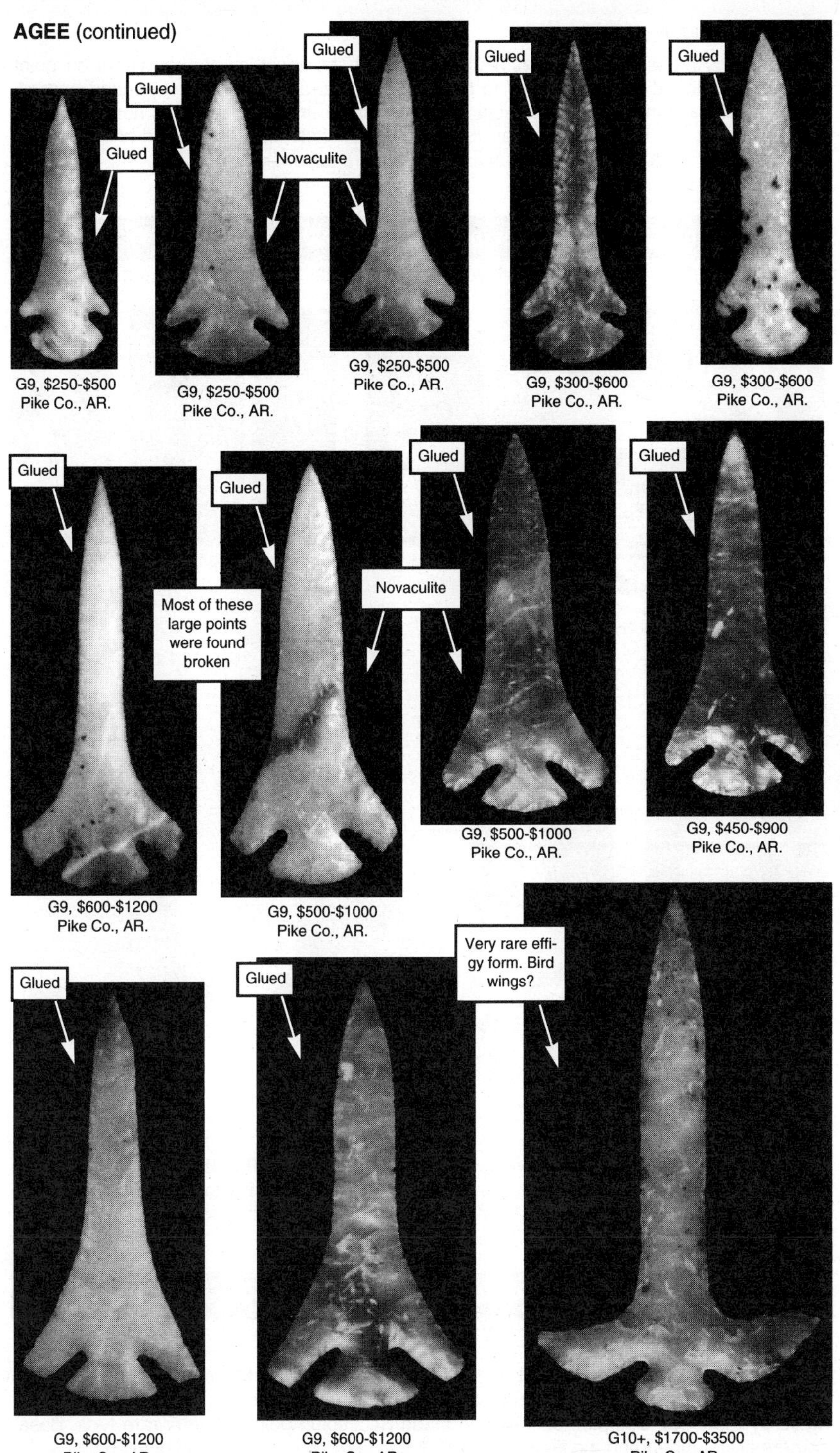

G9, $250-$500
Pike Co., AR.

G9, $250-$500
Pike Co., AR.

G9, $250-$500
Pike Co., AR.

G9, $300-$600
Pike Co., AR.

G9, $300-$600
Pike Co., AR.

G9, $600-$1200
Pike Co., AR.

G9, $500-$1000
Pike Co., AR.

G9, $500-$1000
Pike Co., AR.

G9, $450-$900
Pike Co., AR.

G9, $600-$1200
Pike Co., AR.

G9, $600-$1200
Pike Co., AR.

G10+, $1700-$3500
Pike Co., AR.

AGEE (continued)

LOCATION: Arkansas Caddo sites. **DESCRIPTION:** The finest, most exquisite arrow point made in the United states. A small to medium size, narrow, very thin, expanded barbed, corner notched point. Tips are needle sharp. Some examples are double notched at the base. A rare type that has only been found on a few sites. Total estimated known examples are 1100 to 1200. **I.D. KEY:** Basal form and barb expansion.

ALBA - Woodland to Mississippian, 2000 - 400 B. P.

(Also see Agee, Bonham, Cuney, Hayes, Homan, Keota, Perdiz, Scallorn and Sequoyah)

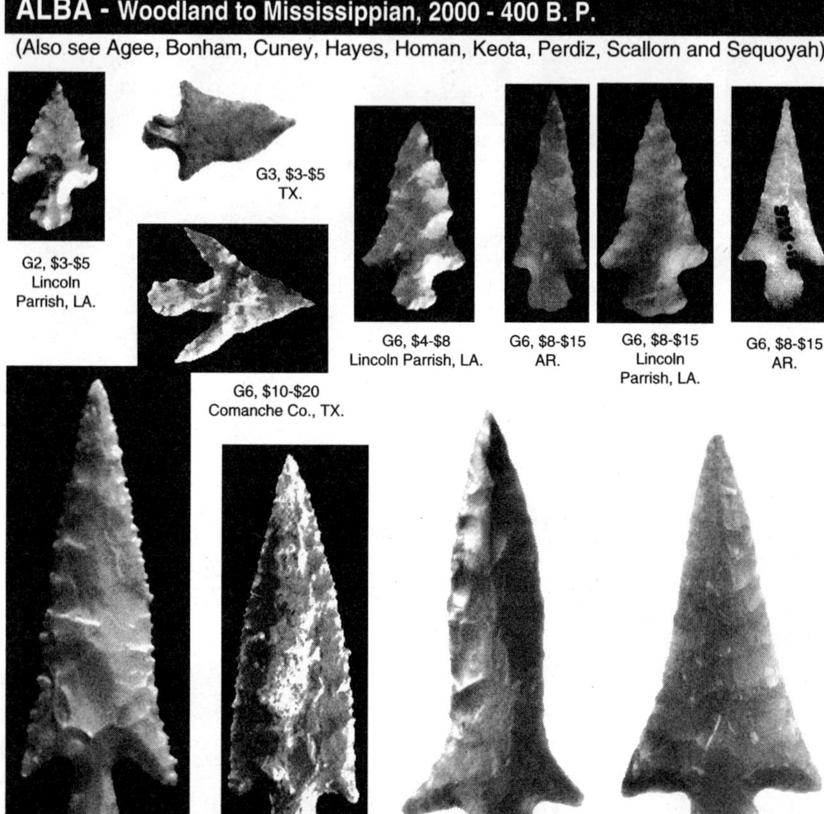

G2, $3-$5 Lincoln Parrish, LA.

G3, $3-$5 TX.

G6, $10-$20 Comanche Co., TX.

G6, $4-$8 Lincoln Parrish, LA.

G6, $8-$15 AR.

G6, $8-$15 Lincoln Parrish, LA.

G6, $8-$15 AR.

G9, $75-$150 Cent. TX.

G8, $50-$100 Cent. TX.

G9, $75-$150 AR.

G9, $75-$150 AR.

LOCATION: Eastern Texas, Arkansas and Louisiana. **DESCRIPTION:** A small to medium size, narrow, well made point with prominent tangs, a recurved blade and a bulbous stem. Some examples are serrated. **I.D. KEY:** Rounded base and expanded barbs.

ALBERTA - Transitional Paleo to Early Archaic, 9500 - 7500 B. P.

(Also see Angostura, Brown's Valley, Clovis, Eden, Plainview and Scottsbluff)

LOCATION: Oklahoma northward to Canada and eastward to Michigan. **DESCRIPTION:** A medium to large size, broad stemmed point with weak, horizontal to tapered shoulders. Made by the Cody Complex people who made Scottsbluff points. A very rare type. Basal corners are rounded and the tip is blunt. **I.D. KEY:** Long, broad stem and blunted tip.

ALBERTA (continued)

G7, $600-$1000
Kay Co., OK.

ALLEN - Transitional Paleo to Early Archaic, 10,000 - 7500 B. P.

(Also see Angostura, Barber, Brown's Valley, Clovis, Golondrina, McKean and Plainview)

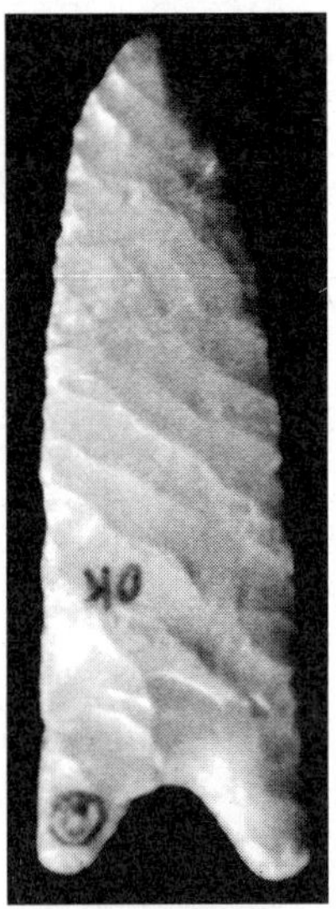

G7, $375-$750
Osage Co., OK.

G7, $500-$1000
Osage Co., Ok.

G5, $150-$300
McIntosh Co., OK.

LOCATION: Midwestern states to Canada. **DESCRIPTION:** A medium to large size, narrow, lanceolate point that has oblique tranverse flaking and a concave base. Basal ears tend to be rounded and the base is ground. **I.D. KEY:** Flaking style and blade form.

ALLEN (continued)

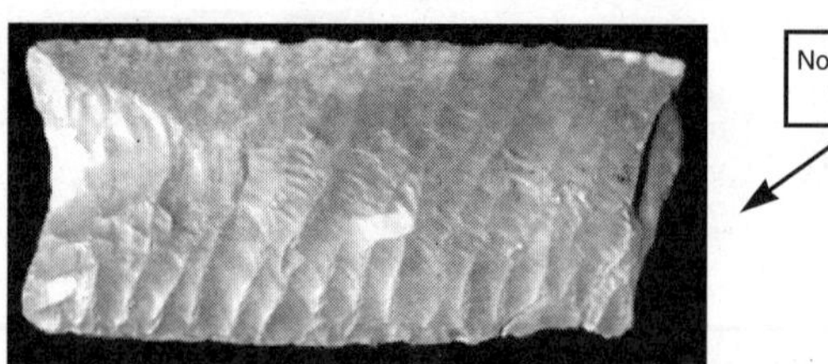

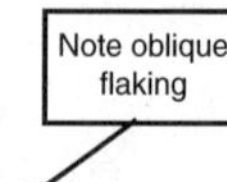

G1, $30-$50
E. Okla. Broken back.

ALMAGRE - Early Archaic, 6000 - 4500 B. P.

(Also see Gary, Hidden Valley, Langtry-Arenosa and Morrow Mountain)

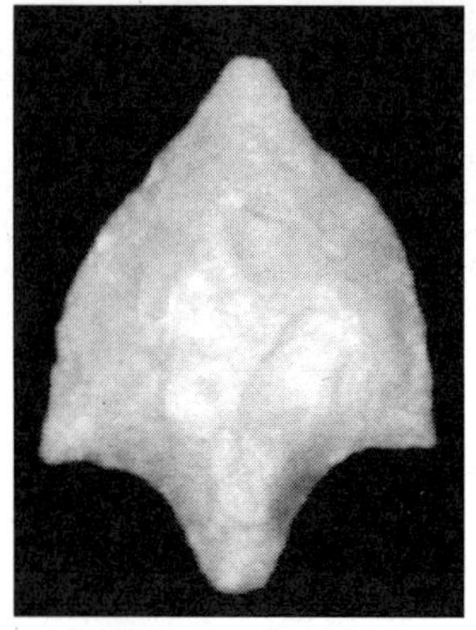

G4, $8-$15
S.W. TX.

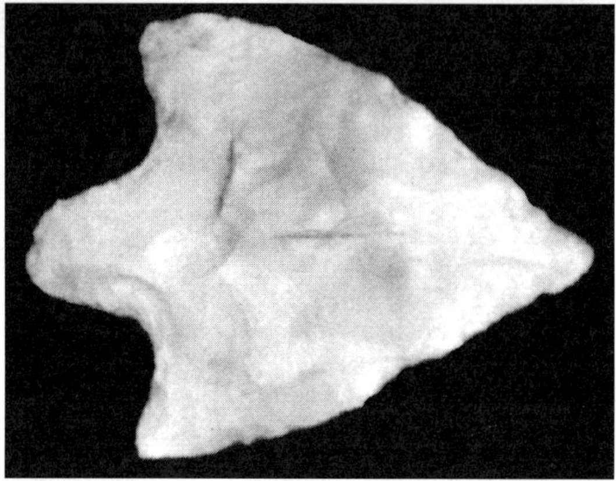

G6, $30-$60
Blanco Co., TX.

G9, $75-$150
Uvalde Co., TX.

G9, $75-$150
Waco, TX.

LOCATION: Midwestern states. **DESCRIPTION:** A broad, triangular point with pointed barbs and a long contracted pointed to rounded base. This point could be a variant of the *Langtry* type.

ANDICE - Early Archaic, 8000 - 5000 B. P.

(Also see Bell, Calf Creek and Little River)

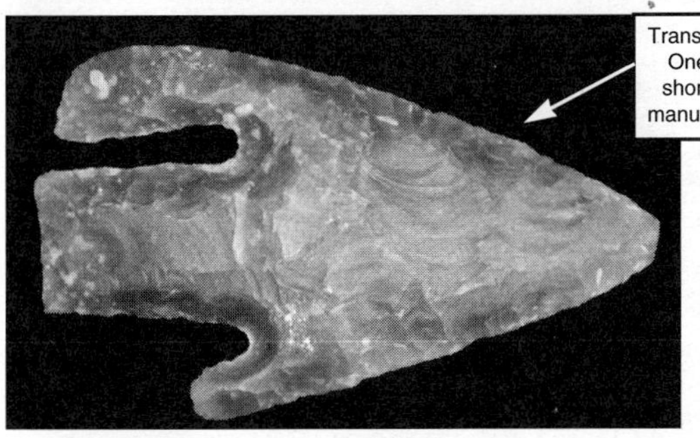

G9, $500-$1000
Wilson Co., TX.

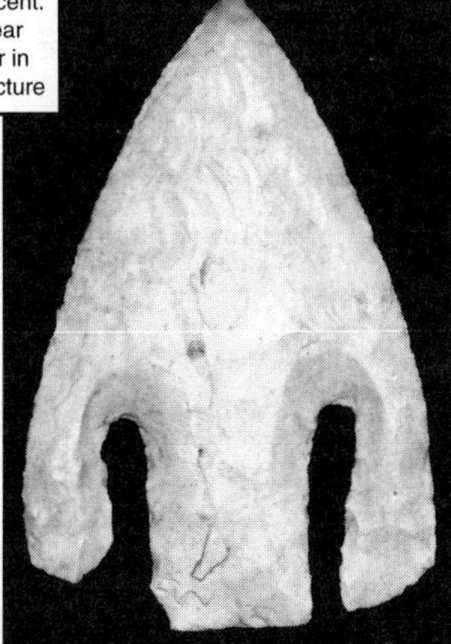

G9, $1000-$2000
Dewitt Co., TX.

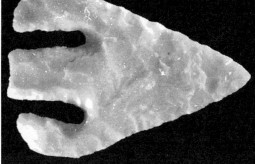

G9, $1500-$3000
Comanche Co., TX.
Excellent quality and thinness.

LOCATION: Southern to Central Texas, Oklahoma and Kansas. **DESCRIPTION:** A broad, thin, large, triangular point with very deep, parallel basal notches. Larger than *Bell* or *Calf Creek* Points. Tangs reach the base. Because of the deep notches, tangs were easily borken off making complete, unbroken specimens rare. **I.D. KEY:** Location and deep parallel basal notches.

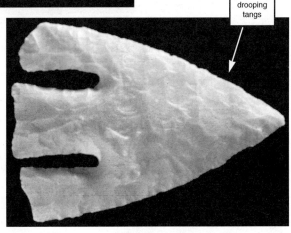

Deep notching producing drooping tangs

G9, $1500-$3000
Lake Summerville, TX.

ANGOSTURA - Transitional Paleo to Middle Archaic, 10,000 - 8000 B. P.

(Also see Agate Basin, Allen, Hell Gap, Lerma, Midland, Milnesand, Plainview & Zella)

ANGOSTURA (continued)

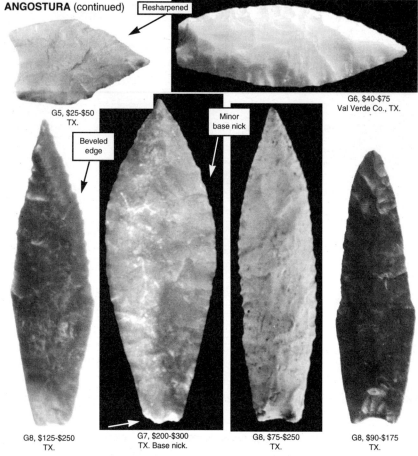

Resharpened

G5, $25-$50
TX.

G6, $40-$75
Val Verde Co., TX.

Beveled edge

Minor base nick

G8, $125-$250
TX.

G7, $200-$300
TX. Base nick.

G8, $75-$250
TX.

G8, $90-$175
TX.

LOCATION: Midwest to Western states. **DESCRIPTION:** A medium to large size, lanceolate blade with a contracting, concave, straight or convex base. Both broad and narrow forms occur. Flaking can be parallel oblique to random. Blades are commonly steeply beveled on one side of each face; some are serrated and most have basal grinding. Formerly called Long points. **I.D. KEY:** Basal form, flaking on blade which can be beveled.

ARENOSA (See Langtry-Arenosa)

ARKABUTLA - Transitional Paleo, 10,000 - 8000 B. P.

(Also see Angostura, Golondrina, Midland, Pelican and Plainview)

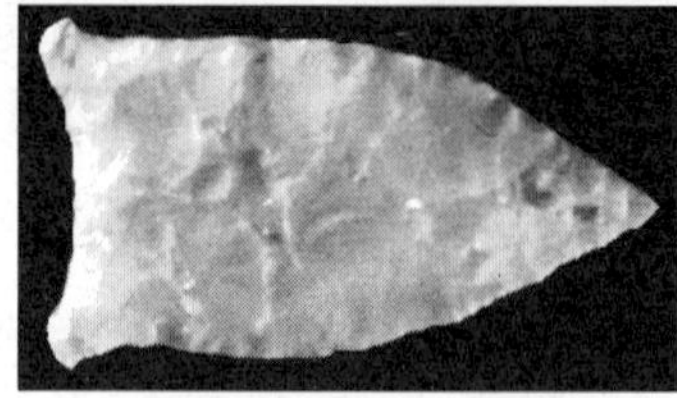

G7, $100-$200
Mineola, TX.

G8, $125-$250
Cent. TX.

ARKABUTLA (continued)

LOCATION: Texas and New Mexico. **DESCRIPTION:** A small to medium size, broad, thin, lanceolate point with expanded auricles. Blade edges recurve into the base which is concave. **I.D. KEY:** Eared basal form.

BAKER - Early Archaic, 8000 - 6000 B. P.

(Also see Jetta, Pedernales and Uvalde)

G5, $20-$35, Comanche Co., TX.

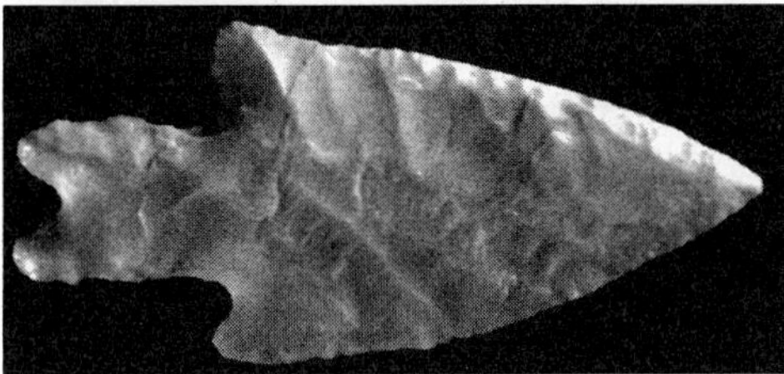

G8, $35-$70
Comanche Co., TX. Note long strikes across face of blade.

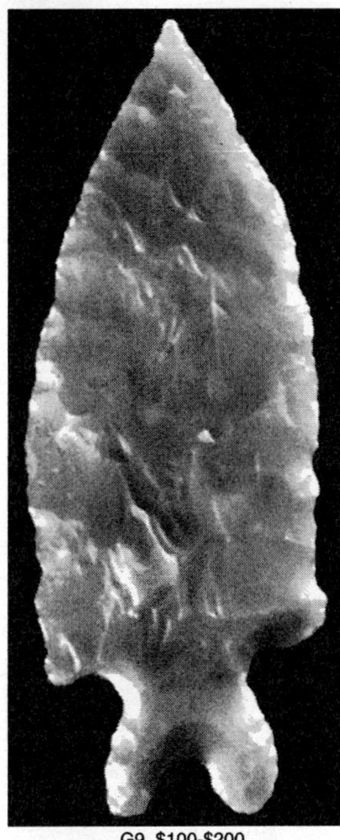

G9, $100-$200
Austin Tx. Georgetown flint.

LOCATION: Southern Midwestern states. **DESCRIPTION:** A medium size, narrow point with a long expanding to parallel stem that is bifurcated. Shoulders are horizontal to slightly barbed. Similar to the *Uvalde* type. **I.D. KEY:** Base extended and bifurcated, early flaking.

SC

BANDY - Early Archaic, 8000 - 5000 B. P.

(Also see Marcos, Marshall and Martindale)

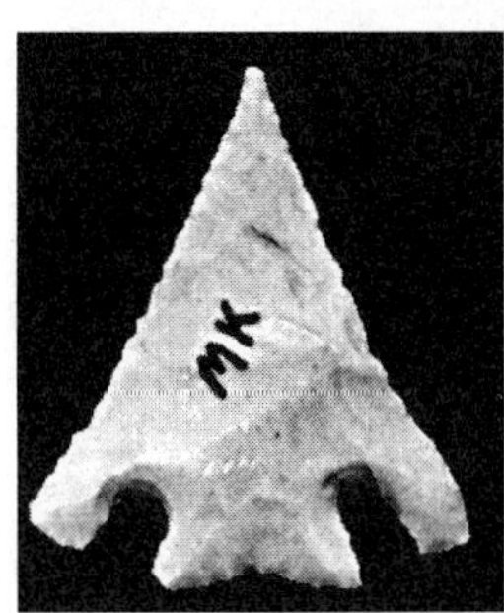

G6, $15-$25
McCullouch Co., TX.

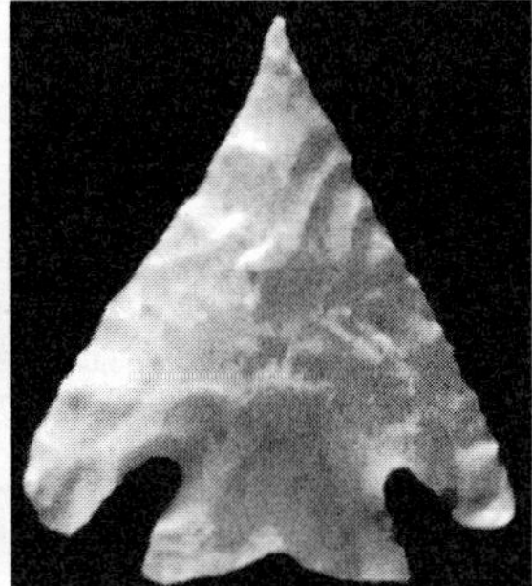

G8, $35-$70
Austin, TX.

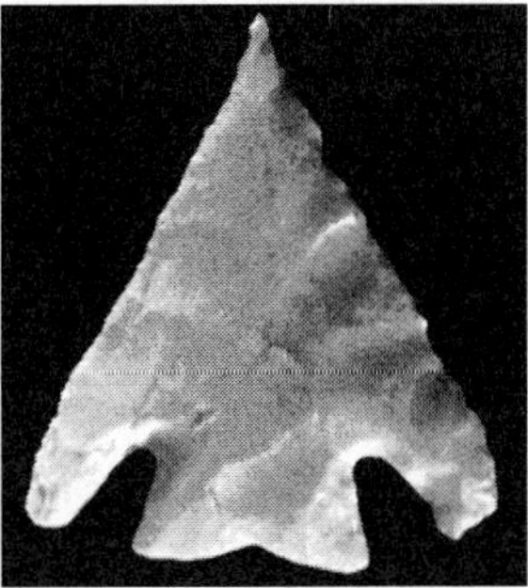

G8, $35-$70
Comanche Co., TX.

LOCATION: Southern Texas. **DESCRIPTION:** A small sized *Martindale* more commonly found in southern Texas. A corner notched to expanded stemmed point. The base is formed by two curves meeting at the center. **I.D. KEY:** Basal form, early flaking.

BARBER - Transitional Paleo, 10,000 - 7000 B. P.

(Also see Allen, Angostura, Clovis, Golondrina, Kinney, McKean and Plainview)

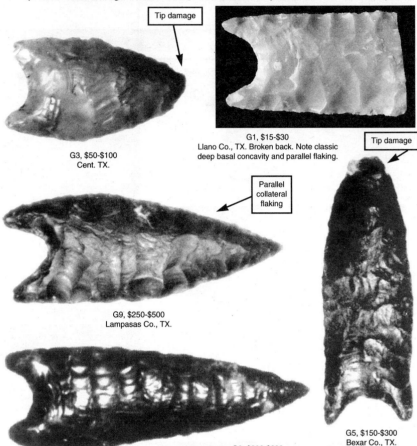

Tip damage

G3, $50-$100
Cent. TX.

G1, $15-$30
Llano Co., TX. Broken back. Note classic deep basal concavity and parallel flaking.

Tip damage

Parallel collateral flaking

G9, $250-$500
Lampasas Co., TX.

G5, $150-$300
Bexar Co., TX.

G9, $300-$600
Llano Co., TX., Sandy Creek.

LOCATION: Central Texas. **DESCRIPTION:** A small to medium size, lanceolate point with a deeply concave base and pointed ears that tend to turn inward. Similar to *Wheeler* points found in the Southeast. Basal area is usually ground. Flaking is early parallel. **I.D. KEY:** Deep basal concavity, parallel flaking.

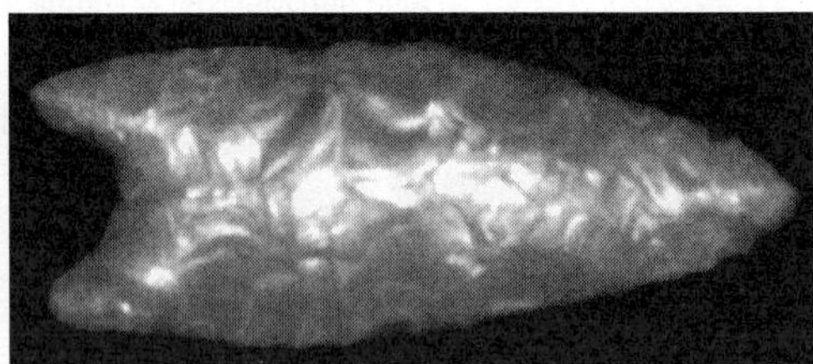

G7, $200-$400, Llano Co., TX.

BASE TANG KNIFE - Late Archaic to Woodland, 4000 - 2000 B. P. o

(Also see Corner Tang, Mid-Back Tang and San Saba)

LOCATION: Central Texas. **DESCRIPTION:** A large size, broad, blade with small basal notches and a concave base. Most examples curve more on one side and are believed to have been used as knives. **I.D. KEY:** Large size, tiny basal notches.

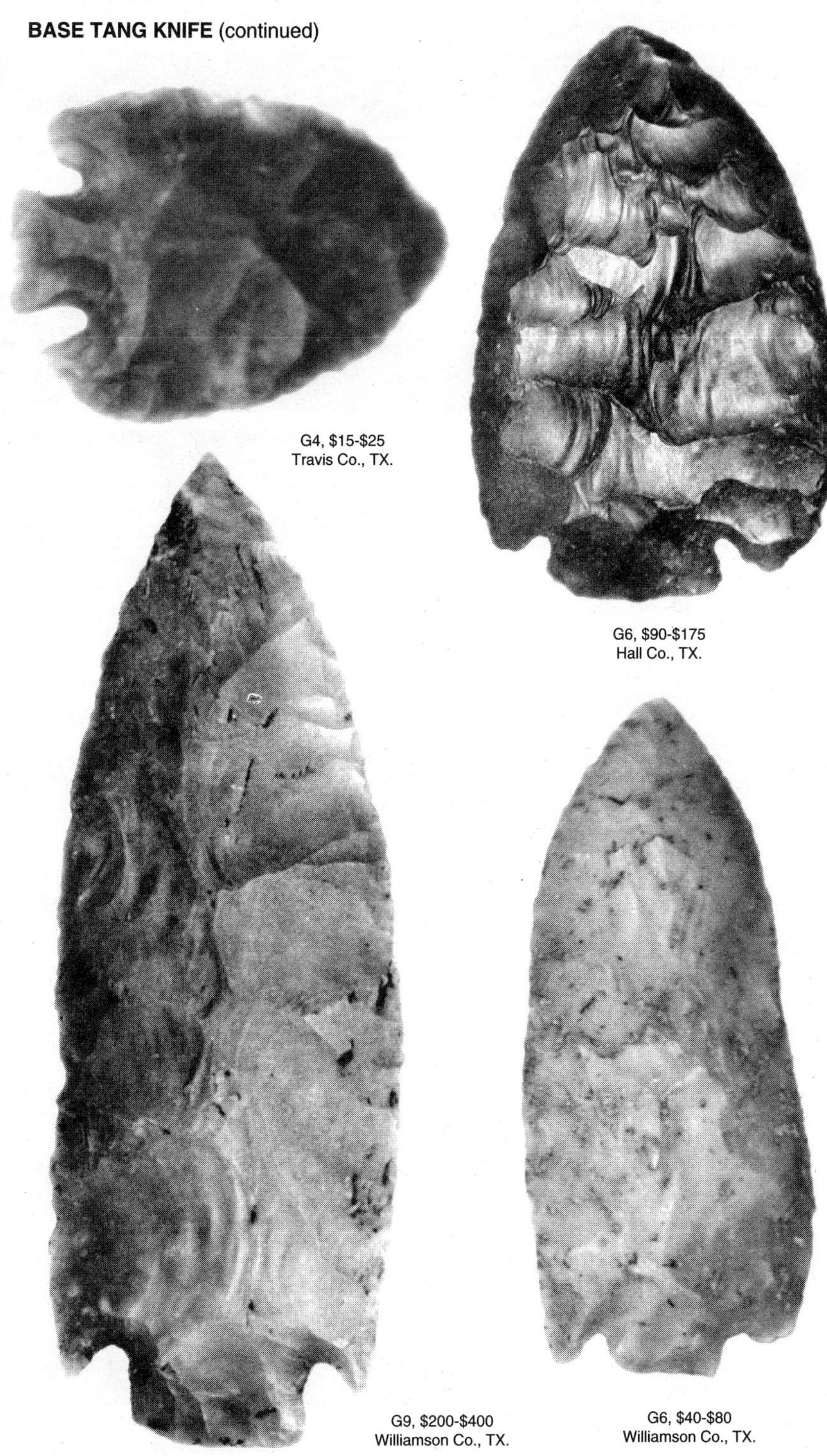

G4, $15-$25
Travis Co., TX.

G6, $90-$175
Hall Co., TX.

G9, $200-$400
Williamson Co., TX.

G6, $40-$80
Williamson Co., TX.

SC

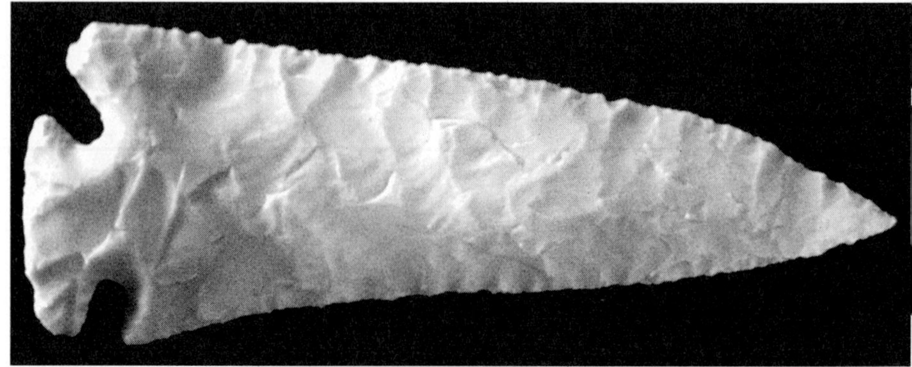

G9, $750-$1500
Smith Co., TX.

G9, $200-$400
TX.

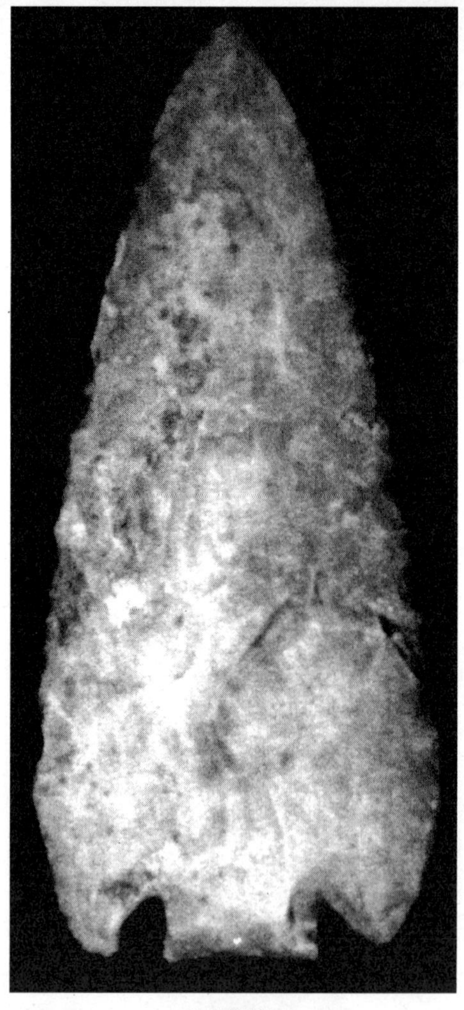

G8, $225-$450
Bandera Co., TX. (Marshall)

BASSETT - Mississippian, 800 - 400 B. P.

(Also see Cliffton, Perdiz, Rockwall and Steiner)

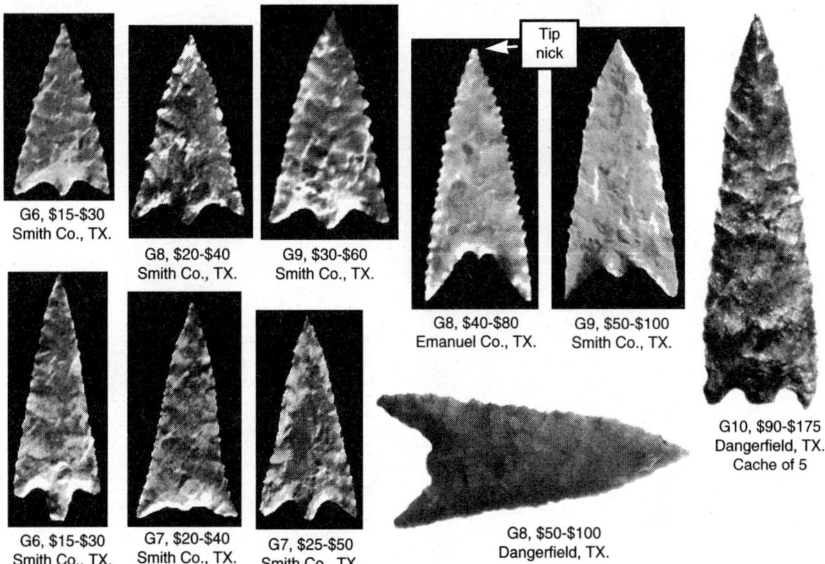

G6, $15-$30
Smith Co., TX.

G8, $20-$40
Smith Co., TX.

G9, $30-$60
Smith Co., TX.

G8, $40-$80
Emanuel Co., TX.

G9, $50-$100
Smith Co., TX.

G10, $90-$175
Dangerfield, TX.
Cache of 5

G6, $15-$30
Smith Co., TX.

G7, $20-$40
Smith Co., TX.

G7, $25-$50
Smith Co., TX.

G8, $50-$100
Dangerfield, TX.

LOCATION: Midwestern states. **DESCRIPTION:** A small size, thin, triangular point with pointed tangs and a small pointed base. High quality flaking is evident on most examples. **I.D. KEY:** Small pointed base.

SC

BELL - Middle Archaic, 7000 - 5000 B. P.

(Also see Andice and Calf Creek).

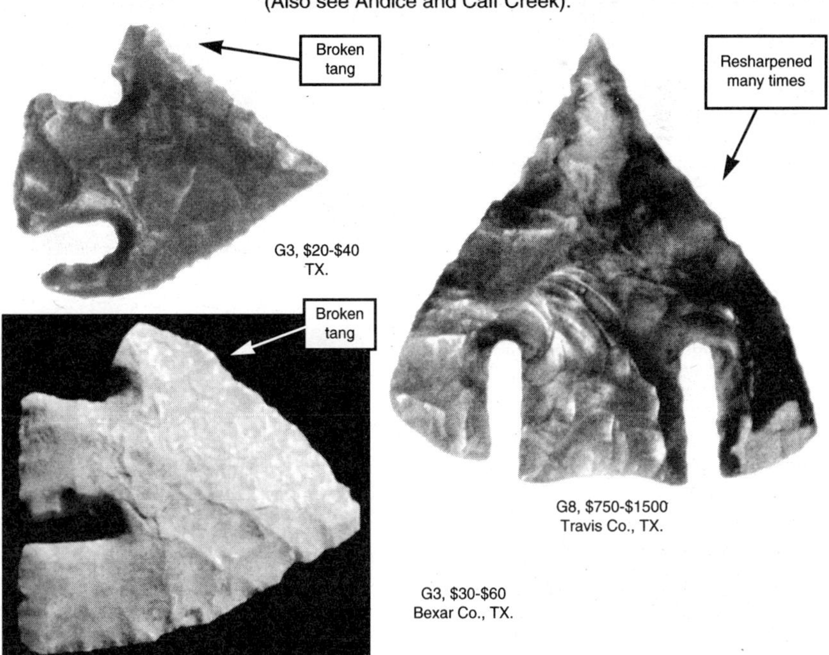

G3, $20-$40
TX.

G8, $750-$1500
Travis Co., TX.

G3, $30-$60
Bexar Co., TX.

Georgetown flint
Shorter basal notching sets the type. *Andice* points have deeper notches.

G10, $3000-$6000
Williamso nCo., TX.
Best known example.

LOCATION: Central Texas. **DESCRIPTION:** A small to medium size point with deep parallel basal notches, but not as deep as in *Andice.* Larger examples usually would fall under *Andice.* Found primarily in Texas. Tangs turn inward at the base. **I.D. KEY:** Shorter tangs and notching.

BIG CREEK - Late Archaic to early Woodland, 3500 - 2500 B. P.

(Also see Ellis, Marcos and Williams)

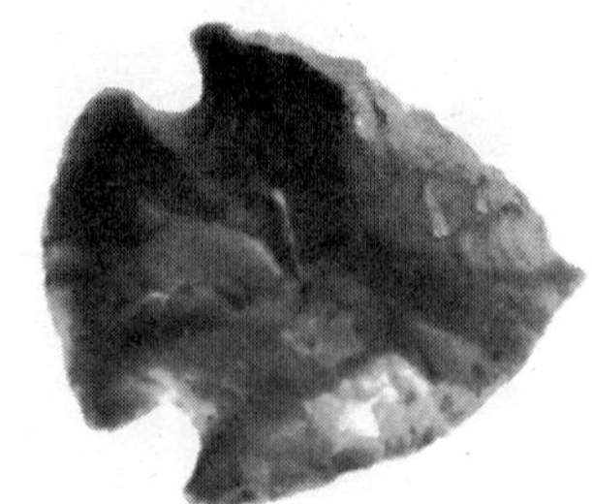

G4, $3-$5
AR.

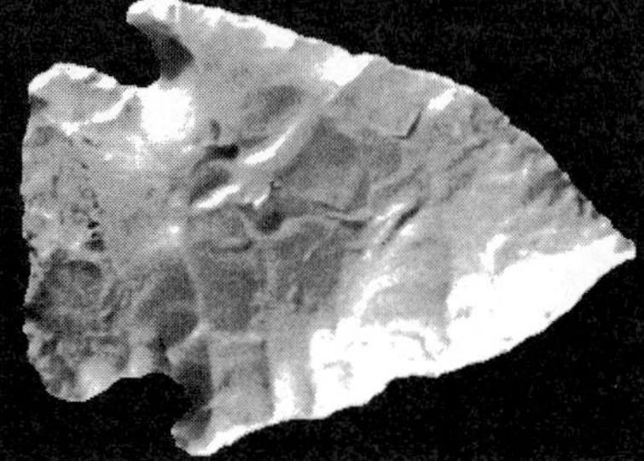

G5, $5-$10
AR.

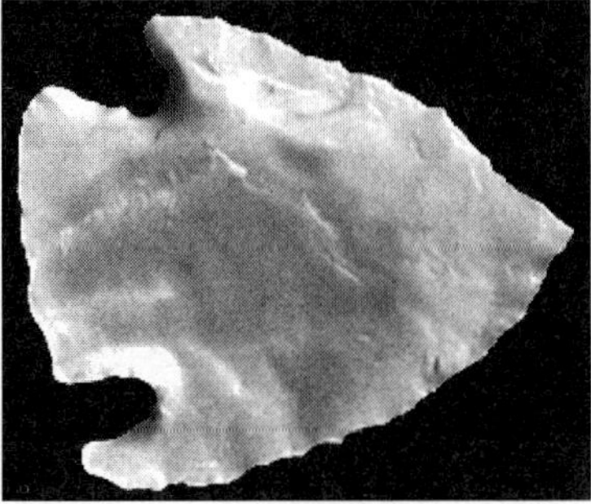

G4, $5-$10
AR.

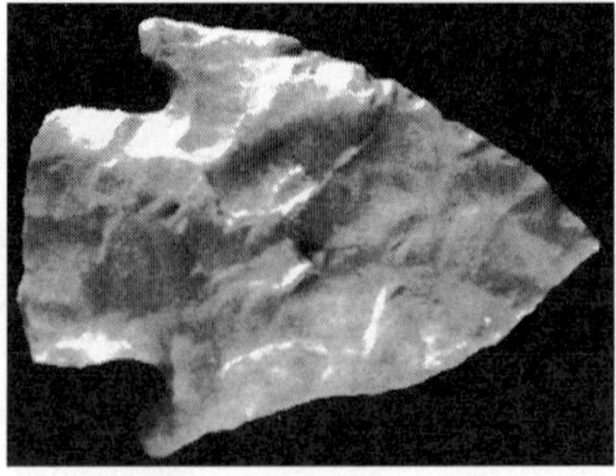

G5, $5-$10
AR.

BIG CREEK (continued)

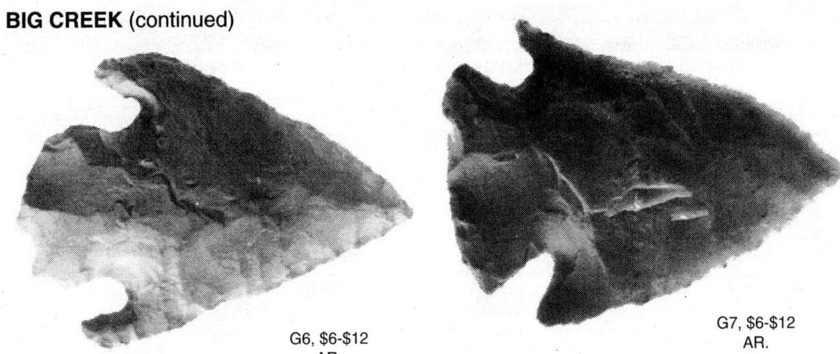

G6, $6-$12
AR.

G7, $6-$12
AR.

LOCATION: Arkansas and surrounding states. **DESCRIPTION:** A small to medium size, short, broad, corner notched point with a bulbous base. Believed to be related to *Marcos* points. The tips are needle sharp on some examples, similar to *Mud Creek* points. Tangs can be weak to very long. Small *Big Slough* of the Southeast would be indistinguishable to this type. **I.D. KEY:** Rounded base and barbs drop.

BIG SANDY - Transitional Paleo to Late Archaic, 10,000 - 3000 B. P.

(Also see Cache River, Frio, Hickory Ridge, Raddatz and Savage Cave)

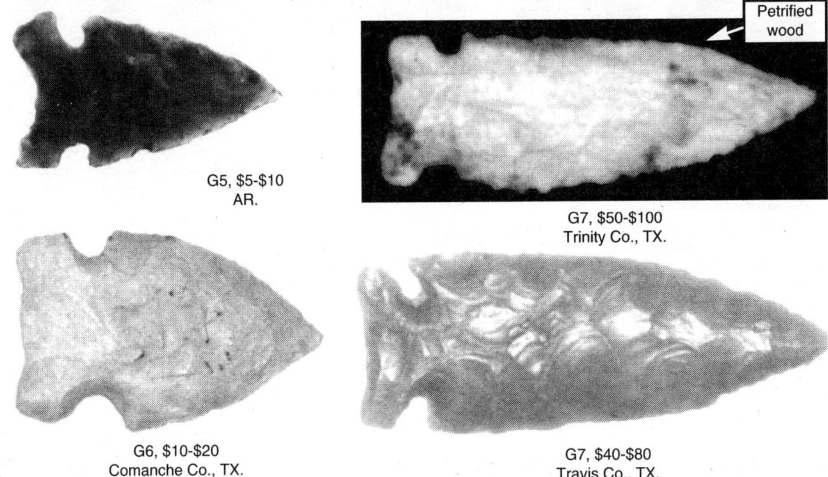

G5, $5-$10
AR.

G7, $50-$100
Trinity Co., TX.

G6, $10-$20
Comanche Co., TX.

G7, $40-$80
Travis Co., TX.

LOCATION: Eastern Texas eastward. **DESCRIPTION:** A small to medium size, side notched point with early forms showing basal grinding, serrations and horizontal flaking. Bases are straight to concave. Deeply concave bases form ears. **I.D. KEY:** Basal form.

BLEVINS - Mississippian, 1200 - 600 B. P.

(Also see Hayes, Howard) and Sequoyah

LOCATION: Midwestern states. **DESCRIPTION:** A small size, narrow spike point with two or more notches on each blade side. The base is diamond shaped. A cross between *Hayes* and *Howard.* **I.D. KEY:** Diamond shaped base.

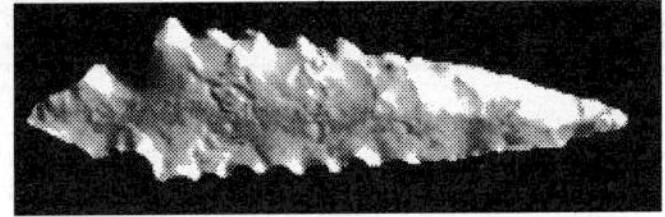

G8, $30-$60
W. AR.

SC

BONHAM - Woodland to Mississippian, 1200 - 600 B. P.

(Also see Alba, Cuney, Hayes, Moran, Perdiz, Rockwall and Scallorn)

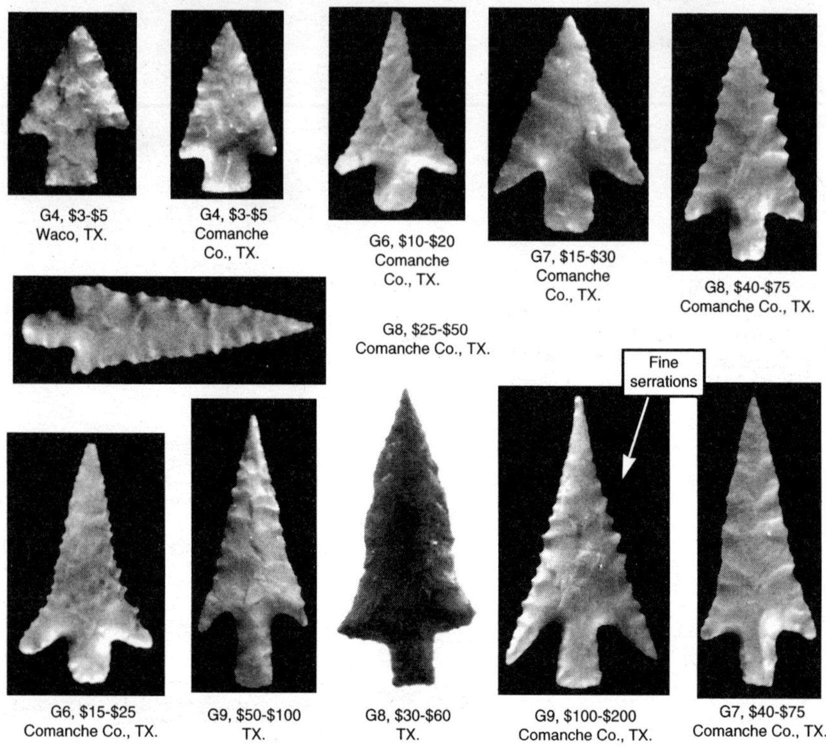

G4, $3-$5 Waco, TX.

G4, $3-$5 Comanche Co., TX.

G6, $10-$20 Comanche Co., TX.

G7, $15-$30 Comanche Co., TX.

G8, $40-$75 Comanche Co., TX.

G8, $25-$50 Comanche Co., TX.

G6, $15-$25 Comanche Co., TX.

G9, $50-$100 TX.

G8, $30-$60 TX.

G9, $100-$200 Comanche Co., TX.

G7, $40-$75 Comanche Co., TX.

LOCATION: Texas and Oklahoma. **DESCRIPTION:** A small to medium size, thin, well made triangular point with a short to long squared or rounded, narrow stem. Many examples are finely serrated. Blade edges are straight, concave, or convex or recurved. Shoulders are squared to barbed. **I.D. KEY:** Long straight base, expanded barbs.

BRAZOS (See Darl Stemmed)

BREWERTON EARED - Middle to Late Archaic, 6000 - 4000 B. P.

(Also see Rice Shallow Side Notched)

LOCATION: Northeast Texas eastward. **DESCRIPTION:** A small size, triangular point with shallow side notches and a concave base.

G7, $3-$5 AR.

BREWERTON SIDE NOTCHED - Middle to Late Archaic, 6000 - 4000 B. P.

(Also see Big Sandy)

LOCATION: Northeast Texas eastward. **DESCRIPTION:** A small size, triangular point with shallow side notches and a concave base.

BREWERTON SIDE NOTCHED (continued)

G2, $1-$2
Friendship Co., AR.

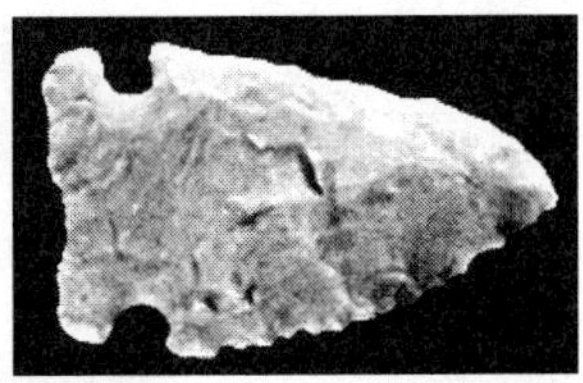

G6, $2-$3
Waco, TX.

BROWNS VALLEY - Transitional Paleo, 10,000 - 8000 B. P.

(Also see Agate Basin, Allen, Angostura, Barber, Clovis, Firstview, Midland and Plainview)

G8, $350-$700
N.E. AR. Translucent patinated Knife River flint. Classic example.

LOCATION: Midwestern states. **DESCRIPTION:** A medium to large, thin, lanceolate blade with usually oblique to horizontal transverse flaking and a concave to straight base which can be ground. A very rare type. **I.D. KEY:** Paleo transverse flaking.

SC

BULVERDE - Middle Archaic to Woodland, 5000 - 1000 B. P.

(Also see Carrolton and Delhi)

G7, $15-$25
TX.

G8, $30-$60
Llano Co., TX.

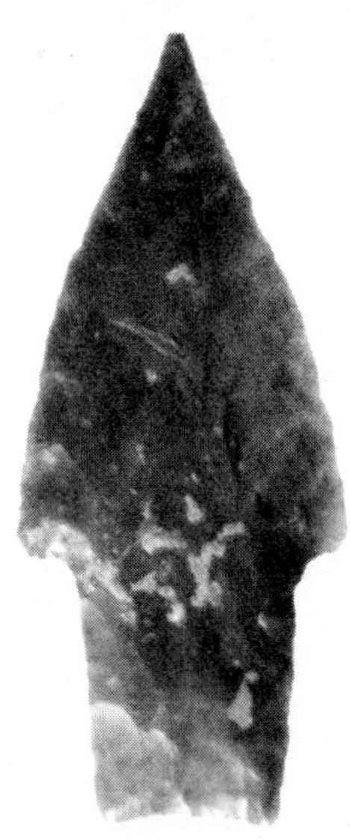

G6, $25-$50
TX.

BULVERDE (continued)

G10, $65-$125
Coryell Co., TX.

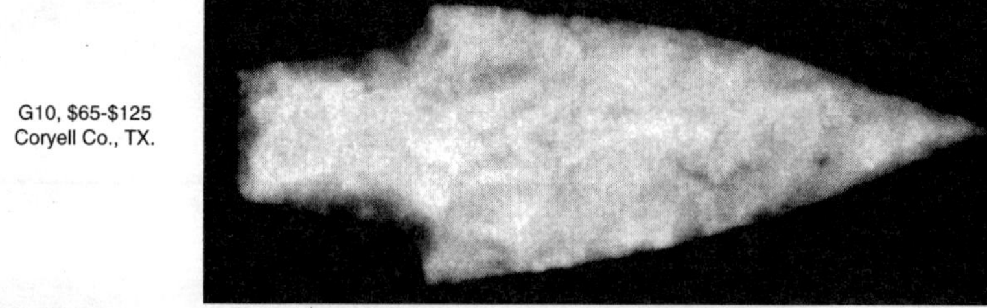

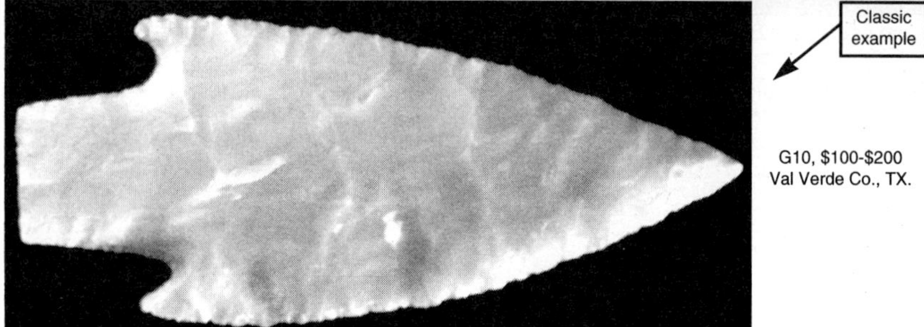

Classic example

G10, $100-$200
Val Verde Co., TX.

LOCATION: Midwestern states. **DESCRIPTION:** A medium size, long, rectangular stemmed point with usually barbed shoulders. Believed to be related to Carrolton.
I.D. KEY: Long, squared base and barbed shoulders.

CACHE RIVER - Transitonal Paleo to Late Archaic, 10,000 - 5000 B. P.

(Also see Big Sandy, Hickory Ridge, Knight Island and White River)

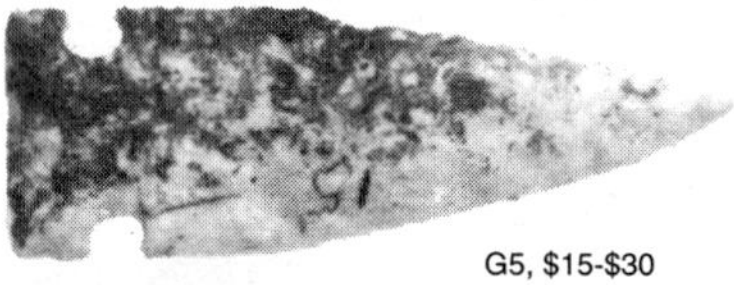

G5, $15-$30
AR.

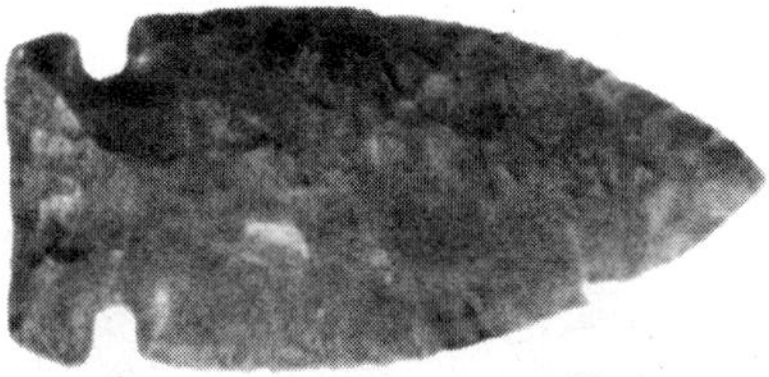

G8, $50-$100
AR.

G6, $15-$30
AR.

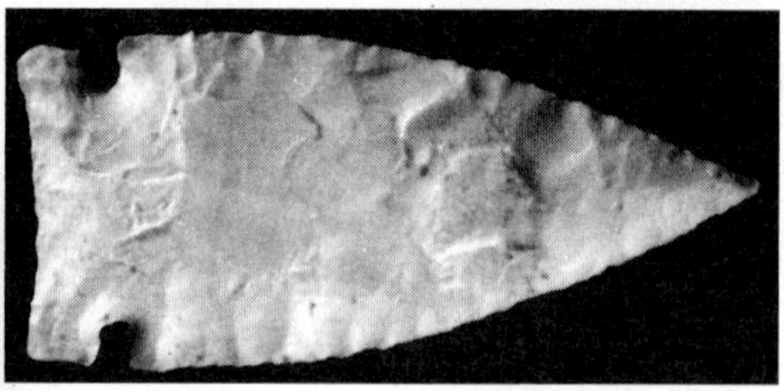

G9, $150-$300
Greene Co., AR.

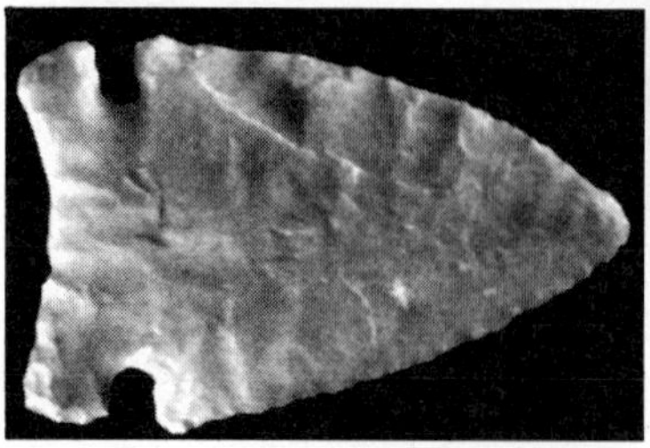

G5, $15-$30
Craighead, AR.

CACHE RIVER (continued)

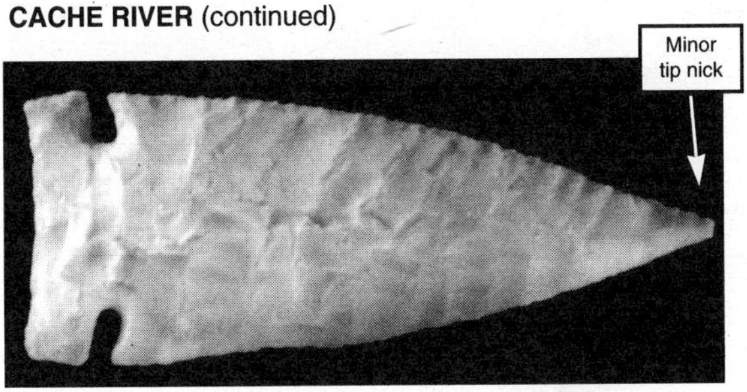

Minor tip nick

G8, \$125-\$250
Greene Co., AR.

G10, \$150-\$300
Greene Co., AR.

G8, \$75-\$150
AR.

Note diagonal flaking

G10, \$300-\$600
Greene Co., AR.

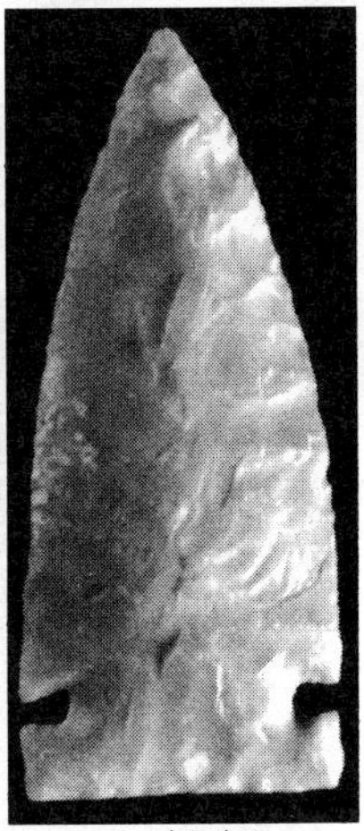

G7, \$40-\$80
AR.

LOCATION: Arkansas to Ohio, West Virginia and Pennsylvania. **DESCRIPTION:** A small to medium size, fairly thin, side-notched, triangular point with a concave base. Blade flaking is of the early parallel type. Could be related to Big Sandy points. Called *Kessell* in West Virginia. **I.D. KEY:** Base form, narrow notched & flaking of blade.

SC

CADDOAN BLADE - Mississippian, 800 - 600 B. P.

(Also see Adena Blade)

IMPORTANT
Caddoan Blade shown 1/2 size

G6, \$150-\$300
AR.

LOCATION: Texas and Arkansas on Caddo culture sites. **DESCRIPTION:** A large size, thin, double pointed, elliptical, ceremonial blade with serrated edges. Examples with basal side notches have been found in Texas. Beware of fakes. **I.D. KEY:** Edgework, flaking style on blade.

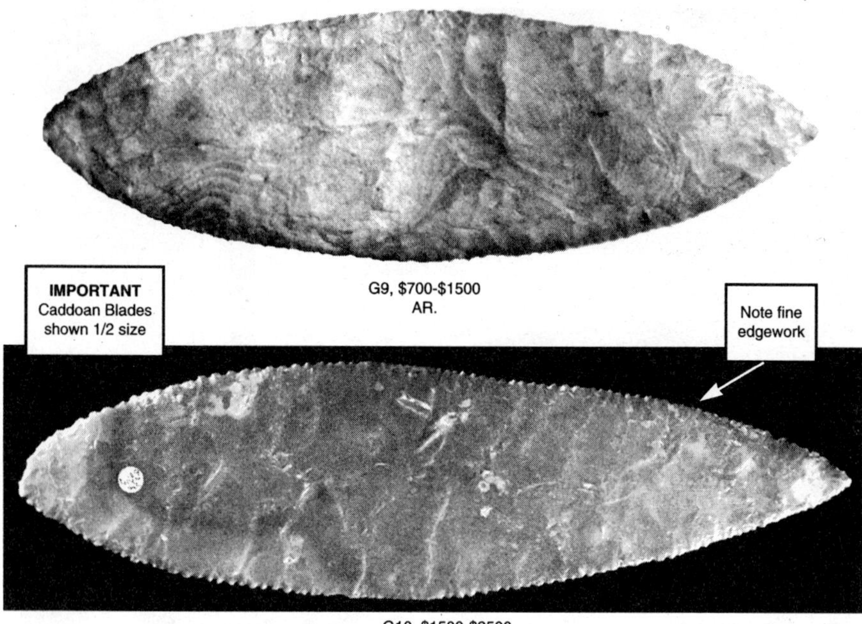

G9, $700-$1500
AR.

G10, $1500-$2500
Little River, AR.

CALF CREEK - Early to Middle Archaic, 8000 - 5000 B. P.

(Also see Andice and Bell)

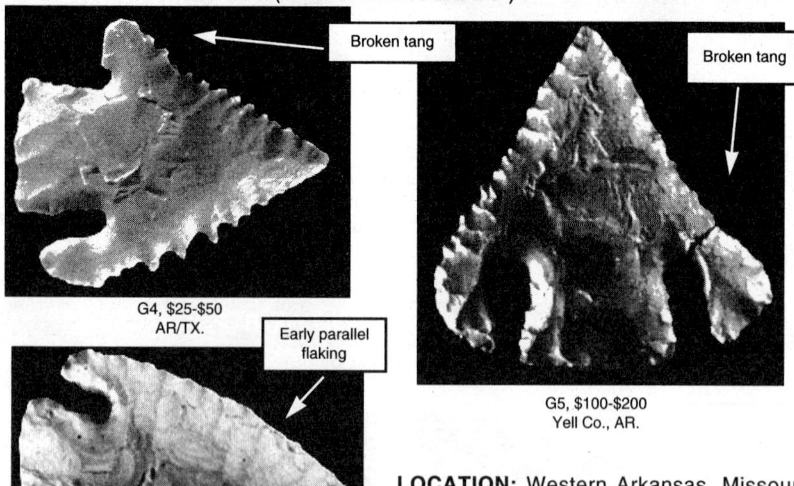

G4, $25-$50
AR/TX.

G5, $100-$200
Yell Co., AR.

G8, $150-$300
AR.

LOCATION: Western Arkansas, Missouri and eastern Oklahoma. **DESCRIPTION:** A medium to large size thin, triangular point with very deep parallel basal notches. *Andice* and *Bell* points, similar in form, are found in Texas. Very rare in type area. **I.D. KEY:** Notches almost straight up.

CALF CREEK (continued)

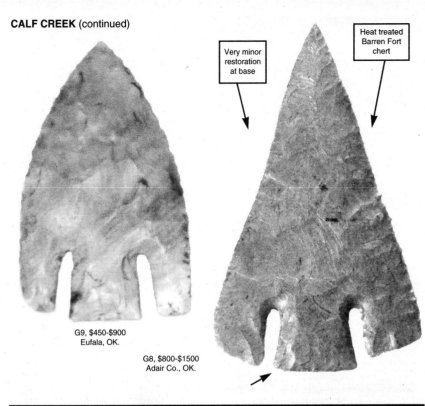

Very minor restoration at base

Heat treated Barren Fort chert

G9, $450-$900
Eufala, OK.

G8, $800-$1500
Adair Co., OK.

SC

CARACARA - Mississippian to Historic, 600 - 400 B. P.

(Also see Huffaker, Reed and Washita)

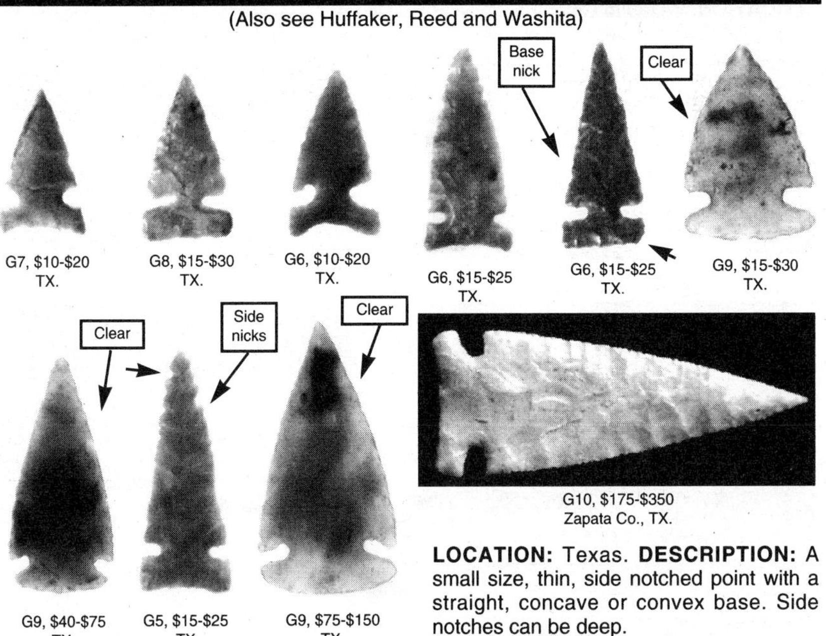

G7, $10-$20 TX. · G8, $15-$30 TX. · G6, $10-$20 TX. · G6, $15-$25 TX. · G6, $15-$25 TX. · G9, $15-$30 TX.

G9, $40-$75 TX. · G5, $15-$25 TX. · G9, $75-$150 TX.

G10, $175-$350
Zapata Co., TX.

LOCATION: Texas. **DESCRIPTION:** A small size, thin, side notched point with a straight, concave or convex base. Side notches can be deep.

CARRIZO - Middle Archaic, 7000 - 4000 B. P.

(Also see Early Triangle, Montell and Tortugas)

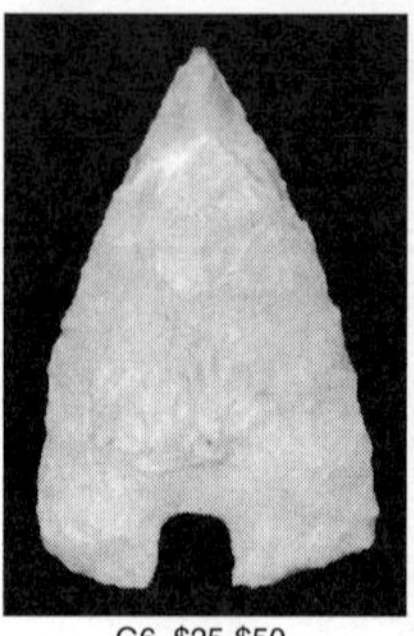

G6, $25-$50
Wilson Co., TX.

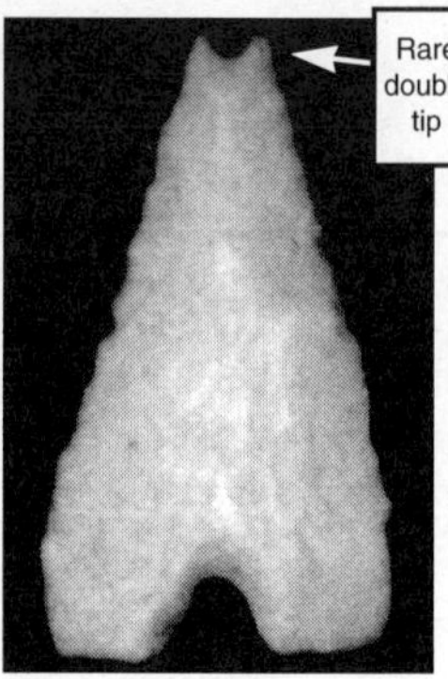

G8, $50-$100
Val Verde Co., TX., Devils River.

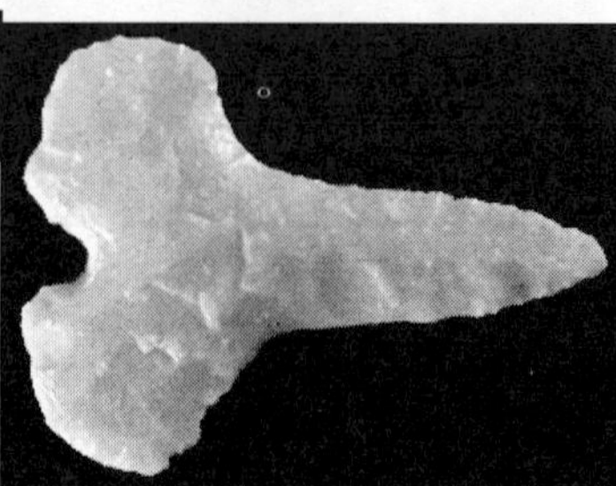

G7, $40-$75, Austin, TX. Drill form. Rare.

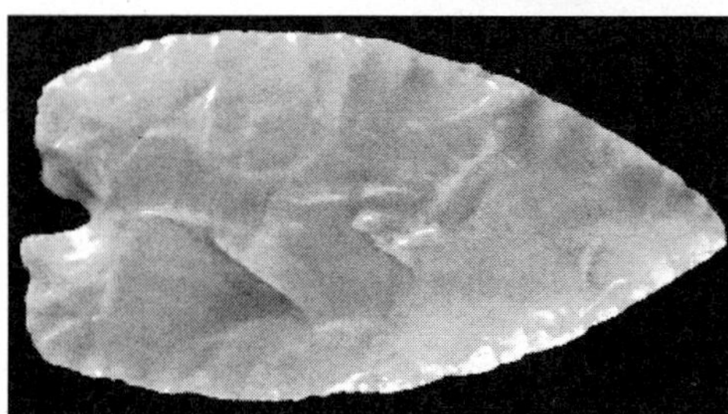

G7, $50-$100, Austin, TX. Rare.

G7, $40-$80
Wilson Co., TX.

LOCATION: Texas to Colorado. **DESCRIPTION:** A small to medium size, triangular point with a deep single notch or a concave indention in the center of the base. Flaking is parallel to random. Blade edges are rarely serrated. **Note:** Some Carrizo's can be resharpened Montells. **I.D. KEY:** Basal notch.

CARROLTON - Middle to Late Archaic, 5000 - 3000 B. P.

(Also see Adena, Bulverde, Dallas and Wells)

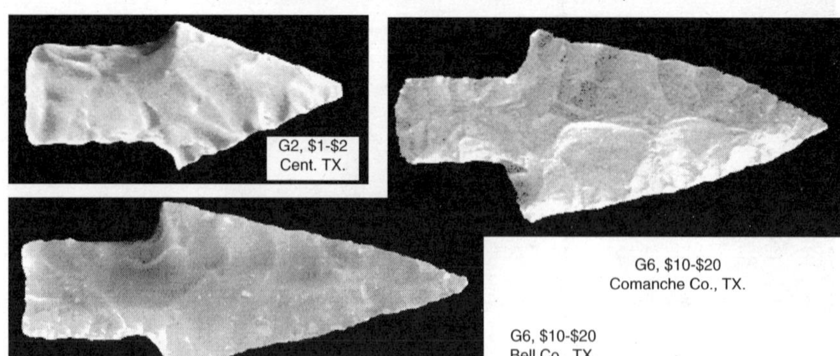

G2, $1-$2
Cent. TX.

G6, $10-$20
Comanche Co., TX.

G6, $10-$20
Bell Co., TX.

CARROLTON (continued)

G7, $15-$30
Central TX.

LOCATION: North Texas. **DESCRIPTION:** A medium to large size, long, parallel stemmed point with a square base. Shoulders are usually tapered. Workmanship is crude to medium grade. Believed to be related to *Bulverde* points.

CASTROVILLE - Late Archaic to Woodland, 4000 - 1500 B. P.

(Also see Lange, Marcos and Marshall)

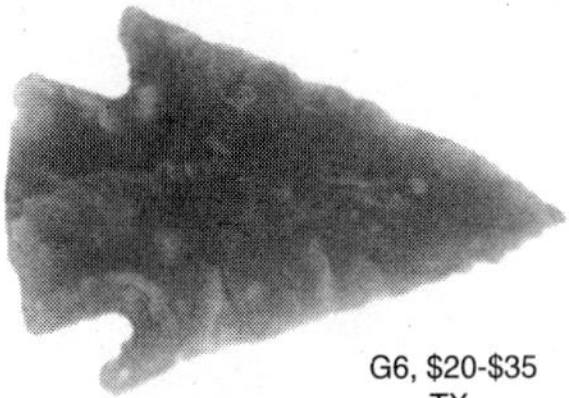

G6, $20-$35
TX.

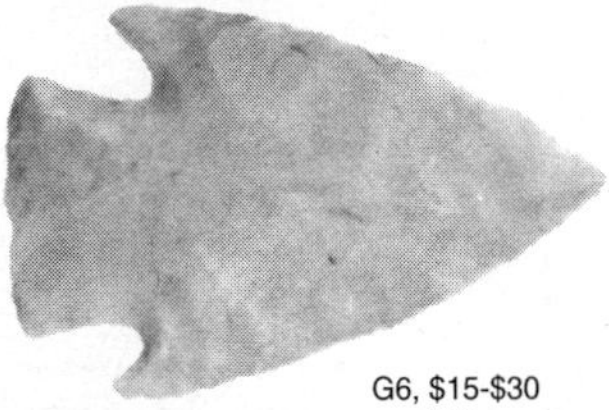

G6, $15-$30
TX.

G6, $25-$50
TX.

Resharpened form

G5, $15-$25
Comanche Co., TX.

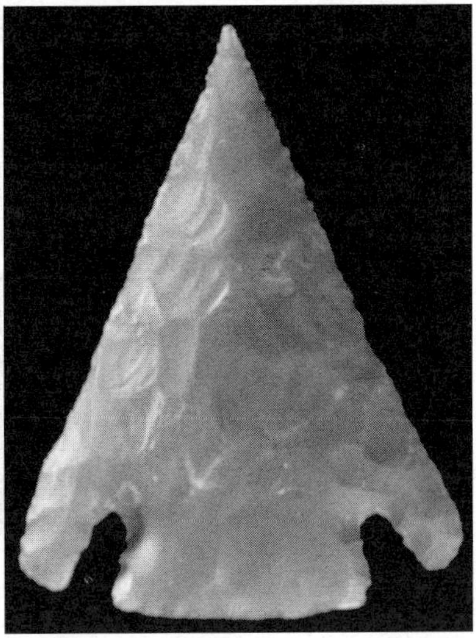

Resharpened into drill form

G8, $75-$150
Kerr Co., TX.

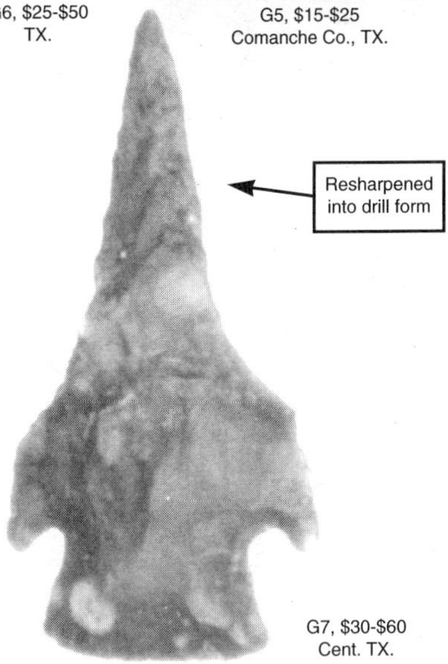

G7, $30-$60
Cent. TX.

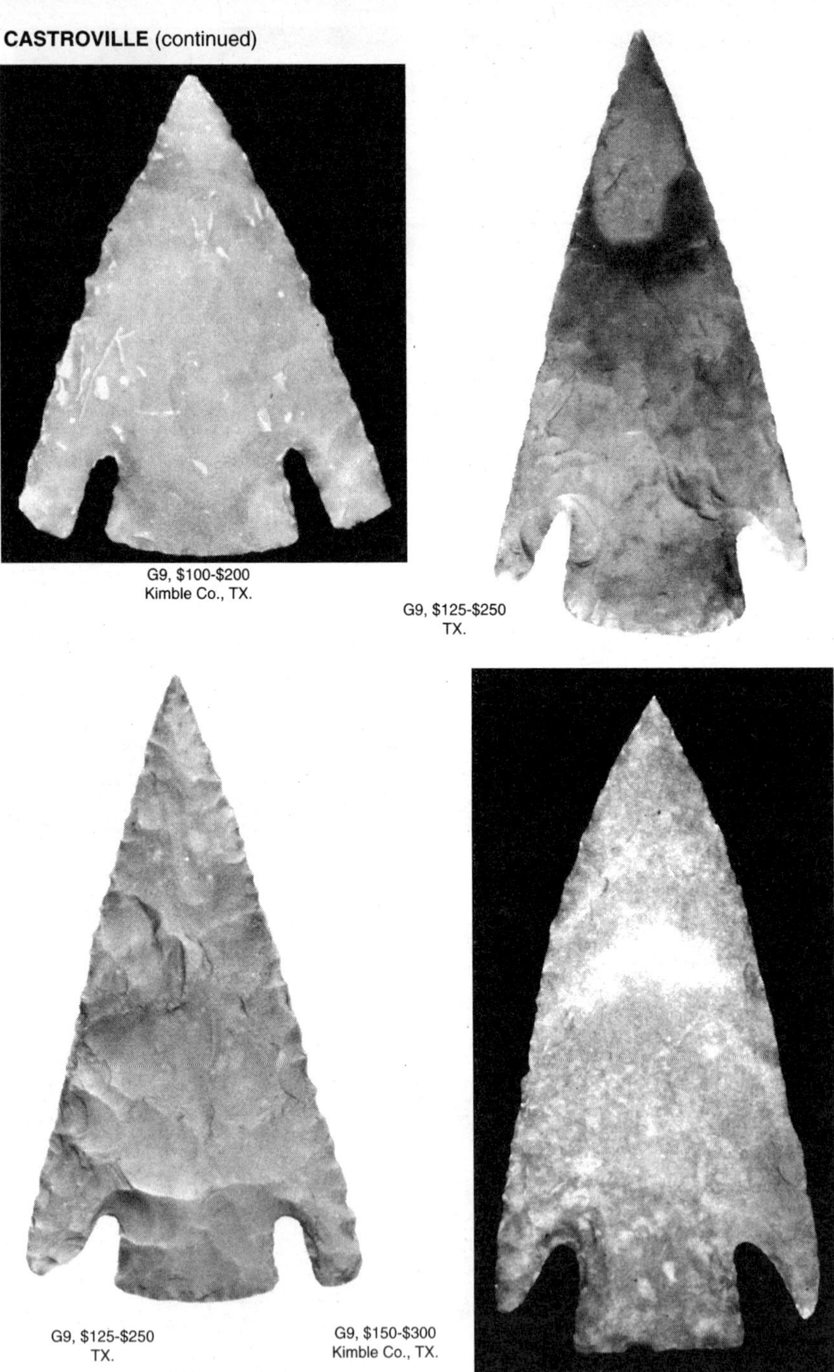

G9, $100-$200
Kimble Co., TX.

G9, $125-$250
TX.

G9, $125-$250
TX.

G9, $150-$300
Kimble Co., TX.

LOCATION: Texas to Colorado. **DESCRIPTION:** A medium to large size, broad, corner notched point with an expanding base and prominent tangs that can reach the basal edge. The base can be straight to convex and is usually broader than in *Lange* and *Marshall.*
I.D. KEY: Broad base, corner notches.

Castroville Base Tang

G9, $140-$275
Kimble Co., TX.

G7, $200-$400
Austin, TX.

CATAHOULA - Mississippian, 800 - 400 B. P.

(Also see Friley, Rockwall and Scallorn)

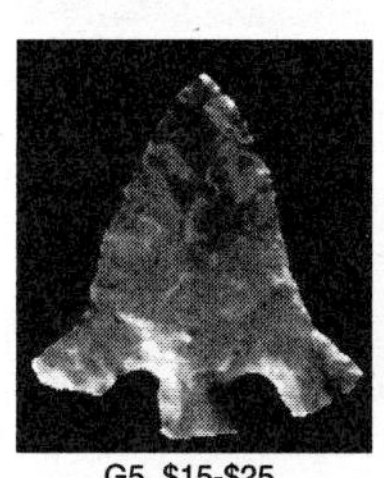

G5, $15-$25
AR.

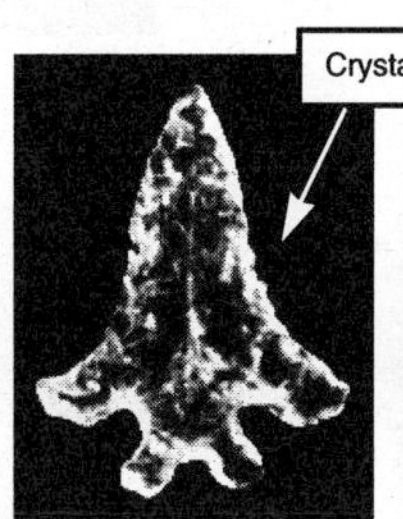

G8, $150-$250
AR.

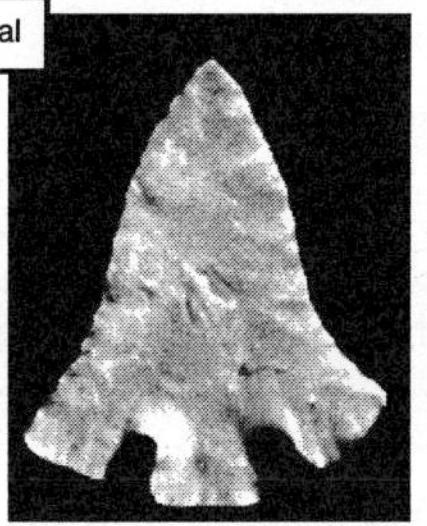

G7, $50-$100
AR.

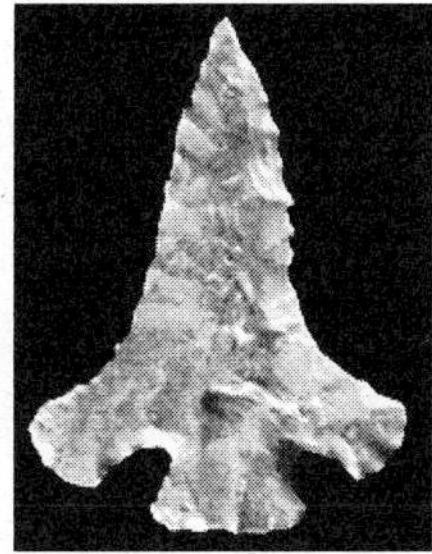

G9, $100-$200
AR.

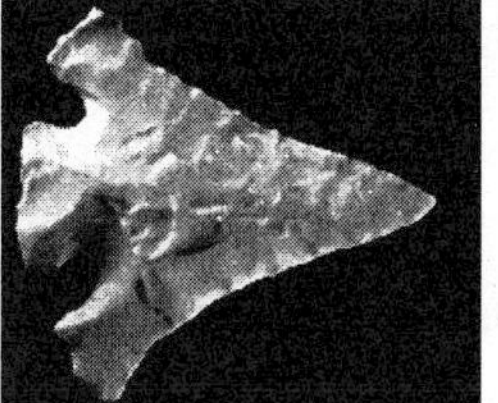

G6, $25-$45
AR.

LOCATION: East Texas, Louisiana to Arkansas. **DESCRIPTION**: A small size, thin, point with broad, flaring, squared tangs. The stem is parallel sided to expanding. The base is straight to concave. **I.D. KEY:** Expanded barbs.

CATAN - Late Archaic to Mississippian, 4000 - 300 B. P.

(Also see Abasolo, Matamoros and Young)

G8, $2-$5 TX.

G5, $2-$5 TX.

G6, $4-$8 TX.

G5, $2-$5 TX.

LOCATION: Southern Texas and New Mexico. **DESCRIPTION**: A small lanceolate point with a rounded base. Large examples would fall under the *Abasolo* type.

CHARCOS - Woodland, 3000 - 2000 B. P.

(Also see Duran, Evans and Sinner)

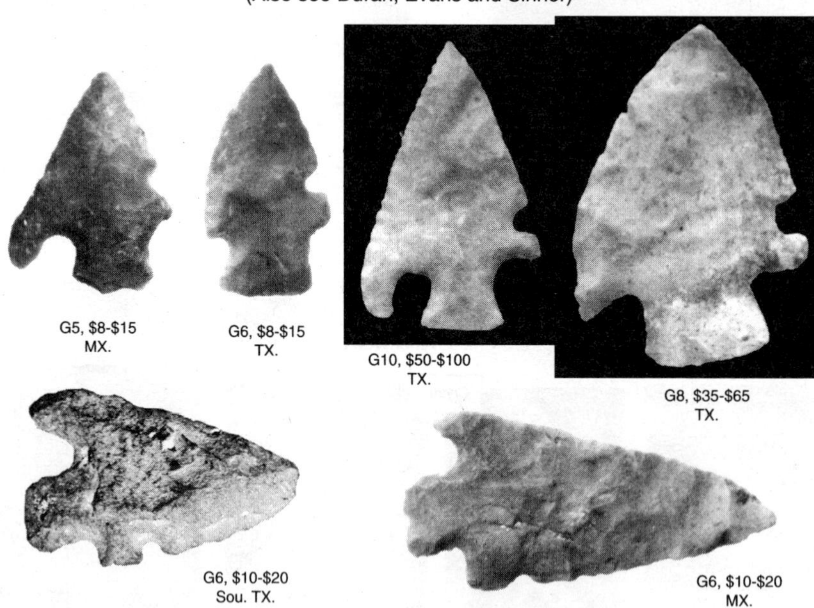

G5, $8-$15 MX.

G6, $8-$15 TX.

G10, $50-$100 TX.

G8, $35-$65 TX.

G6, $10-$20 Sou. TX.

G6, $10-$20 MX.

LOCATION: Northern Mexico into south Texas. **DESCRIPTION:** A small size, thin, single barbed point with a notch near the opposite shoulder. Stem is rectangular. **I.D. KEY:** Asymmetrical form.

CHOPPER - Paleo, 14,000 - 9000 B. P.

(Also see Kerrville Knife)

CHOPPER (continued)

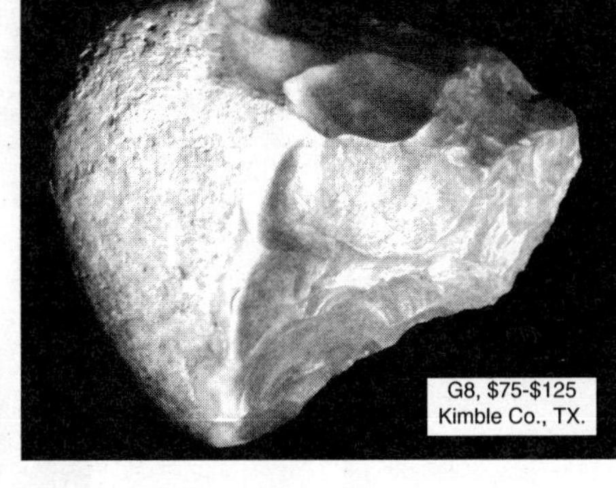
G8, $75-$125
Kimble Co., TX.

LOCATION: Paleo sites everywhere. **DESCRIPTION**: A medium to large size, thick, ovoid hand axe made from local creek or river stones used in the butchering process.

Chopper shown half size

CLIFFTON - Mississippian, 1200 - 500 B. P.

(Also see Bassett)

G6, $.70-$1
Waco, TX.

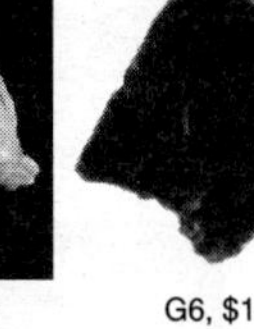
G6, $1-$2
TX.

LOCATION: Central Texas. **DESCRIPTION:** A small size, crude point that is usually made from a flake and is uniface. The base is sharply contracting to pointed.

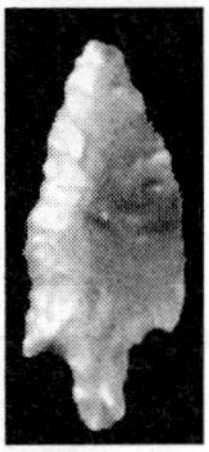

G1, $.50-$1
Waco, TX.

CLOVIS - Early Paleo, 14,000 - 9000 B. P.

(Also see Allen, Angostura, Barber, Browns Valley, Dalton, Golondrina and Plainview)

SC

G7, $125-$250
TX.

G3, $65-$125
TX.

G6, $200-$400
Wilson Co., TX.

Ross County type

G7, $250-$500
Clay Co., AR.

Translucent

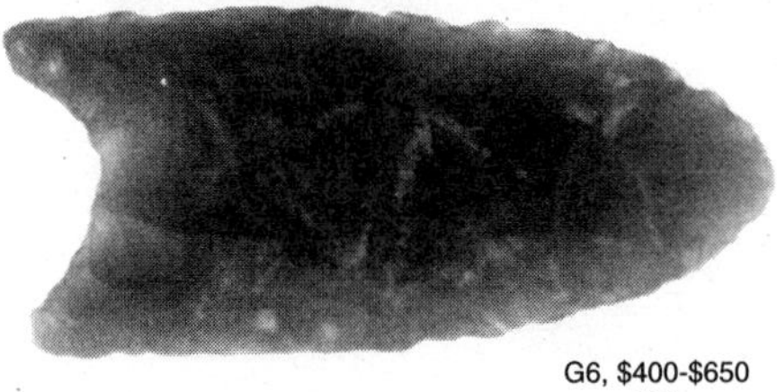

G6, $400-$650
TX.

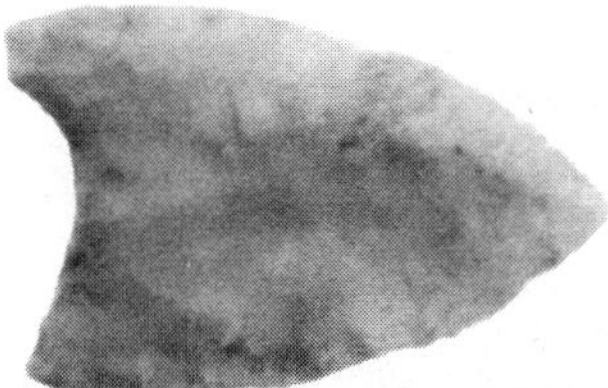

G5, $100-$200
AR.

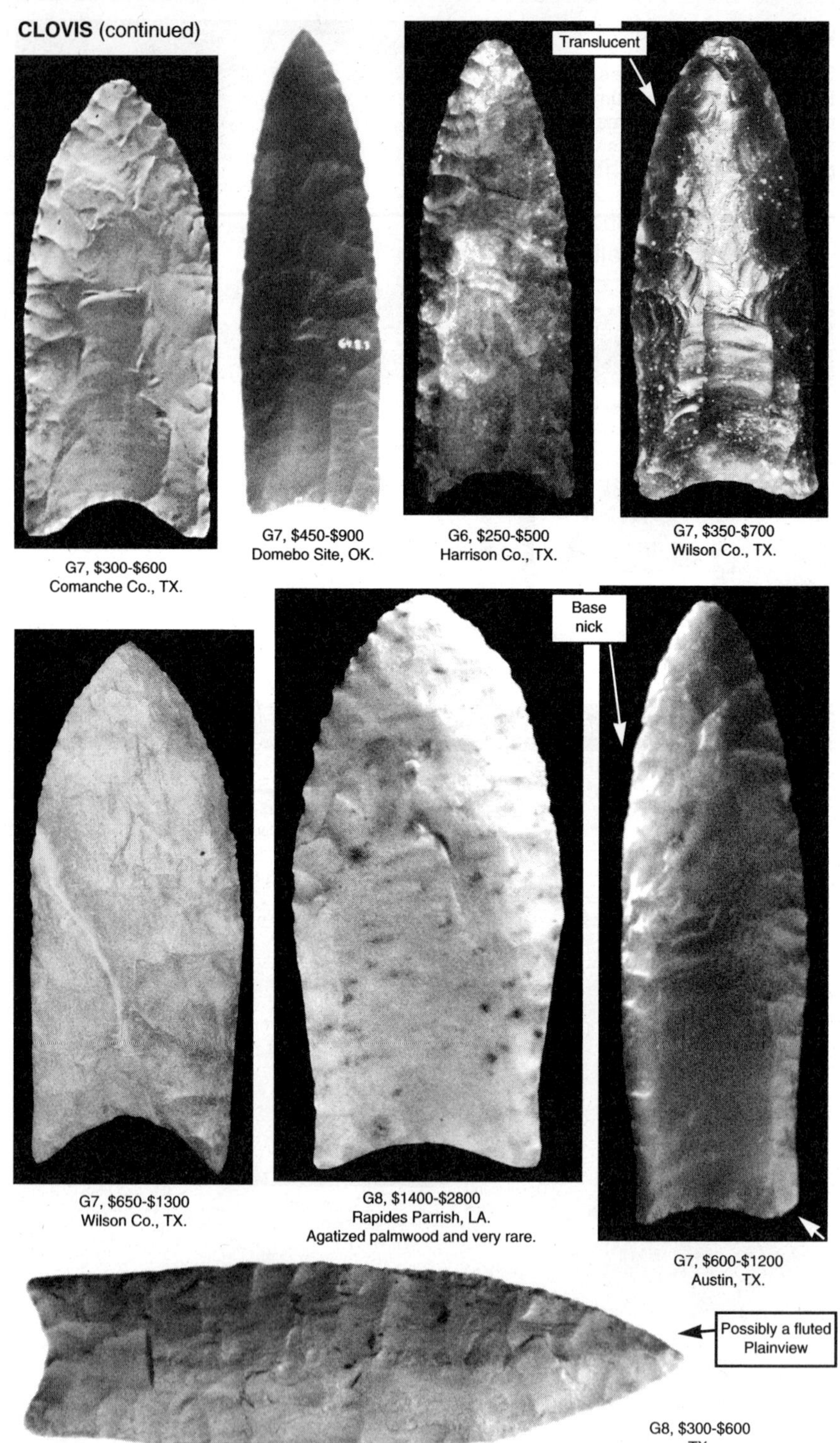

G7, $300-$600
Comanche Co., TX.

G7, $450-$900
Domebo Site, OK.

G6, $250-$500
Harrison Co., TX.

G7, $350-$700
Wilson Co., TX.

G7, $650-$1300
Wilson Co., TX.

G8, $1400-$2800
Rapides Parrish, LA.
Agatized palmwood and very rare.

G7, $600-$1200
Austin, TX.

G8, $300-$600
TX.

G5, $250-$500
TX.

G4, $175-$350
Osage Co., OK.

G6, $600-$1200
Lubbock, TX.

G6, $750-$1500
Lubbock, TX.

G8, $900-$1800
Bastrop Co., TX.

G8, $2000-$4000
Wilson Co., TX.

CLOVIS (continued)

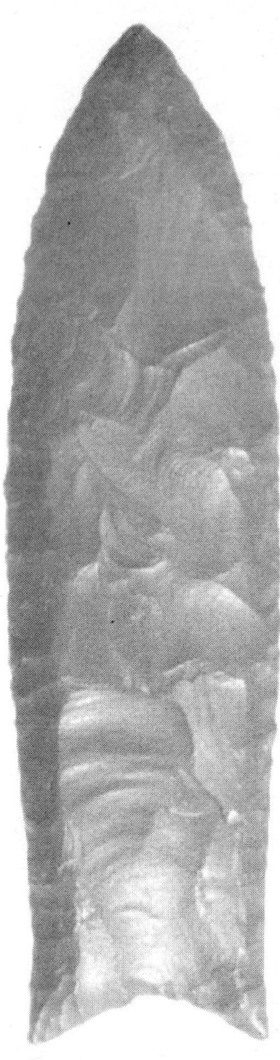

G9, $3000-$5500+
Van Buren, AR.

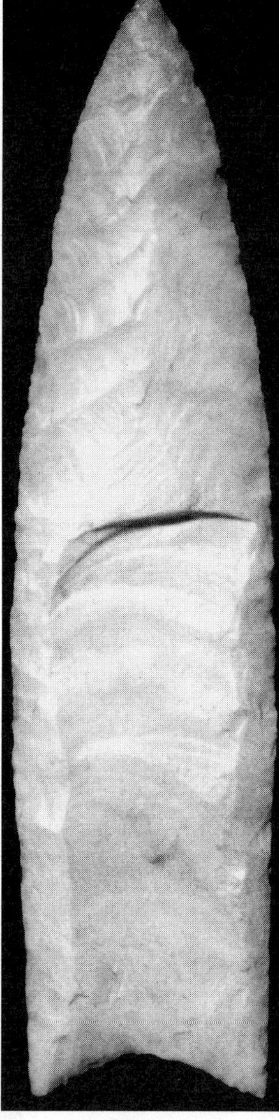

G10, $6,000-$12,000+
Upton Co., TX.

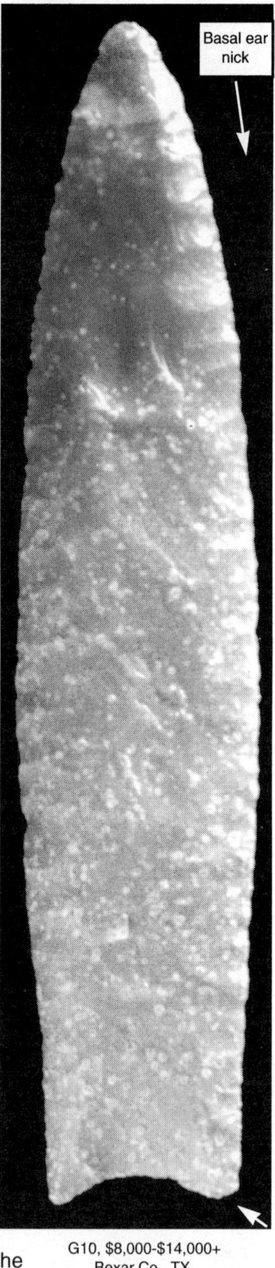

G10, $8,000-$14,000+
Bexar Co., TX.

LOCATION: All of North America. **DESCRIPTION:** A medium to large size, auriculate, fluted, lanceolate point with convex sides and a concave base that is ground. Most examples are fluted on both sides about 1/3 the way up from the base. The flaking can be random to parallel. *Clovis* is the earliest point type in the hemisphere. It is believed that this form was developed in Siberia or China and brought here by early man who crossed the Bering Straits to reach this continent about 12,000 years ago, just before the land bridge disappeared due to the melting of the glaciers. There is no pre-*Clovis* evidence here in the U.S. (no crude forms that pre-date *Clovis). Clovis*-like fluted points have been reported found in China dating to 11-12,000 B.P. *Clovis* has also been found in Alaska and southern Chili in South America. **I.D. Key:** Paleo flaking, shoulders, batan fluting instead of indirect style. **I.D. KEY:** Basal form and fluting.

COAHUILA - Late Archaic to Woodland, 4000 - 2000 B. P.

(Also see Adena, Gary, Hidden Valley and Langtry)

G8, $35-$70
Comanche Co., TX.

LOCATION: Central Texas. **DESCRIPTION:** A medium to large size, narrow point with tapered shoulders and a long, pointed, contracting stem. A scarce type. **I.D. KEY:** Long, pointed stem. Rare type.

CODY KNIFE

(See Red River Knife)

CONEJO - Late Archaic, 4000 - 3000 B. P.

(Also see Bandy, Ellis, Fairland and Marshall)

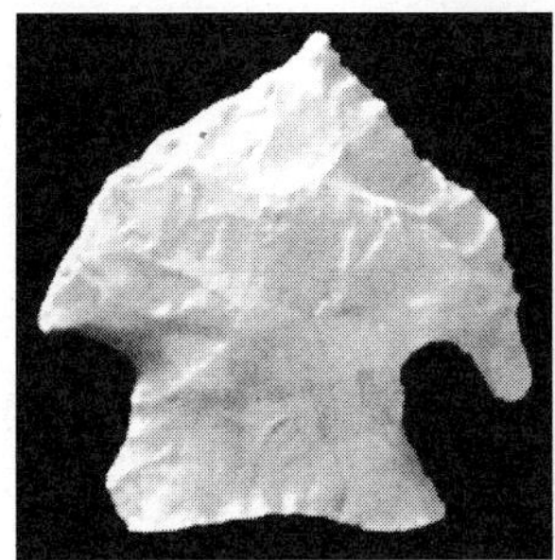

G4, $3-$5
Comanche Co., TX.

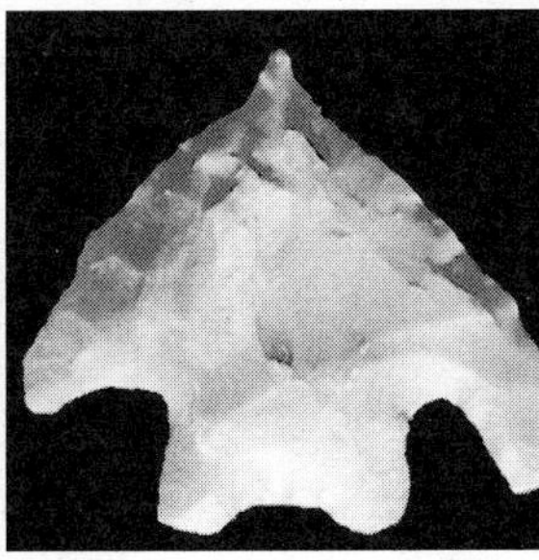

G5, $8-$15
Schleicher Co., TX.

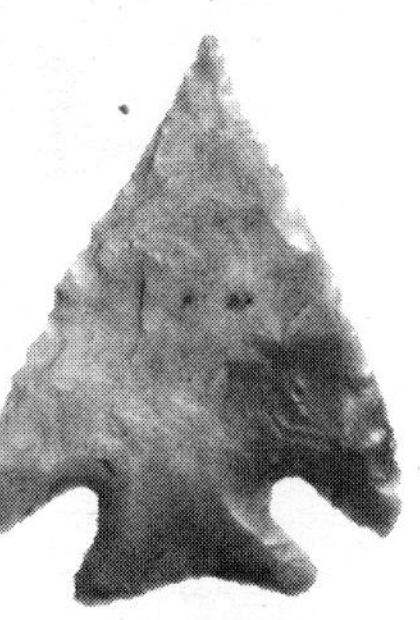

G8, $25-$50
TX.

LOCATION: Texas and New Mexico **DESCRIPTION:** A medium size, corner notched point with an expanding, concave base and shoulder tangs that turn towards the base.

CORNER TANG KNIFE - Late Archaic to Woodland, 4000 - 2000 B. P.

(Also see Base Tang, Crescent Knife and Mid-Back Tang Knife)

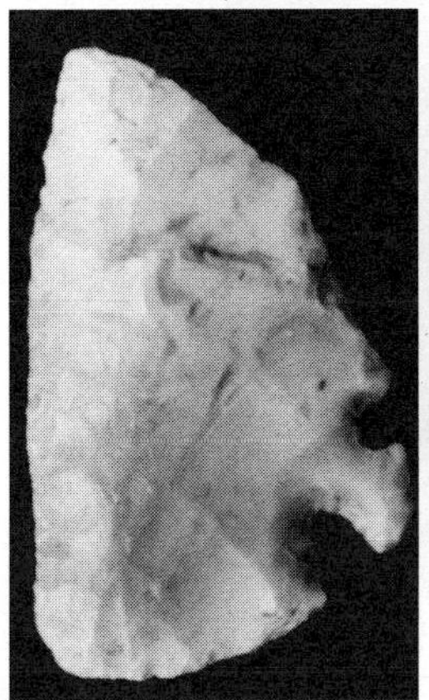

G5, $75-$150
Killeen, TX.

G6, $150-$300
Llano Co., TX.

G9, $400-$750
Comanche Co., TX.

G6, $225-$450
TX.

G7, $250-$500
W. TX.

G8, $300-$600
Wilson Co., TX.

LOCATION: Texas to Oklahoma. **DESCRIPTION:** This knife is notched producing a tang at a corner for hafting to a handle. Tang knives are very rare and have been reproduced in recent years. **I.D. KEY:** Angle of hafting.

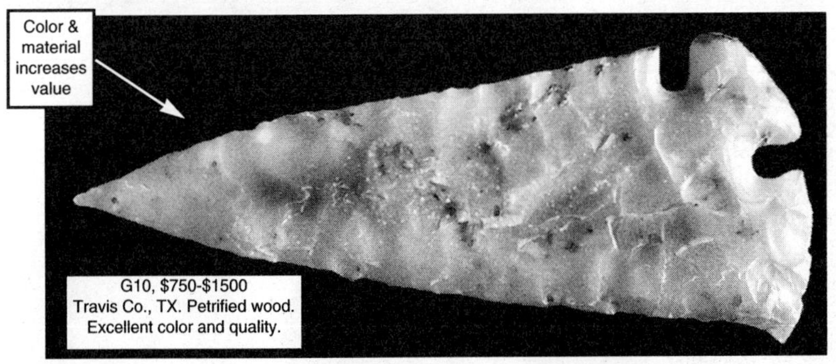

G10, $750-$1500
Travis Co., TX. Petrified wood.
Excellent color and quality.

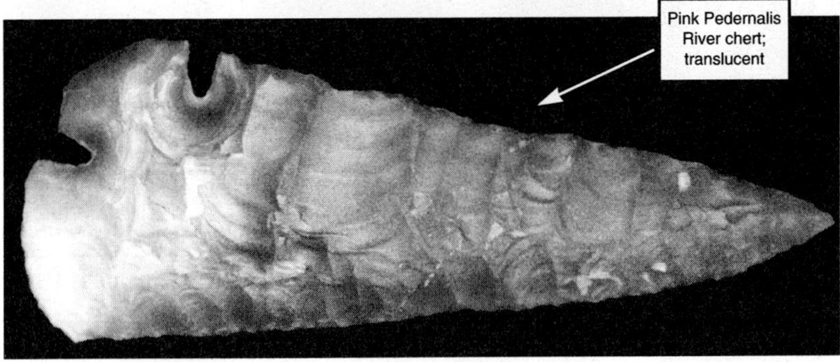

G9, $750-$1500
Bandera Co., TX.

G9, $600-$1200
Kerr Co., TX.

G9, $1000-$2000
Kerr Co., TX.

COVINGTON - Late Archaic, 4000 - 3000 B. P.

(Also see Friday, Gahagan, Sabine, San Saba and San Gabriel)

G6, $50-$100
Kimble Co., TX.

G8, $50-$100
TX.

G8, $50-$100
TX.

G7, $50-$100
TX.,

G5, $40-$75
Junction, TX.

G8 $65-$125
TX.

G7 $100-$200
Williamson Co., TX.

G8 $65-$125
TX.

LOCATION: Texas. **DESCRIPTION:** A medium to large size, thin, lanceolate blade with a broad, rounded base.

CUNEY - Historic, 400 - 200 B. P.

(Also see Bonham, Edwards, Morris, Perdiz, Rockwall and Scallorn)

G5, $8-$15 G5, $8-$15 G8, $35-$50 G5, $8-$15 G7, $15-$30 G5, $8-$15

All Comanche Co., TX.

LOCATION: Midwestern states. **DESCRIPTION:** A small size, well made, barbed, triangular point with a very short, small base that is bifurcated.

CUPP - Late Woodland to Mississippian, 1500 - 600 B. P.

(Also see Gibson, Epps and Motley)

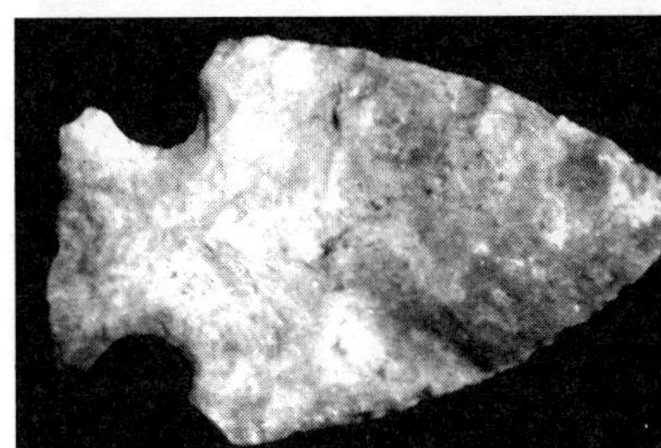

LOCATION: Northern Texas to Kansas to Missouri. **DESCRIPTION:** A medium to large size, narrow point with wide corner notches, shoulder barbs and a convex base. Similar to *Motley,* but the base stem is shorter and broader. *Epps* has square to tapered shoulders, otherwise is identical to *Motley.*

G3, $5-$10
AR.

SC

DALLAS - Late Archaic to Woodland, 4000 - 1500 B. P.

(Also see Carrolton, Dawson, Elam, Travis and Wells)

G4, $1-$2
Waco, TX.

LOCATION: Texas to Oklahoma. **DESCRIPTION:** A small to medium size point with a short blade, weak shoulders, and a long squared stem. Stem can be half the length of the point. Basal area can be ground. **I.D. KEY:** Size, squared stem.

G5, $2-$4
Comanche Co., TX.

G5, $2-$4
Comanche Co., TX.

G5, $2-$4
Comanche Co., TX.

DALTON-BRECKENRIDGE - Early Archaic, 9500 - 5000 B. P.

(Also see Dalton Classic and Meserve)

G4, $20-$35
AR.

LOCATION: Midwestern states, **DESCRIPTION:** A medium to large size, auriculate point with an obvious bevel extending the entire length of the point from tip to base. Similar in form to the *Dalton-Greenbrier*. Basal area is usually ground.

DALTON CLASSIC - Early Archaic, 9500 - 8000 B. P.

(Also see Angostura, Barber, Clovis, Golondrina, Meserve, Plainview and San Patrice)

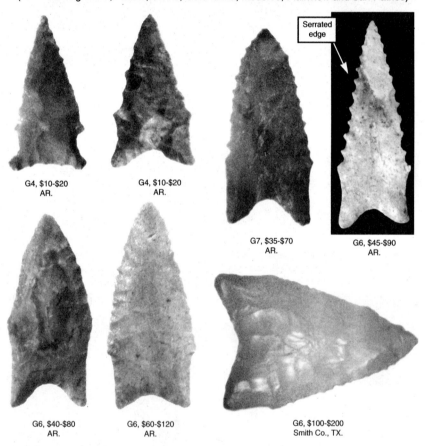

G4, $10-$20
AR.

G4, $10-$20
AR.

G7, $35-$70
AR.

Serrated edge

G6, $45-$90
AR.

G6, $40-$80
AR.

G6, $60-$120
AR.

G6, $100-$200
Smith Co., TX.

LOCATION: Midwestern to Southeastern states. First recognized in Missouri. **DESCRIPTION:** A small to large size, thin, auriculate, fishtailed point. Many examples are finely serrated and exhibit excellent flaking. Some are fluted. Beveling may occur on one side of each face but is usually on the right side. All have basal grinding. This early type spread over most of the Eastern and Midwestern U.S. and strongly influenced many other types to follow.

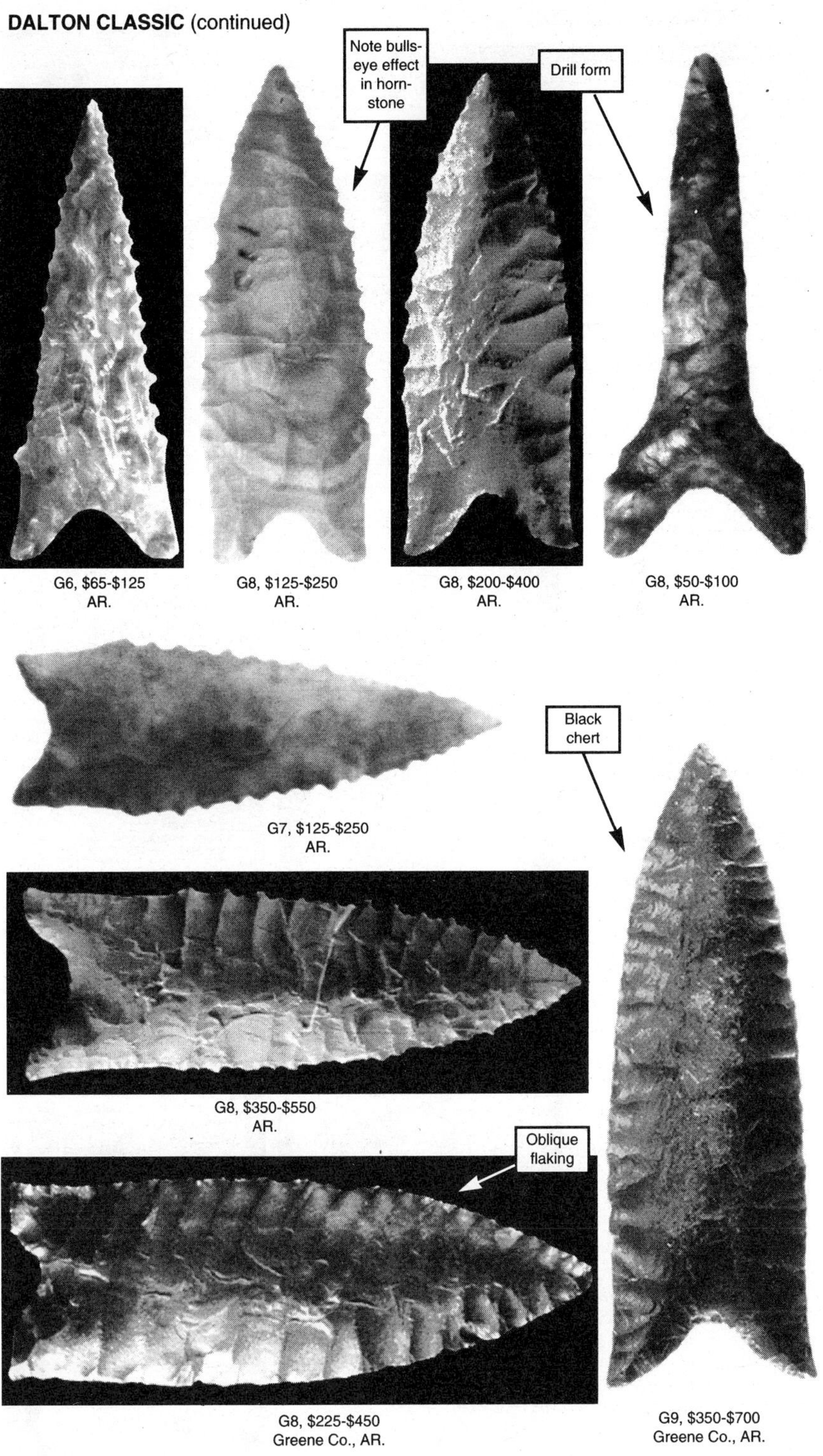

G6, $65-$125
AR.

G8, $125-$250
AR.

G8, $200-$400
AR.

G8, $50-$100
AR.

G7, $125-$250
AR.

G8, $350-$550
AR.

G8, $225-$450
Greene Co., AR.

G9, $350-$700
Greene Co., AR.

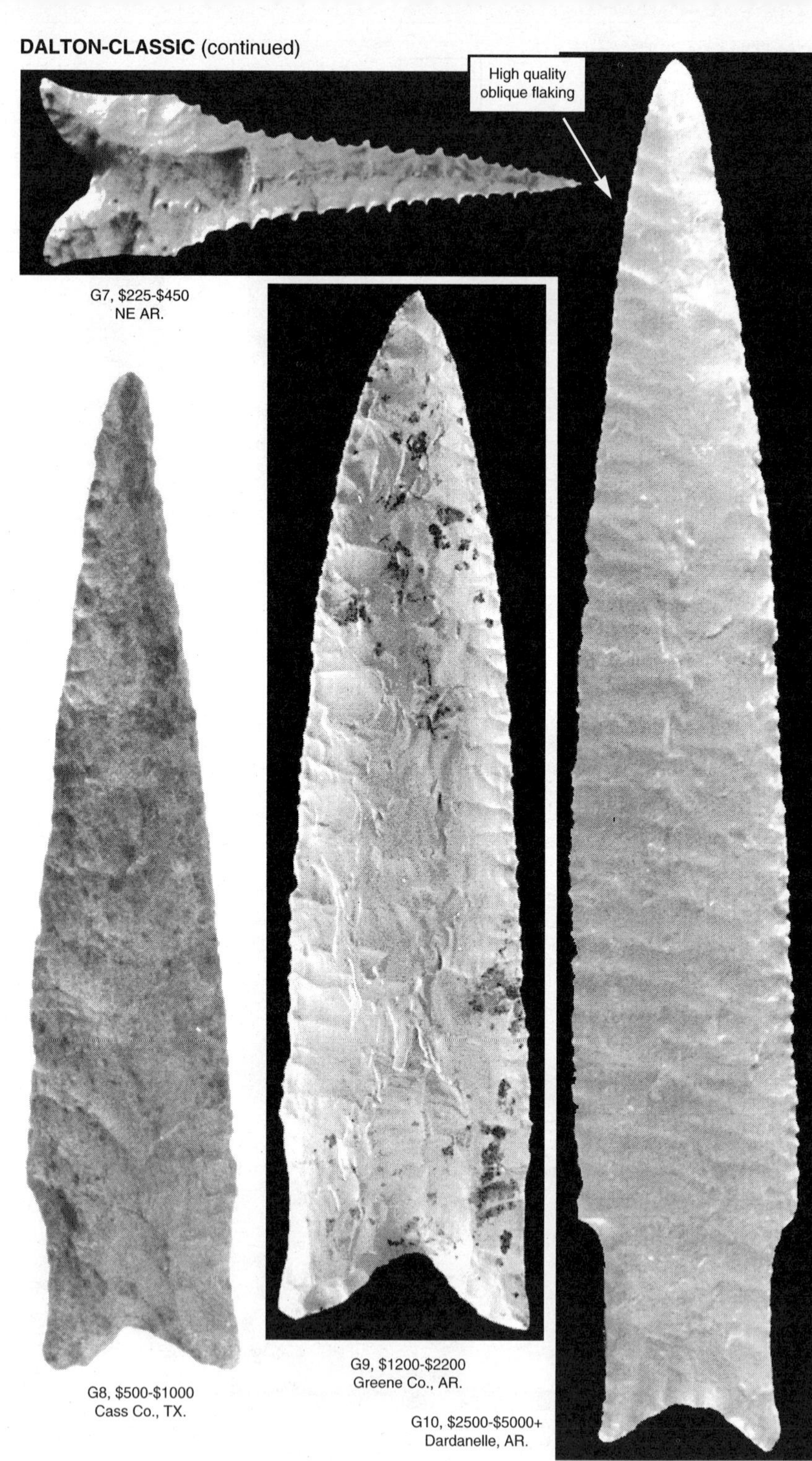

G7, $225-$450
NE AR.

G8, $500-$1000
Cass Co., TX.

G9, $1200-$2200
Greene Co., AR.

G10, $2500-$5000+
Dardanelle, AR.

DALTON-GREENBRIER - Early Archaic, 9500 - 6000 B. P.

(Also see Dalton Breckenridge, Golondrina, Meserve, Pelican and Plainview)

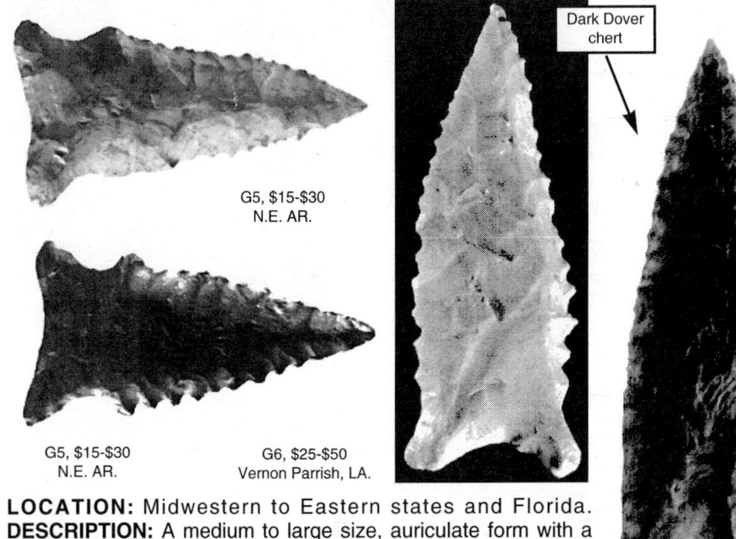

G5, $15-$30
N.E. AR.

G5, $15-$30
N.E. AR.

G6, $25-$50
Vernon Parrish, LA.

G8, $100-$200
N.E. AR.

LOCATION: Midwestern to Eastern states and Florida. **DESCRIPTION:** A medium to large size, auriculate form with a concave base and drooping to expanding auricles. Many examples are serrated, some are fluted on both sides, and all have basal grinding. Resharpened examples are usually beveled on the right side of each face although left side beveling does occur. Thinness and high quality flaking is evident on many examples. This early variation developed in the Arkansas/Kentucky/Tennessee area. **I.D. KEY:** Expanded auricles.

SC

DALTON-HEMPHILL - Early Archaic, 9500 - 6000 B. P.

(Also see Firstview, Hardin and Scottsbluff)

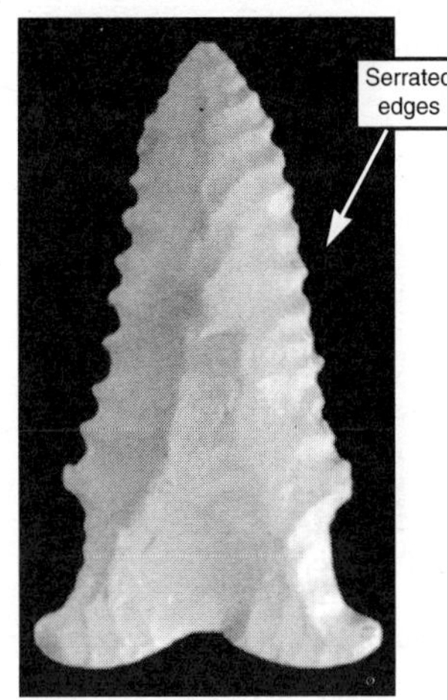

G7, $50-$100
Clay Co., AR.

G5, $40-$80
Comanche Co., TX.

LOCATION: Midwestern to Eastern states. **DESCRIPTION:** A medium to large size point with expanded auricles and horizontal, tapered to weak shoulders. Blade edges are usually serrated and bases are ground. In later times, this variant developed into the *Hemphill* point. **I.D. KEY:** Straightened extended shoulders.

DALTON-HEMPHILL (continued)

Note basal thinning

G7, $100-$200
Stone Co., AR.

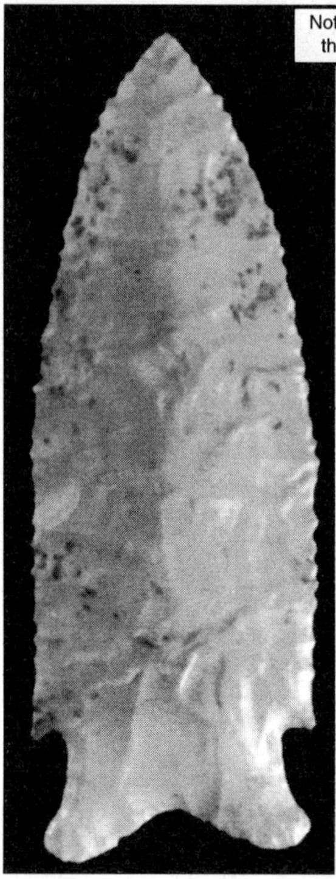

G8, $250-$500
Ozark Co., AR.

G9, $350-$700
Little Rock, AR.

DARDANELLE - Mississippian, 600 - 400 B. P.

(Also see Agee, Keota and Nodena)

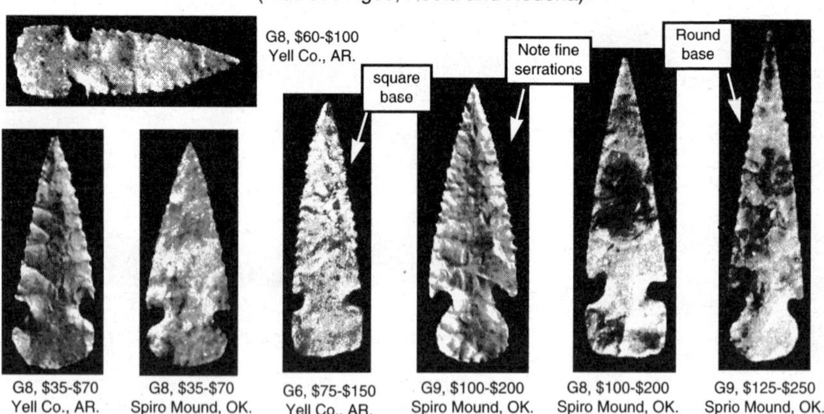

G8, $60-$100
Yell Co., AR.

G8, $35-$70
Yell Co., AR.

G8, $35-$70
Spiro Mound, OK.

G6, $75-$150
Yell Co., AR.

G9, $100-$200
Spiro Mound, OK.

G8, $100-$200
Spiro Mound, OK.

G9, $125-$250
Sprio Mound, OK.

LOCATION: Arkansas to Oklahoma. **DESCRIPTION:** A small to medium size, narrow, thin, serrated, corner or side notched arrow point. Bases can be rounded or square. A *Nodena* variant form with basal notches. This type has been found in caches from the Spiro mound in Oklahoma and from Arkansas. **ID. KEY:** Basal form.

DARL - Woodland, 2500 - 1000 B. P.

(Also see Darl Stemmed, Dawson, Hoxie, Pandale & Zephyr)

G7, $35-$70
Cent. TX.

G7, $50-$100
Austin, TX.

G7, $40-$80
Travis Co., TX.

G6, $40-$75
Milan Co., TX.

G6, $25-$50
Belton, TX.

G8, $65-$125
Zapata Co., TX.

G8, $30-$60
Bastrop Co., TX.

G6, $30-$60
Travis Co., TX.

G8, $65-$125
Austin, TX.

G7, $35-$70
Austin, TX.

SC

LOCATION: Texas to Oklahoma. **DESCRIPTION:** A small to medium size, slender, triangular, expanded to parallel stemmed point. Some have a distinct bevel on one side (right) of each face. Shoulders are tapered to weakly barbed. **I.D. KEY:** Basal form. Bases expand.

DARL BLADE - Woodland, 2500 - 1000 B. P.

(Also see Covington, Friday, Gahagan and Kinney)

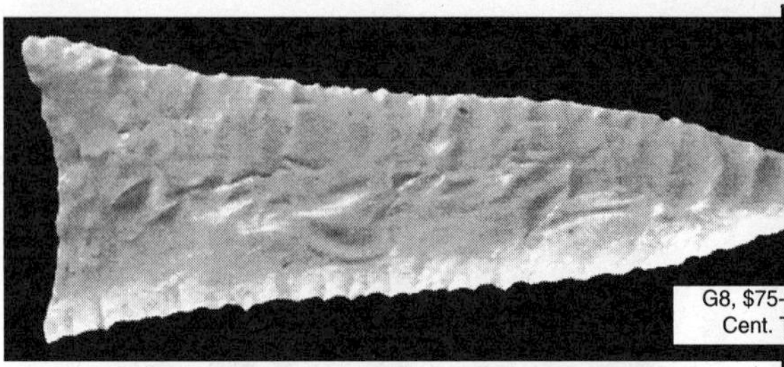

G8, $75-$150
Cent. TX.

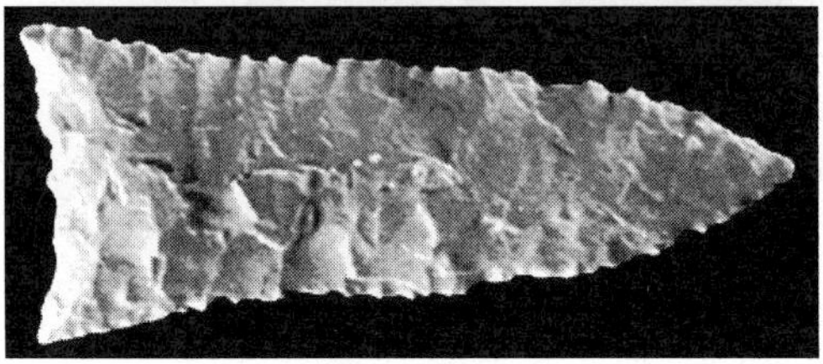

G5, $30-$60
Austin, TX.

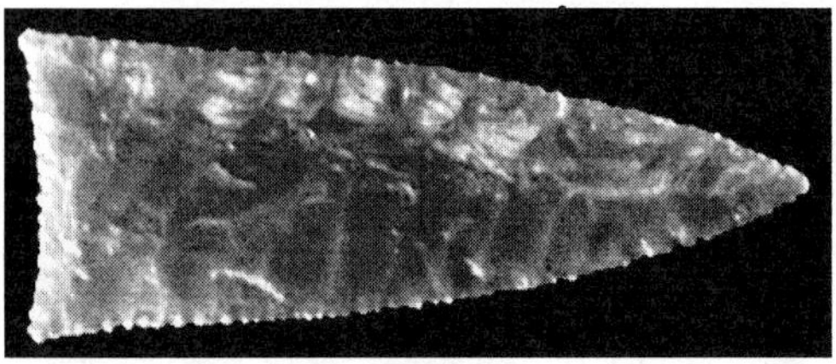

G6, $75-$150
Little River Co., AR.

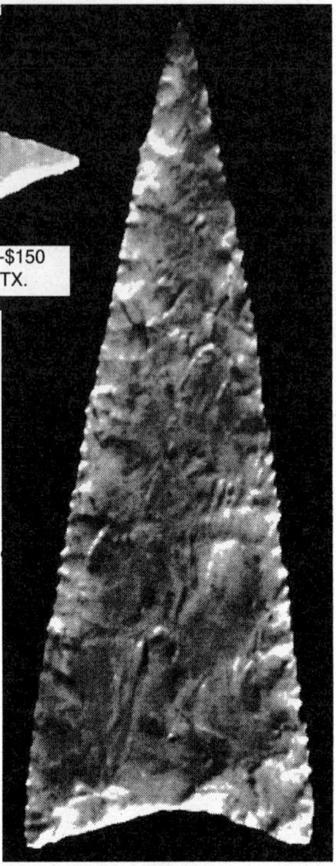

G8, $125-$250
Travis Co., TX.

LOCATION: Texas to Oklahoma. **DESCRIPTION:** A medium to large size, thin, lanceolate blade with typical Darl flaking, fine edgework and a concave to straight base. **I.D. KEY:** Cross section thinness and fine secondary flaking on blade edges.

DARL STEMMED - Early Archaic, 8000 - 5000 B. P.

(Also see Darl, Hoxie and Zephyr)

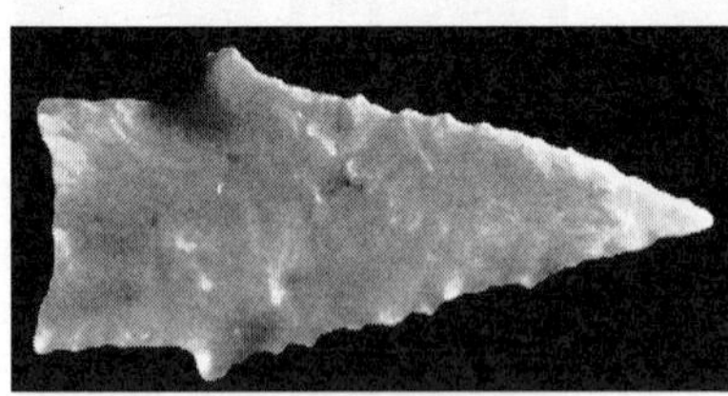

G4, $15-$30
Cent. TX.

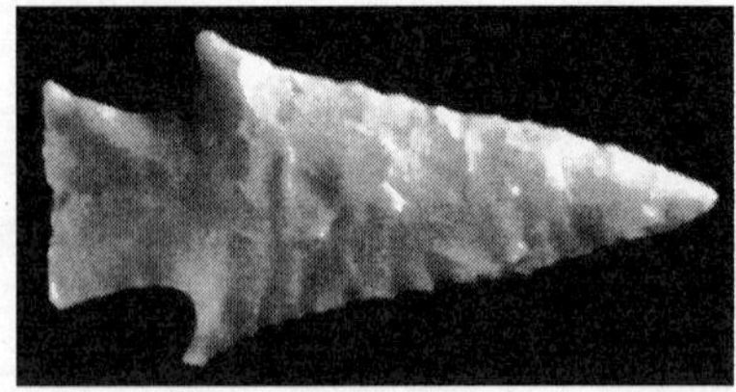

G6, $25-$50
Comanche Co., TX.

LOCATION: Central Texas. **DESCRIPTION:** A medium to large size, narrow point with horizontally barbed shoulders and an expanding to square stem. The blades on most examples are steeply beveled on one side of each face. Flaking is early parallel and is of much higher quality than *Darl.* **I.D. KEY:** Early flaking, straight base.

DARL STEMMED (continued)

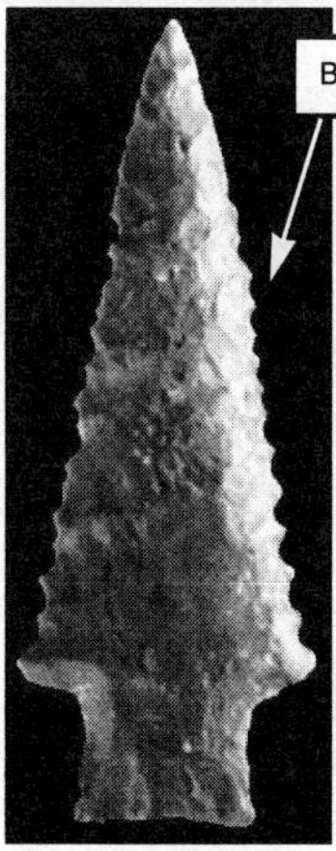

Bevel

G7, $40-$80
Austin Co., TX.

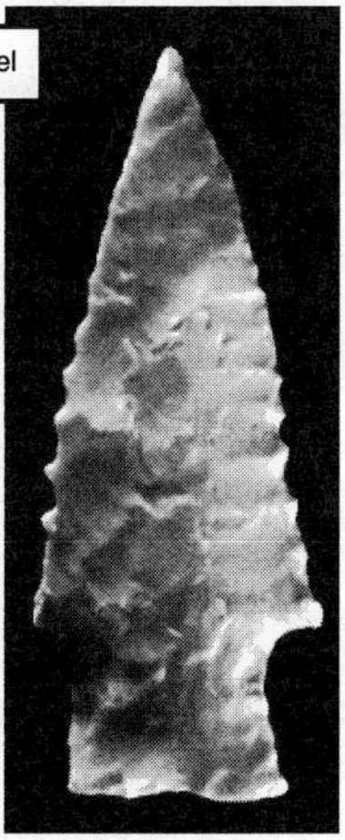

G5, $20-$40
Comanche Co., TX.

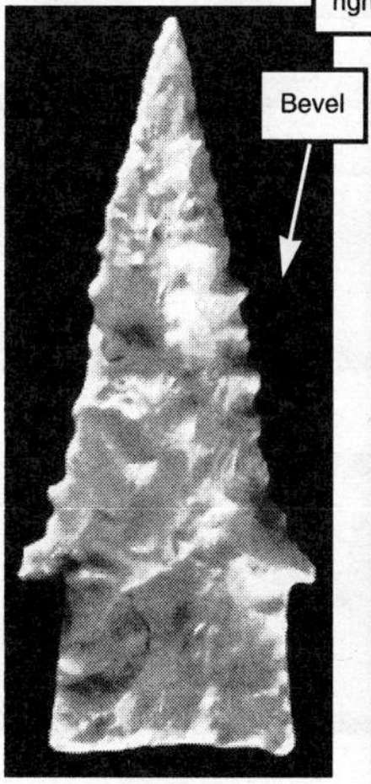

Bevel

G6, $30-$60
Comanche Co., TX.

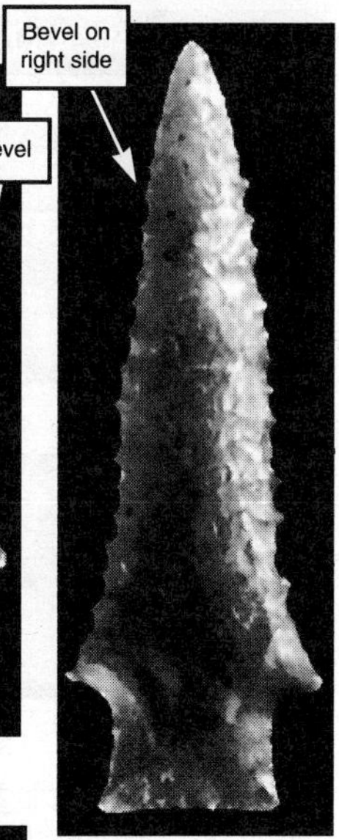

Bevel on right side

G9, $100-$200
Austin, TX.

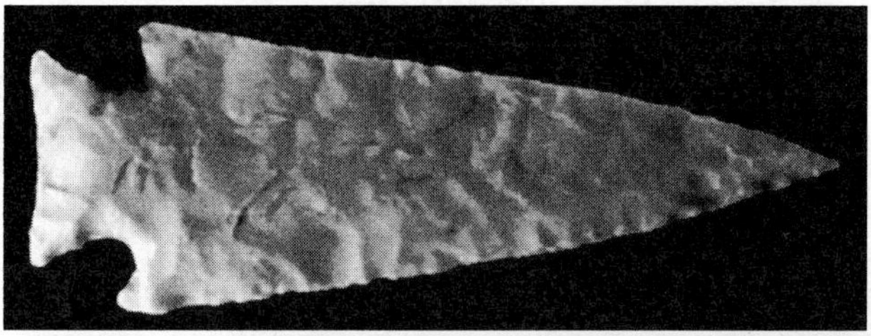

G8, $125-$250
Austin, TX.

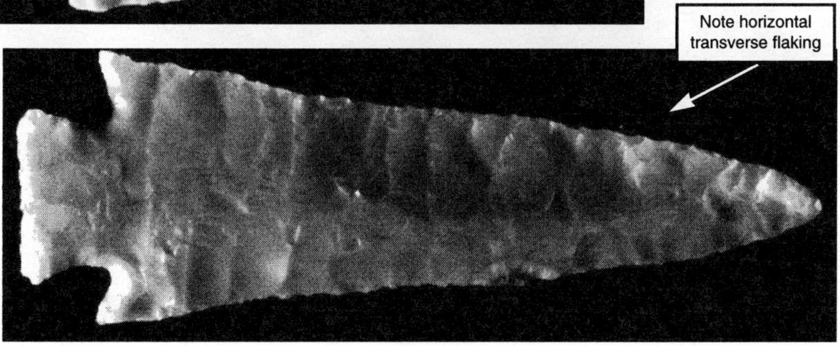

Note horizontal transverse flaking

G9, $150-$300
Austin, TX.

DAWSON - Middle Archaic, 7000 - 4000 B. P.

(Also see Adena, Carrolton, Darl and Wells)

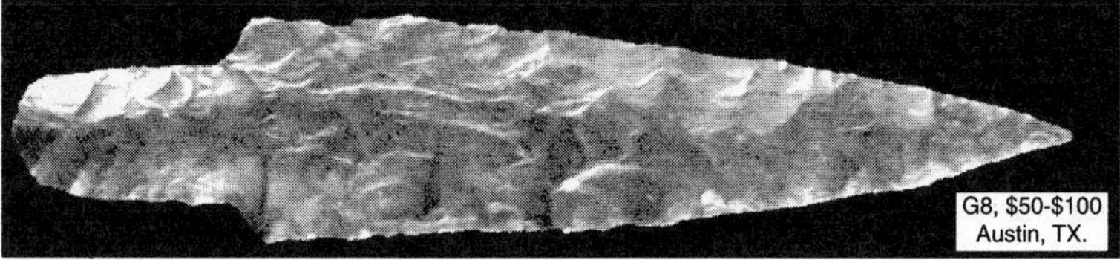

G8, $50-$100
Austin, TX.

LOCATION: Texas. **DESCRIPTION:** A medium size, narrow, stemmed point with strong, tapered shoulders. The base is rounded to square.

DELHI - Late Archaic, 3500 - 2000 B. P.

(Also see Darl and Pontchartrain)

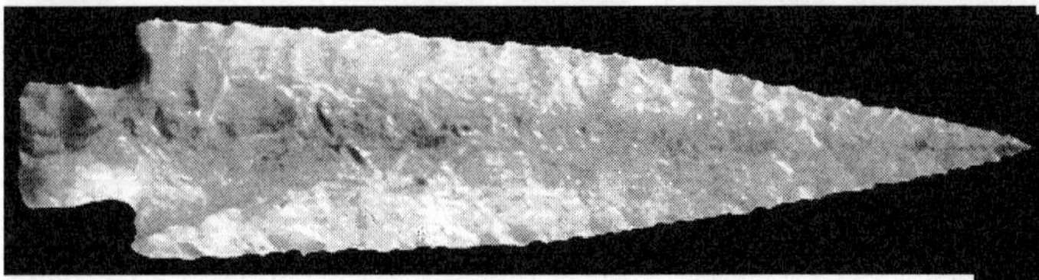

G9, $100-$200
LA.

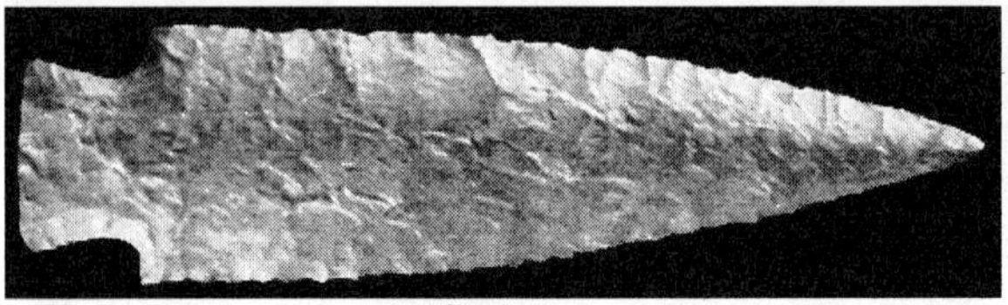

G9, $75-$150
LA.

G9, $75-$150
LA.

LOCATION: Louisiana. **DESCRIPTION:** A medium to large size, narrow, stemmed point with strong, barbed shoulders. The stem can be square or expands and the base is straight to slightly convex.

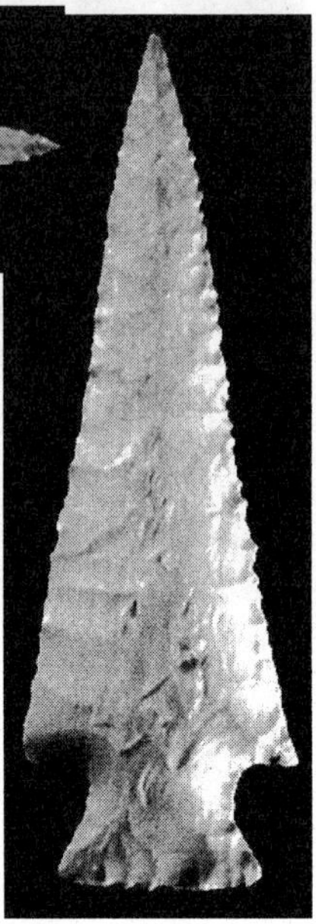

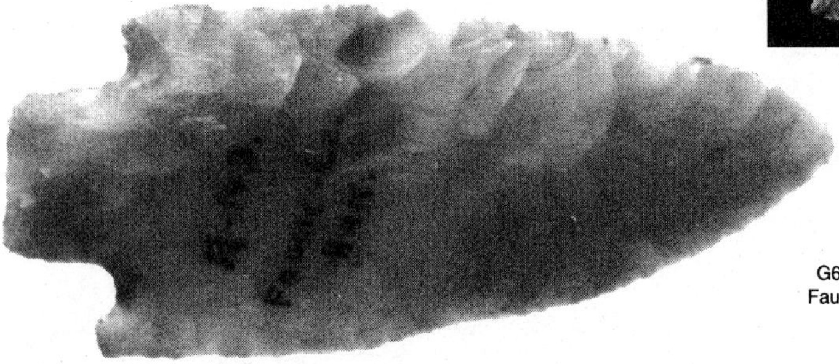

G6, $40-$80
Faulk Co., AR.

DOUBLE TIP (Occurs in Carrizo and Pedernales types)

DOVETAIL - Early Archaic, 9500 - 8000 B. P.

(Also see Gibson and Thebes)

G6, $300-$600
Cherokee Co., TX.

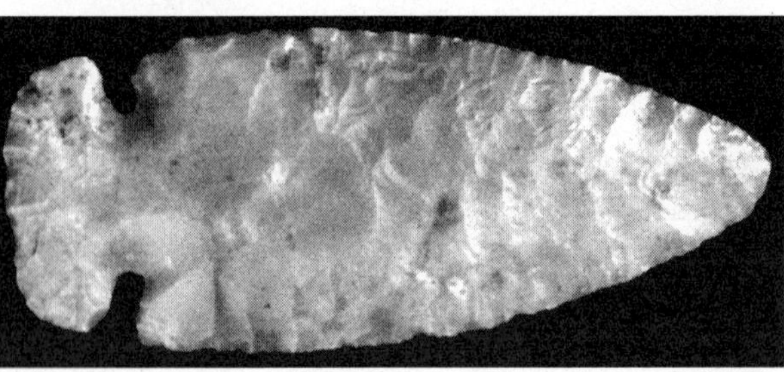

LOCATION: East Texas Eastward. **DESCRIPTION:** Also known as *St. Charles.* A medium to large size, corner notched, dovetailed base point. The blade is beveled on one side of each face on resharpened examples. Bases are ground and can be fractured on both sides or center notched on some examples as found in Ohio. **I.D. KEY:** Dovetailed base, early flaking.

DOVETAIL (continued)

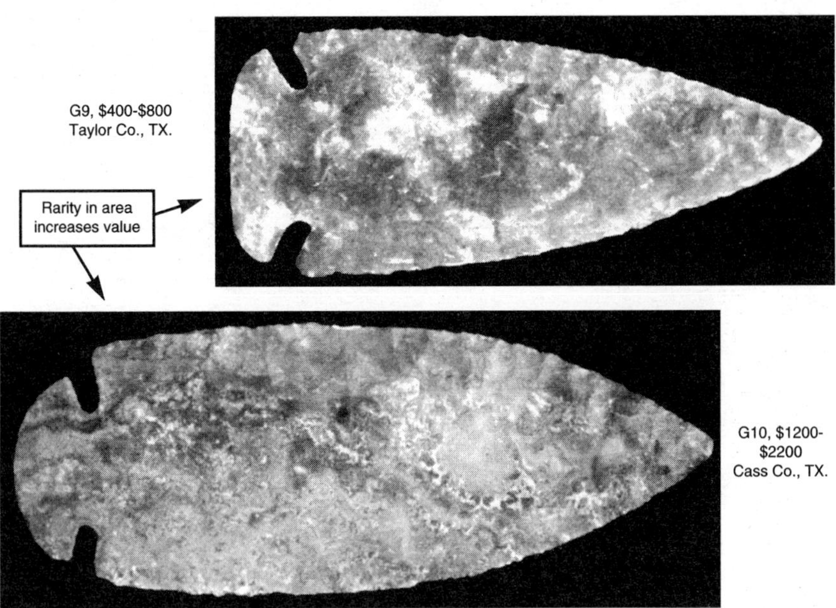

G9, $400-$800
Taylor Co., TX.

G10, $1200-$2200
Cass Co., TX.

DRILL - Paleo to Historic, 14,000 - 200 B. P.

(Also see Perforator and Scraper)

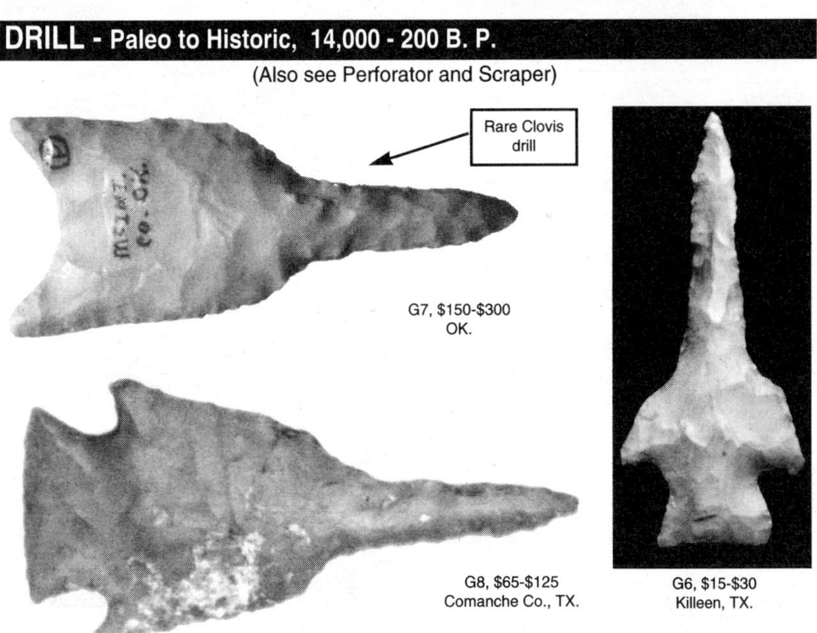

G7, $150-$300
OK.

G8, $65-$125
Comanche Co., TX.

G6, $15-$30
Killeen, TX.

LOCATION: Everywhere. **DESCRIPTION:** Although many drills were made from scratch, all point types were made into the drill form. Usually, heavily resharpened and broken points were salvaged and rechipped into drills. These objects were certainly used as drills (evidence of extreme edge wear), but there is speculation that some of these forms may have been used as pins for clothing, ornaments, ear plugs and other uses.

DRILL (continued)

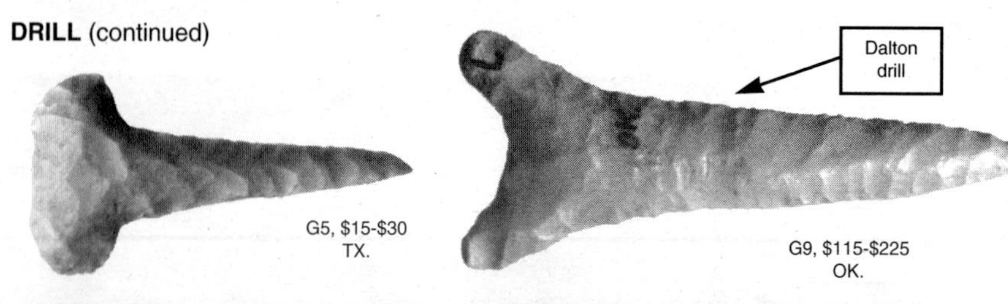

G5, $15-$30
TX.

G9, $115-$225
OK.

DURAN - Woodland, 3000 - 2000 B. P.

(Also see Charcos and Sinner)

G8, $20-$35
TX.

G9, $20-$40
TX.

G9, $15-$30
TX.

G10, $40-$75
TX.

G6, $20-$35
TX.

G7, $40-$75
Zapata Co., TX.

G5, $15-$25
TX.

G7, $20-$40
TX.

LOCATION: Texas. **DESCRIPTION:** A small size, narrow, stemmed point with double notches on each side. Base can be parallel sided to tapered. **I.D. KEY:** Double notches.

EARLY STEMMED - Early Archaic, 9000 - 7000 B. P.

(Also see Brazos, Castroville, Darl Stemmed and Zephyr)

G4, $200-$35
W. TX.

G7, $50-$100
Angelina Co., TX.

G6, $30-$60
Bell Co., TX.

LOCATION: Texas to Oklahoma. **DESCRIPTION:** A medium to large size, broad point with a medium to long expanded stem and shoulder barbs.

G7, $100-$200
Milam Co., TX.

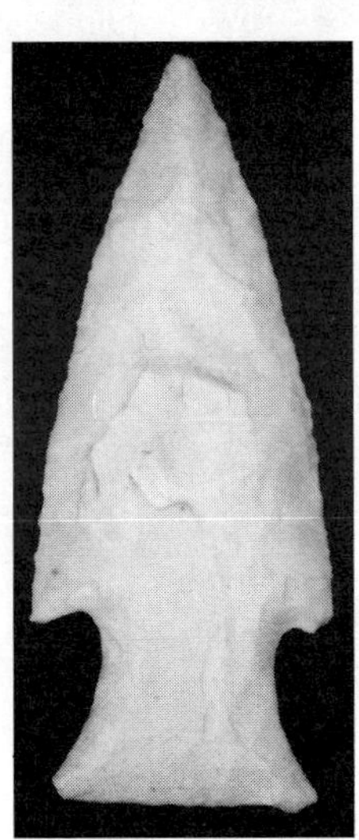

G8, $115-$225
Wilson Co., TX.

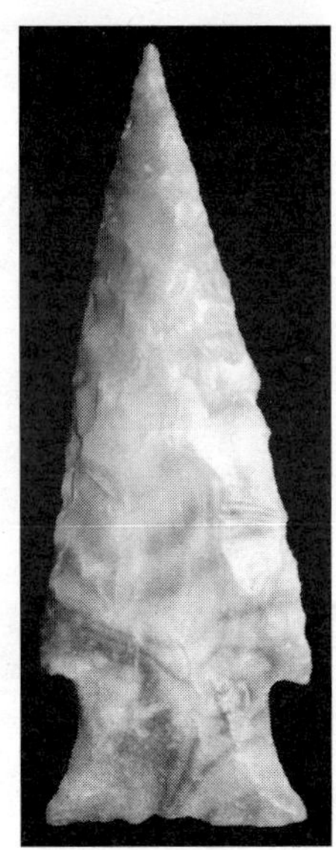

G9, $150-$300
Wilson Co., TX.

EARLY STEMMED LANCEOLATE - Early Archaic, 9000 - 7000 B. P.

(Also see Angostura, Brazos, Castroville, Darl Stemmed, Pontchartrain & Zephyr)

G7, $50-$100
Bell Co., TX.

G6, $30-$60
Bell Co., TX.

G9, $100-$200
Wilson Co., TX.

G3, $20-$40
Wilson Co., TX.

LOCATION: Texas to Oklahoma. **DESCRIPTION:** A medium to large size, narrow lanceolate stemmed point with weak, tapered shoulders.

EARLY TRIANGULAR - Early Archaic, 9000 - 7000 B. P.

(Also see Angostura, Carrizo, Clovis and Tortugas)

G8, $40-$80
Comanche Co., TX.

G6, $25-$50
Comanche Co., TX.

G10, $150-$250
Kinney Co., TX.

G5, $10-$20
TX.

LOCATION: Texas. **DESCRIPTION:** A medium to large size, broad, triangle that is usually serrated. The base is either fluted or has long thinning strikes. Quality is excellent with early oblique transverse flaking and possible right hand beveling. **I.D. KEY:** Basal thinning and edgework.

ECCENTRIC

(See Exotic Forms)

EDGEWOOD - Woodland, 3000 - 1500 B. P.

(Also see Ellis and Fairland)

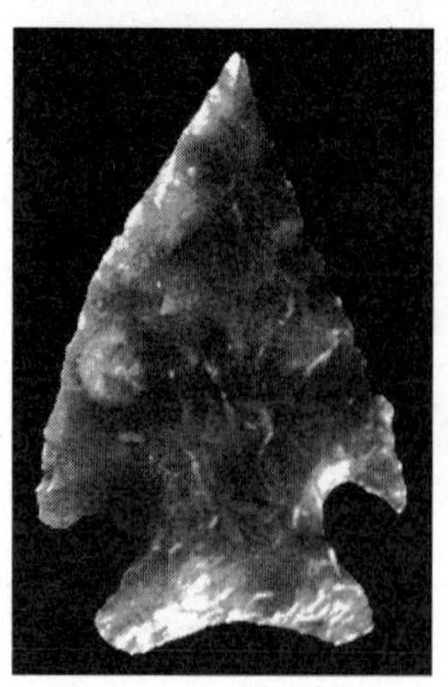

LOCATION: Texas to Oklahoma. **DESCRIPTION:** A small to medium size, expanded stem point with a concave base. Shoulders are barbed to tapered and the base is usually as wide as the shoulders.

G6, $5-$10
Comanche Co., TX.

G4, $3-$5
Killeen, TX.

G4, $2-$4
Cent., TX.

EDGEWOOD (continued)

G6, $8-$15
McIntosh Co., OK.

EDWARDS - Woodland to Mississippian, 2000 - 1000 B. P.

(Also see Cuney, Haskell and Sallisaw)

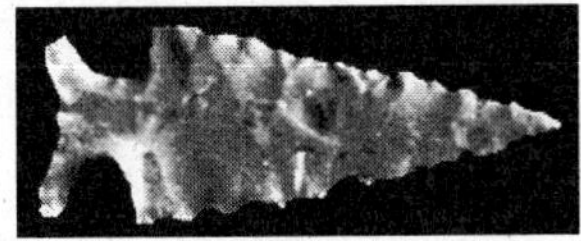
G4, $10-$20
Comanche Co., TX.

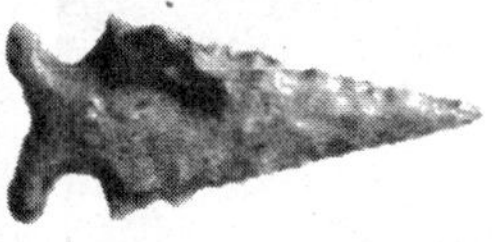
G5, $15-$25
TX.

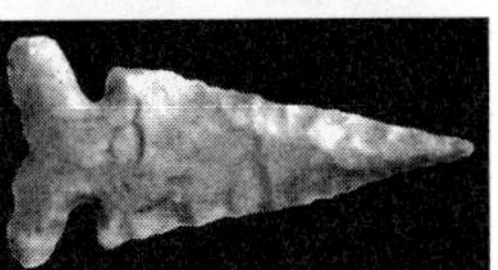
G4, $18-$30
TX.

LOCATION: Texas to Oklahoma. **DESCRIPTION:** A small size, thin, barbed arrow point with long, flaring ears at the base. Some examples are finely serrated. **I.D. KEY:** Basal form and flaking.

ELAM - Late Archaic to Woodland, 4000 - 2000 B. P.

(Also see Dallas, Darl and Ellis)

G6, $3-$5
Comanche Co., TX.

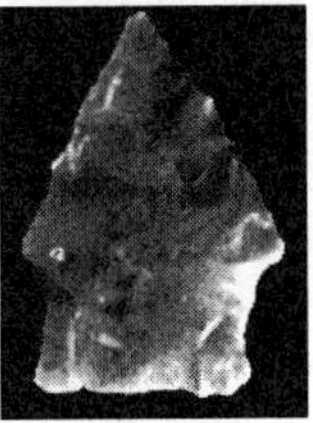
G4, $3-$5
Comanche Co., TX.

G4, $3-$5
Waco, TX.

LOCATION: Texas. **DESCRIPTION:** A small size stubby point with a squared base and weak shoulders.

SC

ELLIS - Late Archaic, 4000 - 2000 B. P.

(Also see Edgewood, Ensor, Godley, Marcos and Scallorn)

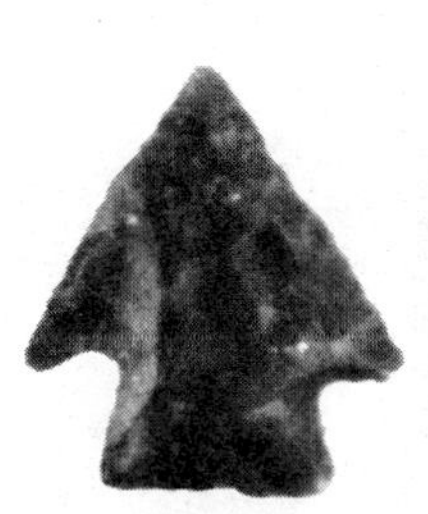
G5, $5-$10
TX.

G4, $3-$5
Comanche Co., TX.

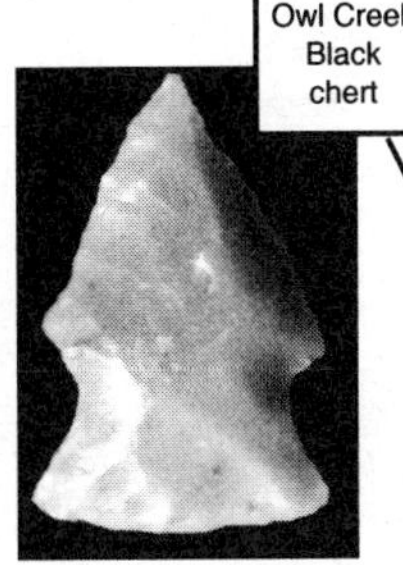
G4, $3-$5
Odessa, TX.

Owl Creek Black chert

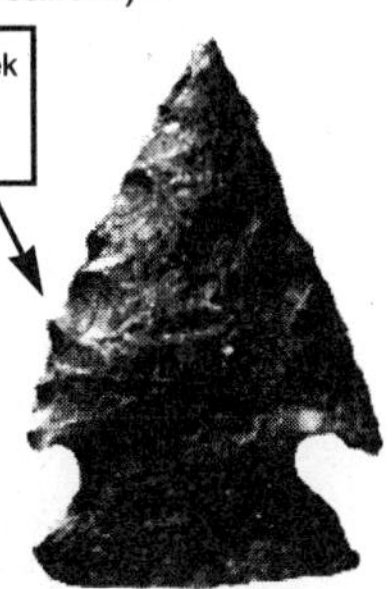
G5, $6-$10
Comanche Co., TX.

LOCATION: Texas, Arkansas to Oklahoma. **DESCRIPTION:** A small to medium size, expanded stemmed to corner notched point with tapered to barbed shoulders. Bases are convex to straight.

ENSOR - Late Archaic to Early Woodland, 4000 - 1500 B. P.

(Also see Ellis, Frio, Marcos and Marshall)

G3, $5-$10
TX.

G7, $10-$20
TX.

G5, $15-$30
Austin, TX.

G5, $20-$40
Cent. TX.

G7, $25-$50
Cent., TX.

G6, $15-$30
Austin, TX.

G8, $30-$60
TX.

G5, $40-$80
Williamson Co., TX.

G5, $25-$50
Austin, TX.

G8, $50-$100
TX.

G5, $15-$30
Bell Co., TX.

G7, $20-$40
Comanche Co., TX.

LOCATION: Texas. **DESCRIPTION:** A medium to large size, thin, well made corner-notched point with a concave, convex or straight base. Some examples are serrated and sharply barbed and tipped. **I.D. KEY:** Thinness, sharp barbs and edgework.

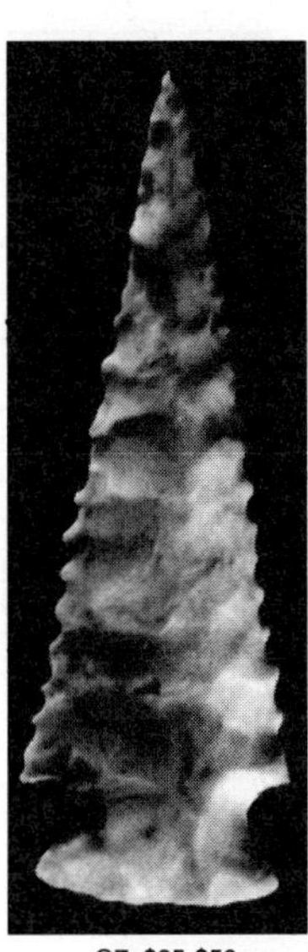
G7, $25-$50
Austin, TX.

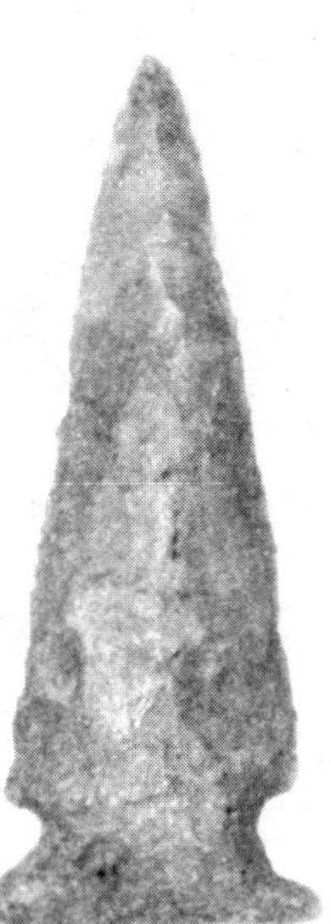
G6, $25-$50
Comanche Co., TX.

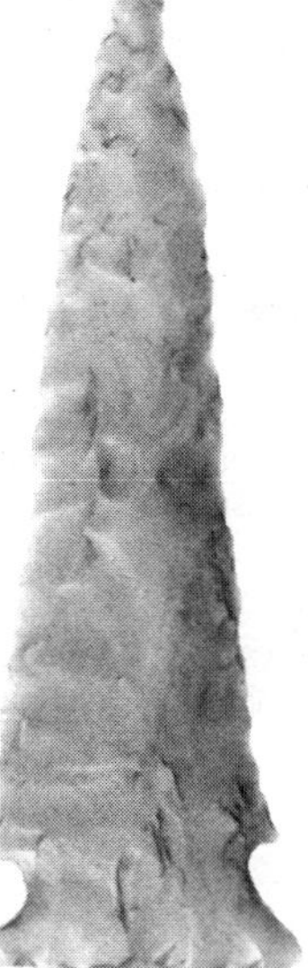
G8, $90-$175
Austin, TX.

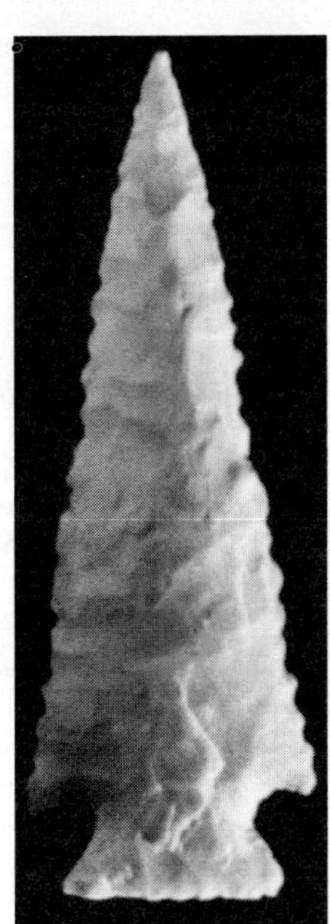
G7, $90-$175
Coryell Co., TX.

ENSOR SPLIT-BASE - Late Archaic to Early Woodland, 4000 - 1500 B. P.

(Also see Frio and Martindale)

LOCATION: Texas. **DESCRIPTION:** Identical to *Ensor* except for the bifurcated base. Look for *Ensor* flaking style. A cross type linking *Frio* with *Ensor*. **I.D. KEY:** Sharp barbs, thinness, edgework and split base.

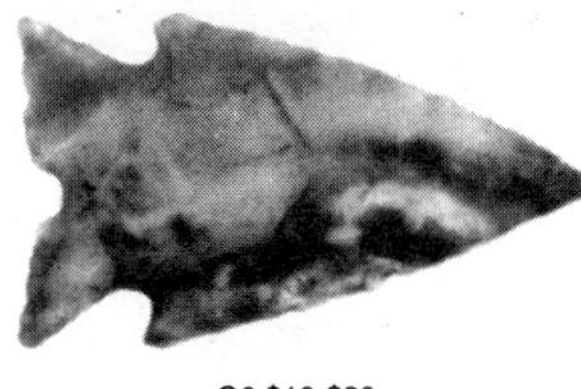
G6 $10-$20
TX.

Owl Creek
Black chert

G9, $125-$250
Comanche Co., TX.

G7, $25-$50
TX.

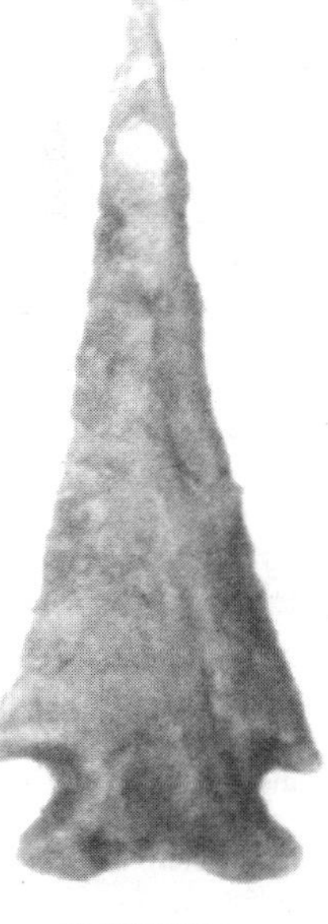
G7, $50-$100
TX.

EPPS - Late Archaic to Woodland, 3500 - 2000 B. P.

(Also see Cupp and Motley)

G3, $1-$2
Comanche
Co., TX.

G5, $4-$8
Waco, TX.

LOCATION: Eastern Texas to Louisiana. **DESCRIPTION:** A medium to large size point with wide corner notches, square to tapered shoulders and a convex base. *Cupp* has barbed shoulders. **I.D. KEY:** Square/tapered shoulders.

EVANS - Late Archaic To Woodland, 4000 - 2000 B. P.

(Also see Charcos, Duran and Sinner)

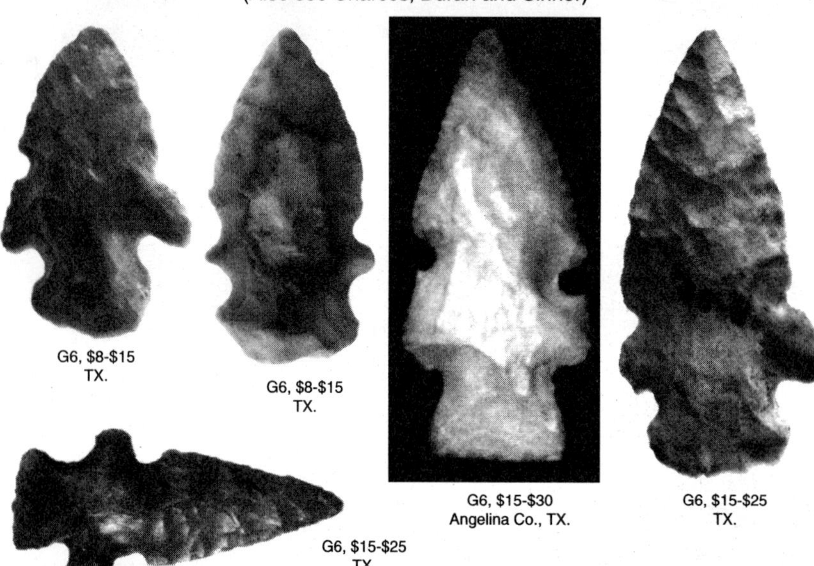

G6, $8-$15
TX.

G6, $8-$15
TX.

G6, $15-$30
Angelina Co., TX.

G6, $15-$25
TX.

G6, $15-$25
TX.

LOCATION: Eastern Texas Eastward to Tennessee. **DESCRIPTION:** A medium to large size stemmed double notched point. The notching occurs somewhere between the tip and shoulders. **I.D. KEY:** Thinness, sharp barbs, edgework and split base.

EXOTIC FORMS - Mid Archaic to Mississippian, 5000 - 1000 B. P.

(Also see Double Tip)

LOCATION: Everywhere **DESCRIPTION:** The forms illustrated here are very rare. Some are definitely effigy forms while others may be no more than the result of practicing how to notch, or unfinished and unintentional doodles.

G4, 10-$20
Cent. AR.

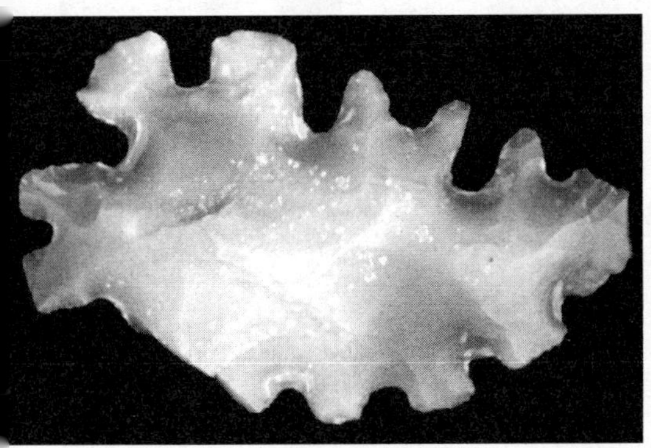

G7, $15-$25
Kimble Co., TX.

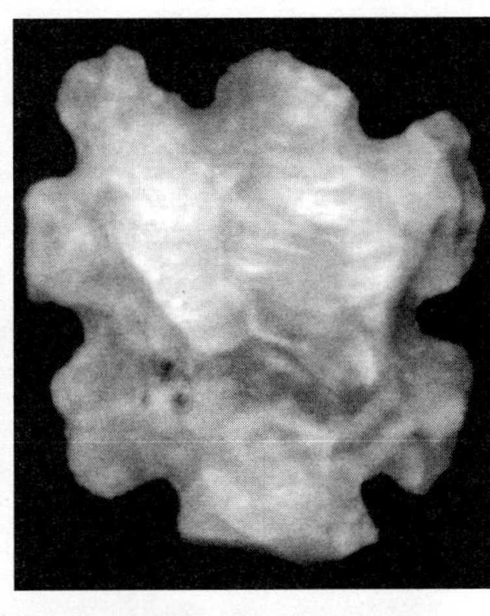

G7, $15-$30
Coleman Co., TX.

FAIRLAND - Woodland, 3000 - 1500 B. P.

(Also see Edgewood, Ellis, Marcos and Marshall)

G6, $10-$20
TX.

G7, $30-$60
Bell Co., TX. Classic.

G5, $30-$60
E. TX.

G6, $20-$40
Austin, TX.

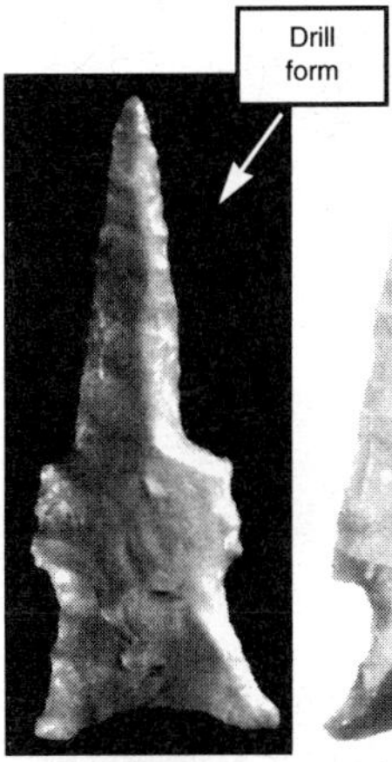

Drill form

G5, $10-$20
Austin, TX.

G6, $30-$60
Killeen, TX.

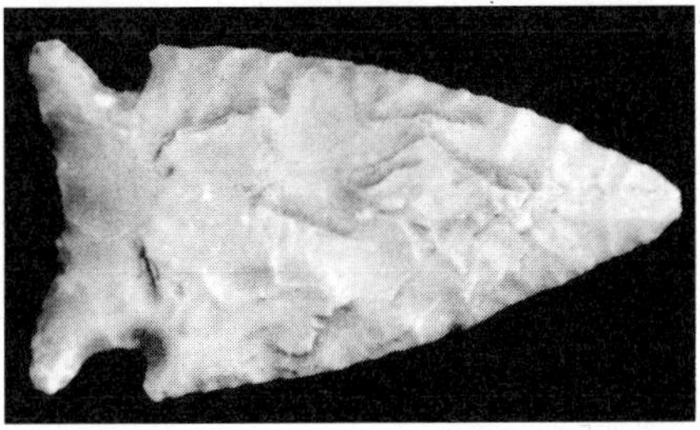

G7, $35-$70
Killeen, TX.

FAIRLAND (continued)

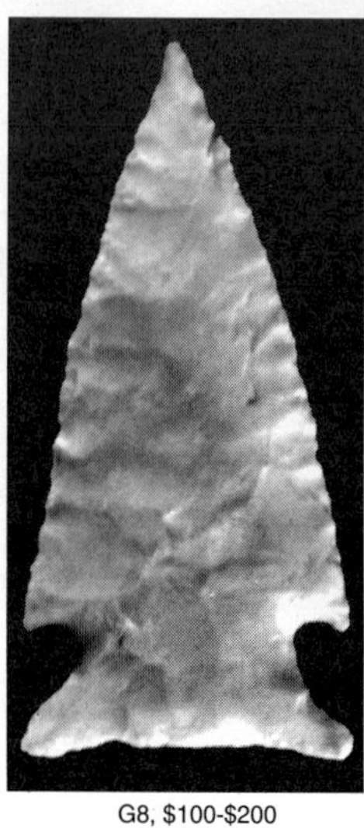

G8, $100-$200
Austin, TX.

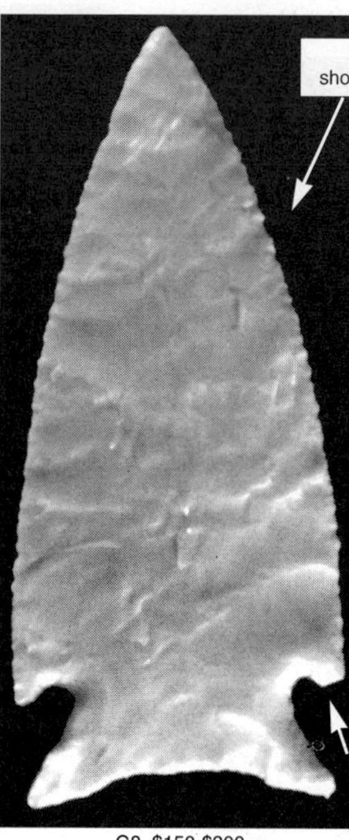
Minor
shoulder nick

G8, $150-$300
Austin, TX.

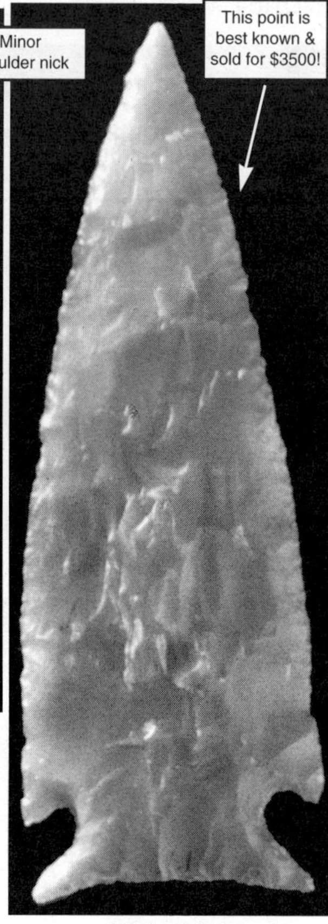
This point is
best known &
sold for $3500!

G10, $2000-$3500
Comanche Co., TX.

LOCATION: Texas, Arkansas to Oklahoma. **DESCRIPTION:** A small to medium size, thin, expanded stem point with a concave base that is usually thinned. Shoulders can be weak and tapered to slightly barbed. The base is broad. **I.D. KEY:** Basal form, systematic form of flaking.

FIGUEROA - Woodland, 3000 - 1500 B. P.

(Also see Big Sandy and Ensor)

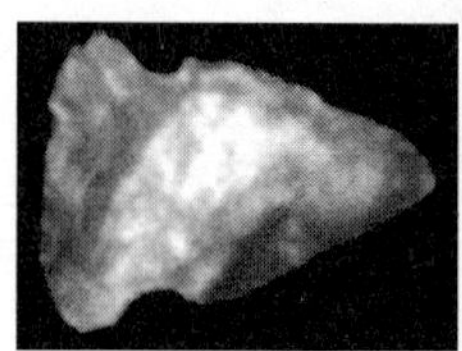

G4, $5-$10
Sou. TX.

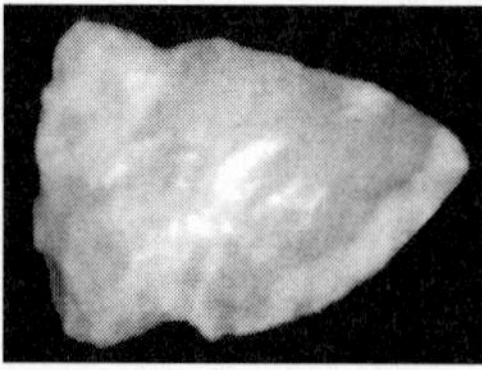

G5, $8-$15
Sou. TX..

LOCATION: Texas. **DESCRIPTION:** A small to medium size side notched to expanded base point with a convex base. Basal corners are the widest part of the point. **I.D. KEY:** Basal form, wide notches.

FIRSTVIEW - Late Paleo, 8700 - 7000 B. P.

(Also see Alberta, Dalton, Eden, Red River and Scottsbluff)

LOCATION: Texas to Colorado. **DESCRIPTION:** A medium to large size lanceolate blade with early paleo flaking and very weak shoulders. A variant of the Scottsbluff type made by the Cody Complex people. Bases are straight and stem sides are parallel. Many examples are median ridged with collateral, parallel flaking. **I.D. KEY:** Broad base, weak shoulders.

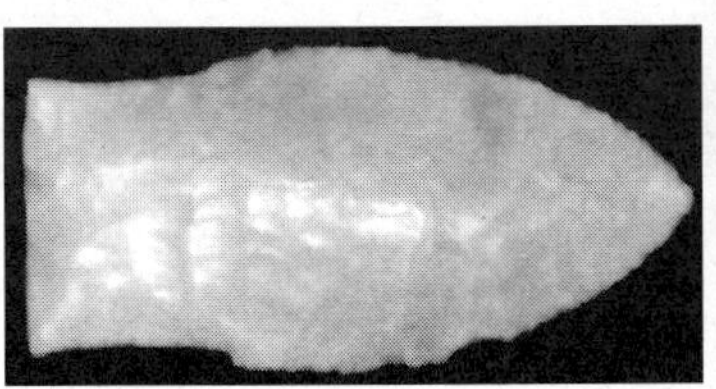

G8, $175-$350
Andrews Co., TX.

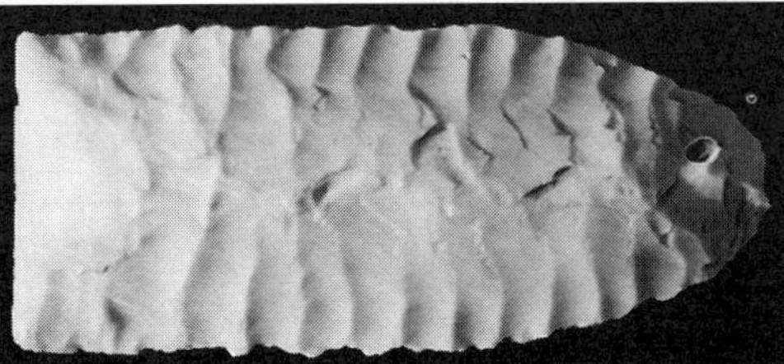

G8, $150-$300
Crosby Co., TX.

G8, $750-$1500
Gillespie Co., TX.

G8, $125-$250
Reeves Co., TX.

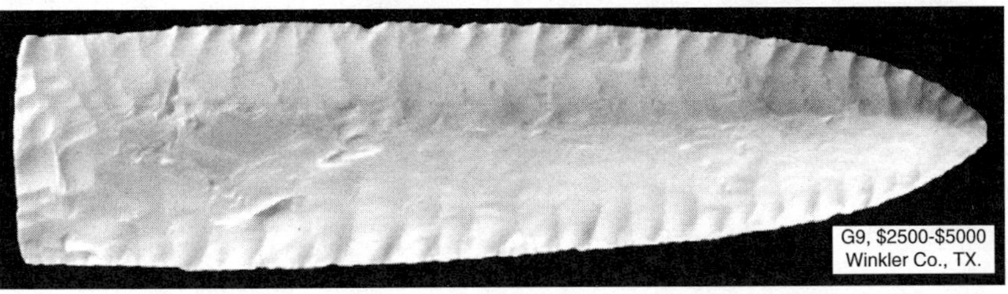

G9, $2500-$5000
Winkler Co., TX.

SC

FOLSOM - Late Paleo, 11,000 - 9000 B. P.

(Also see Arkabutla, Clovis, Golondrina, McKean, Midland and Plainview)

G3, $150-$300
TX.

G5, $200-$400
TX.

G1, $40-$75
Gaines Co., TX.

G7, $850-$1700
W. TX.

G7, $1000-$2000
TX.

G8, $900-$1800
Midland Co., TX.

G8, $1000-$2000
Llano Co., TX.

G8, $1200-$2400
TX.

FOLSOM (continued)

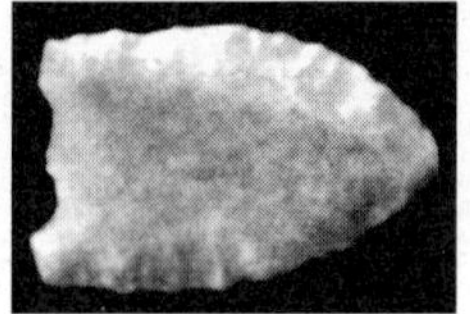

G6, $400-$800
W. TX.

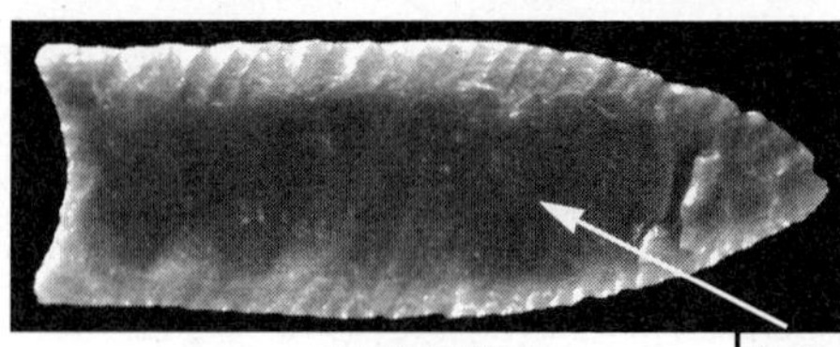

G9, $3000-$5000
Custer Co., OK. Tip nick.

Deep fluting

Rebased from a longer point

Cobble chert

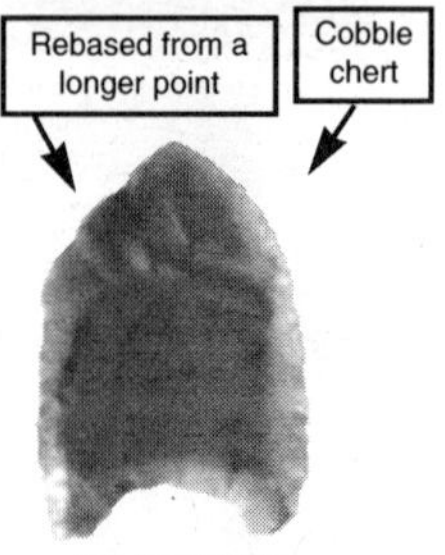

G6, $400-$800
Van Horn, TX.

LOCATION: Texas to Montana to Canada. **DESCRIPTION:** A small to medium size, very thin, high quality, fluted point with contracted, pointed auricles and a concave base. Fluting usually extends the entire length of each face. Blade flaking is extremely fine. The hafting area is ground. A very rare type, even in area of highest incidence. Modern reproductions have been made and extreme caution should be exercised in acquiring an original specimen. Usually found in association with extinct bison fossil remains. **I.D.KEY:** Flaking style (Excessive secondary flaking)

FRESNO - Mississippian, 1200 - 250 B. P.

(Also see Bassett, Friley, Huffaker, Maud and Talco)

G4, $3-$5
TX.

G4, $3-$5
TX.

G10, $60-$120
Nueces Co., TX.

G10, $85-$165
Nueces Co., TX.

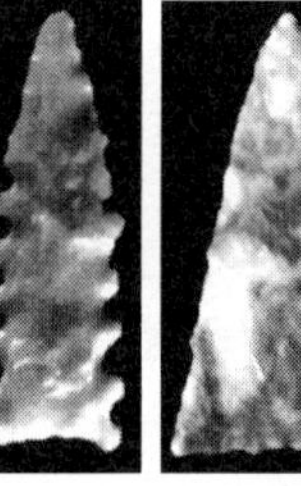

G4, $5-$10
Comanche
Co., TX.

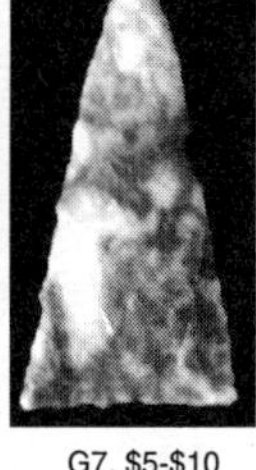

G7, $5-$10
W. OK.

G5, $5-$10
Comanche Co.,
TX.

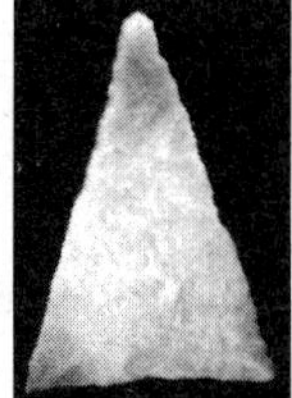

G7, $3-$6
Crane Co., TX.

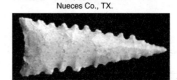

LOCATION: Texas, Arkansas, Oklahoma and New Mexico. **DESCRIPTION:** A small, thin, triangular point with convex to straight sides and a concave to straight base. Many examples are deeply serrated and some are side notched.

FRIDAY - Woodland, 4000 - 1500 B. P.

(Also see Covington, Gahagan, Pandora and Sabine)

G7, $150-$300
Coryell Co., TX.

IMPORTANT:
All Fridays
shown half size

FRIDAY (continued)

G7, $100-$200
Waco, TX.

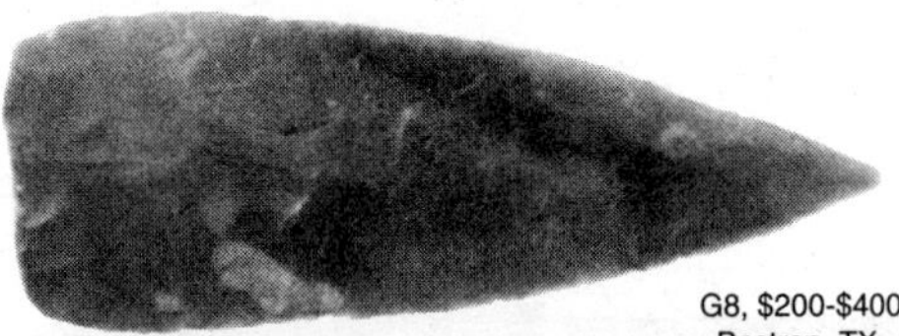

G8, $200-$400
Bastrop, TX.

IMPORTANT:
All Fridays
shown half size

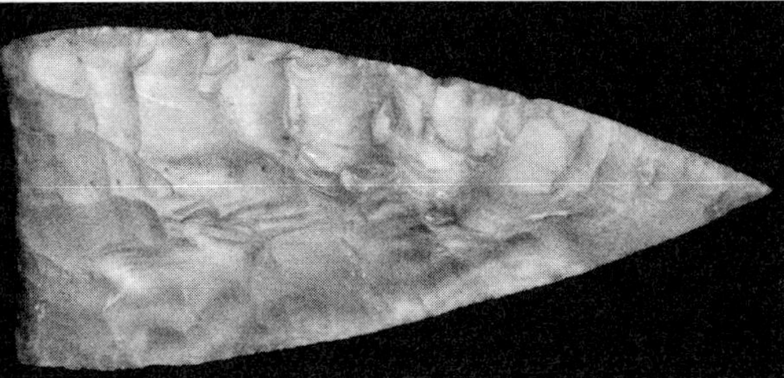

G10, $500-$1000
Kerr Co., TX.

G10, $500-$1000
Cent. TX.

G8, $125-$250
TX.

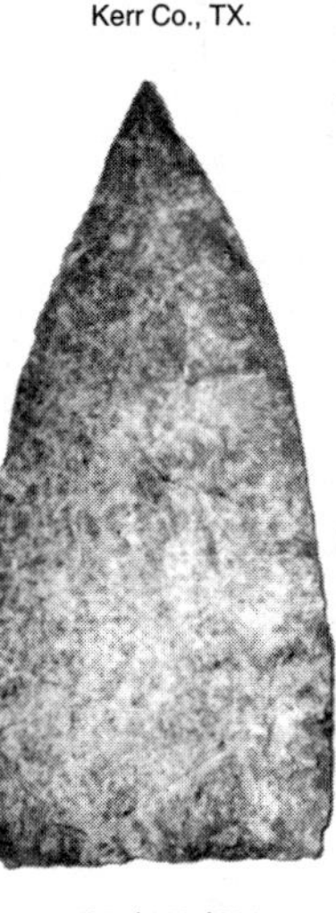

G6, $150-$300
Jonestown, TX.

G7, $225-$450
Bell Co., TX.

SC

LOCATION: Texas to Oklahoma. **DESCRIPTION:** A medium to large, thin, lanceolate blade with recurved sides, sharp corners and a straight base. Flaking quality is excellent.

FRILEY - Late Woodland, 1500 - 1000 B. P.

(Also see Edwards, Fresno, Morris and Steiner)

G3, $3-$5
TX.

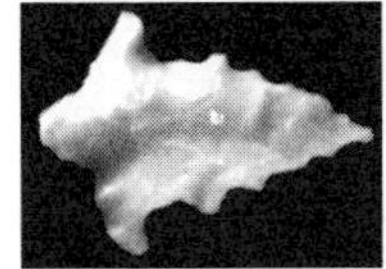

G5, $3-$6
Comanche
Co., TX.

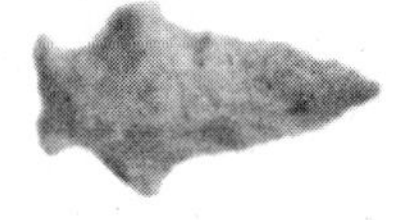

G6, $3-$5
TX.

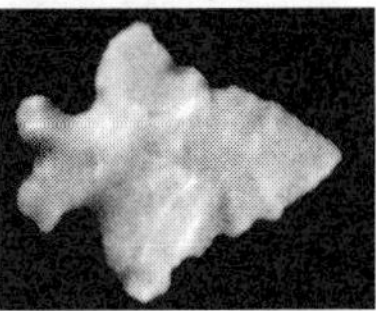

G7, $8-$15
AR.

FRILEY (continued)

LOCATION: East Texas, Arkansas to Louisiana. **DESCRIPTION:** A small size, thin, triangular point with exaggerated shoulders that flare outward and towards the tip. The base can be rounded to eared.

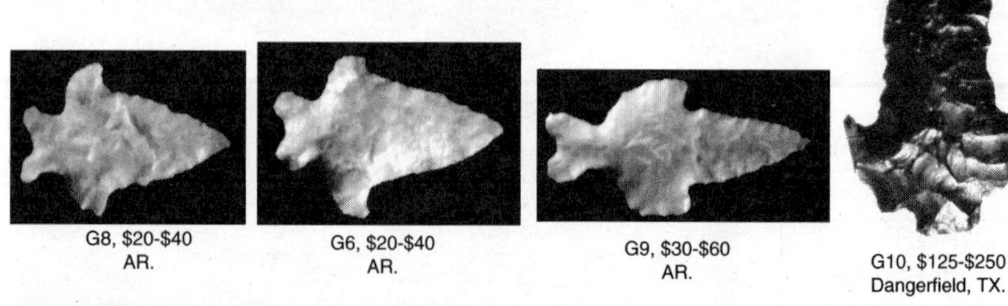

G8, $20-$40
AR.

G6, $20-$40
AR.

G9, $30-$60
AR.

G10, $125-$250
Dangerfield, TX.

FRIO - Middle Archaic to Woodland, 5000 - 1500 B. P.

(Also see Big Sandy, Ensor Split-Base, Fairland, Montell and Uvalde)

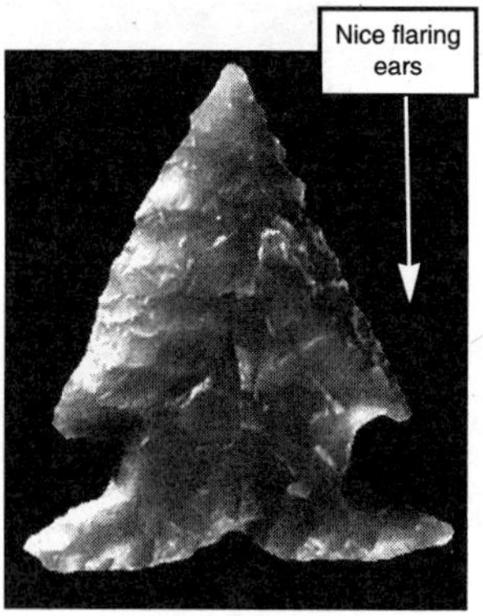

Nice flaring ears

G6, $35-$60
Comanche Co., TX.

G6, $15-$30
Bell Co., TX.

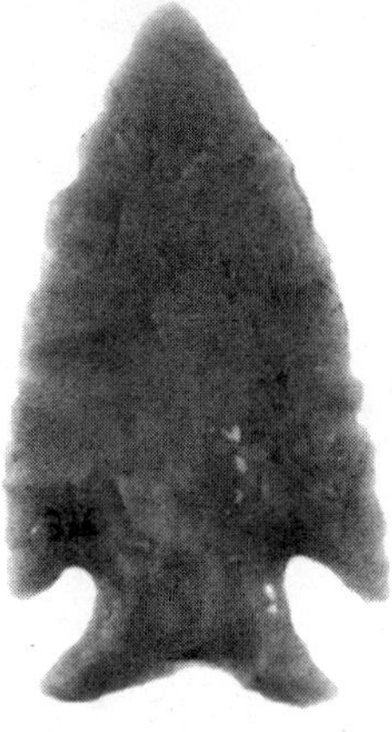

G8, $50-$100
TX.

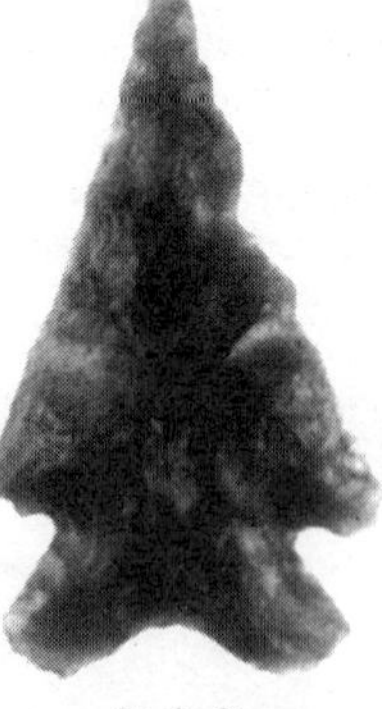

G6, $25-$40
Cent. TX.

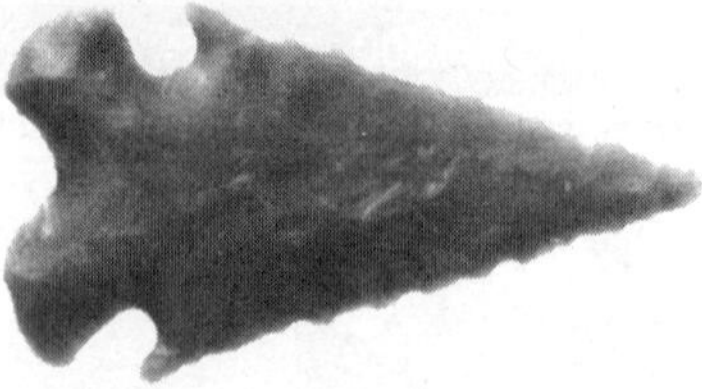

G7, $25-$50
TX.

G5, $4-$8
TX.

LOCATION: Texas to Oklahoma**. DESCRIPTION:** A small to medium size, side to corner-notched point with a concave to notched base that has squared to rounded ears that flare. Some examples can be confused with *Big Sandy Auriculate* forms. **I.D. KEY:** Flaring ears.

FRIO (continued)

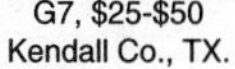
G7, $25-$50
Kendall Co., TX.

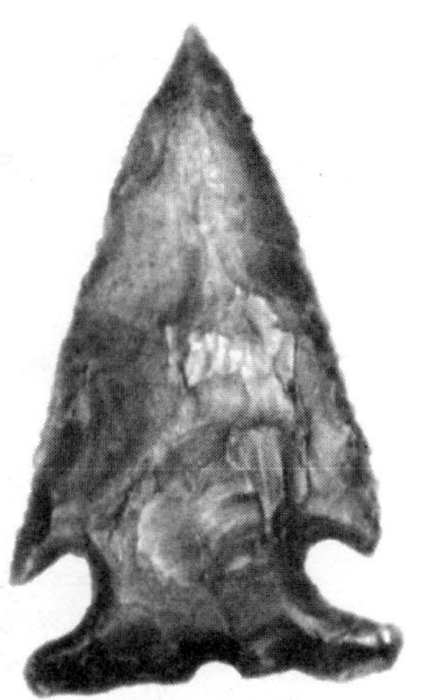

G8, $50-$100
Coryell Co., Tx.

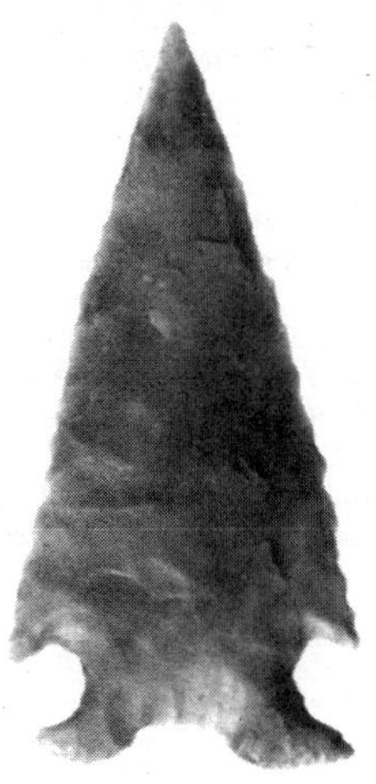

G10, $75-$150
TX.

GAHAGAN - Woodland, 4000 - 1500 B. P.

(Also see Covington, Darl Blade, Friday, Kinney, Mineral Springs, Sabine and San Gabriel)

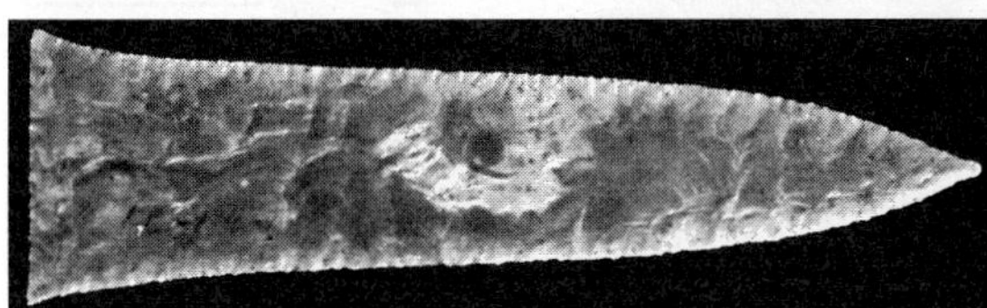

IMPORTANT:
Gahagan
shown half size

G10, $1400-$2500
Little River Co., AR.

LOCATION: Texas. **DESCRIPTION:** A large size, broad, thin, triangular blade with recurved sides and a straight base.

GARY - Late Archaic, 4000 - 1000 B. P.

(Also see Adena, Almagre, Hidden Valley, Langtry and Morrow Mountain)

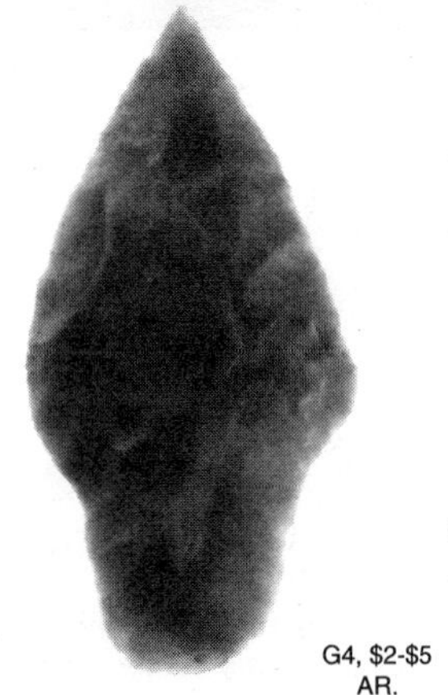

G4, $2-$5
AR.

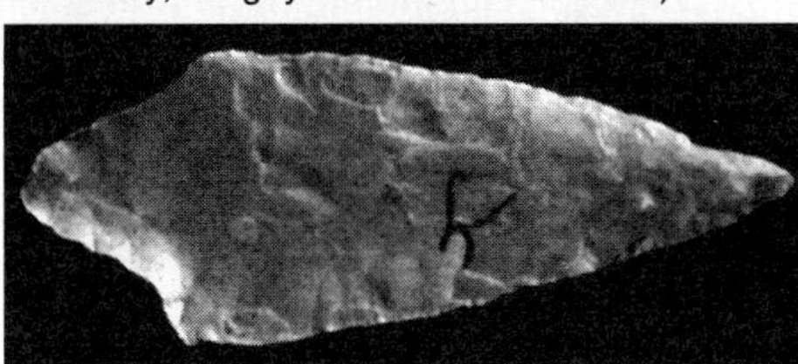

G4, $3-$6
AR.

G4, $3-$6
AR.

GARY (continued)

LOCATION: Mississippi to Oklahoma. **DESCRIPTION:** A medium size, triangular point with a medium to long, contracted, pointed to rounded base. Rarely, the base is straight. Shoulders are usually tapered. **I.D. KEY:** Similar to *Adena,* but thinned more. Another similar form, *Morrow Mountain* has earlier parallel flaking. **I.D. KEY:** Long contracted base.

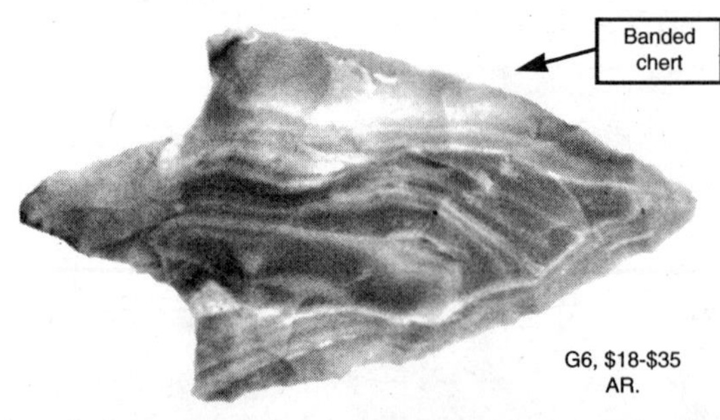

G6, $18-$35
AR.

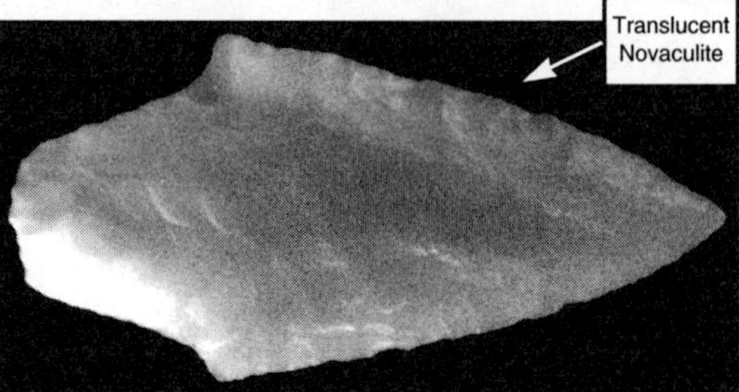

G7, $8-$15
AR.

G8, $90-$175
McIntosh Co., OK.

GARZA - Mississippian to Historic, 500 - 300 B. P.

(Also see Harrell, Lott, Starr and Toyah)

G10, $25-$50
TX.

Chalcedony

Tip nick

G4, $25-$50 TX. | G5, $25-$50 TX. | G9, $25-$50 TX. | G7, $30-$60 TX. | G7, $25-$50 TX. | G9, $25-$50 TX. | G9, $30-$60 TX.

LOCATION: Northern Mexico to Oklahoma. **DESCRIPTION:** A small size, thin, triangular point with concave to convex sides and base that has a single notch in the center. Many examples are serrated. See *Soto* in SW Section.

GIBSON - Mid to Late Woodland, 2000 - 1500 B. P.

(Also see Cupp, Dovetail, Epps and Motley)

LOCATION: Midwestern to Eastern states. **DESCRIPTION:** A medium to large size side to corner notched point with a large, convex base.

G4, $15-$25
Comanche Co., TX.

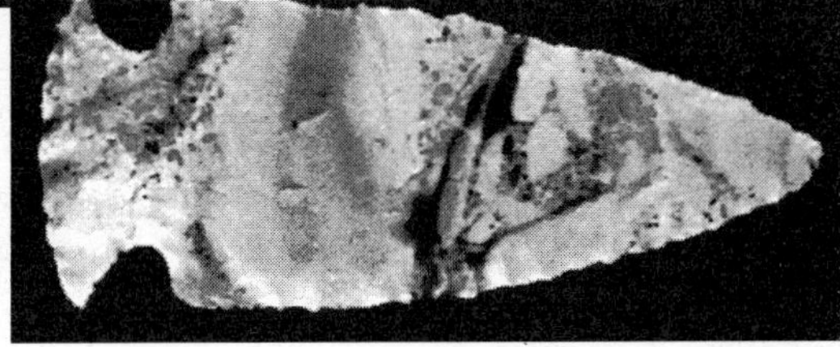

G7, $25-$45
AR.

GODAR - Late Archaic, 4500 - 3500 B. P.

(Also see Big Sandy, Hemphill, Raddatz and Savage Cave)

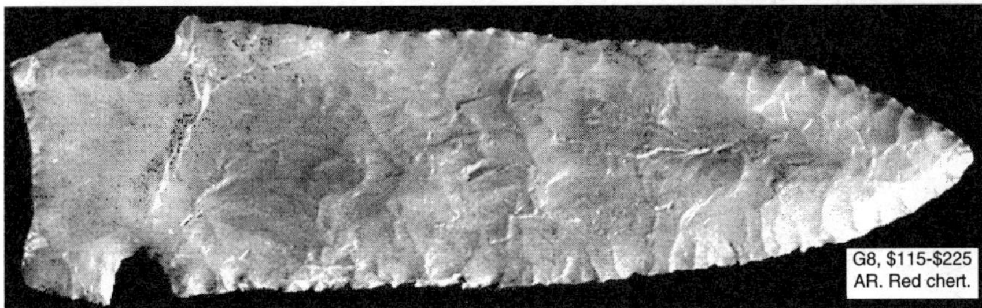

G8, $115-$225
AR. Red chert.

LOCATION: Arkansas to Illinois. **DESCRIPTION:** A medium to large size, narrow to wide, side-notched point with a straight to rounded base. Some examples show parallel flaking.

SC

GODLEY - Woodland, 2500 - 1500 B. P.

(Also see Ellis and Palmillas)

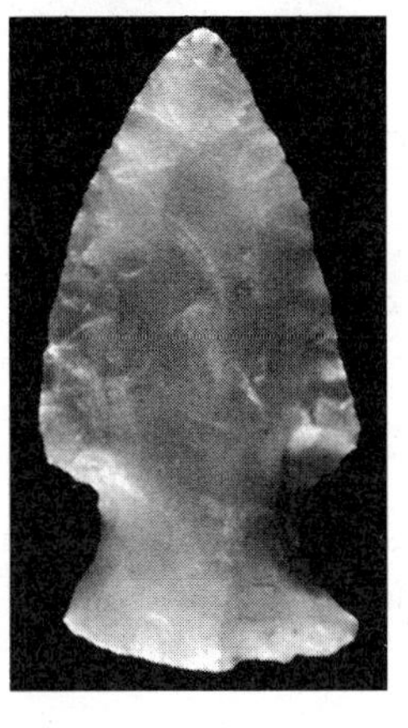

G6, $15-$30
Waco, TX.

G6, $10-$20
AR.

G4, $5-$10
Comanche Co., TX.

GODLEY (continued)

LOCATION: Texas. **DESCRIPTION:** A small to medium size point with broad, expanding side-notches, tapered shoulders and a convex base. Basal area can be ground. Many specimens show unique beveling at the stem, usually from the same side.

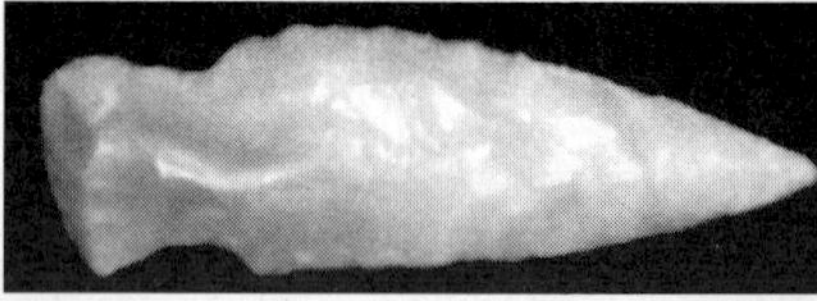

G5, $10-$20
Williamson Co., TX.

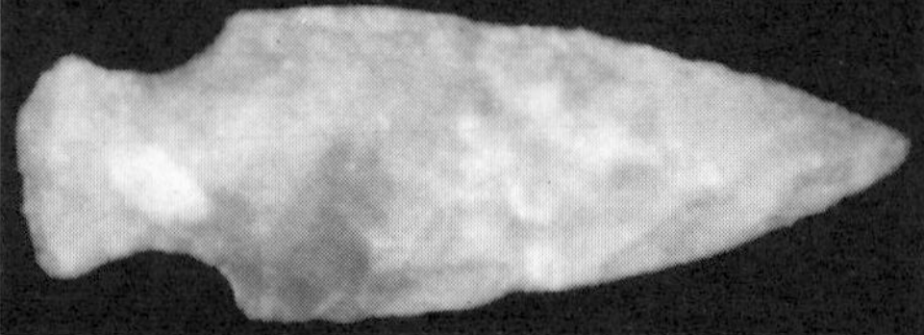

G6, $15-$30
Williamson Co., TX.

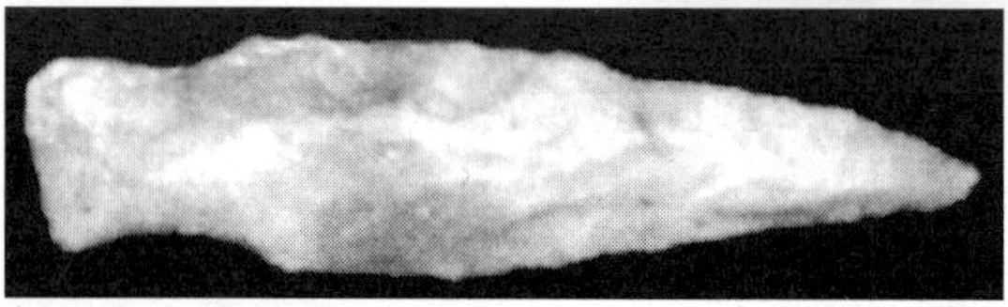

G6, $15-$30
Williamson Co., TX.

GOLONDRINA - Transitional Paleo, 9000 - 7000 B. P.

(Also see Angostura, Arkabutla, Dalton, Midland, Pelican, Plainview & San Patrice)

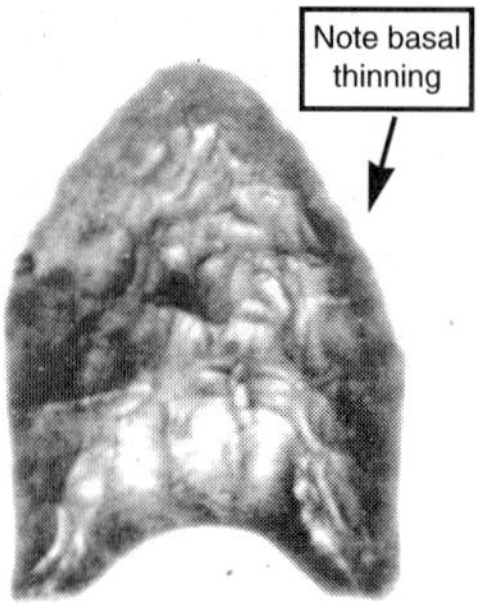

Note basal thinning

G5, $50-$100
Medina Co., TX.

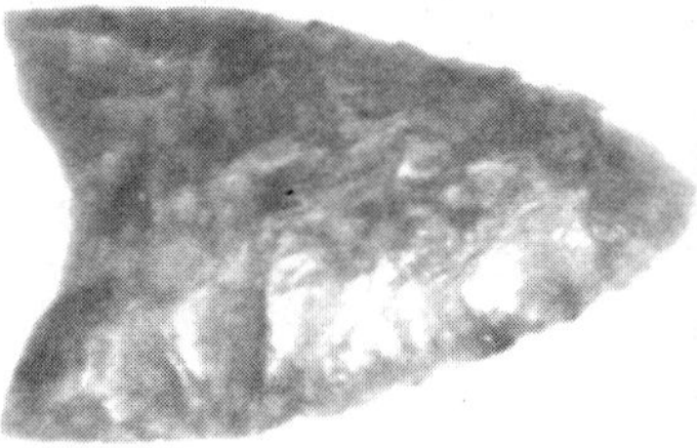

G5, $75-$150
Medina Co., TX.

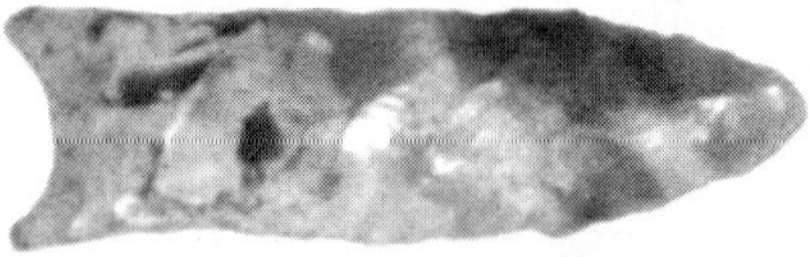

G5, $50-$100
Brady, TX.

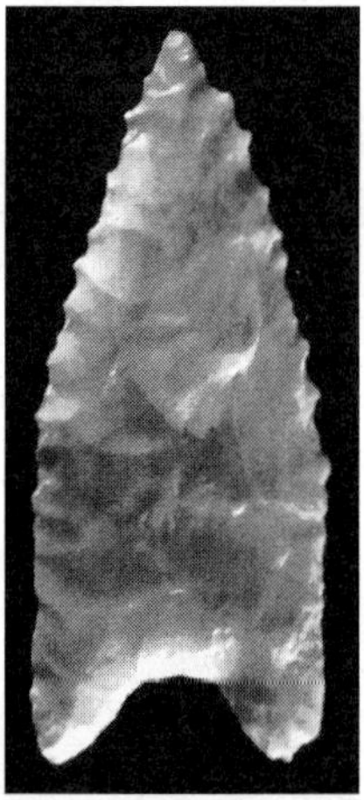

G6, $65-$125
Craighead, AR.

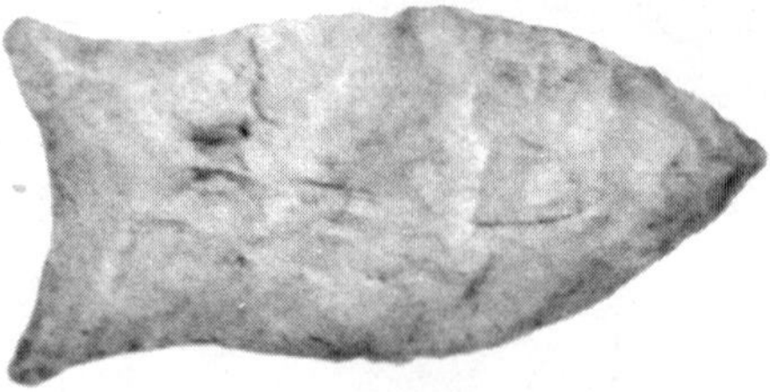

G6, $100-$200
Bowie Co., TX.

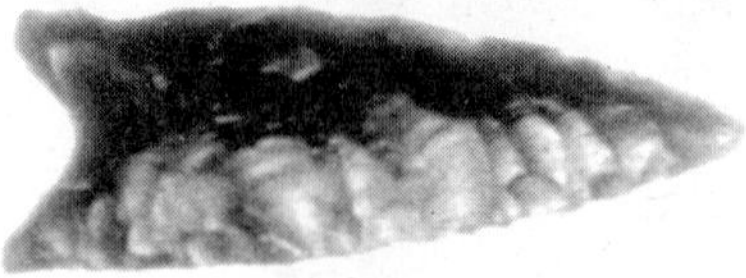

G6, $40-$80
Williamson Co., TX.

LOCATION: Texas, Arkansas to Oklahoma. **DESCRIPTION:** A medium to large size auriculate unfluted point with rounded ears that flare and a deeply concave base. Basal areas are ground. Believed to be related to Dalton. **I.D. Key:** Expanded ears, paleo flaking.

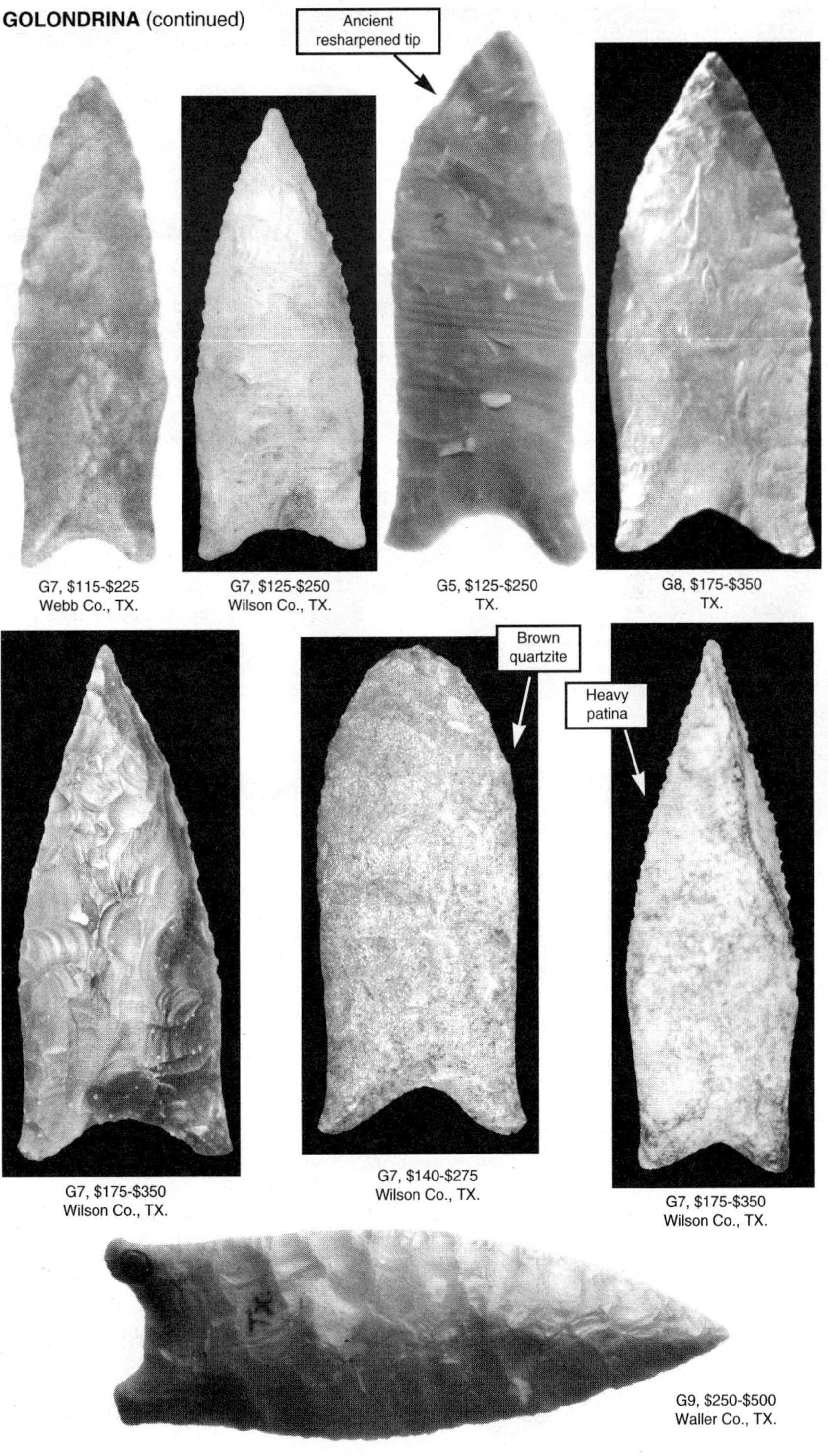

G7, $115-$225
Webb Co., TX.

G7, $125-$250
Wilson Co., TX.

G5, $125-$250
TX.

G8, $175-$350
TX.

G7, $175-$350
Wilson Co., TX.

G7, $140-$275
Wilson Co., TX.

G7, $175-$350
Wilson Co., TX.

G9, $250-$500
Waller Co., TX.

SC

GOWER - Early Archaic, 8000 - 5000 B. P.

(Also see Jetta, Pedernales and Uvalde)

G2, $5-$10
Comanche Co., TX.

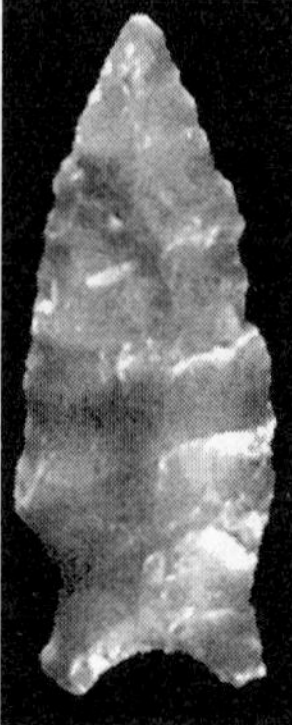

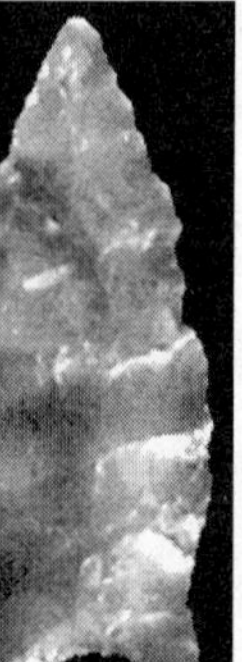

G5, $10-$20
Comanche Co., TX.

G6, $10-$20
Comanche
Co., TX.

G6, $15-$30
Comanche Co., TX.

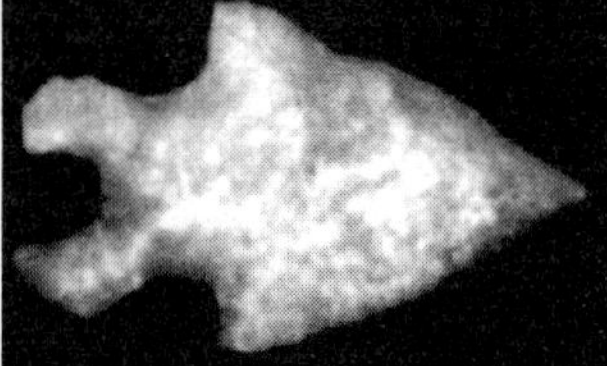

G7, $15-$25
Cent. TX.

G6, $10-$20
Comanche Co., TX.

LOCATION: Texas. **DESCRIPTION:** A medium size, narrow point with weak shoul-drs and a long, deeply bifurcated stem. One or both basal ears turn inward on some examples or flare outward on others. **I. D. Key:** Narrowness, base form.

GOSEN - Paleo, 11,500 - 10,000 B. P.

(Also see Clovis, Midland, Milnesand)

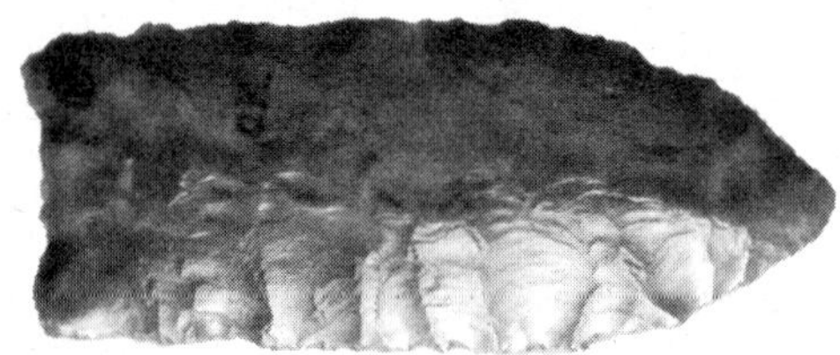

G8, $200-$400
Osage Co., OK.

LOCATION: Oklahoma to Montana. **DESCRIPTION:** A small to medium size, very thin, auriculate point with a concave base. Basal corners slope inward and are rounded. Flaking is oblique to horizontal transverse. A rare type. **I.D. KEY:** Thinness, auricles.

GRAHAM CAVE - Early to Middle Archaic, 9000 - 5000 B. P.

(Also see Big Sandy, Godar and Raddatz)

LOCATION: Midwestern states. **DESCRIPTION:** A medium to large size, narrow, side-notched point with recurved to excurvate sides, pointed basal ears, and a concave base. Some examples are serrated. Bases are ground. **I.D. KEY:** Drooping basal ears.

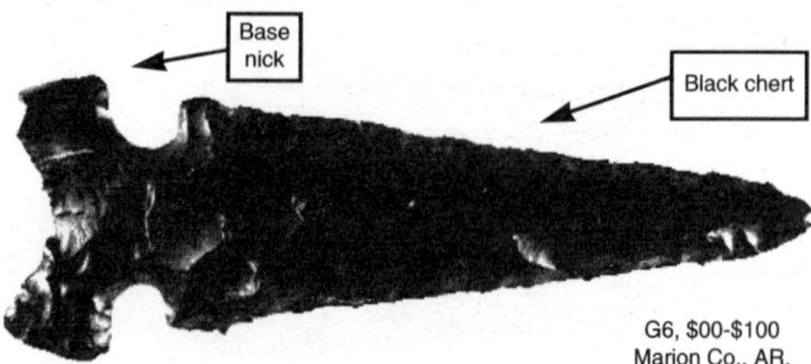

G6, $00-$100
Marion Co., AR.

GRAVER - Paleo to Archaic, 14,000 - 4000 B. P.

(Also see Drill, Perforator and Scraper)

LOCATION: Early man sites everywhere. **DESCRIPTION:** An irregular shaped uniface tool with sharp, pointed projections used for puncturing, incising, tattooing, etc. Some examples served a dual purpose for scraping as well. In later times, *Perforators* took the place of *Gravers.*

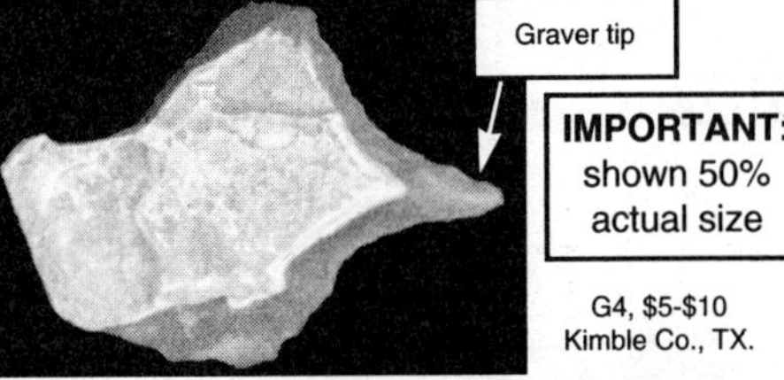

IMPORTANT: shown 50% actual size

G4, $5-$10
Kimble Co., TX.

GUERRERO - Historic, 300 - 100 B. P.

(Also see Guntersville and Maud)

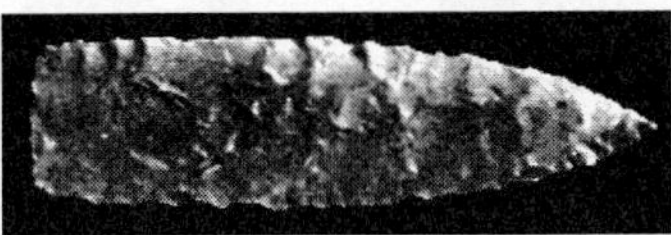

G7, $15-$25
Comanche Co., TX.

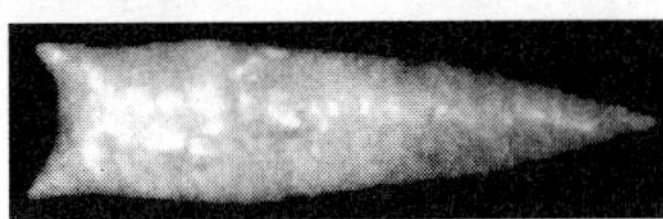

G9, $30-$60
Coke Co., TX.

LOCATION: Texas. **DESCRIPTION:** A small to medium size, narrow, thin, lanceolate point with a straight base. Similar to the Eastern *Guntersville* point. The last stone arrowhead in Texas. Also called "Mission point."

HALE (Bascom) - Late Archaic, 4000 - 3500 B. P.

(Also see Peisker Diamond)

SC

G7, $20-$40
AR.

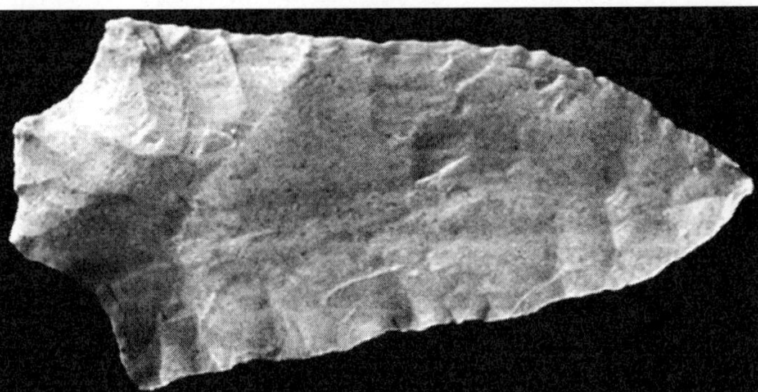

LOCATION: Arkansas into Mississippi. **Description:** A large size, broad point with shoulders tapering to the base which is straight to rounded. Similar to the *Bascom* form found in Alabama and Georgia.

HARAHEY - Mississippian, 700 - 400 B. P.

(Also see Angostura and Lerma)

G6, $100-$200, Cent. TX.

IMPORTANT: All Haraheys shown 50% actual size

G6, $75-$125
Tulsa, OK.

HARAHEY (continued)

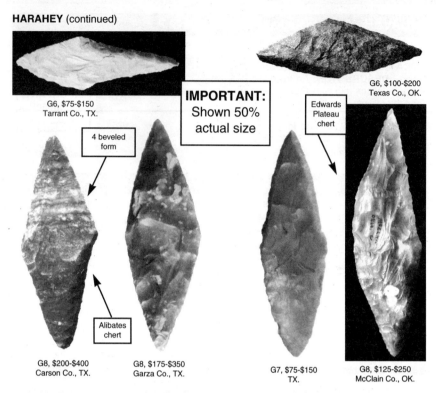

G6, $75-$150
Tarrant Co., TX.

G6, $100-$200
Texas Co., OK.

IMPORTANT:
Shown 50%
actual size

4 beveled form

Alibates chert

Edwards Plateau chert

G8, $200-$400
Carson Co., TX.

G8, $175-$350
Garza Co., TX.

G7, $75-$150
TX.

G8, $125-$250
McClain Co., OK.

LOCATION: Texas to Colorado. **DESCRIPTION:** A large size, double pointed knife that is usually beveled on one or all four sides of each face. The cross section is rhomboid. The true buffalo skinning knife. Found associated with small arrow points in Texas. **I.D. KEY:** Two and four beveled double pointed form.

HARDIN - Early Archaic, 9000 - 6000 B. P.

(Also see Alberta, Dovetail, Kirk and Scottsbluff)

G8, $65-$125
AR.

G9, $400-$800
Angelina Co., TX.

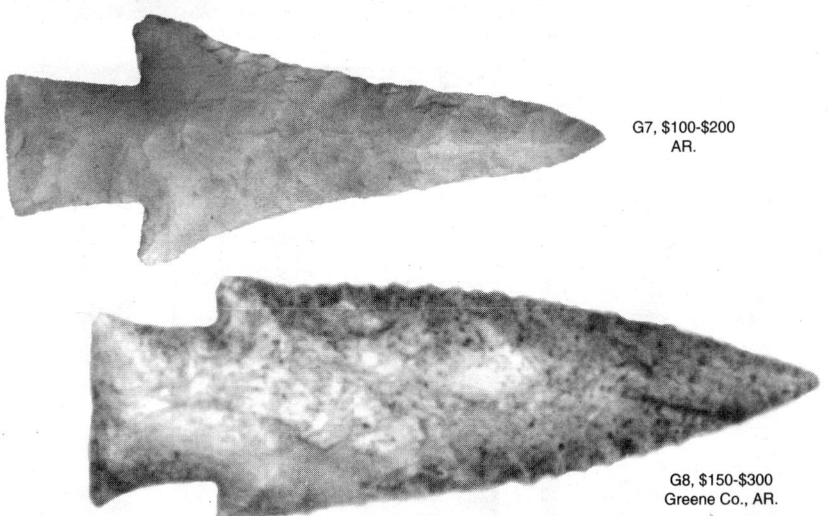

G7, $100-$200
AR.

G8, $150-$300
Greene Co., AR.

LOCATION: Midwestern to Eastern states. **DESCRIPTION:** A large size, well made triangular barbed point with an expanded base that is usually ground. Resharpened examples have one beveled edge on each face. *Hardin* points are believed to have evolved from the *Scottsbluff* type. **I.D. Key:** Notches and stem form.

HARE BIFACE - Late Archaic to Woodland, 3000 - 2000 B. P.

(Also see Covington, Friday, Pandora and San Gabriel)

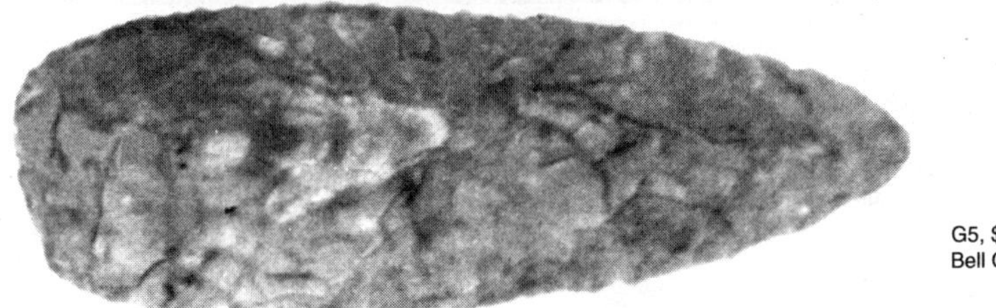

G5, $25-$50
Bell Co., TX.

LOCATION: Texas. **DESCRIPTION:** A medium to large size knife with excurvate sides and a rounded base.

HARRELL - Mississippian to Historic, 900 - 500 B. P.

(Also see Toyah and Washita)

G6, $20-$40
Crand Co., TX.

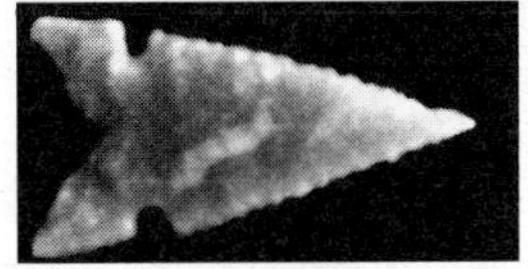

G9, $35-$70
Crane Co., TX.

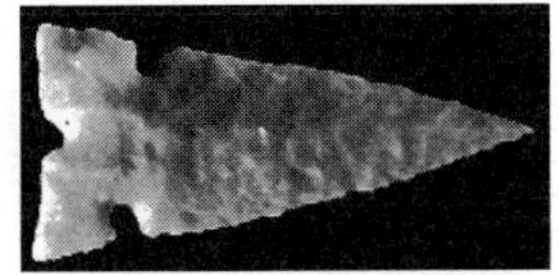

G9, $40-$80
Taylor Co., TX.

LOCATION: Texas to Oklahoma. **DESCRIPTION:** A small size, thin, triangular arrow point with side and basal notches.

HASKELL - Mississippian to Historic, 800 - 600 B. P.

(Also see Edwards, Huffaker, Reed and Toyah)

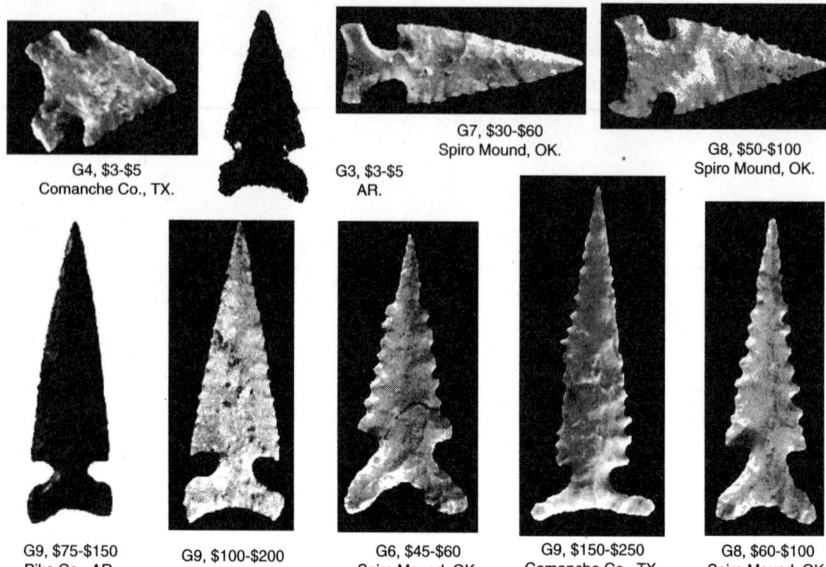

G4, $3-$5
Comanche Co., TX.

G3, $3-$5
AR.

G7, $30-$60
Spiro Mound, OK.

G8, $50-$100
Spiro Mound, OK.

G9, $75-$150
Pike Co., AR.

G9, $100-$200
Spiro Mound, OK.

G6, $45-$60
Spiro Mound, OK.

G9, $150-$250
Comanche Co., TX.

G8, $60-$100
Spiro Mound, OK.

LOCATION: Oklahoma to Arkansas. **DESCRIPTION:** A small size, thin, narrow, triangular, side notched point with a concave base. Rarely, basal tangs are notched.

HAYES - Mississippian, 1200 - 600 B. P.

(Also see Alba, Blevins, Homan, Howard, Perdiz and Sequoyah)

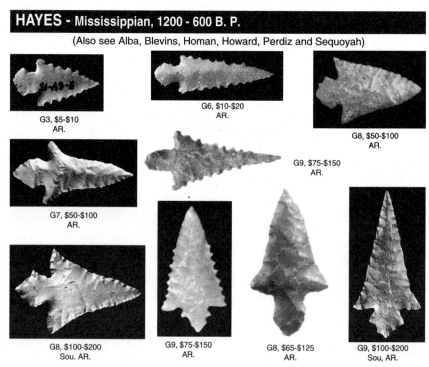

G3, $5-$10
AR.

G6, $10-$20
AR.

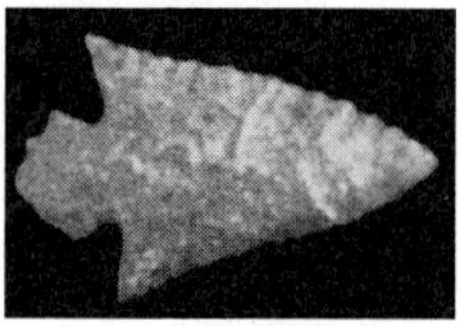

G8, $50-$100
AR.

G7, $50-$100
AR.

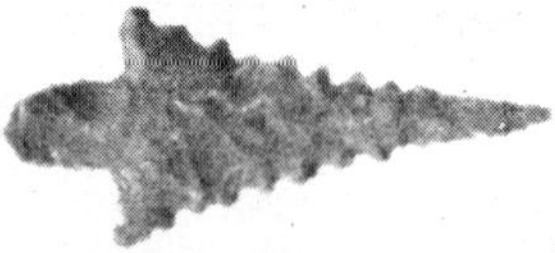

G9, $75-$150
AR.

G8, $100-$200
Sou. AR.

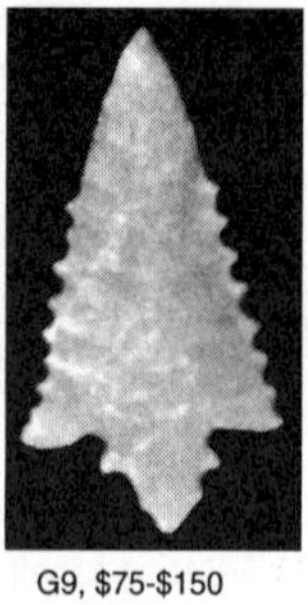

G9, $75-$150
AR.

G8, $65-$125
AR.

G9, $100-$200
Sou, AR.

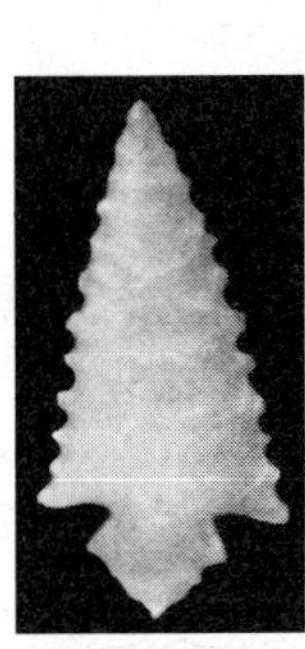

G8, $75-$150
AR.

G7, $40-$80
AR.

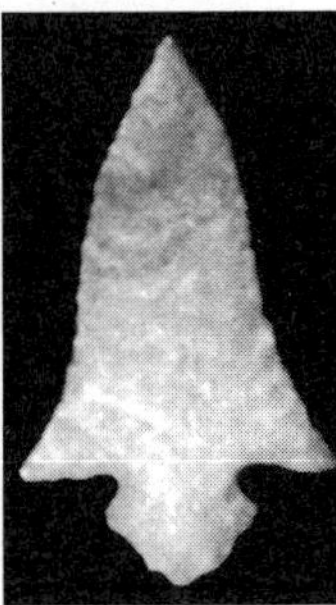

G9, $100-$200
AR.

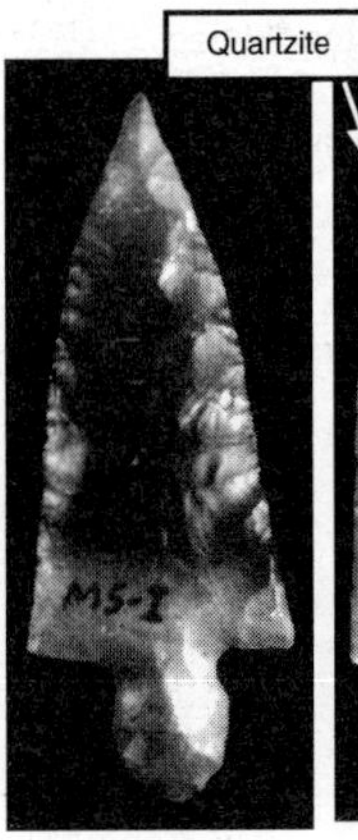

G9, $150-$300
Howard Co., AR.

G9, $125-$250
Howard Co., AR.

LOCATION: Louisiana to Oklahoma. **DESCRIPTION:** A small to medium size, narrow, expanded tang arrow point with a turkeytail base. Blade edges are usually strongly recurved forming sharp pointed tangs. Base is pointed and can be double notched. Some examples are serrated. Has been found in caches. **I.D. KEY:** Diamond shaped base and flaking style.

HELL GAP - Late Paleo, 10,900 - 9000 B. P.

(Also see Agate Basin, Angostura, Midland, Pelican and Rio Grande)

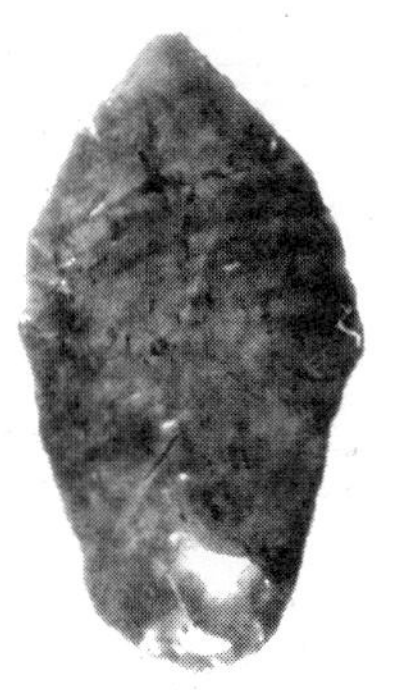

G5, $20-$40
TX.

G5, $30-$60
Midland Co., TX.

G6, $30-$60
Schlleicher Co., TX.

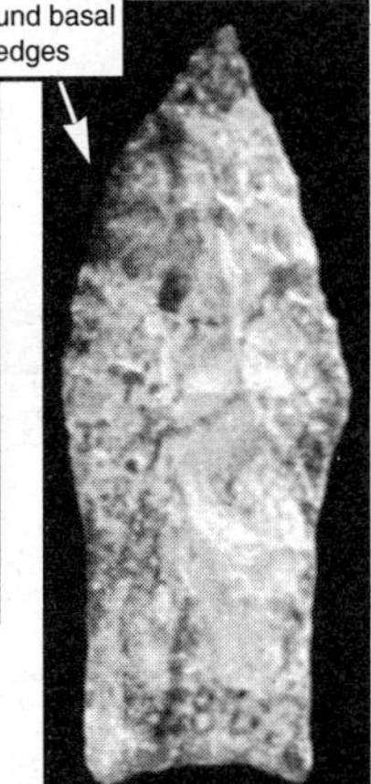

G7, $100-$200
TX.

G7, $150-$250
Tom Greene Co.,
TX.

LOCATION: Texas northward to Canada. **DESCRIPTION:** A medium to large size, lanceolate point with a long, contracting stem. The widest part of the blade is above mid-section. The base is straight to slightly concave and the stem edges are usually ground. **I.D. KEY:** Early flaking and base form.

HELL GAP (continued)

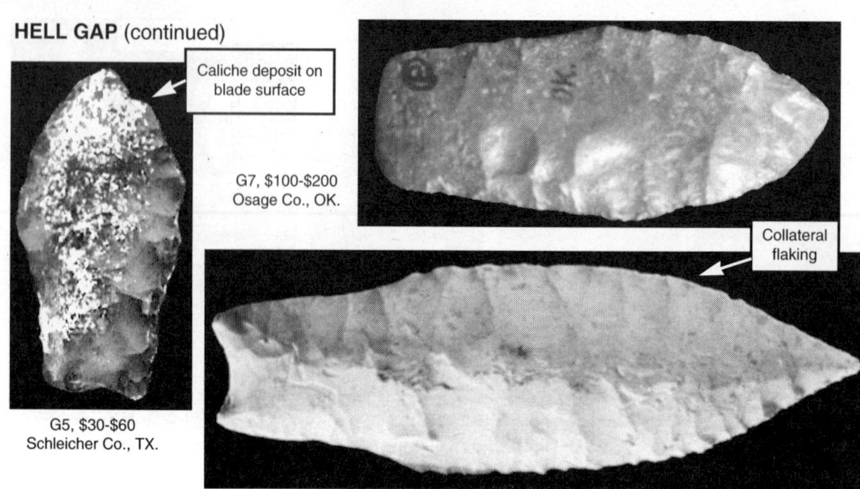

G5, $30-$60
Schleicher Co., TX.

G7, $100-$200
Osage Co., OK.

G10, $250-$500
TX.

HEMPHILL - Middle Archaic, 7000 - 4000 B. P.

(Also see Big Sandy, Dalton-Hemphill, Godar, Graham Cave, Hickory Ridge and Raddatz)

LOCATION: Midwestern to Northeastern states. **DESCRIPTION:** A medium to large size side-notched point with a concave base and parallel to convex sides. These points are usually thinner and of higher quality than the similar *Osceola* type.

G4, $15-$30
Jonesboro, AR.

HICKORY RIDGE - Middle Archaic, 7000 - 4000 B. P.

(Also see Big Sandy, Cache River, Godar, Hemphill, Osceola and Raddatz)

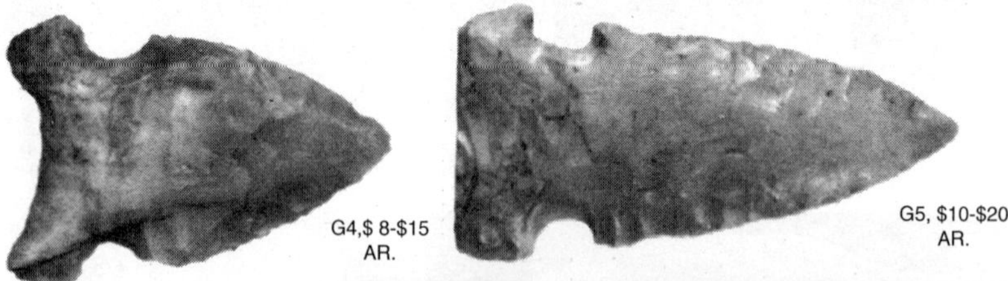

G4,$ 8-$15
AR.

G5, $10-$20
AR.

LOCATION: Arkansas. **DESCRIPTION:** A medium to large size side-notched point. The base is straight to concave and early forms are ground. Basal corners are rounded to square. Side notches are usually wide. **I.D. KEY:** Broad, large side notched point.

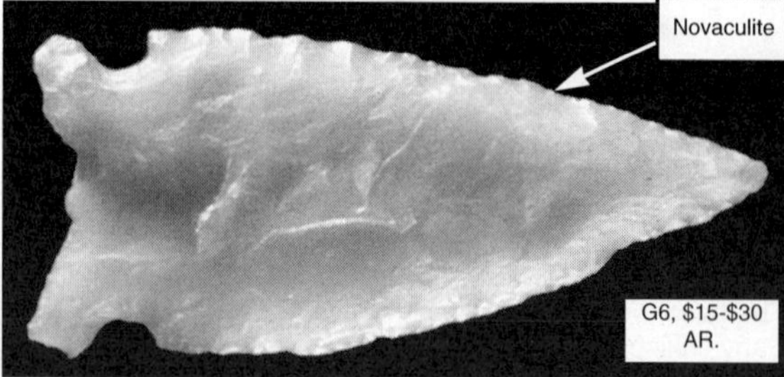

G6, $15-$30
AR.

HIDDEN VALLEY - Early to Middle Archaic, 8000 - 6000 B. P.

(also see Adena Dickson, Gary, Langtry and Morrow Mountain)

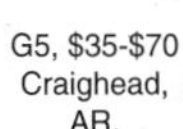

G5, $35-$70
Craighead,
AR.

G7, $25-$50
Craighead, AR.

LOCATION: Arkansas to Wisconsin. **DESCRIPTION:** A medium size point with square to tapered shoulders and a contracting base that can be pointed to straight. Flaking is earlier and more parallel than on *Gary* points. Called *Rice Contrracted Stemmed* in Missouri.

HOLLAND - Early Archaic, 9500 - 7500 B. P.

(also see Alberta, Dalton, Eden, Hardin and Scottsbluff)

G7, $100-$200
AR.

G7, $75-$150
AR.

G9, $300-$600
AR.

LOCATION: Midwestern to Northeastern states. **DESCRIPTION:** A medium to large size broad stemmed point of high quality. Shoulders are weak to nonexistant. Bases can be knobbed to auriculate and are usually ground. Some examples have horizontal to oblique transverse flaking. **I.D. KEY:** Weak shoulders, concave base.

HOMAN - Mississippian, 1000 - 700 B. P.

(Also see Agee, Alba, Hayes, Keota, Perdiz and Scallorn)

HOMAN (continued)

G6, $5-$10
TX.

G5, $5-$10
S.E. OK.

G6, $8-$15
S.E. OK.

G4, $5-$10
Lincoln Parrish, LA.

G6, $10-$20
TX.

G7, $15-$30
Lincoln Parrish, LA.

G4, $3-$5
TX.

LOCATION: Oklahoma to Arkansas. **DESCRIPTION:** A small size expanded barbed arrow point with a bulbous stem. Some tips are mucronate or apiculate. **I.D. KEY:** Bulbous stem.

HOWARD - Mississippian, 700 - 500 B. P.

(Also see Blevins, Hayes and Sequoyah)

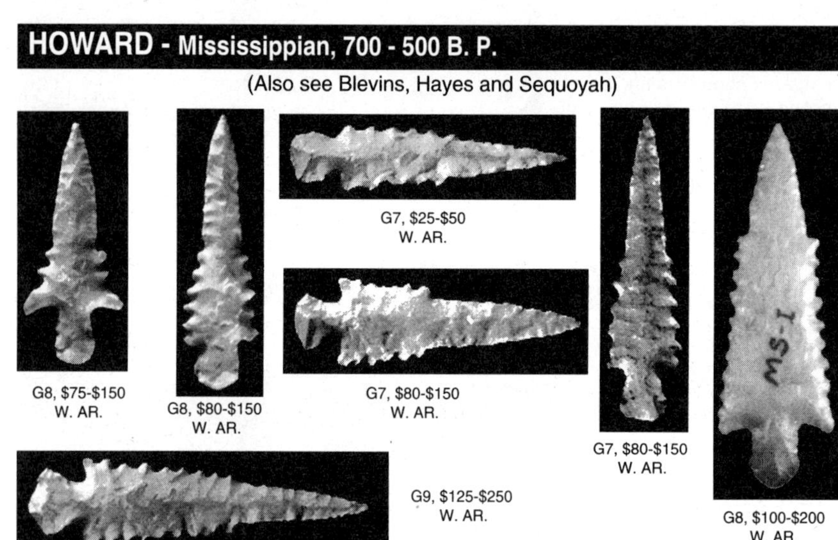

G7, $25-$50
W. AR.

G8, $75-$150
W. AR.

G8, $80-$150
W. AR.

G7, $80-$150
W. AR.

G7, $80-$150
W. AR.

G9, $125-$250
W. AR.

G8, $100-$200
W. AR.

LOCATION: Louisiana to Oklahoma. **DESCRIPTION:** A small size, narrow, spike point with two or more barbs on each side, restricted to the lower part of the point and a parallel to expanding, rounded stem. A Diamond shaped base places the point in the *Blevins* type. **I.D. KEY:** Multiple serrations near the base.

HOXIE - Early Archaic, 8000 - 5000 B. P.

(also see Bulverde, Darl, Brazos, Early Stemmed Lanceolate, Gower and Zephyr)

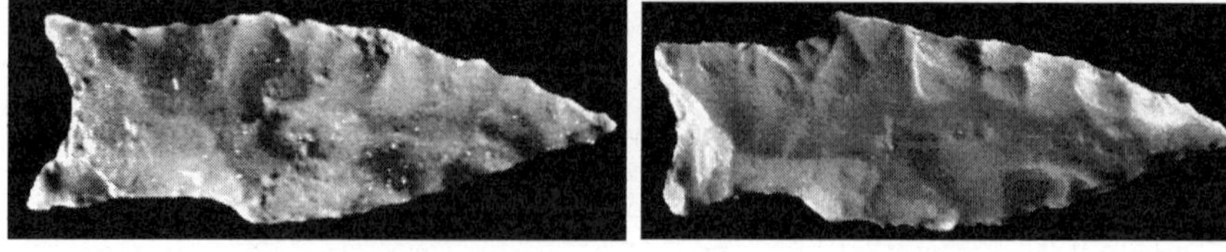

G7, $10-$20
Comanche Co., TX.

G4, $4-$8
Comanche Co., TX.

LOCATION: Texas. **DESCRIPTION:** A medium to large size, narrow point with weak shoulders and a parallel sided, concave base that is ground. Believed to be an early form of *Darl.*

HOXIE (continued)

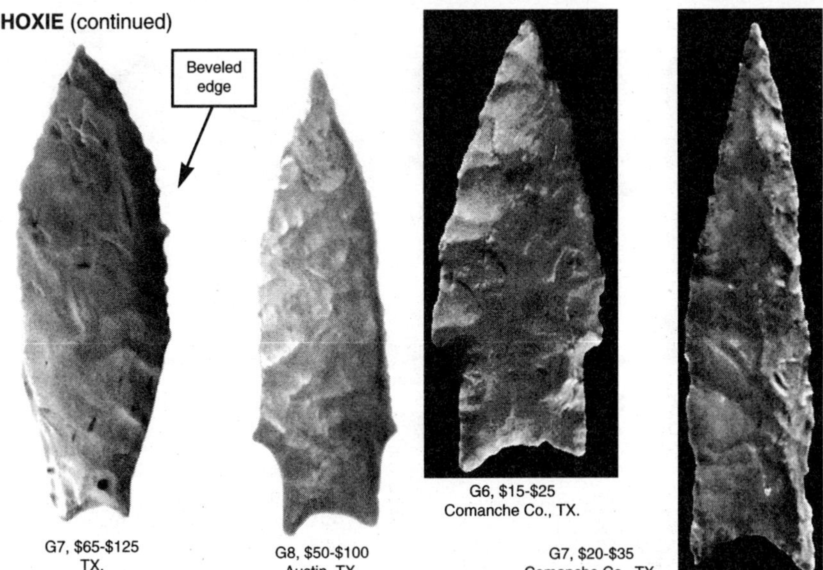

G7, $65-$125
TX.

G8, $50-$100
Austin, TX.

G6, $15-$25
Comanche Co., TX.

G7, $20-$35
Comanche Co., TX.

HUFFAKER - Mississippian, 1000 - 500 B. P.

(Also see Duran, Evans, Fresno, Harrell, Haskell, Sinner and Washita)

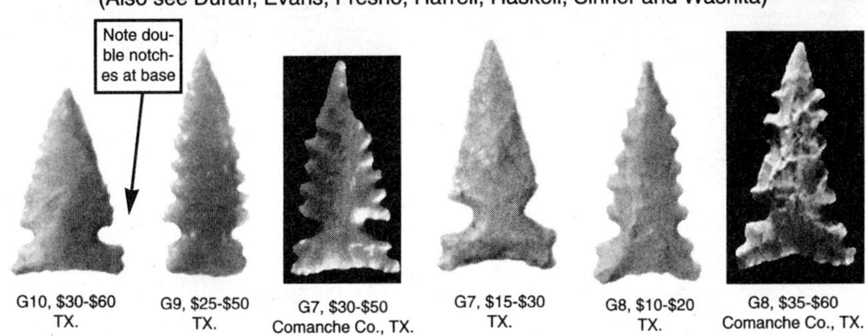

G10, $30-$60
TX.

G9, $25-$50
TX.

G7, $30-$50
Comanche Co., TX.

G7, $15-$30
TX.

G8, $10-$20
TX.

G8, $35-$60
Comanche Co., TX.

SC

LOCATION: Texas northward to Canada**. DESCRIPTION:** A small size triangular point with a straight to concave base and double side notches. Blade edges can be heavily barbed. Bases can have a single notch. **I.D. KEY:** Double notches.

JETTA - Early Archaic, 8000 - 5000 B. P.

(Also see Gower, Pedernales and Uvalde)

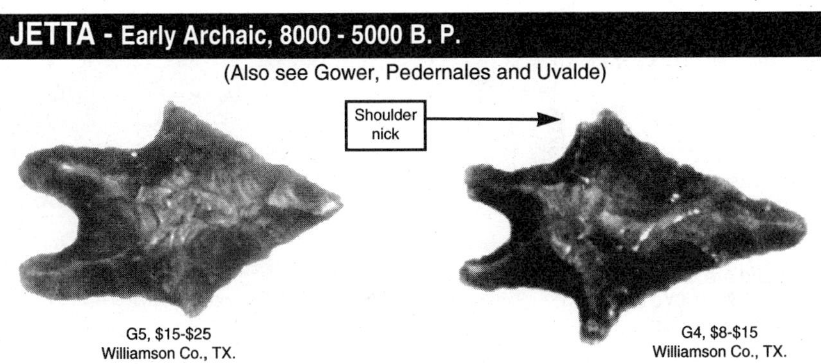

G5, $15-$25
Williamson Co., TX.

G4, $8-$15
Williamson Co., TX.

G10, $200-$400
Three Rivers, TX.

LOCATION: Texas to Oklahoma.. **DESCRIPTION:** A medium to large size point with tapered, horizontal or short pointed shoulders and a deeply notched base. Basal tangs are rounded and the stem is more squared and wider than *Pedernalis.* A very rare type.

G6, $15-$30
McCullough Co., TX.

G8, $150-$300
Wilson Co., TX.

JOHNSON - Early to Middle Archaic, 9000 - 5000 B. P.

(Also see Bulverde and Savannah River)

LOCATION: Mississippi to Oklahoma. **DESCRIPTION:** A medium size, thick, well made, expanded stem point with a broad, short, concave base. Bases are usually thinned and grinding appears on some specimens. Shoulders are slight and are roughly horizontal. **I.D. KEY:** Broad stem that is thinned.

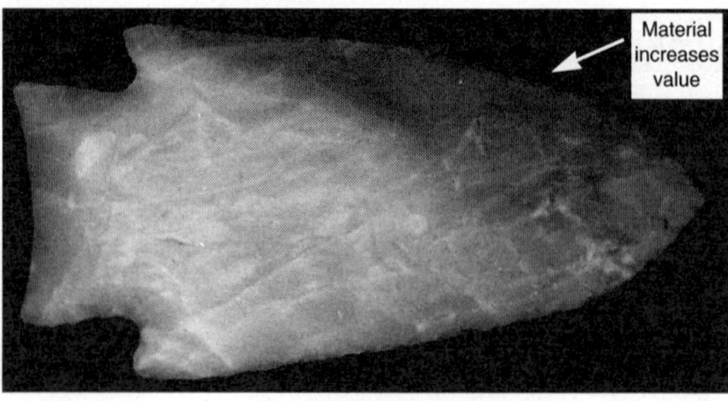

G8, $50-$100
Cent. AR. Novaculite.

G8, $25-$50
Llano, TX.

KEITHVILLE (See San Patrice - Keithville)

KEOTA - Mississippian, 800 - 600 B. P.

(Also see Agee, Alba, Dardanelle, Hayes, Homan and Sequoyah)

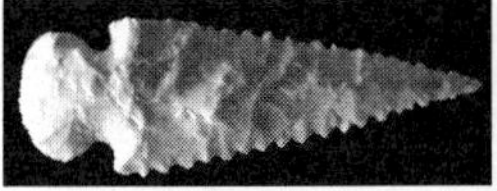

G8, $30-$50
Spiro Mound, OK., Leflore Co.

G9, $45-$85
Spiro Mound, OK.

G9, $45-$85
Spiro Mound, OK.

G9, $45-$85
Spiro Mound, OK.

G8, $35-$65
Spiro Mound, OK.

LOCATION: Texas, Arkansas to Oklahoma. **DESCRIPTION:** A small size, thin, triangular, side to corner-notched point with a rounded, bulbous base. The basal area is large on some specimens. **I.D. KEY:** Large bulbous base.

KERRVILLE KNIFE - Middle to Late Archaic, 5000 - 3000 B. P.

(Also see Scraper)

Shown full size

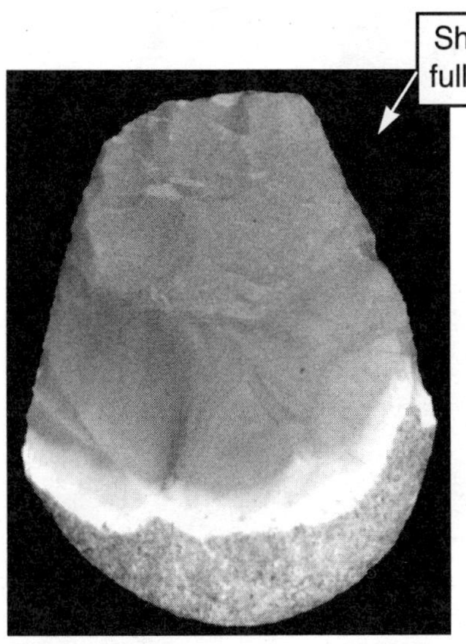

G6, $35-$70
Kimble Co., TX.

A group of Kerrville Knives
from Kerr Co., TX. $50 each.

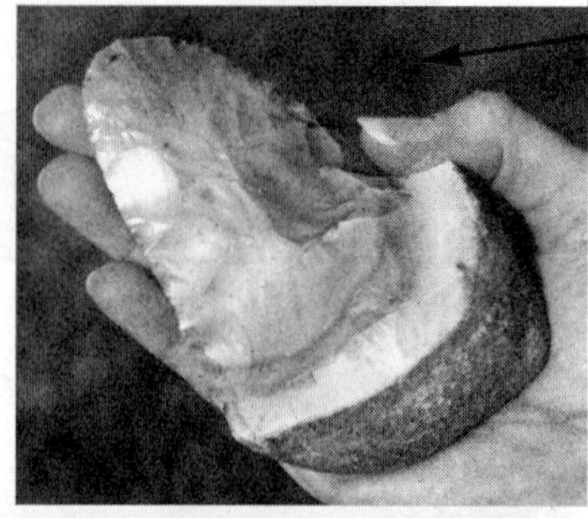

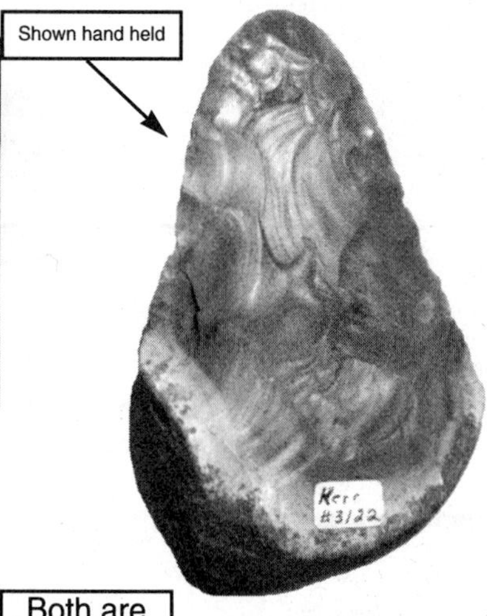

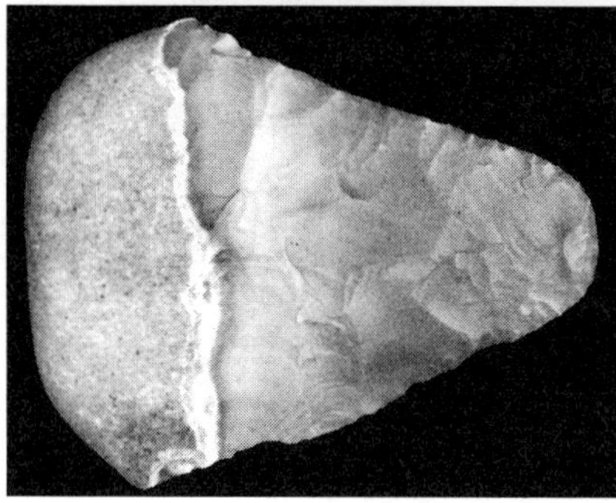

G8, $115-$225
Kimble Co., TX.

Both are shown half size

G8, $115-$225
Kimble Co., TX.

LOCATION: Midwestern states. **DESCRIPTION:** A large size, thick, triangular cutting or chopping tool with straight to slightly convex edges. The original rind occurs at the base.

KINNEY - Middle Archaic, 5000 - 2000 B. P.

(Also see Darl Blade, Early Triangular, Gahagan, Pandora and Tortugas)

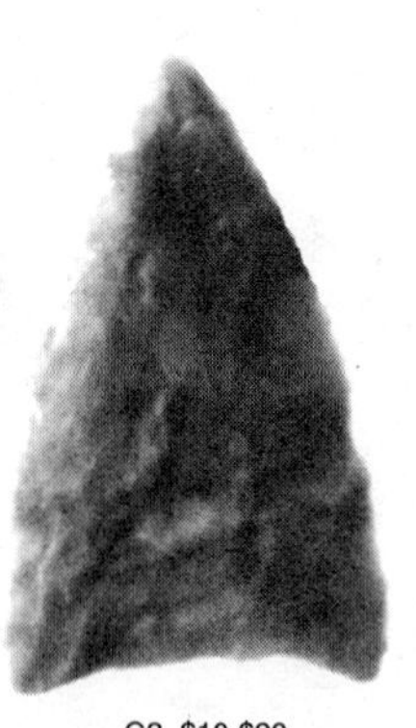

G3, $10-$20
TX.

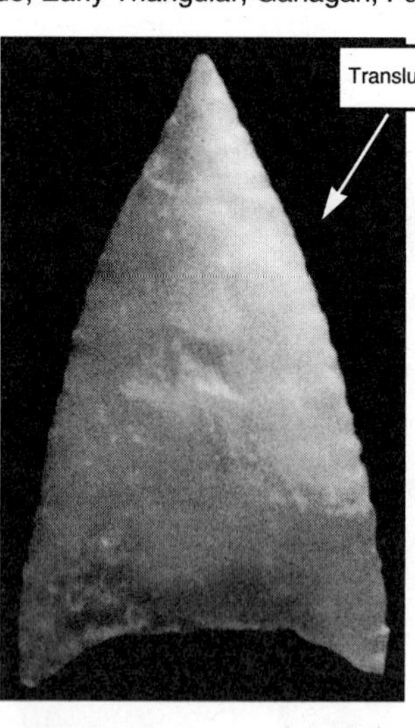

G7, $100-$200
Big Bend, TX.

G5, $25-$50
Killeen, TX.

LOCATION: Texas. **DESCRIPTION:** A medium to large size, thin, broad, lanceolate, well made blade with convex to straight blade edges and a concave base. Basal corners are pointed to rounded. **I.D. KEY:** Broad, concave base.

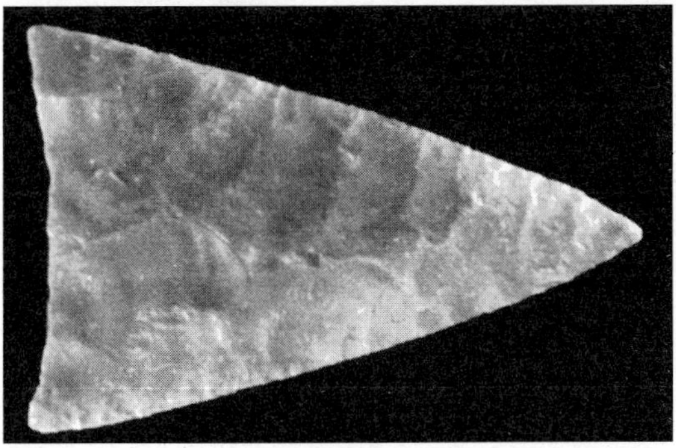

KINNEY (continued)

G7, $100-$200
Austin, TX.

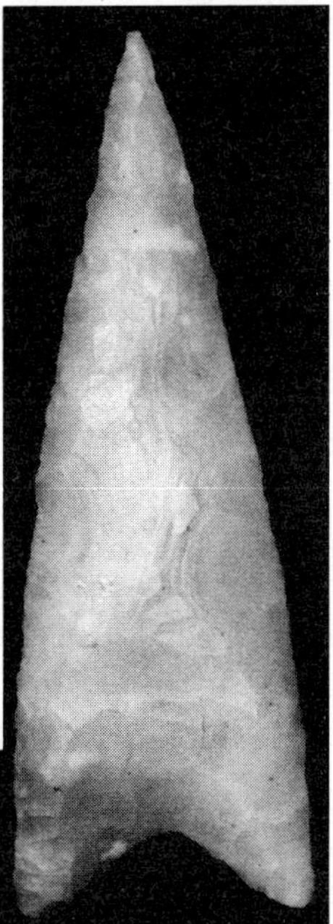

G7, $150-$300
Kerr Co., TX.

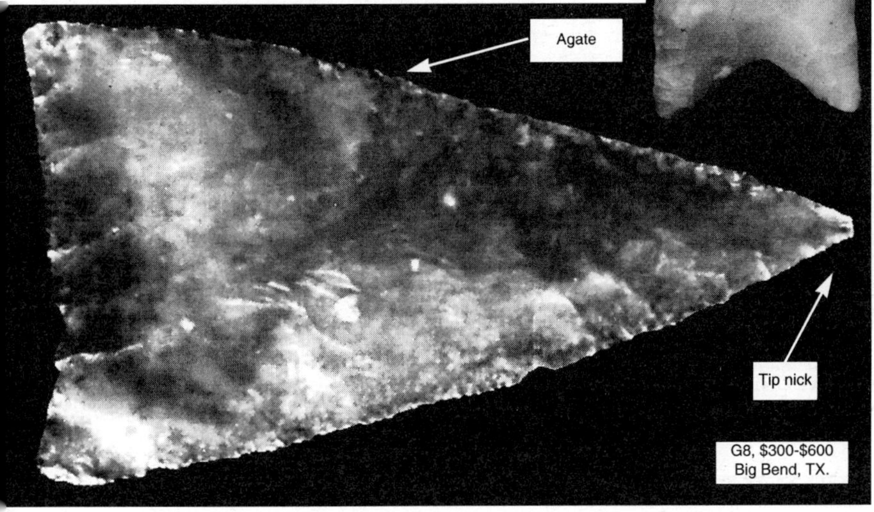

Agate

Tip nick

G8, $300-$600
Big Bend, TX.

KNIGHT ISLAND - Late Woodland, 1500 - 1000 B. P.

(Also see Cache River, Hickory Ridge, Jacks Reef, Reed and White River)

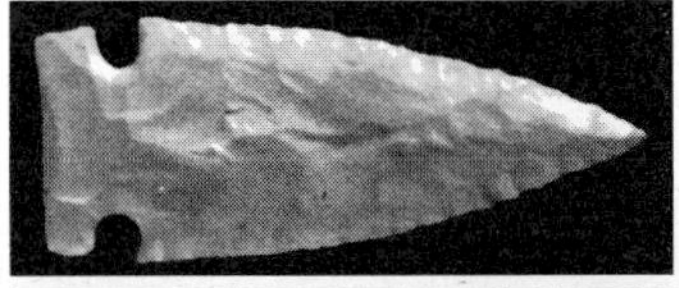

G8, $40-$75
N.E. ARK.

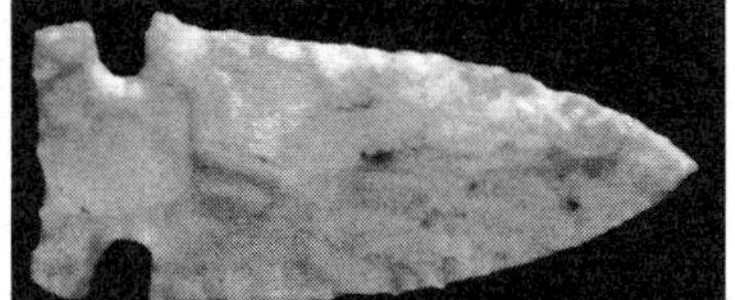

G7, $20-$40
N.E., Ark.

LOCATION: Arkansas to Southeastern states. **DESCRIPTION:** A small to medium size, very thin, narrow, side-notched point with a straight base. Longer examples can have a pentagonal apperarance. Called *Racoon Creek* in Ohio. A side-notched Jacks Reef. **I.D. KEY:** Thinness, basal form. Made by the small triangle point people.

LA JITA - Middle Archaic, 7000 - 4000 B. P.

(Also see Palmillas and Williams)

G6, $20-$40
TX.

G6, $25-$50
Kimble Co., TX.

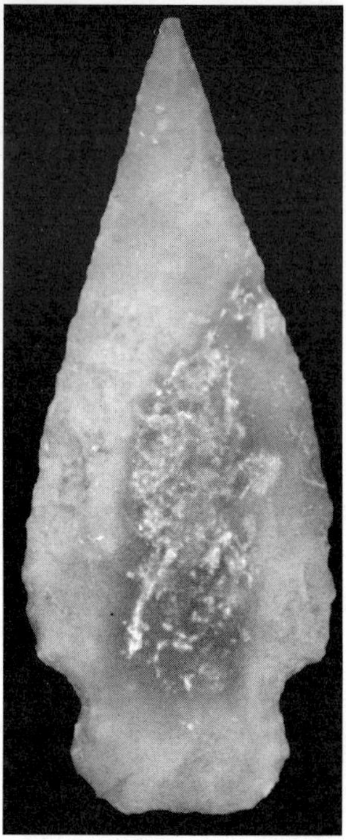

G4, $15-$25
Kimble Co., TX.

G5, $25-$50
Kimble Co., TX.

LOCATION: Texas. **DESCRIPTION:** A medium to large size, broad point with weak shoulders and a broad, bulbous base that expands and has rounded basal corners. **I.D. KEY:** Large bulbous base.

LAMPASAS (See Zephyr)

LANGE - Middle Archaic to Woodland, 6000 - 1000 B. P.

(Also see Bulverde, Castorville, Morrill, Nolan and Travis)

G4, $3-$5
Comanche Co., TX.

G7, $15-$30
Cent. TX.

LOCATION: Louisiana to Texas to Oklahoma. **DESCRIPTION:** A medium to large size, narrow, expanded stem dart point with tapered to horizontal, barbed shoulders and a straight to convex base. **I.D. KEY:** Expanding base, tapered to horizontal shoulders.

LANGE (continued)

Broad base form

G7, $10-$20
Comanche Co., TX.

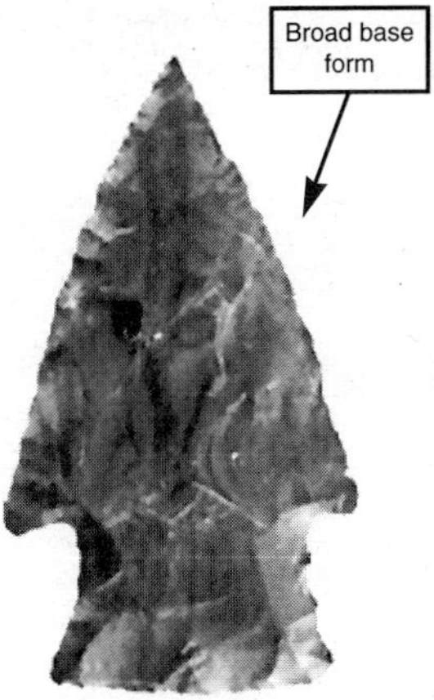

G6, $15-$30
Austin, TX.

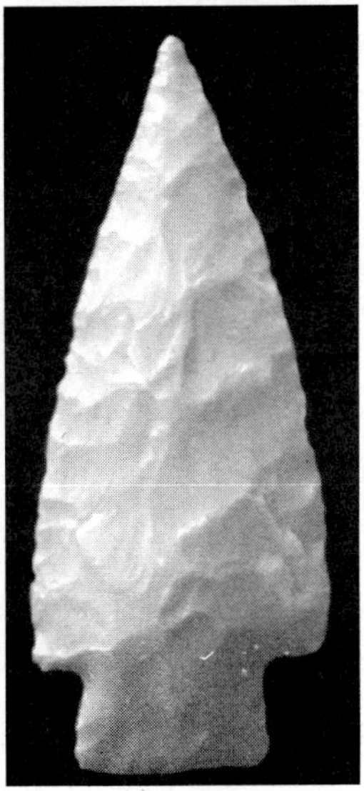

G6, $30-$60
Bexar Co., TX.

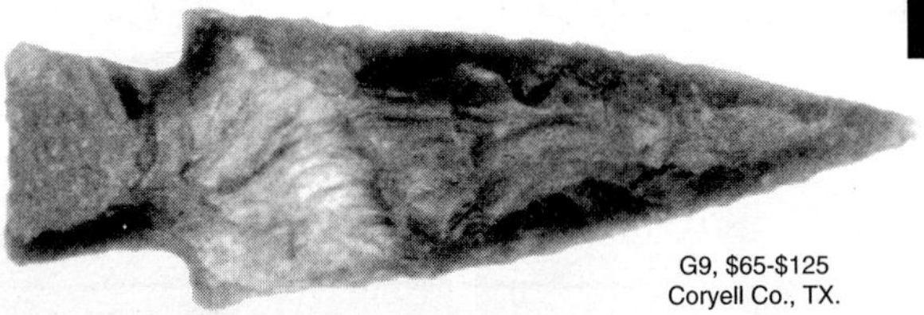

G9, $65-$125
Coryell Co., TX.

SC

G8, $50-$100
Comanche Co., TX.

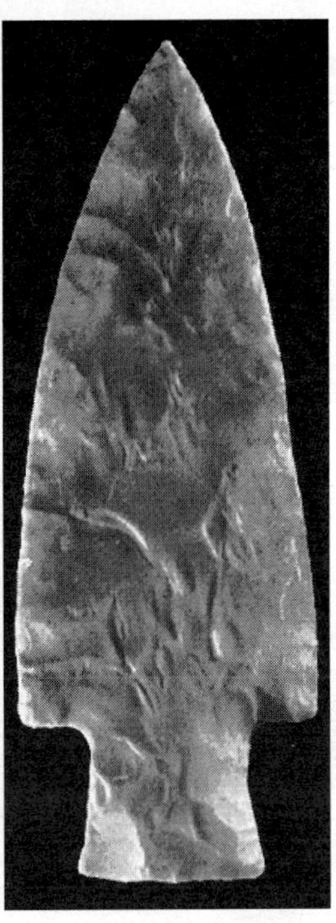

G10, $125-$250
Austin, TX.

G9, $115-$225
Waco, TX.

LANGTRY - Middle Archaic to Woodland, 5000 - 2000 B. P.

(Also see Almagre, Gary, Hidden Valley, Morrow Mountain and Val Verde)

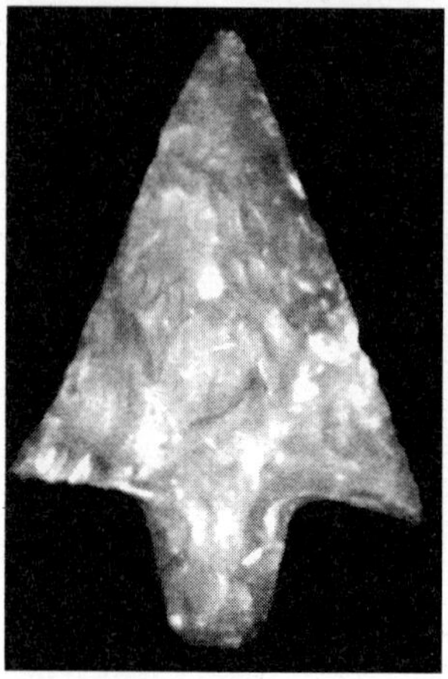

Side damage

G8, $75-$150
Kimble Co., TX.

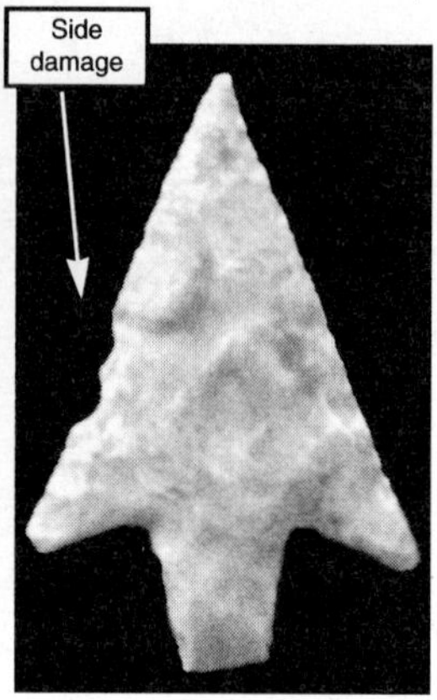

G3, $15-$30
TX.

G7, $45-$90
Bell Co., TX.

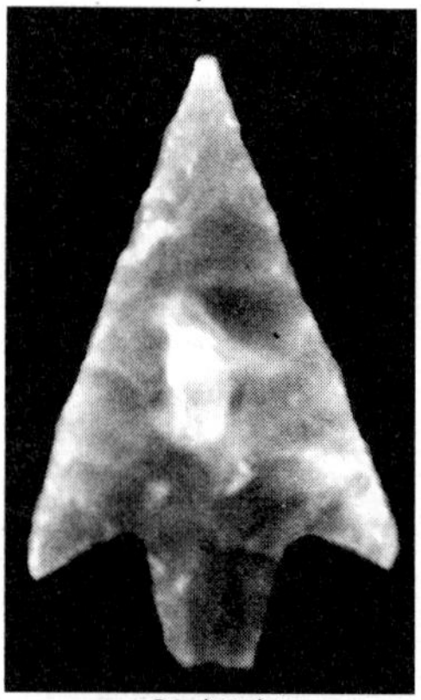

G6, $20-$40
TX.

G8, $65-$125
Zapata Co., TX.

G8, $65-$125
Kimble Co., TX.

LOCATION: Texas to Oklahoma. **DESCRIPTION:** A medium size triangular point with a short to long contracting stem. Shoulders can be square, tapered or strongly barbed. Bases are concave to straight. **I.D. KEY:** Strong barbs, tapered stem.

LANGTRY-ARENOSA - Middle Archaic to Woodland, 5000 - 2000 B. P.

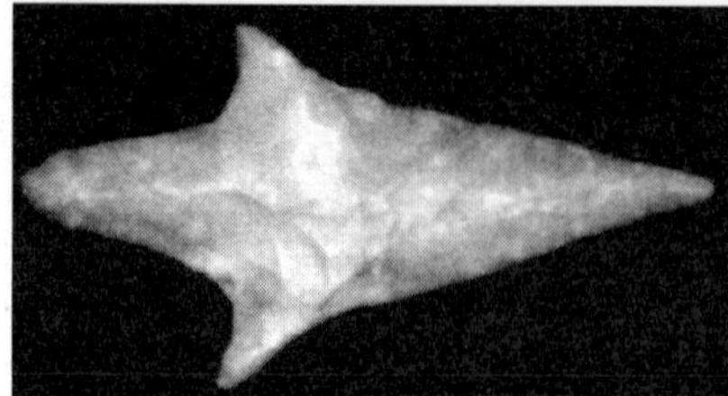

LOCATION: Texas to Oklahoma. **DESCRIPTION:** A variant form of the *Langtry* point which differs in having a pointed to rounded base and strong drooping tangs **I.D. KEY:** Strong barbs, pointed stem.

G8, $65-$125
Crockett Co., TX.

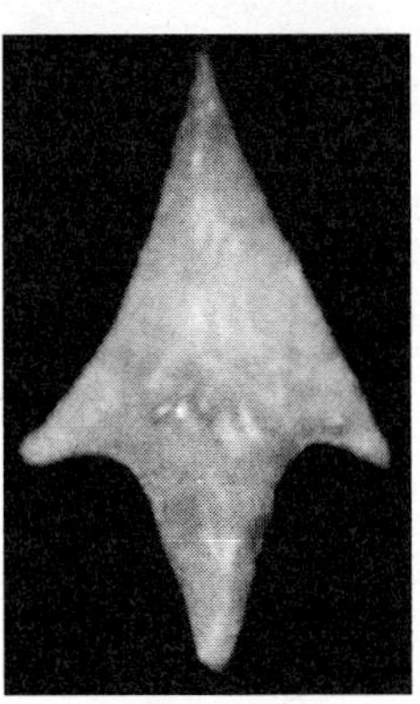
G8, $30-$60
Crockett Co., TX.

G6, $15-$30
TX.

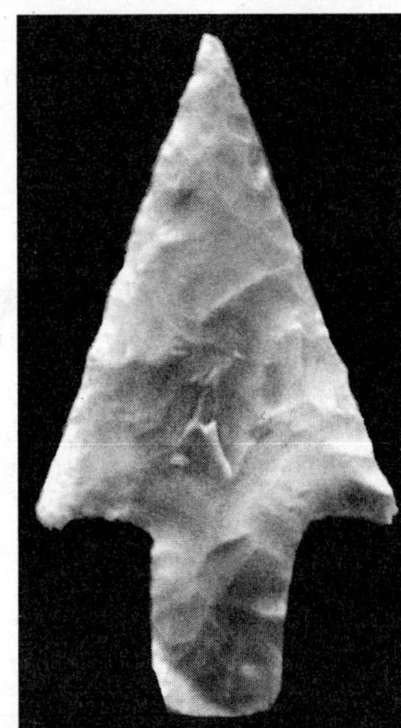
G8, $50-$100
TX.

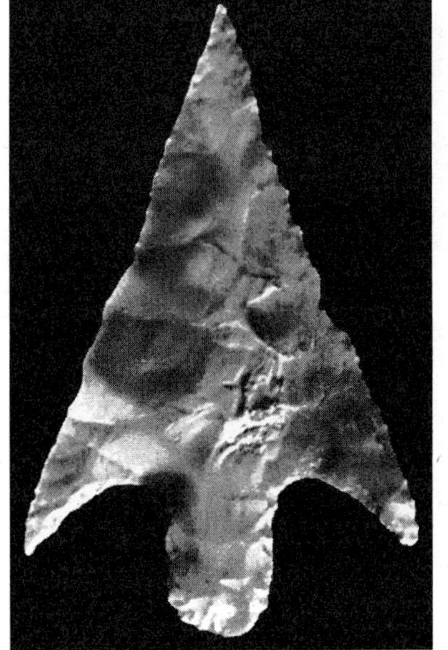
G8, $65-$125
Austin, TX.

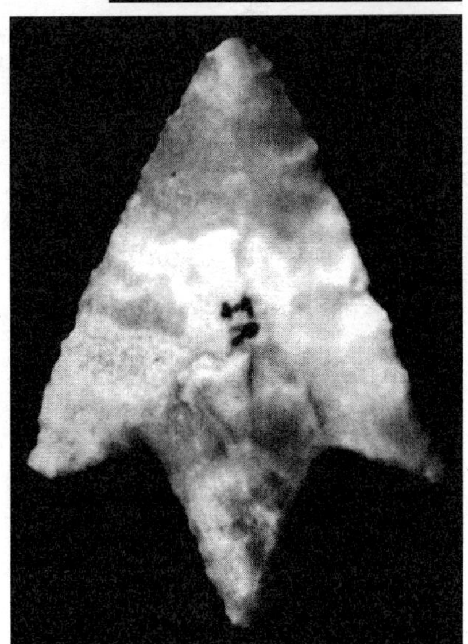
G6, $20-$40
Irion Co., TX.

LERMA POINTED BASE - Middle to Late Archaic, 4000 - 2000 B. P.

(Also see Agate Basin, Angostura and Harahey)

G6, $30-$60
Austin, TX.

LERMA POINTED BASE (continued)

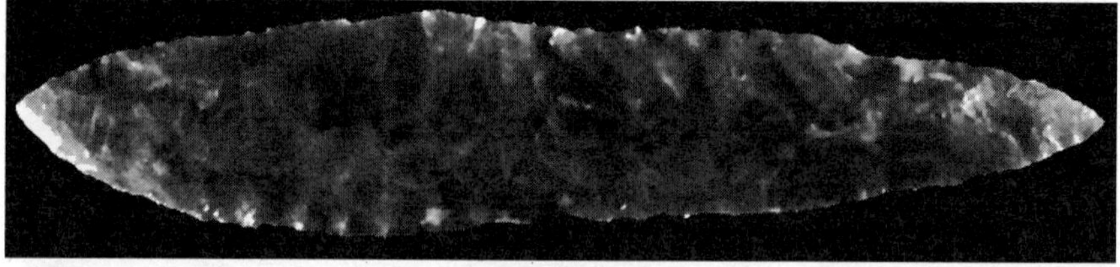

G8, $65-$125
Austin, TX.

LOCATION: Siberia to Alaska, Canada, Mexico, South America and across the U.S. **DESCRIPTION:** A large size, narrow, lanceolate blade with a pointed base. Most are fairly thick in cross section but finer examples can be thin. Flaking tends to be collateral. Basal areas can be ground. Western forms are beveled on one side of each face. Similar forms have been found in Europe and Africa dating back to 20,000 - 40,000 B.P., but didn't enter the U.S. until after the advent of *Clovis.*

LERMA ROUNDED BASE - Middle to Late Archaic, 4000 - 2000 B. P.

(Also see Agate Basin, Angostura, Covington and Harahey)

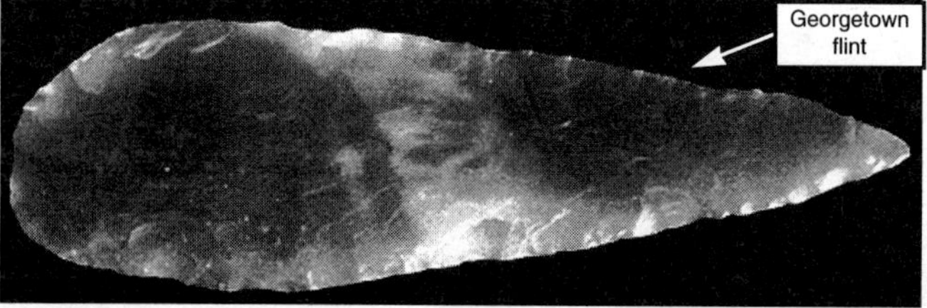

G7, $25-$50
Austin, TX.

LOCATION: Same as pointed base Lerma. **DESCRIPTION:** A large size, narrow, thick, lanceolate blade with a rounded base. Some Western examples are beveled on one side of each face. Flaking tends to be collateral and finer examples are thin in cross section.

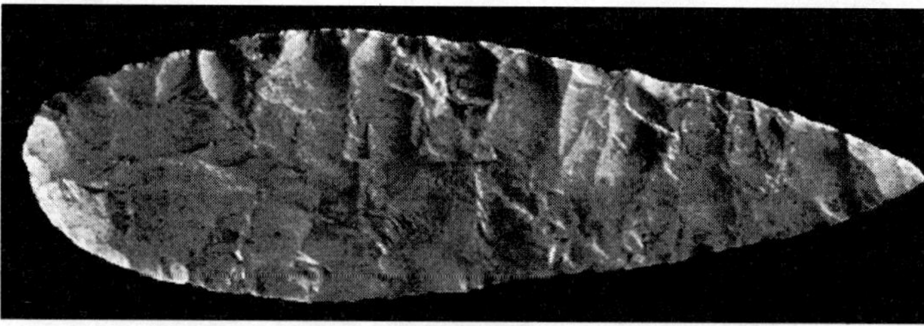

G8, $75-$150
Comanche Co., TX.

LIVERMORE - Mississippian, 1200 - 600 B. P.

(Also see Bassett, Drill and Sequoyah)

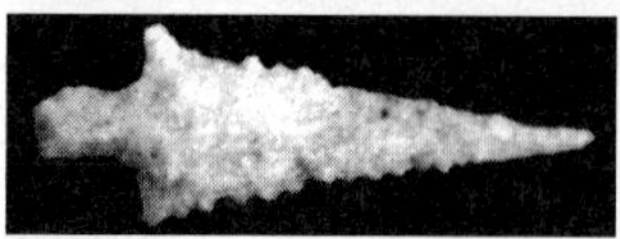

G7, $35-$70
Crane Co., TX.

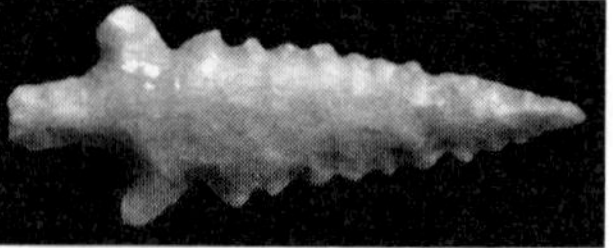

G7, $35-$70
TX.

LOCATION: Texas. **DESCRIPTION:** A small to medium size, very narrow, spike point with wide flaring barbs and a narrow stem that can be short to long. Some examples are serrated. **I.D. KEY:** Extreme narrowness of blade.

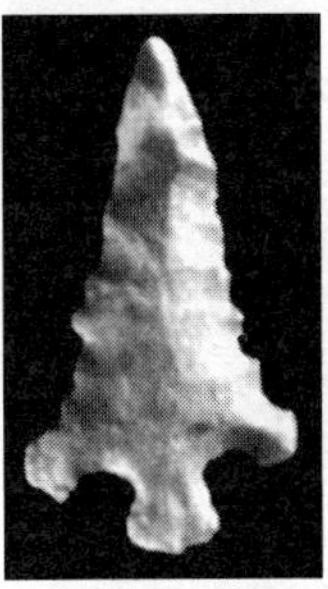
G6, $15-$30
Culberson Co., TX.

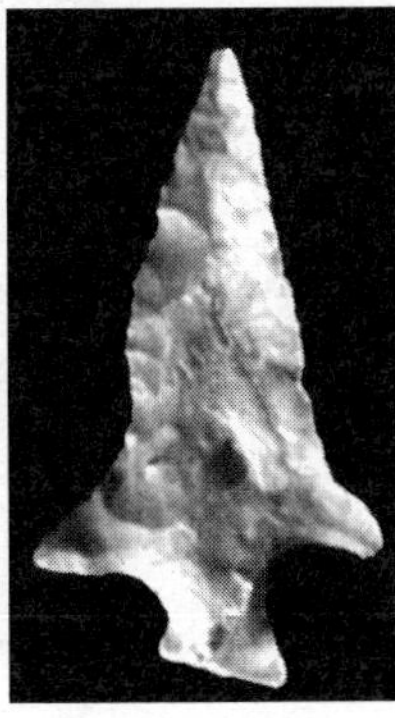
G5, $10-$20
Culberson Co., TX.

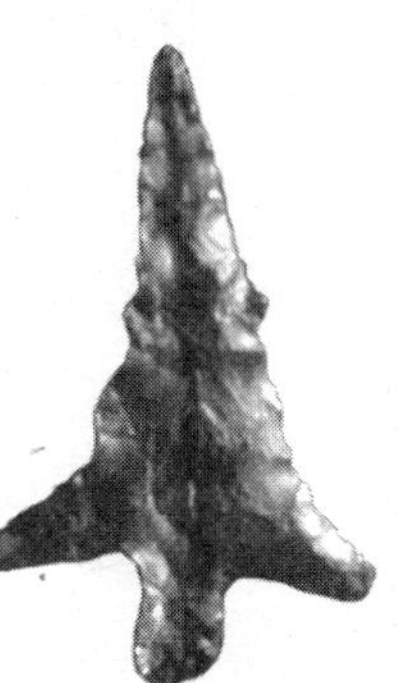
G8, $40-$80
Culberson Co., TX.

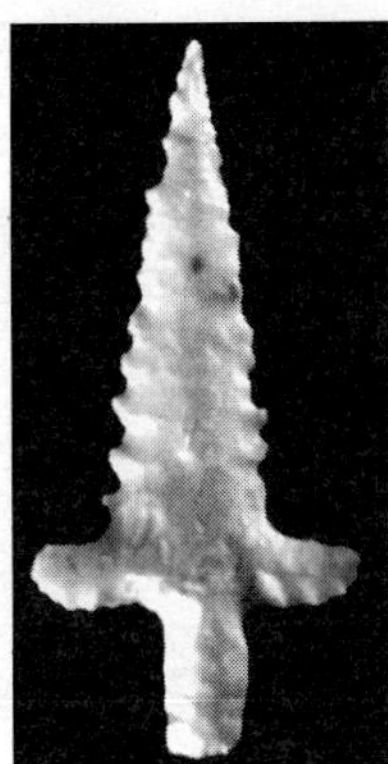
G10, $100-$200
Culberson Co., TX.

G7, $25-$50
Culberson Co., TX.

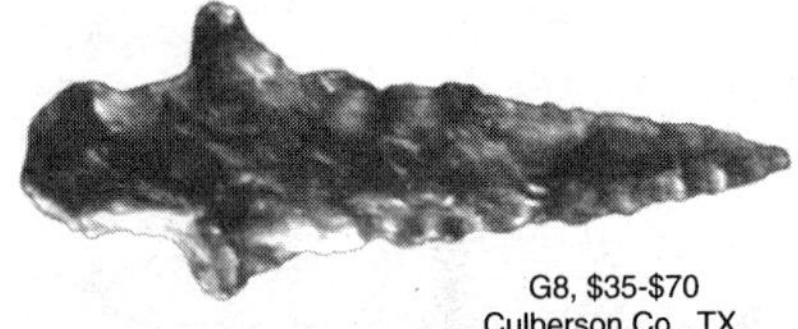
G8, $35-$70
Culberson Co., TX.

LOTT - Mississippian to Historic, 500 - 300 B. P.

(Also see Garza and Harrell)

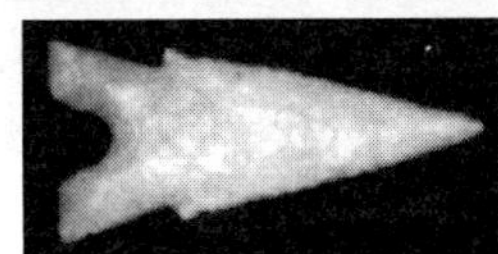
G10, $40-$80
Garza Co., TX.

G9, $30-$60
Garza Co., TX.
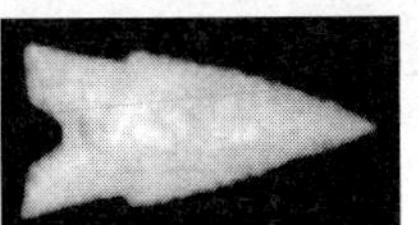

SC

LOCATION: Texas to Arizona. **DESCRIPTION:** A medium size, weakly barbed, thin, arrow point with a bifurcated base. Ears can be long and flare outward. Basal sides and the base are usually straight **I.D. KEY:** Form of ears.

MAHAFFEY - Transitional Paleo-Early Archaic, 10,500 - 8000 B. P.

(Also see Agate Basin and Angostura)

G8, $175-$350
Wilson Co., TX.

LOCATION: Texas, Arkansas to Oklahoma. **DESCRIPTION:** A medium size, ovate point with a rounded base. Widest near the tip, the basal area is usually ground. Believed to be related to the Agate Basin point. **I.D. KEY:** Blade form.

MARCOS - Late Archaic to Woodland, 3500 - 1200 B. P.

(Also see Castroville, Ensor, Fairland and Marshall)

G6, $20-$40
Austin, TX.

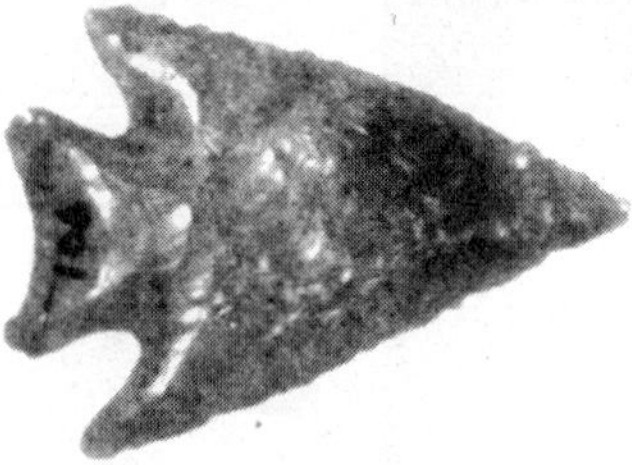

G5, $30-$60
Gray Co., TX.

G6, $40-$75
Bexar Co., TX.

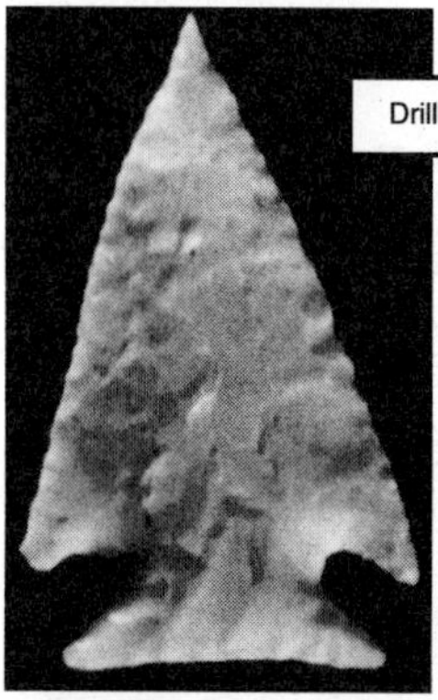

Drill form

G8, $40-$75
Austin, TX.

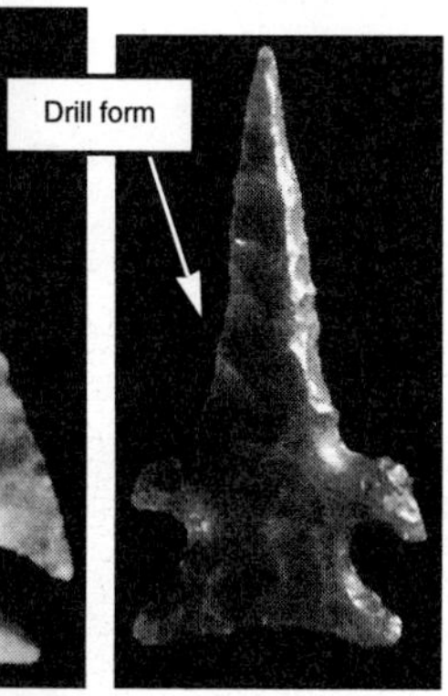

G5, $25-$50
Austin, TX.

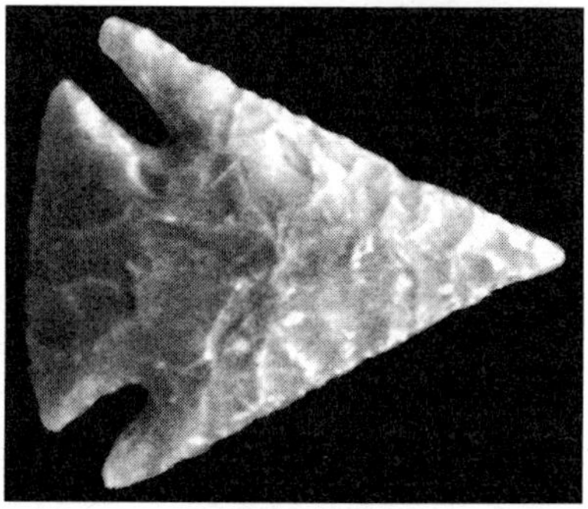

G8, $45-$90
Williams Co., TX. Cache.

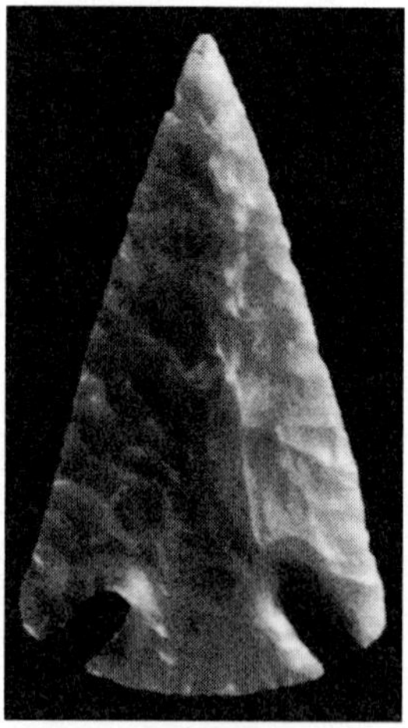

Owl Creek
Black cherk

G8, $65-$125
Austin, TX.

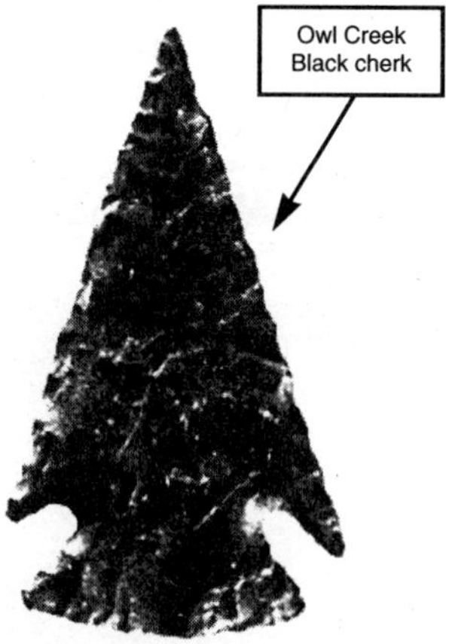

G6, $30-$60
Austin, TX.

G7, $30-$60
Cent. TX.

LOCATION: Texas to Oklahoma. **DESCRIPTION:** A small to medium size, broad, corner notched point with an expanded stem. The blade edges are straight to recurved. Many examples have long barbs and a sharp pointed tip. Bases are convex, straight or concave. **I.D. KEY:** Angle of corner notches.

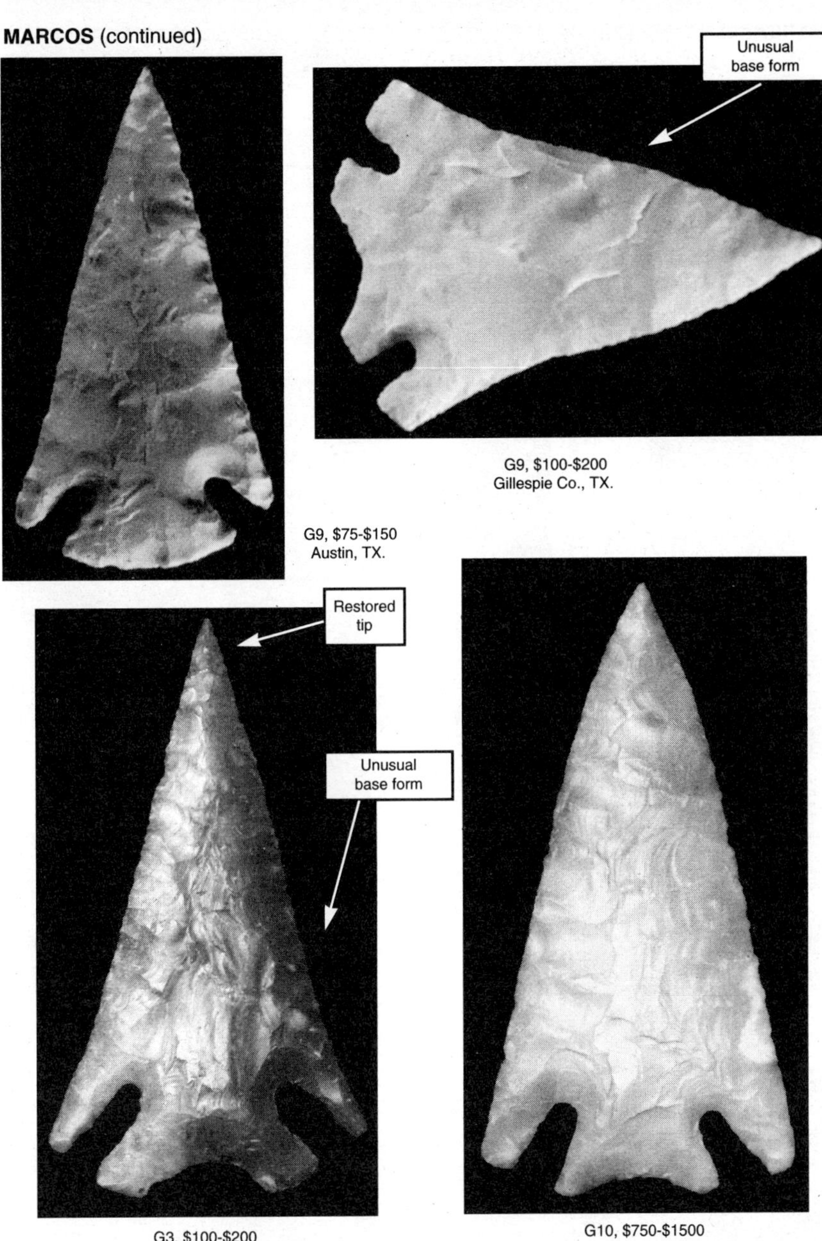

G9, $75-$150
Austin, TX.

G9, $100-$200
Gillespie Co., TX.

G3, $100-$200
Kerr Co., TX.

G10, $750-$1500
Wilson Co., TX.

MARSHALL - Middle Archaic to Woodland, 6000 - 2000 B. P.

(Also see Castroville, Ensor and Marcos)

LOCATION: Texas to Colorado. **DESCRIPTION:** A medium to large size, broad, high quality, corner to basal notched point with long barbs that turn inward towards the base. Notching is less angled than in *Marcos.* **I.D. KEY:** Drooping tangs.

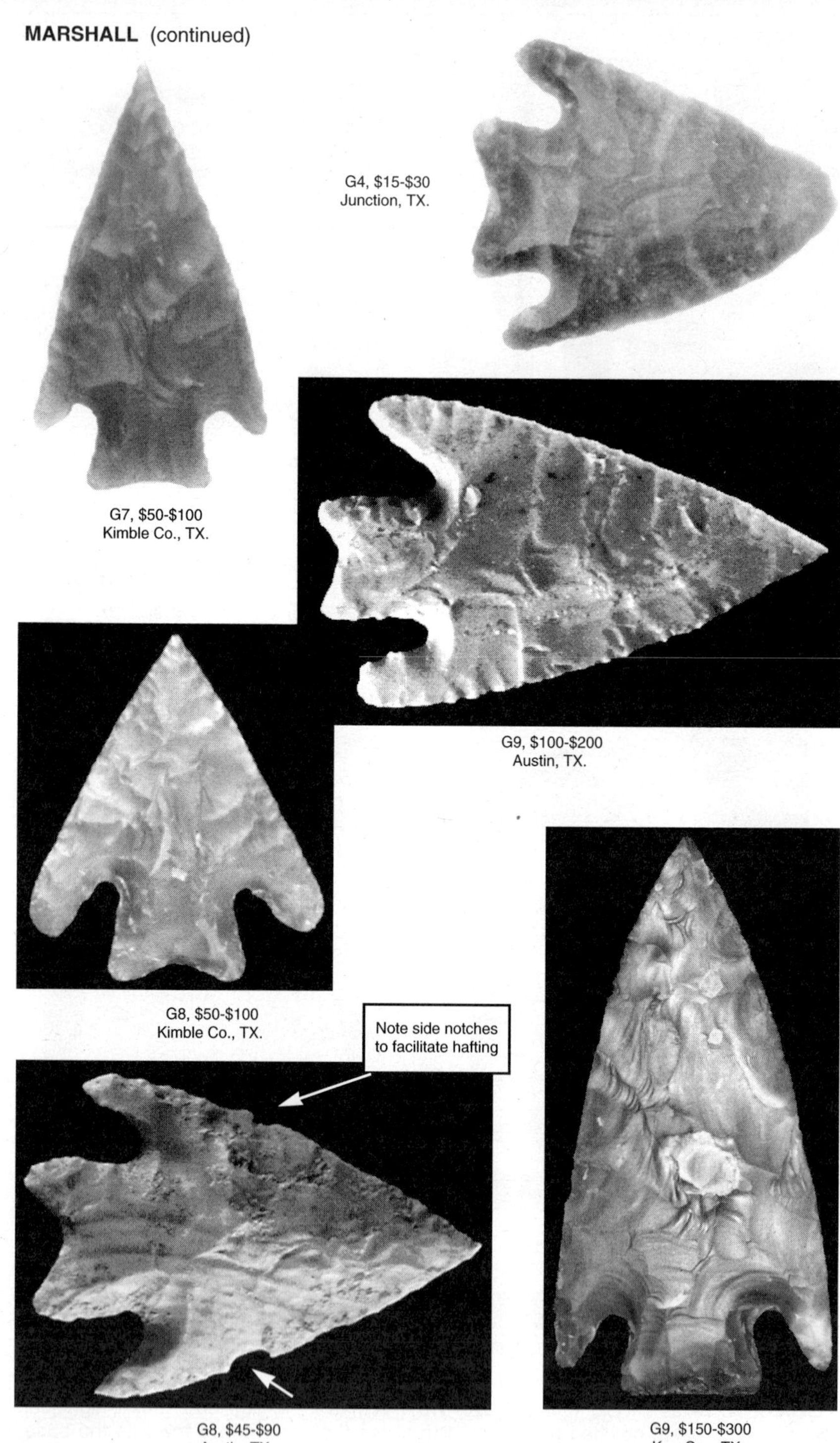
Note side notches to facilitate hafting

G4, $15-$30
Junction, TX.

G7, $50-$100
Kimble Co., TX.

G9, $100-$200
Austin, TX.

G8, $50-$100
Kimble Co., TX.

G8, $45-$90
Austin, TX.

G9, $150-$300
Kerr Co.,, TX.

G8, $65-$125
Kimble Co., TX.

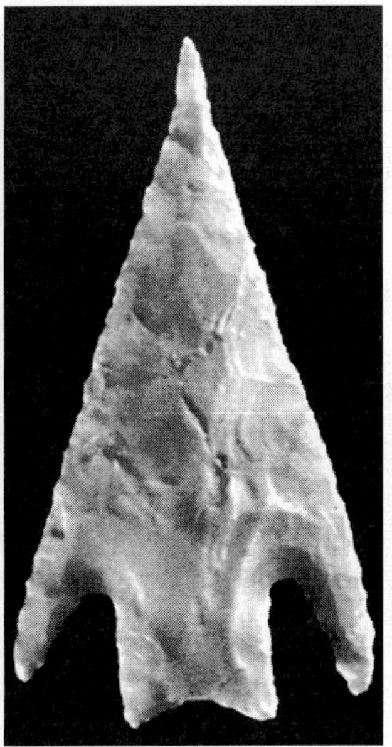
G8, $75-$150
Austin, TX.

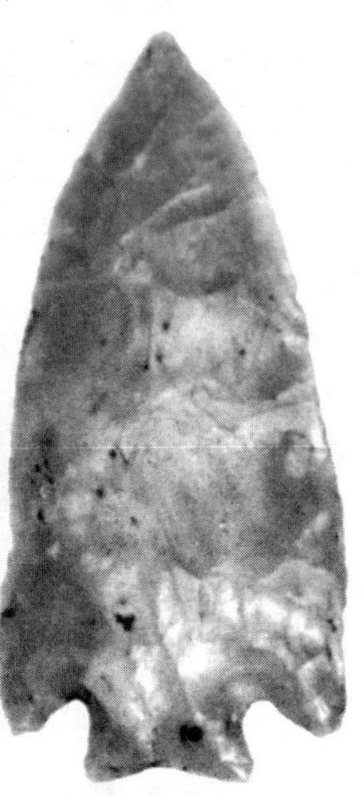
G7, $90-$175
Williamson Co., TX.

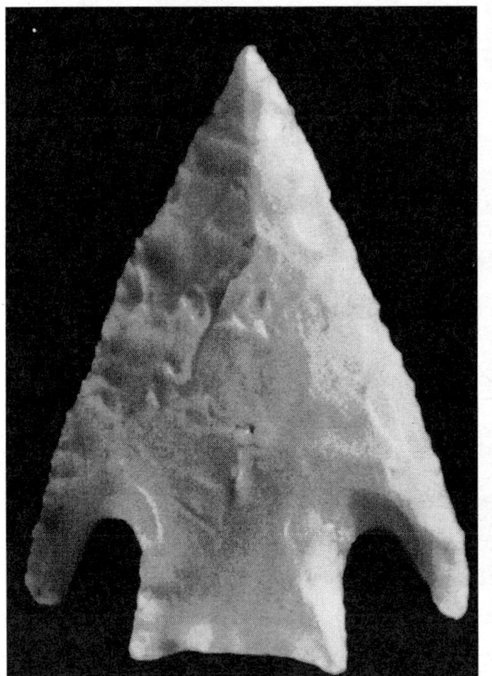
G7, $100-$200
Austin, TX.

G9, $150-$300
Uvalde Co., TX.

G9, $250-$500
Kerr Co., TX.

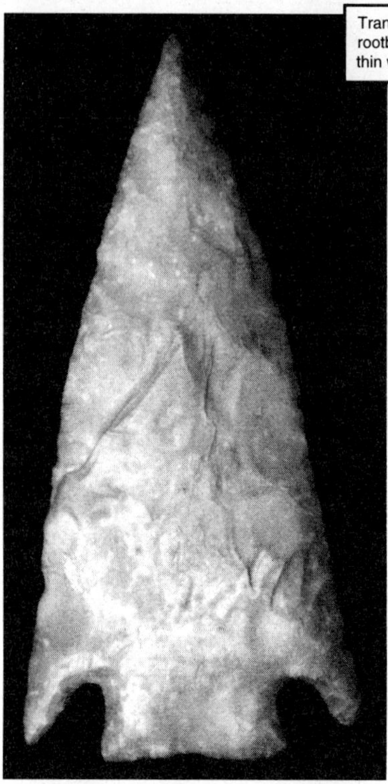

Translucent swirley rootbeer flint; super thin with fine flaking

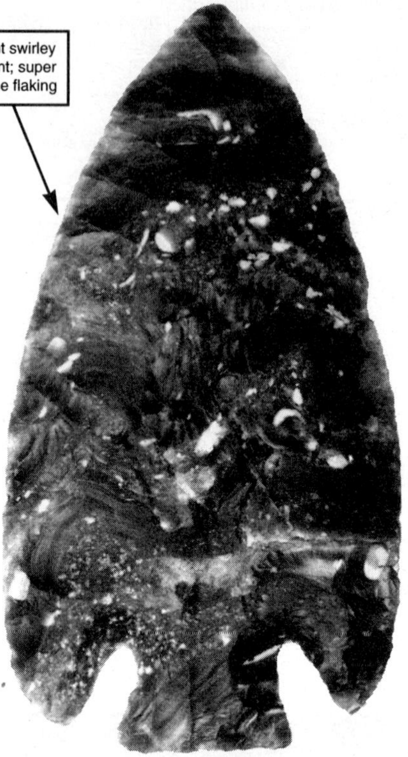

G10+, $1800-$3500
Kerr Co., TX.

MARTINDALE - Early Archaic, 8000 - 5000 B. P.

(Also see Bandy, Marcos and Marshall)

Damaged tip

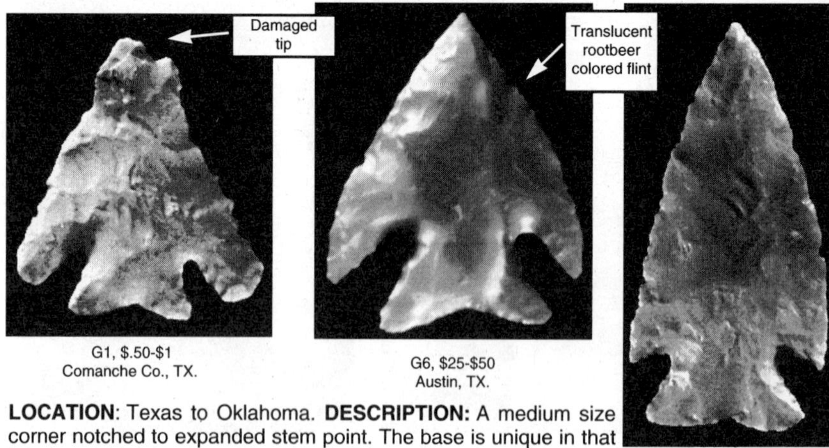

G1, $.50-$1
Comanche Co., TX.

Translucent rootbeer colored flint

G6, $25-$50
Austin, TX.

G6, $20-$40
Austin, TX.

LOCATION: Texas to Oklahoma. **DESCRIPTION:** A medium size corner notched to expanded stem point. The base is unique in that it is formed by two curves meeting at the center. Called *Bandy* in southern Texas. **I.D. KEY:** Basal form, early flaking.

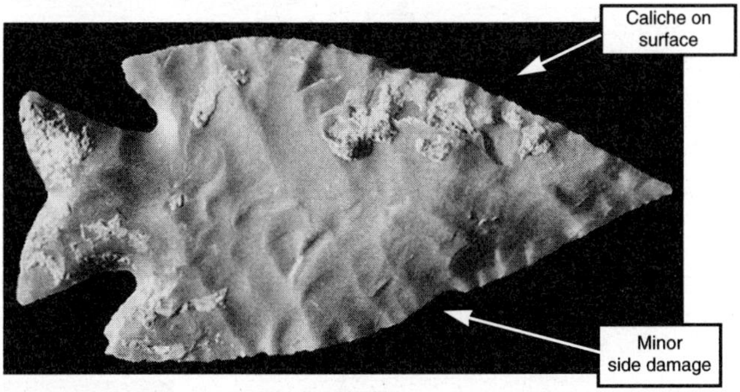

Caliche on surface

Minor side damage

G7, $100-$200
Williamson Co., TX.

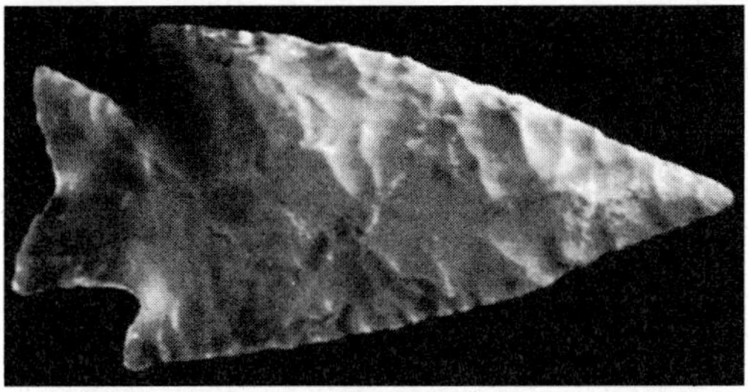

G6, $40-$80
Austin, TX.

G9, $150-$300
Austin, TX.

MATAMOROS - Late Archaic to Mississippian, 3000 - 300 B. P.

(Also see Abasolo, Catan and Tortugas)

G5, $3-$5
TX.

G5, $3-$5
TX.

G5, $3-$5
TX.

G6, $4-$8
TX.

G6, $4-$8
TX.

LOCATION: Texas. **DESCRIPTION:** A small to medium size, broad, triangular point with concave, straight, or convex base. On some excamples, beveling occurs on one side of each face as in *Tortugas* points. Larger points would fall under the *Tortugas* type.

MATANZAS - Mid-Archaic to Mississippian, 4500 - 3000 B. P.

(Also see Palmillas)

MATANZAS (continued)

LOCATION: Arkansas to Missouri. **DESCRIPTION:** A medium size, narrow, side notched dart point with an expanding stem and a straight base.

G7, $15-$30
AR.

MAUD - Mississippian, 800 - 500 B. P.

(Also see Fresno, Starr and Talco)

G7, $10-$20
TX.

G8, $15-$30
TX.

G7, $10-$20
Smith Co., TX.

G8, $15-$25
TX.

G8, $25-$50
TX.

G10, $35-$70
Smith Co., TX.

G9, $65-$125
Red Riv. Co., TX.

G9, $65-$125
Red Riv. Co., TX.

G10, $100-$200
Emanuel Co., TX.

LOCATION: Texas, Arkansas to Oklahoma. **DESCRIPTION:** A small size, thin, triangular arrow point with straight to convex sides and a concave base. Basal corners are sharp. Associated with the Caddo culture in the Midwest. Blades are usually very finely serrated. **I.D. KEY:** Convex sides, sharp basal corners.

MESERVE - Early Archaic, 9500 - 4000 B. P.

(Also see Angostura, Dalton and Plainview)

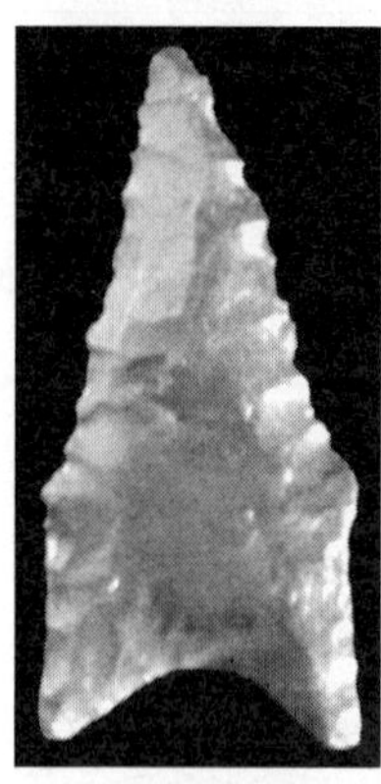

G6, $50-$100
TX.

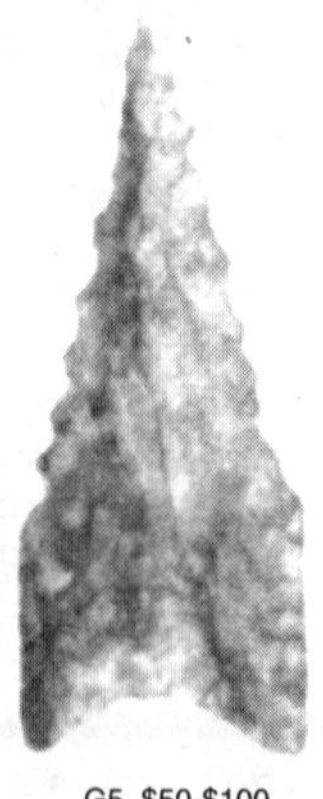

G5, $50-$100
Abilene, TX.

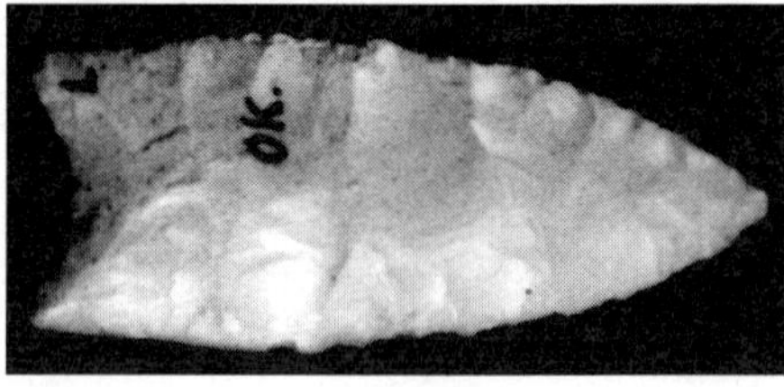

G8, $75-$150
Osage Co., OK.

LOCATION: Texas westward to Arizona and northward to Montana. **DESCRIPTION:** A medium size, auriculate point with a blade that is beveled on one side of each face. Beveling extends into the basal area. This type is related to *Dalton* points.

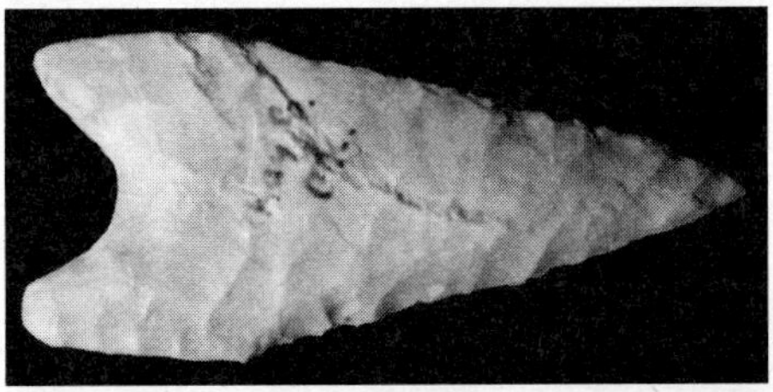

MESERVE (continued)

G5, $20-$40
Abilene, TX.

G8, $75-$150
Kay Co., OK.

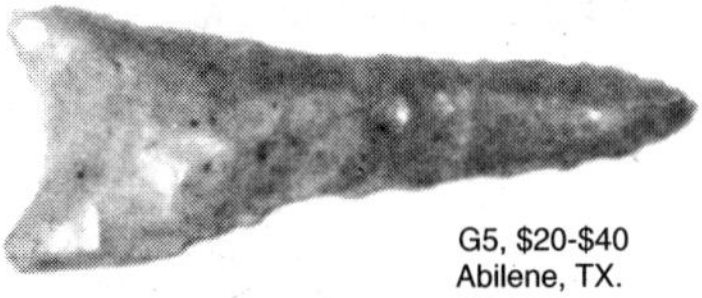

Edgework extends into basal area

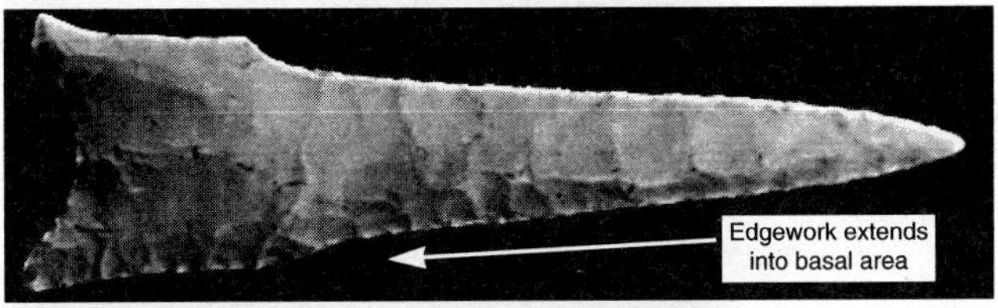

G9, $225-$450, Morris Co., TX. Classic form.

Alibates flint

G7, $75-$150
Osage Co., OK.

G10, $200-$700
Wilson Co., TX.

G9, $175-$350
Osage Co., OK.

SC

MID-BACK TANG - Late Archaic to Woodland, 4000 - 2000 B. P.

(Also see Base Tang Knife and Corner Tang)

G7, $125-$250
Coryell Co., TX.

LOCATION: Texas. **DESCRIPTION:** A variation of the corner tang knife with the hafting area occuring near the center of one side of the blade. A very rare type.

MID-BACK TANG (continued)

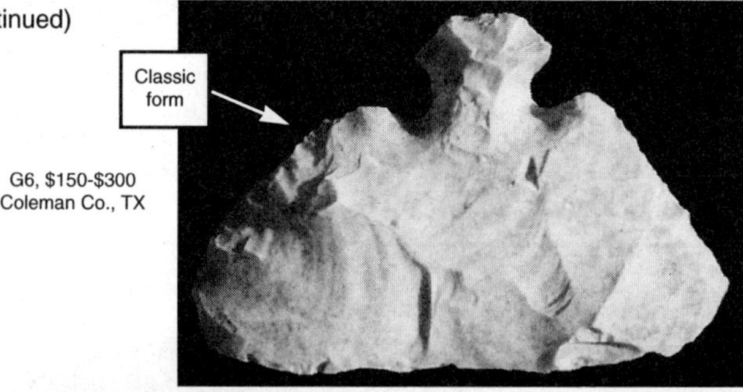

G6, $150-$300
Coleman Co., TX

MIDLAND - Transitional Paleo, 10,700 - 9000 B. P.

(Also see Angostura, Arkabutla, Clovis, Folsom, Milnesand and Plainview)

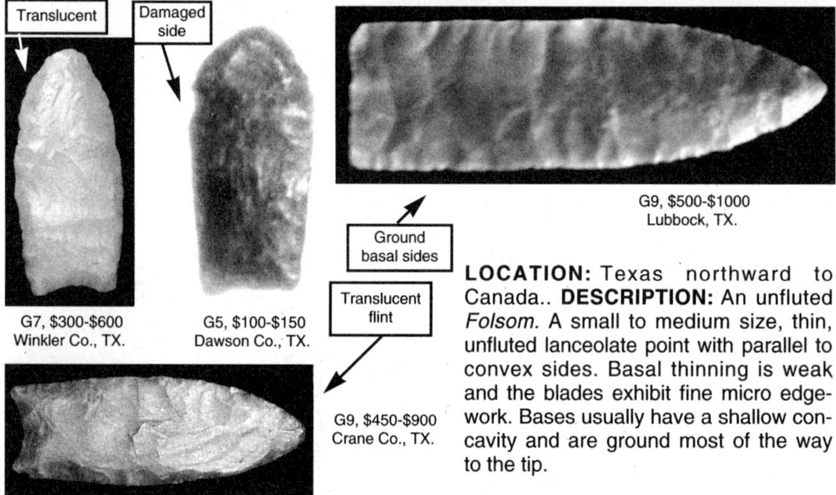

G7, $300-$600
Winkler Co., TX.

G5, $100-$150
Dawson Co., TX.

G9, $500-$1000
Lubbock, TX.

G9, $450-$900
Crane Co., TX.

LOCATION: Texas northward to Canada.. **DESCRIPTION:** An unfluted *Folsom.* A small to medium size, thin, unfluted lanceolate point with parallel to convex sides. Basal thinning is weak and the blades exhibit fine micro edge-work. Bases usually have a shallow concavity and are ground most of the way to the tip.

MILNESAND - Transitional Paleo, 11,000 - 8000 B. P.

(Also see Agate Basin, Angostura, Firstview, Hell Gap and Rio Grande)

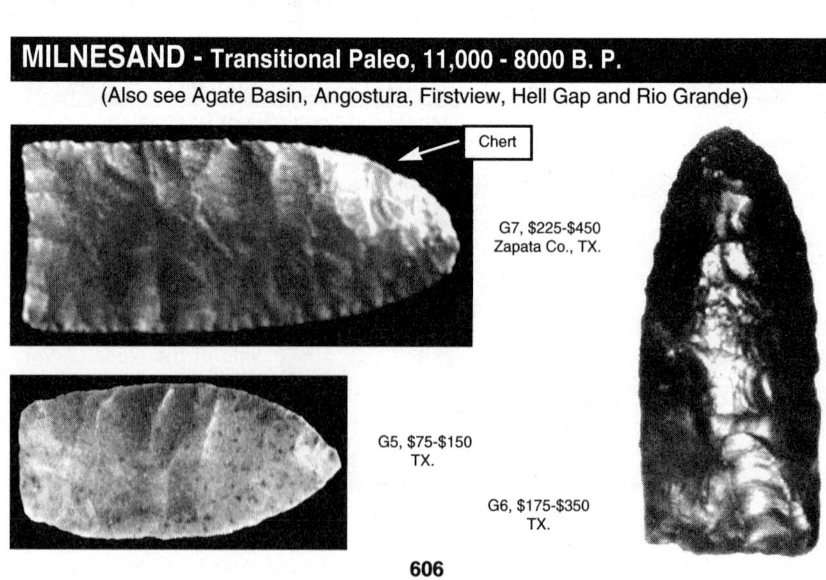

G7, $225-$450
Zapata Co., TX.

G5, $75-$150
TX.

G6, $175-$350
TX.

MILNESAND (continued)

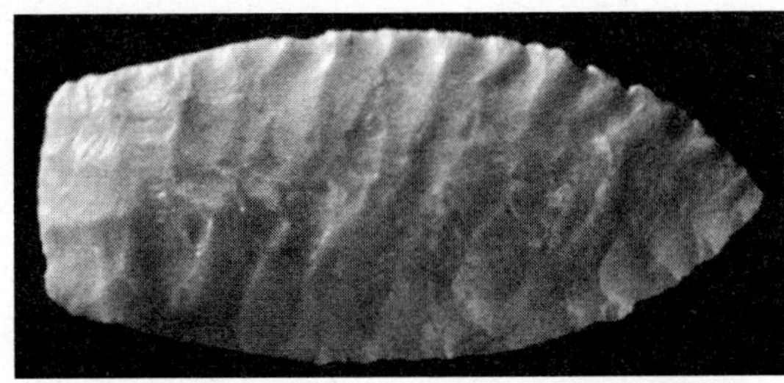
G9, $500-$1000
Terry Co., TX.

LOCATION: Texas, New Mexico, northward to Canada and Alaska. **DESCRIPTION:** A medium size unfluted lanceolate point that becomes thicker and wider towards the tip. The base is basically square and ground. Thicker than *Midland.* **I.D. KEY:** Square base and Paleo flaking.

MINERAL SPRINGS - Mississippian, 1300 - 1000 B. P.

(Also see Gahagan)

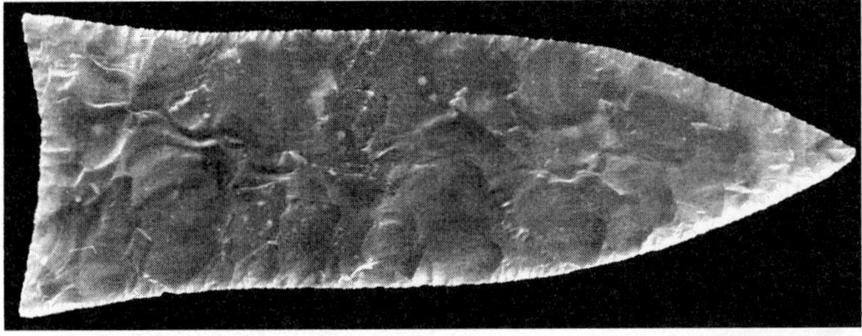
G10, $2500-$4000
Little River Co., AR.
Outstanding quality.

shown half size

LOCATION: Texas, Oklahoma, Arkansas and Louisiana. **DESCRIPTION:** A broad, large size knife with recurved sides, sharp basal corners and a concave base. Some examples have notches at the basal corners.

MONTELL - Mid-Archaic to late Woodland, 5000 - 1000 B. P.

(Also see Ensor Split-Base and Uvalde)

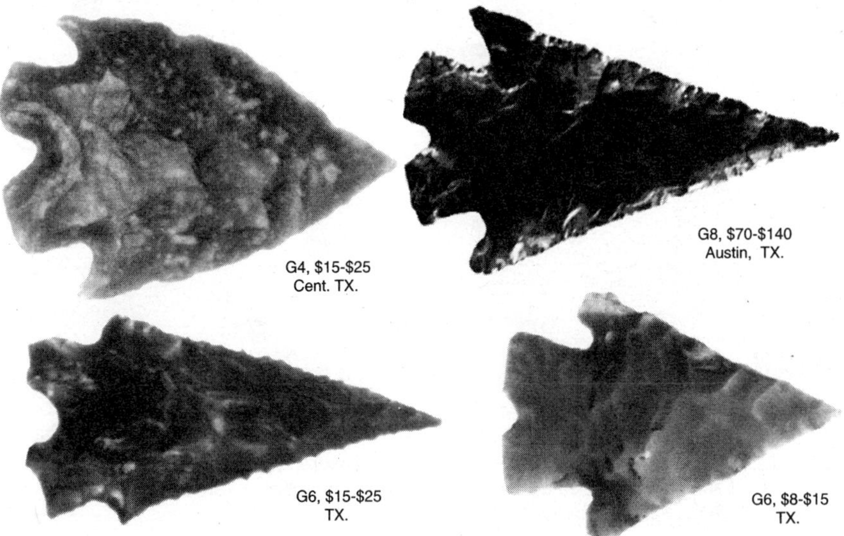
G4, $15-$25
Cent. TX.

G8, $70-$140
Austin, TX.

G6, $15-$25
TX.

G6, $8-$15
TX.

MONTELL (continued)

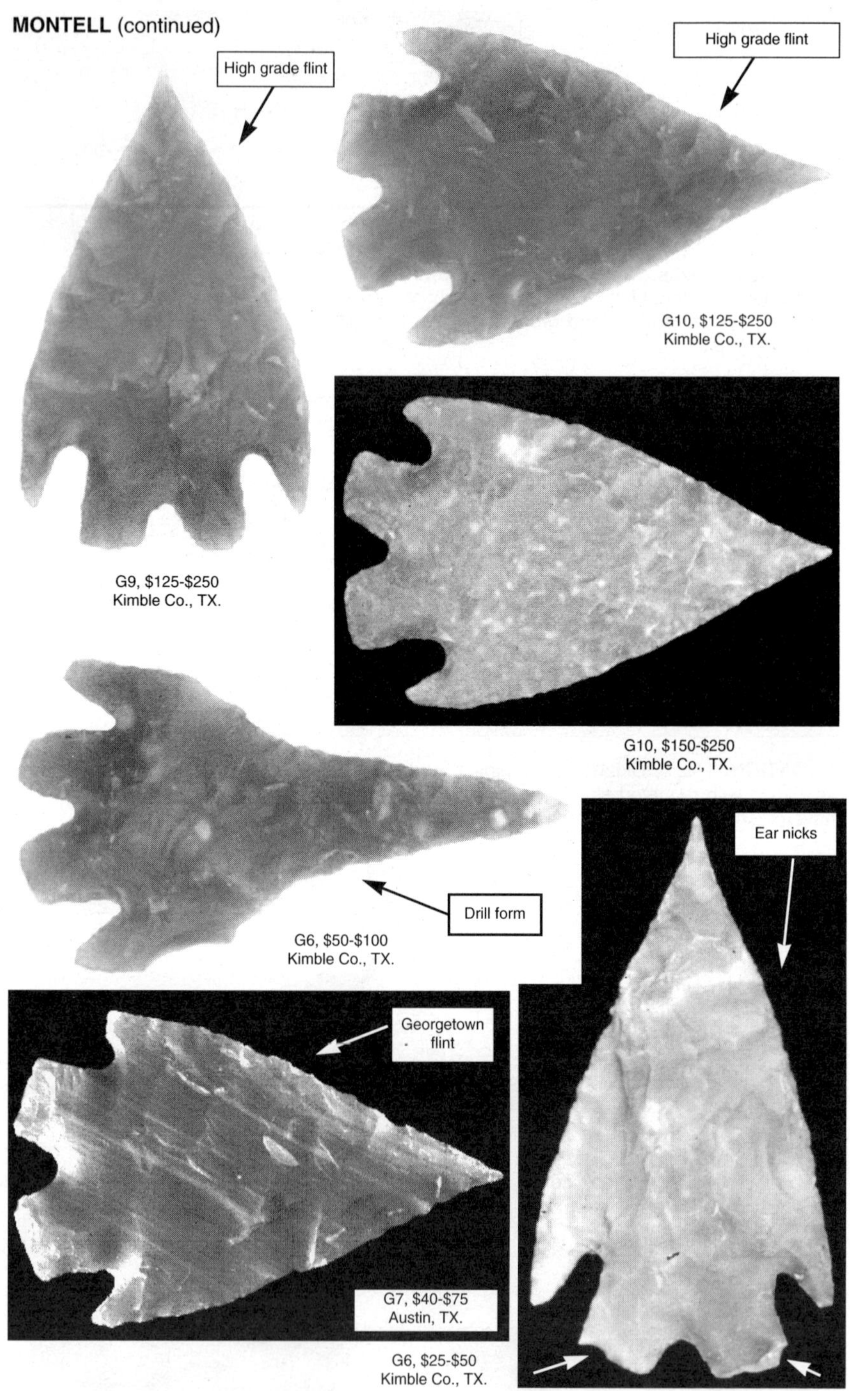

G9, $125-$250
Kimble Co., TX.

G10, $125-$250
Kimble Co., TX.

G10, $150-$250
Kimble Co., TX.

G6, $50-$100
Kimble Co., TX.

G7, $40-$75
Austin, TX.

G6, $25-$50
Kimble Co., TX.

LOCATION: Midwestern states. **DESCRIPTION:** A small to medium size, bifurcated point with barbed shoulders. The ears are usually squared and some examples are beveled on one side of each face and are serrated. **I.D. KEY:** Square basal lobes.

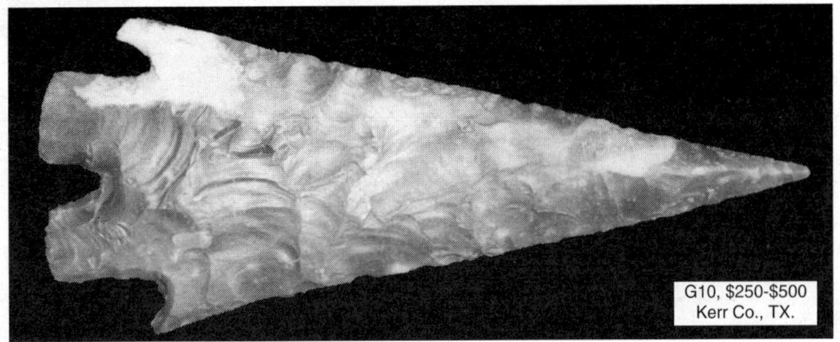
G10, $250-$500
Kerr Co., TX.

MORAN - Woodland-Mississippian, 1200 - 600 B. P.

(Also see Bonham, Rockwall, Sabinal and Scallorn)

G9, $35-$70
TX.

LOCATION: Central Texas. **DESCRIPTION:** A small, thin, barbed arrow point with a narrow, rectangular base. Shoulders barbs are usually sharp.

MORHISS - Late Archaic to Woodland, 4000 - 1000 B. P.

(Also see Adena, Bulverde, Carrolton and Morrill)

G5, $4-$8
Comanche Co., TX.

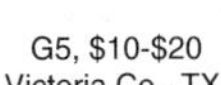
G5, $10-$20
Victoria Co., TX.

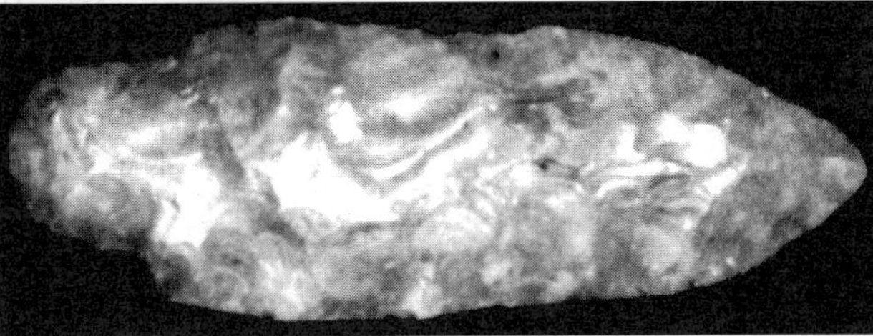

LOCATION: Texas to Oklahoma. **Description:** A medium to large size, thick, long stemmed point with weak shoulders and a convex base.

MORRILL - Woodland, 3000 - 1000 B. P.

(Also see Lange, Wells and Yarbrough)

LOCATION: Texas. **DESCRIPTION:** A medium size, thick, narrow, triangular point with weak, squared shoulders and a long rectangular stem.

MORRILL (continued)

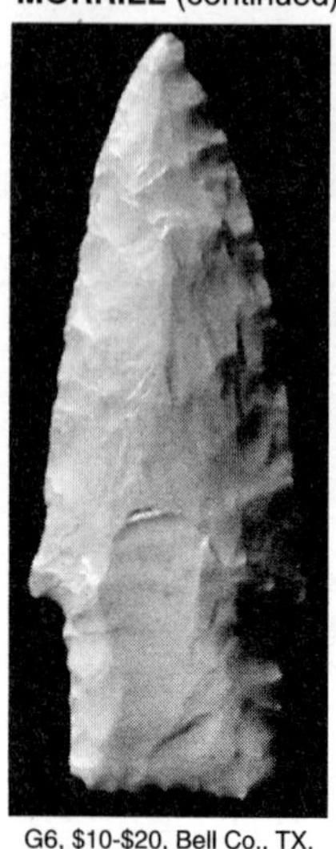

G6, $10-$20, Bell Co., TX.

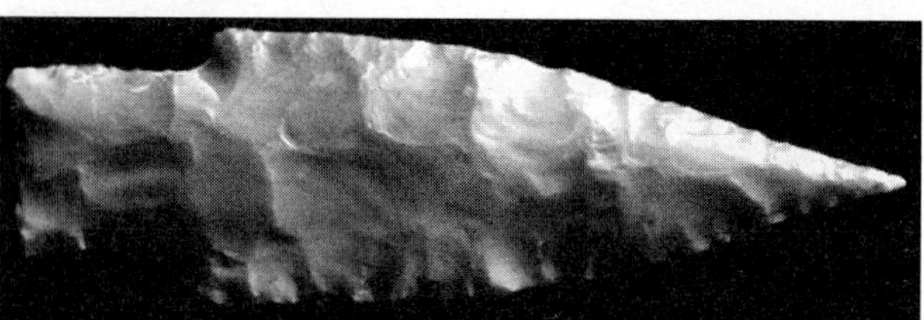

G8, $50-$100, Bell Co., TX.

G7, $30-$60
Llano Co., TX.

MORRIS - Mississippian, 1200 - 400 B. P.

(Also see Cuney, Friley and Sallisaw)

G4, $6-$12
TX.

G4, $15-$30
Spiro Mound, OK

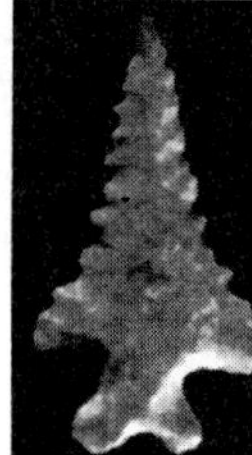

G6, $25-$50
Comanche Co., TX

G5, $25-$40
Spiro Mound, OK

G5, $25-$40
Spiro Mound, OK

G5, $25-$40
McCurtain Co., OK.

LOCATION: Texas to Oklahoma. **DESCRIPTION:** A small size, thin, barbed point with a bifurcated base and rounded ears. Blade edges can be serrated. **I.D. KEY:** Rounded basal ears.

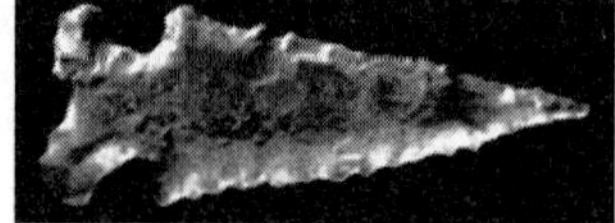

G7,
$30-$60
McCurtain Co., OK.

MORROW MOUNTAIN

(See Hale and Peisker Diamond)

MOTLEY - Middle Archaic to Woodland, 4500 - 1500 B. P.

(Also see Cupp, Epps and Gibson)

G5, $20-$40
Comanche Co., TX.

LOCATION: Arkansas eastward. **DESCRIPTION:** A medium to large size, expanded stemmed to widely corner notched point with strong barbs. The blade edges and the base are convex to straight. **I.D. KEY:** Long, expanding base.

MOTLEY (continued)

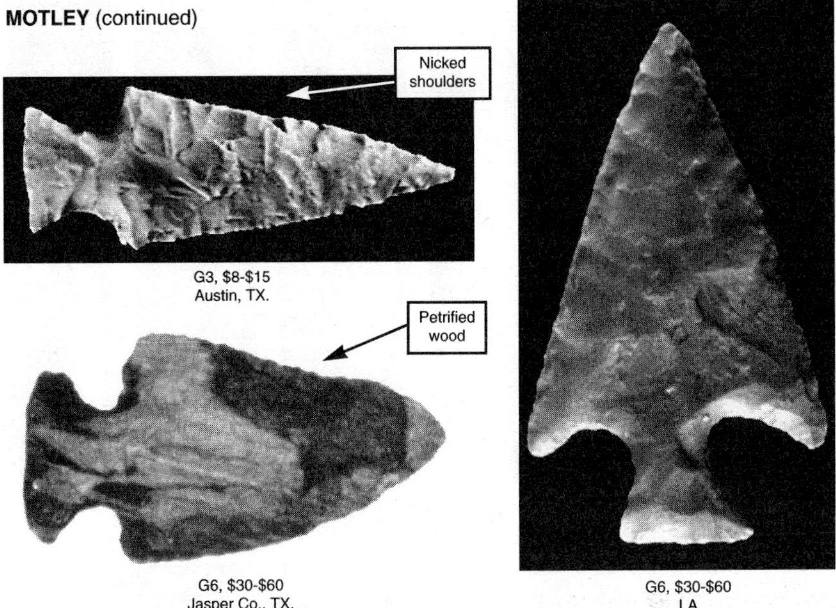

G3, $8-$15
Austin, TX.

G6, $30-$60
Jasper Co., TX.

G6, $30-$60
LA.

NODENA - Mississippian to Historic, 600 - 400 B. P.

(Also see Dardanelle, Guerrero and Guntersville)

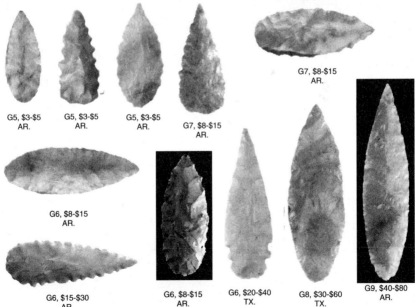

SC

G5, $3-$5
AR.

G5, $3-$5
AR.

G5, $3-$5
AR.

G7, $8-$15
AR.

G7, $8-$15
AR.

G6, $8-$15
AR.

G6, $15-$30
AR.

G6, $8-$15
AR.

G6, $20-$40
TX.

G8, $30-$60
TX.

G9, $40-$80
AR.

LOCATION: Arkansas and Tennessee. **DESCRIPTION:** A small to medium size, narrow, thin, elliptical shaped arrow point with a pointed to rounded base. Some examples have oblique, parallel flaking. Called *Tampa* in Florida. Used by the Quapaw Indians.

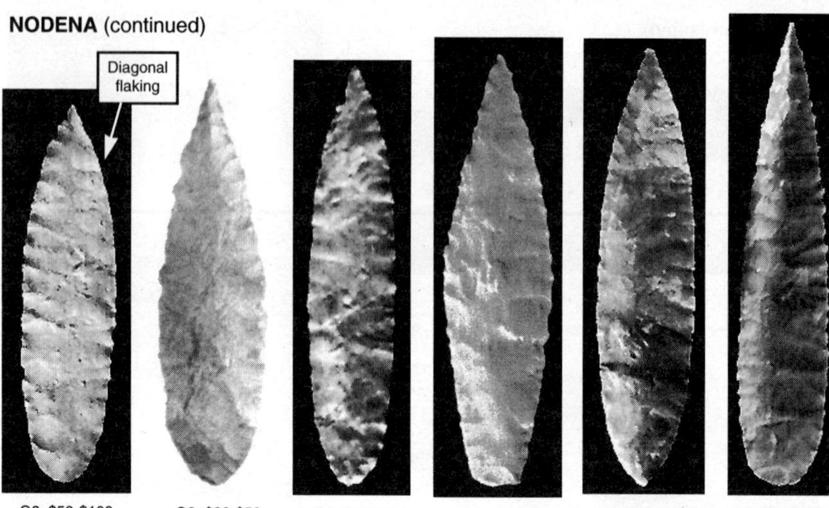

G8, $50-$100
AR.

G8, $30-$50
AR.

G8, $55-$110
AR.

G7, $45-$90
AR.

G8, $65-$130
AR.

G9, $80-$160
AR.

NOLAN - Mid-Archaic, 6000 - 4000 B. P.

(Also see Bulverde, Lange, Travis and Zorra)

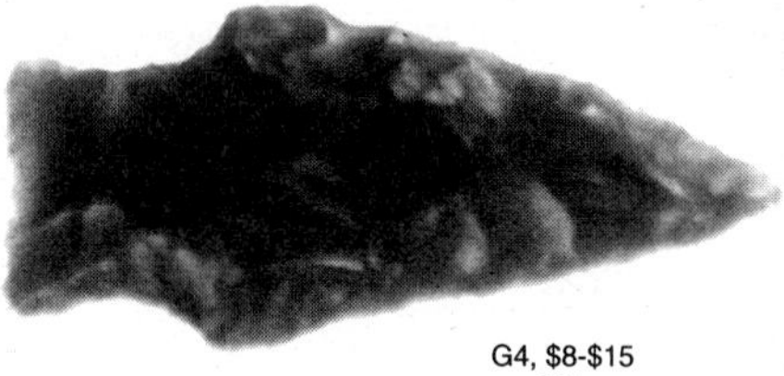

G4, $8-$15
TX.

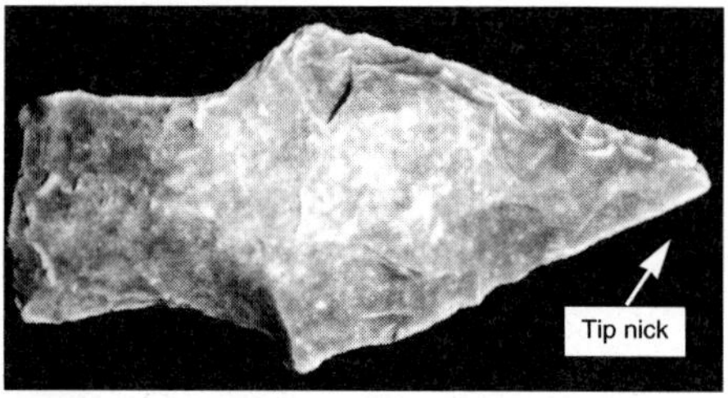

Tip nick

G3, $5-$10
Llano Co., TX.

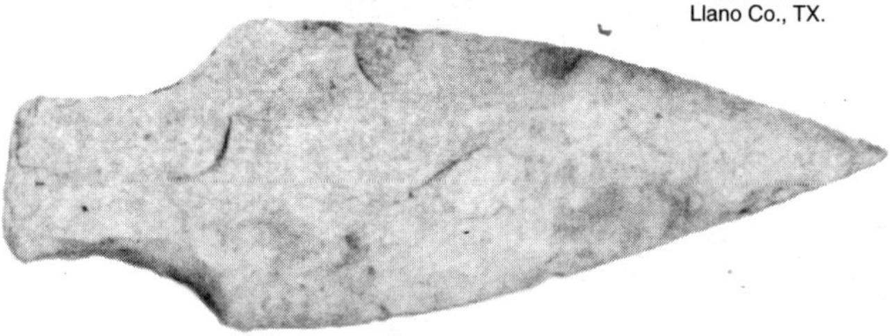

G7, $50-$100
Burnet Co., TX.

G5, $25-$50
Llano Co., TX.

G7, $40-$75
Killeen, TX.

Beleved edge
sets the type

G7, $55-$110
Williamson Co., TX.

G5, $25-$50
TX.

G7, $50-$100
Bell Co., TX.

SC

G8, $75-$150
Austin, TX.

G10, $200-$400
Comanche Co., TX.

G9, $150-$300
Williamson Co., TX.

NOLAN (continued)

LOCATION: Texas to Oklahoma. **DESCRIPTION:** A medium to large size, stemmed point with a needle like point. Shoulders are tapered to rounded. The stem is unique in that it is steeply beveled on one side of each face. **I.D. KEY:** Beveled stem.

OAUCHITA - Woodland, 3000 - 1500 B. P.

(Also see Base Tang and Pontchartrain)

LOCATION: Texas. **DESCRIPTION:** A large, broad, point with a short parallel stem and drooping shoulders.

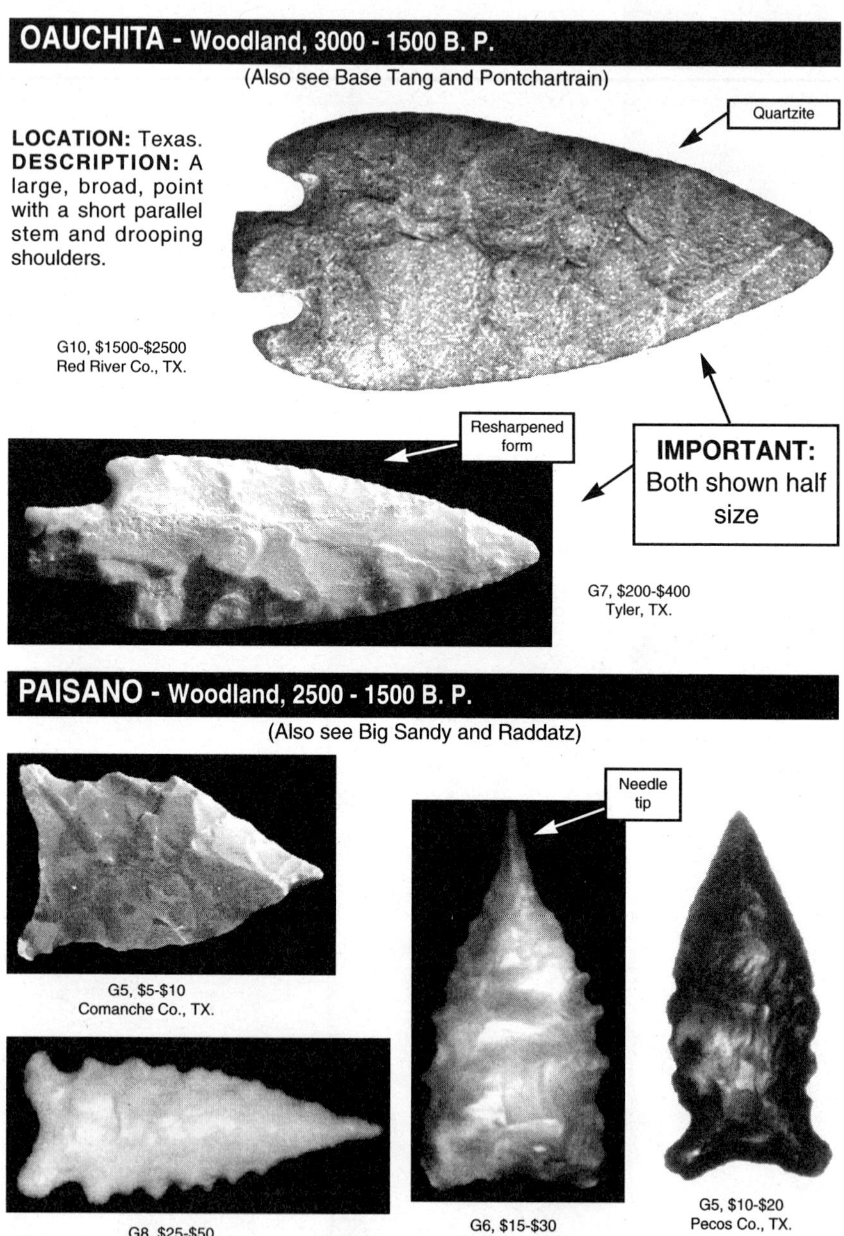

IMPORTANT: Both shown half size

G10, $1500-$2500
Red River Co., TX.

G7, $200-$400
Tyler, TX.

PAISANO - Woodland, 2500 - 1500 B. P.

(Also see Big Sandy and Raddatz)

G5, $5-$10
Comanche Co., TX.

G8, $25-$50
Reeves Co., TX.

G6, $15-$30
Reeves Co., TX.

G5, $10-$20
Pecos Co., TX.

LOCATION: Texas. **DESCRIPTION:** A medium size point with broad side notches forming a squared to auriculate base that is concave.

PAISANO (continued)

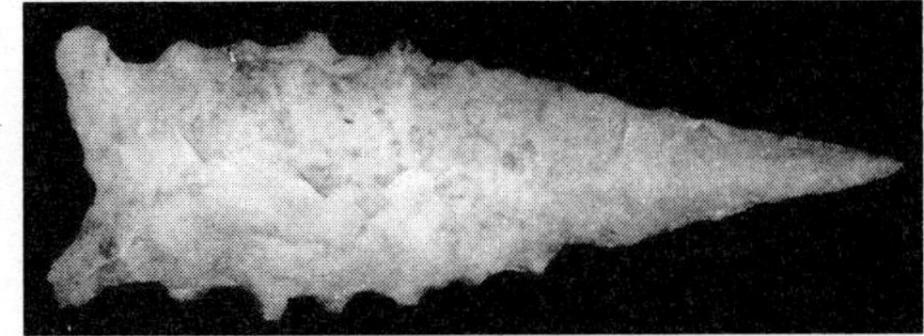

G9, $50-$100
Val Verde Co., TX.

PALEO KNIFE - Transitional Paleo, 10,000 - 8000 B. P.

(Also see Scraper and Square Knife)

G7, $1100-$2200
Amarillo, TX.

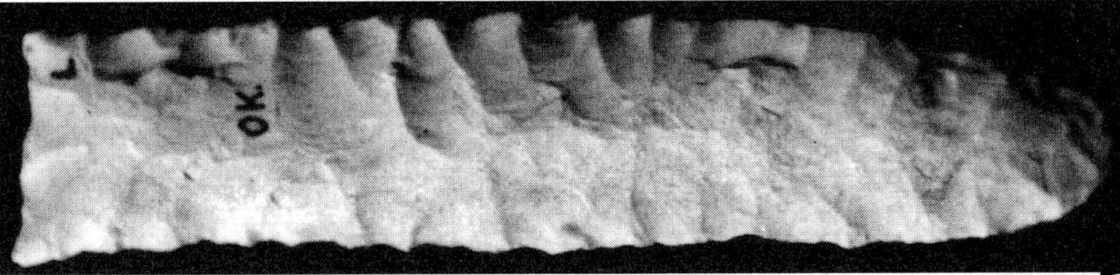

G7, $175-$350
Cherokee Co., OK.

SC

LOCATION: All of North America. **DESCRIPTION:** A large size lanceolate blade finished with broad parallel flakes. These are found on Paleo sites and were probably used as knives.

PALMILLAS - Middle to Late Archaic, 6000 - 3000 B. P.

(Also see Godley and Williams)

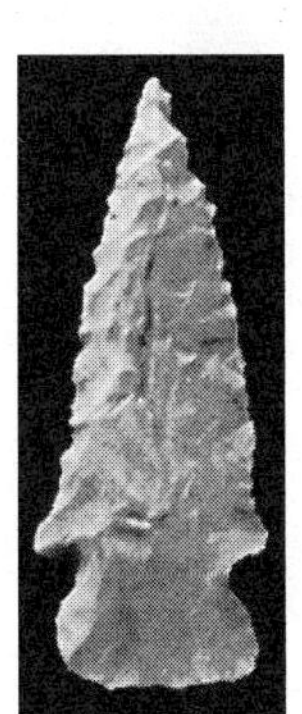

G3, $5-$10
Comanche Co., TX.

G5, $6-$12
Comanche Co., TX.

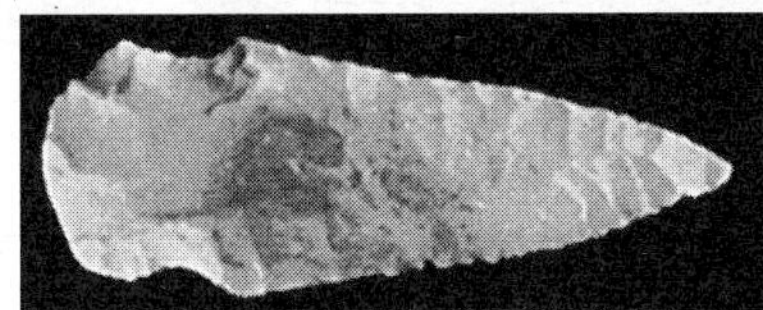

G7, $10-$20
Comanche Co., TX.

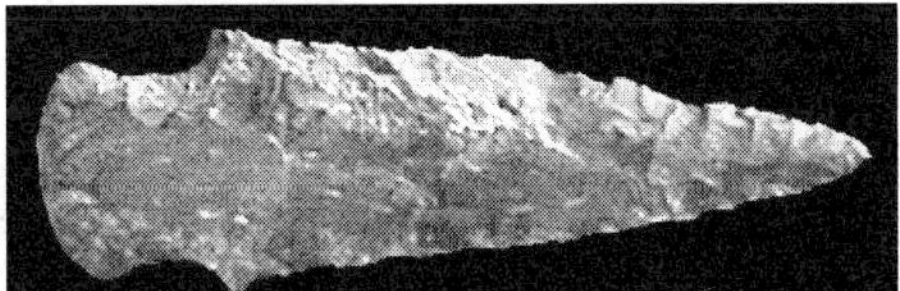

G7, $15-$25
Comanche Co., TX.

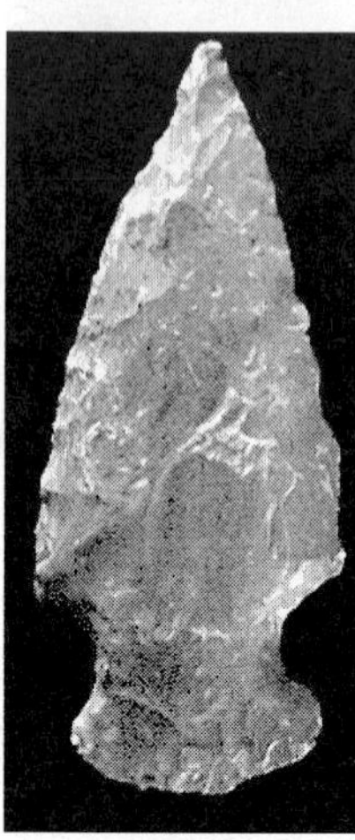

G7, $15-$25
Comanche Co., TX.

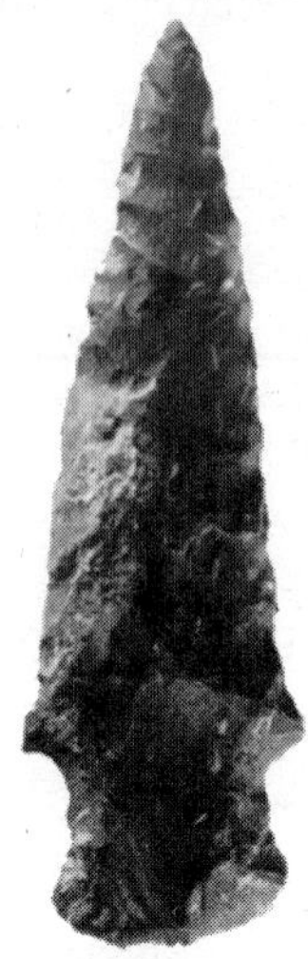

G7, $20-$40
Comanche Co., TX.

G8, $30-$60
Bell Co., TX.

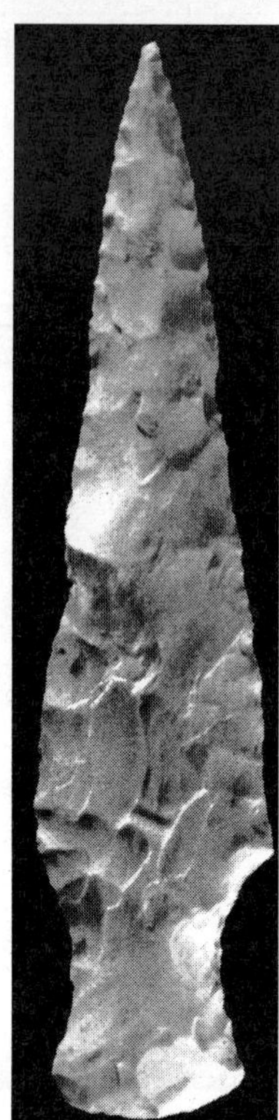

G6, $25-$50
Bell Co., TX.

LOCATION: Texas to Oklahoma. **DESCRIPTION:** A small to medium size triangular point with a bulbous stem. Shoulders are prominent and can be horizontal to barbed or weak and tapered. Stems expand and are rounded. **I.D. KEY:** Bulbous stem.

PANDALE - Middle Archaic, 6000 - 3000 B. P.

(Also see Darl and Travis)

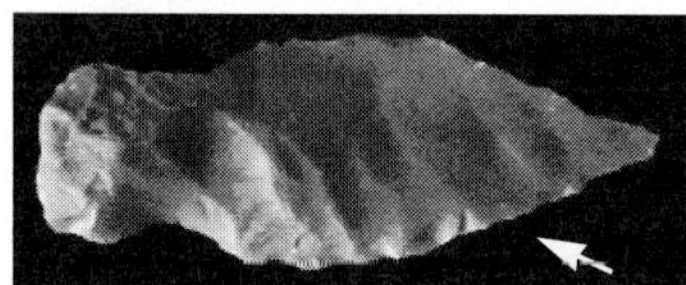

G6, $8-$15
Comanche Co., TX.

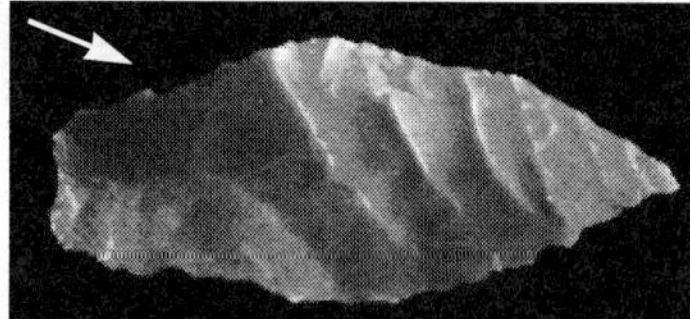

G6, $10-$20
Comanche Co., TX.

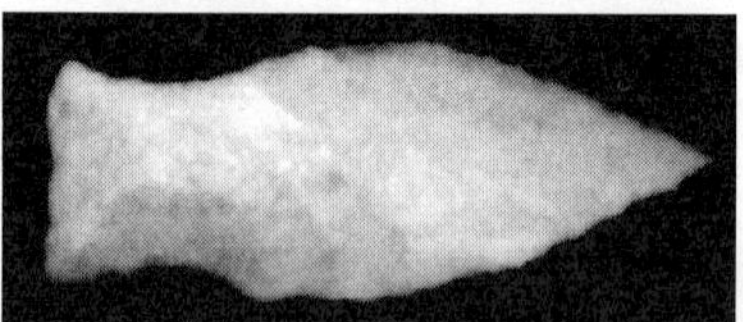

G6, $15-$25
Val Verde Co., TX.

LOCATION: Texas. **DESCRIPTION:** A medium size, narrow, stemmed point or spike with a steepy beveled or torque blade. Some examples show oblique parallel flaking.

PANDORA - Late Archaic to Woodland, 4000 - 1000 B. P.

(Also see Adena Blade, Friday, Kinney and Refugio)

LOCATION: Midwestern states. **DESCRIPTION:** A medium to large size, lanceolate blade with a straight base. Blade edges can be parallel to convex.

G8, $50-$100
TX.

PEDERNALES - Middle Archaic to Woodland, 6000 - 2000 B. P.

(Also see Hoxie, Jetta, Langtry, Montell, Uvalde and Val Verde)

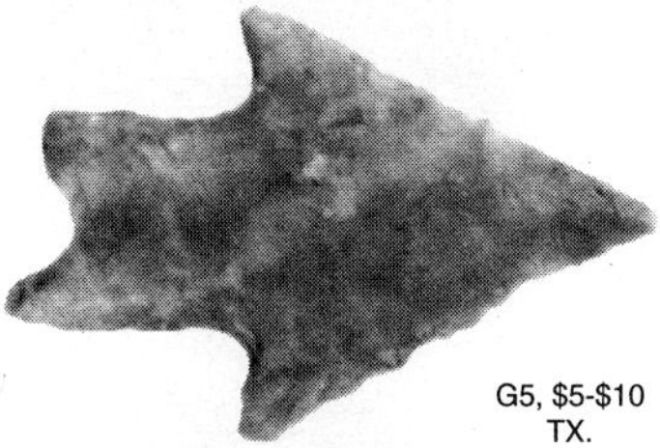

G5, $5-$10
TX.

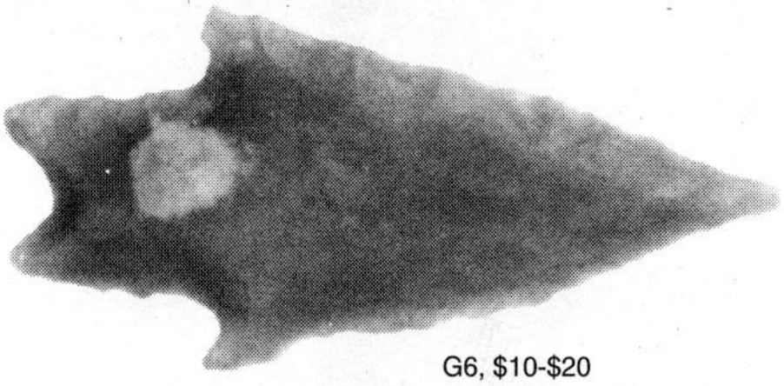

G6, $10-$20
TX.

G6, $15-$25
TX.

G5, $10-$20
TX.

G7, $65-$125
Travis Co., TX.

G6, $15-$30
TX.

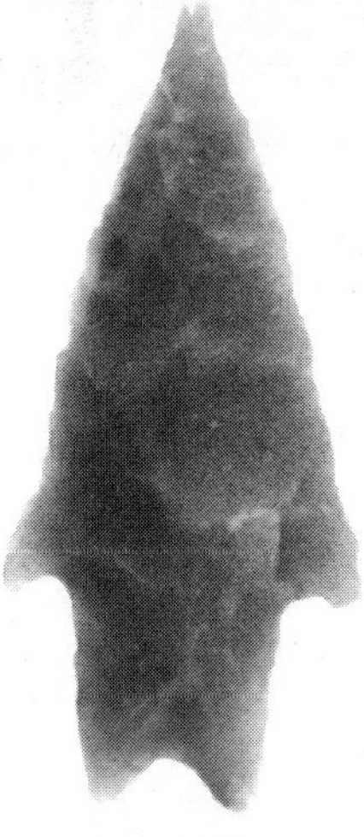

G6, $10-$20
TX.

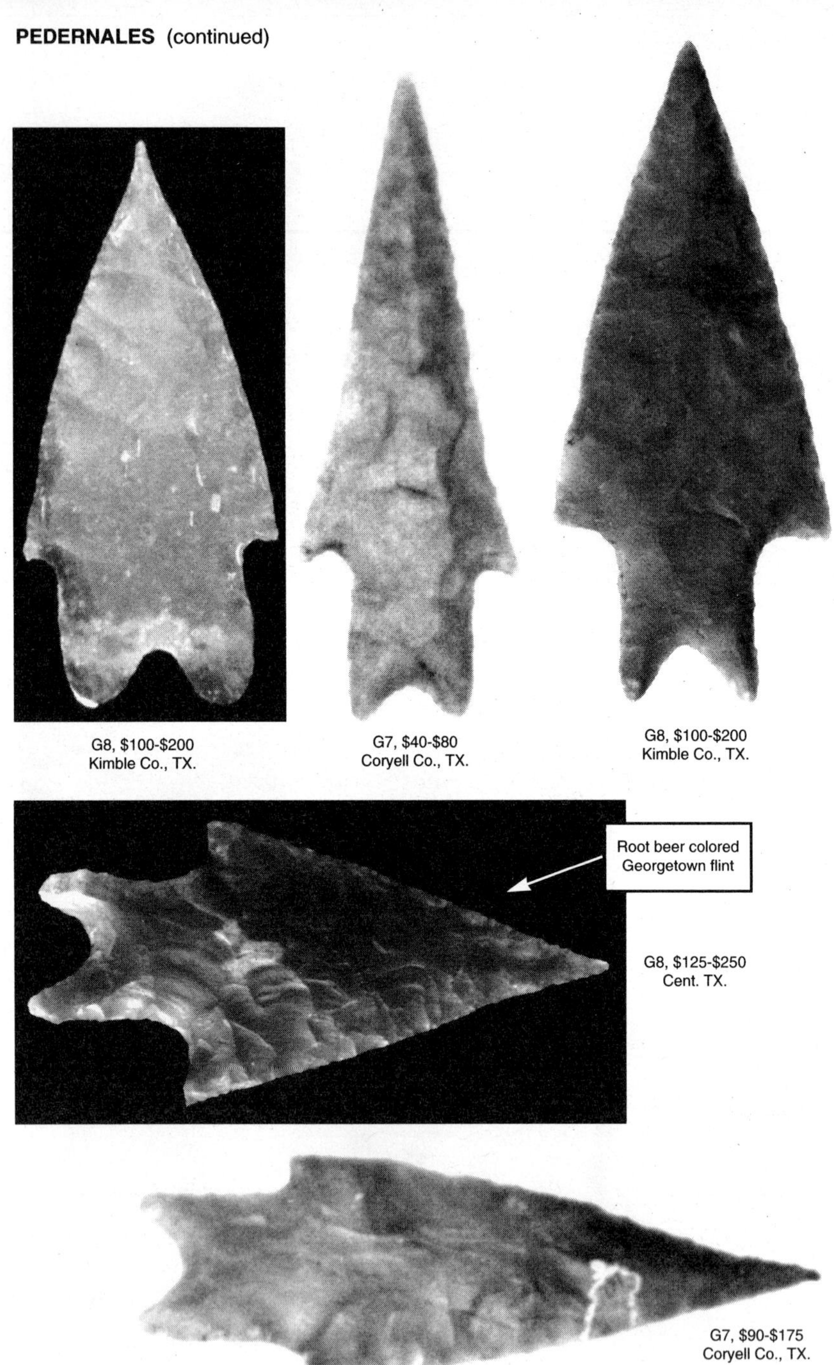

G8, $100-$200
Kimble Co., TX.

G7, $40-$80
Coryell Co., TX.

G8, $100-$200
Kimble Co., TX.

G8, $125-$250
Cent. TX.

G7, $90-$175
Coryell Co., TX.

LOCATION: Texas. **DESCRIPTION:** A medium to large size, thin, usually barbed, point with a broad, long, bifurcated stem. Tangs and tips are very sharp. Blade edges are convex, concave to recurved. These points are of high quality. **I.D. KEY:** Long bifurcated stem.

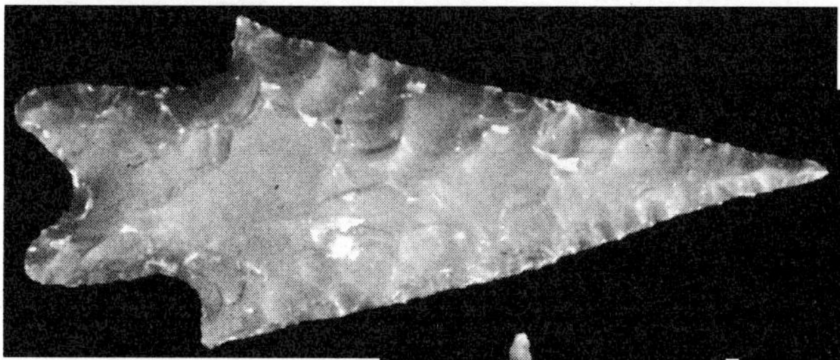

G9, $100-$200
Kimble Co., TX.

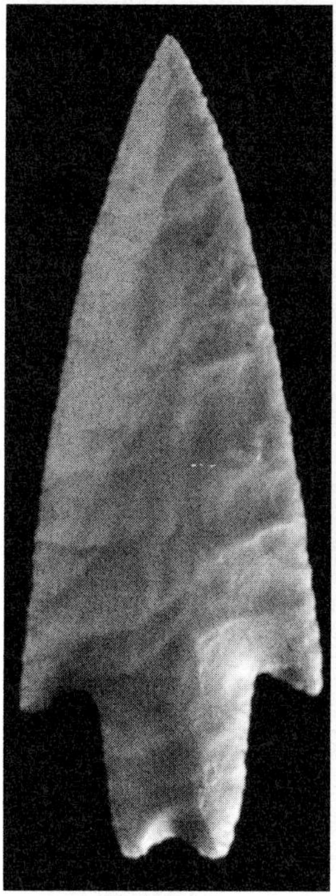

G9, $150-$300
TX.

G7, $125-$250
Kimble Co., TX.

G9, $300-$600
Kimble Co., TX.

G10, $200-$400
Kimble Co., TX.

PEISKER DIAMOND - Woodland, 2500 - 2000 B. P.

(Also see Gary and Hale)

Translucent novaculite

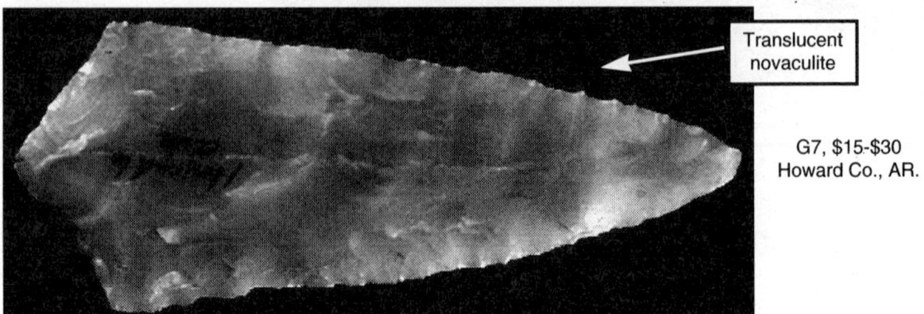

G7, $15-$30
Howard Co., AR.

LOCATION: Illinois, Missouri, Akansas, Kansas into Iowa. **DESCRIPTION:** A large, broad blade with sharp shoulders and a short to moderate contracting base that comes to a point. Blade edges are recurved, convex or straight. Similar in form to the *Morrow Mountain* point found in the Southeast, but not as old. **I.D.KEY:** Contracted "v" base.

PELICAN - Transitional Paleo, 10,000 - 6000 B. P.

(Also see Golondrina, Hell Gap, Midland, Rio Grande and San Patrice)

G8, $100-$200
AR.

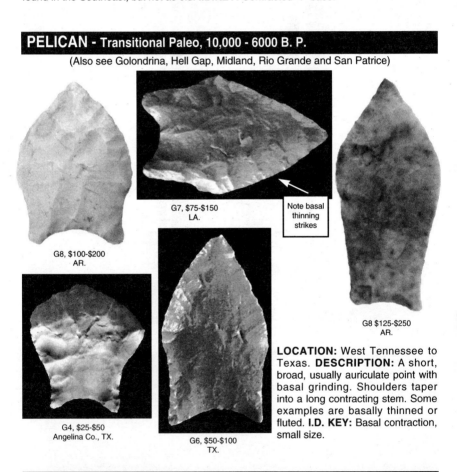

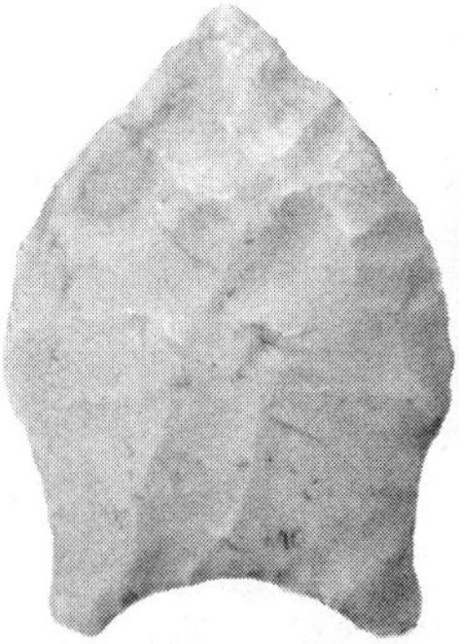

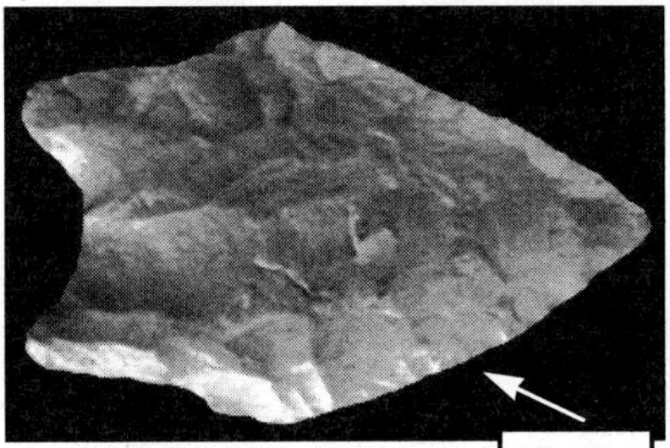

G7, $75-$150
LA.

Note basal thinning strikes

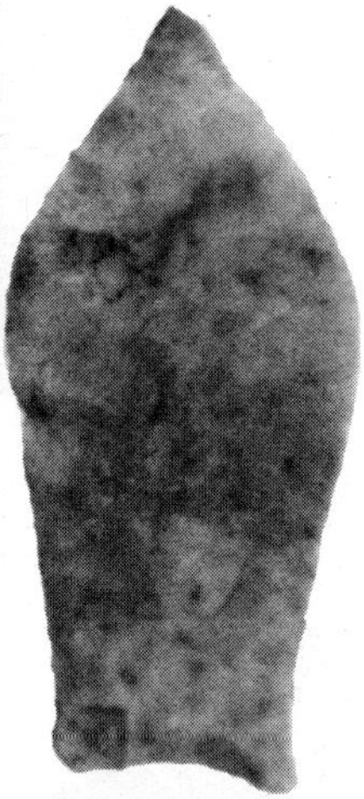

G8 $125-$250
AR.

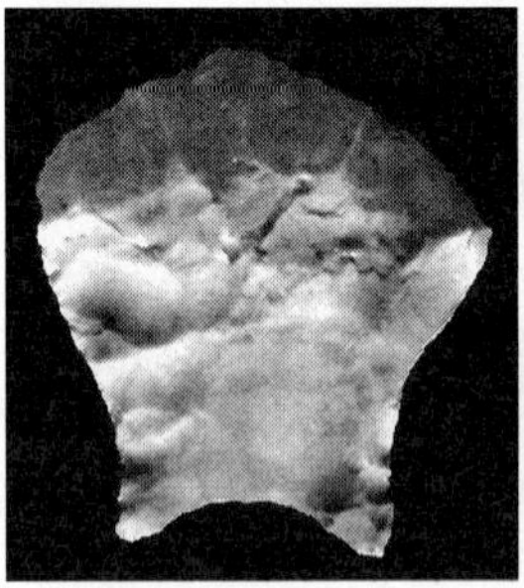

G4, $25-$50
Angelina Co., TX.

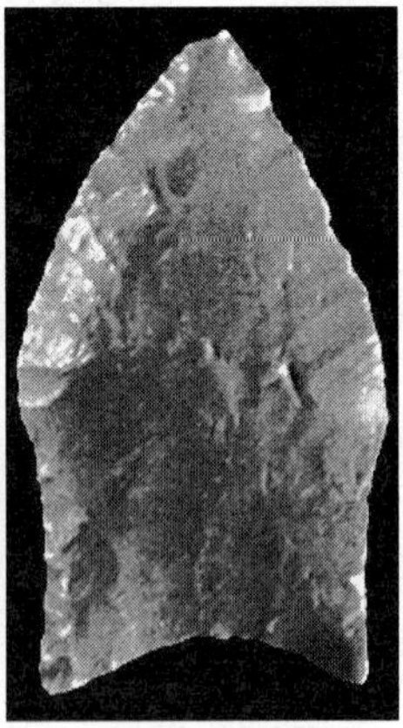

G6, $50-$100
TX.

LOCATION: West Tennessee to Texas. **DESCRIPTION:** A short, broad, usually auriculate point with basal grinding. Shoulders taper into a long contracting stem. Some examples are basally thinned or fluted. **I.D. KEY:** Basal contraction, small size.

PERDIZ - Mississippian, 1000 - 500 B. P.

(Also see Alba, Bassett, Bonham, Cuney, Hayes, Homan and Keota)

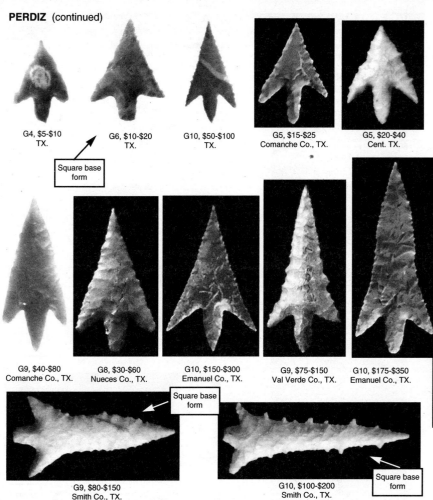

G4, $5-$10
TX.

G6, $10-$20
TX.

Square base form

G10, $50-$100
TX.

G5, $15-$25
Comanche Co., TX.

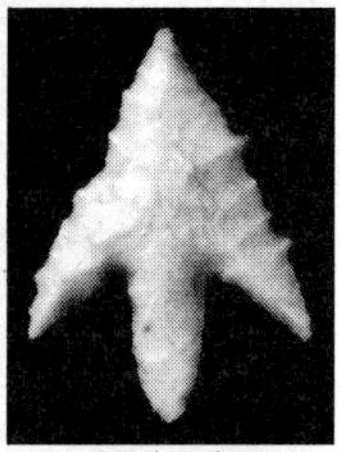

G5, $20-$40
Cent. TX.

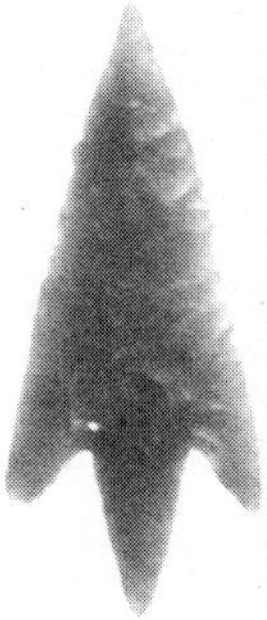

G9, $40-$80
Comanche Co., TX.

G8, $30-$60
Nueces Co., TX.

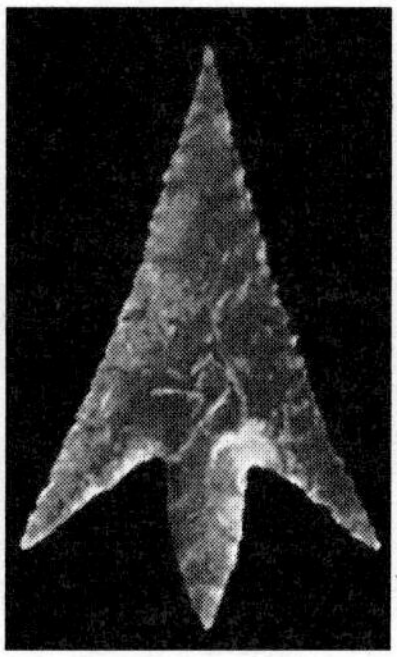

G10, $150-$300
Emanuel Co., TX.

G9, $75-$150
Val Verde Co., TX.

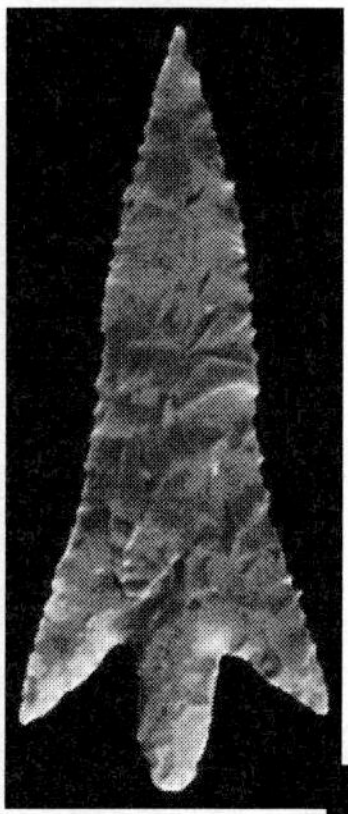

G10, $175-$350
Emanuel Co., TX.

Square base form

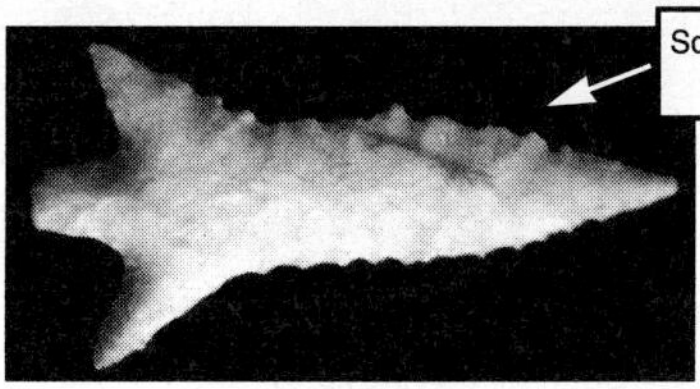

G9, $80-$150
Smith Co., TX.

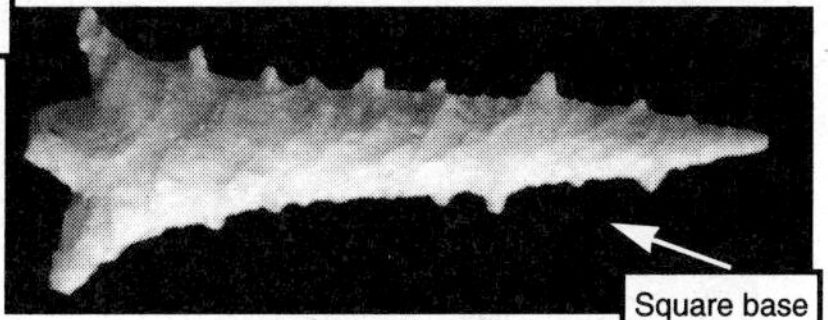

G10, $100-$200
Smith Co., TX.

Square base form

LOCATION: Texas to Oklahoma. **DESCRIPTION:** A small to medium size, thin, narrow, triangular arrow point with pointed barbs and a long, pointed to near pointed stem. Some examples are serrated. Tangs and tips are sharp. **I.D. KEY:** Long pointed stem and barbs.

PERFORATOR - Archaic to Mississippian, 9000 - 400 B. P.

(Also see Drill, Graver and Scraper)

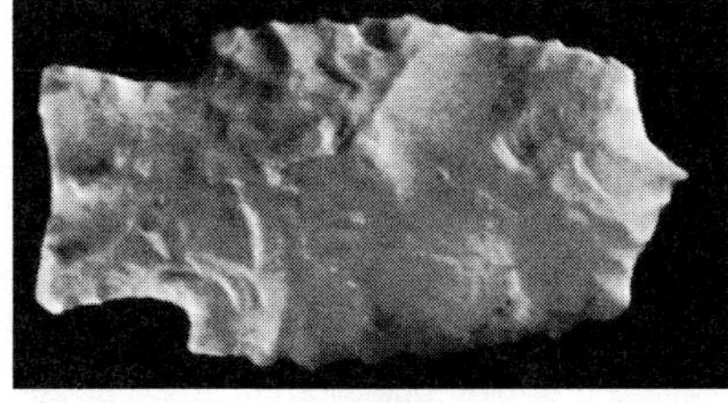

G5, $5-$10
Comanche Co., Tx.

LOCATION: Archaic and Woodland sites everywhere. **DESCRIPTION:** A jabbing projection at the tip would qualify for the type. It is believed that *perforators* were used for tattooing, incising or to punch holes in leather or other materials or objects. Paleo peoples used *Gravers* for the same purpose. All Archaic and Woodland cultures converted their points into this type. Therefore, most point types could occur in this form.

PIKE COUNTY - Early Archaic, 8000 - 5000 B. P.

(Also see Dalton)

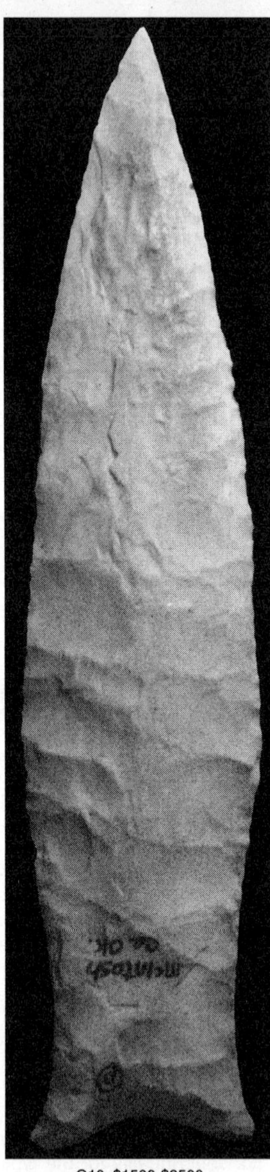

G10, $1500-$2500
McIntosh Co., OK.

LOCATION: Oklahoma, Arkansas into Missouri and Illinois. **DESCRIPTION:** A large size, lanceolate blade with an eared, concave base. Basal area is ground. Related To *Dalton.* **I.D. KEY:** Fishtailed base

PLAINVIEW - Late Paleo, 10,000 - 7000 B. P.

(Also see Angostura, Barber, Brown's Valley, Clovis, Dalton, Golondrina and Midland)

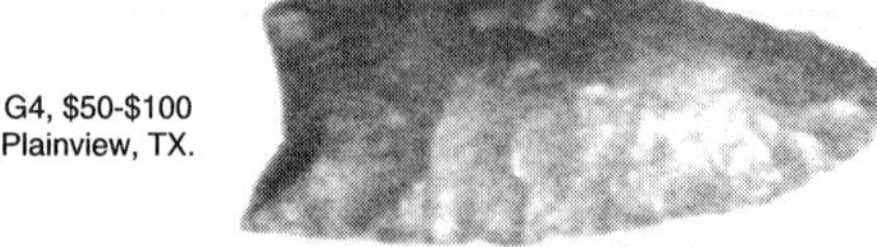

G4, $50-$100
Plainview, TX.

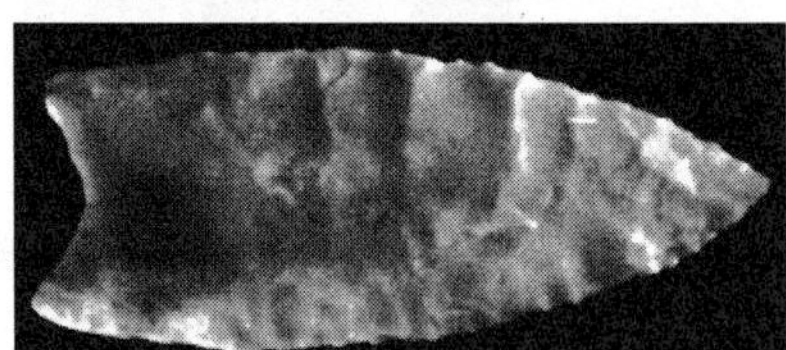

G4, $50-$100
W. TX.

G5, $75-$150
Comanche Co., TX.

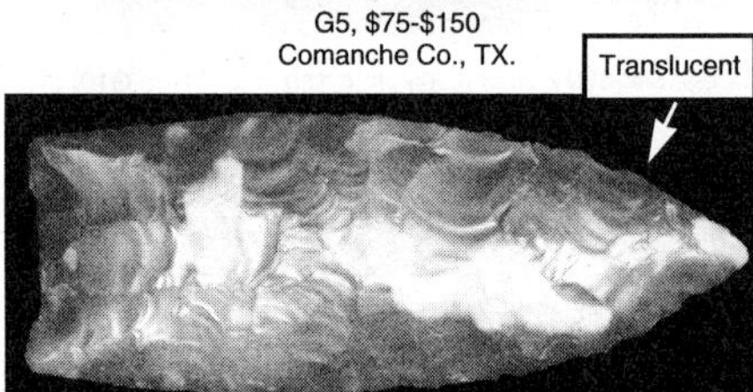

G7, $150-$250
Winkler Co., TX.

G8, $125-$250
Llano Co., TX.

LOCATION: Mexico northward to Canada and Alaska. **DESCRIPTION:** A medium size, thin, lanceolate point with usually parallel sides and a concave base that is ground. Some examples are thinned or fluted and is believed to be related to the earlier *Clovis* and contemporary *Dalton* type. Flaking is of high quality and can be collateral to oblique transverse.

Oblique transverse flaking

Chalcedony

Base nick

G8, $500-$1000
Osage Co., OK.

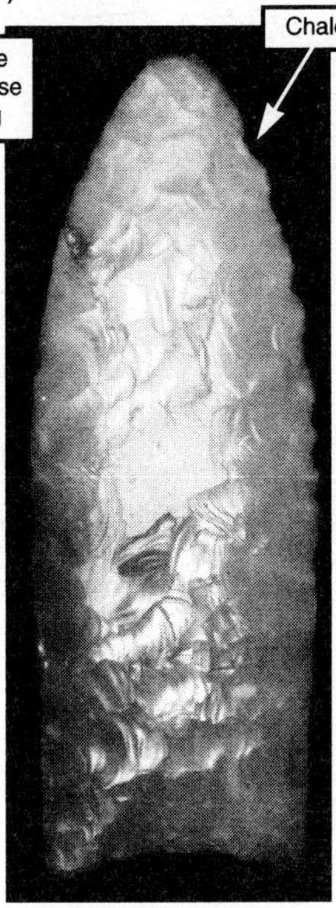

G8, $650-$1300
Bailey Co., TX.

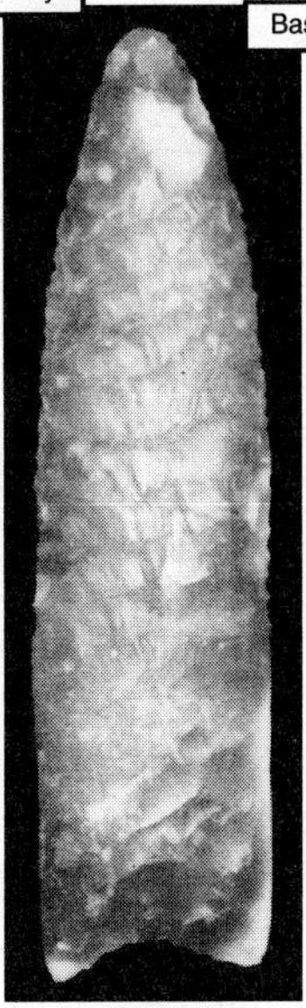

G8, $550-$1100
Wilson Co., TX.

G6, $250-$500
Wilson Co., TX.

SC

Oblique transverse flaking

Oblique transverse flaking

G9, $750-$1500
Osage Co., OK.

G9, $750-$1500
Wilson Co., TX.

G10, $1100-$2200
Mills Co., TX.

G8, $750-$1500
Wilson Co., TX.

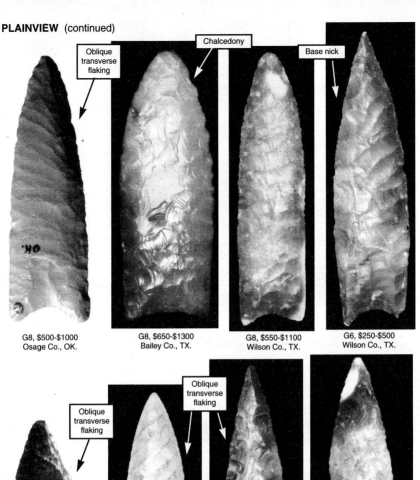

PONTCHARTRAIN (Type I) - Late Archaic to Woodland, 4000 - 2000 B. P.

(Also see Lange, Morrill, Morhiss and Travis)

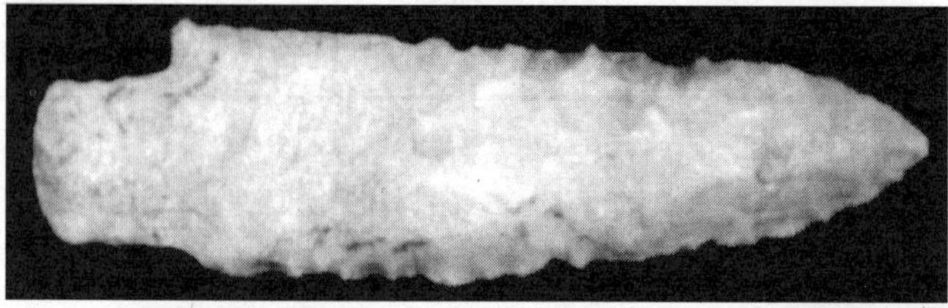

G7, $15-$30
E. TX.

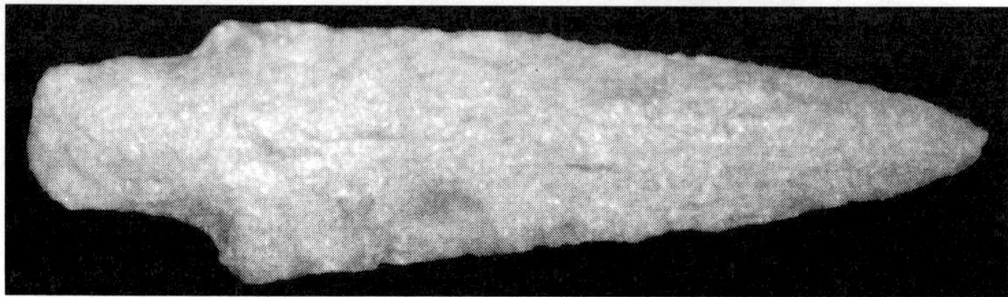

G9, $50-$100
E. TX.

LOCATION: Alabama to Texas. **DESCRIPTION:** A medium to large size, thick, narrow, stemmed point with weak, tapered or barbed shoulders. The stem is parallel sided with a convex to straight base. Some examples are finely serrated and are related and similar to the *Flint Creek* type.

POGO - Woodland to Mississippian, 2000 - 500 B. P.

(Also see Darl, Lange and Travis)

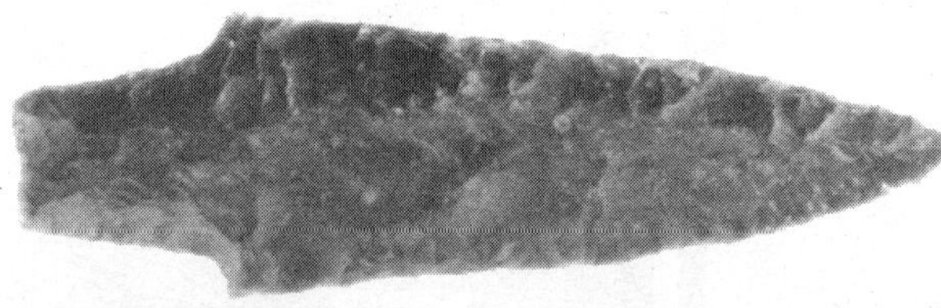

G9, $100-$200
Montgomery Co., TX.

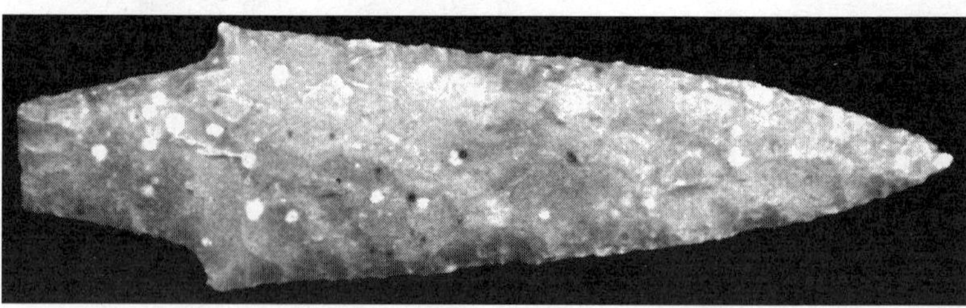

G10, $150-$300
Trinity Co., TX.

LOCATION: Texas. **DESCRIPTION:** A medium to large size contracted stem point with small, tapered shoulders. The base is usually straight.

RADDATZ - Mid-Archaic to Woodland, 5000 - 2000 B. P.

(Also see Big Sandy, Cache River, Hemphill, Hickory Ridge, Osceola and Savage Cave)

G6, $15-$25
Jonesboro, AR.

G5, $10-$20
Jonesboro, AR.

G5, $8-$15
Jonesboro, AR.

LOCATION: Arkansas to Missouri. **DESCRIPTION:** A medium size, side notched point with a concave to straight base. Similar in outline to *Big Sandy* points found in the Southeast.

RED RIVER KNIFE - Transitional Paleo, 9500 - 7000 B. P.

(Also see Alberta, Eden, Firstview and Scottsbluff)

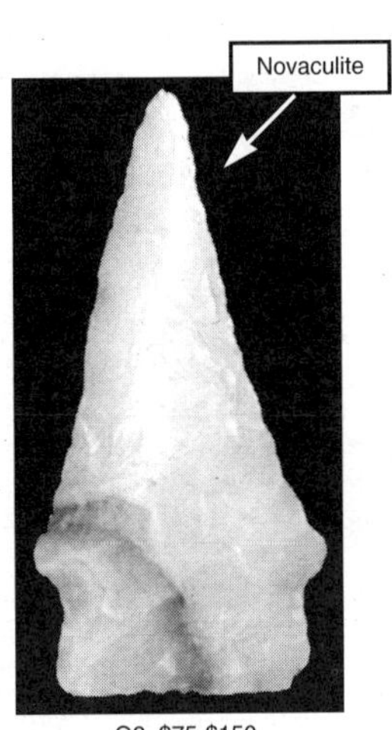

G8, $75-$150
Harrison Co., TX.

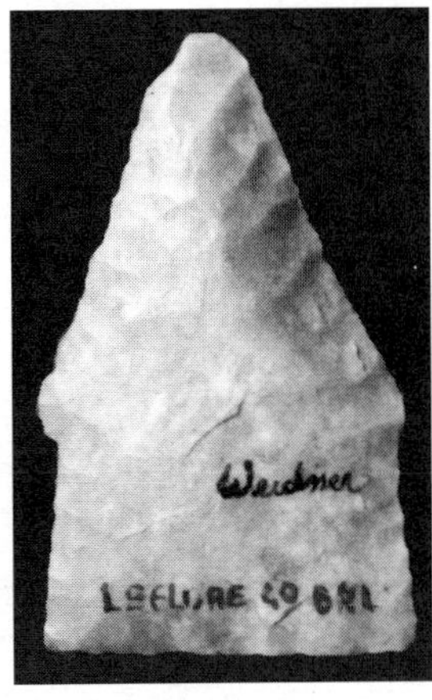

G6, $100-$200
LeFlore Co., OK.

G5, $100-$200
Osage Co., OK.

RED RIVER KNIFE (continued)

G7, $75-$150
S.E. OK.

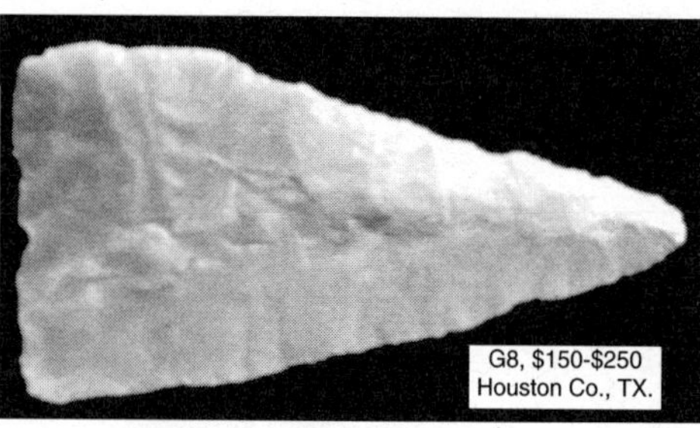
G8, $150-$250
Houston Co., TX.

LOCATION: Texas to Colorado. **DESCRIPTION:** A medium size, asymmetrical blade with weak shoulders and a short, expanding stem. Bases are straight to slightly convex. It has been reported that these knifes were made by the Cody Complex people from Scottsbluff points. Look for early parallel flaking.

REED - Woodland to Mississippian, 1500 - 500 B. P.

(Also see Knight Island and Washita)

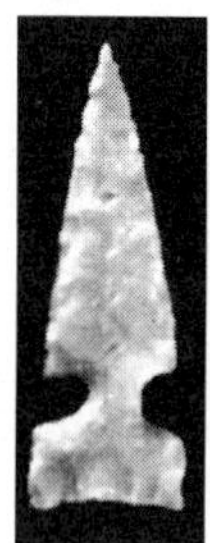
G7, $20-$40
Spiro Md, OK.

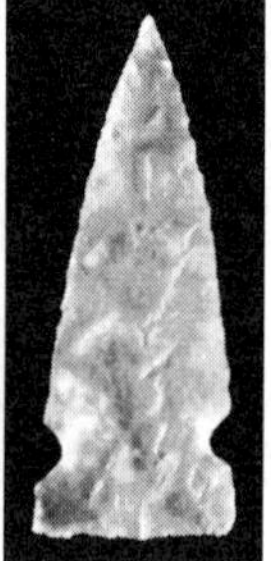
G6, $15-$30
AR.

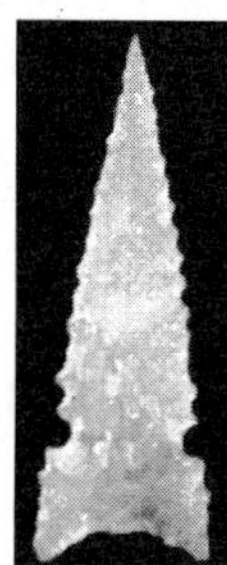
G10, $50-$100
Spiro Md, OK.

G5, $20-$35
Spiro Mound, OK.

G8, $50-$100
AR.

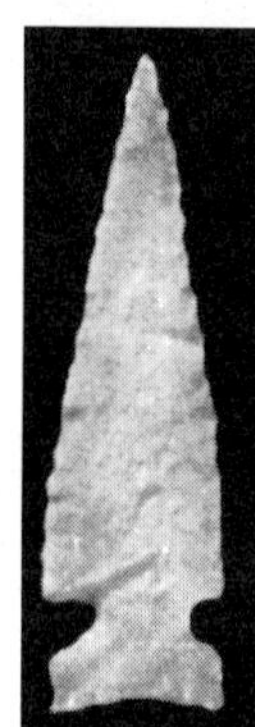
G9, $40-$80
Spiro Mound, OK.

LOCATION: Oklahoma to Arkansas. **DESCRIPTION:** A small size, thin, triangular, side notched point with a straight to concave base. Rarely, serrations occur.

REFUGIO - Middle Archaic, 5000 - 2000 B. P.

(Also see Gahagan, Pandora and Sabine)

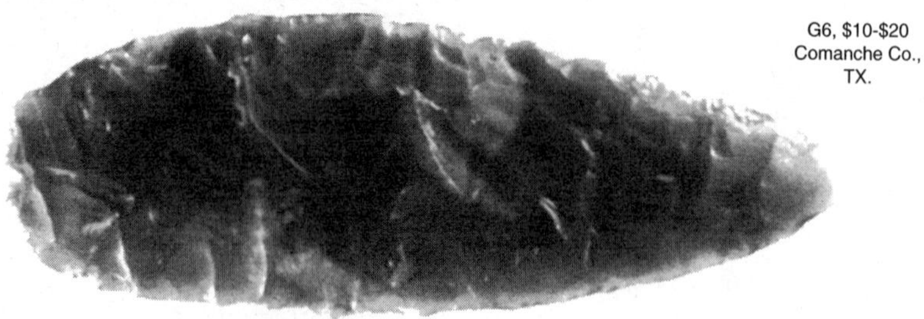
G6, $10-$20
Comanche Co., TX.

LOCATION: Texas. **DESCRIPTION:** A medium to large size, narrow, lanceolate blade with a rounded base.

RICE CONTRACTED STEM (See Hidden Valley)

RICE LOBBED - Early Archaic, 9000 - 5000 B. P.

(Also see Uvalde)

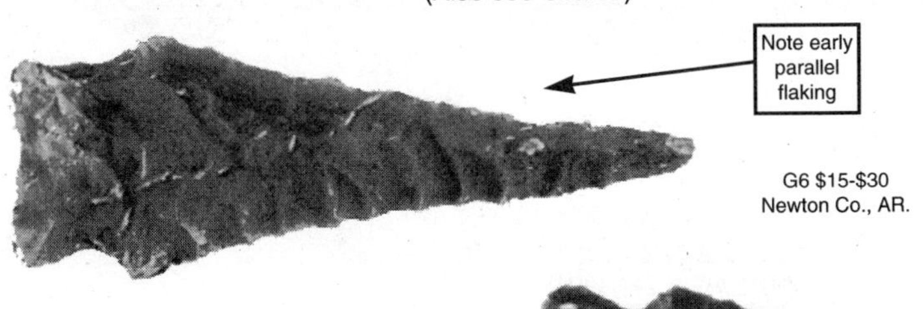

Note early parallel flaking

G6 $15-$30
Newton Co., AR.

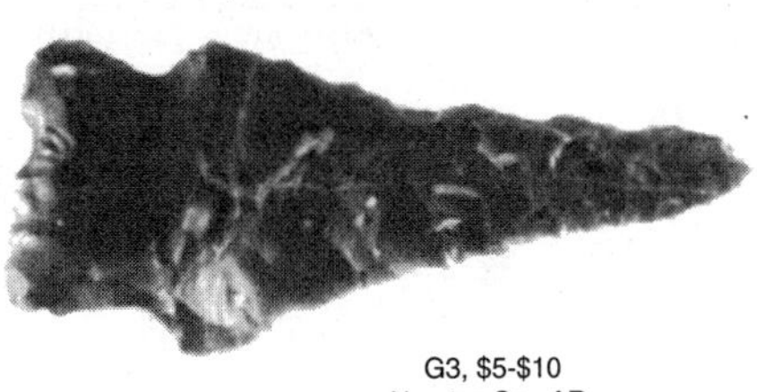

G3, $5-$10
Newton Co., AR.

LOCATION: Oklahoma to Missouri. **DESCRIPTION:** A medium to large size bifurcated to lobed base point with serrated blade edges. The base has a shallow indentation compared to the other bifurcated types. Shoulders are sharp and prominent. Called *Culpepper* Bifurcate in Virginia.

RICE SHALLOW SIDE NOTCHED - Early Archaic, 9000 - 5000 B. P.

(Also see Brewerton Eared)

LOCATION: Oklahoma to Missouri. **DESCRIPTION:** A medium size, broad point with shallow side notches and a convex base.

G4, $6-$10
AR.

SC

RIO GRANDE - Early Archaic, 7500 - 6000 B. P.

(Also see Agate Basin, Angostura, Hell Gap and Pelican)

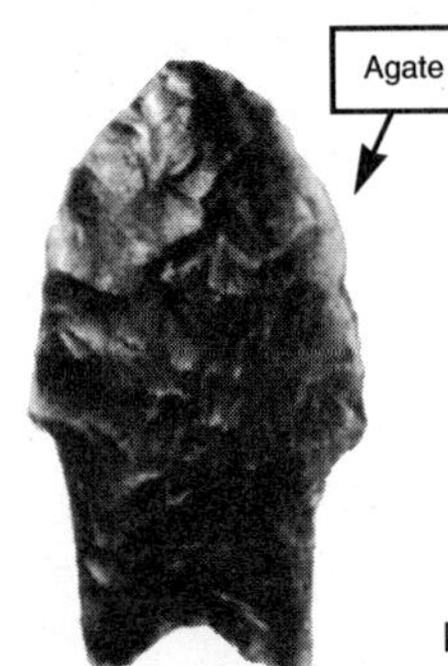

Agate

G6, $30-$60
TX.

G8, $80-$150
Williamson Co., TX.

LOCATION: New Mexico, Texas to Colorado. **DESCRIPTION:** A medium to large size, lanceolate point with tapered shoulders and a long parallel sided to contracting stem. The base can be straight, concave or convex. **I.D. KEY:** Long contracting stem.

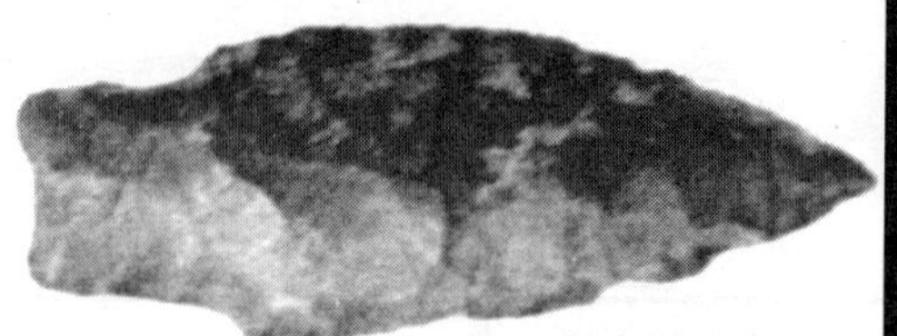

G6, $50-$100
Amarillo, TX.

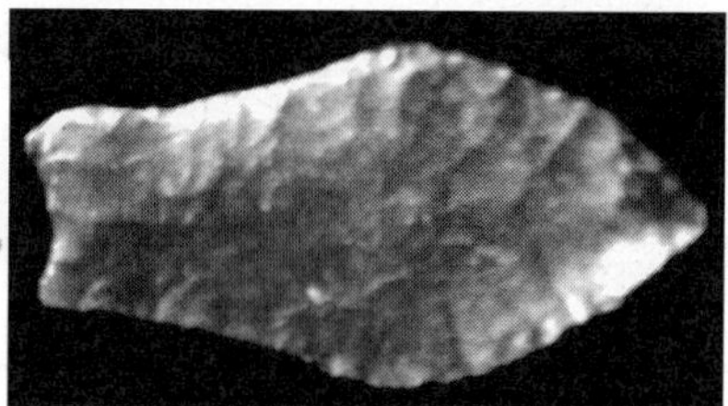

G7, $70-$140
Bailey Co., TX.

ROCKWALL - Late Woodland, 1400 - 1000 B. P.

(Also see Alba, Sabinal, Scallorn and Shumla)

G2, $3-$5
Cent. AR.

G4, $5-$10
Comanche Co., TX.

G7, $15-$30
TX.

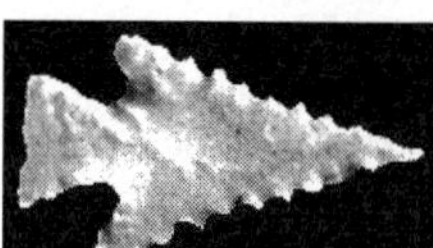

G7, $25-$50
Spiro Mound, OK.

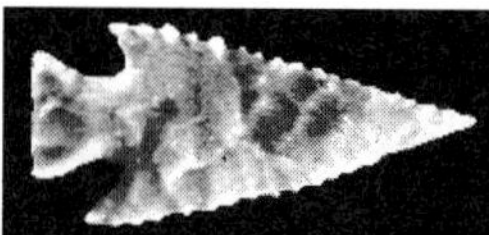

G7, $25-$50
Comanche Co., Tx.

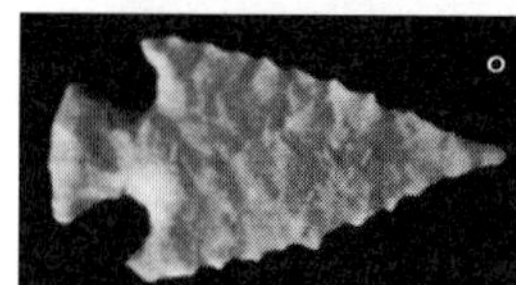

G6, $20-$40
Comanche Co., TX.

G8, $50-$100
Crane Co., TX.

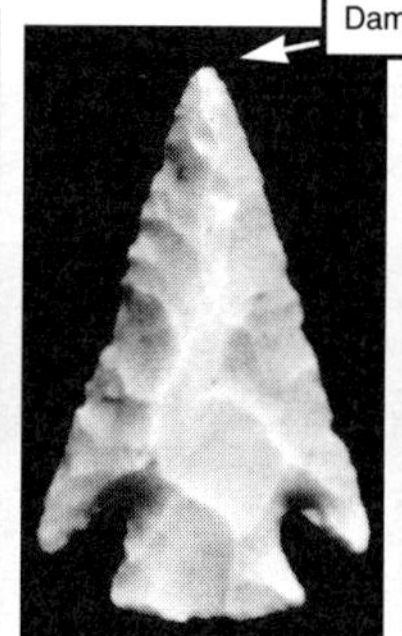

G6, $10-$20
Killeen, TX.

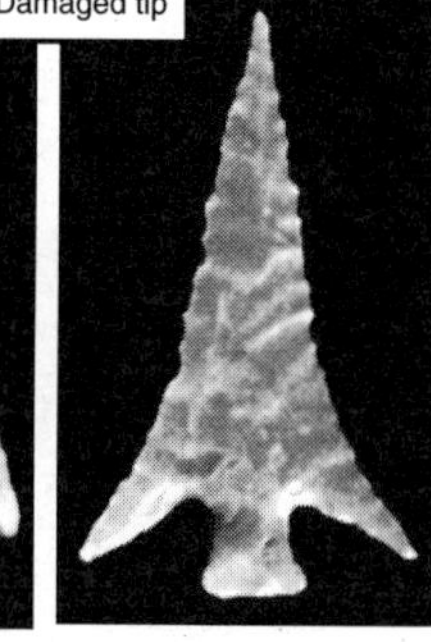

G9, $75-$150
Comanche Co., TX.

LOCATION: Louisiana to Oklahoma. **DESCRIPTION:** A small, thin, triangular arrow point with corner notches. Shoulders are barbed and usually extend almost to the base. Many examples are serrated. Tips and tangs are sharp. **I.D. KEY:** Broad corner ntoches

RODGERS SIDE HOLLOWED - Late Paleo, 10,000 - 8000 B. P.

(Also see Arkabutla, Dalton, Golondrina, Pelican and San Patrice)

G6, $45-$90
Llano Co., Tx.

G10, $200-$300
Lampasas Co., TX. Excellent quality and classic example.

RODGERS SIDE HOLLOWED (continued)

LOCATION: Texas. **DESCRIPTION:** A medium size, broad, unfluted auriculate point which is a variant form of the *San Patrice* type. Base is concave. **I.D. KEY:** Expanding auricles.

ROSS COUNTY (See Clovis)

SABINAL - Mississippian, 1000 - 700 B. P.

(Also see Bonham & Rockwall)

G5, $5-$10
Uvalde Co., TX.

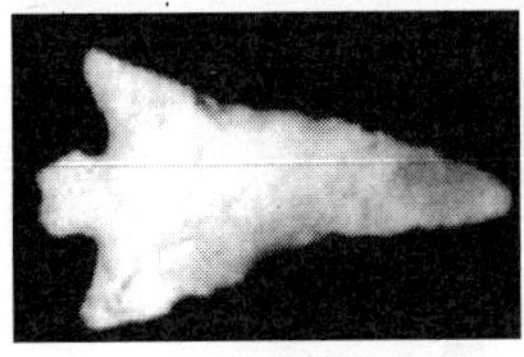

G5, $5-$10
Bandera Co., TX.

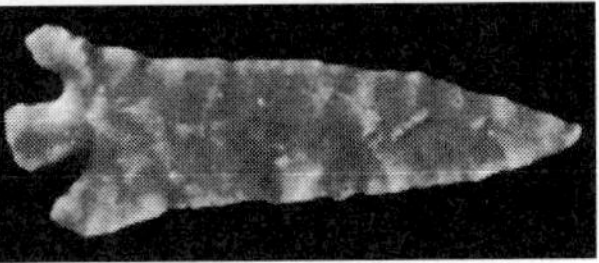

G5, $15-$30
Comanche Co., TX.

LOCATION: Texas. **DESCRIPTION:** A small size, thin basal notched point with shoulders that flare outward and a short expanding to parallel sided stem.

SABINE - Late Archaic to Woodland, 4000 - 2000 B. P.

(Also see Covington, Friday, Gahagan, Refugio and San Gabriel)

G4, $12-$20
Comanche Co., TX.

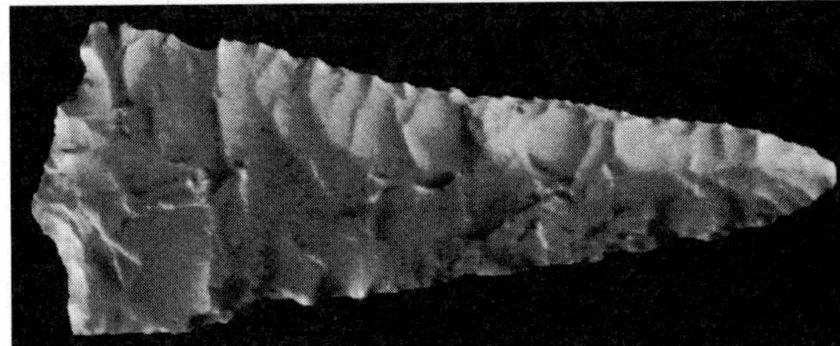

LOCATION: Midwestern states. **DESCRIPTION:** A medium to large size, thin, lanceolate blade with a contracting, rounded to "V" base. Blade edges can be serrated.

SALLISAW - Mississippian, 800 - 600 B. P.

(Also see Edwards, Haskell and Morris)

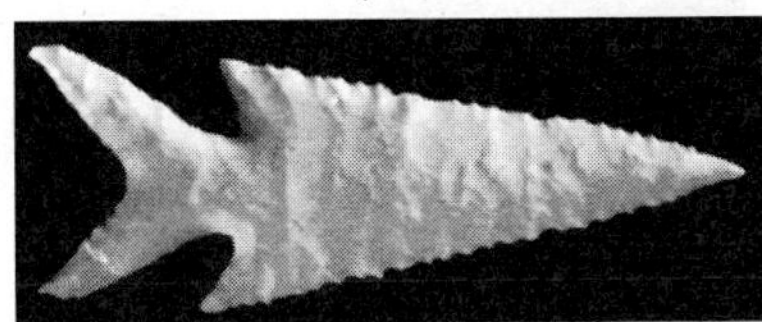

G10, $300-$500
Comanche Co., TX. very thin and excellent quality.

LOCATION: Oklahoma to Arkansas and Texas. **DESCRIPTION:** A small size, thin, serrated, barbed point with long drooping basal tangs and a deeply concave base. A very rare type. **I.D. KEY:** Long drooping ears.

SAN GABRIEL - Woodland 2000 - 1500 B. P.

(Also see Covington, Friday, Gahagan, Kinney and Sabine)

SAN GABRIEL continued)

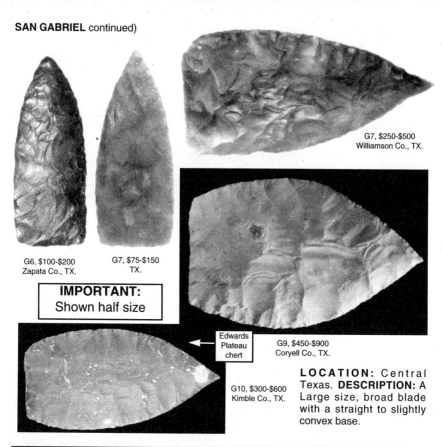

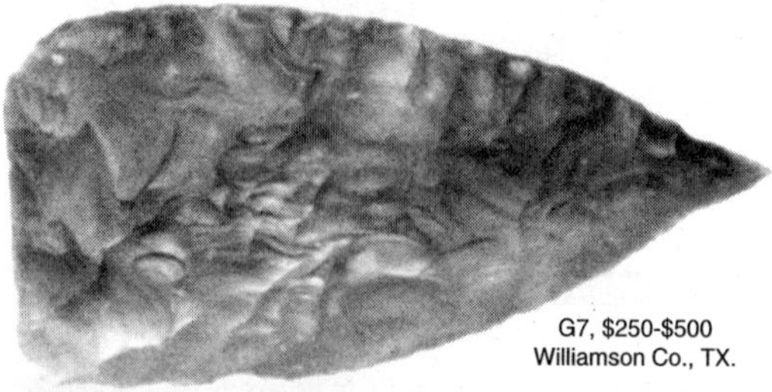

G7, $250-$500
Williamson Co., TX.

G6, $100-$200
Zapata Co., TX.

G7, $75-$150
TX.

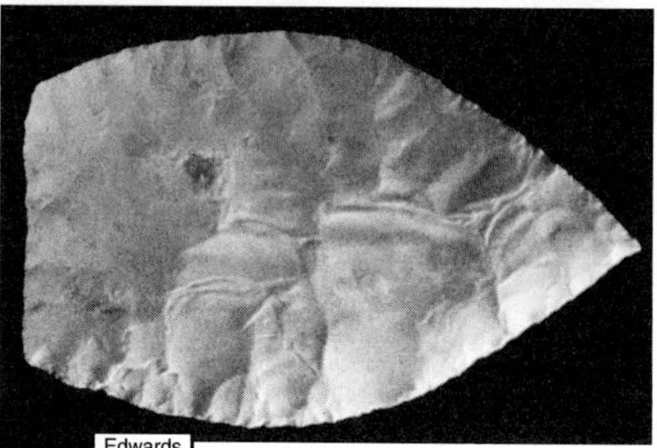

IMPORTANT:
Shown half size

Edwards Plateau chert

G9, $450-$900
Coryell Co., TX.

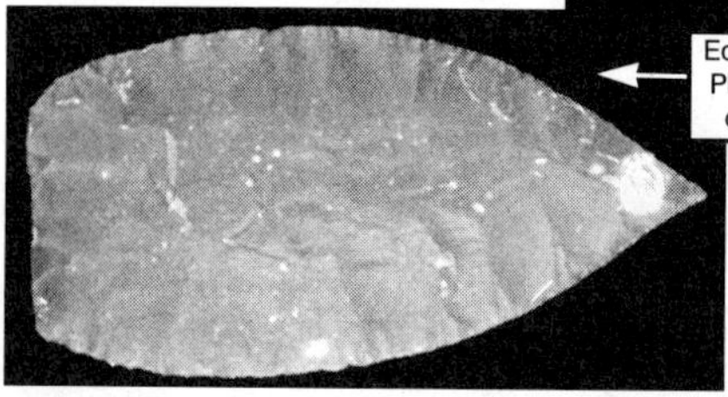

G10, $300-$600
Kimble Co., TX.

LOCATION: Central Texas. **DESCRIPTION:** A Large size, broad blade with a straight to slightly convex base.

SAN PATRICE-HOPE VARIETY - Trans. Paleo, 10,000 - 8000 B. P.

(Also see Dalton, Palmer, Pelican and Rodgers Side Hollowed)

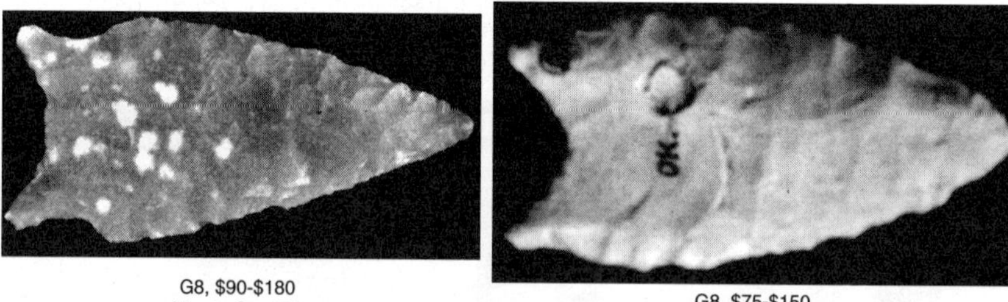

G8, $90-$180
Liberty Co., TX.

G8, $75-$150
Osage Co., OK.

LOCATION: Louisiana to Oklahoma. **DESCRIPTION:** A small size, thin, auriculate point with a concave base. Some examples are thinned from the base. Basal area is longer than the "St. Johns" variety and is usually ground. **I.D. KEY:** Extended auriculate base and small size.

SAN PATRICE-KEITHVILLE - Tran. Paleo, 10,000 - 8000 B. P.

(Also see Dalton, Palmer, Pelican and Rodgers Side Hollowed)

SAN PATRICE-KEITHVILLE (continued)

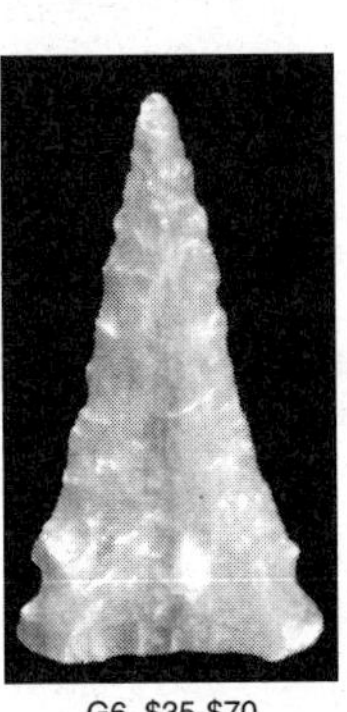

G6, $35-$70
Angelina Co., TX.

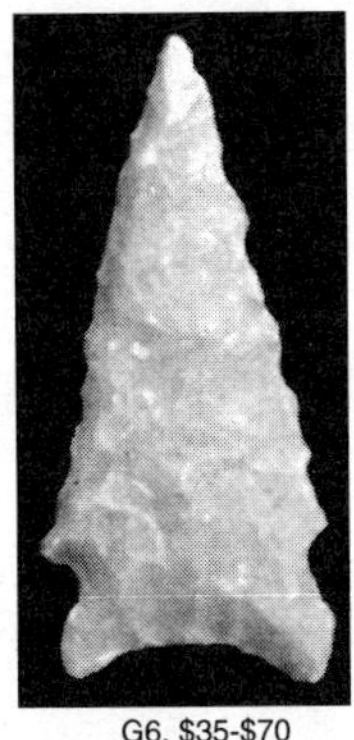

G6, $35-$70
Walker Co., TX.

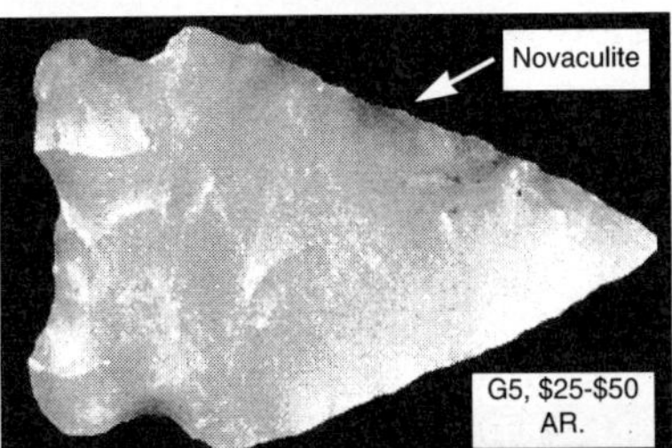

G5, $25-$50
AR.

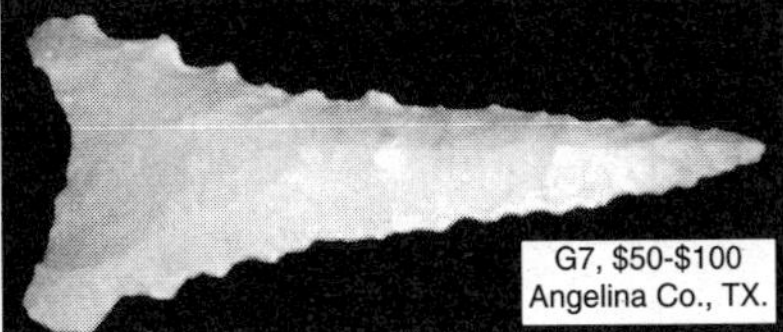

G7, $50-$100
Angelina Co., TX.

LOCATION: Louisiana to Oklahoma. **DESCRIPTION:** A small size, thin, auriculate to side notched point forming a lobed base. Basal area is usually ground. Blade edges can be serrated. **I.D. KEY:** Lobbed base.

SAN PATRICE-ST. JOHNS VARIETY - Tran. Paleo, 10,000 - 8000 B. P.

(Also see Dalton, Palmer, Pelican and Rodgers Side Hollowed)

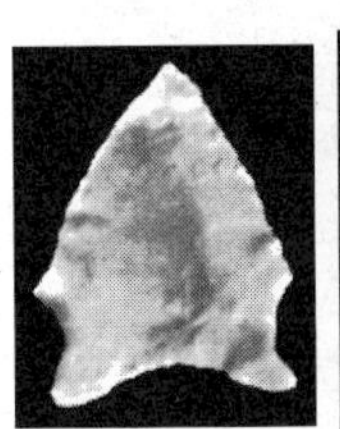

G4, $15-$30
Williamson Co., TX.

G5, $15-$30
Williamson Co., TX.

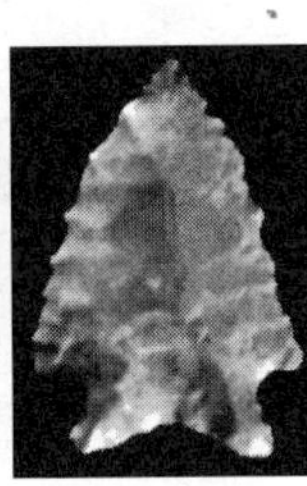

G5, $15-$30
Williamson Co., TX.

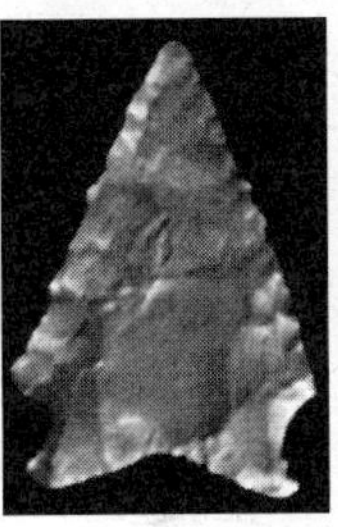

G6, $35-$70
Williamson Co., TX.

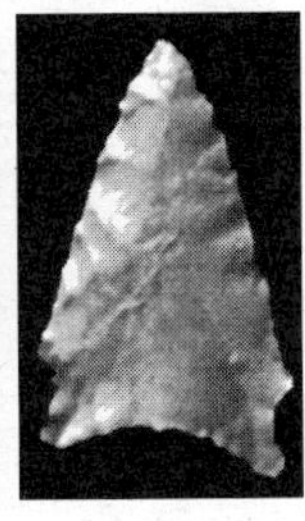

G4, $20-$40
Williamson Co., TX.

G7, $55-$110
Williamson Co., TX.

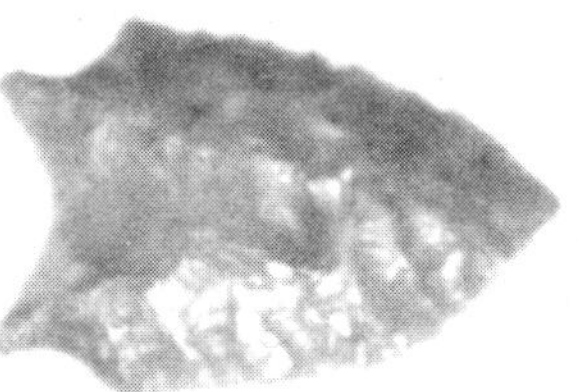

G8, $125-$200
Austin, TX.

G9, $125-$250
NW LA.

LOCATION: Louisiana to Oklahoma. **DESCRIPTION:** A small size, thin, auriculate to side notched point with a short, concave base. Some examples are fluted, others are thinned from the base. Basal area is usually ground. Blade edges can be serrated. **I.D. KEY:** Short auriculate base and small size.

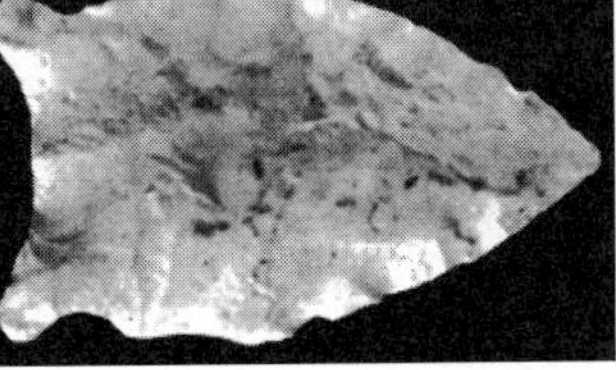

G6, $50-$100
Marksville, LA.

SAN PATRICE-ST. JOHNS VAR. (continued)

G8, $60-$120
Montgomery Co., TX.

SAN SABA - Woodland, 3000 - 2000 B. P.

(Also see Base Tang, Corner Tang and Mid-Back Tang)

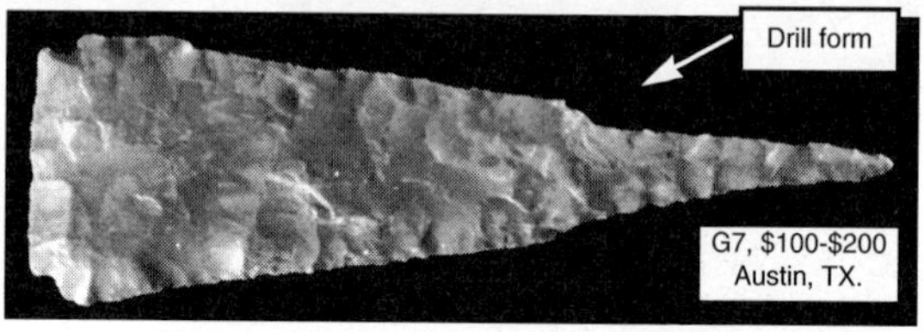

Drill form

G7, $100-$200
Austin, TX.

G6, $75-$150
Williamson Co., TX.

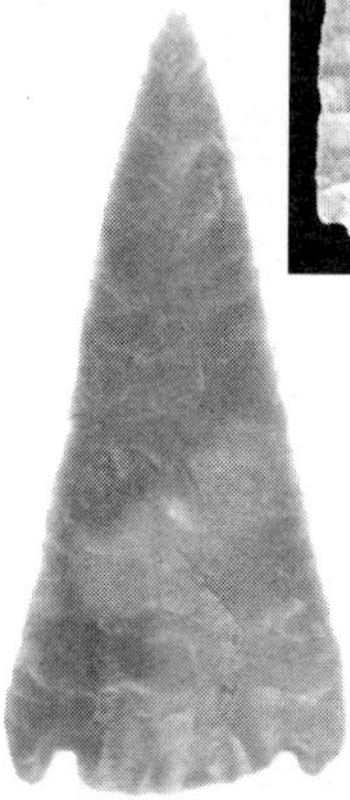

G9, $150-$300
TX.

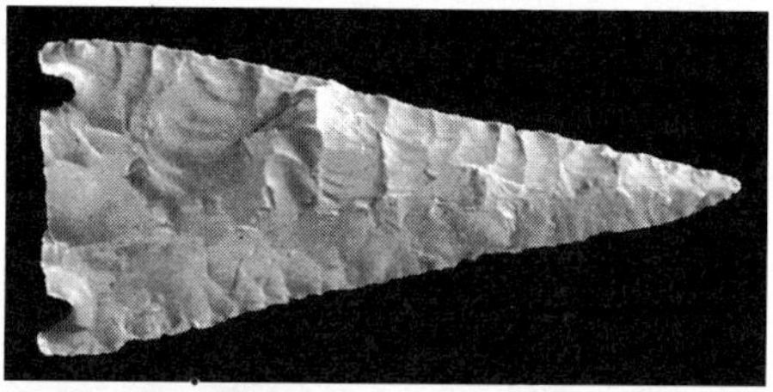

IMPORTANT:
All shown half size

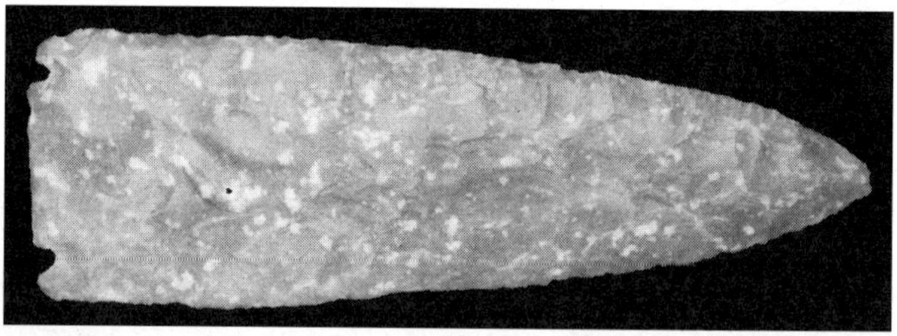

G10, $150-$300
Comanche Co., TX.

G9, $450-$900
Wilson Co., TX.

LOCATION: Texas. **DESCRIPTION:** A large size, triangular blade with shallow, narrow, basal notches. Bases usually are straight. **I.D. KEY:** Small basal notches.

SAVAGE CAVE - Early to Middle Archaic, 7000 - 4000 B. P.

(Also see Big Sandy, Hemphill, Hickory Ridge, Osceola, Raddatz and White River)

LOCATION: Kentucky, Tennessee to Arkansas. **DESCRIPTION:** A medium to large size, broad, side notched point that is usually serrated. Bases are generally straight but can be slightly concave or convex.

G3, $3-$6
N.E. AR.

SAVAGE CAVE (continued)

G6, $8-$15
Jonesboro, AR.

G7, $15-$25
N.E. AR.

SAVANNAH RIVER - Middle Archaic to Woodland, 5000 - 2000 B. P.

(Also see Johnson)

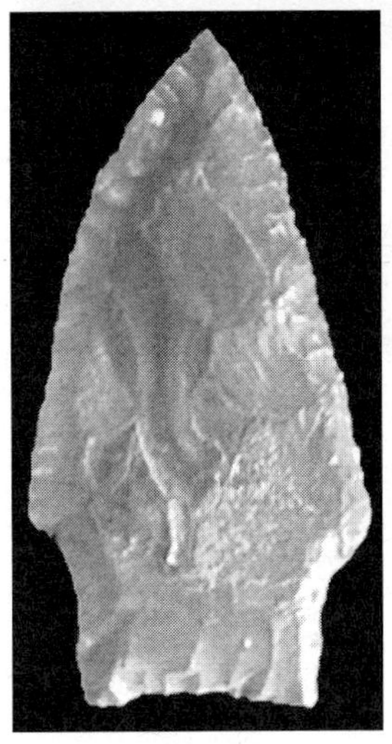

G5, $20-$40
Jonesboro, AR.

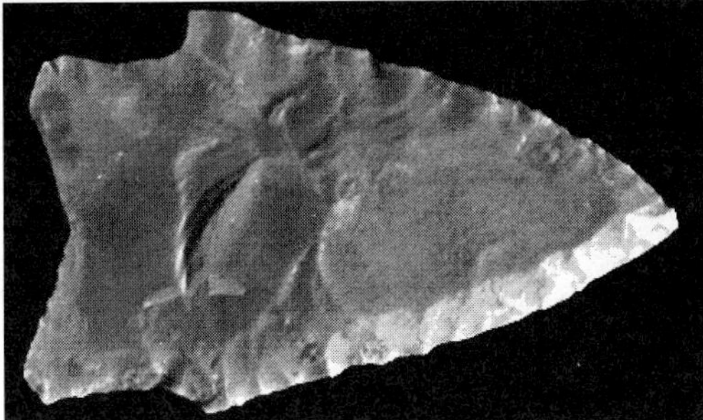

G5, $15-$25
Jonesboro, AR.

LOCATION: Arkansas to Eastern states. **DESCRIPTION:** A medium to large size, straight to contracting stemmed point with a concave to bifurcated base. The shoulders are tapered to square. The stems are narrow to broad. Believed to be related to the earlier *Stanly* point. **I.D. KEY:** Broad, concave base.

SC

SCALLORN - Woodland to Mississippian, 1300 - 500 B. P.

(Also see Alba, Catahoula, Cuney, Ellis, Homan, Keota, Rockwall, Sequoyah and Steiner)

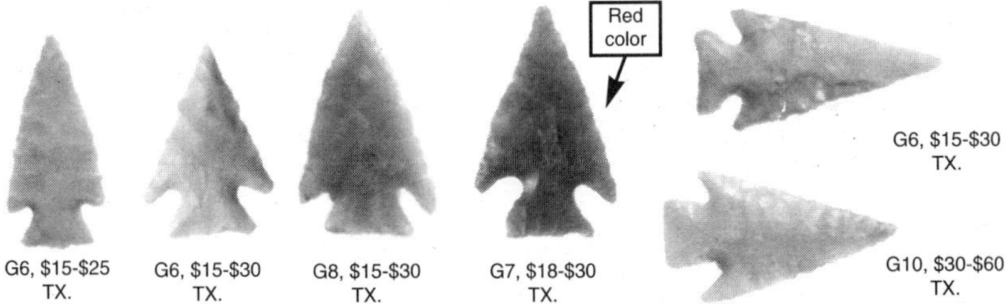

G6, $15-$25
TX.

G6, $15-$30
TX.

G8, $15-$30
TX.

G7, $18-$30
TX.

G6, $15-$30
TX.

G10, $30-$60
TX.

LOCATION: Texas, Oklahoma**. DESCRIPTION:** A small size, corner notched arrow point with a flaring stem. Bases and blade edges are straight, concave or convex and many examples are serrated. Not to be confused with Sequoyah not found in Texas. **I.D. KEY:** Small corner notched point with sharp tangs and tip.

SCALLORN (continued)

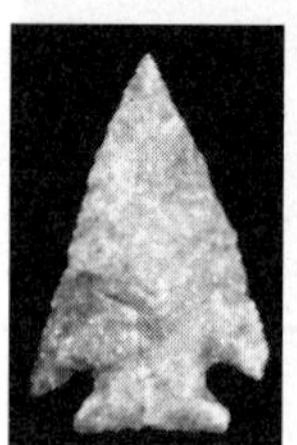
G8, $15-$25
Crane Co., TX.

G7, $15-$25
Comanche Co., TX.

G8, $15-$25
Scallorn Co., TX.

G8, $15-$25
TX.

G8, $20-$40
TX.

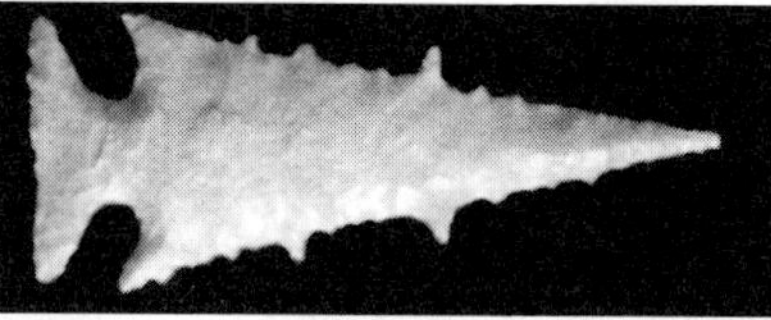
G10, $125-$250
Smith Co., TX.

G8, $20-$40
TX.

G8, $20-$40
TX.

G9, $50-$100
TX.

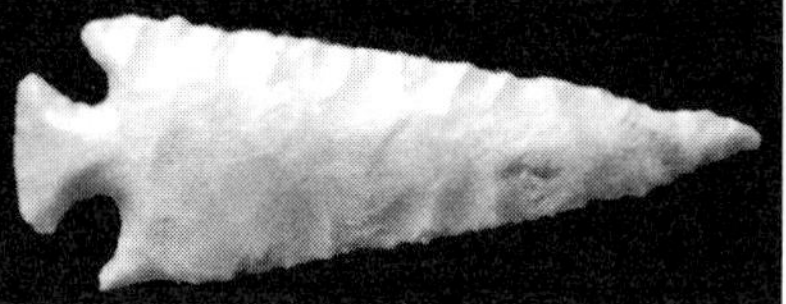
G9, $75-$150
Smith Co., TX.

SCOTTSBLUFF I - Transitional Paleo, 9500 - 7000 B. P.

(Also see Alberta, Cody Knife, Eden, Hardin, Holland and Red River)

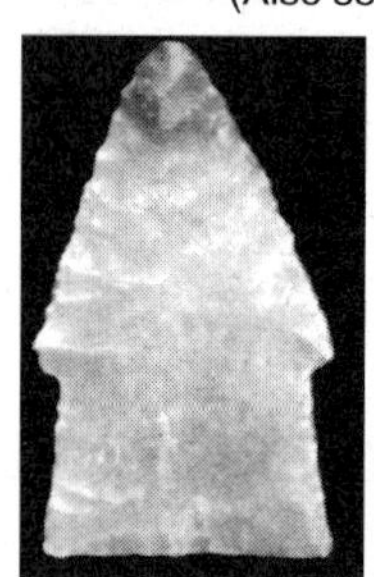
G5, $100-$200
Angelina Co., TX.

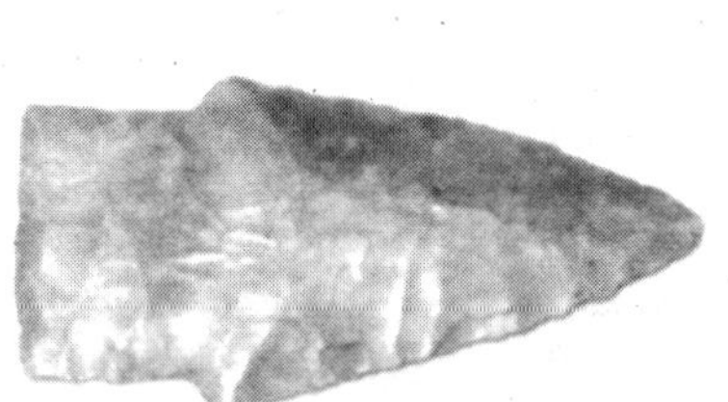
G5, $150-$300
Angelina Co., TX.

G4, $50-$100
Lufkin, TX.

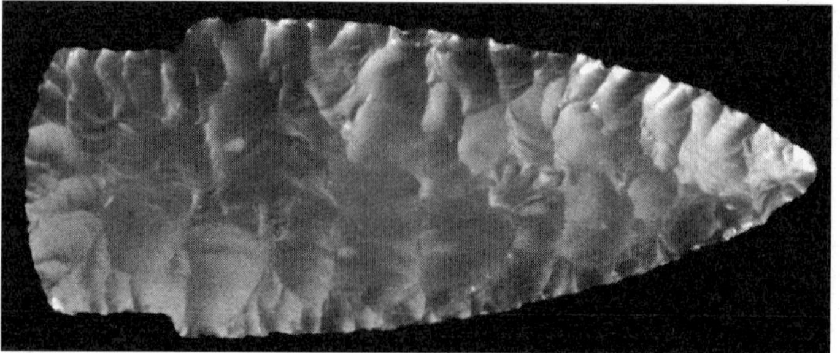
G9, $900-$1800
Angelina Co., TX.

G5, $125-$250
Hamilton Co., TX.

G8, $500-$1000
Wilson Co., TX.

G6, $200-$400
Sabine Co., TX.

G9, $750-$1500
Wilson Co., TX.

G7, $325-$650
Angelina Co., TX.

G6, $250-$450
Monroe, LA.

LOCATION: Louisiana to New Mexico to Canada and the Northwest coast. **DESCRIPTION:** A medium to large size, broad stemmed point with convex to parallel sides and weak shoulders. The stem is parallel to expanding. The basal area is ground. Most examples have horizontal to oblique parallel flaking and are of high quality and thinness. Made by the Cody Complex people. Believed to have evolved into Hardin in later times. **I.D. KEY:** Broad stem, weak shoulders, collateral flaking.

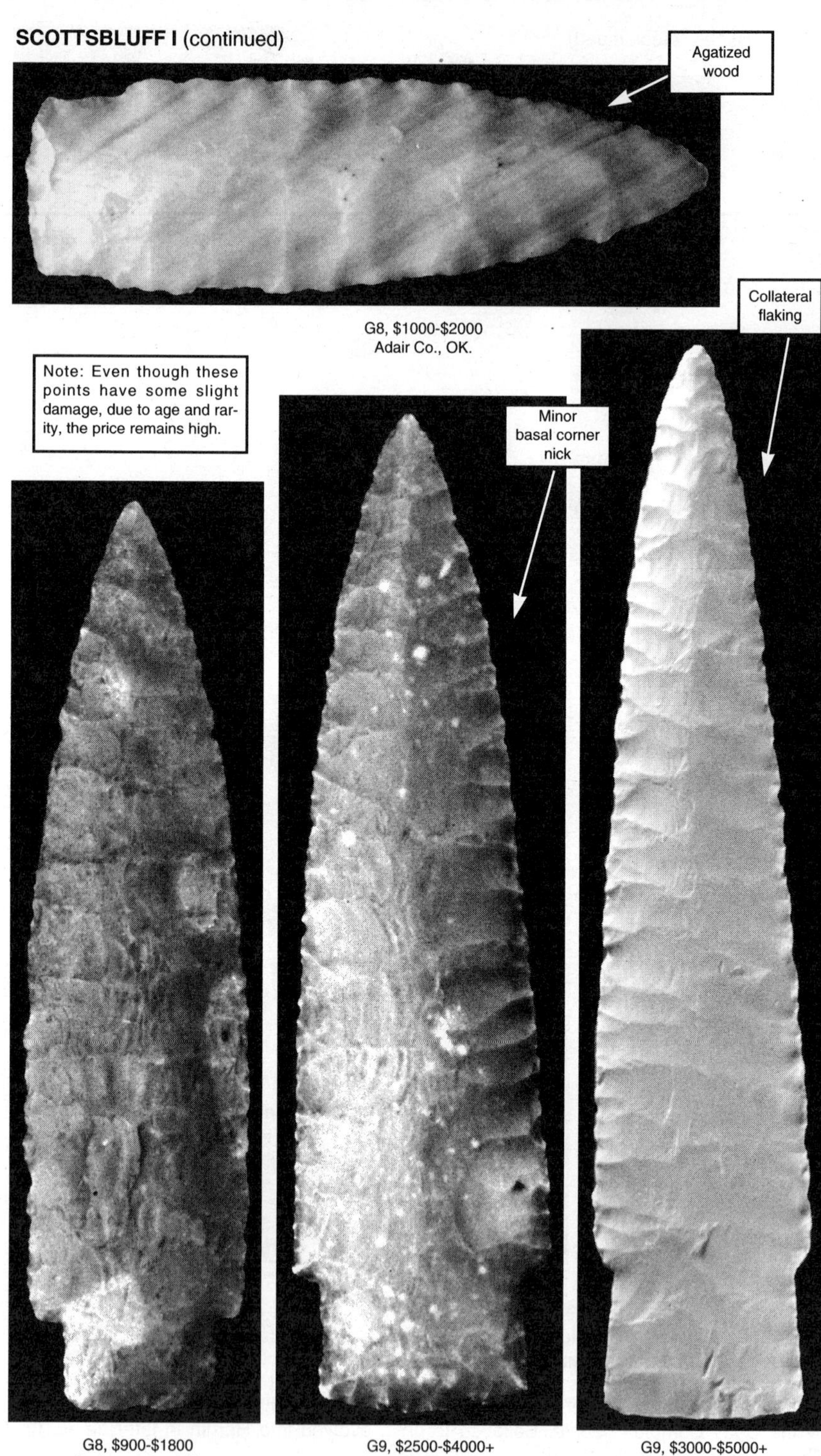
Agatized wood
Collateral flaking
Minor basal corner nick
Note: Even though these points have some slight damage, due to age and rarity, the price remains high.

G8, $1000-$2000
Adair Co., OK.

G8, $900-$1800
Anderson Co., TX.

G9, $2500-$4000+
Polk Co., TX.

G9, $3000-$5000+
N.E. TX.

SCOTTSBLUFF II - Transitional Paleo, 9500 - 7000 B. P.

(Also see Alberta, Cody Knife, Eden, Hardin, Holland and Red River)

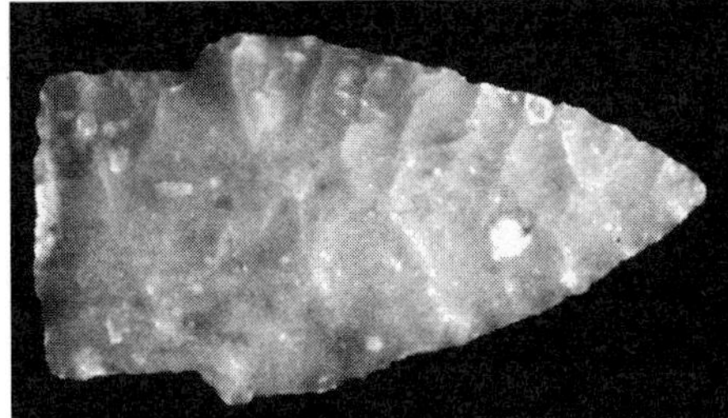

G5, $175-$350
Cent. TX.

LOCATION: Louisiana to New Mexico to Canada to the Northwest coast. **DESCRIPTION:** A medium to large size, broad stemmed point with convex to parallel sides and stronger shoulders than type I. The stem is parallel sided to slightly expanding. The hafting area is ground. Most examples have horizontal to oblique parallel flaking and are of high quality and thinness. Made by the Cody Complex people. **I.D. KEY:** Stronger shoulders.

G7, $375-$750
Montgomery Co., TX.

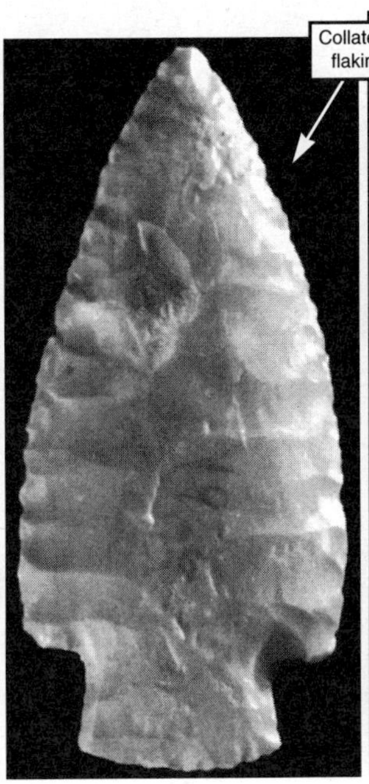

G8, $425-$850
AR.

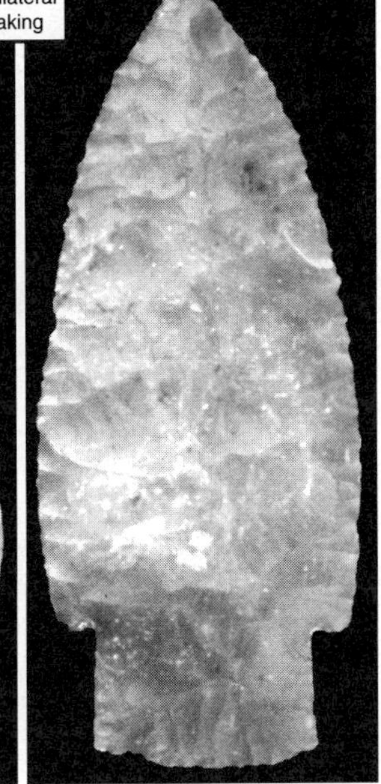

G8, $500-$1000
Angelina Co., TX.

SC

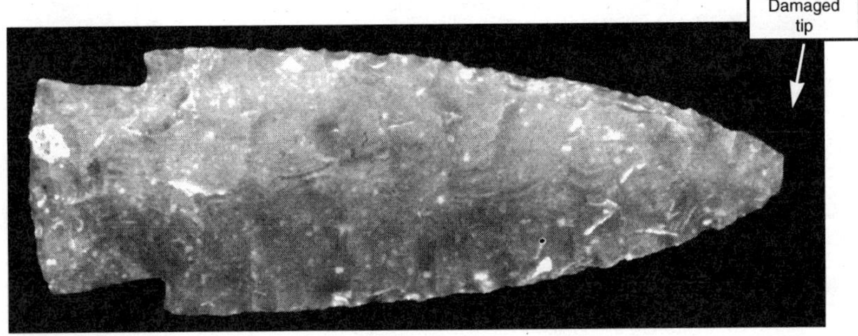

G6, $350-$700
Harris Co., TX.

SCRAPER - Paleo to Archaic, 14,000 - 5000 B. P.

(Also see Drill, Graver, Perforator and Paleo Knife)

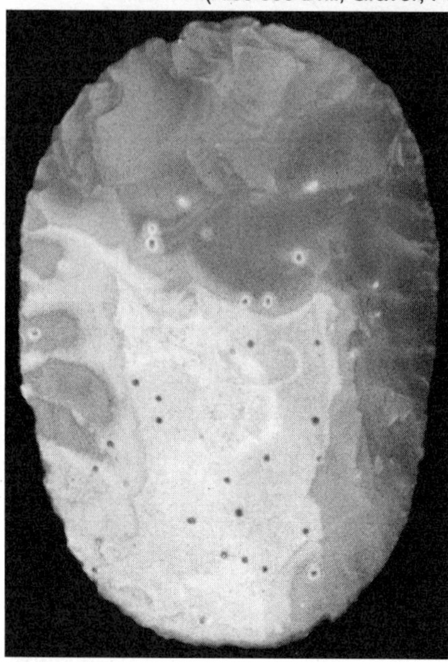

G9, $5-$10
Kimble Co., TX.

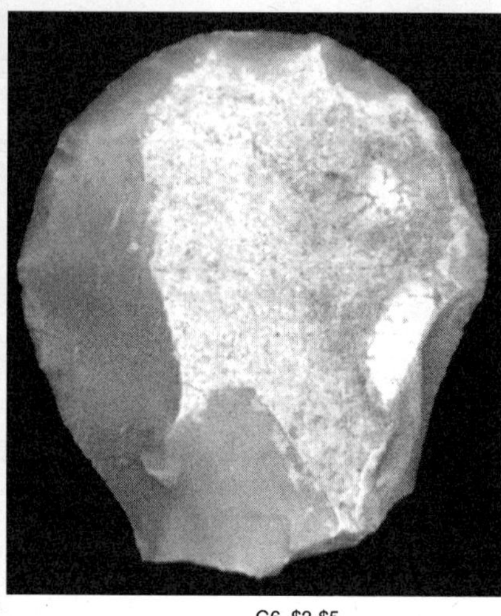

G6, $3-$5
Kimble Co., TX.

LOCATION: Early man sites everywhere. **DESCRIPTION:** Thumb, duckbill and turtleback forms are small to medium size, thick, ovoid shaped, uniface, scraping tools that are steeply beveled, especially at the broadest end. Side scrapers are long hand-held uniface flakes with beveling on all blade edges of one face. Scraping was done primarily from the sides of these blades. Many of these tools were hafted.

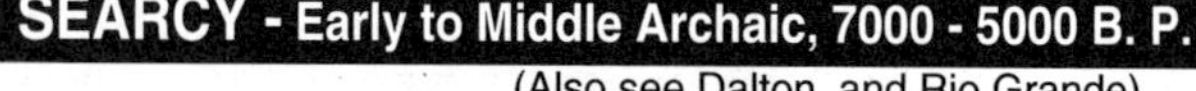

SEARCY - Early to Middle Archaic, 7000 - 5000 B. P.

(Also see Dalton and Rio Grande)

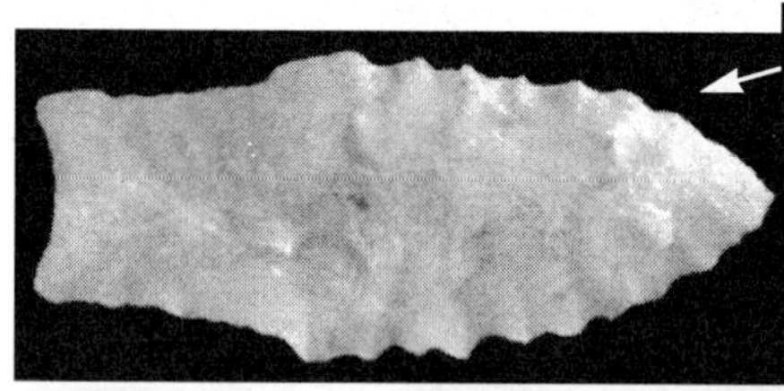

Classic example from type county

G7, $40-$80
Searcy Co., AR.

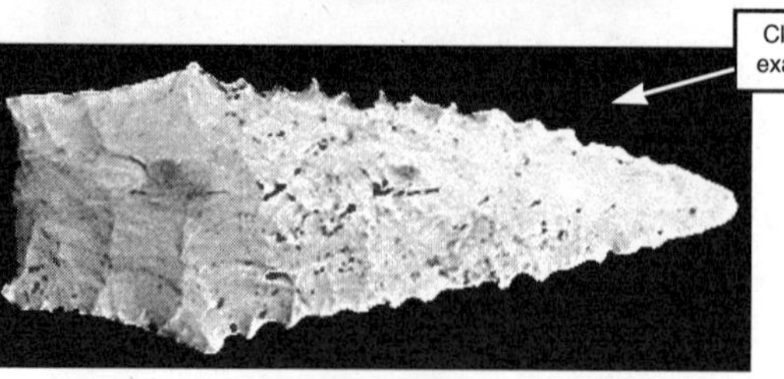

Classic example

G8, $75-$150
Morris Co., TX.

G4, $15-$30
Marion Co., AR.

SEARCY (continued)

LOCATION: Texas, Oklahoma to Missouri to Tennessee. **DESCRIPTION:** A small to medium size, thin, lanceolate point with a squared hafting area. Blade edges are serrated. The base is straight to concave and is usually ground. **I.D. KEY:** Long squared stem, serrations.

G10, $125-$250
Benton Co., AR.

SEQUOYAH - Mississippian, 1000 - 600 B. P.

(Also see Alba, Blevins, Hayes, Homan, Livermore, Scallorn and Steiner)

G5, $8-$15
Spiro Mound, OK.

G6, $15-$25
AR.

G6, $18-$35
AR.

G7, $30-$60
Spiro Mound, OK.

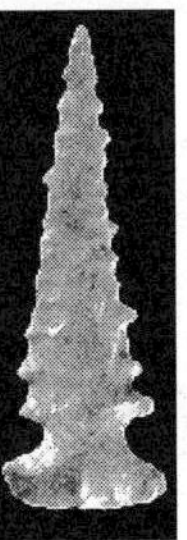
G8, $25-$50
Spiro Mound, OK.

G8, $30-$60
Spiro Mound, OK.

SC

LOCATION: IL, OK, AR, MO. **DESCRIPTION:** A small size, thin, narrow point with coarse serrations and an expanded, bulbous stem. Believed to have been made by Caddo and other people. Named after the famous Cherokee of the same name. **I.D. KEY:** Bulbous base, coarse serrations.

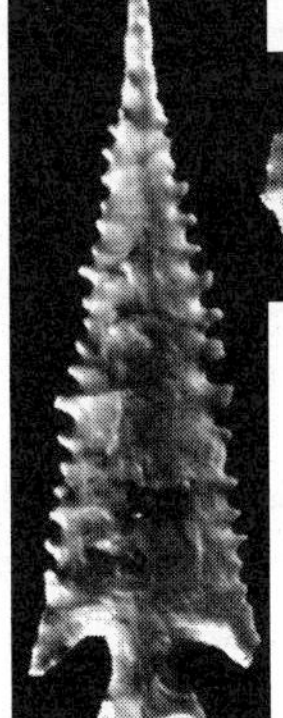
G9, $100-$200
LeFlore Co., OK.

G8, $150-$300
Spiro Mound, OK.

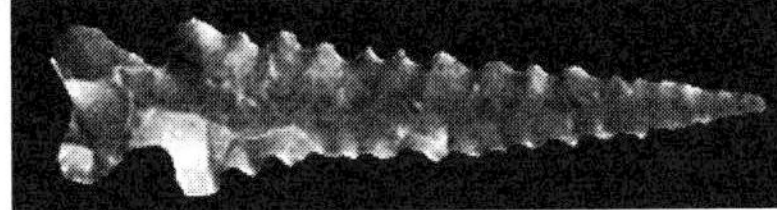
G8, $75-$150
Spiro Mound, OK

SHUMLA - Woodland, 3000 - 1000 B. P.

(Also see Bell, Calf Creek, Marshall and Rockwall)

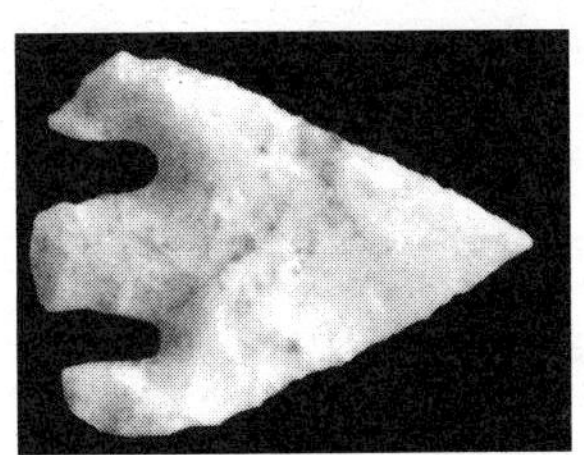
G7, $25-$45
TX.

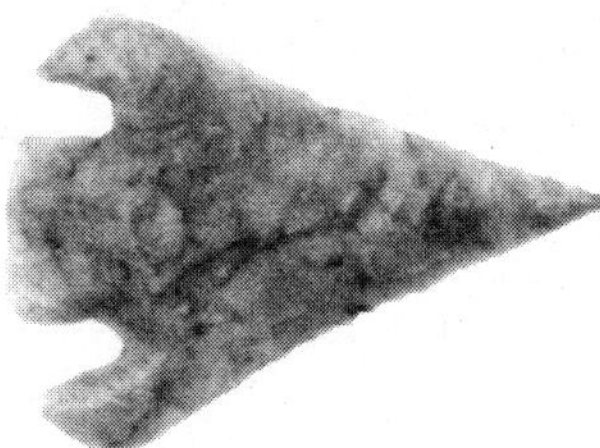
G10, $65-$125
Zapata Co., TX.

G10, $75-$150
Zapata Co., TX.

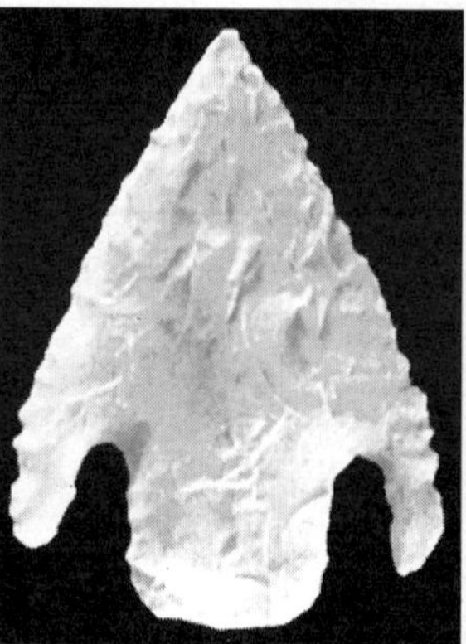
G8, $25-$50
Austin, TX.

G10, $200-$400
Zapata Co., TX.

LOCATION: Texas to Oklahoma**. DESCRIPTION:** A small size, basal notched point with convex, straight or recurved sides. Barbs turn in towards and usually extend to the base.

SINNER - Woodland, 3000 - 2000 B. P.

(Also see Charcos, Duran, Evans and Huffaker)

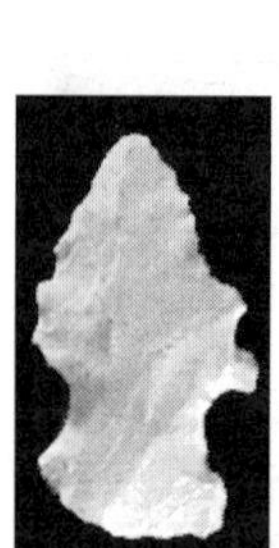
G3, $3-$5
Lincoln Parrish, LA.

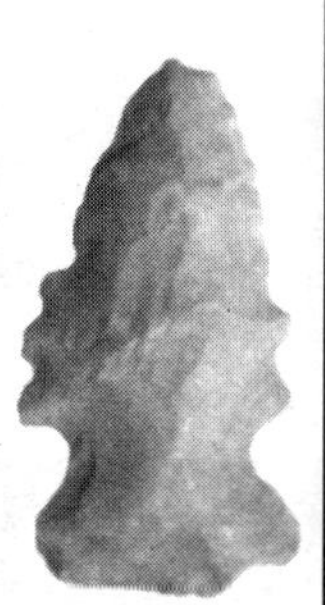
G4, $3-$5
LA.

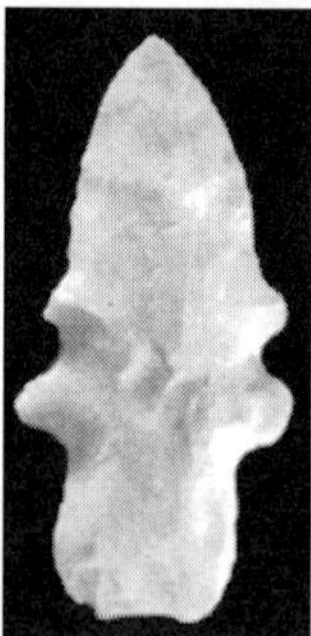
G5, $5-$10
Lincoln Parish, LA.

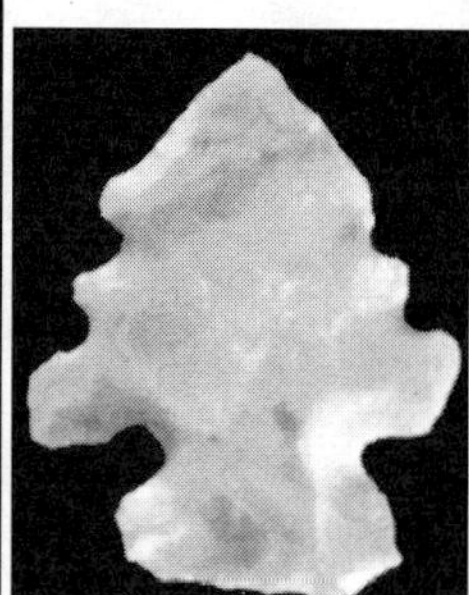
G6, $5-$10
Lincoln Parrish, LA.

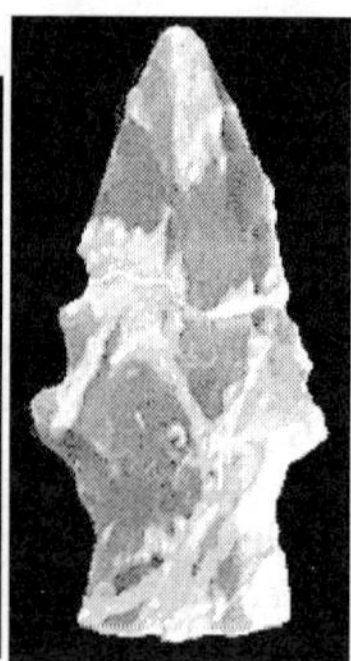
G5, $4-$8
Lincoln Parish, LA.

LOCATION: Louisiana to Texas. **DESCRIPTION:** A medium size, expanded stemmed point with several barbs occurring above the shoulders. **I.D. KEY:** Barbed edges.

SQUARE KNIFE - Late Paleo to Early Archaic, 10,000 - 8000 B. P.

(Also see Angostura, Pandora, Refugio & Victoria)

LOCATION: Texas northward and eastward. **DESCRIPTION:** A medium to large size squared blade that is sometimes fluted from either or both ends on Paleo examples. **I.D. KEY:** Squared form.

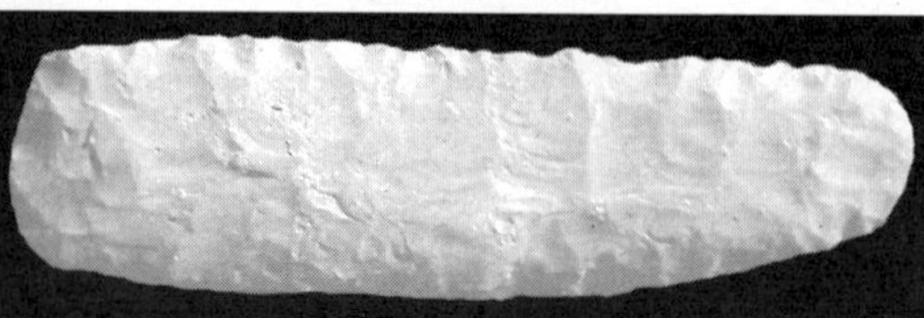
IMPORTANT: Shown half size

G8, $300-$600
Travis Co., TX.

STARR - Mississippian to Historic, 1000 - 250 B. P.

(Also see Maud and Talco)

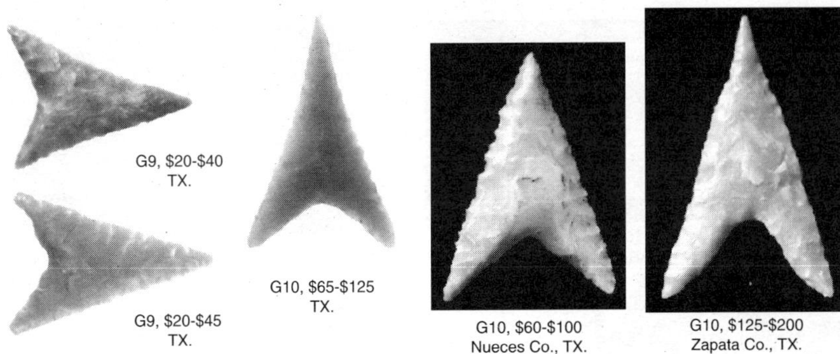

G9, $20-$40 TX.

G9, $20-$45 TX.

G10, $65-$125 TX.

G10, $60-$100 Nueces Co., TX.

G10, $125-$200 Zapata Co., TX.

LOCATION: Texas westward. **DESCRIPTION:** A small size, thin, triangular point with a "V" base concavity. Blade edges can be concave to straight. **I.D. KEY:** "V" base.

STEINER - Mississippian, 1000 - 400 B. P.

(Also see Friley, Scallorn and Sequoyah)

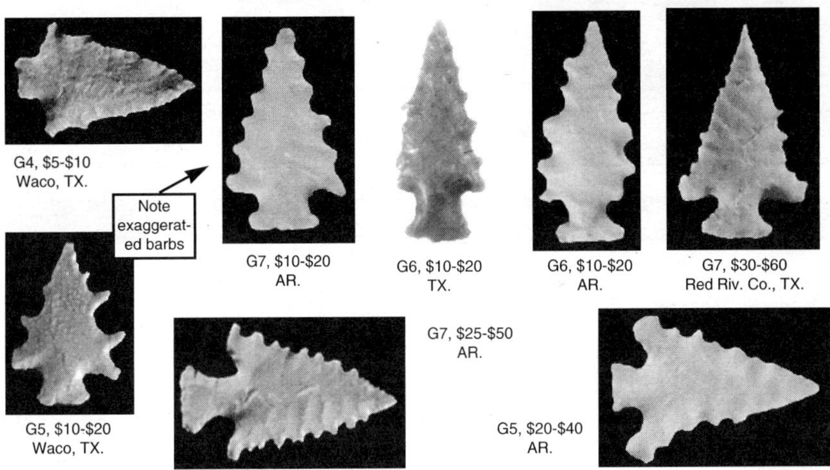

G4, $5-$10 Waco, TX.

G7, $10-$20 AR.

G6, $10-$20 TX.

G6, $10-$20 AR.

G7, $30-$60 Red Riv. Co., TX.

G5, $10-$20 Waco, TX.

G7, $25-$50 AR.

G5, $20-$40 AR.

LOCATION: Mexico, E. Texas into Arkansas. **DESCRIPTION:** A small size, thin, barbed arrow point with strong shoulders. The stem is short and may be horizontal or expanded. **I.D. KEY:** Strong barbs.

STEUBEN - Woodland, 2000 - 1000 B. P.

(Also see Lange, Palmillas and Table Rock)

LOCATION: Arkansas to Illinois. **DESCRIPTION:** A medium to large size, narrow, expanded stem point. shoulders can be tapered to straight. The base is straight to convex. This type is very similar to *Bakers Creek* in the Southeast.

G7, $10-$20 AR.

TABLE ROCK - Late Archaic, 4000 - 3000 B. P.

(Also see Lange, Matanzas, Motley and Steuben)

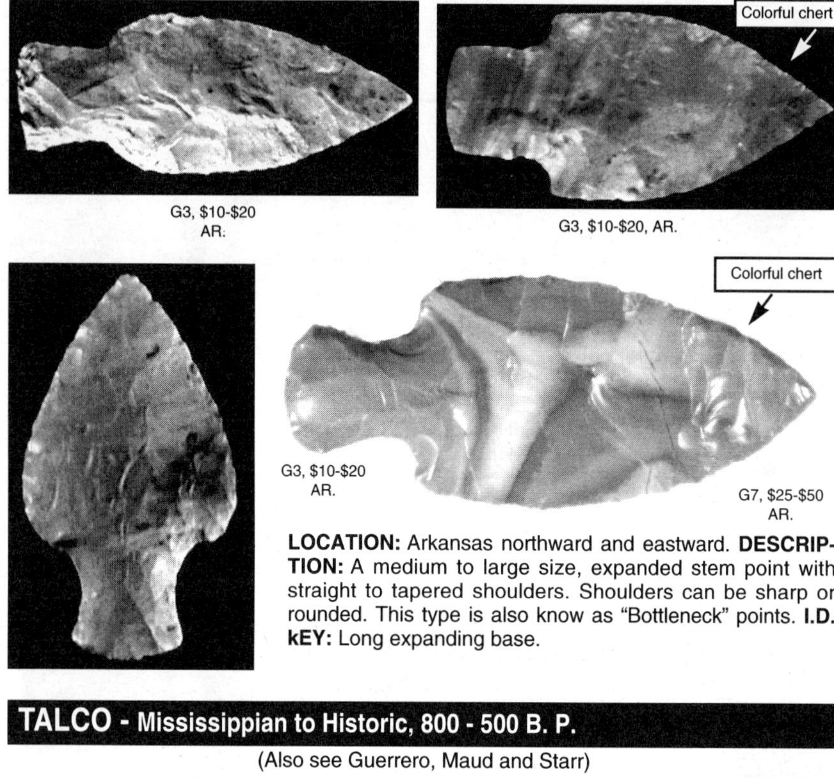

G3, $10-$20
AR.

G3, $10-$20, AR.

G3, $10-$20
AR.

G7, $25-$50
AR.

LOCATION: Arkansas northward and eastward. **DESCRIPTION:** A medium to large size, expanded stem point with straight to tapered shoulders. Shoulders can be sharp or rounded. This type is also know as "Bottleneck" points. **I.D. kEY:** Long expanding base.

TALCO - Mississippian to Historic, 800 - 500 B. P.

(Also see Guerrero, Maud and Starr)

G7, $25-$40
TX.

G8, $30-$60
TX.

G8, $25-$60
TX.

G8, $30-$60
TX.

G9, $40-$80
TX.

G7, $50-$100
Smith Co., TX.

G7, $15-$30
TX.

G6, $15-$25
TX.

G8, $40-$80
TX.

LOCATION: Texas to Oklahoma. **DESCRIPTION:** A small to medium size, thin, narrow, triangular arrow point with recurved sides and a concave base. Blade edges are very finely serrated. On classic examples, tips are more angled than *Maud.* Tips and corners are sharp. This type is found on Caddo and related sites. **I.D. KEY:** Angled tip.

G9, $50-$100
Bowie Co., TX.

G10, $100-$200
Emanuel Co., TX.

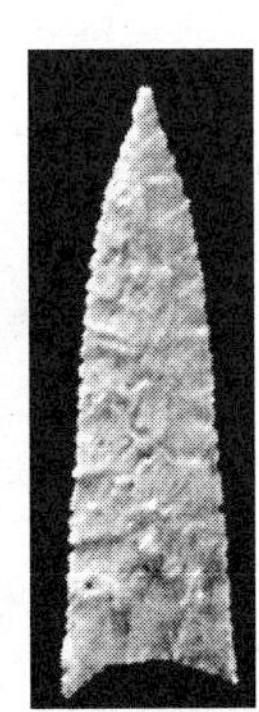

G9, $90-$150
Comanche Co., TX.

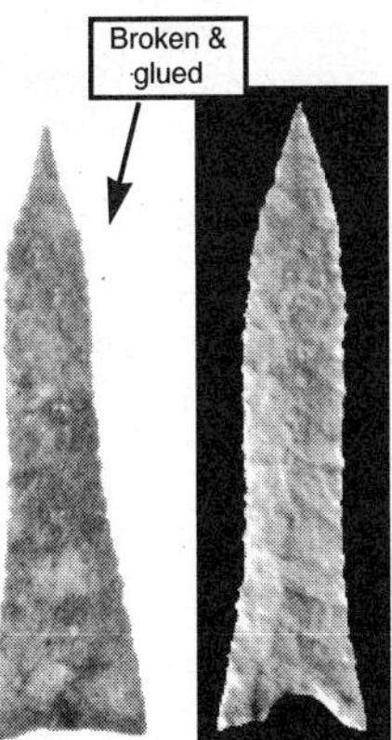

G4, $50-$100
TX.

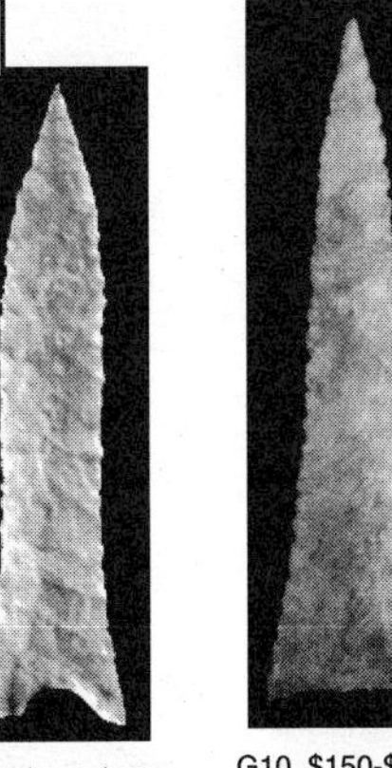

G10, $150-$300
Smith Co., TX.

G10, $150-$300
Pike Co., AR.
Terrell site.

TORTUGAS - Middle Archaic to Woodland, 6000 - 1000 B. P.

(Also see Kinney, Early Triangular and Matamoros)

G8, $20-$40
Mississippi Co., AR.

G4, $5-$10
Cent. TX.

G5, $5-$10
TX.

G6, $10-$20
TX.

G6, $5-$10
TX.

LOCATION: Oklahoma to Tennessee. **DESCRIPTION:** A medium size, fairly thick, triangular point with straight to convex sides and base. Some examples are beveled on one side of each face. Bases are usually thinned. Smaller examples would fall in the *Matamoros* type.

G8, $30-$60
Austin, TX.

SC

TOYAH - Mississippian to Historic, 600 - 400 B. P.

(Also see Garza, Harrell, Huffaker, Morris and Washita)

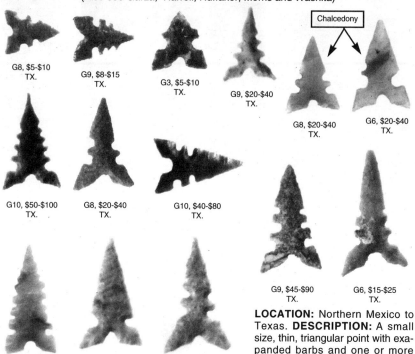

Chalcedony

G8, $5-$10
TX.

G9, $8-$15
TX.

G3, $5-$10
TX.

G9, $20-$40
TX.

G8, $20-$40
TX.

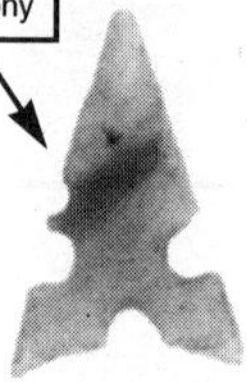

G6, $20-$40
TX.

G10, $50-$100
TX.

G8, $20-$40
TX.

G10, $40-$80
TX.

G9, $45-$90
TX.

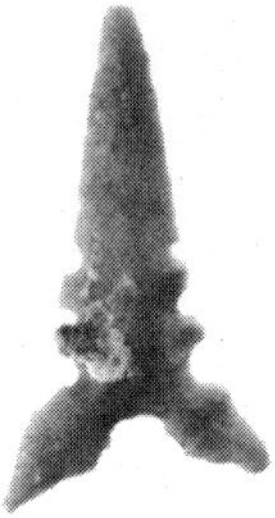

G6, $15-$25
TX.

G9, $50-$100
TX.

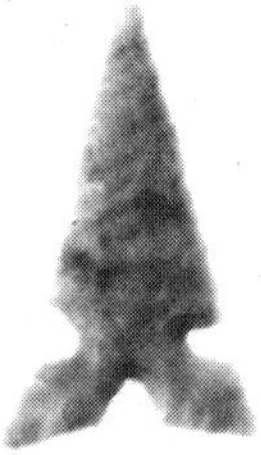

G8, $35-$70
TX.

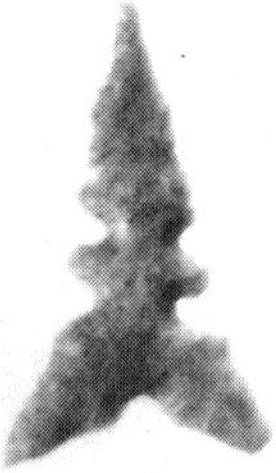

G7, $20-$40
TX.

LOCATION: Northern Mexico to Texas. **DESCRIPTION:** A small size, thin, triangular point with exapanded barbs and one or more notches on each side and a basal notch.

TRADE POINTS - Historic, 400 - 170 B. P.

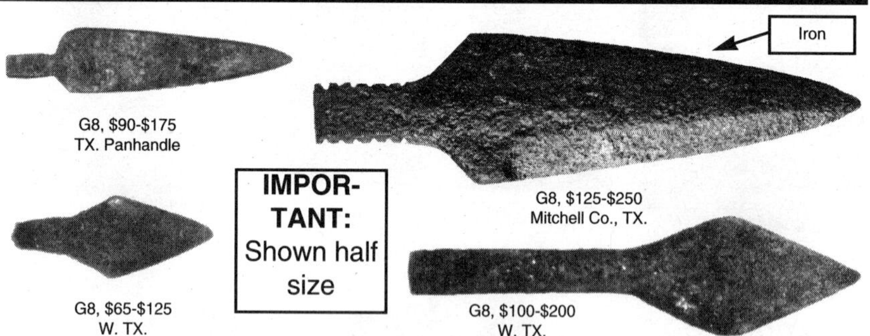

G8, $90-$175
TX. Panhandle

IMPORTANT: Shown half size

G8, $125-$250
Mitchell Co., TX.

G8, $65-$125
W. TX.

G8, $100-$200
W. TX.

LOCATION: All of North America. **DESCRIPTION:** These points were made of copper, iron and steel and were traded to the Indians by the French, British and others from the 1600s to the 1800s.

TRAVIS - Middle-Archaic to Woodland, 5500 - 1000 B. P.

(Also see Darl, Gary, Lange, Nolan and Pandale)

TRAVIS (continued)

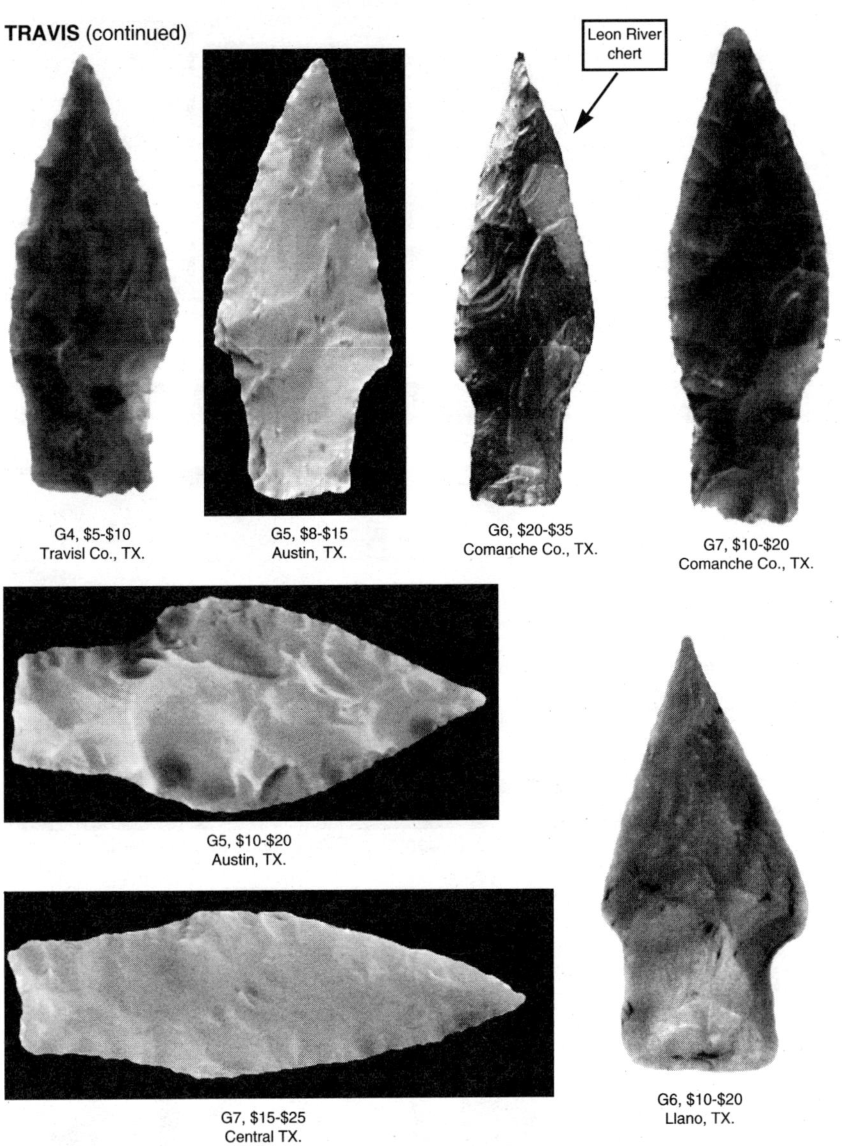

G4, $5-$10
Travisl Co., TX.

G5, $8-$15
Austin, TX.

G6, $20-$35
Comanche Co., TX.

G7, $10-$20
Comanche Co., TX.

G5, $10-$20
Austin, TX.

G6, $10-$20
Llano, TX.

G7, $15-$25
Central TX.

SC

LOCATION: Texas to Oklahoma. **DESCRIPTION:** A small to medium size, narrow point with weak, tapered shoulders and a parallel sided to expanded or contracting stem. The base is straight to convex. Some examples have sharp needle like tips. **I.D. KEY:** Weak, tapered shoulders.

TRINITY - Late Archaic, 4000 - 2000 B. P.

(Also see Ellis, Godley, Halifax and Travis)

LOCATION: Texas to Oklahoma. **DESCRIPTION:** A small to medium size point with broad side notches, weak shoulders and a broad convex base which is usually ground.

TRINITY (continued)

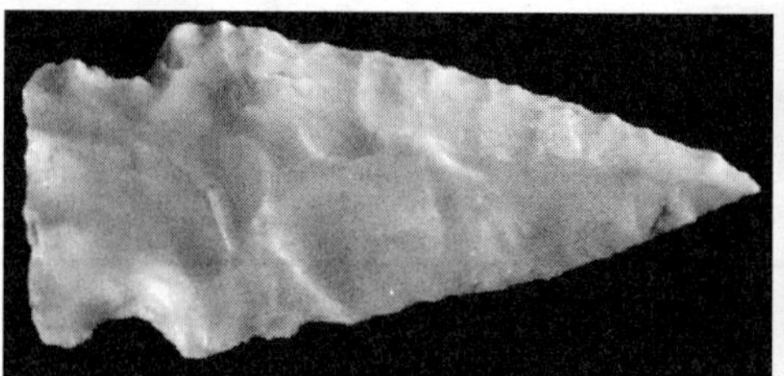

G4, $5-$10
Comanche Co., TX.

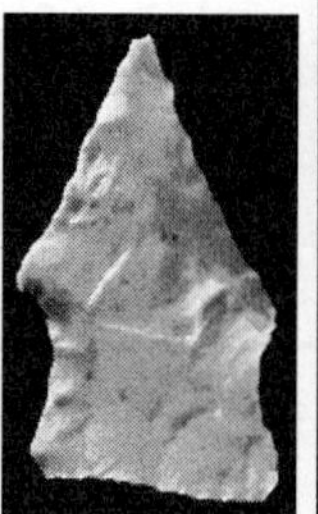

G4, $1-$2
Comanche Co., TX.

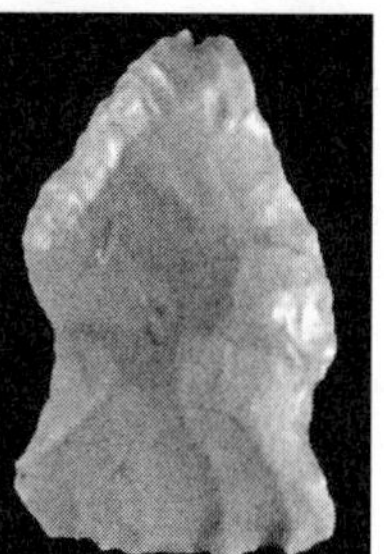

G2, $3-$5
Waco, TX.

TURKEYTAIL (Harrison) - Late Archaic to Woodland, 4000 - 2500 B. P.

(Alse see Adena)

IMPORTANT:
Shown half size

G7, $150-$300
Cache Riv., AR.

LOCATION: Arkansas eastward. **DESCRIPTION:** A medium to very large size, narrow blade with tapered, horizontal or barbed shoulders, and an elongated, diamond-shaped stem in the form of a turkey's tail. Made by the Adena culture. Lengths up to 20 inches known. **I.D. KEY:** Small diamond shaped base.

UVALDE - Middle Archaic to Woodland, 6000 - 1500 B. P.

(Also see Frio, Hoxie, Langtry, Pedernales, Rice Lobbed and Val Verde)

G1, $1-$2
Comanche Co., TX.

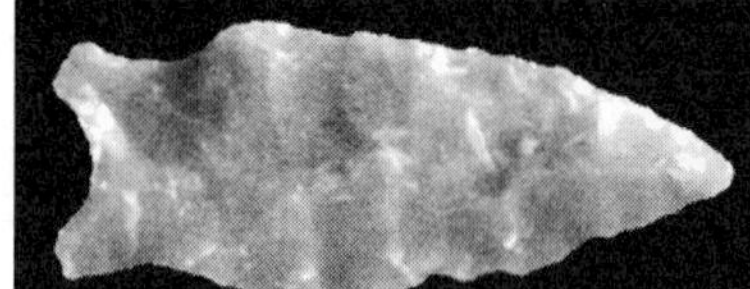

G3, $3-$5
Comanche Co., TX.

G6, $20-$40
Bell Co., TX.

G5, $15-$30
Comanche Co., TX.

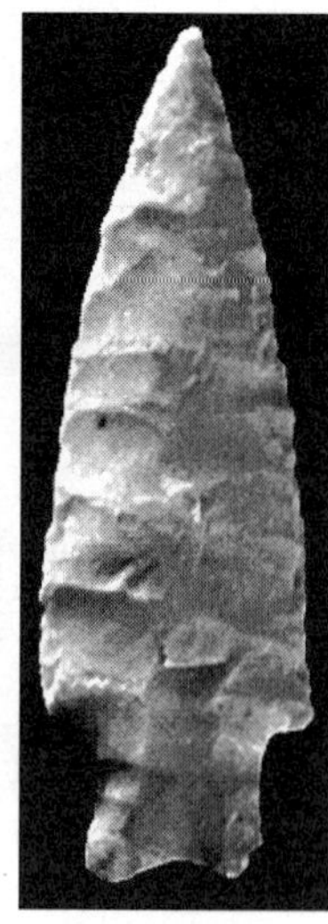

G4, $10-$20
Comanche Co., TX.

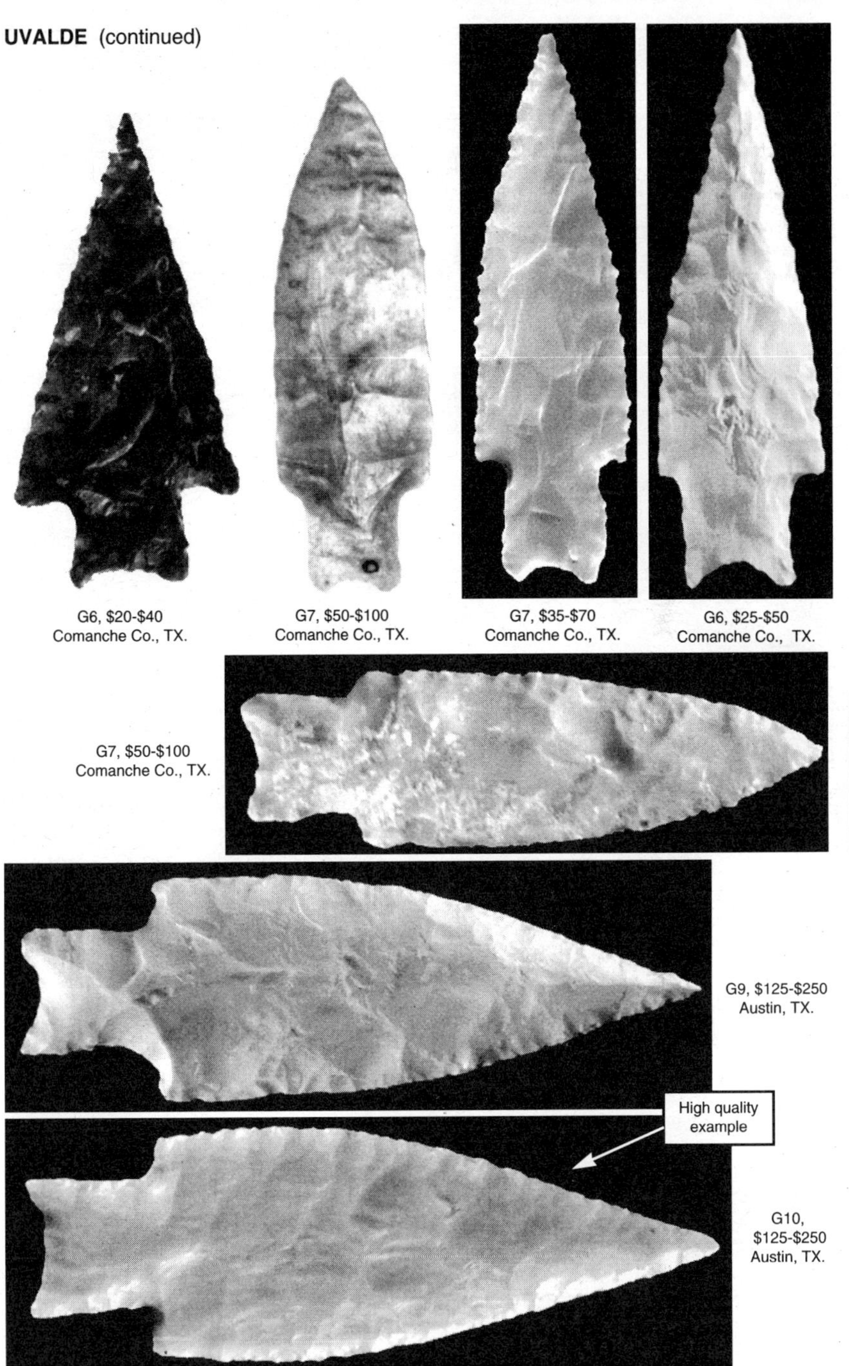

G6, $20-$40
Comanche Co., TX.

G7, $50-$100
Comanche Co., TX.

G7, $35-$70
Comanche Co., TX.

G6, $25-$50
Comanche Co., TX.

G7, $50-$100
Comanche Co., TX.

G9, $125-$250
Austin, TX.

G10,
$125-$250
Austin, TX.

LOCATION: Texas to Oklahoma. **DESCRIPTION:** A medium size, bifurcated stemmed point with barbed to tapered shoulders. Some examples are serrated. The *Frio* point is similar but is usually broader and the ears flare outward more than this type. **I.D. KEY:** Narrow bifurcated stem.

VAL VERDE - Middle to Late Archaic, 5000 - 3000 B. P.

(Also see Langtry, Pedernales and Uvalde)

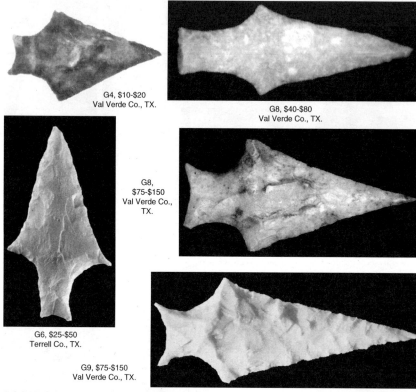

G4, $10-$20
Val Verde Co., TX.

G8, $40-$80
Val Verde Co., TX.

G8,
$75-$150
Val Verde Co.,
TX.

G6, $25-$50
Terrell Co., TX.

G9, $75-$150
Val Verde Co., TX.

LOCATION: Texas. **DESCRIPTION:** A medium size point with outward flaring tapered shoulders, an expanding stem and a concave base. On some examples the basal corners form auricles. **I.D. KEY:** Expanding basal ears, strong shoulders.

VICTORIA - Early Archaic, 8000 - 6000 B. P.

(Also see Angostura and Early Stemmed Lanceolate)

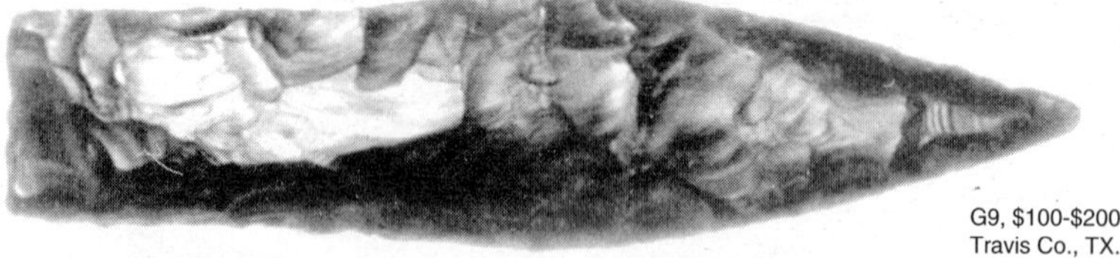

G9, $100-$200
Travis Co., TX.

LOCATION: Texas. **DESCRIPTION:** A medium to large size, narrow, lanceolate blade with a straight base. The hafting area is separated from the blade by weak, tapered shoulders. **I.D. KEY:** "Squared" base.

WASHITA - Mississippian, 800 - 400 B. P.

(Also see Harrell, Keota, Reed and Toyah)

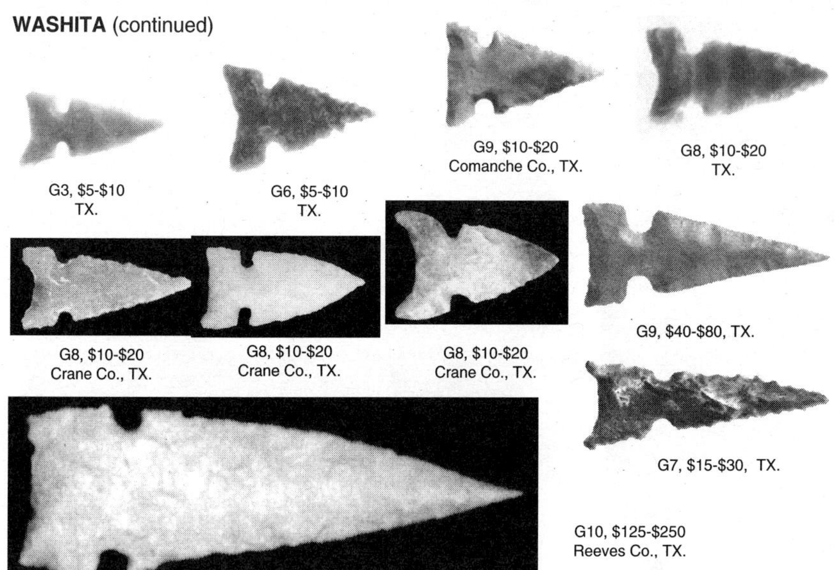

G3, $5-$10
TX.

G6, $5-$10
TX.

G9, $10-$20
Comanche Co., TX.

G8, $10-$20
TX.

G8, $10-$20
Crane Co., TX.

G8, $10-$20
Crane Co., TX.

G8, $10-$20
Crane Co., TX.

G9, $40-$80, TX.

G7, $15-$30, TX.

G10, $125-$250
Reeves Co., TX.

LOCATION: Texas to Oklahoma. **DESCRIPTION:** A small size, thin, triangular side notched arrow point with a concave to straight base. Basal area is usually large in proportion to the blade size. Similar forms occur in the Southwest and Plains states under different names. Concave base forms are called "Peno." **I.D. KEY:** Small triange with side notches.

WELLS - Early to Middle Archaic, 8000 - 5000 B. P.

(Also see Adena, Bulverde, Carrolton and Dawson)

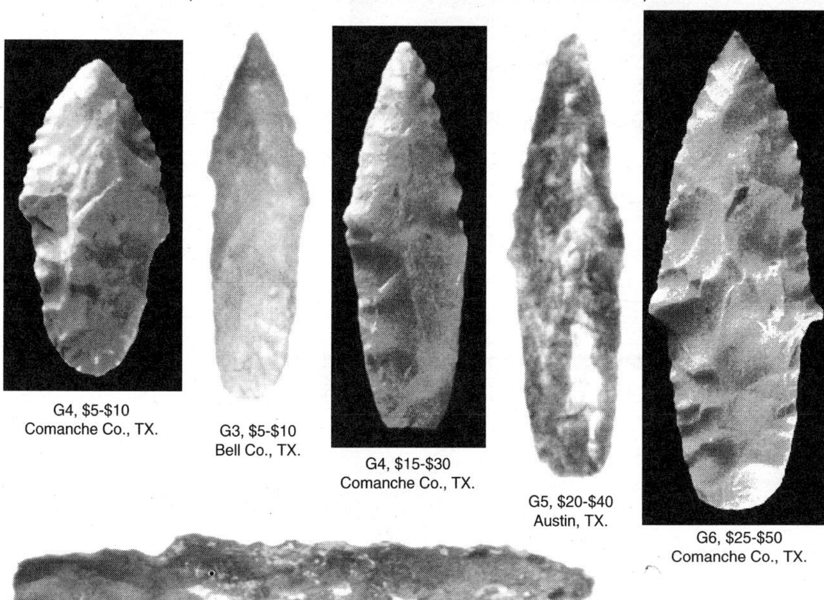

G4, $5-$10
Comanche Co., TX.

G3, $5-$10
Bell Co., TX.

G4, $15-$30
Comanche Co., TX.

G5, $20-$40
Austin, TX.

G6, $25-$50
Comanche Co., TX.

G6, $25-$50
Lampasas, TX.

G7, $25-$50
Bell Co., TX.

G7, $50-$100
Bell Co., TX.

G5, $35-$70
TX.

G5, $25-$45
Austin, TX.

G5, $30-$60
Travis Co., TX.

G8, $50-$100
Williamson Co., TX.

LOCATION: Eastern Texas and Oklahoma. **DESCRIPTION:** A medium to large size, thin, usually serrated point with a long, narrow, contracting to parallel stem that has a rounded to straight base. Shoulders are weak and can be tapered, horizontal or barbed. **I.D. KEY:** Basal form, extended and squared up. Early flaking style.

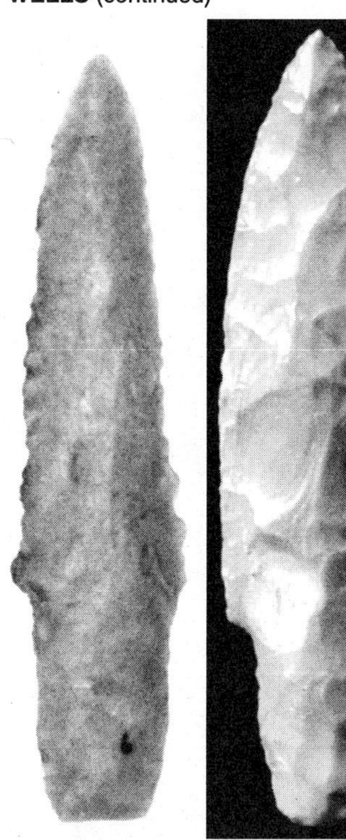
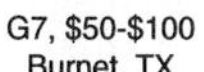

G7, $50-$100
Burnet, TX

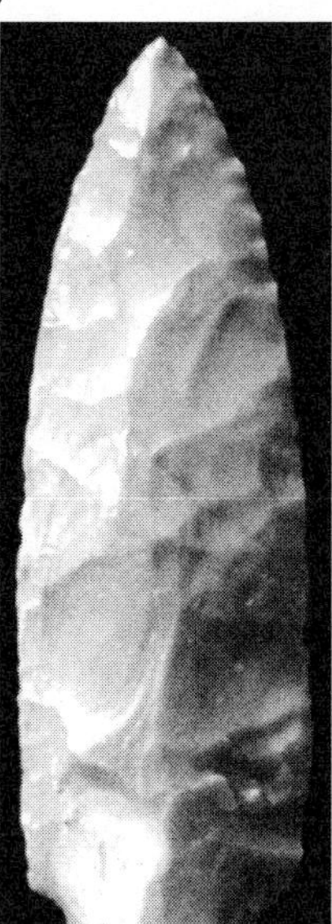

G7, $75-$150
Bexar Co., TX.

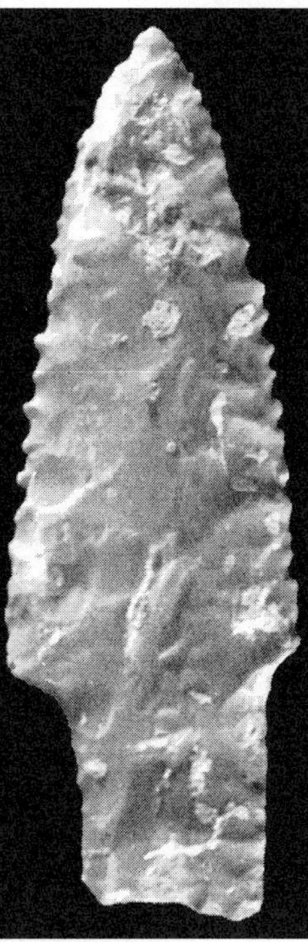

G7, $50-$100
Austin, TX.

G7, $35-$70
Williamson Co., TX.

WHITE RIVER - Middle Archaic to Woodland, 6000 - 1000 B. P.

(Also see Big Sandy, Godar, Hickory Ridge, Osceola and Raddatz)

G8, $125-$250
AR.

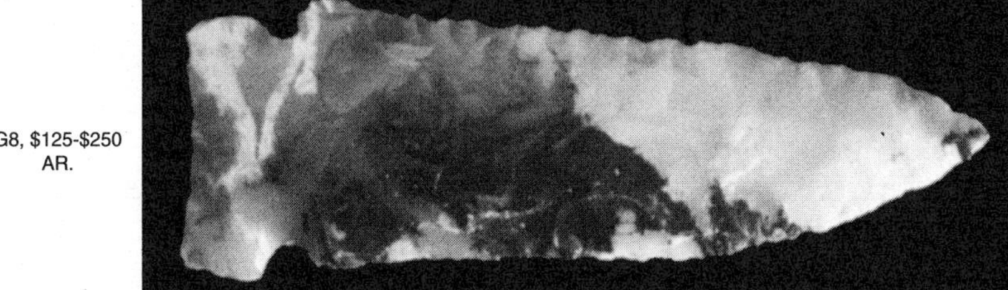

LOCATION: Arkansas, Missouri. **DESCRIPTION:** A medium to large size, narrow, side notched point with a straight to concave base. Blade edges can be serrated.

WILLIAMS - Middle Archaic to Woodland, 6000 - 1000 B. P.

(Also see Castroville, Marcos, Marshall, Palmillas and Shumla)

LOCATION: Texas to Oklahoma. **DESCRIPTION:** A medium to large size, barbed point with an expanded, rounded base. Resharpened examples have tapered shoulders. **I.D. KEY:** Base form, barbs.

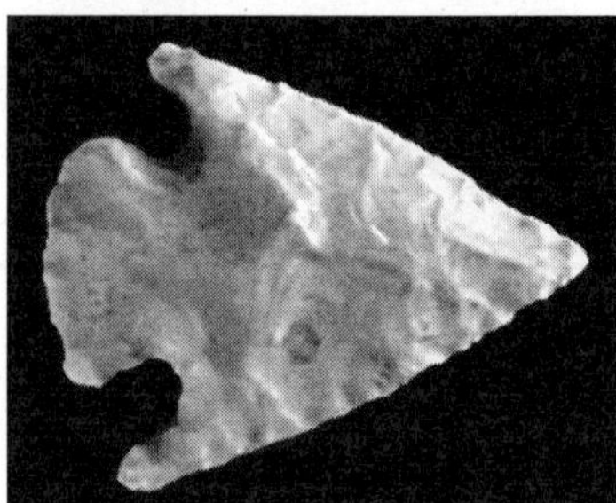

G7, $15-$25
Comanche Co., TX.

G8, $30-$60
Belton, TX.

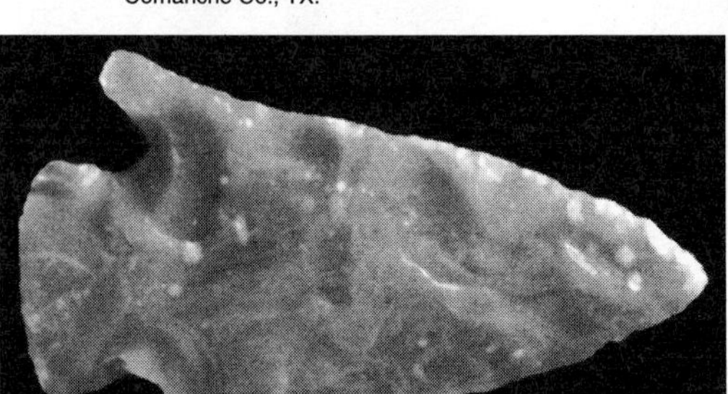

G8, $30-$60
Comanche Co., TX.

G3, $3-$5
Comanche Co., TX.

G7, $35-$70
Austin, Tx.

G8, $100-$200
Coryell Co., TX.

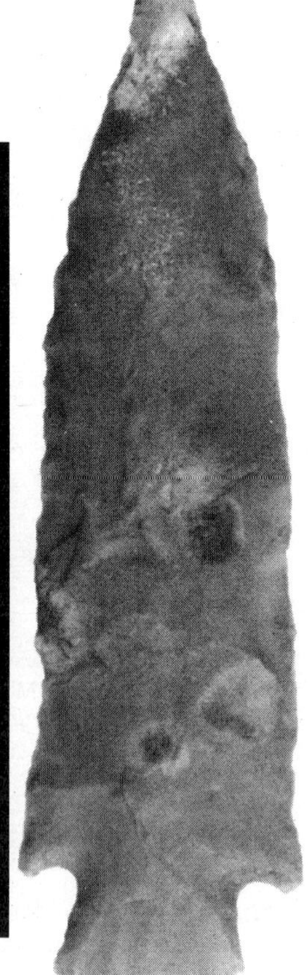

G6, $40-$80
TX.

YARBROUGH - Woodland, 2500 - 1000 B. P.

(Also see Darl, Hoxie, Lange, Travis and Zorra)

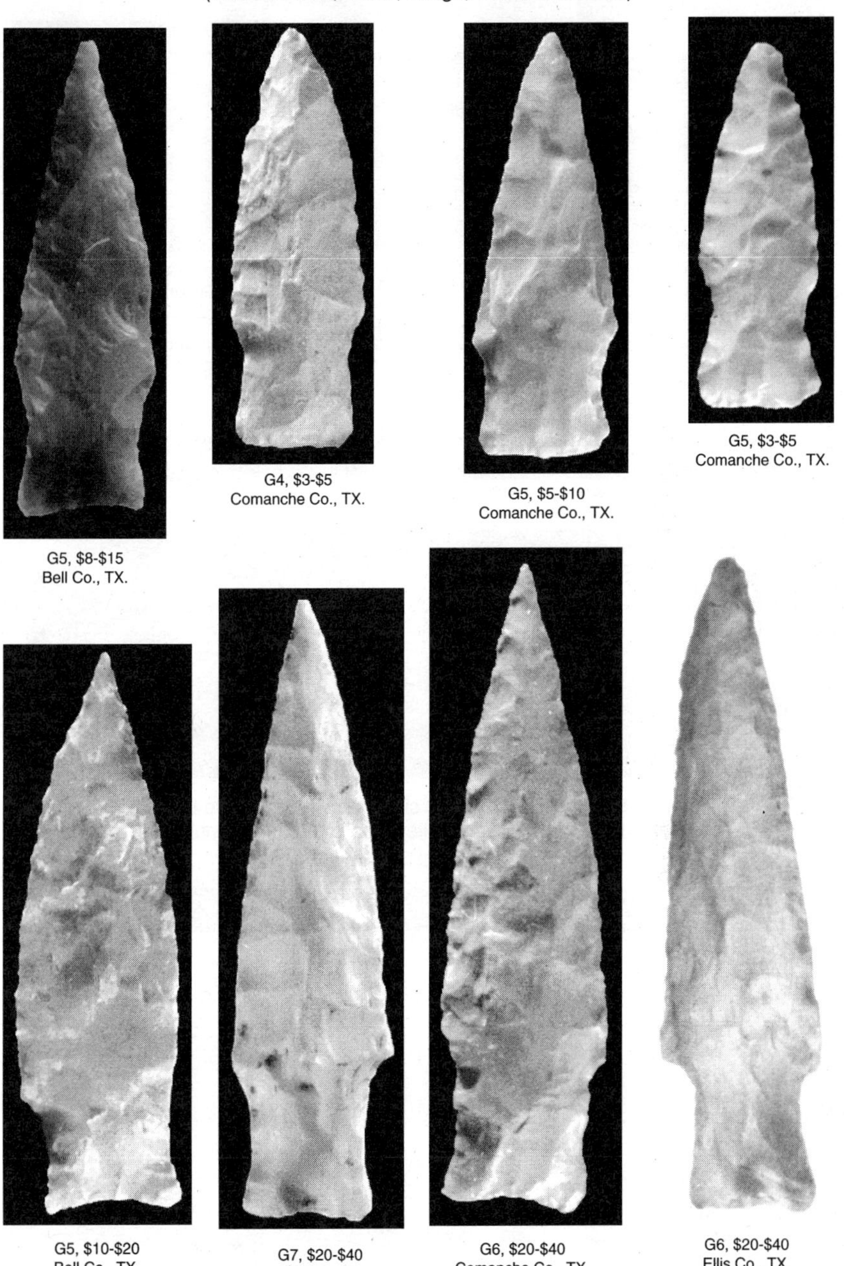

G5, $8-$15
Bell Co., TX.

G4, $3-$5
Comanche Co., TX.

G5, $5-$10
Comanche Co., TX.

G5, $3-$5
Comanche Co., TX.

G5, $10-$20
Bell Co., TX.

G7, $20-$40
Bell Co., Tx.

G6, $20-$40
Comanche Co., TX.

G6, $20-$40
Ellis Co., TX.

SC

LOCATION: Texas to Oklahoma. **DESCRIPTION:** A medium size, narrow point with a long, expanding, rectangular stem that has slightly concave sides. The shoulders are very weak and tapered. The stem edges are usually ground. **I.D. KEY:** Expanding stem.

YOUNG - Mississippian, 1000 - 400 B. P.

(Also see Catan, Clifton, Ebenezer and Morrow Mountain)

G1, $.50-$1
Waco, TX.

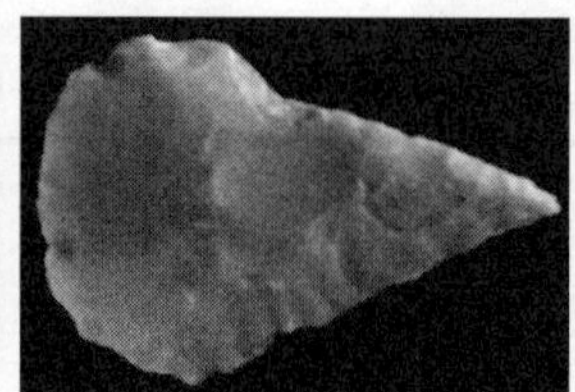
G5, $.50-$1
Comanche Co., TX.

G3, $.50-$1
Comanche Co., TX.

LOCATION: Texas. **DESCRIPTION:** A small size, crudely chipped, elliptical shaped, usually round base point made from a flake. One side is commonly uniface. **I.D. KEY:** Base form, uniface.

ZELLA - Early Archaic, 8500 - 7500 B. P.

(Also see Agate Basin, Angostura and Lerma)

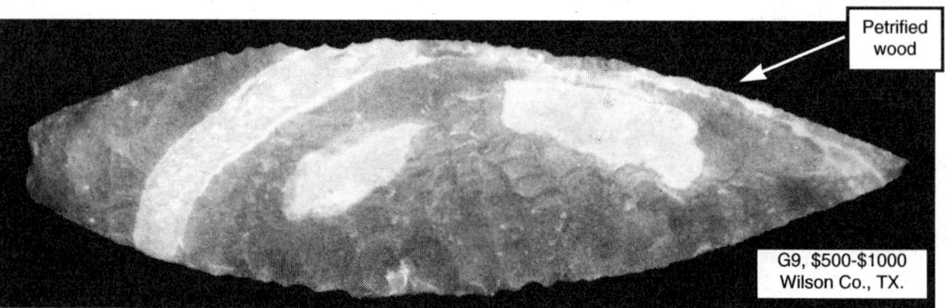

G9, $500-$1000
Wilson Co., TX.

LOCATION: Texas. **DESCRIPTION:** A large size, narrow, lanceolate blade with a rounded to small straight base. Bases are ground. Believed to be a form of Angostura.

ZEPHYR - Early Archaic, 9000 - 6000 B. P.

(Also see Brazos, Darl, Hoxie and Uvalde)

G2, $3-$6
Comanche Co., TX.

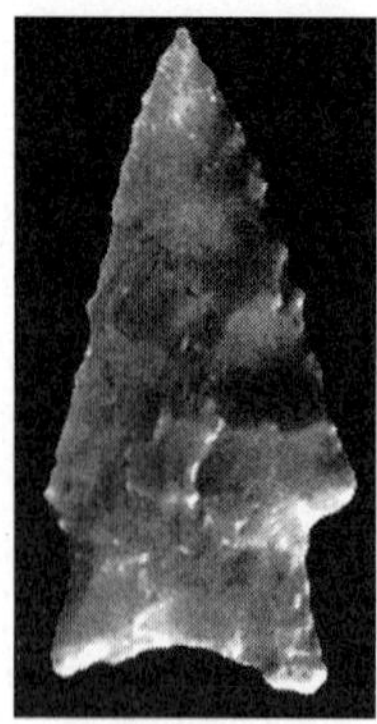
G3, $5-$10
Comanche Co., TX.

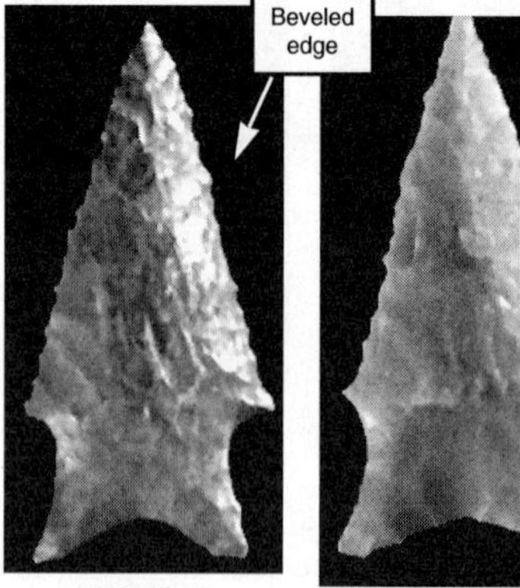

G7, $25-$50
Comanche Co., TX.

G7, $25-$50
Austin, TX.

ZEPHYR (continued)

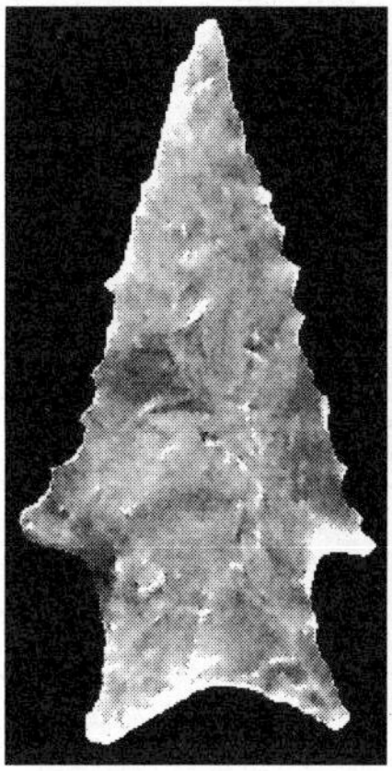

G6, \$15-\$30
Comanche Co., TX.

G6, \$15-\$30
Comanche Co., TX.

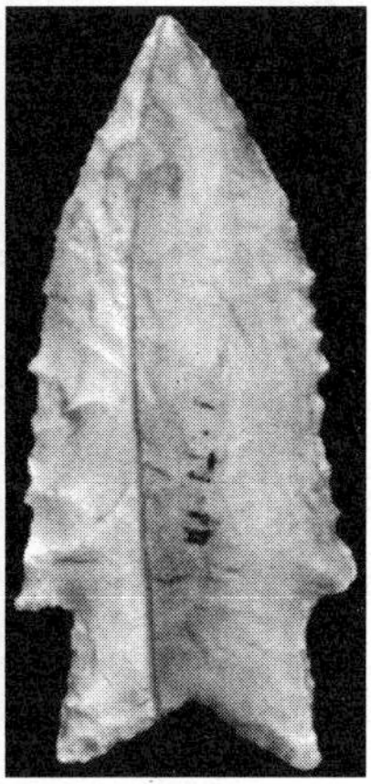

G7, \$25-\$50
Lampasas Co., TX.

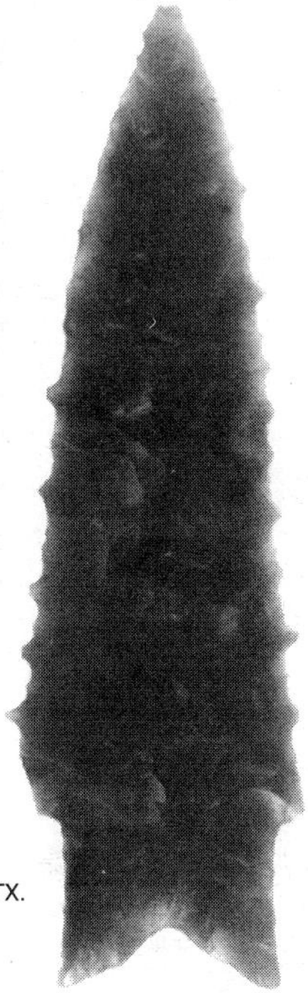

G6, \$35-\$70
TX.

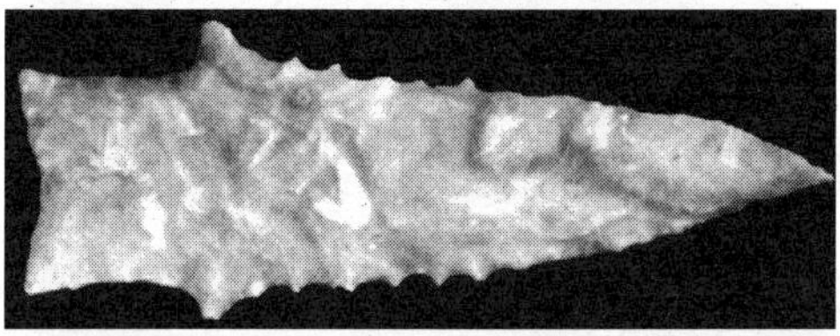

G8, \$65-\$125
Comanche Co., TX.

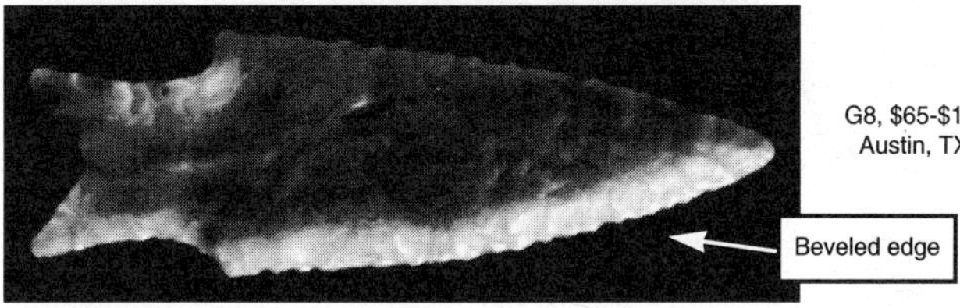

G8, \$65-\$125
Austin, TX.

Beveled edge

SC

LOCATION: Texas. **DESCRIPTION:** A medium to large size, narrow, serrated point with square to tapered, barbed shoulders and an eared base. Blade edges are beveled on one side of each face on resharpened forms. Flaking is of high quality. These points were classified with *Darl* in the past. Also known as *Mahomet* locally. **I.D. KEY:** Fishtail base and serrations.

ZORRA - Middle Archaic, 6000 - 4000 B. P.

(Also see Darl, Lange, Nolan and Travis)

LOCATION: Texas. **DESCRIPTION:** A medium to large size point with tapered shoulders and stem that is usually flat on one face and beveled on both sides of the opposite face. Otherwise identical to *Nolan*. Most have needle tips and good quality flaking. **I.D. KEY:** Base beveling.

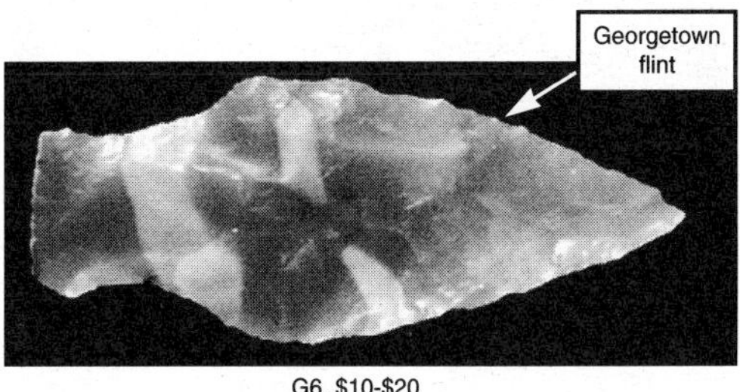

G6, \$10-\$20
Austin, TX.

ZORRA (continued)

G6, $10-$20
Comanche Co., TX.

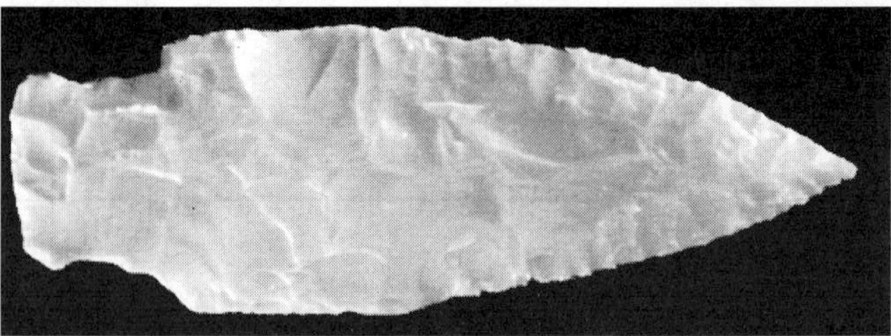

G7, $20-$40
Austin, TX.

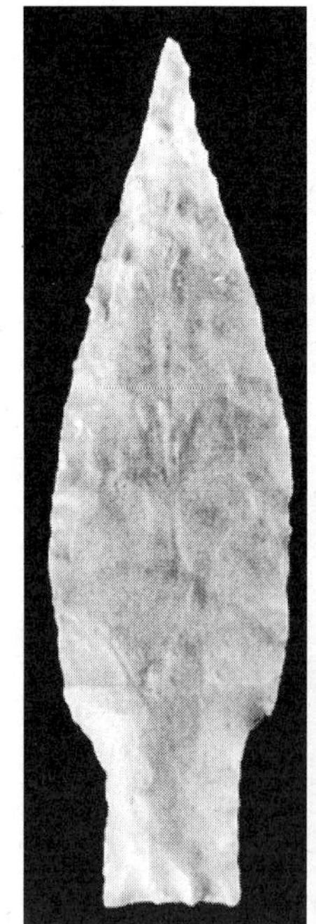

G8, $55-$110
Austin, TX. Classic

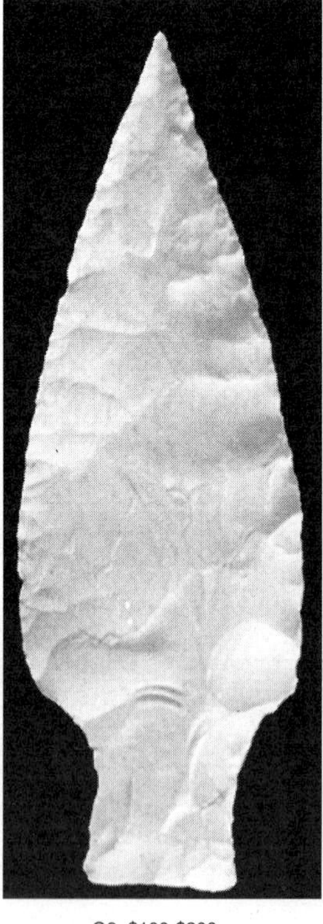

G9, $100-$200
Austin, TX.

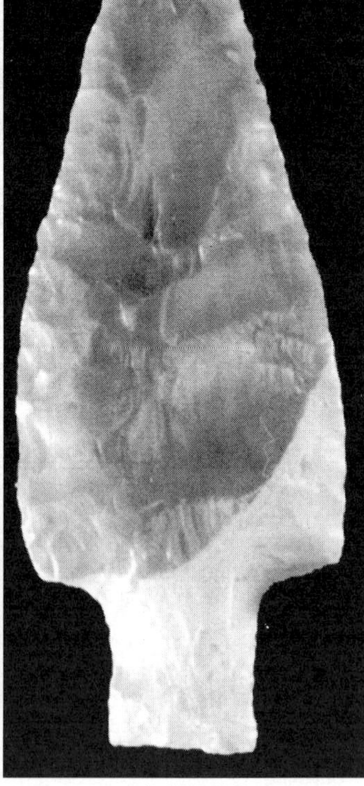

G10, $225-$450
Austin, TX. Excellent quality.

NORTHERN CENTRAL SECTION:

This section includes point types from the following states: Eastern Colorado, Kansas, Illinois, Iowa, Minnesota, Missouri, Nebraska and Wisconsin.

The points in this section are arranged in alphabetical order and are shown **actual size**. All types are listed that were available for photographing. Any missing types will be added to future editions as photographs become available. We are always interested in receiving sharp, black and white or color glossy photos or color slides of your collection. Be sure to include a ruler in the photograph so that proper scale can be determined.

Lithics: Materials employed in the manufacture of point types from this region include: agate, burlington, chalcedony, chert, conglomerate, crystal, flint, jasper, kaolin, Knife River, hornstone, novaculite, petrified wood, quartzite and vein quartz.

Regional Consultant:
Floyd Ritter

Special Advisors:
Tom Davis
Bill Jackson
Glenn Leesman

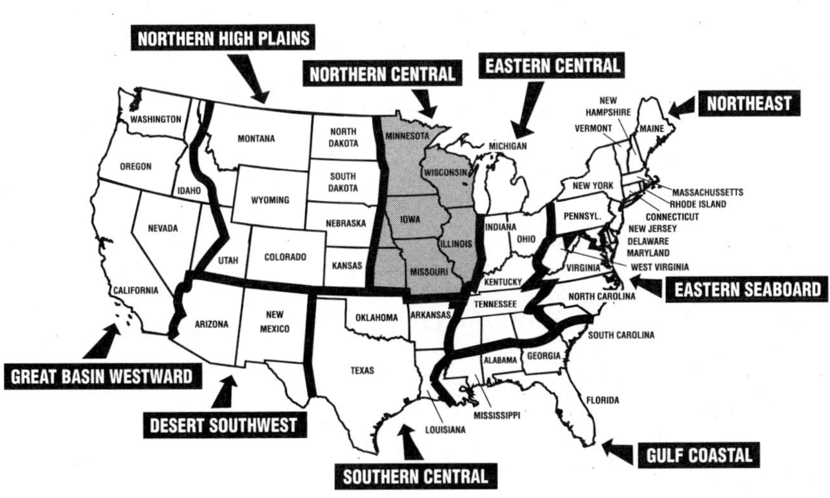

NORTHERN CENTRAL
(Archaeological Periods)

PALEO (14,000 B.P. - 11,000 B.P.)

Beaver Lake
Clovis
Clovis-St. Louis
Cumberland
Cumberland Unfluted
Drill
Folsom

LATE PALEO (12,000 B.P. - 10,000 B.P.)

Hell Gap
Hi-Lo
Plainview
Quad
Square Knife

TRANSITIONAL PALEO (11,000 B.P. - 9,000 B.P.)

Agate Basin
Allen
Angostura
Browns Valley
Eden
Greenbrier
Lerma
Pelican
Scottsbluff Type I & 2

EARLY ARCHAIC (10,000 B.P. - 7,000 B.P.)

Burroughs
Cache River
Calf Creek
Cobbs Triangular
Cossatot River
Dalton Breckenridge
Dalton Classic
Dalton-Hemphill
Dalton-Nuckolls
Dalton-Sloan
Decatur
Dovetail
Fox Valley
Graham Cave
Hardin
Heavy Duty
Hickory Ridge
Holland
Kirk Corner Notched
Lake Erie
Lost Lake
Meserve
Nebo Hill
Osceola
Pike County
Pine Tree Corner Notched
Rice Lobbed
Rochester
St. Charles
Stilwell
Thebes
Warrick

MIDDLE ARCHAIC (7,000 B.P. - 4,000 B.P.)

Afton
Exotic Forms
Ferry
Hemphill
Matanzas
Raddatz
Ramey Knife
Red Ochre
Sedalia
Smith
Stone Square Stem

LATE ARCHAIC (4,000 B.P. - 3,000 B.P.)

Copena Classic
Etley
Evans
Gary
Godar
Helton
Mehlville
Robinson
Table Rock
Turkeytail-Fulton
Turkeytail-Harrison
Wadlow

WOODLAND (3,000 B.P. - 1,300 B.P.)

Adena
Adena Blade
Adena-Dickson
Adena-Narrow Stem
Adena-Notched Base
Adena-Robbins
Adena-Waubesa
Alba
Apple Creek
Carter
Cupp
Gibson
Grand
Hopewell
Kramer
Lehigh
Morse Knife
North
Peisker Diamond
Ross
Snyders
Steuben

MISSISSIPPIAN (1300 B.P. - 400 B.P.)

Agee
Cahokia
Harahey
Harrell
Hayes
Homan
Huffaker
Kay Blade
Lundy
Madison
Nodena
Sequoyah
Washita

HISTORIC (450 B.P. - 170 B.P.)

No types listed.

NORTHERN CENTRAL
THUMBNAIL GUIDE SECTION

The following references are provided to aid the collector in easier and quicker identification of point types. All photos are exactly 30% of actual size and are proportional to each other. Each point pictured in this section represents a classic form for the type. When a match is found, go to the alphabetical location of that type for more examples in actual size.

1 THUMBNAIL GUIDE - AURICULATE FORMS (30% actual size)

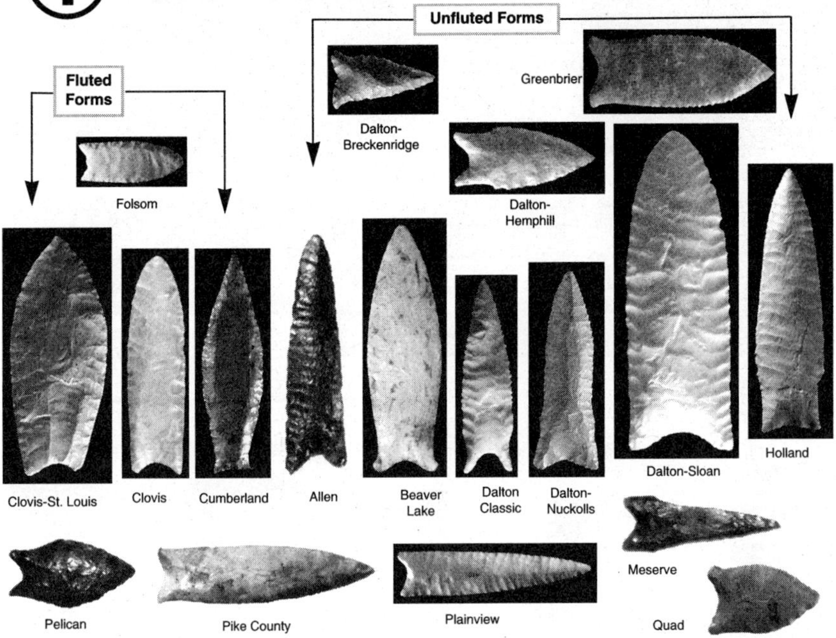

Fluted Forms

Unfluted Forms

Folsom

Dalton-Breckenridge

Greenbrier

Dalton-Hemphill

Clovis-St. Louis

Clovis

Cumberland

Allen

Beaver Lake

Dalton Classic

Dalton-Nuckolls

Dalton-Sloan

Holland

Pelican

Pike County

Plainview

Meserve

Quad

NC

2 THUMBNAIL GUIDE - LANCEOLATE FORMS (30% actual size)

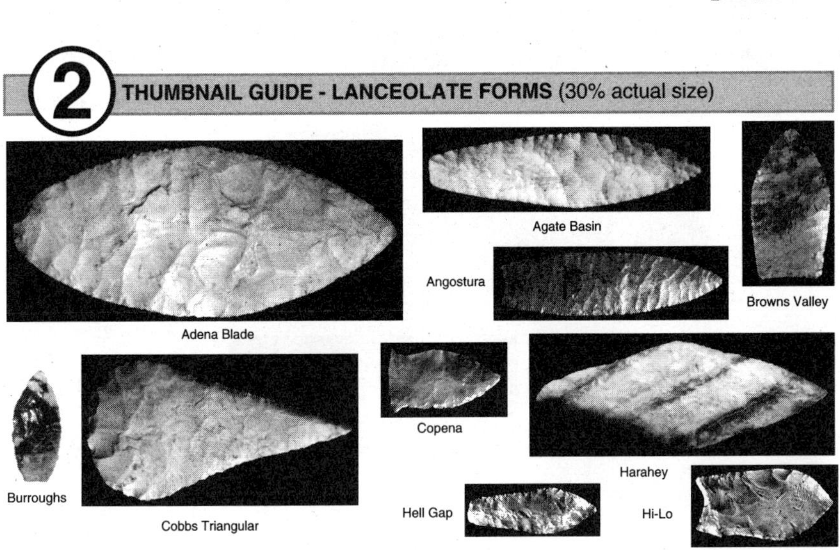

Adena Blade

Agate Basin

Angostura

Browns Valley

Burroughs

Cobbs Triangular

Copena

Harahey

Hell Gap

Hi-Lo

THUMBNAIL GUIDE - Lanceolate forms (continued)

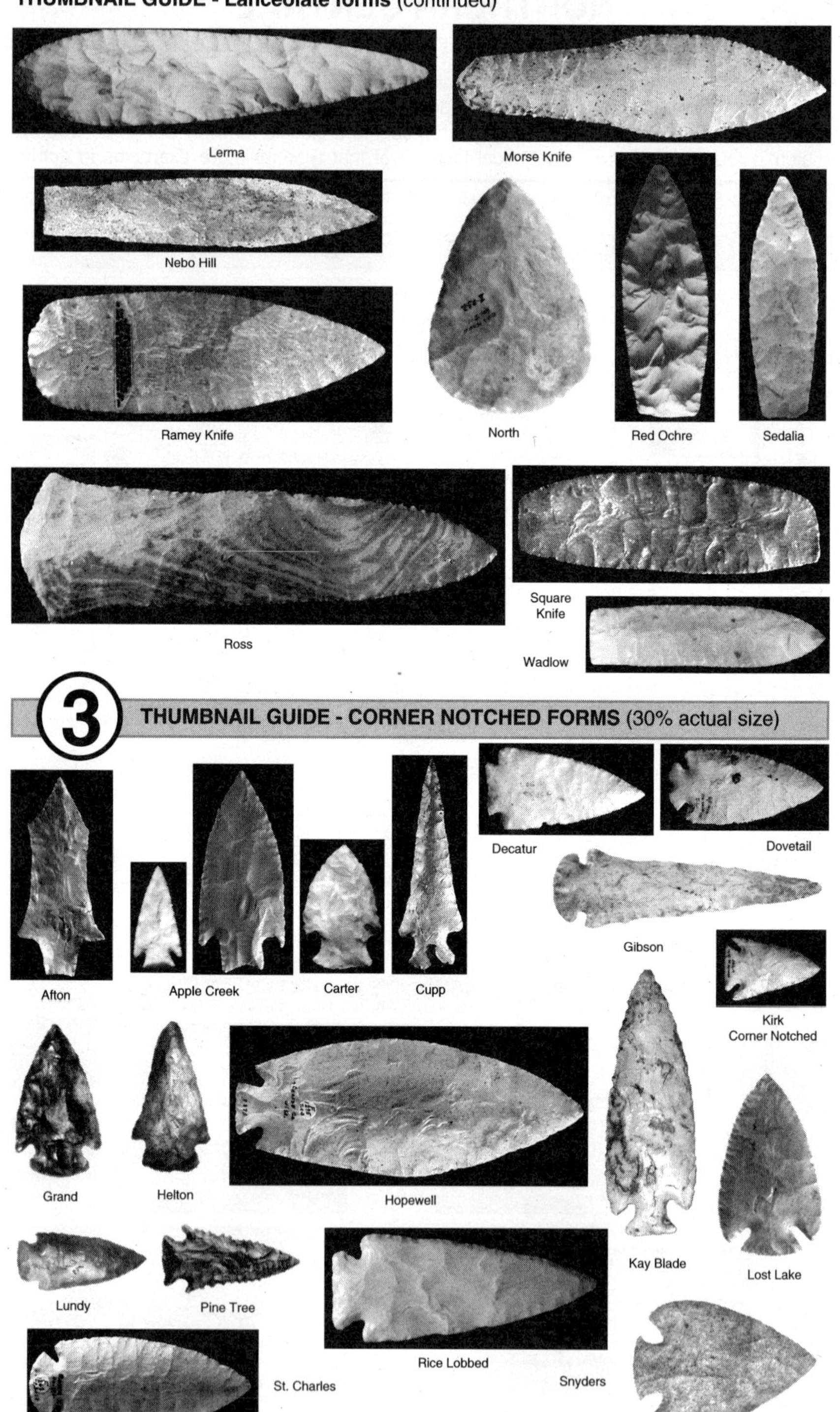

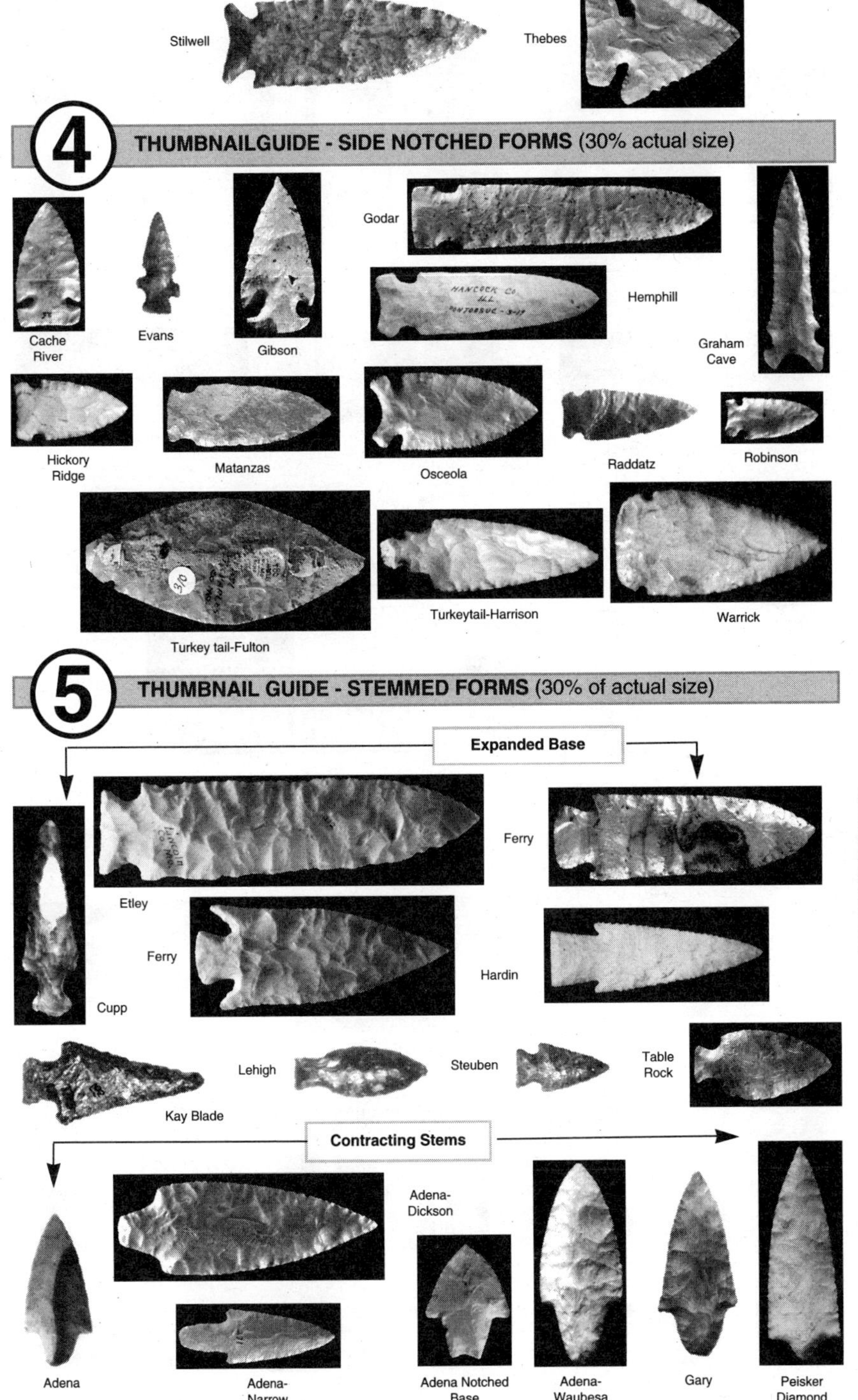
Stilwell
Thebes
4
THUMBNAILGUIDE - SIDE NOTCHED FORMS (30% actual size)
Cache River
Evans
Gibson
Godar
Hemphill
Graham Cave
Hickory Ridge
Matanzas
Osceola
Raddatz
Robinson
Turkey tail-Fulton
Turkeytail-Harrison
Warrick
5
THUMBNAIL GUIDE - STEMMED FORMS (30% of actual size)
Expanded Base
Cupp
Etley
Ferry
Ferry
Hardin
Kay Blade
Lehigh
Steuben
Table Rock
Contracting Stems
Adena
Adena-Dickson
Adena-Narrow
Adena Notched Base
Adena-Waubesa
Gary
Peisker Diamond

THUMBNAIL GUIDE - Stemmed Forms (continued)

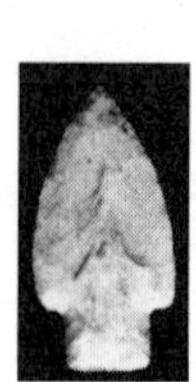
Adena Robbins

Drill

Eden

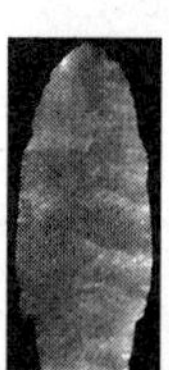
Eden Eared

Heavy Duty

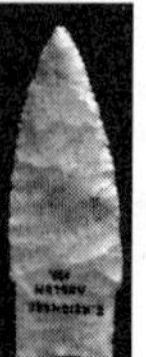
Holland

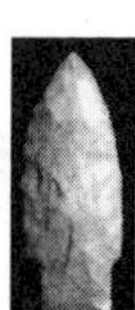
Kramer

Rochester

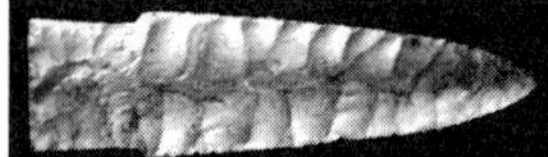
Scottsbluff Type I

Scottsbluff Type II

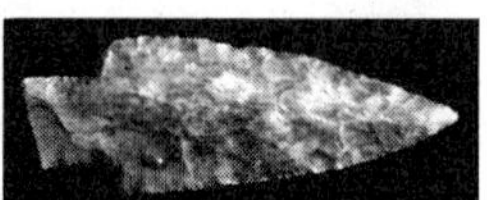
Stone Square Stem

6 THUMBNAIL GUIDE - STEMMED-BIFURCATED FORMS (30% of actual size)

Fox Valley

Lake Erie

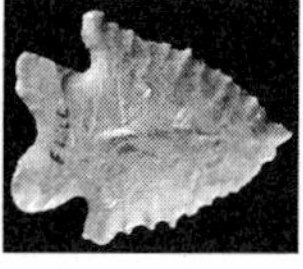
Cossatot River

7 THUMBNAIL GUIDE - BASAL NOTCHED FORMS (30% of actual size)

Calf Creek

Mohlville
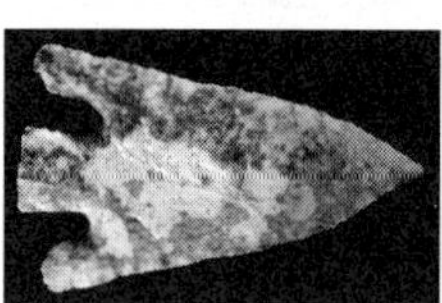

Smith
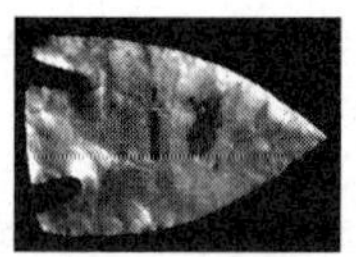

8 THUMBNAIL GUIDE - ARROW POINTS (30% of actual size)

Agee

Alba

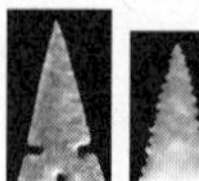

Cahokia

Harrell

Hayes

Homan

Huffaker

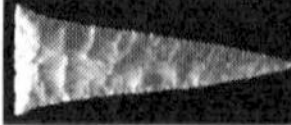
Madison

Nodena

Sequoyah

Washita

ADENA - Late Archaic to late Woodland, 3000 - 1200 B. P.

(see Gary, Kramer and Rochester)

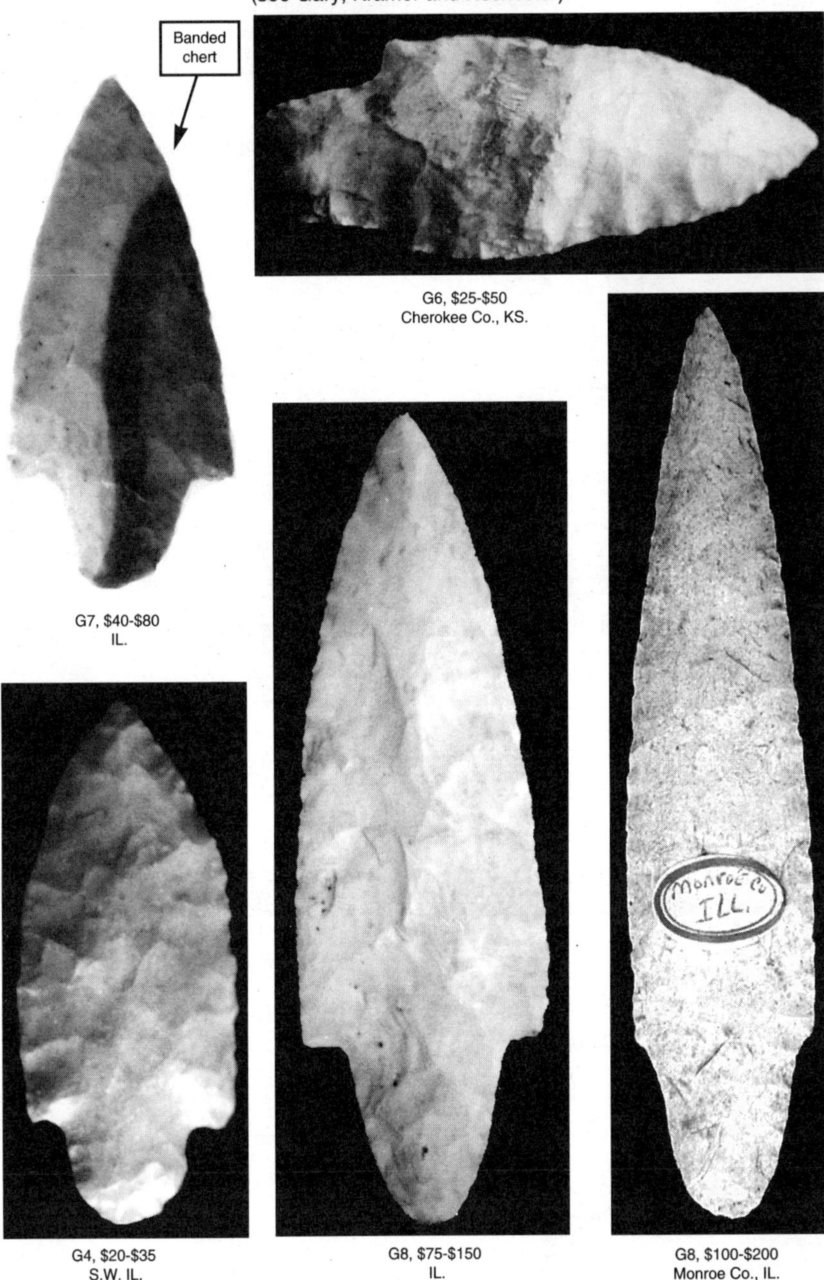

G6, $25-$50
Cherokee Co., KS.

G7, $40-$80
IL.

G4, $20-$35
S.W. IL.

G8, $75-$150
IL.

G8, $100-$200
Monroe Co., IL.

NC

LOCATION: Eastern to Southeastern states. **DESCRIPTION:** A medium to large, thin, narrow, triangular blade that is sometimes serrated, and with a medium to long, narrow to broad rounded "beaver tail" stem. Most examples are from average to excellent quality. Bases can be ground. **I.D. KEY:** Rounded base, Woodland randomflaking.

ADENA BLADE - Late Archaic to Woodland, 3000 - 1200 B. P.

(Also see Lerma, North, Red Ochre)

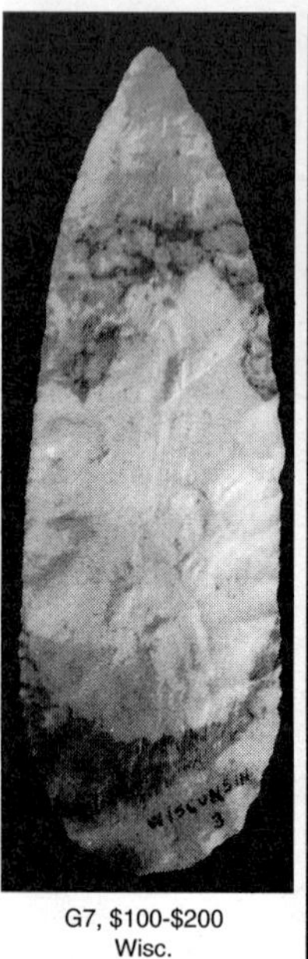

G7, $100-$200
Wisc.

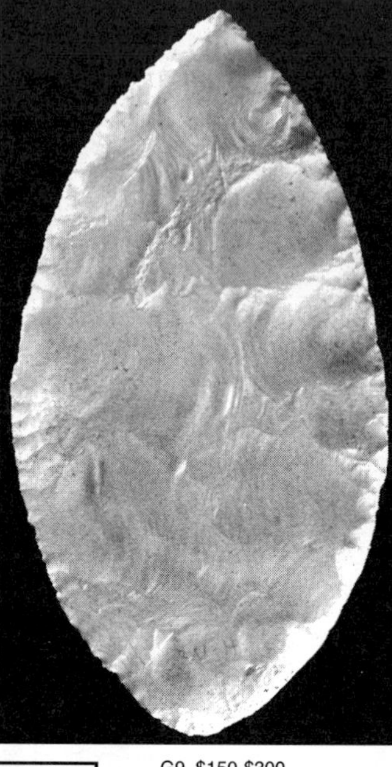

G9, $150-$300
IL.

G9, $180-$350
McLean Co., IL.

IMPORTANT:
Shown half size

LOCATION: Midwestern to Eastern states. **DESCRIPTION:** A large size, thin, broad, ovate blade with a rounded base and is often found in caches. **I.D. KEY:** Random flaking.

ADENA-DICKSON - Woodland, 2500 - 1600 B. P.

(Also see Gary)

G2, $3-$5
Miller Co., MO.

G6, $20-$40
MO.

LOCATION: Midwestern states. **DESCRIPTION:** A medium to large size point with tapered shoulders and a contracting stem. High quality flaking and thinness is evident on most examples. **I.D. KEY:** Basal form.

G5, $30-$60
MO.

G6, $45-$75
IL.

G5, $20-$40
Douglas Co., KS.

G7, $75-$150
IL.,

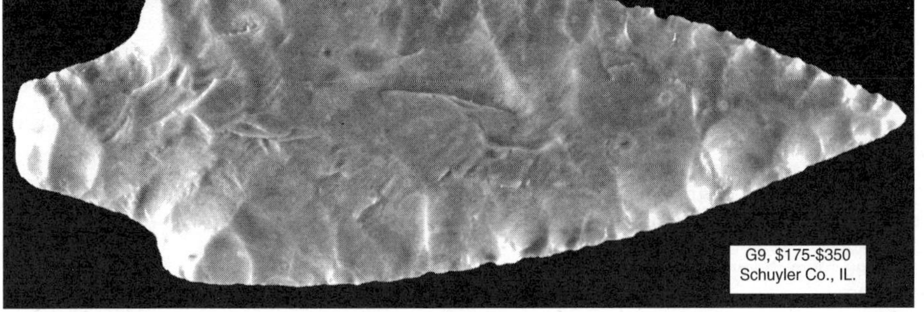

G9, $175-$350
Schuyler Co., IL.

NC

ADENA-NARROW STEM - Late Archaic to Woodland, 3000 - 1200 B. P.

(Also see Adena and Rochester)

G5, $20-$35
IL.

LOCATION: Eastern to Southeastern states. **DESCRIPTION:** A medium to large, thin, narrow triangular blade that is sometimes serrated, and a medium to long, narrow, rounded stem. Most examples are well made. **I.D. KEY:** Narrow rounded base with more secondary work than ordinary Adena.

ADENA-NOTCHED BASE - Late Archaic to Woodland, 3000 - 1200 B. P.

LOCATION: Southeast to midwest. **DESCRIPTION:** Identical to Adena, but with a notched or snapped-off concave base. **I.D. KEY:** Basal form different.

G5, $20-$35
MO.

ADENA ROBBINS - Late Archaic to Woodland, 3000 - 1800 B. P.

(Also see Adena, Kramer and Rochester)

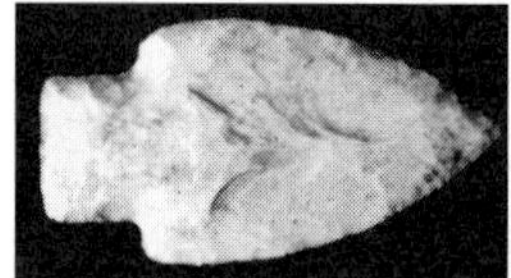

G5, $25-$50
Cherokee Co., KS.

IMPORTANT:
Shown half size

G7, $75-$150
Monroe Co., IL.

LOCATION: Eastern to Southeastern states. **DESCRIPTION:** A large broad, triangular point that is thin and well made with a long, wide, squared stem that is parallel sided. The blade has convex sides and square shoulders. Many examples show excellent secondary flaking on blade ediges. **I.D. KEY:** Squa - red base, heavy secondary flak- ing.

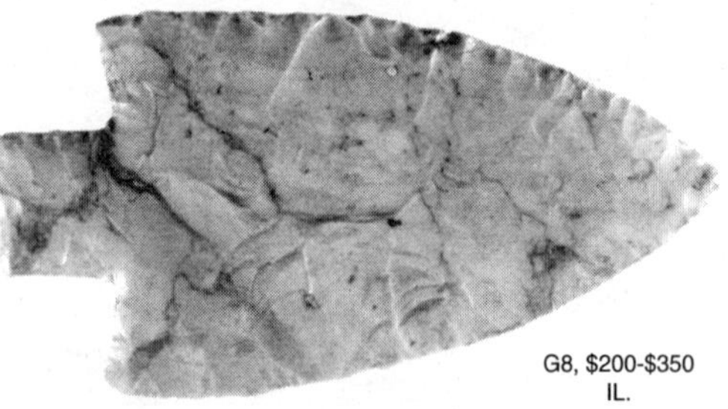

G8, $200-$350
IL.

ADENA-WAUBESA - Woodland, 2500 - 1500 B. P.

(Also see Adena and Gary)

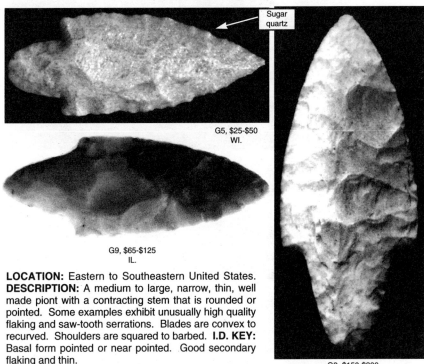

Sugar quartz

G5, $25-$50
WI.

G9, $65-$125
IL.

G9, $150-$300
Sedalia, MO.

LOCATION: Eastern to Southeastern United States. **DESCRIPTION:** A medium to large, narrow, thin, well made piont with a contracting stem that is rounded or pointed. Some examples exhibit unusually high quality flaking and saw-tooth serrations. Blades are convex to recurved. Shoulders are squared to barbed. **I.D. KEY:** Basal form pointed or near pointed. Good secondary flaking and thin.

AFTON - Middle Archaic to early Woodland, 5000 - 2000 B. P.

(Also see Apple Creek, Ferry and Helton)

G4, $15-$30
MO.

G7, $50-$100
MO.

G5, $20-$35
MO.

LOCATION: Midwestern states and is rarely found in some Eastern and Southeastern states. **DESCRIPTION:** A medium to large size pentagonal shaped point with a flaring or corner notched stem. Some examples are base notched and some are stemmed. **I.D. KEY:** Blade form.

AFTON (continued)

G8, $125-$250
MO.

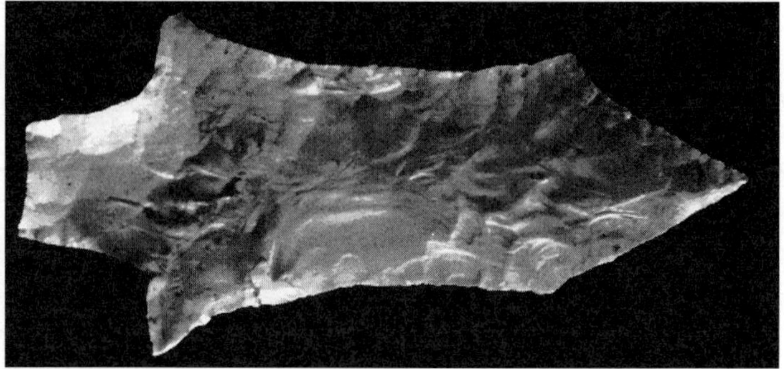

AGATE BASIN - Transitional Paleo to Early Archaic, 10500 - 8000 B. P.

(Also see Allen, Angostura, Burroughs, Eden, Lerma, Nebo Hill and Sedalia)

G5, $50-$100
Riley Co., KS.

Note ancient resharpening above haft

G7, $150-$300
Pike Co., IL.

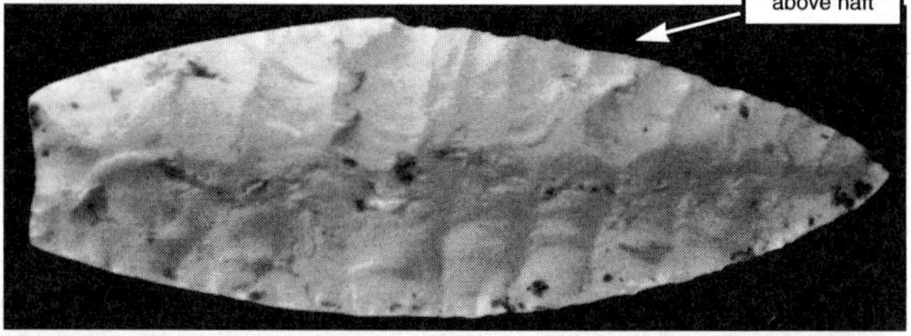

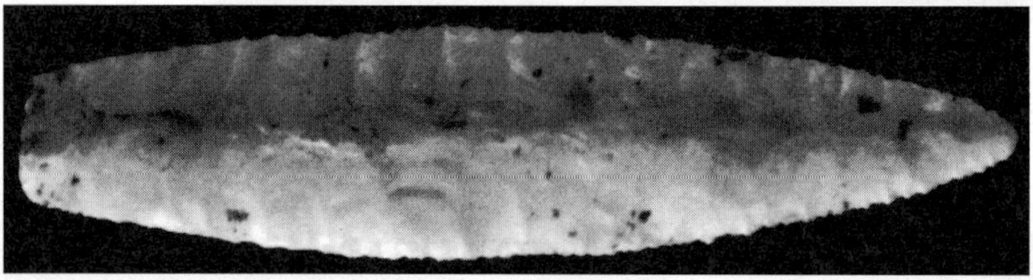

G8, $225-$450
Cent. IA.

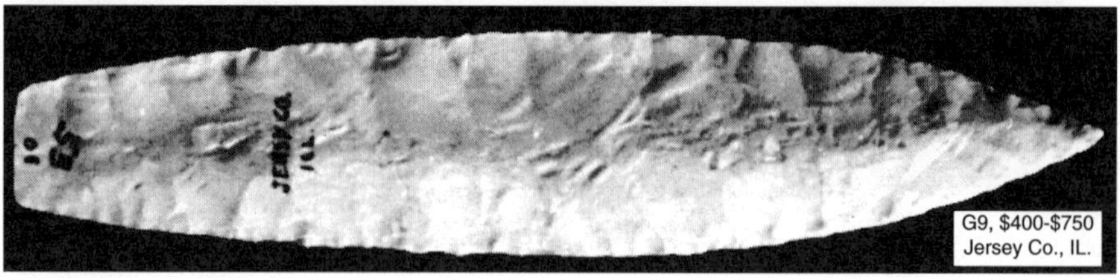

G9, $400-$750
Jersey Co., IL.

LOCATION: Midwestern states. **DESCRIPTION:** A medium to large size lanceolate blade of unusually high quality. Bases are either convex, concave or straight, and are usually ground. Some examples are median ridged and have random to parallel flaking. **I.D. KEY:** Basal form and flaking style.

G8, $400-$800
St. Charles Co., MO.

G9, $500-$1000
Obion Co., IL.

G8, $400-$800
Fulton Co., IL.

G9, $600-$1200
MO.

G10, $1000-$2000
Stephenson Co., IL.

AGEE - Mississippian, 1200 - 700 B. P.

(Also see Alba, Hayes, Homan)

LOCATION: Arkansas; rarely into Missouri and Illinois. **DESCRIPTION:** A small to medium size, narrow, expanded barbed, corner notched point. Tips are needle sharp. Some examples are double notched at the base. A rare type **I.D. KEY:** Basal form and barb expansion.

G5, $90-$150
Cent., MO.

G5, $100-$200
Cent., MO.

G6, $125-$300
Cent., MO.

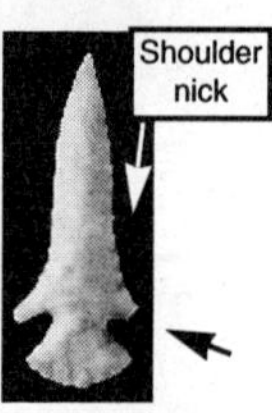

G6, $100-$200
Cent., MO.

ALBA - Woodland to Mississippian, 2000 - 400 B. P.

(Also see Agee, Hayes, Homan and Sequoyah)

G7, $80-$150
IL.

LOCATION: Louisiana, Arkansas into Oklahoma; rarely into Illinois. **DESCRIPTION:** A small to medium size, narrow, well made point with prominent tangs, a recurved blade and a bulbous stem. Some examples are serrated. **I.D. KEY:** Rounded base and expanded barbs.

ALLEN - Transitional Paleo to Early Archaic, 10,000 - 7500 B. P.

(Also see Angostura, Browns Valley, Clovis and Plainview)

LOCATION: Midwestern states to Canada. **DESCRIPTION:** A medium to large size lanceolate point that has oblique tranverse flaking and a concave base. Basal area is ground. **I.D. KEY:** Flaking style and blade form.

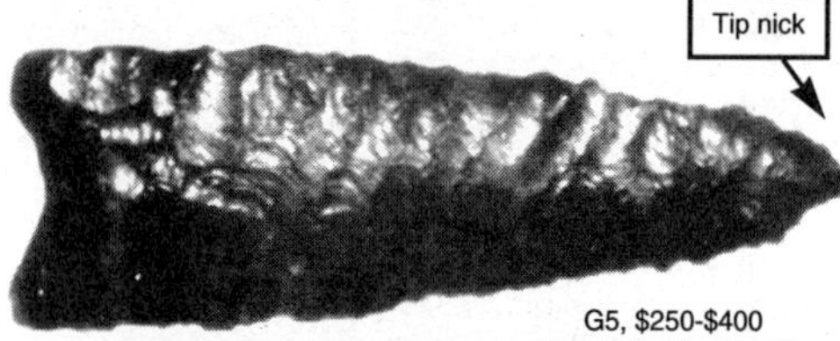

G5, $250-$400
Pottowatomie Co., KS.

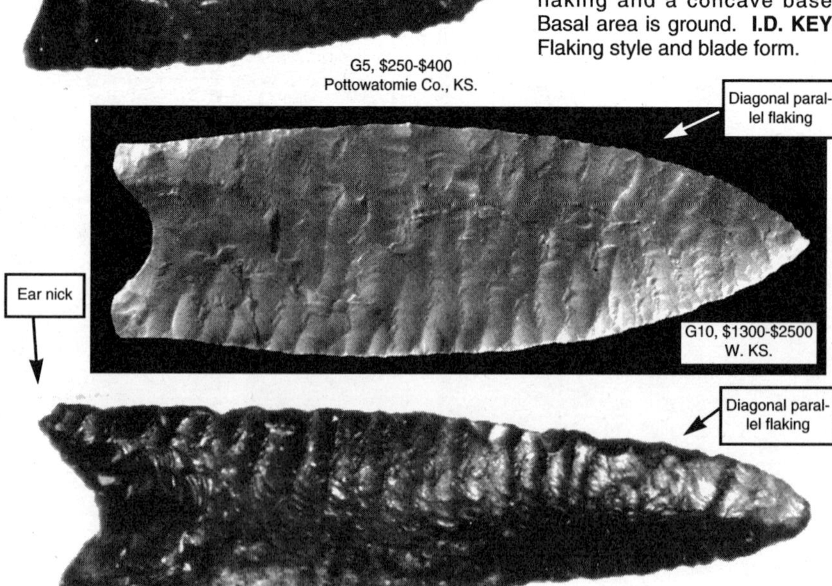

G10, $1300-$2500
W. KS.

G7, $600-$1200
Riley Co., KS.

ANGOSTURA - Transitional Paleo to Middle Archaic, 10,000 - 8000 B. P.

(Also see Agate Basin, Allen and Eden)

G10, $1000-$2000
Cooper Co., MO.

G8, $900-$1700
WI.

G10, $1000-$2000
WI.

NC

LOCATION: Midwest to Western states. **DESCRIPTION:** A medium to large size lanceolate blade with a contracting, concave, straight or convex base. Both broad and narrow forms occur. Flaking can be parallel oblique to random. Blades are commonly steeply beveled on one side of each face; some are serrated and most have basal grinding. Formerly called Long points. **I.D. KEY:** Basal form, flaking on blade which can be beveled.

APPLE CREEK - Late Woodland, 1700 - 1500 B. P.

(Also see Helton, Kirk Corner Notched, Lundy and Pine Tree)

LOCATION: Kansas, Missouri & Illinois. **DESCRIPTION:** A medium to large size, broad, corner notched point with an expanded stem. Barbs are short to moderate. Bases are convex,straight or concave. **I.D. KEY:** Angle of corner notches.

APPLE CREEK (continued)

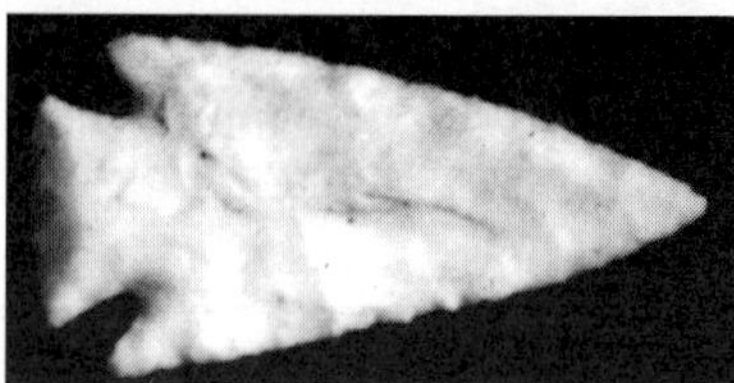
G5, $15-$25
Cherokee Co., KS.

G6, 20-$40
Pettis Co., MO.

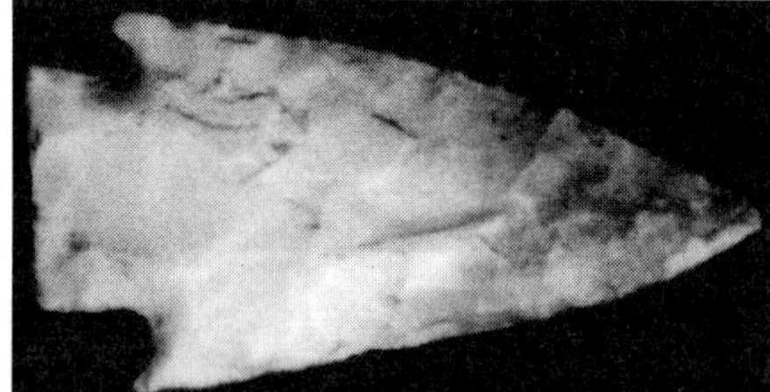
G5, $25-$50
Miller Co., MO.

G7, $75-$150
Dickson Co., MO.

BEAVER LAKE - Paleo, 11,000 - 8000 B. P.

(Also see Clovis, Cumberland, Greenbrier and Quad)

G9, $1500-$2500
IL.

LOCATION: DESCRIPTION: A medium to large size lanceolate blade with flaring ears. Contemporaneous and associated with *Cumberland,* but thinner than unfluted *Cumberlands.* Bases are ground and blade edges are recurved. **I.D. KEY:** Paleo flaking, shoulder area.

BROWNS VALLEY - Transitional Paleo, 10,000 - 8000 B. P.

(Also see Agate Basin, Allen, Angostura, Burroughs, Clovis, Plainview and Sedalia)

BROWNS VALLEY (continued)

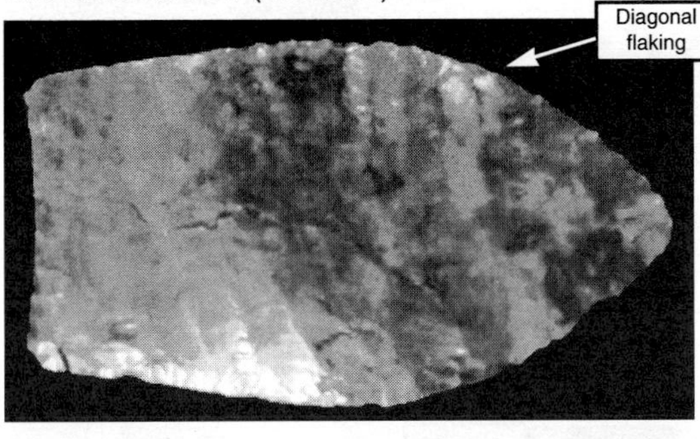

LOCATION: Upper midwestern states. **DESCRIPTION:** A medium to large, thin, lanceolate blade with usually oblique to horizontal transverse flaking and a concave to straight base which can be ground. **I.D. KEY:** Paleo transverse flaking.

G6, $150-$275
Cent. IL. Note oblique parallel flaking which is characteristic of the type.

BURROUGHS - Early Archaic, 8000 - 6000 B. P.

(Also see Agate Basin and Browns Valley

LOCATION: Northern midwestern states. **DESCRIPTION:** A small to medium size, lanceolate point with convex sides and a straight to slightly concave base.

G6, $40-$80
Riley Co., KS.

CACHE RIVER - Early to Middle Archaic, 10,000 - 5000 B. P.

(Also see Godar, Graham Cave, Hickory Ridge, Raddatz and Robinson)

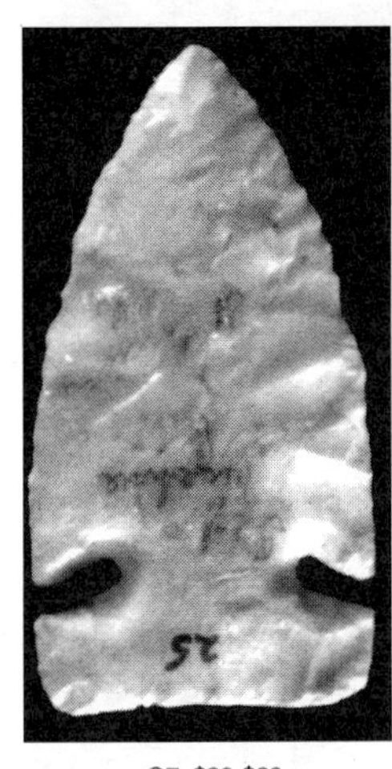

G7, $30-$60
St. Louis, MO.

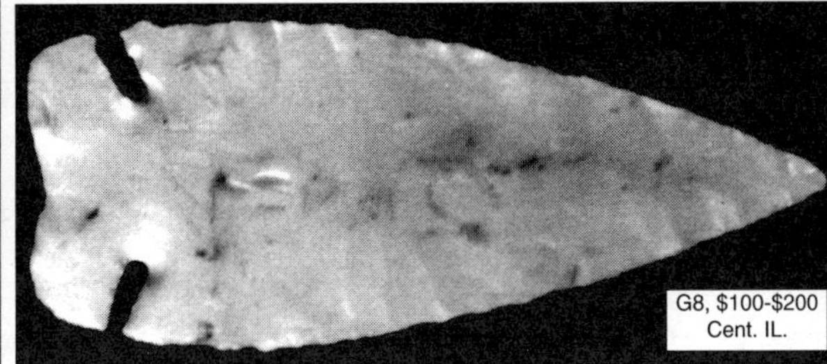

G8, $100-$200
Cent. IL.

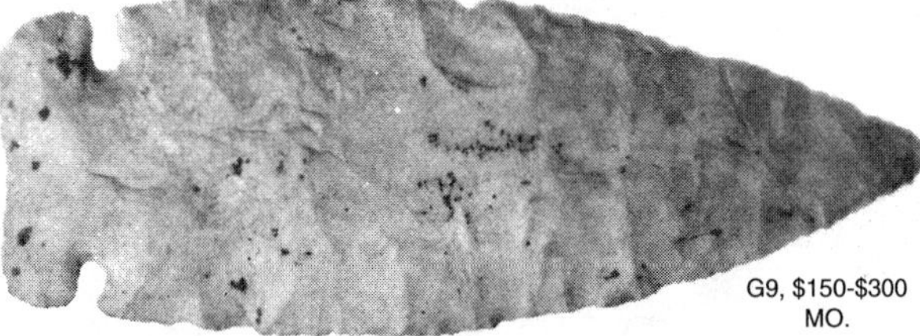

G9, $150-$300
MO.

LOCATION: Midwestern states. **DESCRIPTION:** A small to medium size, fairly thin, side-notched, triangular point with a concave base. Could be related to *Big Sandy* points. **I.D. KEY:** Base form, narrow notched & flaking of blade.

CAHOKIA - Mississippian, 1000 - 500 B. P.

(Also see Harrell, Huffaker, Madison and Washita)

CAHOKIA (continued)

Double notched

Double notched

G5, $15-$25
IL.

G8, $50-$100
IL.

G6, $25-$45
IL.

G7, $25-$45
IL.

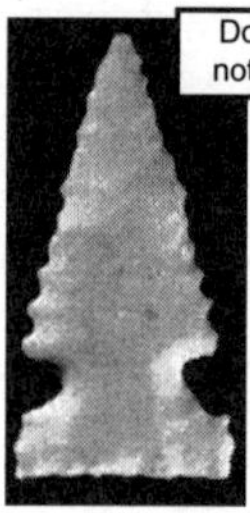

G8, $45-$90
IL.

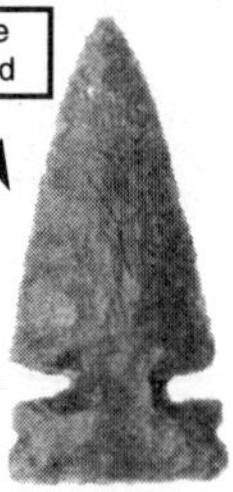

G9, $65-$125
IL.

Double notched

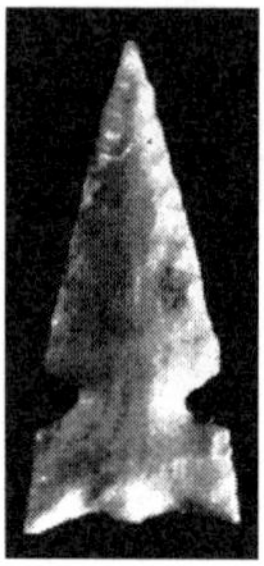

G8, $60-$100
IL.

G9, $80-$150
IL.

G9, $50-$100
IL.

G9, $50-$100
IL.

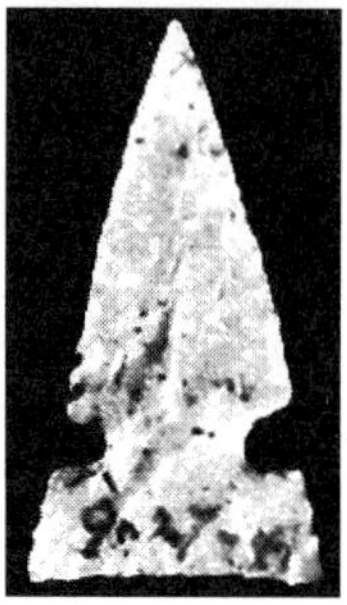

G9, $65-$125
Cent. IL.

The following valuable points are all from the Cahokia type site

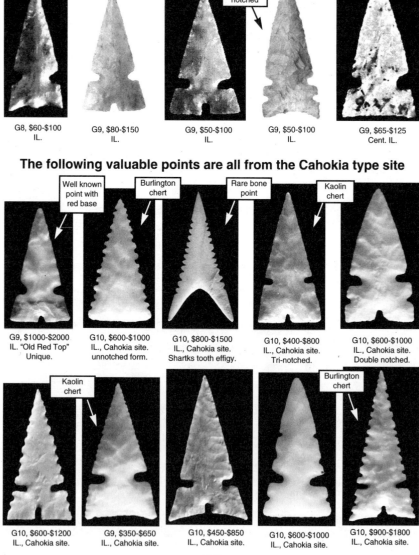

Well known point with red base

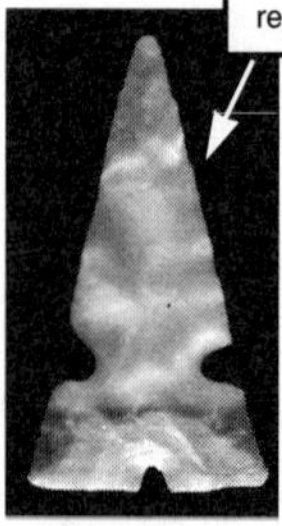

Burlington chert

Rare bone point

Kaolin chert

G9, $1000-$2000
IL. "Old Red Top"
Unique.

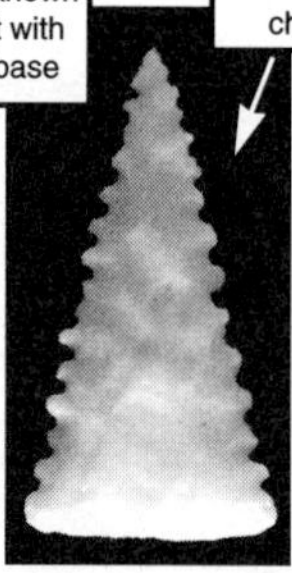

G10, $600-$1000
IL., Cahokia site.
unnotched form.

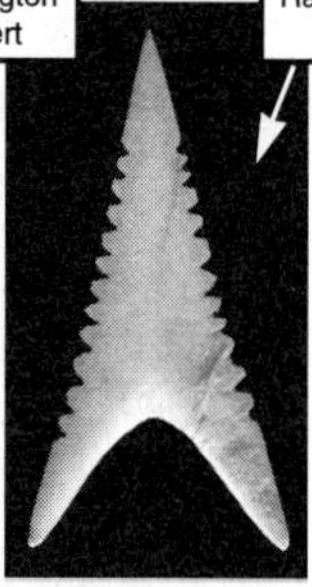

G10, $800-$1500
IL., Cahokia site.
Shartks tooth effigy.

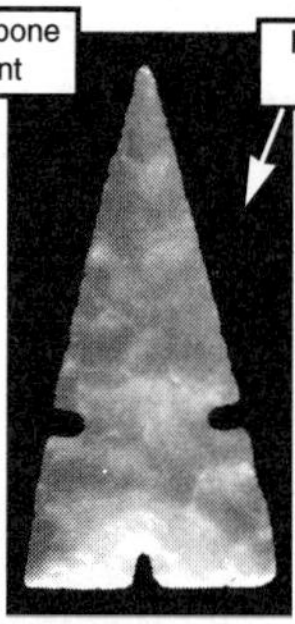

G10, $400-$800
IL., Cahokia site.
Tri-notched.

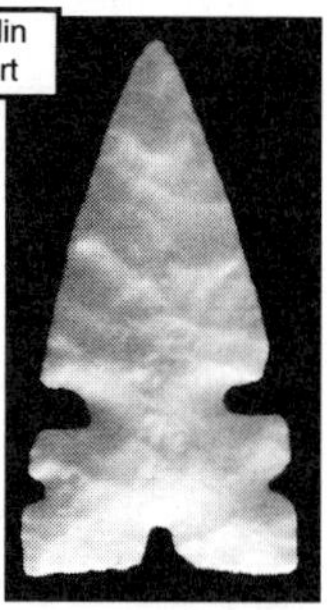

G10, $600-$1000
IL., Cahokia site.
Double notched.

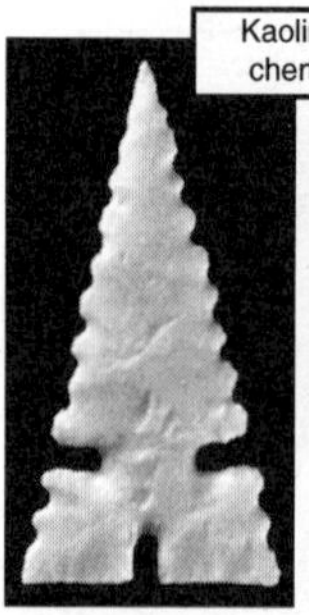

Kaolin chert

Burlington chert

G10, $600-$1200
IL., Cahokia site.

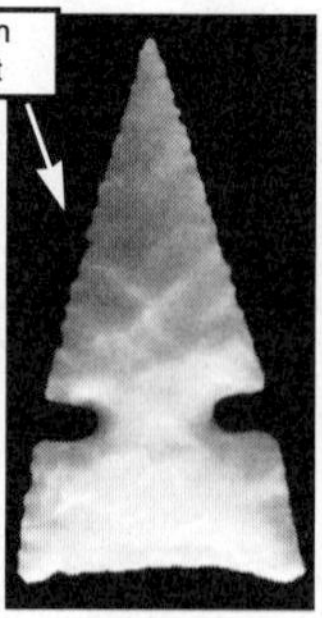

G9, $350-$650
IL., Cahokia site.

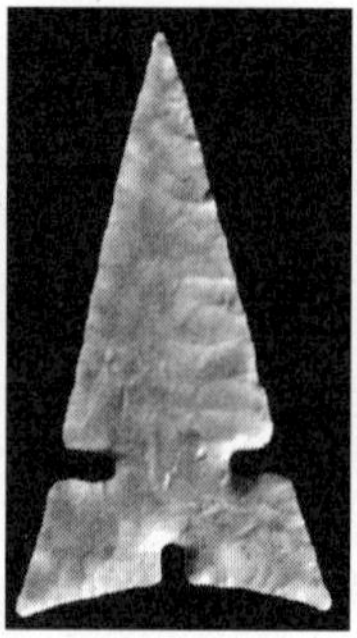

G10, $450-$850
IL., Cahokia site.

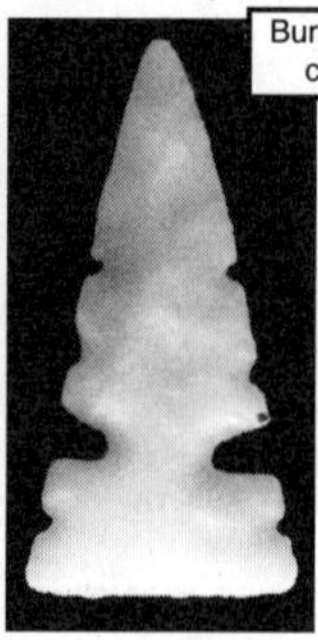

G10, $600-$1000
IL., Cahokia site.

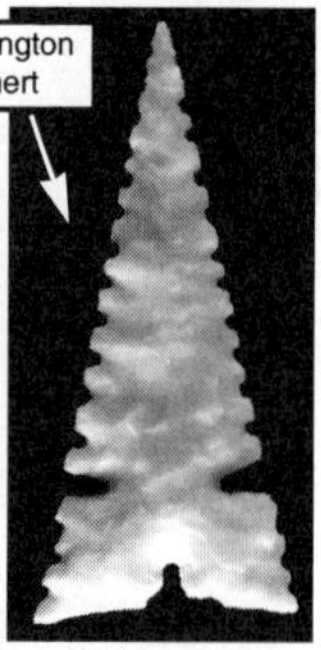

G10, $900-$1800
IL., Cahokia site.

CAHOKIA (continued)

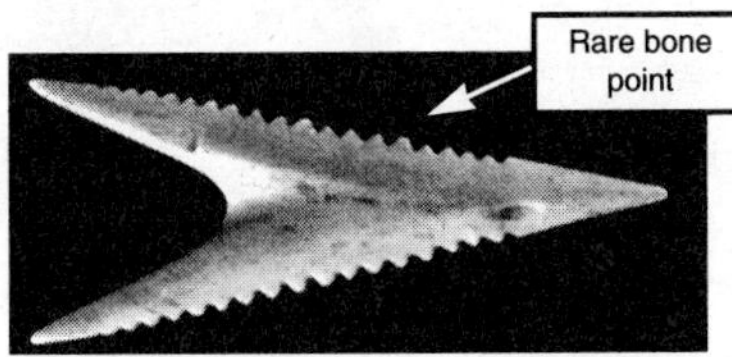

G10, $1000-$1800, IL., Cahokia site.
Caste of very rare bone point. Real point is priced.

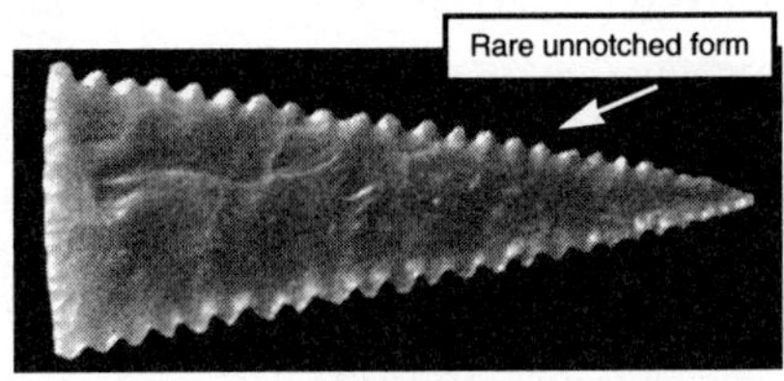

G10, $800-$1500
St. Clair Co., IL. Cahokia site.

LOCATION: Midwestern states. The famous Cahokia mounds are located in Illinois close to the Mississippi river in St. Clair Co. **DESCRIPTION:** A small to medium size, thin, triangular point that can have one or more notches on each blade edge. A rare unnotched serrated form also occurs on the Cahokia site. The base is either plain, has a center notch or is deeply concave. Rarely, they are made of bone. Associated with the Caddo culture.

CALF CREEK - Early to Middle Archaic, 8000 - 5000 B. P.

(Also see Andice and Bell in Southern Central Section)

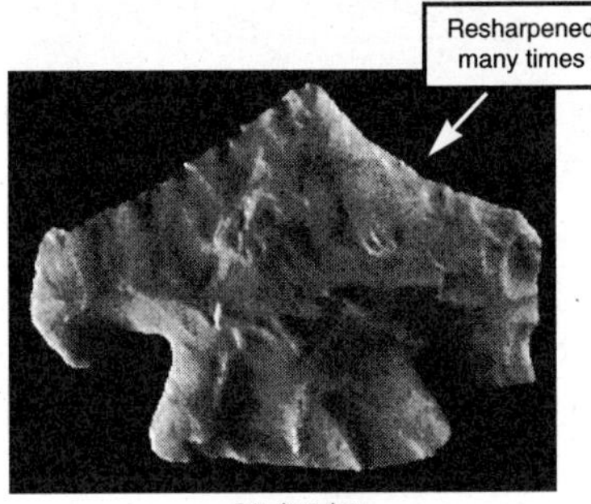

G3, $50-$75
MO. Broken tang.
Heavily resharpened.

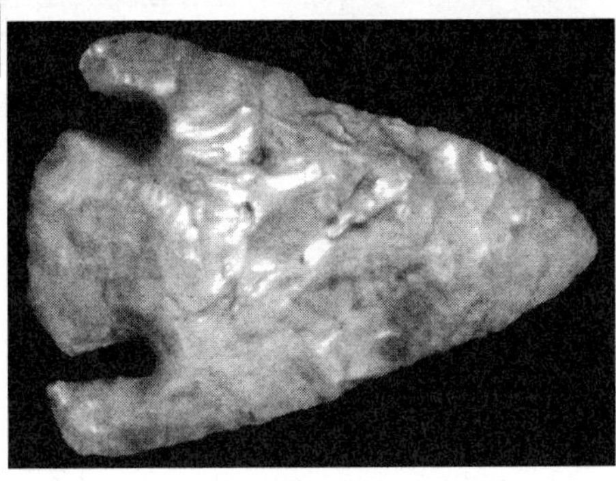

G6, $125-$250
Manhattan, KS.

NC

LOCATION: Texas into Oklahoma, Arkansas, Kansas and Missouri. The type site is in Searcy Co., Arkansas. **DESCRIPTION:** A medium to large size thin, borad, triangular point with very deep parallel basal notches. Related to the *Andice* and *Bell* points found in Texas. Tangs on first-stage examples extended to the base. Very rare in type area. **I.D. KEY:** Notches almost straight up.

G3, $40-$80
MO. Broken tang.

CARTER - (Hopewell) - Woodland, 2500 - 1500 B. P.

(Also see Grand and Snyders)

LOCATION: Illinois. **DESCRIPTION:** A medium to large size, narrow, wide corner to side notched point. Related to the Snyders point.

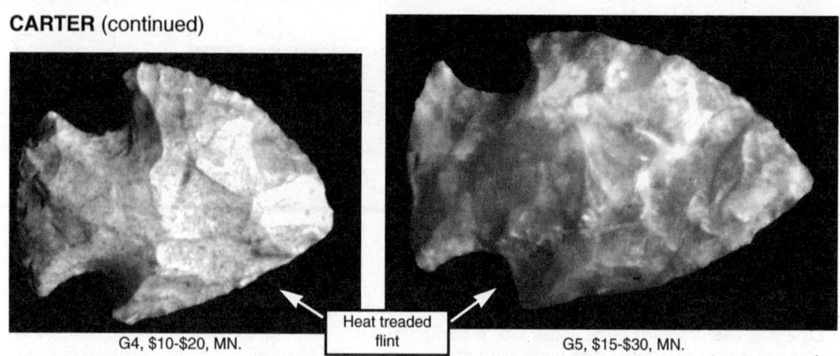

G4, $10-$20, MN.

G5, $15-$30, MN.

CLOVIS - Early Paleo, 14,000 - 10,000 B. P.

(Also see Allen, Angostura, Browns Valley, Cumberland, Dalton, Folsom and Plainview)

Heavily resharpened

G3, $50-$75 IL.

G6, $225-$450 Schuyler Co., IL.

G6, $90-$175 Knox Co., IL.

G4, $100-$200 IL.

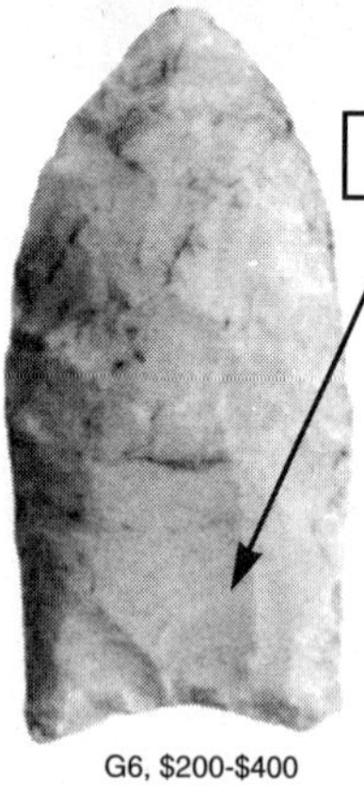

Flute channel

G5, $175-$350 IL.

G6, $200-$400 IL.

G8, $400-$800 IL.

LOCATION: All of North America. **DESCRIPTION:** A medium to large size, auriculate, fluted, lanceolate point with convex sides and a concave base that is ground. Most examples are fluted on both sides about 1/3 the way up from the base. The flaking can be random to parallel. *Clovis* is the earliest point type in the hemisphere. It is believed that this form was developed here after early man crossed the Bering Straits to reach this continent about 50,000 years ago. Current theories place the origin of *Clovis* in the Southeastern U.S. since more examples are found in Florida, Alabama and Tennessee than anywhere else. **I.D. Key:** Paleo flaking, shoulders, batan fluting instead of indirect style.

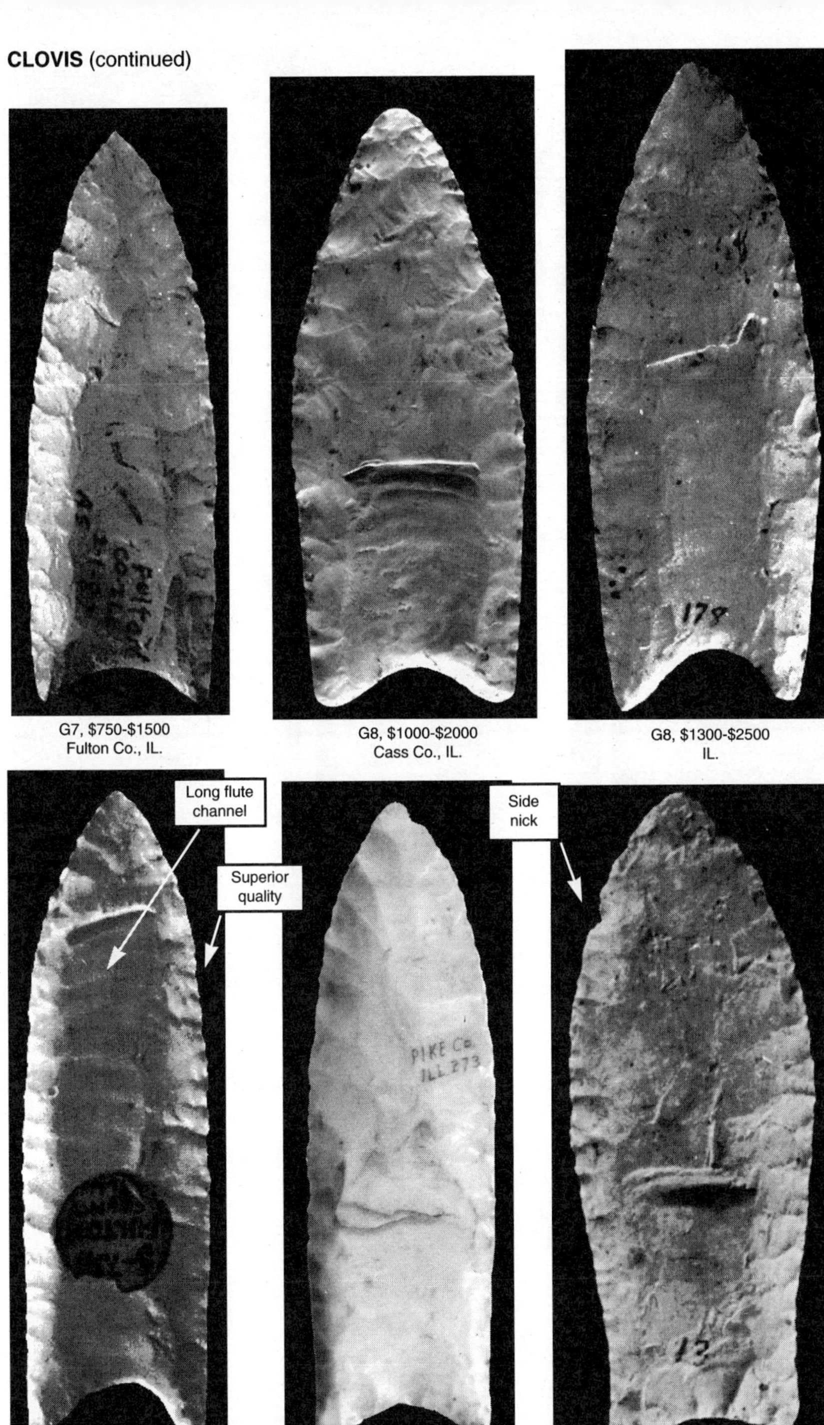

G7, $750-$1500
Fulton Co., IL.

G8, $1000-$2000
Cass Co., IL.

G8, $1300-$2500
IL.

G9, $1500-$3000
Fulton Co., IL.

G8, $700-$1400
Pike Co., IL.

G8, $850-$1700
IL.

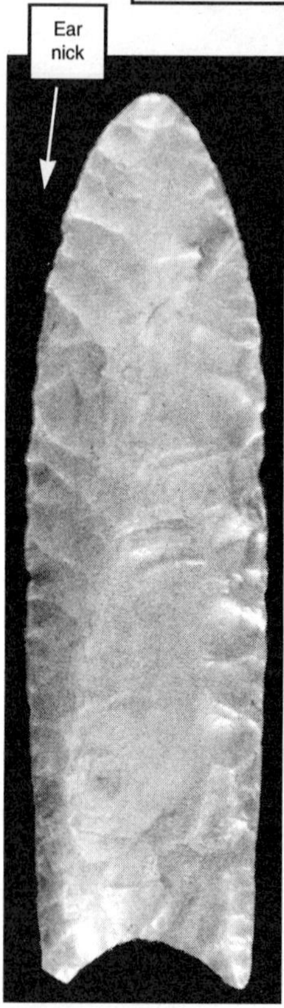

Quartzite Clovis points are uncommon and highly prized by collectors

Ear nick

Quartzite

G8, $1500-$3000
IL.

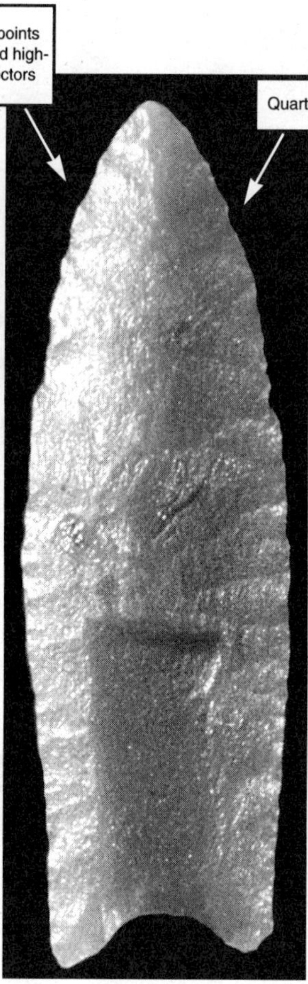

G8, $2500-$4500
Fulton Co., IL.

G9, $3500-$7000
Adams Co., IL.

CLOVIS-ST. LOUIS - Early Paleo, 14,000 - 10,000 B. P.

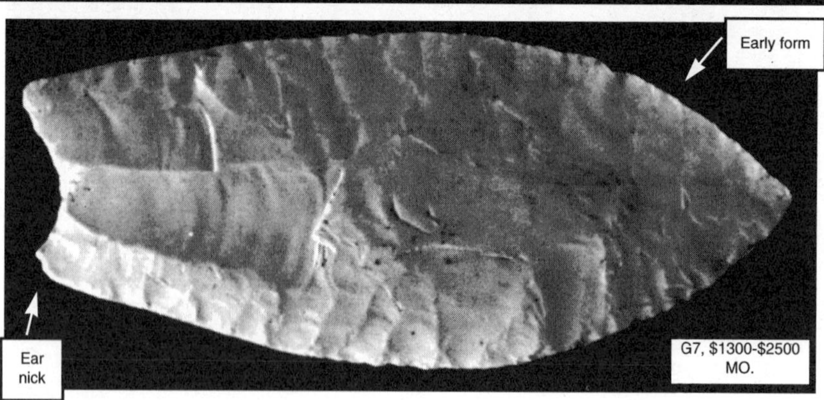

G7, $1300-$2500
MO.

CLOVIS-ST. LOUIS (continued)

LOCATION: The Dakotas, Wisconsin southward to Arkansas and eastward to Michigan. **DESCRIPTION:** A large size, broad, auriculate, fluted, lanceolate point with convex sides and a concave base that is ground. Most examples are fluted on both sides 1/3 or more up from the base. The flaking can be random to parallel. One of the largest *Clovis* forms. **I.D. Key:** Size and broadness.

COBBS TRIANGULAR - Early Archaic, 8000 - 5000 B. P.

(Also see Decatur, Dovetail, Lerma and Lost Lake)

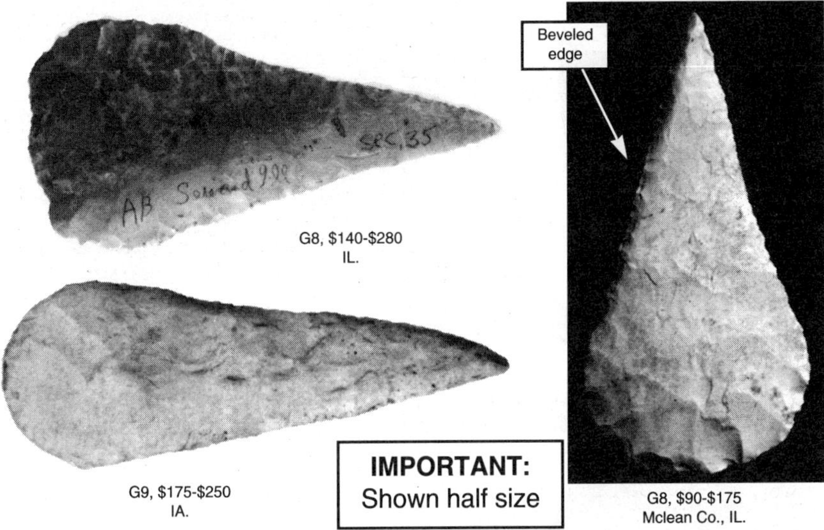

G8, $140-$280
IL.

G9, $175-$250
IA.

G8, $90-$175
Mclean Co., IL.

LOCATION: Southeastern states. **DESCRIPTION:** A medium to large size, thin, lanceolate blade with a broad, rounded to square base. One side of each face is usually steeply beveled. These are un-notched preforms for early Archaic beveled types such as *Decatur, Dovetail, Lost Lake,* etc.

NC

COPENA-CLASSIC - Late Archaic to Woodland, 4000 - 1200 B. P.

LOCATION: DESCRIPTION: A medium to large size, lanceolate point with recurved blade edges and a straight to slightly convex base. This point usually occurs in Woodland burial mounds.

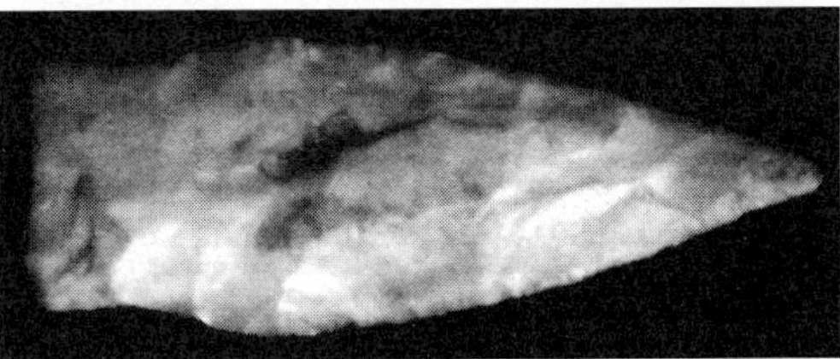

G6, $25-$50
Miller Co., MO.

COSSATOT RIVER - Early Archaic, 9500 - 8000 B. P.

(Also see Fox Valley and Lake Erie)

LOCATION: Missouri into Oklahoma. **DESCRIPTION:** A medium to large size, thin, usually serrated, widely corner notched point with large round to square ears and a deep notch in the center of the base. Bases are usually ground. **I.D. KEY:** Basal notching, early Archaic flaking.

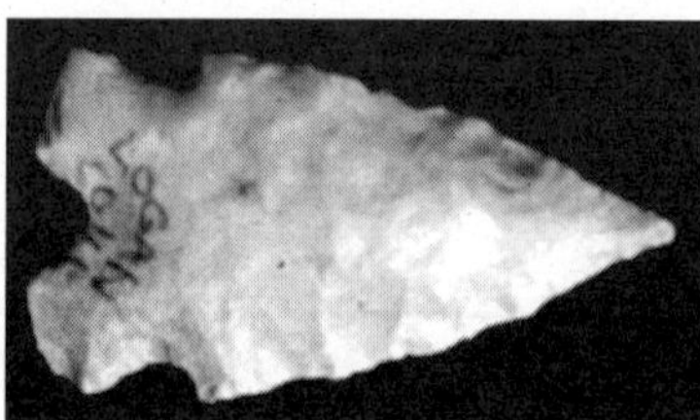

G7, $25-$50
Logan Co., IL.

G7, $40-$75
Logan Co., IL.

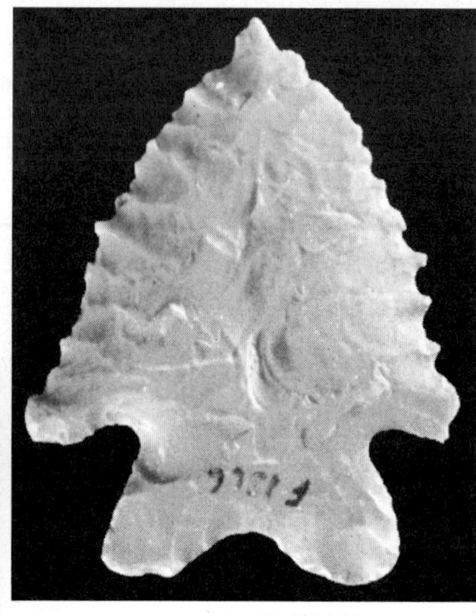

G7, $80-$150
Adams Co., IL.

CUMBERLAND - Paleo, 12,000 - 8000 B. P.

(Also see Beaver Lake, Clovis, Dalton and Quad)

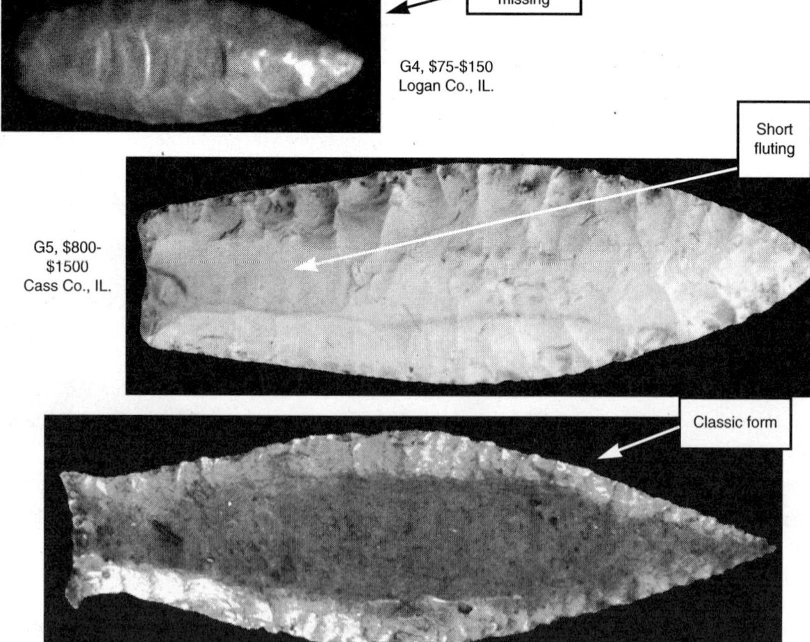

G4, $75-$150
Logan Co., IL.

G5, $800-$1500
Cass Co., IL.

G7, $1500-$3000, Cent. IL.

CUMBERLAND (continued)

LOCATION: Southeastern states into Illinois. Called *Barnes Cumberland* in the Northeast. **DESCRIPTION:** A medium to large size, lanceolate, eared form that is usually fluted on both faces. The fluting and flaking technique is an advanced form as in *Folsom*, with the flutes usually extending the entire length of the blade. Bases are ground on all examples. An unfluted variant which is thicker than *Beaver Lake* has been found. This point is scarce everywhere and has been reproduced in large numbers. **I.D. Key:** Paleo flaking, indirect pressure fluted.

CUMBERLAND UNFLUTED - Paleo, 12,000 - 8000 B. P.

(Also see Beaver Lake, Clovis and Quad)

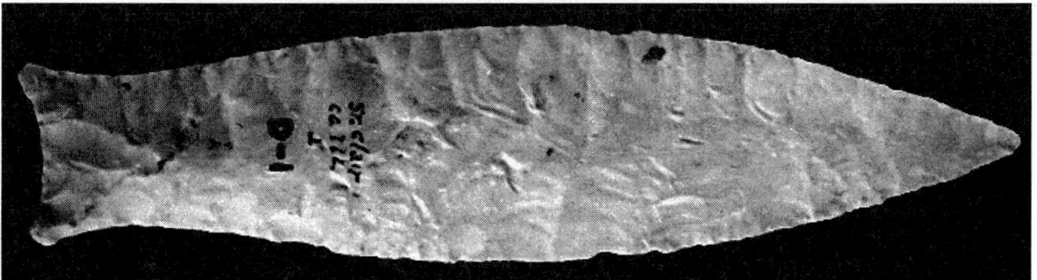

LOCATION: DESCRIPTION: Identical to fluted *Cumberland*, but without the fluting. **Very rare** in the type area. Cross section is thicker than *Beaver Lake*.

G10, $3000-$5000
St. Clair Co., IL.

CUPP - Late Woodland to Mississippian, 1500 - 600 B. P.

(Also see Helton, Kay Blade, Lundy, Snyders, Steuben, Table Rock)

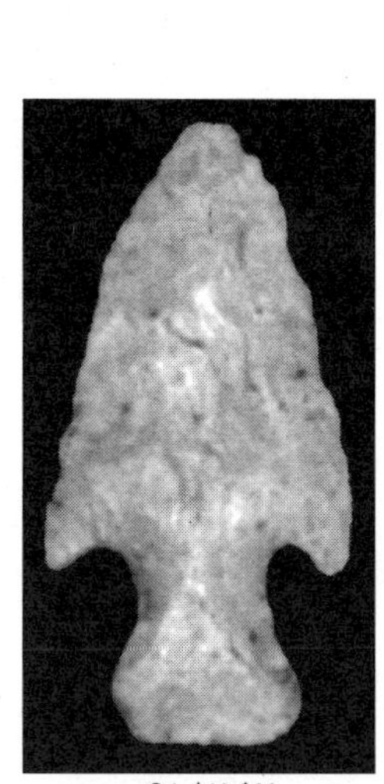

G4, $10-$20
Manhattan, KS.

G6, $15-$30
Riley Co., KS.

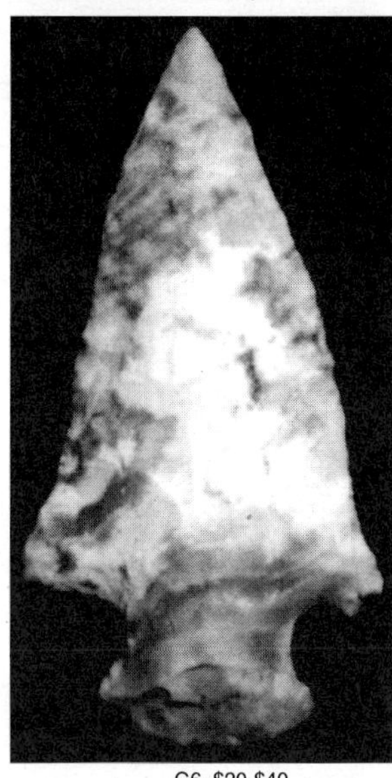

G6, $20-$40
Camden Co., MO.

NC

LOCATION: Eastern states**. DESCRIPTION:** A medium to large size, narrow point with wide corner notches, shoulder barbs and a convex base. Similar to *Motley,* but the base stem is shorter and broader. *Epps* has square to tapered shoulders, otherwise is identical to *Motley.*

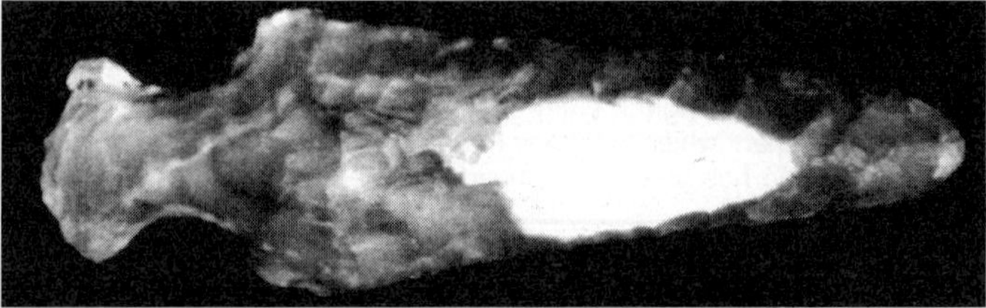

G5, $25-$50
Miller Co., MO.

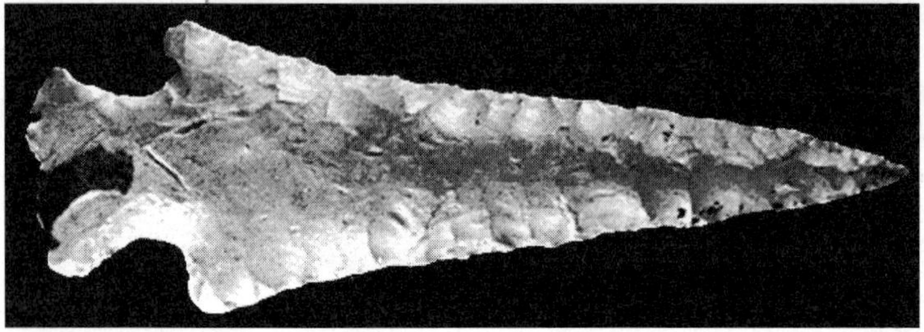

G6, $40-$80
Polk Co., MO.

DALTON-BRECKENRIDGE - Early Archaic, 9500 - 5000 B. P.

(Also see Dalton and Meserve)

LOCATION: Midwestern states, **DESCRIPTION:** A medium to large size, auriculate point with an obvious bevel extending the entire length of the point from tip to base. Similar in form to the *Dalton-Greenbrier*. Basal area is usually ground.

G4, $20-$35
Breckenridge, MO.

DALTON CLASSIC - Early Archaic, 9500 - 8000 B. P.

(Also see Beaver Lake, Greenbrier, Pelican, Plainview and Quad)

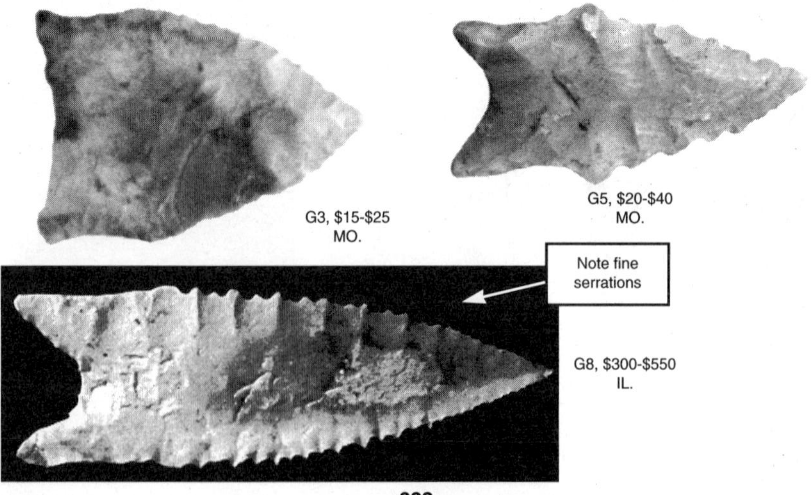

G3, $15-$25
MO.

G5, $20-$40
MO.

G8, $300-$550
IL.

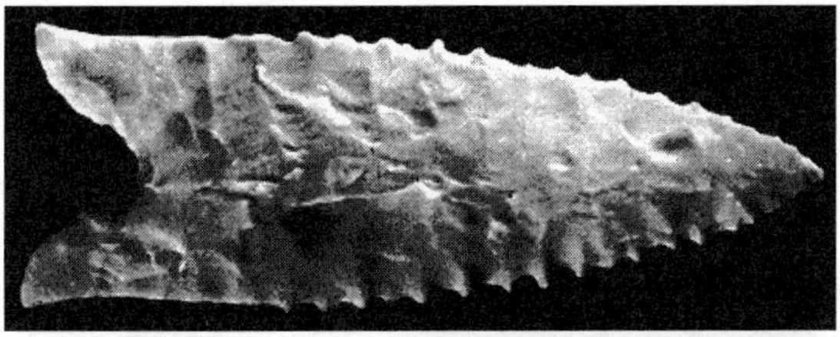

G7, $275-$550
MO.

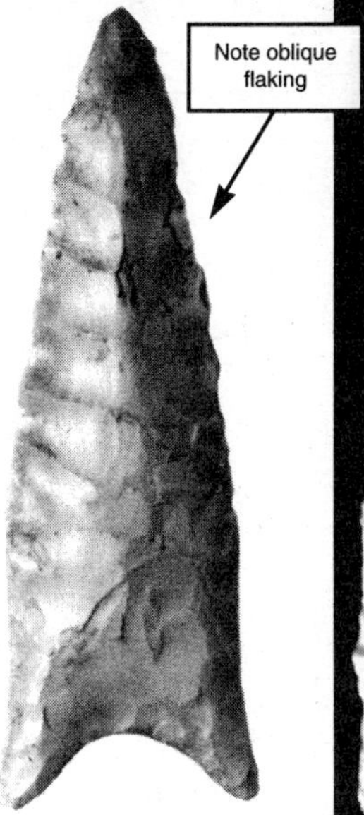

Note oblique flaking

G7, $125-$250
MO.

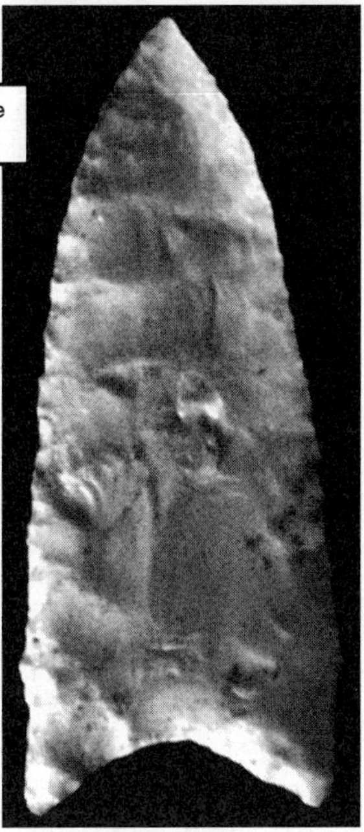

G7, $150-$300
Pike Co., IL.

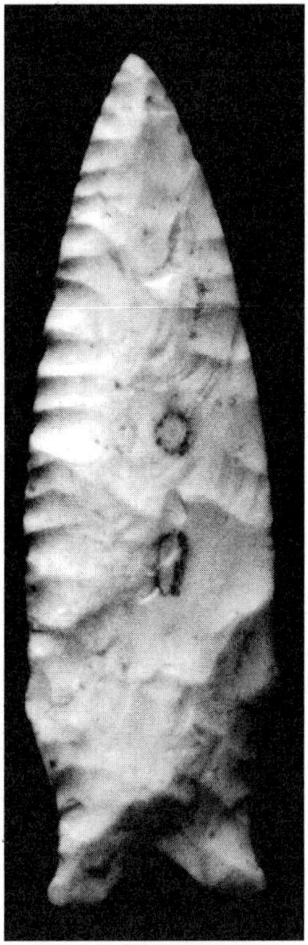

G6, $250-$500
S.W. MO.

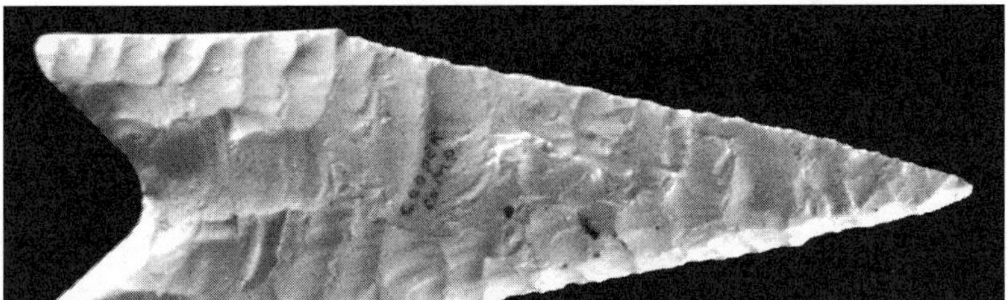

NC

G9, $400-$800
Cooper Co., MO.

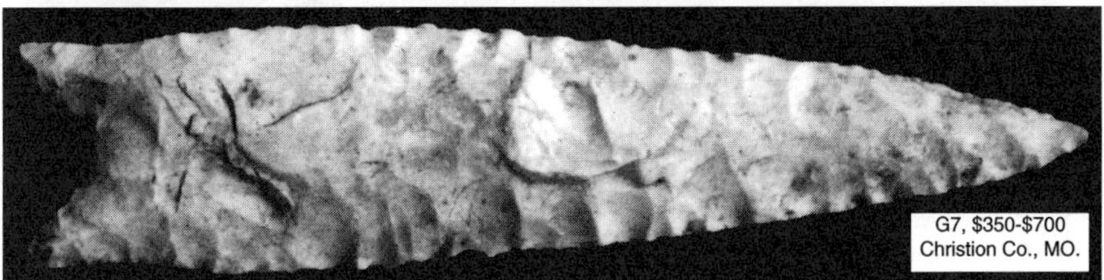

G7, $350-$700
Christion Co., MO.

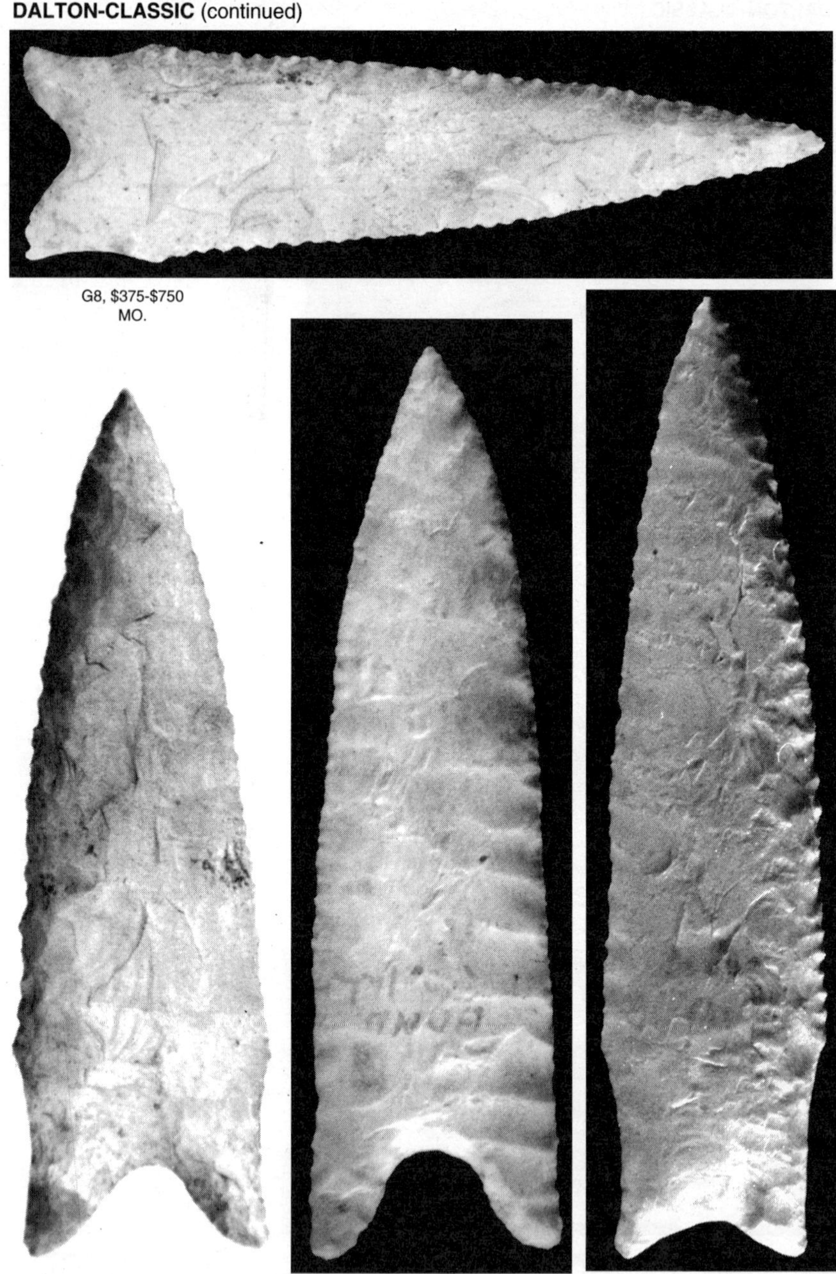

G8, $375-$750
MO.

G8, $450-900
MO.

G9, $900-$1800
Bond Co., IL.

G9, $800-$1600
MO.

LOCATION: Midwestern to Southeastern states. **DESCRIPTION:** A medium to large size, thin, auriculate, fishtailed point. Many examples are finely serrated and exhibit excellent flaking. Beveling may occur on one side of each face but is usually on the right side. All have basal grinding. This early type spread over most of the Eastern and Midwestern U.S. and strongly influenced many other types to follow.

DALTON-HEMPHILL - Late Paleo to Middle Archaic, 9500 - 6000 B. P.

(Also see Holland and Scottsbluff)

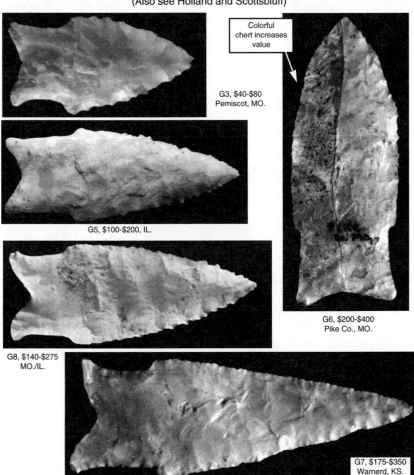

Colorful chert increases value

G3, $40-$80
Pemiscot, MO.

G5, $100-$200, IL.

G6, $200-$400
Pike Co., MO.

G8, $140-$275
MO./IL.

G7, $175-$350
Warnerd, KS.

LOCATION: Midwestern to Eastern states. **DESCRIPTION:** A medium to large size point with expanded aurciles and horizontal, tapered to weak shoulders. Blade edges are usually serrated and bases are ground. In later times, this variant developed into the *Hemphill* point. **I.D. KEY:** Straightened extended shoulders.

DALTON-NUCKOLLS - Late Paleo, 9500 - 5000 B. P.

(Also see Dalton and Holland)

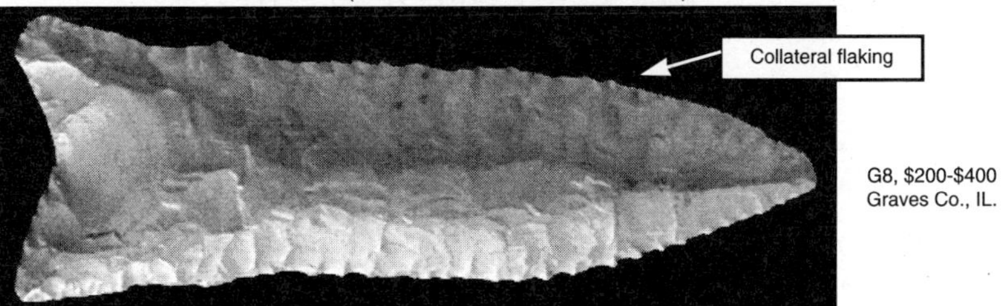

Collateral flaking

G8, $200-$400
Graves Co., IL.

DALTON NUCKOLLS (continued)

LOCATION: Midwestern to Southeastern states. **DESCRIPTION:** A medium to large size variant form, probably occuring from resharpening the *Greenbrier Dalton.* Bases are squared to lobbed to eared, and have a shallow concavity. **I.D. KEY:** Broad base and shoulders, flaking on blade.

DALTON-SLOAN - Late Paleo to Middle Archaic, 9500 - 8000 B. P.

(Also see Allen, Angostura, Dalton, Greenbrier and Plainview)

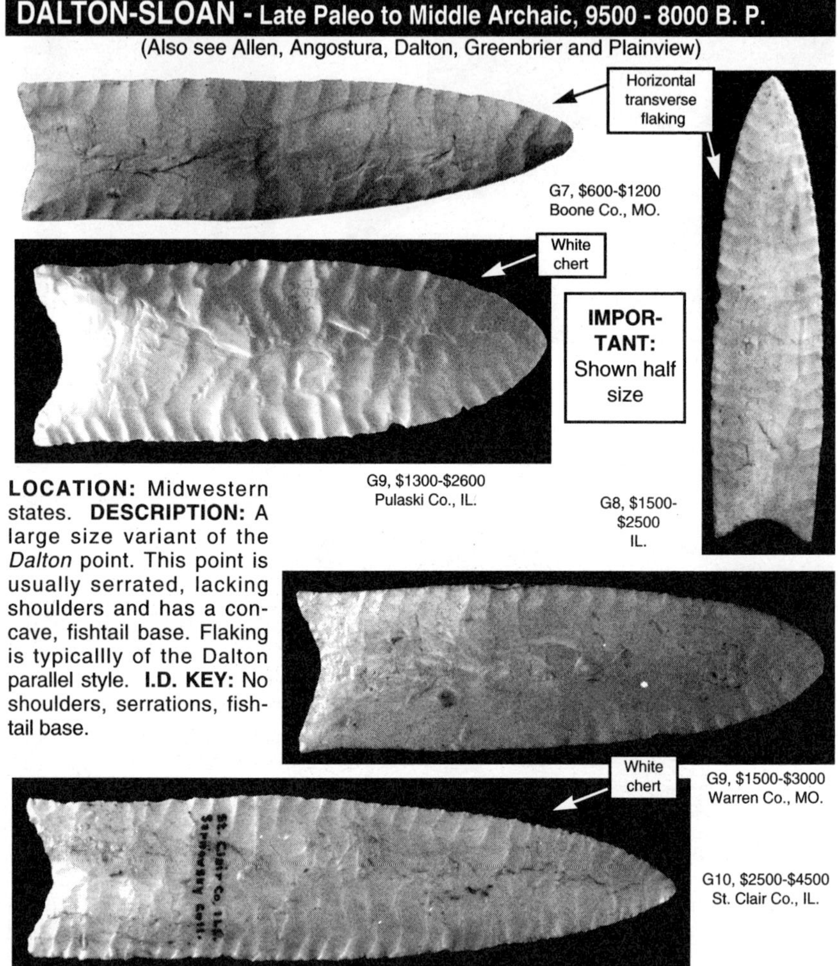

G7, $600-$1200 Boone Co., MO.

G9, $1300-$2600 Pulaski Co., IL.

G8, $1500-$2500 IL.

G9, $1500-$3000 Warren Co., MO.

G10, $2500-$4500 St. Clair Co., IL.

LOCATION: Midwestern states. **DESCRIPTION:** A large size variant of the *Dalton* point. This point is usually serrated, lacking shoulders and has a concave, fishtail base. Flaking is typicallly of the Dalton parallel style. **I.D. KEY:** No shoulders, serrations, fishtail base.

DECATUR - Early Archaic, 9000 - 3000 B. P.

(Also see Cobbs Triangular, Dovetail, Hardin, Kirk and Lost Lake)

LOCATION: Eastern to Midwestern states. **DESCRIPTION:** A small to medium size, serrated, corner notched point that is usually beveled on one side of each face. The base is usually broken off (fractured) by a blow inward from each corner of the stem. Sometimes the sides of the stem and backs of the tang s are also fractured, and in rare cases, the tip may be fractured by a blow on each side directed towards the base. Bases are usually ground and flaking is of high quality. Basal fracturing also occurs in Dovetail, Kirk, Motley and Snyders.

DECATUR (continued)

G4, $15-$30
Fulton Co., IL.

G5, $90-$175
LoganCo., IL.

DOVETAIL - Early Archaic, 9500 - 8000 B. P.

(Also see Cobbs Triangular, Decatur, Gibson, Lost Lake, St. Charles, Thebes and Warrick)

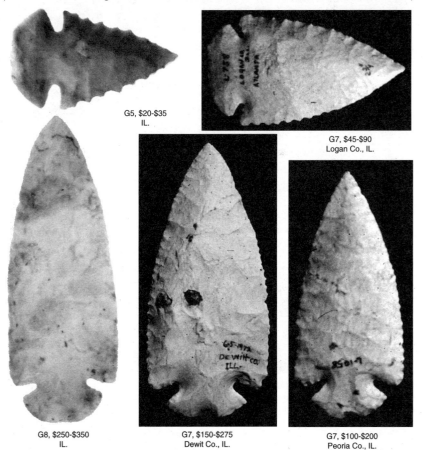

G5, $20-$35
IL.

G7, $45-$90
Logan Co., IL.

NC

G8, $250-$350
IL.

G7, $150-$275
Dewit Co., IL.

G7, $100-$200
Peoria Co., IL.

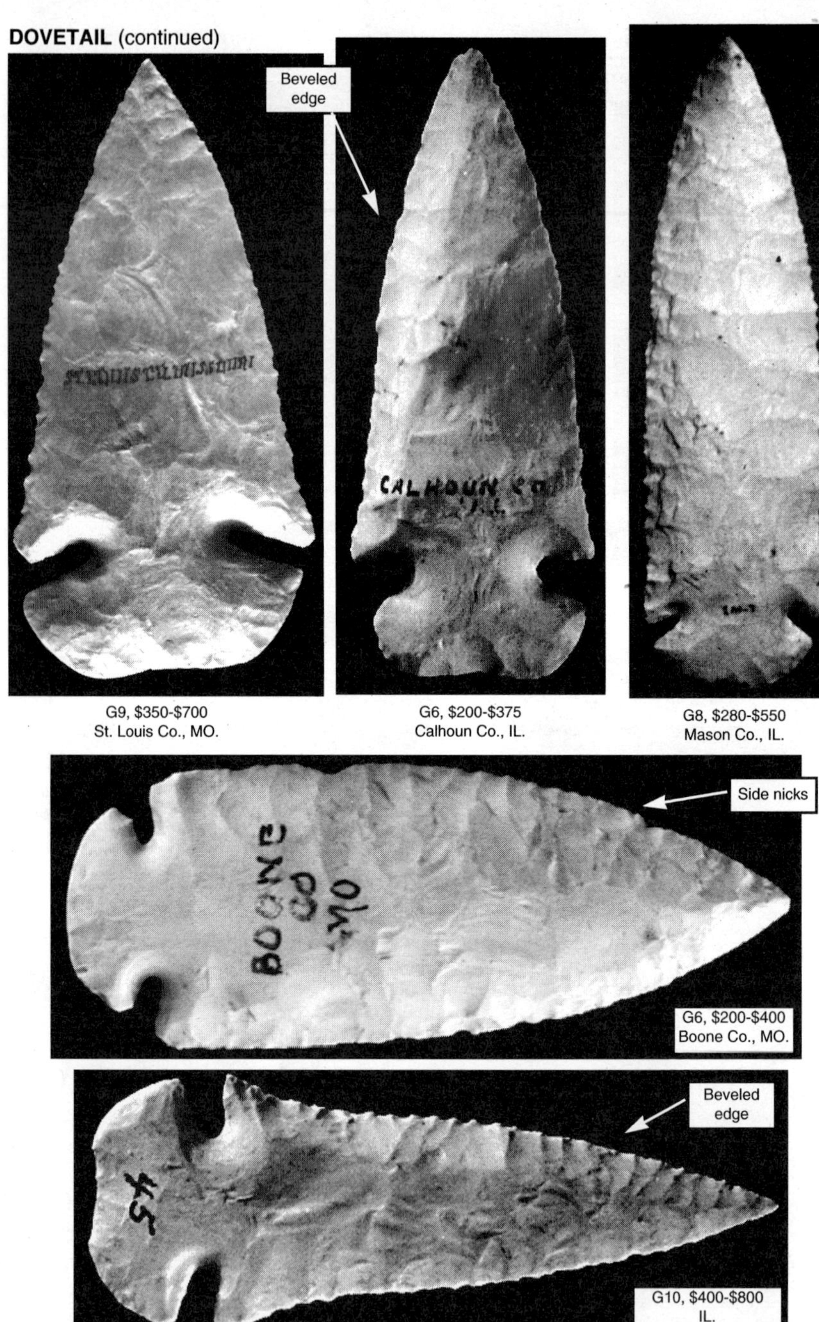

G9, $350-$700
St. Louis Co., MO.

G6, $200-$375
Calhoun Co., IL.

G8, $280-$550
Mason Co., IL.

G6, $200-$400
Boone Co., MO.

G10, $400-$800
IL.

LOCATION: Midwest into the Southeast. **DESCRIPTION:** Also known as *St. Charles.* A medium to large size, corner notched, dovetailed base point. The blade is beveled on one side of each face (usually the left side) on resharpened examples. Bases are always convex. Straight bases would place a point into the *Lost Lake* type. Bases are ground and can be fractured on both sides or center notched on some examples. **I.D. KEY:** Dovetailed base.

DOVETAIL (continued)

G10, \$800-\$1500
Madison Co., IL.

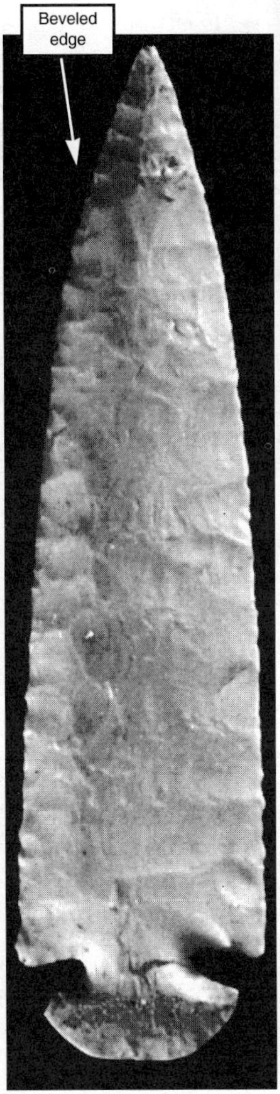

Beveled edge

Beveled edge

NC

G8, \$600-\$1200
IL.

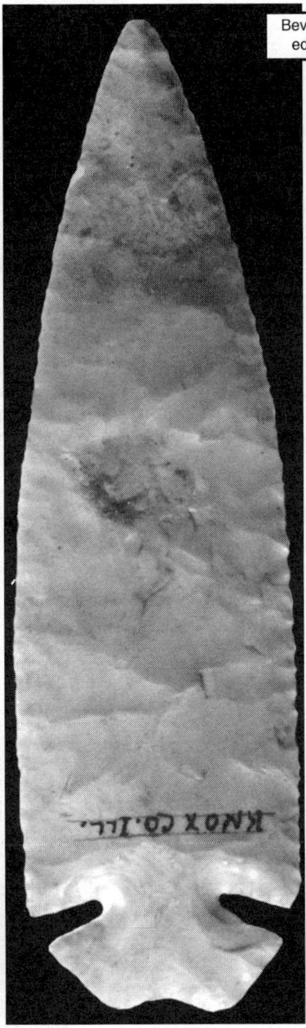

G9, \$1000-\$2000
Knox Co., IL.

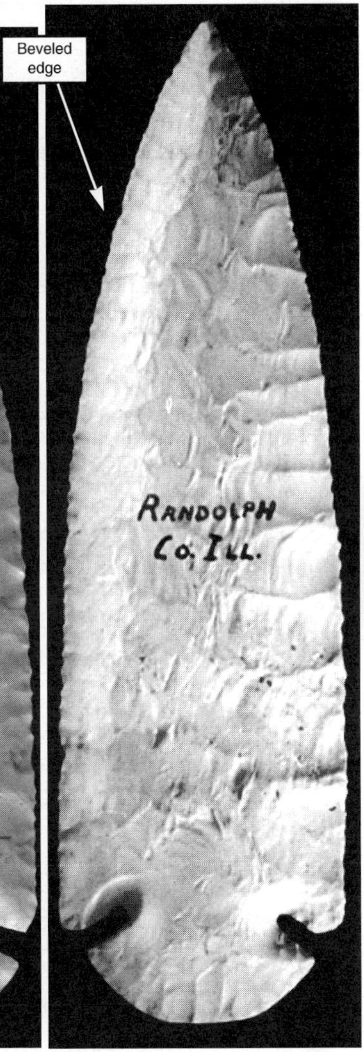

G9, \$1500-\$2500
Randollph Co., IL.

DRILL - Paleo to Historic, 14,000 - 200 B. P.

(Also see Scraper)

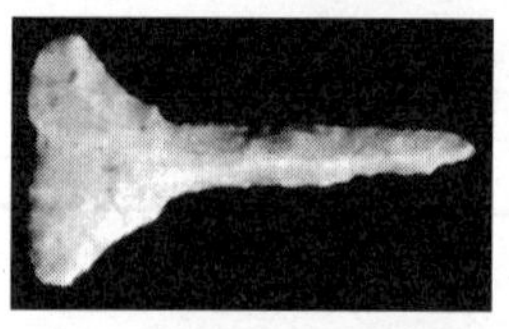

G5, $8-$15
Logan Co., IL.

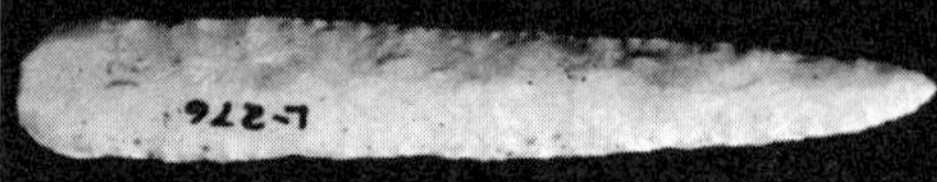

G8, $20-$35
Logan Co., IL.

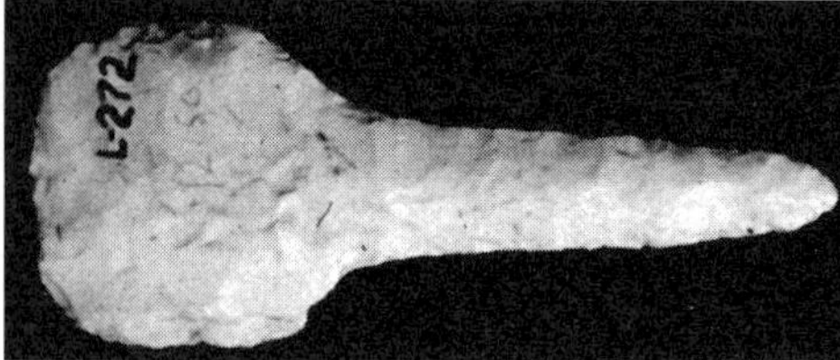

G7, $25-$50
Logan Co., IL.

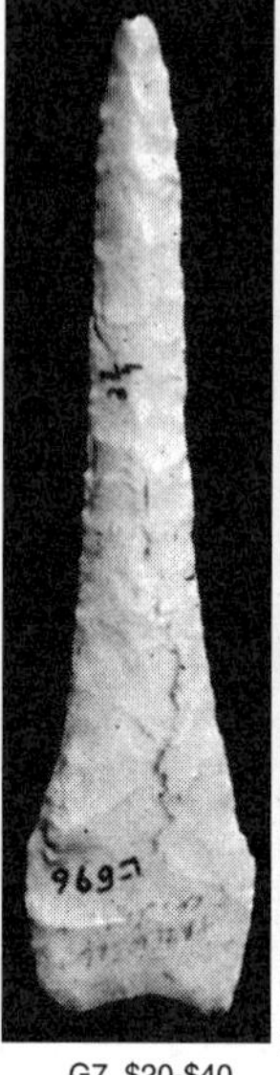

G7, $20-$40
Tazewell Co., IL.

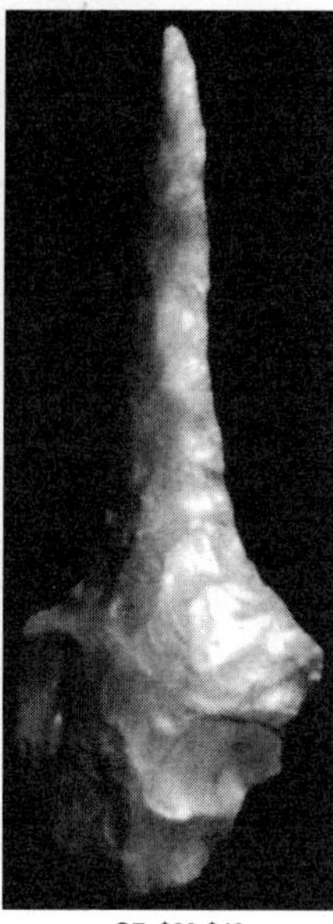

G7, $20-$40
Miller Co., MO.

LOCATION: Everywhere. **DESCRIPTION:** Although many drills were made from scratch, all point types were made into the drill form. Usually, heavily resharpened and broken points were salvaged and rechipped into drills. These objects were certainly used as drills (evidence of extreme edge wear), but there is speculation that some of these forms may have been used as pins for clothing, ornaments, ear plugs and other uses.

EDEN - Transitional Paleo to Early Archaic, 9500 - 7500 B. P.

(Also see Agate Basin, Angostura, Holland, Scottsbluff and Sedalia)

G6, $150-$300
W. MO.

Eden Eared form
G5, $125-$250
Rock Co., WI.

LOCATION: Midwestern states. **DESCRIPTION:** A medium to large size, narrow, lanceolate blade with a straight to concave base. Many examples have a median ridge and collateral to oblique parallel flaking. Bases are usually ground. **I.D. KEY:** Weak shoulders.

EDEN (continued)

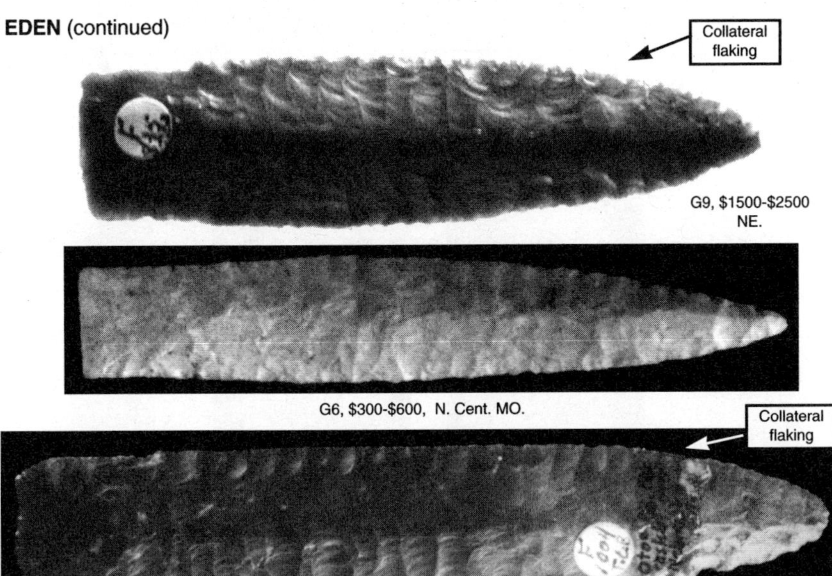

G9, $1500-$2500
NE.

G6, $300-$600, N. Cent. MO.

G9, $1500-$3000
Otoe Co., NE.

ETLEY - Late Archaic, 4000 - 2500 B. P.

(Also see Hardin, Mehlville, Smith, Stilwell, Stone Square Stem and Wadlow)

IMPORTANT:
All Etleys shown half size

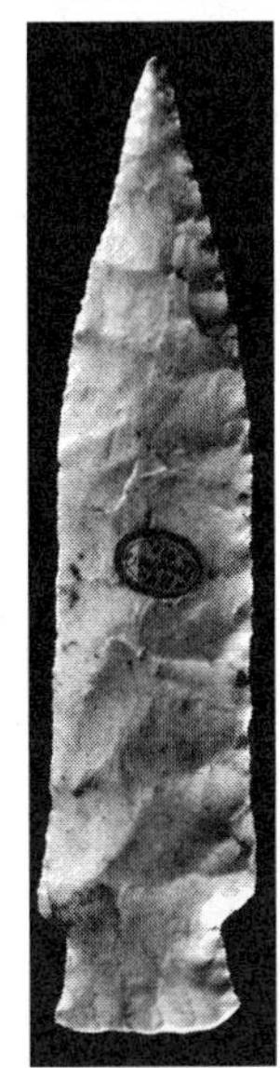

G9, $250-$500
Lincoln Co., MO.

G8, $250-$450
MO.

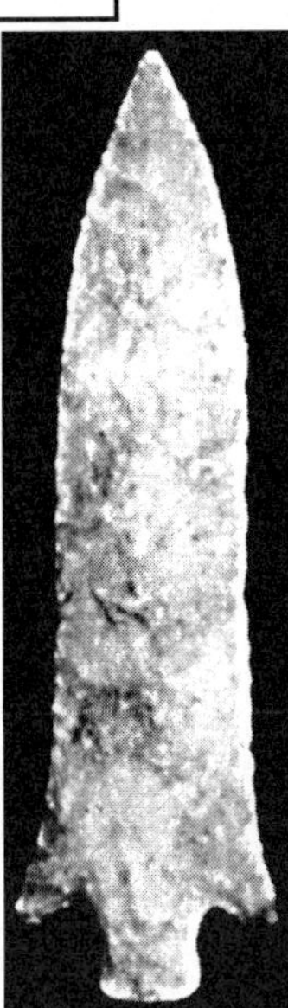

G9, $250-$500
IL.

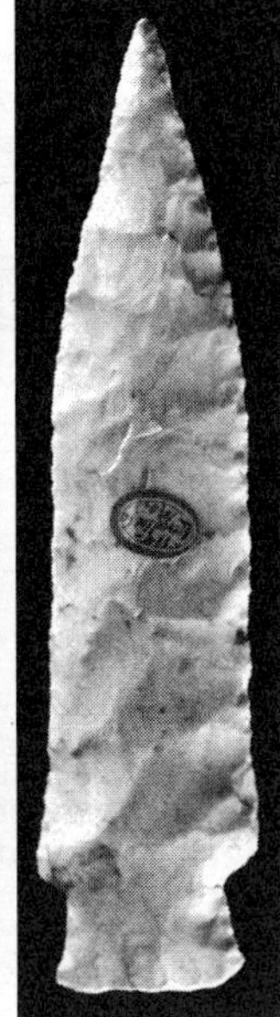

G8, $250-$400
Lincoln Co., MO.

G8, $200-$400
MO.

IMPORTANT:
Shown half size

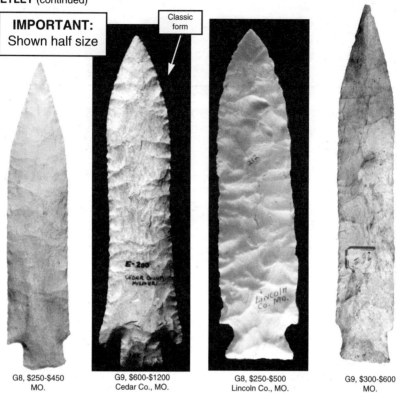

Classic form

G8, $250-$450
MO.

G9, $600-$1200
Cedar Co., MO.

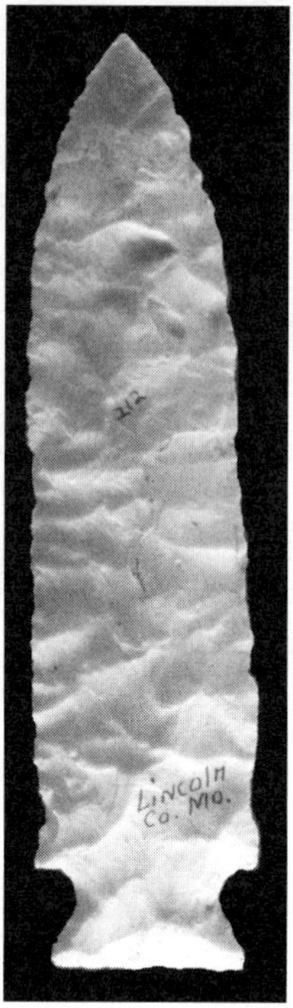

G8, $250-$500
Lincoln Co., MO.

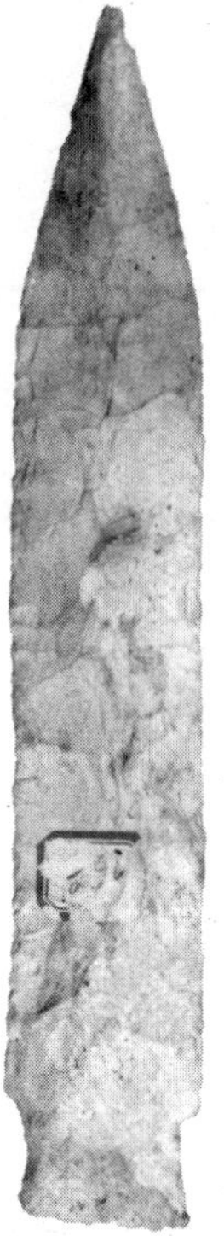

G9, $300-$600
MO.

LOCATION: Midwestern states.The Etley site is in Calhoun Co., IL. Many *Wadlow* points were found there which is the preform for this type. **DESCRIPTION:** A large, narrow, blade with an angular point, recurved blade edges, a short, expanded stem and a straight to slightly convex base. Shoulders usually expand but have a tendency to point inward towards the base. **I.D. KEY:** Large size, barbs, narrow blade.

EVANS - Late Archaic to Woodland, 4000 - 2000 B. P.

(Also see Hickory Ridge and Turkeytail)

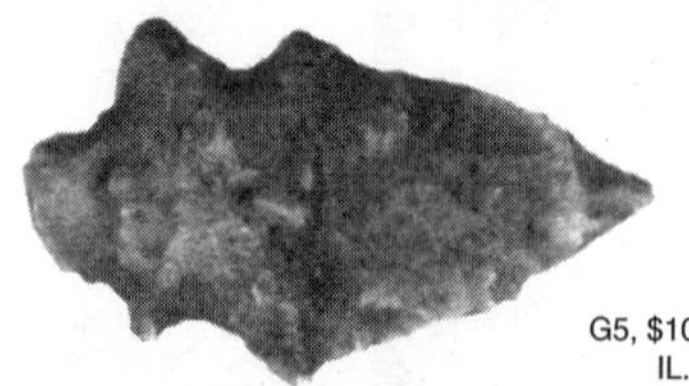

G5, $10-$20
IL.

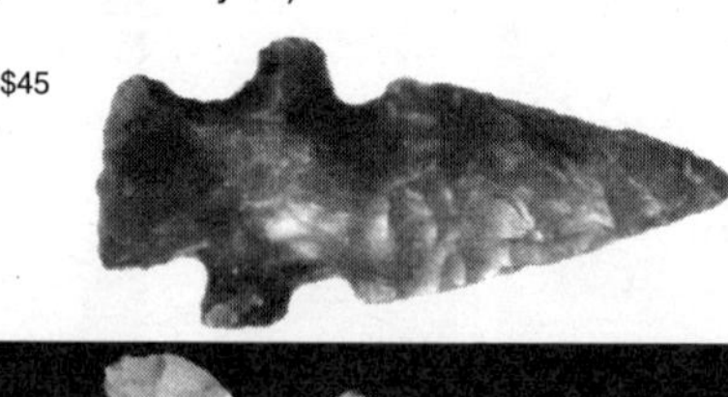

G6, $25-$45
MO.

LOCATION: Midwestern to Southeastern states. **DESCRIPTION:** A medium to large size stemmed point that is notched on each side somewhere between the point and shoulders. A similar form is found in Ohio and called *Ohio Double-Notched.*

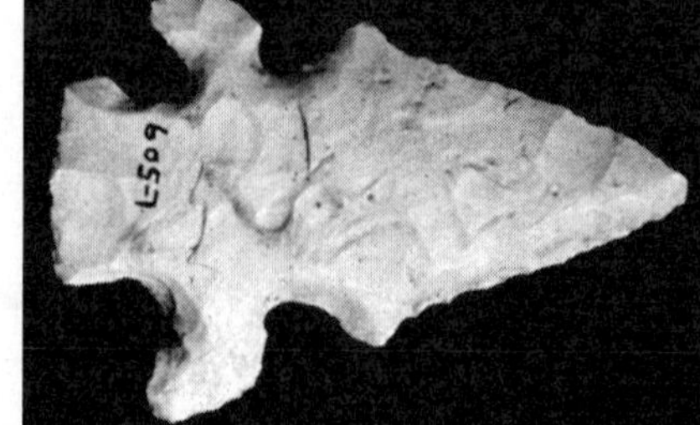

G7, $50-$100
Mason Co., IL.

EXOTIC FORMS - Archaic-Mississippian, 5000 - 1000 B. P.

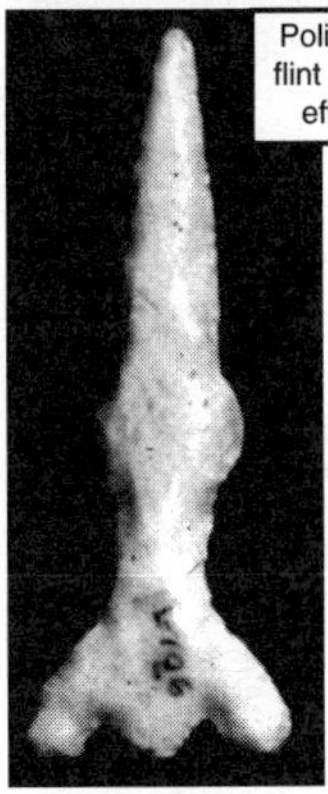

Polished flint lizard effigy

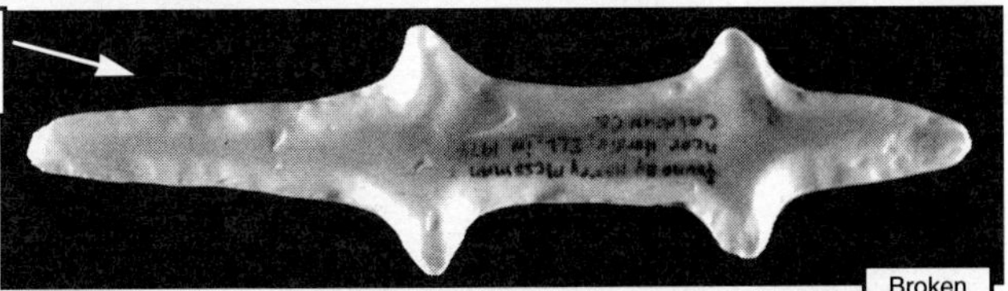

G8, $600-$1300
Calhoun Co., IL.

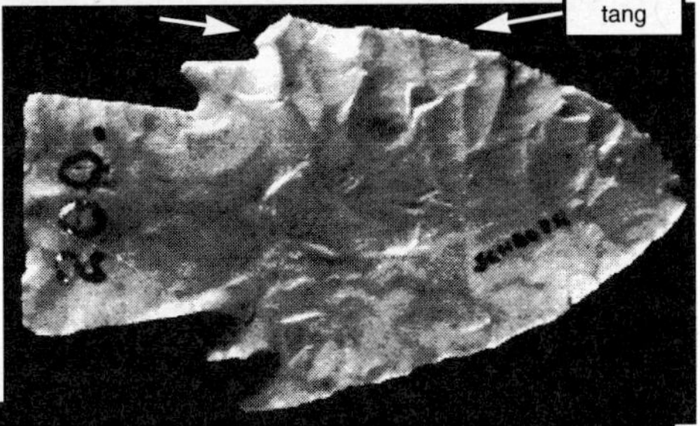

Broken tang

Hardin form

G5, $100-$190
Montgomery Co., MO.

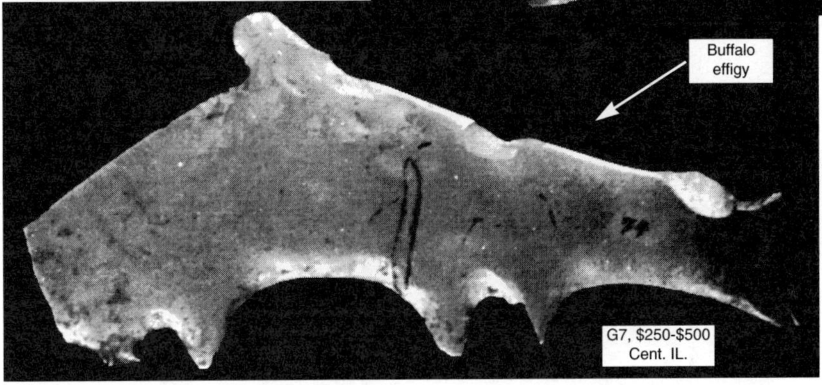

G5, $75-$150
Fulton Co., IL.

Buffalo effigy

G7, $250-$500
Cent. IL.

LOCATION: Everywhere. **DESCRIPTION:** The forms illustrated on this and the following pages are very rare. Some are definitely effigy forms while others may be no more than unfinished and unintentional doodles.

NC

FERRY - Middle to late Archaic, 5500 - 4500 B. P.

(Also see Hardin, Kirk Corner Notched and Stilwell)

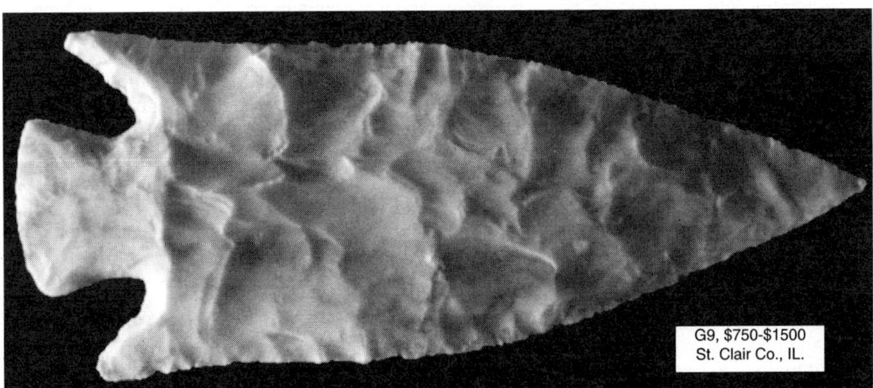

G9, $750-$1500
St. Clair Co., IL.

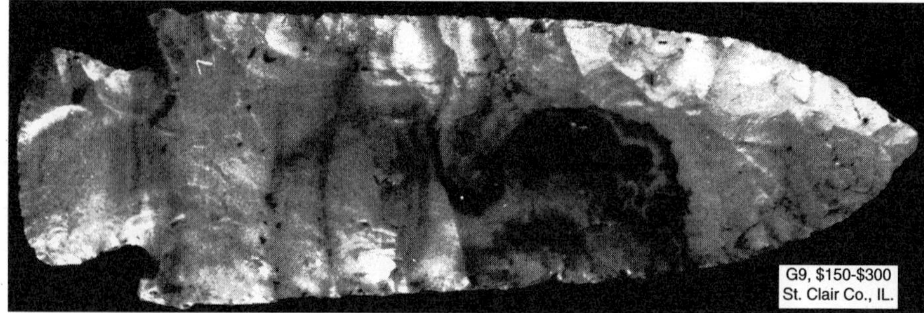

G9, $150-$300
St. Clair Co., IL.

LOCATION: Illinois and Missouri. **DESCRIPTION:** A medium to large size, broad, stemmed point with a bulbous base. The blade is convex to recurved. The shoulders are barbed. **I.D. KEY:** Basal form and barbs.

FOLSOM - Paleo, 11,000 - 9000 B. P.

(Also see Clovis and Cumberland)

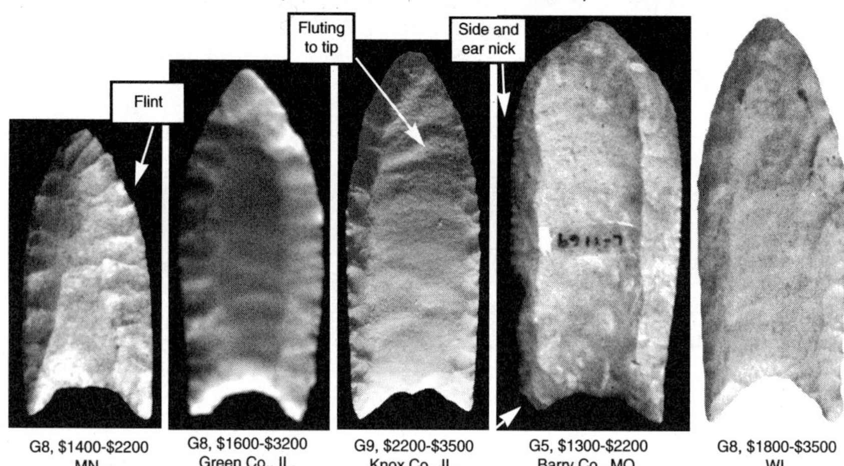

G8, $1400-$2200 MN. | G8, $1600-$3200 Green Co., IL. | G9, $2200-$3500 Knox Co., IL. | G5, $1300-$2200 Barry Co., MO. | G8, $1800-$3500 WI.

LOCATION: N. Indiana Westward to Texas, northward to the Dakotas and West to Montana. **DESCRIPTION:** A small to medium size, thin, high quality, fluted point with contracted to slightly expanding, pointed auricles and a concave base. Fluting usually extends the entire length of each face. Blade flaking is extremely fine. The hafting area is ground. A very rare type, even in area of highest incidence. Modern reproductions have been made and extreme caution should be exercised in acquiring an original specimen. Usually found in association with extinct bison fossil remains. **I.D. KEY:** Thinness and flaking style (Excessive secondary flaking). **NOTE:** A *Folsom* site was recently found on the Tippecanoe River in N. Indiana. *Clovis* and *Beaver Lake* were also found there.

FOX VALLEY - Early to Middle Archaic, 9000 - 4000 B. P.

(Also see Kirk, Lake Erie and Cossatot River)

LOCATION: Midwestern to Eastern states. **DESCRIPTION:** A small size, triangular point with flaring shoulders and a short bifurcated stem. Shoulders are sometimes clipped winged and have a tendency to turn towards the tip. Blades exhibit early parallel flaking and the edges are usually serrated. **I.D. KEY:** Bifurcated base and barbs.

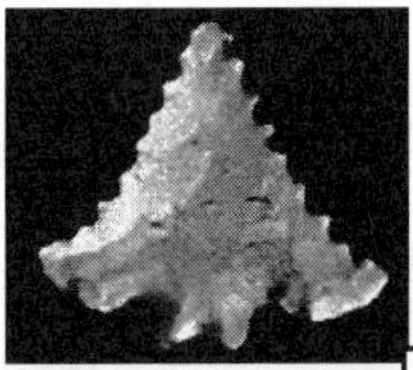

Classic form

G5, $25-$50
IL.

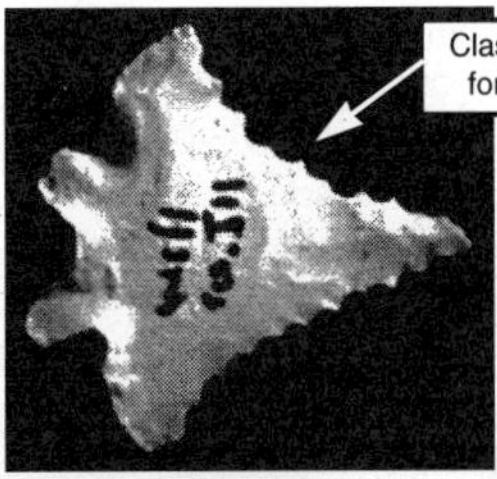

Classic form

G8,
$50-$100
Will Co., IL.

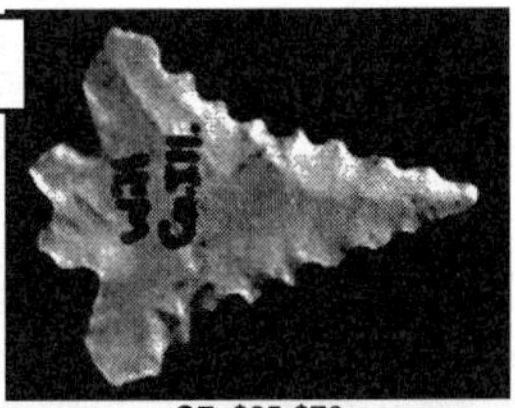

G7, $35-$70
Will Co., IL.

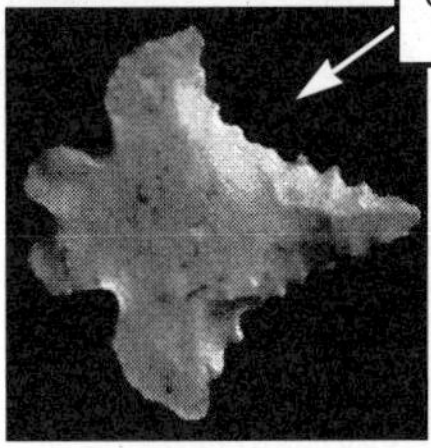

G8, $60-$100
IL.

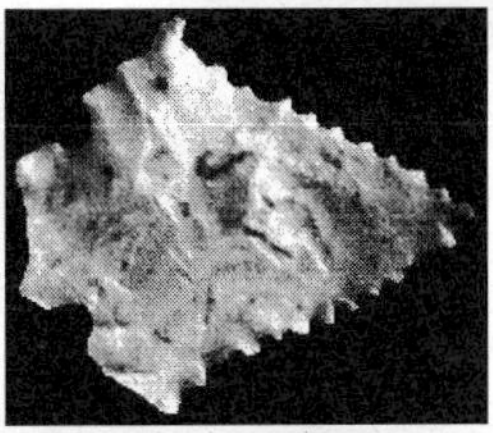

G6, $25-$50
IL.

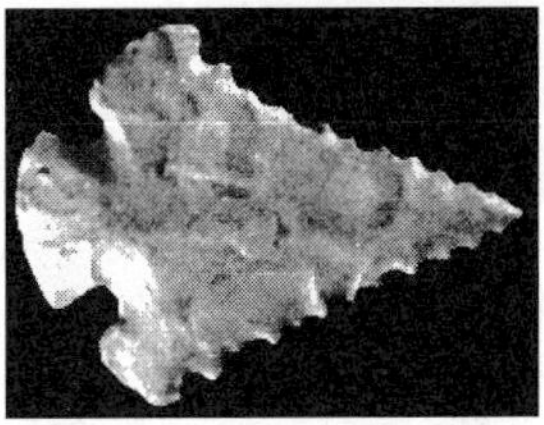

G7, $30-$60
IL.

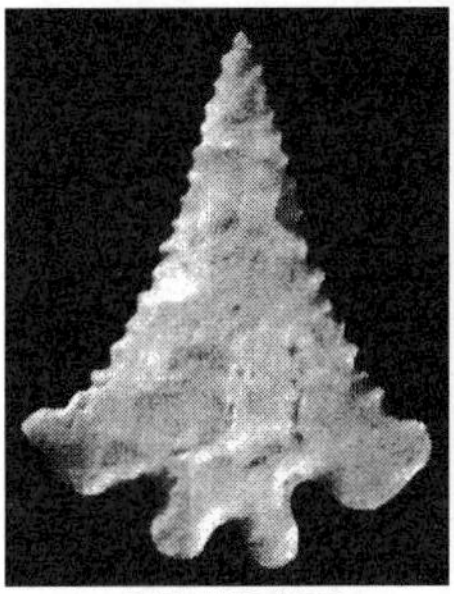

G10, $150-$250
IL. Classic.

G6, $25-$45
IL.

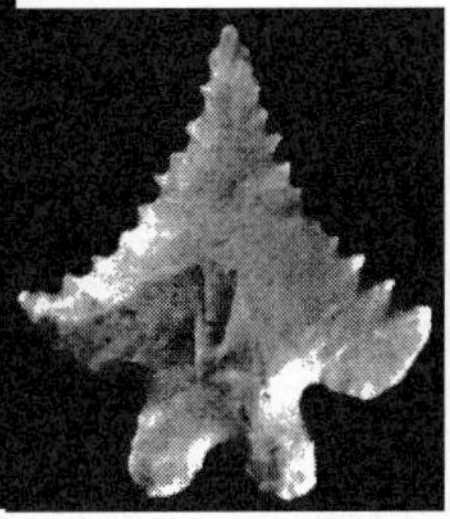

G10, $150-$250
IL. Classic.

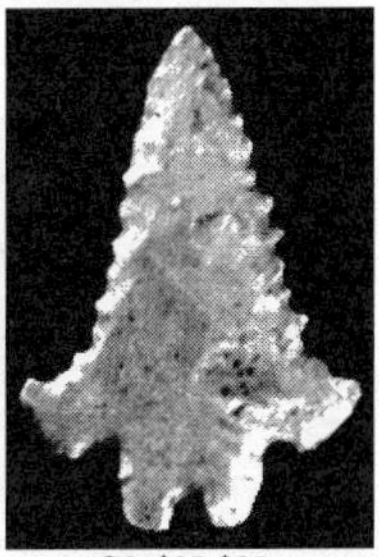

G8, $35-$65
IL. Classic.

GARY - Late Archaic, 4000 - 1000 B. P.

(Also see Adena and Peisker Diamond)

G6, $8-$15
KS.

G6, $15-$30
MO.

G8, $30-$50
MO.

GARY (continued)

LOCATION: Midwestern to Southwestern states. **DESCRIPTION:** A medium size, triangular point with a medium to long, contracted, pointed to rounded base. Shoulders are usually tapered. **I.D. KEY:** Similar to *Adena*, but thinned more.

GIBSON - Mid to late Woodland, 2000 - 1500 B. P.

(Also see Cupp, Dovetail and St. Charles)

LOCATION: Midwestern to Eastern states. Gibson mound group (1969), type site in Calhoun Co., IL. **DESCRIPTION:** A medium to large size side to corner notched point with a large, convex base.

G8, $60-$120
Blackjack, MO.

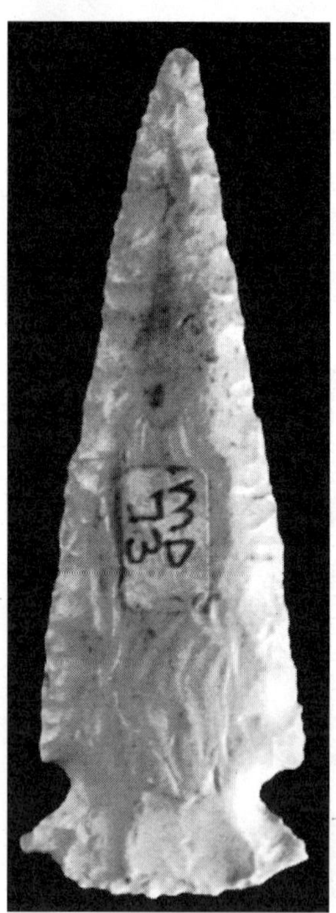

G6, $40-$65
Walworth Co., WI.

G8, $80-$125
IL.

G7, $75-$150
MO.

GODAR - Late Archaic, 4500 - 3500 B. P.

(Also see Hemphill, Hickory Ridge, Osceola and Raddatz)

GODAR (continued)

LOCATION: Midwestern states. **DESCRIPTION:** A medium to large size, narrow to wide, side-notched point with a straight to rounded base. Some examples show parallel flaking.

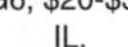

G6, $20-$35
IL.

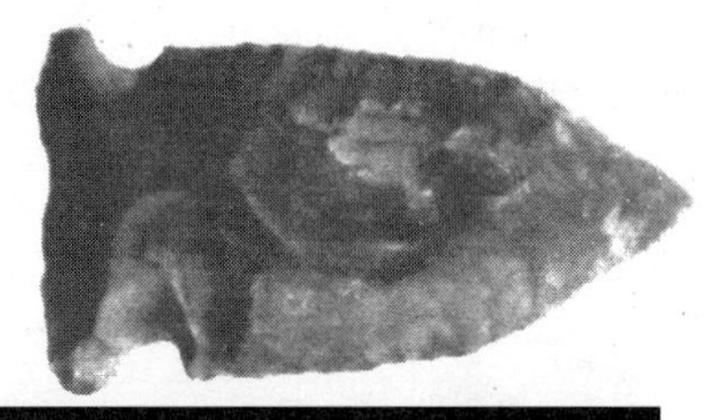

G6, $140-$275
Warren Co., MO.

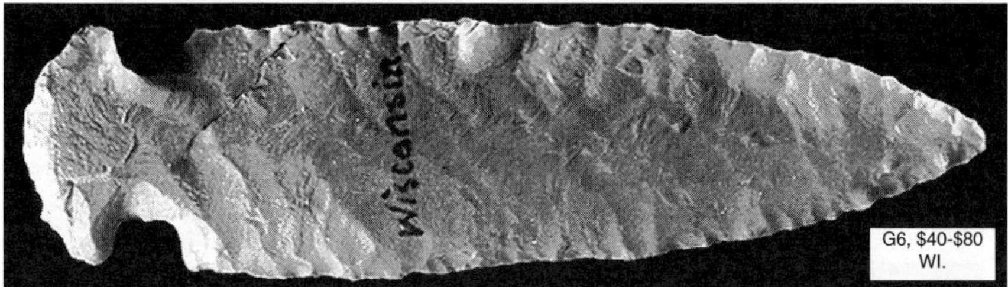

G6, $40-$80
WI.

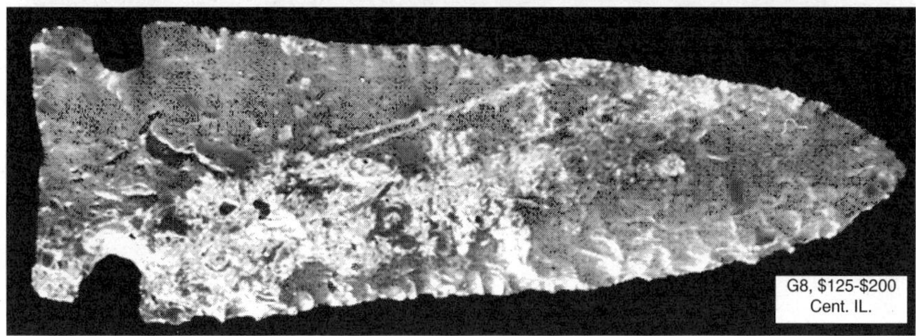

G8, $125-$200
Cent. IL.

GRAHAM CAVE - Early to Middle Archaic, 9000 - 5000 B. P.

(Also see Godar, Hemphill, Osceola and Raddatz)

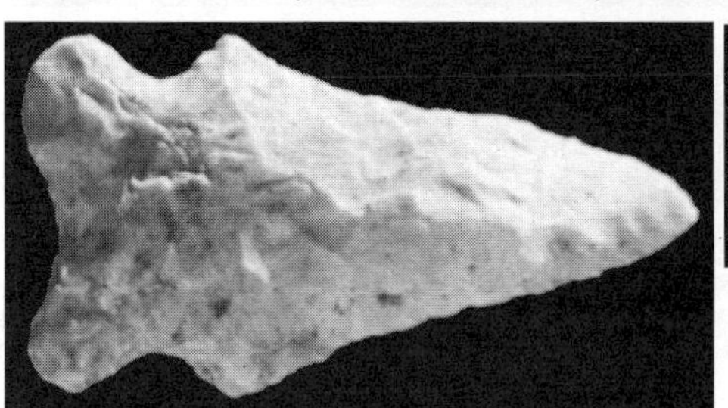

G5, $40-$75
Alexander Co., IL.

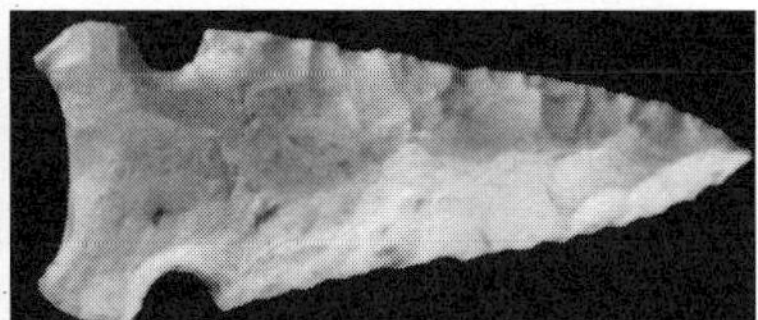

G5, $35-$65
MO.

G5, $40-$75
IL.

LOCATION: Midwestern states. **DESCRIPTION:** A medium to large size, narrow, side-notched point with recurved sides, pointed auricles, and a concave base. Rarely, examples have been found fully fluted.

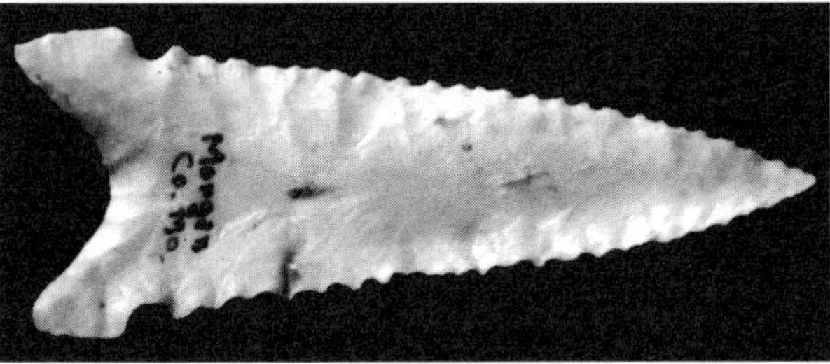

G9, $200-$400
Morgan Co., MO.

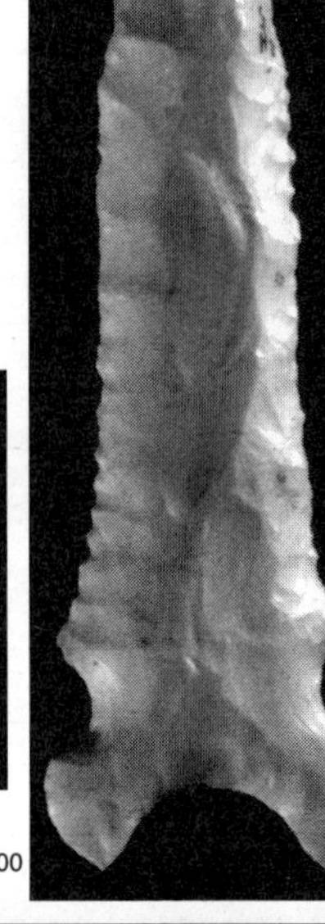

G8, $250-$500
Peoria, IL.

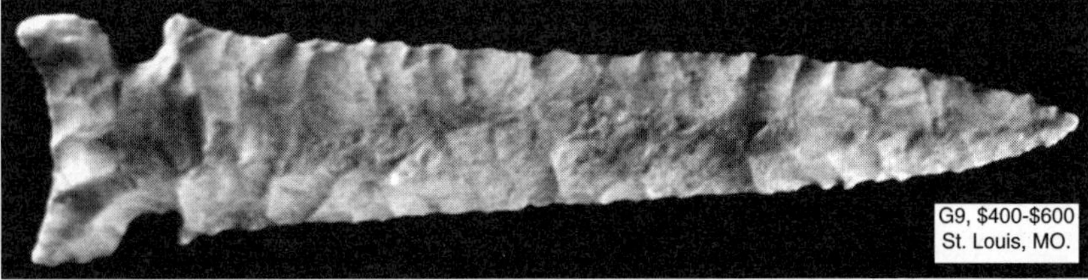

G9, $400-$600
St. Louis, MO.

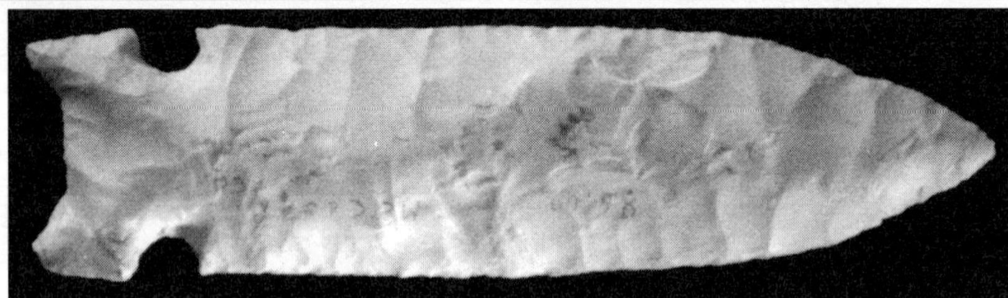

G8, $250-$500
McClean Co., IL.

G7, $125-$250
IL.

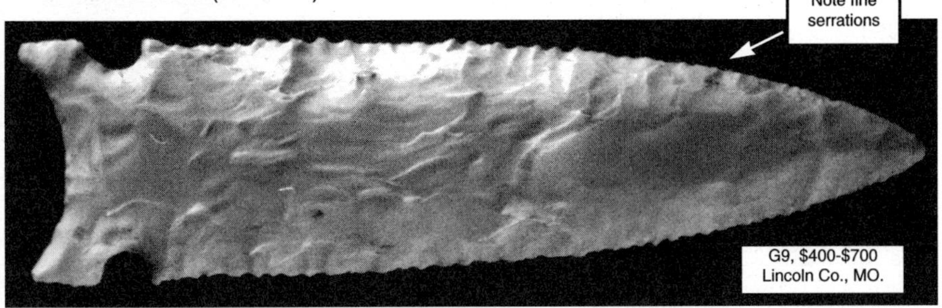

G9, $400-$700
Lincoln Co., MO.

GRAND- Mid-Woodland, 1800 - 1600 B. P.

(Also see Carter, Helton, Kirk Corner Notched, Lost Lake, Lundy and Snyders)

LOCATION: Oklahoma, Kansas. **DESCRIPTION:** A medium sized, broad, corner notched point with barbed shoulders and an expanding, convex base. Basal corners can be sharp. **I.D. KEY:** Width of blade, corner notching.

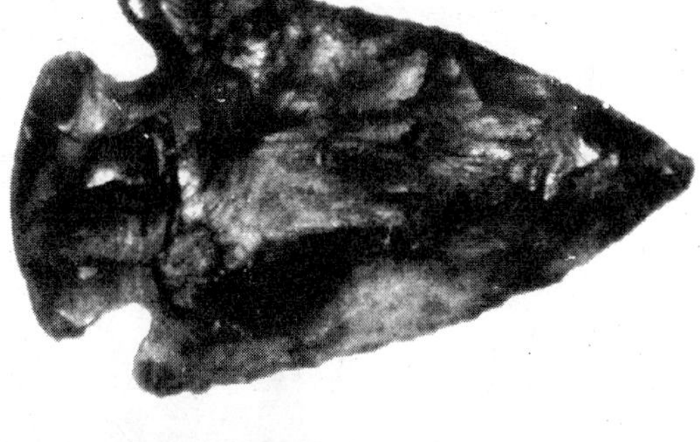

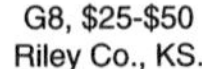

G8, $25-$50
Riley Co., KS.

GREENBRIER - Transitional Paleo 9500 - 6000 B. P.

(Also see Dalton and Pine Tree)

Colorful
bands

G5, $40-$75
MO./IL.

G10, $225-$450
MO. Colorful.

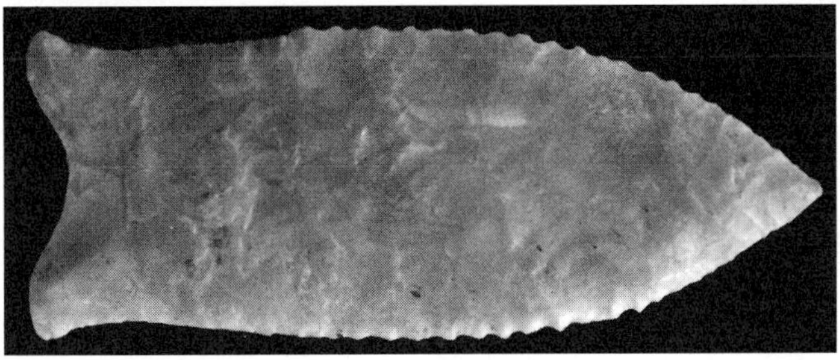

G10, $600-$1200
IL.

GREENBRIER (continued)

G8, $300-$600
Adams Co., IL.

LOCATION: Southeastern to Midwestern states. **DESCRIPTION:** A medium to large size, auriculate point with tapered shoulders and broad, weak side notches. Blade edges are usually finely serrated. The base can be concave, lobbed, eared, straight or bifurcated and is ground. Early examples can be fluted. This type developed from the *Dalton* point as well as directly from the *Clovis* point, and later evolved into other types such as the *Pine Tree* point. **I.D. KEY:** Heavy grinding in shoulders, good secondary edgework.

HARAHEY - Mississippian, 700 - 350 B. P.

(Also see Morse Knife)

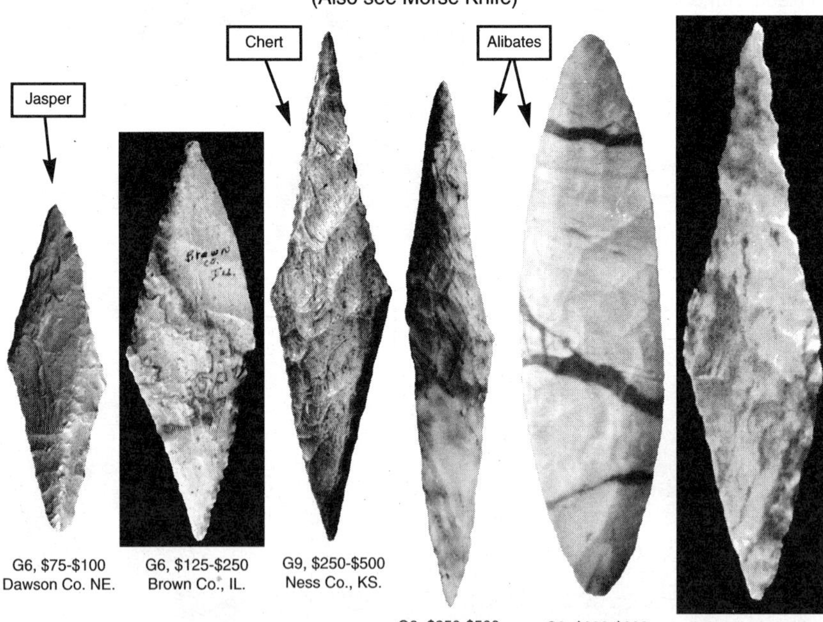

G6, $75-$100
Dawson Co. NE.

G6, $125-$250
Brown Co., IL.

G9, $250-$500
Ness Co., KS.

G8, $250-$500
Comanche Co., KS.

G9, $300-$600
IA.

G7, $150-$300
W. Cent. KS.

Alibates

G9, $250-$500
Hamilton Co., KS.

IMPORTANT:
All Haraheys
shown half size

HARAHEY (continued)

LOCATION: Midwestern states to Texas. **DESCRIPTION:** A large size, double pointed knife that is usually beveled on one or all four sides of each face. The cross section is rhomboid. **I.D. Key:** Rhomboid cross section, two and four beveled form.

HARDIN - Early Archaic, 9000 - 6000 B. P.

(Also see Dovetail, Ferry, Kirk, Lost Lake, Scottsbluff and Stilwell)

G5, $20-$40
WI.

G9, $65-$125
IL.

G5, $75-$150
Logan Co., IL.

G6, $40-$75
IL.

G6, $125-$250
Cent.IL.

G5, $100-$200
IL.

G6, $75-$150
Calhoun Co., IL.

LOCATION: Midwestern to Eastern states. **DESCRIPTION:** A large size, well made triangular barbed point with an expanded base that is usually ground. Resharpened examples have one beveled edge on each face. This type is believed to have evolved from the *Scottsbluff* type. **I.D. Key:** Notches and stem form.

HARDIN (continued)

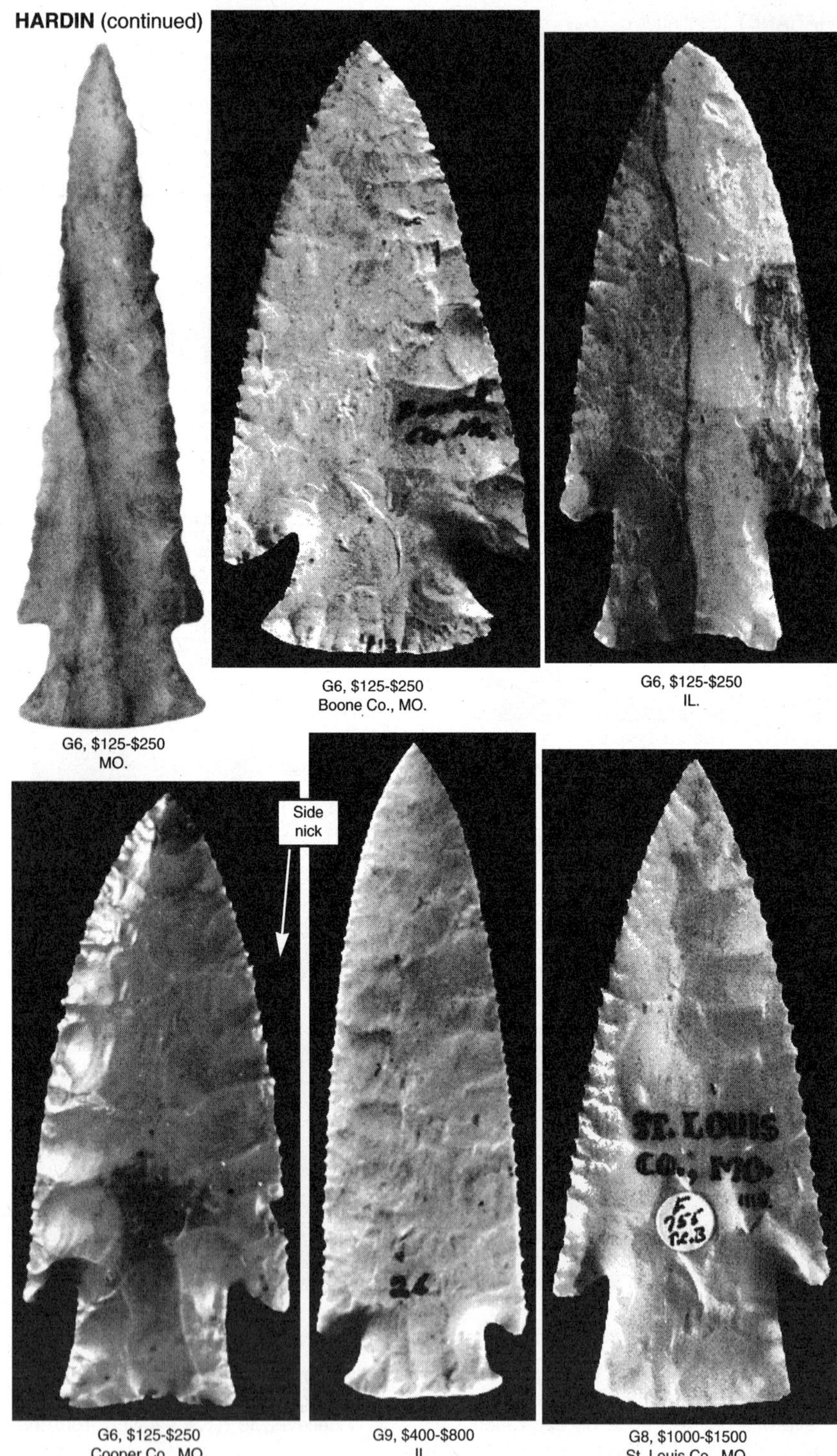

G6, $125-$250
MO.

G6, $125-$250
Boone Co., MO.

G6, $125-$250
IL.

G6, $125-$250
Cooper Co., MO.

G9, $400-$800
IL.

G8, $1000-$1500
St. Louis Co., MO.

G10, $500-$1000
IL.

G8, $600-$1200
Kennert Co., MO.

G8, $500-$1000
IL.

G9, $800-$1500
IL.

G9, $600-$1200
IL.

HARDIN (continued)

G8, $250-$500
MO.

G8, $275-$550
IL.

G8, $400-$800
MO.

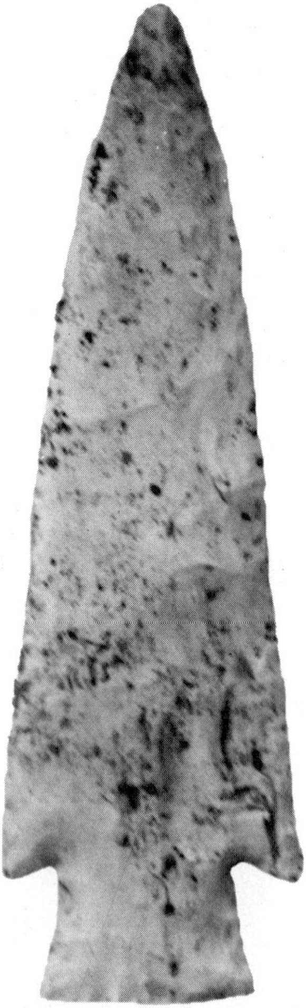

G8, $200-$400
MO.

HARRELL- Mississippian, 900 - 500 B. P.

(Also see Cahokia, Huffaker and Washita)

G5, $20-$40
IL.

G5, $20-$40
IL.

G5, $20-$40
Pottowatomie Co., KS.

G4, $15-$25
IL.

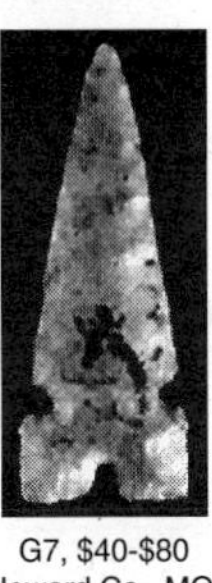
G7, $40-$80
Howard Co., MO.

G7, $40-$80
Riley Co., KS.

LOCATION: Midwestern states. **DESCRIPTION:** A small, thin, triangular arrow point with side and basal notches. Basal ears can be pointed. Bases are usually deeply concave with a basal notch. **I.D. KEY:** Triple notching.

HAYES - Mississippian, 1200 - 600 B. P.

(Also see Alba, Homan and Sequoyah)

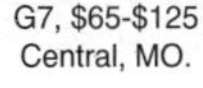
G7, $65-$125
Central, MO.

G10, $115-$225
IL.

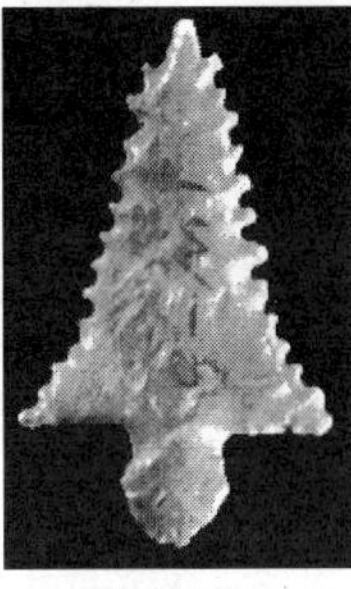
G9, $90-$175
IL.

G9, $150-$300
IL.

LOCATION: Midwestern states. **DESCRIPTION:** A small to medium size, narrow, expanded tang point with a turkeytail base. Blade edges are usually strongly recurved forming sharp pointed tangs. Base is pointed and can be double notched. Some examples are serrated. **I.D. KEY:** Pointed base and flaking style.

NC

HEAVY DUTY - Early to Middle Archaic, 7000 - 5000 B. P.

(Also see Rochester, Stone Square Stem)

G5, $40-$75
Schuyler Co., IL.

LOCATION: Eastern to Midwestern states. **DESCRIPTION:** A medium to large size, thick, serrated point with a parallel stem and a straight to slightly concave base. **I.D. KEY:** Base, thickness, flaking.

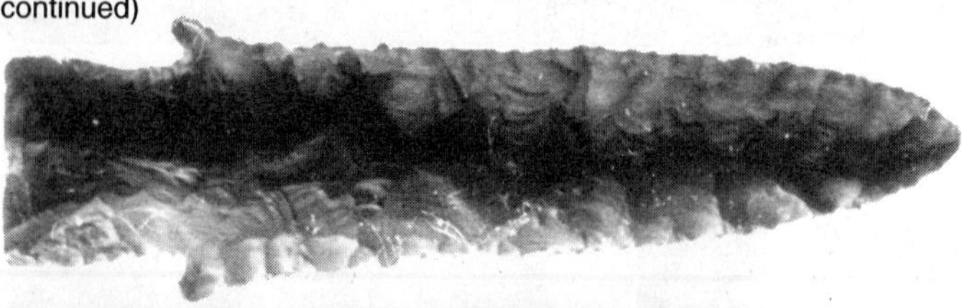

G7, $150-$200
Cent. IL.

G9, $100-$200
Dewitt Co., IL.

HELL GAP - Late Paleo, 10,900 - 9000 B. P.

(Also see Agate Basin, Burroughs and Angostura)

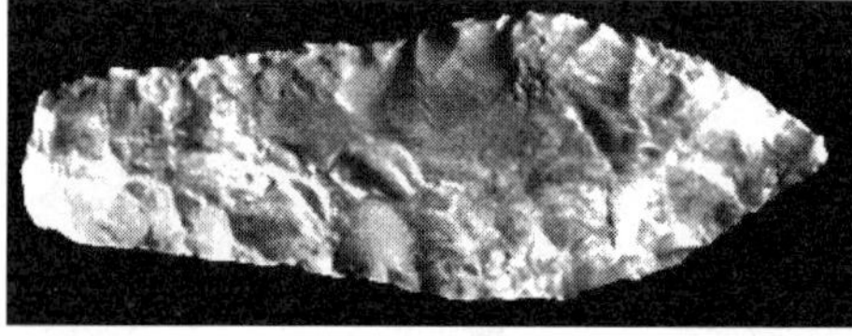

G7, $150-$250
MO.

LOCATION: Midwestern to Western states. **DESCRIPTION:** A medium to large size, lanceolate point with a long, contracting stem. The widest part of the blade is above the mid-section. The base is straight to slightly concave and the stem edges are usually ground. **I.D. KEY:** Early flaking and base form.

HELTON - Late Archaic to early Woodland, 4000 - 2500 B. P.

(Also see Apple Creek, Kay Blade, Lehigh and Lundy)

LOCATION: Midwestern states. **DESCRIPTION:** A medium to large size, broad, point with a short, expanding stem. Shoulders are horizontal to barbed and the base is convex. **I.D. KEY:** Base form.

G6, $20-$40
Riley Co., KS.

HEMPHILL - Mid toLate Archaic, 7000 - 5000 B. P.

(Also see Godar, Graham Cave, Osceola and Raddatz)

LOCATION: Midwestern to Northeastern states. Type site-Brown Co., IL. Associated with the Old Copper & Red Ochre culture. **DESCRIPTION:** A medium to large size side-notched point with a concave base and parallel to convex sides. These points are usually thinner and of higher quality than the similar *Osceola* type.

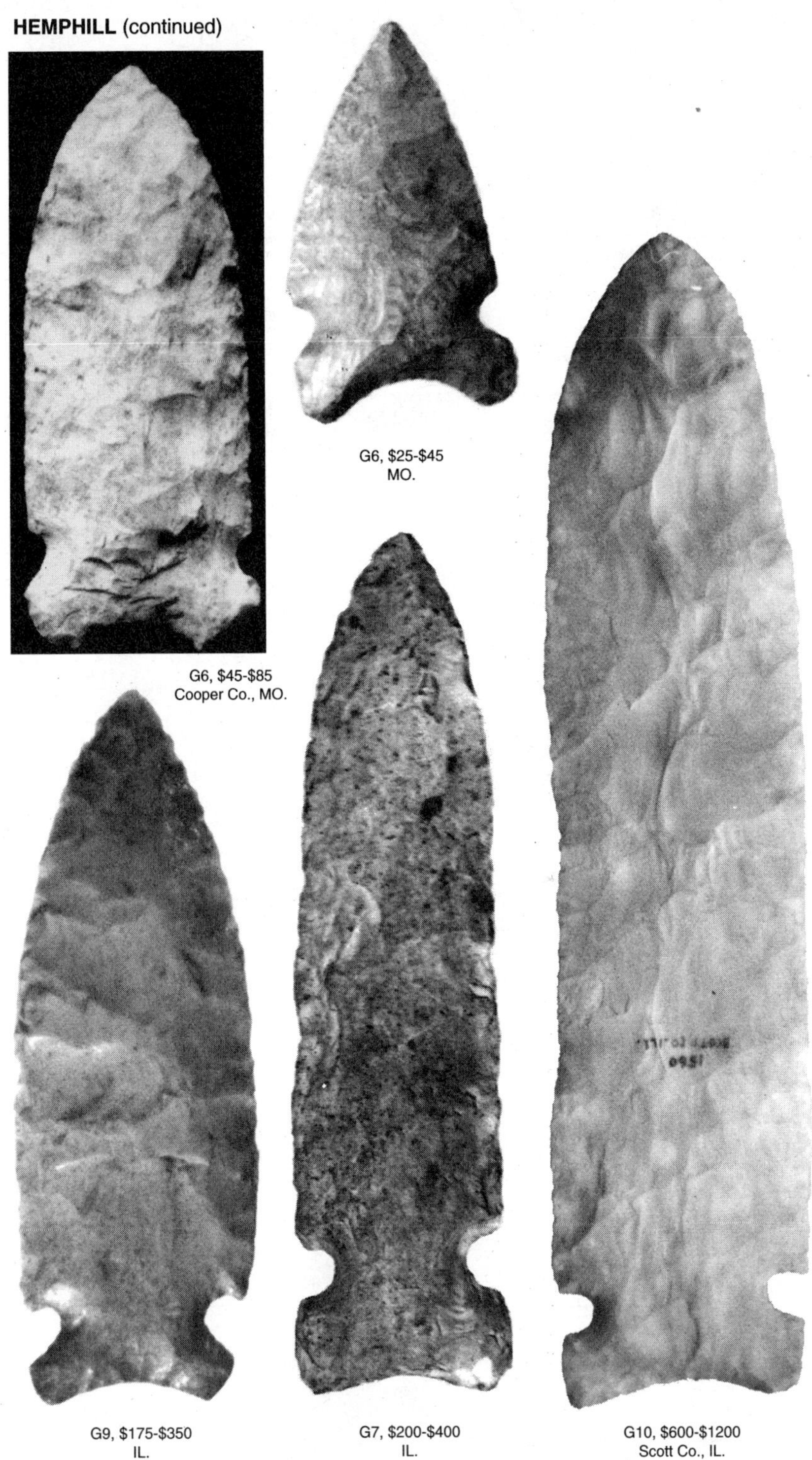

G6, $25-$45
MO.

G6, $45-$85
Cooper Co., MO.

G9, $175-$350
IL.

G7, $200-$400
IL.

G10, $600-$1200
Scott Co., IL.

HI-LO - Late Paleo, 10,000 - 8000 B. P.

(Also see Angostura and Browns Valley)

LOCATION: Midwestern states. **DESCRIPTION:** A medium to large size, broad, eared, lanceolate point with a concave base. Believed to be related to *Plainview* and *Dalton* points.

G7, $125-$250
MO.

HICKORY RIDGE - Early Archaic, 7000 - 5000 B.P.

(Also see Godar, Hemphill, Osceola, Raddatz and Robinson)

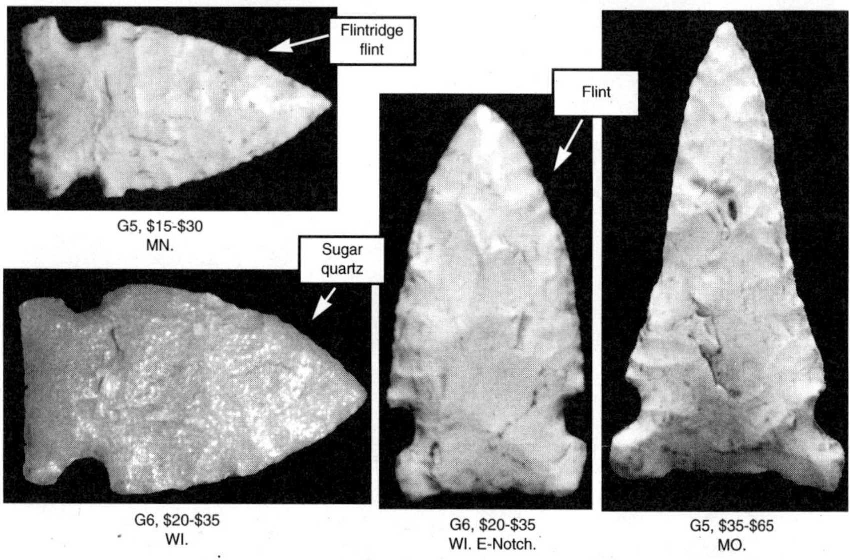

G5, $15-$30
MN.

G6, $20-$35
WI.

G6, $20-$35
WI. E-Notch.

G5, $35-$65
MO.

LOCATION: Missouri to Arkansas. **DESCRIPTION:** A medium to large size side notched point with a straight to slightly concave base

HOLLAND - Early Archaic, 9500 - 7500 B. P.

(Also see Dalton, Eden, Hardin and Scottsbluff)

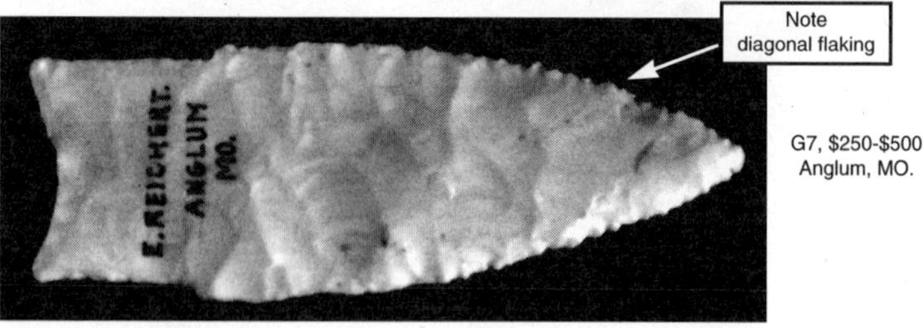

G7, $250-$500
Anglum, MO.

G6, $125-$250
Pike Co., IL.

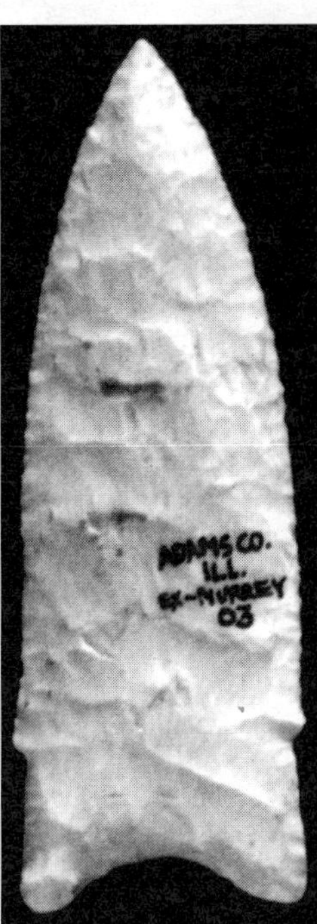

G8, $275-$550
Adams Co., IL.

G6, $100-$200
McClean Co., IL.

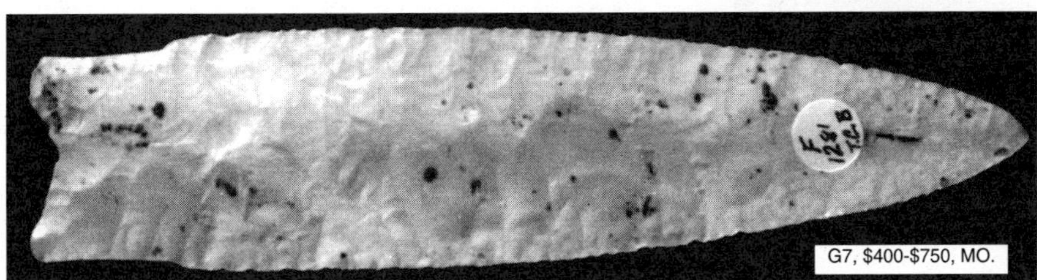

G7, $400-$750, MO.

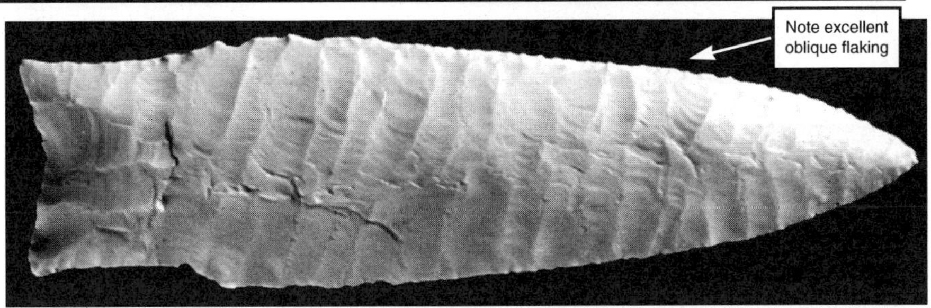

G9, $2000-$3500, Cooper Co., MO., Cast. Actual point is priced.

LOCATION: Midwestern states. **DESCRIPTION:** A medium to large size lanceolate blade that is very well made. Shoulders are weak to nonexistant. Bases can be knobbed to auriculate and are usually ground. Some examples have horizontal to oblique transverse flaking. **I.D. KEY:** Weak shoulders, concave base.

Thin, and excellent quality

Note parallel diagonal flaking

G7, $400-$600
Nebo, IL.

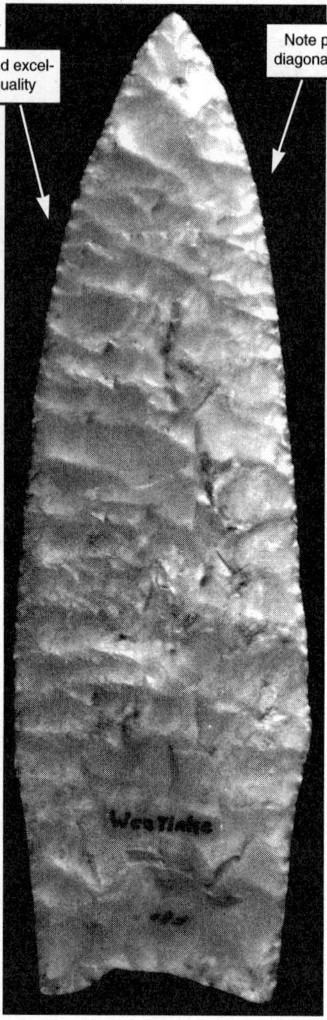

G10, $2000-$3800
St. Louis Co., MO.

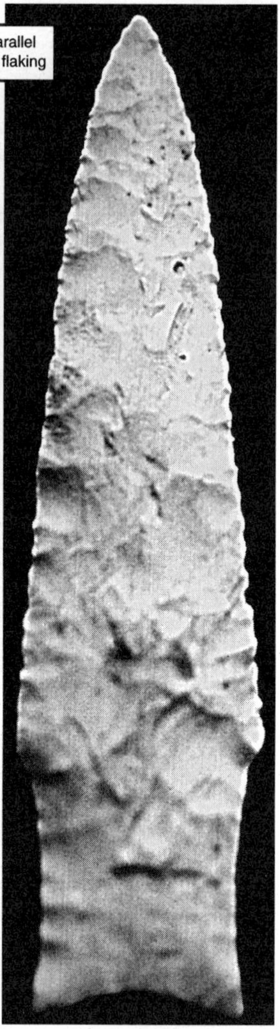

G8, $450-$900
St. Charles Co., MO.

HOMAN - Mississippian, 1000 - 700 B. P.

(Also see Agee, Alba, Hayes and Sequoyah)

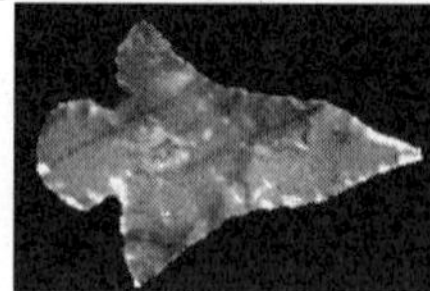

LOCATION: Northwest to Midwestern states. **DESCRIPTION:** A small size expanded barb point with a bulbous stem. Some tips are mucronate or apiculate.

G6, $35-$65
IL.

HOPEWELL - Woodland, 2500 - 1500 B. P.

(Also see Carter, Dovetail, Gibson, North, St. Charles and Snyders)

LOCATION: Midwestern to Eastern states. **DESCRIPTION:** A large size, broad, corner notched point that is similar to *Snyders.* Made by the Hopewell culture.

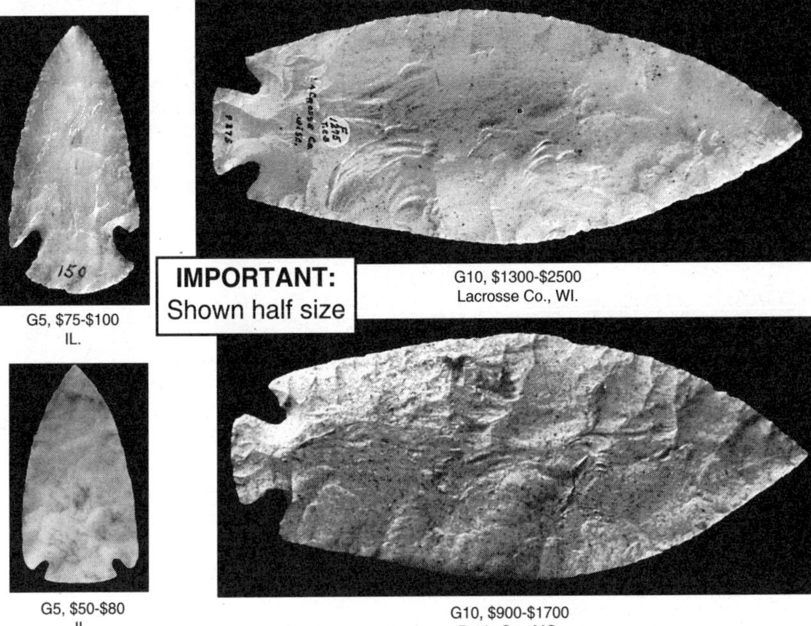

G5, $75-$100
IL.

G10, $1300-$2500
Lacrosse Co., WI.

G5, $50-$80
IL.

G10, $900-$1700
Pettis Co., MO.

HUFFAKER - Mississippian, 1000 - 500 B. P.

(Also see Cahokia, Evans and Washita)

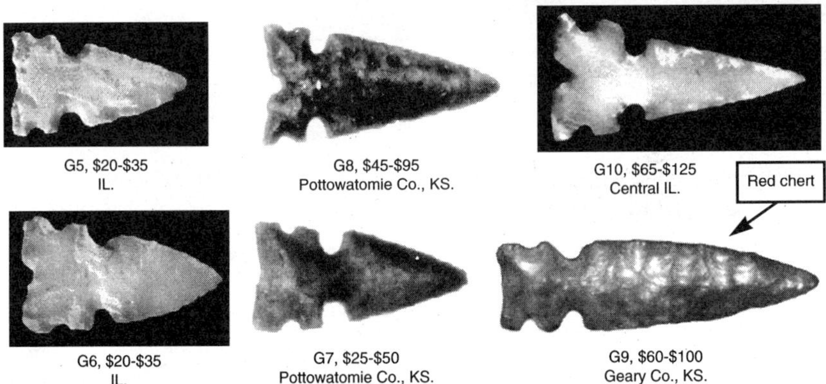

G5, $20-$35
IL.

G8, $45-$95
Pottowatomie Co., KS.

G10, $65-$125
Central IL.

G6, $20-$35
IL.

G7, $25-$50
Pottowatomie Co., KS.

G9, $60-$100
Geary Co., KS.

LOCATION: Midwestern states. **DESCRIPTION:** A small size triangular point with a straight to concave base and double side notches. Bases can have a single notch.

KAY BLADE - Mississippian, 1000 - 600 B. P.

(Also see Cupp, Helton, Kramer, Lundy and Lehigh)

LOCATION: Midwestern states. **DESCRIPTION:** A medium to large size point with a long expanding stem and barbed shoulders. Used by the Mississippian, Caddoan people.

KAY BLADE (continued)

G6, $35-$60
Douglas Co., KS.

G7, $150-$300
St. Louis Co., MO.

KIRK CORNER NOTCHED - Early to Middle Archaic, 9000 - 6000 B. P.

(Also see Apple Creek, Decatur, Dovetail, Lost Lake, Pine Tree, St. Charles & Stilwell)

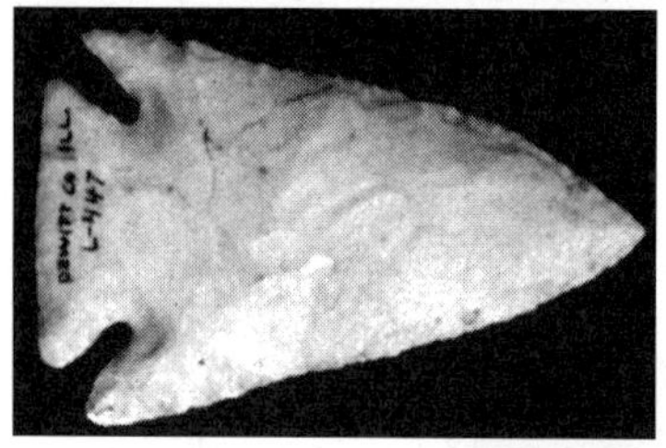

G8, $75-150
Dewitt Co., IL.

G5, $20-$40
IL.

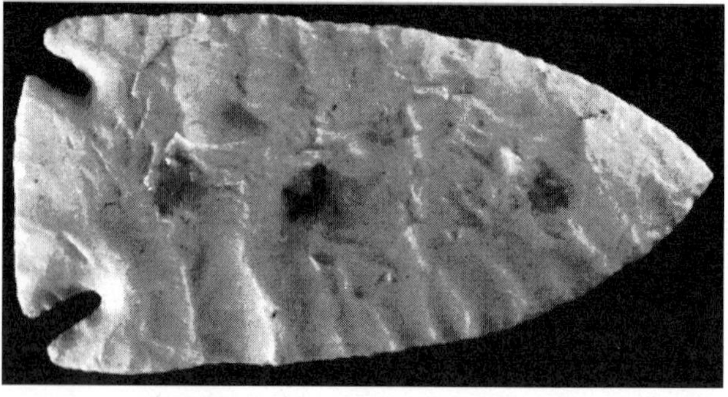

G8, $125-$250
Calhoun, Co., IL.

LOCATION: Southeastern states. **DESCRIPTION:** A medium to large size, corner notched point. Blade edges can be convex to recurved and are finely serrated on many examples. The base can be convex, concave, straight or auriculate. Points that are beveled on one side of each face would fall under the *Lost Lake* type. **I.D. KEY:** Secondary edgework.

KIRK CORNER NOTCHED (continued)

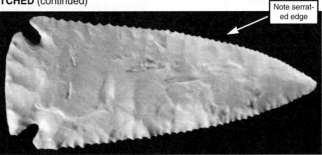

Note serrat-
ed edge

G8, $125-$250
IL.

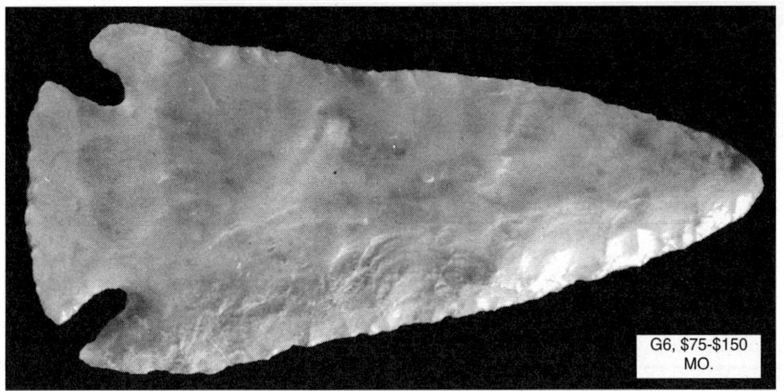

G6, $75-$150
MO.

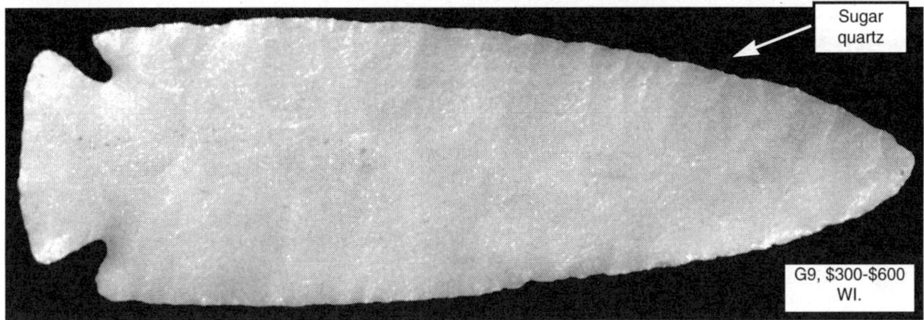

Sugar
quartz

G9, $300-$600
WI.

NC

KRAMER - Woodland, 3000 - 2500 B. P.

(Also see Adena Robbins, Helton, Lehigh, Rochester and Stone Square Stem)

G4, $8-$15
Miller Co., MO.

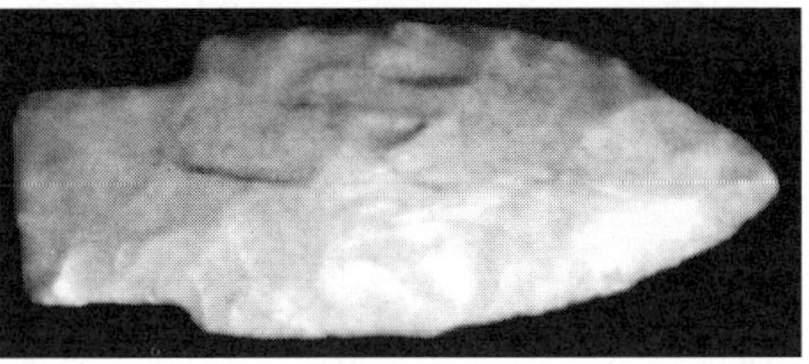

G7, $20-$35
Miller Co., MO.

LOCATION: Midwest. **DESCRIPTION:** A medium size, narrow point with weak shoulders that are tapered to horizontal and a long rectangular stem. Stems are usually ground. **I.D. KEY:** Rectangular stem.

KRAMER (continued)

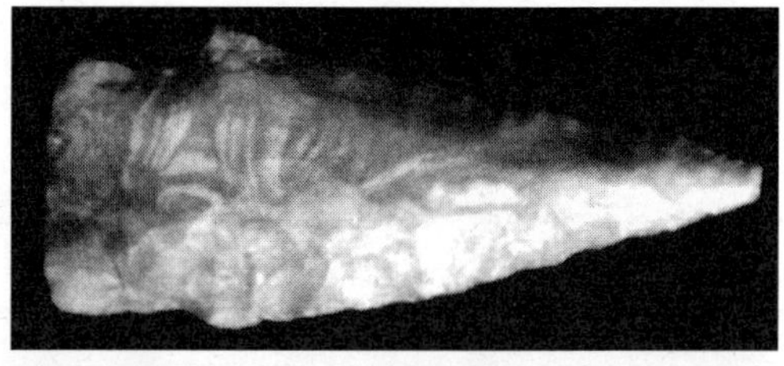

G6, $15-$25
Miller Co., MO.

LAKE ERIE - Early to Middle Archaic, 9000 - 5000 B. P.

(Also see Cossatot River and Fox Valley)

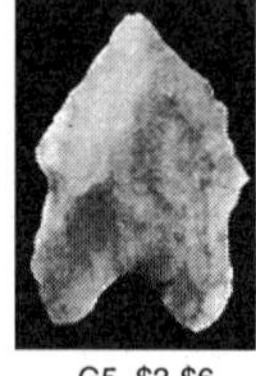

G5, $3-$6
IL.

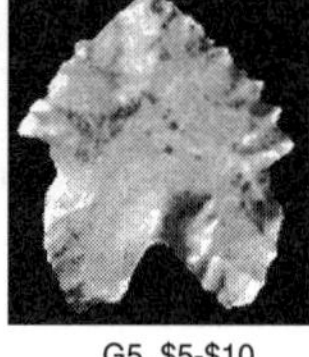

G5, $5-$10
IL.

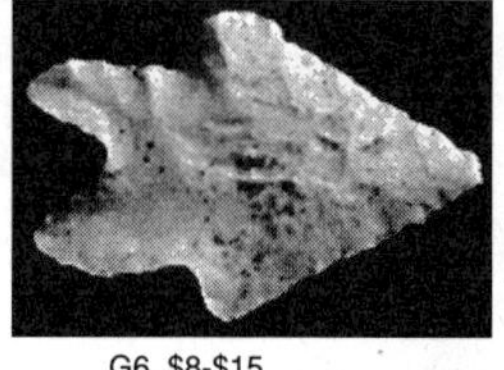

G6, $8-$15
IL.

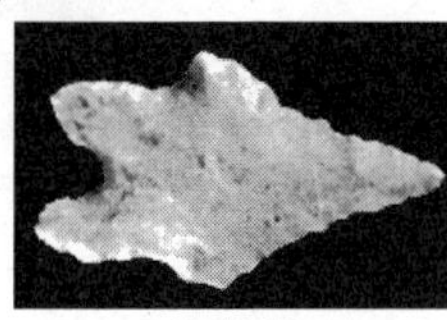

G4, $1-$3
IL.

LOCATION: Northeastern states. **DESCRIPTION:** A small to medium size, thin, deeply notched or serrated, bifurcated stemmed point. The basal lobes are parallel with a tendency to turn inward and are pointed. The outward sides of the basal lobes are usually fractured from the base towards the tip and can be ground.

G5, $6-$12
IL.

LEHIGH - Woodland, 2500 - 1500 B. P.

(Also see Helton, Kay Blade, Kramer, Lundy and Steuben)

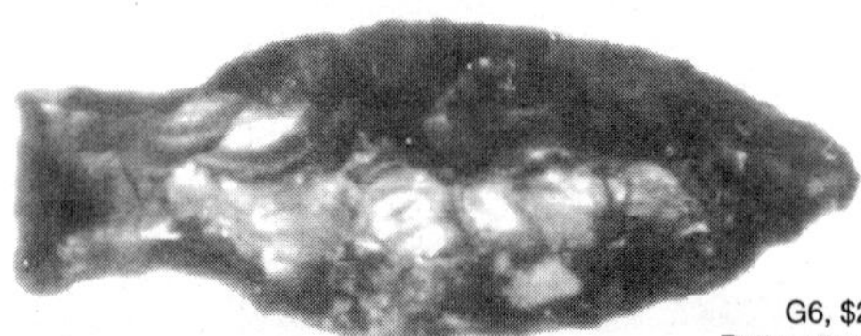

G6, $20-$40
Pottowatomie Co., KS.

LOCATION: Midwest. **DESCRIPTION:** A medium to large size, narrow point with tapered shoulders and a long expanding stem. Bases are straight. **I.D. KEY:** Long expanding stem.

LERMA - Transitional Paleo to Middle Archaic, 10,000 - 5000 B. P.

(Also see Agate Basin, Burroughs and Sedalia)

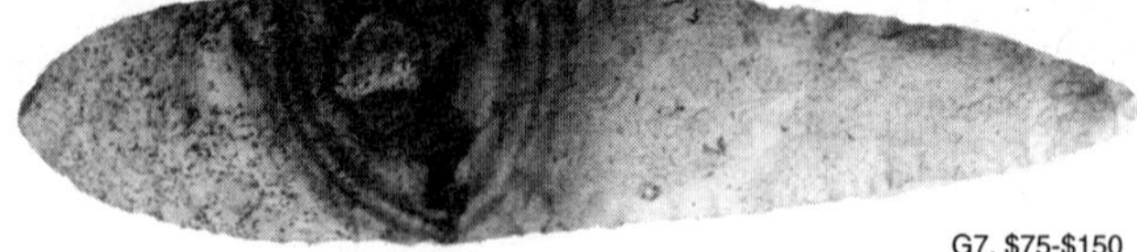

G7, $75-$150
MO.

IMPORTANT: Shown half size

LOCATION: Siberia to Alaska, Canada, Mexico, South America and across the U.S. **DESCRIPTION:** A large size, narrow, lanceolate blade with a pointed base. Most are fairly thick in cross section but finer examples can be thin. Flaking tends to be collateral. Basal areas can be ground. Western forms are beveled on one side of each face. Similar forms have been found in Europe and Africa dating back to 20,000 - 40,000 B.P., but didn't enter the U.S. until after the advent of *Clovis.*

LERMA (continued)

IMPORTANT:
Shown half size

G8, $90-$180
IL.

G8, $100-
$190
Cent. MO.

LOST LAKE - Early Archaic, 9000 - 6000 B. P.

(Also see Dovetail, Hardin, Kirk Corner Notched and Thebes)

G7, $125-$225
St. Clair Co., IL.

G6, $100-$200
Anna, IL.

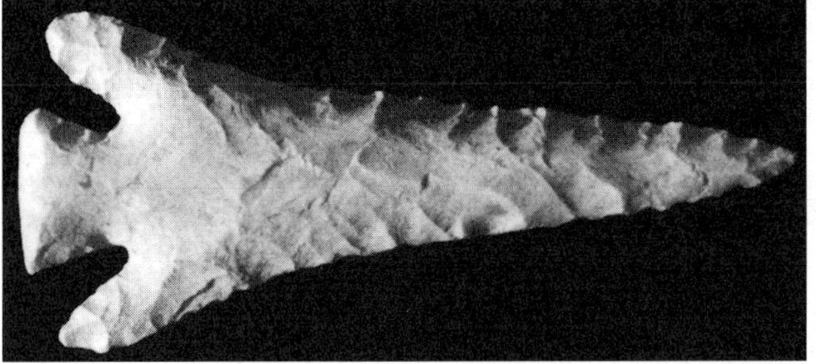

G8, $150-$300
MO.

NC

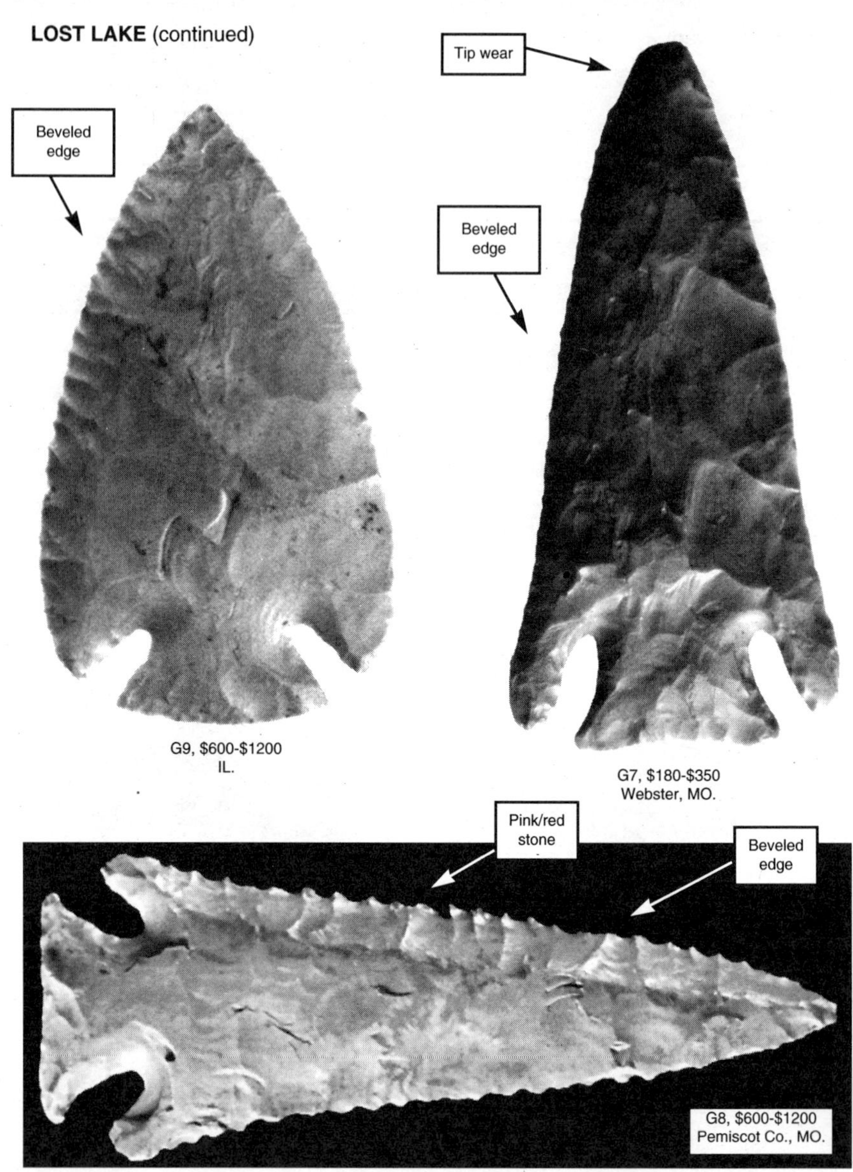

G9, $600-$1200
IL.

G7, $180-$350
Webster, MO.

G8, $600-$1200
Pemiscot Co., MO.

LOCATION: DESCRIPTION: A medium to large size, broad, corner notched point that is beveled on one side of each face. The beveling continues when resharpened and creates a flat rhomboid cross section. Most examples are finely serrated and exhibit high quality flaking and symmetry. **I.D. KEY:** Notching, secondary edgework is always opposite creating at least slight beveling on one side of each face.

LUNDY- Late Caddoan, 800 - 600 B. P.

(Also see Helton, Kay Blade, Lehigh, Steuben and Table Rock)

LOCATION: Midwestern states. **DESCRIPTION:** A small to medium size, narrow, corner notched point with barbed shoulders and a convex base.

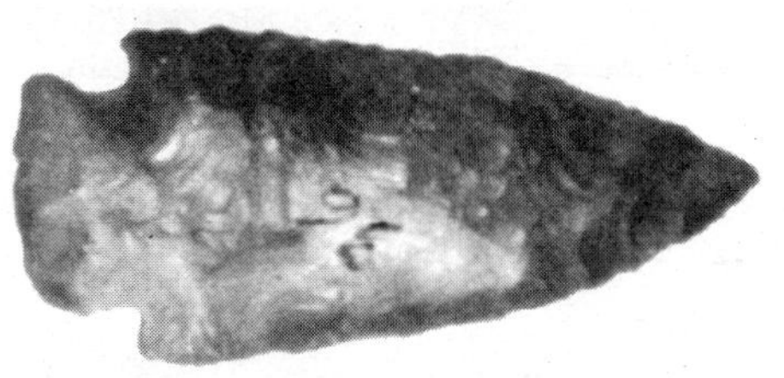
G6, $15-$30
Geary Co., KS.

MADISON - Mississippian, 1100 - 200 B. P.

(Also see Cahokia)

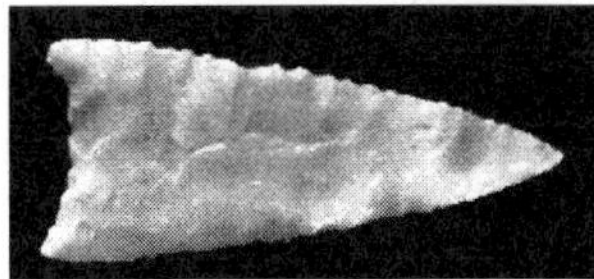
G7, $8-$12
MO.

G10, $150-$300
IL., Cahokia site.
Titterington form.

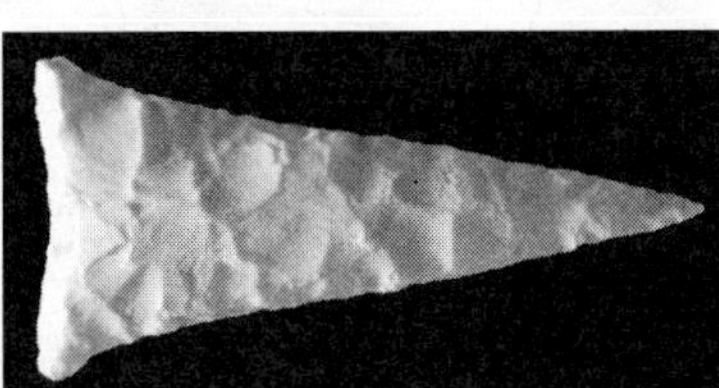

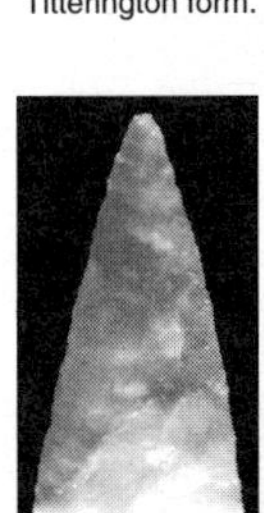
G4, $5-$8
Madison Co., IL.

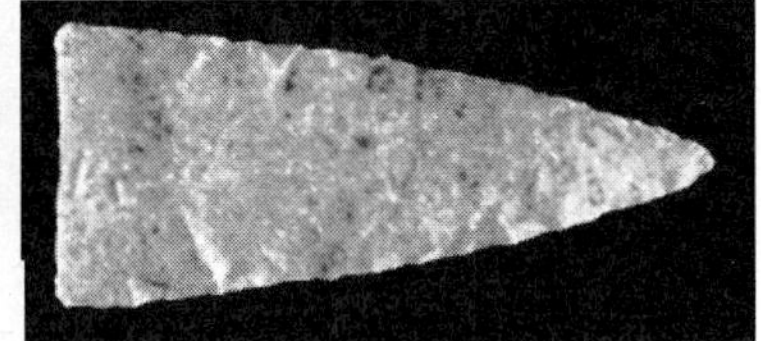
G8, $12-$20
Central IL.

LOCATION: Coincides with the Mississippian culture in the Eastern states. Type site-Madison Co., IL. Found at Cahokia mounds. Un-notched *Cahokias.* Used by the Kaskaskia tribe into the 1700s. **DESCRIPTION:** A small to medium size, thin, triangular point with usually straight sides and base. Some examples are notched on two to three sides. Many are of high quality and some are finely serrated.

G10, $1000-$1800, IL.
Cahokia site. Largest known Titterington form.

MATANZAS - Mid-Archaic to Woodland, 4500 - 2500 B. P.

(Also see Carter, Cupp, Hickory Ridge, Kirk Corner Notched)

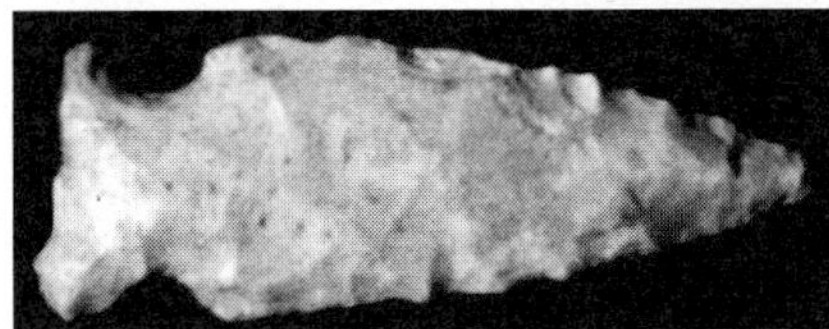

LOCATION: Midwestern states. **DESCRIPTION:** A small to medium size, narrow, side notched point with a concave, convex or straight base.

G4, $5-$10
WI. Chert.

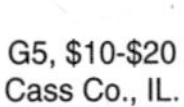
G5, $10-$20
Cass Co., IL.

MEHLVILLE - Late Archaic, 4000 - 3000 B. P.

(Also see Etley and Smith)

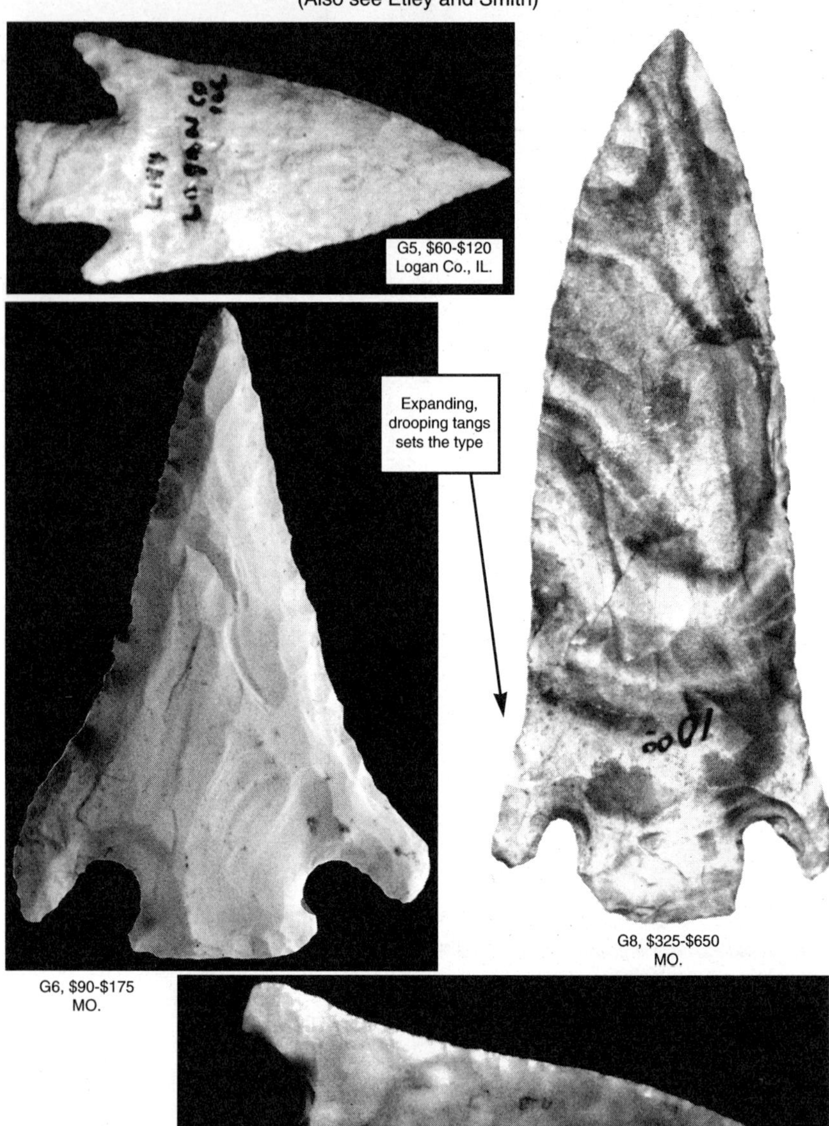
Expanding, drooping tangs sets the type

G5, $60-$120
Logan Co., IL.

G8, $325-$650
MO.

G6, $90-$175
MO.

G8, $300-$600
Cent. IL.

LOCATION: Midwestern states. **DESCRIPTION:** A large size, broad, point with expanding shoulders and a squared base. The long barbs give the appearance of basal notching. **I.D. KEY:** Expanding barbs.

MESERVE - Early Archaic, 9500 - 4000 B. P.

(Also see Dalton, Greenbrier and Plainview)

LOCATION: Midwestern states to Texas and west to Montana. **DESCRIPTION:** A medium size auriculate point with a blade that is beveled on one side of each face. Beveling extends into the basal area.Related to Dalton points. **I.D. KEY:** Beveling into the base.

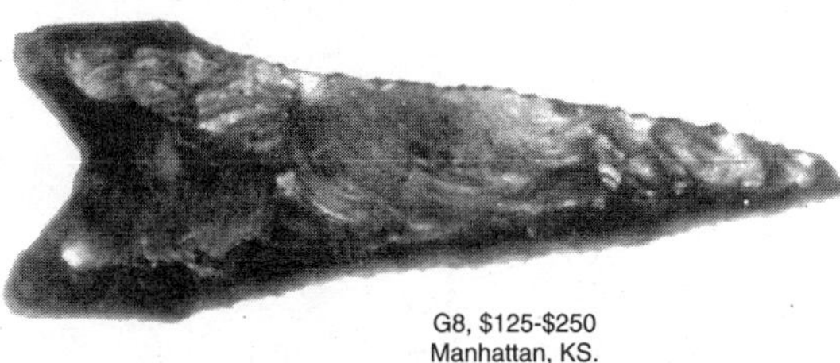

G8, $125-$250
Manhattan, KS.

MORSE KNIFE - Woodland, 3000 - 1500 B. P.

(Also see Harahey, Ramey Knife and Red Ochre)

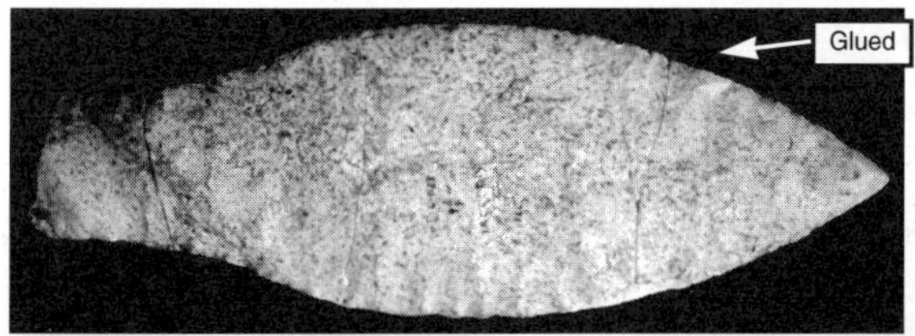

IMPORTANT
All Morse knives are shown 1/2 size

G3, $200-$400
Iroqois Co., IL.

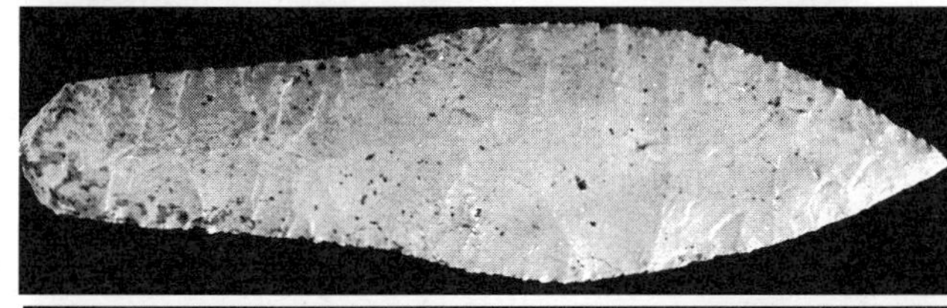

G9, $600-$1200
LaSalle Co., IL.

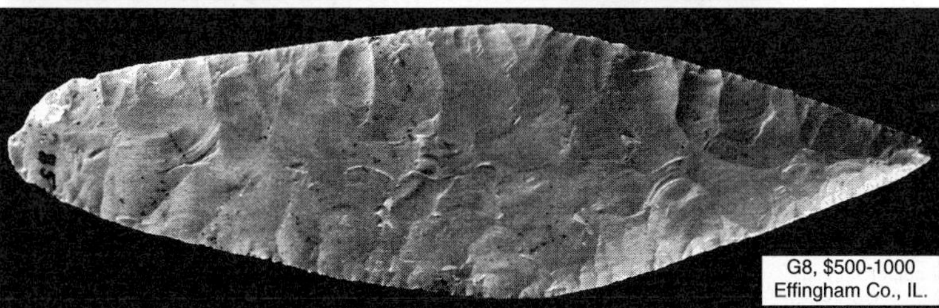

G8, $500-1000
Effingham Co., IL.

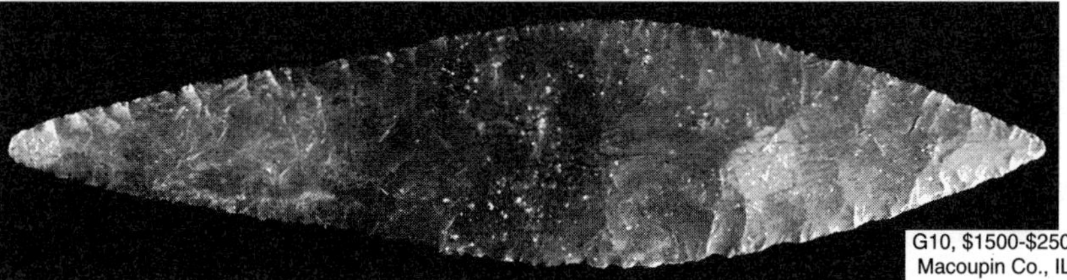

G10, $1500-$2500
Macoupin Co., IL.

NC

MORSE KNIFE (continued)

LOCATION: Midwestern states. **DESCRIPTION:** A large lanceolate blade with a long contracting stem and a rounded base. The widest part of the blade is towards the tip.

NEBO HILL - Early Archaic, 7500 - 6000 B. P.

(Also see Agate Basin, Burroughs, Eden, Lerma and Sedalia)

G6, $40-$75
MO.

G8, $50-$100
IL.

LOCATION: Central states. **DESCRIPTION:** A large size, narrow, thick, lanceolate blade with convex sides that gently taper to the base. On some examples, the basal area is determined by the presence of slight shoulders. Collateral flaking does occur on some examples.

NODENA - Mississippian to Historic, 600 - 400 B. P.

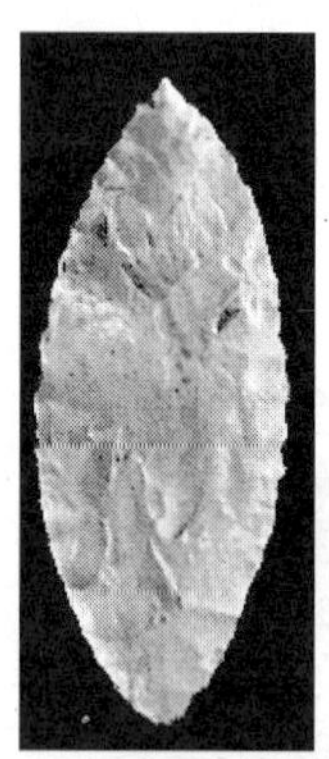

G7, $25-$50
Pemiscot, MO.

G7, $30-$60
Pemiscot, MO.

G7, $40-$75
Pemiscot, MO.

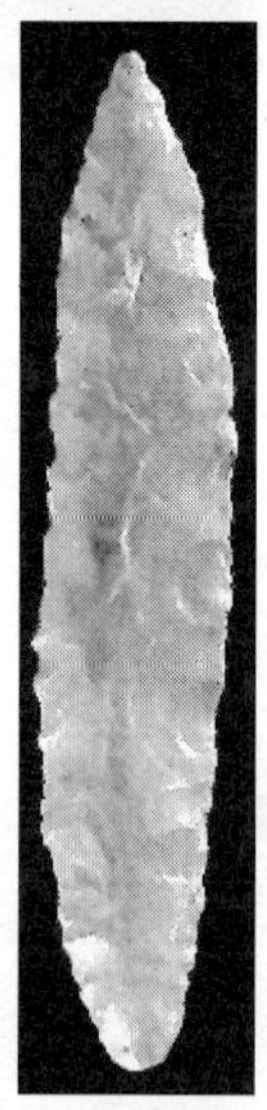

G7, $40-$80
IL.

LOCATION: Midwestern states. **DESCRIPTION:** A small to medium size, narrow, thin elliptical shaped arrow point with a pointed to rounded base. Some examples have oblique, parallel flaking.

NORTH - Woodland, 2200 - 1600 B. P.

(Also see Hopewell and Snyder)

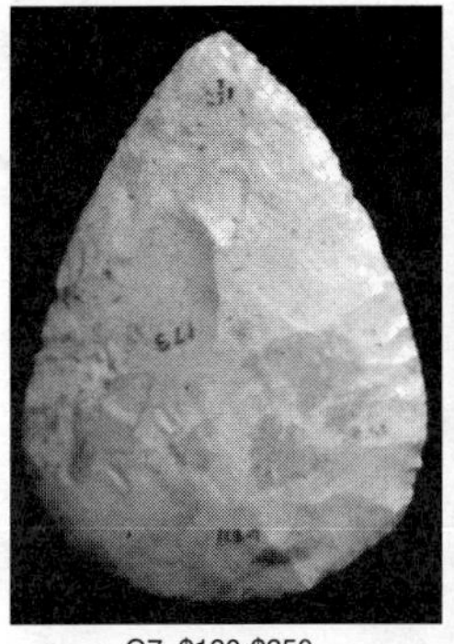
G7, $180-$350
Logan Co., IL.

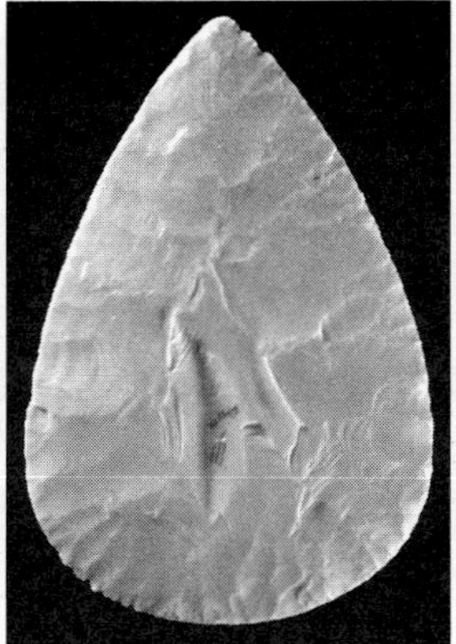
G10, $300-$600
Madison Co., IL.

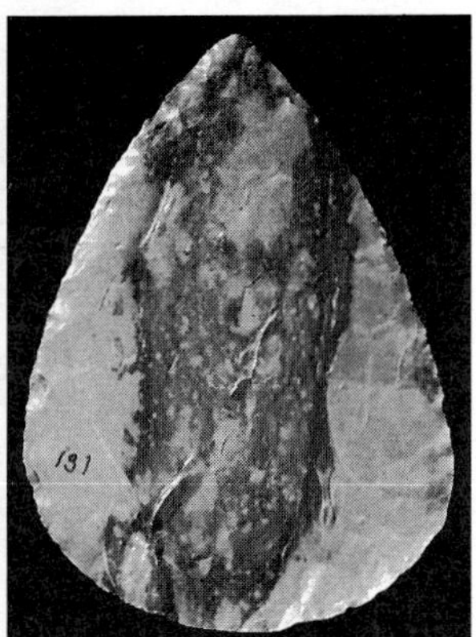
G9, $250-$500
Osage Co., MO.

G7, $100-$200
Scott Co., IL.

G9, $300-$600
Lincoln Co., MO.

IMPORTANT:
All Norths
shown 1/2 size

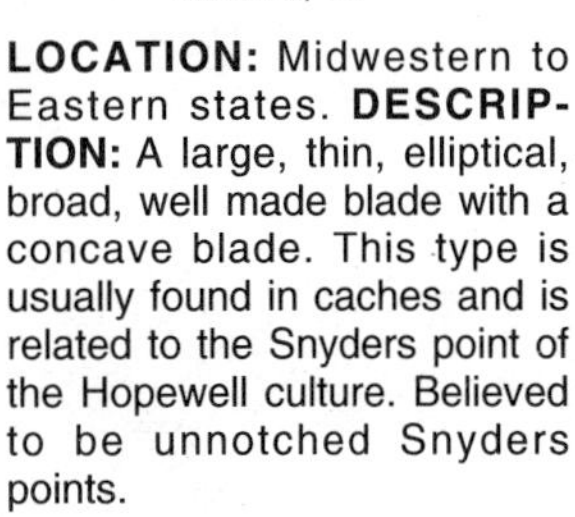
LOCATION: Midwestern to Eastern states. **DESCRIPTION:** A large, thin, elliptical, broad, well made blade with a concave blade. This type is usually found in caches and is related to the Snyders point of the Hopewell culture. Believed to be unnotched Snyders points.

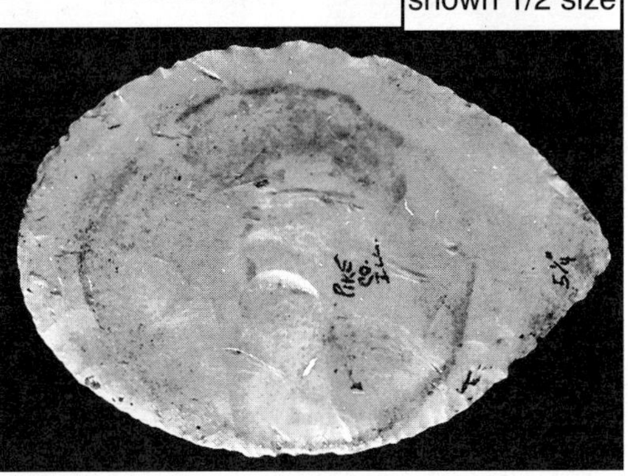
G9, $300-$600
Pike Co., IL.

NC

OSCEOLA - Early to Middle Archaic, 7000 - 5000 B. P.

(Also see Cache River, Godar, Graham Cave, Hemphill and Raddatz)

LOCATION: Midwestern to Southeastern states. **DESCRIPTION:** A large size, narrow, side notched point with parallel sides on longer examples and a straight to concave to notched base which could be ground. **I.D. KEY:** Always has early flaking to the middle of the blade.

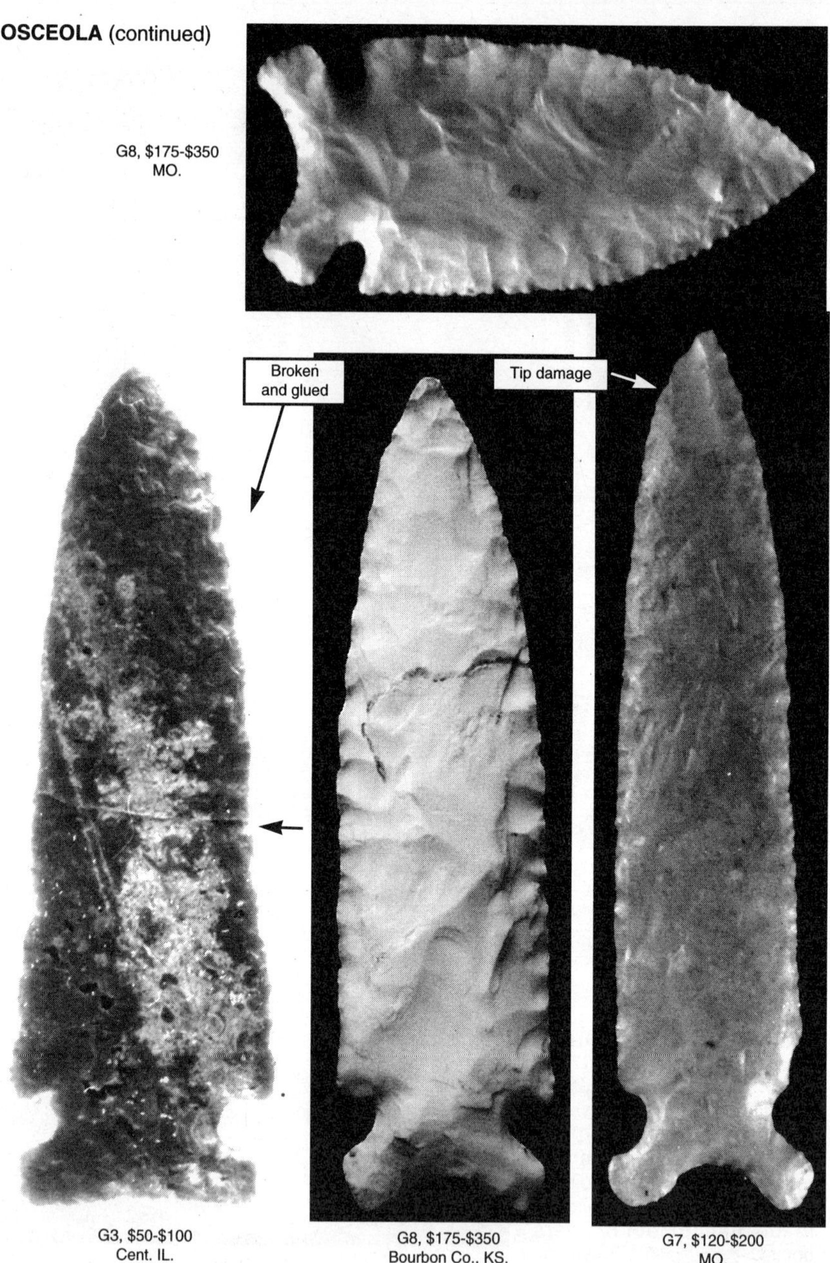

G8, $175-$350
MO.

G3, $50-$100
Cent. IL.

G8, $175-$350
Bourbon Co., KS.

G7, $120-$200
MO.

PEISKER DIAMOND - Woodland, 2500 - 2000 B. P.

(Also see Adena and Gary)

LOCATION: Illinois, Missouri, Kansas into Iowa. **DESCRIPTION:** A large, broad blade with sharp shoulders and a short to moderate contracting base that comes to a point. Blade edges are recurved, convex or straight. Similar in form to the *Morrow Mountain* point found in the Southeast, but not as old. **I.D.KEY:** Contracted base, pointed base.

PEISKER DIAMOND (continued)

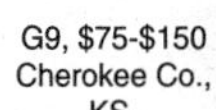
G9, $75-$150
Cherokee Co.,
KS.

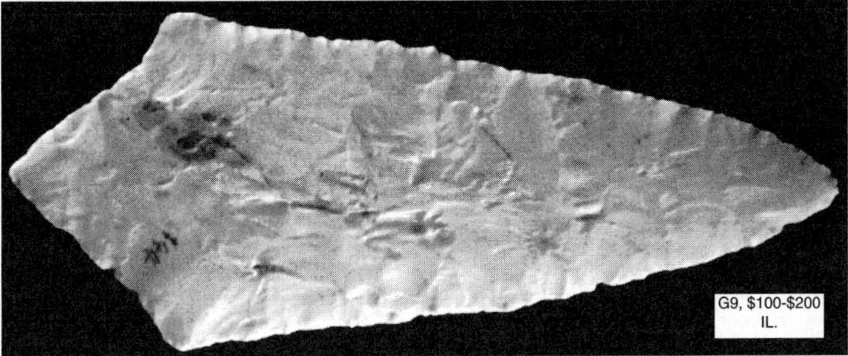
G9, $100-$200
IL.

PELICAN - Transitional Paleo, 10,000 - 6000 B. P.

(Also see Beaver Lake, Dalton, Greenbrier and Holland)

LOCATION: Louisiana, Texas, Arkansas into Kansas. **DESCRIPTION:** A medium size auriculate point with recurved sides. The base is concave with edge grinding. **I.D. KEY:** Basal contraction.

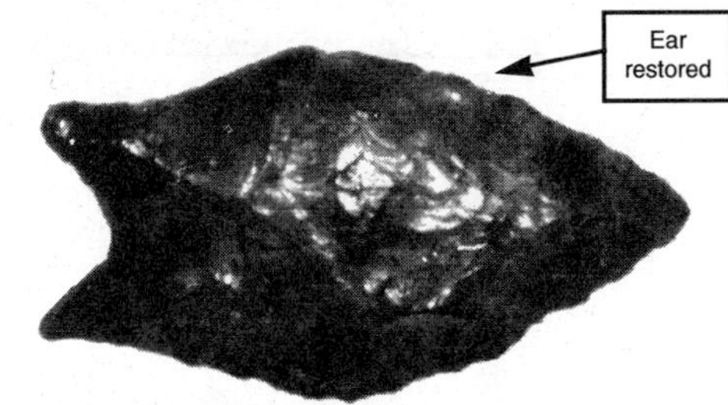

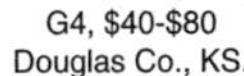
G4, $40-$80
Douglas Co., KS.

PIKE COUNTY - Early Archaic, 9500 - 7500 B. P.

(Also see Dalton, Greenbrier and Holland)

G7, $600-$1200
Pike Co., MO.

LOCATION: Midwestern states. **DESCRIPTION:** A medium to large size, lanceolate blade with an eared, fishtail base. Basal area is ground. Related to Dalton.

PINE TREE CORNER NOTCHED - Early Archaic, 8000 - 5000 B. P.

(Also see Kirk and Lost Lake and Stilwell)

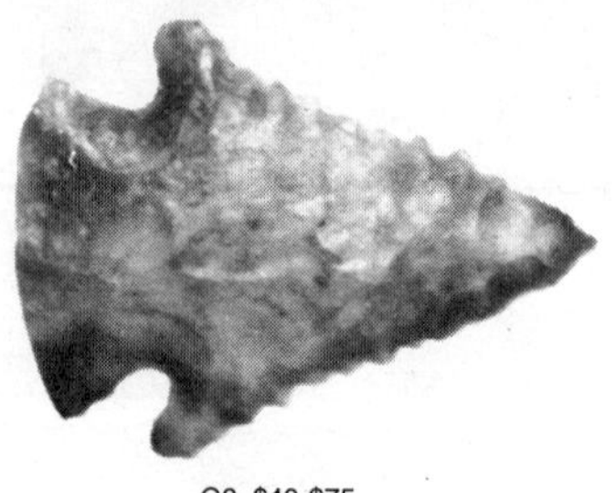

G8, $40-$75
IL.

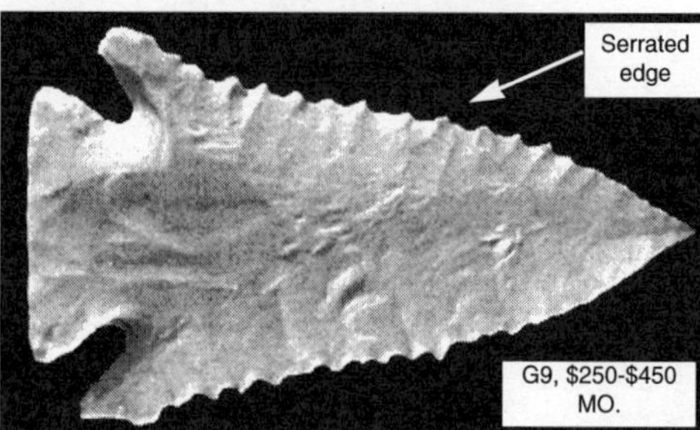

G9, $250-$450
MO.

LOCATION: DESCRIPTION: A small to medium size, thin, corner notched point with a concave, convex, straight, bifurcated or auriculate base. Blade edges are usually serrated and flaking is parallel to the center of the blade. The shoulders expand and are barbed. The base is ground. Small examples would fall under the *Palmer* typer**. I.D. KEY:** Archaic flaking to the center of each blade.

Serrated
edge

G8, $150-$300
MO.

PLAINVIEW - Late Paleo, 10,000 - 7000 B. P.

(Also see Angostura, Browns Valley, Clovis, Cumberland and Dalton)

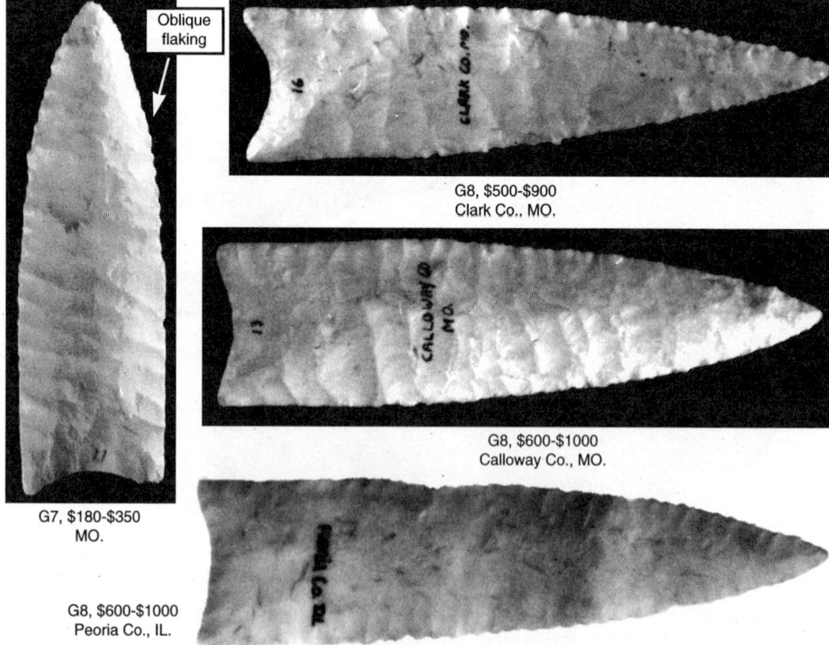

G8, $500-$900
Clark Co., MO.

G8, $600-$1000
Calloway Co., MO.

G7, $180-$350
MO.

G8, $600-$1000
Peoria Co., IL.

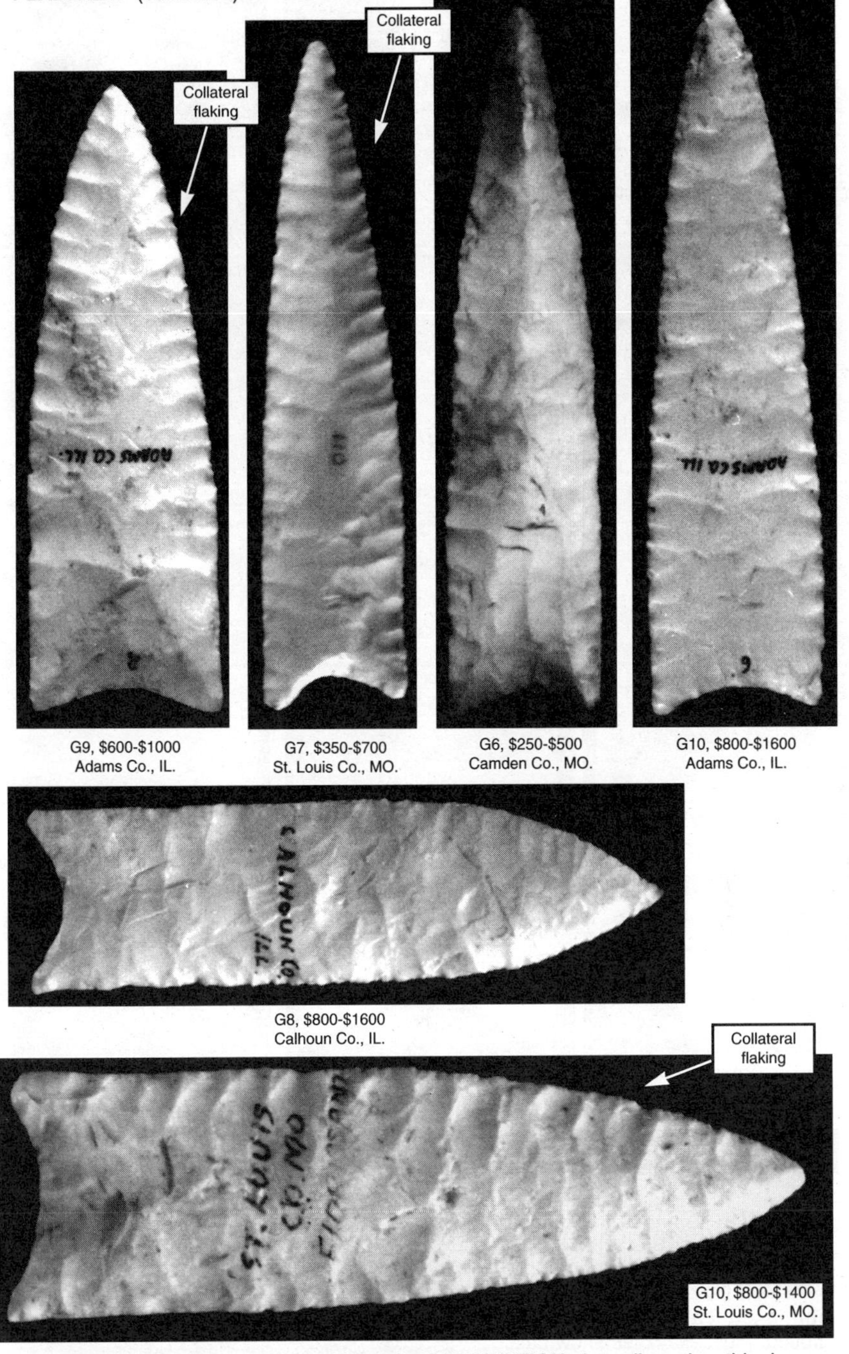

G9, $600-$1000
Adams Co., IL.

G7, $350-$700
St. Louis Co., MO.

G6, $250-$500
Camden Co., MO.

G10, $800-$1600
Adams Co., IL.

G8, $800-$1600
Calhoun Co., IL.

G10, $800-$1400
St. Louis Co., MO.

LOCATION: Midwestern states and Canada. **DESCRIPTION:** A medium size, thin, lanceolate point with usually parallel sides and a concave base that is ground. Some examples are thinned or fluted and is believed to be related to the earlier *Clovis* and contemporary *Dalton* type. Flaking is of high quality and can be collateral to oblique transverse.

Collateral flaking

G10, $2000-$3500
E. Prairie, MO.

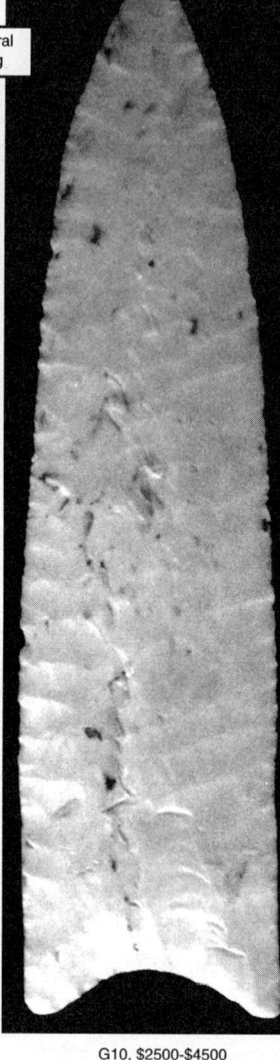

G10, $2500-$4500
Jefferson Co., MO.

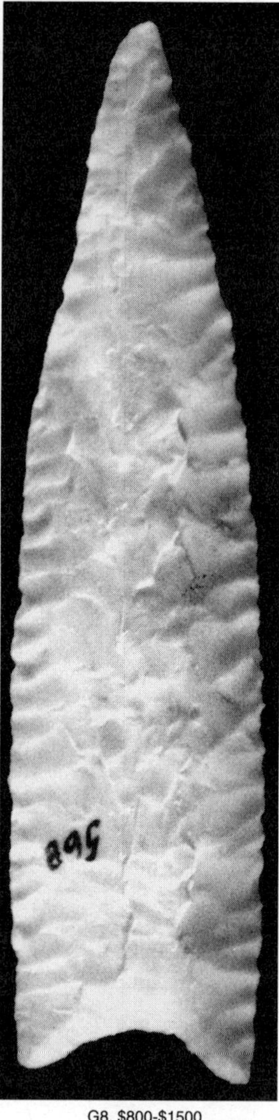

G8, $800-$1500
MO.

QUAD - Late Paleo, 10,000 - 6000 B. P.

(Also see Beaver Lake, Clovis and Cumberland)

LOCATION: Southeastern states into Missouri. **DESCRIPTION:** A medium to large size lanceolate point with flaring "squared" auricles and a concave base which is ground. Most examples show basal thinning and some are fluted. Believed to be related to the earlier Cumberland point. **I.D. KEY:** Paleo flaking, squarish auricles.

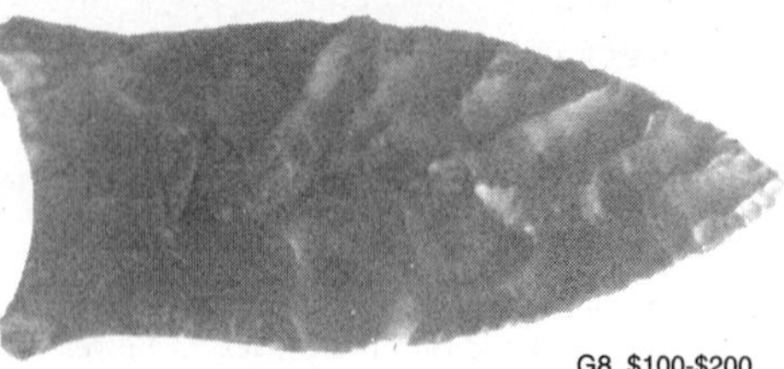

G8, $100-$200
MO.

QUAD (continued)

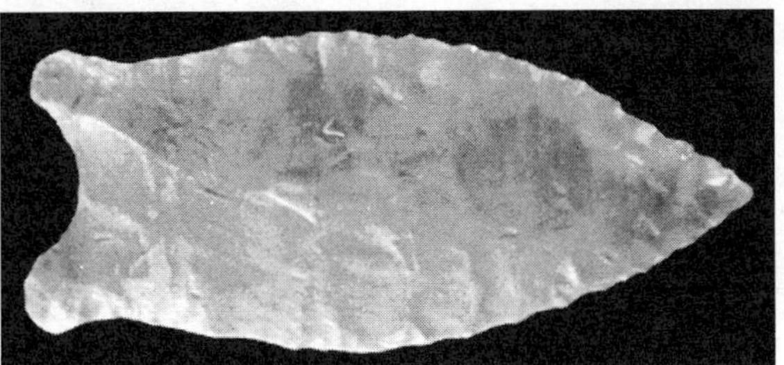

G8, $250-$500
Cape Girardeau Co., MO.

G5, $65-$125
Franklin Co., MO.

RADDATZ - Mid-Archaic to Woodland, 5000 - 2000 B. P.

(Also see Godar, Graham Cave, Hemphill, Hickory Ridge and Osceola)

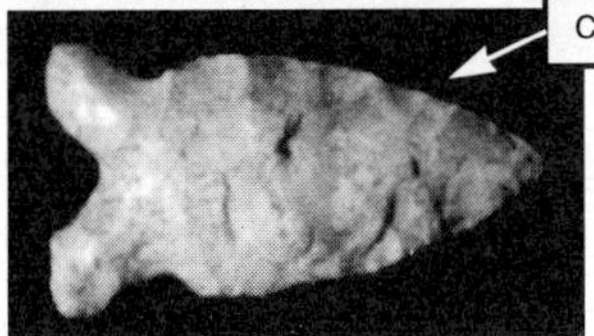

G4, $8-$15
WI.

G5, $20-$35
Sedalia, MO.

LOCATION: Illinois and Missouri. **DESCRIPTION:** A medium size, side notched point with a concave to striaght base. Similar in outline to *Hickory Ridge* points centered in Arkansas.

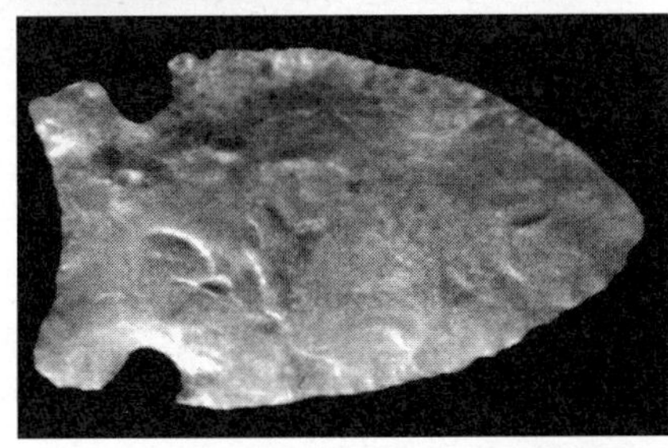

G6, $25-$45
MO.

RAMEY KNIFE- Mid-Archaic, 5000 - 4000 B. P.

(Also see Morse knife and Red Ochre)

IMPORTANT:
Shown half size

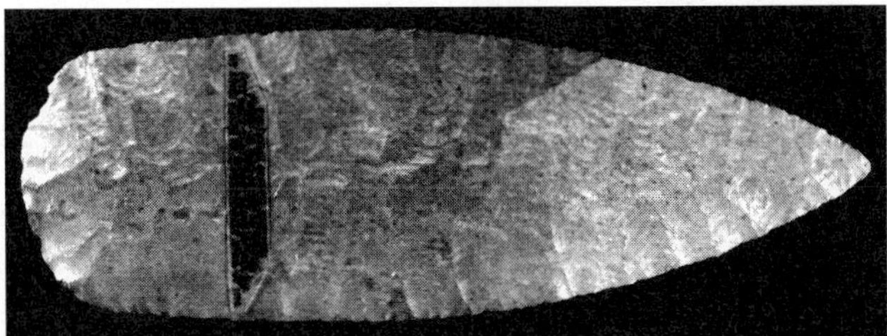

G8, $900-$1800
Calloway Co., MO.

LOCATION: Midwestern states. **DESCRIPTION:** A large size, broad, lanceolate blade with a rounded base and high quality flaking.

IMPORTANT:
Shown half size

G6, $1000-$2000 Madison Co., IL.

G10, $2500-$4500, Brown Co., IL.

G10, $1500-$3000, St. Clair Co., IL.

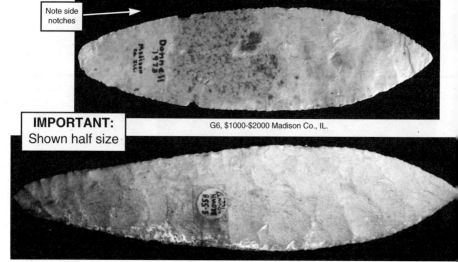

RED OCHRE - Mid to Late Archaic, 5000 - 3000 B. P.

(Also see Adena Blade, Sedalia and Wadlow)

G5, $20-$40
St. Clair Co., IL.

LOCATION: Midwestern to Southeastern states. Type site-St. Louis MO. Named by Scully ('51)- Red Ochre Mound in Fulton Co., MO. **DESCRIPTION:** A large, thin, broad blade with a contracting basal area. The base is convex to straight. Very similar to *Wadlow* which has the parallel sides. Possibly related to the *Turkeytail* type.

IMPORTANT:
All Red Ochres shown half size

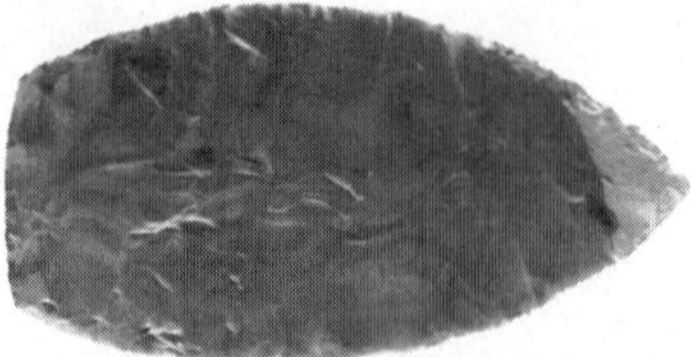

G8, $40-$80
Sikeston, MO.

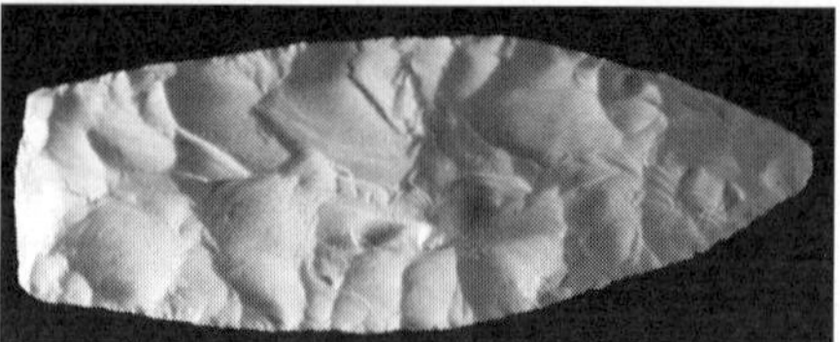

G6, $40-$80
St. Clair Co., IL. Cache

RAMEY KNIFE (con tinued)

IMPORTANT:
All Red Ochres shown half size

G10, $300-$600
St. Clair Co., IL.

RICE LOBBED - Early Archaic, 9000 - 5000 B. P.

(Also see Grand, Helton and Lundy)

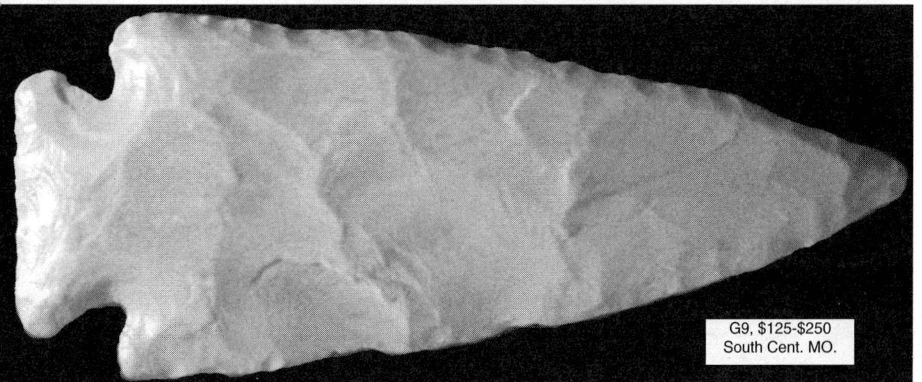

G9, $125-$250
South Cent. MO.

LOCATION: Midwestern to Northeastern states. **DESCRIPTION:** A medium to large size bifurcated to lobbed base point with serrated blade edges. The base has a shallow indentation compared to the other bifurcated types. Shoulders are sharp and prominent.

G4, $12-$20
Stone Co., MO.

ROBINSON - Late Archaic, 4000 - 3000 B. P.

(Also see Cache River, Hickory Ridge and Raddatz)

LOCATION: DESCRIPTION: A small to medium size, narrow, side-nothced point with a straight to concave base. **I.D. KEY:** Size, small basal notches.

G6, $25-$40
MO.

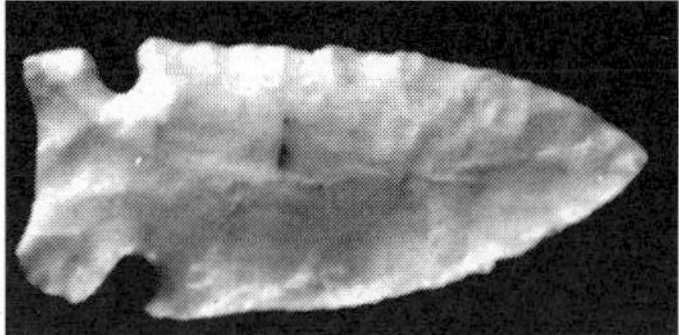

ROCHESTER - Early Archaic, 8000 - 6000 B. P.

(Also see Adena Robbins and Kramer)

ROCHESTER (continued)

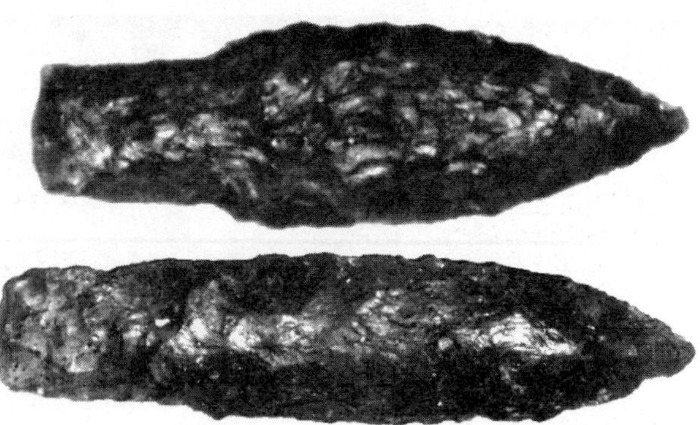

G6, $30-$50
Pottowatomie Co., KS.

LOCATION: Midwestern states. **DESCRIPTION:** A medium to large size, narrow point with weak, tapered shoulders and a long rectangular stem.

G6, $45-$90
Riley Co., KS.

ROSS- Woodland, 2500 - 1500 B. P.

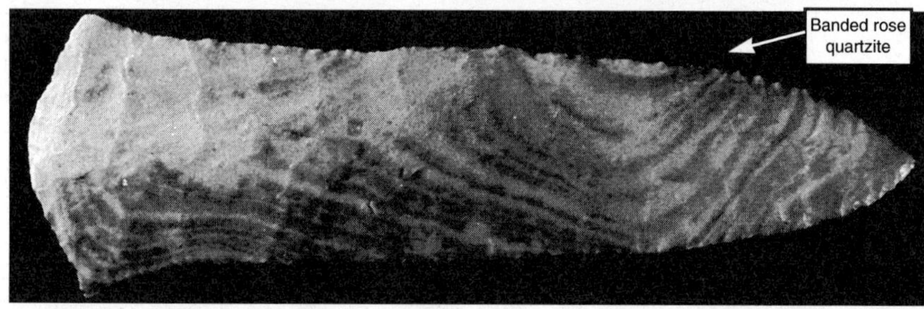

IMPORTANT: Shown half size

G10, $3000-$6000
Kent Co., MI. 9-3/4" long

LOCATION: Midwestern to Eastern states. **DESCRIPTION:** A large size ceremonial blade with an expanded, rounded base. Some examples have a contracting "V" shapened base.

ROSS COUNTY

(See Clovis)

ST. CHARLES - Early Archaic, 9500 - 8000 B. P.

(Also see Dovetail, Gibson, Grand, Helton, Kirk Corner Notched and Lost Lake)

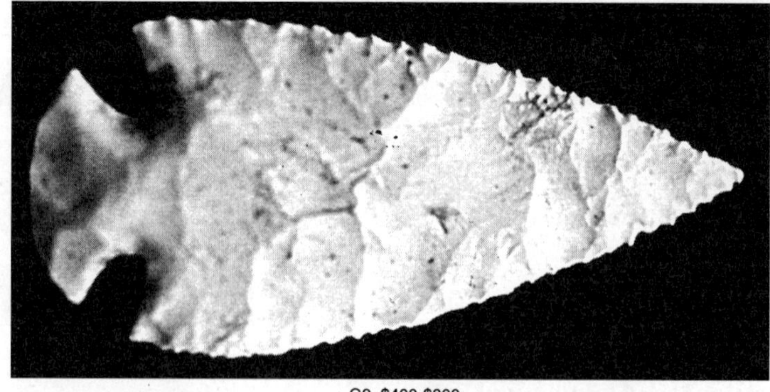

G9, $400-$800
S.W. MO.

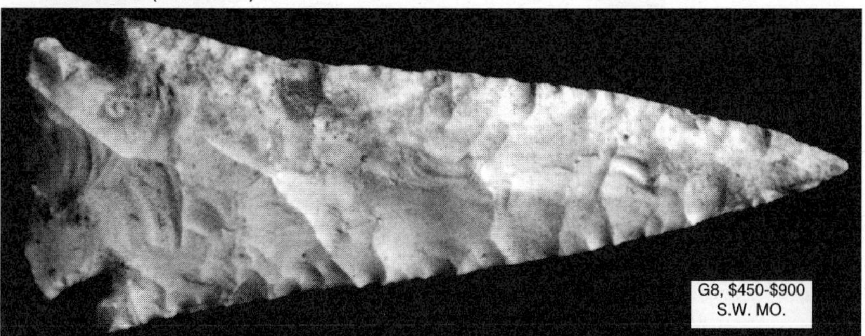

G8, $450-$900
S.W. MO.

LOCATION: Midwestern to Eastern states. **DESCRIPTION:** Also known as *Dovetail.* A medium to large size, broad, thin, elliptical, corner notched point with a dovetail base. Blade edges are beveled on opposite sides when resharpened. The base is convex and most examples exhibit high quality flaking. There is a rare variant that has the barbs clipped (clipped wing) as in the *Decatur* type. There are many variations on base style from bifurcated to eared, rounded or squared. Base size varies from small to very large. **I.D. KEY:** Dovetailed base.

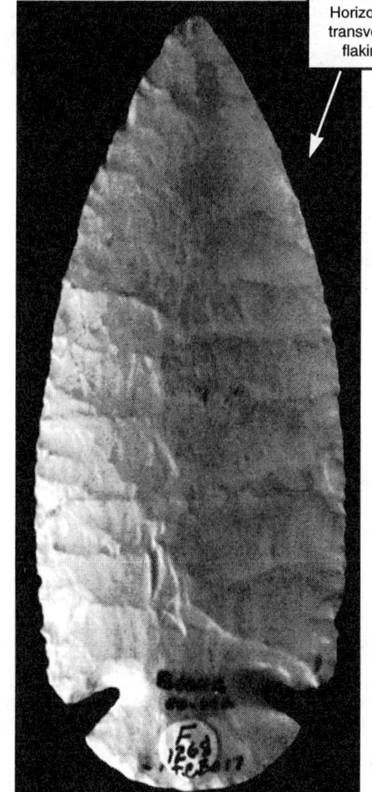

G10, $1000-$2000
Boone Co., MO.

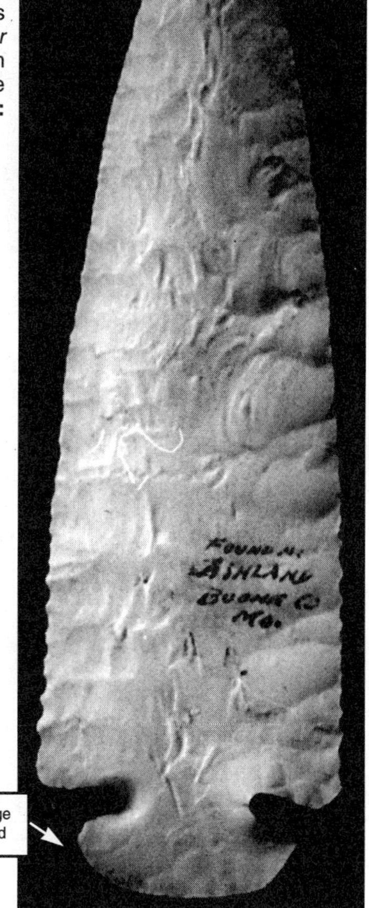

G10, $1600-$3000
Boone Co., MO.

NC

ST. CHARLES
(continued)

IMPORTANT:
Shown half
size

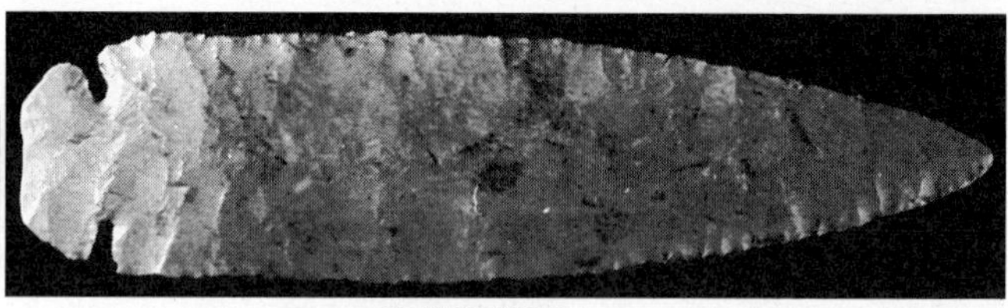

G9, $1000-$2000
Madison Co., IL.

SCOTTSBLUFF I - Transitional Paleo, 9500 - 7000 B. P.

(Also see Eden, Hardin, Holland and Stone Square Stem)

Oolithic flint

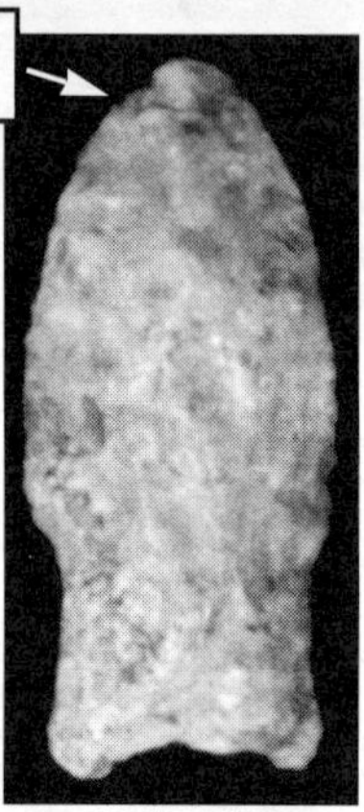

G3, $75-$150
Riley Co., KS.

G6, $180-$350
Riley Co., KS.

G4, $125-$250
MN.

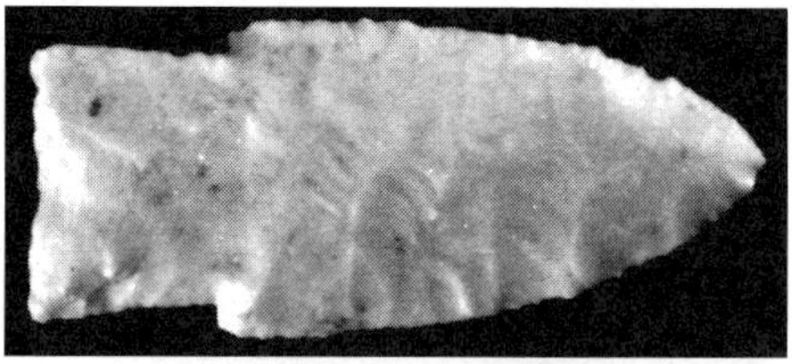

G6, $200-$400
MO.

Edge wear

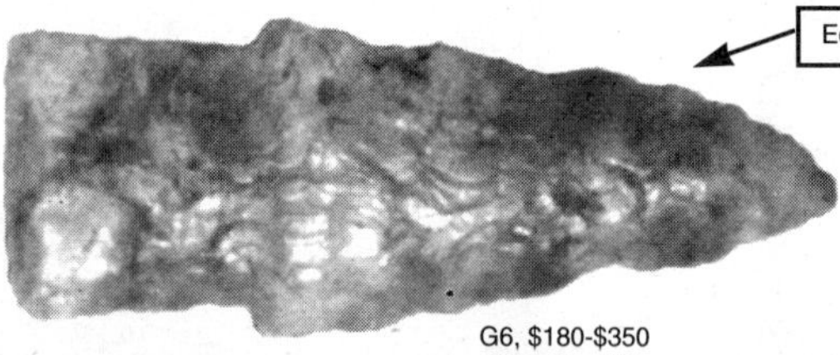

G6, $180-$350
Riley Co., KS.

Collateral flaking

G8, $600-$1200
MO.

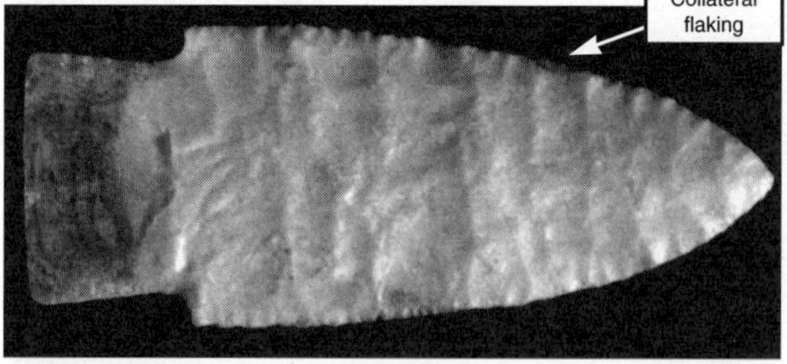

G9, $600-$1200
Kansas City, MO.

LOCATION: Midwestern states. **DESCRIPTION:** A medium to large size, broad stemmed point with convex to parallel sides and weak shoulders The stem is parallel sided to expanding.The hafting area is ground. Made by the Cody Complex people. Believed to have evolved into *Hardin* in later times. Most examples have horizontal to oblique parallel flaking and are of high quality and thinness.

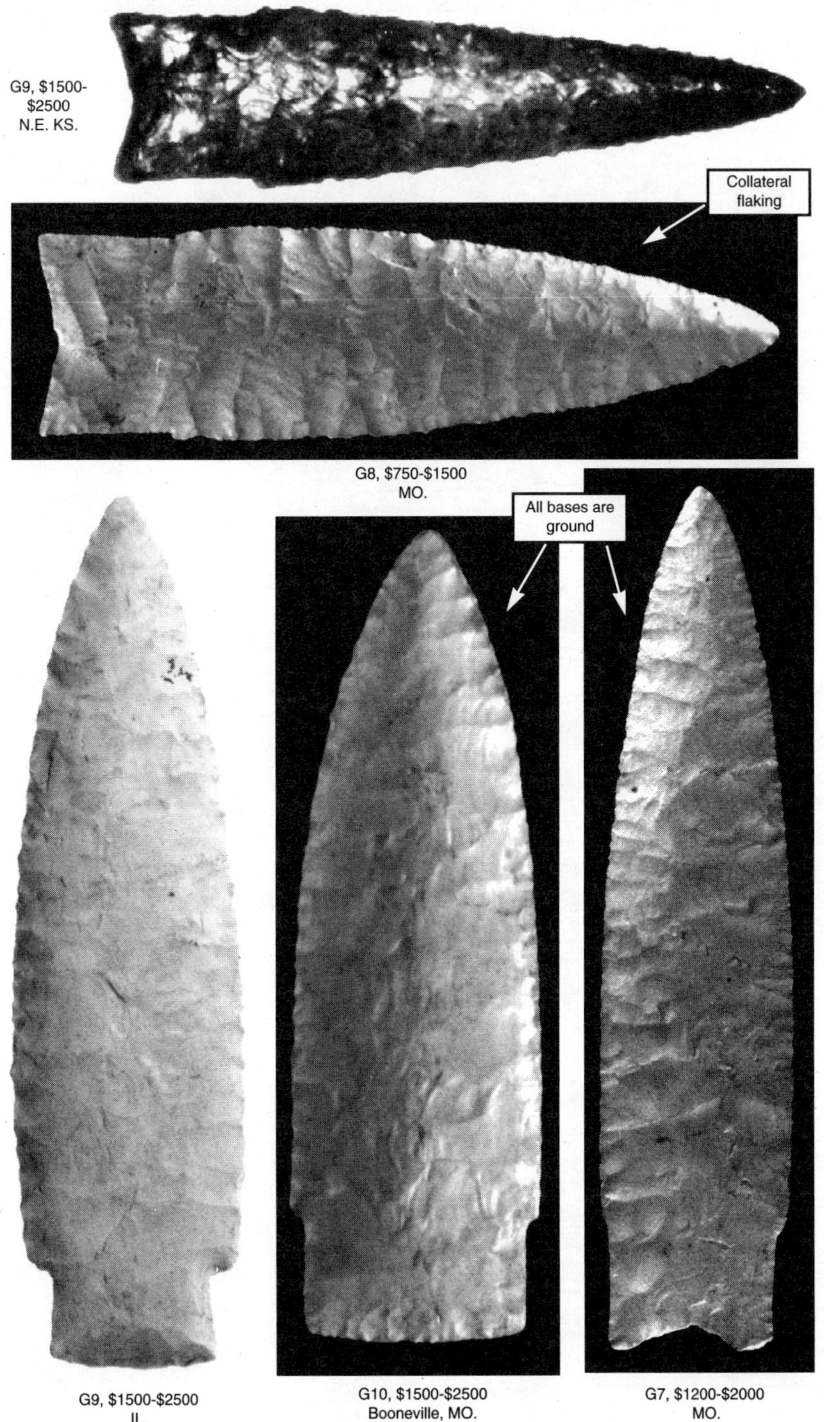

G9, $1500-$2500
N.E. KS.

G8, $750-$1500
MO.

G9, $1500-$2500
IL.

G10, $1500-$2500
Booneville, MO.

G7, $1200-$2000
MO.

SCOTTSBLUFF II - Late Paleo, 9500 - 7000 B. P.

(Also see Hardin and Holland)

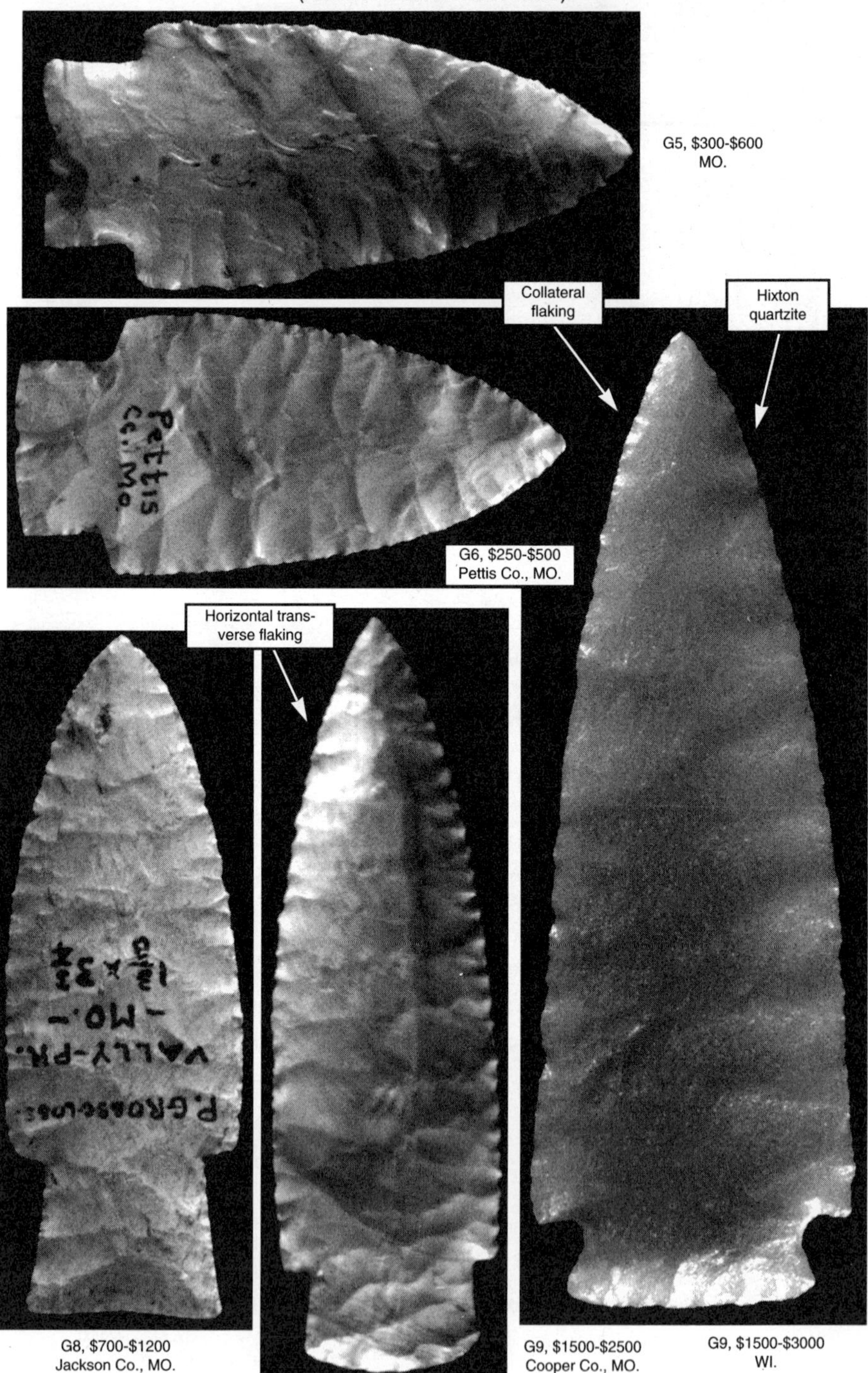

G5, $300-$600 MO.

G6, $250-$500 Pettis Co., MO.

G8, $700-$1200 Jackson Co., MO.

G9, $1500-$2500 Cooper Co., MO.

G9, $1500-$3000 WI.

SCOTTSBLUFF I (continued)

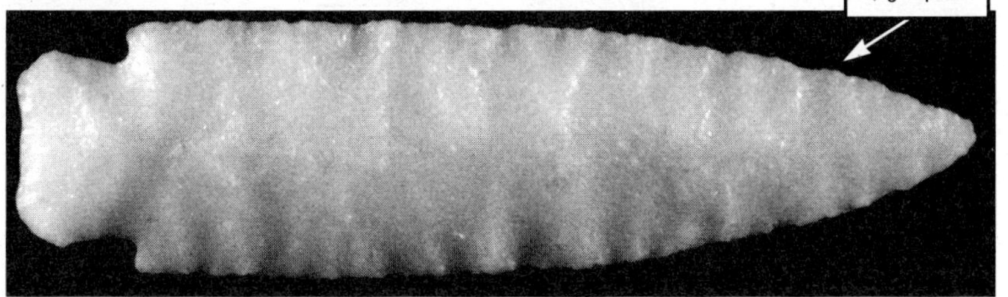

G7, $1500-$2500
MO.

LOCATION: Midwestern states. **DESCRIPTION:** A medium to large size triangular point with shoulders a little stronger than on Type I and a broad parallel sided/expanding stem.

SEDALIA - Mid-Late Archaic, 5000 - 3000 B. P.

(Also see Agate Basin, Burroughs, Lerma, Nebo Hill and Red Ochre)

G6, $65-$125
Cooper Co., MO.

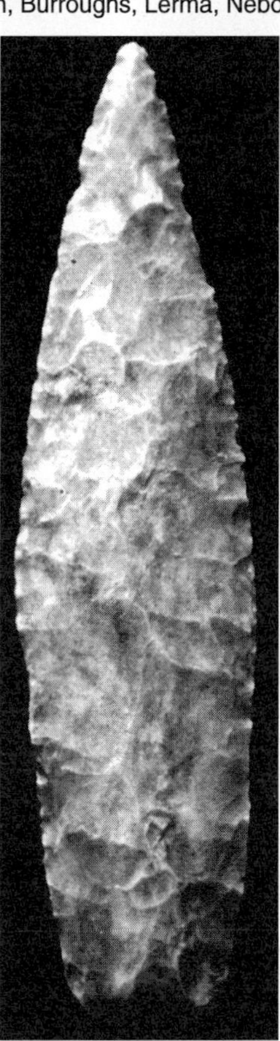

G7, $65-$125
Pettis Co., MO.

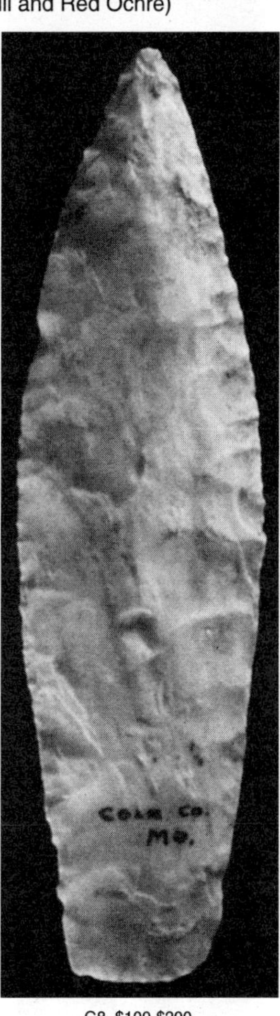

G8, $100-$200
Cole Co., MO.

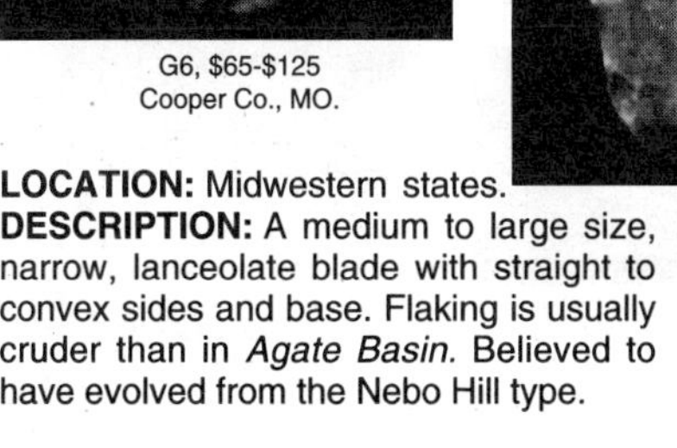

LOCATION: Midwestern states.
DESCRIPTION: A medium to large size, narrow, lanceolate blade with straight to convex sides and base. Flaking is usually cruder than in *Agate Basin.* Believed to have evolved from the Nebo Hill type.

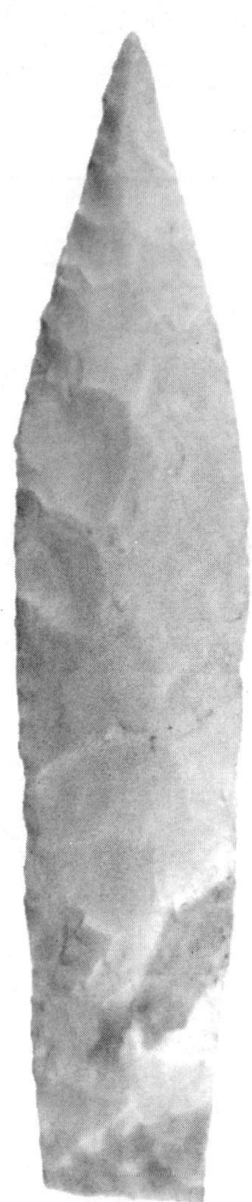

G10, $125-$250
MO.

G8, $150-$250
MO.

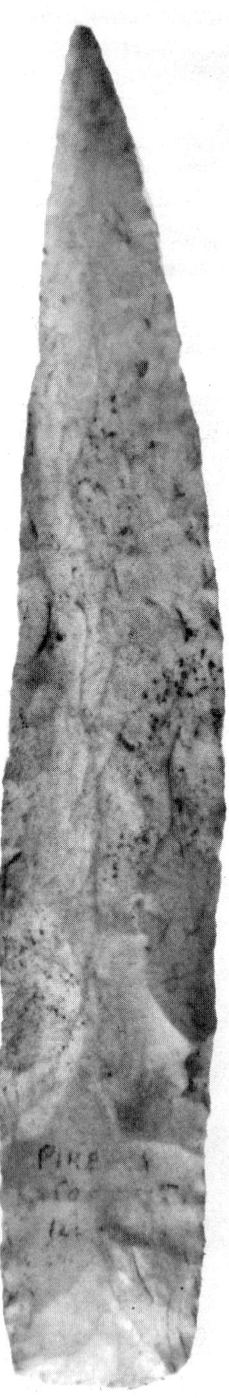

G10, $350-$700
Pike Co., IL.

SEQUOYAH - Mississippian, 1000 - 600 B. P.

(Also see Alba, Hayes and Homan)

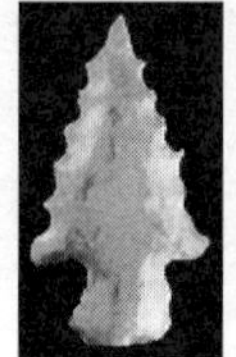

G5, $15-$25 ea.
St. Louis Co., MO.

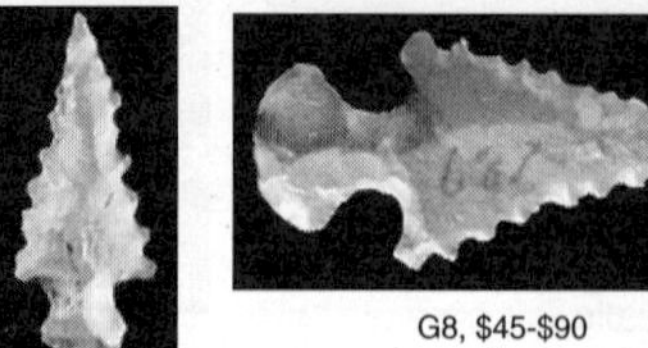

G8, $45-$90
IL.

SEQUOYAH (continued)

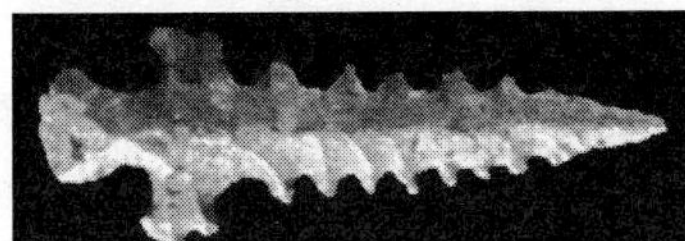
G9, $80-$150
IL.

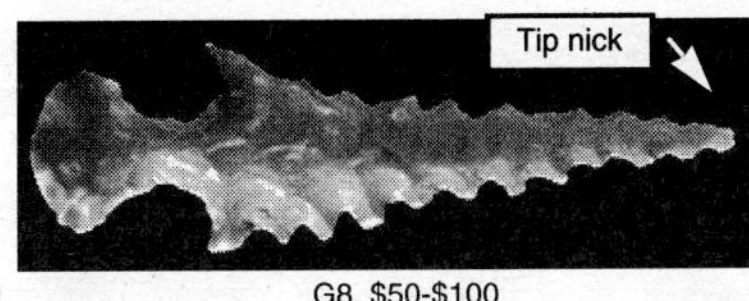

G8, $50-$100
IL.

LOCATION: IL, OK, AR, MO. **DESCRIPTION:** A small size, thin, narrow point with coarse serrations and an expanded, bulbous stem. Believed to have been made by Caddo and other people. Associated with Mississippian Caddo culture sites. Named after the famous Cherokee of the same name. **I.D. KEY:** Bulbous base, coarse serrations.

SMITH - Middle Archaic, 7000 - 4000 B. P.

(Also see Etley and Mehlville)

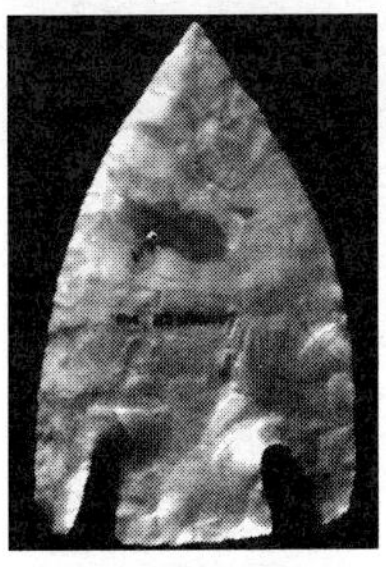
G8, $200-$400
Advance, MO.

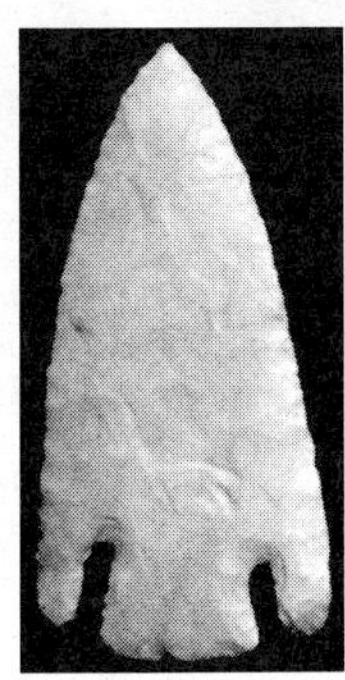
G9, $300-$550
Menard Co., IL.

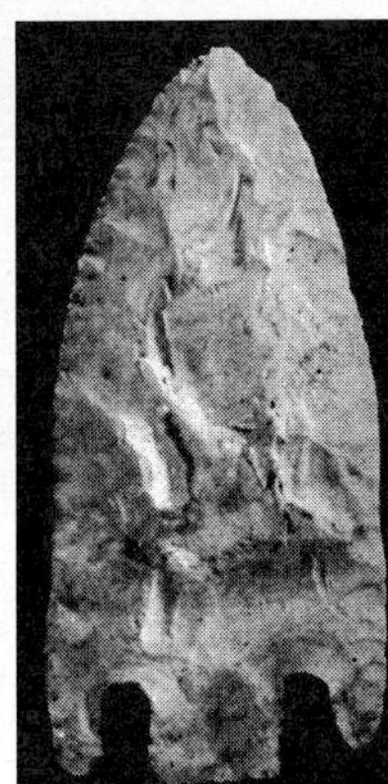
G7, $225-$450
Howard Co., MO.

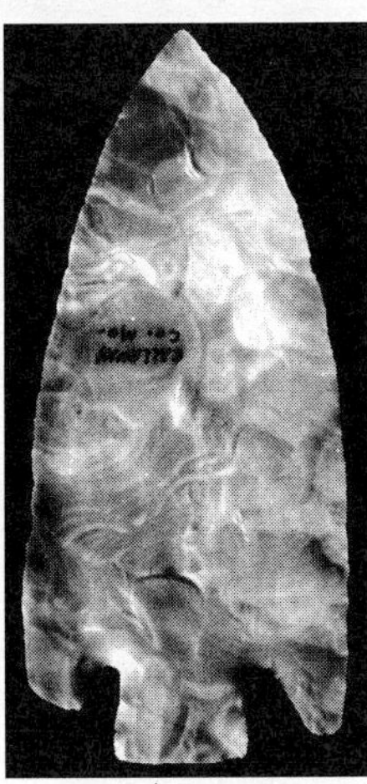
G8, $300-$600
Calloway Co., MO.

IMPORTANT:
All Smiths shown half size

NC

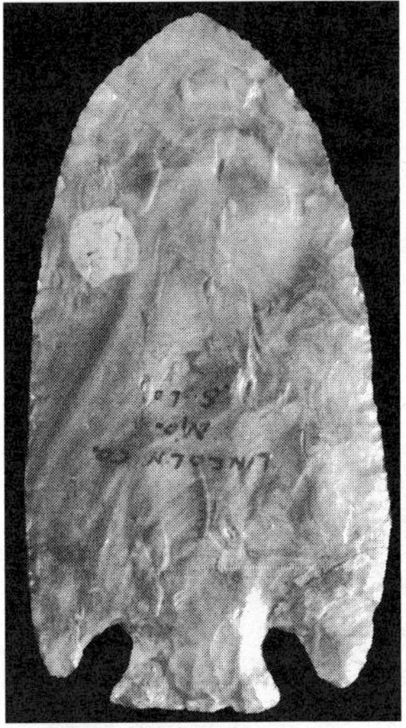
G9, $450-$900
Lincoln Co., MO.

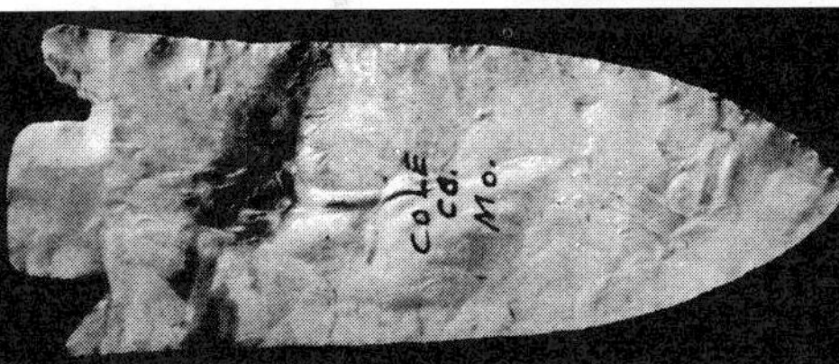

G10, $700-$1200
Cole Co., MO.

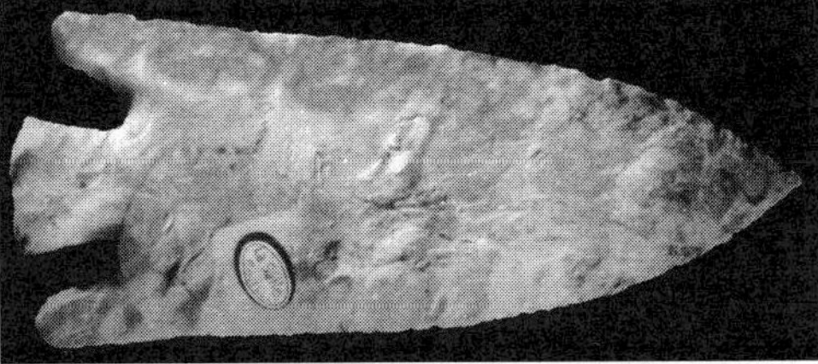
G9, $400-$800, Lasalle Co., IL.

LOCATION: Midwestern states. **DESCRIPTION:** A very large size, broad, point with long parallel shoulders and a squared to slightly expanding base. Some examples may appear to be basally notched due to the long barbs.

(Also see Carter, Grand, Helton, Hopewell and North)

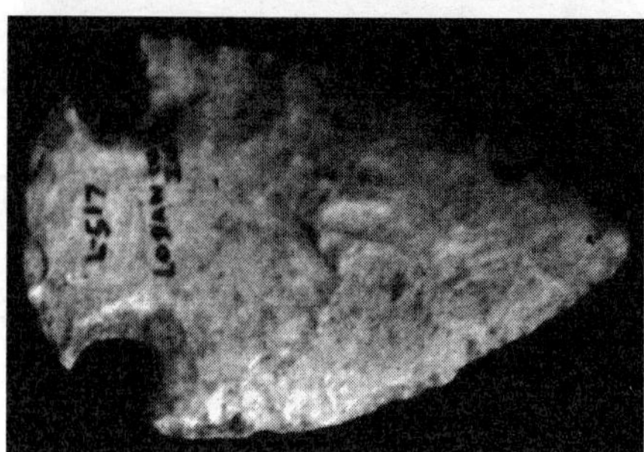

G6, $75-$150
Logan Co., IL.

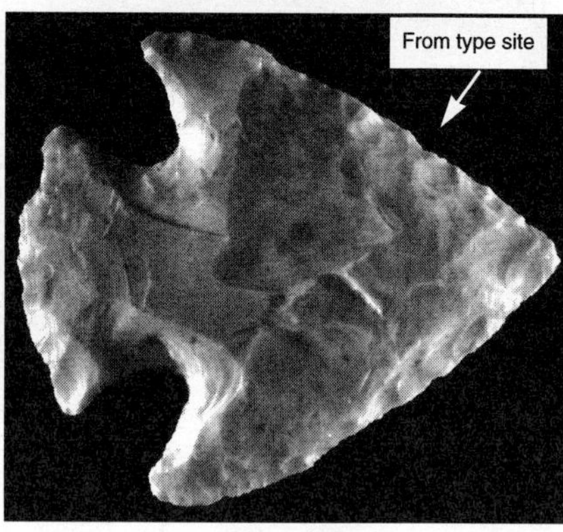

G7, $150-$250
Calhoun Co., IL.

G8, $100-$200
Livingston Co., IL.

LOCATION: Midwestern to Eastern states. Type site located in Calhoun IL., IL. **DESCRIPTION:** A medium to large size, broad, thin, wide corner notched point of high quality. Blade edges and base are convex. Many examples have intentional fractured bases. Made by the Hopewell culture.This point has been reproduced in recent years. **I.D. KEY:** Size and broad corner notches.

IMPORTANT: All Snyders points on this page shown actual size

G8, $300-$600
IL.

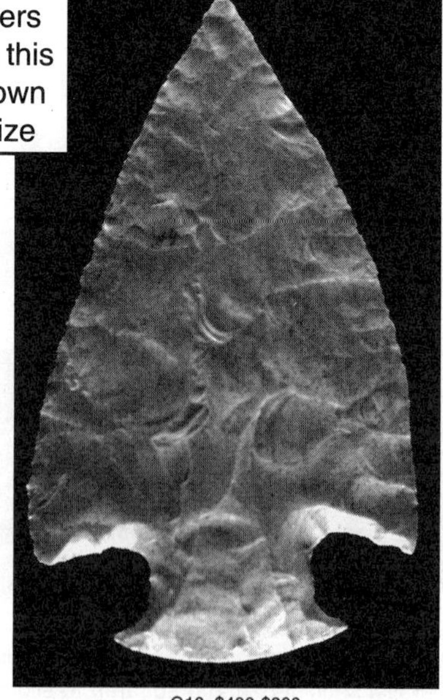

G10, $400-$800
Greene Co., IL.

G6, $125-$250, Morgan Co., IL.

G8, $175-$350
St. Clair Co., IL.

G7, $140-$275
McLean Co., IL.

G6, $250-$500
IL.

G10, $250-$400
IL.

G7, $275-$550
Lincoln Co., MO.

G7, $250-$500
IL.

G8, $170-$325
IL.

IMPORTANT:
All Snyders points on this page shown half size

G8, $300-$600
Greene Co., IL.

G9, $600-$1200
IL.

G8, $350-$700
IL.

SQUARE KNIFE - Late Paleo to Early Archaic, 10,000 - 8000 B. P.

(Also see Angostura, Red Ochre and Wadlow)

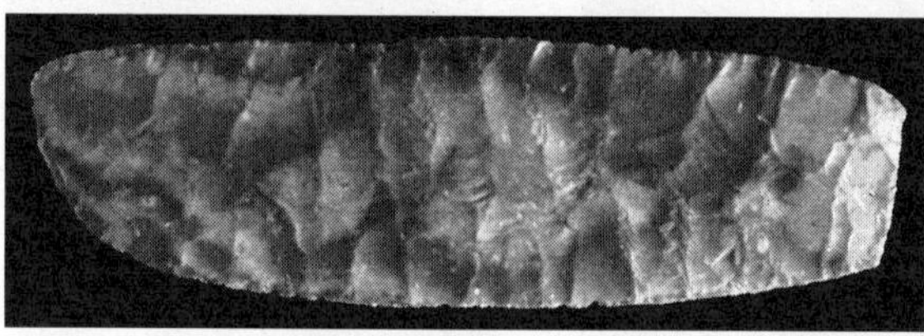

G9, $300-$600
Douglas Co., KS. Classic. Cache blade.

LOCATION: Midwestern states. **DESCRIPTION:** A medium to large size squared blade that is sometimes fluted from either or both ends on Paleo examples.

IMPORTANT: shown half size

STEUBEN- Woodland, 2000 - 1000 B. P.

(Also see Carter, Hardin, Lehigh, Matanzas, Steuben and Table Rock)

G5, $15-$25
Miller Co., MO.

G4, $8-$15
N.E. KS.

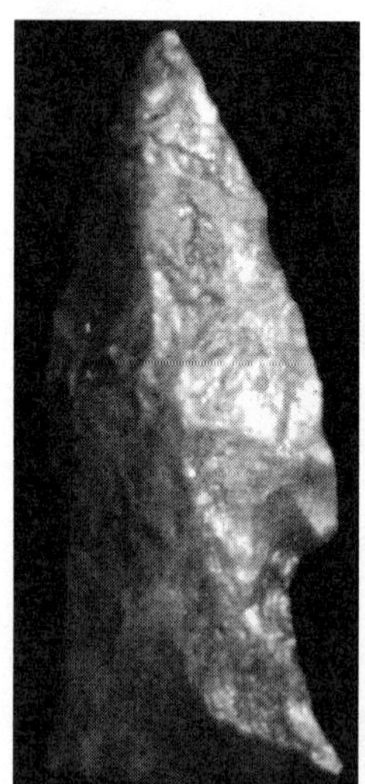

G6, $20-$40
Boone Co., MO.

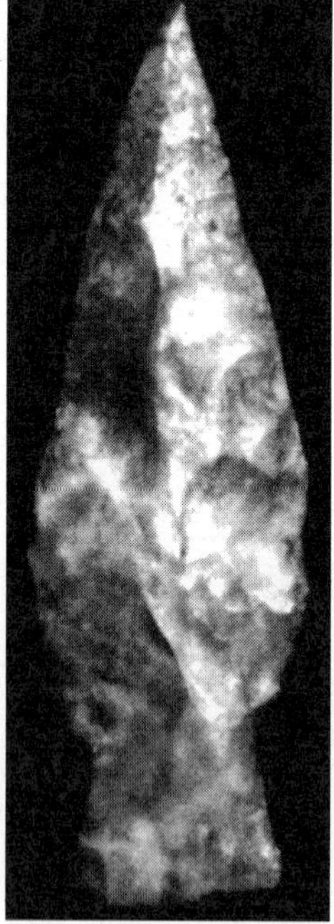

G7, $30-$60
Miller Co., MO.

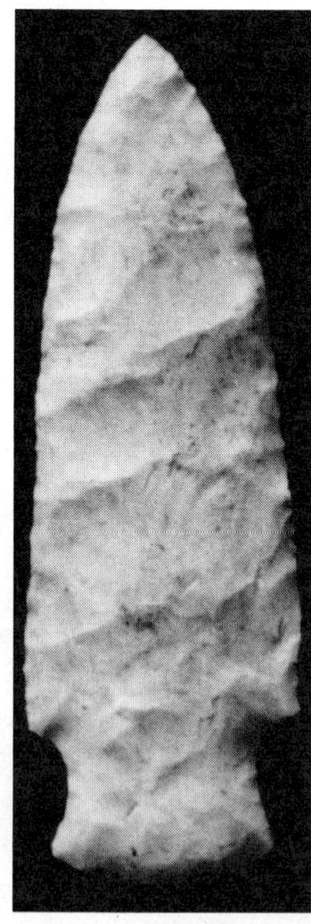

G9, $50-$100
Cherokee Co., KS.

LOCATION: Midwestern states. **DESCRIPTION:** A medium to large size, narrow point with tapered to horizontal shoulders and a medium to long expanding stem. The base is straight to convex. **I.D. KEY:** Long expanded stem.

STILWELL - Early Archaic, 9000 - 7000 B. P.

(Also see Kirk Corner Notched and Pine Tree)

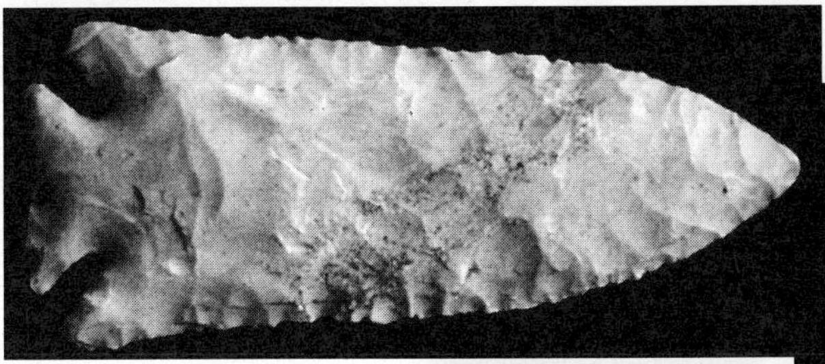

G8, $150-$300
Cherokee Co., KS.

G7, $65-$125
IL.

G8, $225-$450
IL.

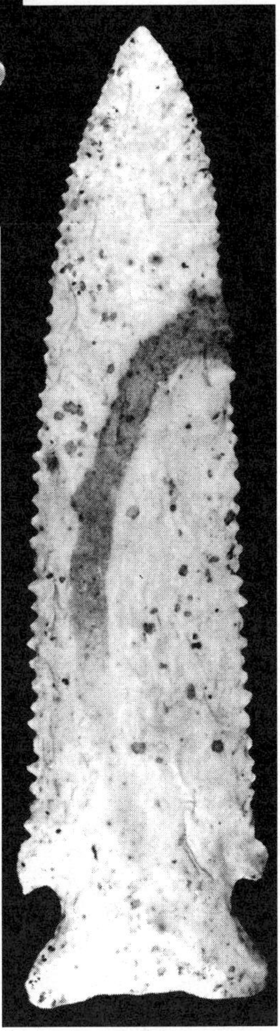

G9, $450-$900
Henry Co., IA.

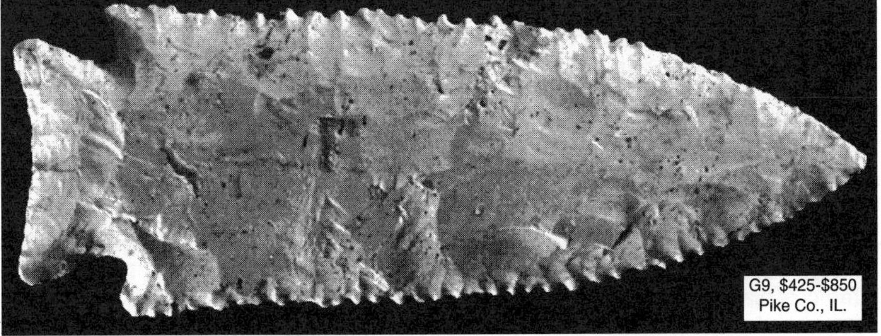

G9, $425-$850
Pike Co., IL.

NC

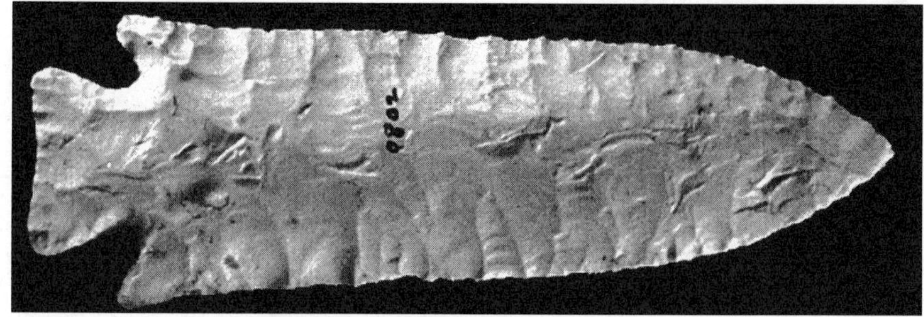

G9, $400-$800
Adams Co., IL.

G10, $1500-$2500
Stoddard Co., MO.

LOCATION: Midwestern to Eastern states. **DESCRIPTION:** A medium to large size, corner notched point with usually serrated blade edges. The shoulders are barbed. The base is concave to eared and ground. The blade edges are convex, parallel or recurved. This type may be related to *Kirk.*

STONE SQUARE STEM - Middle Archaic, 6000 - 4000 B. P.

(Also see Etley, Heavy Duty, Kramer and Rochester)

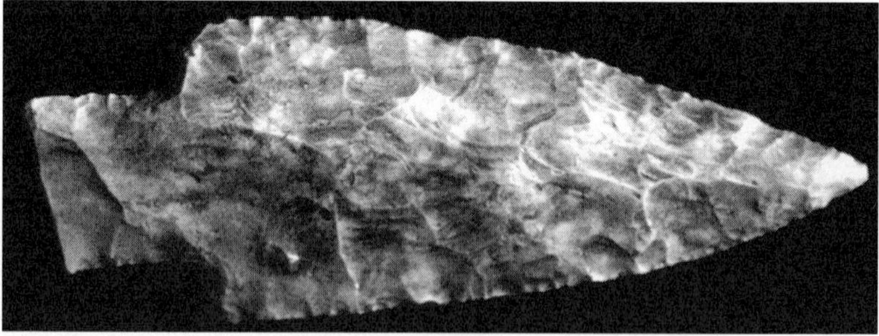

G8, $75-$150
Pettis Co., MO.

LOCATION: Midwestern states. Type site is in Stone Co., MO. **DESCRIPTION:** A medium to large size, broad stemmed point. Blade edges are convex to recurved. The shoulders are horizontal to barbed and the base is square to slightly expanding with a prominent stem.

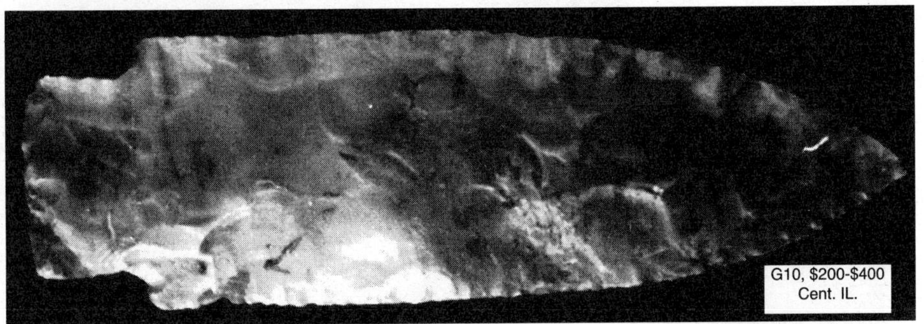

G10, $200-$400
Cent. IL.

TABLE ROCK - Late Archaic, 4000 - 3000 B. P.

(Also see Kay Blade, Lehigh and Steuben)

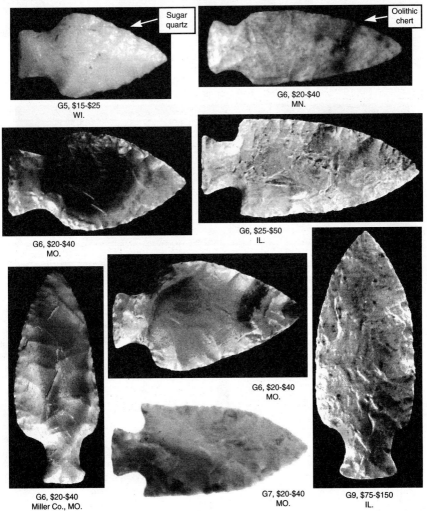

Sugar quartz

G5, $15-$25
WI.

Oolithic chert

G6, $20-$40
MN.

G6, $20-$40
MO.

G6, $25-$50
IL.

G6, $20-$40
MO.

G6, $20-$40
Miller Co., MO.

G7, $20-$40
MO.

G9, $75-$150
IL.

NC

TABLE ROCK (continued)

G6, $25-$50
MO.

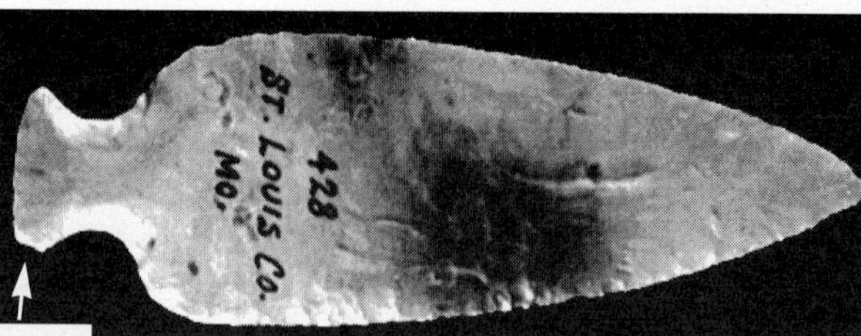

Base nick

G7, $40-$75, St. Louis Co., MO.

G8, $75-$150, St. Louis Co., MO.

LOCATION: Midwestern to Northeastern states. **DESCRIPTION:** A medium to large size, expanded stem point with straight to tapered shoulders. Shoulders can be sharp or rounded. This type is also known as a "Bottleneck" point.

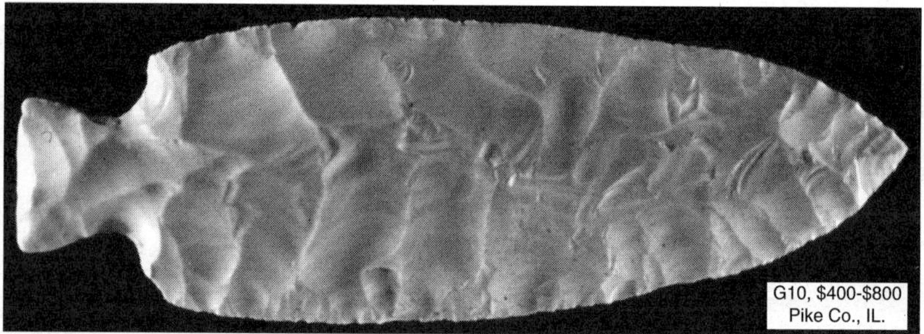

G10, $400-$800
Pike Co., IL.

THEBES - Early Archaic, 10,000 - 8000 B. P.

(Also see Dovetail, Lost Lake and Stilwell)

G6, $125-$200
IL.

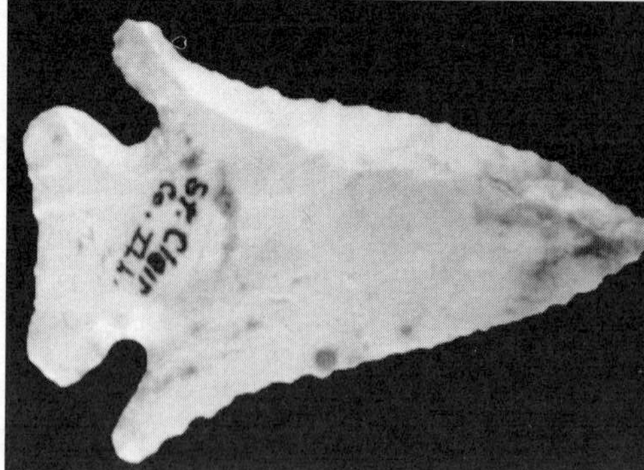

G8, $125-$200
St. Clair Co., IL.

G6, $300-$600
IL.

G6, $45-$90
IL.

G8, $175-$350
White Co., IL.

G9, $300-$600
Cass Co., IL.

G8, $300-$550
IL.

THEBES (continued)

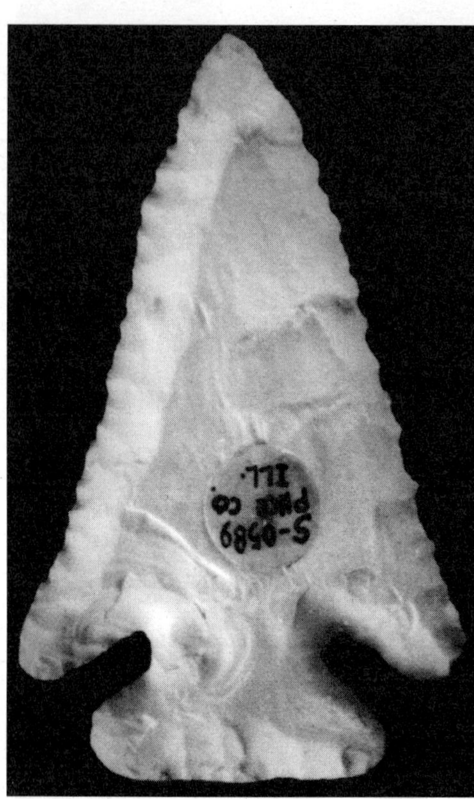

G8, $400-$800
Pike Co., IL.

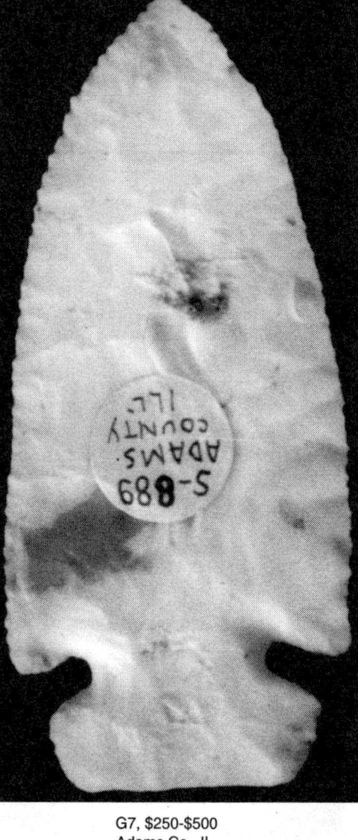

G7, $250-$500
Adams Co., IL.

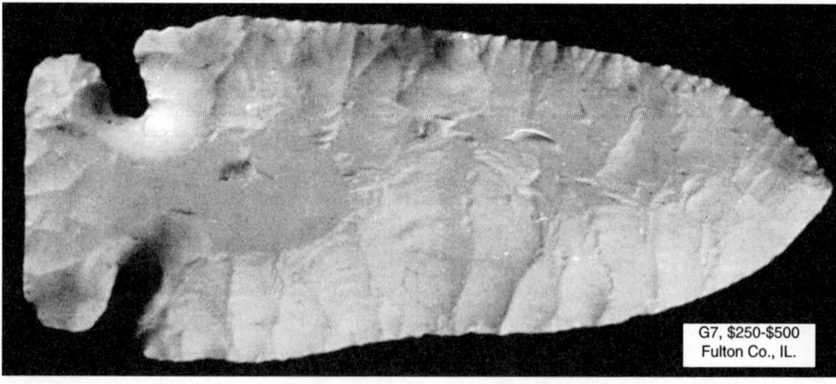

G7, $250-$500
Fulton Co., IL.

LOCATION: Midwestern states. **DESCRIPTION:** A medium to large size, wide, blade with deep, angled side notches that are parallel sided and squared. Resharpened examples have beveling on one side of each face. The bases of this type have broad proportions and are concave, straight or convex and are ground. Some examples have unusual side notches called Key notch. This type of notch is angled into the blade to produce a high point in the center, forming the letter E. See *Big Sandy E-Notched.*

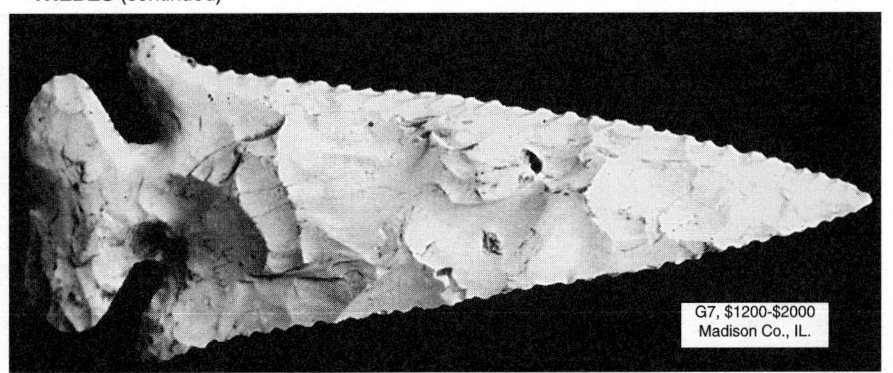

G7, $1200-$2000
Madison Co., IL.

G7, $250-$500
Adams Co., IL.

TURKEYTAIL-FULTON- Late Archaic to Woodland, 4000 - 2500 B. P.

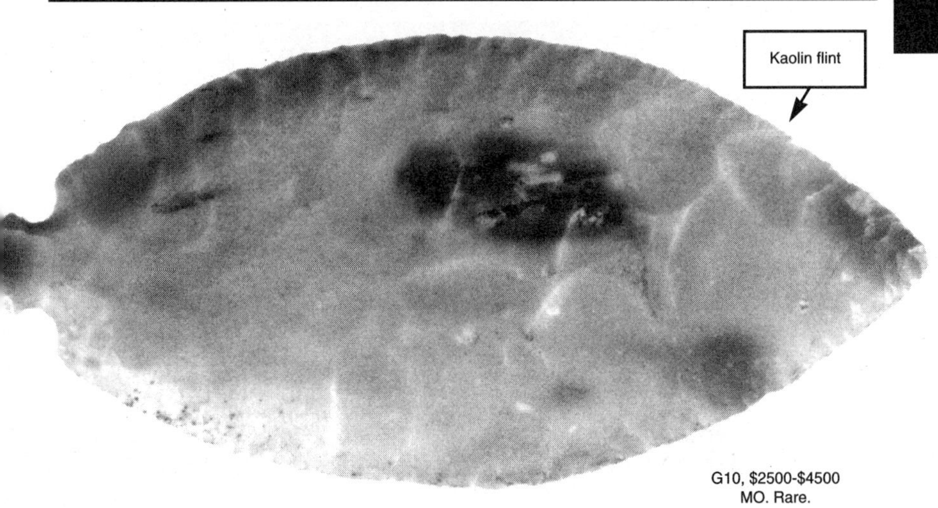

G10, $2500-$4500
MO. Rare.

G8, $800-$1400
St. Charles Co., MO.

LOCATION: Midwestern to Eastern states. **DESCRIPTION:** A medium to large size, wide, thin, elliptical blade with shallow notches very close to the base. This type is usually found in caches and has been reproduced in recent years. Made by the Adena culture. Found in late *Benton* caches in Mississippi carbon dated to about 4000 B.P.

TURKEYTAIL-HARRISON - Late Archaic to Woodland, 4000 - 2500 B. P.

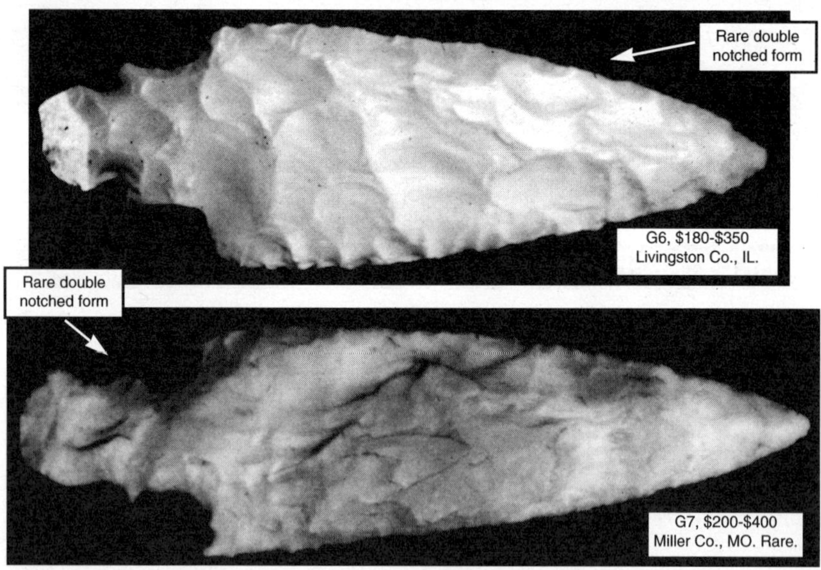

G6, $180-$350
Livingston Co., IL.

G7, $200-$400
Miller Co., MO. Rare.

LOCATION: Midwestern to Eastern states. **DESCRIPTION:** A medium to large size, narrow, elliptical tapered, horizontal or barbed shoulders, and an elongated, diamond-shaped stem in the form of a turkey's tail. Large examples may have fine pressure flaking on one edge of each face. Made by the Adena culture. Lengths up to 20 inches know.

WADLOW - Late Archaic, 4000 - 2500 B. P.

(Also see Cobbs Triangular, Etley and Red Ochre)

G9, $250-$500
Ralls Co., MO.

G6, $175-$350
MO.

G5, $50-$100
MO.

G8, $75-$150
IL.

G8, $1500-$3000
Cooper Co., MO.

LOCATION: Midwestern states.Type site-The Etley site, Calhoun Co., IL. Walter Wadlow first discovered this form in 1939, Jersey Co., IL. **DESCRIPTION:** A large to very large size, broad, parallel sided blade with a straight to convex base. The preform for the *Etley* point.

WADLOW (continued)

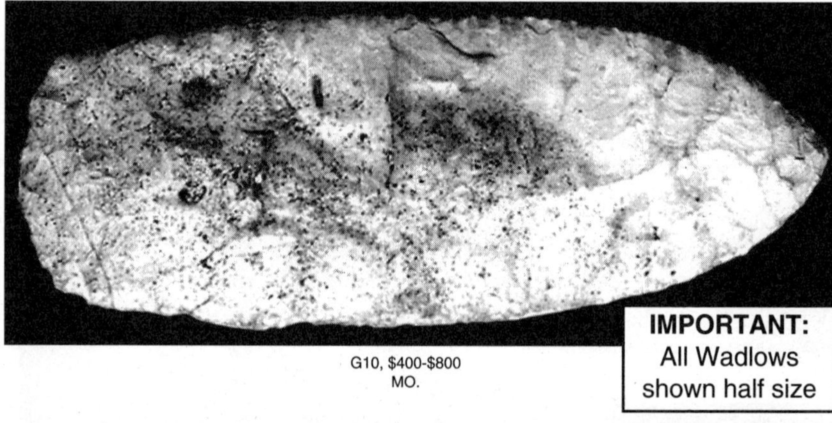

G10, $400-$800
MO.

IMPORTANT:
All Wadlows
shown half size

WARRICK - Early Archaic, 9000 - 5000 B. P.

(Also see Cobbs Triangular, Dovetail)

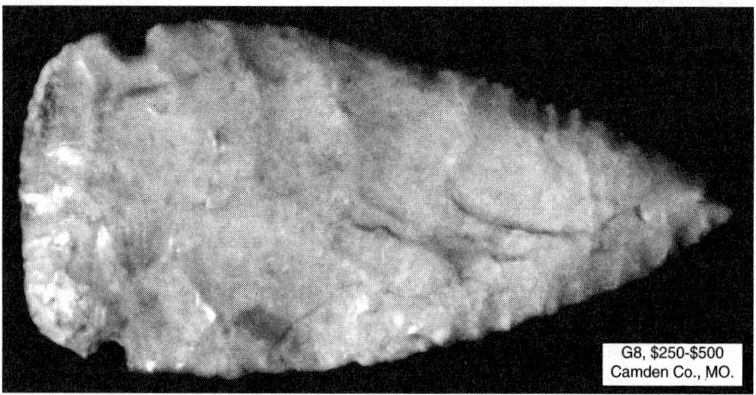

G8, $250-$500
Camden Co., MO.

LOCATION: Midwestern states. **DESCRIPTION:** A small size, thin, triangular side notched arrow point with a concave base. Basal area is usually large in proportion to the blade size.

WASHITA - Mississippian, 800 - 400 B. P.

(Also see Cahokia and Huffaker)

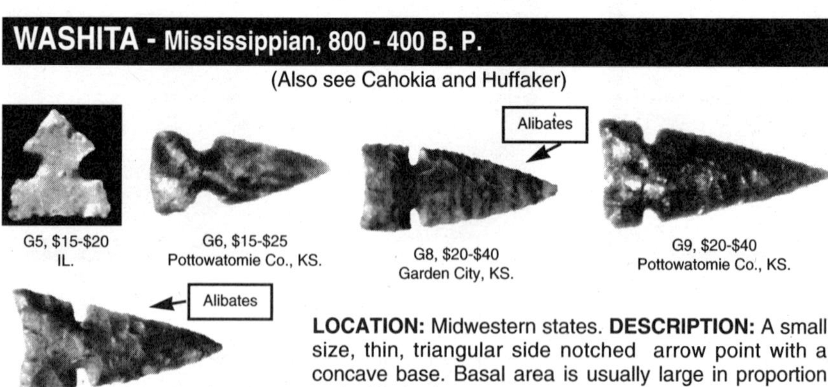

G5, $15-$20
IL.

G6, $15-$25
Pottowatomie Co., KS.

G8, $20-$40
Garden City, KS.

G9, $20-$40
Pottowatomie Co., KS.

G10, $125-$250
Garden City, KS.

LOCATION: Midwestern states. **DESCRIPTION:** A small size, thin, triangular side notched arrow point with a concave base. Basal area is usually large in proportion to the blade size.

DESERT SOUTHWEST SECTION:

This section includes point types from the following states: Arizona, Colorado, Nevada, New Mexico, Texas, Utah and from Mexico

The points in this section are arranged in alphabetical order and are shown **actual size**. All types are listed that were available for photographing. Any missing types will be added to future editions as photographs become available. We are always interested in receiving sharp, black and white or color glossy photos or color slides of your collection. Be sure to include a ruler in the photograph so that proper scale can be determined.

Lithics: Materials employed in the manufacture of projectile points from this region are: agate, basalt, chalcedony, chert, jasper, obsidian, petrified wood, quartzite, siltstone.

Important sites: Clovis (Paleo), Blackwater Draw, NM. Folsom (Paleo), Folsom NM. Sandia (Paleo), Sandia Cave, NM.

SPECIAL SENIOR ADVISOR:
Charles D. Meyer

Other advisors:
John Byrd
William H. "Bill" Dickey
George E. Johnston
William J. "Bill" Creighton
Jeb Taylor

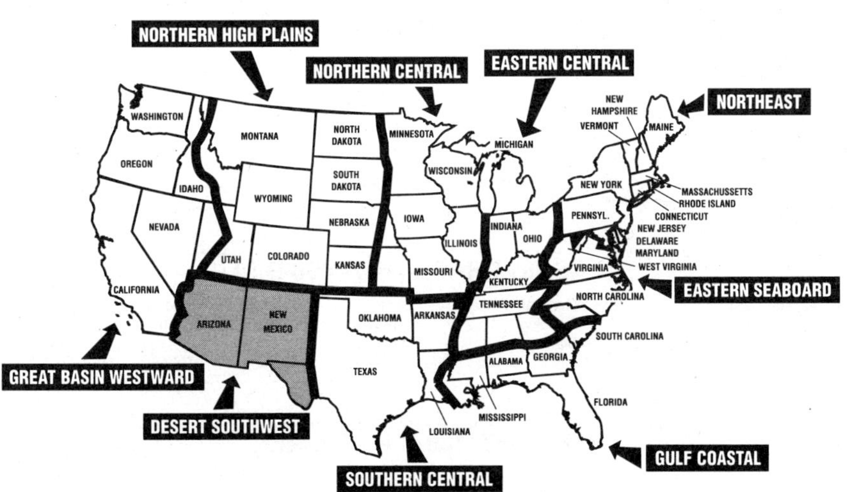

SW

DESERT SOUTHWEST POINT TYPES

(Archaeological Periods)

PALEO (14,000 B.P - 8,000 B.P.)

Clovis
Drill
Folsom
Midland
Milnesand
Sandia

EARLY ARCHAIC (10,500 B.P - 5,500 B.P.)

Agate Basin
Allen
Angostura
Augustin
Bat Cave
Datil
Eden
Escobas
Firstview
Hell Gap
Lake Mohave
Lancet
Matamoros
McKean
Meserve
Mount Albion
Pelona
Rio Grande
San Jose
Scottsbluff
Silver Lake
Texcoco
Ventana-Amargosa

MIDDLE ARCHAIC (5,500 B.P - 3,300 B.P.)

Chiricahua
Duncan
Gatecliff
Gypsum Cave
Hanna
Lerma
Matamoros
McKean
Neff
Squaw Mountain
Triple T
Val Verde

LATE ARCHAIC (3,500 B.P - 2,300 B.P.)

Bajada
Basal Double Tang
Catan
Conejo
Duran
Elko Corner Notched
Elko Eared
Maljamar
Martis
Patticus
San Pedro
Sierra Stemmed
Yavapai

DESERT TRADITIONS:
TRANSITIONAL (2,300 B.P - 1600 B.P.)

Figueroa
Humboldt
Humboldt Constricted Base

DEVELOPMENTAL (1600 - 700 B.P)

Ahumada
Bull Creek
Colonial
Deadman's
Dry Prong
Eastgate Split-Stem
Gila Butte
Hohokam
Nawthis
Parowan
Rose Springs Corner Notched
Rose Springs Contracted Base
Rose Springs Side Notched
Sacaton
Salado
Santa Cruz
Snaketown
Soto
Temporal
Truxton

CLASSIC PHASE (700 - 400 B.P)

Cottonwood Leaf
Cottonwood Triangle
Desert-Delta
Desert-General
Desert-Redding
Desert-Sierra
Garza
Lott
Mescal Knife
Red Horn
Toyah

HISTORIC (400 B.P - Present)

Papago
Trade

DESERT SOUTHWEST
THUMBNAIL GUIDE SECTION

The following references are provided to aid the collector in easier and quicker identification of point types. All photos are exactly 30% of acutal size and are proportional to each other. Each point pictured in this section represents a classic form for the type. When a match is found, go to the alphabetical location of that type for more examples in true actual size.

1 THUMBNAIL GUIDE - AURICULATE FORMS (30% actual size)

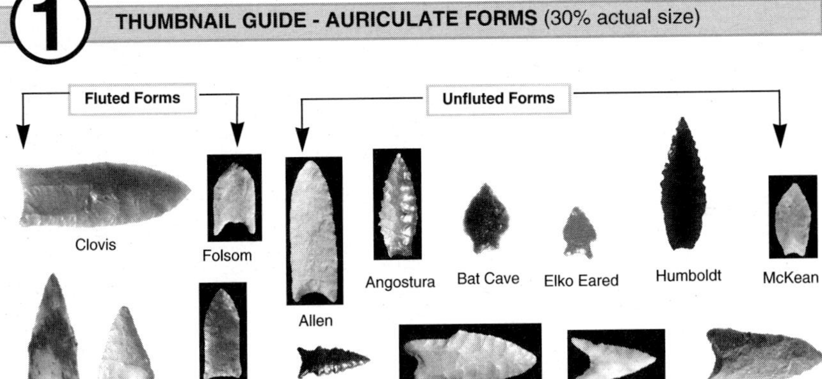

2 THUMBNAIL GUIDE - LANCEOLATE FORMS (30% actual size)

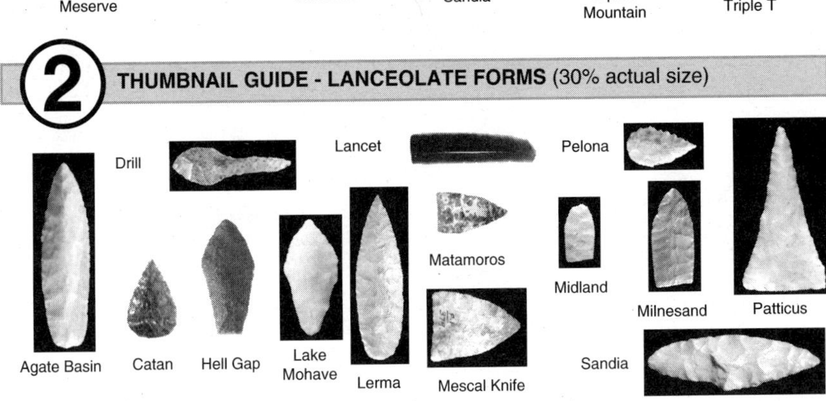

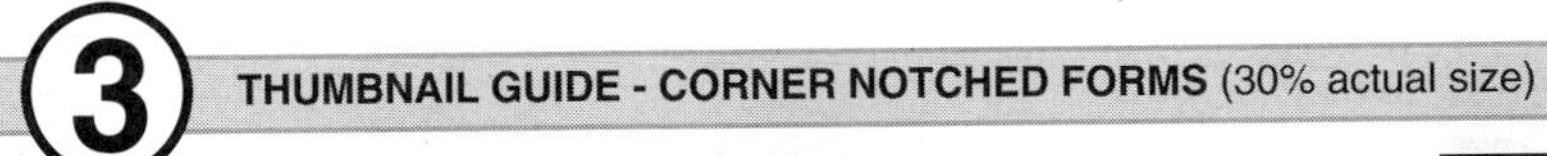

3 THUMBNAIL GUIDE - CORNER NOTCHED FORMS (30% actual size)

Elko Corner

Mount Albion

Rose Springs

Texcoco

4 THUMBNAILGUIDE - SIDE NOTCHED FORMS (30% actual size)

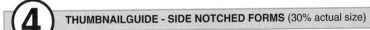

Rose Springs

San Jose

San Pedro

Squaw Mountain

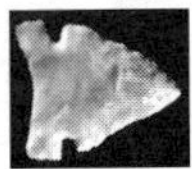

Texcoco

SW

5 THUMBNAIL GUIDE - STEMMED FORMS (30% of actual size)

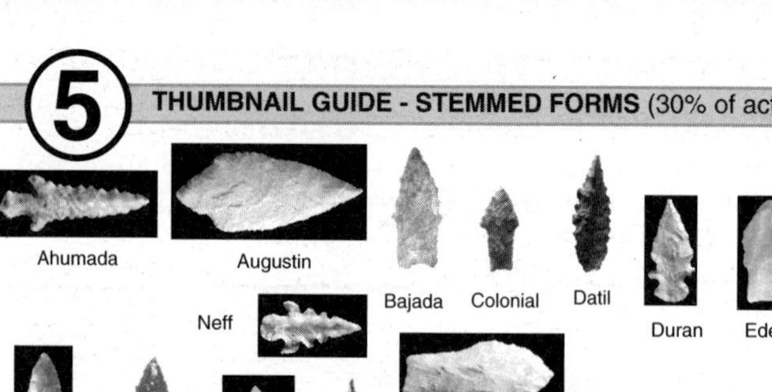

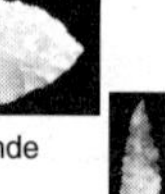

Ahumada, Augustin, Bajada, Colonial, Datil, Duran, Eden, Escobas, Figueroa, Neff, Firstview, Gatecliff, Gypsum Cave, Maljamar, Rio Grande, Rose Springs Contracted, Scottsbluff, Sierra Stemmed, Silver Lake, Trade, Truxton, Val Verde, Ventana-Amargosa, Yavapai

6 THUMBNAIL GUIDE - STEMMED-BIFURCATED FORMS (30% of actual size)

Chiricauha, Conejo, Duncan, Eastgate Split Stem, Hanna

7 THUMBNAIL GUIDE - BASAL NOTCHED FORMS (30% of actual size)

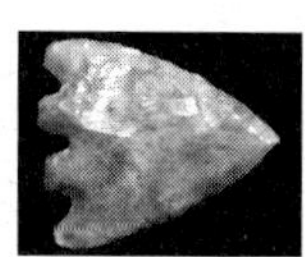
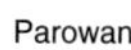

Basal Double Tang, Parowan

8 THUMBNAIL GUIDE - ARROW POINTS (30% of actual size)

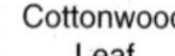

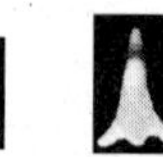

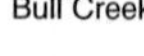

Cottonwood Leaf, Bull Creek, Cottonwood Triangle, Deadman's, Desert Delta, Desert General, Desert Redding, Desert Sierra, Dry Prong, Garza, Gila Butte, Nawthis, Sacaton, Rose Springs, Temporal, Hohokam, Lott, Papago, Red Horn, Salado, Santa Cruz, Snaketown, Soto, Toyah

AGATE BASIN - Early Archaic, 10,500 - 10,000 B.P.

(Also see Allen, Angostura, Lerma)

G4, $75-$150
Yavapai Co.,
AZ.

G7, $100-$200
NM

G8, $150-$300
Chaves Co., NM

LOCATION: New Mexico eastward to Pennsylvania. **DESCRIPTION:** A medium to large size lanceolate blade of high quality. Bases are either convex, concave or straight and are usually ground. Some examples are median ridged. **I.D. KEY:** Basal form and flaking style.

AHUMADA - Desert Tradition-Developmental Phase, 1250 - 1100 B.P.

(Also see Maljamar, Neff and Truxton)

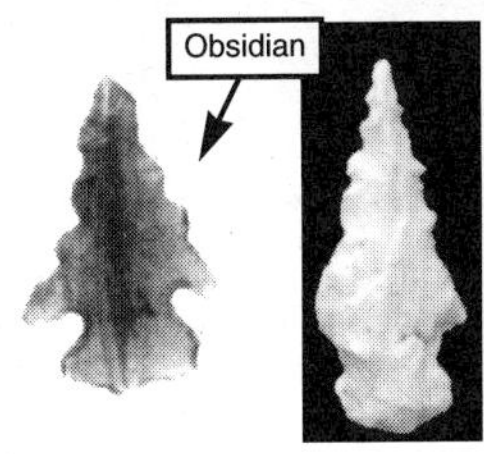

G7, $20-$40
Cochise Co., AZ

G3, $2-$5
Luna Co., NM.

G3, $5-$10
Apache Co., AZ

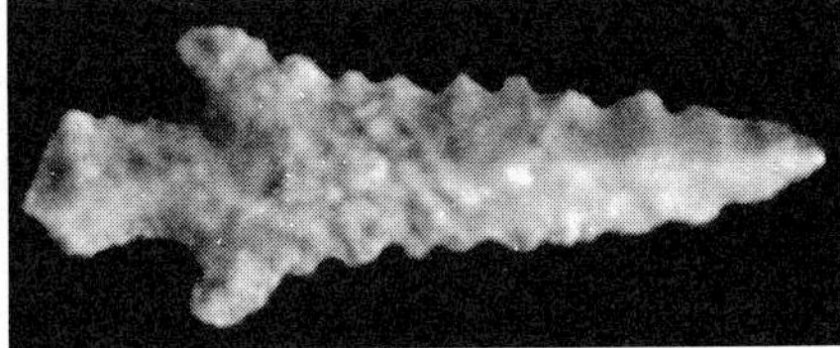

G7, $20-$40
Pinal Co., AZ

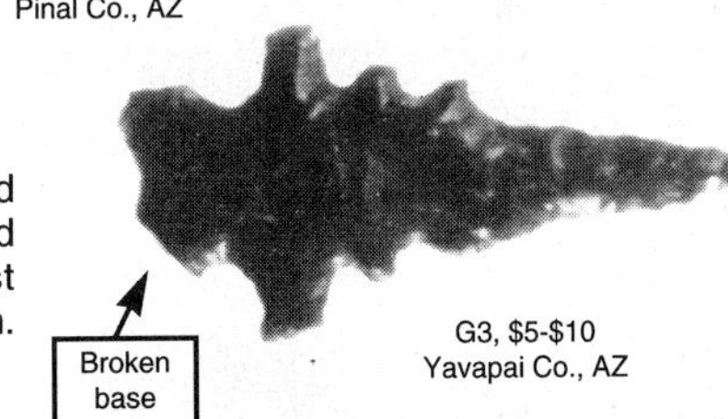

G3, $5-$10
Yavapai Co., AZ

LOCATION: Arizona, New Mexico and Mexico. **DESCRIPTION:** A corner notched arrow point with a triangular blade; almost always serrated and with an expanding stem. **I.D. KEY:** Fan shaped stem and serrations.

SW

ALLEN - Early Archaic, 10,000 - 9500 B.P.

(Also see Angostura, Clovis, Humboldt and McKean)

LOCATION: New Mexico to Canada. **DESCRIPTION:** A small to medium size lanceolate point that has oblique transverse flaking and a ground concave base. **I.D. KEY:** Flaking style and blade form.

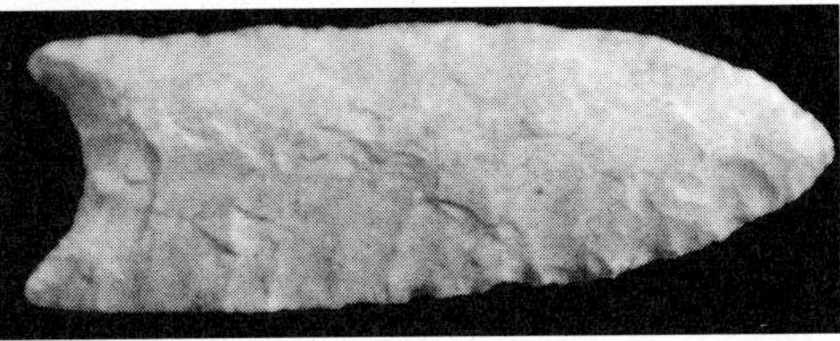

G8, $250-$500
Chaves Co., NM

ALLEN (continued)

G2, $50-$100
NM.

ANGOSTURA - Early Archaic, 10,000 - 8000 B.P.

(Also see Allen, Clovis and Humboldt)

G3, $30-$60
S.W. CO.

G1, $20-$40
CO. Broken back.

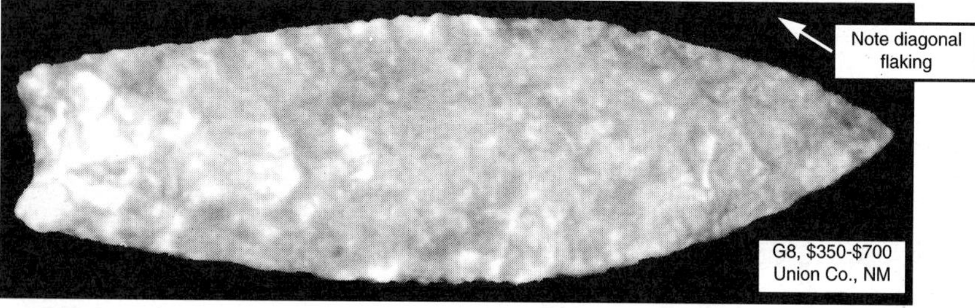

G8, $350-$700
Union Co., NM

LOCATION: Southwestern states. **DESCRIPTION:** A medium to large size lanceolate blade of unusually high quality. Bases are either convex, concave or straight and are usually ground. Most examples have oblique transverse flaking. **I.D. KEY:** Basal form and flaking style.

AUGUSTIN - Early to Middle Archaic, 7000- 5000 B.P.

(Also see Gypsum Cave, and Santa Cruz)

G6, $20-$40
Cochise Co., AZ.

G4, $10-$20
Hidalgo Co., NM.

G4, $10-$20
Yavapai Co., AZ.

G5, $15-$30
Yavapai Co., AZ.

G7, $20-$40
NM.

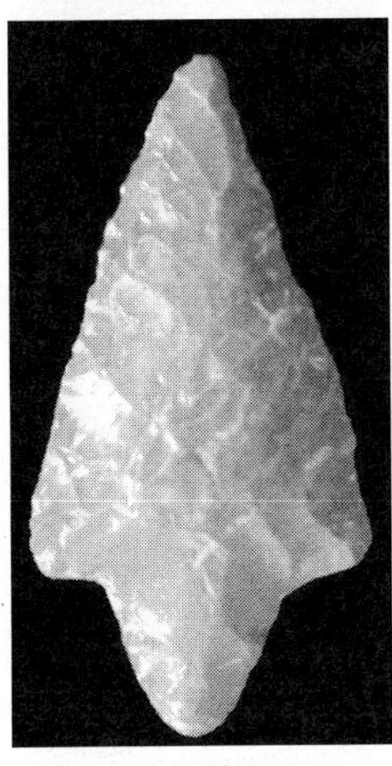

G9, $75-$150
Luna Co., NM.

G4, $25-$50
Luna Co.,
NM.

G5, $40-$80
Pima Co., AZ.

G6, $25-$50
Cochise Co., AZ.

LOCATION: The southern portion of the southwestern states and northern Mexico. **DESCRIPTION:** A small to medium sized dart/knife point with a broad triangular blade and a contracting, rounded to pointed stem and obtuse shoulders. The *Gypsum Cave* point may be a westerly and northerly extension of this point. **I.D. KEY:** Contracting base.

BAJADA - Late Archaic to Developmental Phase, 3000 - 1000 B.P.

(Also see Conejo, Duncan, Escobas and Hanna)

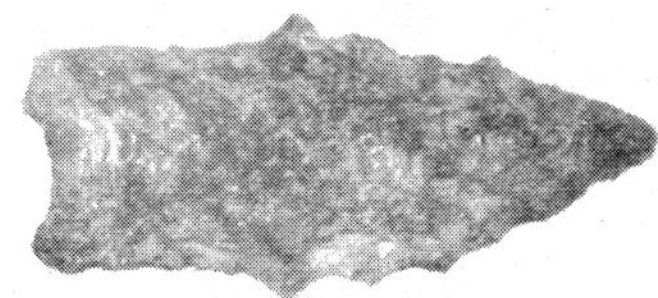

G8, $20-$40
Mohave Co., AZ.

LOCATION: Northern Arizona to Colorado. **DESCRIPTION:** A medium sized birfurcated, stemmed point with weak shoulders and serrated blade edges. **I.D. KEY:** Long concave stem.

BASAL DOUBLE TANG - Late Archaic, 3500 - 2300 B.P.

(Also see Parowan)

LOCATION: Southern Arizona, New Mexico and northern Mexico. **DESCRIPTION:** A medium sized dart/knife point which is basally notched, and then with the stem bifurcated. Worn out examples appear as a lanceolate blade with a notched basal edge. **I.D. KEY:** Triple basal notches.

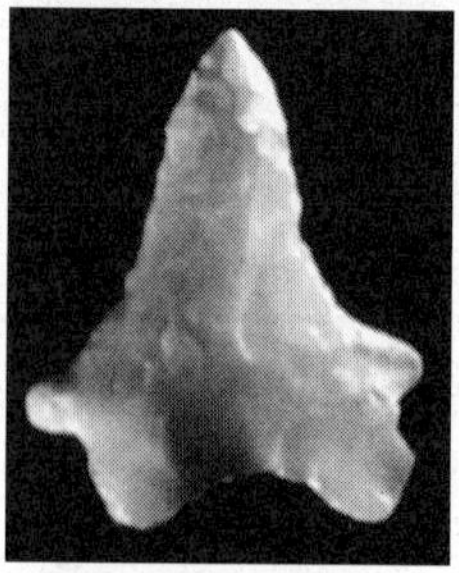

Base nick

G6, $15-$30
San Luis Potosi, MX.

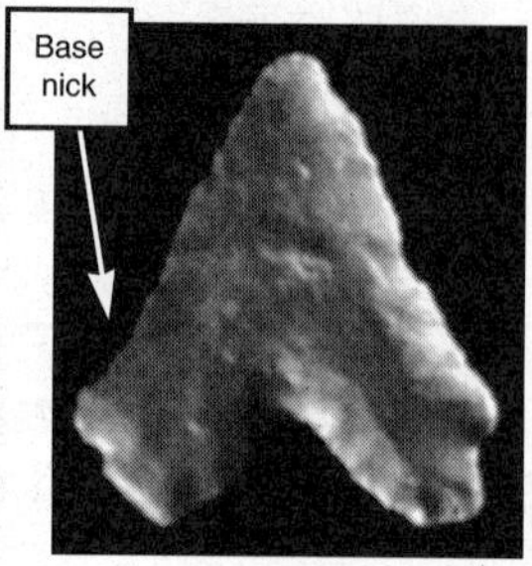

G3, $4-$8
San Luis Potosi, MX.

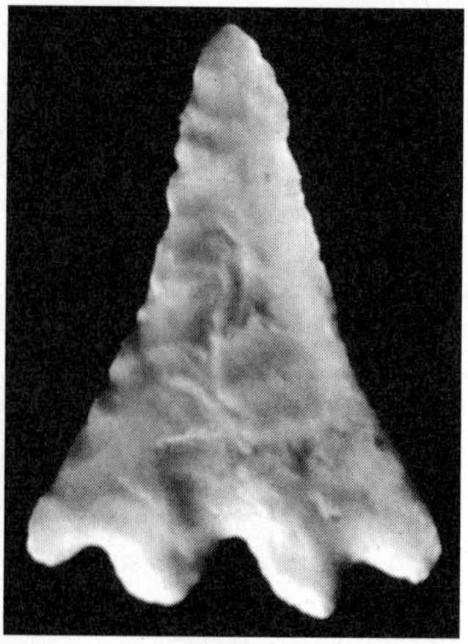

G8, $40-$75
San Luis Potosi, MX.

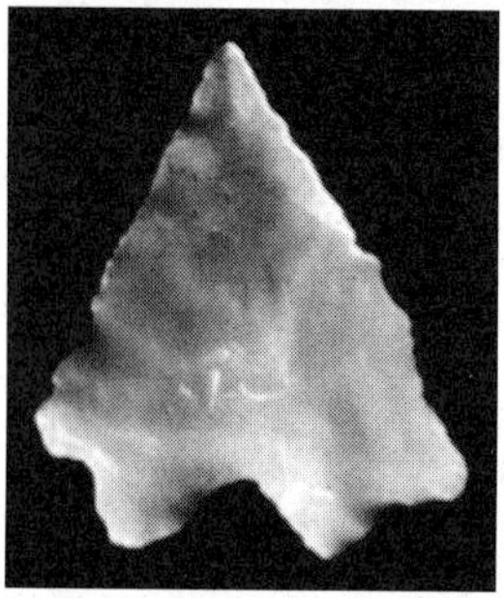

G4, $10-$20
San Luis Potosi, MX.

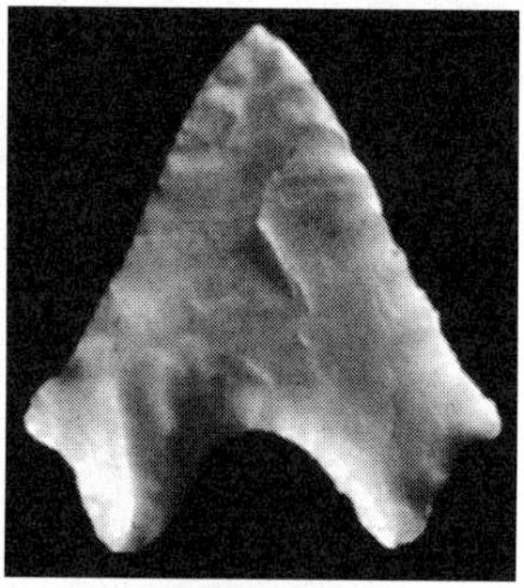

G9 $25-$50
San Luis Potosi, MX.

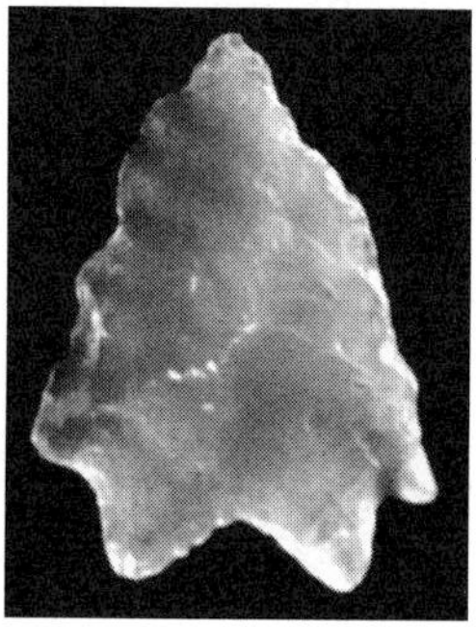

G5, $10-$20
San Luis Potosi, MX.

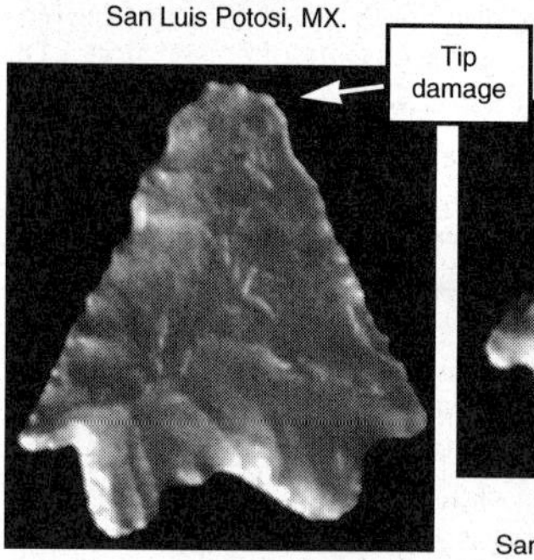

Tip damage

Tip damage

G3 $3-$5
San Luis Potosi, MX.

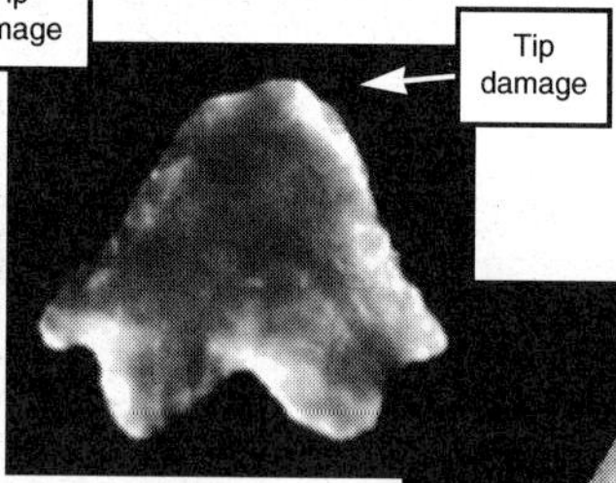

G2, $1-$2
San Luis Potosi, MX.

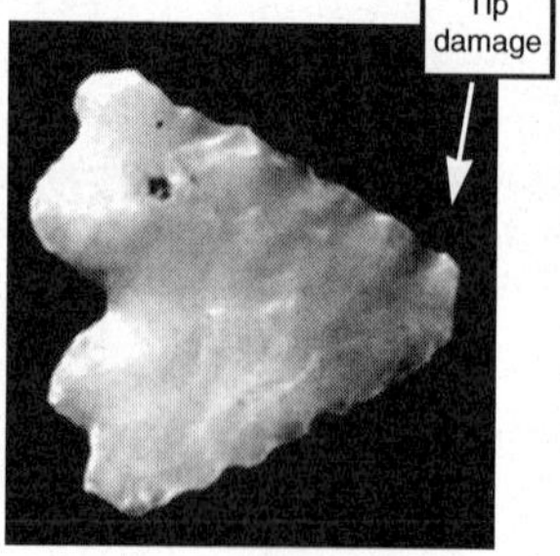

Pristine example

Tip damage

G3, $2-$4
San Luis Potosi, MX.

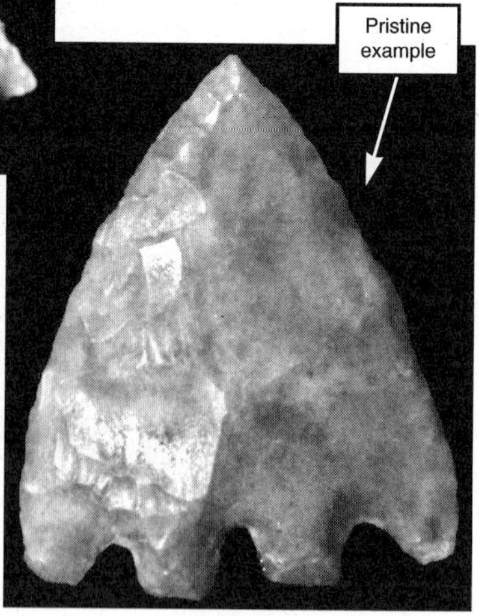

G8, $50-$100
Pinal Co., AZ.

BAT CAVE - Early Archaic, 9000 - 8000 B.P.

(Also see Humboldt)

G4, $10-$20
Yavapai Co., AZ.

G6, $30-$60
Yavapai Co., AZ.

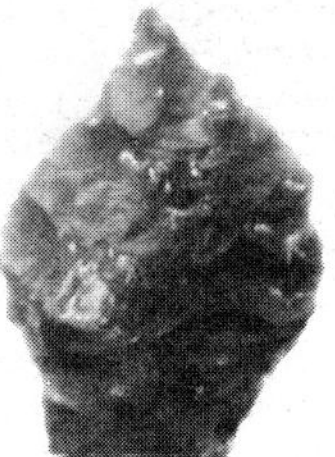
G5, $15-$30
Yavapai Co., AZ.

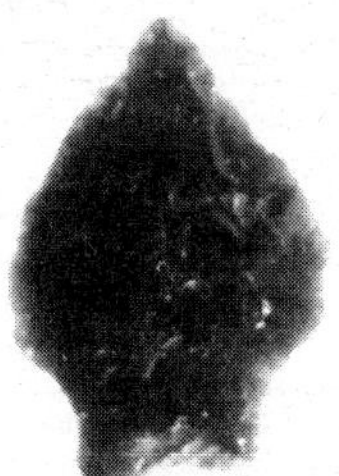
G5, $15-$30
Yavapai Co., AZ.

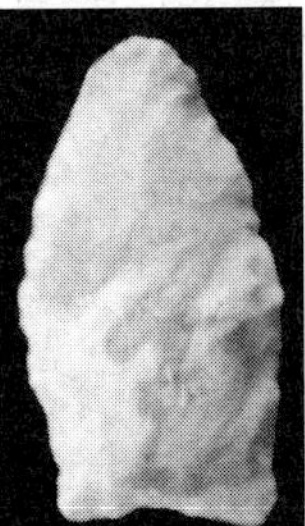
G6, $25-$45
Cochise Co., AZ.

LOCATION: The southwestern states and northern Mexico. **DESCRIPTION:** A small, lanceolate dart/knife with convex blade edges, constricting toward the base to form small, flaring ears. The basal edge is slightly concave and is well thinned. **I.D. KEY:** Waisted appearance and small, flaring ears.

BULL CREEK - Desert Traditions-Developmental Phase, 950 - 700 B.P.

(Also see Cottonwood, Desert and Red Horn)

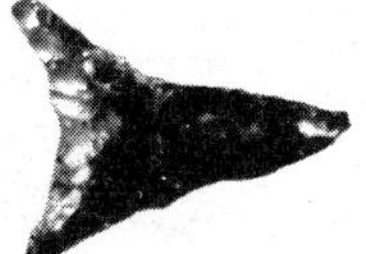
G4 $12-$20
Mojave Co., AZ.

G7, $40-$60
Mojave Co., AZ.

G6, $25-$45
Mojave Co., AZ

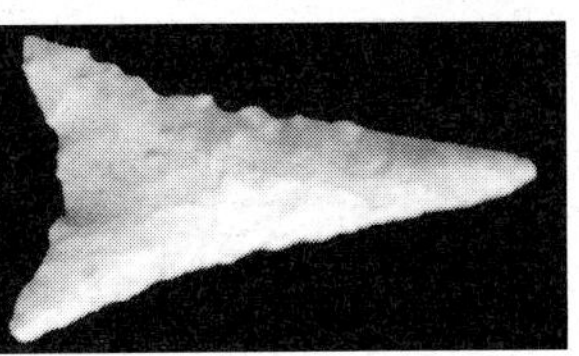
G8, $40-$75
Pima Co., AZ.

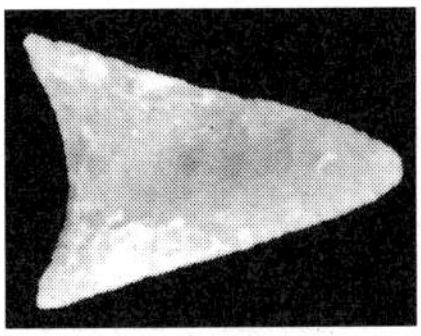

G9, $60-$100
Luna Co., NM.

LOCATION: Northern Arizona, southern Utah and northeastern Nevada. **DESCRIPTION:** A long, thin triangular arrow point with a deeply concave basal edge. They are sometimes serrated. Some examples have been shortened by resharpening. **I.D. KEY:** Isosceles triangle shape and concave base.

SW

CATAN - Late Archaic, 3000 - 1000 B.P.

(Also see Cottonwood Leaf and Matamoros)

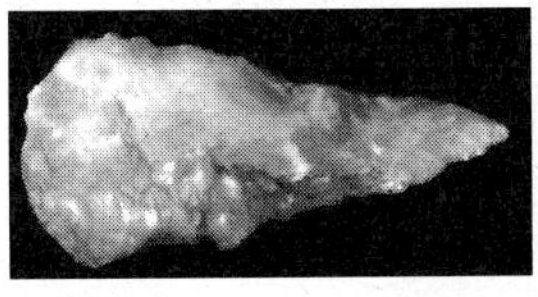
G2, $1-$2
S.W. CO.

G4, $2-$4
S. W. CO.

G5, $3-$6
S.W. CO.

LOCATION: Texas to Colorado. **DESCRIPTION:** A small size ovoid point with a rounded base.

CHIRICAHUA - Middle Archaic, 5000 - 4000 B.P.

(Also see Cottonwood Triangle and Desert)

Basalt

G3, \$2-\$4
Cochise Co., AZ.

G3, \$2-\$4
Cochise Co., AZ.

G6, \$8-\$15
Cochise Co., AZ.

G5, \$6-\$12
Cochise Co., AZ.

G5, \$8-\$16
S.W. CO.

Basalt

Rare double tip

dinged

G6, \$10-\$20
Cochise Co., AZ.

G6, \$10-\$20
AZ.

G6, \$6-\$12
Mojave Co., AZ

G5, \$20-\$40
Cochise Co., AZ.

G9, \$35-\$70
Cochise Co., AZ.

G6, \$15-\$30
Cochise Co.,
AZ.

LOCATION: New Mexico, Arizona, southern California and northern Mexico. **DESCRIPTION:** A small to medium sized dart/knife point with side notches and a concave base, producing an eared appearance. **I.D. KEY:** Generally ears are "rounded" in appearance.

CLOVIS - Early Paleo, 14,000 - 10,000 B.P.

(Also see Allen, Angostura, Folsom, Meserve and Sandia)

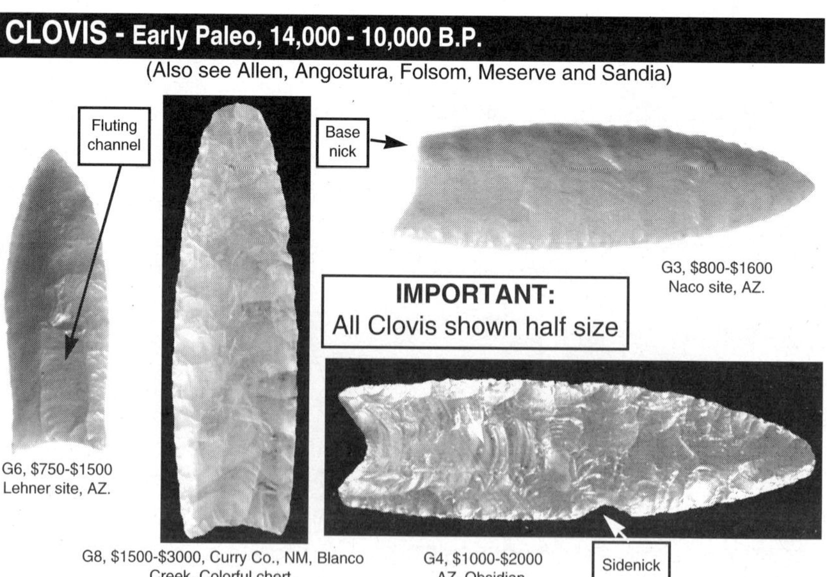

G6, \$750-\$1500
Lehner site, AZ.

G8, \$1500-\$3000, Curry Co., NM, Blanco Creek. Colorful chert.

G3, \$800-\$1600
Naco site, AZ.

G4, \$1000-\$2000
AZ. Obsidian.

CLOVIS (continued)

G7, $1800-$3500
Blackwater Draw, NM. Clovis type site. Black obsidian.

IMPORTANT:
All Clovis shown half size

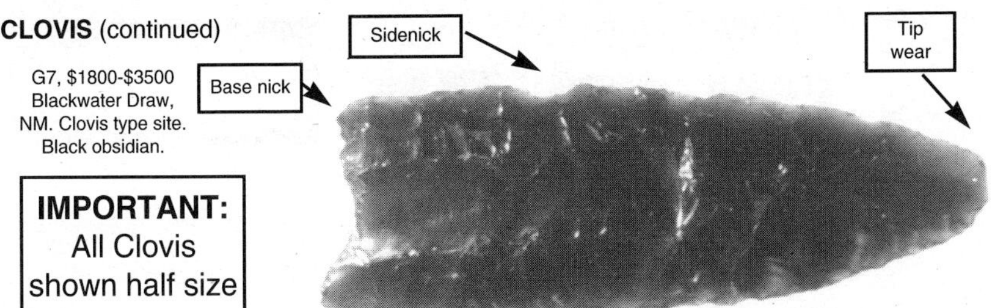

LOCATION: All of North America. Named after Clovis, New Mexico near where these fluted projectile points were found. **DESCRIPTION:** A medium to large size, auriculate, fluted, lanceolate point with a convex base that is ground. Most examples are fluted on both sides about 1/3 the way up from the base. *Clovis* is the earliest known point type in the hemisphere. The first *Clovis* find associated with Mastodons was in 1979 at Mastodon State Park, Jefferson Co., MO. in the Kimmswick bone bed dated to 12,000 B.P. The origin of Clovis is a mystery as there is no pre-*Clovis* evidence here (crude forms that pre-date Clovis). **I.D. KEY:** Paleo flaking, basal ears, batan fluting instead of indirect style.

COLONIAL - Desert Traditions-Transitional & Developmental Phases, 1200 - 900 B.P.

(Also see Ventana-Amargosa and Yavapai))

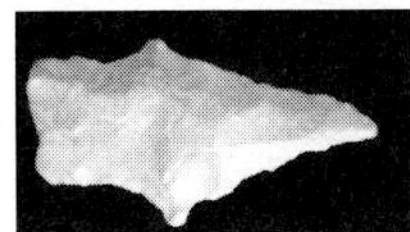

G3, $3-$6
Yavapai Co., AZ.

G6, $18-$35
Yavapai Co., AZ.

LOCATION: Most of Arizona and into the edges of contiguous states. **DESCRIPTION:** A small arrow point with a triangular blade and an exceptionally long, narrow, rectangular stem. The point has obtuse shoulders. **I.D. KEY:** Rectangular stem longer than the blade portion of the point.

CONEJO - Late Archaic, 3500 - 2300 B.P.

(Also see Val Verde)

CONEJO (continued)

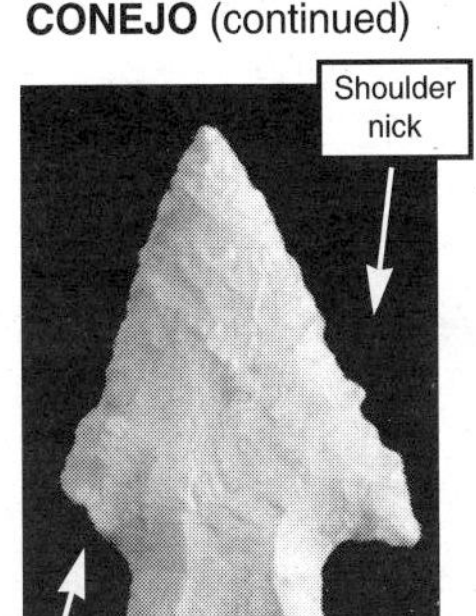

G3, $4-$8
Luna Co., NM.

G7, $30-$60
Luna Co., NM.

LOCATION: Extreme western Texas and most of New Mexico. **DESCRIPTION:** A corner notched dart/knife with convex blade edges, short barbs and a short, straight stem. The basal edge may be straight or concave.

SW

COTTONWOOD LEAF - Desert Traditions-Classic/Historic Phases, 700 - 200 B.P.

(Also see Catan, Datil and Pelona)

COTTONWOOD LEAF (continued)

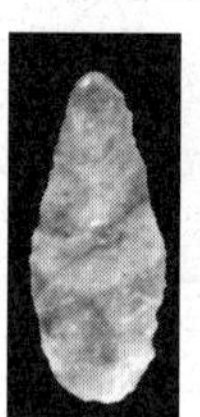
G6, $5-$10
Pima Co., AZ.

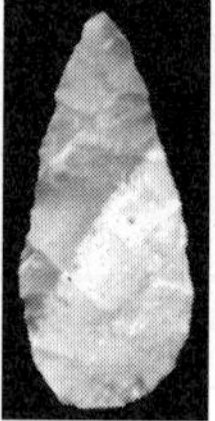
G7, $25-$50
Apache Co., AZ.

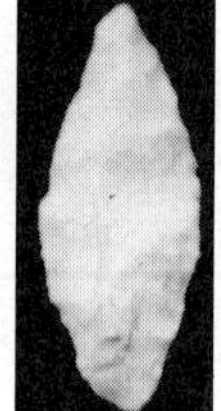
G2, $.50-$1
Mojave Co., AZ.

G8, $25-$50
Pima Co., AZ.

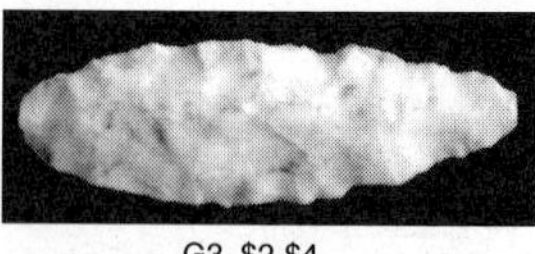
G3, $2-$4
Pima Co., AZ.

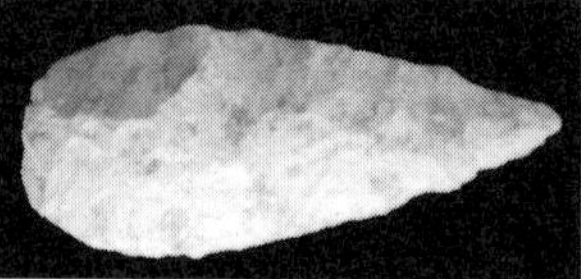
G7, $20-$40
Yavapai Co., AZ.

LOCATION: Arizona and westward into California and Nevada. **DESCRIPTION:** A small, thin, leaf shaped arrow point that resembles a long tear-drop. The base is rounded. **I.D. KEY:** Size and blade form.

COTTONWOOD TRIANGLE - Desert Traditions-Classic and Historic Phases, 700 - 200 B.P.

(Also see Cottonwood Leaf, Desert and Red Horn)

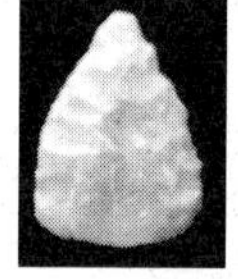
G6, $8-$15
Cochise Co., AZ.

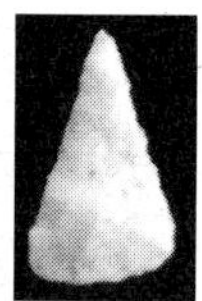
G4, $3-$5
Cochise Co., AZ.

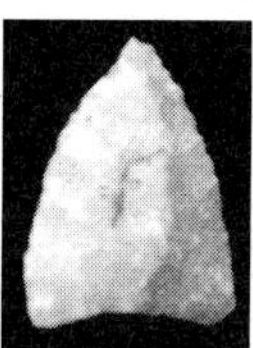
G2, $1-$2
Cochise Co., AZ.

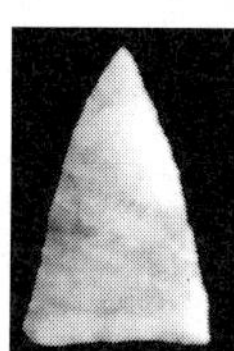
G6, $10-$20
Cochise Co., AZ.

G4, $3-$5
Pima Co., AZ.

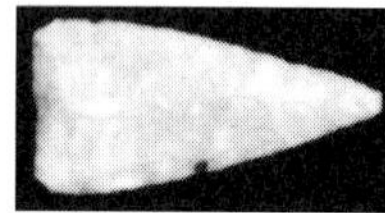
G2, $1-$2
Pima Co., AZ.

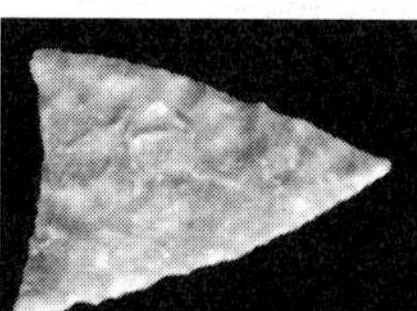
G6, $15-$30
Cochise Co., AZ.

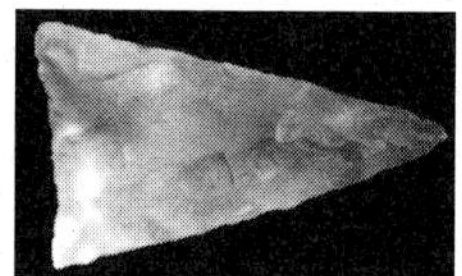
G6, $15-$30
Mojave Co., AZ.

G5, $8-$15
Pima Co., AZ.

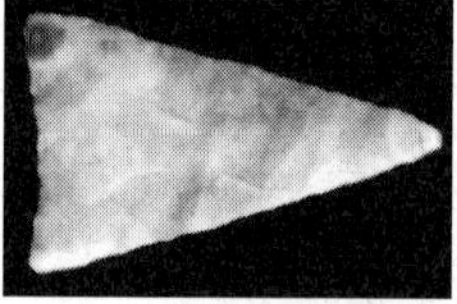
G6, $15-$30
Cochise Co., AZ.

G5, $6-$12
Yavapai Co., AZ.

LOCATION: Arizona and westward into California and Nevada. **DESCRIPTION:** A small, thin triangular arrow point with a straight to slightly convex basal edge. **I.D. KEY:** Size and blade form.

DATIL - Early Archaic, 7000 - 6000 B. P.

(Also see Cottonwood Leaf and Truxton)

DATIL (continued)

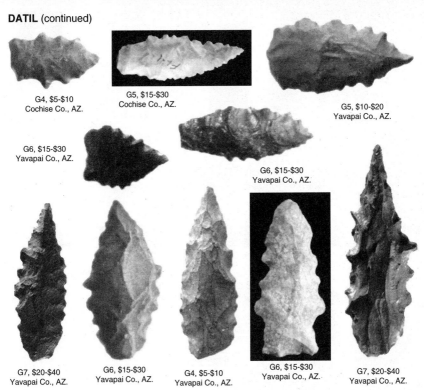

G4, $5-$10
Cochise Co., AZ.

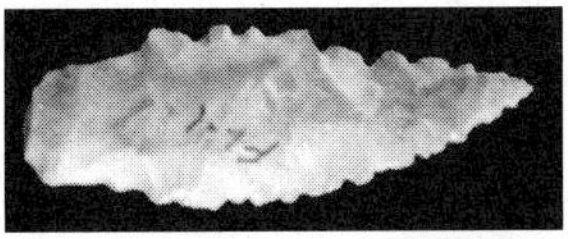

G5, $15-$30
Cochise Co., AZ.

G5, $10-$20
Yavapai Co., AZ.

G6, $15-$30
Yavapai Co., AZ.

G6, $15-$30
Yavapai Co., AZ.

G7, $20-$40
Yavapai Co., AZ.

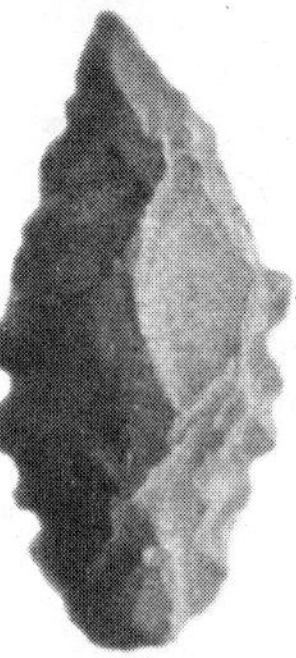

G6, $15-$30
Yavapai Co., AZ.

G4, $5-$10
Yavapai Co., AZ.

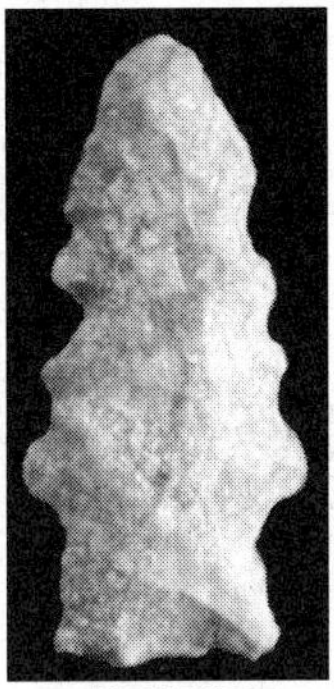

G6, $15-$30
Yavapai Co., AZ.

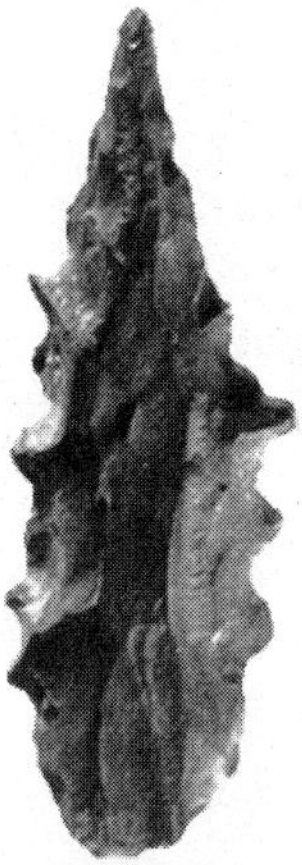

G7, $20-$40
Yavapai Co., AZ.

LOCATION: The southern portion of the southwestern states. **DESCRIPTION:** A small dart/knife with long, narrow, heavily serrated blade edges. The stem is short and rectangular to rounded. Shoulders are straight to obtuse and are very small to non-existent in relation to the overall size of the point.

DEADMAN'S - Desert Traditions-Developmental Phase, 1600 - 1300 B. P.

(Also see Gila Butte and Rose Springs)

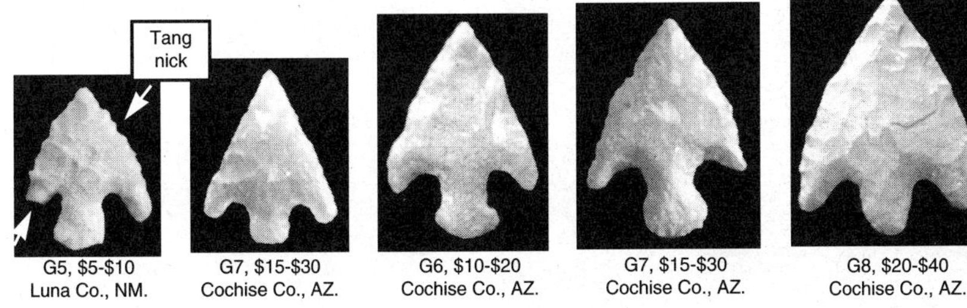

G5, $5-$10
Luna Co., NM.

G7, $15-$30
Cochise Co., AZ.

G6, $10-$20
Cochise Co., AZ.

G7, $15-$30
Cochise Co., AZ.

G8, $20-$40
Cochise Co., AZ.

LOCATION: Southeastern Arizona, southern New Mexico and western Texas. **DESCRIPTION:** A small arrow point with very deep basal notches creating a long, straight to slightly bulbous stem with a rounded basal edge. The blade is triangular. **I.D. KEY:** Long stem and barbs.

DESERT DELTA - Desert Traditions-Classic to Historic, 700 - 200 B. P.

(Also see Hohokam, Sacaton, Salado and Temporal)

DESERT DELTA (continued)

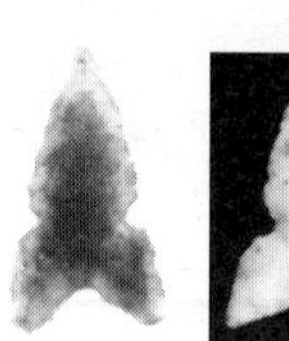
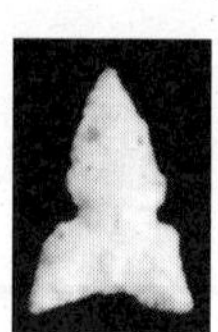

G6, $5-$10 Cochise Co., AZ. | G3, $3-$6 Apache Co., AZ. | G4, $5-$10 Yavapai Co., AZ. | G7, $15-$30 Pima Co., AZ. | G7, $15-$30 AZ. | G7, $20-$40 AZ. | G7, $20-$40 Cochise Co., AZ.

LOCATION: Most of Arizona and contiguous states to the west. **DESCRIPTION:** A small arrow point with straight blade edges, side notches and a deeply concave to V-shaped basal edge. **I.D. KEY:** V-shaped basal edge.

DESERT GENERAL-Desert Traditions-Classic to Historic,700-200 B. P.

(Also see Hohokam, Sacaton and Salado)

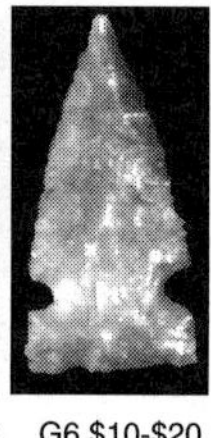
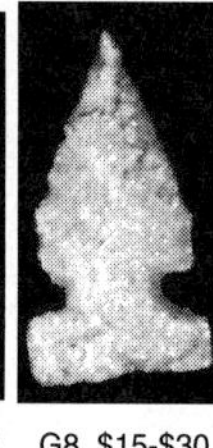

G2, $2-$4 NM. | G4, $5-$10 AZ. | G2, $2-$4 AZ. | G6, $10-$20 S.W. CO. | G6,$10-$20 S.W. CO. | G8, $15-$30 S.W. CO. | G2, $2-$4 S.W. CO. | G9, $30-$60 Yuma Co., AZ.

LOCATION: Most of Arizona and contiguous states to the west. **DESCRIPTION:** A small arrow point with convex blade edges, side notches and a straight to slightly concave basal edge. **I.D. KEY:** Straight to concave base.

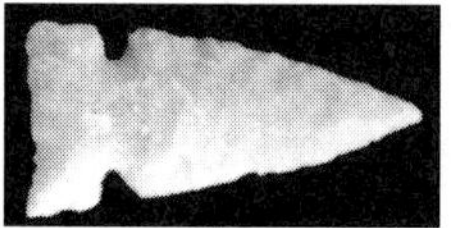

G8, $25-$50 Cochise Co., AZ.

DESERT REDDING-Desert Traditions-Classic to Historic, 700-200 B. P.

(Also see Hohokam, Sacaton, Salado and Temporal)

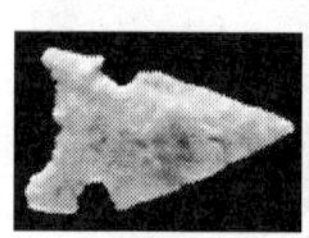

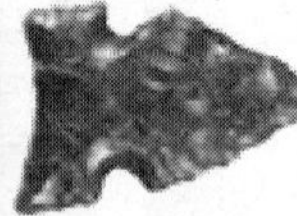
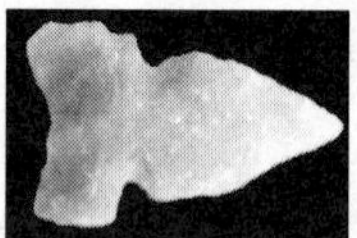

G4, $5-$10 NM. | G6, $8-$15 NM. | G6, $8-$15 AZ. | G5, $6-$10 Pima Co., AZ. | G7, $12-$25 Pima Co., AZ.

LOCATION: Most of Arizona and contiguous states to the west. **DESCRIPTION:** A small arrow point with convex sides, diagonal side notches and a concave basal edge which is narrower than the shoulders **I.D. KEY:** Narrow basal edge.

DESERT SIERRA - Desert Traditions-Classic to Historic, 700-200 B. P.

(Also see Hohokam and Sacaton)

DESERT SIERRA (continued)

G5, $5-$10
S.W. CO.

G6, $8-$15
AZ.

G6, $8-$15
S.W. CO.

G6, $8-$15
AZ.

G6, $8-$15
S.W. CO.

G6, $10-$20
AZ.

G6, $10-$20
AZ.

G6, $8-$15
AZ.

G6, $10-$20
AZ.

G6, $10-$20
AZ.

G7, $15-$30
AZ.

LOCATION: Most of Arizona and contiguous states to the west. **DESCRIPTION:** A small arrow point with straight sides, a straight basal edge and a basal notch. **I.D. KEY:** Triangular tri-notched point.

DRILL - Paleo to Historic, 14,000 - 850 B.P.

(Also see Lancet)

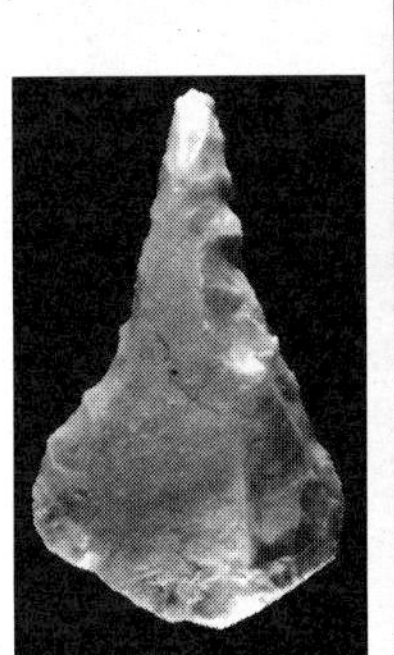

G4, $5-$10
Mojave Co., AZ.

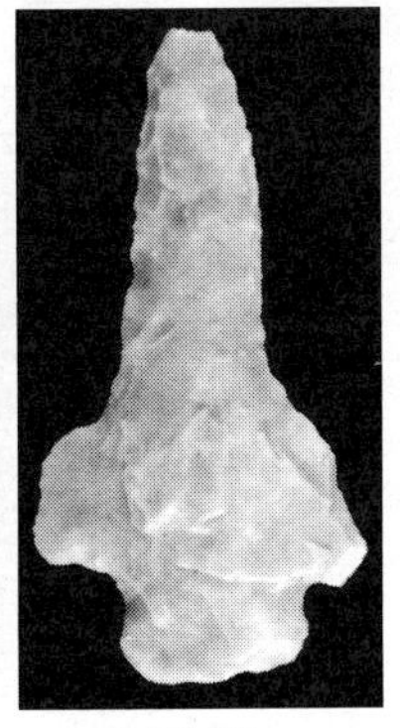

5, $10-$20
Mojave Co., AZ.

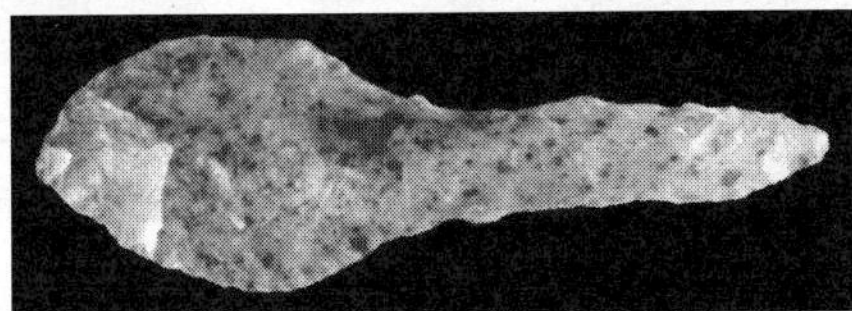

G8, $20-$40
Mojave Co., AZ.

LOCATION: Throughout north America. **DESCRIPTION:** Although many drills were made from scratch, all point types were made into the drill form. Usually, heavily resharpened and broken points were salvaged and rechipped into drills. **I.D. KEY:** Narrow blade form.

SW

DRY PRONG - Desert Traditions, 1000 - 850 B.P.

(Also see Desert, Sacaton and Temporal)

G5-6 average, Apache Co.AZ. 6 point cache. Value of cache of 6 points $180.

LOCATION: East central Arizona and west central New Mexico. **DESCRIPTION:** A small, narrow triangular arrow point with side notches and one or two additional side notches on one side of the blade. Some examples do not have the extra notch(es) and must be found in association with the extra notch variety to be typed as *Dry Prong* points. **I.D. KEY:** The extra side notch(es).

DRY PRONG (continued)

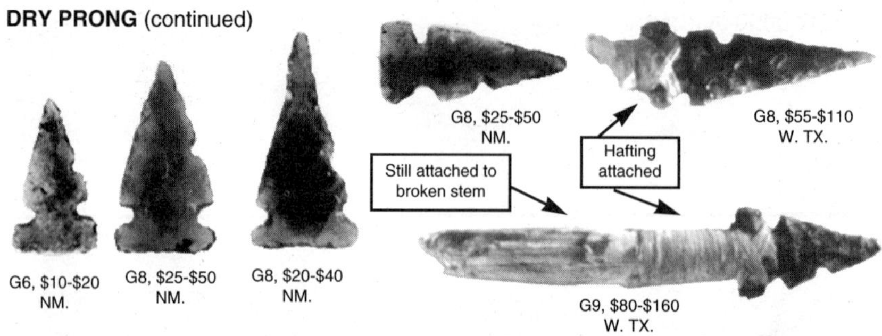

G6, $10-$20
NM.

G8, $25-$50
NM.

G8, $20-$40
NM.

G8, $25-$50
NM.

G8, $55-$110
W. TX.

G9, $80-$160
W. TX.

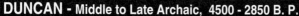

DUNCAN - Middle to Late Archaic, 4500 - 2850 B. P.

(Also see Bajada, Escobas and Hanna)

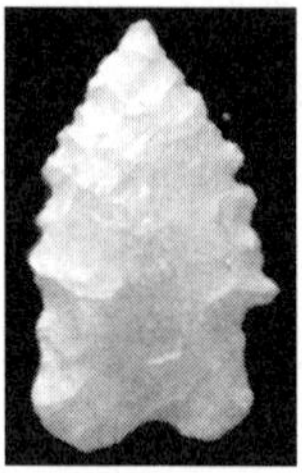

Chalcedony

G7, $15-$30
Apache Co., AZ.

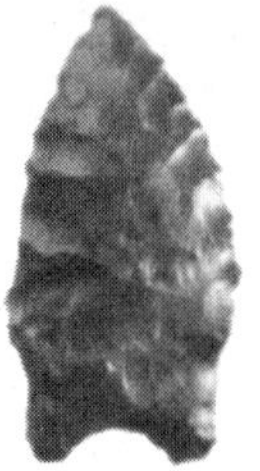

G7, $10-$20
Yavapai Co., AZ.

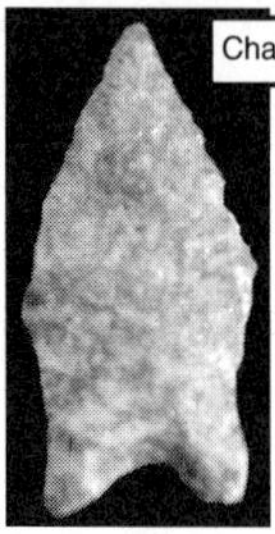

G8, $20-$40
Pinal Co., AZ.

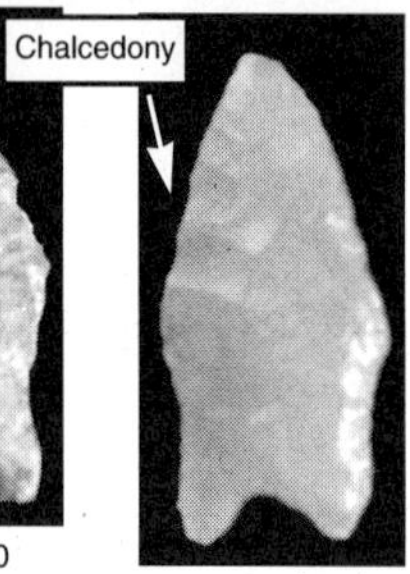

G6, $10-$20
Cochise Co., AZ.

G5, $6-$12
Apache Co., AZ.

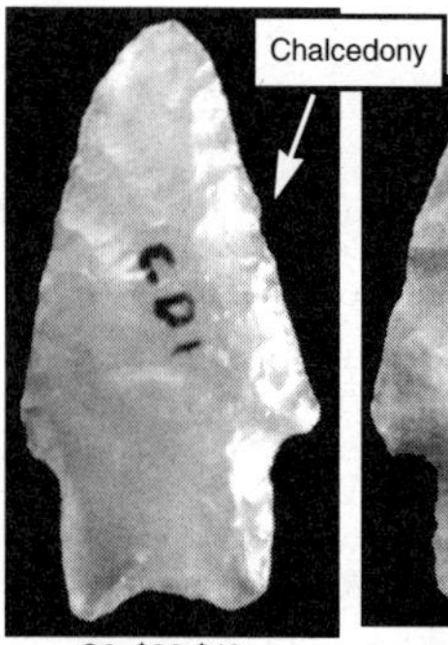

Chalcedony

Tip nick

G8, $20-$40
Mojave Co., AZ.

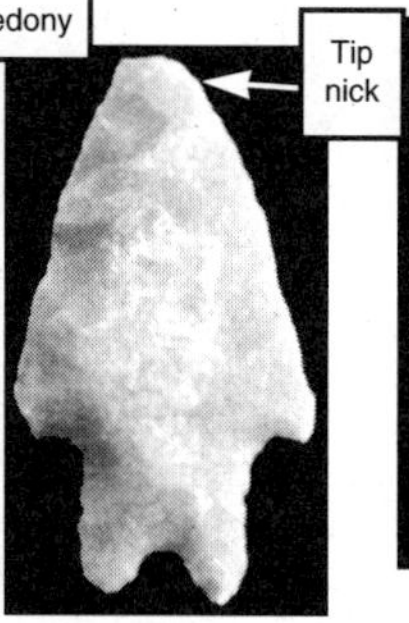

G5, $10-$20
Apache Co., AZ.

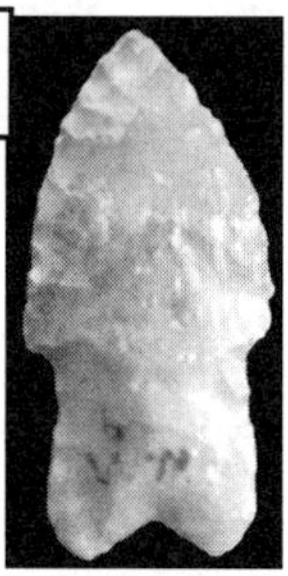

G8, $20-$40
Yavapai Co., AZ.

LOCATION: Northern Arizona to Canada on the north and to eastern Oklahoma on the east. **DESCRIPTION:** A small to medium sized dart/knife point with a triangular blade and angular shoulders. The stem is straight with a V-shaped notch in the basal edge. Stem edges are usually ground. **I.D. KEY:** Straight stem edges.

DURAN - Late Archaic to Transitional Phase, 3000 - 2000 B. P.

(Also see Maljamar, Neff and Truxton)

G6, $20-$40
San Luis Potosi, MX.

G6, $15-$30
San Luis Potosi, MX.

G6, $15-$30
San Luis Potosi, MX.

LOCATION: Texas into Mexico. **DESCRIPTION:** A small size, narrow, stemmed point with double to multiple notches on each side. Base can be parallel sided to tapered with rounded basal corners. **I.D. KEY:** Double notches, round base.

EASTGATE SPLIT-STEM - Desert Traditions-Developmental Phase, 1400 - 1000 B. P.

(Also see Conejo, Duncan, Elko and Hanna)

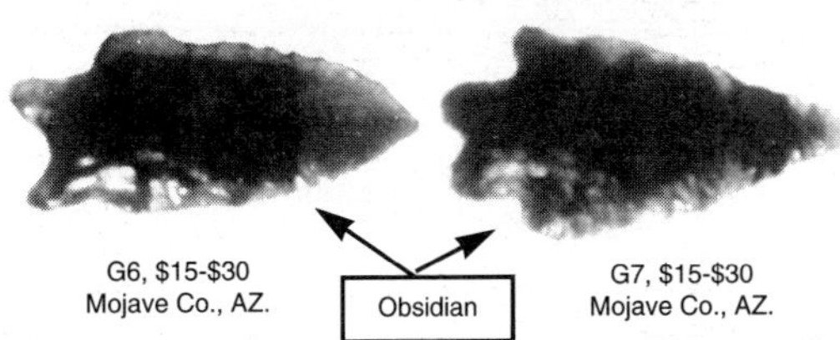

G6, $15-$30
Mojave Co., AZ.

Obsidian

G7, $15-$30
Mojave Co., AZ.

LOCATION: Arizona to Washington. **DESCRIPTION:** A corner to base notched arrow point with a triangular blade and a straight to slightly expanding stem with a basal notch. **I.D. KEY:** The basal notch differentiates it from other *Eastgate* points.

EDEN - Early Archaic, 9500 - 7500 B. P.

(Also see Firstview and Scottsbluff)

LOCATION: Southwest to northern and midwestern states. **DESCRIPTION:** A medium to large size, narrow, lanceolate blade with a straight to concave base and almost unnoticable shoulders. Many examples have a median ridge and collateral oblique parallel flaking. Bases are usually ground. **I.D. KEY:** Narrowness, weak shoulders.

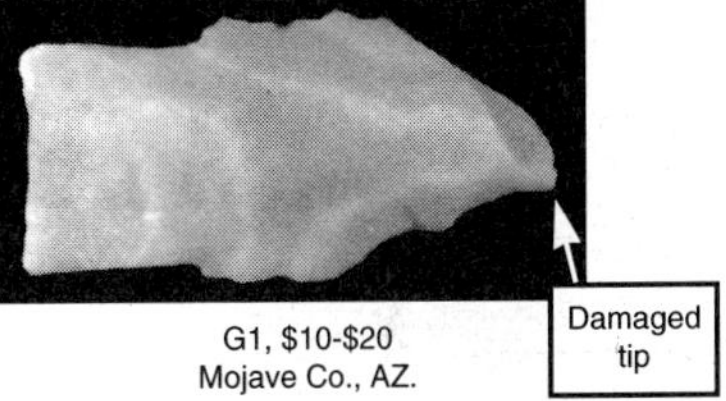

G1, $10-$20
Mojave Co., AZ.

Damaged tip

ELKO CORNER NOTCHED - Mid-Archaic to Developmental Phase, 3500 - 1200 B.P.

(Also see Eastgate and Mount Albion)

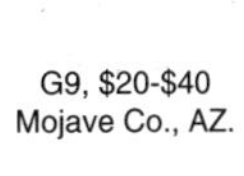

G9, $20-$40
Mojave Co., AZ.

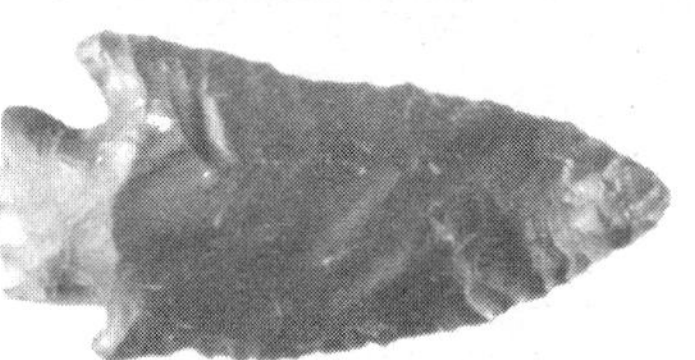

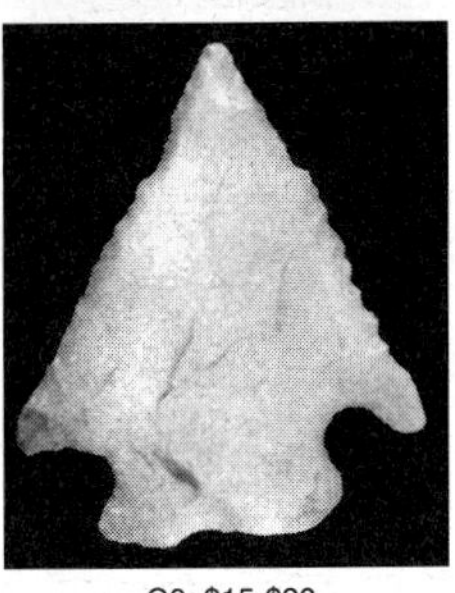

G9, $15-$30
Mojave Co., AZ.

LOCATION: Great Basin into Arizona. **DESCRIPTION:** a small to large size, thin, corner notched dart point with shoulder tangs and a convex, concave or auriculate base. Shoulders and tips are sharp. Some examples exhibit excellent parallel flaking on blade edges. **I.D. KEY:** Corner notches, sharp tangs.

SW

ELKO EARED - Mid-Archaic to Developmental Phase, 3500 - 1200 B.P.

(Also see Eastgate)

Tang damage

G5, $5-$10
Mojave Co., AZ.

LOCATION: Great Basin into Arizona. **DESCRIPTION:** a small to large size, thin, corner notched dart point with shoulder tangs and an eared base. Basal ears are usually exaggerated and corners and tips are sharp. Some examples exhibit excellent parallel flaking on blade edges. **I.D. KEY:** Expanding to drooping ears.

ESCOBAS - Mid-Archaic, 6500 - 5000 B. P.

(Also see Bajada, Colonial, Duncan, Hanna and San Jose)

LOCATION: Southwestern states. **DESCRIPTION:** A small, long stemmed point with weak shoulders, serrated edges and a concave base. **I.D. KEY:** Long straight stem; concave base; serrations.

G6, $20-$40
Chinle, AZ.

FIGUEROA - Transitional Phase, 2200 B. P.

(Also see Mount Albion, San Pedro and Val Verde)

LOCATION: Western Texas, New Mexico and Arizona. **DESCRIPTION:** A dart/knife point with medium-wide side notches, an expanding stem and a convex basal edge. **I.D. KEY:** Wide side notches, convex base.

G4, $10-$20
Chnile, AZ.

G6, $25-$50
Chnile, AZ.

FIRSTVIEW - LATE PALEO, 8700 - 8050 B. P.

(Also see Eden and Scottsbluff)

LOCATION: Extreme western Texas into New Mexico and southern Colorado. **DESCRIPTION:** A lanceolate point with slightly convex blade edges, slight shoulders and a rectangular stem. Shoulders are sometimes absent from resharpening. It generally exhibits parallel-transverse flaking. **I.D. KEY:** A diamond shaped cross-section.

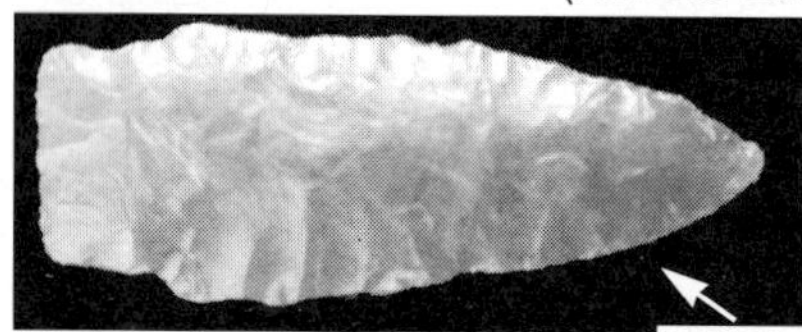

G9, $400-$800
Chaves Co., NM.

FOLSOM - PALEO, 11,000 - 10,000 B. P.

(Also see Allen, Angostura, Clovis, McKean and Midland)

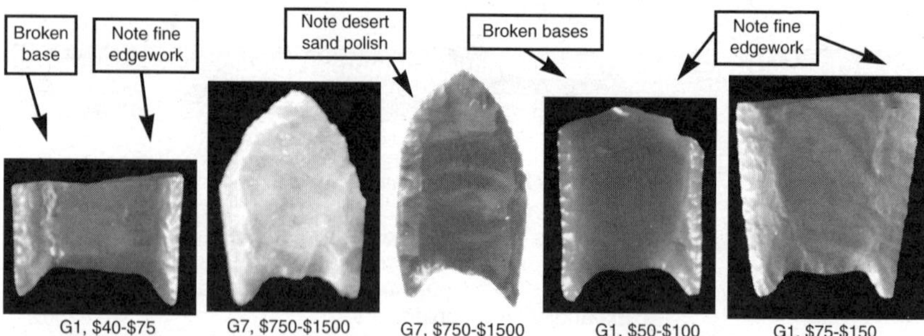

G1, $40-$75
El Paso Co., TX.

G7, $750-$1500
Chaves Co., NM.

G7, $750-$1500
El Paso Co., TX.

G1, $50-$100
El Paso Co., TX.

G1, $75-$150
El Paso Co., TX.

FOLSOM (continued)

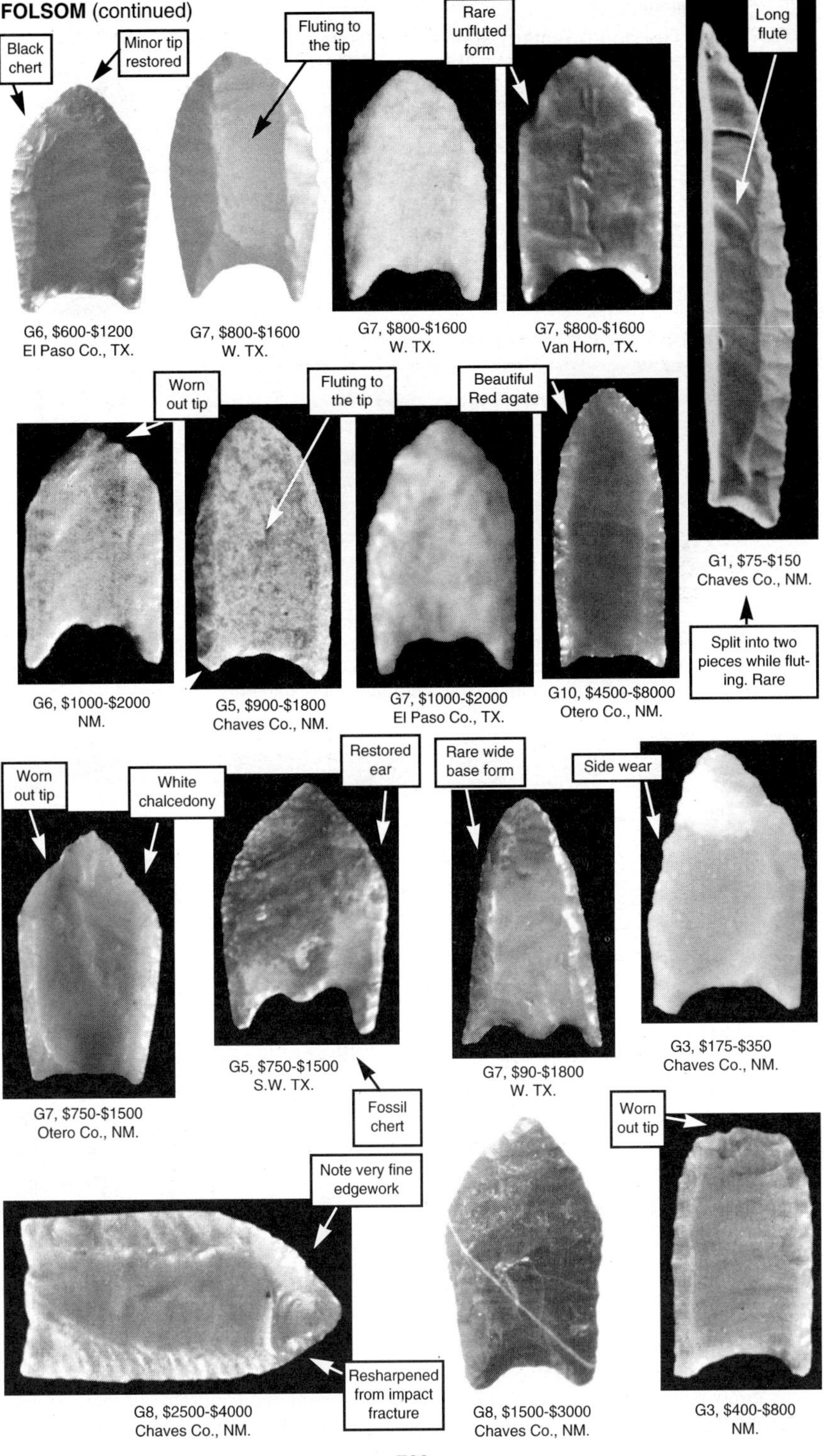

G6, $600-$1200
El Paso Co., TX.

G7, $800-$1600
W. TX.

G7, $800-$1600
W. TX.

G7, $800-$1600
Van Horn, TX.

G1, $75-$150
Chaves Co., NM.

G6, $1000-$2000
NM.

G5, $900-$1800
Chaves Co., NM.

G7, $1000-$2000
El Paso Co., TX.

G10, $4500-$8000
Otero Co., NM.

G7, $750-$1500
Otero Co., NM.

G5, $750-$1500
S.W. TX.

G7, $90-$1800
W. TX.

G3, $175-$350
Chaves Co., NM.

G8, $2500-$4000
Chaves Co., NM.

G8, $1500-$3000
Chaves Co., NM.

G3, $400-$800
NM.

SW

FOLSOM (continued)

G8, $1500-$3000
NM.

LOCATION: The southwestern states and as far north as Canada and east to northern Indiana. Type site is a bison kill site near Folsom, NM, where 24 fluted *Folsom* points were excavated in 1926-1928. Being the first fluted point named, for years all fluted points were called *Folsom*. **DESCRIPTION:** A very thin, small to medium sized, lanceolate point with convex to parallel edges and a concave basal edge creating sharp ears or basal corners. Most examples are fluted from the basal edge to nearly the tip of the point. They do rarely occur unfluted. Workmanship is very fine and outstanding. Most examples found have worn out tips or were rebased from longer points that broke at the haft. **I.D. KEY:** Micro secondary flaking, pointed auricles.

GARZA - Desert Traditions-Classic Phase, 500 - 300 B.P.

(Also see Lott, Soto and Toyah)

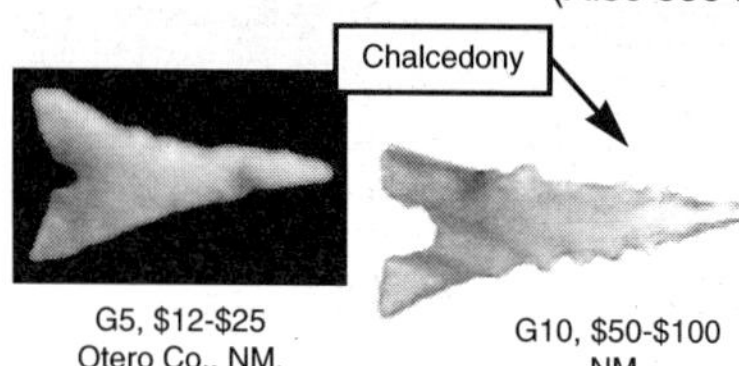

G5, $12-$25
Otero Co., NM.

G10, $50-$100
NM.

G8, $35-$70
MX, Chihuahua

G9, $40-$80
NM.

LOCATION: Western Texas and southern New Mexico. **DESCRIPTION:** A small, thin, triangular arrow point. Blade edges vary from convex to concave and can be serrated. The basal edge is deeply concave and notched, creating long, thin ears.

GATECLIFF- Mid to late Archaic, 5000 - 3000 B. P.

(Also see Elko and Gypsum Cave)

LOCATION: Great Basin into Arizona. **DESCRIPTION:** A medium to large size stemmed dart point that occurs in two forms. One form has a contracted base and barbed shoulders. The second form has a contracted base that is bifurcated or deeply concave and shoulder barbs. Believed to evolve into *Elko* points.

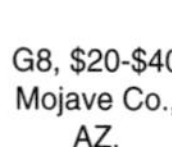

G8, $20-$40
Mojave Co.,
AZ.

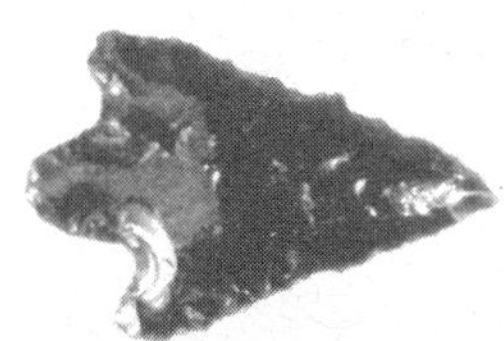

GILA BUTTE - Desert Traditions-Developmental Phase,1500 - 1300 B. P.

(Also see Santa Cruz)

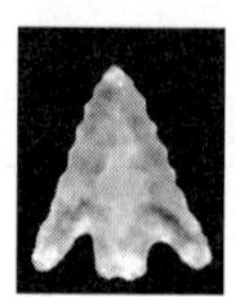

G9, $40-$75
Mojave Co., AZ.

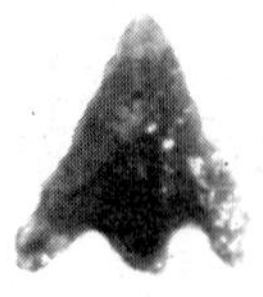

G4, $8-$15
Yavapai Co., AZ.

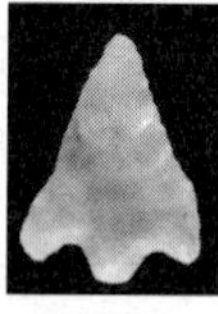

G8, $30-$60
Mojave Co., AZ.

G6, $20-$40
Mojave Co., AZ.

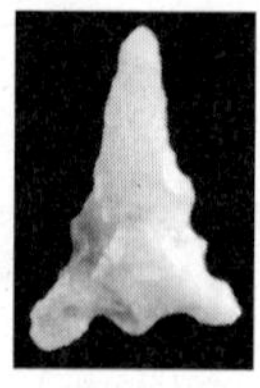

G6, $12-$25
Mojave Co., AZ.

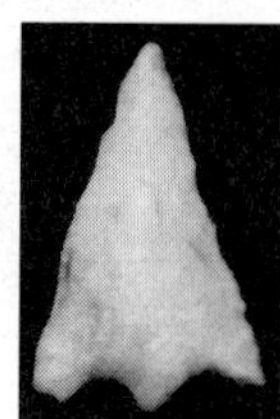

G4, $8-$15
Mojave Co., AZ.

LOCATION: Arizona ranging into adjacent parts of contiguous states. **DESCRIPTION:** A small arrow point with basal notching which creates barbs ranging from shallow to deep. The stem may be pointed or truncated. **I.D.KEY:** Basal notches.

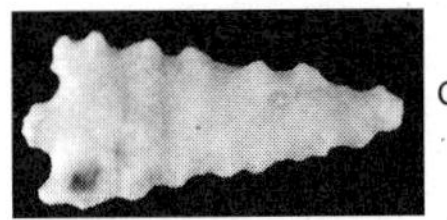

G3, $6-$10 Mojave Co., AZ.

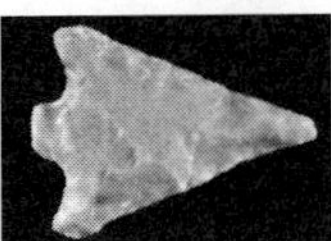

G9, $30-$60 Mojave Co., AZ.

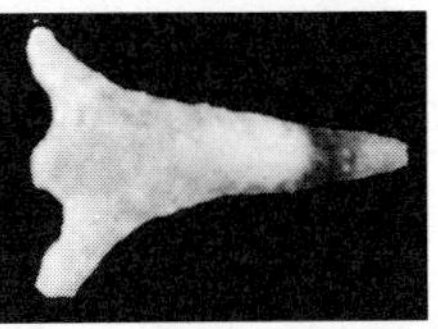

G7, $20-$40 Mojave Co., AZ.

GYPSUM CAVE - Middle Archaic, 5000 - 3300 B. P.

(Also see Augustin, Gatecliff, Parowan and Santa Cruz)

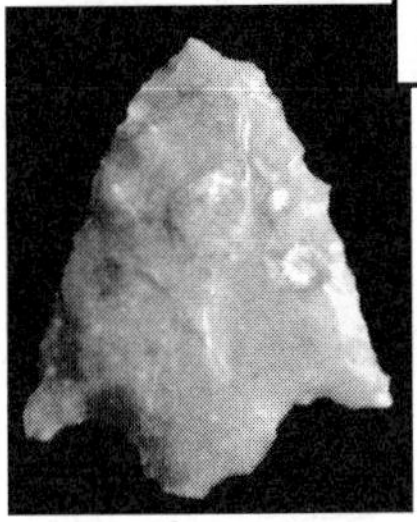

G3, $5-$10 Cohonino Co., AZ.

Preform for type

G6, $15-$30 Mojave Co., AZ.

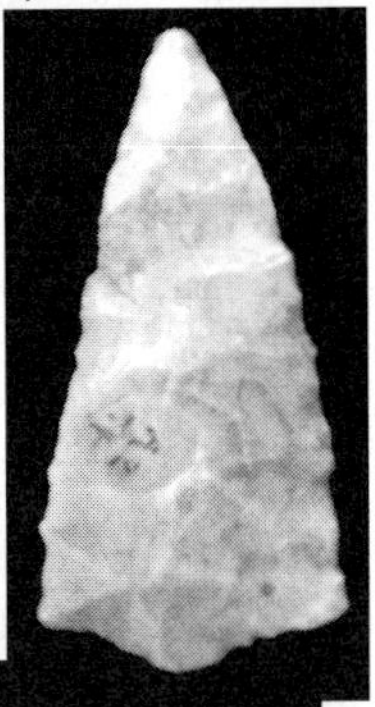

G7, $40-$80 Mojave Co., AZ.

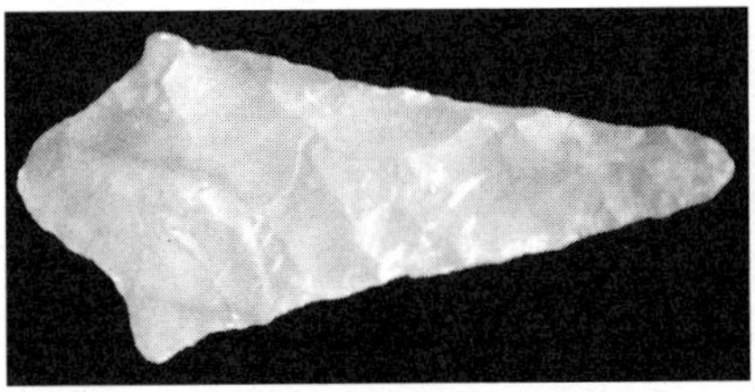

G9, $50-$100 Mojave Co., AZ.

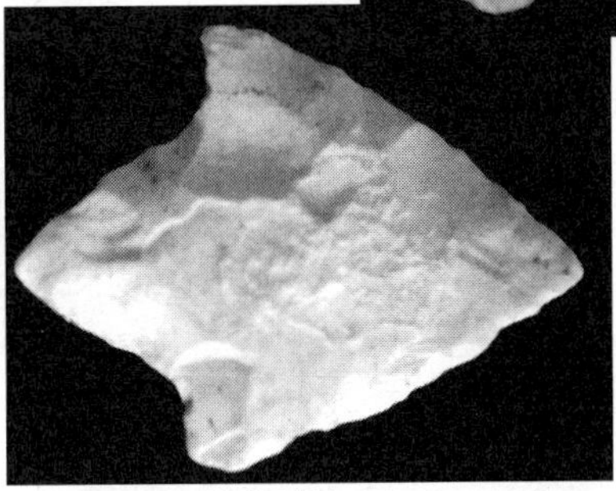

G6, $20-$40 Yavapai Co., AZ.

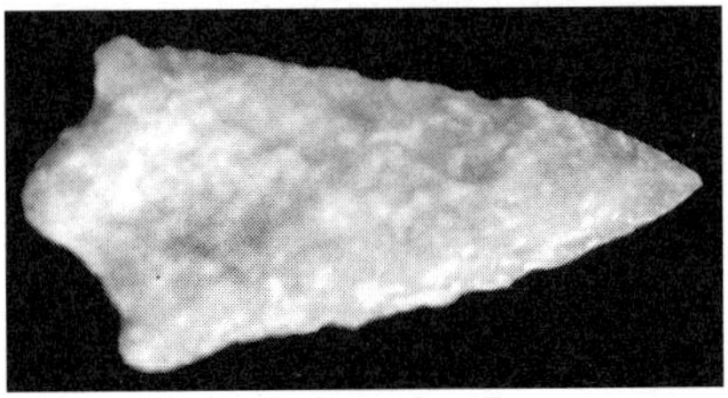

G8, $40-$80, Mojave Co., AZ.

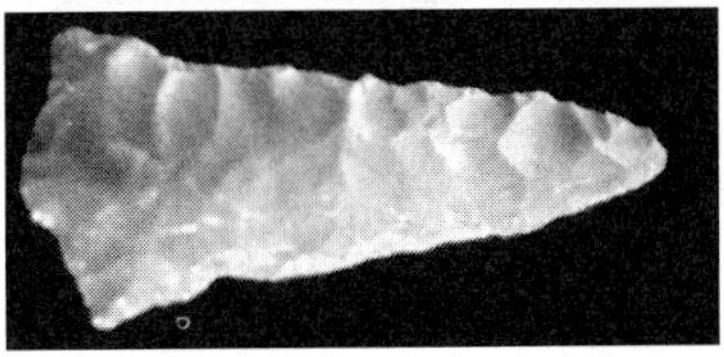

G6, $25-$50, Cohonino Co., AZ.

LOCATION: Northwestern Arizona and into contiguous states to the west and north. **DESCRIPTION:** A medium sized dart/knife with straight blade edges and a short stem which contracts to a rounded point. The shoulders are obtuse. This point may be a northerly and westwardly extension of the *Augustin* point, though, in general, it seems to have better workmanship. **I.D. KEY:** Stubby stem.

HANNA - Middle to Late Archaic, 4500 - 2850 B. P.

(Also see Chiricahua, Duncan and Squaw Mountain)

LOCATION: Southwestern states and north as far as Canada and east as far as Nebraska. **DESCRIPTION:** A small dart/knife with obtuse shoulders and an expanding stem which is notched to produce diagonally projecting ears. **I.D. KEY:** Expanding stem.

G8, $30-$60
Mojave Co., AZ.

G4, $8-$15
Yavapai Co., AZ.

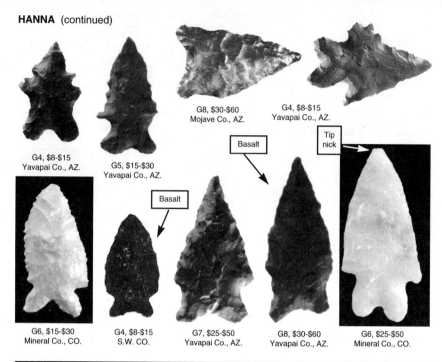

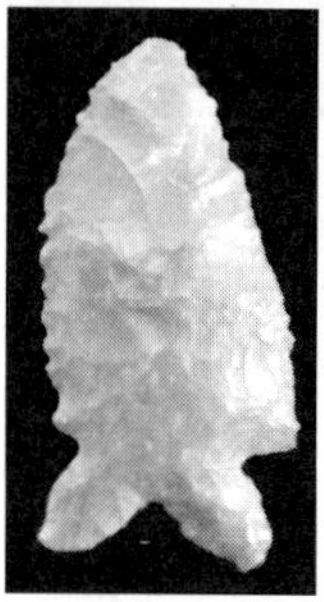

G4, $8-$15
Yavapai Co., AZ.

G5, $15-$30
Yavapai Co., AZ.

Basalt

Tip nick

Basalt

G6, $15-$30
Mineral Co., CO.

G4, $8-$15
S.W. CO.

G7, $25-$50
Yavapai Co., AZ.

G8, $30-$60
Yavapai Co., AZ.

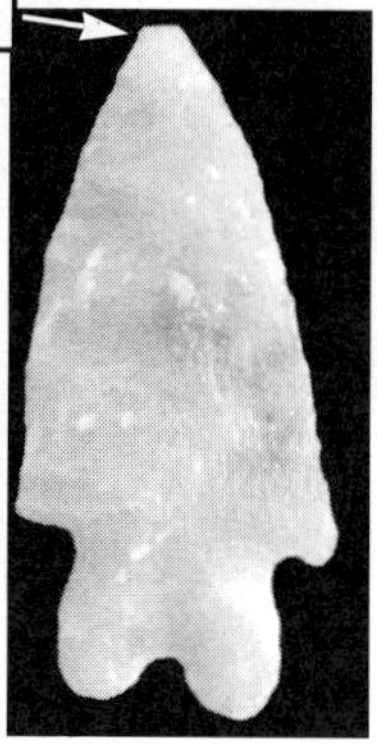

G6, $25-$50
Mineral Co., CO.

HELL GAP - Late Paleo, 10,900 - 9500 B. P.

(Also see Agate Basin, Angostura and Rio Grande)

G7, $75-$150
Pima Co., AZ.

G7, $100-$200
S.W., CO.

LOCATION: Colorado northward to the Dakotas and Canada and eastward to Texas. **DESCRIPTION:** A medium size lanceolate point with a long, contracting basal stem and a short, stubby tip. Bases are generally straight and are ground. High quality flaking. **I.D. KEY:** Long stem.

HOHOKAM - Desert Traditions-Developmental Phase, 1200 - 1000 B. P.

(Also see Datil, Desert, Dry Prong and Salado)

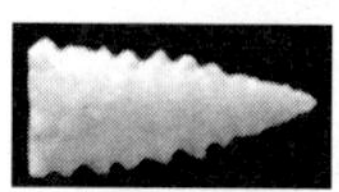

G8 $20-$40
Cedar Ridge, AZ.

G6, $15-$30
Yavapai Co., AZ.

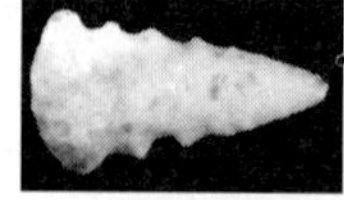

G5, $10-$20
Apache Co, AZ.

G9, $25-$50
Yavapai Co., AZ.

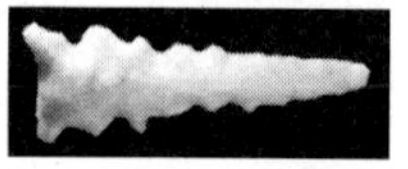

G4, $10-$20
Cedar Ridge, AZ.

G9, $25-$50
Gila Riv., AZ.

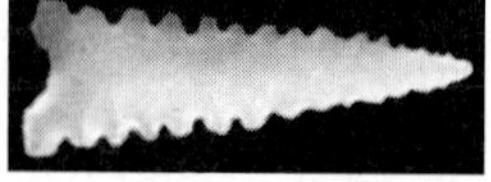

HOHOKAM (continued)

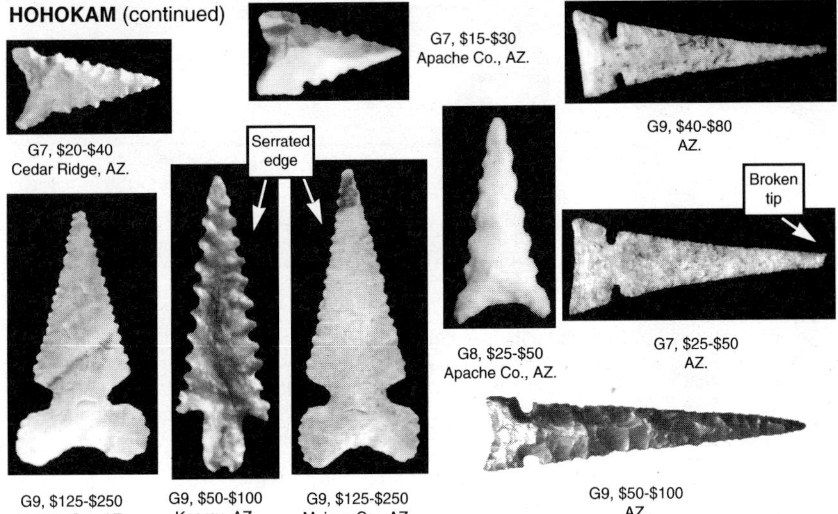

G7, $15-$30
Apache Co., AZ.

G9, $40-$80
AZ.

G7, $20-$40
Cedar Ridge, AZ.

G8, $25-$50
Apache Co., AZ.

G7, $25-$50
AZ.

G9, $125-$250
Mojave Co., AZ.

G9, $50-$100
Kearny, AZ.

G9, $125-$250
Mojave Co., AZ.

G9, $50-$100
AZ.

LOCATION: Most of Arizona. **DESCRIPTION:** A short to long, narrow, triangular arrow point which is generally well made. It may or may not have side notches, can be stemmed, and is usually serrated. **I.D.KEY:** Most often made of obsidian.

HUMBOLDT - Transitional Phase, 2000 - 1500 B. P.

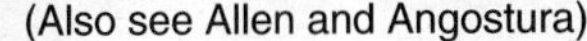

(Also see Allen and Angostura)

G6, $25-$50
Mojave Co., AZ.

G7, $35-$70
NM.

G6, $15-$30
Mojave Co., AZ.

LOCATION: Great Basin states, esp. Nevada. **DESCRIPTION:** A small to medium size, narrow, lanceolate point with a constricted, concave base. Basal concavity can be slight to extreme. **I.D. KEY:** Base form.

SW

HUMBOLDT-CONSTRICTED BASE - Transitional Phase, 2000 - 1500 B.P.

(Also see Allen, Angostura, Cascade, Early Leaf, McKean and Wheeler)

G3, $5-$10
NM.

LOCATION: Great Basin states, esp. Nevada. **DESCRIPTION:** A small to medium size, narrow, lanceolate point with a constricted, concave base. Basal concavity can be slight to extreme.

LAKE MOHAVE - Paleo, 13,200 - 10,000 B.P.

(Also see Silver Lake)

LAKE MOHAVE (continued)

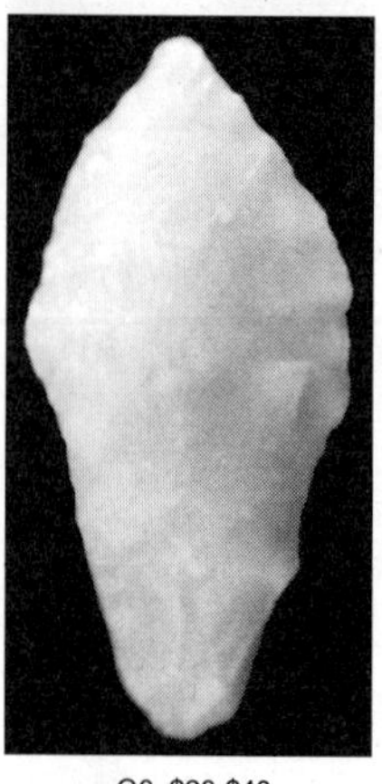

G6, $20-$40
Navajo Co., AZ.

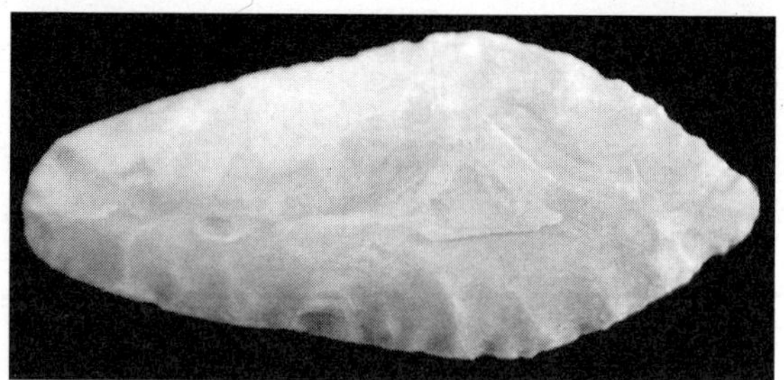

G9, $75-$150
Chaves Co., NM.

LOCATION: Southern California into Arizona and the Great Basin. **DESCRIPTION:** A medium sized, narrow, parallel to contracting stemmed point with weak, tapered to no shoulders. Stem is much longer than the blade. Some experts think these points are worn out *Parman* points. **I.D.KEY:** Long stem, very short blade.

LANCET- All Periods from Paleo to Historic

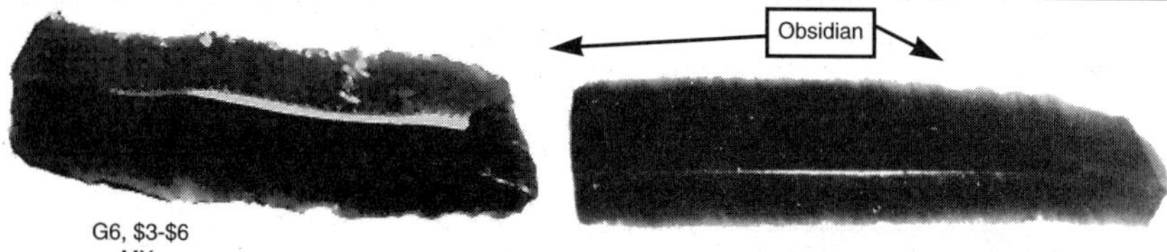

G6, $3-$6
MX.

G6, $4-$8, Chaves Co., NM.

LOCATION: Over the entire U.S. **DESCRIPTION:** This artifact is also known as a lammeler flake blade and was produced by knocking a flake or spall off a parent stone. Most of the western examples are of obsidian. Perhaps the best known of the type were those made and used by the Hopewell people in the midwest. **I.D.KEY:** Double uniface and the presence, generally, of the parent stone showing on one face.

LERMA - Middle to Late Archaic, 4000 - 3000 B. P.

(Also see Agate Basin, Angostura, Catan and Datil)

G4, $8-$15
Cochise Co., AZ.

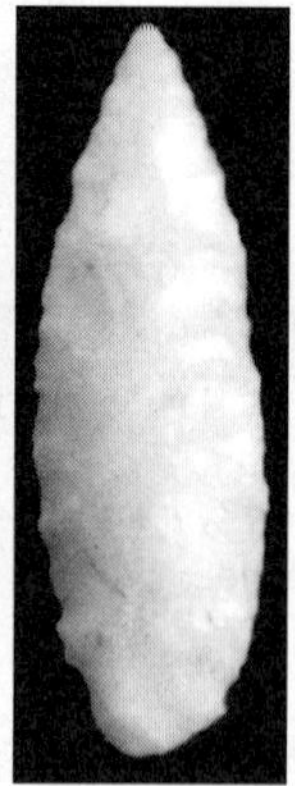

G7, $20-$40
Pima Co., AZ.

G5, $15-$30
Cochise Co., AZ.

G6, $15-$30
Cochise Co., AZ.

G8, $35-$70
Mojave Co., AZ.

LERMA (continued)

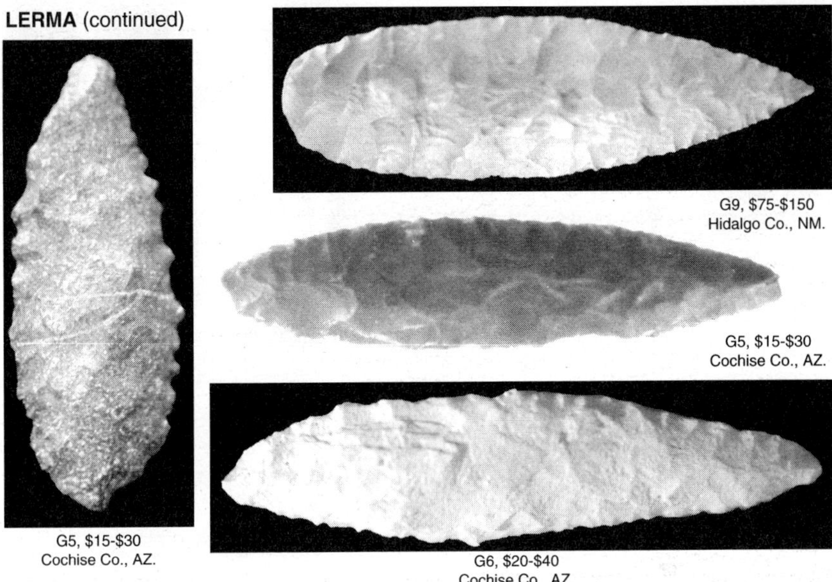

G9, $75-$150
Hidalgo Co., NM.

G5, $15-$30
Cochise Co., AZ.

G5, $15-$30
Cochise Co., AZ.

G6, $20-$40
Cochise Co., AZ.

LOCATION: From central Texas westward through New Mexico and into eastern Arizona. Examples of *Lerma* points from further east are, most likely, Guilford points. **DESCRIPTION:** A long ovoid with a rounded to somewhat pointed basal edge.

LOTT - Desert Traditions-Classic Phase, 500 - 300 B.P.

(Also see Garza, Soto and Toyah)

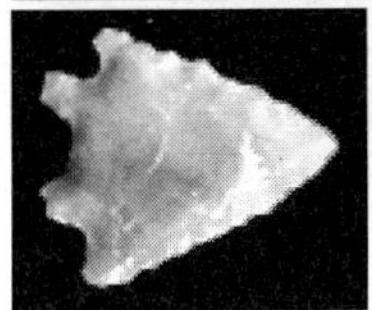

G4, $15-$30
Apache Co., AZ.

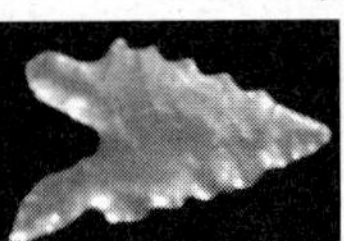

G5, $10-$20
MX, chihuahua

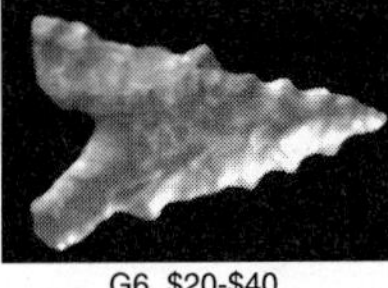

G6, $20-$40
MX, chihuahua

LOCATION: Arizona to Texas. **DESCRIPTION:** A medium size , weakly barbed point with a bifurcated base. Ears can be long and flare outward.

MALJAMAR - Late Archaic, 3500 - 2300 B. P.

(Also see Ahumada, Mount Abion, Neff, San Jose and Truxton)

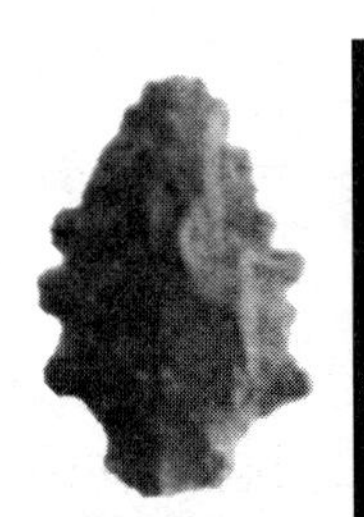

G3, $3-$6
Cochise Co., AZ.

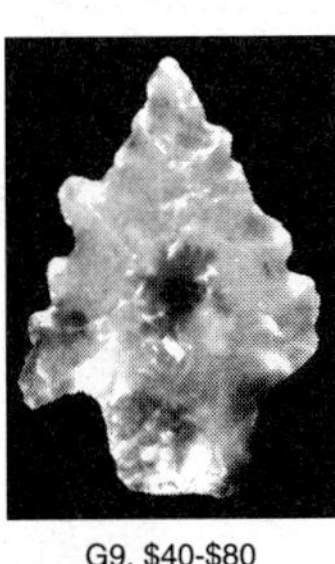

G9, $40-$80
Hidalgo Co., NM.

G5, $25-$50
Otero Co., NM.

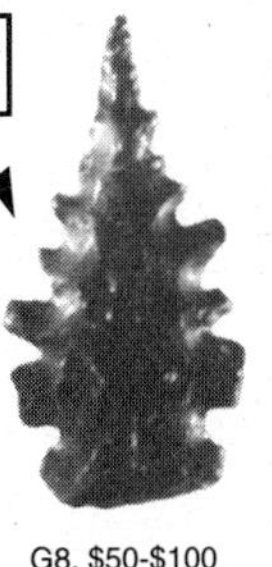

Barbed edges

G8, $50-$100
Otero Co., NM.

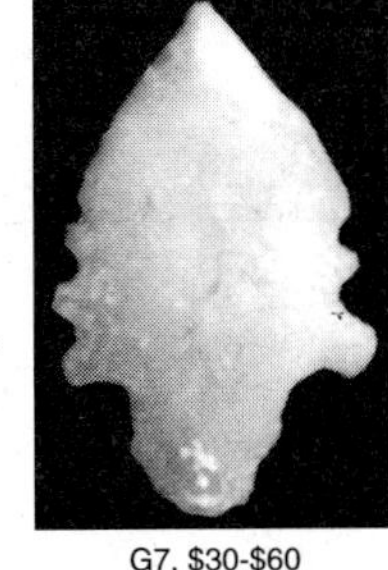

G7, $30-$60
Luna Co., NM.

LOCATION: Southeastern New Mexico and extreme western Texas. **DESCRIPTION:** A small side notched dart point with a rounded to pointed stem. They are serrated, sometimes heavily, and can acquire extra notches along the blade edges. Similar to *Duran* and *Sinner* found in Texas. **I.D.KEY:** Multiple notching.

SW

MALJAMAR (continued)

Barbed edges

G6, $25-$50
Otero Co., NM.

G8, $65-$125
Otero Co., NM.

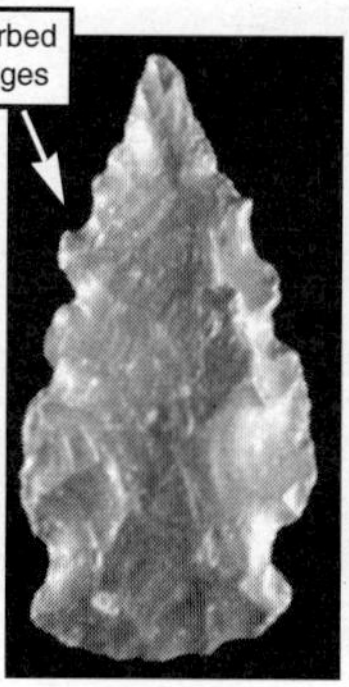

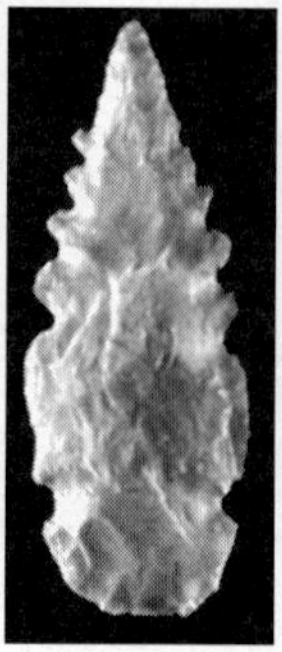

G8, $65-$125
Otero Co., NM.

G8, $35-$70
Otero Co., NM.

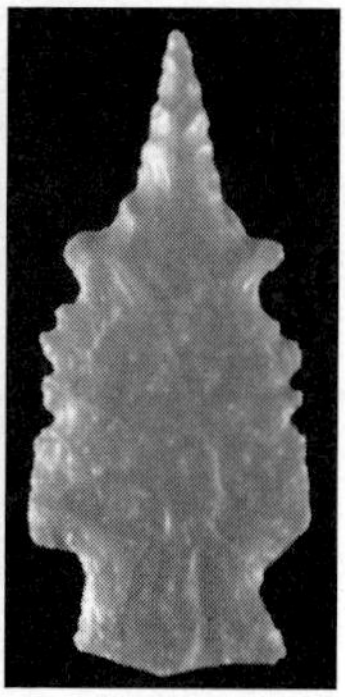

G8, $100-$200
Otero Co., NM.

Exceptional size

G9, $150-$300
Otero Co., NM.

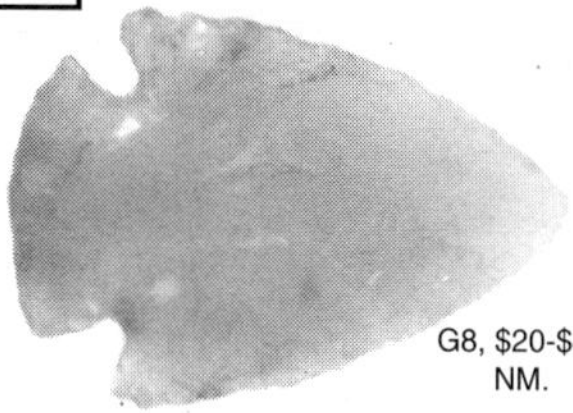

G8, $20-$40
NM.

MARTIS - Late Archaic, 3000 - 1500 B. P.

(Also see Figueroa and Mount Albion)

LOCATION: Western Arizona northward into the Great Basin. **DESCRIPTION:** A medium size corner to side notched point with small, tapered to horizontal shoulders.

MATAMOROS - Late Archaic to Classic Phase, 3000 - 400 B. P.

(Also see Catan, Mescal and Patticus)

G9, $30-$60
Mojave Co., AZ.

G8, $15-$30
Cochise Co., AZ.

G7, $12-$25
W. TX.

LOCATION: Western Texas into Arizona. **DESCRIPTION:** A small to medium size, broad, triangular point with concave, straight, or convex base. On some examples, beveling occurs on one side of each face as in *Tortugas* points. **I.D. KEY:** Triangular form.

MCKEAN- Mid to late Archaic, 4500 - 2500 B. P.

(Also see Allen, Folsom and Midland)

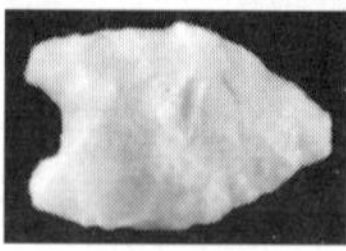

G4, $8-$15
Mojave Co., AZ.

G6, $20-$40
Mojave Co., AZ.

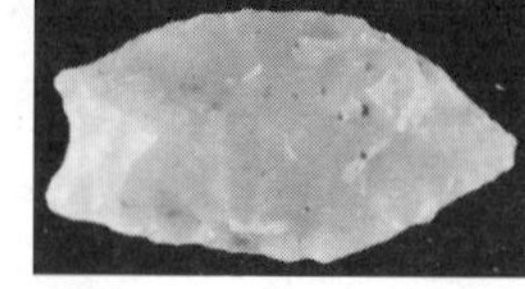

G6, $20-$40
Mojave Co., AZ.

LOCATION: Arizona to Montana. **DESCRIPTION:** A small to medium size, narrow, basal notched point. No basal grinding is evident. Similar to the much earlier *Wheeler* point of the Southeast. Basal ears are rounded to pointed. Flaking is more random although earlier examples can have parallel flaking. **I.D. KEY:** Narrow lanceolate with notched base.

MESCAL KNIFE - Desert Traditions- Classic and Historic Phases, 700 B. P. to historic times

(Also see Matamoros, Meserve, Midland and Patticus)

LOCATION: Southwestern states. **DESCRIPTION:** A well made triangular blade which was hafted horizontally along one edge.

G9, $100-$200
Yavapai Co., AZ.

MESERVE - Late Paleo, 9500 - 8500 B.P.

(Also see Allen, Angostura and Midland)

G5, $20-$40
S.W. CO.

G5, $30-$60
Luna Co., NM.

G5, $30-$60
NM.

G9, $125-$250
CO.

G9, $200-$400
Apache Co., AZ.

LOCATION: Throughout the U.S. from the Rocky Mountains to the Mississippi River. **DESCRIPTION:** A member of the *Dalton* Family. Blade edges are straight to slightly concave with a straight to very slightly concave sided stem. They are basally thinned and most examples are beveled and have light serrations on the blade edges. The basal edge is concave. **I.D. KEY:** Squared , concave base.

SW

MIDLAND - Paleo, 10,700 - 10,400 B. P.

(Also see Folsom, Mescal Knife, McKean and Milnesand)

G5, $75-$150
NM.

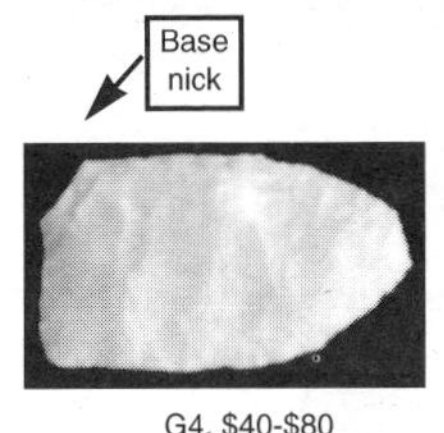

G4, $40-$80
W. TX.

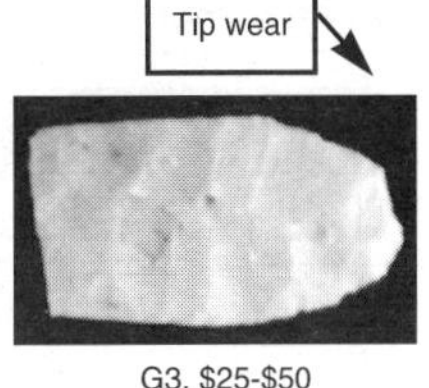

G3, $25-$50
W. TX.

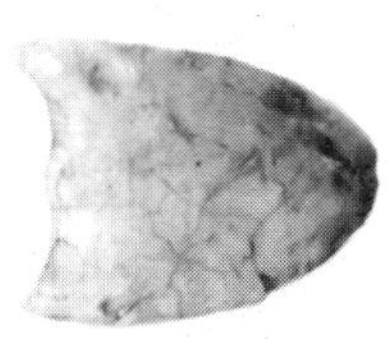

G5, $150-$300
NM.

MIDLAND (continued)

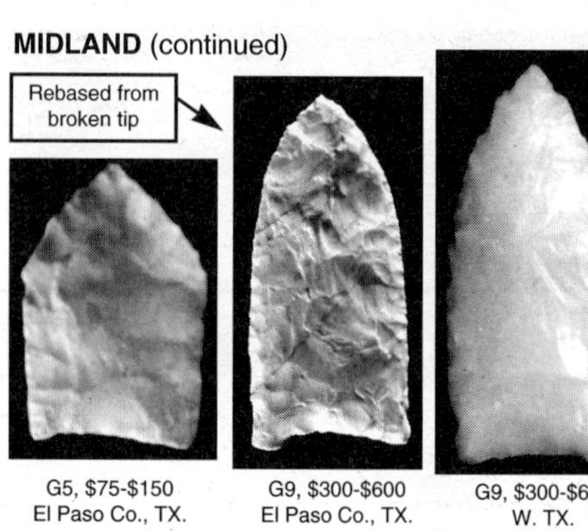

G5, $75-$150
El Paso Co., TX.

G9, $300-$600
El Paso Co., TX.

G9, $300-$600
W. TX.

G9, $300-$600
W. TX.

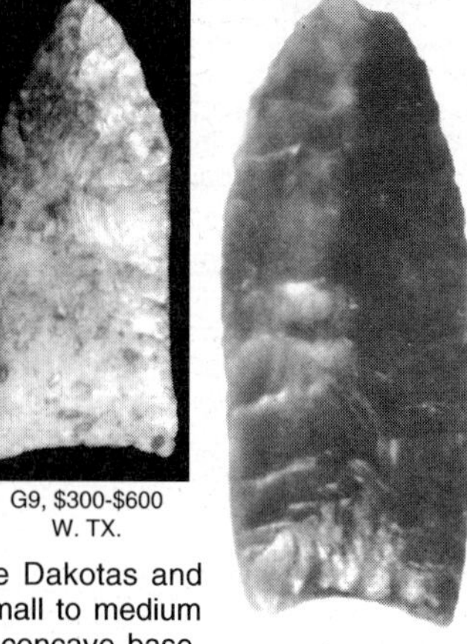

G9, $400-$800
W. TX.

LOCATION: New Mexico northward to Montana, the Dakotas and Minnesota. **DESCRIPTION:** An unfluted *Folsom.* A small to medium size, thin, unfluted lanceolate point with a straight to concave base. Basal thinning is weak and the blades exhibit fine, micro edgework. Bases are ground.

MILNESAND - Transitional Paleo, 11,000 - 8000 B. P.

(Also see Folsom and Midland)

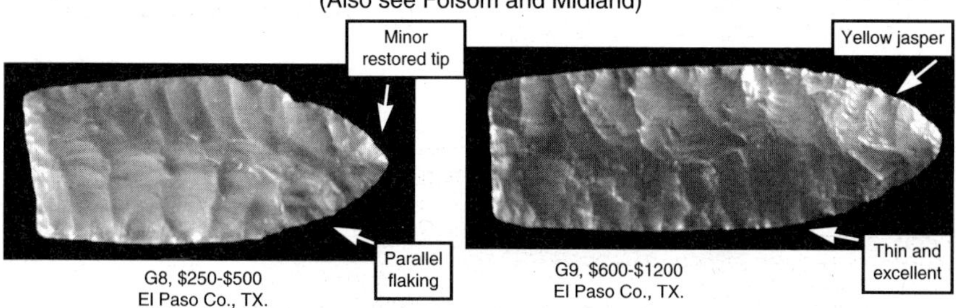

G8, $250-$500
El Paso Co., TX.

G9, $600-$1200
El Paso Co., TX.

LOCATION: Texas, New Mexico northward to Canada. **DESCRIPTION:** medium size unfluted lanceolate point that becomes thicker and wider towards the tip. The base is basically square and ground. Thicker than *Midland.* A scarce type. **I.D. KEY:** Square base and Paleo parallel flaking.

MOUNT ALBION - Early to Middle Archaic, 5800 - 5350 B. P.

(Also see Elko Corner Notched, Figueroa, Martis and San Pedro)

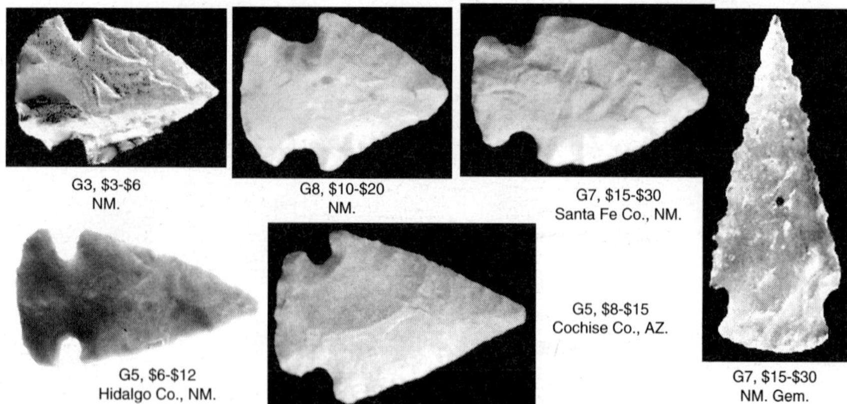

G3, $3-$6
NM.

G8, $10-$20
NM.

G7, $15-$30
Santa Fe Co., NM.

G5, $6-$12
Hidalgo Co., NM.

G5, $8-$15
Cochise Co., AZ.

G7, $15-$30
NM. Gem.

MOUNT ALBION (continued)

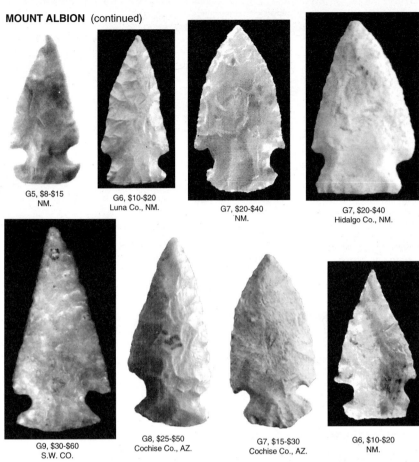

G5, $8-$15
NM.

G6, $10-$20
Luna Co., NM.

G7, $20-$40
NM.

G7, $20-$40
Hidalgo Co., NM.

G9, $30-$60
S.W. CO.

G8, $25-$50
Cochise Co., AZ.

G7, $15-$30
Cochise Co., AZ.

G6, $10-$20
NM.

LOCATION: Northeastern Arizona, southeastern Utah, northern New Mexico and southern Colorado. **DESCRIPTION:** A medium sized dart/knife with small side to corner notches, an expanded stem and convex blade edges. The basal edge is convex. **I.D. KEY:** Large expanded, convex base

NAWTHIS- Developmental Phase, 1100 - 700 B.P.

(Also see Desert, Red Horn, Rose Springs Side Notched and Sacaton)

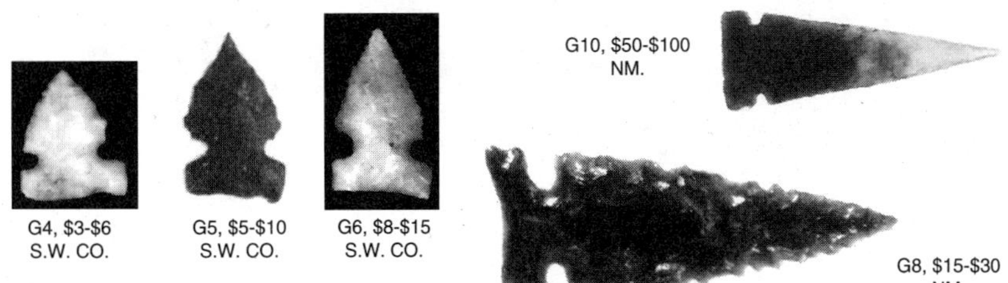

G10, $50-$100
NM.

G4, $3-$6
S.W. CO.

G5, $5-$10
S.W. CO.

G6, $8-$15
S.W. CO.

G8, $15-$30
NM.

LOCATION: Northern New Mexico into Colorado. **DESCRIPTION:** A well made, side notched arrow point. It is triangular in shape with deep, narrow notches placed low on the blade. **I.D. KEY:** Low, deep and narrow side notches.

NEFF - Late Archaic, 3500 - 2300 B. P.

(Also see Ahumada, Duran, Escobas, Maljamar and San Jose)

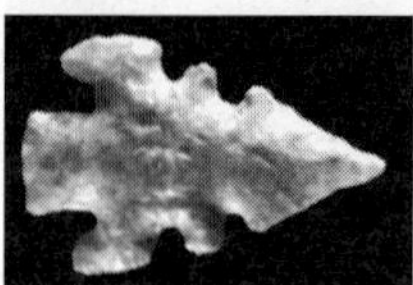

G8, $50-$100
Chaves Co., NM.

G8, $85-$175
Chaves Co., NM.

G8, $75-$150
Chaves Co., NM.

G9, $125-$250
Chaves Co., NM.

LOCATION: Eastern New Mexico and western Texas. **DESCRIPTION:** A small to medium sized dart/knife with an expanded stem, drooping shoulders and multiple notches between the shoulders and tip. Another variation similar to *Duran* and *Sinner* found in Texas. **I.D. KEY:** Large expanded, convex base

PAPAGO - Historic Phase, 400 B. P.

(Also see Cottonwood)

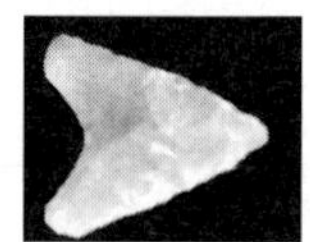

G8, $5-$10
Mojave Co., AZ.

G4, $1-$3
Yavapai Co., AZ.

G8, $8-$15
Yavapai Co., AZ.

G8, $6-$12
Mojave Co., AZ.

LOCATION: Arizona and northern Mexico. **DESCRIPTION**: A small, triangular arrow point which can range from crudely made to very well made. The base is slightly to deeply concave. It is often made on a flake. **I.D. KEY:** Concave base.

PAROWAN - Desert Traditions-Developmental Phase, 1300 - 800 B. P.

(Also see Basal Double Tang, Gila Butte and Santa Cruz)

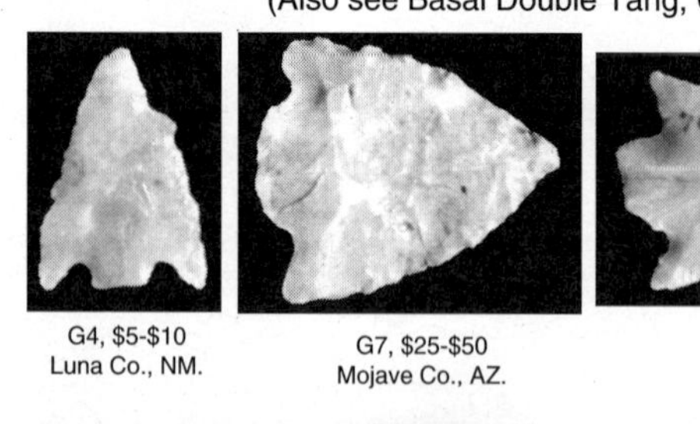

G4, $5-$10
Luna Co., NM.

G7, $25-$50
Mojave Co., AZ.

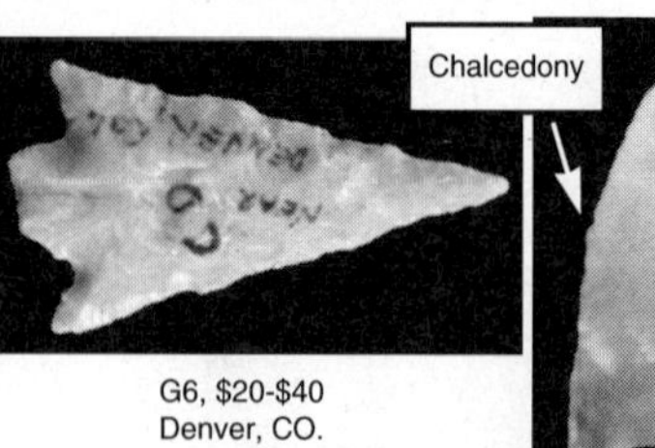

G6, $20-$40
Denver, CO.

Chalcedony

G9, $25-$50
Apache Co., AZ..

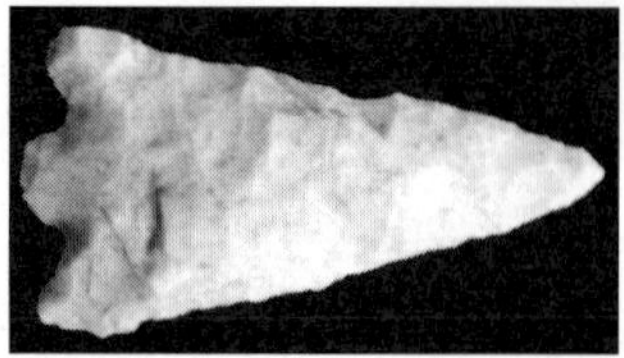

G4, $10-$20
CO.

G5, $15-$30
Mojave Co., AZ.

PAROWAN (continued)

G7, $20-$40
Apache Co., AZ.

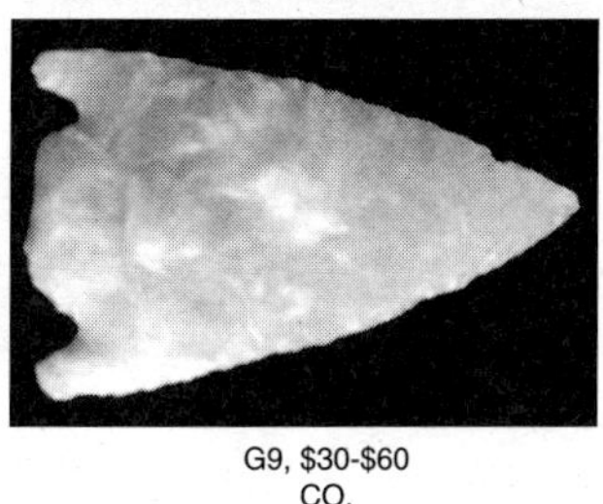

G9, $30-$60
CO.

LOCATION: Southern Utah, northern Arizona and into Nevada. **DESCRIPTION**: A medium to large triangular arrow point with two shallow basal notches creating a short straight to contracting stem. **I.D. KEY:** Stem and barbs are the same length.

PATTICUS - Late Archaic, 3500 - 2300 B. P.

(Also see Mescal Knife and Matamoros)

G6, $20-$40
Mojave Co., AZ.

G7, $25-$50
Mojave Co., AZ.

LOCATION: Northwestern Arizona and, possibly, into adjacent areas of contiguous states. **DESCRIPTION**: A large, asymmetrical to triangular knife form which may have been hafted horizontally. The blade is very thin and flat for its size.

PELONA - Early to Middle Archaic, 6000 - 4000 B. P.

(Also see Cottonwood, Lerma)

G7, $15-$30
Cochise Co., AZ. Used as graver.

G6, $10-$20
Apache Co., AZ.

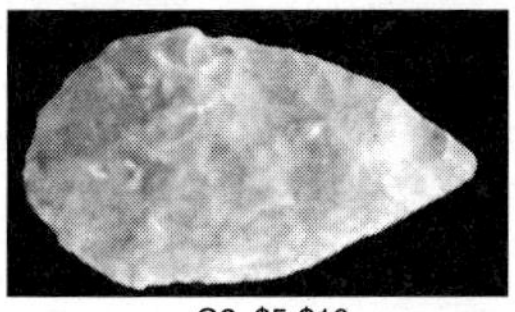

G3, $5-$10
Cochise Co., AZ.

LOCATION: Southern Arizona, southwestern New Mexico and southeastern California. **DESCRIPTION:** Ranges from lozenge to ovoid in shape. It may have serrations on the blade, or, less frequently, on the hafting area, or, in most cases, not serrated.

PELONA (continued)

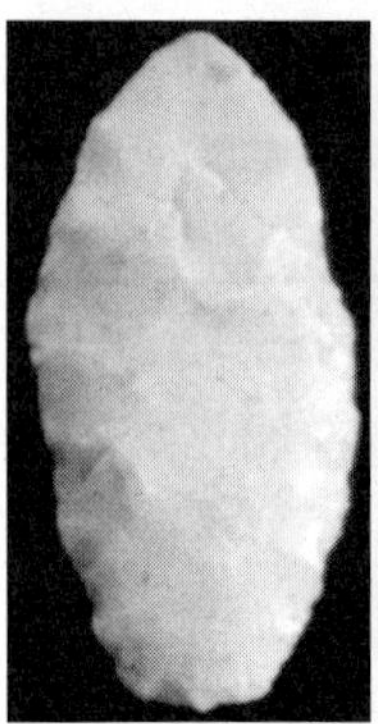
G3, $5-$10
Apache Co., AZ.

G7, $25-$50
Apache Co., AZ.

G4, $6-$12
Yavapai Co., AZ.

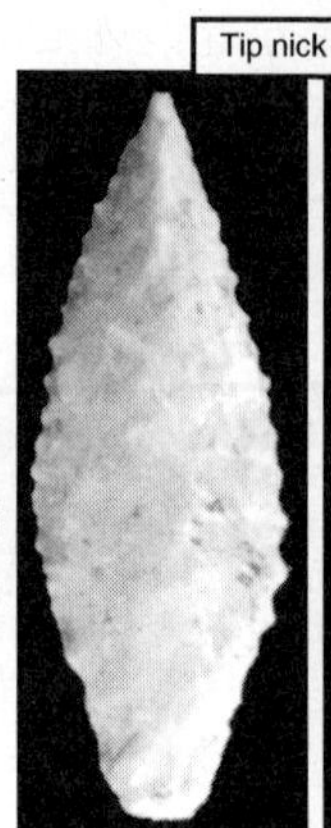
G9, $30-$60
Apache Co., AZ.

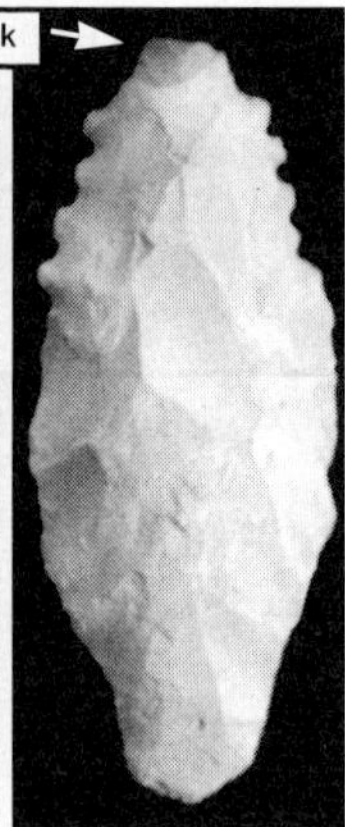

G5, $10-$20
Apache Co., AZ.

RED HORN - Classic to Historic Phase, 700 - 400 B. P.

(Also see Desert and Rose Springs Side Notched)

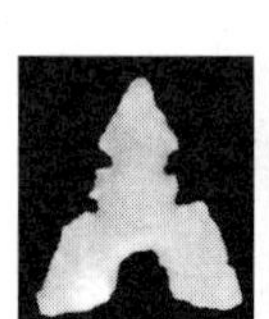
G5, $8-$15
Mojave Co., AZ.

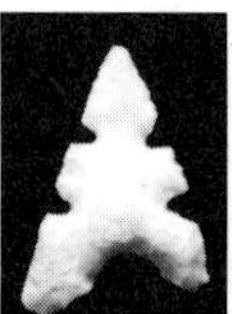
G4, $6-$12
Mojave Co., AZ.

G6, $10-$20
Mojave Co., AZ.

G5, $8-$15
Yavapai Co., AZ.

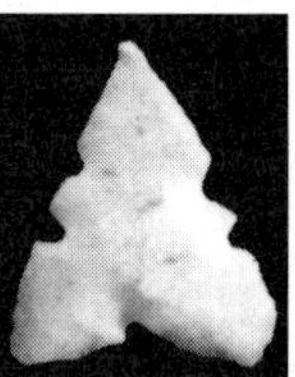
G6, $12-$25
Navajo Co., AZ.

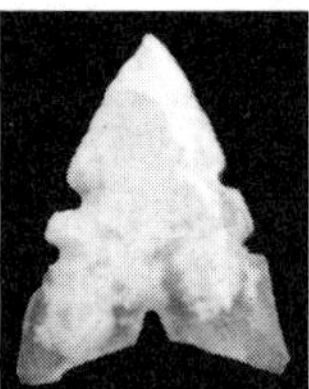
G8, $25-$50
Navajo Co., AZ.

LOCATION: Most of Arizona, southern New Mexico, southwestern Texas and northern Mexico. **DESCRIPTION:** A small, triangular arrow point with a deep basal notch and multiple side notches, most often with two pairs of side notches but examples with three pairs are not uncommon. Blade edges are generally straight. **I.D. KEY:** Multiple side notches.

RIO GRANDE - Early Archaic, 7500 - 6000 B. P.

(Also see Agate Basin, Angostura, Hell Gap, Lake Mohave and Pelican)

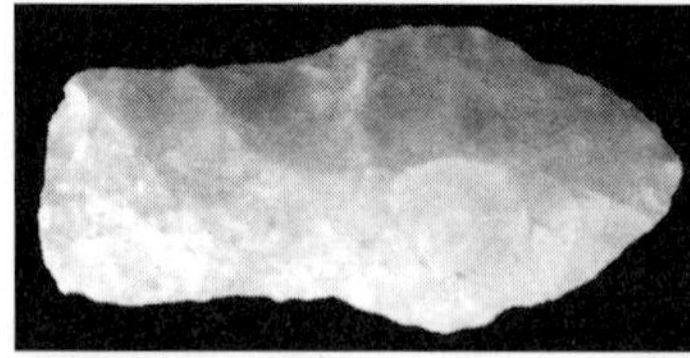
G6, $18-$35
Chaves Co., NM.

G7, $35-$70
Sante Fe, NM.

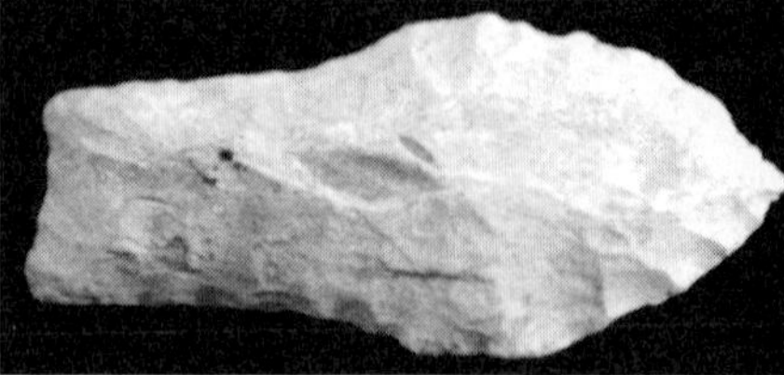
G7, $25-$50
NM.

LOCATION: Southern Colorado, New Mexico and western Texas. **DESCRIPTION:** A lanceolate point with a relatively long stem formed by obtuse shoulders. The stem contracts slightly and stem edges are ground. **I.D. KEY:** The shoulders are more pronounced then on *Hell Gap* points.

ROSE SPRINGS CONTRACTED STEM - Developmental Phase, 1600 - 700 B. P.

(Also see Datil and Gypsum Cave))

G6, $5-$10
Pinal Co., AZ.

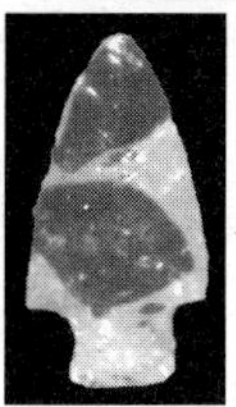
G6, $5-$10
Mojave Co., AZ.

G6, $10-$20
UT.

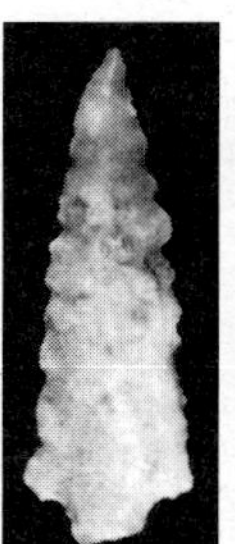
G6, $5-$10
Mojave Co., AZ.

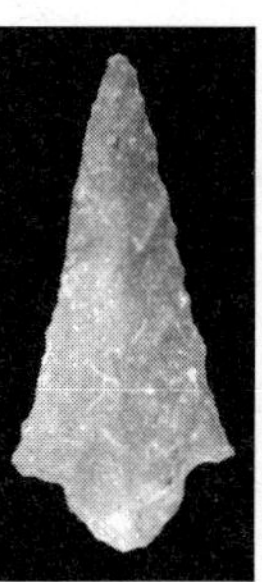
G6, $5-$10
Mojave Co., AZ.

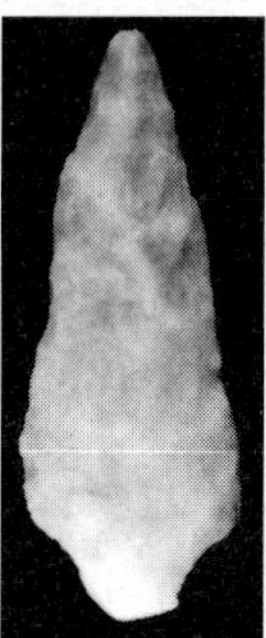
G6, $5-$10
Pima Co., AZ.

LOCATION: Arizona and New Mexico northward. **DESCRIPTION:** A small size, thin, light weight, arrow point with a short, contracted stem. Stem base can be straight to rounded. **I.D. KEY:** Short contracting stem.

ROSE SPRINGS CORNER NOTCHED - Developmental Phase, 1600 - 700 B. P.

(Also see Desert)

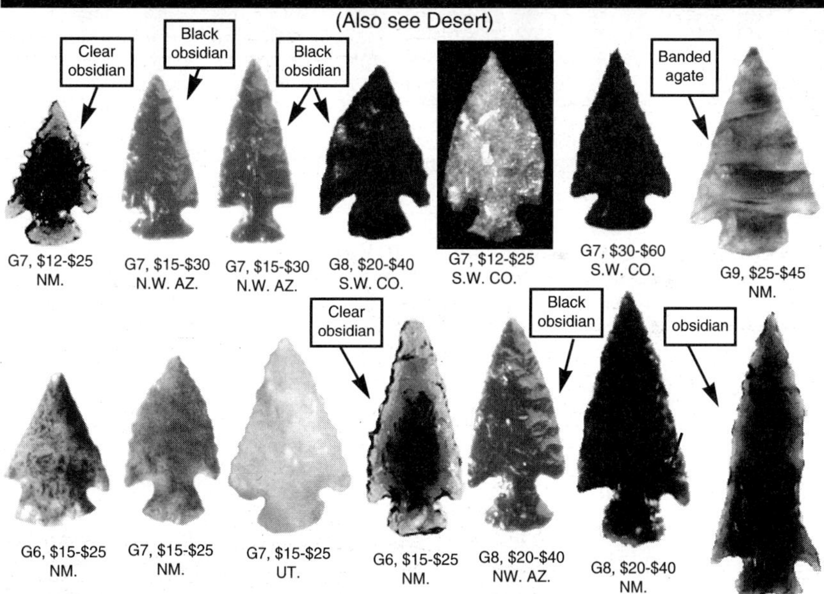

G7, $12-$25 NM. G7, $15-$30 N.W. AZ. G7, $15-$30 N.W. AZ. G8, $20-$40 S.W. CO. G7, $12-$25 S.W. CO. G7, $30-$60 S.W. CO. G9, $25-$45 NM.

G6, $15-$25 NM. G7, $15-$25 NM. G7, $15-$25 UT. G6, $15-$25 NM. G8, $20-$40 NW. AZ. G8, $20-$40 NM. G7, $20-$40 NM.

LOCATION: Arizona and New Mexico northward. **DESCRIPTION:** A small size, thin, light weight, corner notched arrow point. Notching is usually wide producing sharp tangs. Base corners are sharp to rounded. **I.D. KEY:** Size, broad corner notches.

SW

ROSE SPRINGS SIDE NOTCHED - Developmental Phase, 1600 - 700 B. P.

(Also see Deser and Red Horn)

ROSE SPRINGS SIDE NOTCHED (continued)

LOCATION: Arizona and New Mexico northward. **DESCRIPTION:** A small size, thin, light weight, side side notched arrow point. Bases are straight to slightly convex or concave. **I.D. KEY:** Small size, side notches.

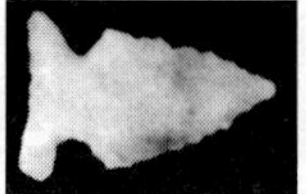

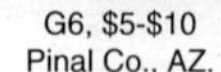

G6, $5-$10
Pinal Co., AZ.

G6, $5-$10
NM.

SACATON - Desert Traditions-Developmental Phase, 1100 - 900 B. P.

(Also see Desert, Dry Prong and Temporal)

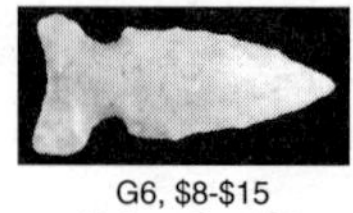

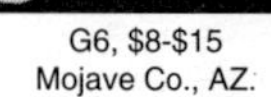

G6, $8-$15
Mojave Co., AZ.

G8, $20-$40
NM.

Clear obsidian

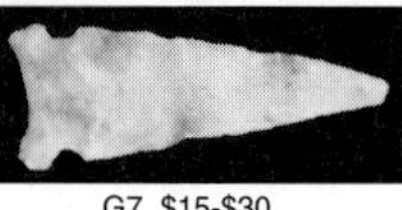

G7, $15-$30
Apache Co., AZ.

LOCATION: Arizona and central and southwestern New Mexico. **DESCRIPTION:** A small, triangular arrow point with relatively large side notches placed close to the basal edge. The base is the widest part of the point and is slightly concave. **I.D. KEY:** Wide base.

SALADO - Developmental Phase, 1500 - 1000 B.P.

(Also see Desert and Hohokam)

G6, $8-$15
Cedar
Ridge, AZ.

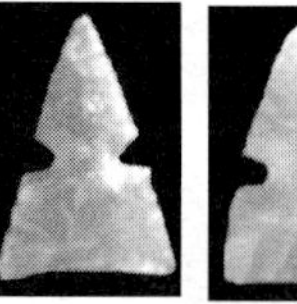

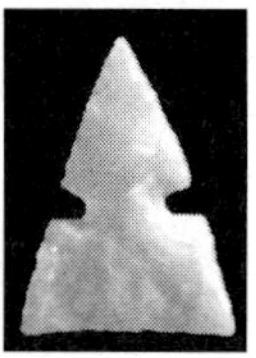

G7, $10-$20 ea.
Cedar Ridge, AZ.

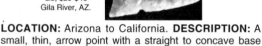

G9, $20-$30
Cedar Ridge, AZ.

G7, $15-$30
Cedar Ridge, AZ.

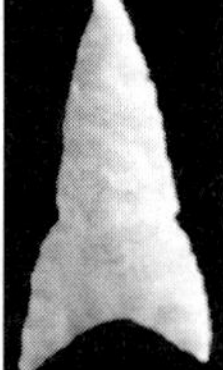

G8, $20-$40
Gila River, AZ.

G8, $20-$40
Gila River, AZ.

LOCATION: Arizona to California. **DESCRIPTION:** A small, thin, arrow point with a straight to concave base and tiny side notches set well up from the base. Related to *Hohokam*. **I.D. KEY:** Large basal area. See *Panoche* in California.

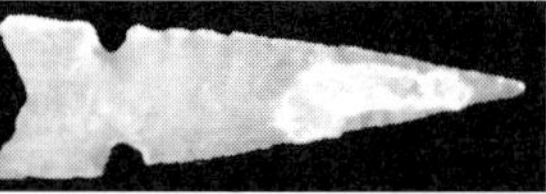

G9, $25-$50
Cedar Ridge, AZ.

SAN JOSE - Early Archaic, 6000 - 5000 B. P.

(Also see Bajada, Chiricahua, Escobas, Hanna, Maljamar, Meserve, Neff and Snaketown)

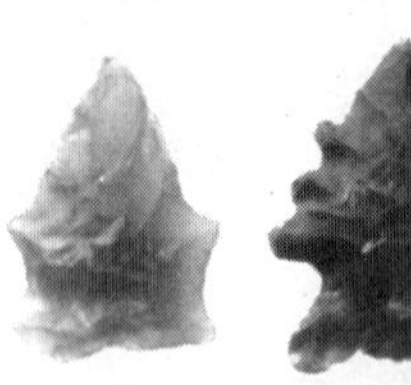

G2, $2-$5
Yavapai Co., AZ.

G5, $5-$10
Yavapai Co., AZ.

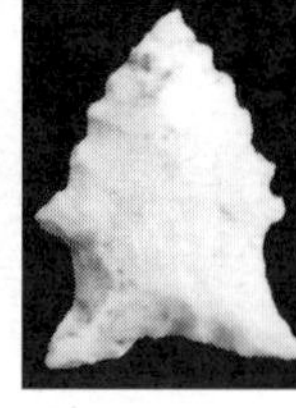

G6, $15-$30
Apache Co., AZ.

G5, $5-$10
Yavapai Co., AZ.

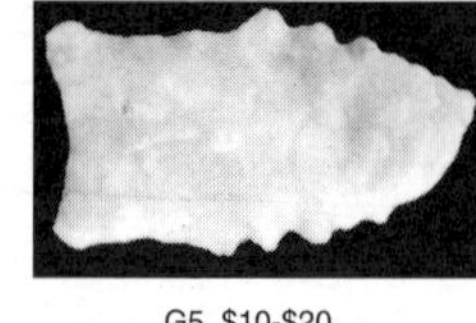

G5, $10-$20
Apache Co., AZ.

Shoulders gone from resharpening

G4, $5-$10
Cochise Co., AZ.

G9, $50-$100
Yavapai Co., AZ.

SAN JOSE (continued)

G7, $35-$70
Chinle, AZ.

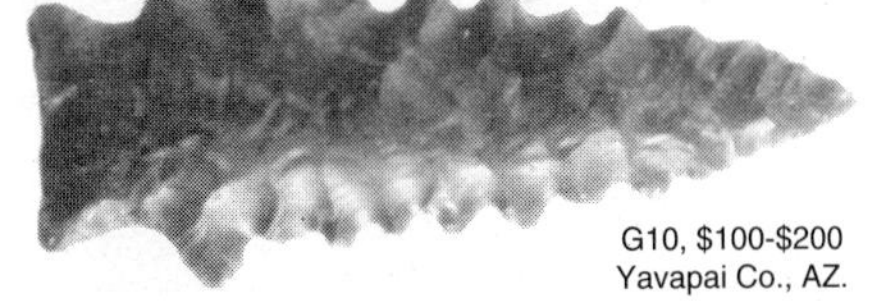

G10, $100-$200
Yavapai Co., AZ.

LOCATION: Arizona and New Mexico. **DESCRIPTION:** A small dart/knife with wide, shallow side notches. The shoulders are obtuse and the blade edges always have relatively large serrations. **I.D. KEY:** Large serrations.

SAN PEDRO - Late Archaic, 2500 - 1800 B. P.

(Also see Mount Albion and Yavapai Stemmed)

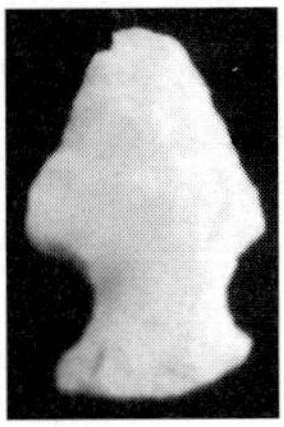

G3, $2-$4
Navajo Co., AZ.

G3, $2-$4
Cochise Co., AZ.

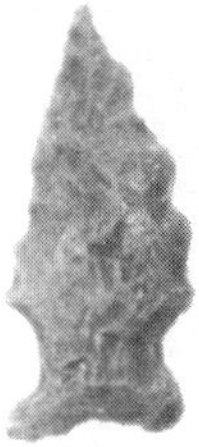

G5, $10-$20
Cochise Co., AZ.

G3, $3-$6
Cochise Co., AZ.

G5, $8-$15
Yavapai Co., AZ.

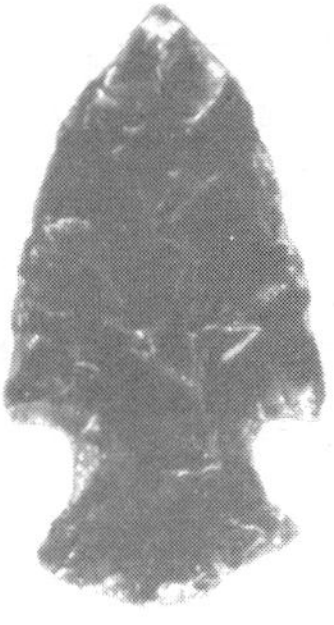

G6, $10-$20
Cochise Co., AZ.

Base nick

G5, $8-$15
Yavapai Co., AZ.

G10, $40-$80
Mojave Co., AZ.

G6, $15-$30
Chinle, AZ.

G5, $8-$15
Yavapai Co., AZ.

Basalt

G6, $15-$30
Yavapai Co., AZ.

G5, $15-$30
NM.

LOCATION: New Mexico, Arizona and northern Mexico. **DESCRIPTION:** A small to medium sized dart/knife made on a triangular preform and having side notches which begin at the basal corners and range from shallow to as deep as wide. Blade edges may be lightly serrated and the basal edge is straight to slightly convex.

SW

SANDIA - Paleo, 14,000 - 10,000 B. P.

(Also see Clovis and Folsom)

G9, type I, $500-$1000 Sandia Mtns, NM. (shot from cast of real point from the type site discovered between 1936 and 1940)

G6, type II, $350-$700 Sandia Mtns, NM. (shot from cast of real point from the type site)

G8, type II, $500-$1000 Yuma Co., AZ.

G9, type III, $750-$1500 Sandia Mtns, NM. (shot from cast of real point from the type site)

LOCATION: Type site is Sandia Mtns., New Mexico, south of Albuquerque. **DESCRIPTION:** This point occurs in three forms: The first form is a narrow, elliptical shape with only one shoulder and a rounded base. The second form has a slightly concave base, otherwise it is the same as the first form. The third form has a deeply concave base with drooping auricles. This, as well as the second form, have been found fluted on one or both faces. This type is extremely rare everywhere and may be later than *Clovis.* Another site with datable contex has not yet been found. Originally (questionably?) carbon dated to 20,000 B.P. **I.D. KEY:** Single shoulder.

SANTA CRUZ -Desert Traditions-Developmental Phase, 1400-600 B. P.

(Also see Augustin and Gypsum Cave)

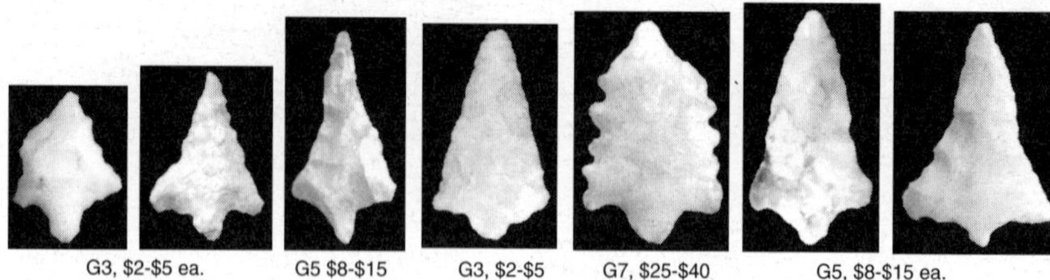

G3, $2-$5 ea. Apache Co., AZ.

G5 $8-$15 Cochise Co., AZ.

G3, $2-$5 Mojave Co., AZ.

G7, $25-$40 Apache Co., AZ.

G5, $8-$15 ea. Apache Co., AZ.

LOCATION: Arizona and contiguous parts of adjoining states. **DESCRIPTION:** A small, triangular arrow point with straight to obtuse shoulders and a short, tapering stem. **I.D. KEY:** Tiny, triangular stem.

SCOTTSBLUFF II - Transitional Paleo, 9500 - 8500 B. P.

(Also see Eden and Firstview)

IMPORTANT: Shown half size

G8, $800-$1500, Taos, NM.

LOCATION: Midwestern states. **DESCRIPTION:** A medium to large size triangular point with shoulders a little stronger than on Type I and a broad parallel sided/expanding stem.

SIERRA STEMMED- Late Archaic, 2800 - 1700 B. P.

(Also see Silver Lake)

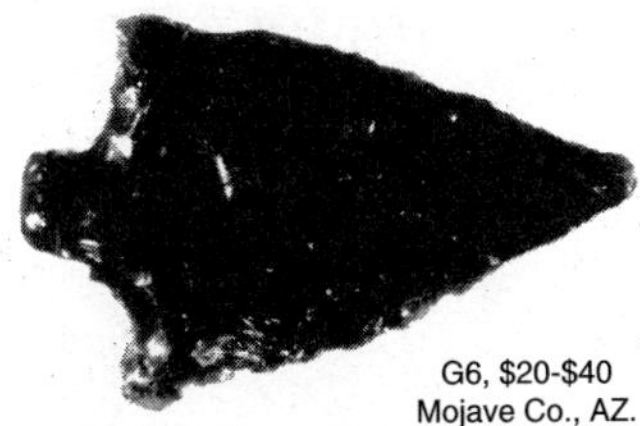

G6, $20-$40
Mojave Co., AZ.

LOCATION: Arizona. **DESCRIPTION:** A medium size stemmed point with tapered to horizontal shoulders and a contracting stem.

SILVER LAKE- Early Archaic, 11,000 - 7000 B. P.

(Also see Colonial, Firstview, Lake Mohave and Yavapai)

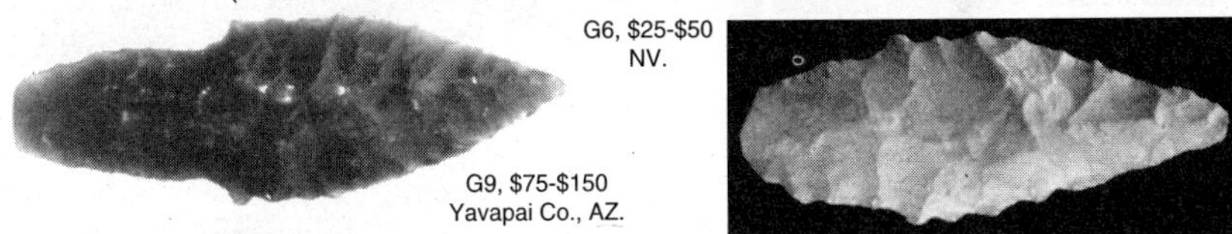

G9, $75-$150
Yavapai Co., AZ.

G6, $25-$50
NV.

LOCATION: Arizona, Nevada to California. **DESCRIPTION:** A medium to large size, stemmed point with weak, tapered shoulders and usually a serrated edge. The stem can be up to half its length. The base is usually rounded and ground. **I.D. KEY:** Long stem, weak shoulders.

SNAKETOWN-Desert Traditions-Developmental Phase, 1200-1050 B. P.

(Also see Hohokam)

G5, $25-$50
Yavapai Co., AZ.

Broken tip

G8, $75-$150
Yavapai Co., AZ.

G9, $100-$200
Phoenix, AZ.

LOCATION: Arizona. **DESCRIPTION:** A very rare, ceremonial form of *Hohokam* arrow point. The stem is straight to expanded and sometimes concave to bifurcated and has large serrations on both sides of the blade. Some examples are serrated on the lower half of the point. **I.D. KEY:** Narrowness, length, broad serrations.

SOTO- Developmental Phase, 1000-700 B. P.

(Also see Garza, Lott and Toyah)

Fine serrations

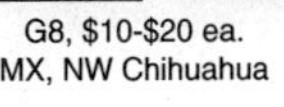

G8, $10-$20 ea.
MX, NW Chihuahua

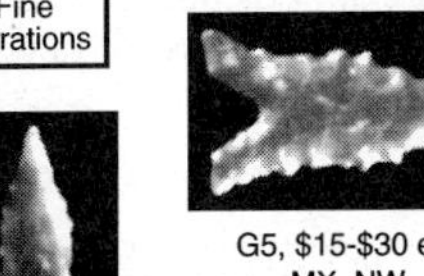

G5, $15-$30 ea.
MX, NW
Chihuahua

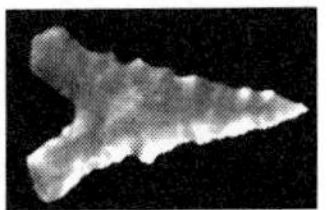

G8, $20-$40
MX, NW Chihuahua

SOTO (continued)

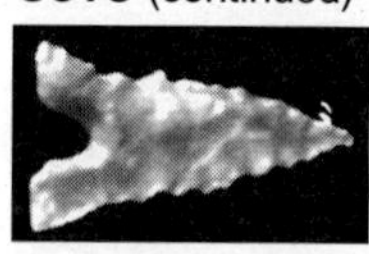

G9, $20-$40
MX, NW Chihuahua

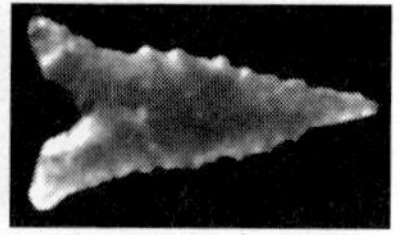

G9, $25-$50 ea.
MX, NW Chihuahua

LOCATION: NW Chihuahua Mexico. **DESCRIPTION:** A small, serrated arrow point with expanding ears, weak shoulders and a concave base. Most are made of agate and jasper. Similar to Garza & Toyah. **I.D. KEY:** Thinness, drooping ears.

SQUAW MOUNTAIN - Middle Archaic, 5000 - 3000 B. P.

(Also see Hanna and San Jose)

G4, $5-$10
Nanajo Co., AZ.

G5, $10-$20
Cohise Co., AZ.

G7, $25-$50
Cochise Co., AZ.

G6, $20-$40
Pinal Co., AZ.

G6, $20-$40
Cochise Co., AZ.

G8, $25-$50
Apache Co., AZ.

G6, $20-$40
Yavapai Co., AZ.

G4, $12-$25
Yavapai Co., AZ.

LOCATION: Southwestern states. **DESCRIPTION:** A triangular form with wide, shallow side notches and a deep basal concavity which creates highly exaggerated basal tangs. Tangs are rounded to pointed. **I.D. KEY:** Exaggerated tangs.

TEMPORAL - Desert Traditions-Developmental Phase, 1000 - 800 B. P.

(Also see Desert, Dry Prong and Sacaton)

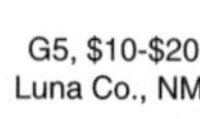

G5, $10-$20
Luna Co., NM.

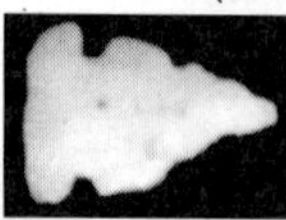

G5, $10-
$20, NM.

G7, $15-$30
NM.

LOCATION: New Mexico, Arizona and western Texas. **DESCRIPTION:** A small side notched arrow point with one or two extra notches on one side. It is triangular with straight sides and a convex basal edge. Notches are narrow and deeper than they are wide. **I.D. KEY:** Rounded or rocker like basal edge.

TEXCOCO - Late Archaic, 6000 - 5000 B.P.

(Also see Elko Corner Notched, Martis and Mount Albion)

TEXCOCO (continued)

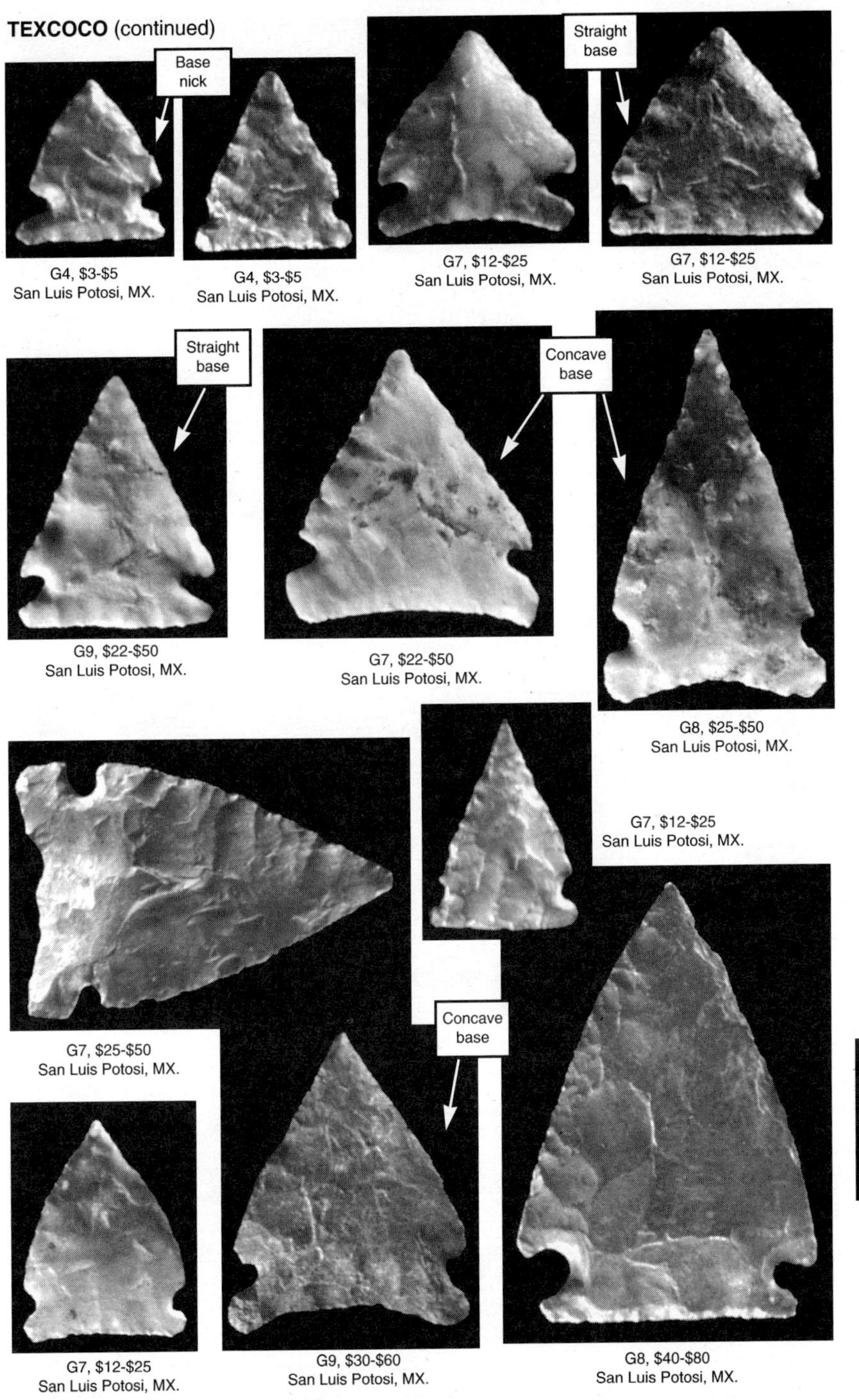

G4, $3-$5
San Luis Potosi, MX.

G4, $3-$5
San Luis Potosi, MX.

G7, $12-$25
San Luis Potosi, MX.

G7, $12-$25
San Luis Potosi, MX.

G9, $22-$50
San Luis Potosi, MX.

G7, $22-$50
San Luis Potosi, MX.

G8, $25-$50
San Luis Potosi, MX.

G7, $12-$25
San Luis Potosi, MX.

G7, $25-$50
San Luis Potosi, MX.

G7, $12-$25
San Luis Potosi, MX.

G9, $30-$60
San Luis Potosi, MX.

G8, $40-$80
San Luis Potosi, MX.

SW

LOCATION: Central Mexico. **DESCRIPTION:** A triangular, wide based, thin, flat, corner to side notched point. The base is straight to concave. **I.D. KEY:** Width and thinness.

TOYAH- Desert Traditions-Late Classic Phase, 600 - 400 B. P.

(Also see Desert)

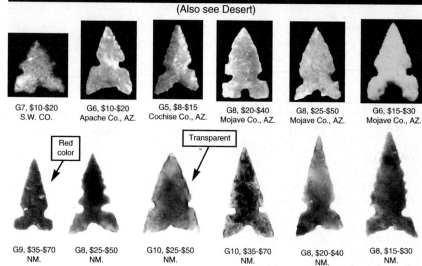

G7, $10-$20
S.W. CO.

G6, $10-$20
Apache Co., AZ.

G5, $8-$15
Cochise Co., AZ.

G8, $20-$40
Mojave Co., AZ.

G8, $25-$50
Mojave Co., AZ.

G6, $15-$30
Mojave Co., AZ.

Red color

Transparent

G9, $35-$70
NM.

G8, $25-$50
NM.

G10, $25-$50
NM.

G10, $35-$70
NM.

G8, $20-$40
NM.

G8, $15-$30
NM.

LOCATION: Arizona, New Mexico and western Texas. **DESCRIPTION:** A small triangular arrow point with straight blade edges, side notches, and a concave base which often has a further central notch. Variations of this point may have multiple sets of side notches.

TRADE - Historic, 400 - 170 B. P.

G4, $15-$30
S.W. CO.

G5, $25-$50
S.W. CO.

G3, $10-$20
S.W. CO.

G6, $25-$50
S.W. CO.

G5, $25-$50
S.W. CO.

G7, $30-$60
S.W. CO.

Serrated base

G8, $35-$70
S.W. CO.

G8, $75-$150
S.W. CO.

LOCATION: All over North America. **DESCRIPTION:** These points were made of copper, iron, and steel and were traded to the Indians by the French, British and others from the 1600s to the 1800s. Examples have been found all over the United States.

TRIPLE T - Middle Archaic, 5400 - 5000 B. P.

(Also see Meserve)

G6, $15-$30
Yavapai Co., AZ.

G5, $12-$25
Yavapai Co., AZ.

LOCATION: Western Arizona and into Nevada. **DESCRIPTION:** A medium sized lanceolate point with convex sides, a concave basal edge and rounded basal corners. A variation of the *Humboldt.*

TRUXTON - Desert Traditions-Developmental Phase, 1500 - 1000 B. P.

(Also see Duran and Maljamar)

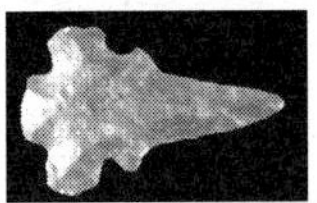
G4, $6-$12
Mojave Co., AZ.

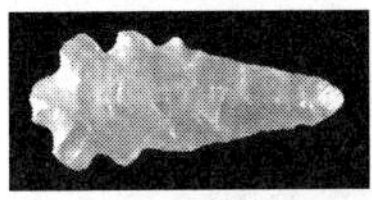
G4, $8-$15
Mojave Co., AZ.

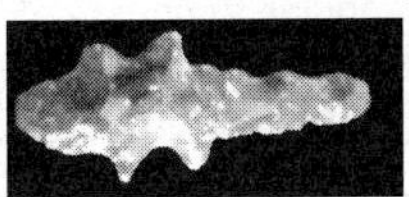
G4, $5-$10
Navajo Co., AZ.

G6, $20-$40
Mojave Co., AZ.

G5, $12-$25
Mojave Co., AZ.

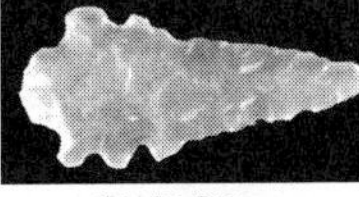
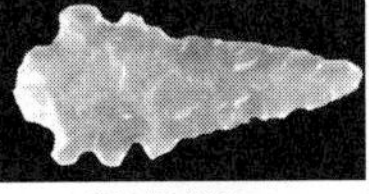
G4, $8-$15
Mojave Co., AZ.

LOCATION: Northern Arizona and possibly into adjacent states. **DESCRIPTION:** A small arrow point with a short stem, most often with a convex basal edge. The central portion of the blade has multiple notches and the tip of the blade is straight sided converging to a sharply pointed tip.

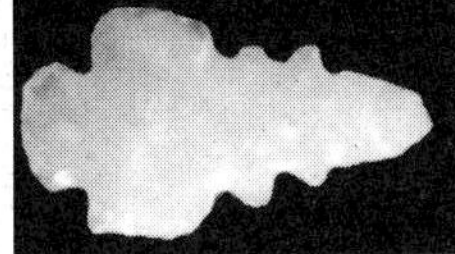
G6, $20-$40
Apache Co., AZ.

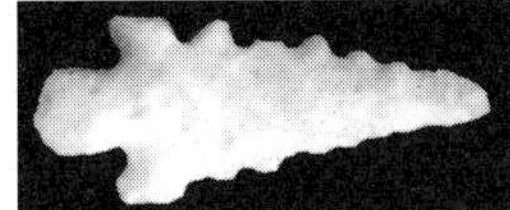
G7, $25-$50
Apache Co., AZ.

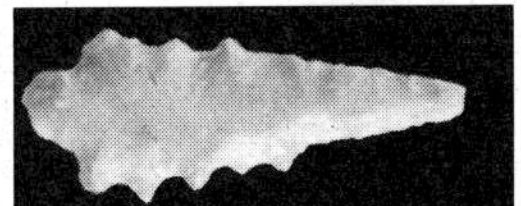
G4, $8-$15
Apache Co., AZ.

VAL VERDE - Mid-late Archaic, 5000 - 3000 B.P.

(Also see Figueroa)

LOCATION: Northern Arizona and possibly into adjacent states. **DESCRIPTION:** A medium size dart point with a short, expanding stem, most often with a concave basal edge. Shoulders are obtuse and blade edges are straight to concave or recurved. Rarely, it occurs with a chisel tip. **I.D. KEY:** "Swallow tail" stem.

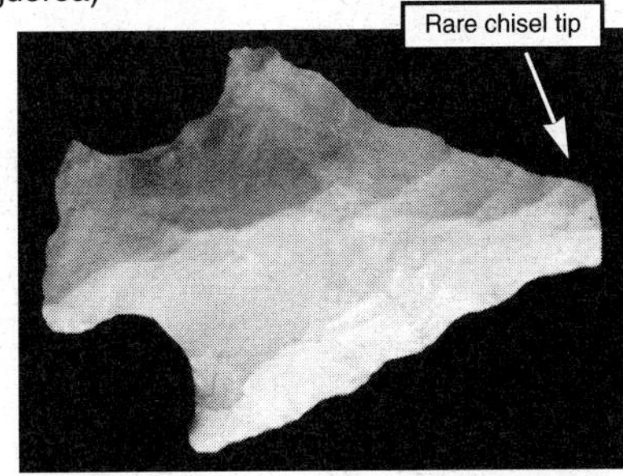

G6, $20-$40
Cochise Co., AZ.

SW

VENTANA-AMARGOSA - Early Archaic, 7000 - 5000 B. P.

(Also see Colonial and Yavapai Stemmed)

G4, $5-$10
Yavapai Co., AZ.

G5, $8-$15
Cochise Co., AZ.

G3, $3-$6
Cochise Co., AZ.

G5, $10-$20
Yavapai Co., AZ.

G4, $6-$12
Cochise Co., AZ.

LOCATION: Arizona and contiguous parts of adjacent states. **DESCRIPTION:** A small to medium sized dart/knife with a triangular blade with straight to slightly convex edges and straight to angular shoulders. The stem is parallel sided and rectangular to square. The basal edge is straight to rounded. **I.D. KEY:** A very square appearing stem.

G4, $8-$15
Cochise Co., AZ.

YAVAPAI - Late Archaic to Transitional, 3300 - 1000 B. P.

(Also see Colonial and Ventana-Amargosa)

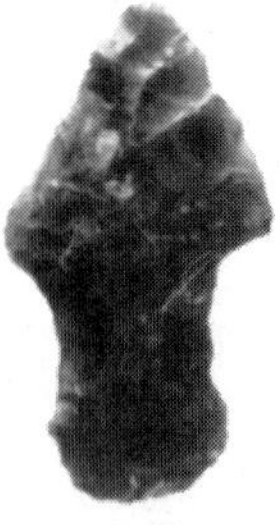

G3, $5-$10
Yavapai Co., AZ.

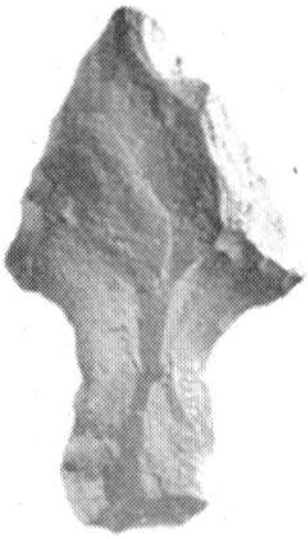

G3, $5-$10
Yavapai Co., AZ.

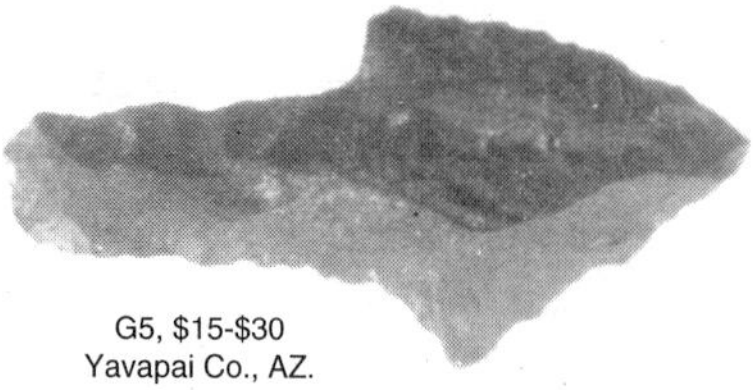

G5, $15-$30
Yavapai Co., AZ.

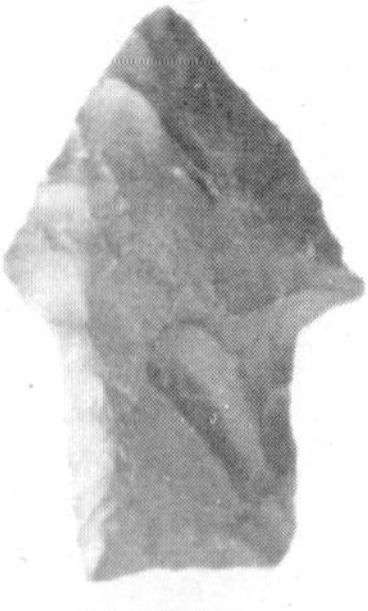

G4, $10-$20
Cochise Co., AZ.

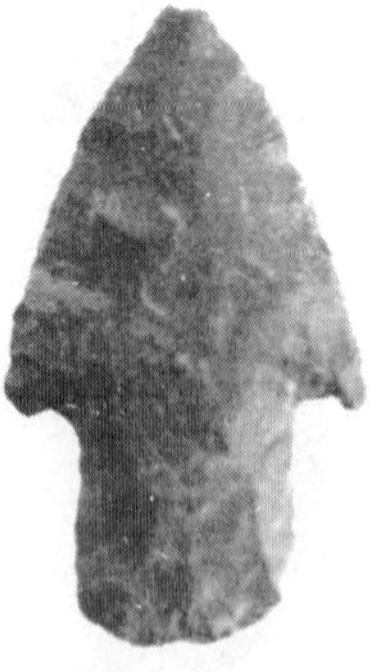

G5, $15-$30
Yavapai Co., AZ.

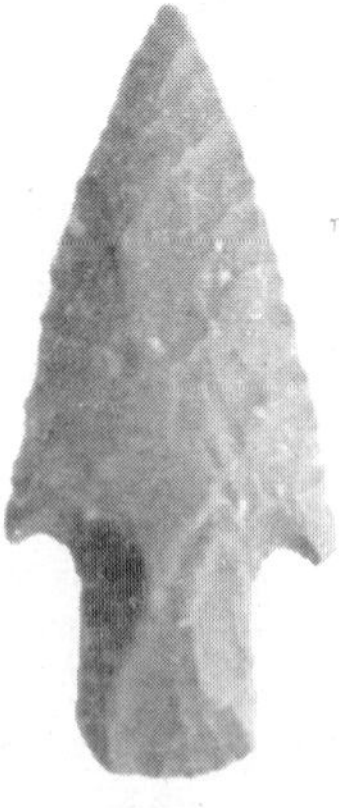

G6, $15-$30
Yavapai Co., AZ.

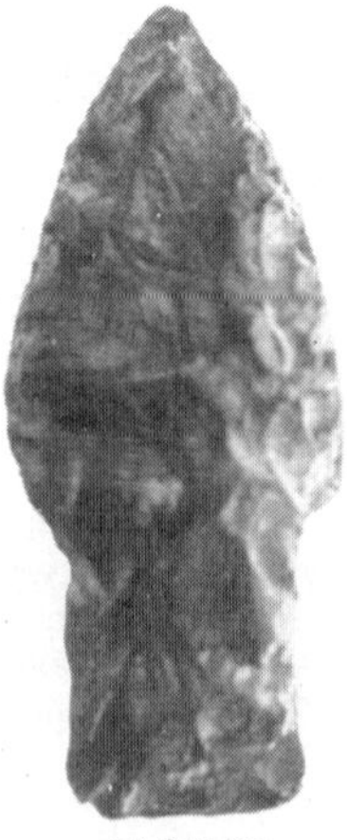

G6, $15-$30
Yavapai Co., AZ.

LOCATION: Arizona and contiguous areas of adjacent states. **DESCRIPTION:** A medium sized dart point with a triangular blade and obtuse to lightly barbed shoulders. The stem is rectangular to slightly tapering or slightly expanding and longer than wide. The basal edge is straight to slightly concave or convex. **I.D. KEY:** Stem longer than wide.

NORTHERN HIGH PLAINS SECTION:

This section includes point types from the following states:
Colorado, Idaho, Kansas, Montana, Nebraska, North Dakota, South Dakota Utah and Wyoming

The points in this section are arranged in alphabetical order and are shown **actual size**. All types are listed that were available for photographing. Any missing types will be added to future editions as photographs become available. We are always interested in receiving sharp, black and white or color glossy photos or color slides of your collection. Be sure to include a ruler in the photograph so that proper scale can be determined.

Lithics: Materials employed in the manufacture of projectile points from this region are: agate, basalt, chert, Dendritic chert, Flat Top chert, Flint, Knife River flint, obsidian, petrified wood, porcellanite, siltstone, Swan River chert and quartzite.

Regional Consultant:
John Byrd

Special Advisors:
Jerry Cubbuck, John Grenawalt, Charles Shewey,
Jeb Taylor, Greg Truesdell

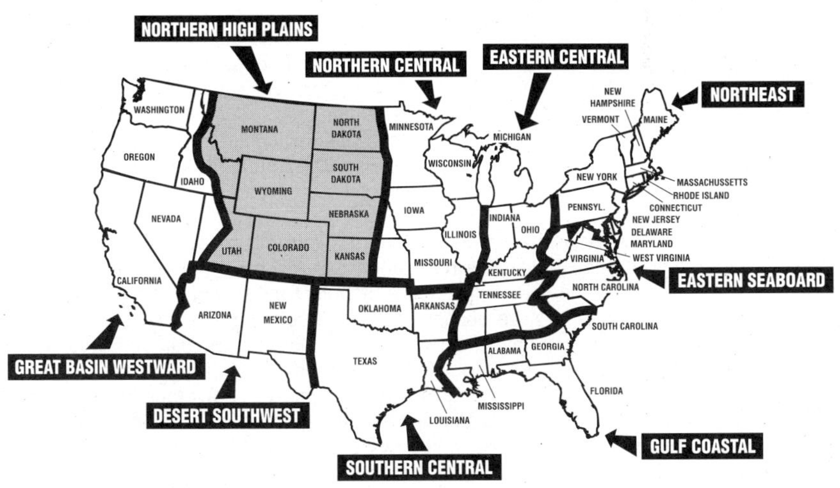

NP

HUNTING THE BUFFALO JUMPS

By John Byrd

Throughout all of the 14,000 plus years that prehistoric peoples lived in the geographical area now known as Montana, hunting has been the primary subsistence base. The open prairie grass lands and abundant water found in the eastern three quarters of this region provided an ideal habitat for all manner of grazing herd animals. Chief among these were the bison and later the buffalo, both of which were favorite prey for these early hunters.

To a limited degree, mass kills of these herds by coordinated communal hunting techniques were employed from the earliest of times. However, the sheer number of these kill sites dramatically increased around 1,200 to 1,300 years ago. Interestingly enough, this fits the time period when the bow and arrow technology was replacing the atlatl and a number of these kill sites will show evidence of use with both weapon types. The systematic use of this hunting method continued up until the 1600s when horses finally became readily available to the Indian population.

Digging in the bone beds of this Montana Buffalo Jump has yielded many fine projectile points.

The technique employed was usually very similar from one location to another. Small groups of between 10 and 100 animals were gathered from their grazing areas or intercepted going to or from water. They were then driven or stampeded to the site chosen as the kill area (no small task given the nature of these animals). This actual kill would either be a low cliff 10 to 50 feet high or more frequently a steep bank or low lying depression. In the later cases, a stout corral was built to contain the herd long enough to complete the slaughter. The intent was not necessarily to kill the animals from the drop over a cliff or down a bank, but rather to injure them severely enough that they were easier to kill with the weapons available.

Example of Buffalo Jump located in Montana. Animals were driven over this cliff for slaughter.

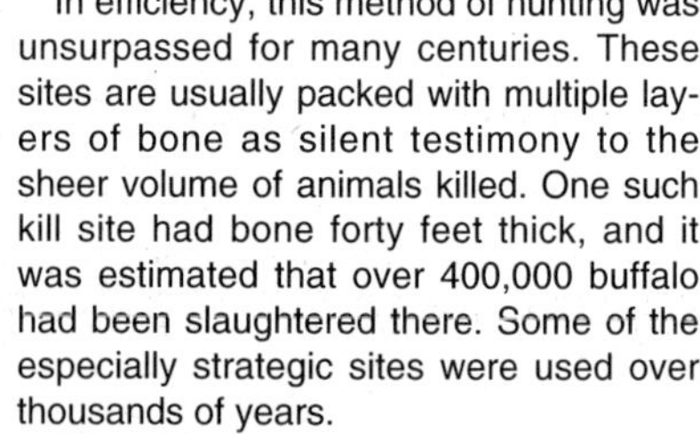

In efficiency, this method of hunting was unsurpassed for many centuries. These sites are usually packed with multiple layers of bone as silent testimony to the sheer volume of animals killed. One such kill site had bone forty feet thick, and it was estimated that over 400,000 buffalo had been slaughtered there. Some of the especially strategic sites were used over thousands of years.

Of course, to kill these creatures a vast number of projectiles were used and many of these were either lost, damaged or left behind. Since the 1930s these kill sites have been popular locations for collectors and archaeologists alike. Many hundreds of thousands of projectile points have been found and placed in collections from what have become commonly referred to as "Buffalo Jumps". The highest percentage of these are true arrow points rather than the dart points used by the earlier atlatl. The very small size of these "arrowheads" is surprising to many people when considering the large stature of the animal being hunted. The average length will be between 3/4" and 1 1/4" with examples as small as 1/4" not being uncommon. Specimens that are over 1 1/2" are relatively scarce and very sought after. Many people who do not know the difference refer to these small arrow points as "bird points" which is completely erroneous. It was not the size that made these arrowheads effective on large animals but rather their ability to penetrate into the vital organs.

NORTHERN HIGH PLAINS POINT TYPES
(Archaeological Periods)

PALEO (14,000 B. P. - 8,000 B. P.)

Agate Basin
Alberta
Alder Complex
Allen
Angostura
Bat Cave
Browns Valley
Clovis
Clovis-Colby
Dalton
Drill
Eden
Firstview
Folsom
Goshen
Graver
Green River
Hell Gap
Holland
Lancet
Lovell
Meserve
Midland
Milnesand
Plainview
Scottsbluff I & II
Scraper
Simonsen
Square Knife

EARLY ARCHAIC (8,000 B. P. - 5,500 B. P.)

Archaic Knife
Archaic Side Notched
Archaic Triangle
Bitterroot
Cody Knife
Corner Tang
Hawkens
Logan Creek
Lookingbill
Mount Albion
Mummy Cave
Plains Knife
Rio Grande

MIDDLE ARCHAIC (5,500 B. P. - 3,300 B. P.)

Base Notch
Base Tang Knife
Buffalo Gap
Duncan
Elko
Hanna
Hanna-Northern
Lerma
Mallory
McKean
Mid-Back Tang
Oxbow
Pelican Lake
Pelican Lake-Harder Variety
Pinto Basin
Yonkee

LATE ARCHAIC (3,300 B. P. - 2,300 B. P.)

Plains Side Notched

DESERT TRADITIONS

TRANSITIONAL PHASE (2,300 B. P. - 1,600 B. P.)

Samantha Dart
Side Knife

DEVELOPMENTAL PHASE (1,600 B. P. - 700 B. P.)

Avonlea-Carmichael
Avonlea-Classic
Avonlea-Gull Lake
Avonlea-Timber Ridge
Besant
Besant Knife
Eastgate
Emigrant
High River
Hog Back
Horse Fly
Huffaker
Irvine
Lewis
Nanton
Paskapoo
Pekisko
Plains Side Notched
Plains Triangular
Prairie Side Notched
Rose Springs
Samantha-Arrow
Sattler
Side Knife
Sonota
Stott
Swift Current
Tompkins
Washita
Washita Northern

CLASSIC PHASE (700 B. P. - 400 B. P.)

Cottonwood Leaf
Cottonwood Triangle
Desert-General
Desert Sierra
Desert Stemmed
Harahey

HISTORIC PHASE (400 B. P. - Present)

Billings
Cut Bank
Cut Bank Jaw Notched
Trade Points

NORTHERN HIGH PLAINS
THUMBNAIL GUIDE SECTION

The following references are provided to aid the collector in easier and quicker identification of point types. All photos are exactly 30% of actual size and are proportional to each other. Each point pictured in this section represents a classic form for the type. When a match is found, go to the alphabetical location of that type for more examples in actual size.

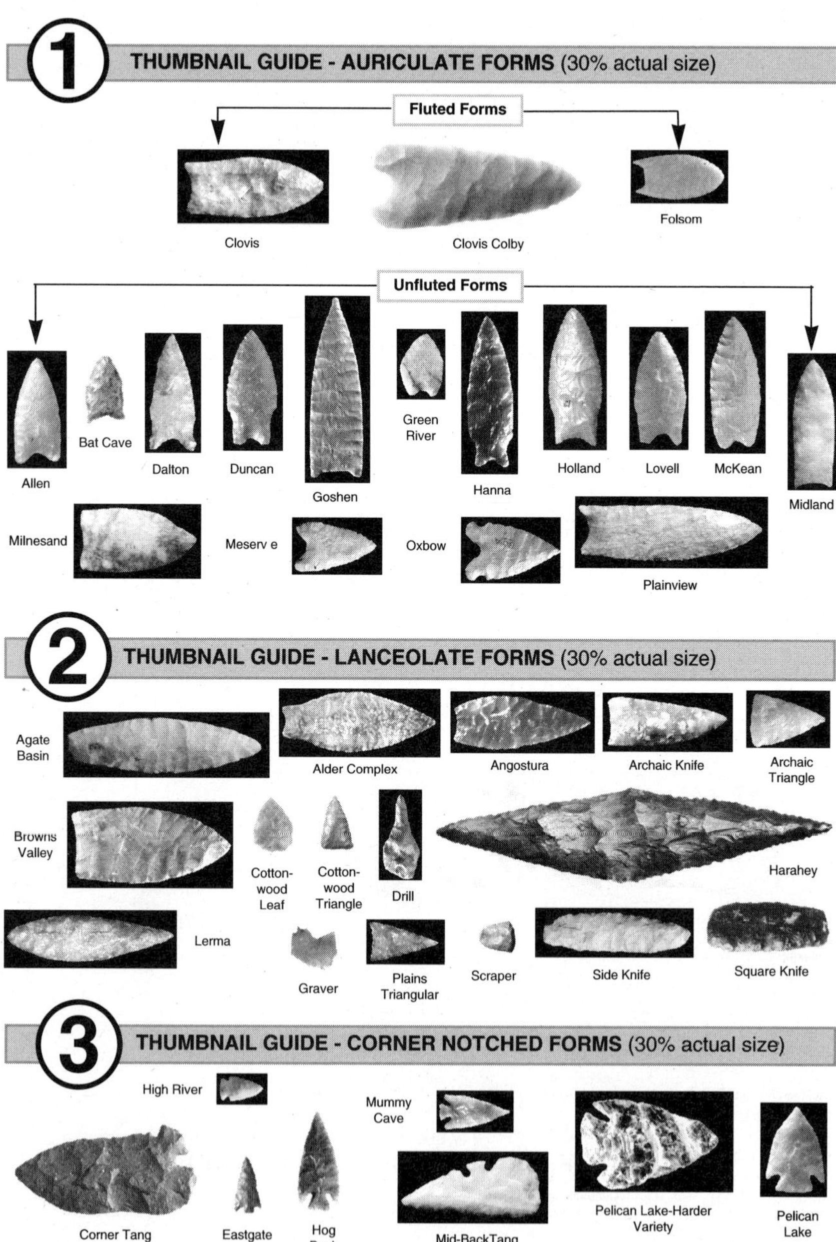

4 THUMBNAIL GUIDE - SIDE NOTCHED FORMS (30% actual size)

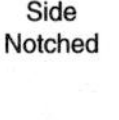

Avonlea-Timber Ridge, Avonlea-Classic, Archaic Side Notched, Avonlea-Carmichael, Avonlea-Gull Lake, Besant, Besant, Besant Knife, Billings, Bitterroot, Buffalo Gap, Cut Bank, Cut Bank Jaw Notched, Huffaker

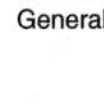
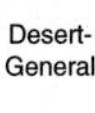

Desert-General, Desert-Sierra, Emigrant, Hawkens, Irvine, Lancet, Lewis, Logan Creek, Looking Bill, Mallory

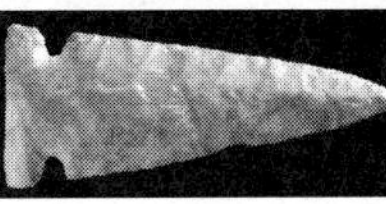

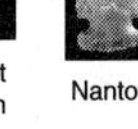

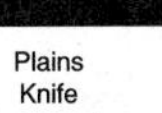
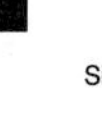

Mount Albion, Nanton, Paskapoo, Pekisko, Plains Knife, Plains Side Notched, Simonsen, Prarie Side Notched

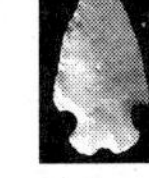

Samantha Arrow, Samantha Dart, Sonota, Stott, Swift Current, Washita, Washita-Northern, Yonkee

5 THUMBNAIL GUIDE - STEMMED FORMS (30% of actual size)

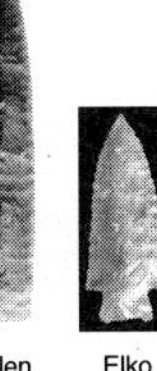

Duncan, Alberta, Base Tang Knife, Besant, Cody Knife, Desert Stemmed, Eastgate, Eden, Elko, Firstview, Hanna, Hanna-Norternh

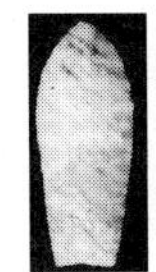

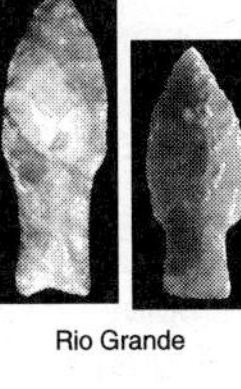
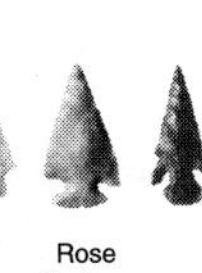

Hell Gap, Horse Fly, Pinto Basin, Rio Grande, Rose Springs, Sattler, Scottsbluff I, Scottsbluff II, Trade

NP

AGATE BASIN - Transitional Paleo to Early Archaic, 10,500 - 8000 B. P.

(Also see Alder Complex, Angostura, Browns Valley and Eden)

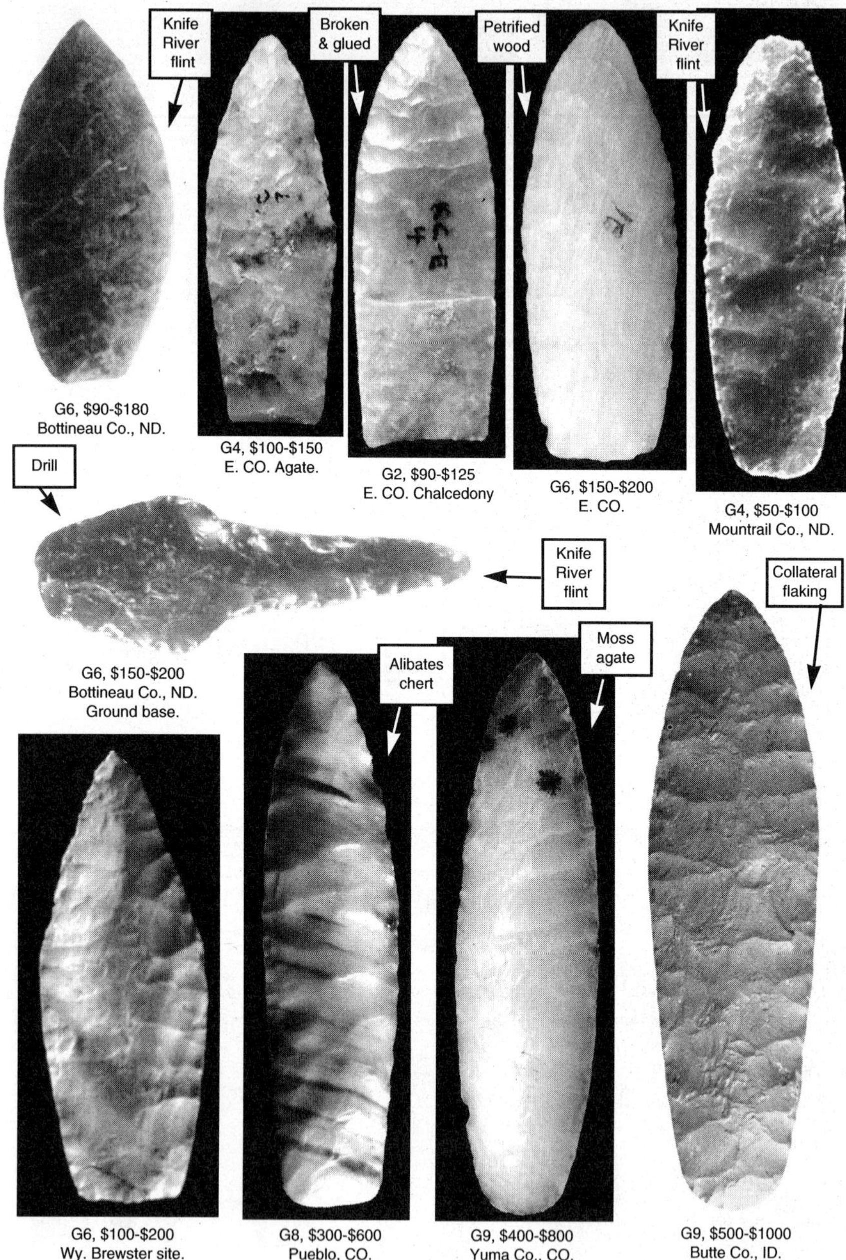

G6, $90-$180
Bottineau Co., ND.

G4, $100-$150
E. CO. Agate.

G2, $90-$125
E. CO. Chalcedony

G6, $150-$200
E. CO.

G4, $50-$100
Mountrail Co., ND.

G6, $150-$200
Bottineau Co., ND.
Ground base.

G6, $100-$200
Wy. Brewster site.

G8, $300-$600
Pueblo, CO.

G9, $400-$800
Yuma Co., CO.

G9, $500-$1000
Butte Co., ID.

LOCATION: Northern states from Pennsylvania to western states. **DESCRIPTION:** A medium to large size lanceolate blade of unusually high quality. Bases are either convex, concave or straight, and are usually ground. Some examples are median ridged and have random to parallel flaking. **I.D. KEY:** Basal form and flaking style.

AGATE BASIN (continued)

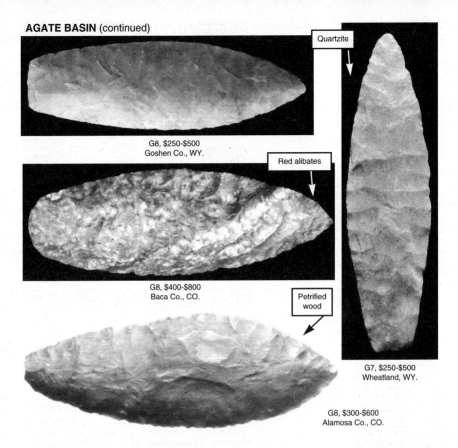

G8, $250-$500
Goshen Co., WY.

Quartzite

G7, $250-$500
Wheatland, WY.

Red alibates

G8, $400-$800
Baca Co., CO.

Petrified wood

G8, $300-$600
Alamosa Co., CO.

ALBERTA - Transitional Paleo to Early Archaic, 9500 - 7000 B. P.

(Also see Cody Knife, Eden, Rio Grande and Scottsbluff)

G5, $100-$200
WY.

G3, $75-$150
Lewis & Clark Co., MT.

G3, $75-$150
E. CO.

G6, $180-$350
Adams Co., CO.

ALBERTA (continued)

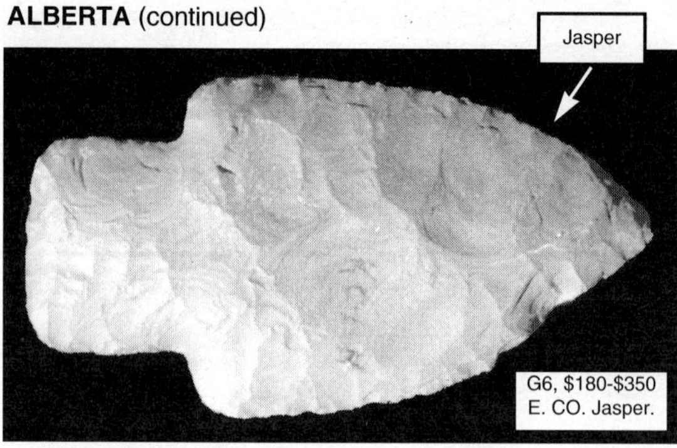

G6, $180-$350
E. CO. Jasper.

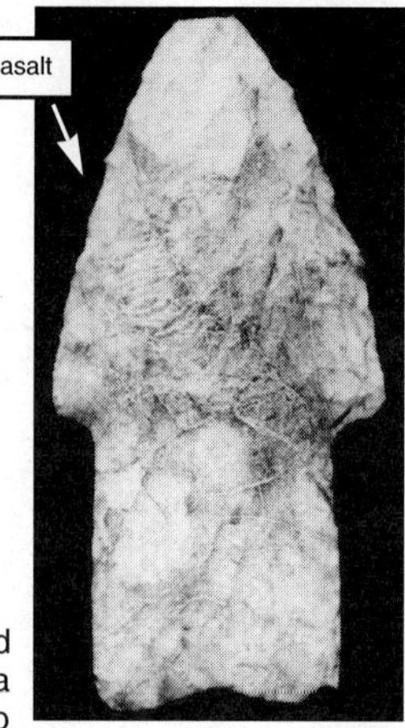

G4, $125-$250
E. CO. Basalt.

LOCATION: Northern states from Michigan to Montana and Nevada. **DESCRIPTION:** A medium to large size point with a broad, long parallel stem and weak shoulders. Believed to belong to the Cody Complex and is related to the *Eden* and *Scottsbluff* type. **I.D. KEY:** Long stem, weak shoulders.

ALDER COMPLEX - Paleo, 9500 - 8000 B. P.

(Also see Agate Basin, Browns Valley, Clovis, Dalton, Green River and Lovell)

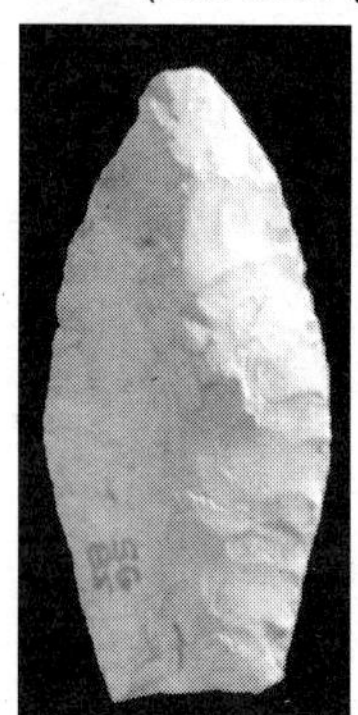

G8, $300-$600
Park Co., MT.

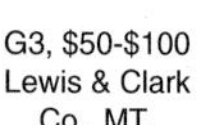

G3, $50-$100
Lewis & Clark
Co., MT.

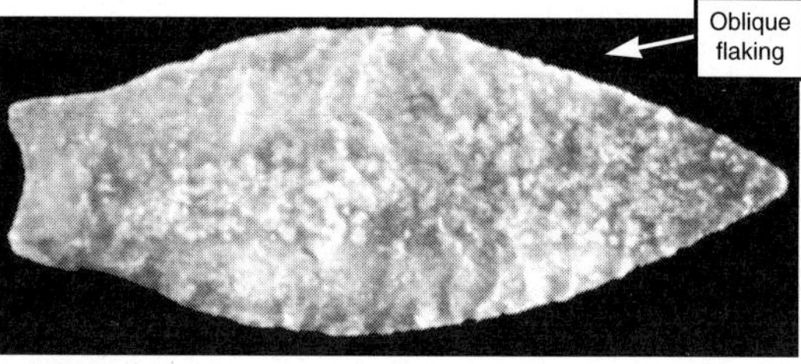

LOCATION: Plains states. **DESCRIPTION:** A medium to large size unfluted lanceolate point of high quality with convex sides and a straight to concave base. Flaking is usually the parallel oblique type. Basal areas are ground. **I.D. KEY:** Basal form and flaking style.

ALLEN - Transitional Paleo to Early Archaic, 10,000 - 9500 B. P.

(Also see Alder Complex, Browns Valley, Clovis, Dalton, Goshen, Green River and Lovell)

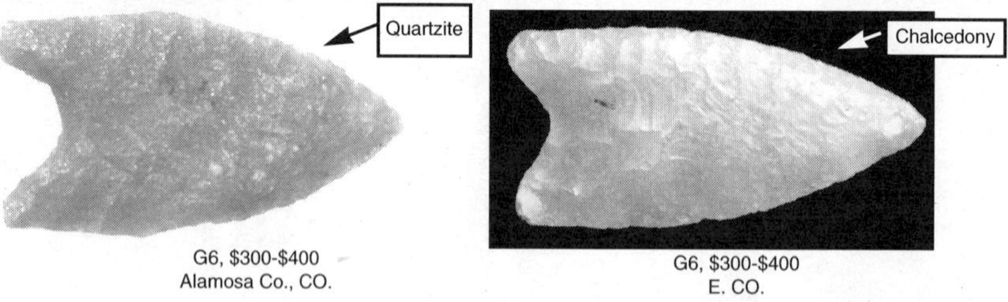

G6, $300-$400
Alamosa Co., CO.

G6, $300-$400
E. CO.

LOCATION: Plains states. Named after Jimmy Allen of Wyoming. **DESCRIPTION:** A medium to large size lanceolate point that has oblique tranverse flaking and a concave base with usually rounded ears. Basal area is ground. **I.D. KEY:** Basal form and flaking style.

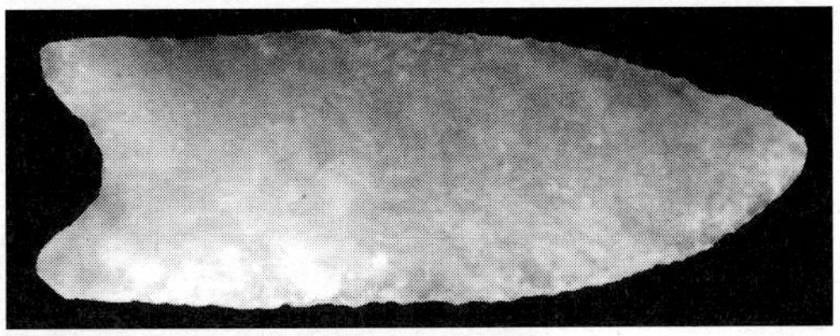

G8, $300-$600
Morgan Co., CO.

G2, $50-$100
E. CO.

ANGOSTURA - Transitional Paleo to Early Archaic, 9000 - 7500 B. P.

(Also see Alder Complex, Allen, Browns Valley, Clovis, Dalton and Goshen)

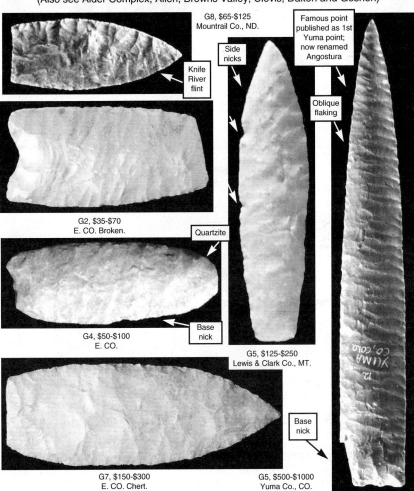

G8, $65-$125
Mountrail Co., ND.

Knife
River
flint

G2, $35-$70
E. CO. Broken.

Quartzite

Base
nick

G4, $50-$100
E. CO.

Side
nicks

G5, $125-$250
Lewis & Clark Co., MT.

Famous point
published as 1st
Yuma point;
now renamed
Angostura

Oblique
flaking

Base
nick

G7, $150-$300
E. CO. Chert.

G5, $500-$1000
Yuma Co., CO.

NP

ANGOSTURA (continued)

Oblique flaking
Oblique flaking
Knife River flint

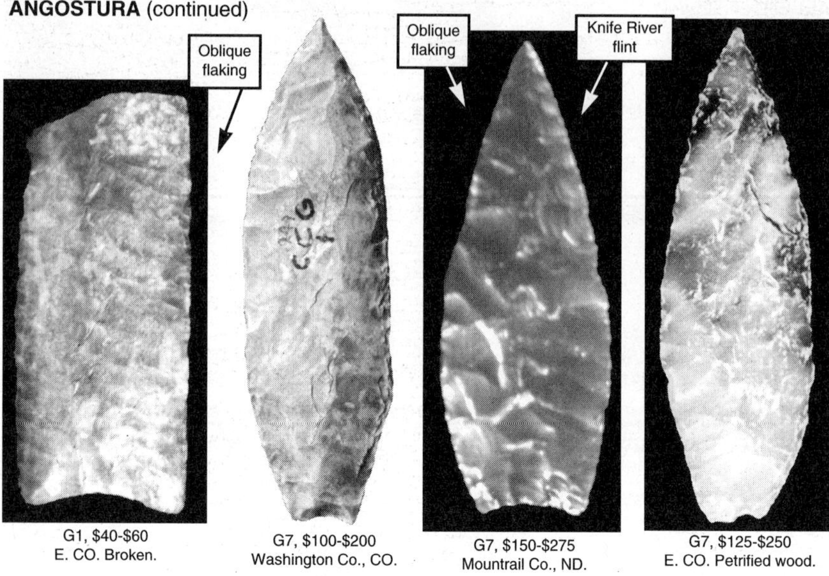

G1, $40-$60
E. CO. Broken.

G7, $100-$200
Washington Co., CO.

G7, $150-$275
Mountrail Co., ND.

G7, $125-$250
E. CO. Petrified wood.

LOCATION: Plains states. **DESCRIPTION:** A medium to large size lanceolate blade of unusually high quality. Bases are either convex, concave or straight and are usually ground. Most examples have oblique transverse flaking. **I.D. KEY:** Basal form and flaking style.

ARCHAIC KNIFE - Early to Middle Archaic, 6000 - 4000 B. P.

(Also see Harahey, Plains Knife and Plains Triangular)

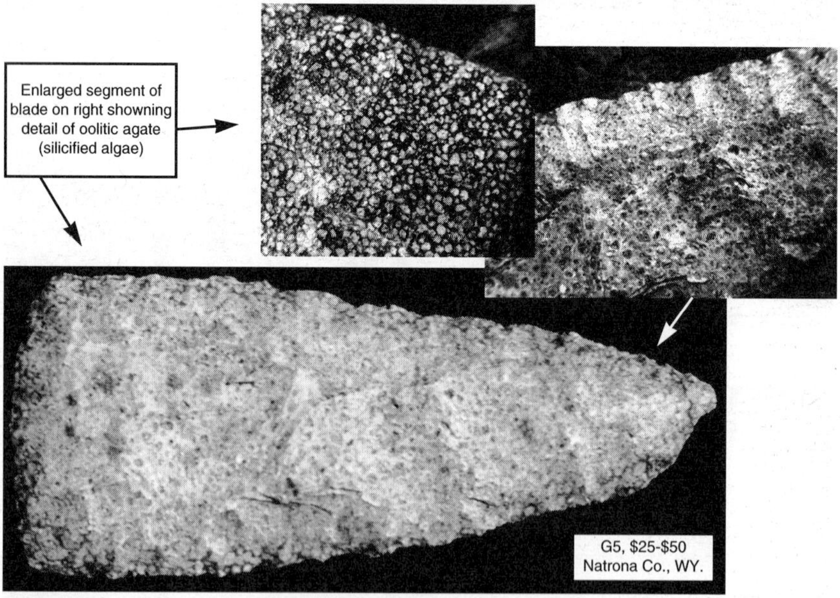

Enlarged segment of blade on right showning detail of oolitic agate (silicified algae)

G5, $25-$50
Natrona Co., WY.

LOCATION: Plains states. **DESCRIPTION:** A medium to large triangular blade with a concave to straight base. **I.D. KEY:** Large triangle with early flaking.

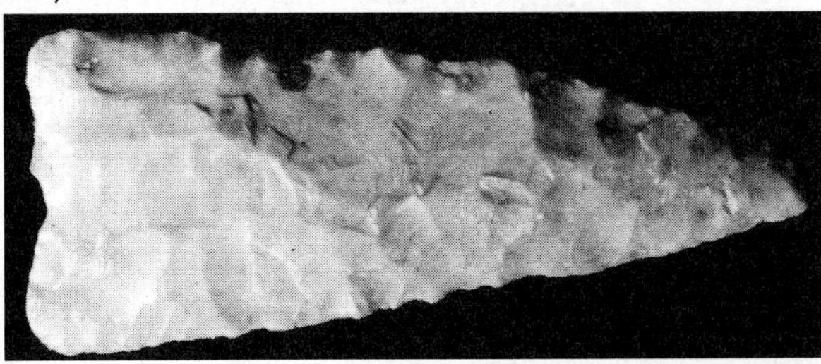

G5, $15-$30
E. CO.

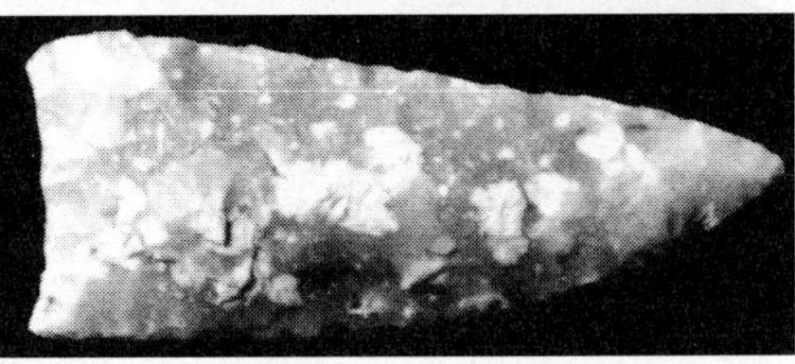

G5, $12-$20
E. CO.

G5, $8-$15
E. CO.

ARCHAIC SIDE NOTCHED - Early to Middle Archaic, 6000 - 4000 B. P.

(Also see Besant, Bitterroot and Plains Knife)

G5, $30-$60
E. Co.

Knife River flint

G6, $50-$100
Lewis & Clark Co., MT.

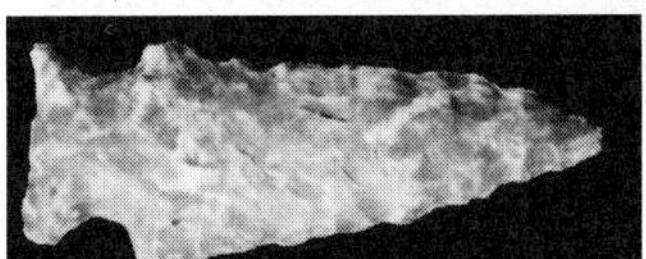

G5, $10-$20
E. CO.

G7, $65-$125
Mountrail Co., ND.

LOCATION: Northern Plains states. **DESCRIPTION:** A small to medium size, narrow, side-notched point with early flaking.

ARCHAIC TRIANGLE - Early to Middle Archaic, 6000 - 4000 B. P.

(Also see Cotton Wood and Plains Triangular)

G6, $10-$20
Lewis & Clark
Co., MT.

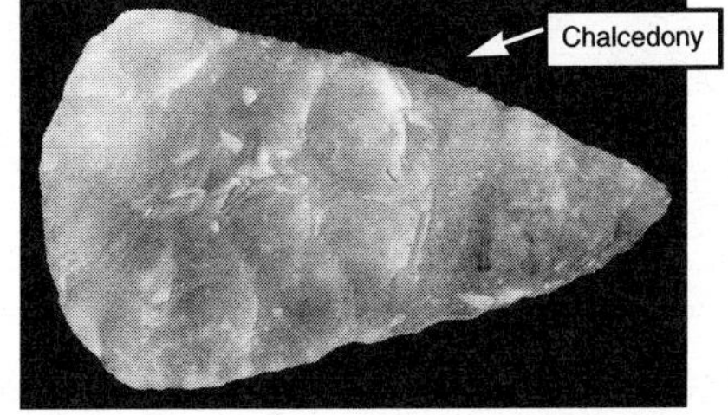

Chalcedony

G7, $15-$30
E. CO.

LOCATION: Plains states. **DESCRIPTION:** A small size triangular point that shows early flaking. **I.D. KEY:** Triangle with early flaking.

NP

AVONLEA-CARMICHAEL - Developmental, 1300 - 400 B. P.

(Also see High River, Irvine, Lewis, Nanton, Pekisko, Swift Current and Tompkins)

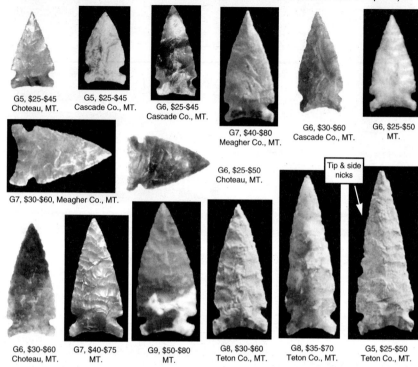

G5, $25-$45 Choteau, MT.

G5, $25-$45 Cascade Co., MT.

G6, $25-$45 Cascade Co., MT.

G7, $40-$80 Meagher Co., MT.

G6, $30-$60 Cascade Co., MT.

G6, $25-$50 MT.

G7, $30-$60, Meagher Co., MT.

G6, $25-$50 Choteau, MT.

Tip & side nicks

G6, $30-$60 Choteau, MT.

G7, $40-$75 MT.

G9, $50-$80 MT.

G8, $30-$60 Teton Co., MT.

G8, $35-$70 Teton Co., MT.

G5, $25-$50 Teton Co., MT.

LOCATION: Plains states. **DESCRIPTION:** A small size, very thin, high quality arrow point with shallow side notches close to the base which is concave. The blade is constructed with broad, parallel flakes that extend to the center. Quality is slightly lower than the other forms of this type. Frequently found on Bison kill sites. **I.D. KEY:** Low side notches, very thin.

AVONLEA-CLASSIC - Developmental Phase, 1300 - 400 B. P.

(Also see High River, Irvine, Lewis, Nanton, Pekisko, Swift Current and Tompkins)

G6, $20-$30 Meagher Co., MT.

G6, $20-$30 Meagher Co., MT.

G5, $10-$20 Phillips Co., MT.

G6, $20-$40 Meagher Co., MT.

G6, $20-$40 Meagher Co., MT.

G8, $25-$50 Cascade Co., MT.

LOCATION: Plains states. **DESCRIPTION:** A small size, very thin, high quality arrowpoint with shallow side notches close to the base which is concave. High quality parallel flaking is evident on the blade. Found at Bison kill sites. **I.D. KEY:** Low side notches, very thin.

AVONLEA CLASSIC (continued)

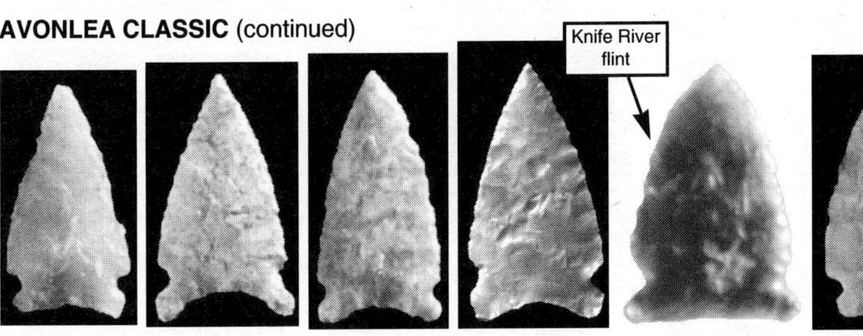

G6, $20-$30 Phillips Co., MT. G8, $30-$60 Meagher Co., MT. G6, $20-$40 Meagher Co., MT. G6, $20-$40 Meagher Co., MT. G6, $20-$30 Meagher Co., MT. G6, $20-$30 Meagher Co., MT.

AVONLEA-GULL LAKE - Developmental Phase, 1800 - 400 B. P.

(Also see Besant, High River, Irvine, Lewis, Nanton, Pekisko, Swift Current and Tompkins)

Black obsidian

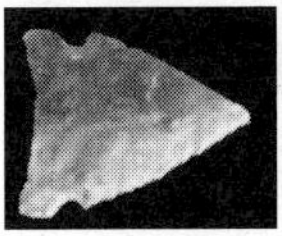

G5, $15-$30 Meagher Co., MT.

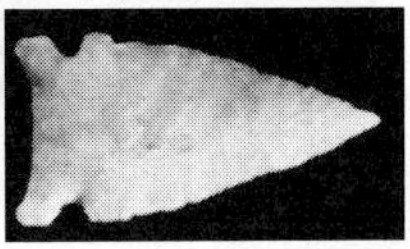

G7, $30-$60 Meagher Co., MT.

G8, $30-$60 Cascade Co., MT.

G7, $50-$80 Meagher Co., MT.

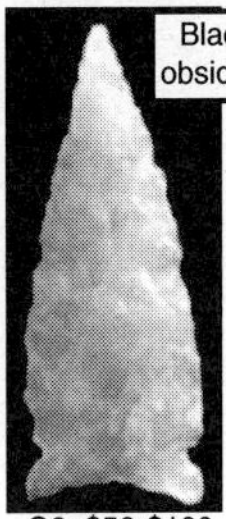

G9, $50-$100 Meagher Co., MT.

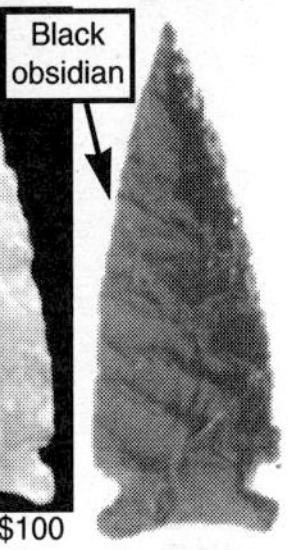

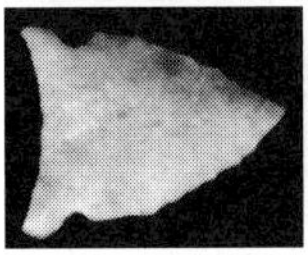

G9, $50-$100 Meagher Co., MT.

G6, $20-$40 Cascade Co., MT.

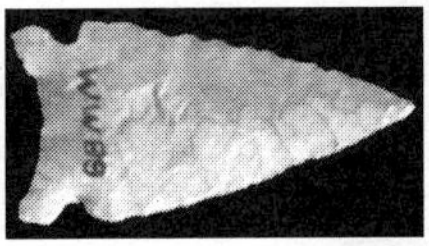

G7, $35-$70 Phillips Co., MT.

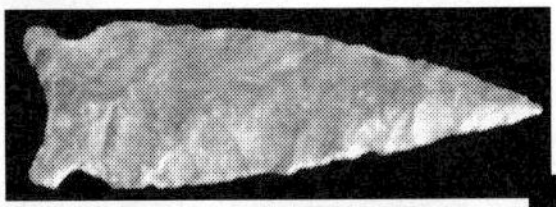

G7, $40-$80 Meagher Co., MT.

G7, $35-$70 Choteau, MT.

G9, $80-$150 Cascade Co., MT.

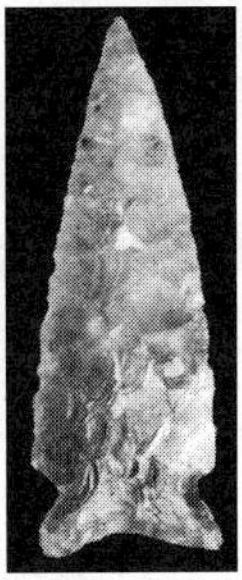

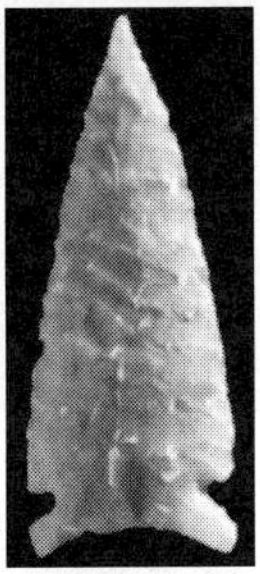

G9, $80-$150 Cascade Co., MT.

G10, $150-$300 Meagher Co., MT. Best known example.

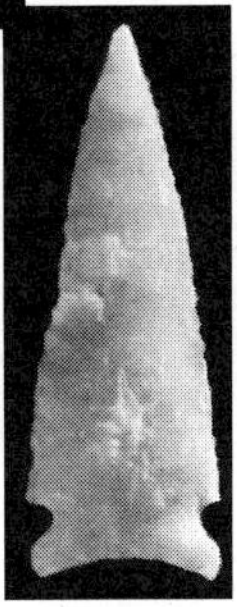

G10, $80-$150 Cascase Co., MT.

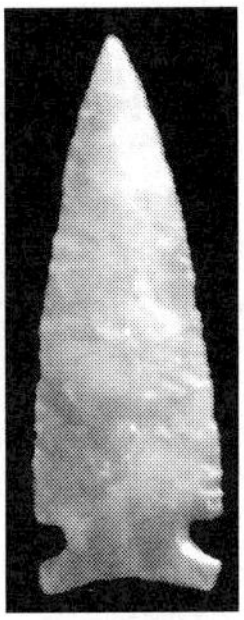

G10, $80-$150 Meagher Co., MT.

LOCATION: Plains states. **DESCRIPTION:** A small to medium size, thin, high quality point with shallow notches located close to the base. The earliest form for the type. Carefully controlled parallel flaking was used in the construction. Some examples have basal grinding. The earliest forms of this variety were dart points changing into arrow points at a later time. Believed to be related to the *Besant* type. **I.D. KEY:** Basal form and flaking style.

AVONLEA-TIMBER RIDGE - Developmental to Historic Phase, 1300 - 400 B. P.

(Also see Besant, High River, Irvine, Nanton, Pekisko, Swift Current and Tompkins)

AVONLEA-TIMBER RIDGE (continued)

G4, $10-$20
Cascade Co., MT.

G5, $15-$30
Cascade Co., MT.

G5, $15-$30
Cascade Co., MT.

G5, $15-$30
Cascade Co., MT.

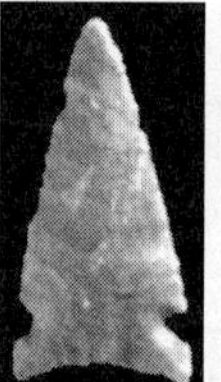

G5, $20-$40
Cascade Co., MT.

G6, $25-$45
Peck Res., MT.

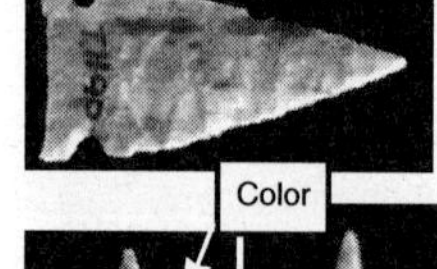

G6, $30-$60
Cascade Co.,
MT.

G6, $30-$60
Meagher Co., MT.

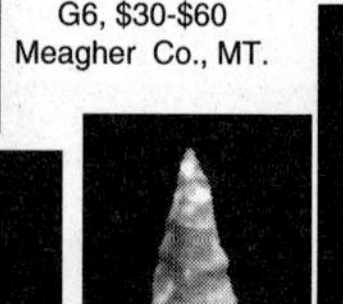

Color

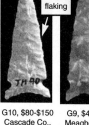

G10, $50-$100
Cascade Co.,
MT.

G9, $50-$100
Meagher Co.,
MT.

G8, $40-$80
Peck Res., MT.

Parallel
flaking

G10, $80-$150
Cascade Co.,
MT.

G9, $40-$80
Meagher Co.,
MT.

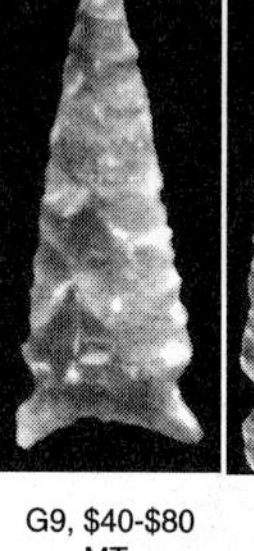

G9, $40-$80
MT.

G9, $90-$180
Saco, MT.

LOCATION: Northern Plains states. **DESCRIPTION:** A small size, very thin, narrow, arrow point with shallow side notches close to the base. Bases can be straight to concave. Corners of ears are sharper than the other varieties.

BASE TANG KNIFE - Middle Archaic to Transitional Phase, 4000 - 2000 B. P.

(Also see Cody Knife, Corner Tang and Mid-Back Tang)

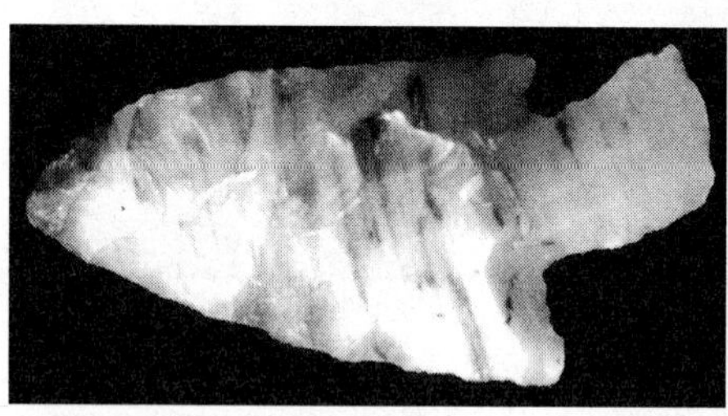

G6, $50-$100
E. CO. Petrified wood.

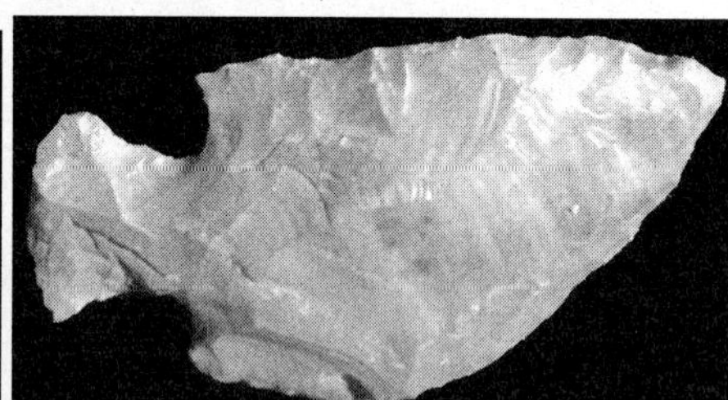

G6, $50-$100
E. CO. Petrified wood.

LOCATION: Northern Plains states. **DESCRIPTION:** A medium to large size shouldered point with a long stem meeting the base at a sharp angle. **I.D. KEY:** Asymmetrical from.

BAT CAVE - Late Paleo, 9000 - 8000 B. P.

(Also see Alder complex, Angostura and Midland)

G6, $15-$30
W. CO.

BAT CAVE (continued)

LOCATION: Southwest to Mexico. **DESCRIPTION:** A small lanceolate dart/knife with convex blade edges, constricting toward the base to form small, flaring ears. Base is concave and well thinned. **I.D. KEY:** Waisted app. and small, flaring ears.

BESANT - Developmental Phase, 1600 - 1400 B. P.

(Also see Avonlea and Pelican Lake)

Agate

G2, \$2-\$5
Mandan, ND.

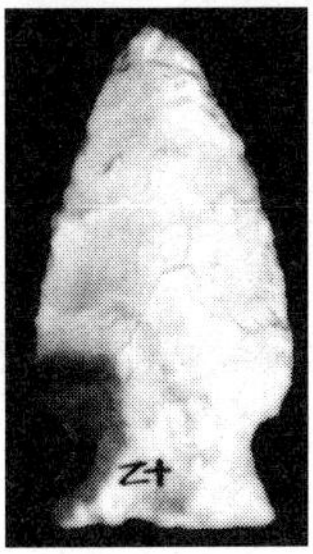

G3, \$5-\$10
Phillips Co., MT.

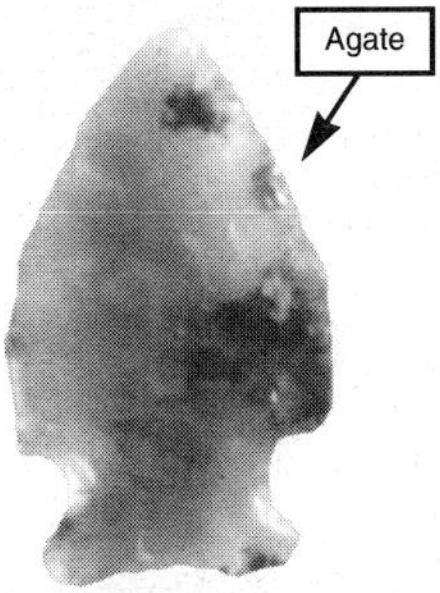

G6, \$40-\$75
Mountrail Co., ND.

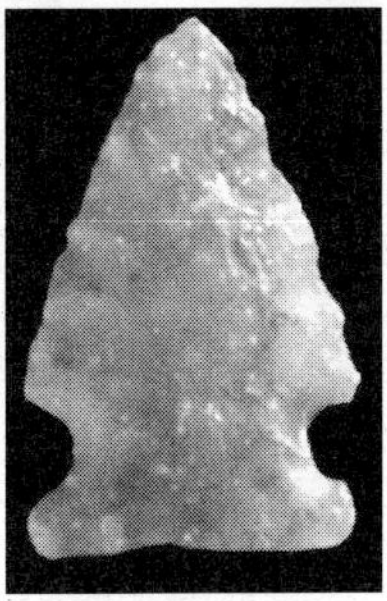

G6, \$20-\$35
Meagher Co., MT.

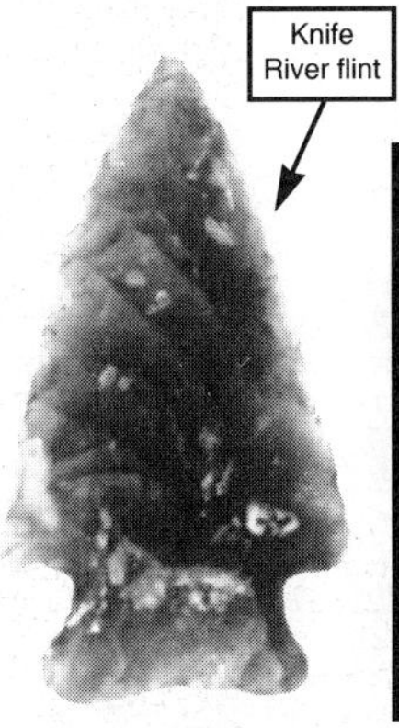

Knife River flint

Knife River flint

G8, \$85-\$150
Harding Co., SD.

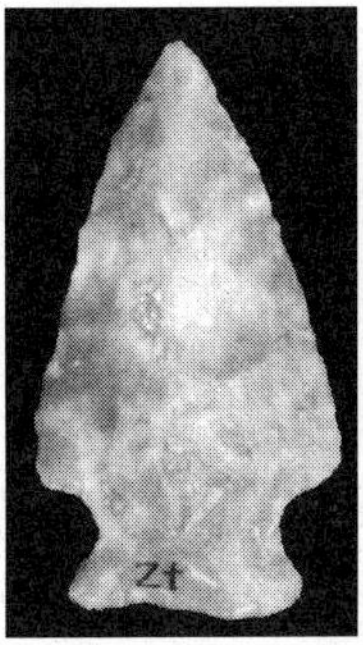

G6, \$35-\$65
Phillips Co., MT.

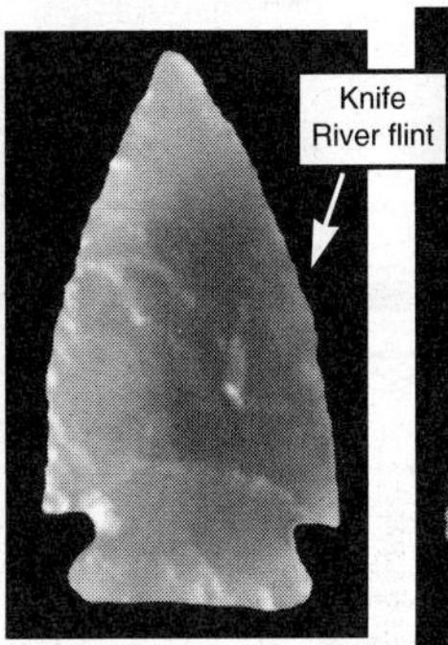

G6, \$35-\$65
Mountrail Co., ND.

G8, \$85-\$125
Meagher Co., MT.

Clear agate

G7, \$35-\$65
Zortman, MT.

G8, \$85-\$125
Meagher Co., MT.

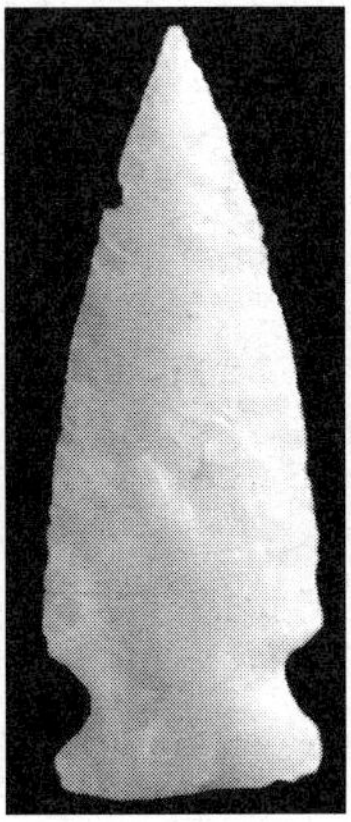

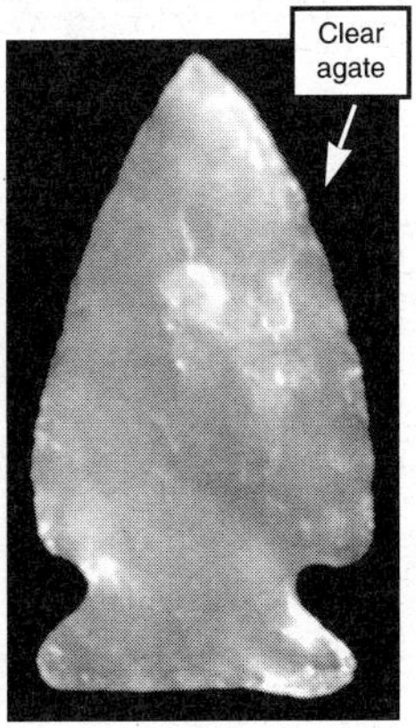

G8, \$85-\$125
Meagher Co., MT.

G7, \$45-\$90
Mountrail Co., ND.

NP

BESANT (continued)

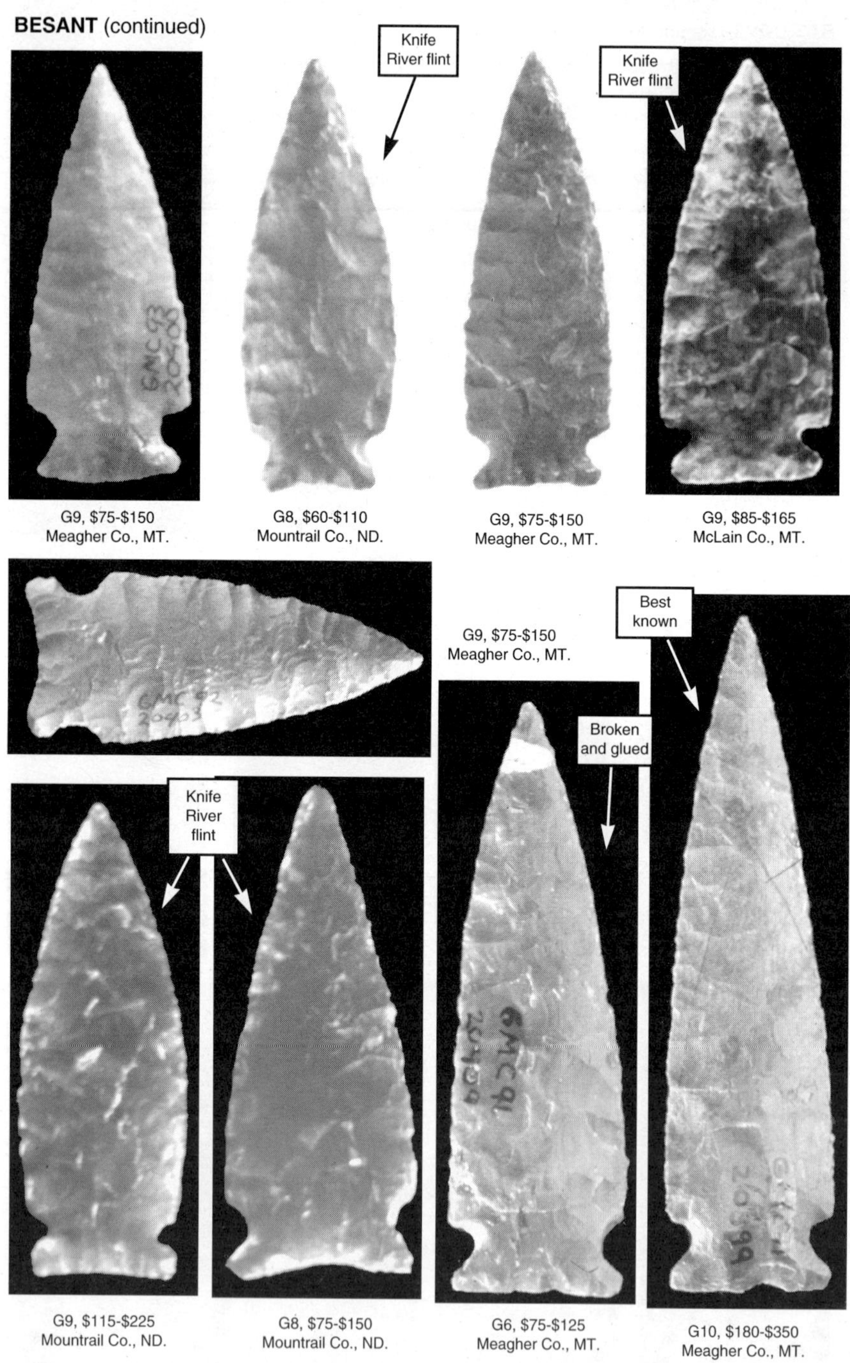

G9, $75-$150
Meagher Co., MT.

G8, $60-$110
Mountrail Co., ND.

G9, $75-$150
Meagher Co., MT.

G9, $85-$165
McLain Co., MT.

G9, $75-$150
Meagher Co., MT.

G9, $115-$225
Mountrail Co., ND.

G8, $75-$150
Mountrail Co., ND.

G6, $75-$125
Meagher Co., MT.

G10, $180-$350
Meagher Co., MT.

LOCATION: Northern Plains states. **DESCRIPTION:** A small to medium size, high quality corner to side notched dart point. Notches occur close to the base. The base is straight to convex. Believed to be related to the Avonlea type and the earlier Pelican lake type. Shoulders are tapered to straight.

BESANT KNIFE - Developmental Phase, 1600 - 1400 B. P.

(Also see Plains Knife)

G10, $300-$600
Douglas Co., ND.

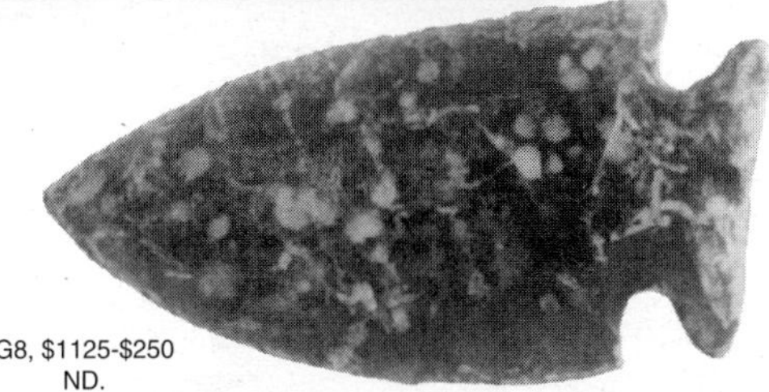

G8, $1125-$250
ND.

LOCATION: Northern Plains states. **DESCRIPTION:** A medium to large size asymmetrical knife with wide corner to side notches. On some examples the blade leans heavily to one side. **I.D.KEY:** Symmetry of blade and notches.

BILLINGS - Historic Phase, 300 - 200 B. P.

(Also see Desert Sierra, Emigrant and Mallory)

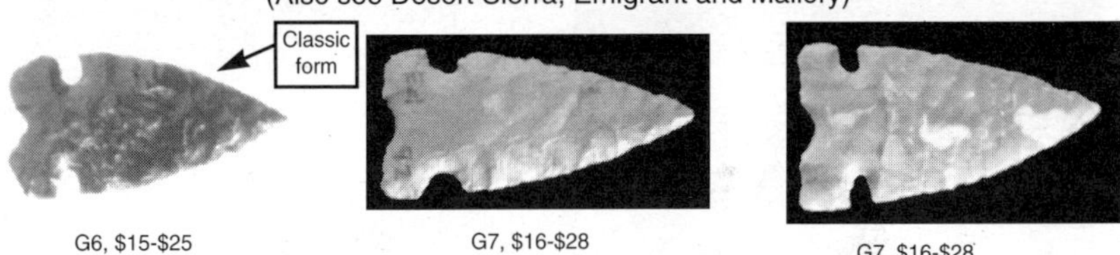

G6, $15-$25
Meagher Co., MT.

G7, $16-$28
Teton Co., MT.

G7, $16-$28
Teton Co., MT.

LOCATION: Northern Plains states. **DESCRIPTION:** A small size, thin, tri-notched arrow point with rounded basal corners. Flaking quality is excellent. If basal corners are pointed the type would be *Emigrant*.

BITTERROOT - Early to Middle Archaic, 7000 - 5000 B. P.

(Also see Archaic Side Notched, Hawkens, Lookingbill and Logan Creek)

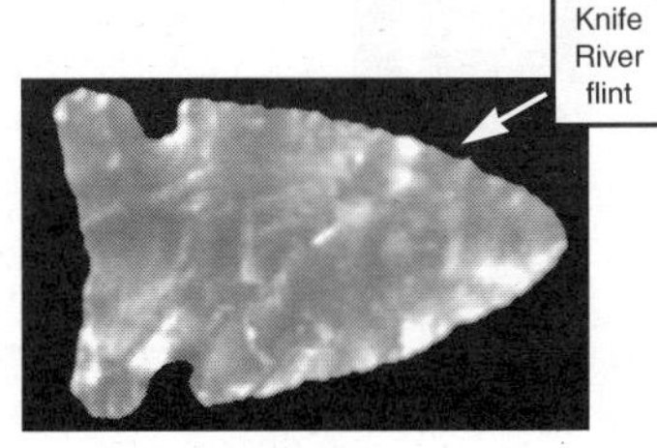

G6, $30-$55
Mountrail Co., ND.

LOCATION: Northern Plains states. **DESCRIPTION:** A small to medium size, short, broad, side notched point with a concave to convex base. Notches are placed at an angle into each side of the blade. Early Archaic flaking is evident on many examples.

NP

BITTERROOT (continued)

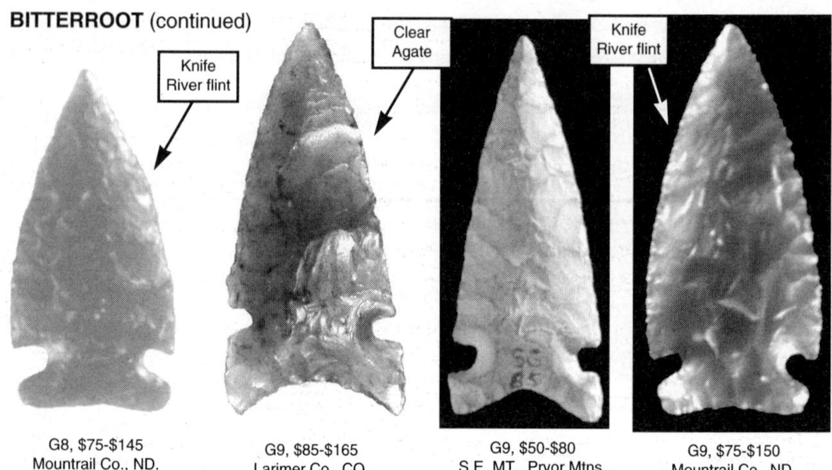

G8, $75-$145
Mountrail Co., ND.

G9, $85-$165
Larimer Co., CO.

G9, $50-$80
S.E. MT., Pryor Mtns.

G9, $75-$150
Mountrail Co., ND.

BROWNS VALLEY - Transitional Paleo, 10,000 - 8000 B. P.

(Also see Agate Basin, Alder Complex, Allen, Angostura, Goshen and Lovell)

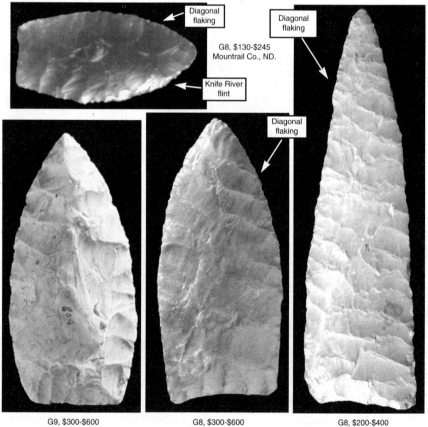

Diagonal flaking

Knife River flint

G8, $130-$245
Mountrail Co., ND.

Diagonal flaking

Diagonal flaking

G9, $300-$600
Meagher Co., MT.

G8, $300-$600
Cascade Co., MT.

G8, $200-$400
E. CO. Jasper.

BROWNS VALLEY (continued)

LOCATION: Midwest to Northern Plains states. **DESCRIPTION:** A medium to large, thin, lanceolate blade with usually oblique to horizontal transverse flaking and a concave to straight base which can be ground. **I.D.KEY:** Paleo transverse flaking.

BUFFALO GAP - Middle Archaic, 5500 - 3500 B. P.

(Also see Bitterroot and Desert Side Notched)

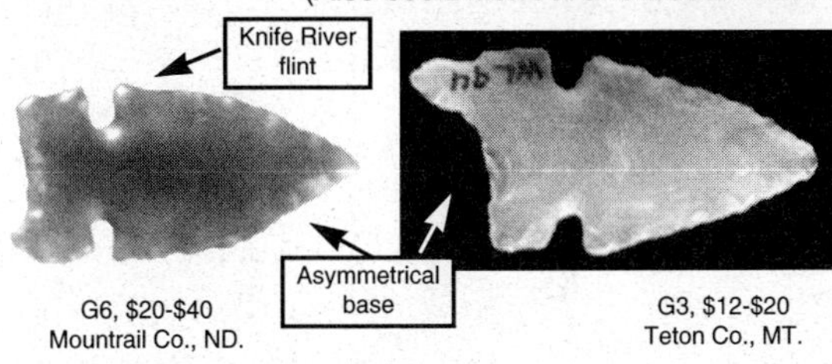

Knife River flint
Asymmetrical base
G6, $20-$40
Mountrail Co., ND.

G3, $12-$20
Teton Co., MT.

LOCATION: Northern Plains states. **DESCRIPTION:** A medium size, thin, side notched triangular point with a concave base. Basal corners are asymmetrical with one higher than the other. **I.D. KEY:** Asymmetrical basal corners.

CLOVIS - Paleo, 14,000 - 9000 B. P.

(Also see Alder Complex, Allen, Angostura, Dalton, Folsom, Goshen and Plainview)

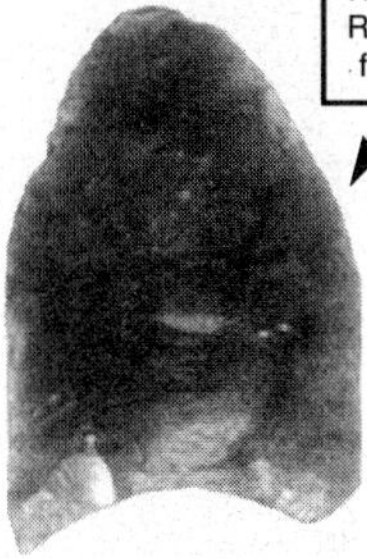

Knife River flint
G3, $150-$285
Bottineau Co., ND.

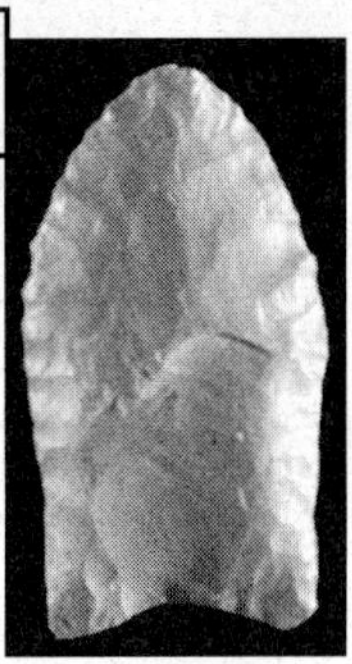

G5, $175-$225
Pine Ridge, SD.
Bison kill site.

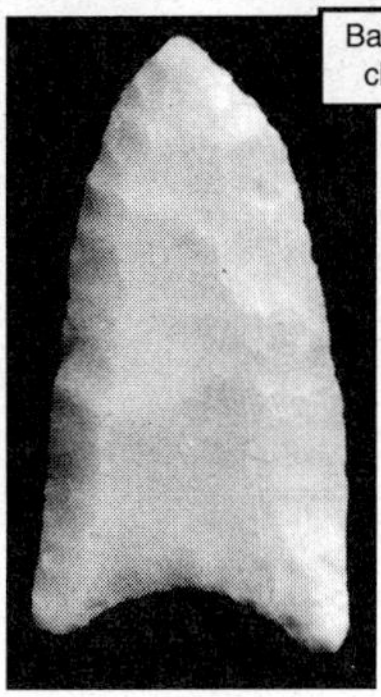

G4, $100-$200
E. CO.

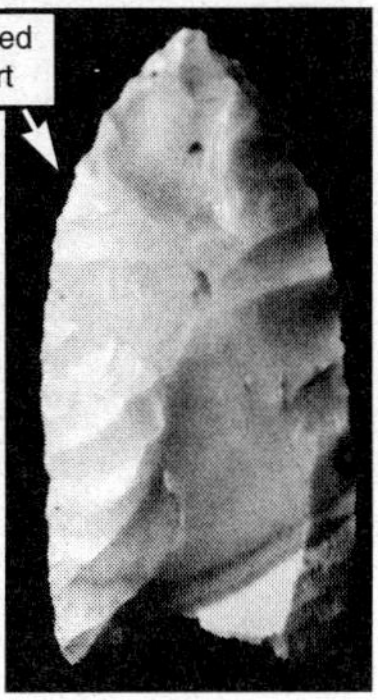

Banded chert
G7, $175-$225
Laramie, WY.

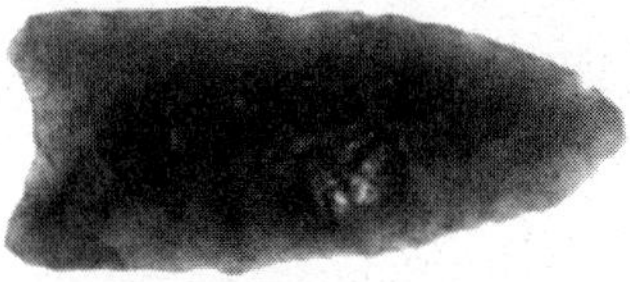

G6, $275-$550
CO.

G6, $125-$250
Teton Co., MT.

Petrified wood
G6, $180-$350
E. CO.

Knife River flint
G7, $250-$500
ND.

NP

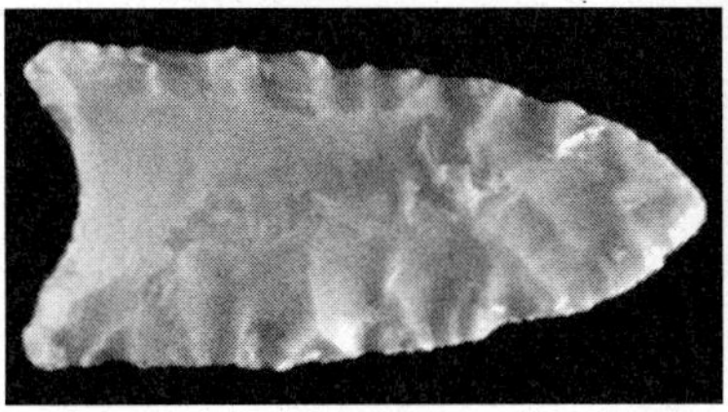

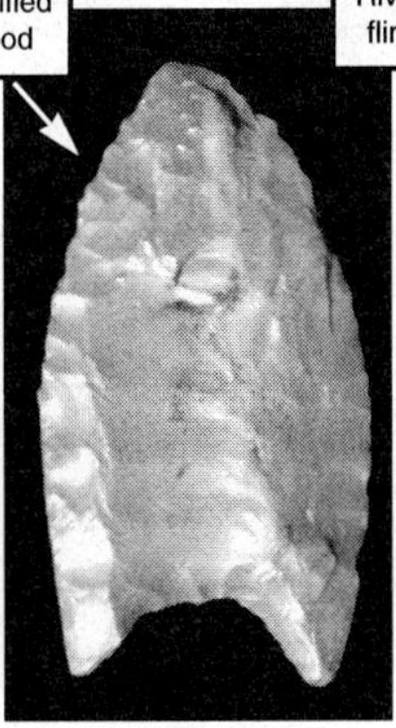

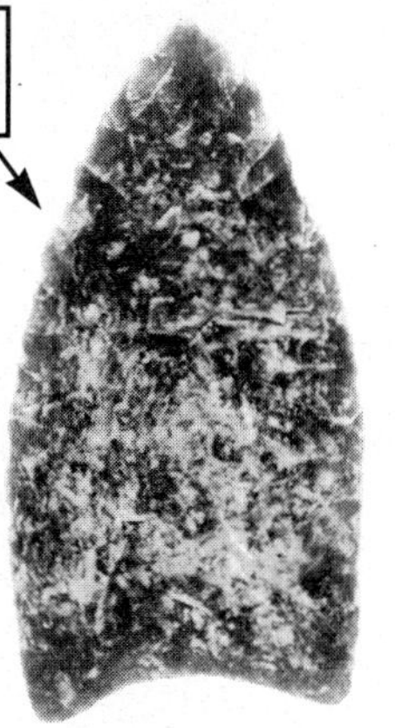

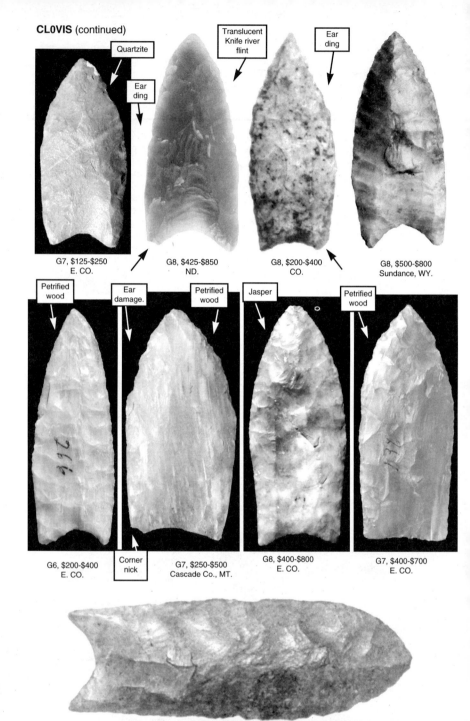

Quartzite

Ear ding

G7, $125-$250
E. CO.

Translucent Knife river flint

G8, $425-$850
ND.

Ear ding

G8, $200-$400
CO.

G8, $500-$800
Sundance, WY.

Petrified wood

G6, $200-$400
E. CO.

Ear damage.

Petrified wood

Corner nick

G7, $250-$500
Cascade Co., MT.

Jasper

G8, $400-$800
E. CO.

Petrified wood

G7, $400-$700
E. CO.

G8, $500-$1000
Yankton, SD.

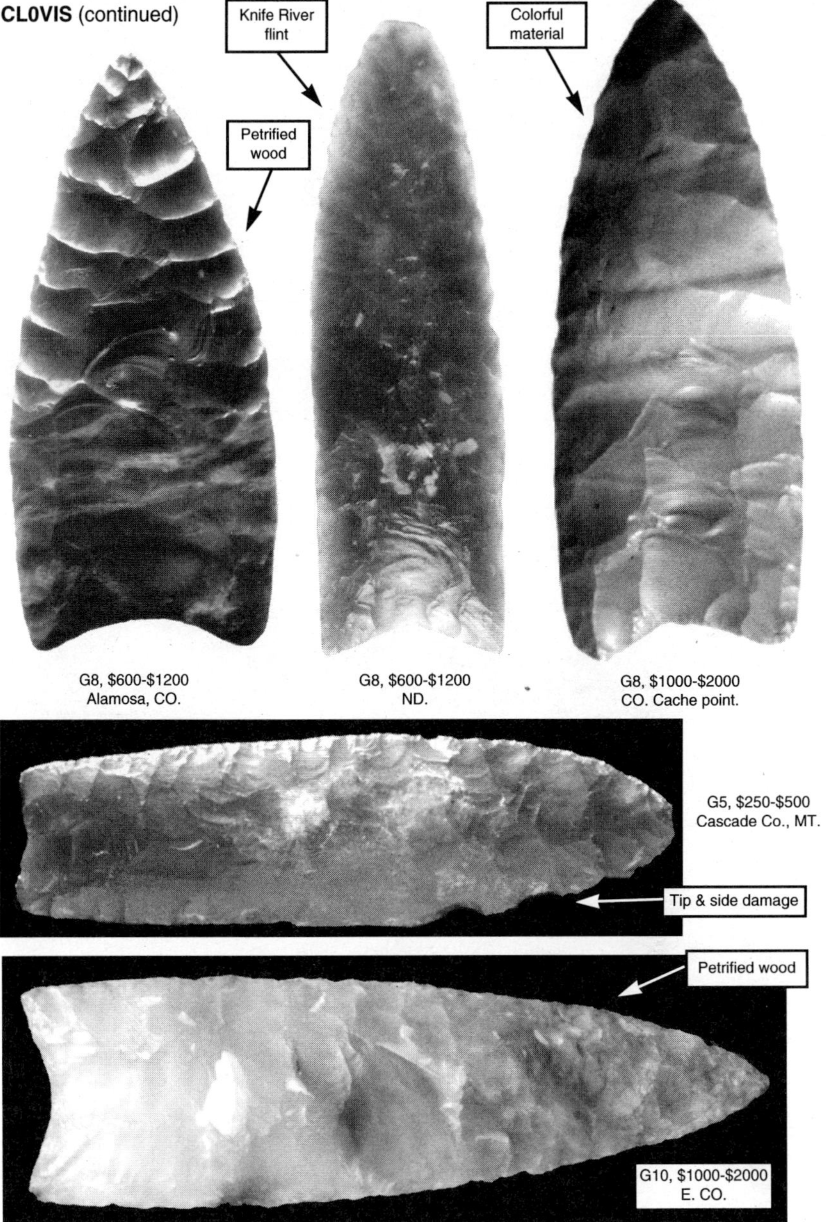

G8, \$600-\$1200
Alamosa, CO.

G8, \$600-\$1200
ND.

G8, \$1000-\$2000
CO. Cache point.

G5, \$250-\$500
Cascade Co., MT.

G10, \$1000-\$2000
E. CO.

LOCATION: All of North America. **DESCRIPTION:** A medium to large size, auriculate, fluted, lanceolate point with convex sides and a concave base that is ground. Most examples are fluted on both sides about 1/3 the way up from the base. The flaking can be random to parallel. Clovis is the earliest point type in the hemisphere. It is believed that this form was developed in Siberia or China and brought here over the land bridge that crossed the Bering Straits 12,000 years ago. There is no evidence of pre-Clovis technology here. The first Clovis find associated with Mastodon was in 1979 at Mastodon State Park, Jefferson Co., MO. in the Kimmswick bone bed dated to 12,000 B.P. **I.D. KEY:** Paleo flaking, shoulders, batan fluting instead of indirect style.

G10, $2000-$4000
N.E. UT., Fenn cache.

CLOVIS-COLBY - Paleo, 12,700 - 10,000 B. P.

(Also see Alder Complex, Allen, Angostura, Folsom, Goshen, Midland and Plainview)

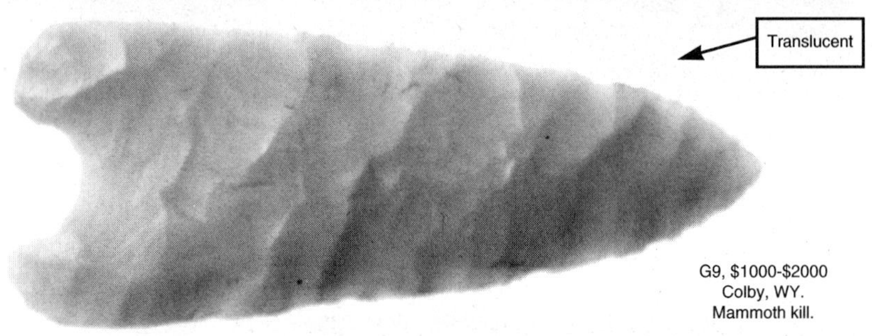

G9, $1000-$2000
Colby, WY.
Mammoth kill.

LOCATION: Northern Plains states. **DESCRIPTION:** Rebased Clovis points. A later form for the type. A medium to large size, auriculate, fluted, lanceolate point with convex sides and a deep, concave base that is ground. Most examples are fluted on both sides up to about 1/3 the way from the base. The flaking can be random to parallel. Has been found associated with bison and mammoth remains. Clovis is the earliest point type in the hemisphere. **I.D. KEY:** Paleo flaking, shoulders, batan fluting instead of indirect style.

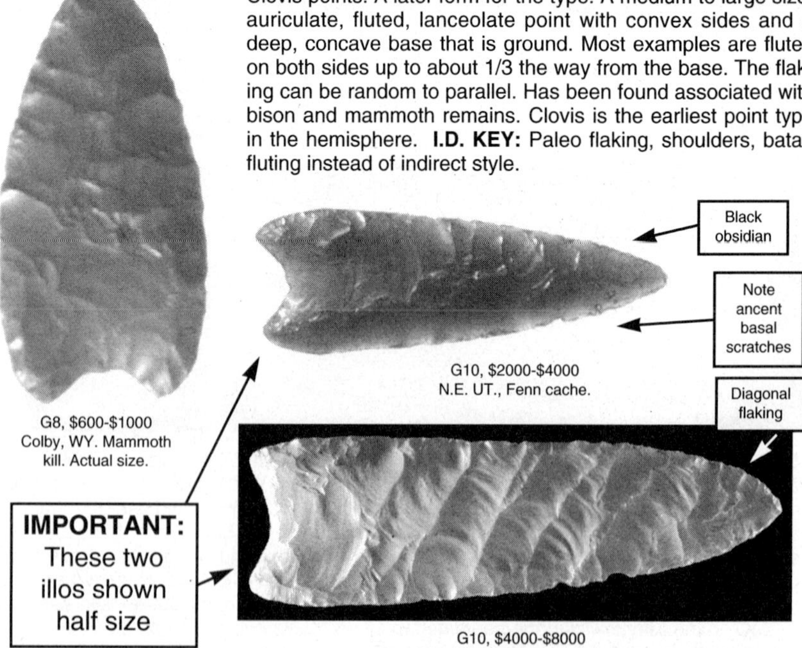

G8, $600-$1000
Colby, WY. Mammoth
kill. Actual size.

G10, $2000-$4000
N.E. UT., Fenn cache.

G10, $4000-$8000
N.E. UT., Fenn cache. Unique.

CODY KNIFE - Early to Middle Archaic, 8000 - 5000 B. P.

(Also see Base-Tang Knife, Corner Tang, Eden, Mid-Back Tang and Scottsbluff)

G5, $125-$250
E. CO.

G9, $2000-$3500
ND.

G5, $115-$225
Caribou Co., ID.

G10, $3800-$7500
Yuma, CO. (Classic)

G7, $200-$400
E. CO.

G7, $180-$300
ND.

NP

LOCATION: Northern Plains states. **DESCRIPTION:** A medium to large size asymmetrical blade with one or two shoulders and a medium to short stem. Stem edges are ground on early examples. Made by the Cody complex people who made *Scottsbluff* points. Flaking is similar to the *Scottsbluff* type and some examples were made from *Scottsbluff* points. **I.D. KEY:** Paleo flaking, asymmetrical form.

CODY KNIFE (continued)

G7, $325-$650
ND.

CORNER TANG KNIFE - Early to Middle Archaic, 8000 - 5000 B. P.

(Also see Base-Tang Knife, Eden and Scottsbluff)

G3, $10-$20
Weld Co., CO.

G7, $200-$400
Alamosa, CO.

LOCATION: Arizona northward. **DESCRIPTION:** A small to medium size triangular point with a straight, slightly convex or concave base. Basal corners tend to be sharp.

COTTONWOOD LEAF - Classic to Historic Phase, 700 - 200 B. P.

(Also see Archaic Triangle and Plains Trianglular)

G2, $4-$6, CO.

G2, $4-$6
Alamosa, CO.

G3, $5-$8, CO.

G6, $6-$12, Morton Co., ND.
Knife River flint.

G2, $4-$6
Weld Co., CO.

G6, $10-$12
Lewis & Clark Co., MT.

G5, $8-$10
Lewis & Clark Co., MT.

LOCATION: Arizona northward. **DESCRIPTION:** A small to medium size triangular arrow point with a rounded base.

COTTONWOOD TRIANGLE - Classic to Historic Phase, 700 - 200 B. P.

(Also see Archaic Triangle and Plains Trianglular)

G2, $4-$6, CO.

G2, $4-$6, CO.

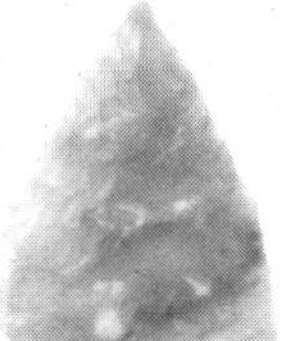

G4, $5-$9, CO.

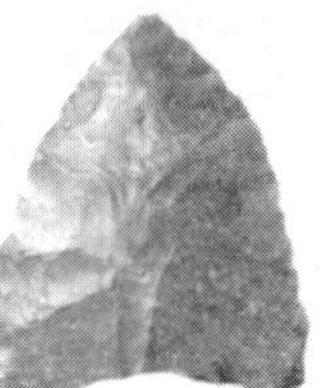

G3, $6-$10, CO.

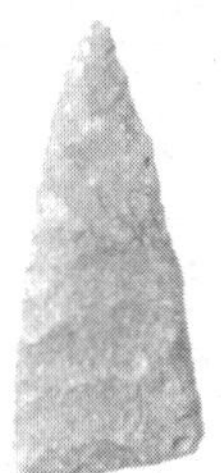

G2, $4-$6, CO.

LOCATION: Arizona northward. **DESCRIPTION:** A small to medium size triangular point with a straight, slightly convex or concave base. Basal corners tend to be sharp.

CUT BANK - Historic Phase, 300 - 200 B. P.

(Also see Buffalo Gap, Desert, Emigrant, Paskapoo, Pekisko and Plains Side Notched)

G5, $10-$20 (Classic)
Cascade Co., MT.

G4, $10-$20
Great Falls, MT.

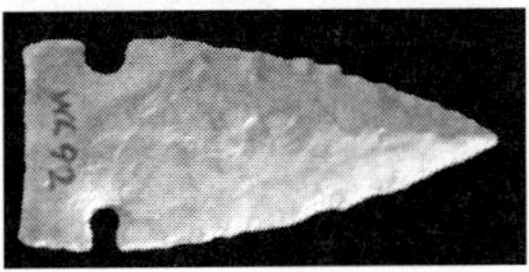

G8, $25-$45
Lewis & Clark Co., MT.

LOCATION: Northern Plains states. **DESCRIPTION:** A small size, thin, triangular point with deep, narrow side notches and a straight to concave base.

CUT BANK JAW-NOTCHED - Historic Phase, 300 - 200 B. P.

(Also see Buffalo Gap, Desert, Emigrant, Paskapoo, Pekisko and Plains Side Notched)

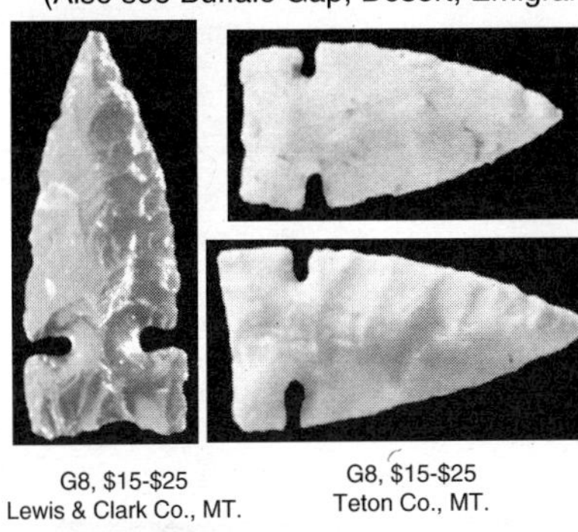

G8, $15-$30
Lewis & Clark
Co., MT.

G8, $15-$25
Lewis & Clark Co., MT.

G8, $15-$25
Teton Co., MT.

G8, $15-$25
Weld Co., CO.

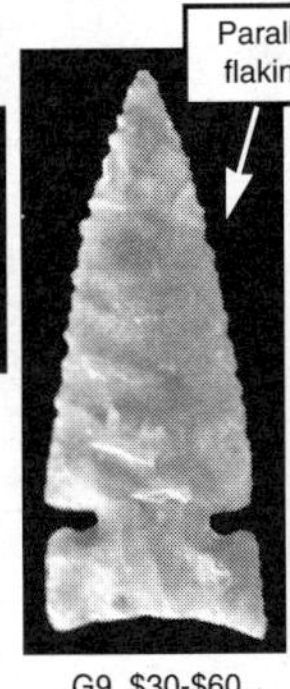

G9, $30-$60
Teton Co., MT.

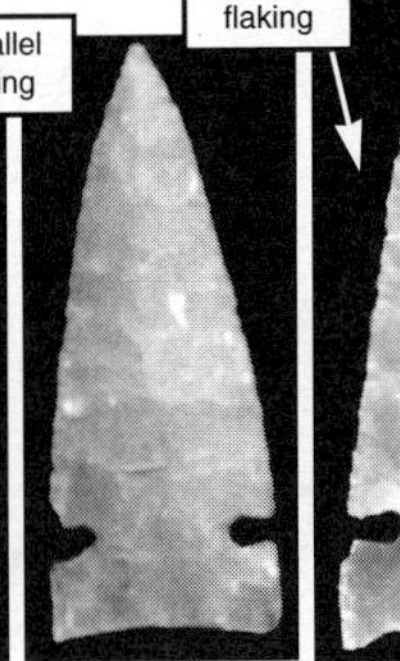

G8, $20-$40
MT.

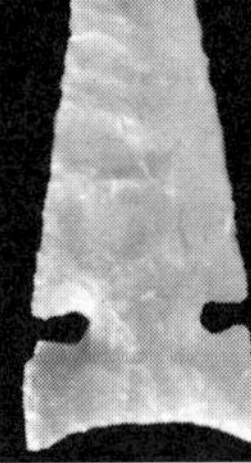

G9, $30-$60
Teton Co., MT.

NP

LOCATION: Northern Plains states. **DESCRIPTION:** A small size, thin, triangular point with deep, narrow side notches that expand towards the center of the blade. Base can be straight to concave. Flaking is of high quality, usually oblique parallel struck from the edge to the center of the blade.

DALTON - Late Paleo, 10,000 - 8000 B. P.

(Also see Alder Complex, Allen, Clovis, Folsom, Goshen and Meserve)

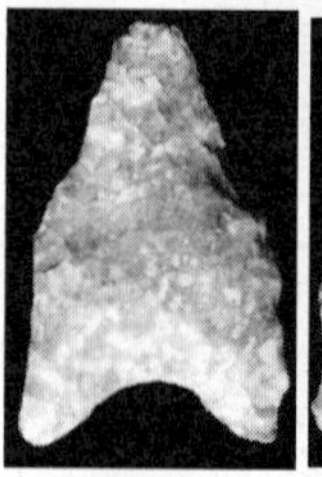

G2, $15-$25
E. CO. Alibates.

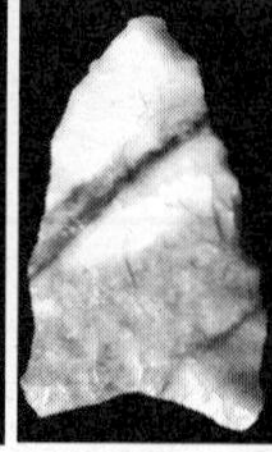

G2, $15-$25
E. CO. Alibates.

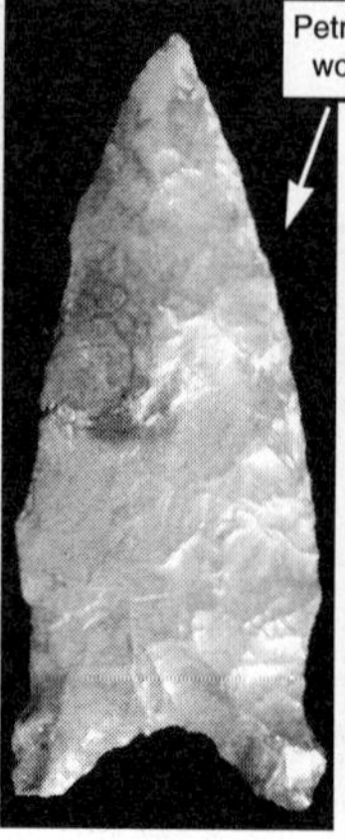

G6, $40-$80
E. CO.

G8, $125-$250
Weld Co., CO.

G9, $175-$350
Weld Co., CO.

LOCATION: Focused in Missouri, but extends to the Plains and into the Southeastern states. **DESCRIPTION:** A small to large size, thin, auriculate, fishtailed point. Many examples are finely serrated and exhibit excellent flaking. Beveling may occur on one side of each face. All have basal grinding. Early examples may be fluted. **I.D. KEY:** Basal ears.

DESERT-GENERAL - Classic to Historic Phase, 700 - 200 B. P.

(Also see Bitterroot, Buffalo Gap, Cold Springs, Emigrant, Irvine, Plains Side Notched and Swift Current)

G2, $2-$4
CO.

G4, $2-$4
CO.

G7, $5-$8
CO.

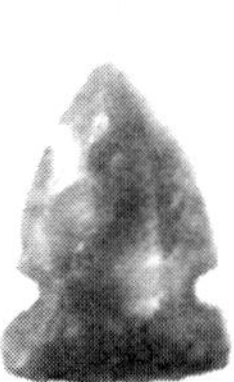

G7, $10-$15
CO.

G5, $6-$12
CO.

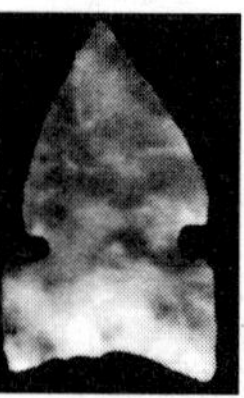

G5, $8-$15
Weld Co., CO.

G5, $15-$30
CO.

LOCATION: Arizona northward and westward. **DESCRIPTION:** A small, thin, side notched point with a straight, convex or concave base. Blade edges can be serrated. Reported to have been used by the Shoshoni Indians of the Historic period.

DESERT-SIERRA - Late Archaic to Historic Phase, 2500 - 400 B. P.

(Also see Billings and Emigrant)

LOCATION: Northern Plains to California to Arizona. **DESCRIPTION:** A small, thin, tri-notched point with a concave to straight base. Blade edges can be serrated.

G6, $10-$20
CO.

DESERT STEMMED- Late Archaic to Historic Phase, 2500 - 400 B. P.

LOCATION: Northern Plains to California to Arizona. **DESCRIPTION:** A small, narrow, serrated dart point with a narrow, expanding base. Shoulders are horizontal and pointed.

G6, $10-$20
Alamosa, CO.

DRILL - Paleo to Historic Phase, 14,000 - 200 B. P.

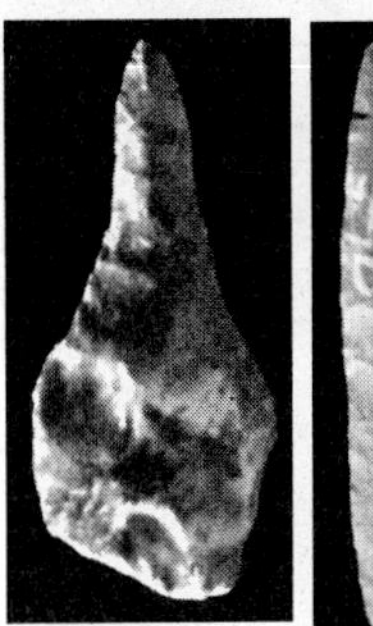

G3, $5-$10
Lewis & Clark Co., MT.

G4, $8-$15
Lewis & Clark Co., MT.

G5, $15-$30
Morton Co., ND.

LOCATION: Throughout North America. **DESCRIPTION:** Although many drills were made from scratch, all point types were made into the drill form. Usually, heavily resharpened and broken points were salvaged and rechipped into drills. **I.D.KEY:** Narrow blade form.

G7, $20-$40
Morgan Co., CO.

DUNCAN - Middle to Late Archaic, 4500 - 2850 B. P.

(Also see Hanna)

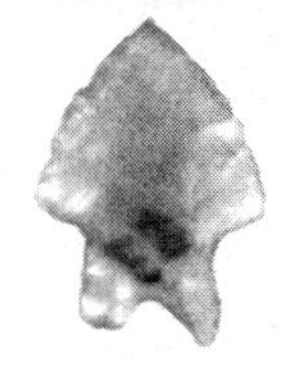

G4, $20-$35
CO. Gem.

G4, $8-$12
Sundance, WY.

G5, $15-$25
Dillon, MT.

G5, $20-$35
Moorcroft, WY.

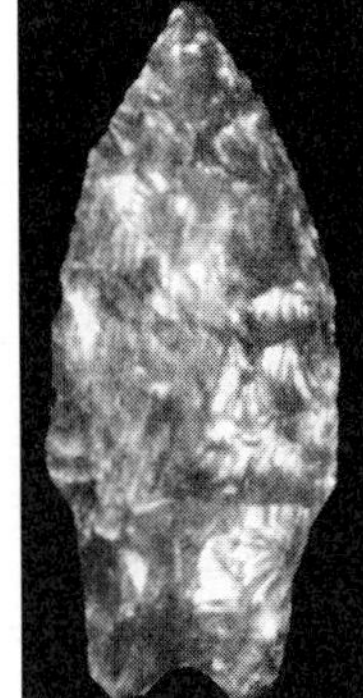

G5, $12-$25
Morgan Co., CO.

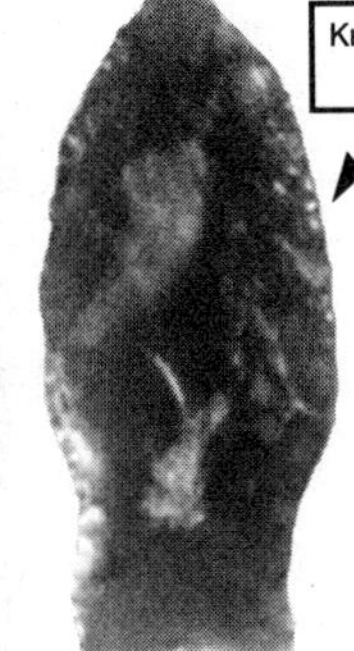

G7, $30-$55
Mountrail Co., ND.

G4, $10-$20
Pryor Mtns., MT.

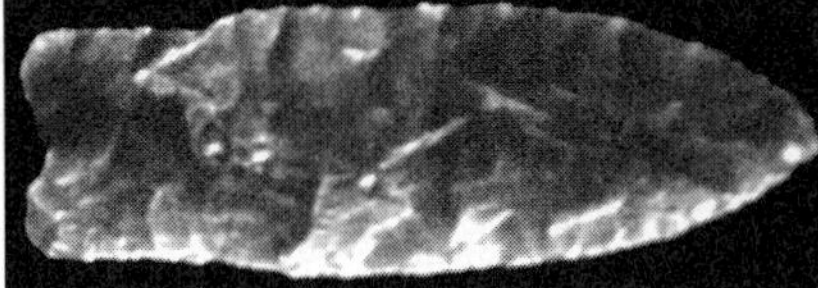

G8, $40-$75
Mountrail Co., ND.

NP

DUNCAN (continued)

G4, $10-$20
E. CO.

Petrified wood

G8, $40-$80
Morgan Co., CO.

Thin cross section

G9, $40-$80
Casper, WY.

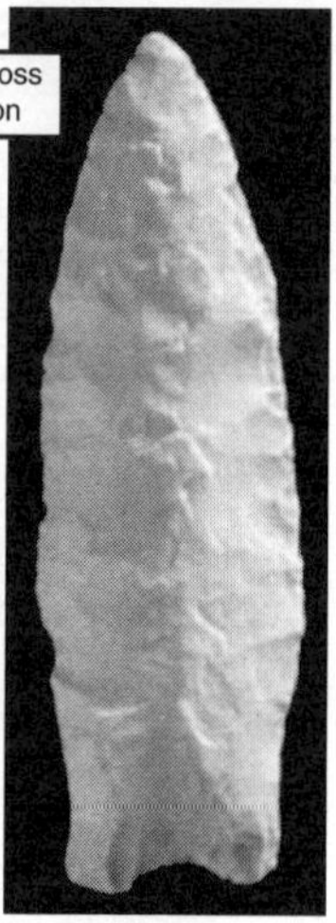

G8, $25-$50
Lewis & Clark Co., MT.

G8, $30-$60
Lewis & Clark Co., MT.

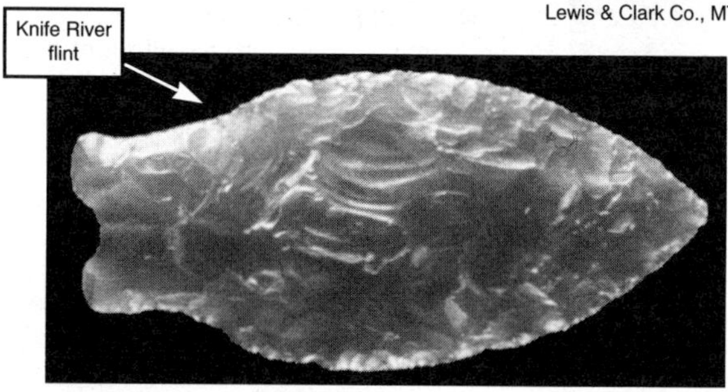

Knife River flint

G9, $75-$150
Jamestown, ND.

Quartzite

G9, $40-$80
Casper, WY. Quartzite.

LOCATION: Northern Arizona to Canada and to eastern Oklahoma. **DESCRIPTION:** A small to medium size dart/knife point with a triangular blade and angular shoulders. The stem is straight with a V-shaped notch in the basal edge. Stem edges are usually ground. **I.D.KEY:** Straight stem edges.

EASTGATE - Developmental Phase, 1400 - 1000 B. P.

(Also see Mummy Cave, Pelican Lake and Rose Springs)

G4, $5-$10
Alamosa, CO.

LOCATION: Great Basin to Northern Plains states. **DESCRIPTION:** A small, thin, triangular corner notched arrow point with a short parallel sided to expanding stem. Barbs can be pointed or square.

EASTGATE (continued)

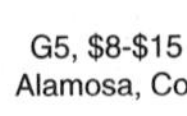

G5, $8-$15
Alamosa, Co.

G5, $8-$15
Alamosa, CO.

EDEN - Transitional Paleo to Early Archaic, 9500 - 7500 B. P.

(Also see Agate Basin, Alder Complex, Angostura, Browns Valley and Scottsbluff)

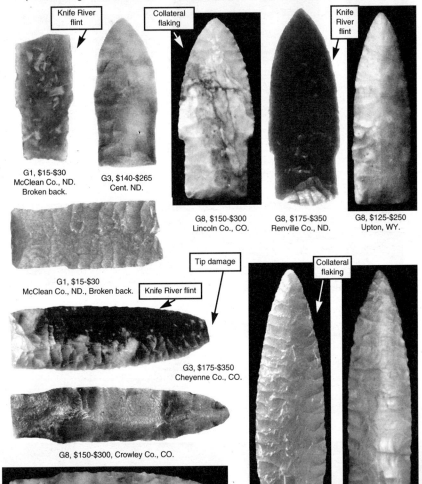

Knife River flint

G1, $15-$30
McClean Co., ND.
Broken back.

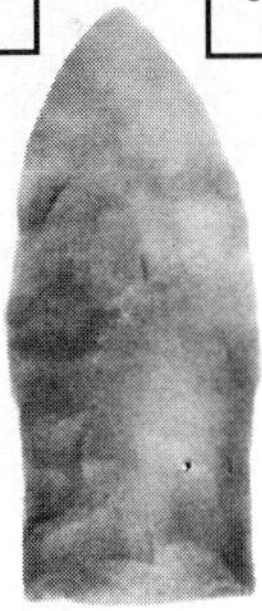

G3, $140-$265
Cent. ND.

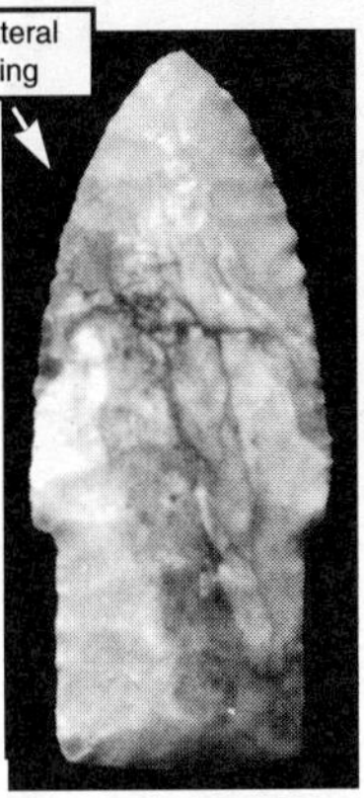

Collateral flaking

G8, $150-$300
Lincoln Co., CO.

G8, $175-$350
Renville Co., ND.

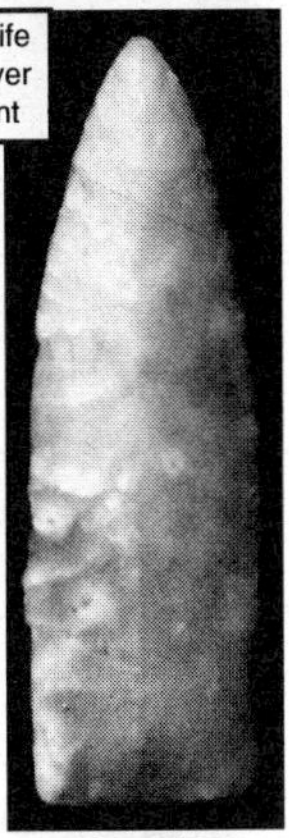

Knife River flint

G8, $125-$250
Upton, WY.

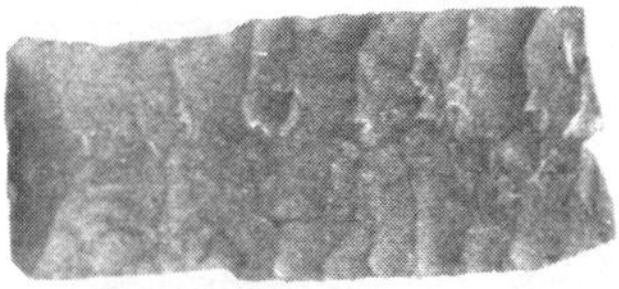

G1, $15-$30
McClean Co., ND., Broken back.

Tip damage

Knife River flint

G3, $175-$350
Cheyenne Co., CO.

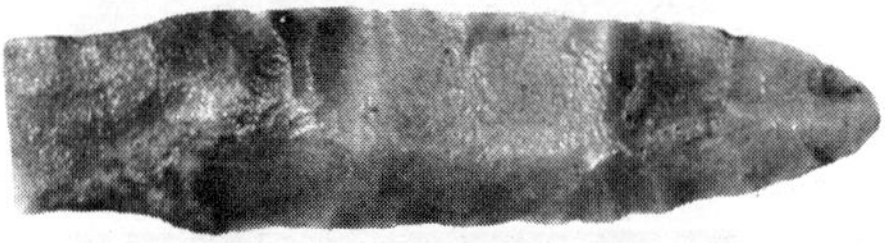

G8, $150-$300, Crowley Co., CO.

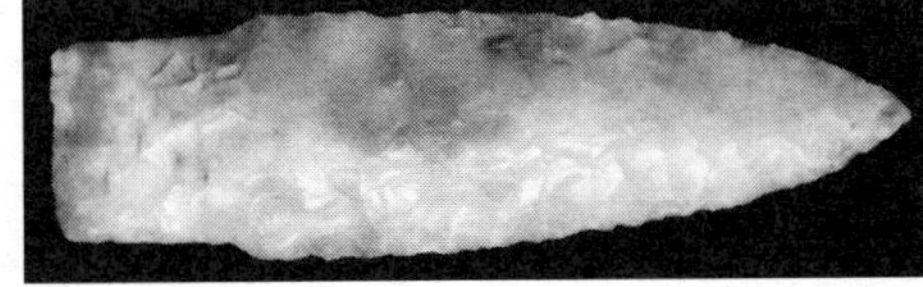

G8, $200-$400, Sagauche Co., CO.

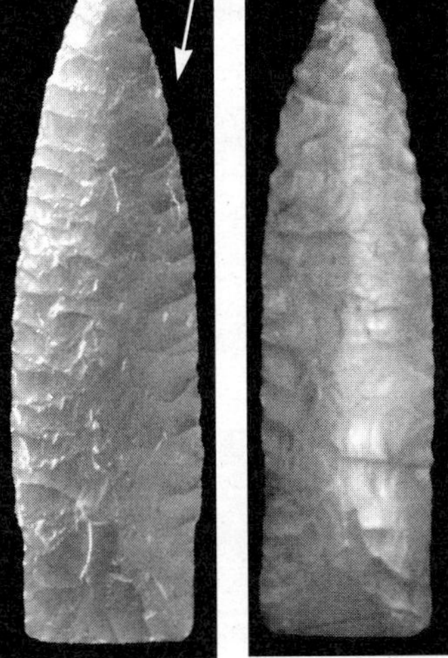

G8, $300-$600
Meagher Co., MT.

G7, $250-$500
Yuma Co., CO.

NP

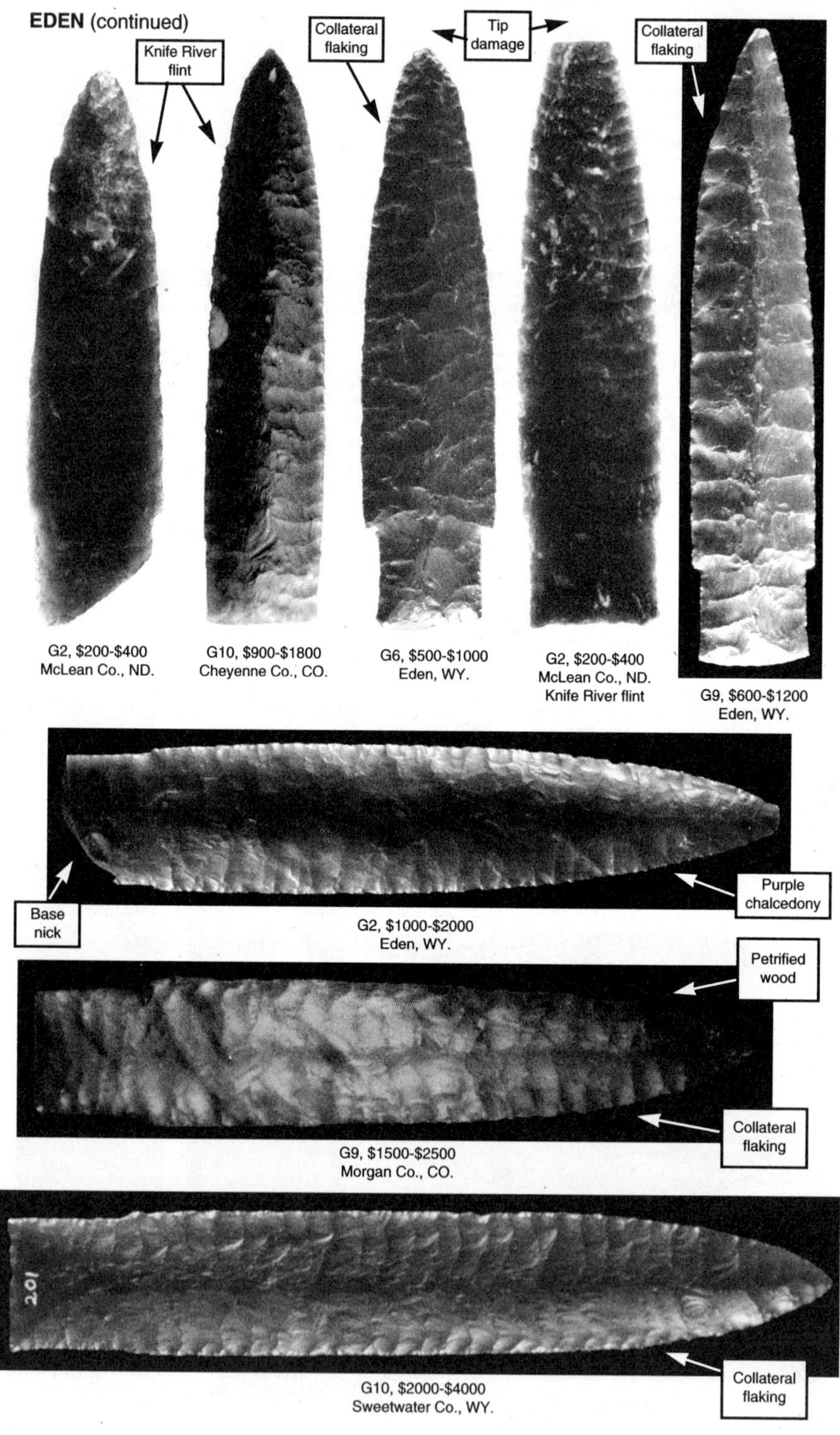

G2, $200-$400
McLean Co., ND.

G10, $900-$1800
Cheyenne Co., CO.

G6, $500-$1000
Eden, WY.

G2, $200-$400
McLean Co., ND.
Knife River flint

G9, $600-$1200
Eden, WY.

G2, $1000-$2000
Eden, WY.

G9, $1500-$2500
Morgan Co., CO.

G10, $2000-$4000
Sweetwater Co., WY.

EDEN (continued)

LOCATION: Northern Plains to Midwestern states. **DESCRIPTION:** A medium to large size, narrow, stemmed point with very weak shoulders and a straight to convex base. Basal sides are parallel to slightly expanding. Many examples have a median ridge and collateral to oblique parallel flaking. Bases are usually ground. A Cody Complex point. **I.D. KEY:** Paleo flaking, narrowness.

ELKO - Mid-Archaic to Developmental Phase, 3500 - 2000 B. P.

(Also see Mummy Cave, Pelican Lake and Rose Springs)

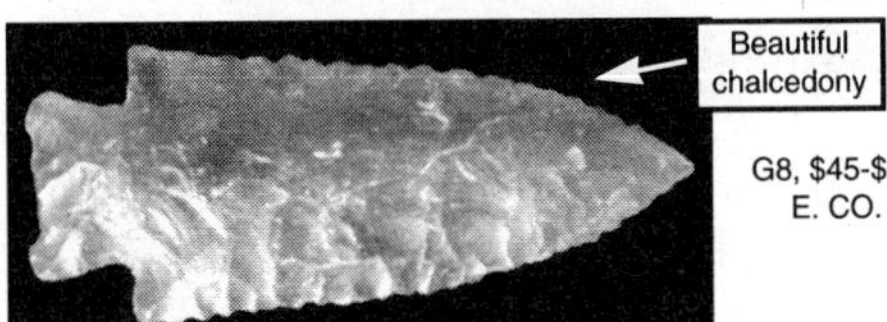

G8, $45-$75
E. CO.

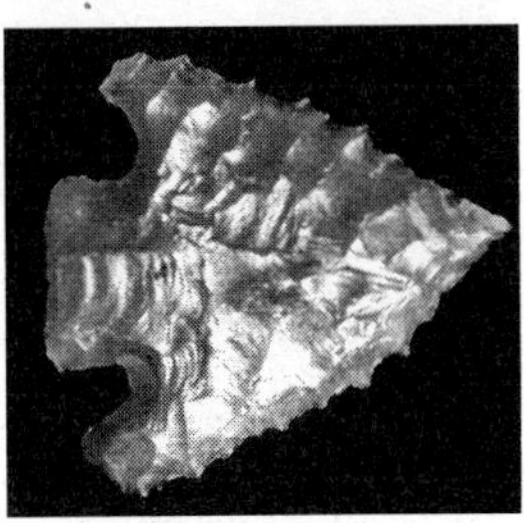

G8, $20-$40
Sweetwater Co., WY.

LOCATION: Northwestern states. **DESCRIPTION:** A medium to large size, narrow, stemmed to side notched point with convex to straight sides. Bases are parallel to bulbous to expanding. Blade edges are usually serrated. **I.D. KEY:** Narrow blade, short stem.

EMIGRANT - Developmental Phase, 900 - 400 B. P.

(Also see Billings, Bitterroot, Buffalo Gap, Cut Bank, Desert, Plains Side Notched and Swift Current)

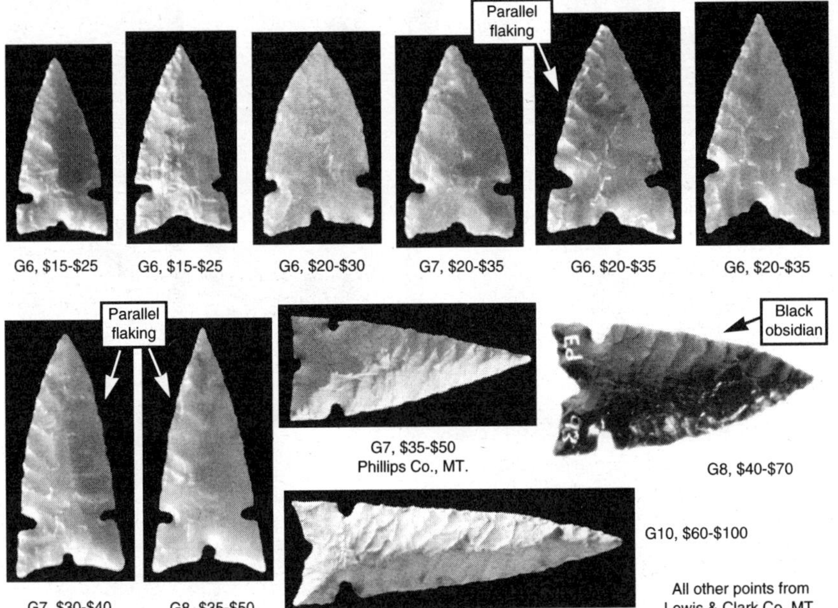

G6, $15-$25 G6, $15-$25 G6, $20-$30 G7, $20-$35 G6, $20-$35 G6, $20-$35

G7, $30-$40 G8, $35-$50

G7, $35-$50
Phillips Co., MT.

G8, $40-$70

G10, $60-$100

All other points from
Lewis & Clark Co. MT.

NP

LOCATION: Northern Plains states. **DESCRIPTION:** A small, thin, tri-notched point with a straight to convex base. Blade edges can be serrated. Basal corners are sharp to pointed. Widest at the base, this point has excellent flaking, usually of the oblique transverse variety.

FIRSTVIEW - Late Paleo, 8700 - 8000 B. P.

(Also see Alberta, Alder Complex, Cody Knife, Eden and Scottsbluff)

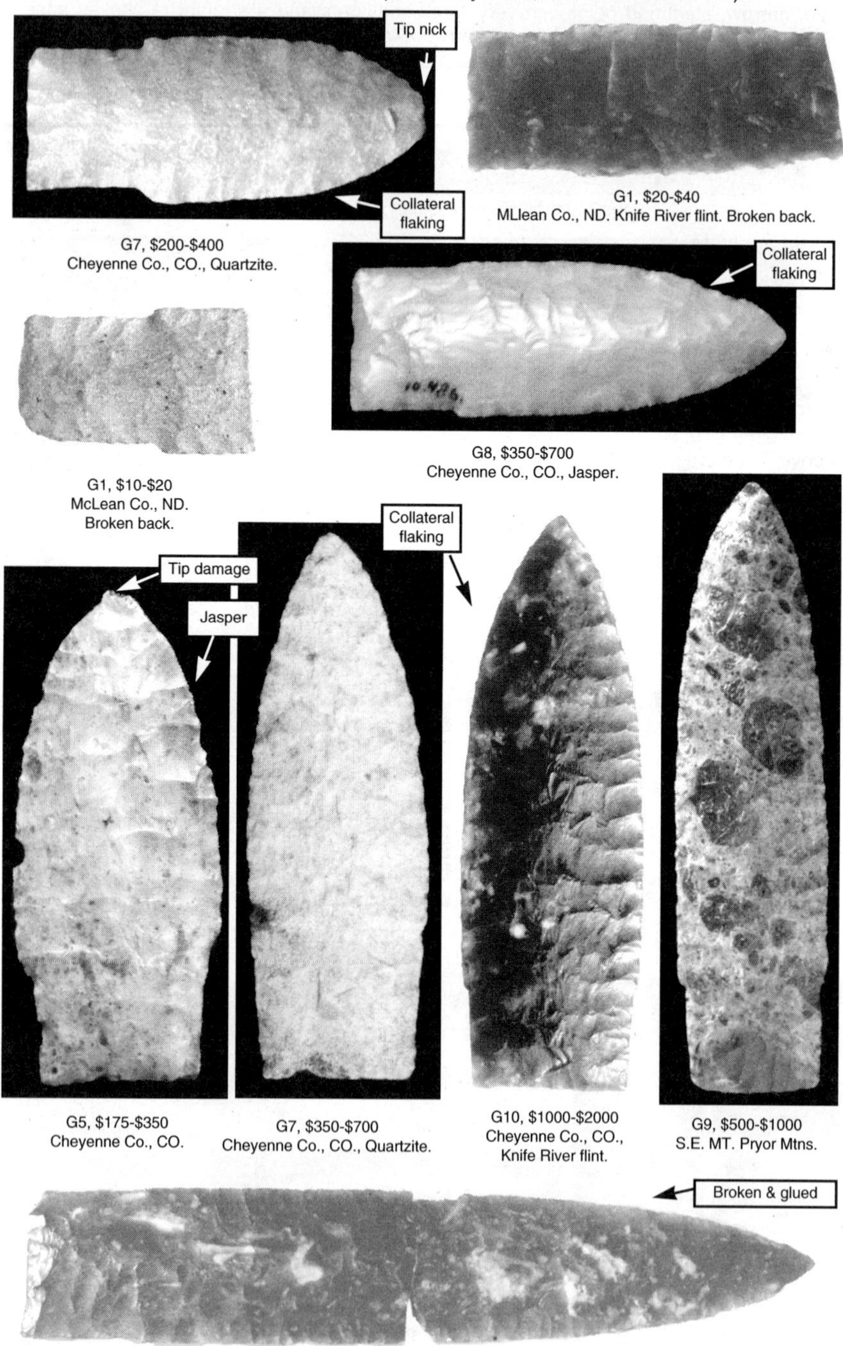

G7, $200-$400
Cheyenne Co., CO., Quartzite.

G1, $20-$40
MLlean Co., ND. Knife River flint. Broken back.

G1, $10-$20
McLean Co., ND.
Broken back.

G8, $350-$700
Cheyenne Co., CO., Jasper.

G5, $175-$350
Cheyenne Co., CO.

G7, $350-$700
Cheyenne Co., CO., Quartzite.

G10, $1000-$2000
Cheyenne Co., CO.,
Knife River flint.

G9, $500-$1000
S.E. MT. Pryor Mtns.

G1, $125-$250
McLean Co., ND. Knife River flint.

FIRSTVIEW (continued)

LOCATION: Colorado, Western Texas and New Mexico. **DESCRIPTION:** A medium to large size lanceolate point with slightly convex blade edges, slight shoulders and a rectangular stem. Shoulders are sometimes absent from resharpening. It generally exhibits parallel-transverse flaking. A variant form of the Scottsbluff type made by Cody Complex people. **I.D. KEY:** Weak shoulders, diamond shaped cross-section.

FOLSOM - Paleo, 11,000 - 9000 B. P.

(Also see Alder Complex, Clovis, Goshen, Green River, Midland and Milnesand)

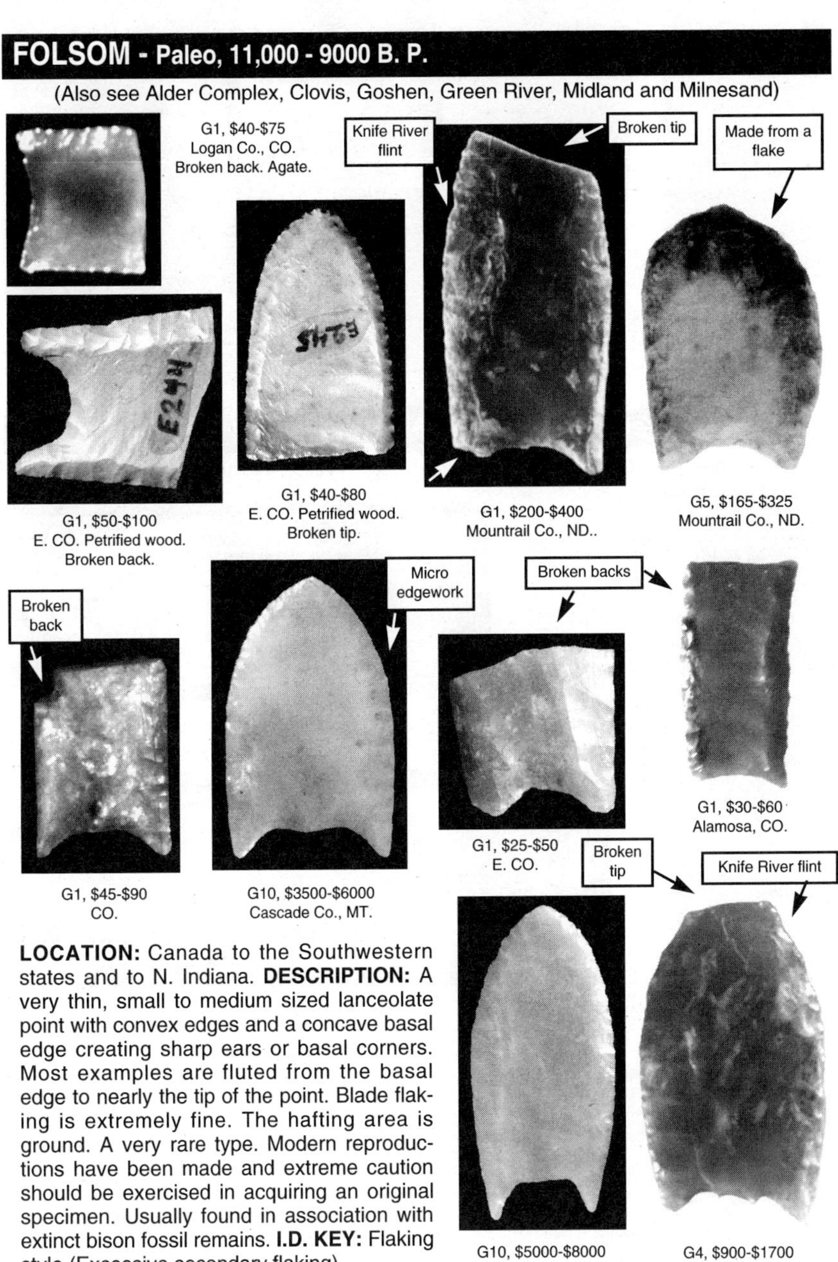

G1, $40-$75
Logan Co., CO.
Broken back. Agate.

G1, $50-$100
E. CO. Petrified wood.
Broken back.

G1, $40-$80
E. CO. Petrified wood.
Broken tip.

G1, $200-$400
Mountrail Co., ND..

G5, $165-$325
Mountrail Co., ND.

G1, $45-$90
CO.

G10, $3500-$6000
Cascade Co., MT.

G1, $25-$50
E. CO.

G1, $30-$60
Alamosa, CO.

LOCATION: Canada to the Southwestern states and to N. Indiana. **DESCRIPTION:** A very thin, small to medium sized lanceolate point with convex edges and a concave basal edge creating sharp ears or basal corners. Most examples are fluted from the basal edge to nearly the tip of the point. Blade flaking is extremely fine. The hafting area is ground. A very rare type. Modern reproductions have been made and extreme caution should be exercised in acquiring an original specimen. Usually found in association with extinct bison fossil remains. **I.D. KEY:** Flaking style (Excessive secondary flaking).

G10, $5000-$8000
Broadwater Co., MT.

G4, $900-$1700
Mountrail Co., ND.

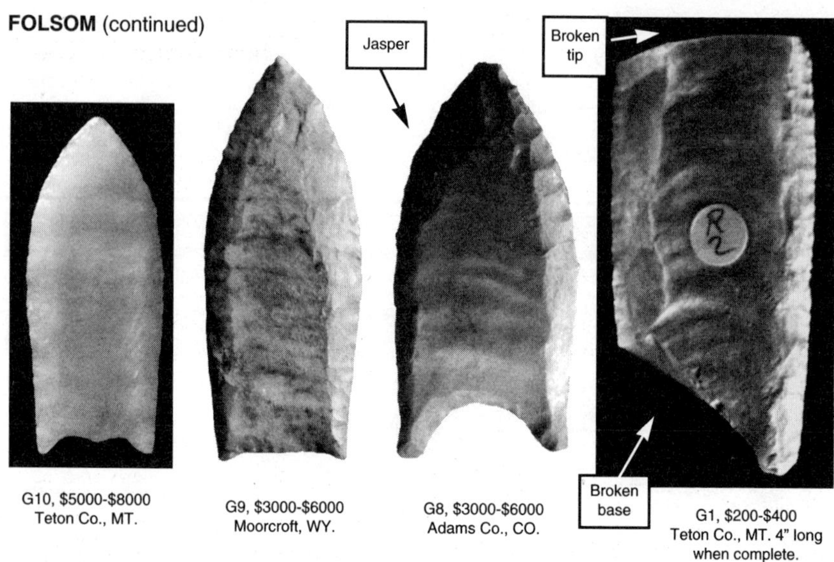

G10, $5000-$8000
Teton Co., MT.

G9, $3000-$6000
Moorcroft, WY.

G8, $3000-$6000
Adams Co., CO.

G1, $200-$400
Teton Co., MT. 4" long when complete.

GOSHEN - Paleo, 11,500 - 10,000 B. P.

(Also see Alder Complex, Clovis, Folsom, Green River, Midland and Milnesand)

G1, $15-$25
Casper, WY., Broken Back.

G9, $800-$1500
E. CO., Chalcedony.

G1, $15-$25
Casper, WY., Broken back.

G10, $1500-$2500
Carter Co., MT.

G7, $250-$500
WY.

LOCATION: Northern Plains states. **DESCRIPTION:** A small to medium size, very thin, auriculate point with a concave base. Basal corners slope inward and are rounded. Basal area is ground. Flaking is oblique to horizontal transverse. A very rare type. **I.D. KEY:** Thinness, auricles.

GRAVER - Paleo to Archaic, 14,000 - 4000 B. P.

(Also see scraper)

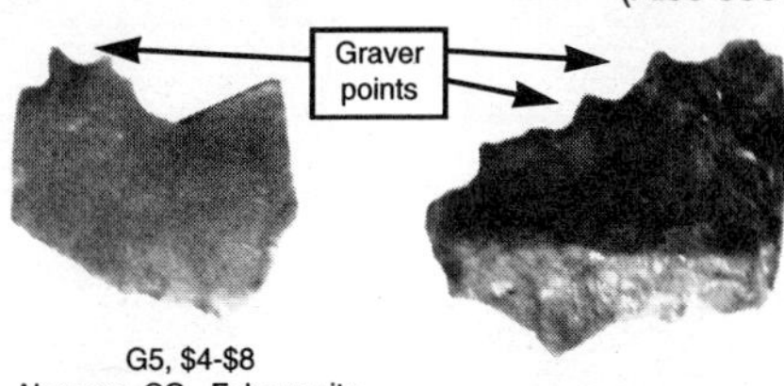

LOCATION: Early man sites everywhere. **DESCRIPTION:** An irregular shaped uniface tool with sharp, pointed projections used for puncturing, incising, tattooing, etc.

G5, $4-$8
Alamosa, CO., Folsom site.

G6, $5-$10
Alamosa, CO., Folsom site.

GREEN RIVER - Paleo, 11,500 - 10,000 B.P.

(Also see Alder Complex, Clovis, Folsom, Green River, Midland and Milnesand)

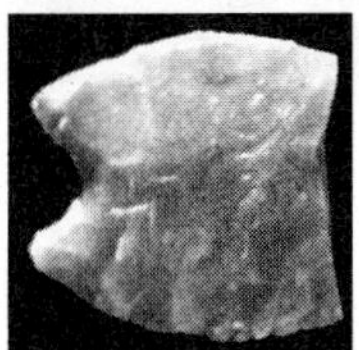

G1, $15-$25
Casper, WY.,
Broken Back.

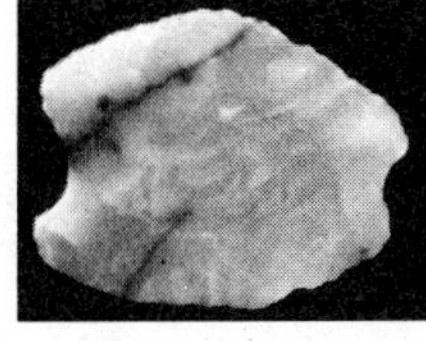

G1, $25-$40
Casper, WY.,
Tip damage.

LOCATION: Northern Plains states. **DESCRIPTION:** A small, very thin, auriculate point with contracting, almost pointed auricles and a small, deep basal concavity. **I.D. KEY:** Thinness, auricles.

HAFTED KNIFE (See Side Knife)

HANNA - Middle to Late Archaic, 4500 - 2850 B. P.

(Also see Duncan)

G5, $12-$20
CO.

G6, $10-$18
CO.

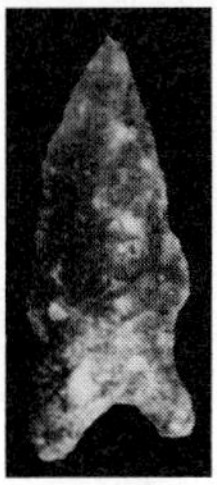

G6, $8-$15
Weld Co., CO.

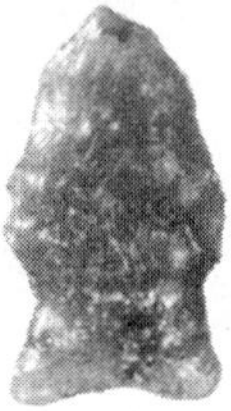

G4, $6-$10
CO.

G5 $15-$25
Lewis & Clark Co. MT.

Petrified wood

G5, $15-$30
Weld Co., CO.

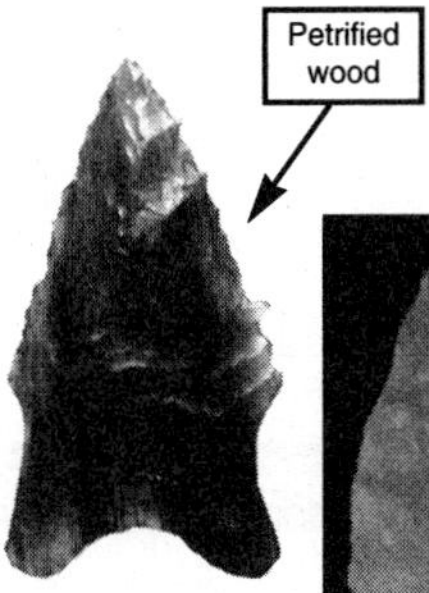

G7, $30-$60
Alamosa, CO.

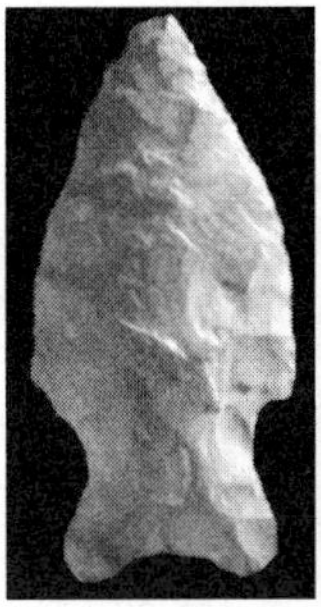

G7, $20-$35
Lewis & Clark Co., MT.

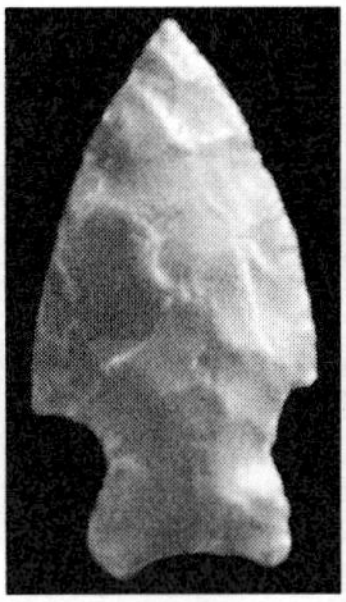

G7, $25-$45
Lewis & Clark
Co., MT.

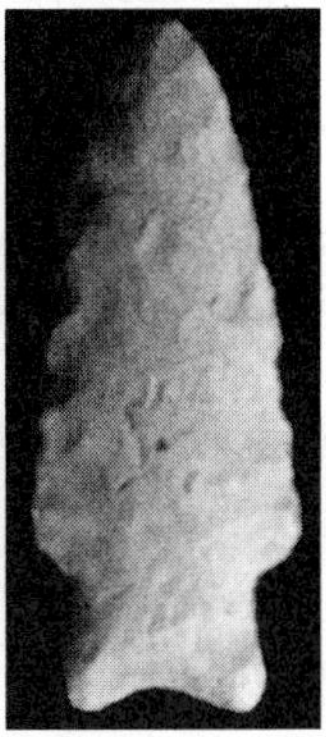

G6, $20-$40
Moorcroft, WY.

G5, $15-$30
Moorcroft, WY.

NP

HANNA (continued)

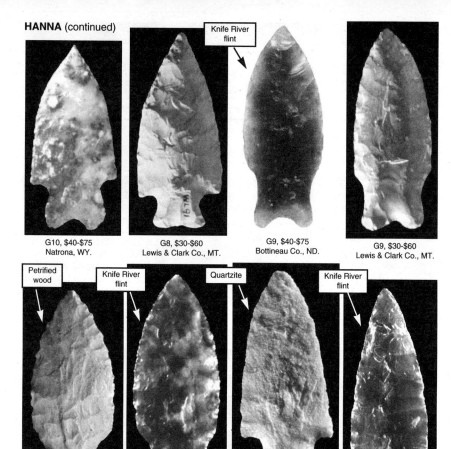

Knife River flint

G10, $40-$75
Natrona, WY.

G8, $30-$60
Lewis & Clark Co., MT.

G9, $40-$75
Bottineau Co., ND.

G9, $30-$60
Lewis & Clark Co., MT.

Petrified wood

Knife River flint

Quartzite

Knife River flint

G7, $35-$70
Adams Co., CO.

Basal grinding

G8, $40-$80
Bottineau Co., ND.

G7, $25-$50
Casper, WY.

Basal grinding

G9, $75-$145
Bottineau Co., ND.

LOCATION: Nebraska to Canada and as far south as the Southwestern states. **DESCRIPTION:** A small to medium size, narrow, bifurcated stemmed dart/knife point with tapered to horizontal shoulders and an expanding stem which is notched to produce diagonally projecting rounded "ears". **I.D. KEY:** Expanding stem.

HANNA NORTHERN - Middle to Late Archaic , 4500 - 3000 B. P.

(Also see Duncan)

LOCATION: Northern Plains states to Canada. **DESCRIPTION:** A small to medium size, narrow, long stemmed point with tapered to horizontal shoulders. Stem can be bifurcated.

G6, $25-$50
Alberta, Canada.

HARAHEY - Classic Phase, 700 - 350 B. P.

(Also see Archaic Knife)

Beveled on 4 sides

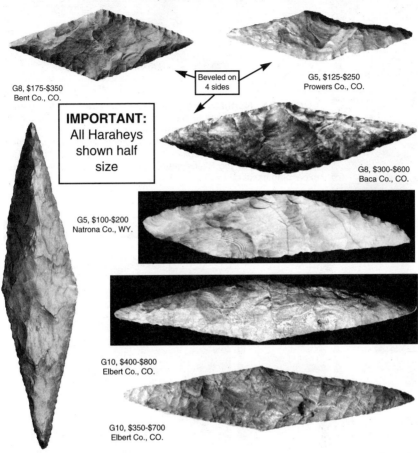

G8, $175-$350
Bent Co., CO.

G5, $125-$250
Prowers Co., CO.

IMPORTANT: All Haraheys shown half size

G8, $300-$600
Baca Co., CO.

G5, $100-$200
Natrona Co., WY.

G10, $400-$800
Elbert Co., CO.

G10, $350-$700
Elbert Co., CO.

G10, $450-$900
Natrona Co., WY.

LOCATION: Northern Plains states to Texas to Illinois to Canada. **DESCRIPTION:** A large size, double pointed knife that can be beveled on two to four edges. The cross section is rhomboid. **I.D. Key:** Rhomboid cross section.

HAWKENS - Early to Middle Archaic, 7000 - 5000 B. P.

(Also see Besant, Logan Creek and Lookingbill)

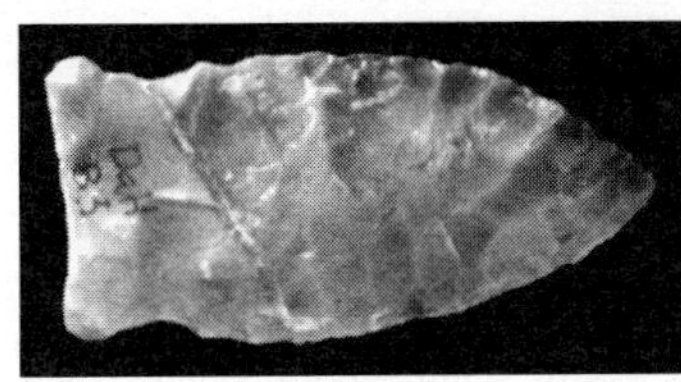

G7, $100-$200
Teton Co., MT.

G6, $100-$200
Meagher Co., MT.

NP

HAWKENS (continued)

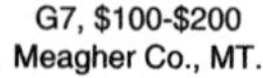

G7, $100-$200
Meagher Co., MT.

G8, $250-$500
Meagher Co., MT.

LOCATION: Northern Plains state. Type site is in Wyoming. **DESCRIPTION:** A small to medium size, narrow point with broad, shallow side notches and an expanding stem. Blade flaking is of high quality and is usually the oblique to horizontal parallel type. Along with *Logan Creek* and *Loogkingbill* this is one of the earliest side-notched points of the Plains states. **I.D. KEY:** Broad side notches, expanding base.

HELL GAP - Late Paleo, 10,900 - 9000 B. P.

(Also see Agate Basin, Angostura, Browns Valley and Rio Grande)

G5, $90-$180
Washington Co., CO.

G5, $90-$180
Weld Co., CO.

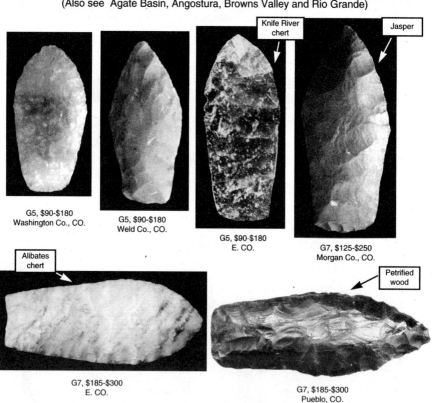

Knife River chert

G5, $90-$180
E. CO.

Jasper

G7, $125-$250
Morgan Co., CO.

Alibates chert

G7, $185-$300
E. CO.

Petrified wood

G7, $185-$300
Pueblo, CO.

LOCATION: Northern Plains states to Canada. **DESCRIPTION:** A medium to large size, narrow, long stemmed point with weak, tapered shoulders. Base can be concave, convex or straight. The basal area is usually ground. **I.D. KEY:** Early flaking and base form.

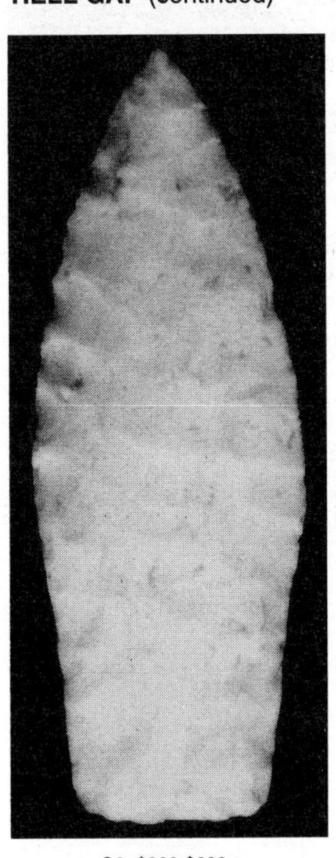

G8, $300-$600
Goshen Co., WY.

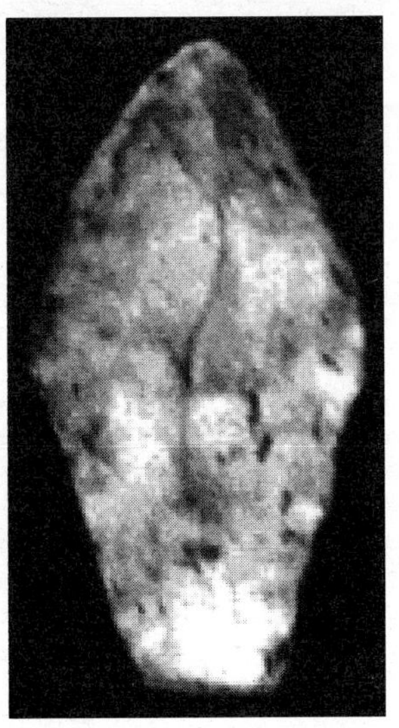

G7, $50-$100
MN.

G9, $350-$700
Lincoln Co., CO.
Flat top Chalcedony

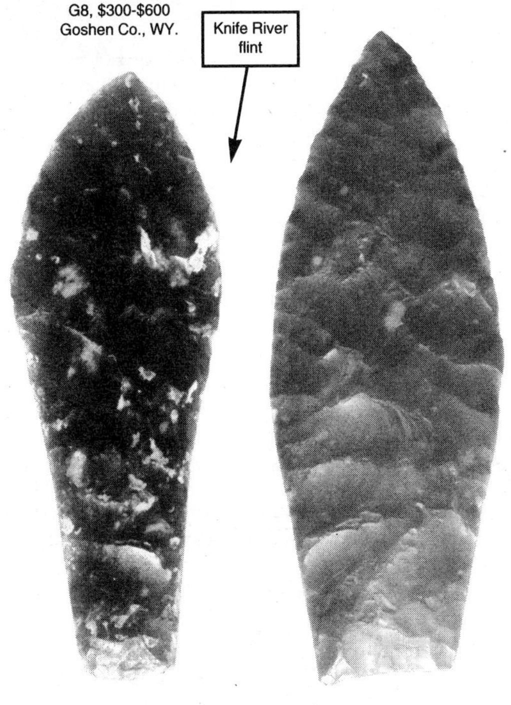

G9, $425-$850
ND.

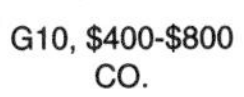

G10, $400-$800
CO.

G7, $150-$250
Lewis & Clark Co., MT.

NP

HIGH RIVER - Developmental Phase, 1300 - 800 B. P.

(Also see Avonlea, Hog Back, Pelican Lake and Samantha)

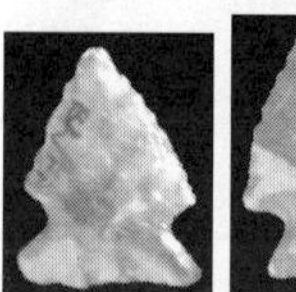
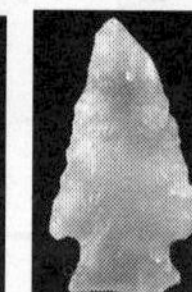

G4, $4-$7 ea.
Ft. Peck Res., MT.

G3, $3-$6
UT.

G7, $8-$15
Meagher Co., MT.

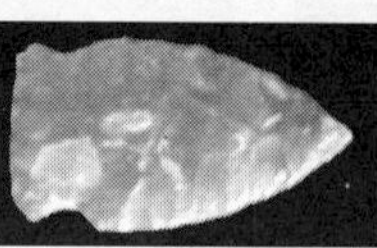

G7, $8-$15
Meagher Co., MT.

G8, $15-$20
Meagher Co., MT.

LOCATION: Northern Plains states to Canada. **DESCRIPTION:** A small, thin, corner notched triangular arrowpoint with a straight to convex base. Basal grinding is evident on some specimens. **I.D. KEY:** Small corner notched point.

HOG BACK - Developmental Phase, 1300 - 1000 B. P.

(Also see Mummy Cave, Pelican Lake and Samantha)

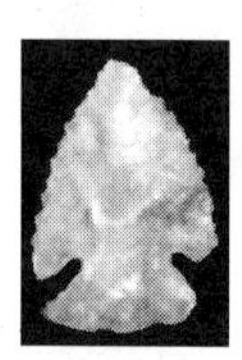

G7, $10-$15
CO.

G5, $10-$15
Alamosa, CO.

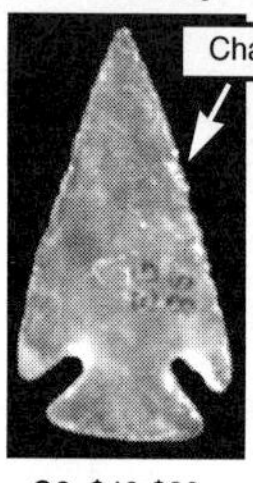

Chalcedony

G8, $40-$80
S.E. MT.

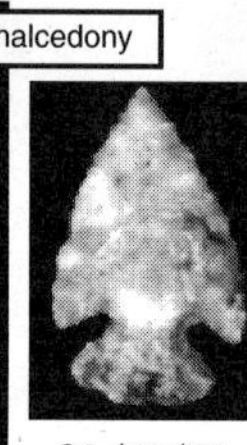

G6, $10-$20
CO.

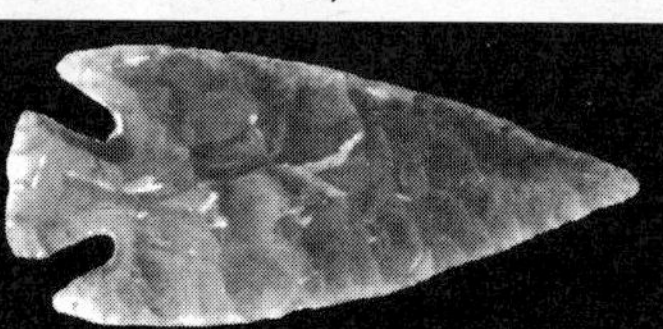

G8, $50-$100
Sweetwater Co.,
WY.

G6, $10-$20, CO.

LOCATION: Northern Plains states to Canada. **DESCRIPTION:** A small, thin, corner notched triangular arrowpoint with barbed shoulders and a convex base. The preform is ovoid and blade edges can be serrated. **I.D. KEY:** Small corner notched point, barbs.

HOLLAND - Transitional Paleo, 9500 - 200 B. P.

(Also see Dalton, Eden, Firstview and Scottsbluff)

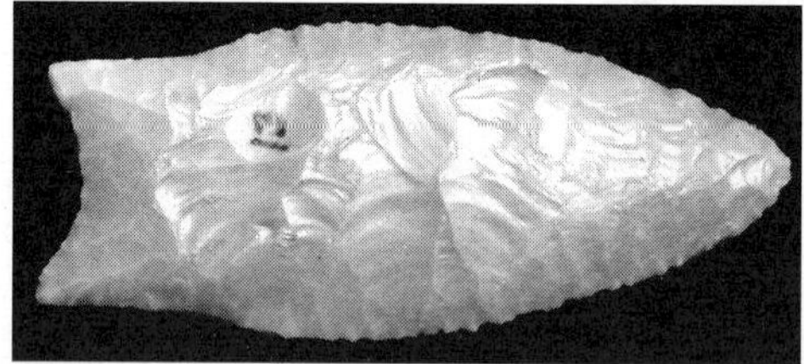

LOCATION: Northern Plains states. **DESCRIPTION:** A medium to large size lanceolate blade with weak to tapered shoulders. Bases can be knobbed to auriculate and are ground. **I.D. KEY:** Weak shoulders, concave base.

G7, $125-$250
Cheyenne Co., CO.

HORSE FLY - Developmental Phase, 1500 - 1000 B. P.

(Also see High River and Lewis)

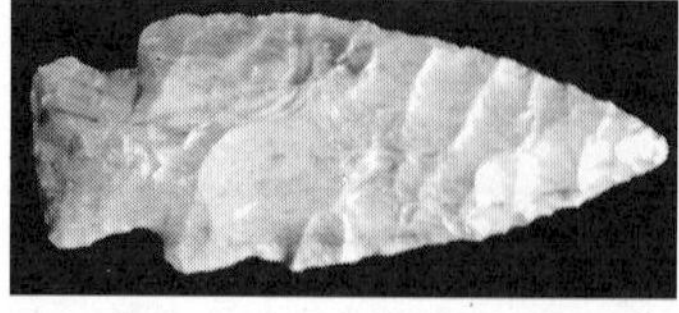

G7, $20-$30
E. CO.
Petrified
wood.

LOCATION: Colorado. **DESCRIPTION:** A medium to large size, narrow, stemmed point with a short, expanding stem and a straight to slightly convex base. Shoulders are horizontal to slightly barbed. **I.D. KEY:** Short, expanding stem.

HUFFAKER - Developmental Phase, 1000 - 500 B. P.

(Also see Desert and Washita)

LOCATION: Midwest to Northern Plains states. **DESCRIPTION:** A small size, thin, arrowpoint with a straight to concave base and double side notches. Bases can have a single notch. **I.D. KEY:** Double side notches.

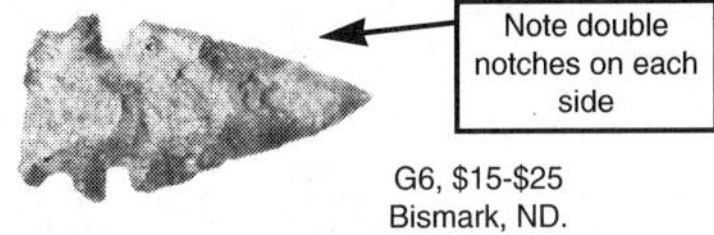

Note double notches on each side
G6, $15-$25
Bismark, ND.

IRVINE - Developmental Phase, 1400 - 800 B. P.

(Also see Avonlea, Bitterroot, Emigrant, Plains Side Notched and Samantha)

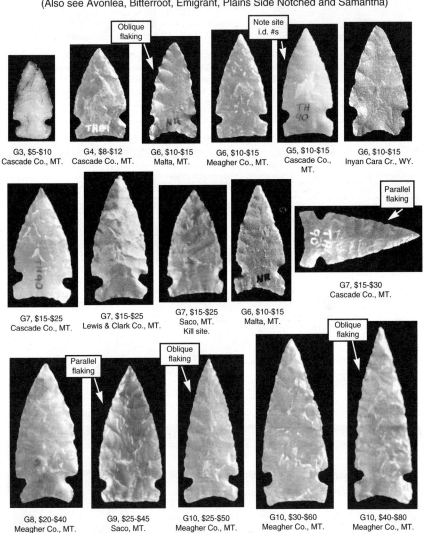

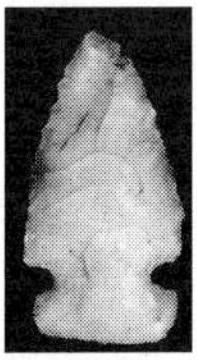

G3, $5-$10
Cascade Co., MT.

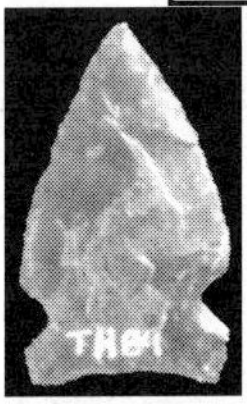

G4, $8-$12
Cascade Co., MT.

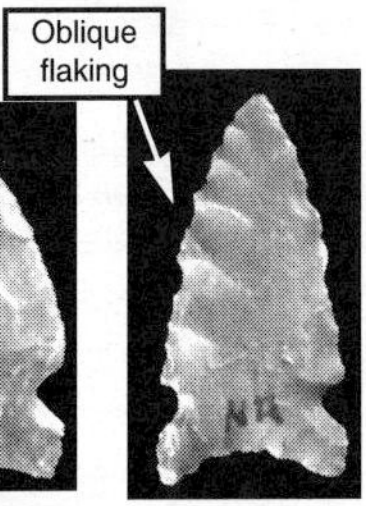

Oblique flaking
G6, $10-$15
Malta, MT.

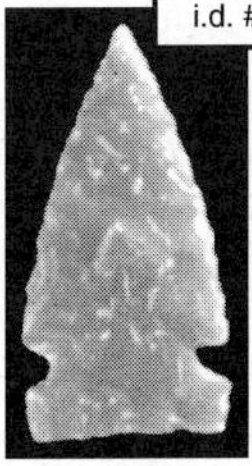

G6, $10-$15
Meagher Co., MT.

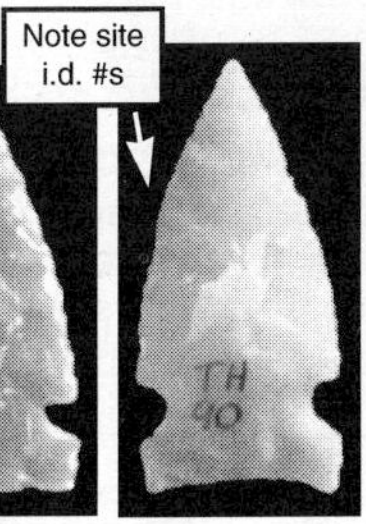

Note site i.d. #s
G5, $10-$15
Cascade Co., MT.

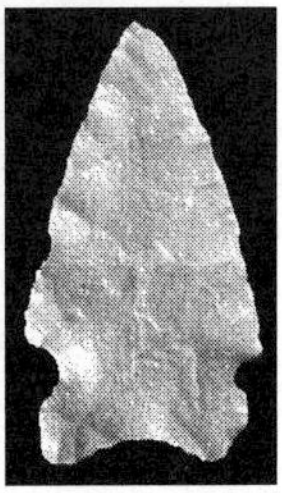

G6, $10-$15
Inyan Cara Cr., WY.

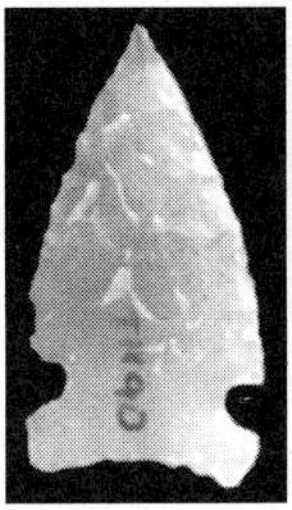

G7, $15-$25
Cascade Co., MT.

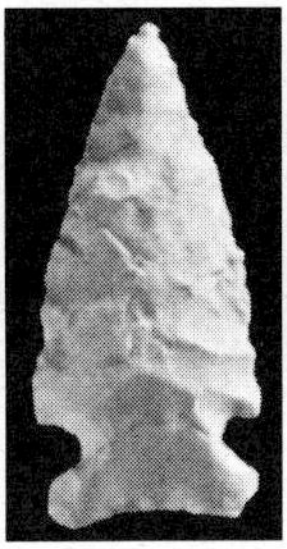

G7, $15-$25
Lewis & Clark Co., MT.

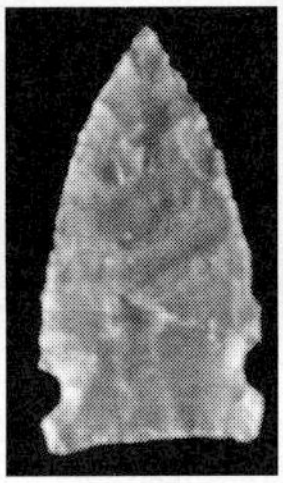

G7, $15-$25
Saco, MT.
Kill site.

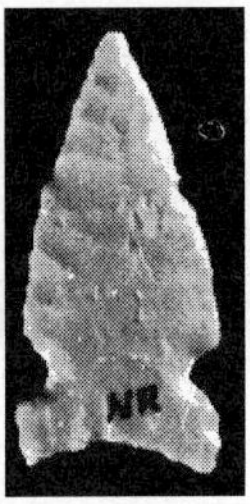

G6, $10-$15
Malta, MT.

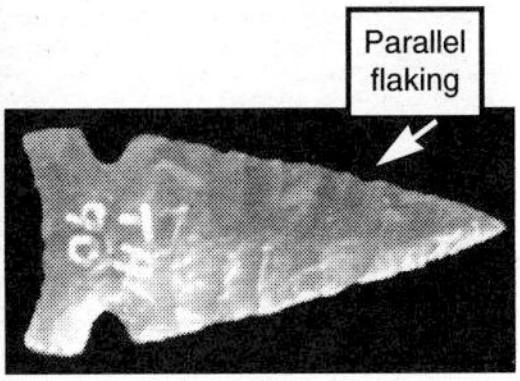

Parallel flaking
G7, $15-$30
Cascade Co., MT.

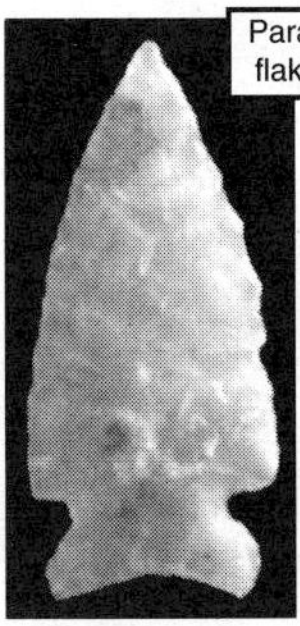

G8, $20-$40
Meagher Co., MT.

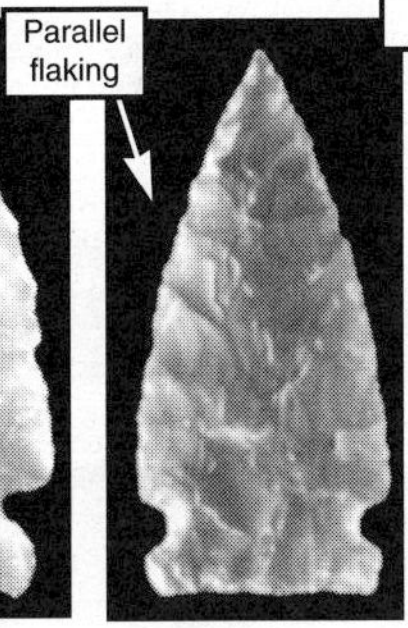

Parallel flaking
G9, $25-$45
Saco, MT.

Oblique flaking
G10, $25-$50
Meagher Co., MT.

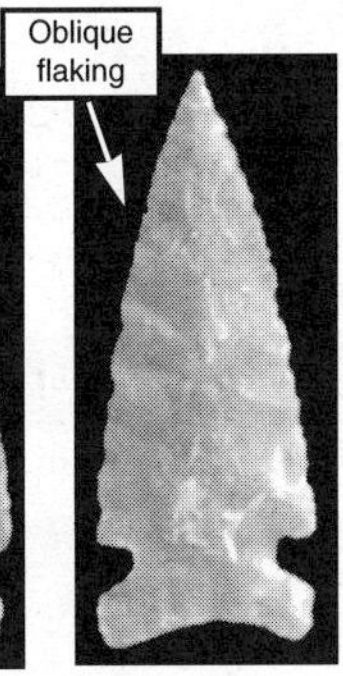

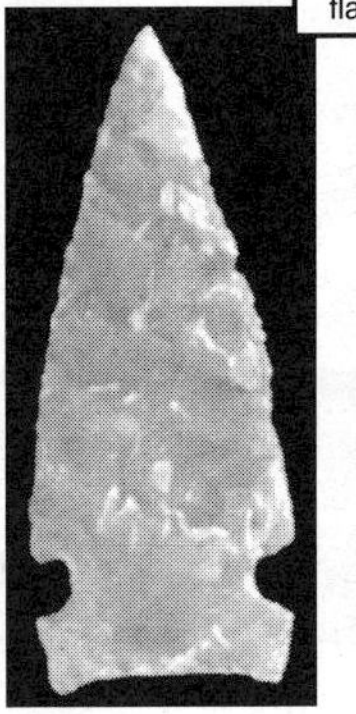

G10, $30-$60
Meagher Co., MT.

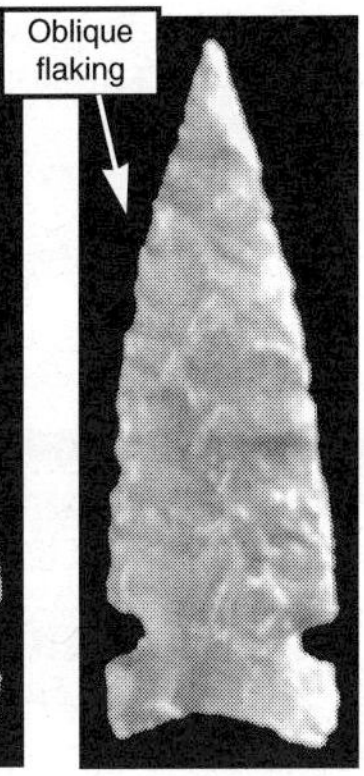

Oblique flaking
G10, $40-$80
Meagher Co., MT.

LOCATION: Northern Plains states. **DESCRIPTION:** A small size, thin, side notched arrowpoint with a concave base. The notching is distinct forming squarish basal ears. **I.D. KEY:** Square basal ears.

NP

LANCET - Paleo to Historic Phase, 14,000 - 200 B. P.

(Also see Drill and Scraper)

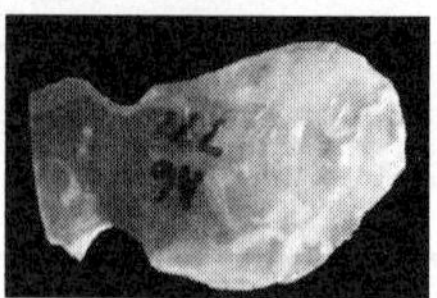

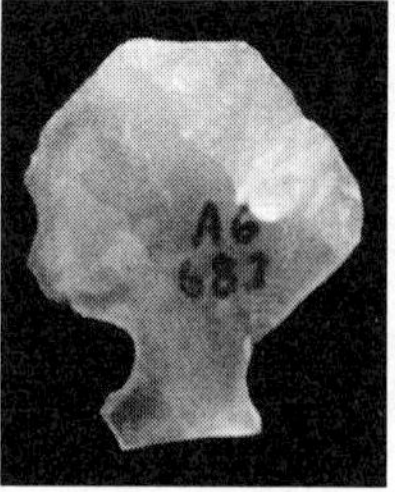

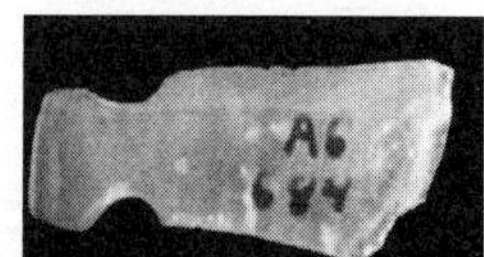

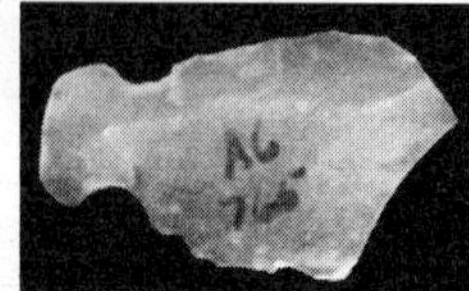

G7, $8-$12 ea.
Lewis & Clark Co., MT.

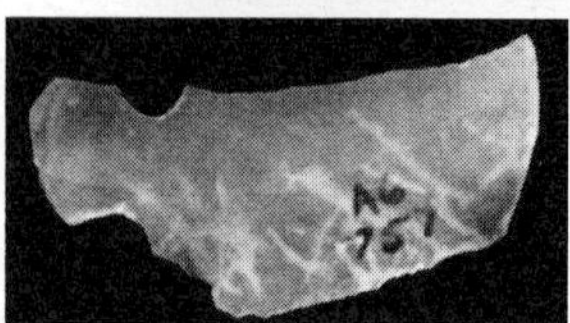

LOCATION: Everywhere. **DESCRIPTION:** Also known as a lammeler flake blade, it was produced by striking a flake or spall off a parent stone and was used as a knife for cutting. Some examples are notched for hafting. Recent experiments proved that these knives were sharper than a surgeon's scapel. Similar to *burins* which are fractured at one end to produce a sharp point.

LERMA - Mid-Archaic, 4000 - 3000 B. P.

(Also see Agate Basin, Angostura and Harahey)

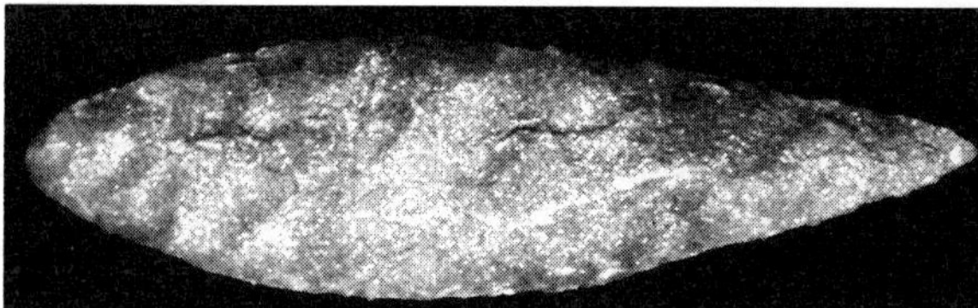

G8, $40-$80
Weld Co., CO.

LOCATION: Arizona to Texas to Northern Plains states. **DESCRIPTION:** A medium to large size lanceolate point with a pointed to rounded base. Beveling can occur on one side of each face. **I.D. KEY:** Lanceolate form.

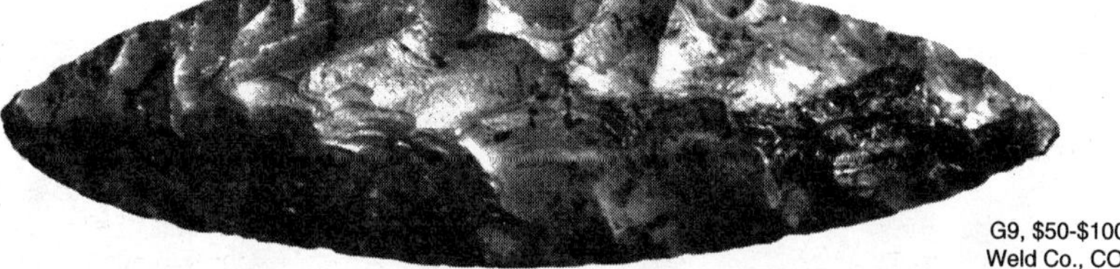

G9, $50-$100
Weld Co., CO.

LEWIS - Developmental to Historic Phase, 1400 - 400 B. P.

(Also see Avonlea, High River, Irvine, Nanton, Paskapoo, Swift Current and Tompkins)

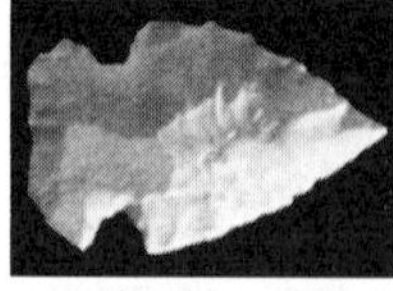

G5, $5-$10
Lewis & Clark Co., MT.

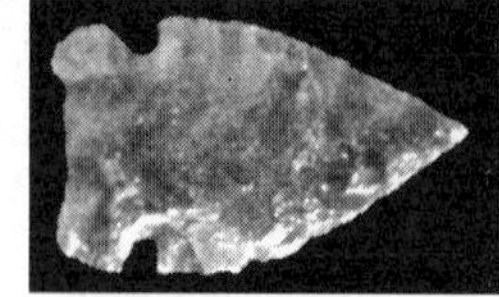

G6, $6-$12
Lewis & Clark Co., MT.

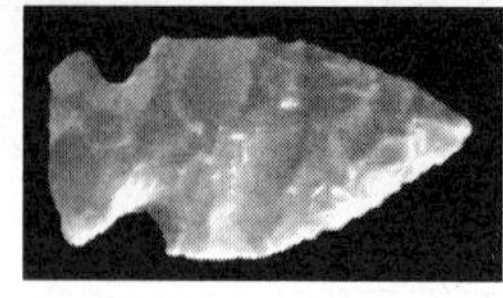

G6, $6-$12
Phillips Co., MT.

LEWIS (continued)

G6, $10-$20
Phillips Co., MT.

G6, $10-$20
Phillips Co., MT.

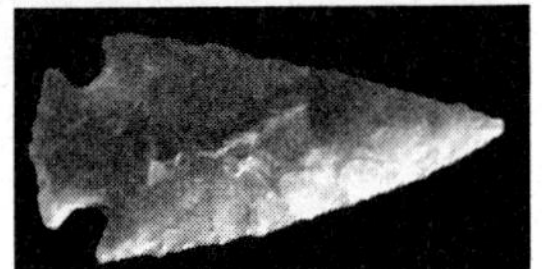

G6, $10-$20
Meagher Co., MT.

LOCATION: Midwestern to Northern Plains states. **DESCRIPTION:** A small to medium size, thin, side notched point with a convex to concave base. The width of the base is less than the shoulders and the basal corners are rounded. Some specimens have basal grinding.

LOGAN CREEK - Early to Middle Archaic, 7000 - 5000 B. P.

(Also see Hawkens and Lookingbill)

G6, $12-$20
WY.

G5, $10-$15
Pryor Mtns, MT. Tip nick.

G8, $70-$135
Douglas Co., ND.

G7, $60-$115
Bottineau Co., ND.

G6, $10-$20
WY.

LOCATION: Midwestern to Northern Plains states. **DESCRIPTION:** A medium to large size, broad side-notched point with a straight, concave or convex base. Along with *Hawkens* and *Lookingbill* , this is one of the earliest side-notched points of the Plains states. Oblique to horizontal blade flaking is evident. **I.D.KEY:** Broad side-notches close to the base, early flaking.

LOOKINGBILL - Early to Middle Archaic, 7000 - 5000 B. P.

(Also see Hawkens and Logan Creek)

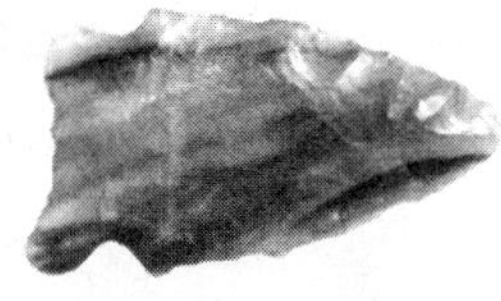

G7, $20-$30
CO.

LOCATION: Midwestern to Northern Plains states. **DESCRIPTION:** A medium to large size, broad side-notched point with a straight to concave base. Along with *Hawkens* and *Logan Creek* this is one of the earliest side-notched point of the Plains states. **I.D.KEY:** Broad side notches close to the base, parallel flaking.

NP

LOOKINGBILL (continued)

G7, $15-$30
Tongue Riv., WY.

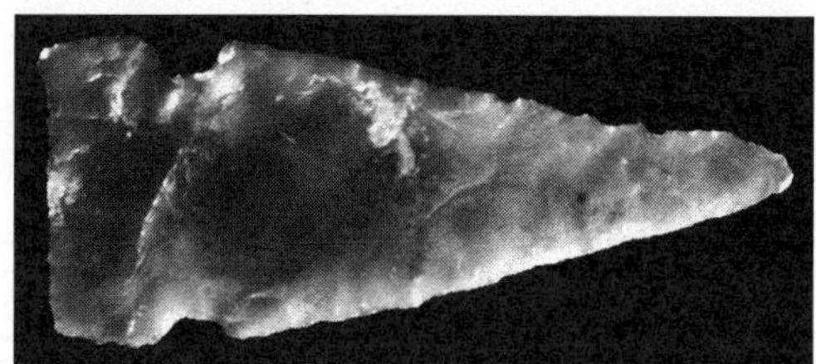
G7, $35-$70
N. Cent. S.D.

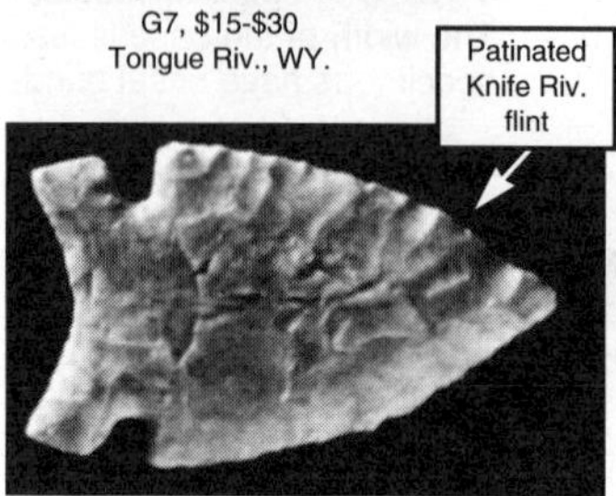

G8, $45-$85
Jamestown, ND.

G10, $100-$200
Nashua, MT. Tongue River.

LOVELL - Transitional Paleo to Early Archaic, 8500 - 8000 B. P.

(Also see Agate Basin, Alder Complex, Clovis, Folsom, Goshen and Green River)

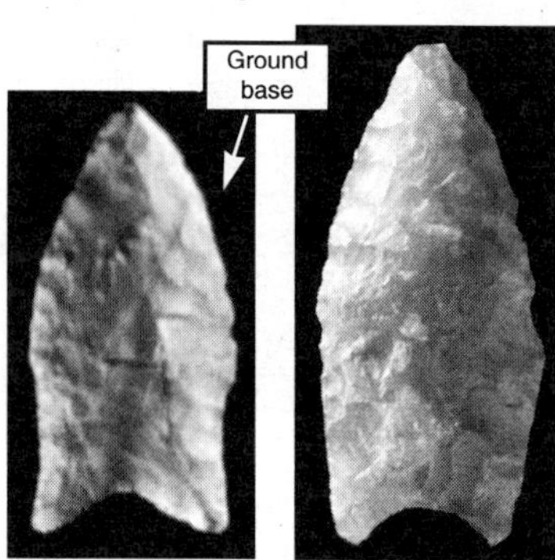

G7, $40-$75
Mountrail Co., ND.

G6, $50-$100
Lewis & Clark Co., MT.

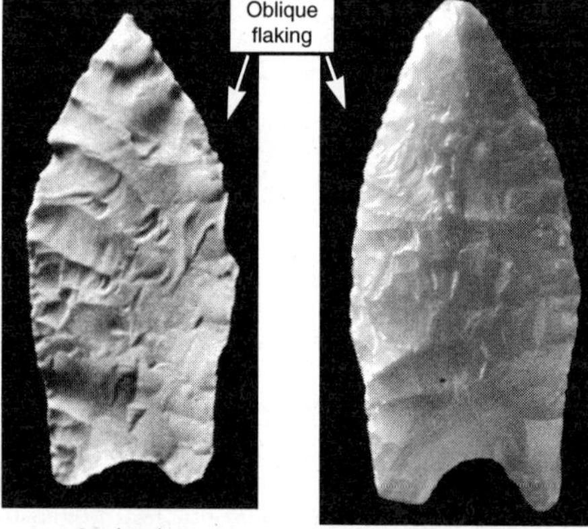

G6, $40-$75
Lewis & Clark Co., MT.

G5, $100-$200
Lewis & Clark Co., MT.

LOCATION: Northern Plains states. **DESCRIPTION:** A small to medium size, narrow, unfluted lanceolate point with a straight to concave base. Blade edges recurve towards the base on most examples. Random to oblique or horizontal parallel flaking occurs. **I.D. KEY:** Form and basal constriction.

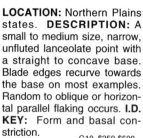

G10, $250-$500
Broadwater Co., MT.

MALLORY - Middle to Late Archaic, 4000 - 3000 B. P.

(Also see Billings, Bitterroot, Emigrant and Lookingbill)

MALLORY (continued)

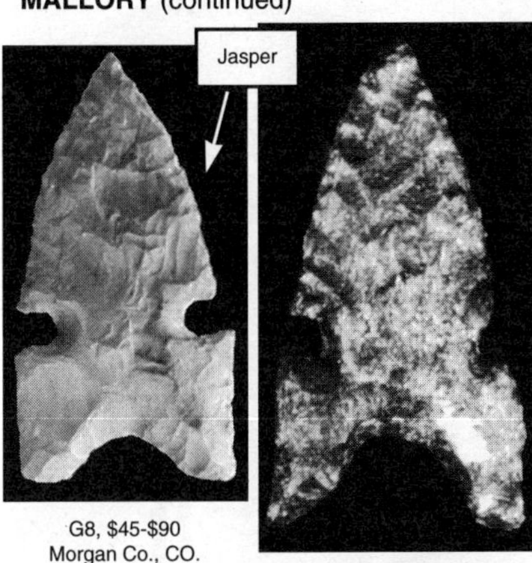

G8, $45-$90
Morgan Co., CO.

G8, $45-$90
Morgan Co., CO.

G8, $45-$90
Morgan Co., CO.

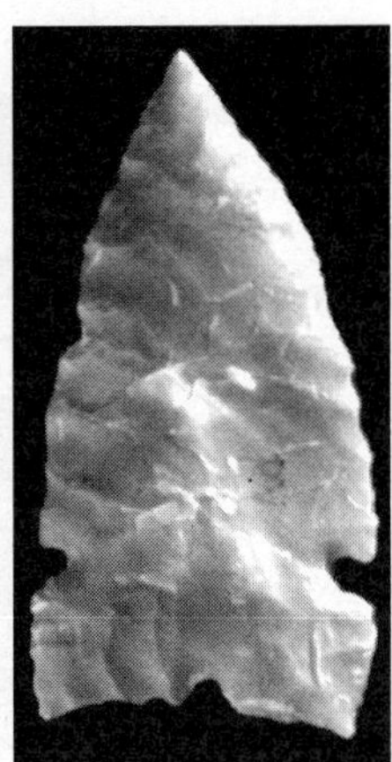

G10, $45-$90
Teton Co., MT.

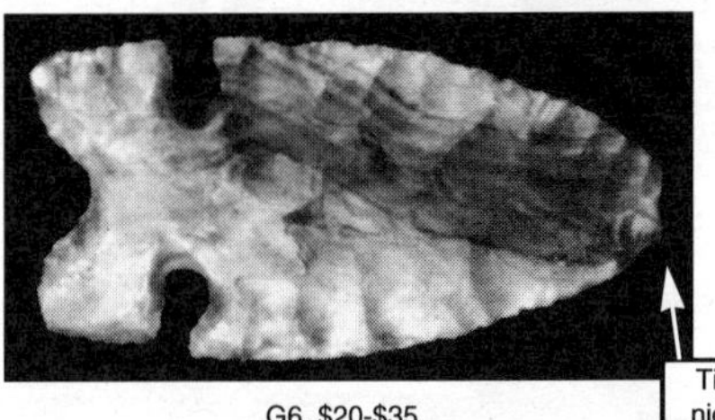

G6, $20-$35
Morgan Co., CO.

LOCATION: Northern Plains states. **DESCRIPTION:** A small to medium size, broad, tri-notched to side notched point with a concave base and sharp basal corners. Side notches occur high up from the base. **I.D. KEY:** Size and tri-notching.

MCKEAN - Middle to Late Archaic, 4500 - 2500 B. P.

(Also see Folsom, Goshen, Green River and Lovell)

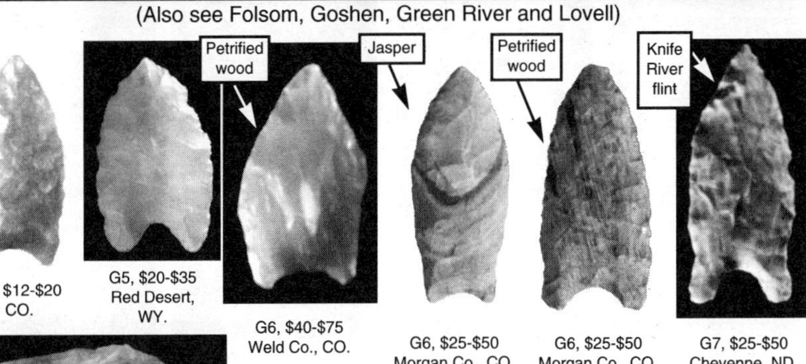

G5, $12-$20
CO.

G5, $20-$35
Red Desert,
WY.

G6, $40-$75
Weld Co., CO.

G6, $25-$50
Morgan Co., CO.

G6, $25-$50
Morgan Co., CO.

G7, $25-$50
Cheyenne, ND.

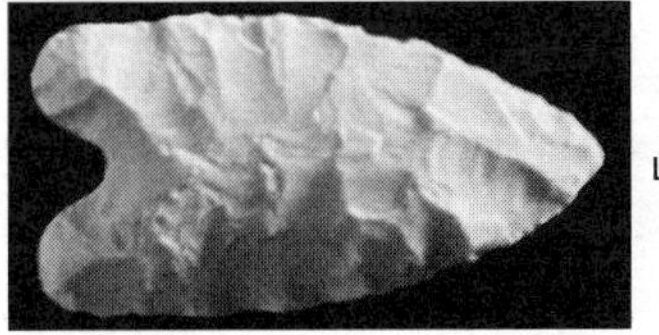

G8, $40-$75
Weld Co., CO.

G8, $40-$75
Lewis & Clark
Co., MT.

LOCATION: Northern Plains states. Type site is in N.E. Wyoming. **DESCRIPTION:** A small to medium size, narrow, basal notched point. No basal grinding is evident. Similar to the much earlier *Wheeler* points of the Southeast. Basal ears are rounded to pointed. Flaking is more random although earlier examples can have parallel flaking. **I.D. KEY:** Narrow lanceolate with notched base.

NP

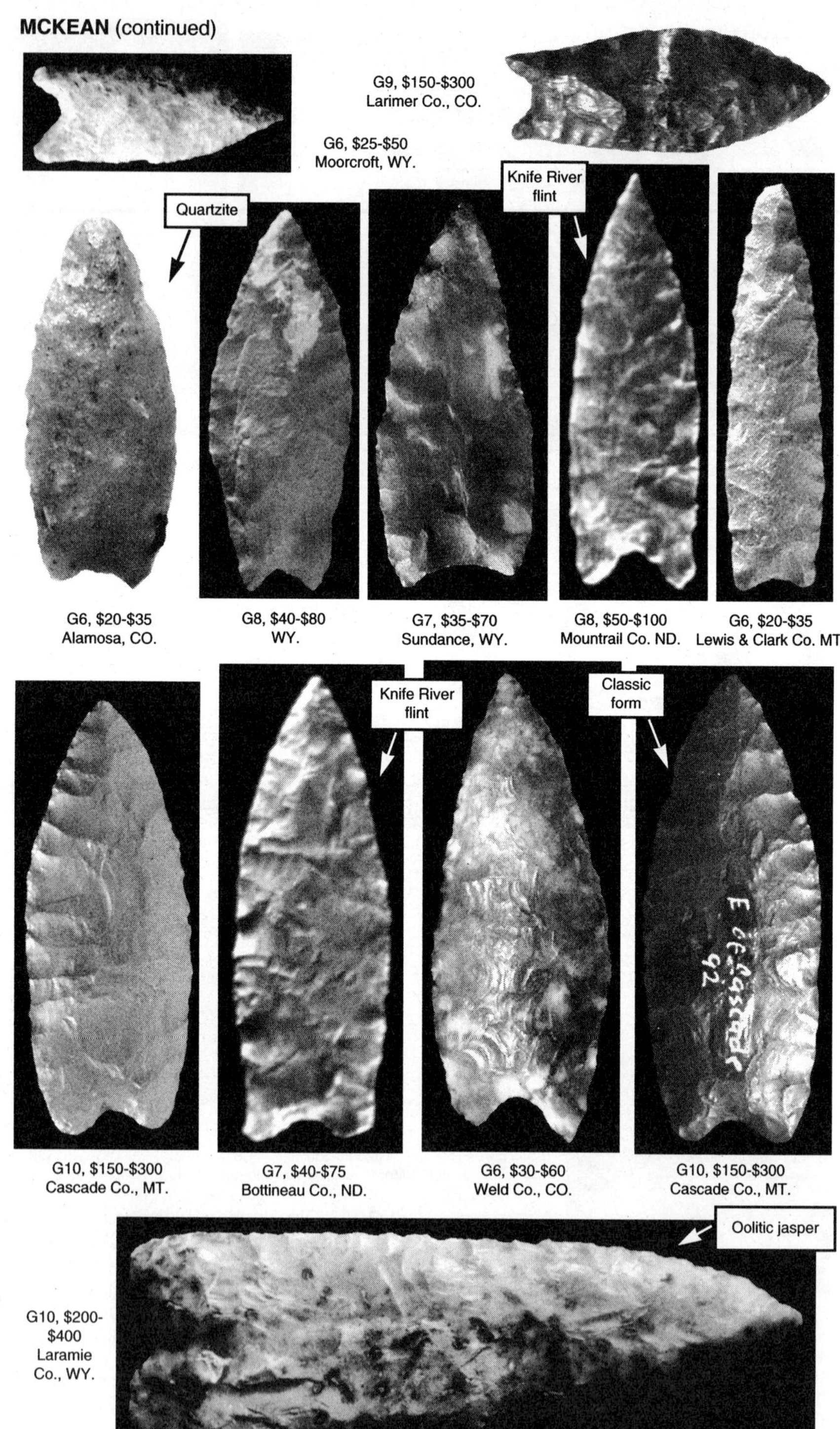

G9, $150-$300
Larimer Co., CO.

G6, $25-$50
Moorcroft, WY.

G6, $20-$35
Alamosa, CO.

G8, $40-$80
WY.

G7, $35-$70
Sundance, WY.

G8, $50-$100
Mountrail Co. ND.

G6, $20-$35
Lewis & Clark Co. MT.

G10, $150-$300
Cascade Co., MT.

G7, $40-$75
Bottineau Co., ND.

G6, $30-$60
Weld Co., CO.

G10, $150-$300
Cascade Co., MT.

G10, $200-$400
Laramie Co., WY.

MESERVE - Late Paleo, 9500 - 8500 B. P.

(Also see Clovis, Dalton, Folsom, Goshen and Lovell)

Obsidian

Quartzite

Beveled edge

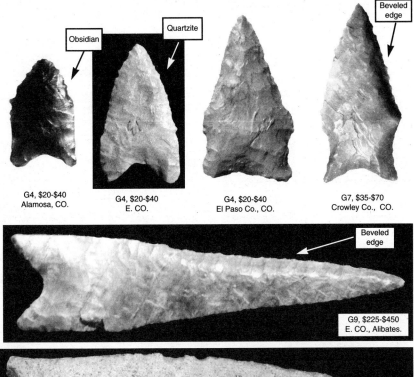

G4, $20-$40
Alamosa, CO.

G4, $20-$40
E. CO.

G4, $20-$40
El Paso Co., CO.

G7, $35-$70
Crowley Co., CO.

Beveled edge

G9, $225-$450
E. CO., Alibates.

G8, $150-$300
Lincoln Co., CO.

LOCATION: Throughout the U.S. from the Rocky Mountains to the Mississippi River. **DESCRIPTION:** A member of the *Dalton* family. Blade edges are straight to slightly concave with a straight to very slightly concave sided stem. They are basally thinned and most examples are beveled and have light serrations on the blade edges. Beveling extends to the basal area. **I.D. KEY:** Beveling into base.

MID-BACK TANG - Middle Archaic to Transitional Phase, 4000 - 2000 B. P.

(Also see Base Tang Knife, Cody Knife and Corner Tang)

LOCATION: Midwestern states and Canada. **DESCRIPTION:** A variation fo the corner tang knife with the hafting area occuring near the center of one side of the blade. **I.D. KEY:** Tang in center of blade.

MID-BACK TANG (continued)

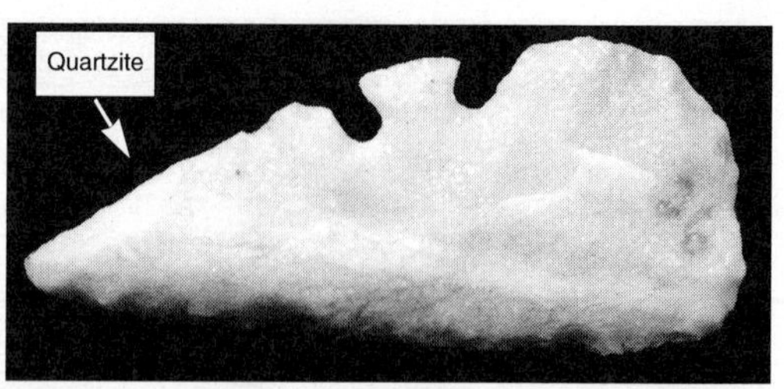

G7, $200-$400
E. CO.

MIDLAND - Transitional Paleo, 10,700 - 9000 B. P.

(Also see Alder Complex, Clovis, Folsom, Goshen and Milnesand)

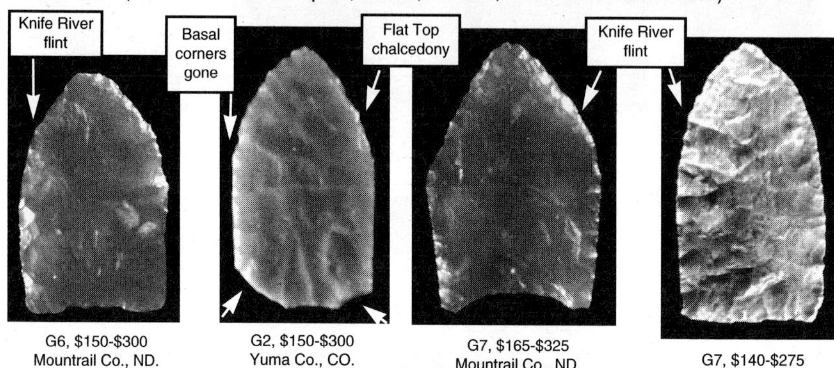

G6, $150-$300
Mountrail Co., ND.

G2, $150-$300
Yuma Co., CO.

G7, $165-$325
Mountrail Co., ND.

G7, $140-$275
Mountrail Co., ND.

G7, $225-$450
Morgan Co., CO.

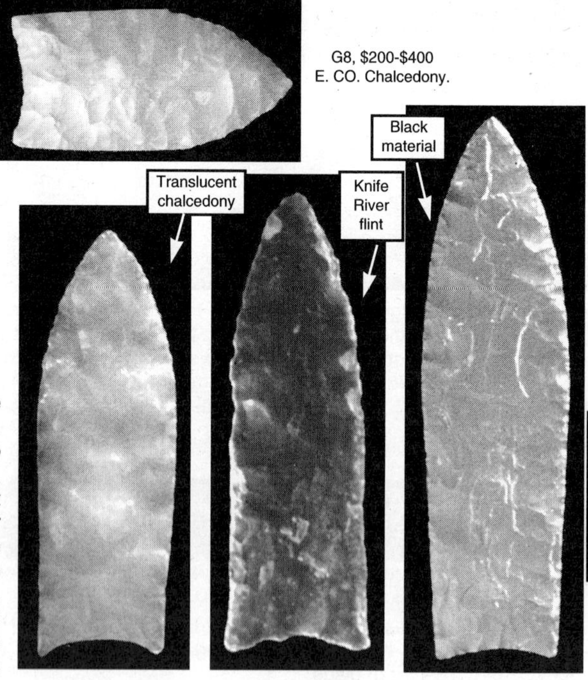

G8, $200-$400
E. CO. Chalcedony.

G10, $450-$900
S.W. MT., Ruby Valley.

G9, $325-$650
Mountrail Co., ND.

G10, $900-$1500
Dillon, MT.

LOCATION: Texas to the Northern Plains states. **DESCRIPTION:** A small to medium size, very thin, unfluted lanceolate point with the widest part near the tip. Believed to be unfluted *Folsoms.* Bases have a shallow concavity. Basal thinning is weak and the blades exhibit fine micro-edgework. **I.D. KEY:** Form and thinness.

MILNESAND - Paleo, 11,000 - 9500 B. P.

(Also see Alder Complex and Midland)

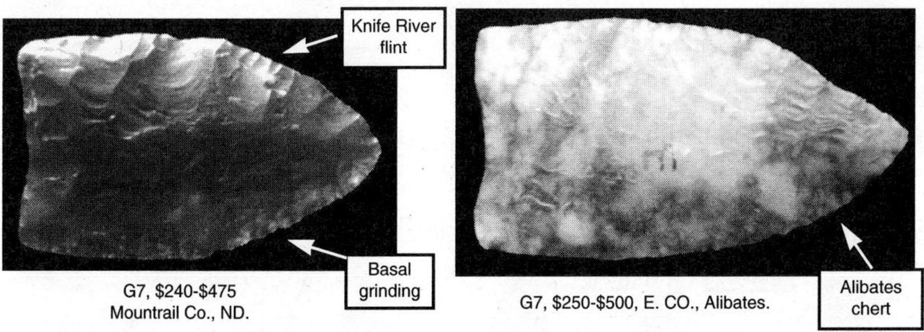

G7, $240-$475
Mountrail Co., ND.

G7, $250-$500, E. CO., Alibates.

LOCATION: North Dakota to Colorado to west Texas and eastern New Mexico. **DESCRIPTION:** A lanceolate point with parallel to very slightly convex blade edges. The basal edge is straight and is beveled and ground, as are the stem edges. Thicker than *Midland.* **I.D. KEY:** Thickness and Paleo parallel flaking.

MOUNT ALBION - Early to Middle Archaic, 5800 - 5500 B. P.

(Also see Besant)

G3, $4-$8
Weld Co., CO.

G3, $4-$8
Weld Co., CO.

G3, $3-$6
Weld Co., CO.

G3, $3-$6
Weld Co., CO.

G4, $6-$12
Weld Co., CO.

G3, $4-$8
Weld Co., CO.

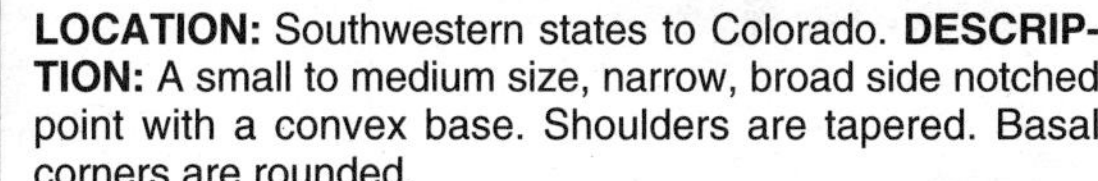

G6, $6-$12
Weld Co., CO.

LOCATION: Southwestern states to Colorado. **DESCRIPTION:** A small to medium size, narrow, broad side notched point with a convex base. Shoulders are tapered. Basal corners are rounded.

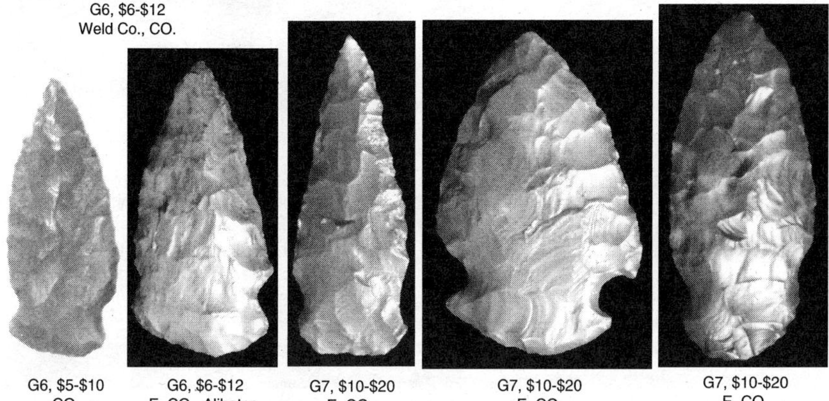

G6, $5-$10
CO.

G6, $6-$12
E. CO., Alibates.

G7, $10-$20
E. CO.,

G7, $10-$20
E. CO.

G7, $10-$20
E. CO.

NP

MUMMY CAVE - Early to Middle Archaic, 7500 - 5000 B. P.

(Also see Hog Back and Pelican Lake)

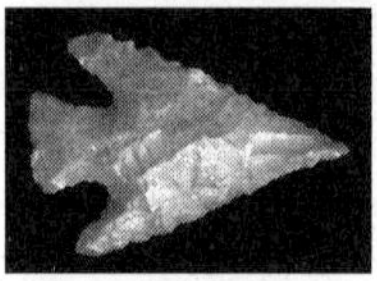

G9, $25-$50
Grand Co., UT.

G9, $20-$40
UT.

G9, $25-$50
Bent/Crowley Co., CO.

G5, $15-$30
Grand Co., UT.

Broken shoulder

G6, $12-$20
CO.

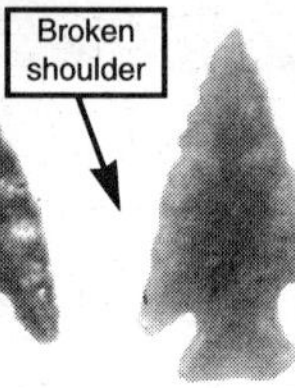

Broken base

G4, $4-$8
CO., Gem.

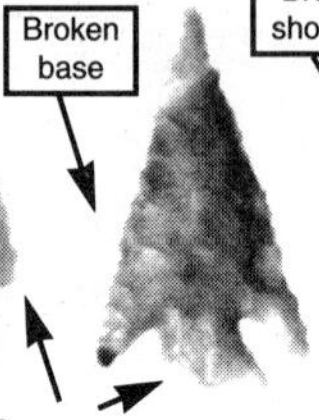

Broken shoulder

G2, $4-$8
CO.

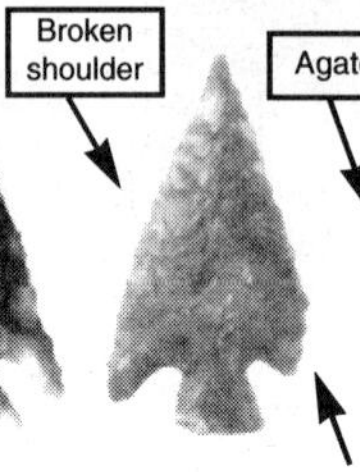

Agate

G4, $5-$10
CO.

Broken shoulder

G8, $20-$40
CO. Agate.

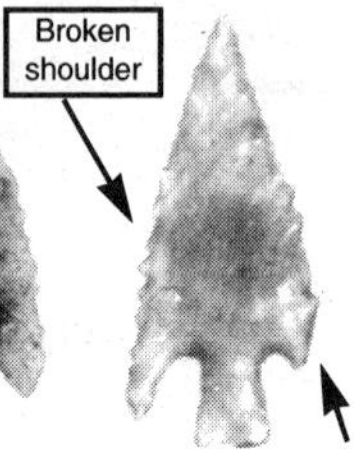

G4, $5-$10
CO.

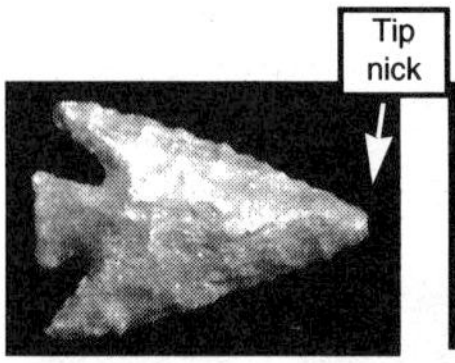

Tip nick

G7, $12-$25
CO.

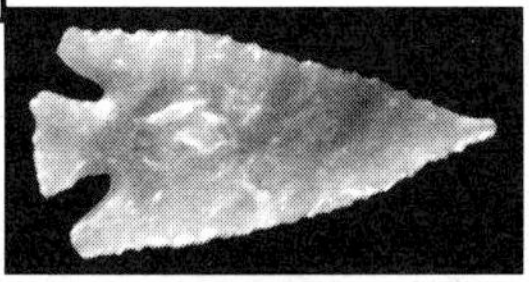

G10, $30-$60
Casper, WY.

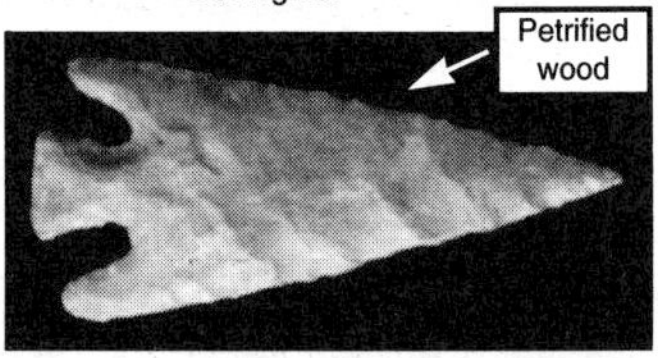

Petrified wood

G10, $50-$100
Weld Co., CO.

LOCATION: Northern Plains states. **DESCRIPTION:** A small size, thin, corner notched point with sharp, pointed tangs and an expanding base. Blade edges can be serrated. **I.D. KEY:** Thinness, sharp tangs, early flaking.

NANTON - Developmental to Historic Phase, 1400 - 300 B. P.

(Also see Avonlea, Cut Bank, Pekisko, Irvine and Swift Current)

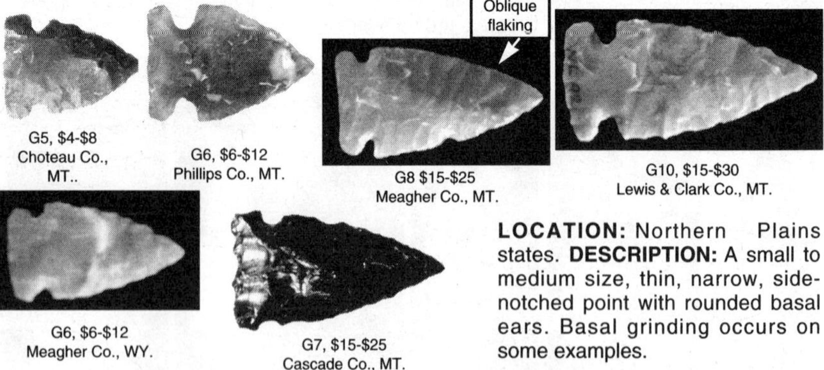

G5, $4-$8
Choteau Co., MT..

G6, $6-$12
Phillips Co., MT.

G8 $15-$25
Meagher Co., MT.

G10, $15-$30
Lewis & Clark Co., MT.

G6, $6-$12
Meagher Co., WY.

G7, $15-$25
Cascade Co., MT.

LOCATION: Northern Plains states. **DESCRIPTION:** A small to medium size, thin, narrow, side-notched point with rounded basal ears. Basal grinding occurs on some examples.

OXBOW - Middle Archaic, 5500 - 5000 B. P.

(Also see Dalton and McKean)

OXBOW (continued)

G5, $8-$15
Weld Co., CO.

G5, $10-$20
Cascade, WY.

G5, $10-$20
Weld Co., CO.

G6, $15-$30
Moorcorft, WY.

G8, $35-$65
Mountrail Co., ND. Gem.

G7, $40-$80
Jamestown, ND.

G6, $25-$45
Mountrail Co., ND.

G8, $30-$60
Divide Co., ND.

G8, $40-$75
Mountrail Co., ND.

G10, $45-$85
Mountrail Co., ND.

G10, $65-$115
Mountrail Co., ND.

G6, $15-$25
Broadwater Co., MT.

G7, $20-$35
Divide Co., ND.

G8, $65-$115
Mountrail Co., ND.

G10, $65-$125
Meagher Co., WY.

G8, $40-$75
Mountrail Co., ND.

G9, $65-$125
Bottineau Co., ND.

NP

OXBOW (continued)

G8, $35-$70
Broadus, MT.

G10, $115-$225
Bottineau Co., ND.

G10, $65-$125
Pollack, SD.

G10, $85-$165
Bottineau Co., ND.

LOCATION: Northern Plains states and Canada. **DESCRIPTION:** A small to medium size, side notched, auriculate point with a concave to bifurcated base that may be ground. Ears are squared to rounded and extend outward or downward from the base. Flaking is random to parallel oblique. **I.D. KEY:** Basal form.

PASKAPOO - Developmental to Classic Phase, 1000 - 400 B. P.

(Also see Cut Bank, Irvine, Nanton, Pekisko and Plains Side Notched)

G6, $8-$15
Choteau, MT.

G8, $10-$18
Lewis & Clark Co., MT.

G6, $8-$15
Lewis & Clark Co., MT.

G8, $15-$30
Lewis & Clark Co., MT.

G10, $20-$35
Meagher Co., MT.

G8, $15-$25
Ft. Peck Res., MT.

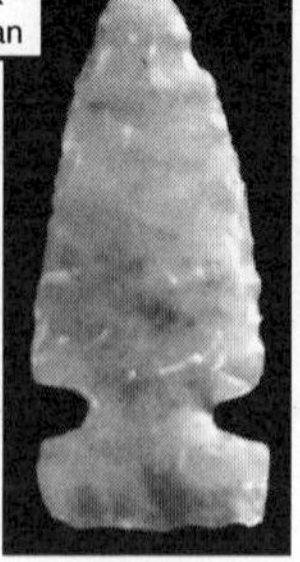

G10, $22-$50
Lewis & Clark Co., MT.

G10, $20-$40
Cascade, MT.

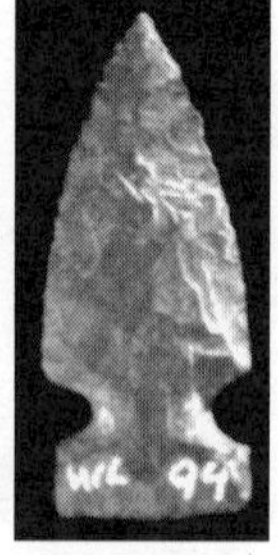

G10, $20-$40
Lewis & Clark Co., MT.

G8, $20-$35
Meagher Co., MT.

PASKAPOO (continued)

LOCATION: Northern Plains states. **DESCRIPTION:** A small to medium size, thin point with side-notches that occur higher up from the base than other Plains forms. The base is straight with rounded corners and are usually ground.

PEKISKO - Developmental to Historic Phase, 800 - 400 B. P.

(Also see Buffalo Gap, Cut Bank, Nanton and Paskapoo)

G3, $3-$6
Cascade Co., MT.

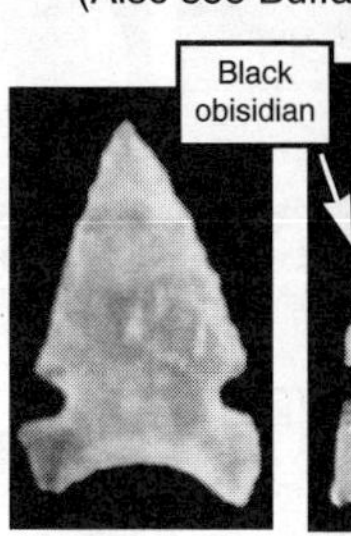

G6, $5-$10
Meagher Co., MT.

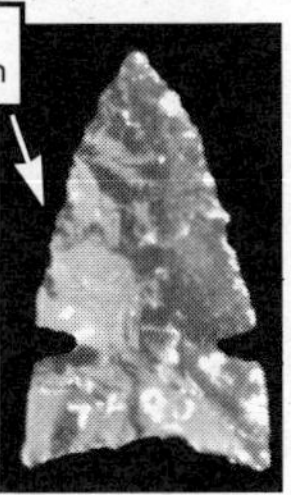

G6, $10-$20
Cascade Co., MT.

G6, $10-$20
Lewis & Clark Co., MT.

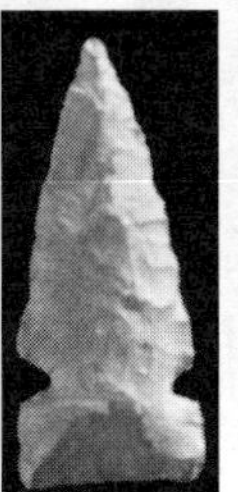

G6, $8-$15
Cascade Co., MT.

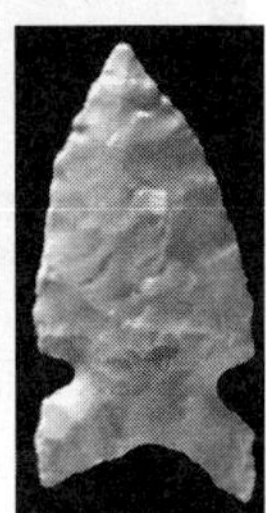

G6, $8-$15
Cascade Co., MT.

LOCATION: Northern Plains states. **DESCRIPTION:** A small to medium size, thin, triangular arrow point with v-notches on both sides above the base. Bases are concave to straight and are as wide as the shoulders. **I.D.KEY:** v-notches.

G6, $10-$20
Great Falls, MT.

G6, $10-$20
Cascade Co., MT.

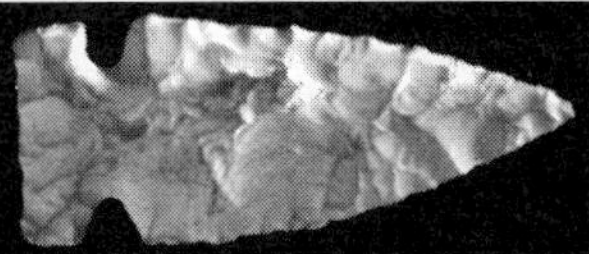

G10, $25-$45
Cascade Co., MT., Porcellanite.

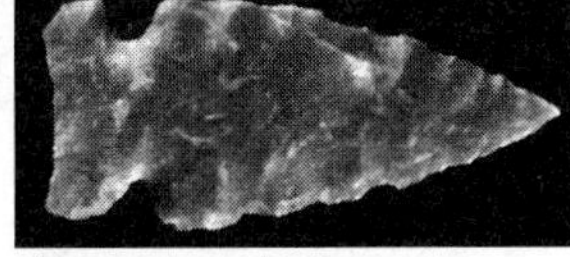

G8, $15-$25
Great Falls, MT.

PELICAN LAKE - Middle Archaic to Transitional Phase, 3500 - 2200 B. P.

(Also see Desert, Elko, Hog Back and Samantha)

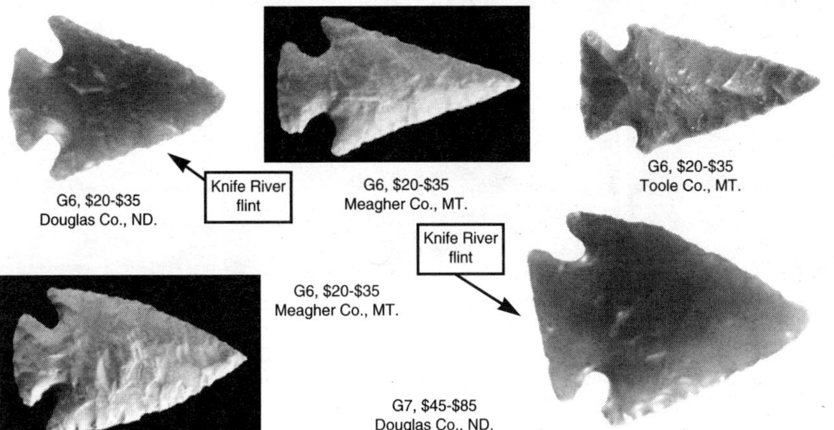

G6, $20-$35
Douglas Co., ND.

G6, $20-$35
Meagher Co., MT.

G6, $20-$35
Toole Co., MT.

G6, $20-$35
Meagher Co., MT.

G7, $45-$85
Douglas Co., ND.

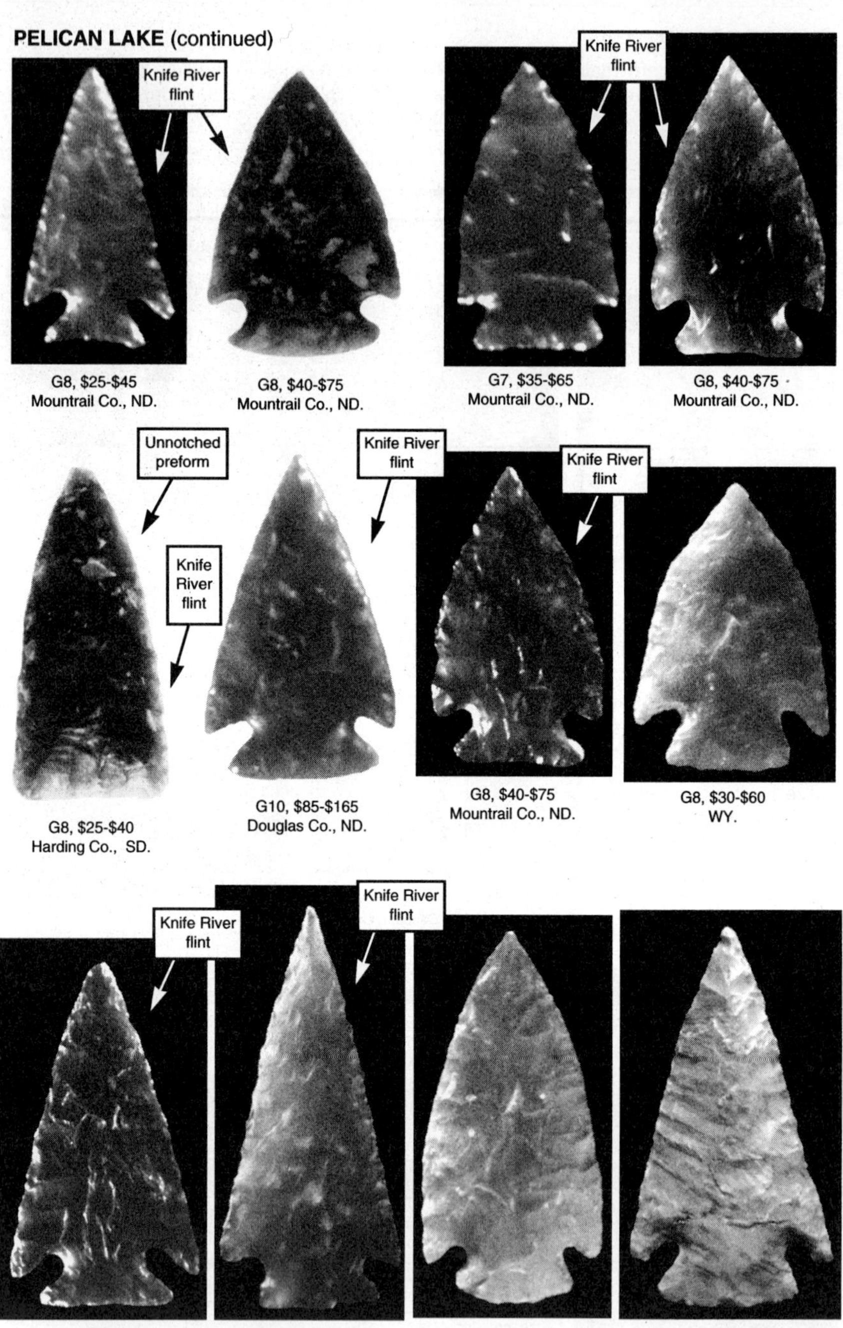

G8, $25-$45
Mountrail Co., ND.

G8, $40-$75
Mountrail Co., ND.

G7, $35-$65
Mountrail Co., ND.

G8, $40-$75
Mountrail Co., ND.

G8, $25-$40
Harding Co., SD.

G10, $85-$165
Douglas Co., ND.

G8, $40-$75
Mountrail Co., ND.

G8, $30-$60
WY.

G9, $65-$135
Mountrail Co., ND.

G7, $35-$65
Mountrail Co., ND.

G10, $40-$80
Casper, WY.

G10, $50-$100
E. CO.

LOCATION: Northern Plains states to Canada. **DESCRIPTION:** A small to medium size, thin, corner notched point with a straight to convex, expanding base. Tangs are usually pointed. Grinding may occur in notches and around base. Believed to have evolved into the *Samantha Dart* point. **I.D. KEY:** Sharp tangs.

PELICAN LAKE (continued)

Flat Top
chalcedony

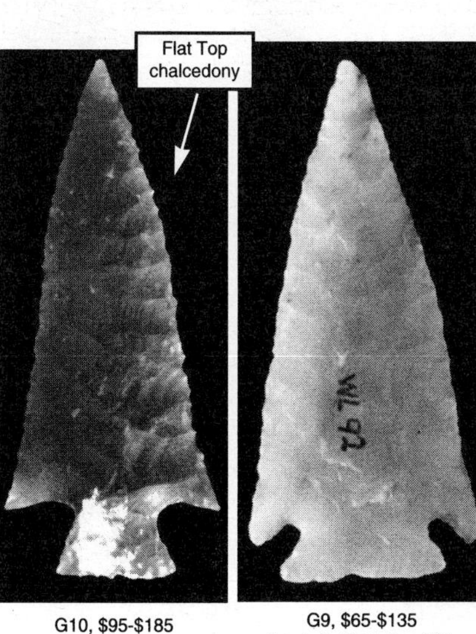

G10, $95-$185
Weld Co., CO.

G9, $65-$135
Lewis & Clark Co., MT.

Knife River
flint

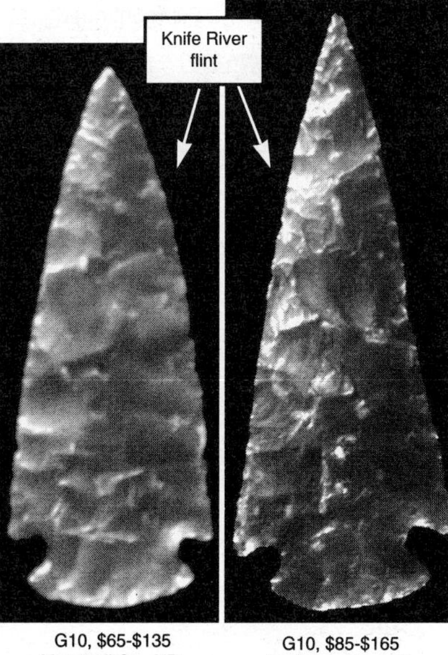

G10, $65-$135
Mountrail Co., ND.

G10, $85-$165
Bottineau Co., ND.

PELICAN LAKE-HARDER VARIETY - Late Archaic, 3500 - 3000 B. P.

(Also see Base Notched, Mount Albion and Samantha Dart)

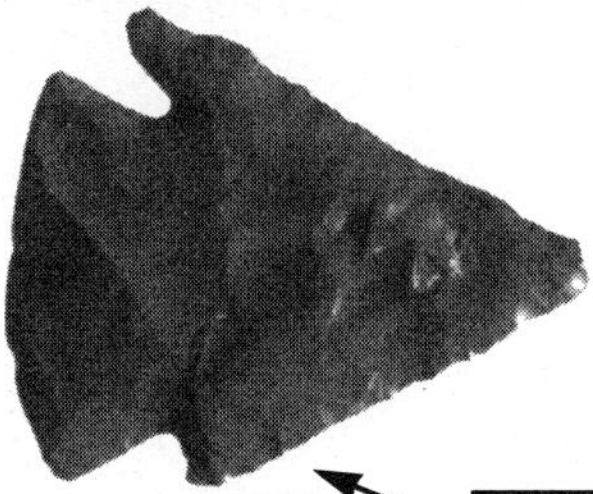

Shoulder
nick

G4, $15-$25
Weld Co., CO.

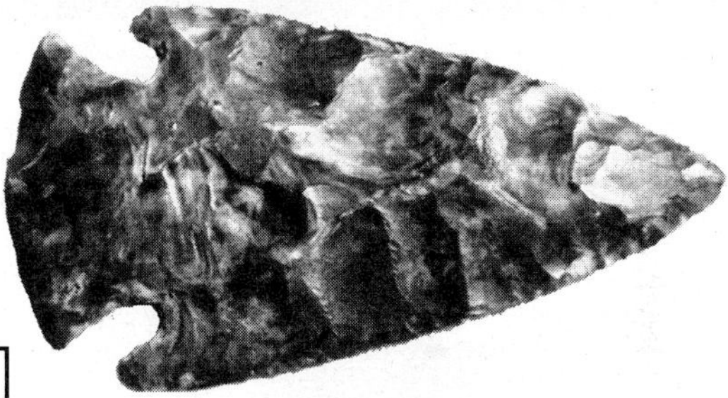

G9, $65-$135
Dolores Co., CO.

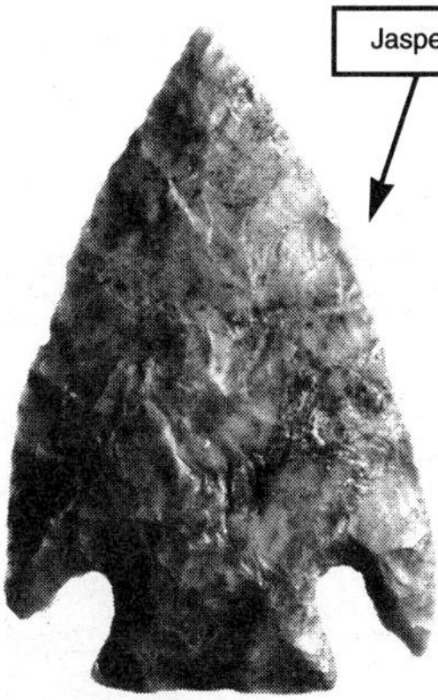

Jasper

G7, $35-$70
Alamosa, CO.

Chert
Tip
nick

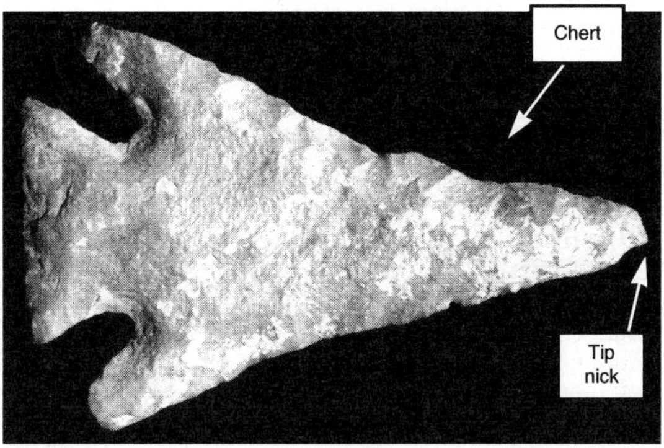

G6, $25-$50
E. CO.

PELICAN LAKE HARDER (continued)

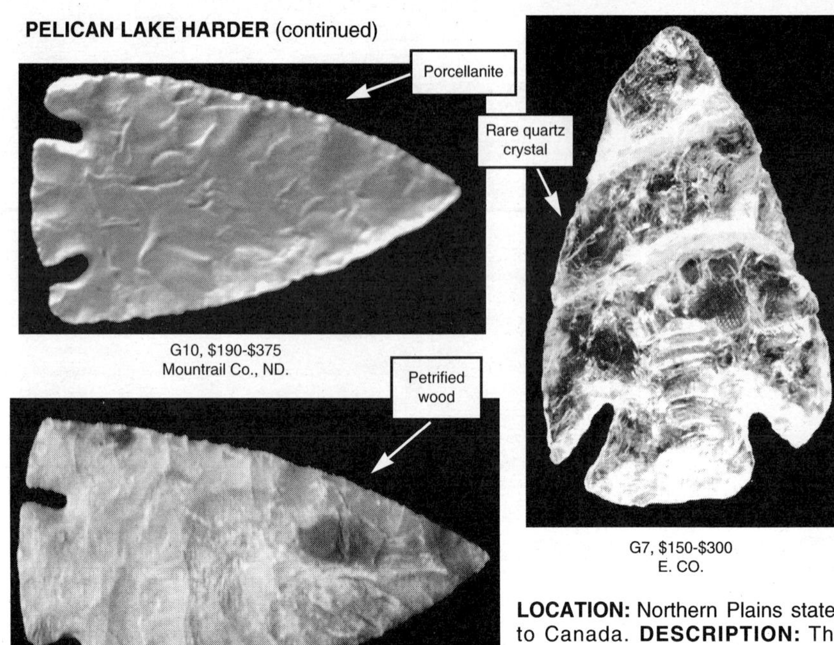

G10, $190-$375
Mountrail Co., ND.

G7, $150-$300
E. CO.

G10, $225-$450
Boar's Tusk, WY.

LOCATION: Northern Plains states to Canada. **DESCRIPTION:** The earliest form of the type. A medium size corner to base notched point with a convex base. Tangs are sharp to squared and the base that is usually ground is convex.

PINTO BASIN - Mid to Late Archaic, 4500 - 4000 B. P.

(Also see Lovell and McKean)

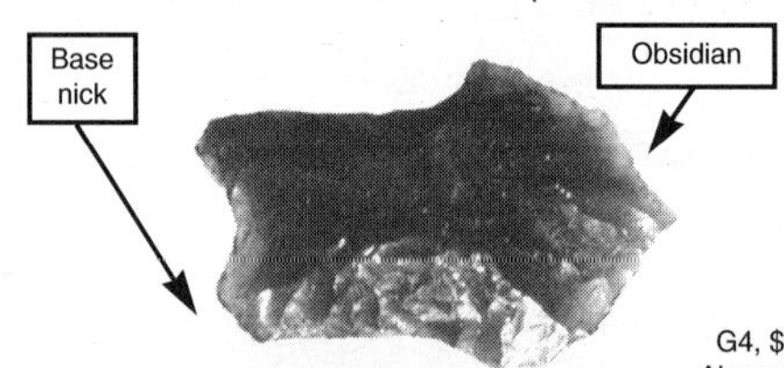

G4, $5-$10
Alamosa, CO.

LOCATION: Great Basin into the plains states. **DESCRIPTION:** A medium size, narrow, auriculate point. Shoulders can be tapered, horizontal or barbed. Bases are deeply bifurcated. Ears can be parallel to expanding. **I.D. KEY:** Long pointed ears.

PLAINS KNIFE - Early to Middle Archaic, 6000 - 4000 B. P.

(Also see Archaic Knife, Archaic Side, Bitterroot, Logan Creek, Lookingbill and Mallory)

LOCATION: Northern Plains states. **DESCRIPTION:** A medium to large size, triangular, side-notched point with a straight to concave base. Flaking is horizontal transverse. The widest part of the point is at the basal corners. Bases are ground. **I.D. KEY:** Size, wide base.

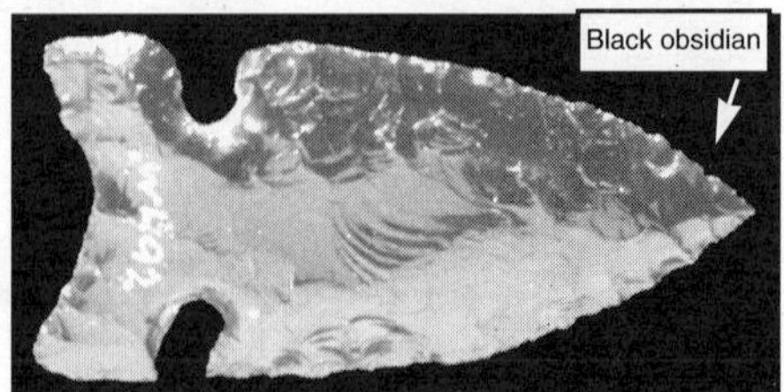

G8,$ 30-$60
Lewis & clark Co., MT.

G9,$ 65-$125
Lincoln Co., MT.

G4,$50-$100
Phillips Co., MT.

PLAINS SIDE NOTCHED - Developmental to Classic Phase, 1000 - 500 B. P.

(Also see Bitterroot, Buffalo Gap, Cut Bank, Desert, Nanton, Paskapoo and Pekisko)

G3, $4-$8
Teton Co., MT.

G3, $4-$10
Morton Co., ND.

G7, $10-$20
Morton Co., ND.

G7, $15-$20
Weld Co., CO.

G7, $15-$25
Weld Co., CO.

G7, $15-$25
Morton Co., ND.

G8, $20-$35
Casper, WY.

G9, $25-$50
Weld Co., CO.

G8, $30-$60
MT.

G7, $15-$25
Cascade Co., MT.

LOCATION: Northern Plains states. **DESCRIPTION:** A small to medium size, thin, triangular, side-notched arrow point with a concave base. Notches are narrow and occur high up from the base. Basal corners are usually sharp and blade edges are not serrated. Many have been dug in buffalo kill sites. **I.D. KEY:** Notches.

PLAINS SIDE NOTCHED (continued)

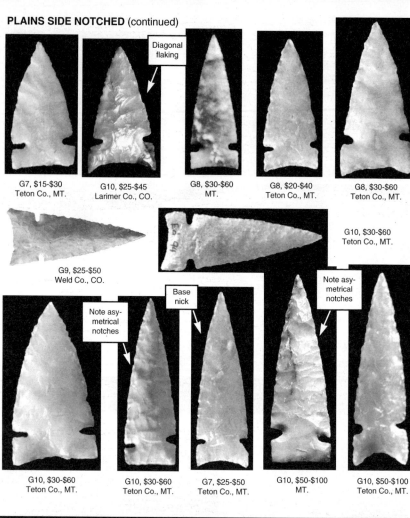

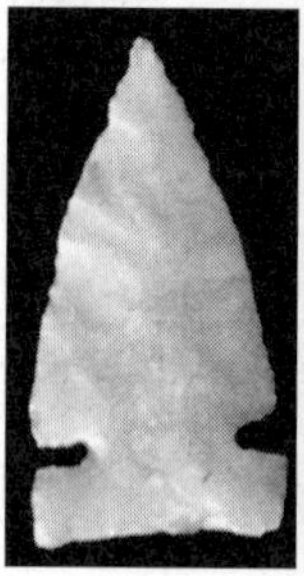

Diagonal flaking

G7, $15-$30
Teton Co., MT.

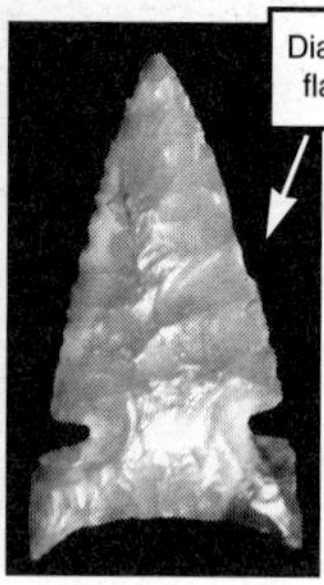

G10, $25-$45
Larimer Co., CO.

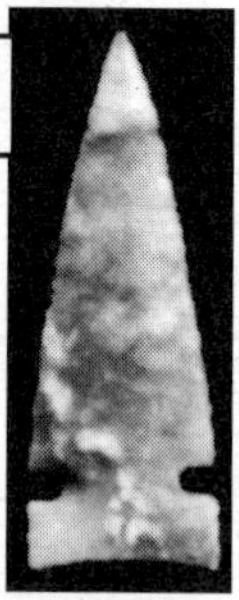

G8, $30-$60
MT.

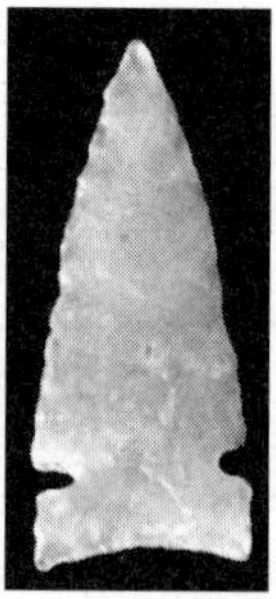

G8, $20-$40
Teton Co., MT.

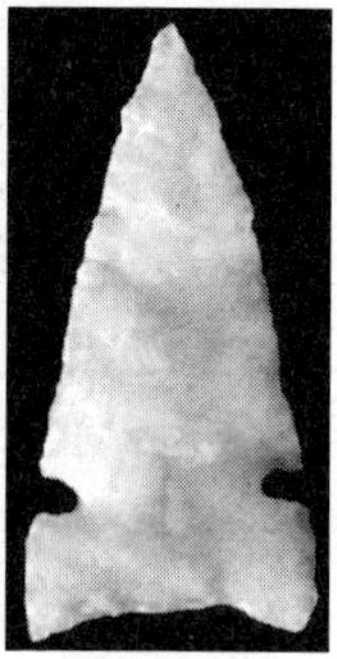

G8, $30-$60
Teton Co., MT.

G9, $25-$50
Weld Co., CO.

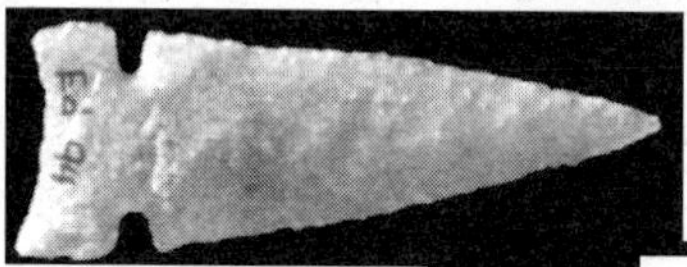

G10, $30-$60
Teton Co., MT.

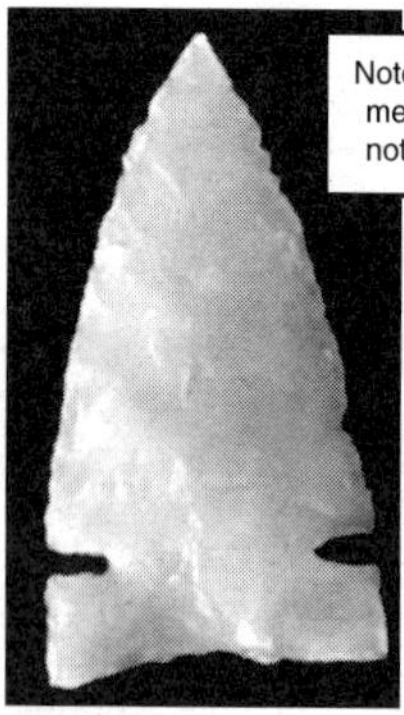

Note asymmetrical notches

Base nick

Note asymmetrical notches

G10, $30-$60
Teton Co., MT.

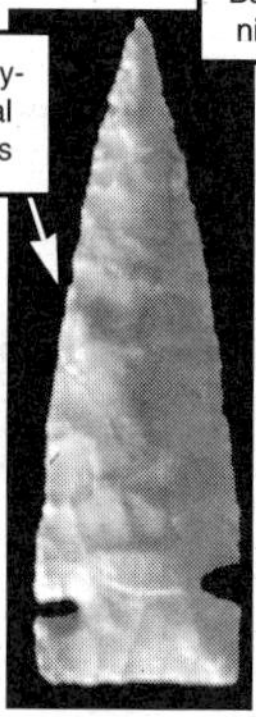

G10, $30-$60
Teton Co., MT.

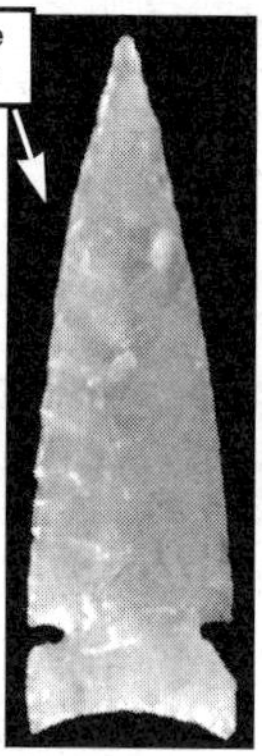

G7, $25-$50
Teton Co., MT.

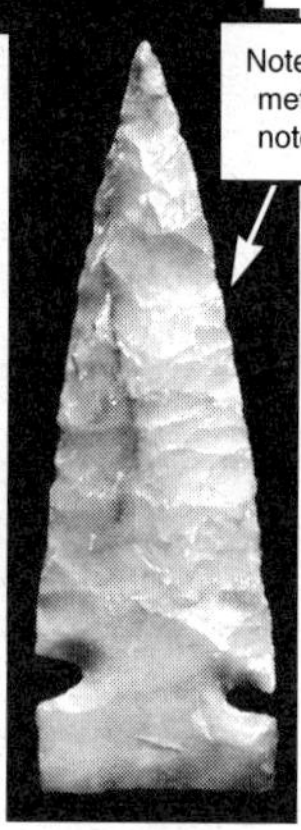

G10, $50-$100
MT.

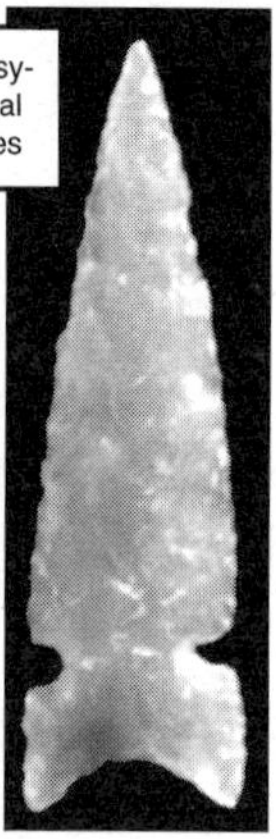

G10, $50-$100
Teton Co., MT.

PLAINS TRIANGULAR - Developmental to Classic Phase, 1000 - 500 B. P.

(Also see Cottonwood)

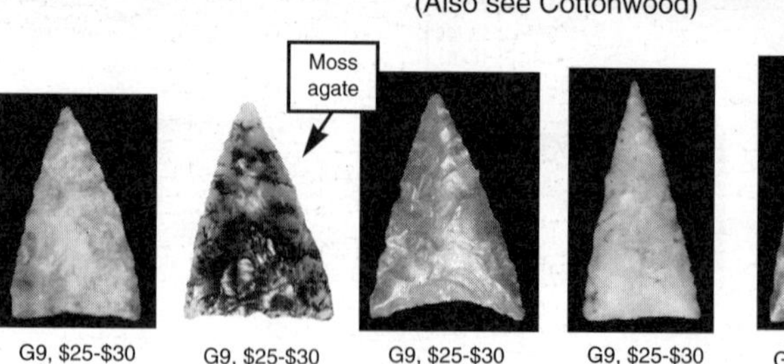

Knife River flint

G9, $25-$30
Bismarck, ND.

G9, $25-$30
Bismarck, ND.

G9, $25-$30
Bismarck, ND.

G9, $25-$30
Bismarck, ND.

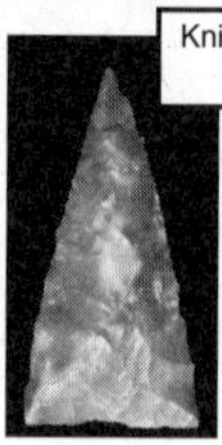

G9, $25-$30
Bismarck, ND.

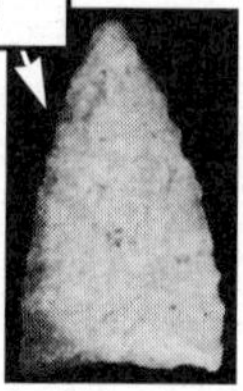

G9, $25-$30
Bismarck, ND.

LOCATION: Northern Plains states. **DESCRIPTION:** A small size, thin, triangular point with a straight to concave base and sharp basal ears. **I.D. KEY:** Small triangle

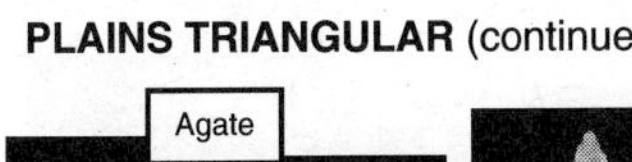

PLAINS TRIANGULAR (continued)

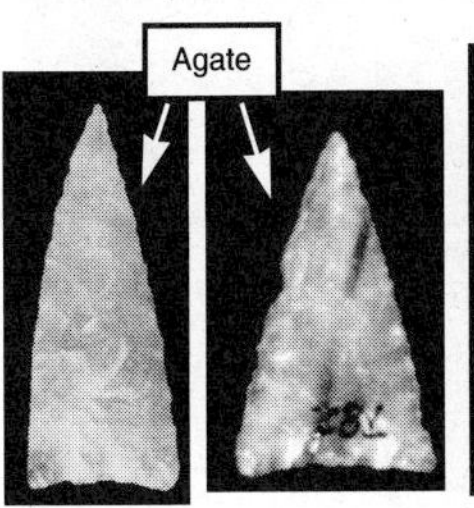

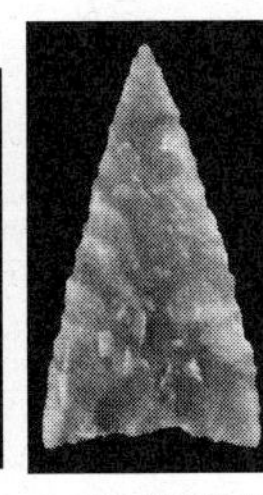

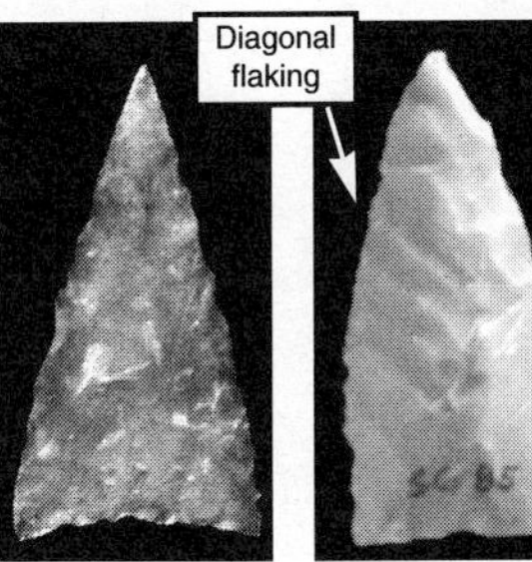

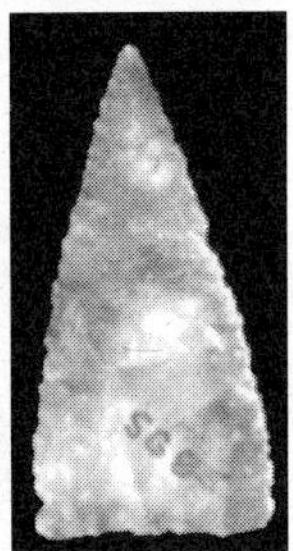

G7, $10-$20
E. CO.,

G8, $10-$20
Mobridge, SD.

G9, $15-$25
Bismarck, ND.

G9, $15-$30
Bismarck, ND.

G9, $15-$30
S.E. MT.

G8, $15-$25
S.E. MT., Pryor Mtns.

PLAINVIEW - Late Paleo to Early Archaic, 10,000 - 7000 B. P.

(Also see Clovis, Folsom, Goshen, Lovell and Midland)

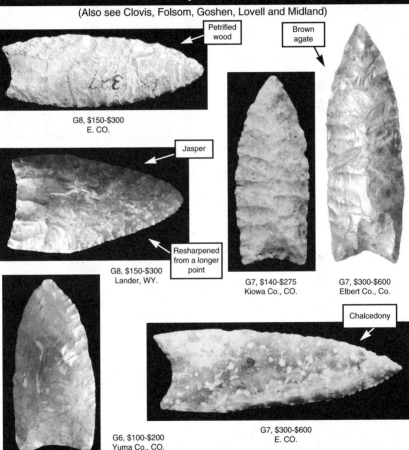

Petrified wood

G8, $150-$300
E. CO.

Brown agate

Jasper

Resharpened from a longer point

G8, $150-$300
Lander, WY.

G7, $140-$275
Kiowa Co., CO.

G7, $300-$600
Elbert Co., Co.

Chalcedony

G6, $100-$200
Yuma Co., CO.

G7, $300-$600
E. CO.

NP

LOCATION: Colorado eastward. **DESCRIPTION:** A medium to large size, thin, lanceolate point with usually parallel sides and a concave base that is ground. Some examples are thinned or fluted and is believed to be related to the earlier *Clovis* and contemporary *Dalton* type. Flaking is of high quality and can be collateral to oblique transverse. A cross type between *Clovis* and *Dalton*. **I.D. KEY:** Basal form and parallel flaking.

PLAINVIEW (continued)

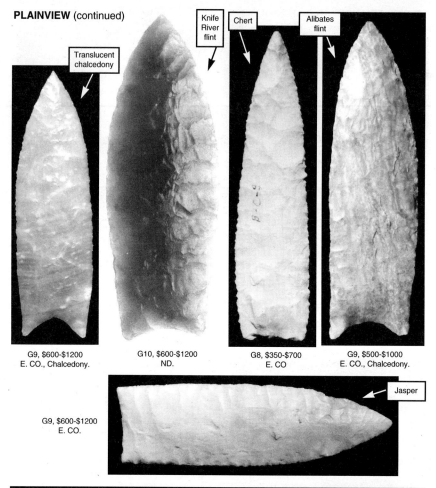

Translucent chalcedony

Knife River flint

Chert

Alibates flint

G9, \$600-\$1200
E. CO., Chalcedony.

G10, \$600-\$1200
ND.

G8, \$350-\$700
E. CO

G9, \$500-\$1000
E. CO., Chalcedony.

Jasper

G9, \$600-\$1200
E. CO.

PRAIRIE SIDE NOTCHED - Developmental Phase, 1300 - 800 B. P.

(Also see Irvine, Nanton, Paskapoo, Pekisko and Plains Side Notched)

G5, \$10-\$12
Phillips Co., MT.

G5, \$12-\$20
Phillips Co., MT.

G5, \$12-\$20
Phillips Co., MT.

G5, \$10-\$20
Morton Co., ND.

G5, \$12-\$20, Phillips Co., MT.

G5, \$12-\$20
Phillips Co., MT.

G5, \$12-\$20
Bismark, ND.

LOCATION: Northern Plains states. **DESCRIPTION:** A medium size triangular point with broad side notches. Bases are straight to slightly convex.

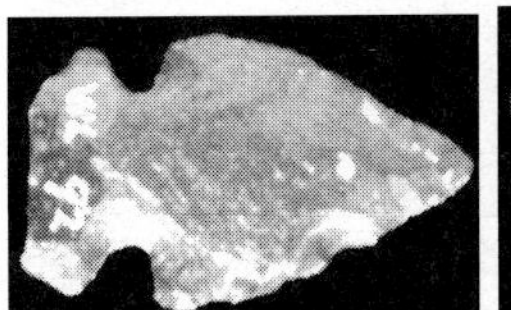

PRAIRIE SIDE NOTCHED (continued)

G6, $10-$20
Lewis & Clark Co., MT.

G6, $10-$20
Lewis & Clark Co., MT.

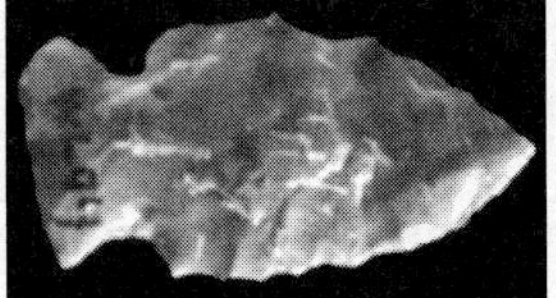

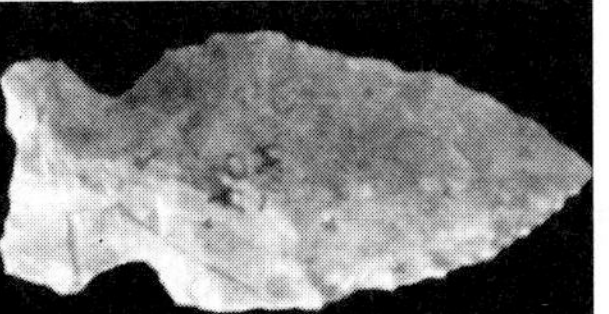

G7, $15-$25
Lewis & Clark Co., MT.

RIO GRANDE - Early Archaic, 7500 - 6000 B. P.

(Also see Hell Gap)

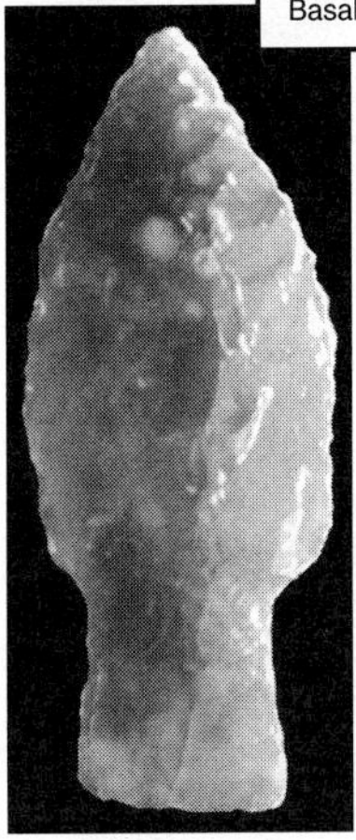

G7, $125-$250
Yuma Co., CO.

Basalt

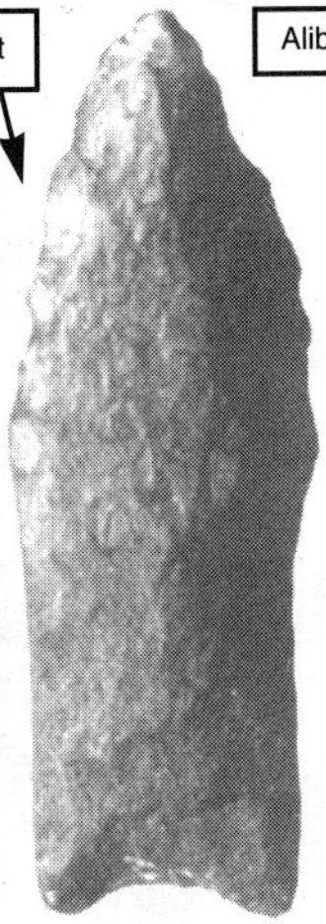

G7, $125-$250
Alamosa, CO.

Alibates

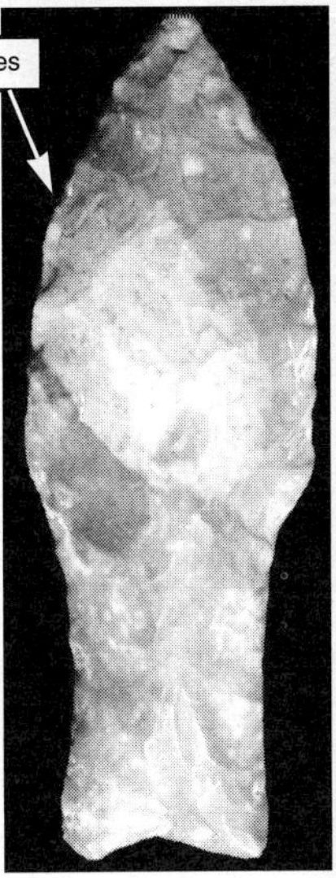

G8, $200-$400
E. CO.

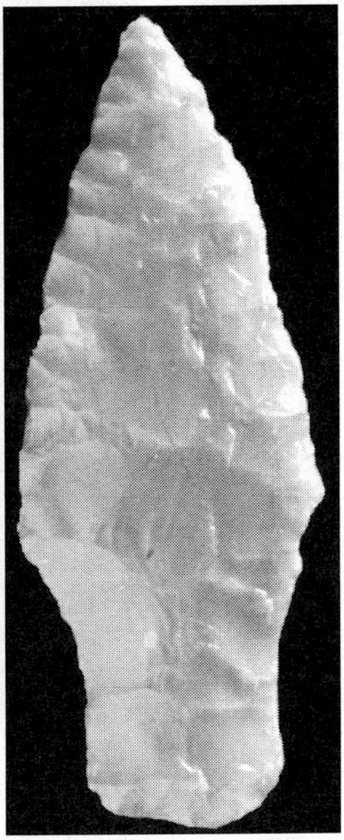

G7, $150-$300
Cascade Co., MT.

Basalt

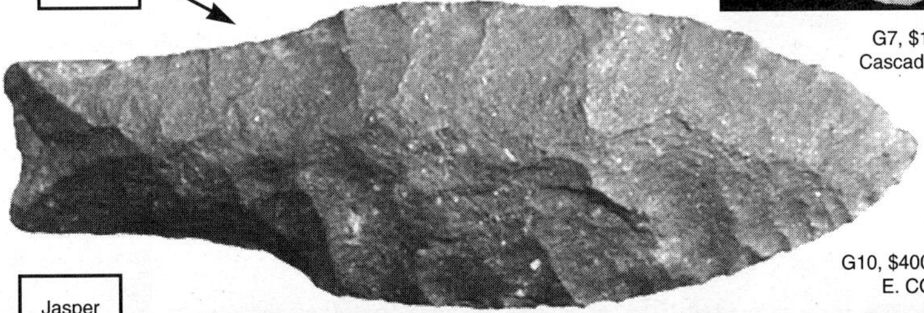

G10, $400-$800
E. CO.

Jasper

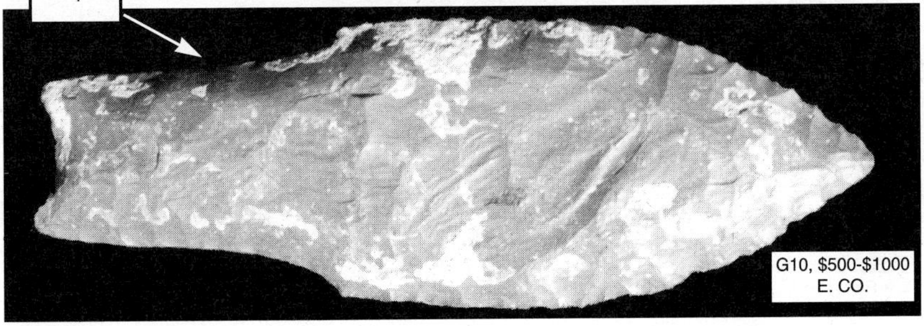

G10, $500-$1000
E. CO.

NP

RIO GRANDE (continued)

LOCATION: Sou. Colorado into western Texas. **DESCRIPTION:** A lanceolate point with a relatively long stem formed by tapered shoulders. The stem contracts slightly and edges are ground. **I.D. KEY:** Shoulders more pronounced than on *Hell Gap* points.

ROSE SPRINGS - Developmental to Historic Phase, 1600 - 700 B. P.

(Also see Mummy Cave)

G7, $8-$12
Alamosa, CO.

G7, $6-$12
Alamosa, CO.

G7, $8-$15
Alamosa, CO.

G6, $8-$15
Alamosa, CO.

G6, $8-$15
Alamosa, CO.

G6, $10-$20
Alamosa, CO.

LOCATION: Great Basin Northward. **DESCRIPTION:** A small to medium size arrowpoint that occurs as corner, side or expanded to contracted stemmed.

SAMANTHA-ARROW - Developmental Phase, 1500 - 1200 B. P.

(Also see Avonlea, High River, Lewis and Tompkins)

G5, $6-$12
Tiber Res., MT.

G5, $8-$15
CO.

G6, $15-$25
Tiber Res., MT.

G6, $15-$25
Tiber Res., MT.

G7, $25-$45
Tiber Res., MT.

G7, $25-$45
Meagher Co., MT.

G9, $40-$75
Tiber Res., MT.

G7, $25-$45
Tiber Res., MT.

G6, $20-$35
Tiber Res., MT.

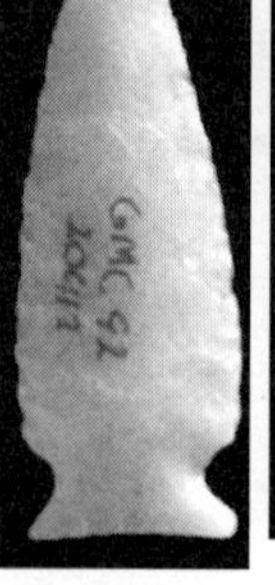

G10, $50-$100
Meagher Co., MT.

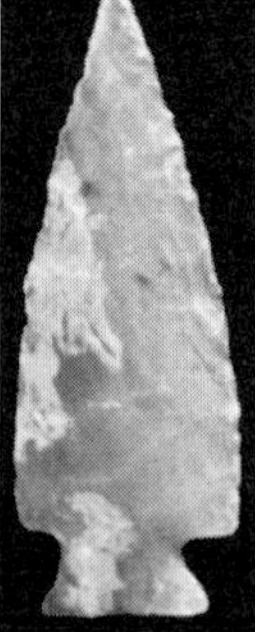

G10, $50-$100
Lewis & Clark Co., MT.

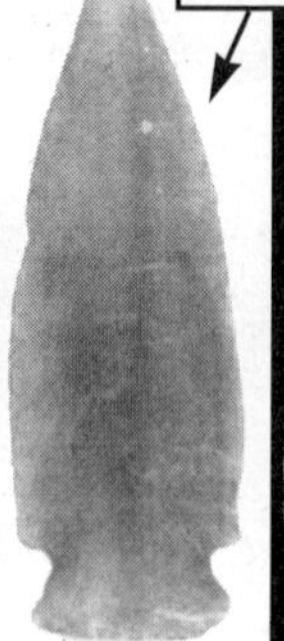

G10, $65-$135
Mountrail Co., ND.

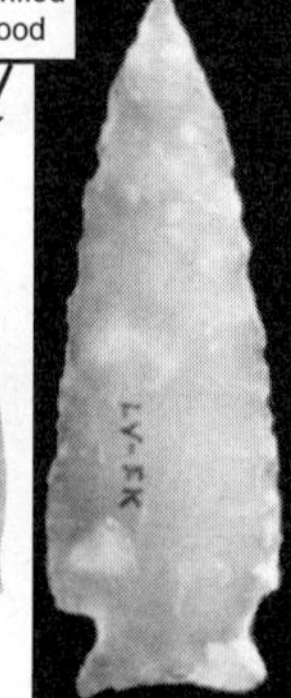

G10, $50-$100
Tiber Res., MT.

SAMANTHA ARROW (continued)

LOCATION: Canada to the Northern Plains states. **DESCRIPTION:** A small to medium size, narrow, thin, corner to side-notched arrow point. Flaking is random to oblique transverse. Related and developed from the earlier *Samantha Dart* point. Shoulders are tapered and the stem expands to a straight to slightly concave base.

SAMANTHA-DART - Transitional to Developmental Phase, 2200 - 1500 B. P.

(Also see Besant and Pelican Lake)

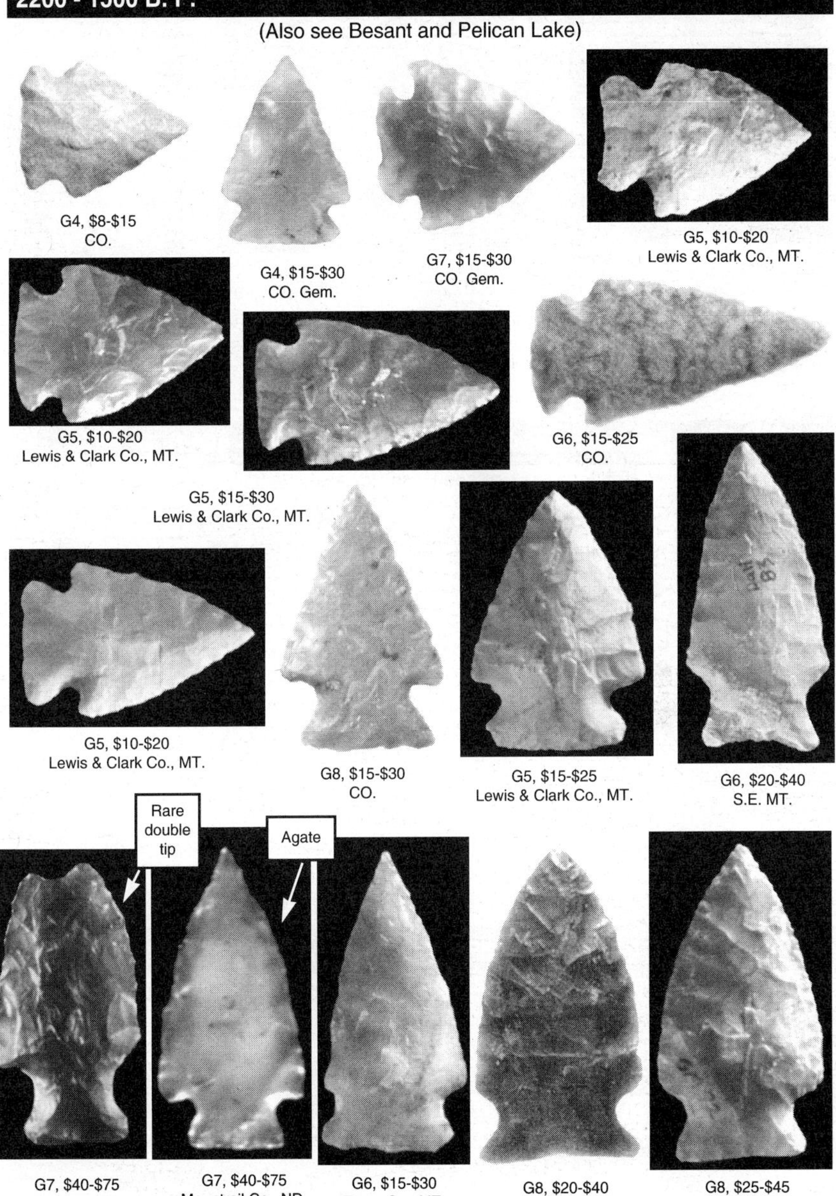

G4, $8-$15
CO.

G4, $15-$30
CO. Gem.

G7, $15-$30
CO. Gem.

G5, $10-$20
Lewis & Clark Co., MT.

G5, $10-$20
Lewis & Clark Co., MT.

G5, $15-$30
Lewis & Clark Co., MT.

G6, $15-$25
CO.

G5, $10-$20
Lewis & Clark Co., MT.

G8, $15-$30
CO.

G5, $15-$25
Lewis & Clark Co., MT.

G6, $20-$40
S.E. MT.

G7, $40-$75
Jamestown, ND.

G7, $40-$75
Mountrail Co., ND.

G6, $15-$30
Teton Co., MT.

G8, $20-$40
Pollack, SD.

G8, $25-$45
Meagher Co., MT.

NP

SAMANTHA-DART (continued)

G8, $45-$85
Renville Co., ND.

G7, $25-$50
Phillips Co., MT.

G7, $30-$60
Lewis & Clark Co., MT.

G10, $150-$300
Adams Co., CO.

LOCATION: Canada to the Northern Plains states. **DESCRIPTION:** A medium to large size, corner to side-notched point with with horizontal, tapered or slightly barbed shoulders. Believed to have evolved from the *Pelican Lake* type.

SATTLER - Developmental to Historic Phase, 1400 - 400 B. P.

(Also see Rose Springs)

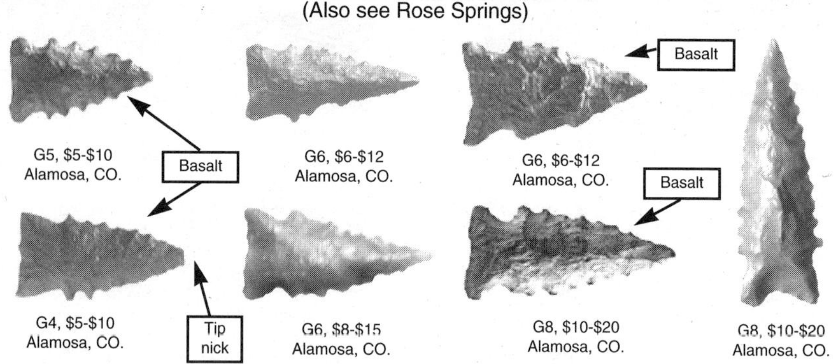

G5, $5-$10
Alamosa, CO.

G6, $6-$12
Alamosa, CO.

G6, $6-$12
Alamosa, CO.

G4, $5-$10
Alamosa, CO.

G6, $8-$15
Alamosa, CO.

G8, $10-$20
Alamosa, CO.

G8, $10-$20
Alamosa, CO.

LOCATION: Sou. Colorado. **DESCRIPTION:** A small size, thin, serrated arrowpoint with an expanded base. Base is straight to concave. Tips are sharp.

SCOTTSBLUFF I - Transitional Paleo to Early Archaic, 9500 - 7000 B. P.

(Also see Alberta, Cody Knife, Eden, Firstview and Hell Gap)

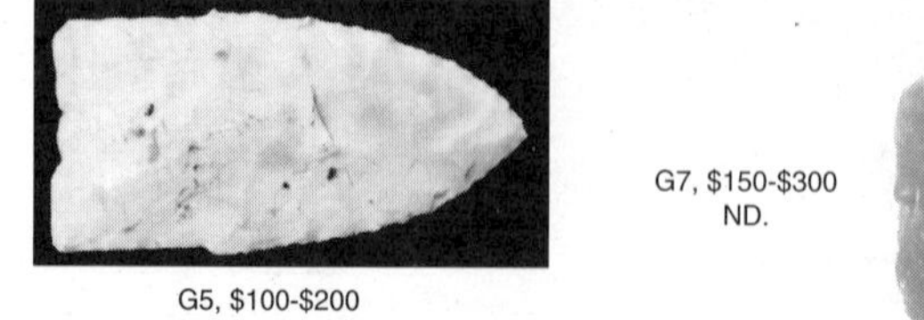

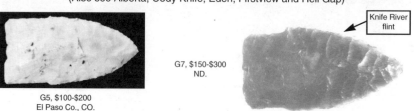

G5, $100-$200
El Paso Co., CO.

G7, $150-$300
ND.

Knife River flint

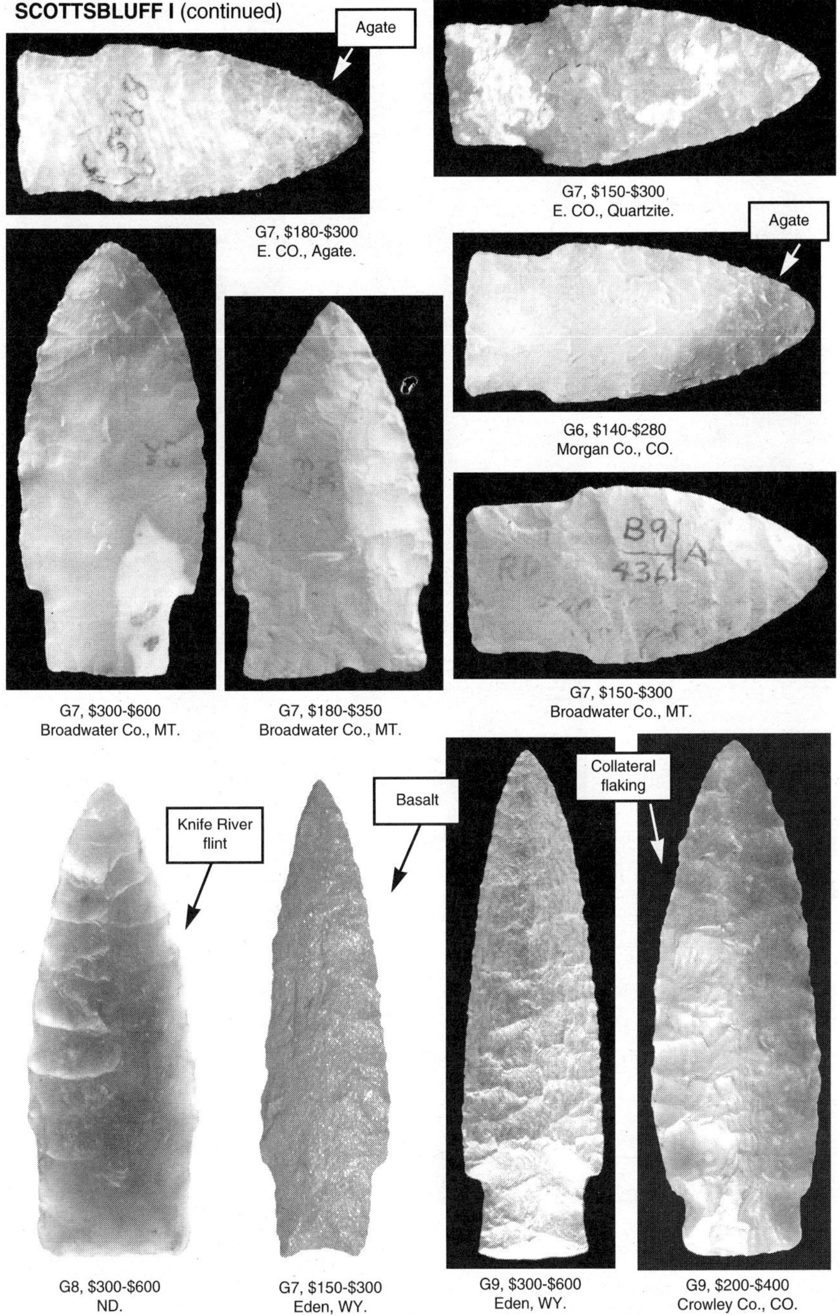

G7, $180-$300
E. CO., Agate.

G7, $150-$300
E. CO., Quartzite.

G6, $140-$280
Morgan Co., CO.

G7, $300-$600
Broadwater Co., MT.

G7, $180-$350
Broadwater Co., MT.

G7, $150-$300
Broadwater Co., MT.

G8, $300-$600
ND.

G7, $150-$300
Eden, WY.

G9, $300-$600
Eden, WY.

G9, $200-$400
Crowley Co., CO.

LOCATION: Midwestern states to Texas and Colorado. **DESCRIPTION:** A medium to large size, broad, stemmed point with parallel to convex sides and weak shoulders. The stem is parallel sided or expands slightly. The base is straight to concave. Made by the Cody complex people. Flaking is of the high quality parallel horizontal to oblique transverse type. Bases are ground. **I.D. KEY:** Broad stem, weak shoulders.

SCOTTSBLUFF I (continued)

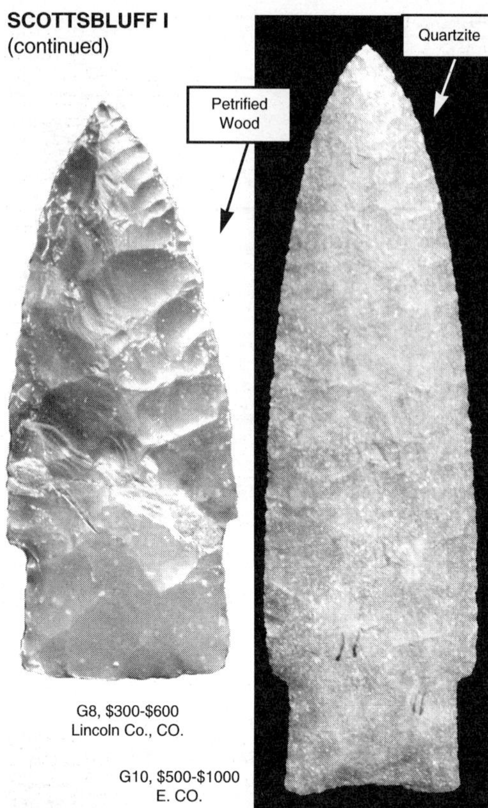

G8, $300-$600
Lincoln Co., CO.

G10, $500-$1000
E. CO.

SCOTTSBLUFF II (continued)

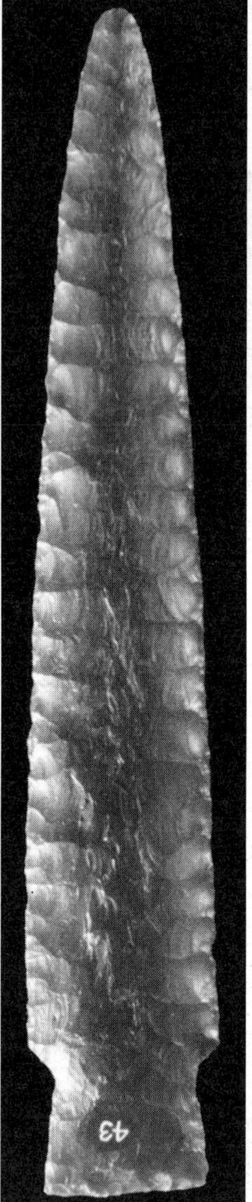

G10, $1500-$3000
Beaverhead Co., MT.

SCOTTSBLUFF II - Late Paleo to Early Archaic, 9500 - 7000 B. P.

(Also see Alberta, Cody Knife, Eden and Hell Gap)

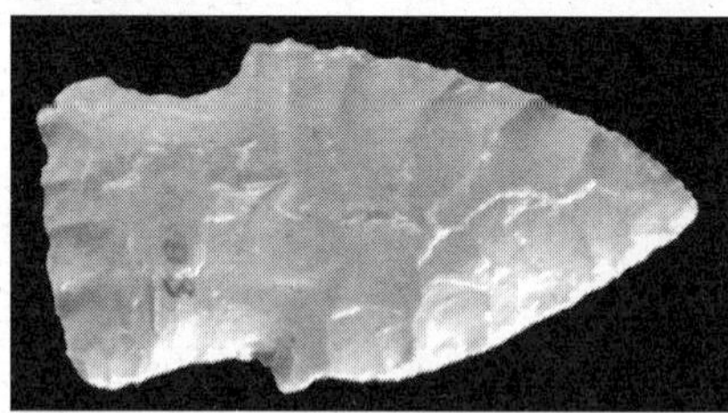

G5, $100-$200
Phillips Co., MT.

LOCATION: Midwestern states to Texas and Colorado. **DESCRIPTION:** A medium to large size triangular point with shoulders a little stronger than on Type I and a broad parallel sided/expanding stem that is ground. **I.D. KEY:** Broad stem, stronger shoulders.

SCRAPER - Paleo to Middle Archaic, 14,000 - 5000 B. P.

(Also see Drill, Hafted Knife, Paleo Knife and Scraper)

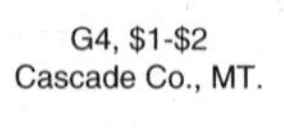

G4, $1-$2
Cascade Co., MT.

SCRAPER (continued)

LOCATION: All early-man sites. **DESCRIPTION:** Thumb, duckbill and turtleback forms are small to medium size, thick, ovoid shaped, uniface, scraping tools that are steeply beveled, especially at the broadest end. Side scrapers are long hand-held uniface flakes with beveling on all blade edges of one face. Scraping was done primarily from the sides of these blades. Many of these tools were hafted.

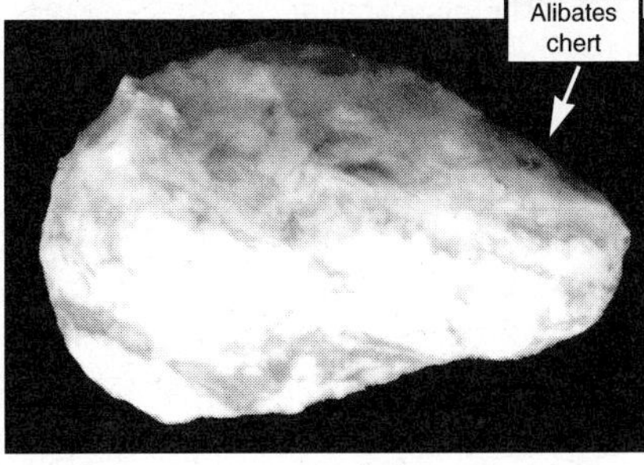

G8, $3-$5
Cheyenne Co., WY.

SIDE NOTCH (See Archaic Side Notch)

SIDE KNIFE - Transitional to Historic Phase, 2300 - 500 B. P.

(Also see hafted arrowheads illustrated under various types)

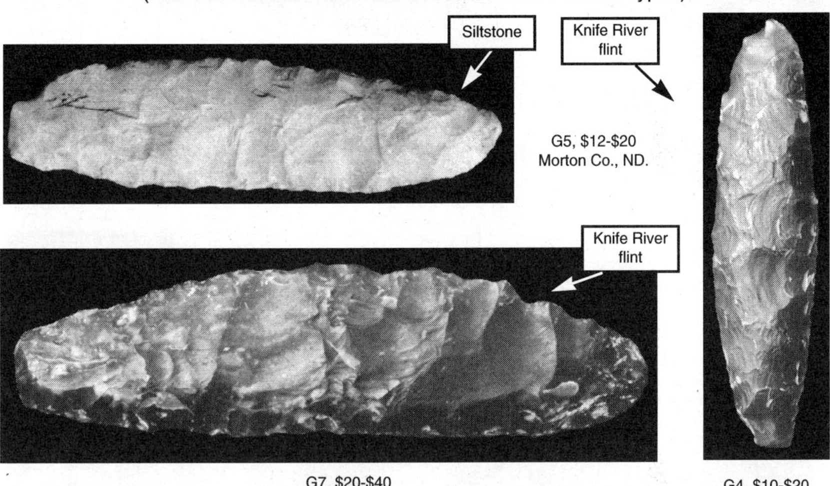

G5, $12-$20
Morton Co., ND.

G7, $20-$40
Morton Co., ND.

G4, $10-$20
Morton Co., ND.

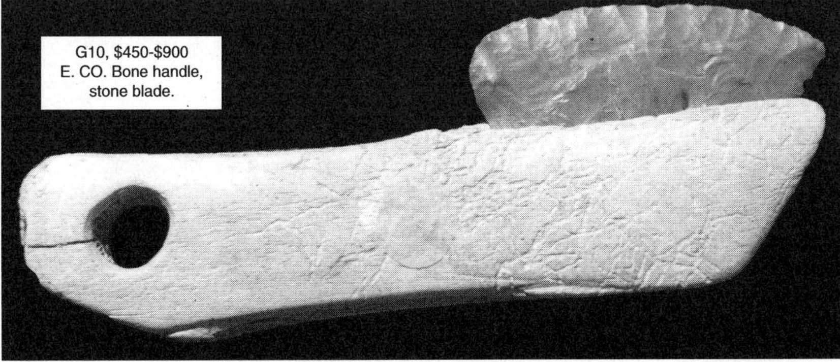

G10, $450-$900
E. CO. Bone handle, stone blade.

NP

LOCATION: Northern Plains states. **DESCRIPTION:** Very rare examples of hafted knives, both in a bone handle and found perfectly preserved. Asphaltum or pitch was used as an adhesive to glue the stone tool in the handle. Gut and plant fibers were also used when needed to bind the hafting.

G10, $400-$800
ND. 500-800 years old.

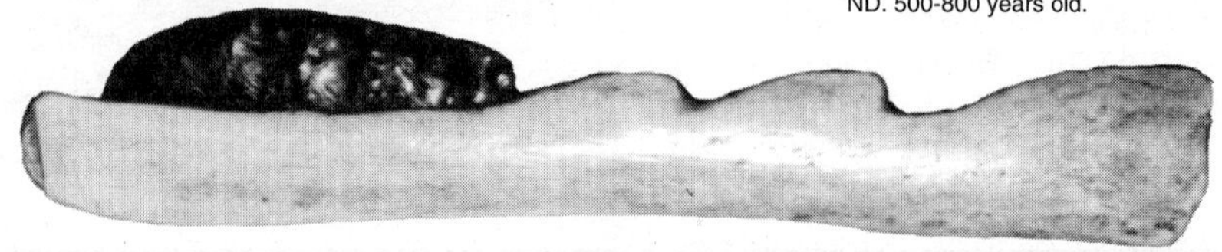

SIMONSEN - Early Archaic, 8500 - 7000 B. P.

(Also see Besant and Bitterroot)

LOCATION: Canada to the Northern Plains states. **DESCRIPTION:** A small to medium size, side-notched point with a concave base. Notching can be shallow to deep. Basal ears can be rounded to squared.

G6, $20-$40
Cascade Co., MT.

SONOTA - Developmental to Classic Phase, 1000 - 400 B. P.

(Also see Besant and Bitterroot)

G8, $65-$125
Mountrail Co., ND.

G8, $40-$75
Mountrail Co., ND.

G10, $115-$225
Bottineau Co., ND.

G9, $165-$325
McKenzie Co., ND.

G9, $180-$350
McLean Co., ND.

LOCATION: Canada to the Northern Plains states. **DESCRIPTION:** A small to medium size, thin, side to corner-notched point with a concave base. Base usually is not as wide as the shoulders.

SQUARE KNIFE - Paleo to Early Archaic, 10,000 - 8000 B. P.

(Also see Drill, Hafted Knife and Scraper)

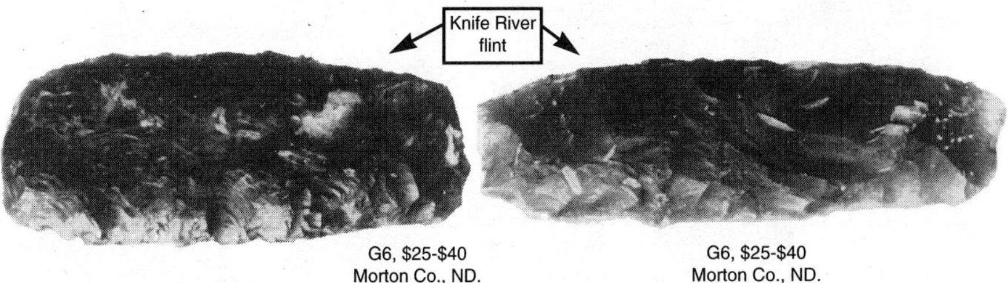

G6, \$25-\$40
Morton Co., ND.

G6, \$25-\$40
Morton Co., ND.

LOCATION: Canada to the Northern Plains states. **DESCRIPTION:** A small to medium size, side-notched point with a concave base.

STOTT - Developmental to Classic Phase, 1300 - 600 B. P.

(Also see Besant, Bitterroot, Nanton, Paskapoo, Pekisko and Tompkins)

G5, \$4-\$8
Lewis & Clark Co., MT.

G6, \$5-\$10
Phillips Co., MT.

G6, \$4-\$8
Lewis & Clark Co., MT.

G5, \$4-\$8
Meagher Co., MT.

G9, \$20-\$40
Sweetwater Co., WY.

LOCATION: Canada to the Northern Plains states. **DESCRIPTION:** A small size, v-notched point with a convex base. Size of base is large in proportion the the blade size. **I.D. KEY:** V-notches, large base.

SWIFT CURRENT - Developmental Phase, 1300 - 800 B. P.

(Also see Avonlea, Cut Bank, Irvine and Pekisko)

G5, \$8-\$15
Augusta, MT.

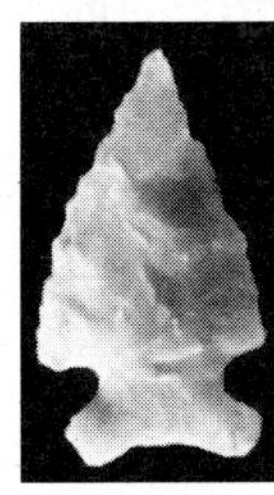

G6, \$10-\$20
Lewis & Clark Co., MT.

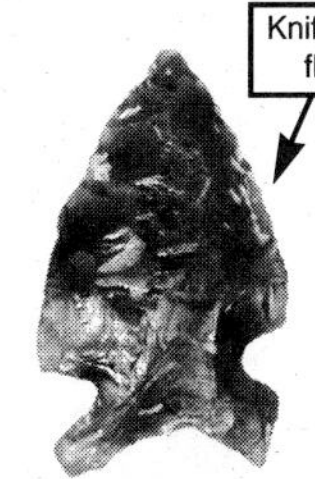

G6, \$10-\$20
Phillips Co., MT.

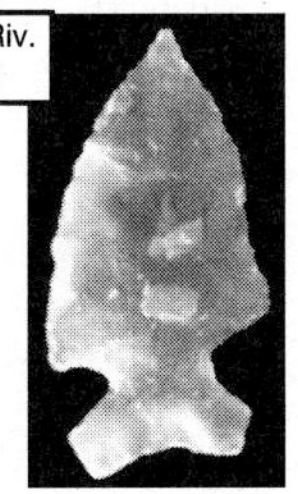

G6, \$8-\$15
Lewis & Clark Co., MT.

G6, \$10-\$20
Nelson Res., MT.

LOCATION: Northern Plains states. **DESCRIPTION:** A small size, thin, serrated, side notched arrow point with a concave base. Ancient buffalo jump kill sites have been discovered in the Plains states where this type is found. Early man drove the buffalo over cliffs and into corrals for easy killing. **I.D. KEY:** Drooping ears.

SWIFT CURRENT (continued)

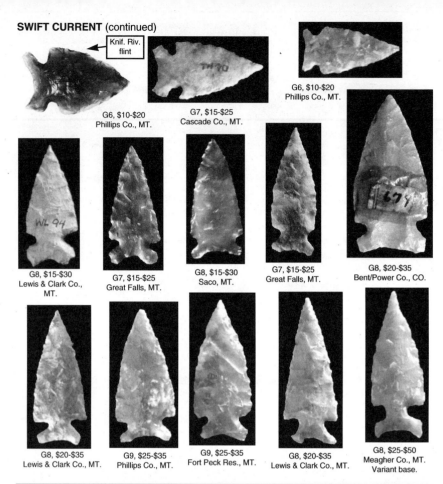

Knif. Riv. flint

G6, $10-$20
Phillips Co., MT.

G7, $15-$25
Cascade Co., MT.

G6, $10-$20
Phillips Co., MT.

G8, $15-$30
Lewis & Clark Co., MT.

G7, $15-$25
Great Falls, MT.

G8, $15-$30
Saco, MT.

G7, $15-$25
Great Falls, MT.

G8, $20-$35
Bent/Power Co., CO.

G8, $20-$35
Lewis & Clark Co., MT.

G9, $25-$35
Phillips Co., MT.

G9, $25-$35
Fort Peck Res., MT.

G8, $20-$35
Lewis & Clark Co., MT.

G8, $25-$50
Meagher Co., MT.
Variant base.

TOMPKINS - Developmental Phase, 1200 - 800 B. P.

(Also see Cut Bank, High River, Irvine, Nanton, Pekisko, Paskapoo, Prairie Side Notched and Swift Current)

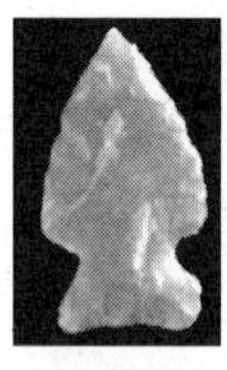

G6, $4-$8
Phillips Co., MT.

G6, $4-$8
Choteau Co., MT.

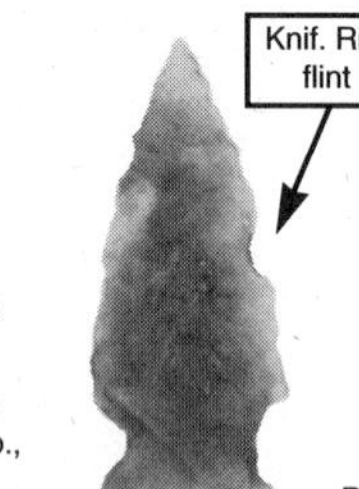

Knif. Riv. flint

G6, $5-$10
Phillips Co., MT.

LOCATION: Northern Plains states. **DESCRIPTION:** A small size, thin, serrated, side to corner notched arrow point with a concave base. On some examples, one notch is from the corner and the other definitely from the side. Some have basal grinding. Found on ancient Buffalo jump kill sites.

TRADE POINTS - Classic to Historic Phase, 400 - 170 B. P.

These points were made of copper, iron, and steel and were traded to the Indians by the French, British and others from the 1600s to the 1800s. Examples have been found all over the United States.

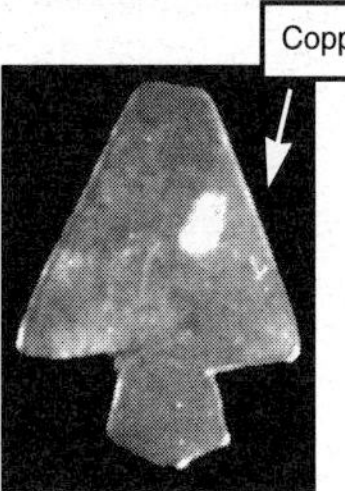

G2, $20-$35
Mountrail Co., ND.

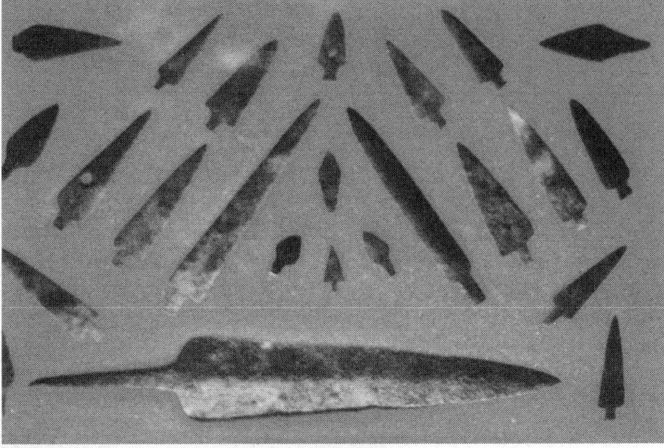

Weld Co., CO. A collection of trade points. The long lance is 12" in length.

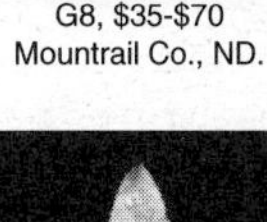

G8, $35-$70
Mountrail Co., ND.

G6, $20-$40
Lewis & Clark Co., MT.

G9, $65-$125
Meagher Co., MT.

G9, $75-$150
Meagher Co., MT.

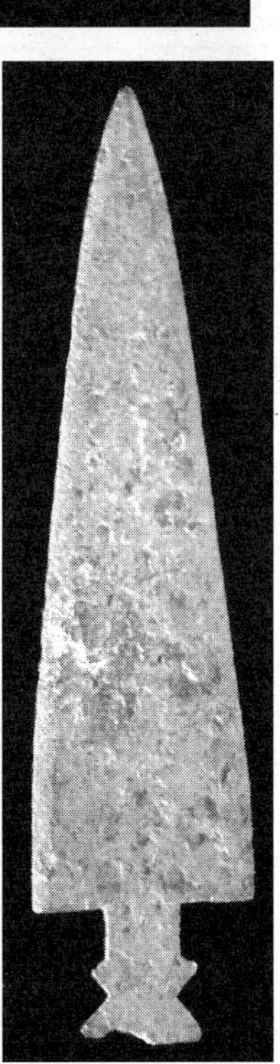

G10, $100-$200
Cascade Co., MT.

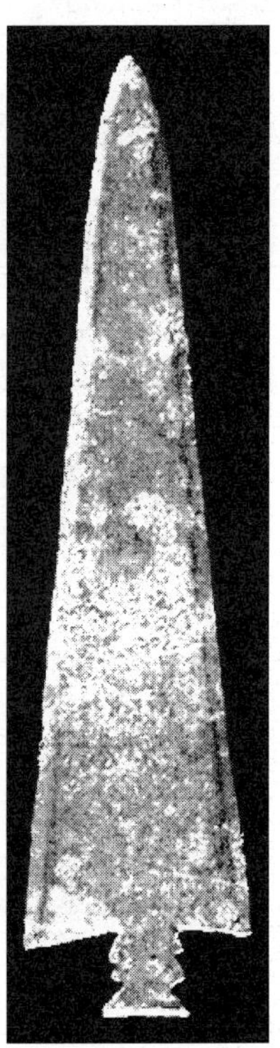

G10, $125-$250
Cheyenne, MT. Little Big Horn site. ca. 1850/Iron.

WASHITA - Classic Phase, 800 - 400 B. P.

(Also see Desert)

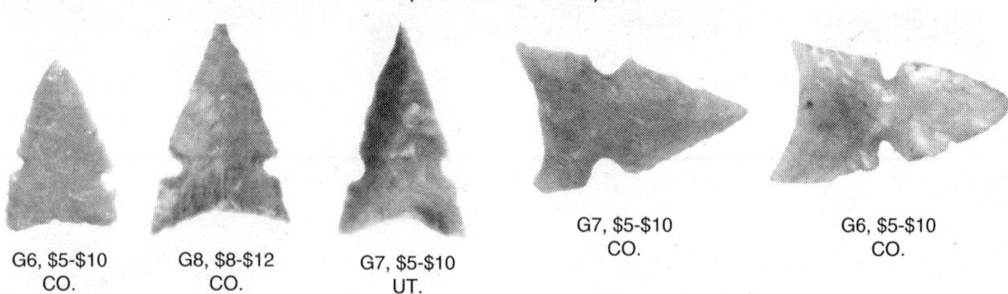

G6, $5-$10
CO.

G8, $8-$12
CO.

G7, $5-$10
UT.

G7, $5-$10
CO.

G6, $5-$10
CO.

LOCATION: Northern Plains states to the Southwest and eastward to Oklahoma. **DESCRIPTION:** A small size, thin, side notched arrow point with a concave base and sharp basal corners. Notches usually occur far up from the base.

WASHITA-NORTHERN - Developmental to Classic Phase, 800 - 400 B. P.

(Also see Desert)

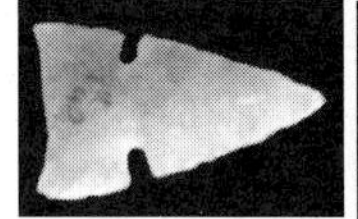

G6, $20-$25
Cascade Co., MT.

G6, $20-$25
Cascade Co., MT.

G6, $20-$25
Bismark, ND.

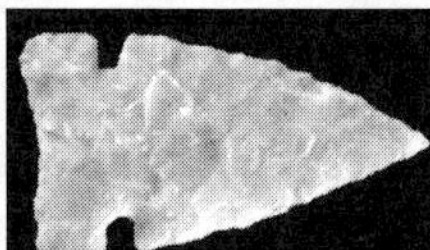

G6, $15-$20
Great Falls, MT.

G6, $20-$25
Lewis & Clark
Co., MT.

LOCATION: Northern Plains states. **DESCRIPTION:** A small size, thin, triangular side notched arrow point with a concave base. Basal area is usually large in proportion to the blade size. Basal corners are sharp. Notches are narrow.

YONKEE - Middle to Late Archaic, 4500 - 2500 B. P.

(Also see Besant and Bitterroot)

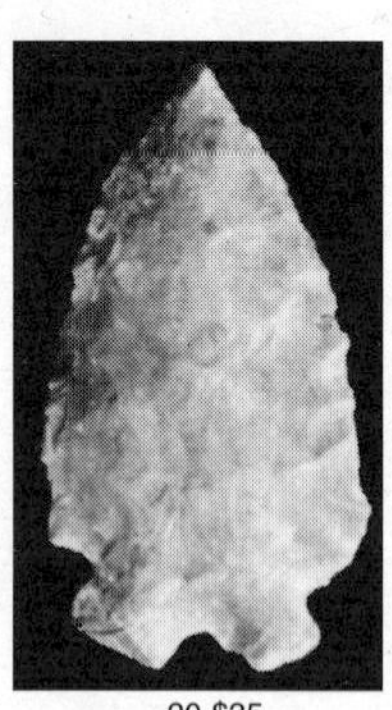

20-$35
Moorcroft, WY.

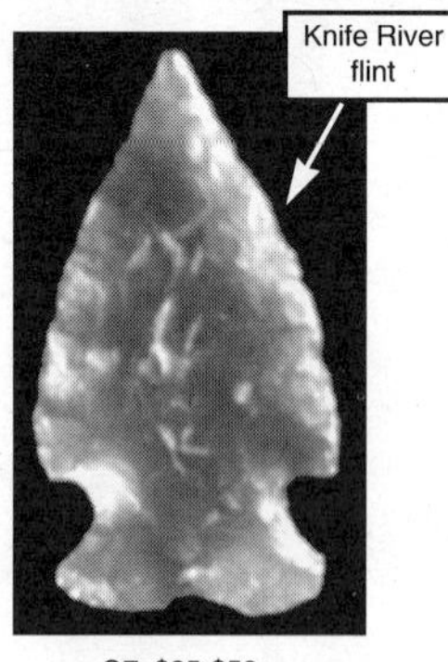

G7, $25-$50
Mountrail Co., ND.

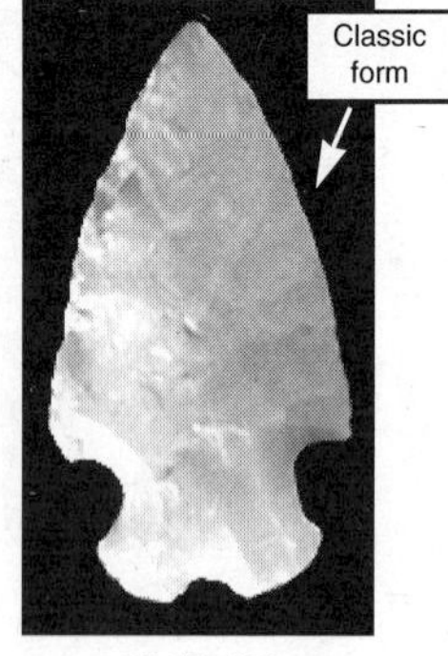

G7, $25-$50
Lewis & Clark Co., MT.

LOCATION: Northern Plains states. **DESCRIPTION:** A medium size, narrow point that is corner or side-notched. The base is concave to bifurcated forming ears. Shoulders are slightly barbed to horizontal. Found in conjunction with McKean points on Bison jump-kill sites. **I.D. KEY:** Lobed ears.

GREAT BASIN WESTWARD SECTION:

This section includes point types from the following states:
California, Idaho, Nevada, Oregon, Utah, Washington

The points in this section are arranged in alphabetical order and are shown **actual size**. All types are listed that were available for photographing. Any missing types will be added to future editions as photographs become available. We are always interested in receiving sharp, black and white or color glossy photos or color slides of your collection. Be sure and include a ruler in the photograph so that proper scale can be determined.

Lithics: Materials employed in the manufacture of projectile points from this region are: obsidian, basalt, dacite and ignumbrite with lesser amounts of agate, jasper, chert, chalcedony, opal, petrified wood.

Important sites: Clovis: Borax Lake, N. California., Wenatchee Clovis cache, WA.

Regional Consultant:
Jeb Taylor

Special Advisors:
John Byrd
Bill & Donna Jackson
Ben E. Stermer
Gregory J. Truesdell

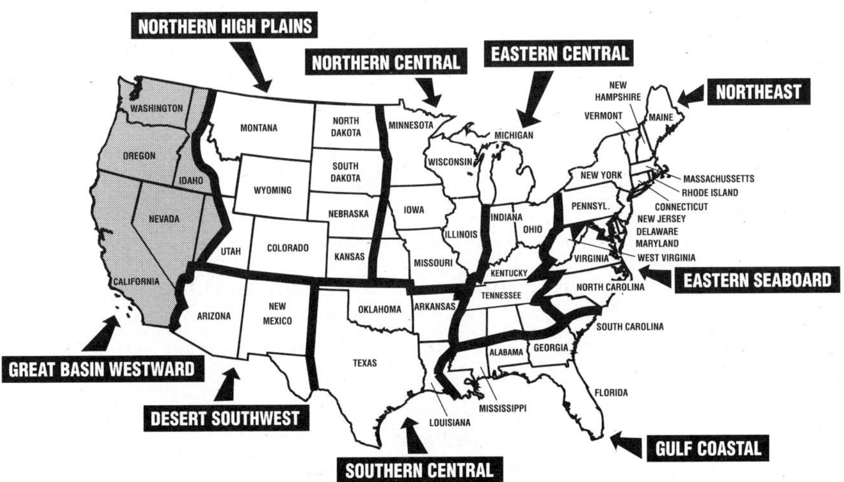

GB

GREAT BASIN WESTWARD POINT TYPES
(Archaeological Periods)

PALEO (14,000 B. P. - 8,000 B. P.)

Black Rock Concave
Chindadn
Chopper
Clovis
Cougar Mountain
Crescent
Drill
Graver
Haskett
Lake Mohave
Paleo Knife
Parman
Scraper
Silver Lake
Spedis
Sub-Triangular

EARLY ARCHAIC (10,500 B. P. - 5,500 B. P.)

Alberta
Bitterroot
Cascade
Chumash
Chumash Knife
Cody Complex
Cody Complex Knife
Early Eared
Early Leaf
Early Stemmed Lanceolate
Firstview
Humboldt Constricted Base
Humboldt Expanded Base
Humboldt Triangular
Northern Side Notched
Owl Cave
Pryor Stemmed
Square Knife
Wahmuza
Wendover
Windust
Windust Knife
Ytias

MIDDLE ARCHAIC (5,500 B. P. - 3,300 B. P.)

Base Tang Knife
Cold Springs
Gatecliff
Pinto Basin
Rabbit Island
Triple "T"

LATE ARCHAIC (3,500 B. P. - 2,300 B. P.)

Elko
Elko Corner Notched
Elko Eared
Elko Split-Stem
Exotic Forms
Pismo
Quilomene Bar

DESERT TRADITIONS:

TRANSITIONAL PHASE (2,300 B. P. - 1,600 B. P.)

Hafted Knife
Snake River

DEVELOPMENTAL PHASE (1,600 B. P. - 700 B. P.)

Alkali
Bear River
Bone Pin
Buck Gulley
Calapooya
Canalino
Dagger
Eastgate
Eastgate Split-Stem
Gold Hill
Gunther
Gunther Triangular
Hell's Canyon Basal Notched
Hell's Canyon Corner Notched
Panoche
Rose Springs
Uinta
Wallula
Washita
Wintu

CLASSIC PHASE (700 B. P. - 400 B. P.)

Columbia Mule Ear
Columbia Plateau
Cottonwood Leaf
Cottonwood Triangle
Desert Delta
Desert General
Desert Redding
Desert Sierra
Plateau Pentagonal

HISTORIC (400 B. P. - Present)

Bear
Ground Stone
Ishi
Kavik
Klickitat
Nottoway
Stockton
Trade Points

GREAT BASIN WESTWARD
THUMBNAIL GUIDE SECTION

The following references are provided to aid the collector in easier and quicker identification of point types. All photos are exactly 30% of actual size and are proportional to each other. Each point pictured in this section represents a classic form for the type. When a match is found, go to the alphabetical location of that type for more examples in true actual size.

1 THUMBNAIL GUIDE - AURICULATE FORMS (30% actual size)

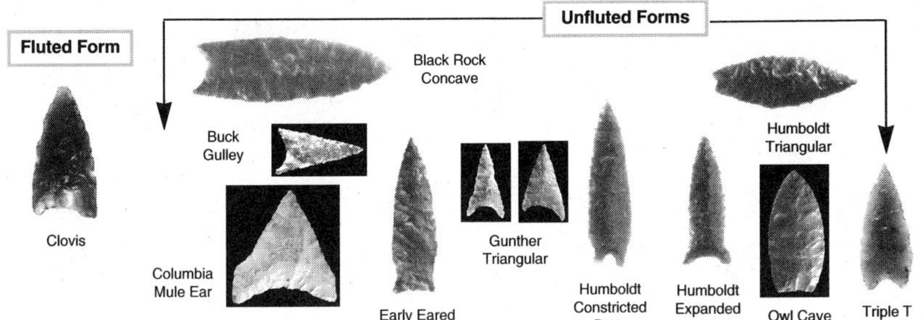

2 THUMBNAIL GUIDE - LANCEOLATE FORMS (30% actual size)

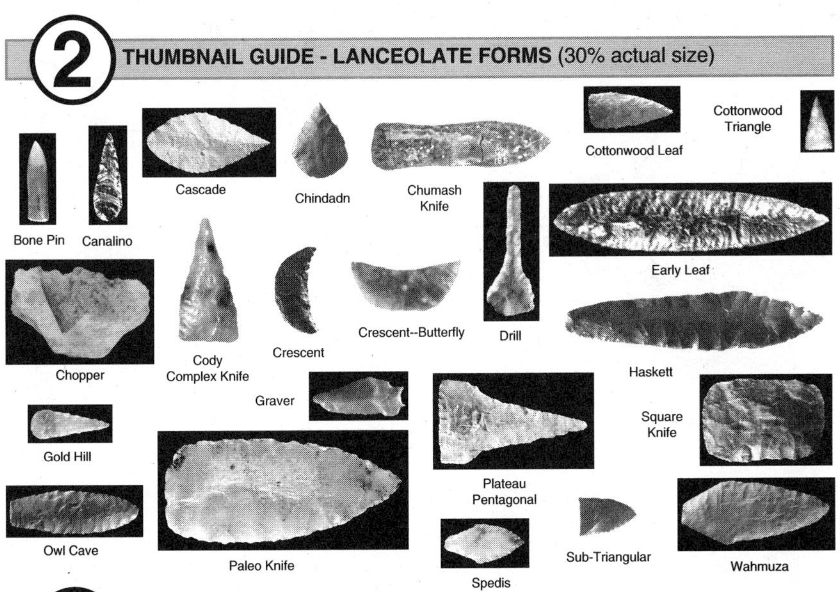

3 THUMBNAIL GUIDE - CORNER NOTCHED FORMS (30% actual size)

Elko Corner Notched

Elko Eared

Elko Eared Double Tip

Hell's Canyon Corner Notched

Quillomene Bar

Snake River

Snake River

Rose Springs

4 THUMBNAIL GUIDE - SIDE NOTCHED FORMS (30% actual size)

Base Tang Knife
Bear River
Bitterroot
Calapooya
Cold Springs
Desert Delta
Northern (Wolf Ears)
Northern
Desert General
Desert Redding
Desert Sierra
BASAL NOTCHED FORM
Panoche
Rose Springs
Stockton
Uinta
Wintu
Ytias
Eastgate
Hell's Canyon

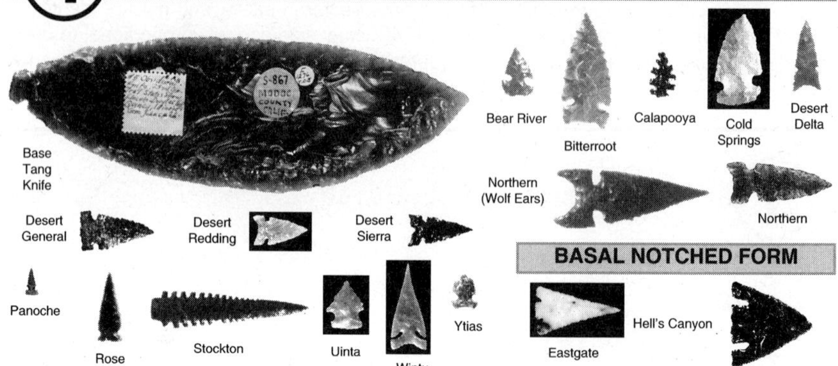

5 THUMBNAIL GUIDE - STEMMED FORMS (30% of actual size)

Bear
Dagger
Eastgate
Elko
Exotic
Alberta
Alkali
Calapooya
Columbia Plateau
Cody Complex
Pryor Stemmed
Rose Springs
Firstview
Silver Lake
Gunther
Kavik
Klickitat
Nottoway
Parman
Trade Points
Wallula
Wallula
Wallula Double Tip
Wendover
Windust Knife
Windust
Contracting Stems
Cougar Mountain
Ground Stone
Early Stemmed
Gatecliff
Lake Mohave
Chumash
Parman
Pismo
Rabbit Island

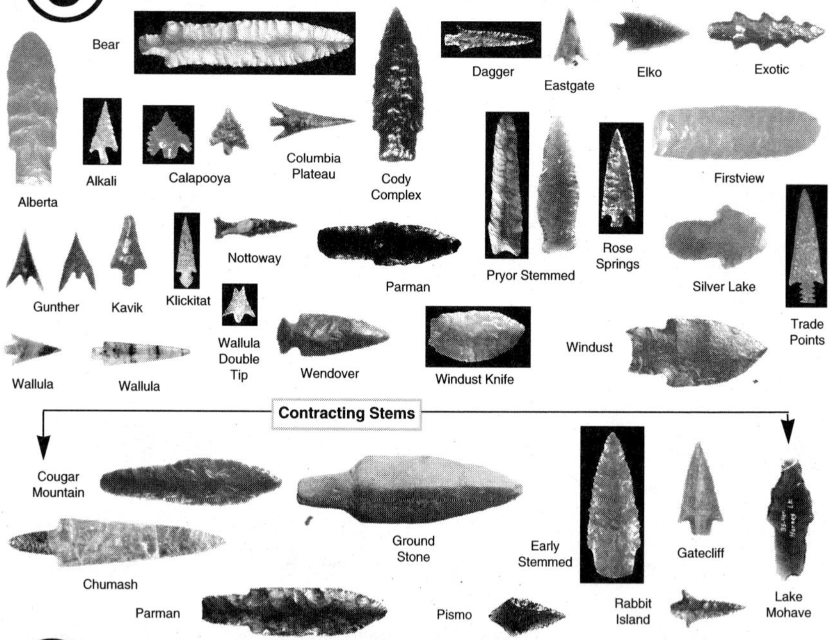

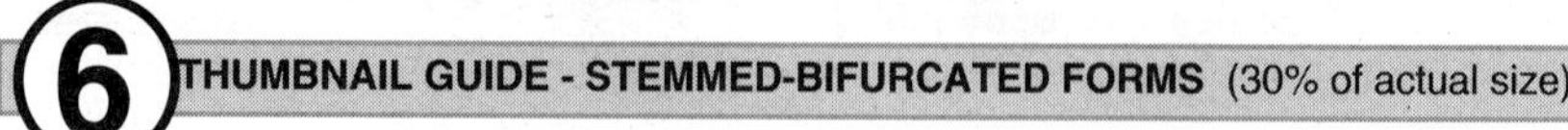

6 THUMBNAIL GUIDE - STEMMED-BIFURCATED FORMS (30% of actual size)

Eastgate Split-Stem
Columbia Plateau
Elko Split Stem
Gatecliff
Pinto Basin
Windust

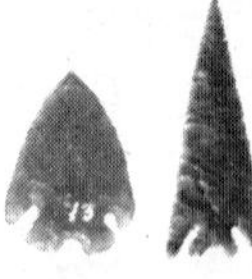

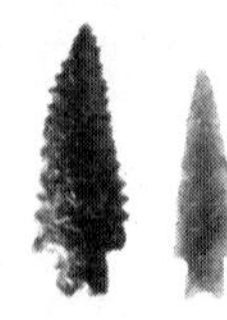

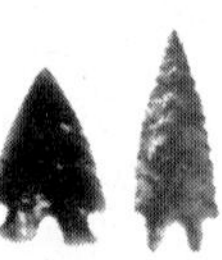

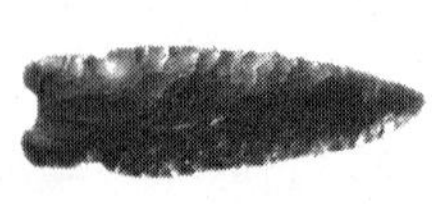

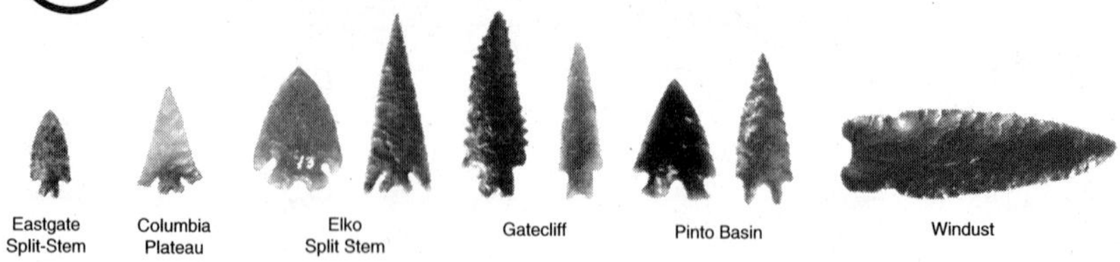

ALBERTA - Transitional Paleo-Early Archaic, 9500 - 7000 B. P.

(Also see Cody Complex)

Ground stem

Obsidian

G6, $125-$250
Warner Valley, OR.

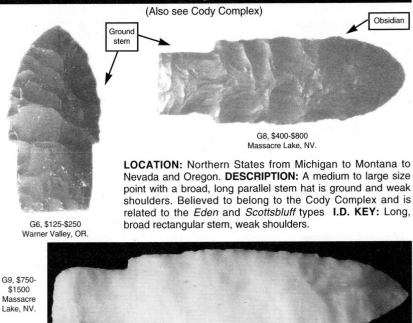

G8, $400-$800
Massacre Lake, NV.

LOCATION: Northern States from Michigan to Montana to Nevada and Oregon. **DESCRIPTION:** A medium to large size point with a broad, long parallel stem hat is ground and weak shoulders. Believed to belong to the Cody Complex and is related to the *Eden* and *Scottsbluff* types **I.D. KEY:** Long, broad rectangular stem, weak shoulders.

G9, $750-$1500
Massacre Lake, NV.

Ground base

ALKALI - Developmental to Classic Phase, 1500 - 500 B. P.

(Also see Colonial, Eastgate, Elko and Rose Springs)

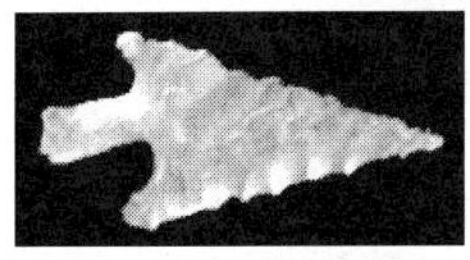

G6, $6-$10
Butte Falls, OR.

G7, $25-$50
Hart Lake, OR.

LOCATION: California to Canada. **DESCRIPTION:** A small size, barbed arrow point with a long parallel sided stem. This type was included with *Rose Springs* in early reports. **I.D. KEY:** Flaking style and long stem.

BASE TANG KNIFE - Late Archaic-Transitional, 4000 - 2000 B. P.

Obsidian

IMPORTANT Shown 1/2 actual size

G10, $500-$1000
Modoc Co., CA.

LOCATION: California. **DESCRIPTION:** A large size elliptical blade with a very small side notched base. Similar to the Turkeytail point found in the East. **I.D. KEY:** Large, broad blade with side notches close to the base.

BEAR - Historic Phase, 300 - 200 B. P.

(Also see Kavik, Lake Mohave, Parman, Silver Lake, Wendover)

Tip nick

Flint

Tip nick

G4, $10-$20 Point Hope, Alaska

G7, $20-$40 Point Hope, Alaska

G6, $15-$30 High Arctic, Alaska

G6, $15-$25 High Arctic, Alaska

G5, $20-$35 Point Hope, Alaska

G5, $20-$35 St. Lawrence, Island, Alaska

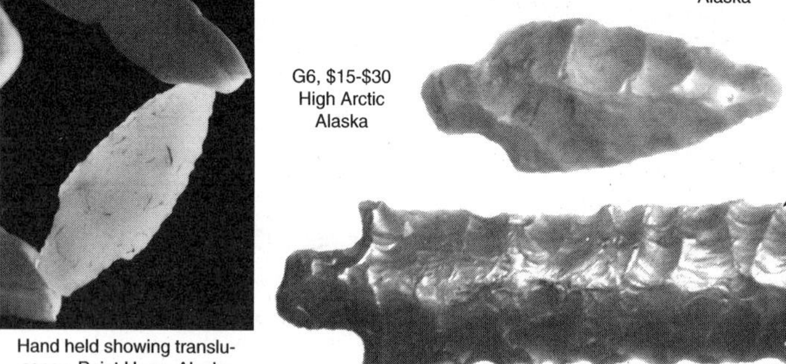

Hand held showing translucency, Point Hope, Alaska

G6, $15-$30 High Arctic Alaska

Parallel flaking

G8, $75-$150 St. Lawrence Island, Alaska

Parallel flaking

G9, $190-$375 Alaska

LOCATION: Alaska. **DESCRIPTION:** A medium to large size, narrow point with a parallel sided, narrow stem. Parallel flaking is common. The stem is moderately long. **I.D. KEY:** Long, narrow stemmed point.

BEAR RIVER - Developmental to Classic Phase, 1300 - 400 B. P.

(Also see Desert, Emigrant, Rose Spring)

G6, $15-$25 Gooding Co., ID.

G9, $20-$40 Gooding Co., ID.

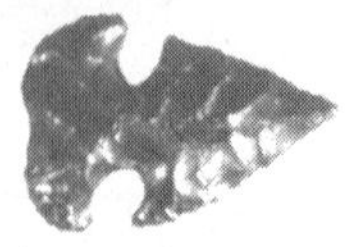

G9, $20-$40 Gooding Co., ID.

BEAR RIVER (continued)

LOCATION: Great Basin area. Found in the Fremont area of Utah into SW Idaho. **DESCRIPTION:** A small size, thin, side-notched arrow point with deep notches. The base is large in relation to its overall size. Basal corners are rounded. **I.D. KEY:** Large base, small overall size.

BITTERROOT - Early to middle Archaic, 7500 - 5000 B. P.

(Also see Desert, Emigrant, Northern Side Notched, & Swift Current)

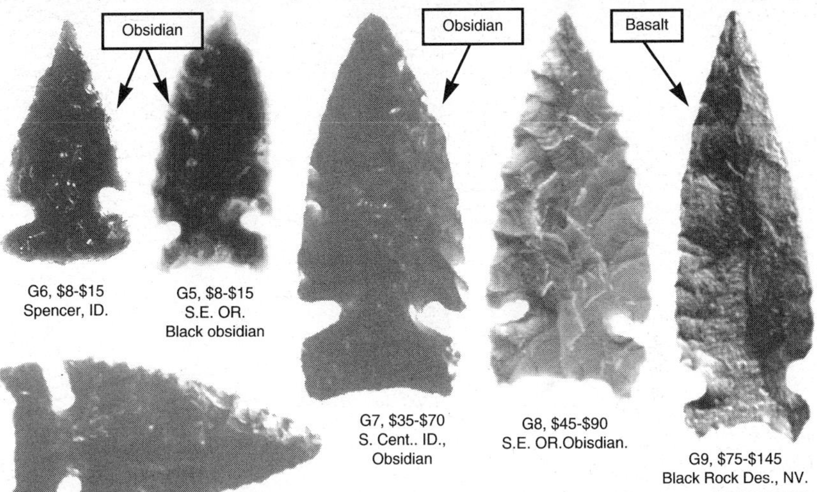

G6, $8-$15
Spencer, ID.

G5, $8-$15
S.E. OR.
Black obsidian

G7, $35-$70
S. Cent.. ID.,
Obsidian

G8, $45-$90
S.E. OR.Obisdian.

G9, $75-$145
Black Rock Des., NV.

G6, $15-$30
S. ID., Obsidian

G7, $20-$40
S.E. OR. Thorn Lake

LOCATION: Northwestern states. **DESCRIPTION:** A variant of the *Northern Side Notched.* A medium size side-notched point with a straight, concave or convex base. Notches are placed at an angle into each side of the blade. Early Archaic flaking is evident on many examples.

BLACK ROCK CONCAVE - Paleo, 11,000 - 10,500 B. P.

(Also see Clovis, Goshen and Humboldt)

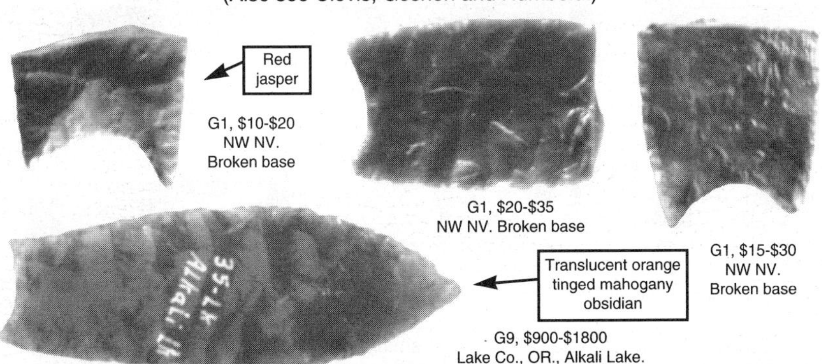

G1, $10-$20
NW NV.
Broken base

G1, $20-$35
NW NV. Broken base

G1, $15-$30
NW NV.
Broken base

G9, $900-$1800
Lake Co., OR., Alkali Lake.

LOCATION: NW Nevada and SE Oregon. An extremely rare type with few complete examples known. **DESCRIPTION:** A medium size, thin, lanceolate point with a concave base. Basal edges are usually ground. Blade flaking is horizontal transverse. Similar in flaking style and form to *Midland* and *Goshen* points and is considered to be the unfluted *Folsom* of the Great Basin. **I.D. KEY:** Micro secondary flaking, ground basal sides.

BLACK ROCK CONCAVE (continued)

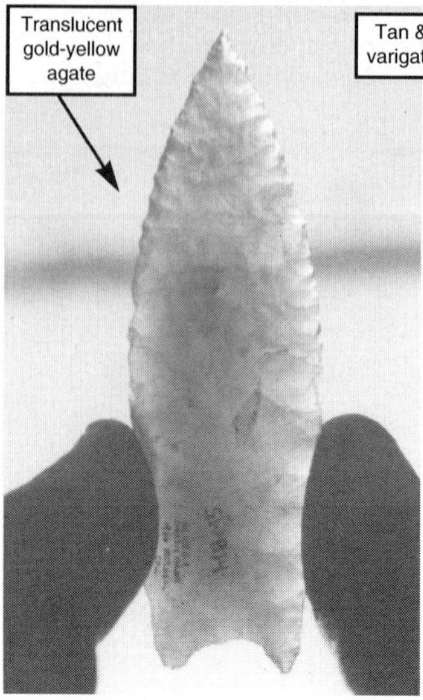

Translucent gold-yellow agate

Tan & orange varigated agate

Unique-retipped using the burin spall technique

Basalt

G10, $1100-$2200
Black Rock Desert, NV.
Hand held with back lighting

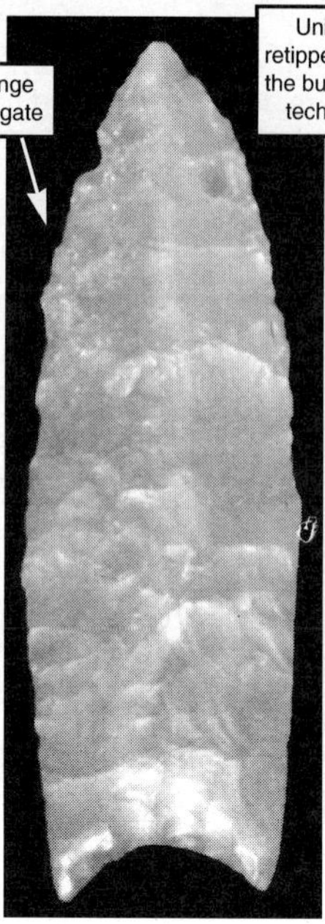

Ground basal areas

G9, $1200-$2000
Black Rock Desert, NV.
Soldier Meadows

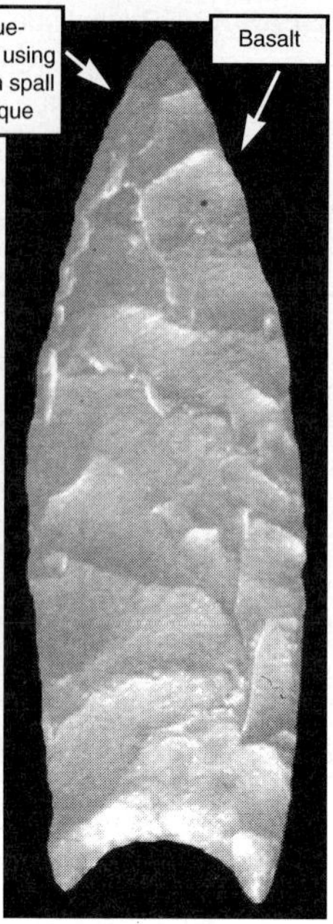

G9, $900-$1800
Lake Co., OR.

BONE PIN - Developmental to Historic Phase, 1500 - 300 B. P.

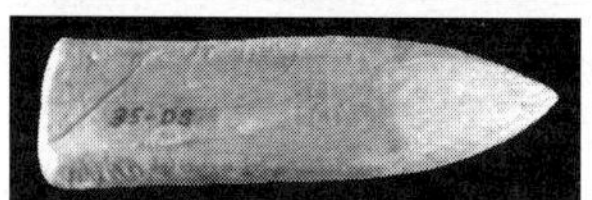

G9, $25-$40
Lane Co., OR.

LOCATION: Oregon. **DESCRIPTION:** A small size, rounded, point crafted from bone.

BUCK GULLEY - Developmental to Historic Phase, 1500 - 300 B. P.

(Also see Canalino, Cottonwood and Gold Hill)

G5, $12-$20
Santa Barbara Co., CA.

G7, $20-$35
Los Angeles Co., CA.

G7, $20-$35
Santa Barbara Co., CA.

G8, $20-$35
Los Angeles Co., CA.

G9, $35-$70
Santa Barbara Co., CA.

LOCATION: California. **DESCRIPTION:** A small size, thin, triangular arrow point with a shallow to deep concave base. Some are serrated. Also known as *Canalino Triangular* or *Coastal Cottonwood.*

CALAPOOYA - Developmental to Historic Phase, 1000 - 200 B. P.

(Also see Columbia Plateau, Gunther, and Winitu)

CALAPOOYA (continued)

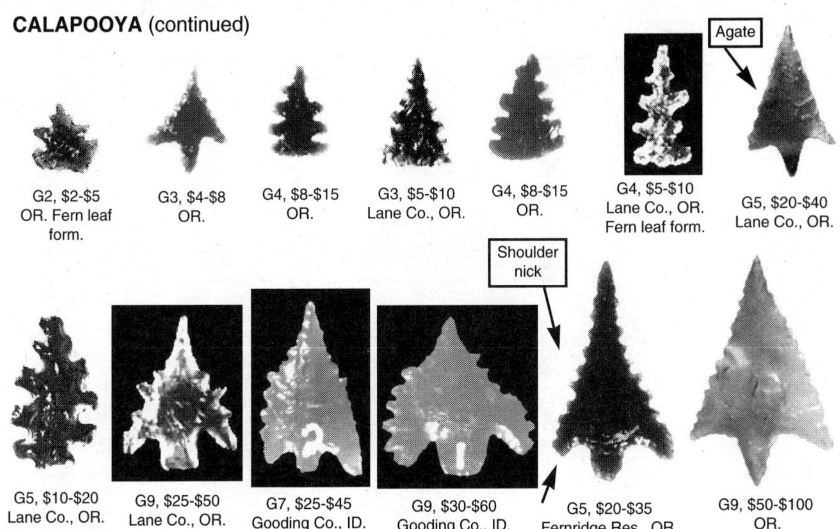

G2, $2-$5 OR. Fern leaf form.

G3, $4-$8 OR.

G4, $8-$15 OR.

G3, $5-$10 Lane Co., OR.

G4, $8-$15 OR.

G4, $5-$10 Lane Co., OR. Fern leaf form.

G5, $20-$40 Lane Co., OR.

G5, $10-$20 Lane Co., OR. Fern leaf form.

G9, $25-$50 Lane Co., OR.

G7, $25-$45 Gooding Co., ID.

G9, $30-$60 Gooding Co., ID.

G5, $20-$35 Fernridge Res., OR.

G9, $50-$100 OR.

LOCATION: Oregon, Columbia River basin. **DESCRIPTION:** A small size, thin, dart point with serrated to strongly barbed blade edges. Stems are short and slightly contracting or expanding and shoulders are strong. The barbed edge variant is called a *Fern Leaf* point.

CANALINO - Developmental to Historic Phase, 800 - 200 B. P.

(Also see Buck Gulley, Cottonwood and Gold Hill)

G9, $25-$45 Los Angeles Co., CA.

G8, $18-$35 Los Angeles Co., CA. Banded shale.

G7, $15-$25 Los Angeles Co., CA.

LOCATION: Coastal southern California. **DESCRIPTION:** A small to medium size lanceolate point with a rounded base. Similar to the *Gold Hill* point found in Oregon. Also known as the *Coastal Cottonwood* point.

CASCADE - Paleo to Early Archaic, 8000 - 6000 B. P.

(Also see Early Leaf, Early Stemmed, Haskett, Parman and Windust)

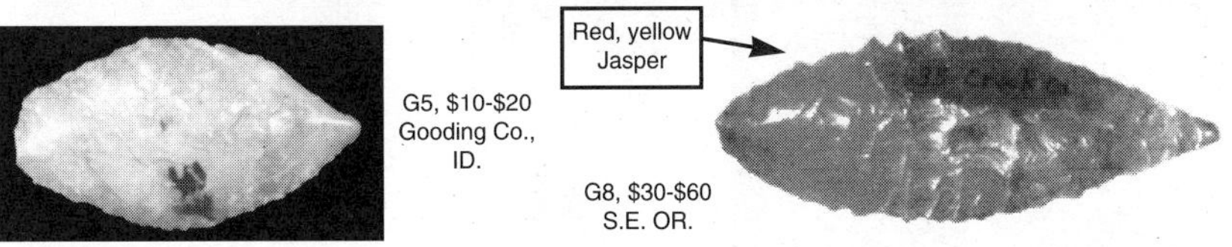

G5, $10-$20 Gooding Co., ID.

G8, $30-$60 S.E. OR.

LOCATION: Great Basin to Washington. **DESCRIPTION:** A medium to large size, narrow, thin blade that usually exhibits oblique parallel flaking. Base can be convex to pointed. The famous Paulina Creek Dietz Cascade cache of 2130 blades was found in Oregon in 1961. **I.D. Key**: Lanceolate form, oblique, parallel flaking.

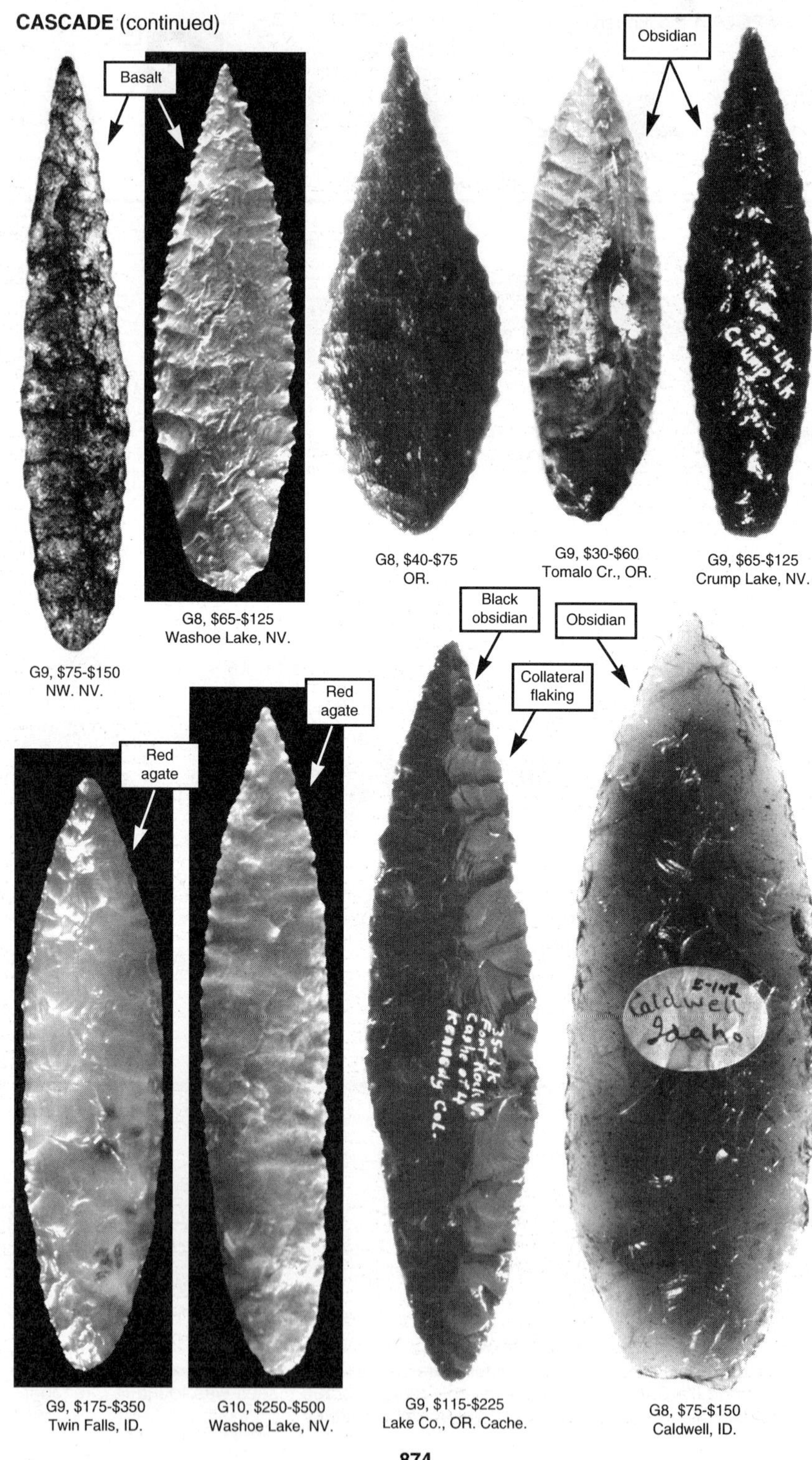

G9, $75-$150
NW. NV.

G8, $65-$125
Washoe Lake, NV.

G8, $40-$75
OR.

G9, $30-$60
Tomalo Cr., OR.

G9, $65-$125
Crump Lake, NV.

G9, $175-$350
Twin Falls, ID.

G10, $250-$500
Washoe Lake, NV.

G9, $115-$225
Lake Co., OR. Cache.

G8, $75-$150
Caldwell, ID.

CHINDADN - Paleo, 11,300 - 11,000 B. P.

(Also see Cascade,Clovis and Sub-Triangular)

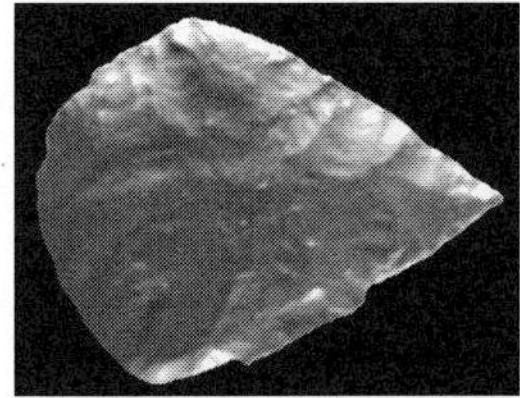

G8, $25-$50
Nenana Valley, AK.

LOCATION: Alaska. **DESCRIPTION:** A small size, broad, thin, ovate point made from a flake that has a convex base. Made during the Nenana occupation. **I.D. Key**: Broad, ovate form.

CHOPPER - Paleo, 14,000 - 10,000 B. P.

(Also see Scraper)

LOCATION: California. **DESCRIPTION:** A medium to large size, thick, early chopping and pounding tool. Most are irregular shaped to oval to circular.

G6, $25-$50 ea.
San Bernadino, CA.

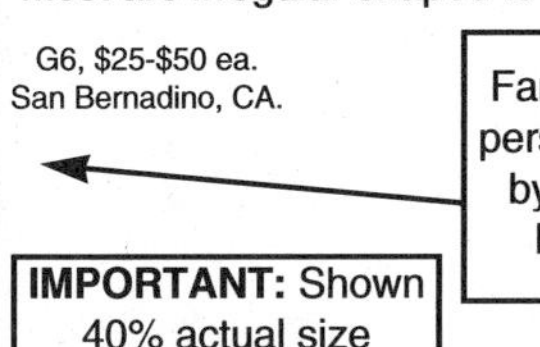

Famed Calico site choppers dated to 50,000 B.P. by L.S.B. Leakey, San Bernadino Co., CA.

IMPORTANT: Shown 40% actual size

CHUMASH - Early to Middle Archaic, 9000 - 5000 B. P.

(Also see Early Stemmed, Parman)

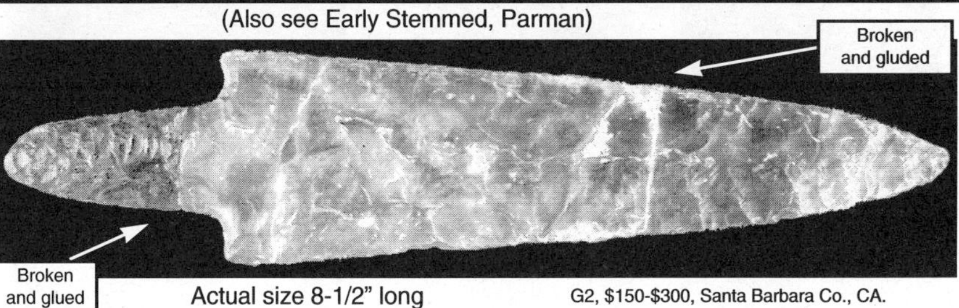

Actual size 8-1/2" long

G2, $150-$300, Santa Barbara Co., CA.

LOCATION: California. **DESCRIPTION:** A large size, long stemmed, narrow point with square shoulders and a long, narrow, rounded base.

CHUMASH KNIFE - Early to Middle Archaic, 9000 - 5000 B. P.

(Also see Chumash)

G2, $100-$200
Santa Barbara Co., CA.

Actual size 7-1/2" long

LOCATION: California. **DESCRIPTION:** A large size, lanceolate blade that expands towards the base, hafted and used as a knife. Residue of tar is still on the handle.

CLOVIS - Paleo, 14,000 - 10,000 B. P.

(Also see Black Rock Concave, Cascade and Humboldt)

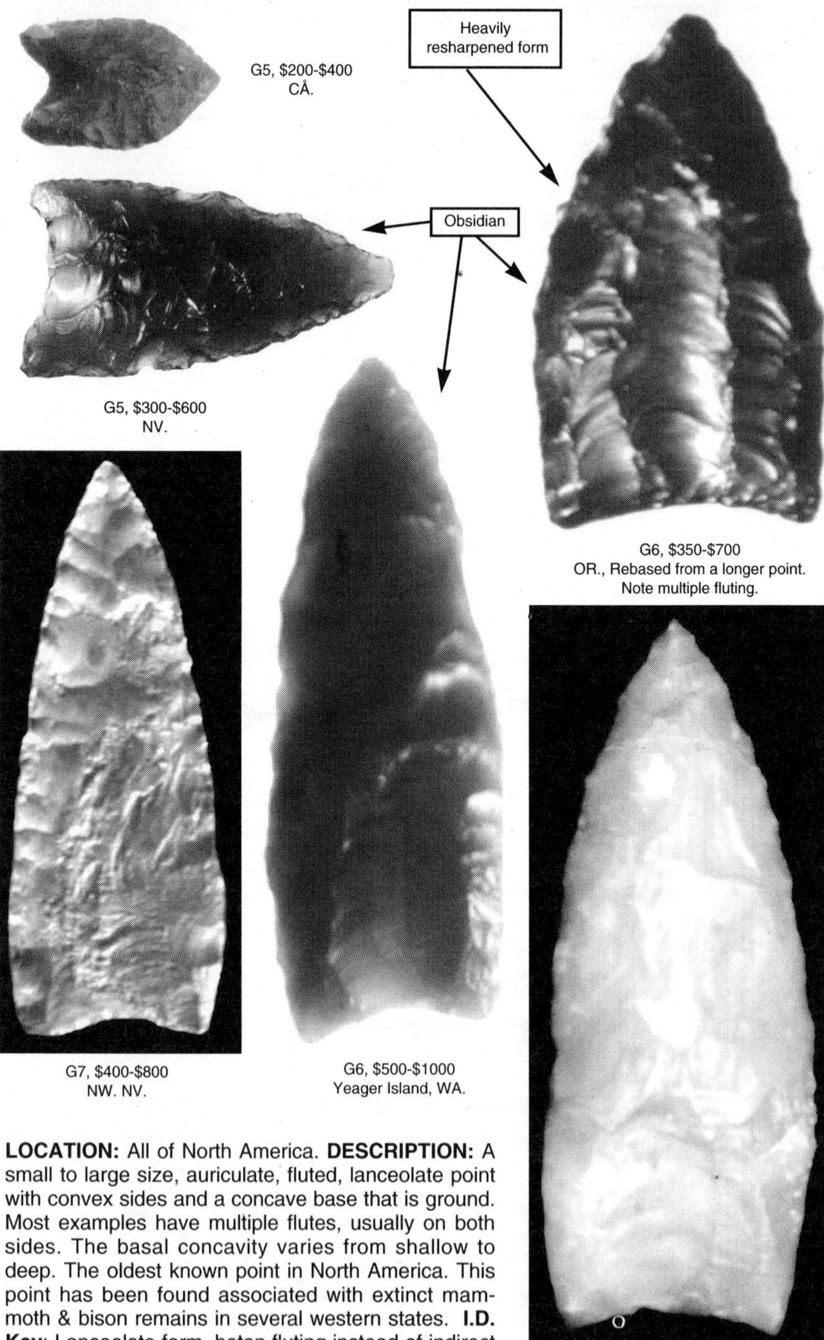

G5, $200-$400
CA.

G5, $300-$600
NV.

G6, $350-$700
OR., Rebased from a longer point. Note multiple fluting.

G7, $400-$800
NW. NV.

G6, $500-$1000
Yeager Island, WA.

G8, $600-$1200
Double O Flats, OR.

LOCATION: All of North America. **DESCRIPTION:** A small to large size, auriculate, fluted, lanceolate point with convex sides and a concave base that is ground. Most examples have multiple flutes, usually on both sides. The basal concavity varies from shallow to deep. The oldest known point in North America. This point has been found associated with extinct mammoth & bison remains in several western states. **I.D. Key**: Lanceolate form, batan fluting instead of indirect style.

CLOVIS (continued)

SHOWN HALF SIZE

Largest Clovis point known. Actual size is 9-1/2" long

Note unusual barbed edges

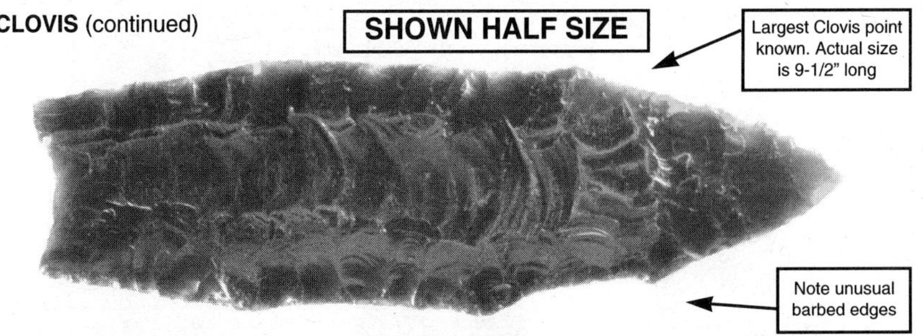

G10, $9,000-$18,000

Douglas Co., WA. Obsidian. This point was probably used as a knife. It was found next to an extinct bison trail close to where the Wenatchee Clovis site is located.

CODY COMPLEX - Early Archaic, 9500 - 7000 B. P.

(Also see Alberta, Cody Knife and Firstview)

G1, $5-$10
NW NV.
Broken base.

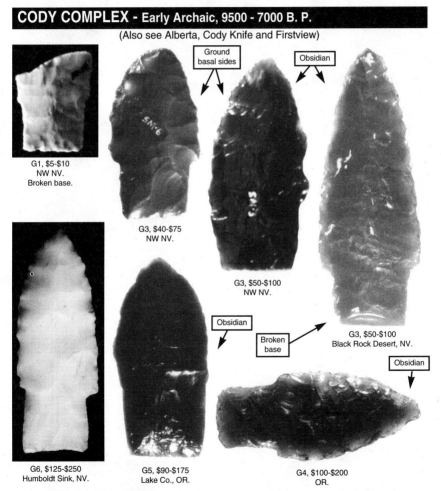

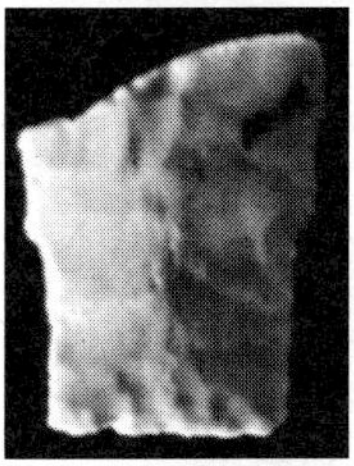

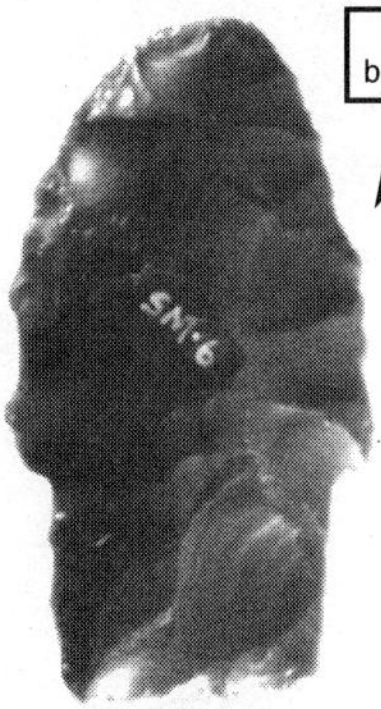

Ground basal sides

G3, $40-$75
NW NV.

Obsidian

G3, $50-$100
NW NV.

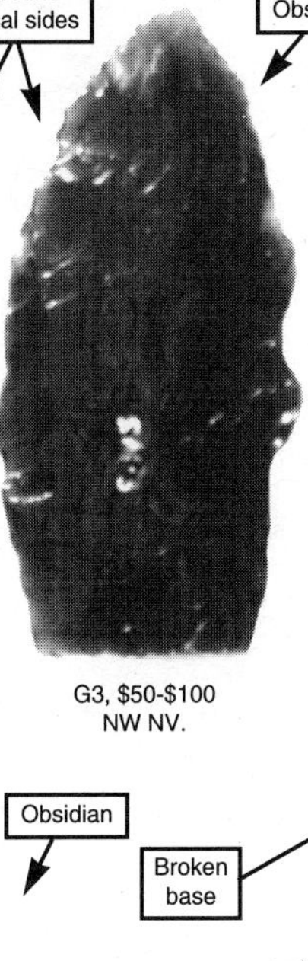

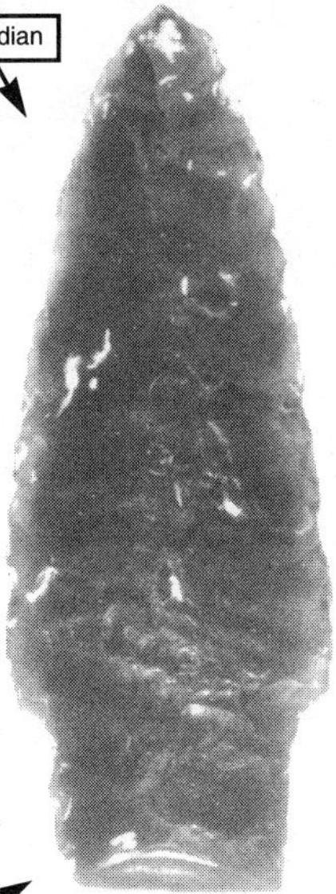

Broken base

G3, $50-$100
Black Rock Desert, NV.

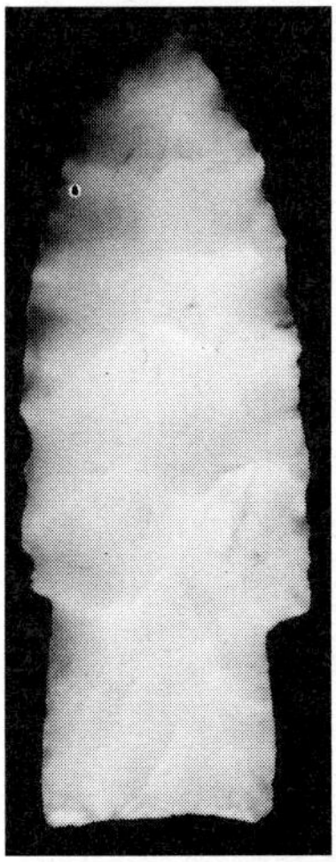

G6, $125-$250
Humboldt Sink, NV.

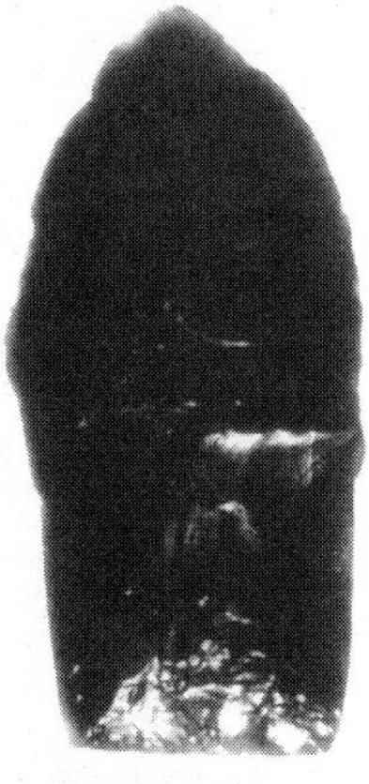

Obsidian

G5, $90-$175
Lake Co., OR.

Obsidian

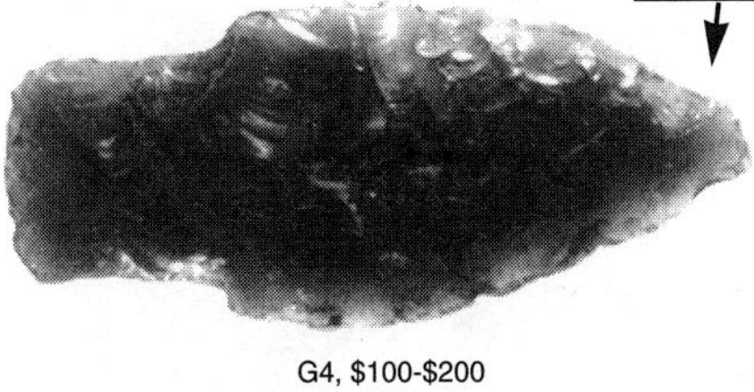

G4, $100-$200
OR.

LOCATION: Western Oregon into Idaho, Nevada and Montana. **DESCRIPTION:** A medium to large size, broad, stemmed point with weak shoulders and a broad parallel sided to expanding stem that is ground. Flaking is usually the horizontal to oblique style. Type names are *Eden, Firstview* and *Scottsbluff.* **I.D. KEY:** Early flaking, square stem.

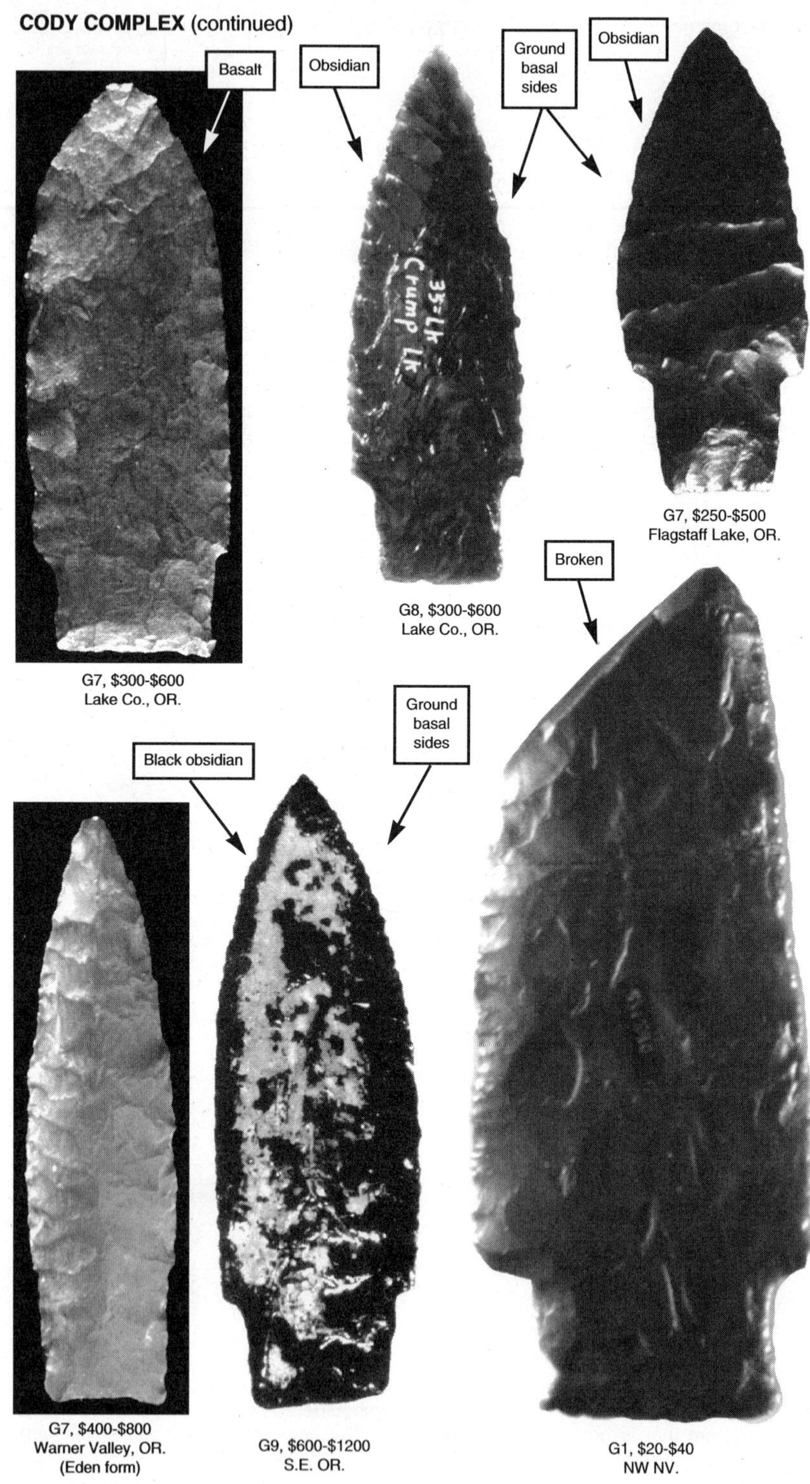

G7, $300-$600
Lake Co., OR.

G8, $300-$600
Lake Co., OR.

G7, $250-$500
Flagstaff Lake, OR.

G7, $400-$800
Warner Valley, OR.
(Eden form)

G9, $600-$1200
S.E. OR.

G1, $20-$40
NW NV.

CODY COMPLEX KNIFE - Early Archaic, 9500 - 7000 B. P.

(Also see Cody Complex)

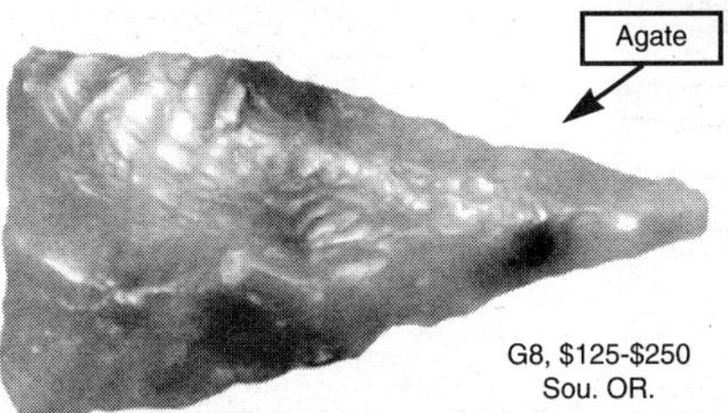

G8, $125-$250
Sou. OR.

LOCATION: Oregon and Washington. **DESCRIPTION:** A medium to large size, well made, triangular knife with a broad base. Resharpened examples have prominent shoulders forming a pentagonal form. **I.D. KEY:** Early flaking, pentagonal form.

COLD SPRINGS - Middle Archaic, 5000 - 4000 B. P.

(Also see Bitterroot, Buffalo Gap, Desert Side-Notched)

G4, $8-$15
Snake Riv., OR.

G5, $8-$15
Umatilla, OR.

LOCATION: Oregon and Washington. **DESCRIPTION:** A small to medium size broadly side-notched point with a straight to convex base.

COLUMBIA MULE EAR - Classic Phase, 700 - 400 B. P.

(Also see Plateau Pentagonal)

G6, $25-$50
Wasco Co., OR.

G4, $25-$45
Wasco Co., OR.

G8, $75-$150
Wasco Co., OR. Classic form.

LOCATION: Oregon and Washington. **DESCRIPTION:** A small to medium size, well made, triangular knife with a broad base. Resharpened examples have prominent shoulders forming a pentagonal form. Used by the Umatilla tribe. Found only along the Columbia River in Washington & Oregon. **I.D. KEY:** Pentagonal form.

COLUMBIA MULE EAR (continued)

G8, $45-$90
Wasco Co., OR.

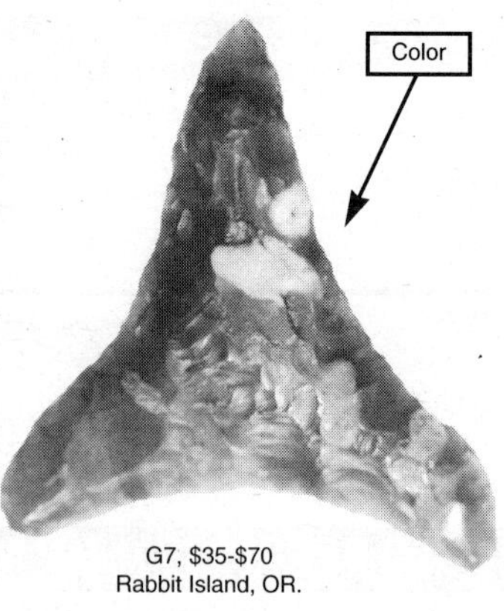

G7, $35-$70
Rabbit Island, OR.

COLUMBIA PLATEAU - Classic to Historic Phase, 500 - 200 B. P.

(Also see Eastgate, Gatecliff, Gunther, Molalla and Wallula)

Color

G4, $15-$30
OR.

G7, $40-$80
WA. Gem.

Agate

G8, $40-$80
OR/WA. Gem.

G7, $35-$70
Umatilla Co., OR.

G8, $40-$80
WA. Gem.

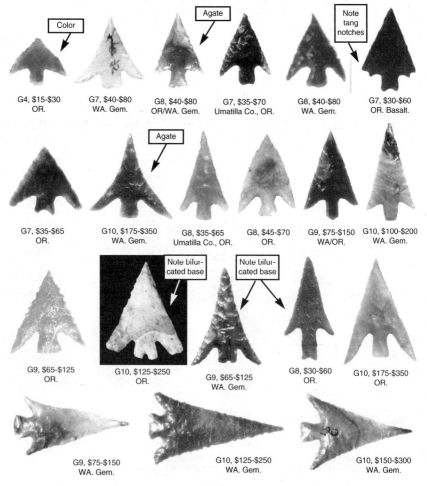

Note tang notches

G7, $30-$60
OR. Basalt.

G7, $35-$65
OR.

Agate

G10, $175-$350
WA. Gem.

G8, $35-$65
Umatilla Co., OR.

G8, $45-$70
OR.

G9, $75-$150
WA/OR.

G10, $100-$200
WA. Gem.

G9, $65-$125
OR.

Note bifurcated base

G10, $125-$250
OR.

Note bifurcated base

G9, $65-$125
WA. Gem.

G8, $30-$60
OR.

G10, $175-$350
OR.

G9, $75-$150
WA. Gem.

G10, $125-$250
WA. Gem.

G10, $150-$300
WA. Gem.

COLUMBIA PLATEAU (continued)

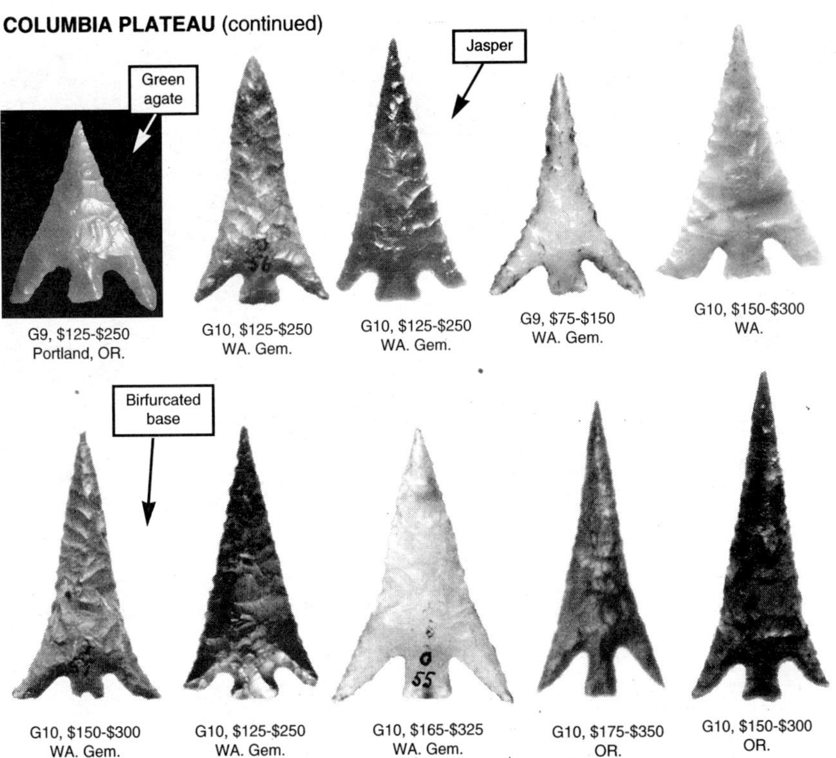

G9, $125-$250 Portland, OR.

G10, $125-$250 WA. Gem.

G10, $125-$250 WA. Gem.

G9, $75-$150 WA. Gem.

G10, $150-$300 WA.

G10, $150-$300 WA. Gem.

G10, $125-$250 WA. Gem.

G10, $165-$325 WA. Gem.

G10, $175-$350 OR.

G10, $150-$300 OR.

LOCATION: Columbia river in Oregon and Washington. **DESCRIPTION:** A small size, thin, triangular point with strong barbs and a short, expanding to parallel sided stem. Shoulder barbs are usually pointed and can extend to the base. Blade edges can be serrated and the base can be bifurcated.

COTTONWOOD LEAF - Classic to Historic Phase, 700 - 200 B. P.

(Also see Canalino, Cottonwood Triangle)

Gem

G6, $10-$20 OR.

G6, $4-$8 NV.

G6, $8-$15 NV.

G6, $15-$25 Asotin Co., WA.

G4, $5-$10 CA.

G8, $20-$40 NV.

Caramel color

G9, $20-$40 OR.

G5, $2-$5 UT.

COTTONWOOD LEAF (continued)

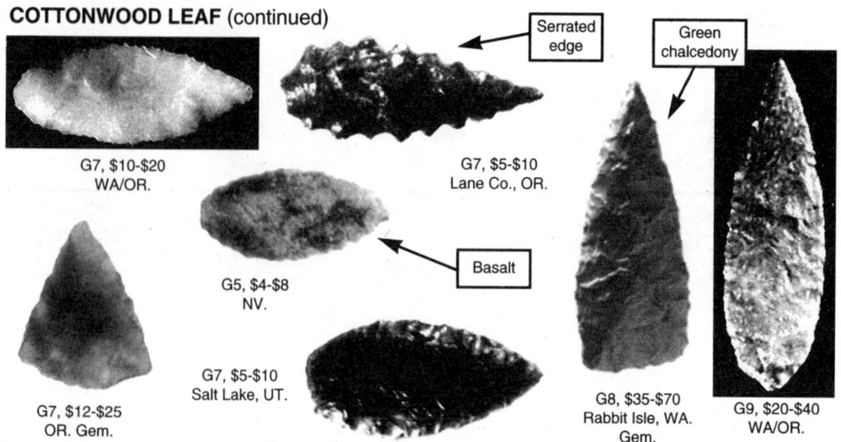

G7, $10-$20
WA/OR.

G7, $5-$10
Lane Co., OR.

G5, $4-$8
NV.

G7, $12-$25
OR. Gem.

G7, $5-$10
Salt Lake, UT.

G8, $35-$70
Rabbit Isle, WA.
Gem.

G9, $20-$40
WA/OR.

LOCATION: Great Basin states northward. **DESCRIPTION:** A small size, thin, ovoid point with a convex base. Similar to the Nodena type from Arkansas. **I.D. KEY:** Small ovoid form.

COTTONWOOD TRIANGLE - Classic to Historic Phase, 700 - 200 B. P.

(Also see Cottonwood Leaf)

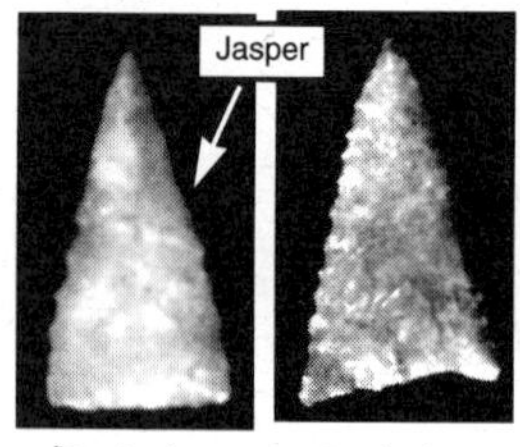

G6, $6-$10
Bonner Co., ID.

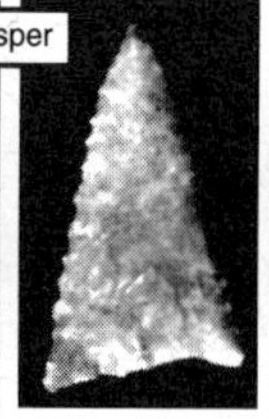

G5, $3-$5
Bonner Co., ID.

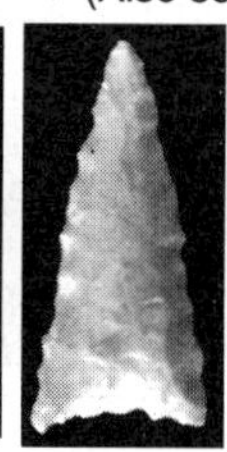

G5, $6-$15
Bonner Co., ID.

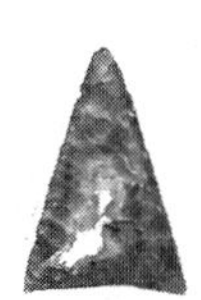

G4, $5-$8
Santa Barbara
Co., CA.

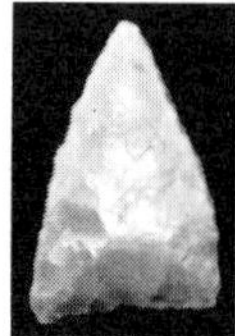

G6, $6-$12
Reno, NV.

G6, $8-$15
WA/OR.

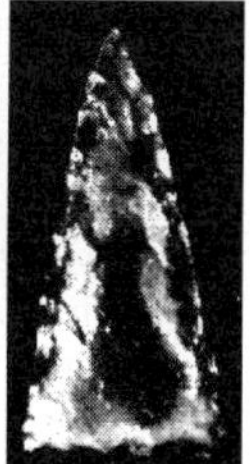

G6, $12-$20
Los Angeles Co., CA.
Banded shale.

LOCATION: Great Basin states northward. **DESCRIPTION:** A small to medium size, thin, triangular point with a straight to concave base. Basal corners are sharp to rounded. **I.D. KEY:** Small triangle form.

G8, $8-$15
NV.

COUGAR MOUNTAIN - Paleo, 10,000 - 9000 B. P.

(Also see Cody Complex, Lind Coulee, Lake Mohave and Parman)

G1, $8-$15
Lake Co., OR.
Broken stem.

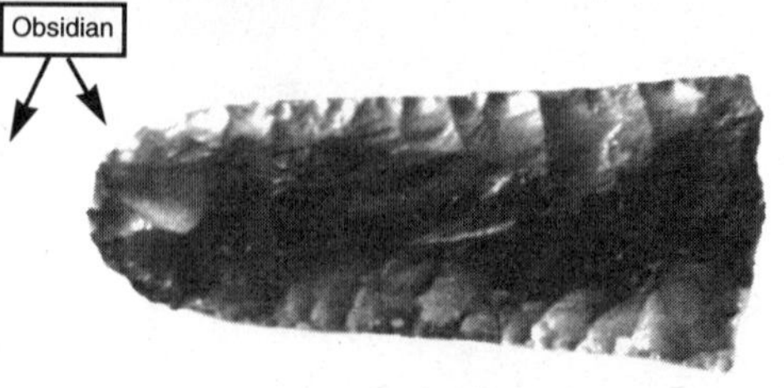

G1, $15-$30
NW NV., broken stem

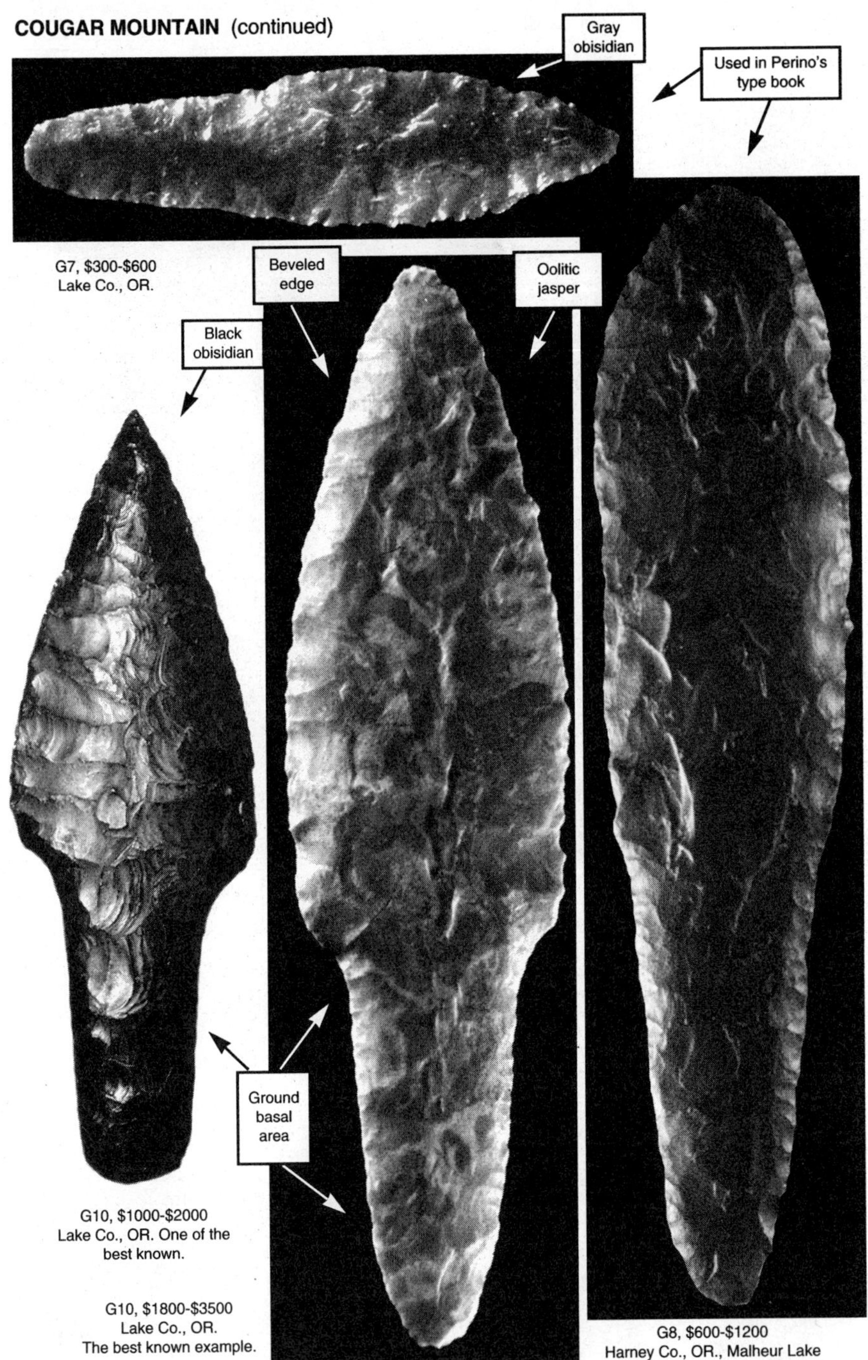

G7, $300-$600
Lake Co., OR.

G10, $1000-$2000
Lake Co., OR. One of the best known.

G10, $1800-$3500
Lake Co., OR.
The best known example.

G8, $600-$1200
Harney Co., OR., Malheur Lake

LOCATION: Southern Oregon, NW Nevada. **DESCRIPTION:** A large size, long stemmed form with weak tapered shoulders and a convex base. Basal area is ground. Associated with *Haskett* points found on the same sites. The earliest points found at Cougar Mountain Cave in Southern Oregon. Very rare. **I.D. KEY:** Long tapered stem.

COUGAR MOUNTAIN (continued)

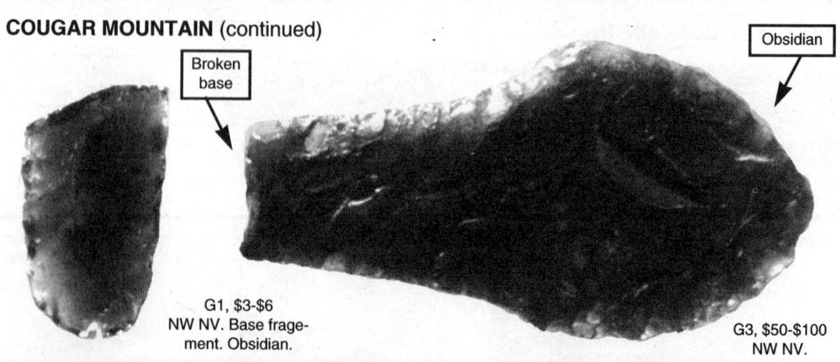

G1, $3-$6
NW NV. Base frage-
ment. Obsidian.

G3, $50-$100
NW NV.

CRESCENT - Paleo, 11,000 - 10,500 B. P.

(Also see Lind Coulee)

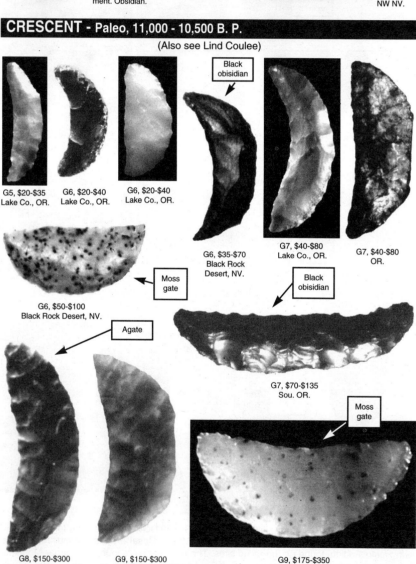

G5, $20-$35
Lake Co., OR.

G6, $20-$40
Lake Co., OR.

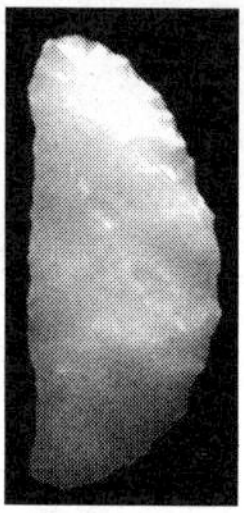

G6, $20-$40
Lake Co., OR.

G6, $35-$70
Black Rock
Desert, NV.

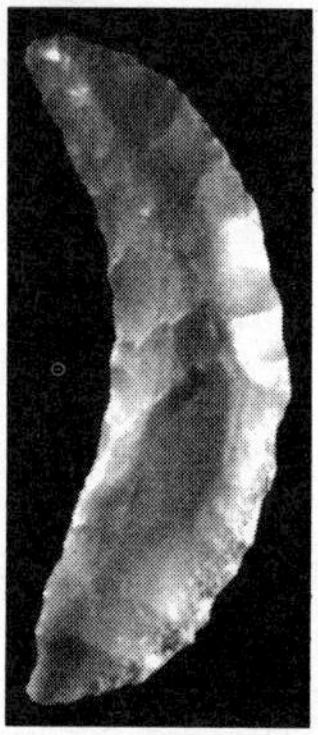

G7, $40-$80
Lake Co., OR.

G7, $40-$80
OR.

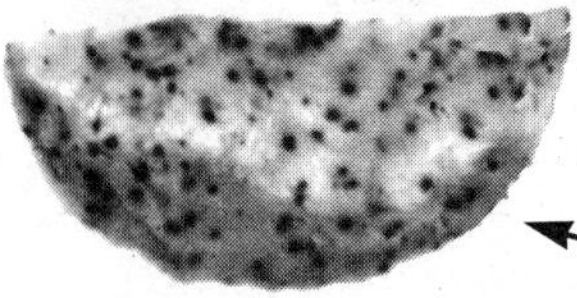

G6, $50-$100
Black Rock Desert, NV.

G7, $70-$135
Sou. OR.

G8, $150-$300
Black Rock Desert, NV.

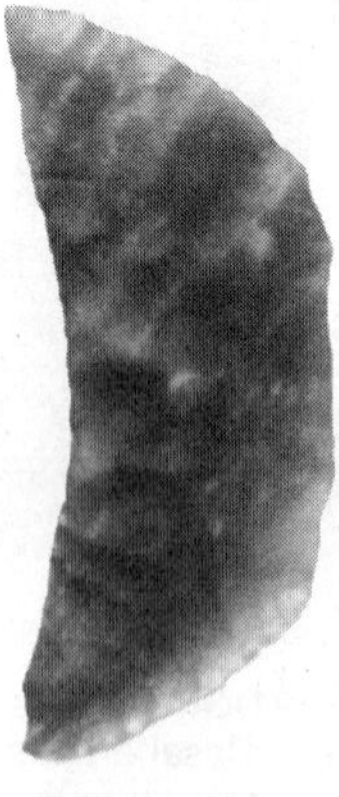

G9, $150-$300
Black Rock Desert, NV.

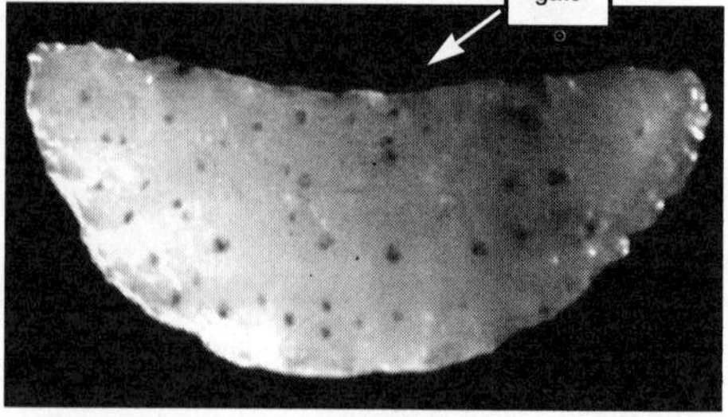

G9, $175-$350
NW NV.

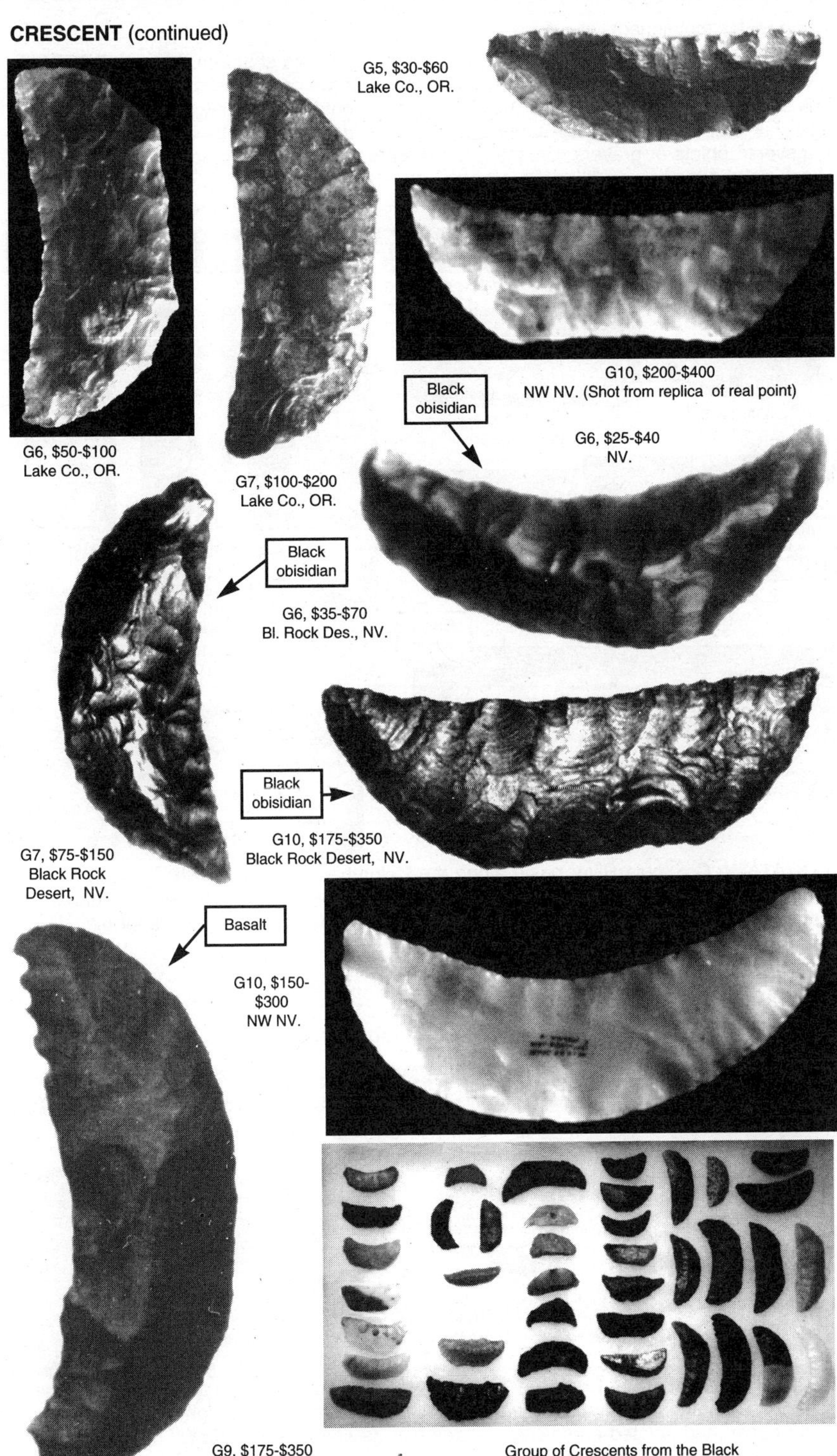

G5, $30-$60
Lake Co., OR.

G6, $50-$100
Lake Co., OR.

G7, $100-$200
Lake Co., OR.

G10, $200-$400
NW NV. (Shot from replica of real point)

G6, $25-$40
NV.

G6, $35-$70
Bl. Rock Des., NV.

G7, $75-$150
Black Rock
Desert, NV.

G10, $175-$350
Black Rock Desert, NV.

G10, $150-
$300
NW NV.

G9, $175-$350
Black Rock Desert, NV.

Group of Crescents from the Black
Rock Desert region, NW Nevada.

CRESCENT (continued)

LOCATION: *Black Rock Concave* sites in NW Neveda and southern Oregon. **DESCRIPTION:** Crescent moon to butterfly shaped, Crescents are controversial with different theories as to their use. The earlier forms show grinding on the edge only at the center of both sides as well as one or more burinated tips. Possible use could be as knives, scrapers, transverse points or gravers. Crescent forms were found at the Paleo *Lind Coulee* site in Washington state.

DAGGER - Developmental to Classic Phase, 1200 - 400 B. P.

(Also see klickatat)

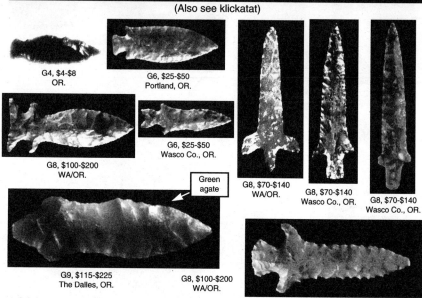

G4, $4-$8
OR.

G6, $25-$50
Portland, OR.

G8, $100-$200
WA/OR.

G6, $25-$50
Wasco Co., OR.

G8, $70-$140
WA/OR.

G8, $70-$140
Wasco Co., OR.

G8, $70-$140
Wasco Co., OR.

Green agate

G9, $115-$225
The Dalles, OR.

G8, $100-$200
WA/OR.

LOCATION: Columbia River basin along the Columbia River. **DESCRIPTION:** A small to medium size, narrow, thin, barbed point. Bases vary from being bifurcated to expanded to contracted. These are variant forms of the *Klickitat* Dagger. **I.D. KEY:** Blade form.

DAGGER (see Klickitat)

DESERT CORNER NOTCHED (see Elko Corner Notched)

DESERT DELTA - Classic to Historic Phase, 700 - 200 B. P.

(Also see Bitterroot, Buffalo Gap, Cold Spring, Emigrant, & Northern Side Notched)

G7, $10-$20
OR.

G7, $10-$20
OR.

G7, $10-$20
Twin Falls Co., ID.

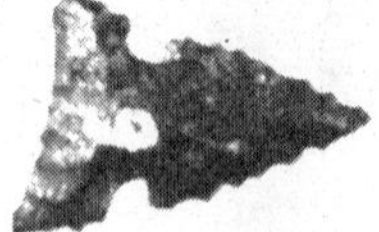

G8, $15-$25
Gooding Co., ID.

G8, $15-$30
WA.

LOCATION: Great Basin westward. **DESCRIPTION:** A small, thin, triangular, side notched arrow point with a deeply concave base, straight blade edges and pointed ears. Blade edges can be serrated. **I.D. KEY:** Small triangle, side notched form.

DESERT DELTA (continued)

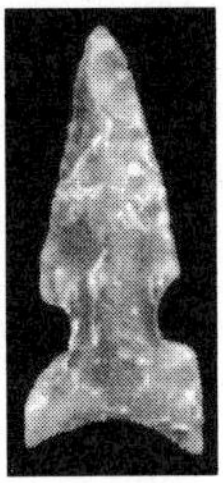

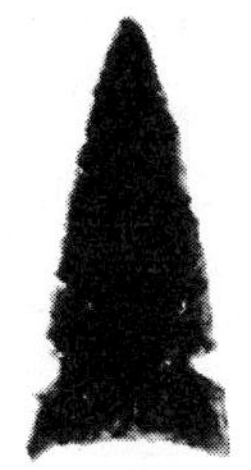

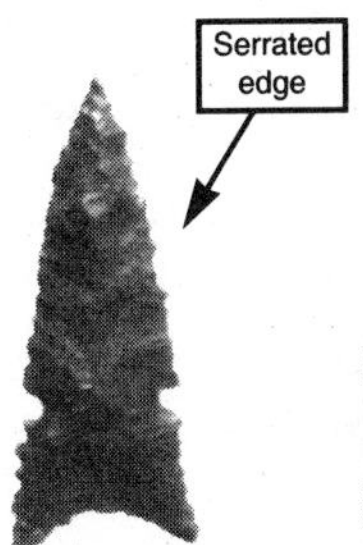

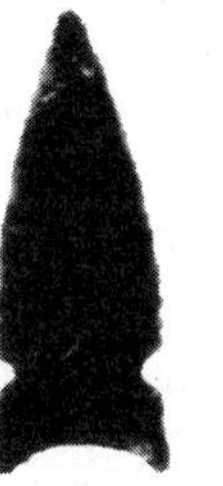

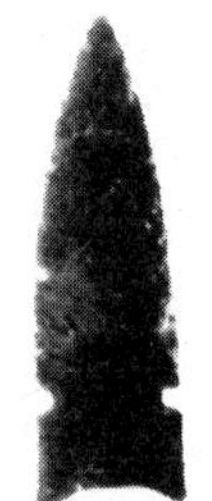

G6, $8-$10
Monterey Co., CA.

G6, $8-$15
Klamath Co., OR.

Serrated
edge

G9, $45-$90
CA.

G10, $60-$120
OR.

G10, $75-$150
OR.

DESERT GENERAL - Classic to Historic Phase, 700 - 200 B. P.

(Also see Bitterroot, Buffalo Gap, Cold Spring, Emigrant, Northern Side Notched & Wintu)

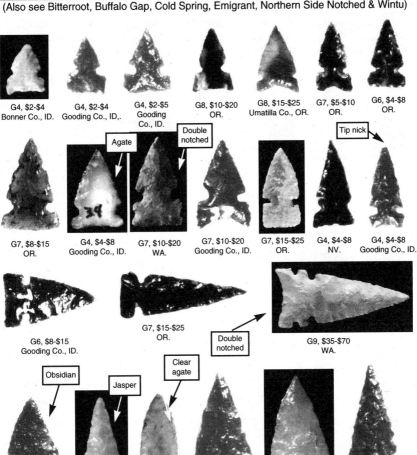

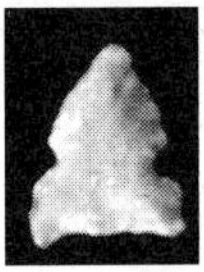

G4, $2-$4
Bonner Co., ID.

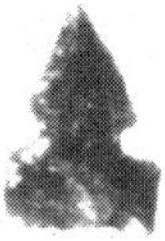

G4, $2-$4
Gooding Co., ID,.

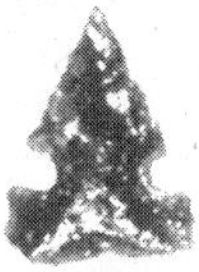

G4, $2-$5
Gooding
Co., ID.

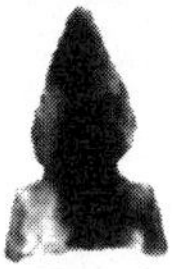

G8, $10-$20
OR.

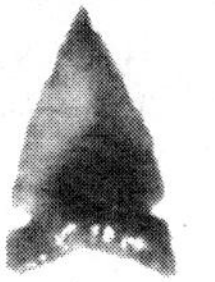

G8, $15-$25
Umatilla Co., OR.

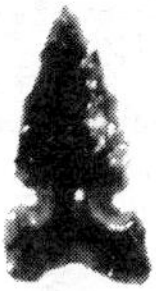

G7, $5-$10
OR.

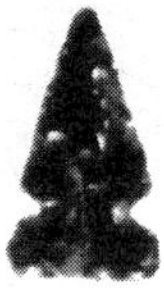

G6, $4-$8
OR.

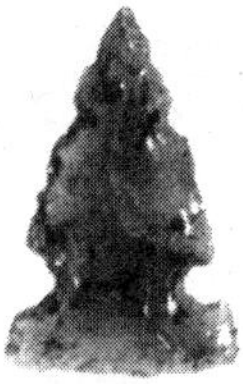

G7, $8-$15
OR.

Agate

G4, $4-$8
Gooding Co., ID.

Double
notched

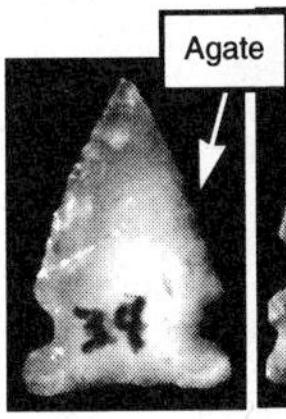

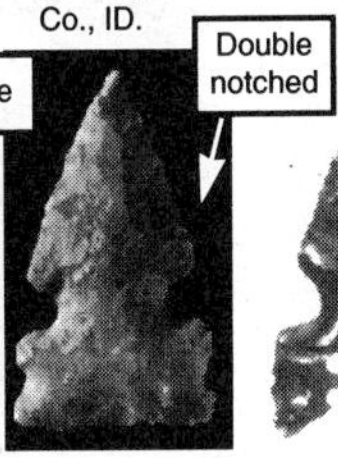

G7, $10-$20
WA.

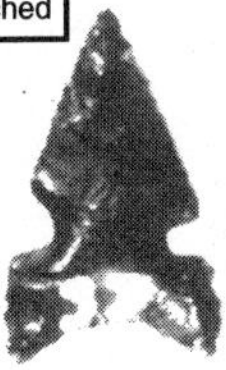

G7, $10-$20
Gooding Co., ID.

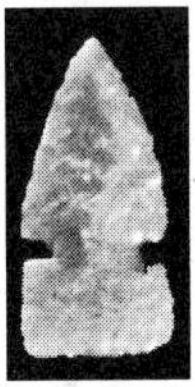

G7, $15-$25
OR.

G4, $4-$8
NV.

Tip nick

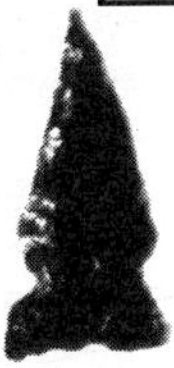

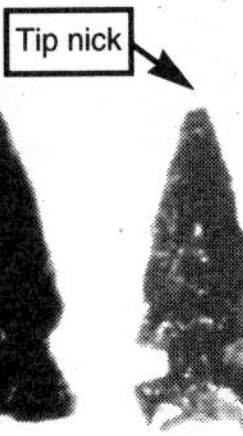

G4, $4-$8
Gooding Co., ID.

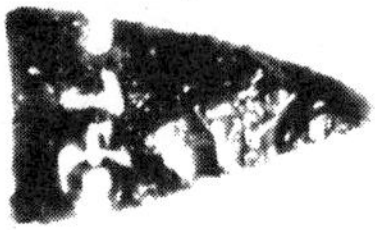

G6, $8-$15
Gooding Co., ID.

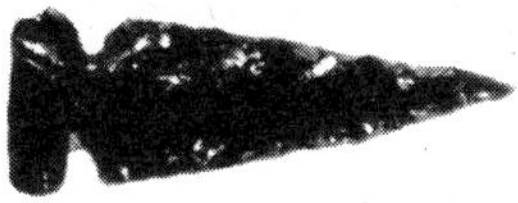

G7, $15-$25
OR.

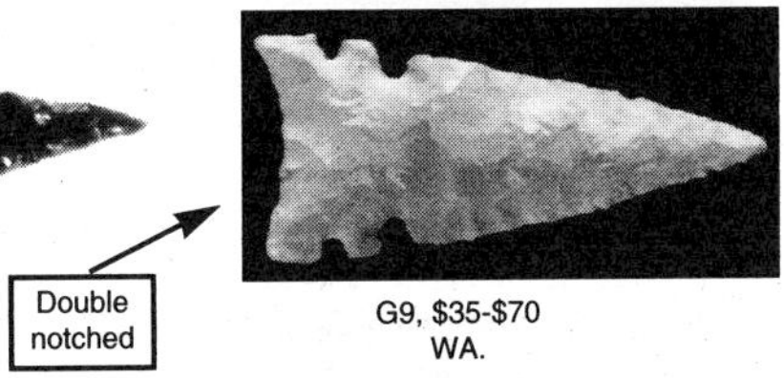

Double
notched

G9, $35-$70
WA.

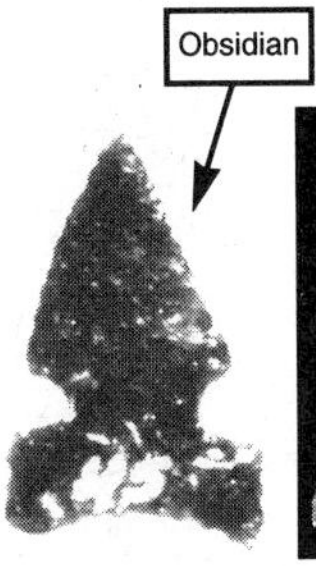

Obsidian

G8, $15-$30
Gooding Co., ID.

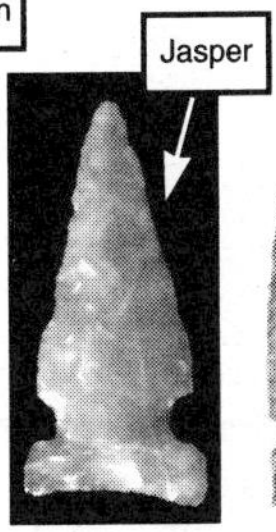

Jasper

G5, $8-$15
Bonner Co., ID.

Clear
agate

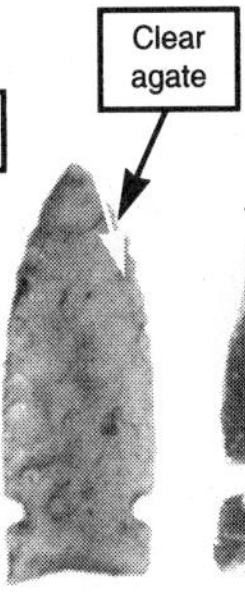

G10, $45-$90
OR.

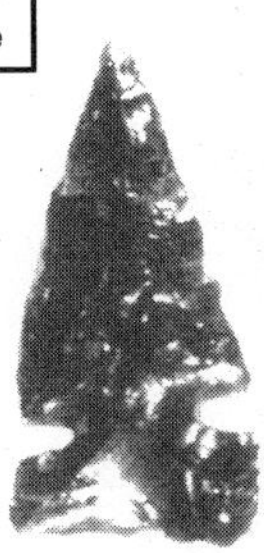

G5, $4-$8
Gooding Co., ID.

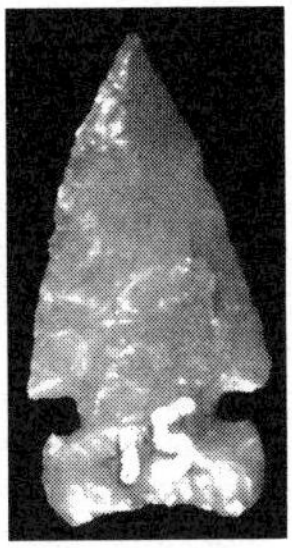

G8, $15-$25
Gooding Co., ID.

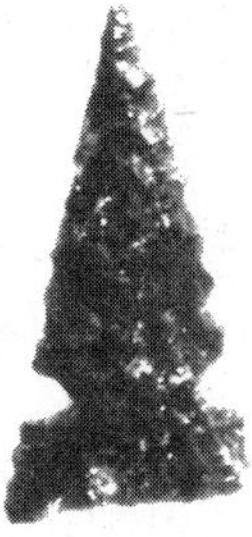

G6, $10-$20
Gooding Co., ID.

DESERT GENERAL (continued)

LOCATION: Great Basin westward. **DESCRIPTION:** A small, thin, side notched arrow point with a straight to slightly concave base. Blade edges can be serrated. Similar to the Reed point found in Oklahoma. Reported to have been used by the Shoshoni Indians of the historic period.

DESERT REDDING - Classic to Historic Phase, 700 - 200 B. P.

(Also see Bitterroot, Buffalo Gap, Cold Spring & Northern Side Notched)

G7, $5-$10
Twin Falls Co., ID.

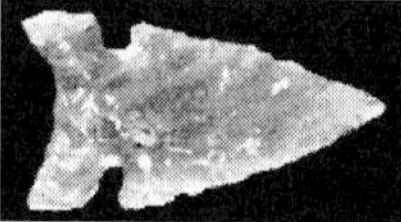

G8, $8-$15
Klamath Co., OR.

LOCATION: Great Basin westward. **DESCRIPTION:** A small, thin, side notched arrow point with a concave base. Blade edges curve into the base and can be serrated. Reported to have been used by the Shoshoni Indians of the historic period.

DESERT - SIERRA VARIETY - Classic to Historic Phase, 700 - 200 B. P.

(Also see Bitterroot, Buffalo Gap, Cold Spring and Northern Side Notched)

G6, $10-$15
WA.

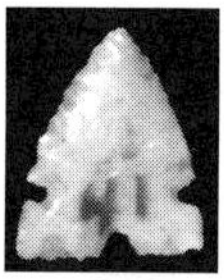

G6, $8-$10
NV.

G9, $15-$30
OR.

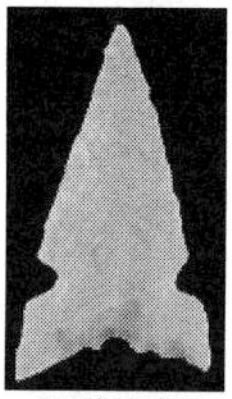

G9, $15-$30
Humboldt Co., NV.

Jasper

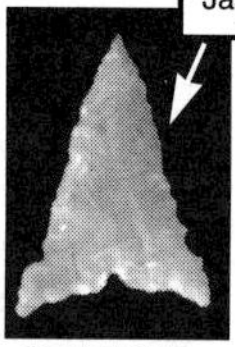

G8, $10-$20
Bonner Co., ID.

G4, $5-$10
Gooding Co., ID.

G8, $15-$30
SW NV.

G10, $65-$125
OR.

G7, $10-$20
Twin Falls Co., ID.

G8, $20-$40
Klamath Co., OR.

G4, $6-$10
Lake Co., OR.

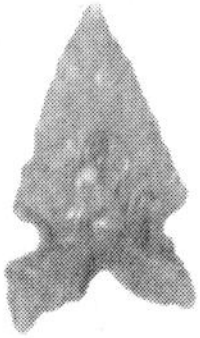

G4, $4-$8
OR.

G4, $5-$10
OR.

G5, $6-$10
Lake Co., OR.

Agate

G7, $10-$20
Reno, NV.

G3, $3-$6
UT.

G9, $65-$125
Twin Falls Co., ID.

G7, $20-$35
Klamath Co., OR.

G8, $25-$50
Warner Valley, OR.

G8, $35-$65
Twin Falls Co., ID.

LOCATION: Great Basin westward. **DESCRIPTION:** A small size, thin, triangular side and basal notched arrow point with destinctive basal pointed barbs and a basal notch. **I.D. KEY:** Triple notches, pointed basal corners.

DOUBLE TIP

(See Elko Eared and Wallula)

DRILL - Paleo to Historic Phase, 14,000 - 200 B. P.

(Also see Addison Micro-Drill)

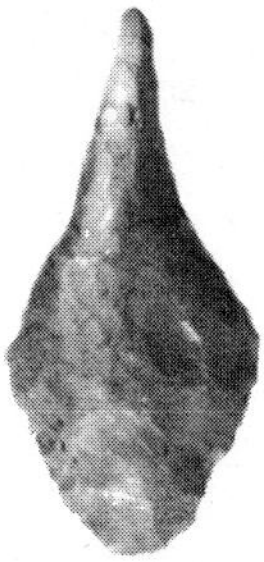

G3, $4-$8
St. Lawrence Isle, AK.

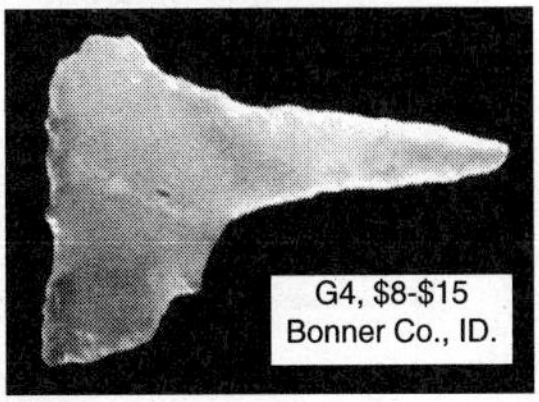

G4, $8-$15
Lane Co., OR.

G5, $8-$15
UT.

G5, $8-$15
OR.

G4, $8-$15
Bonner Co., ID.

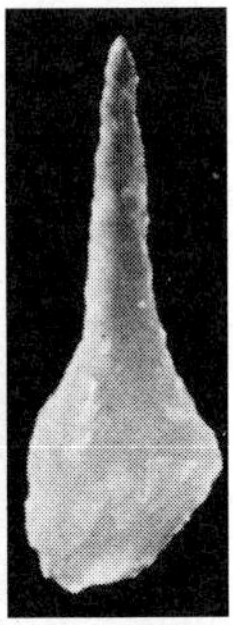

G5, $8-$15
Bonner Co., ID.

G4, $10-$10
WA.

G4, $10-$15
St. Lawrence Isle, AK.

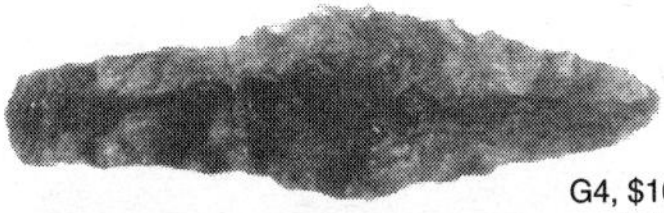

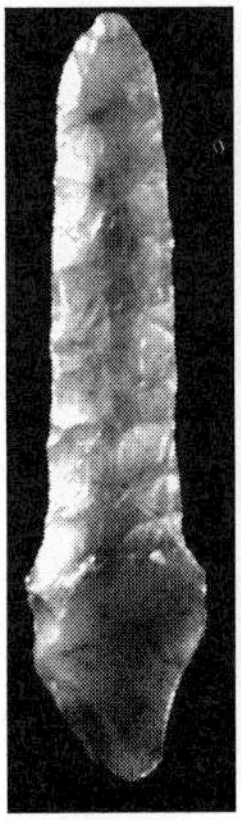

G5, $8-$15
Bonner Co., ID.

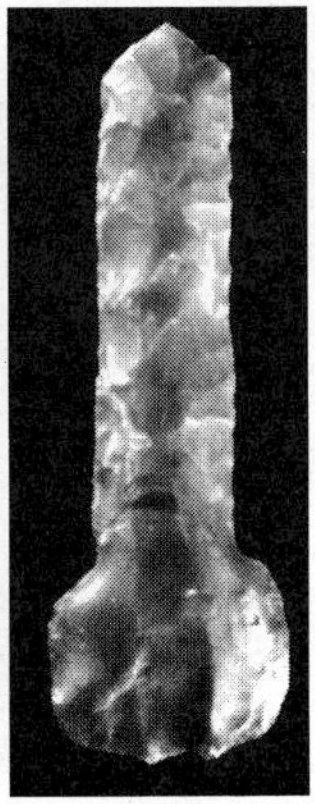

G7, $15-$30
Bonner Co., ID.

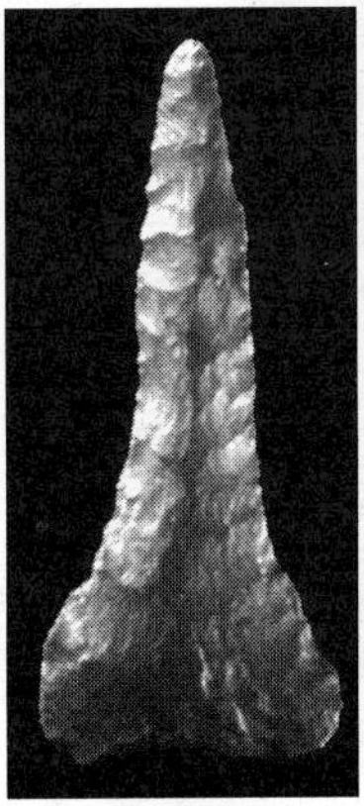

G6, $12-$20
Bonner Co., ID.

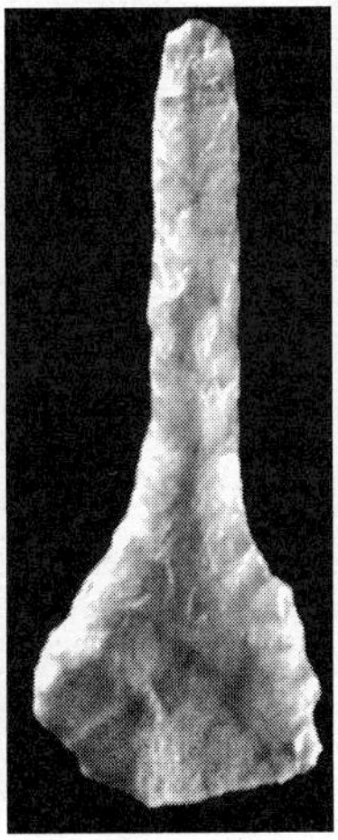

G7, $15-$30
Bonner Co., ID.

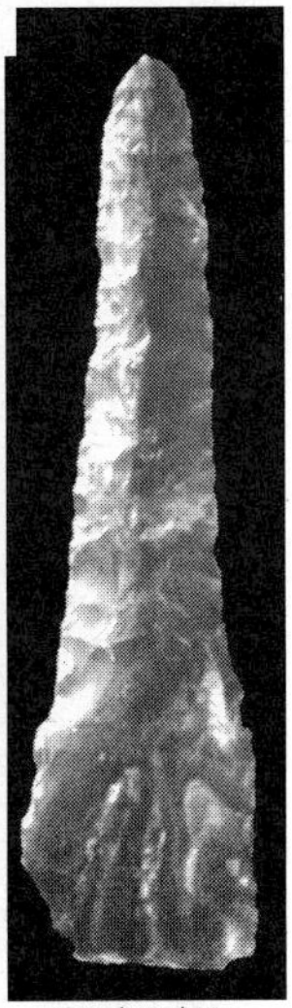

G6, $15-$30
Bonner Co., ID.

LOCATION: Everywhere. **DESCRIPTION:** Although many drills were made from scratch, all point types were made into the drill form. Usually, heavily resharpened and broken points were salvaged and rechipped into drills. These objects were certainly used as drills (evidence of extreme edge wear), but there is speculation that some of these forms may have been used as pins for clothing, ornaments, ear plugs and other uses.

EARLY EARED - Early to Middle Archaic, 8000 - 5000 B. P.

(Also see Early Stemmed , Pryor Stemmed)

G9, $100-$200
Black Rock Desert, NV.

LOCATION: Great Basin westward. **DESCRIPTION:** A medium size, thin, lanceolate point with broad, shallow side notches expanding into rounded ears that may be ground. The base is concave. **I.D. KEY:** Base form.

EARLY LEAF - Early to Middle Archaic, 8000 - 5000 B. P.

(Also see Cascade, Early Stemmed and Lerma)

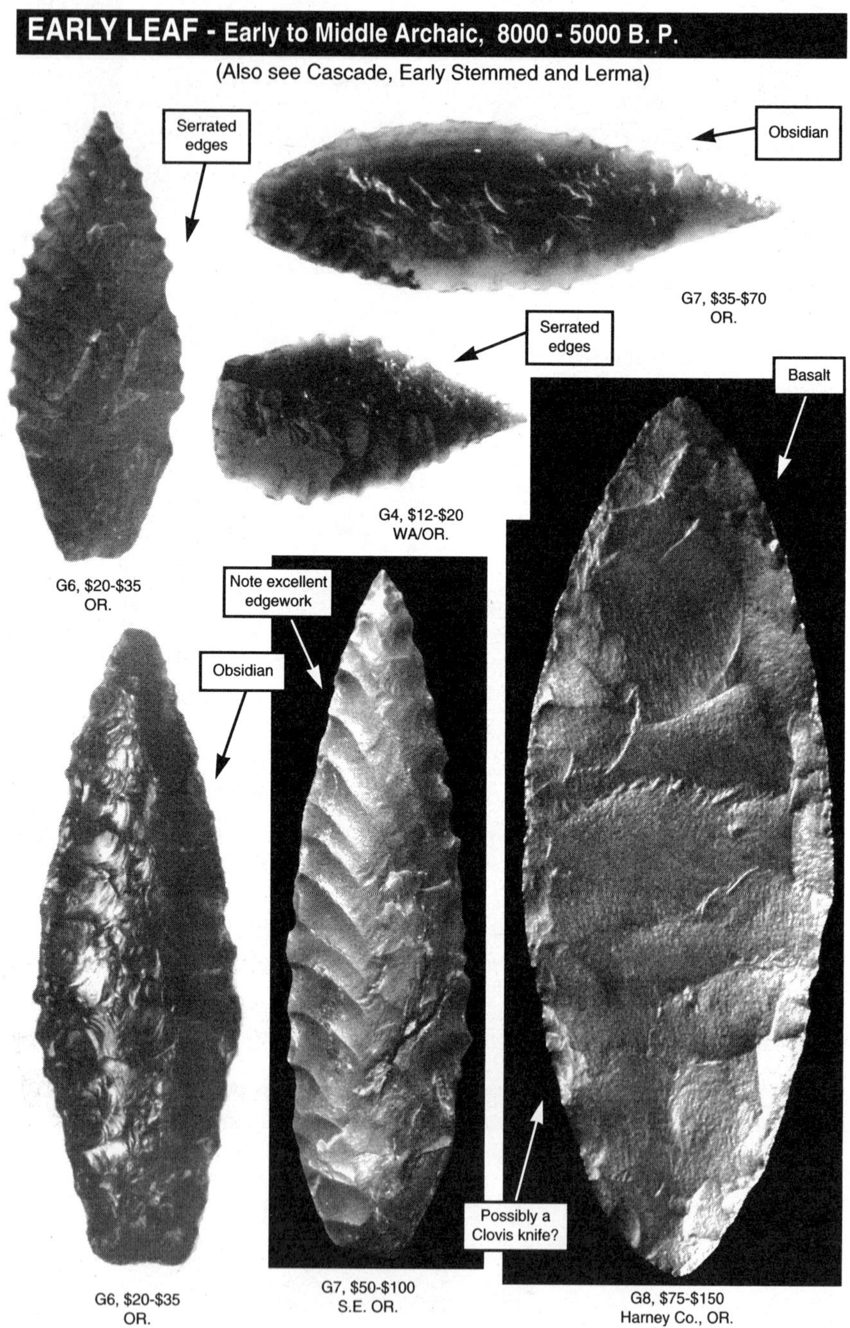

G7, $35-$70
OR.

G4, $12-$20
WA/OR.

G6, $20-$35
OR.

G6, $20-$35
OR.

G7, $50-$100
S.E. OR.

G8, $75-$150
Harney Co., OR.

EARLY LEAF (continued)

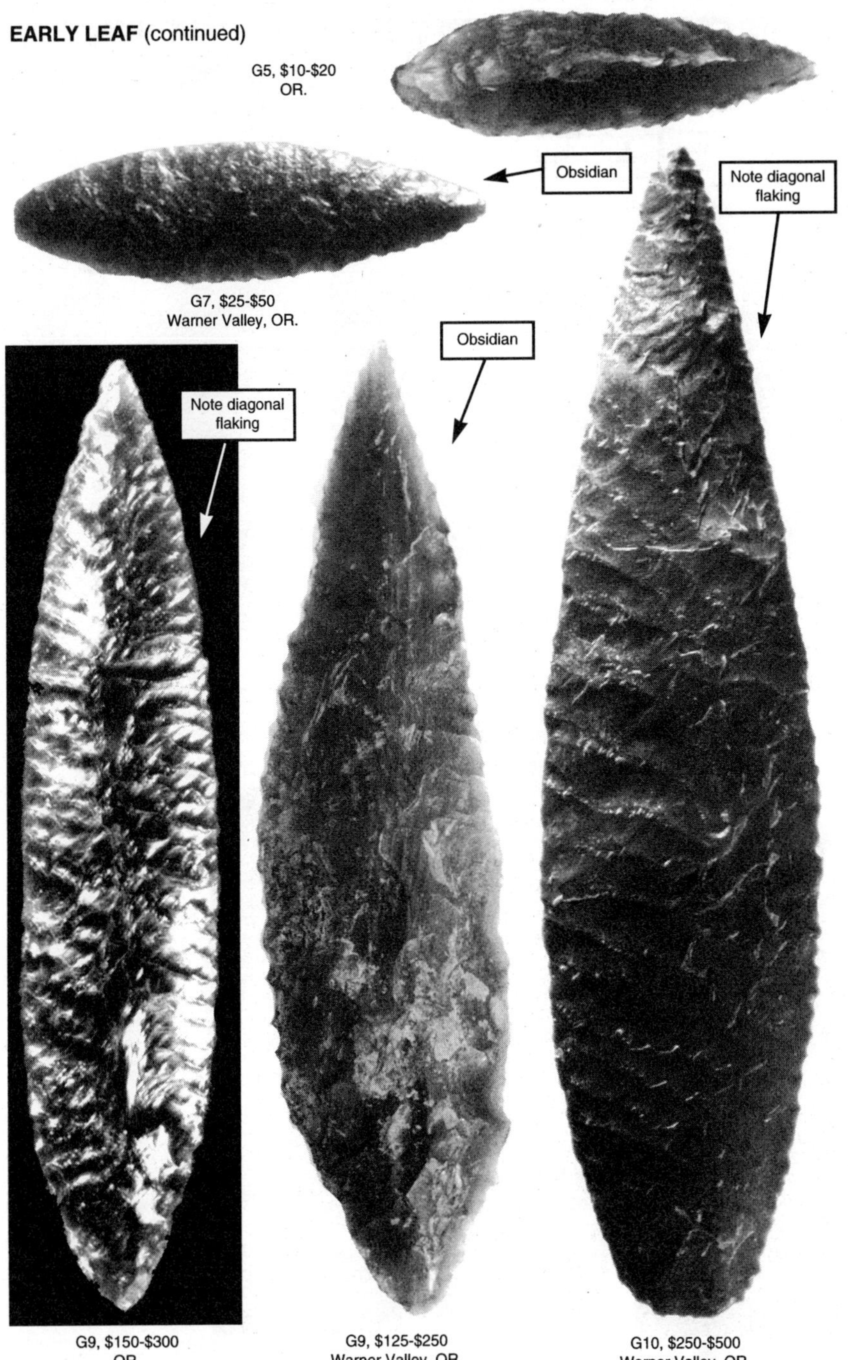

G5, $10-$20
OR.

G7, $25-$50
Warner Valley, OR.

G9, $150-$300
OR.

G9, $125-$250
Warner Valley, OR.

G10, $250-$500
Warner Valley, OR.

LOCATION: Great Basin to Washington. **DESCRIPTION:** A medium to large size lanceolate point with a convex or pointed base. Early parallel flaking is evident on most examples. These and the Early Stemmed haven't been officially named yet. Some could be early Cascade forms

EARLY STEMMED-LANCEOLATE - Early to Middle Archaic, 8000 - 5000 B. P.

(Also see Cascade, Early Leaf, Lind Coulee, Parma, Silver Lake, Windust)

Yellow jasper

Basal grinding

Clear obsidian

G7, $15-$30
Lake Co., OR.

G7, $25-$45
Deschutes Co., OR.

G6, $10-$20
Warner Valley, OR.

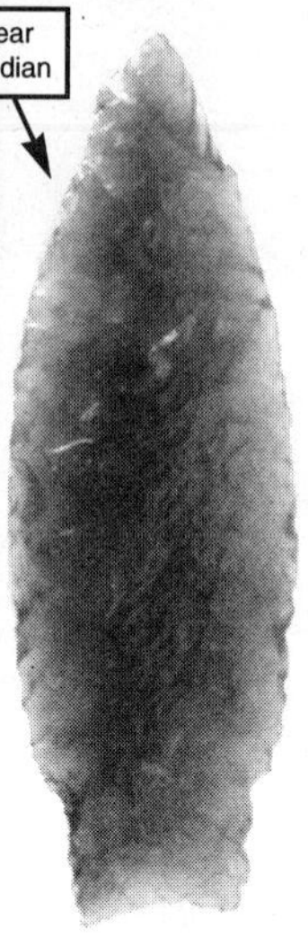

G6, $15-$30
Warner Valley, OR.

G7, $15-$30
Warner Valley, OR.

Diagonal flaking

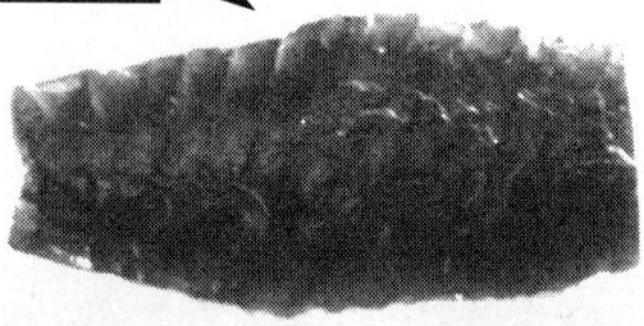

G1, $2-$4
Warner Valley, OR.
Broken back.

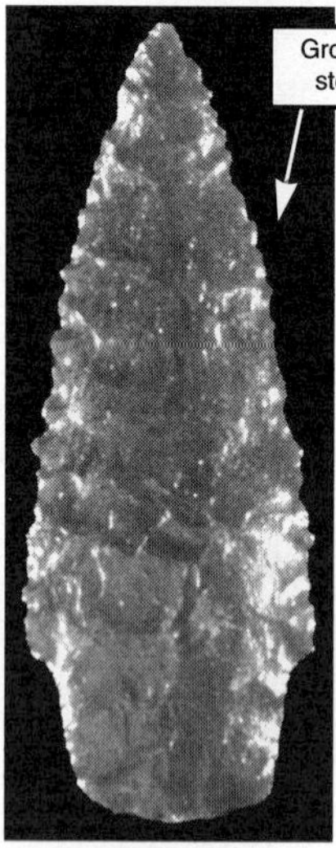

Ground stem

Obsidian

G8, $30-$60
Jefferson Co., OR.

G8, $30-$60
Deschutes Co., OR.

G7, $15-$30
Warner Valley, OR.

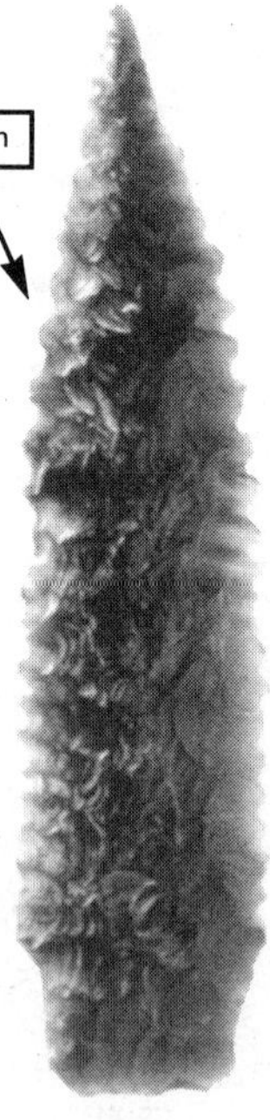

G9, $45-$85
Warner Valley, OR.

LOCATION: Northwestern states. **DESCRIPTION:** A medium to large size lanceolate point with weak, tapered shoulders and a parallel to contacting stem that can be convex to straight. Early parallel flaking is evident on most examples and stems are ground.

EASTGATE - Developmental to Classic Phase, 1400 - 400 B. P.

(Also see Columbia Plateau, Eastgate, Elko, Gunther, Rogue River, Rose Springs, Wallula)

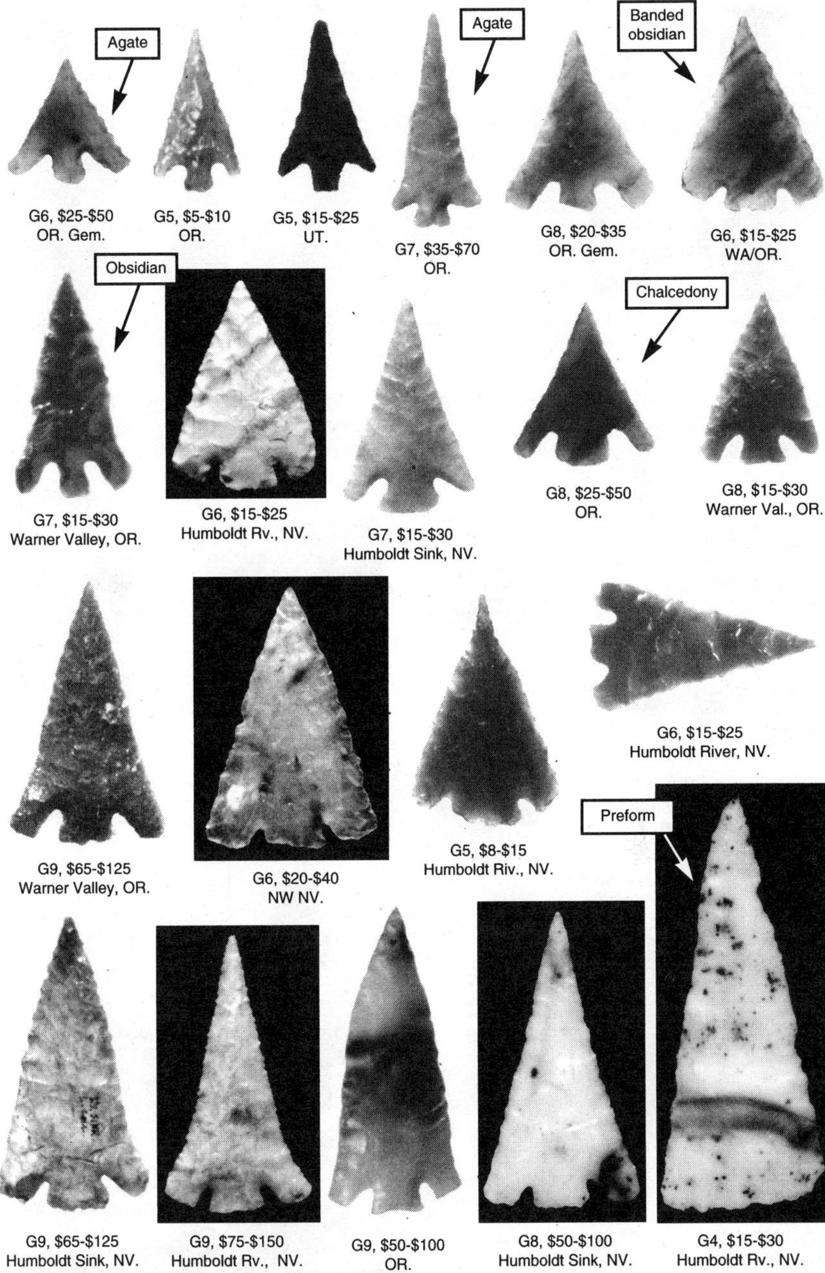

G6, $25-$50 OR. Gem.

G5, $5-$10 OR.

G5, $15-$25 UT.

G7, $35-$70 OR.

G8, $20-$35 OR. Gem.

G6, $15-$25 WA/OR.

G7, $15-$30 Warner Valley, OR.

G6, $15-$25 Humboldt Rv., NV.

G7, $15-$30 Humboldt Sink, NV.

G8, $25-$50 OR.

G8, $15-$30 Warner Val., OR.

G9, $65-$125 Warner Valley, OR.

G6, $20-$40 NW NV.

G5, $8-$15 Humboldt Riv., NV.

G6, $15-$25 Humboldt River, NV.

G9, $65-$125 Humboldt Sink, NV.

G9, $75-$150 Humboldt Rv., NV.

G9, $50-$100 OR.

G8, $50-$100 Humboldt Sink, NV.

G4, $15-$30 Humboldt Rv., NV.

LOCATION: Great Basin westward. **DESCRIPTION:** A small, thin, triangular corner-notched arrow point with a short parallel sided to expanded stem. Barbs can be pointed or squared and usually extend to base.

EASTGATE (continued)

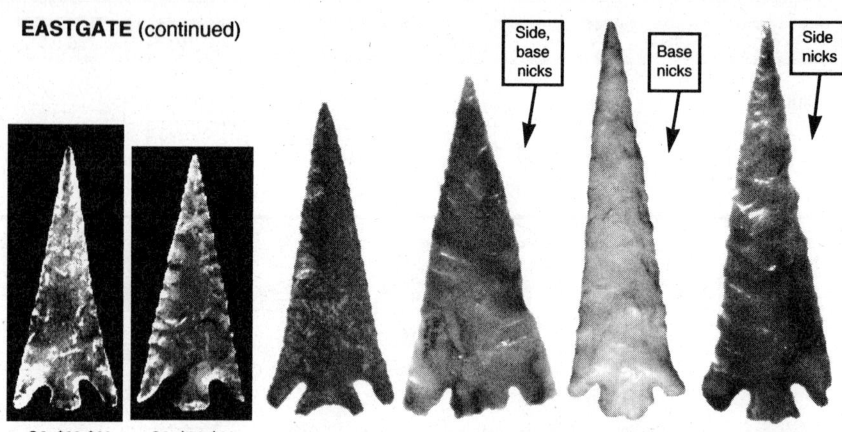

G8, $30-$60
WA/OR.

G8, $30-$60
WA/OR.

G8, $35-$70
Warner Val., OR.

Side, base nicks

G5, $20-$40
Humboldt Rv., NV.

Base nicks

G6, $25-$50
Warner Val., OR.

Side nicks

G5, $20-$40
Washoe Lake, NV.

EASTGATE SPLIT STEM - Developmental to Classic Phase, 1400 - 400 B. P.

(Also see Columbia Plateau, Rogue River, Wallula)

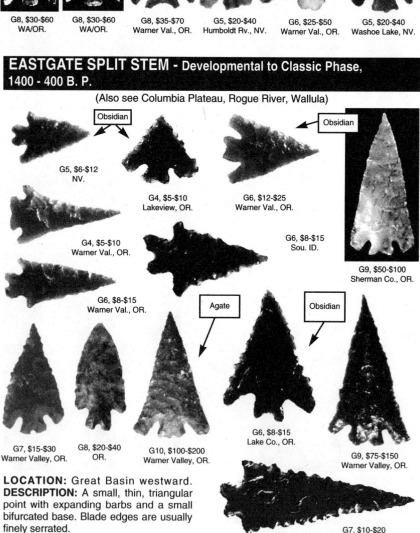

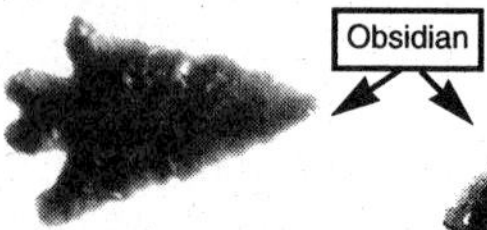

Obsidian

G5, $6-$12
NV.

G4, $5-$10
Lakeview, OR.

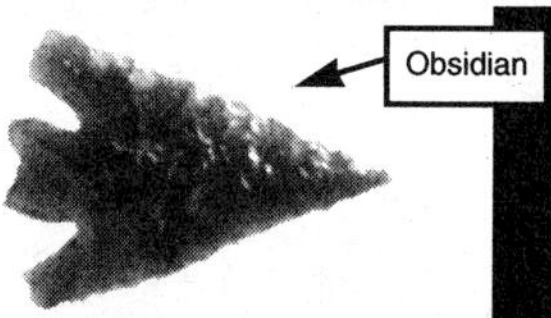

Obsidian

G6, $12-$25
Warner Val., OR.

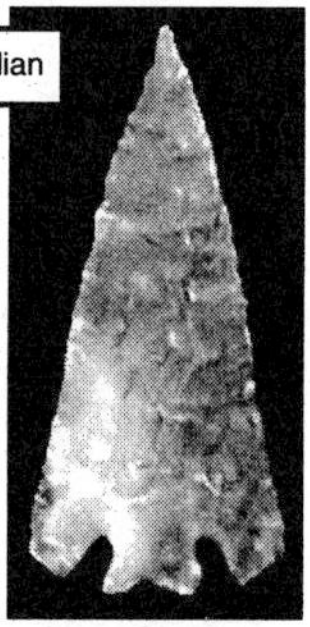

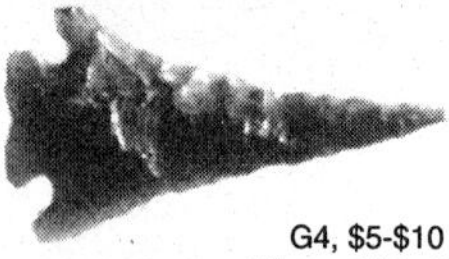

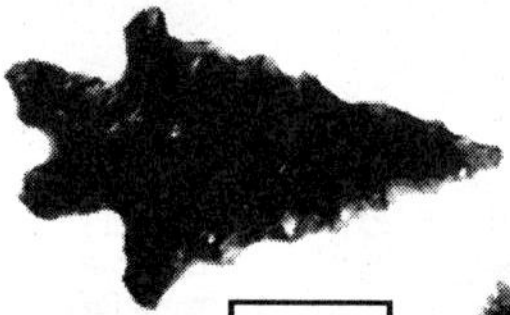

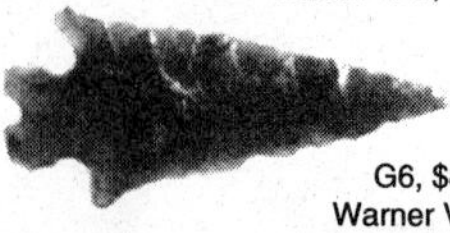

G9, $50-$100
Sherman Co., OR.

G4, $5-$10
Warner Val., OR.

G6, $8-$15
Sou. ID.

G6, $8-$15
Warner Val., OR.

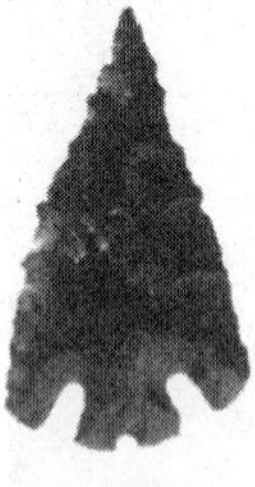

G7, $15-$30
Warner Valley, OR.

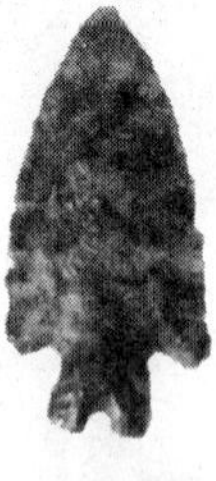

G8, $20-$40
OR.

Agate

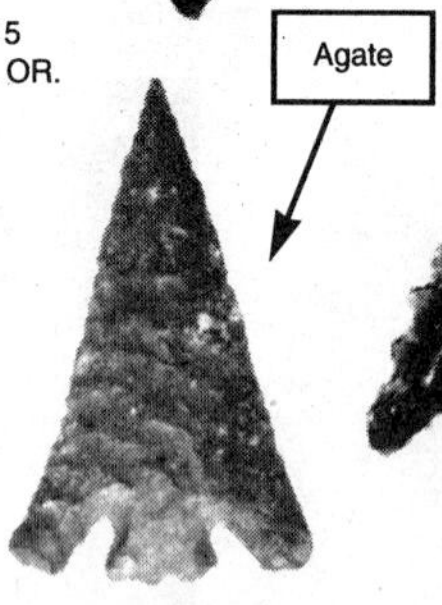

G10, $100-$200
Warner Valley, OR.

Obsidian

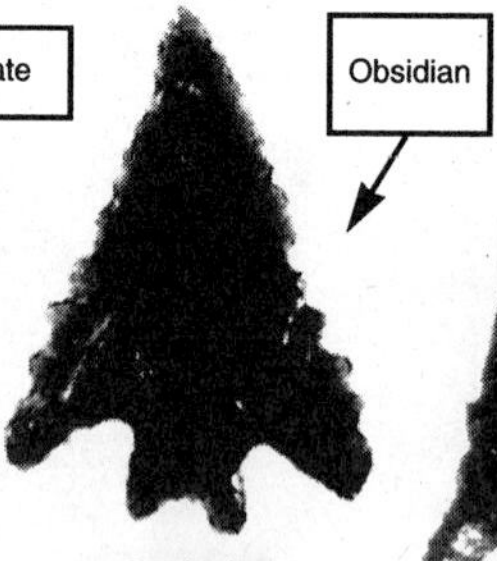

G6, $8-$15
Lake Co., OR.

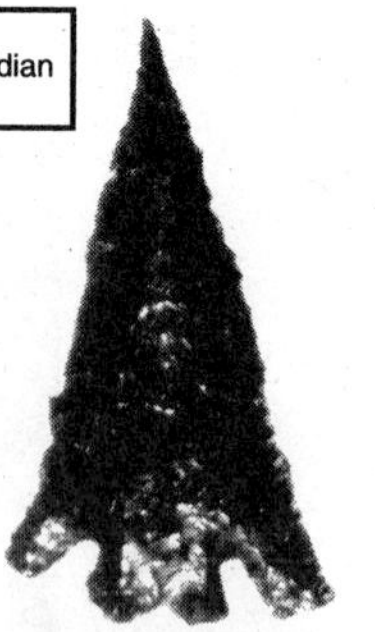

G9, $75-$150
Warner Valley, OR.

LOCATION: Great Basin westward. **DESCRIPTION:** A small, thin, triangular point with expanding barbs and a small bifurcated base. Blade edges are usually finely serrated.

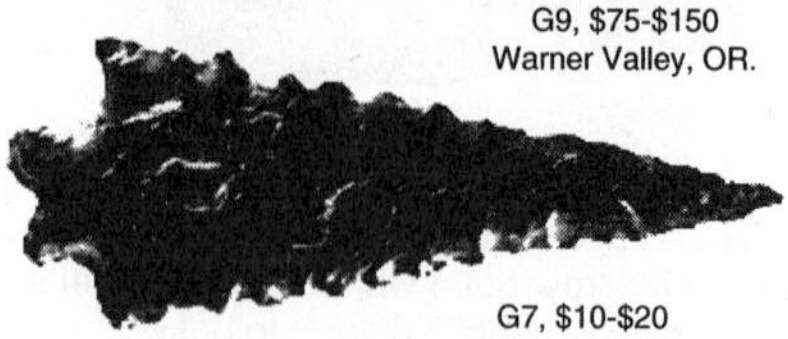

G7, $10-$20
Lake Co., OR.

EDEN (See Cody Complex)

ELKO - Middle Archaic to Developmental Phase, 3500 - 1200 B. P.

(Also see Hell's Canyon, Mummy Cave, Quillomene Bar and Rose Springs)

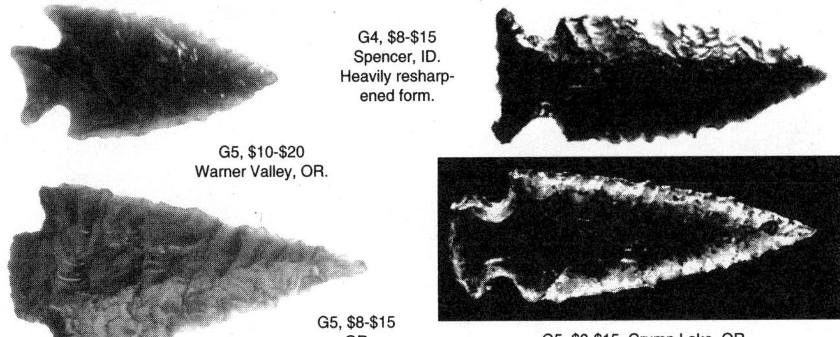

G4, $8-$15
Spencer, ID.
Heavily resharpened form.

G5, $10-$20
Warner Valley, OR.

G5, $8-$15
OR.

G5, $8-$15, Crump Lake, OR.

LOCATION: Great Basin westward. **DESCRIPTION:** A medium to large size, narrow, stemmed to side notched point with convex to straight sides. Bases are parallel to bulbous. Blade edges are usually serrated.

ELKO CORNER NOTCHED - Middle Archaic to Developmental Phase, 3500 - 1200 B. P.

(Also see Columbia Plateau, Eastgate & Hell's Canyon)

G8, $10-$20
OR.

G6, $5-$10
Gooding Co., ID.

G9, $30-$60
Clearwater Co., ID.

G5, $5-$10
NV.

G6, $8-$15
Gooding Co., ID.

G6, $10-$20
Gooding Co., ID.

Obsidian

Basalt

G7, $15-$25
Storey Co., NV.

G6, $8-$15
Gooding Co., ID.

G6, $15-$25
Gooding Co., ID.

G6, $10-$20
OR.

G4, $10-$20
Gooding Co., ID.

Obsidian

Obsidian

G4, $6-$12
Warner Val., OR.

G9, $30-$60
Warner Val., OR.

G9, $30-$60
Warner Valley, OR.

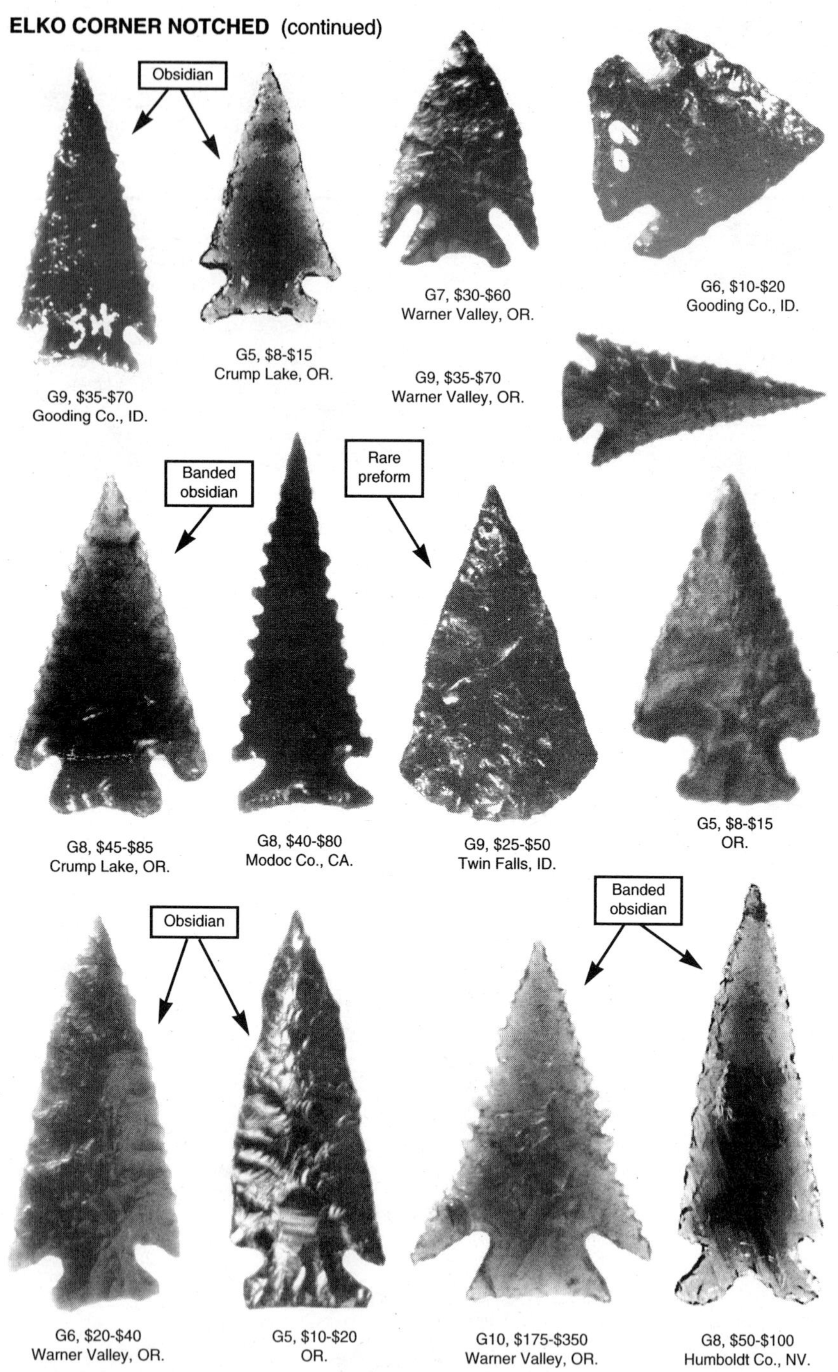

G9, $35-$70
Gooding Co., ID.

G5, $8-$15
Crump Lake, OR.

G7, $30-$60
Warner Valley, OR.

G6, $10-$20
Gooding Co., ID.

G9, $35-$70
Warner Valley, OR.

G8, $45-$85
Crump Lake, OR.

G8, $40-$80
Modoc Co., CA.

G9, $25-$50
Twin Falls, ID.

G5, $8-$15
OR.

G6, $20-$40
Warner Valley, OR.

G5, $10-$20
OR.

G10, $175-$350
Warner Valley, OR.

G8, $50-$100
Humboldt Co., NV.

LOCATION: Great Basin westward. **DESCRIPTION:** A small to large size, thin, corner notched dart point with shoulder tangs and a convex, concave or auriculate base. Shoulders and tips are sharp. Some examples exhibit excellent parallel flaking on blade edges.

ELKO CORNER NOTCHED (continued)

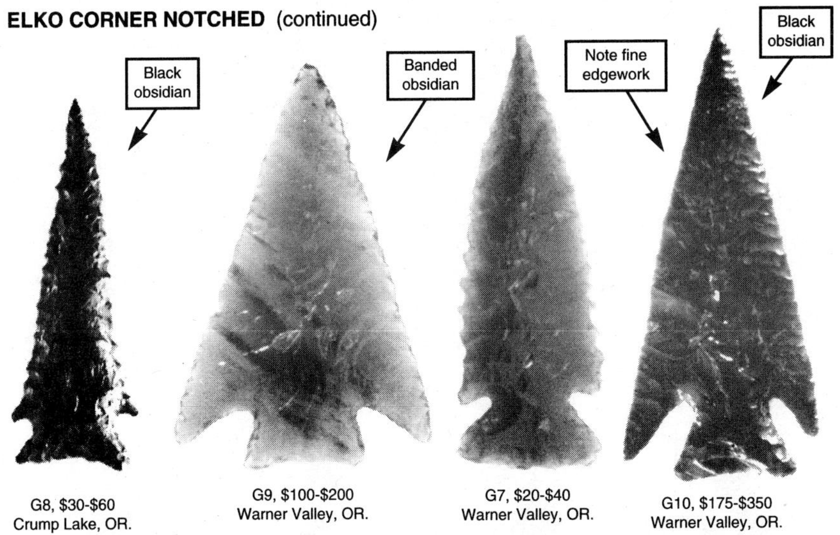

G8, $30-$60
Crump Lake, OR.

G9, $100-$200
Warner Valley, OR.

G7, $20-$40
Warner Valley, OR.

G10, $175-$350
Warner Valley, OR.

ELKO EARED - Middle Archaic to Developmental Phase, 3500 - 1200 B. P.

(Also see Eastgate and Elko Corner Notched)

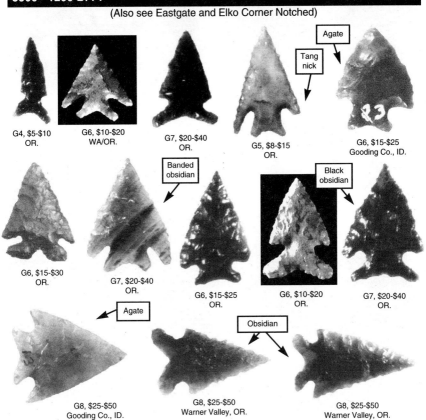

Tang nick

Agate

G4, $5-$10
OR.

G6, $10-$20
WA/OR.

G7, $20-$40
OR.

G5, $8-$15
OR.

G6, $15-$25
Gooding Co., ID.

Banded obsidian

Black obsidian

G6, $15-$30
OR.

G7, $20-$40
OR.

G6, $15-$25
OR.

G6, $10-$20
OR.

G7, $20-$40
OR.

Agate

Obsidian

G8, $25-$50
Gooding Co., ID.

G8, $25-$50
Warner Valley, OR.

G8, $25-$50
Warner Valley, OR.

ELKO EARED (continued)

G8, $35-$70
Warner Valley, OR.

G8, $40-$75
Warner Valley, OR.

G8, $35-$70
Warner Valley, OR.

G8, $25-$50
Warner Valley, OR.

G9, $75-$150
Warner Valley, OR.

G8, $35-$70
Modoc Co., CA.

G9, $100-$200
Warner Valley, OR.

G10, $150-$300
Lake Co., OR.

G10, $150-$300
Lake Co., OR.

G9, $90-$175
Warner Valley, OR.

G10, $140-$275
Warner Valley, OR.

G10, $200-$400
Reno, NV.

LOCATION: Great Basin westward. **DESCRIPTION:** A small to large size corner notched point with shoulder tangs and an eared base. Basal ears are usually exaggerated, and corners and tips are sharp. Some examples exhibit excellent parallel flaking on blade edges.

ELKO EARED (continued)

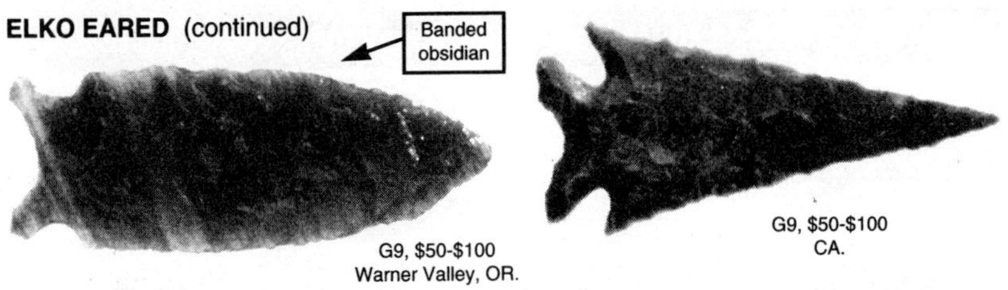

G9, $50-$100
Warner Valley, OR.

G9, $50-$100
CA.

ELKO SPLIT STEM - Middle Archaic to Developmental Phase, 3500 - 1200 B. P.

(Also see Eastgate, Elko Corner Notched and Elko Eared)

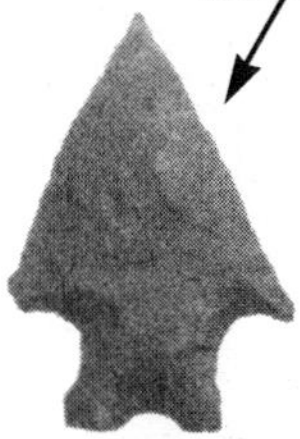

Basalt

G3, $5-$10
OR.

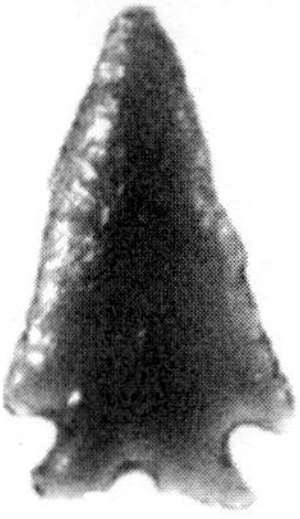

G5, $6-$12
OR.

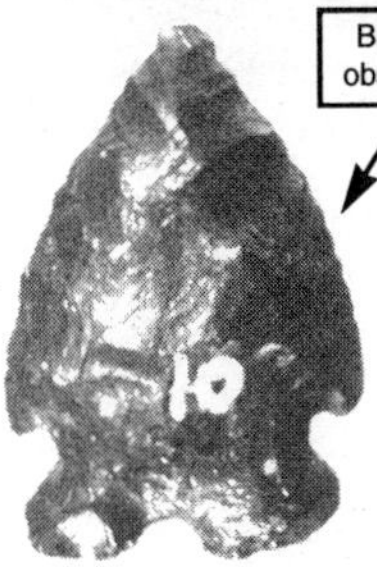

Brown
obsidian

G6, $10-$20
Gooding Co., ID.

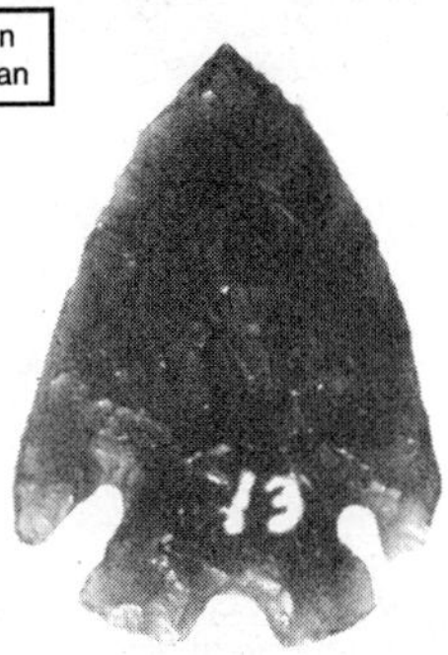

G8, $35-$65
Gooding Co., ID.

Unusual
base form

G6, $20-$35
Goose Lake, CA.

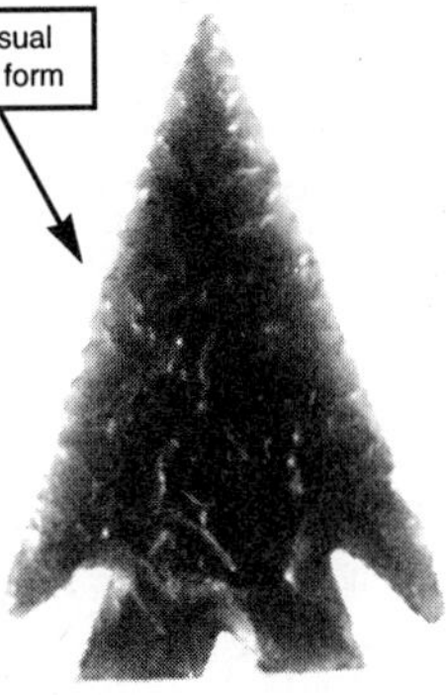

G10, $125-$250
Crump Lake, OR.

G8, $15-$25
Crump Lake, OR.

G6, $20-$35
Goose Lake, CA.

Purple agate

G10, $150-$300
Lake Co., OR.

G8, $30-$60
OR.

LOCATION: Great Basin westward. **DESCRIPTION:** A small to large size corner notched point with shoulder tangs and a short base that is bifurcated. Shoulders are rounded to sharp. Some examples exhibit excellent parallel flaking on blade edges. Believed to have evolved from the earlier Gatcliff point.

EXOTIC FORMS - Late Archaic to Developmental, 3000 - 1000 B. P.

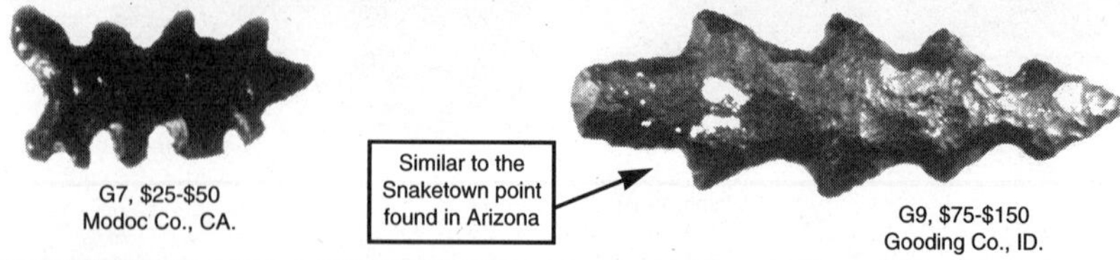

G7, $25-$50
Modoc Co., CA.

G9, $75-$150
Gooding Co., ID.

LOCATION: Everywhere. **DESCRIPTION:** The forms illustrated are rare. Some are definitely effigy forms or exotic point designs while others may be no more than unfinished and unintentional dodles.

FIRSTVIEW - Late Paleo, 8700 - 8000 B. P.

(Also see Alberta, Cody Complex)

G7, $300-$600
Massacre Lake, NV.

LOCATION: Great Basin into the Plains states. **DESCRIPTION:** A medium to large size lanceolate point with slight shoulders and a rectangular stem that is ground. Shoulders are sometimes absent from resharpening. Most examples exhibit excellent parallel transverse flaking. A variant form of the Scottsbluff type made by the Cody Complex people. I.D. KEY: Weak shoulders, diamond shaped cross-section.

GATECLIFF - Middle to Late Archaic, 5000 - 3000 B. P.

(Also see Eastgate, Pismo, Rabbit Island)

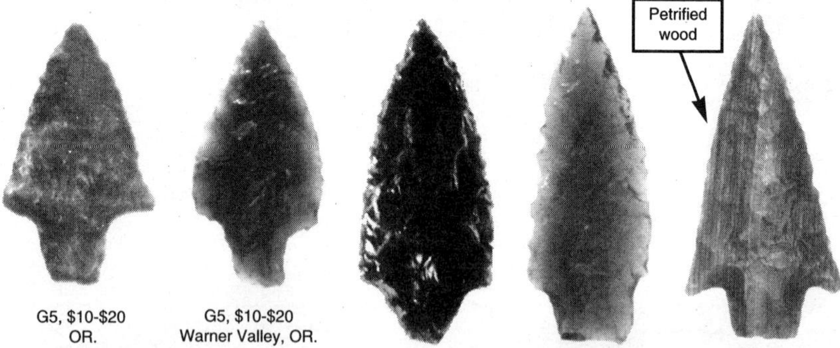

G5, $10-$20
OR.

G5, $10-$20
Warner Valley, OR.

G4, $10-$18
Black Rock Desert, NV.

G6, $12-$20
Warner Val., OR.

G10, $65-$125
OR. Gem.

LOCATION: Great Basin westward. **DESCRIPTION:** A medium to large size stemmed dart point that occurs in two forms. One form has a contracted base and barbed shoulders. The second form has a contracted base that is bifurcated or deeply concave and shoulder barbs. Believed to evolve into Elko points.

G7, $15-$25
Warner Valley, OR.

G6, $20-$40
Black Rock Desert, NV.

G6, $10-$20
Fort Hall, ID.

G8, $30-$60
Warner Valley, OR.

G10, $100-$200
Warner Valley, OR.

GOLD HILL - Developmental to Historic Phase, 800 - 200 B. P.

(Also see Canalino)

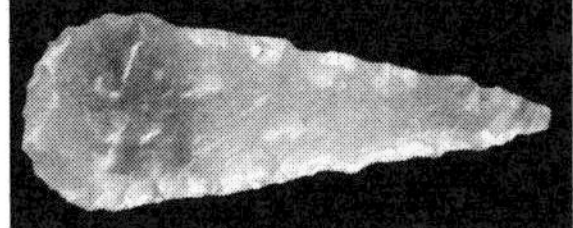
G6, $8-$15
Coquille Riv., OR.

LOCATION: Oregon. **DESCRIPTION:** A small to medium size lanceolate point with a rounded base. Similar in form to Canalino found in southern California.

GRAVER - Paleo to Archaic, 14,000 - 4000 B. P.

(Also see Drill and Scraper)

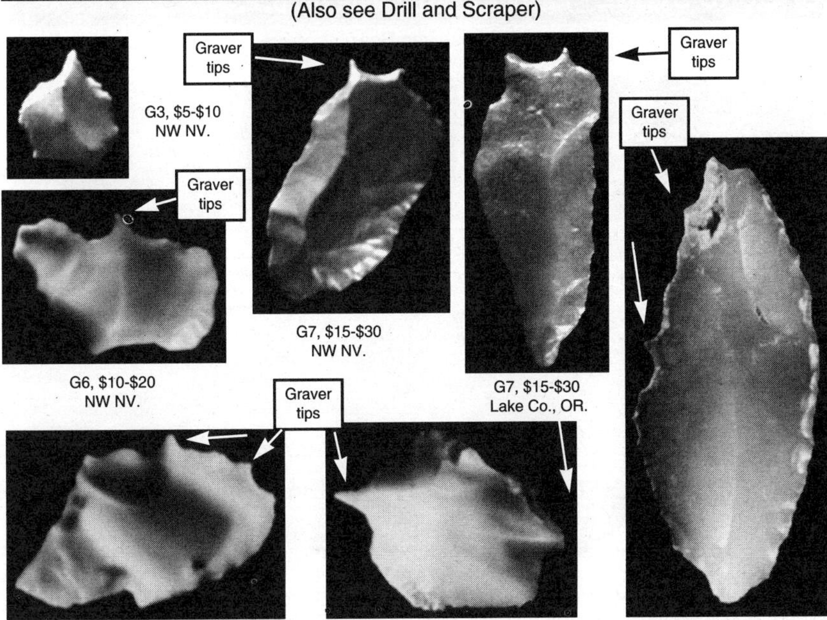

G3, $5-$10
NW NV.

G7, $15-$30
NW NV.

G6, $10-$20
NW NV.

G7, $15-$30
Lake Co., OR.

G6, $15-$25
NW NV.

G5, $8-$15
NW NV.

G8, $20-$40
Lake Co., OR.

GRAVER (continued)

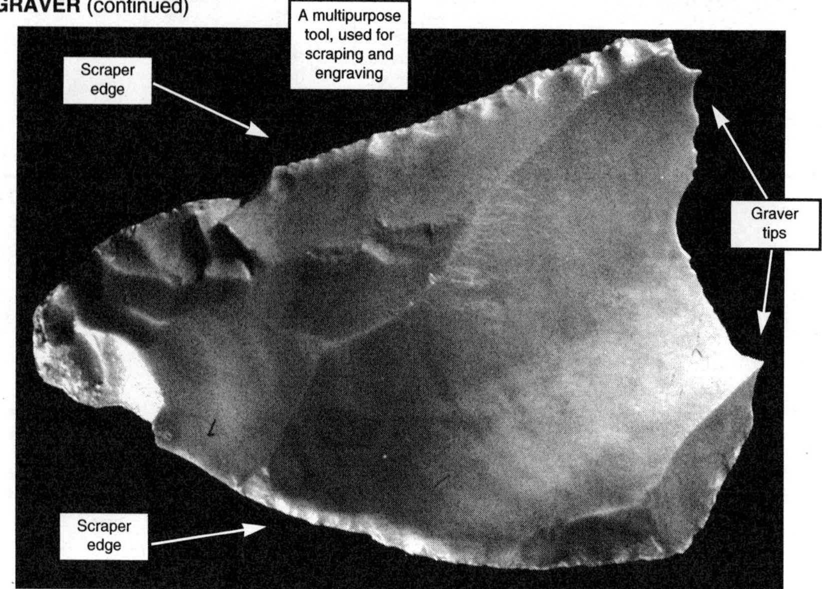

G10, $45-$90
Lake Co., OR., Alkali Lake.

LOCATION: Paleo and Archaic sites everywhere. **DESCRIPTION:** An irregular shaped uniface tool with sharp, pointed projections used for puncturing, incising, tattooing, etc. Some examples served a dual purpose for scraping as well. Gravers have been found on *Black Rock Concave* sites in the Great Basin.

GROUND STONE - Historic Phase, 300 - 100 B. P.

(Also see Bear)

G4, $10-$20
AK.

G5, $15-$25
AK.

G6, $30-$60
AK.

LOCATION: Alaska. **DESCRIPTION:** A medium to large size, stemmed point made from stone. Some examples have a median ridge running along the center of the blade. These points were probably used as harpoons by the Eskimos along the coastal waters.

GROUND STONE (continued)

G8, $40-$75
AK.

GUNTHER - Developmental to Historic Phase, 1000 - 200 B. P.

(Also see Columbia Plateau, Deadman, Molalla and Wallula)

Tip nick

Green agate

G6, $25-$40
OR.

G6, $20-$35
SW OR.

G9, $75-$150
OR.

G9, $75-$150
OR.

G9, $75-$150
OR.

Petrified wood

G8, $50-$100
OR.

G8, $35-$70
OR.

G7, $45-$90
OR.

G6, $20-$35
OR.

G9, $125-$250
OR.

G9, $100-$200, OR.

G10, $125-$250
OR.

G9, $75-$150
OR.

G9, $75-$150
OR.

G9, $80-$160
OR.

G9, $85-$170
OR.

G10, $150-$300
OR.

G9, $100-$200
OR.

G9, $100-$200
SW OR.

GUNTHER (continued)

LOCATION: Great Basin westward. **DESCRIPTION:** A small to medium size, thin, broad, triangular point with long barbs that extend to and beyond the base. The blade sides are straight to concave and the stem is parallel sided to slightly contracting or expanding. These points exhibit high quality flaking. Other local names used for this type are "Camas Valley," "Mad River," "Molalla," "Roger River," and "Shasta."

GUNTHER TRIANGULAR - Developmental to Historic Phase, 1000 - 200 B. P.

(Also see Cottonwood)

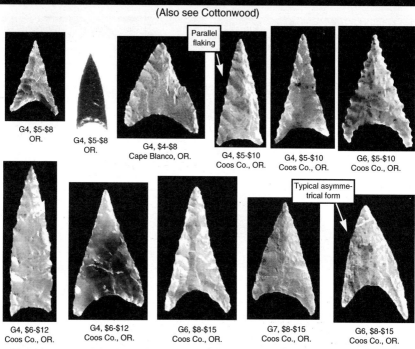

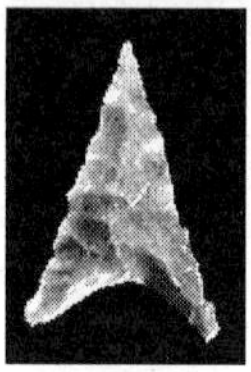

Parallel flaking

G4, $5-$8
OR.

G4, $5-$8
OR.

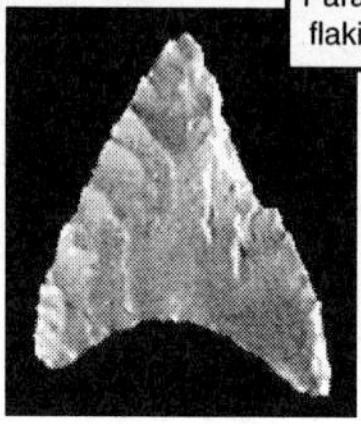

G4, $4-$8
Cape Blanco, OR.

G4, $5-$10
Coos Co., OR.

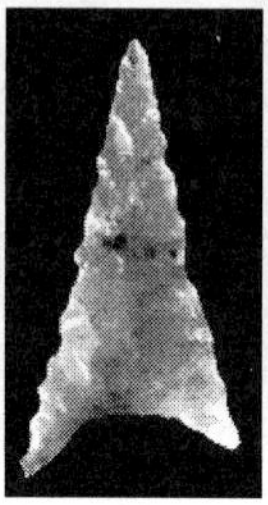

G4, $5-$10
Coos Co., OR.

G6, $5-$10
Coos Co., OR.

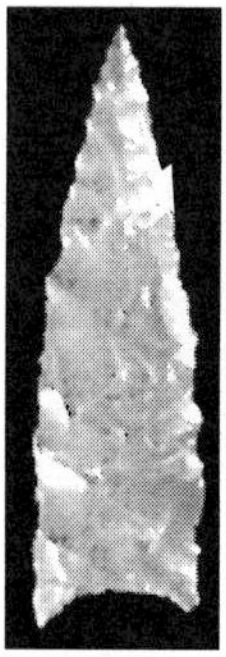

Typical asymmetrical form

G4, $6-$12
Coos Co., OR.

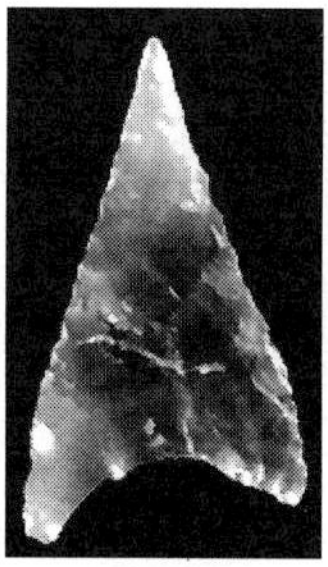

G4, $6-$12
Coos Co., OR.

G6, $8-$15
Coos Co., OR.

G7, $8-$15
Coos Co., OR.

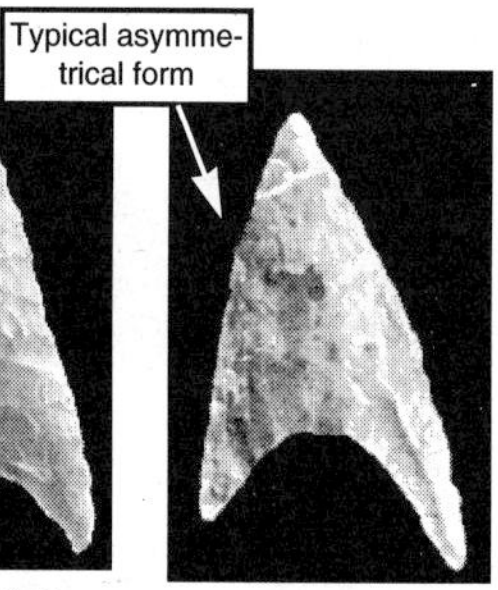

G6, $8-$15
Coos Co., OR.

LOCATION: Great Basin westward. **DESCRIPTION:** A small to medium size, thin, triangular point with basal barbs that can be asymmetrical with one longer than the other. The basal ears have a tendency to turn in towards the base which is concave. Early forms are called U-Back locally.

HAFTED KNIFE -Transitional-Historic Phase, 2300 - 500 B. P.

(Also see Hafted Knife in Northern High Plains section)

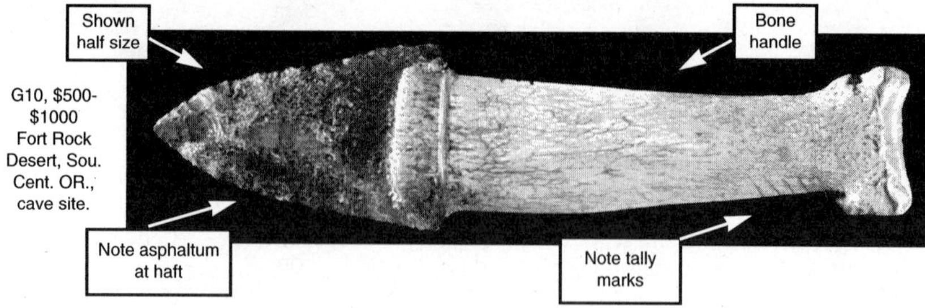

G10, $500-$1000
Fort Rock Desert, Sou. Cent. OR., cave site.

HAFTED KNIFE (continued)

LOCATION: Great Basin westward. **DESCRIPTION:** Due to the dry climate in this region, completely hafted arrows and knives have been found in dry caves. The above example has a flaked stone blade glued with asphaltum and lashed on the bone handle. Sinew, gut and rawhide were used for lashing as well as fibers from hair and plants (grasses, tree bark, yucca, vines, etc.).

HASKETT - Late Paleo, 10,000 - 9000 B. P.

(Also see Cougar Mountain, Cascade and Humboldt)

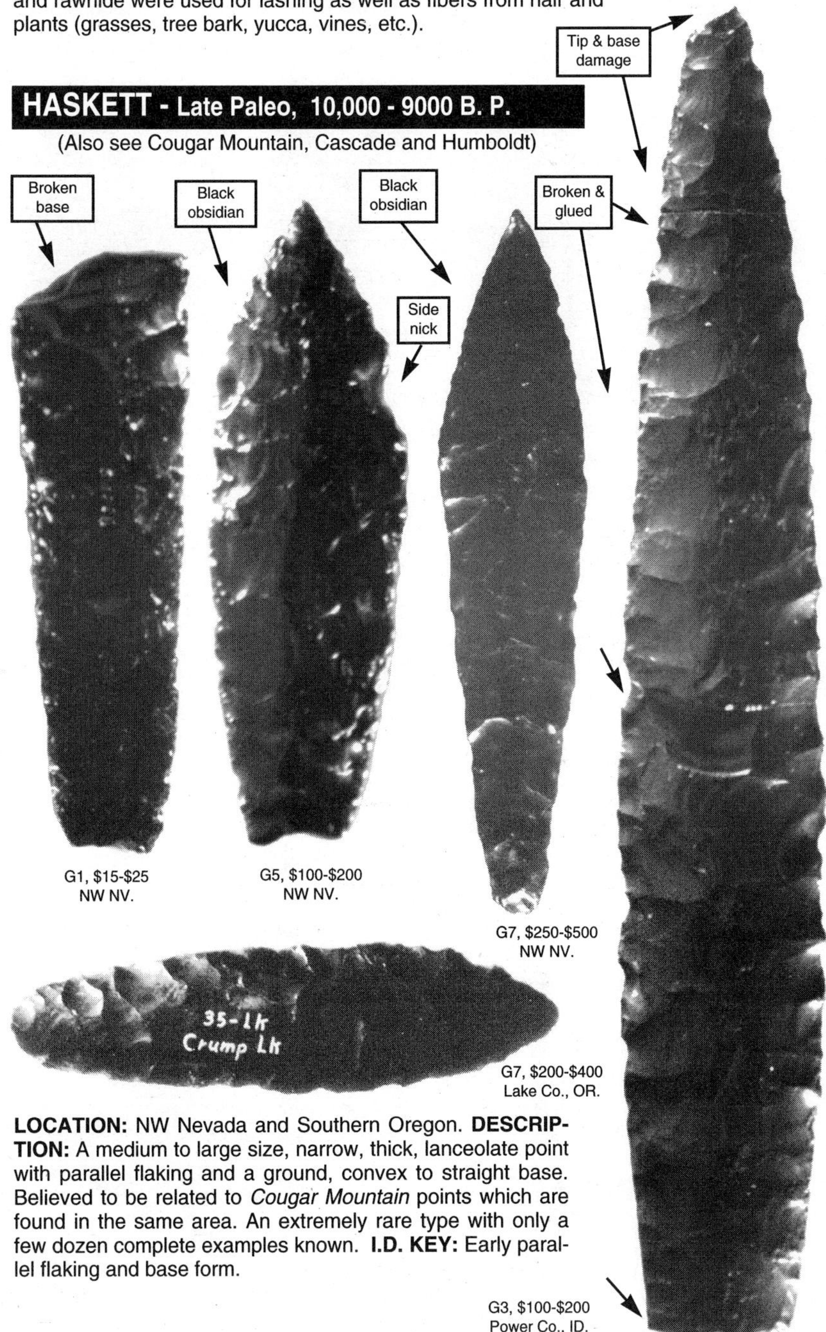

G1, $15-$25
NW NV.

G5, $100-$200
NW NV.

G7, $250-$500
NW NV.

G7, $200-$400
Lake Co., OR.

LOCATION: NW Nevada and Southern Oregon. **DESCRIPTION:** A medium to large size, narrow, thick, lanceolate point with parallel flaking and a ground, convex to straight base. Believed to be related to *Cougar Mountain* points which are found in the same area. An extremely rare type with only a few dozen complete examples known. **I.D. KEY:** Early parallel flaking and base form.

G3, $100-$200
Power Co., ID.

Beautiful red stripe, scheen obsidian

This point is complete. The bottom half is shown for the exquisite material.

Black obsidian

Gray obsidian

Basal grinding

G7, $150-$300
NW NV.

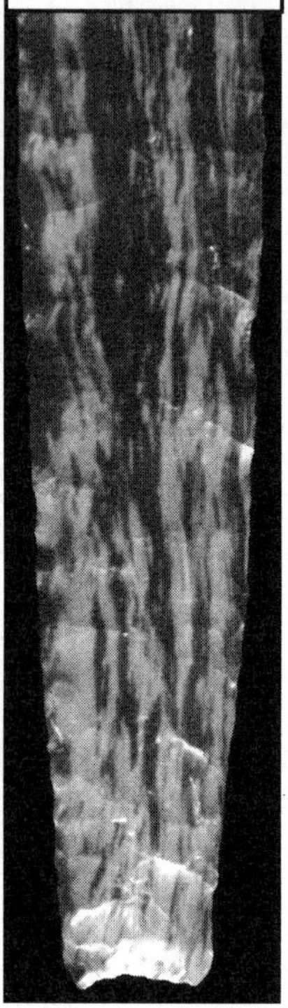

G10, $2500-$5000+
NW NV. 8-3/8" long

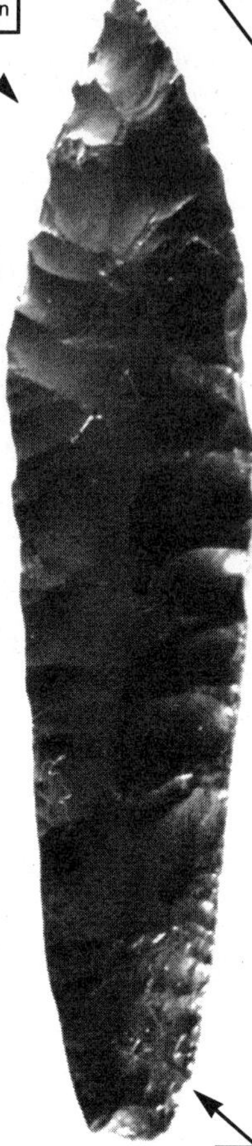

G9, $400-$800
Power Co., ID.

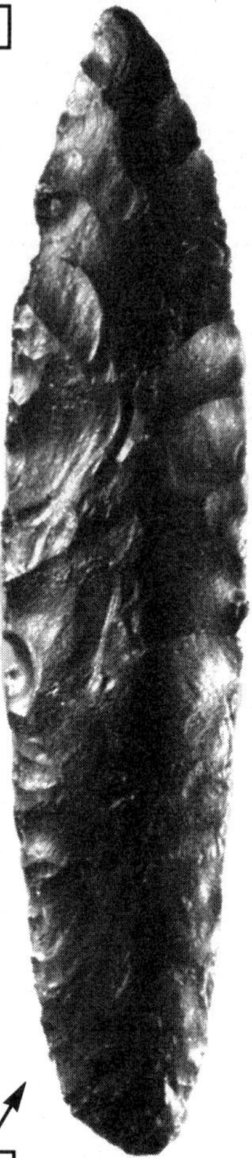

G8, $300-$600
Lake Co., OR.

HELL'S CANYON BASAL NOTCHED - Developmental to Historic Phase, 1200 - 200 B. P.

(Also see Elko Corner Notched and Quillomene Bar)

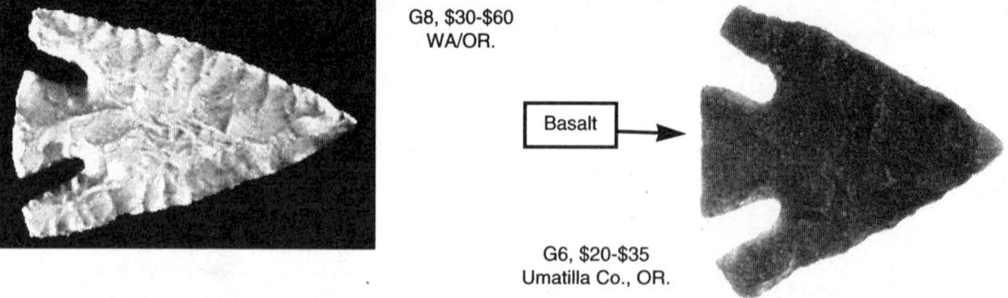

G8, $30-$60
WA/OR.

G6, $20-$35
Umatilla Co., OR.

LOCATION: Great Basin westward. **DESCRIPTION:** A medium to large size, broad, basal notched point with tangs usually dropping to the base line.

HELL'S CANYON BASAL NOTCHED (continued)

Black obsidian

G8, $30-$60
Warner Valley, OR.

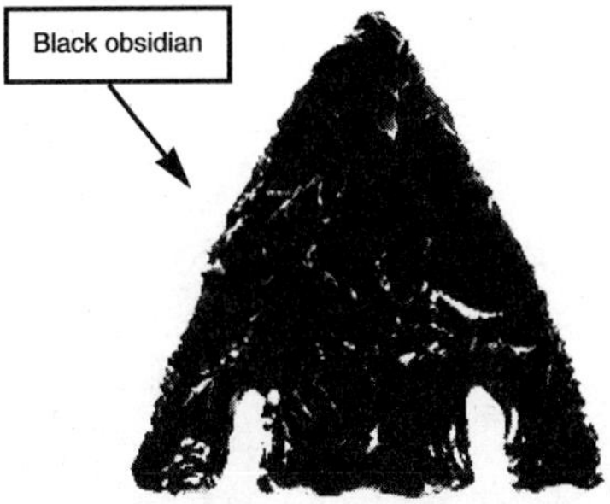

G8, $45-$90
Lake Co., OR.

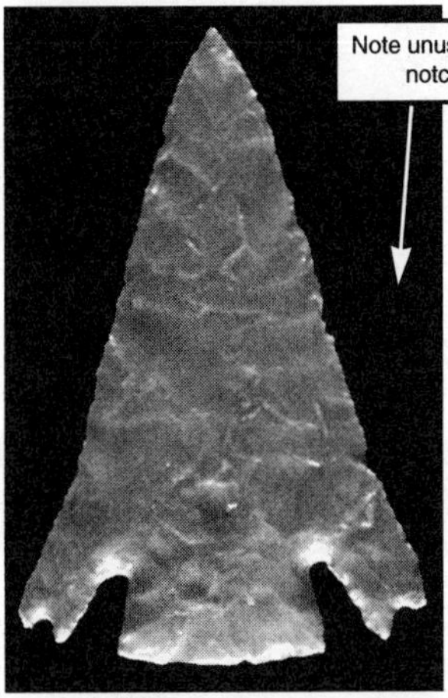

Note unusual tang notches

Agate

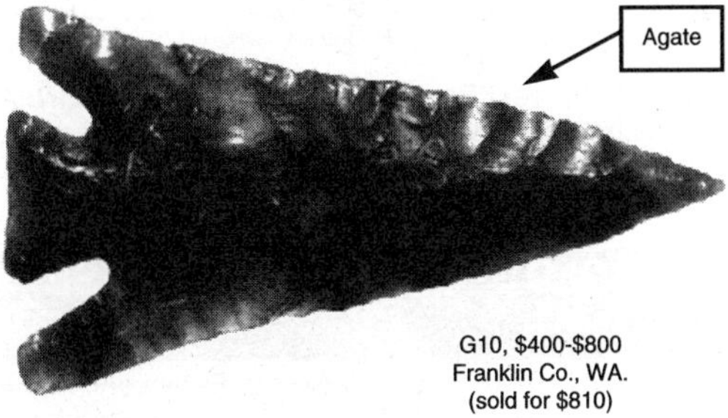

G10, $400-$800
Franklin Co., WA.
(sold for $810)

G10, $200-$400
Klameth Co., OR.

HELL'S CANYON CORNER NOTCHED - Developmental to Historic, Phase, 1200 - 200 B. P.

(Also see Elko Corner Notched & Quillomene Bar)

G6, $10-$20
OR.

G6, $15-$25
Gooding Co., ID.

G8, $20-$30
OR.

G6, $15-$25
OR.

G6, $15-$30
Bonner Co., ID.

G5, $20-$35
Gooding Co., ID.

G6, $15-$25
OR. Gem.

HELL'S CANYON CORNER NOTCHED (continued)

G5, $15-$25
OR. Gem.

G4, $15-$25
Umatilla Riv., OR.

G4, $15-$25
Twin Falls Co., ID.

G8, $40-$80
McNary Dam, OR. Agate.

LOCATION: Great Basin westward. **DESCRIPTION:** A medium to large size, broad, corner notched point with barbed shoulders and an expanding stem. Shoulder barbs are rounded. First recognized and found on Hell's Canyon Reservoir in Idaho.

HUMBOLDT - CONSTRICTED BASE - Early to mid-Archaic, 7000 - 5000 B. P.

(Also see Early Leaf, Pinto Basin)

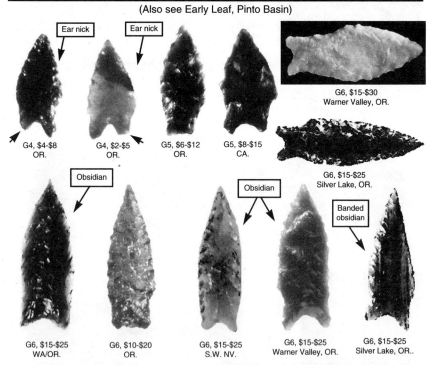

Ear nick

Ear nick

G4, $4-$8
OR.

G4, $2-$5
OR.

G5, $6-$12
OR.

G5, $8-$15
CA.

G6, $15-$30
Warner Valley, OR.

G6, $15-$25
Silver Lake, OR.

Obsidian

Obsidian

Banded obsidian

G6, $15-$25
WA/OR.

G6, $10-$20
OR.

G6, $15-$25
S.W. NV.

G6, $15-$25
Warner Valley, OR.

G6, $15-$25
Silver Lake, OR..

LOCATION: Great Basin states, esp. Nevada. **DESCRIPTION:** A small to medium size, narrow, lanceolate point with a constricted, concave, eared base. Some examples have faint shoulders. Parallel, oblique flaking occurs on many examples.

HUMBOLDT-CONSTRICTED BASE (continued)

Tip nick

Parallel oblique flaking

Parallel oblique flaking

Obsidian

Obsidian

Obsidian

G7, $25-$50
Warner Valley, OR.

G7, $20-$40
Warner Valley, OR.

G9, $125-$200
Warner Valley, OR.

G8, $40-$75
Warner Valley, OR.

G9, $100-$200
Warner Valley, OR.

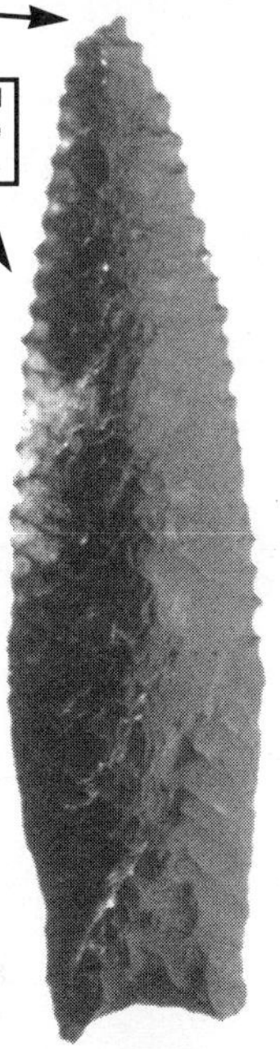

G8, $125-$250
Warner Valley, OR.

HUMBOLDT-EXPANDED BASE - Early Archaic, 8000 - 6000 B. P.

(Also see Bat Cave and Black Rock Concave)

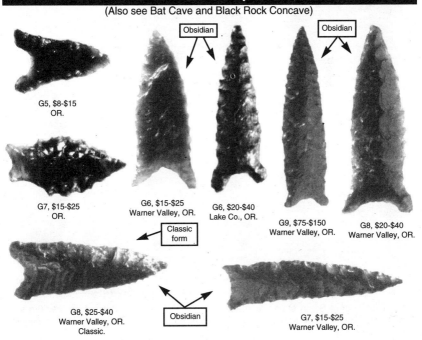

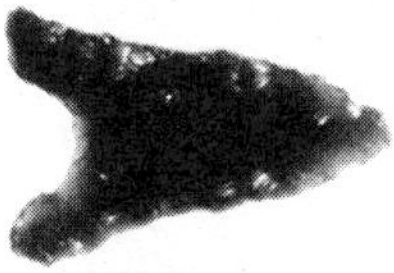

Obsidian

Obsidian

G5, $8-$15
OR.

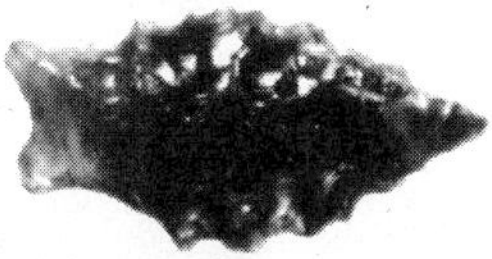

G7, $15-$25
OR.

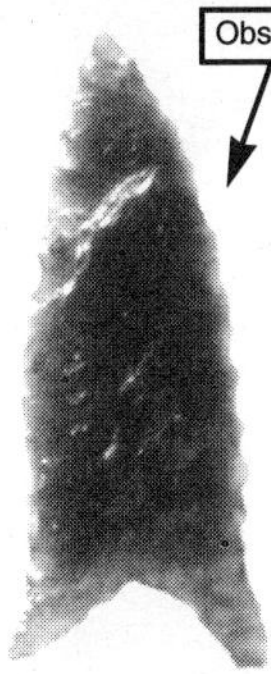

G6, $15-$25
Warner Valley, OR.

G6, $20-$40
Lake Co., OR.

G9, $75-$150
Warner Valley, OR.

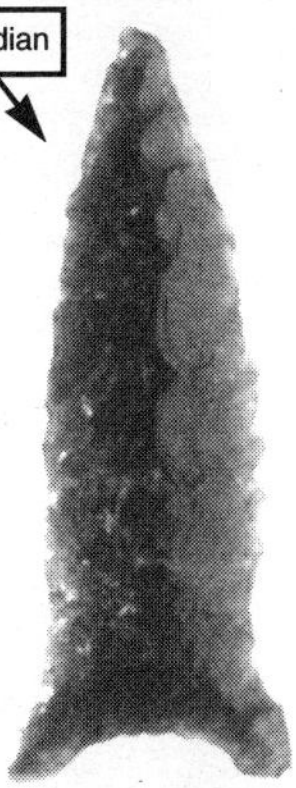

G8, $20-$40
Warner Valley, OR.

Classic form

Obsidian

G8, $25-$40
Warner Valley, OR.
Classic.

G7, $15-$25
Warner Valley, OR.

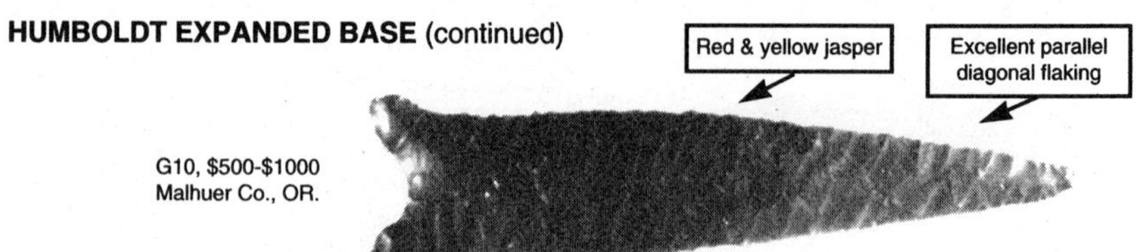

G10, $500-$1000
Malhuer Co., OR.

LOCATION: Great Basin states, esp. NW Nevada. **DESCRIPTION:** A small to medium size, narrow, lanceolate point with an expanded, eared, concave base. Some examples show excellent parallel flaking. An early form of Humboldt.

HUMBOLDT-TRIANGULAR - Mid-late Archaic, 7000 - 5000 B. P.

(Also see Black Rock, Cascade, Clovis, Early Leaf)

G6, $9-$18
OR.

G6, $10-$20
Gooding Co., ID.

G6, $10-$20
CA.

G8, $15-$30
NV.

G6, $10-$20
Warner Val., OR.

G6, $15-$30
Warner Valley, OR.

G6, $15-$30
Warner Valley, OR.

G6, $25-$40
Humboldt Co., NV.

G6, $15-$30
Washoe Lake, NV.

G6, $15-$30
Humboldt Co., NV.

G6, $15-$30
Warner Val., OR.

G7, $20-$40
Warner Val., OR.

G7, $20-$40
Gooding Co., ID.

G9, $25-$50
Warner Valley, OR.

LOCATION: Great Basin states, esp. Nevada. **DESCRIPTION:** A small to medium size, narrow, lanceolate point with a tapered, concave base. Basal concavity can be slight to extreme. Many examples have high quality oblique parallel flaking.

G8, $25-$50
Warner Valley, OR.

G9, $50-$100
Humboldt Sink, NV.

G6, $25-$50
Warner Valley, OR.

G10, $400-$800
Modoc Co., CA.

G8, $40-$80
Lake Co., OR.

G8, $65-$125
Nixon, NV.

G10, $550-$1100
Warner Valley, OR.

G10, $500-$1000
Black Rock Desert, NV.

G10, $750-$1500
CA.

HUMBOLDT TRIANGULAR (continued)

G10, $150-$300
CA.

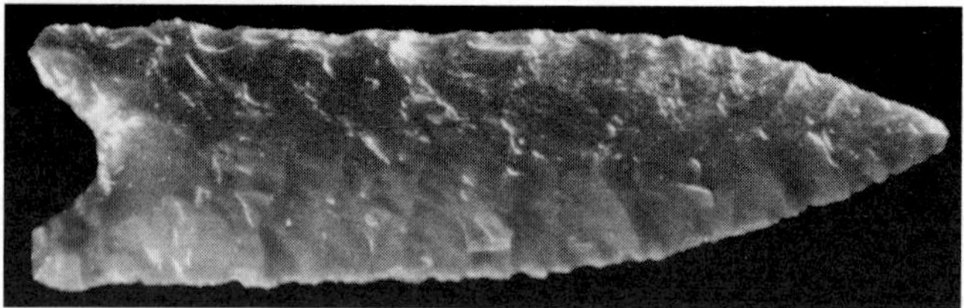

ISHI - Historic Phase, 100 - 80 B.P.

Very rare. Real examples would need excellent provenance

G10, $750-$1500
CA. 1911

LOCATION: Northern California. **DESCRIPTION:** A medium size, thin, corner to side notched point with deep notches set close to the base. Bases vary from concave to convex. Ishi, known as the last wild Indian in North America and the last survivor of his tribe, in fear for his life, turned himself in to the local authorities in Oroville, California. The year was 1911. The University of California museum offered him sanctuary for the rest of his life. While there, he knapped arrowpoints which were given to friends and acquaintances he met at the museum. For more information, read "Ishi in Two Worlds", 1963, University of Calif. Press at Berkeley.

KAVIK - Historic Phase, 300 - 200 B.P.

(Also see Bear)

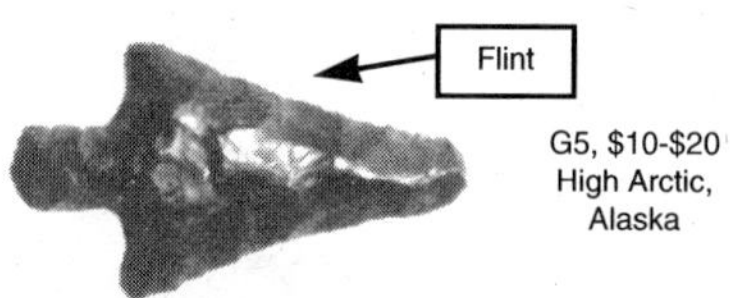

G5, $10-$20
High Arctic,
Alaska

LOCATION: Alaska. **DESCRIPTION:** A medium size stemmed point with the blade expanding towards the base. Shoulders are horizontal and the stem is narrow and parallel sided. Base is straight to convex. **ID. KEY:** Base and shoulder form.

KLICKITAT - Historic Phase, 300 - 160 B.P.

(Also see Dagger)

G6, $35-$50
Jake Co., OR.
Cache point.

G7, $75-$150
WA. Gem.

G7, $50-$100
OR.

G6, $45-$70
OR.

G6, $45-$70
WA. Gem.

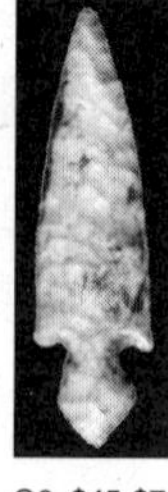

G6, $45-$70
Wasco Co., OR.

G6, $65-$130
Lake Co.,
OR. cache

G7, $75-$150
Wasco Co.,
OR.

KLI CKITAT (continued)

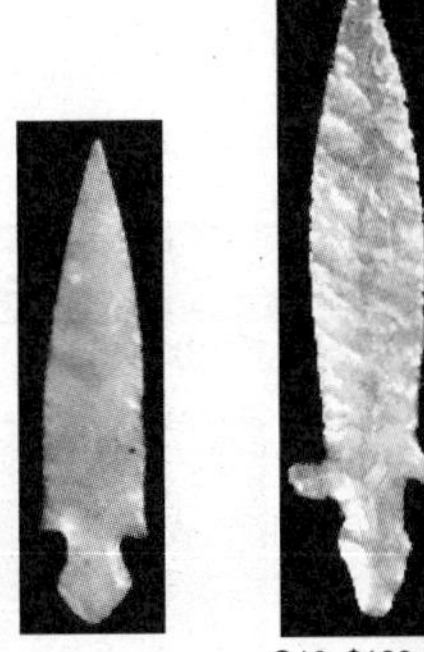

G9, $100-$200
Wasco Co., OR.

G10, $180-$375
Wasco Co., OR.
Red & green agate.

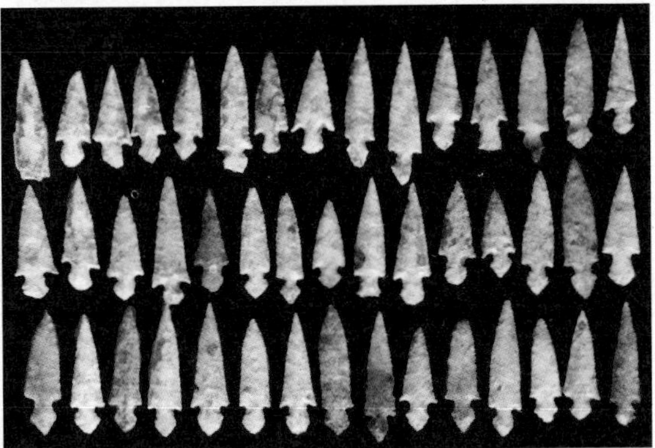

The above photograph illustrates a cache of Klickitat points found on the Columbia River in Washington. This point is similar to Hayes and other point types found further East.

LOCATION: The Columbia River in Oregon and Washington. **DESCRIPTION:** A small size, narrow, thin, lanceolate, barbed point with a diamond shaped base. Some examples have excellent oblique, parallel flaking. Other base forms would fall under the Dagger type.

LAKE MOHAVE - Paleo to Early Archaic, 13,200 - 7000 B. P.

(Also see Lind Coulee, Parman, Silver Lake and Windust)

G6, $25-$50
Lake Co., OR.

G4, $20-$40
Lake Co., OR.

G7, $35-$70
Black Rock Desert, NV.

G7, $50-$100
Humboldt Co., NV.

G7, $75-$150
Harney Lake, OR.

LOCATION: S.E. Calif. to Sou. Oregon. Type site: S.E. California. **DESCRIPTION:** A medium size, narrow, parallel to contracting stemmed point with none to weak tapered shoulders. Stem is much longer than the blade. Basal sides are ground. Most examples are worn-out, resharpened points. Found with Butterfly Crescents. Associated with Bison hunting. One of the oldest dated projectile point types in the Great Basin. Carbon dated to 13,200 B.P. Variants exist where a burin was removed from opposite sides of the tip, called chisel tips. This type may prove to be worn-out *Parmans*.

LIND COULEE

(See Parman)

MOLALLA (See Gunther)

MULE EAR (See Columbia Mule Ear)

NEWBERRY (See Pismo)

NORTHERN SIDE NOTCHED - Paleo to late Archaic, 9000 - 3000 B. P.

(Also see Bitterroot, Buffalo Gap, Cold Springs, Desert, Emigrant)

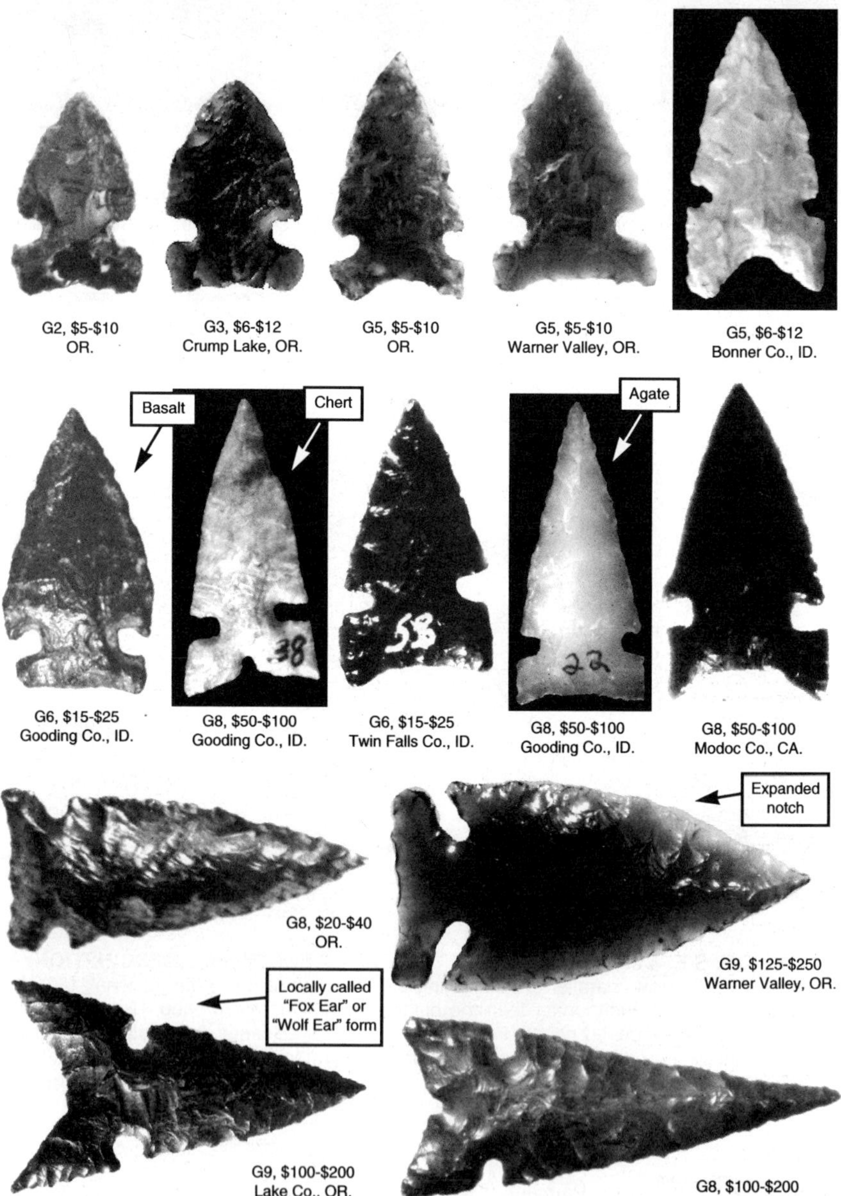

G2, $5-$10 OR.

G3, $6-$12 Crump Lake, OR.

G5, $5-$10 OR.

G5, $5-$10 Warner Valley, OR.

G5, $6-$12 Bonner Co., ID.

G6, $15-$25 Gooding Co., ID.

G8, $50-$100 Gooding Co., ID.

G6, $15-$25 Twin Falls Co., ID.

G8, $50-$100 Gooding Co., ID.

G8, $50-$100 Modoc Co., CA.

G8, $20-$40 OR.

G9, $125-$250 Warner Valley, OR.

G9, $100-$200 Lake Co., OR.

G8, $100-$200 CA.

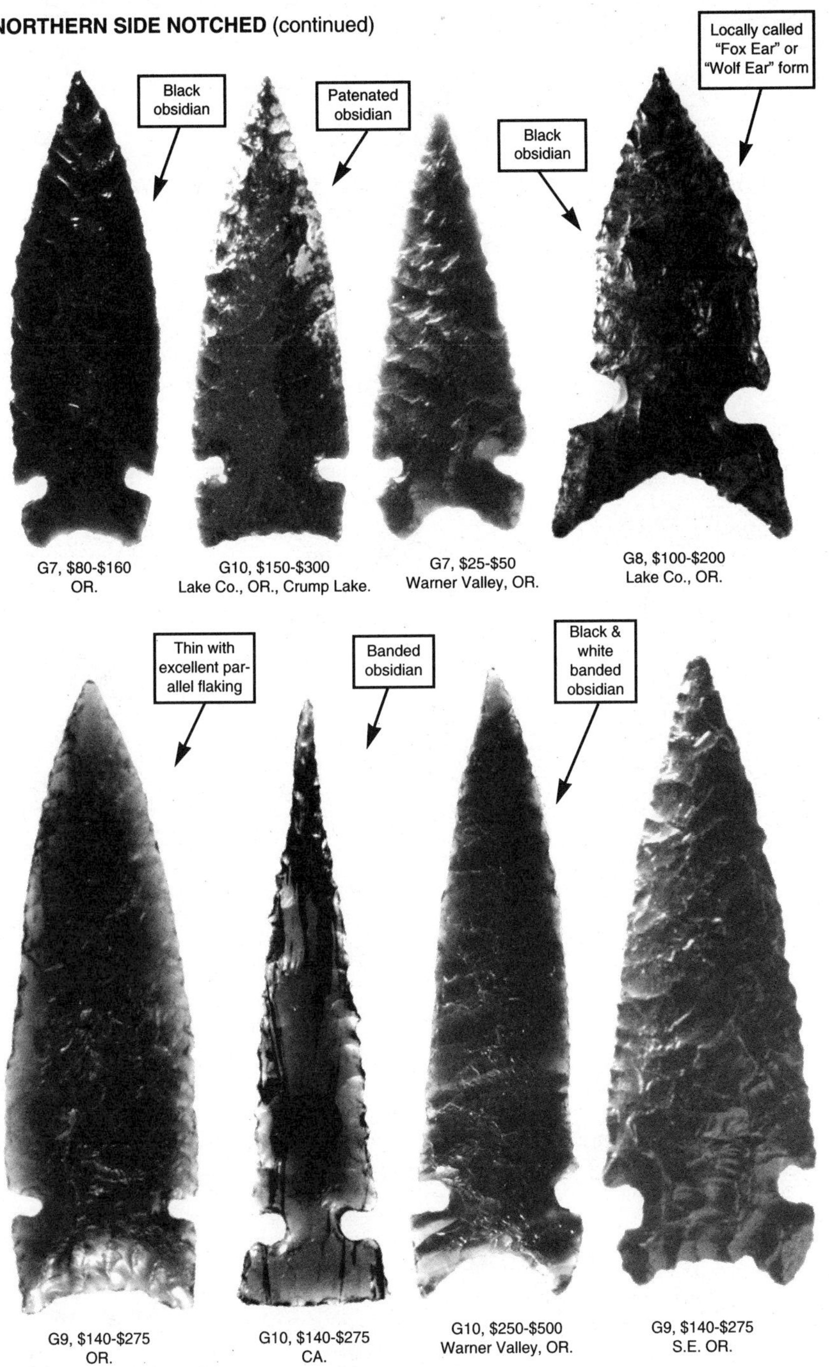

G7, $80-$160
OR.

G10, $150-$300
Lake Co., OR., Crump Lake.

G7, $25-$50
Warner Valley, OR.

G8, $100-$200
Lake Co., OR.

G9, $140-$275
OR.

G10, $140-$275
CA.

G10, $250-$500
Warner Valley, OR.

G9, $140-$275
S.E. OR.

LOCATION: Great Basin westward. **DESCRIPTION:** A medium to large size, narrow side-notched point with early forms showing basal grinding and parallel flaking. Bases are usually concave to eared. Shoulders are tapered to horizontal. **I.D. KEY:** Broad side notched point.

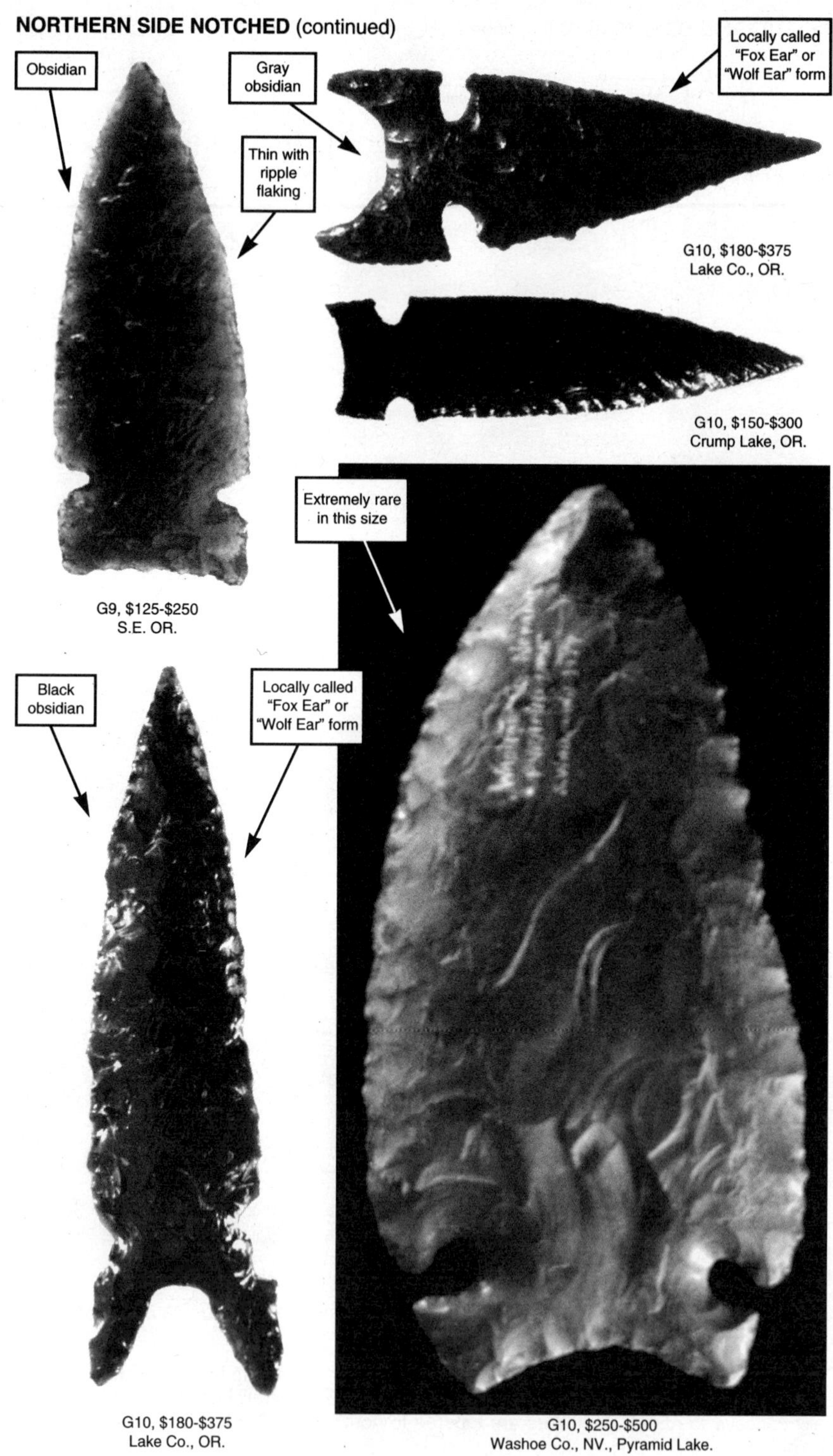

G10, $180-$375
Lake Co., OR.

G10, $150-$300
Crump Lake, OR.

G9, $125-$250
S.E. OR.

G10, $180-$375
Lake Co., OR.

G10, $250-$500
Washoe Co., NV., Pyramid Lake.

NOTTOWAY - Historic Phase, 300 - 160 B. P.

(Also see Dagger and Klickitat)

G8, $20-$35
OR.

LOCATION: Great Basin westward. **DESCRIPTION:** A medium size, narrow, thin, arrowpoint with tapered shoulders and a long, expanded base. **I.D. KEY:** Large basal area.

OWL CAVE - Late Paleo, 9500 - 9000 B. P.

(Also see Cody Complex, Haskett and Pryor Stemmed)

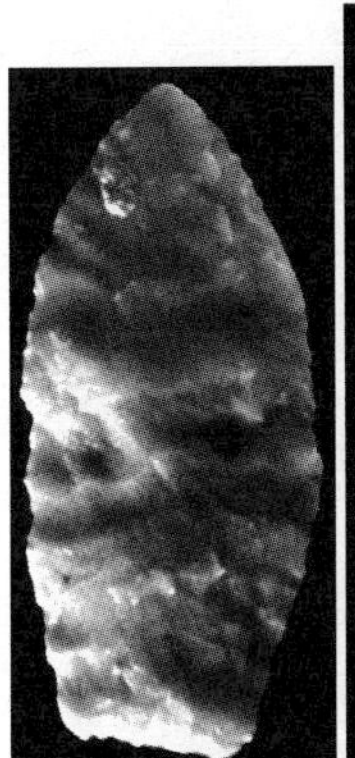

G5, $25-$50
Bonner Co., ID.

G9, $75-$150
Caribou Co., ID.

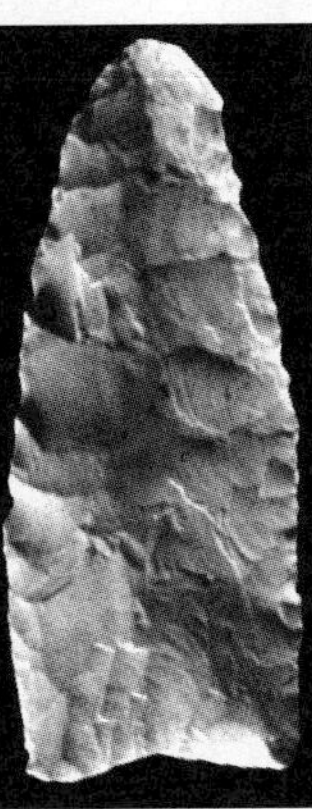

G6, $30-$60
Bonner Co., ID.

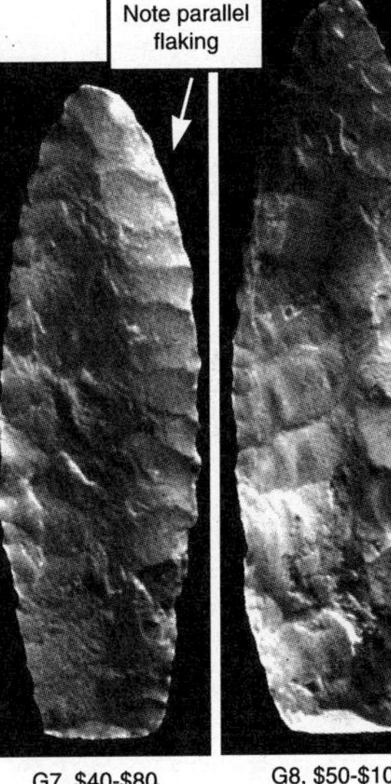

G7, $40-$80
Bonner Co., ID.

G8, $50-$100
Bonner Co., ID.

LOCATION: The Wasden Site in southern Idaho is the type area. **DESCRIPTION:** A medium size, narrow, lanceolate point with a straight to concave base. Blade edges are convex. Basal sides are ground. **I.D. KEY:** Basal form and flaking style.

PALEO KNIFE - Paleo, 10,000 - 8000 B. P.

(Also see Lind Coulee and Windust)

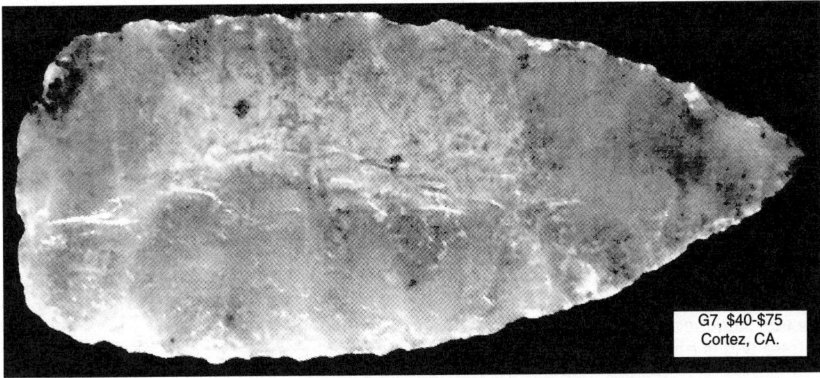

G7, $40-$75
Cortez, CA.

LOCATION: Great Basin westward. **DESCRIPTION:** A medium to large size, broad, lanceolate blade with a rounded base. Look for parallel horizontal flaking.

PANOCHE - Developmental Phase, 1500 - 1000 B. P.

(Also see Desert)

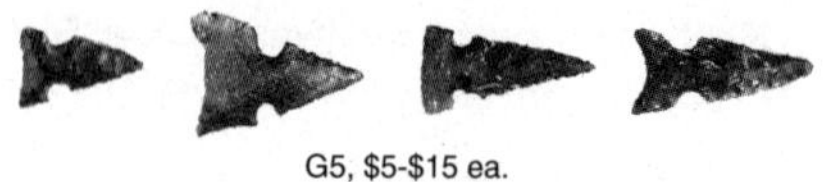

G5, $5-$15 ea.
Monterey, CA.

LOCATION: Panoche Reservoir in California. **DESCRIPTION:** A small size, thin side notched arrow point with a straight to concave base. Similar to *Salado* found further East.

PARMAN - Late Paleo, 10,500 - 9000 B. P.

(Also see Cougar Mountain, Early Stemmed, Lake Mohave, and Silver Lake)

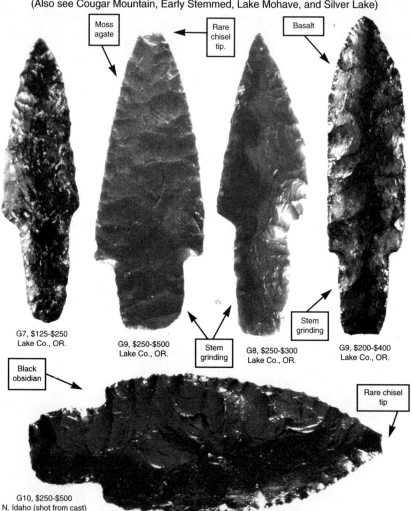

Moss agate

Rare chisel tip.

Basalt

G7, $125-$250
Lake Co., OR.

G9, $250-$500
Lake Co., OR.

Stem grinding

G8, $250-$300
Lake Co., OR.

Stem grinding

G9, $200-$400
Lake Co., OR.

Black obsidian

Rare chisel tip

G10, $250-$500
N. Idaho (shot from cast)

LOCATION: NW Nevada and southern Oregon. **DESCRIPTION:** A medium size, long contracted stemmed point with tapered to squared shoulders. The Basal area is rounded to square and is ground. Flaking is random. Heavily resharpened examples may be the same as *Lake Mohave* points. A very rare type. Occurs in chisel tip along with *Lake Mohave* and *Windust*. Believed to have possibly evolved into *Lind Coulee* and other types. **I.D.KEY:** Long stem that is ground.

PARMAN (continued)

Brown chert

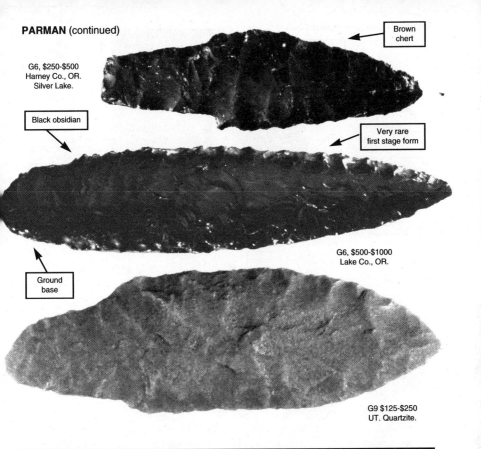

G6, $250-$500
Harney Co., OR.
Silver Lake.

Black obsidian

Very rare first stage form

G6, $500-$1000
Lake Co., OR.

Ground base

G9 $125-$250
UT. Quartzite.

PINTO BASIN - Middle to late Archaic, 4500 - 2500 B. P.

(Also see Eastgate Bifurcated, Elko, Gatecliff and Humboldt)

G8, $20-$35
Warner Valley, OR.

G5, $10-$20
Warner Valley, OR.

G6, $15-$25
Gooding Co., ID.

G6, $15-$25
Warner Valley, OR.

G5, $10-$20
OR.

G8, $20-$35
Warner Valley, OR.

G7, $25-$50
Warner Valley, OR.

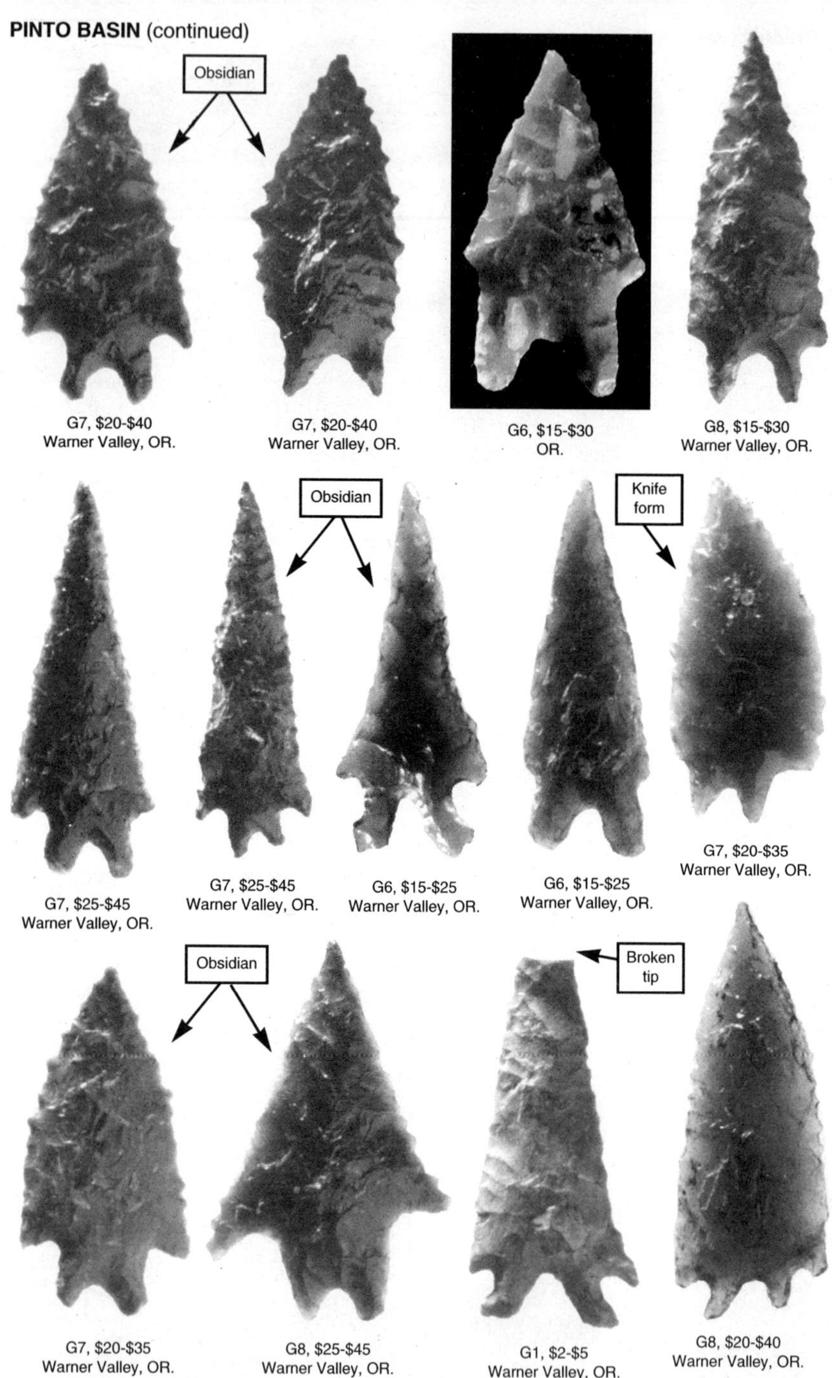

G7, $20-$40
Warner Valley, OR.

G7, $20-$40
Warner Valley, OR.

G6, $15-$30
OR.

G8, $15-$30
Warner Valley, OR.

G7, $25-$45
Warner Valley, OR.

G7, $25-$45
Warner Valley, OR.

G6, $15-$25
Warner Valley, OR.

G6, $15-$25
Warner Valley, OR.

G7, $20-$35
Warner Valley, OR.

G7, $20-$35
Warner Valley, OR.

G8, $25-$45
Warner Valley, OR.

G1, $2-$5
Warner Valley, OR.

G8, $20-$40
Warner Valley, OR.

LOCATION: Great Basin states. **DESCRIPTION:** A medium sized, narrow, auriculate point. Shoulders can be tapered, horizontal or barbed. Bases are deeply bifurcated. Ears can be parallel to expanding. Most examples show excellent flaking. **I.D. KEY:** Long pointed ears.

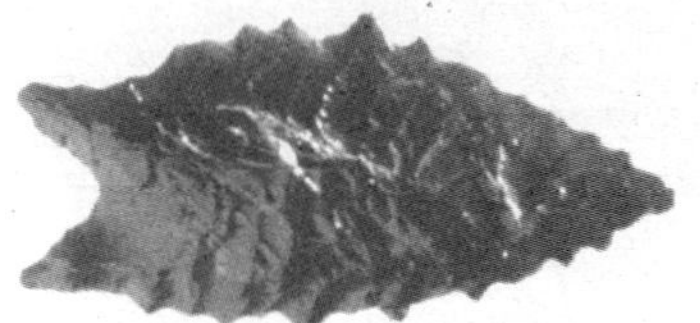

G7, $20-$40
Warner Valley, OR.

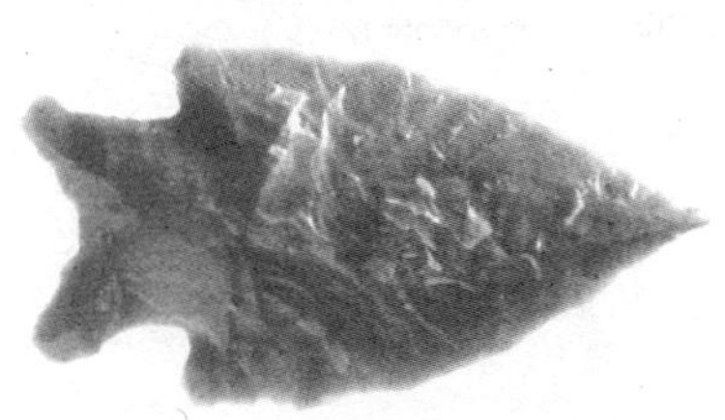

G7, $20-$40
Warner Valley, OR.

G9, $40-$80
Warner Valley, OR.

Basalt

G8, $65-$125
Wasco Lake, NV.

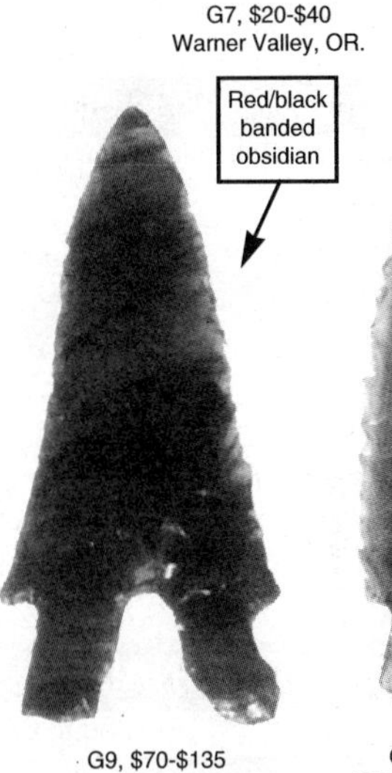

G9, $70-$135
OR.

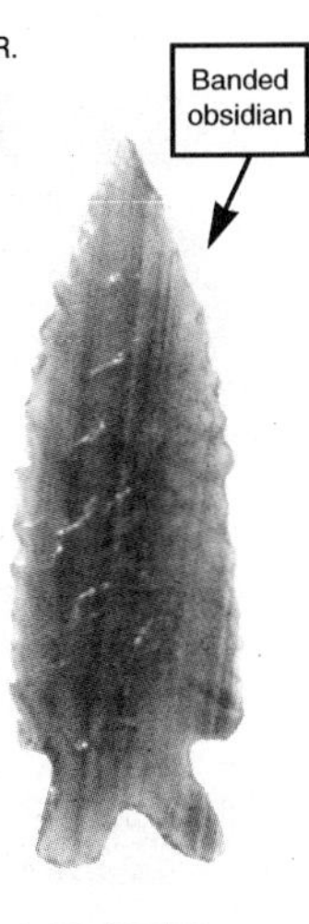

G8, $25-$50
Warner Valley, OR.

Banded
obsidian

G10, $90-$175
CA.

G10, $50-$100
S.E. OR.

G10, $90-$175
Humboldt Sink, NV.

G10, $90-$175
Lake Co., OR.

GB

PINTO BASIN (continued)

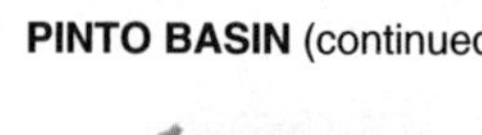

G9, $40-$80
Warner Valley, OR.

G9, $45-$85
Lake Co., Crump Lake, OR.

PISMO - Middle Archaic to Classic Phase, 3500 - 400 B. P.

(Also see Gatecliff, Gypsum Cave, Pelona, Spedis, Rabbit Island)

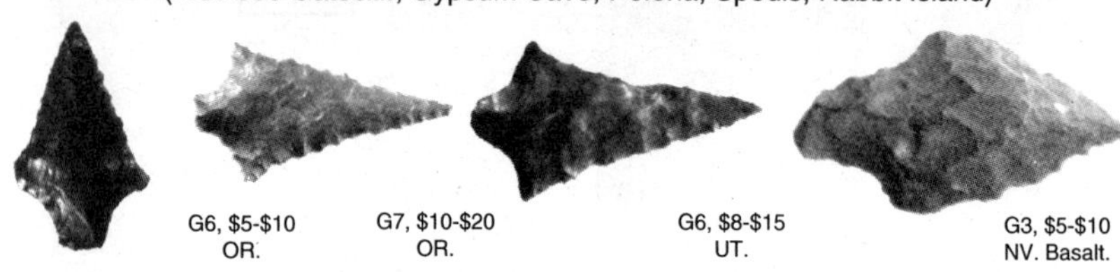

G6, $5-$10
OR.

G7, $10-$20
OR.

G6, $8-$15
UT.

G3, $5-$10
NV. Basalt.

LOCATION: A California type that may extend eastward. **DESCRIPTION:** A small to medium size, serrated point with a long contracted base that can be rounded or pointed. Shorter examples can be diamond shaped. Also called *Newberry.*

PLATEAU PENTAGONAL - Classic Phase, 700 - 400 B. P.

(Related to Columbia Mule Ear)

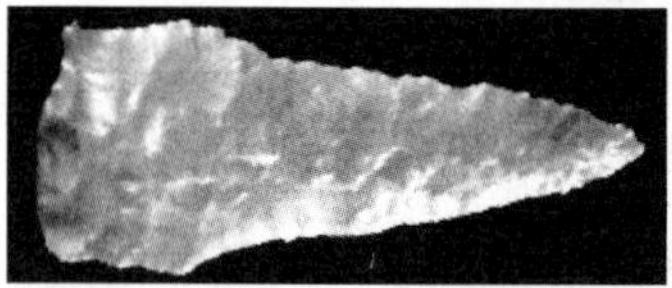

G3, $5-$10
Blalock Isle, OR.

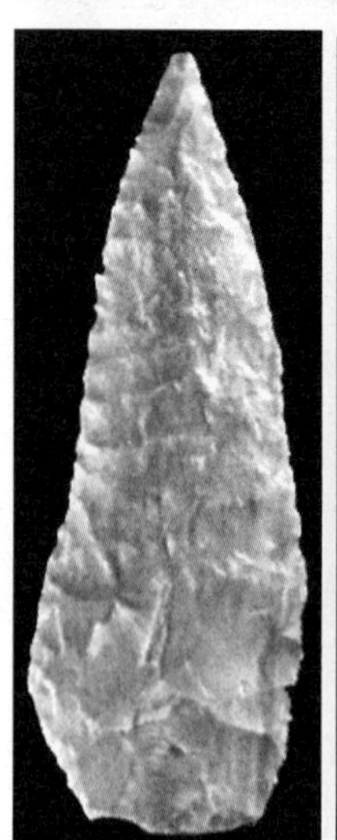

G4, $15-$25
Wasco Co., OR.

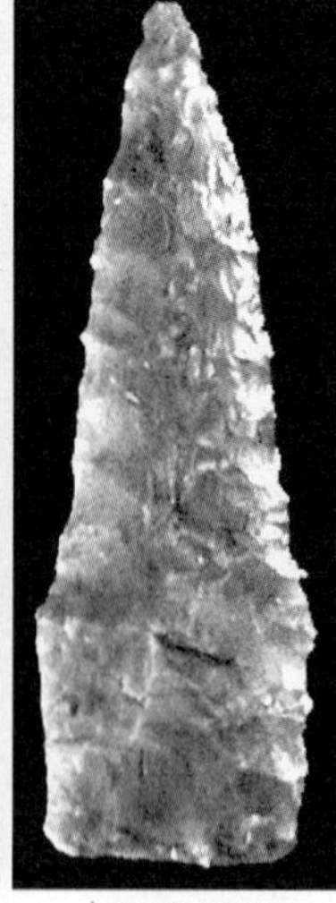

G6, $20-$35
Wasco Co., OR.

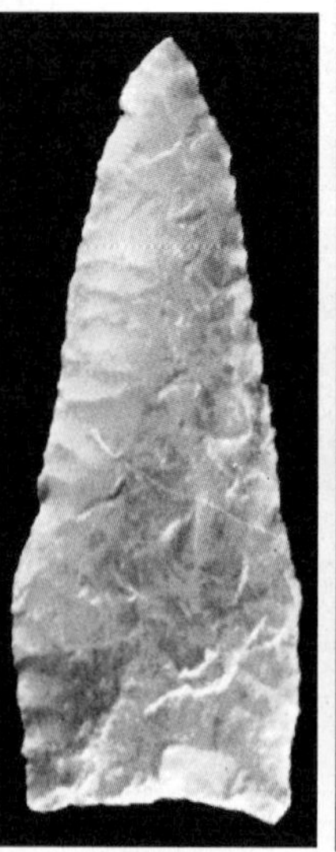

G6, $20-$35
NV. Basalt.

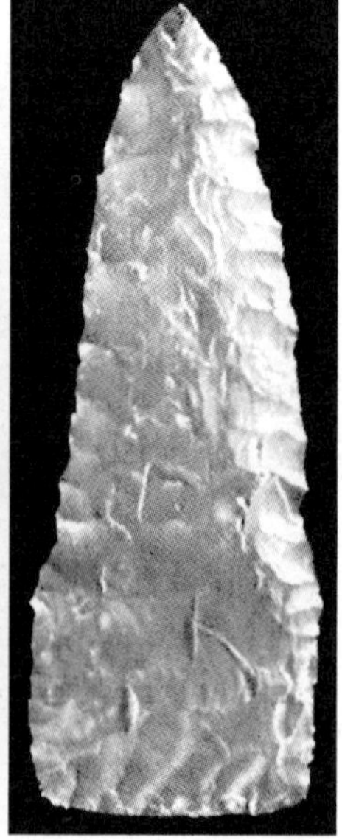

G7, $30-$60
NV. Basalt.

PLATEAU PENTAGONAL (continued)

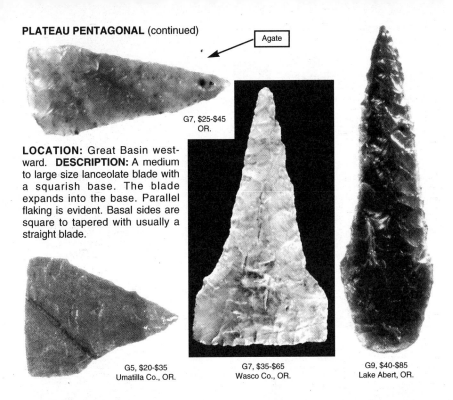

Agate

G7, $25-$45
OR.

LOCATION: Great Basin westward. **DESCRIPTION:** A medium to large size lanceolate blade with a squarish base. The blade expands into the base. Parallel flaking is evident. Basal sides are square to tapered with usually a straight blade.

G5, $20-$35
Umatilla Co., OR.

G7, $35-$65
Wasco Co., OR.

G9, $40-$85
Lake Abert, OR.

PRYOR STEMMED - Early Archaic, 8000 - 7000 B. P.

(Also see Cody Complex, Owl Cave and Parman)

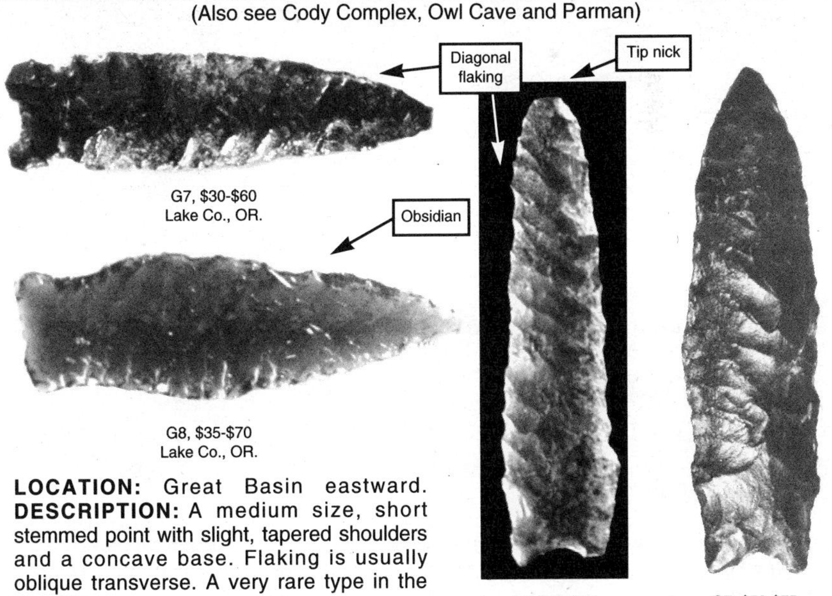

G7, $30-$60
Lake Co., OR.

G8, $35-$70
Lake Co., OR.

LOCATION: Great Basin eastward. **DESCRIPTION:** A medium size, short stemmed point with slight, tapered shoulders and a concave base. Flaking is usually oblique transverse. A very rare type in the Great Basin.

G6, $25-$50
Lake Co., OR.

G7, $50-$75
Lake Pend Oreill, ID.

PRYOR STEMMED (continued)

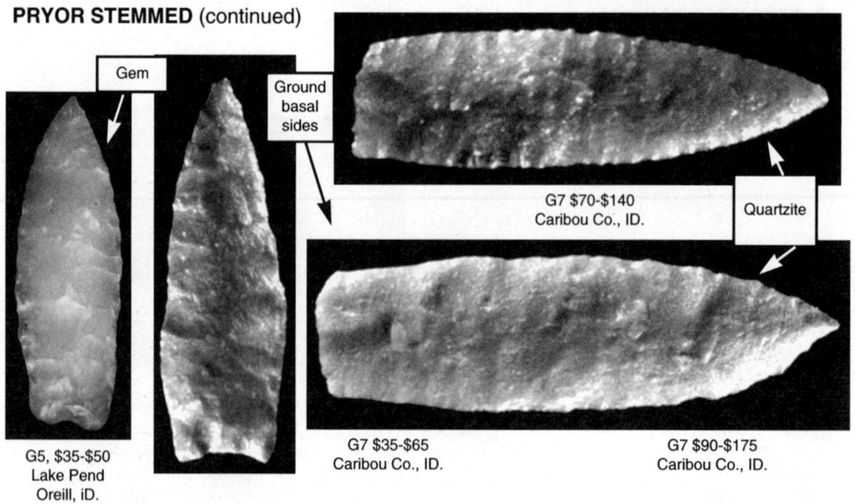

G5, $35-$50 Lake Pend Oreill, iD.

G7 $70-$140 Caribou Co., ID.

G7 $35-$65 Caribou Co., ID.

G7 $90-$175 Caribou Co., ID.

QUILOMENE BAR - Late Archaic to Transitional Phase, 3000 - 2000 B. P.

(Also see Elko Corner Notched & Hell's Canyon)

G6, $15-$25 Gooding Co., ID.

G7 $20-$35 Gooding Co., ID.

G7 $25-$45 WA.

G7 $20-$35 Bonner Co., ID.

LOCATION: Columbia River in Oregon and Washington. **DESCRIPTION:** A medium size base to corner notched point. The classic form has a convex base. The stem is straight to expanded.

RABBIT ISLAND - Middle to late Archaic, 4000 - 2500 B. P.

(Also see Gatecliff, Gypsum Cave, Pismo & Spedis)

G8, $15-$25 OR. , Columbia River

G8, $25-$50 Umatilla Co., OR. Gem.

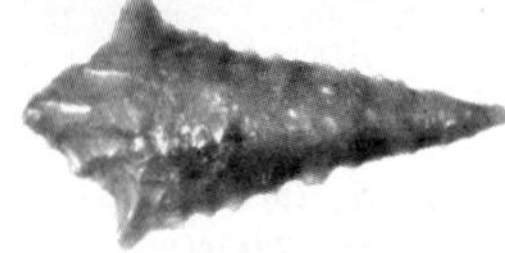

G9, $35-$70 Umatilla Co., OR. Gem.

LOCATION: Columbia River of Oregon and Washington. **DESCRIPTION:** A medium size, thick, contracted stemmed point with tapered, pointed shoulders and a short base that can be pointed or rounded. Blade edges can be serrated.

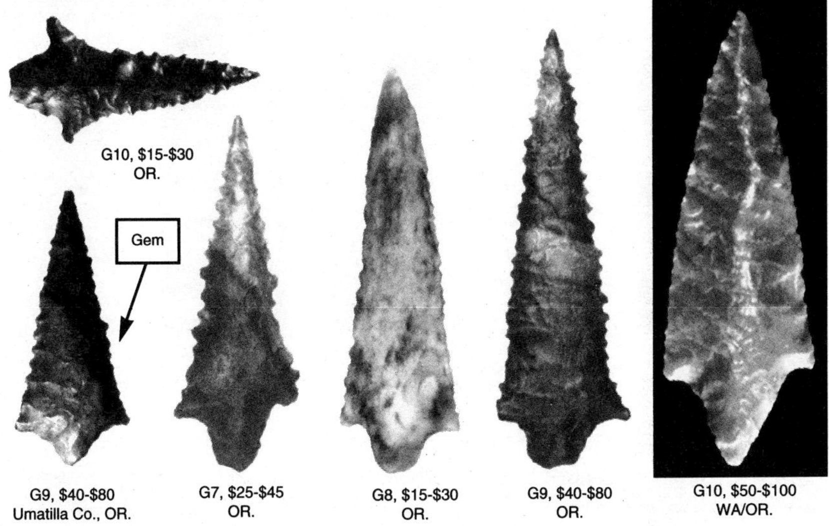

G10, $15-$30 OR.

G9, $40-$80 Umatilla Co., OR.

G7, $25-$45 OR.

G8, $15-$30 OR.

G9, $40-$80 OR.

G10, $50-$100 WA/OR.

ROGUE RIVER

(See Gunther)

ROSE SPRINGS - Developmental to Classic Phase, 1100 - 600 B. P.

(Also see Colonial, Eastgate, Elko, Mummy Cave & Wendover)

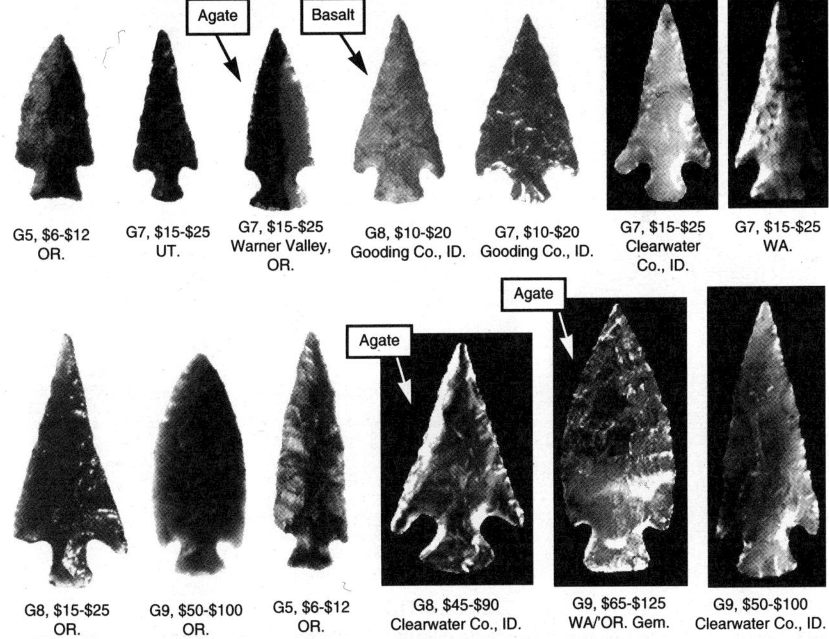

G5, $6-$12 OR.

G7, $15-$25 UT.

G7, $15-$25 Warner Valley, OR.

G8, $10-$20 Gooding Co., ID.

G7, $10-$20 Gooding Co., ID.

G7, $15-$25 Clearwater Co., ID.

G7, $15-$25 WA.

G8, $15-$25 OR.

G9, $50-$100 OR.

G5, $6-$12 OR.

G8, $45-$90 Clearwater Co., ID.

G9, $65-$125 WA/'OR. Gem.

G9, $50-$100 Clearwater Co., ID.

LOCATION: Great Basin westward. **DESCRIPTION:** Several forms are known. A small to medium size, narrow, corner, side or expanded to contracted stemmed arrow point. Side notches are very distinctive in that they are very close to the base.

ROSE SPRINGS (continued)

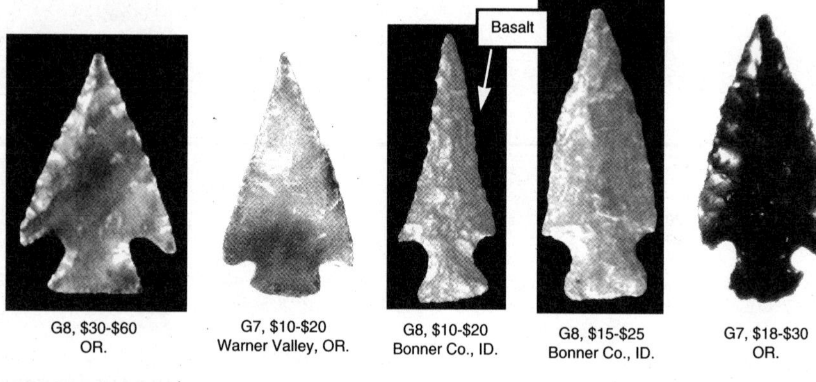

G8, $30-$60
OR.

G7, $10-$20
Warner Valley, OR.

G8, $10-$20
Bonner Co., ID.

G8, $15-$25
Bonner Co., ID.

G7, $18-$30
OR.

SCOTTSBLUFF

(See Cody Complex)

SCRAPER- Paleo to Developmental Phase, 14,000 - 1000 B. P.

(Also see Drill, Graver, Paleo Knife)

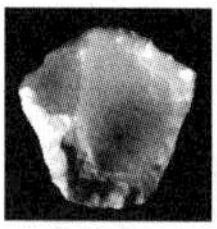

G4, $2-$4
Lake Co., OR.

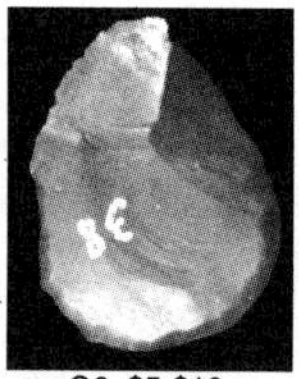

G6, $5-$10
Gooding Co., ID.

IMPORTANT:
All scrapers
shown half size

G7, $8-$15
Lake Co., OR.

G8, $15-$25
Lake Co., OR., Christmas Lake

Dated to over
10,000 B.P.

Cougar
Mountain site

G10 $25-$50
Lake Co., OR.

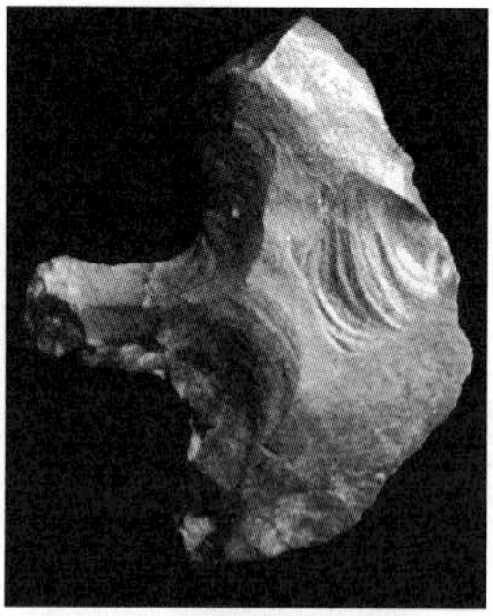

G4, $10-$20
Henry's Lake, ID.

G8, $20-$40
Lake Co., OR., Alkali Lake.

LOCATION: All early-man sites. **DESCRIPTION:** Thumb, duckbill and turtleback forms are small to medium size, thick, ovoid shaped, uniface, scraping tools that are steeply beveled, especially at the broadest end. Side scrapers are long to oval hand-held uniface flakes with beveling on the edges intended for use. Scraping was done primarily from the sides of these blades. Some of these tools were hafted.

SILVER LAKE - Late Paleo to Early Archaic, 11,000 - 7000 B. P.

(Also see Cody Complex, Early Stemmed, Lake Mohave, Parman)

G8, $30-$60
Warner Valley, OR.

G6, $25-$50
Massacre Lake, NV.

LOCATION: Great Basin westward. **DESCRIPTION:** A small to medium size, narrow point with slight to moderate tapered to square shoulders and a long, contracting stem that is ground. **I.D. KEY:** Long stem, weak shoulders.

SNAKE RIVER - Late Archaic to Developmental Phase, 2000 - 1000 B. P.

(Also see Columbia Plateau, Eastgate, Elko, Hell's Canyon, Mummy Cave & Wendover)

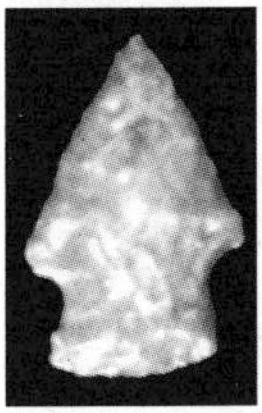

Petrified wood

Yellow agate

G3, $4-$8
Bonner Co., ID.

G5, $8-$15
Bonner Co., ID.

G8, $30-$60
Umatilla, OR.

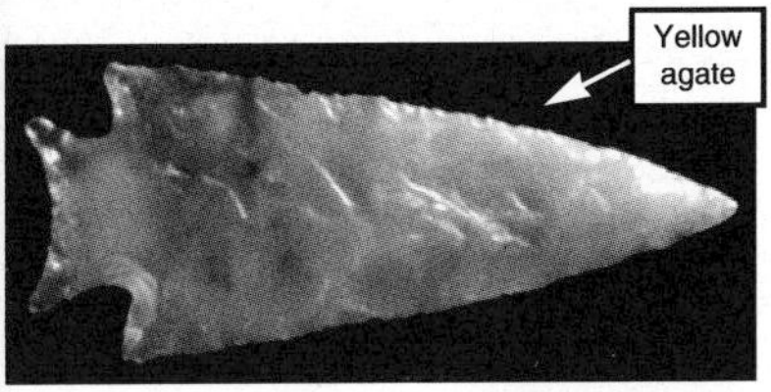

G10, $75-$150
Blalock Isle, WA.

Basalt

G6, $10-$20
Bonner Co., ID.

G7, $15-$30
McNary Dam, OR.

G8, $25-$45
Twin Falls Co., ID.

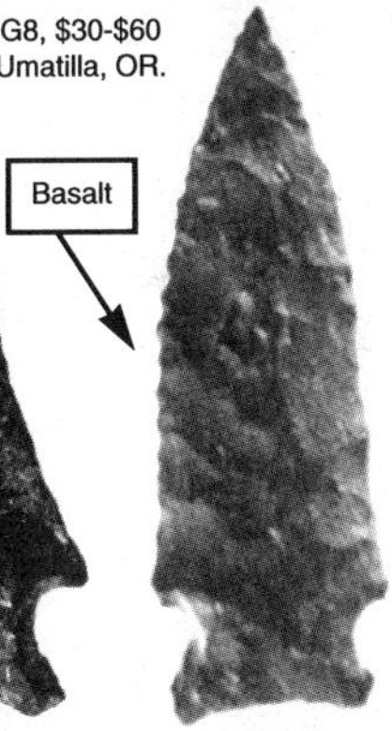

G8, $40-$80
Black Rock Desert, NV.

G6, $15-$30
Kettle Falls, OR.

LOCATION: Great Basin westward. **DESCRIPTION:** A small to medium size barbed, corner, side or expanded to contracted stemmed dart point. Bases are usually straight to concave.

SPEDIS - Paleo, 10,000 - 8000 B. P.

(Also see Cascade, Gypsum Cave, Pismo and Rabbit Island)

LOCATION: Oregon and Washington, Columbia River basin. **DESCRIPTION:** A small to medium size, thin, narrow, lanceolate point with a contracting basal area. Base can be concave or convex. Oblique parallel flaking occurs on some examples. Single shoulder examples occur.

SPEDIS (continued)

Agate

G8, $30-$40
Wasco Co., OR.

G7, $30-$60
OR.

G6, $15-$25
Wasco Co., OR.

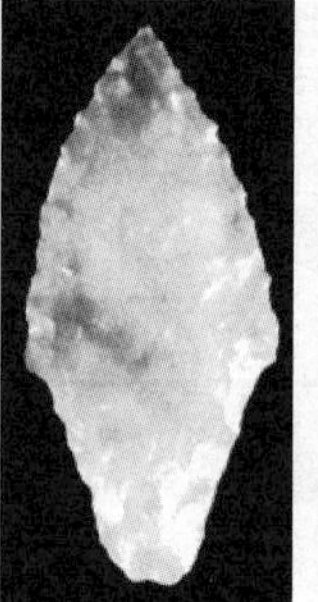

G8, $30-$60
Lake Co., OR.

G8, $50-$100
Wasco Co., OR.

SQUARE KNIFE - Early Archaic, 8000 - 5000 B. P.

(Also see Drill, Scraper, Paleo Knife)

LOCATION: Great Basin westward. **DESCRIPTION:** A medium to large size squared blade that is beveled on all four sides for cutting. **I.D. KEY:** Squared form.

G6, $10-$20
Lake Co., OR., Christmas Lake.

STOCKTON - Historic Phase, 400 - 200 B. P.

(Also see Snake River)

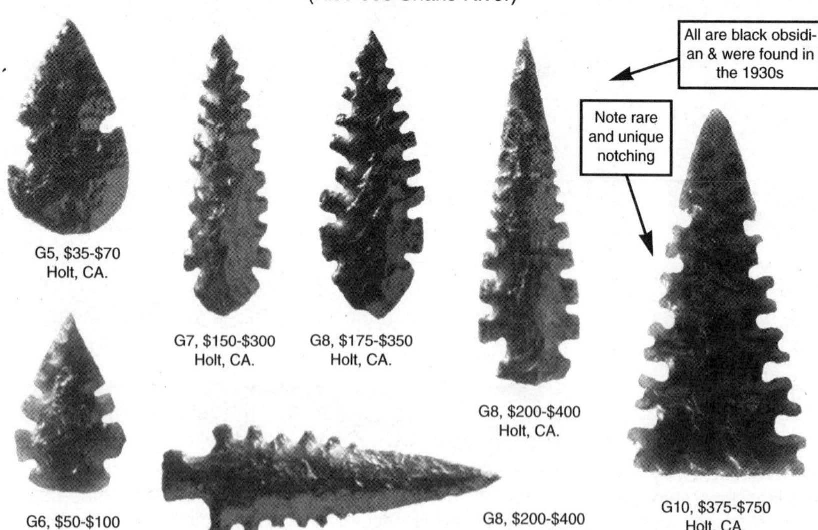
All are black obsidian & were found in the 1930s
Note rare and unique notching

G5, $35-$70
Holt, CA.

G7, $150-$300
Holt, CA.

G8, $175-$350
Holt, CA.

G8, $200-$400
Holt, CA.

G6, $50-$100
Holt, CA.

G8, $200-$400
Holt, CA.

G10, $375-$750
Holt, CA.

STOCKTON (continued)

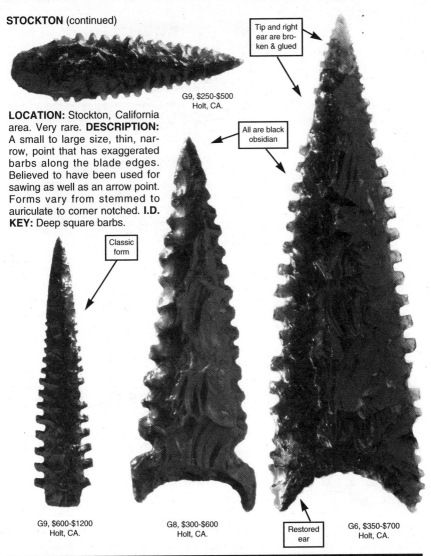

Tip and right ear are broken & glued

G9, $250-$500
Holt, CA.

LOCATION: Stockton, California area. Very rare. **DESCRIPTION:** A small to large size, thin, narrow, point that has exaggerated barbs along the blade edges. Believed to have been used for sawing as well as an arrow point. Forms vary from stemmed to auriculate to corner notched. **I.D. KEY:** Deep square barbs.

All are black obsidian

Classic form

G9, $600-$1200
Holt, CA.

G8, $300-$600
Holt, CA.

Restored ear

G6, $350-$700
Holt, CA.

SUB-TRIANGULAR - Paleo, 11,300 - 11,000 B. P.

(Also see Black Rock Concave, Cascade and Chindadn)

G8, $25-$50
Nenana Valley,
south central AK.

LOCATION: Alaska. **DESCRIPTION:** A small size, broad, thin, triangular point made from a flake that has a straight to slightly concave base. Made during the Nenana occupation. **I.D. Key**: Broad triangle.

TRADE POINTS - Classic to Historic Phase, 400 - 170 B.P.

LOCATION: These points were made of copper, iron, and steel and were traded to the Indians by the French, British and others from the 1600s to the 1800s. Examples have been found all over the United States. Forms vary from triangular to conical to stemmed.

TRADE POINTS (continued)

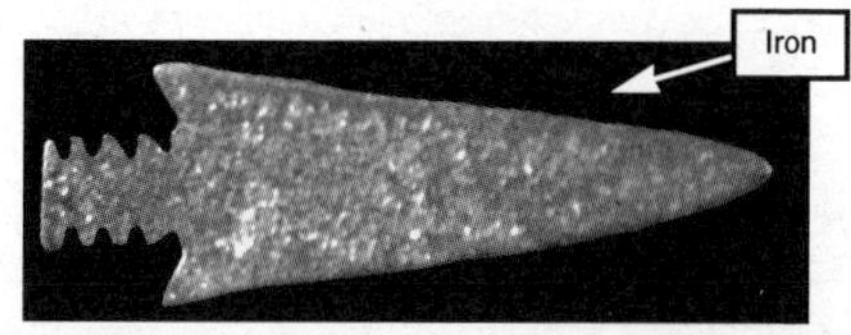

G8, $30-$60
Bonner Co., ID.

TRIPLE "T" - Middle Archaic, 5500 - 5000 B. P.

(Also see Black Rock, Cascade, Early Stemmed, Humboldt)

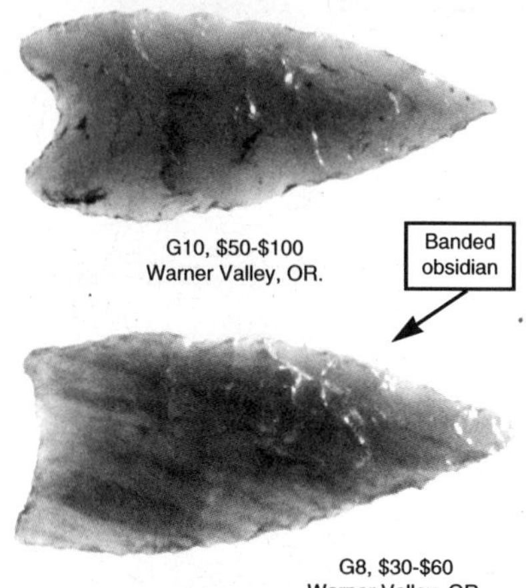

G10, $50-$100
Warner Valley, OR.

G8, $30-$60
Warner Valley, OR.

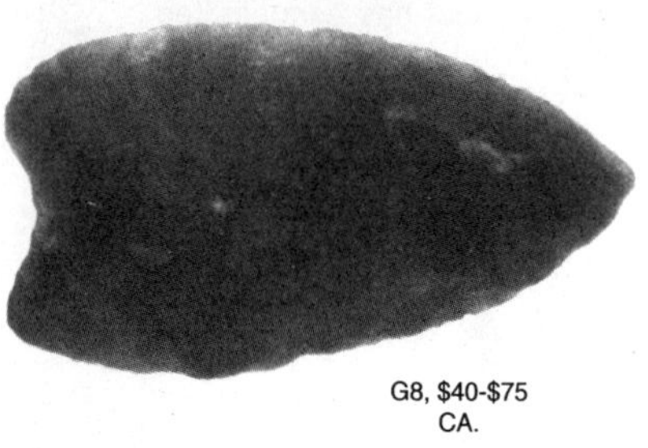

G8, $40-$75
CA.

LOCATION: Great Basin westward. **DESCRIPTION:** A medium size, lanceolate point with rounded basal corners and a concave base. Blade edges curve from point to base. Another variation of the Humboldt series.

UINTA - Developmental Phase, 1200 - 800 B. P.

(Also see Desert General and Ytias)

G4, $3-$6
Bonner Co., ID.

LOCATION: Great Basin westward. **DESCRIPTION:** A small to medium size triangular point with side notches close to the base. Bases are straight to slightly convex or concave.

WAHMUZA - Transitional Paleo, 9000 - 8000 B. P.

(Also see Owl Cave and Pryor Stemmed)

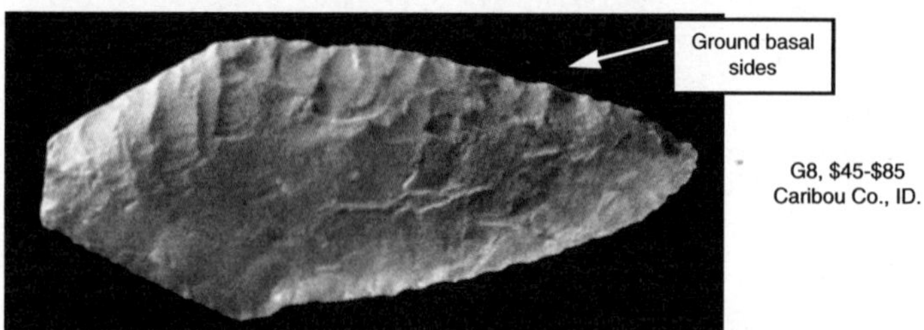

G8, $45-$85
Caribou Co., ID.

LOCATION: Great Basin area. **DESCRIPTION:** A medium size lanceolate point with a long, straight sided, tapered base that is ground. The basal edge is straight. **I.D. KEY:** pronounced contracting base.

WALLULA - Developmental to Historic Phase, 1000 - 200 B. P.

(Also see Columbia Plateau, Eastgate, Rabbit Island, Rose Spring,)

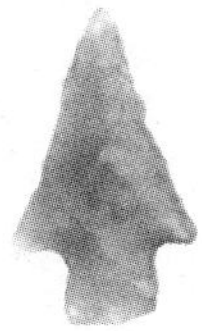

G6, $20-$35
OR. Gem.

G8, $25-$50
OR.

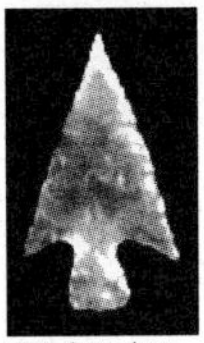

G8, $35-$65
Umatilla Co., OR.

G7, $20-$35
WA.

G7, $25-$45
Wasco Co., OR.

G7, $15-$30
OR..

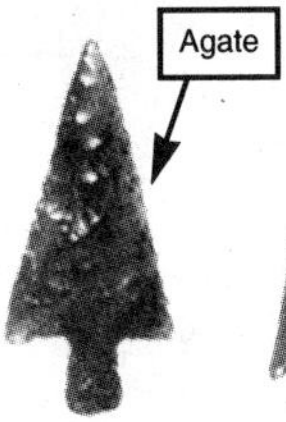

Agate

Gem

Gem

Gem

G8, $28-$55
Umatilla Co., OR.

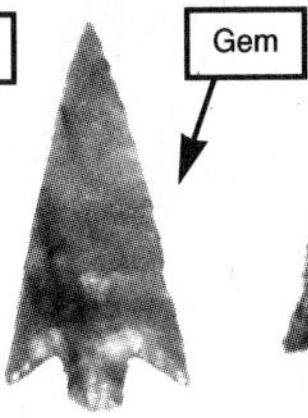

G8, $40-$55
Franklin Co., WA.

G8, $20-$40
John Day Rv., OR.

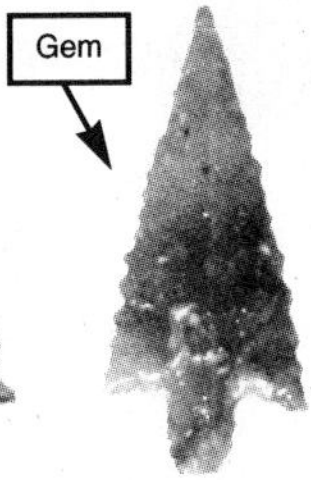

G5, $38-$75
Umatilla Co., OR.

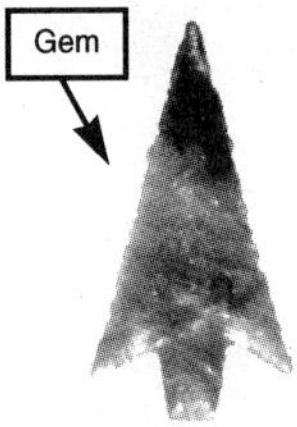

G9, $50-$100
Franklin Co., WA.

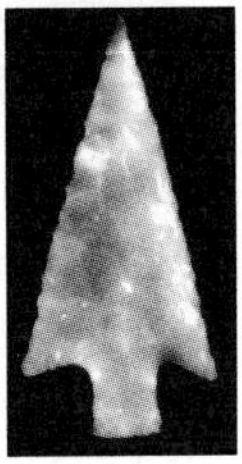

G9, $38-$75
The Dalles, OR.

G8, $30-$55
Warner Valley, OR.

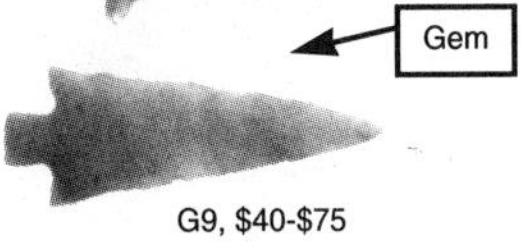

Gem

G9, $40-$75
OR.

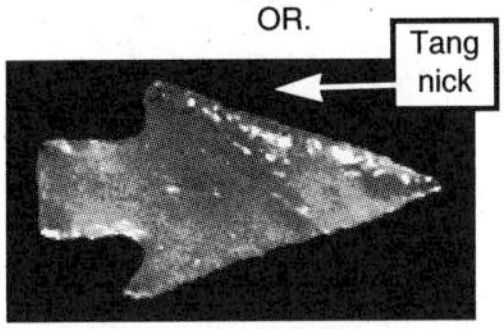

Tang
nick

Gem

Colorful
agate

G5, $15-$30
OR. Gem.

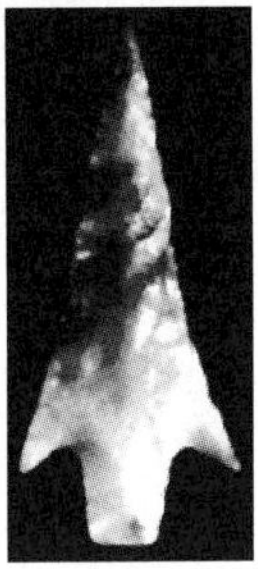

G9, $30-$60
Clearwater Co., ID.

G9, $65-$125
OR.

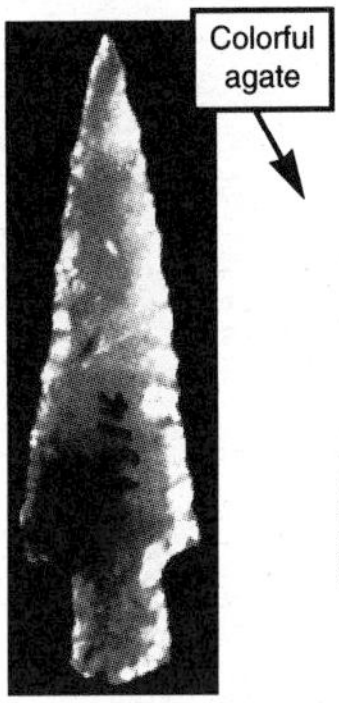

G7, $25-$50
Clearwater Co., ID.

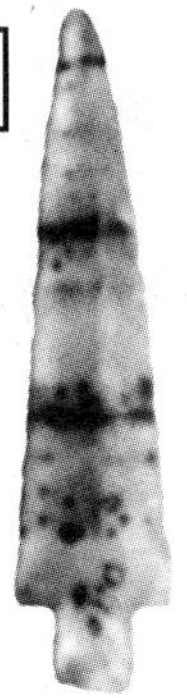

G10, $60-$100
OR.

LOCATION: Columbia River basin of Oregon and Washington. **DESCRIPTION:** A small size, thin, stemmed, arrow point usually with barbs. The base can be expanding, bulbous or contracting. Shoulders are usually barbed but can be horizontal. Blade edges can be serrated.

WENDOVER - Early to middle Archaic, 7000 - 5000 B. P.

(Also see Bitterroot, Eastgate and Rose Springs)

LOCATION: Great Basin westward. **DESCRIPTION:** A medium size, narrow, small, expanded stemmed dart point with a convex base. Blade edges can be serrated. Found in association with Buffalo jump kill sites. Early man drove herds through a prepared pathway into a prepared corral or over an unsuspected cliff ledge. The wounded animals were then easily slaughtered.

G3, $5-$10
NV. Basalt.

WENDOVER (continued)

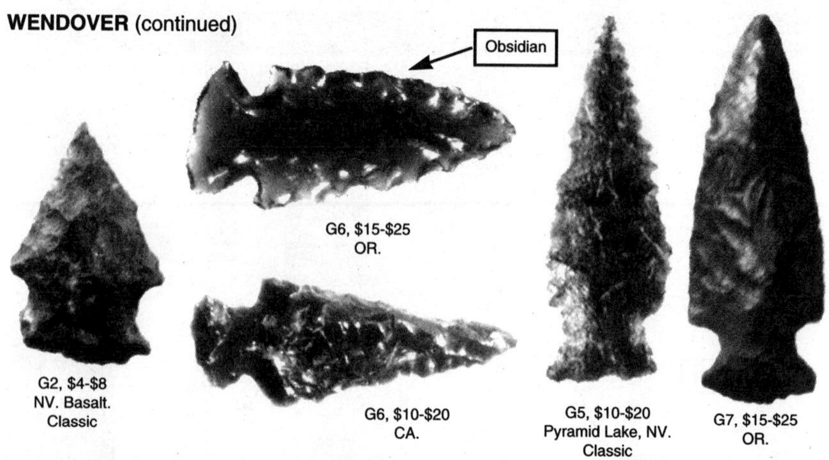

G6, $15-$25
OR.

G2, $4-$8
NV. Basalt.
Classic

G6, $10-$20
CA.

G5, $10-$20
Pyramid Lake, NV.
Classic

G7, $15-$25
OR.

WINDUST - Paleo to Early Archaic, 10,200 - 7500 B. P.

(Also see Early Stemmed, Lake Mojave, Lind Coulee, Parman and Silver Lake)

Jasper; knife form

G6, $15-$25
Bonner Co., ID.

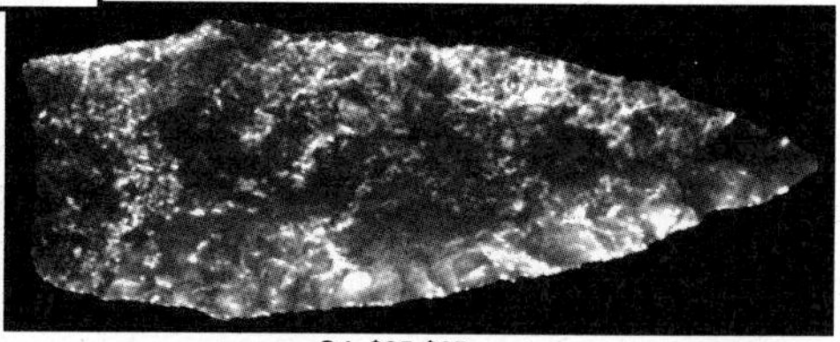

G4, $35-$65
Lake Co., OR.

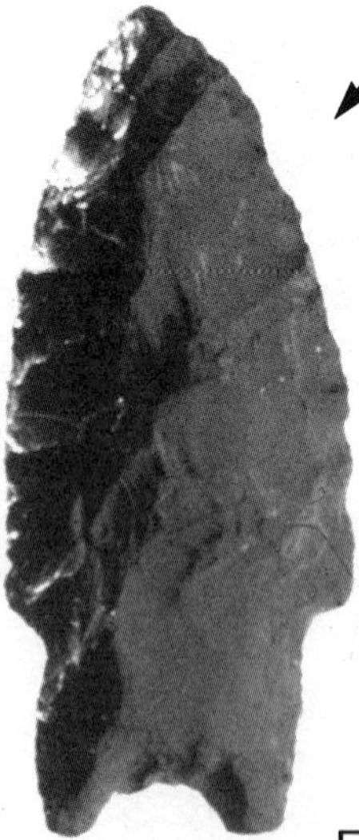

Obsidian

Classic form

Basalt

Basal grinding

Basal grinding

G9, $175-$350
Warner Valley, OR.

G9, $140-$275
Lake Co., OR.
Christmas Lake

G6, $65-$125
Bonner Co., ID.

WINDUST (continued)

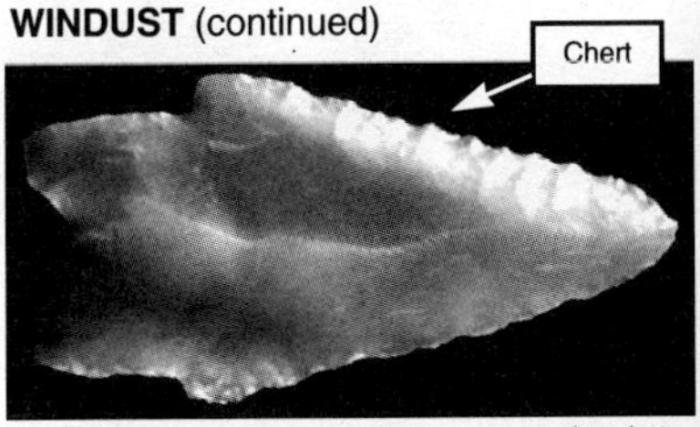

Chert

G5, $35-$50
Bonner Co., ID.

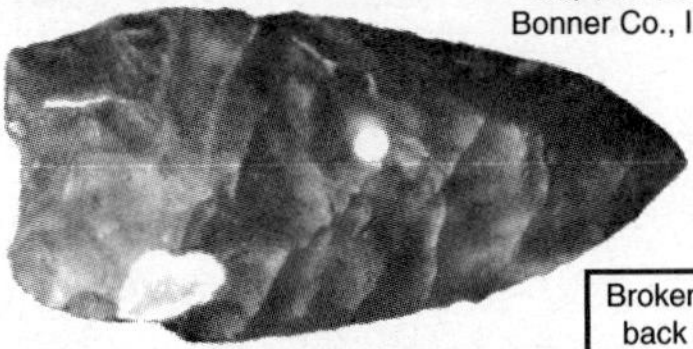

Basal grinding

G5, $35-$50
Bonner Co., ID.

Broken back

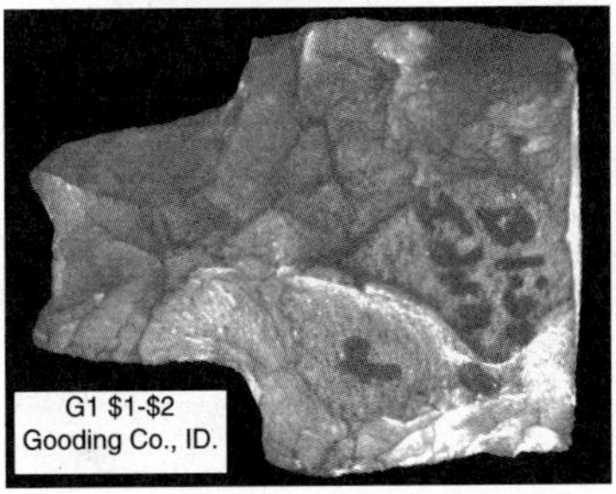

G1 $1-$2
Gooding Co., ID.

G9, $200-$400
Lake Co., OR.

G10, $300-$600
S.E. OR. Classic form.

LOCATION: Oregon and Washington. **DESCRIPTION:** A medium size, broad point that has weak shoulders and a stemmed, concave basal area. Basal concavity can be shallow to deep. Some examples are non-stemmed with a concave base. Basal area can be ground. Chisel tips occur along with *Lake Mojave* and *Parman* points.

WINTU - Developmental to Historic Phase, 1000 - 200 B. P.

(Also see Desert Side Notched)

LOCATION: Central California **DESCRIPTION:** A rare, thin, needle tipped point with unique upward sloping, narrow side notches and a concave base. Usually made of jasper and obsidian.

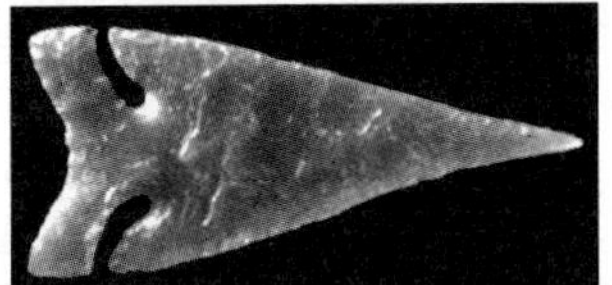

G10, $75-$150
Redding, CA.

YTIAS - Paleo to middle Archaic, 11000 - 5000 B. P.

(Also see Cold Springs, Northern)

G3, $3-$5 ea., Santa Barbara, CA.

LOCATION: Central California **DESCRIPTION:** A small side notched dart point with a straight to concave base. Most examples have been resharpened many times from longer points.

SEEING

This edition of The Overstreet Indian Arrowheads Identification and Price Guide is available with two covers. One (right) can be found in traditional bookstores and the other (facing page) is available exclusively from Gemstone Publishing, relic dealers and specialty shops. Don't be confused...other than the covers, these are the same book. Both covers are available directly from Gemstone Publishing.

The Confident Collector
6th EDITION
THE OVERSTREET
INDIAN ARROWHEADS
IDENTIFICATION AND PRICE GUIDE
Folsom - the rarest of the fluted points!
ROBERT M. OVERSTREET

Bookstore Cover

DOUBLE?

To order, call Toll Free (888) 375-9800 Ext. 249 or fax (410) 560-7143. $24.00 each (plus $4.00 Shipping & Handling for the first book, $1.50 for each additional book). Be sure to specify which cover you want. You can mail your order to Arrowhead Guide #6, Gemstone Publishing, Inc., 1966 Greenspring Drive, Suite LL3, Timonium, MD 21093. We accept Visa, MasterCard, Checks & Money Orders. Discounts available for quantity purchase.

Specialty Cover

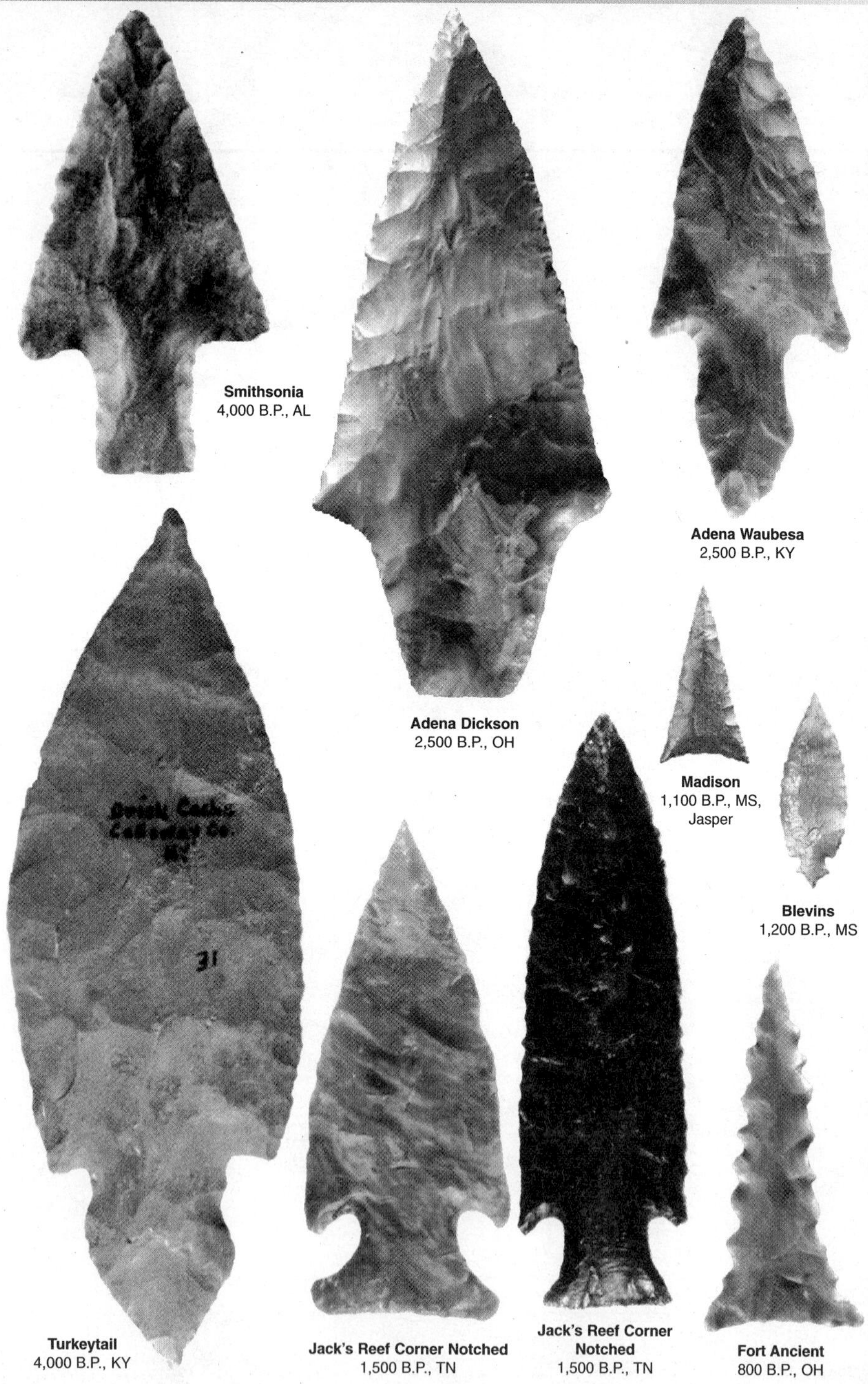

Smithsonia
4,000 B.P., AL

Adena Dickson
2,500 B.P., OH

Adena Waubesa
2,500 B.P., KY

Madison
1,100 B.P., MS, Jasper

Blevins
1,200 B.P., MS

Turkeytail
4,000 B.P., KY

Jack's Reef Corner Notched
1,500 B.P., TN

Jack's Reef Corner Notched
1,500 B.P., TN

Fort Ancient
800 B.P., OH

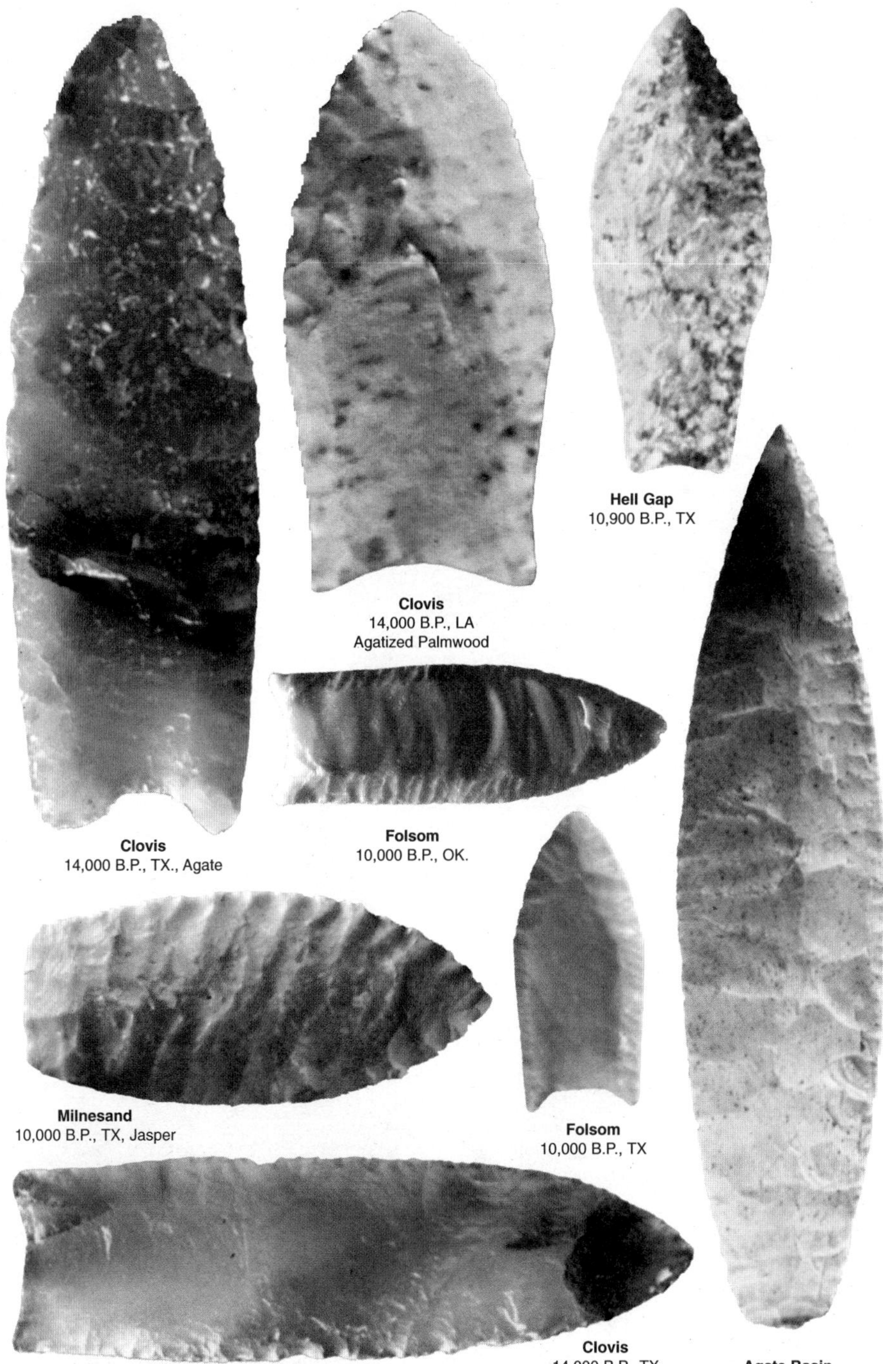

Clovis
14,000 B.P., TX., Agate

Clovis
14,000 B.P., LA
Agatized Palmwood

Hell Gap
10,900 B.P., TX

Folsom
10,000 B.P., OK.

Milnesand
10,000 B.P., TX, Jasper

Folsom
10,000 B.P., TX

Clovis
14,000 B.P., TX
Agate

Agate Basin
10,500 B.P., TX

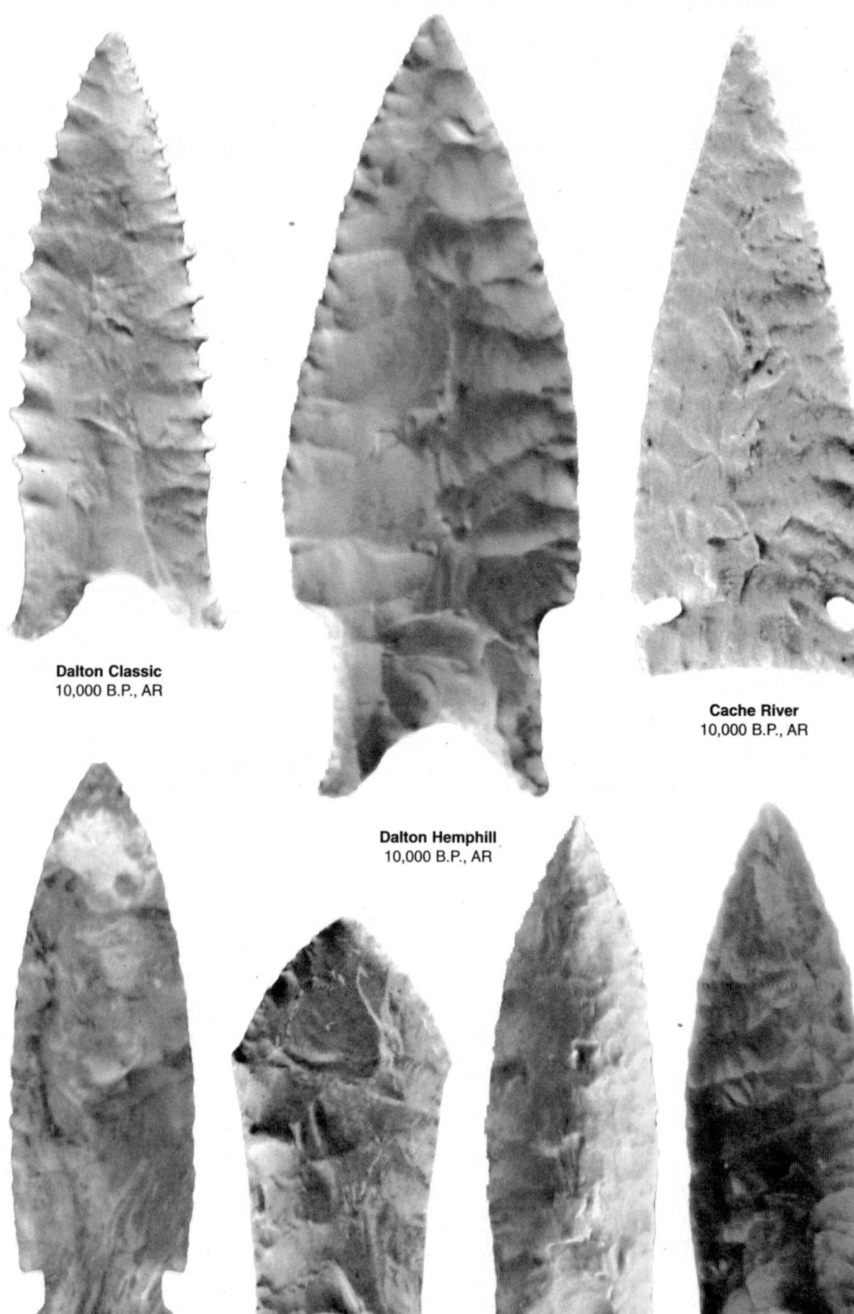

Dalton Classic
10,000 B.P., AR

Dalton Hemphill
10,000 B.P., AR

Cache River
10,000 B.P., AR

Hardin
10,000 B.P., TX
Petrified wood

Pelican
10,000 B.P., LA

Plainview
10,000 B.P., TX

Plainview
10,000 B.P., TX

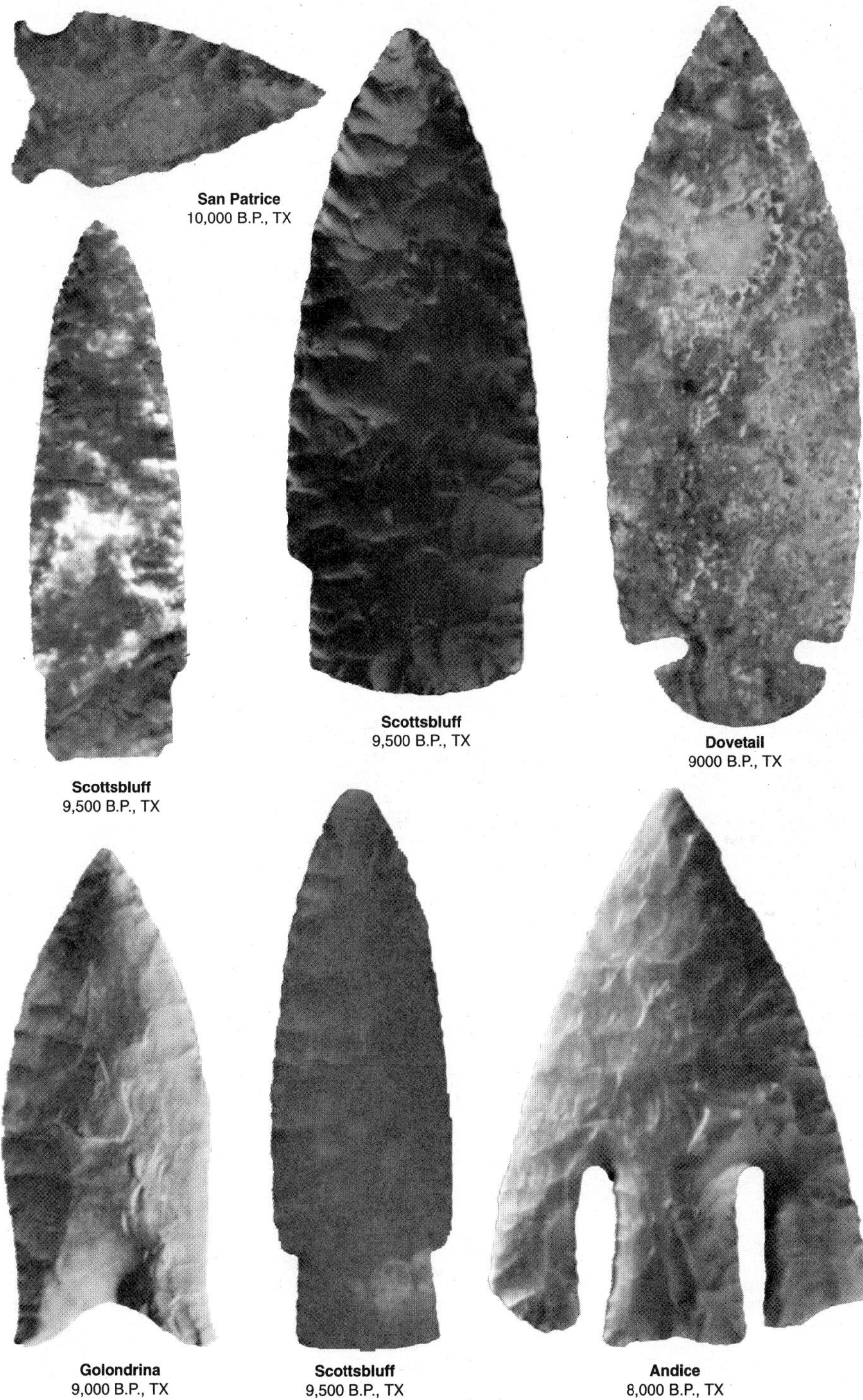

San Patrice
10,000 B.P., TX

Scottsbluff
9,500 B.P., TX

Dovetail
9000 B.P., TX

Scottsbluff
9,500 B.P., TX

Golondrina
9,000 B.P., TX

Scottsbluff
9,500 B.P., TX

Andice
8,000 B.P., TX

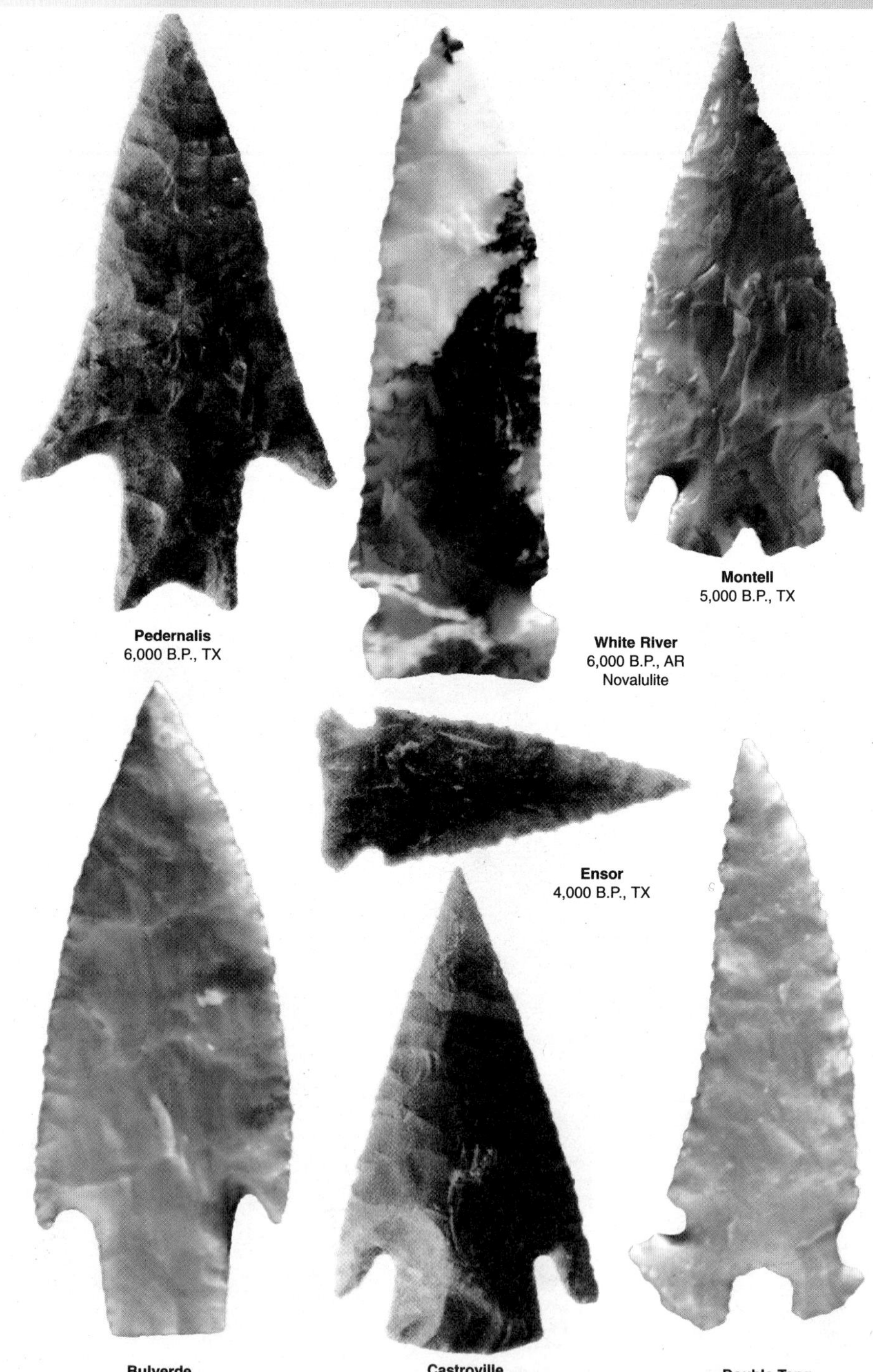

Pedernalis
6,000 B.P., TX

White River
6,000 B.P., AR
Novalulite

Montell
5,000 B.P., TX

Ensor
4,000 B.P., TX

Bulverde
5,000 B.P., TX

Castroville
4,000 B.P., TX

Double Tang
4000 B.P., TX

Ensor Split Base
4,000 B.P., TX

Marcos
3,500 B.P., TX

Polo
4,000 B.P., TX

Delhi
3,500 B.P., LA

Delhi
3,500 B.P., LA

San Saba
3,000 B.P., TX

Fairland
3,000 B.P., TX

SOUTH CENTRAL POINT TYPES

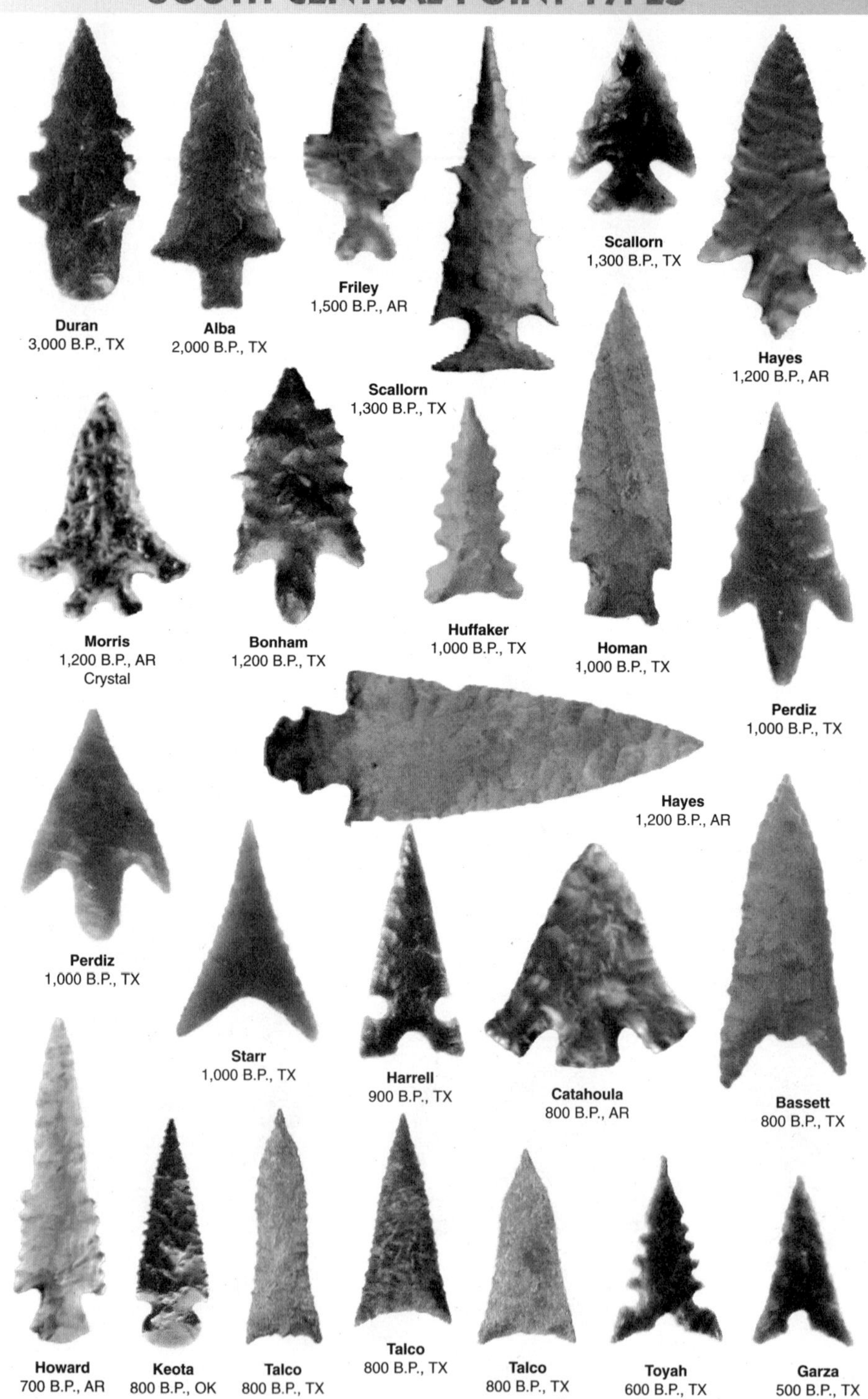
Duran
3,000 B.P., TX
Alba
2,000 B.P., TX
Friley
1,500 B.P., AR
Scallorn
1,300 B.P., TX
Scallorn
1,300 B.P., TX
Hayes
1,200 B.P., AR
Morris
1,200 B.P., AR
Crystal
Bonham
1,200 B.P., TX
Huffaker
1,000 B.P., TX
Homan
1,000 B.P., TX
Perdiz
1,000 B.P., TX
Hayes
1,200 B.P., AR
Perdiz
1,000 B.P., TX
Starr
1,000 B.P., TX
Harrell
900 B.P., TX
Catahoula
800 B.P., AR
Bassett
800 B.P., TX
Howard
700 B.P., AR
Keota
800 B.P., OK
Talco
800 B.P., TX
Talco
800 B.P., TX
Talco
800 B.P., TX
Toyah
600 B.P., TX
Garza
500 B.P., TX

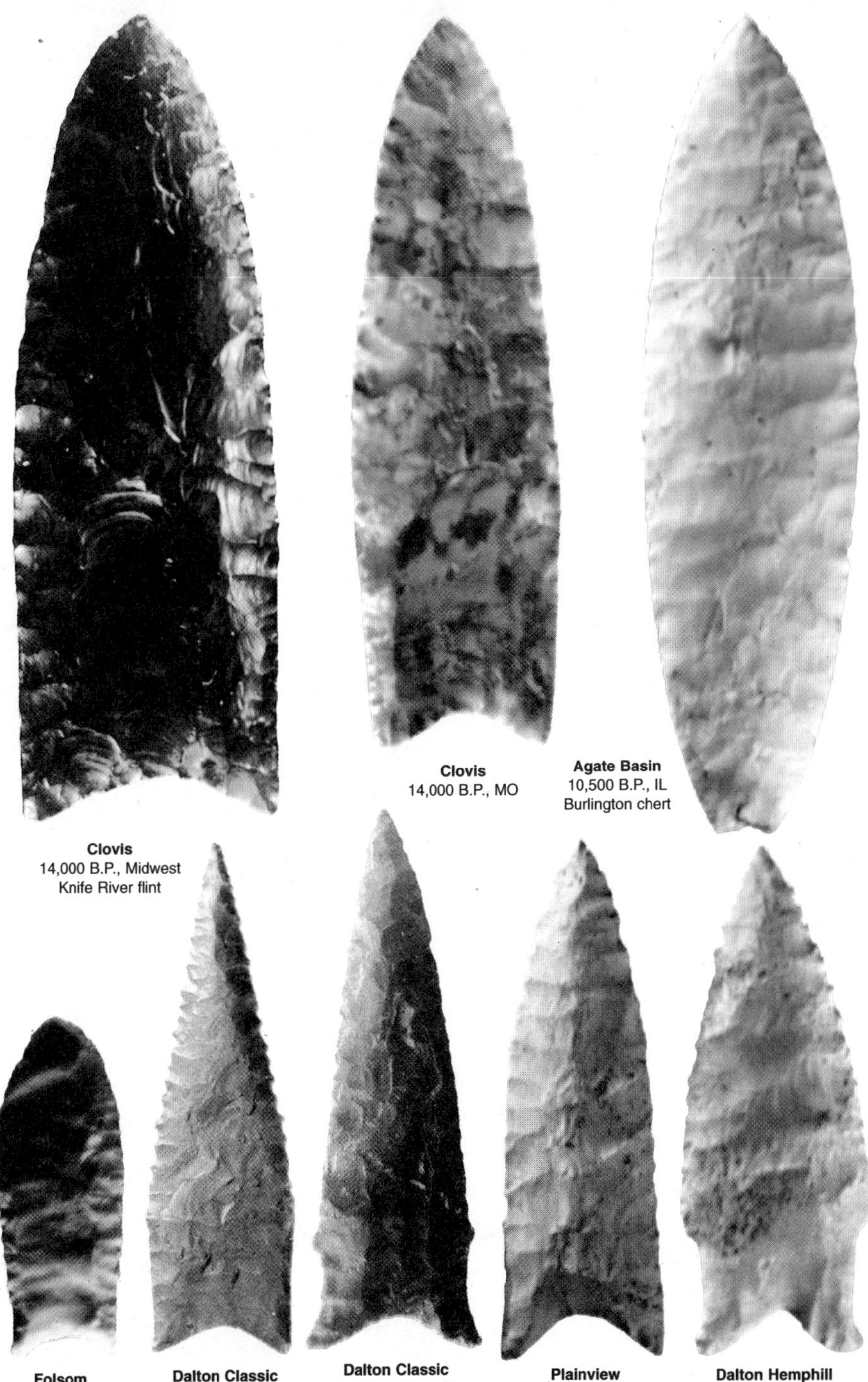

Clovis
14,000 B.P., Midwest
Knife River flint

Clovis
14,000 B.P., MO

Agate Basin
10,500 B.P., IL
Burlington chert

Folsom
10,000 B.P., IL

Dalton Classic
10,000 B.P., IL

Dalton Classic
10,000 B.P., MO

Plainview
10,000 B.P., IL

Dalton Hemphill
10,000 B.P., MO

Dalton Classic
10,000 B.P., IL

Hardin
10,000 B.P., MO

Scottsbluff
9,500 B.P., Wis.
Sugar quartz

Cahokia
1000 B.P., IL
Kaolin chert

Madison, 1,100 B.P., IL
Tittertington form

Hardin
10,000 B.P., IL

Snyders, 2,500 B.P., IL

DESERT SW POINT TYPES

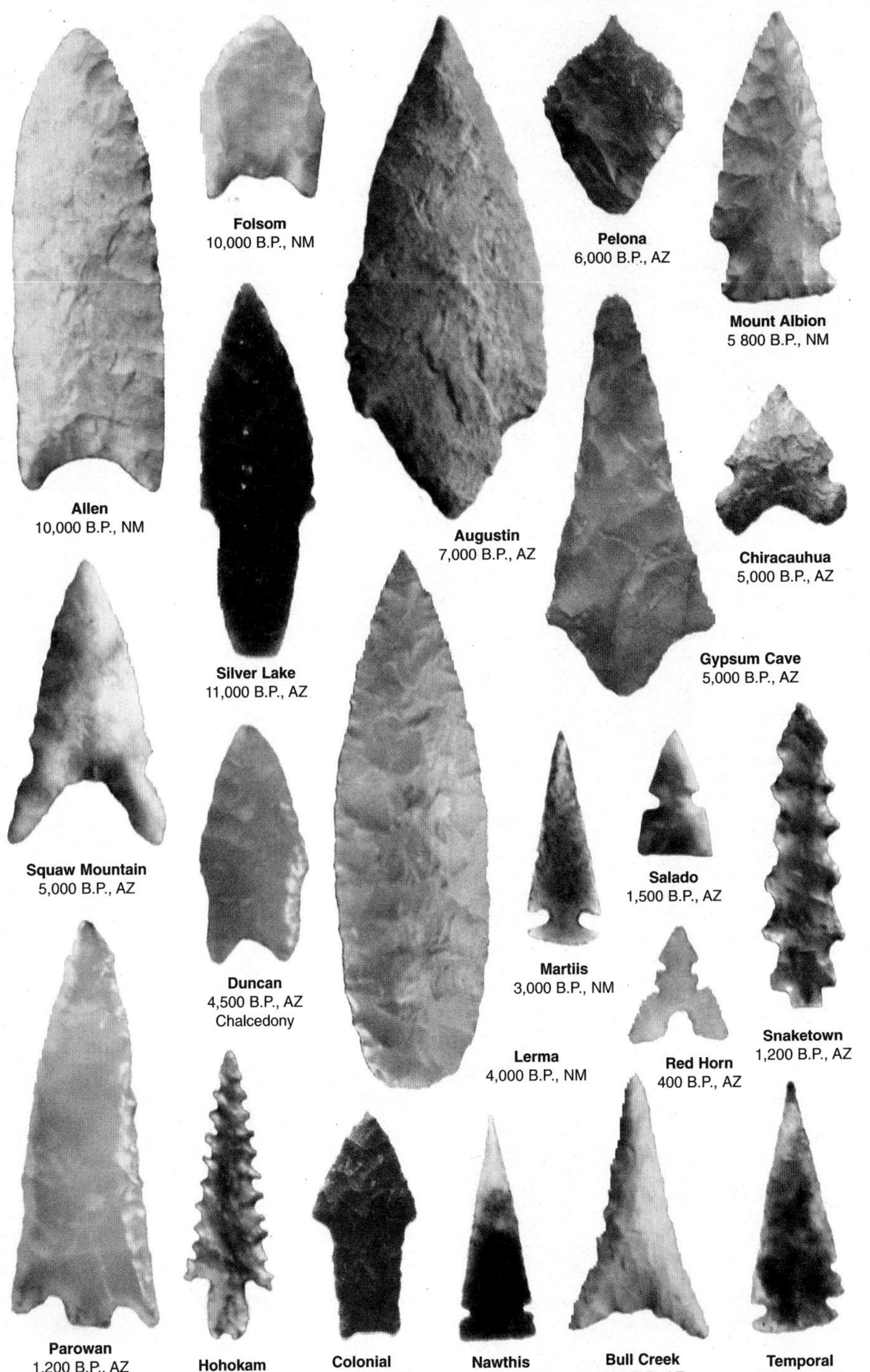

Allen
10,000 B.P., NM

Folsom
10,000 B.P., NM

Silver Lake
11,000 B.P., AZ

Augustin
7,000 B.P., AZ

Pelona
6,000 B.P., AZ

Mount Albion
5 800 B.P., NM

Chiracauhua
5,000 B.P., AZ

Gypsum Cave
5,000 B.P., AZ

Squaw Mountain
5,000 B.P., AZ

Duncan
4,500 B.P., AZ
Chalcedony

Lerma
4,000 B.P., NM

Martiis
3,000 B.P., NM

Salado
1,500 B.P., AZ

Red Horn
400 B.P., AZ

Snaketown
1,200 B.P., AZ

Parowan
1,200 B.P., AZ
Chalcedony

Hohokam
1,200 B.P., AZ

Colonial
1,200 B.P., AZ

Nawthis
1,100 B.P., NM

Bull Creek
950 B.P., AZ

Temporal
600 B.P., NM

Clovis
14,000 B.P., MT

Clovis
14,000 B.P., MT

Goshen
11,500 B.P., WY

Folsom
10,000 B.P., WY

Folsom
10,000 B.P., MT

Midland
10,000 B.P., MT

Scottsbluff
9,500 B.P., MT

Browns Valley
10,000 B.P., MT

Alberta
9,000 B.P., WY

Alder Complex
9,500 B.P., MT.

Eden
9,500 B.P., MT

Eden
9,500 B.P., MT

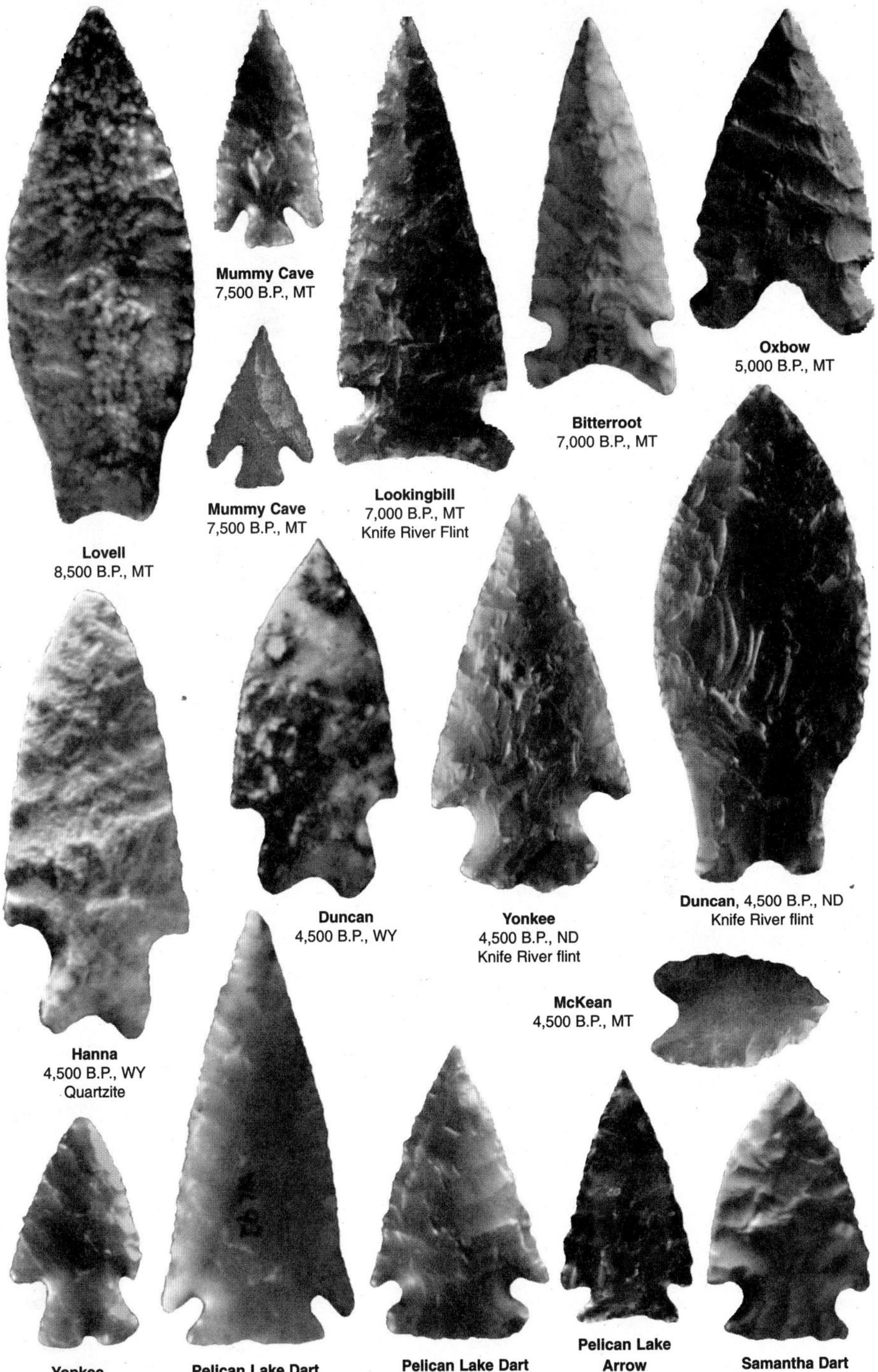

Mummy Cave
7,500 B.P., MT

Lookingbill
7,000 B.P., MT
Knife River Flint

Bitterroot
7,000 B.P., MT

Oxbow
5,000 B.P., MT

Mummy Cave
7,500 B.P., MT

Lovell
8,500 B.P., MT

Duncan
4,500 B.P., WY

Yonkee
4,500 B.P., ND
Knife River flint

Duncan, 4,500 B.P., ND
Knife River flint

McKean
4,500 B.P., MT

Hanna
4,500 B.P., WY
Quartzite

Yonkee
4,500 B.P., WY

Pelican Lake Dart
3,500 B.P., MT

Pelican Lake Dart
3,500 B.P., MT

Pelican Lake Arrow
2,500 B.P., MT

Samantha Dart
2,200 B.P., MT

N. HIGH PLAINS POINT TYPES

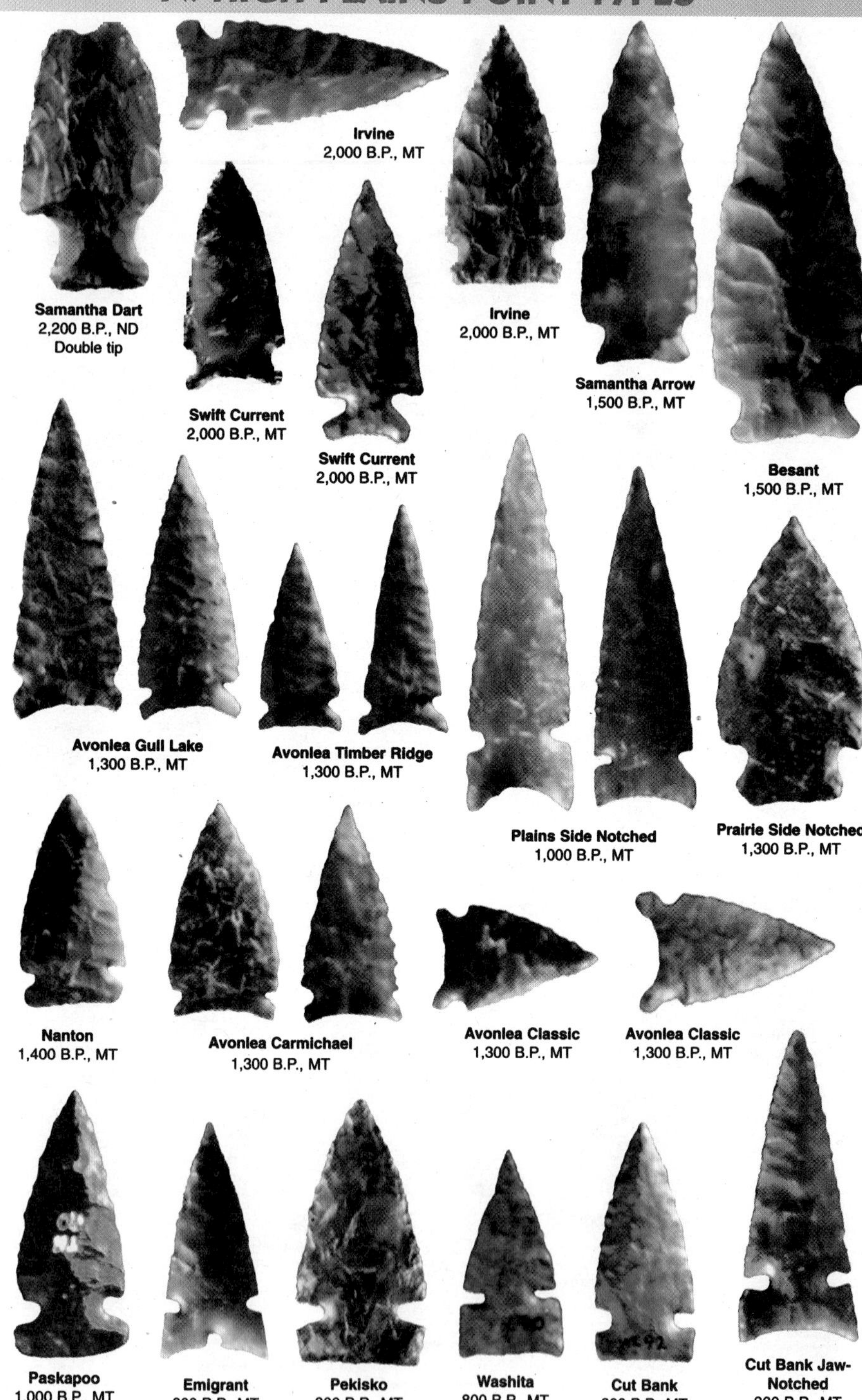

Samantha Dart
2,200 B.P., ND
Double tip

Irvine
2,000 B.P., MT

Swift Current
2,000 B.P., MT

Swift Current
2,000 B.P., MT

Irvine
2,000 B.P., MT

Samantha Arrow
1,500 B.P., MT

Besant
1,500 B.P., MT

Avonlea Gull Lake
1,300 B.P., MT

Avonlea Timber Ridge
1,300 B.P., MT

Plains Side Notched
1,000 B.P., MT

Prairie Side Notched
1,300 B.P., MT

Nanton
1,400 B.P., MT

Avonlea Carmichael
1,300 B.P., MT

Avonlea Classic
1,300 B.P., MT

Avonlea Classic
1,300 B.P., MT

Paskapoo
1,000 B.P., MT

Emigrant
900 B.P., MT

Pekisko
800 B.P., MT

Washita
800 B.P., MT

Cut Bank
300 B.P., MT

Cut Bank Jaw-Notched
300 B.P., MT

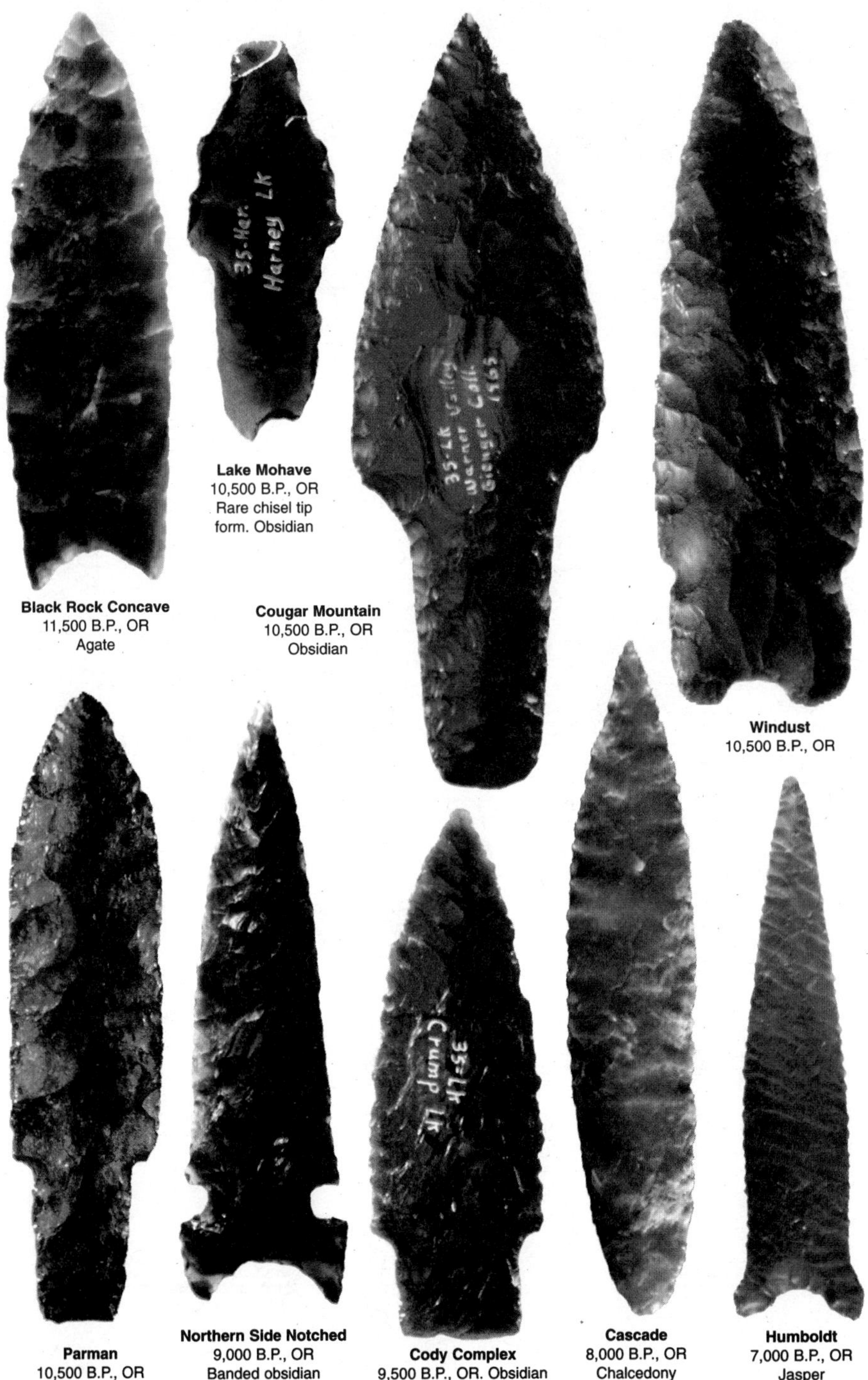

Black Rock Concave
11,500 B.P., OR
Agate

Lake Mohave
10,500 B.P., OR
Rare chisel tip form. Obsidian

Cougar Mountain
10,500 B.P., OR
Obsidian

Windust
10,500 B.P., OR

Parman
10,500 B.P., OR

Northern Side Notched
9,000 B.P., OR
Banded obsidian

Cody Complex
9,500 B.P., OR. Obsidian

Cascade
8,000 B.P., OR
Chalcedony

Humboldt
7,000 B.P., OR
Jasper

GREAT BASIN WESTWARD POINT TYPES

Rabbit Island
6,000 B.P., OR
Elko Eared
4,000 B.P., OR
Agate
Elko Corner Notched
4,000 B.P., OR
Mahagony obsidian
Bitterroot
7,000 B.P., OR
Humboldt
7,000 B.P., OR
Obsidian
Columbia Plateau
2,000 B.P., WA
Snake River
2,000 B.P., OR
Agate
Pinto Basin
4,000 B.P., OR, Obsidian
Walulla
1,000 B.P., OR
Columbia Plateau
2,000 B.P., WA
Klickatat
300 B.P., OR
Hell's Canyon
1,200 B.P., WA
Agate
Walulla
1,000 B.P., OR
Calapooya
1,000 B.P., OR
Cottonwood
700 B.P., OR
Agate
Stockton
400 B.P., CA
Obsidian
Klickatat
300 B.P., OR

CHRONOLOGY/TERMINOLOGY

IMPORTANT EVENTS IN THE HISTORY OF EARLY MAN

It is a clearly established fact that the Indian (or man), in the Western Hemisphere, did not originate from those sources that have long been proposed and advocated by non-scientific theories. Such theories as the lost continent of Mu, the lost tribe of Israel, the sunken continent of Atlantis, the Vikings, The Phoenicians, the Polynesians, lost Egyptian seamen, etc. can only be considered as legends of Western man's origins and have no true basis in fact.

Evidence now clearly indicates that neither the Indian himself, nor his prehistoric ancestor, such as Cro-Magnon, Neanderthal, Peking, Java, Swanscomb, and many others, evolved in the Western Hemisphere. But rather (it is generally accepted), that whoever he was or wherever he came from, he appeared as a full fledged Homo Sapien (man), and entered the unpopulated new world of our Western Hemisphere. He is still with us today.

Likewise, it is generally accepted, with few reservations, that his ancestor the American Indian (and later the American Eskimo), was none other than the Mongolian peoples. There now seems to be little or no reluctance to accept this theory as to the origin of the American Indians' ancestry.

From a genetic point of view, the evidence is overwhelming; scant beard, prominent cheekbones, straight black coarse hair, broad face, large torso, short legs, dark brown-red skin, a tendency to slanted eyes and epicanthus fold.

These nomadic people followed herds of mammoth elephants and other animals, as the herds moved to new grazing lands. The herds were prey and without them early man starved.

These ancestors of the American Indian migrated from inner Mongolia to the Western Hemisphere by way of the Alaskan land bridge that came into being during the glacier epochs. This land-bridge was over a thousand miles wide and was the direct result of a large percentage of the oceans being tied up in glacier ice and snow. This ice and snow (several miles thick in places), was so vast that the resultant weight-burden was great enough that the continents themselves were actually depressed into the Earth's mantle.

The Indians of North America peopled two continents and filled its earth, sea, rivers and sky with a pantheon of Spirits and Gods long before the Bronze Age had even dawned in Europe and Asia.

The men of profound knowledge in Europe overlooked an enormous truth while trying to explain the origins of the Indian within the context of the Bible, which was the basic document of European thought. In truth, the New World contained as varied, and as complex, human societies and communities as did the Old World, but this thought was unacceptable to the Old World.

When Hernando Cortes invaded the Aztecs of Mexico, he encountered an empire that boasted astronomy, writing, a calendar more accurate than that of Europe, monumental architecture, a floating capital city with causeways, canals, and a vast and complex monarchy that ruled thousands of square miles, with millions of people in a number of different tribes.

Francisco Pizarro encountered much of these same cultural advances when he invaded the Incas of Peru. Here the business of a monarchy was more complex due to the empire's incredible size, varied cultures, and the inhospitable Andes Mountain range.

These and other Indians of North, Central and South America are a source of wonder, awe and puzzlement to the savants of Europe. Who were these people? Where did they come from? What was their history?

For nearly two centuries, answers to these questions remained unanswered, or rather farfetched. But, beginning with Thomas Jefferson, an inquiry into questions of American Indian cultural history was done in a systematic and scientific way. Such a detailed approach could be expected of Jefferson since he was known worldwide as "The Renaissance Man".

The course of search, study and inquiry has been arduous, steep and involved. Due to the immensity of the subject, and the nature of the scholarly discipline required, entirely new methods and records of archaeological techniques had to be developed. New date, hypotheses and ideas are constantly examined, compared and re-examined. We now know much, but many old (and new) questions remain for future generations to answer.

Please note that this chronology is obviously subject to critique, revision and correction. Indulgence is a must. Compiling this listing and the research was, as the saying goes, "like putting shoes on a running horse."

As archaeological money and interest increase, as methods and techniques are developed and improved, along with the inclusion of such fields as paleoanthropology, geochemistry, the pedology, the palynology, and others, we are covered each day with a mass of theories, proofs, facts and evidence. We are now rapidly learning about man, his origin, and his history.

For this reason, the chronology that follows includes the total picture of man in order to lead up to one of man's descendants who was the progenitor, or ancestor of our special interest, the American Indian.

CHRONOLOGY

3,750,000 B.P.-Dr. Mary D. Leaky of the National Geographic Society, discovers five foot prints of an ancient man. The mud prints turned out to be fossilized, stone imbedded prints of this age. The prints found at Laetoeli, Tanzania were of an individual who was four feet tall.

3,350,000 B.P.-The earliest know fossil remains of ancient humans discovered by Mary Leaky in December, 1974, in the area called Laetoeli, 25 miles from Olduvai Gorge in Tanzania. The date was proven by radio isotope techniques on fossilized teeth and jawbones of eleven different individuals.

3,000,000 B.P. -Dr. Donald C. Johanson and a team at Hadar, Ethopia in 1974 discover "Lucy", a partial female skeleton. Other finds of 60 individuals there and at Laetoli, Tanzania, led to the naming of a new species of Hominidae, Australopithecus afarensis.

2,500,000 B.P. -Stone tools, similar to the Oldowan tools found in Ethiopia, appear.

2,000,000 B.P -In 1924 a skull of this age was found in a South African cave by Professor Raymond Dart, of the Department of Anatomy at Witwatersand at Johannesburg, South Africa. It is the skull of a six year old child, gathered with other fossils from the limestone quarry which had exposed the cave. Later Professor Dart announced his discovery as the famous Taung Child, which he named Australopithecus africanus. Overnight, the 32-year old Dart was a celebrity.

1,500,000 B.P.- The skull of a Homo Erectus boy is found (in 70 pieces), and fitted together by Richard Leakey, and Kamoya Kimeu near West Turkana, Kenya.

1,500,000 B.P.- Fossilized footprints of ancient man were discovered along the shore of Lake Turkana in northern Kenya. These footprints were discovered in July and August of 1978, by Dr. Anna K. Behrensmeyer of Yale University and the University of California. Announced by the National Science Foundation, the ancient footprints were made by an individual who was 5 feet 6 inches tall and weighed 120 lbs.

1,500,000 B.P.-Man's first standardized tool, the handaxe, appeared. The earlier ones were crudely chipped and called abbevillain, and the later forms were more elegant and called acheulian and chellean.

1,500,000 B.P.-First documented evidence of man using or playing with fire. C.K. Brain (Transvaal Museum in Pretoria) and Andrew Sillen (Univ. of Cape Town) found bone fragments which indicate that fire was used for warmth, cooking, or keeping wild beasts away at the site in Kenya.

1,200,000 B.P. -The Ice Age begins. First Glacier movement South.

800,000 B.P. -The oldest unquestionable site of hominid occupation in Europe is Soleihac, the Massif Central of France. Based on many tools found there.

500,000 B.P. -Northeast of Madrid Spain, at Ambrona and Torralba, on the Spanish plain, butchering sites of Mammoth elephants were found. Excavations by anthropologists Clark Howell and Leslie Freeman revealed thousands of stone tools, traces of fires and well preserved elephant bones and tusks.

400,000 B.P. -At the Terra Amata site on the French Riviera, a foot print of Homo Erectus is unearthed in 1966.

300,000 B.P. -Swanscombe skull fragments, Britain's oldest know human remains, are so dated.

160,000 B.P.-Utility flake tools were in wide use. These Middle Paleolithic tools were known as mousterian and levalloisian.

125,000 B.P.-Neanderthal Man appears on the scene in Europe, based on finds in the Neander Valley near Dusseldorf in Germany starting in 1956.

120,000 B.P.-Excavations at the mouth of the Klasies River in South Africa indicate that ancient people lived there at this time. The occupational levels are as distinct as the layers of a cake and reveal much about our ancestors of that period.

60,000 B.P.-Carbon-14 dates on wood remains unearthed at Amersfoart, Netherlands.

60, 000 B.P.-Kebara Cave, overlooking an Isreali banana plantation, has yielded a Neanderthal burial dating back to this time.

50,000 B.P.-Fragments of anatomically modern humans, found in caves at Klasies River mouth on South Africa's Indian Ocean coast are dated back to this period in the past.

50,000 B.P. -Excavations by an Isreali-French team in 1983, at the Kebara Cave on Israel's Mount Carmel, reveals for the record that at this early time, deliberate burials were already in vogue.

50,000 B.P. -In 1951, Ralph and Rose Solecki, excavating in Shanidar Cave in Iran for the Smithsonian discovers several remains of Neanderthal Man dating to this age. Remains of a variety of small plant pollen gave clues that certain mortuary rites (flowers) already had begun. Now referred to as the "Flower People".

47,000 B.P. -Start of the Paleolithic Age.

47,000 B.P.-Modern man, Homo Sapiens, appears in Europe.

47,000 B.P.-Pedra Furada in Northeast Brazil has a huge rock shelter with cave painting of deer, birds, armadillos, stick figure people, hunting, sex and childbirth. Niede Guidon of the Institute of Advanced Social Science in Paris believes this site was occupied at the same time Neanderthals were living in Europe.

42,000 B.P.-Modern man, Homo Sapiens, appears in the Middle East.

41,000 B.P. -A fossilized skull with many stone implements was found at the Florisbad site near Bloemfortein, South Africa, and has been given this tentative date.

40,000 B.P. -Late Paleolithic flaked tools known as Solutrean Perigondian and Aurignacian appeared (Similar to the later Lerma type of the new world.)

40,000 B.P. -At Orogrande cave in southern New Mexico, archaeologist Richard Mac Neish uncovered chipped stones and the toe bone of a horse with a spear point embedded in it; also found was a fireplace with human fingerprints in the clay.

37,000 B.P. -Carbon test on charcoal from firepits near Lewisville, Texas suggest that man was in that part of North America by this time.

34,160 B.P. -Charcoal from a fire pit in a rock shelter in Brazil give a radio carbon test date of 34,160 B.P. discovered in 1986.

33,000 B.P. -A peat bog site was discovered by Tom Dillehay of the University of Kentucky at Monte Verde, west of the Andes in south-central Chile. Many items were found in excellent condition under the bog including plant remains, wooden artifacts, digging sticks, mortars, spear tips and building foundations. 65 plant species with 15 plants having medicinal properties still used by local Indians today were found.

32,000 B.P. -A wealth of ornaments, tools, and animal remains points to a complex of early Ice Age people located on the windswept steps of Kostienki along the Dan River in the U.S.S.R. These Siberian shelters were mostly made of mammoth tusks, bones, large mandibles and hides.

32,000 B.P. -An ivory carved body of a man, dating to this time was found in a cave at Hohlenstein, West Germany. Years after the discovery, a small lion muzzle was found at the same site and the same level. They fit together. This is the oldest anthropomorphic figure known.

32,000 B.P. -It is now generally agreed that prehistoric people had invented the bow and arrow by this time. This enabled man to much improve his standards of living by increasing his ability to kill animals from a distance. The Egyptians were the first to adopt the bow and arrow as a standard weapon of war, quickly followed by the neighboring countries.

32,000 B.P. -In Brazil, excavations by N. Guidon have revealed remains dating back to 32,000 B.P. And 27,000 B.P. in a rock shelter located in an arid polygon in the state of piaui. The deep levels of Toco-do-Boqueirac-da-Pedra-Furado produced find in support of these dates. Other caves in the same area lend further support to these dated eras.

30,000 B.P. -Neanderthal man appears to be fading from the scene in Europe.

27,000 B.P. -Jacques Cinq-Mars of the Archaeological Survey of Canada has found evidence of episodic human activity at Bluefish Caves in the Yukon. He also found the leg bone of a mammoth from which flakes were chipped. Also, broken mammoth bones were found at Old Crow Basin.

26,000 B.P. -This seems to be the approximate period of time in which Ice Age man began to create works of art with his hands. Of course, those which have lasted long enough for us to find are made of ivory. A small bust of an Ice Age male was found in 1890 in Dolri Vestonice. Starting in 1920, archaeologists have found many additional items of Ice Age man's art at this site. The very realistic likeness of an Ice Age man has recently been re-examined by Alexander Marshook after special request for his evaluation. Exhaustive tests reveal the age of this eight-centimeter Czechoslovakian art at this date.

26,000 B.P. One of the earliest known statues of man was discovered at Brno, Czechoslovakia. This rare human symbol is unique in that it has a mobile left arm, was carved of ivory, and touched with ocher.

23,800 B.P. Material felt to be of human origin is charcoal from an ancient lake bed deposit near Tule Springs, Nevada. Carbon-14 test indicates age of more than 23,800 years old.

22,000 B.P. At Valsequillo, Mexico, geologically dated artifacts suggest man's presence in Middle America at this date.

20,000 B.P. - Cro-Magnon man invents the bone needle, followed by the spear thrower, the bone fish hook, the bow and arrow(millennia later in Europe), musical instruments of bone and decorative ornaments.

20,000 B.P. - Despite hazards brought about by glaciers that gripped North America, Paleo man continued to flood across the land bridge from Asia. Ice-Age hunters, armed with fragile spears, pursued the Woolly Mammoth elephant which stood 13 feet in height. Their descendants peopled the western Hemisphere from Alaska and The Bering Sea, south to Terre del Fuego at the southern tip of South America.

20,000 B.P. -In southwestern Pennsylvania a jagged overhang juts out from a sand stone cliff. In this shelter archaeologists have evidence of human occupation many millenniums ago. A piece from a mat or basket woven 19,600 years ago and hearths, stone tools, and deer bones lined with knife marks were found there. Dubbed "Meadowcroft", the resident hunters-gatherers traded with others in areas we know as Ohio and West Virginia.

20,000 B.P. -In July 1953, Keith Glasscock, amateur archaeologist, finds fluted points and bones of an ancient man at Scharbauer Ranch near Midland, Texas. The Smithsonian Institute announced a year later that these bones and points date back to this time.

20,000 B.P. -Pikimachay (Cave of the Fleas) is located in the temperate basin of Ayacucho, Peru, at an altitude of 9,400 ft. In this harsh environment the cave deposits indicate human occupation until 12,000 B.P. and indicates the Indian's adaptability for the 8,000 year period.

18,000 B.P. -A Paleolithic camp beneath an overhanging rock bluff near Les Eyzies was long used as an Atlantic Salmon fishing camp.

17,000 B.P.-At Laguna Beach, California a human skull was found that dates to 15,000 years B.P. the oldest human remains yet found in North America.

15,500 B.P.-Stone-Age man leaves his pre-historic cave paintings on the wall in Lascaux Cave in Southwestern France and other caves in Europe. Amazingly accurate, it is man's first attempt at the art of depicting living creatures. His earlier forms of art were decorative for himself and for his weapons.

15,000 B.P.-Excavated at Malta, Siberia, an ivory plaque incised with dots may have been an early attempt at a calendar or of record keeping.

15,000 B.P.-The global Ice Age ends although some glaciers persisted to 11,000 B.P. Last retreat of the glaciers, raising the global ocean level by 300 feet, and flooding the coastal areas of all continents.

15, 000 B. P..-Mesolithic Period significant by Magdalenian burins and lancets.

14,000 B.P.-Discovered in 1912, the Tuc d'Audoubert cave in the French Pyrenees has been found to contain statues of hand shaped bison molded of wet clay and dated to this time.

14, 000 B.P.-A spectacular discovery was made in Chile by T. Dillehay and a Chilean team of archaeologists. The remains of an encampment of mastodon hunters previously unknown in South America dated to 14,000 B.P. and found in a peat bog. There were 14 dwellings made of wood and skin housing about 56 people for many seasons. The occupants did not use worked of flaked points. The hunting weapons were stone balls (the oldest baolas in Americas).

14,000 B.P.-Small bands of early man in South America hunted horse, mastodon and giant sloth (all later extinct) in this period. These hunters did note use bifacial stone points, nor did they use flaked or delicately fashioned tools in general. A. Kriger referred to this in 1964 as the "pre-Projectile Phase" on the South American scene, characterized by the absence of bifacial points. It appears that these early South American hunters were very few in number and had not yet mastered the technique of the pressure flaking art.

13, 500 B.P.-Artistic caveman wall art on a sandstone tablet was found in Enlene Cave in the French Pyrenees. Found by Robert Begouen and Jean Clottes.

13,000 B.P.-Taima-taima in northwest Venezuela contains the remains of a mastodon elephant slain at this approximate date. Spear points and tools were also found by archaeologist Ruth Gruhn of the University of Alberta at Edmonton.

13,000 B.P.-Part of a fossilized jaw bone was found south of the equatorial sites in Kenya and Uganda. Believed to be the earliest known and first example of what scientists call Miocene Hominoids. Called "otavipithecus Namibiensis," the fossil, like those from East Africa, is one of the closest to the evolutionary split, says researcher Glen Conroy, Professor of anatomy and anthropology at Washington Medical School in St. Louis.

12,000 B.P.-In 1924, a fluted point campsite was found by C.C. Coffin in eastern Colorado. Over a decade later, bison bones were found during excavation. The points found here were of the same type found one year later on the Folsom site.

12,000 B.P.-In 1925, the Folsom site was found by George McJunkin near Folsom, New Mexico. The remains of Ice Age bison were found with fluted projectile points, the first proof that early man hunted bison.

12,000 B.P.-Midland, Texas. A skull of Midland Man was found and dated back to 12,000 years ago.

12,000 B.P.-In 1987, Moises Aquirre dug up an enormous Clovis spear point. He and his foreman, Mark Mickles, of the R. and R. Orchard, at Wenatchee, Washington, by day's end had found 19 stone tools and 6 large Clovis spearpoints. This was confirmed in 1988 by subsequent excavations in a formal archaeological dig by Dick Daughtery of Washington State University. The largest number of Clovis points ever found (20) in one place, authenticated, with one matched pair 9 inches long, are the largest ever found. They are excellent in workmanship and made of translucent chalcedony.

12,000 B.P.-In 1927, Anna Le Guillion Mitchell-Hedges, adopted daughter of F.A.. Mitchell-Hedges, found a skull of human size and appearance. Carved from a single piece of clear crystal, it is an object unlike any other on earth. Shrouded in mysticism, it was found in the ruins of the Bubaantun Tomb in a large Myan citadel located in Honduras.

11,200 B.P.-In 1936, the Clovis site was found near Clovis, New Mexico. The area is called Llano Estacado. The location excavated was called Blackwater Draw No. 1 where Clovis fluted points were found with mammoth bones, and identified as a "kill" site. Radiocarbon dates are: Clovis level-11,200 B.C., Folsom, Midland level- 10,300 B.P.; Agate Basin level-9,800 B.P.

12,000 B.P.-In Colorado, the Dent Site produced Clovis points in association with debris that dates back to this time.

11,000 B.P.-Last major advance of the glacier period's ice sheet nears present day Milwaukee, Wisconsin.

11,000 B.P.-Unmistakable recent evidence of human occupations found in Fells' Cave, near the Strait of Magellon in Chile. Already, the wanderers who crossed the land bridge from Asia into Alaška had traversed two continents and arrived at the southernmost tip of South America.

11,000 B.P.-In Flint Run, Virginia, numerous quarries and campsites were dated from 9,000 B.P.

10,600 B.P.-At Debert, Nova Scotia, 4,000 fling tools and hunting points (Dalton variants) were found and dated to 10,600 years old.

10,400 B.P.-Burial discovered at Buhl site in western Idaho with a chisel tip Parman point. Unique and contro versial in that the skeleton was caucasian. Carbon dated to this time.

10,240 B.P.-A man of Mongolian decent was found entombed in a lake at Warm Mineral Springs, Florida, in association with a Sabre Tooth Tiger and a Giant Ground Sloth. A spear thrower or atlatl was also found. Carbon-14 dating of this age was obtained. It is not known If the American Indians invented the atlatl themselves or acquired it by way of Asia. A revolutionary improvement for the Indian. This allowed for increasing the impact energy by 200 times as well as extending the range.

10,000 B.P.-Start of the Mesolithic Age.

10,000 B.P.-In Schrabauer, Texas, a woman's skull was found that dated to 8,000 B.P.

10,000 B.P.-At the Hell Gap Site in Eastern Wyoming, Agate Basin, Alberta and Hell Gap points are found.

10,000 B.P.-In 1951, the Quad site on Beaver Creek near Decatur, Alabama, two miles from the Tennessee River, was discovered, producing a new type the Quad point.

10,000 B.P.-In 1936 Sandia Cave in the Sandia Mountains near Albuquerque, New Mexico was hunted by Kenneth Davis. He found relics there abd took them to Dr. Hibben of the University of New Mexico, who excavated the cave. About 19 Sandia points were found, and a radiocarbon date of 19,000 B.P. was reported in the earliest levels, but is today belived to be much later.

10,000 B.P.-Wyoming Thunderbird site. Clovis type projectile points, fragments, and flint napping evidence dated.

10.000 B.P.-Modoc Rock Shelter in Southern Illinois, yielded evidence of early man at the lower levels of the cave-like site.

10.000 B.P.-Footprints of ancient man were found in the mud of a cave in France.

10,000 B.P.-In 1951, the Bull Brooks site, near Ipswich, Massachussets (Essex County), was found to produce fluted points. Radiocarbon dated at 10,000 B.P., these Paleo points were brought to light by William Eldridge as well as Tony, Frank, Joseph and Nicola Vaccaro. Their help and cooperation with John and Beth Brimes (Peabody Museum staff members) clearly establishes Paleo culture in New England. This is a classic example of how persistent and determined amature archaeologists such as Eldridge and the Vaccaro brothers can add much to our knowledge of early man.

10,000 B.P.-An archaeological survey of the Shattuck farm near Andover, Massachussetts revealed that this site has a complex record of cultures of the Archaic and Woodland periods. Now known as the Andover Technological Center, this site has produced 77 known extensive private collections and added much to the cultural knowledge of the Archaic and Woodland periods in Massachusetts.

10,000 B.P.-First known site in America of a maritime adaptation is that of Anangula on the Aleutian Islands. Microlithic tools and microdrills in evidence suggest their wide use in the working of bone and ivory.

9,415 B.P.-In 1940 the Nevada State Park Commission had archeologists Georgia N. & S.M. Wheeler checking caves near Fallon, Nevada for ancient burials. A mummy was found in "Spirit Cave" wrapped in a mat made of tules that was wrapped again in a fur blanket. Woven bags were also found. This is the oldest munny found in North America.

9,000 B.P.-In Fort Rock Cave, Oregon, sandals made of shredded sagebrush bark are found which date back 90 centuries ago.

8,400 B.P.-Numerous excavations in Utah's Hogup Cave revealed hunting and gathering evidence of Indians using this site as a shelter for both seasonal hunts as well as a permanent dwelling place.

8,000 B.P.-In 1956, the Pine Tree site on Beaver Creek near Decatur, Alabama, west of the Quad site, was excavated, naming the Pine Tree point.

7,210 B.P.-In Windover, Florida, 170 individuals were found in a peat bog and carbon dated to this time. Unique in all history is that ancient human brain tissue was found still in an excellent state of preservation. This allowed biologists from the University of Florida at Gainesville to study actual DNA from human brain cells of the first Americans. Finely woven fabrics made from palm fronds were also preserved for study.

7,000 B.P.-Evidence points to this date as the start of corn (maize) as a food product-cultivated by the Indians in Mexico. Maize was the end product of cross-breeding corn grass with tripsacum and teosinte.

7,000 B.P.-Neolithic ware of the stone implements appears. Agriculture and metal working begins.

7,000 B.P.-In the early 1930's the Eden site near Eden, Wyoming, was found. The site was excavated and Eden points were found with fossil bison. Radiocarbon dated at 7,000 B.P.

7,000 B.P.- In 1932, the Scottsbluff site was found in Scottsbluff County, Nebraska. The site was excavated and Scottsbluff points were found with fossil bison. A radiocarbon date of 7,000 B.P. was obtained for this site.

6,500 B.P.-Start of the Copper Age

6,000 B.P.-Shoreline villages of long term occupation at Cape Kiusensfenn, Alaska.

5,600 B.P.-Building of the great Egyptian pyramids begins.

5,500 B.P.-Start of the Bronze Age

5,500 B.P.-Invention of the wheel in the Caucasus, or in Mesopotania.

5,000 B.P.-Earliest evidence of corn in North America was discovered in Bat Cave, New Mexico, and dates back 5,000 years.

5,000 B.P.-Wyoming's Mummy Cave yields evidence of 5,000 years of human habitations and 38 layers of artifacts including agate projectile points in one of the topmost layers.

5,000 B.P.-Weapons, tools and ornaments are hammered from nuggets of copper by Indians of the Great Lakes area.

5,000 B.P.-A recent series of archaeological finds in South America shows that the Incas were merely the final act in the many civilizations of the Andes. New excavations reveal stone pyramids and monuments back to this date along with seeds, potatoes and fragments of nets and fabrics.

5,000 B.P.-12 large wooden boats were found at Abydos, Egypt in 1991. 50 to 60 feet long, these boats are the earliest royal ships ever found, the greatest number of ancient ships ever found at one site and the oldest boats ever found anywhere. The site is 280 miles south of Cairo and 8 miles from the Nile River. Each boat was inside a mud brick coffin and buried in a pit with pottery. The boats were to serve as magical vehicles to transport the dead pharaohs through the sky. Found by David O'Conner, curator of the Egyptian section of the University Museum of Pennsylvania and the Egyptian Antiquities Organization.

5,000 B.P.-Johan Reinhard with Chicago's Field Museum of Natural History in La Paz, Bolivia has been studying high-altitude ceremonial sites in the Andean peaks. It seems that the Inca Indians believed these high peaks were their ancestors, who had to be venerated by sacrifice. Reinhard located, studied and excavated hundreds of "offerings" and human sacrifices to these Inca gods. The sites are located on almost inaccessible peaks and crags, at heights of 17,000 to 22,000 feet. the Incas built ceremonial centers here in the rock and gravel, so isolated that they were undisturbed for 500 to 1,000 years. At these antiseptic, very high altitudes, the site and mummified contents were actually in a "deep freeze" locale. The cold is so extreme that even the flesh on the mummies is well preserved. Young women, boys and girls were sacrificed here. Blood types, diseases and last food consumed before death was discernible.

4,600 B.P.-In 1991 a frozen and mummified prehistoric man was found at an elevation of 10,500 feet in a melting Similaur glacier in the Alps on the Italian side. Dated from the Neolithic age, a pure copper axe (not bronze), a bow, quiver, arrows, flint knife, and flint fire starter with kindling in a leather pouch were found with the remains. This is the oldest naturally preserved corpse ever found of a European man.

4,500 B.P.-Clay tablets found in northwestern Syria reveal that an ancient city named Ebla once rivaled Egypt and Mesopotamia as major powers of the ancient world. Dr. Paolo Matthiae of the University of Rome, while on an archaeological mission in Syria, discovered more than 15,000 cuneiform tablets in a mound called Tell Markdikh. The early Bronze Age city of Ebla is clearly stated many times. The cities of Sodom and Gomorrah as well as Iram, a city mentioned in the Koran, are referred to for the first time.

4,500 B.P.-A giant fish weir was built near Boston, Massachussetts.

4,400 B.P.-Records and relics found in Peru take the record of Western man, the Indian, back to still further distant epochs about the year 2,400 B.C.

4,000 B.P.-Finds on the surface and later archaeological digs in recent decades date the inhabitation of Russell Cave in Alabama.

4, 000 B.P.-Mashkan-Shapin, a Mesopotamian city is discovered in January of 1989. Found by Archaeologist Elizabeth C. Stone of the State University of New York at Stony Brook.

3,800 B.P.-Tell Leilan, a Mesopotamian city is discovered in 1985 and dated to this time.

3,600 B.P.-Bronze Age in China begins

3,600 B.P.-Start of the Iron Age

3,500 B.P.-Near the confluence of the Arkansas and Mississippi River in Louisiana, the Poverty Point Culture evolved. This enigmatic cultural site is one square mile in size, but contains six miles of ridges built by hauling in 1,500,000,000 pounds of dirt by hand.

3,000 B.P.-The Maya culture begins which lasted for 2,000 years.

3,000 B.P.-In late 1989, Richard Hansen, who discovered the ancient Mayan city of Nakbe, unearthed another significant city of Nakbe in that it is built over an even earlier Mayan village dating back to 1,000 B.C. that had been preserved underneath it like a modern-day Pompeii.

3,000 B.P.-Rise of the Adena culture in Ohio. A turkey-tail point (Adena Culture) made of Indiana hornstone found in Indiana was dated to 3,000 years ago.

2,600 B.P.-Advent of Stonehenge on the Salisbury Plain in England.

2,600 B.P.-The Mayan Indian calendar of the Central American Indian began in 613 B.C. (based on actual Mayan calendar date).

2,600 B.P.-Tikal, a Mayan super city begins, consisting of 3,000 constructions in a 6 square mile area, with more than 10,000 earlier structures lying beneath these. Here stands the tallest ancient structure made by Indians in the Western Hemisphere, erected in 741 A.D.. This culture lasted through to 900 A.D..

2,600 B.P.-In a remote Guatamalan jungle in 1989, Richard Hanson, U.C.L.A. archaeologist, excavated what may be the oldest known Mayan center of civilization. Known as Nakbe, it consists of 75 major structures and hundreds of mounds and has been dated to this time.

2,600 B.P.-In 1932, a great treasure was discovered at Monte Alban (Olmec Culture). Found were over 500 pieces of Mixtec jewelry, including gold, silver, jade, turquoise, rock crystal and intrically carved bone.

2,600 B.P.-At Copan "City of Kings" in Honduras, William L. Fash, Jr. of Northern Illinois Univ., and Ricardo Agurcias Fasquelle of the Honduran Institute of Anthropology discovered a Mayan temple. this buried temple had 200-250 years of construction beneath it and three major structures atop it. The 18 by 12 meter temple had been completely plastered over and sealed up before the later temples were built over it. In the temple were found nine eccentric flints of intricate quality with scarps of cloth wrapping clinging to their surface. Each piece was individually wrapped and bundled together.

2,500 B.P.-The Bow is introduced in North America, after having been used in Europe for several thousand years.

2,290 B.P.-The National Geographic Society discovers a Mayan monument in the Yucatan in 1939, which bears the date of Nov. 4th, 291 B.C. (spinden Correlation), the earliest known work dated by man himself found in the new world thus far.

2,250 B.P.-Rise of Olmec civilization and culture of Central America.

2.000 B.P.-In 1837, a woman's body was found in Haraldskjaer Fen, Denmark in a peat bog, perfectly preserved with hair, clothes, and skin all intact. On May 8th, 1950, Tollund Man was found in a peat bog near Aarhu, Denmark. He was so perfectly preserved that the undigested remains of his last meal were still in his digestive tract. With more discoveries, these bog people were dated to 1500 to 2000 years old.

2,000 B.P.-In 1954 the Camp Creek site in Greene County, Tennessee, at the convergence of Camp Creek and the Nolichucky River, was excavated. Camp Creek and Nolichucky points found here became new types. Radiocarbon dates of 2,000 B.P. were acquired.

2,000 B.P.-The Snaketown site of Hohokam culture near Gila, Arizona yields some 3,000 beautifully chipped arrowheads in one ceremonial area. Called Sawtooth Icicles, they are of unique beauty. the World's first acid etching was done by the Hohokam.

1,700 B.P.-Known as the "Moche" a culture of Indians in the Lambrayeuqe valley of Peru lived by farming the land from about A.D. 100 to A. D. 800. Ever since 1532, when the Spanish appeared, their tombs have been looted for gold and artifacts even to this day. In February 1987, some looters were caught with part of their bounty. Investigations by authorities and the Bruning Museum of Peru resulted in the discovery of an ancient tomb never before opened. Now considered one of the richest and most significant tombs ever found in the Americas, this excavation reveals much about the clutter of the "Moche".

1,500 B.P.-At Lake Titicaca, in Bolivia, the Andean Empire of the Tiahuanaco flourished. Their knowledge of hydrology and farming to produce irrigated fields outproduced modern farming methods by a yield seven times as great. This was done without modern farm technology and equipment by using the Tiahuanaco technique of raised fields and water channels.

1,500 B.P.-A recent dig in South America has uncovered a Peruvian King Tut in an elaborate tomb containing his 1,500 year old remains. Buried with him were hundred of priceless gold and silver artifacts.

24 A.D.-In 1890, Frank H. Cushing of the Smithsonian Institution discovers and partially excavates the site of Key Marco, Florida. He finds several hundred wooden artifacts and works of art over 1,000 years old still preserved.

100 A.D-Rise of the Culture preceding the Aztecs, known as Teotihuacan (Yucatan). This civilization built the two famous structures known as The Pyramid of the Sun and The Pyramid of the Moon, the first great city in the New World.

100 A.D.-Caracol, an ancient Mayan city, flourishes. Remains of buildings at this city in the Yucatan were taller than any building in the Americas until the construction in 1896 of the Flatiron building in New York City.

200 A.D.-Rise of the Hopewell Culture in midwestern United States.

200 A.D.-Largest effigy mound in America was built, the Serpent Mound in Ohio.

575 A.D.-Zimbabwe, the mystery city of Southern Rhodesia is dated by Carbon-14 tests.

600-1200 A.D.-Mississippian ceremonial centers evolved rapidly in the Southeast. Spiro in Oklahoma, Etowah in Georgia, and Cahokia near St. Louis, all of whose names are legendary.

879 A.D.-A stela bearing this Mayan date(converted) was found at Chichen Itza. This Mayan city was a center of advanced civilization. Here was the sacred sacrificial Cenote (lake) where children were sacrificed amid great treasure and artifacts.

900 A.D.-The Turks develop an advanced bow and arrow. Their laminated bows were made of a combination of special woods, animal horns and tendons.

924 A.D.-In 1924, L.L. Loud, of the University of California, found several duck decoys in Lovelock Cave in Northwestern Nevada. Dated at 1,000 years of age, these decoys were made of bouyant rushes, and some were covered with duck feathers; more proof of the masterful adaptions made by the American Indians.

1000 A.D.-The sophisticated pre-Inca Indians created the incredible giant art of Peru's Nazea plain. Giant spiders, repitiles, birds, insects, fish and monkeys are included with lines and geometrical figures so vast that they were not discernible until the advent of aircraft.

1064 A.D.-Construction of the Tenayuca Pyramid (The Pyramid of Serpents), near present day Mexico City.

1100 A.D.-The crossbow becomes the most popular weapon in Europe. It fired a smaller and shorter arrow, but it was a deadly and accurate projectile called a bolt.

1100 A.D.-The rise of the Toltec civilization and culture in Mexico.

1100 A.D.-Wetherill and Mason, in December 1888, discover the cliff dwellings at Mesa Verde, Colorado built nearly 800 years earlier by the Anasazi. This one site had 23 kivas and 200 rooms.

1100 A.D.-Cahokia, in Illinois, becomes the largest town in North America.

1100 A.D.-Pueblo Bonito, in New Mexico, becomes the largest in Pueblo village in North America.

1200 A.D.-Easter Island statues were erected.

1200 A.D.-Rise of the civilization and culture of the Aztecs.

1200-1400 A.D.-The large Mississippian town of Moundville in western Alabama flourishes.

1325 A.D.-Founding by the Aztecs of Tenochititlan (now Mexico City), built on a marshy island in Lake Texacoco. Alliance with Texacoco and Tlacopan, along with subjugation of Tlatelelco, forged the highest civilization in the Western Hemisphere prior to the advent of Columbus. By the time of its conquest by Hernando Cortes, this city had a population of 300,000. A city of canals and causeways, its beauty awed the Spanish Conquistadors as they were aware that no city in Europe could compare to it. the Spaniards promptly proceeded to destroy it.

1438 A.D.-Dawn of the Inca Empire in Peru. Forged by the emperor Pachacuti, ninth in the dynasty of Incas, lords of Cuzco.

1492 A.D.-Christopher Columbus lands at San Salvador and claims all land in the Western world for Spain.

1500 A.D.-A bison kill site was discovered in 1969 by a surveying crew laying out an interstate just east of Sundance Wyoming. Now known as the "Vore Buffalo Jump" this site has revealed that between 1500 and 1800 A.D. an estimated 20,000 animals died and were butchered here by the Indians. The bison were periodically driven by the Indians over a 55 foot drop in small groups, as needed for food and etc. The drop killed, injured, or stunned the bison for slaughter. This site was used by the Arapaho, Cheyenne, Kiowa, Apache, Crowe, Shoshone and the Sioux Indians.

1519 A.D.-On Good Friday, Hernando Cortes, with 508 soldiers, 16 horses, and 14 cannon landed at San Juan de Ulua (modern day Vera Cruiz). From here Cortes started the looting and destruction of an innocent people consisting of many cultures and civilizations, not to end until 1525 A.D. with the conquest of the Maya (Guatemala).

1540 A.D.-The earlier Mississippian ceremonial centers were quickly followed by satellite cultures such as Hiwassee Island, Citico, and Tellico in Tennessee. Weeded Island, Coles creek, Natchez Coosa, and Ocmulgee complexes were next. Many of these were encountered by Desoto on his explorations, including the older Etowah center at Cartersville, Georgia.

1540 A.D.-Hernando DeSoto, the Spaniard explorer, seeking gold, starts his explorations at the Southeastern areas of what is now Florida, Georgia, Alabama, Tennessee, and Mississippi as well as touching the western areas of North and South Carolina. As a result of this expedition, the Indian population in the Southeast was nearly wiped out within 10 years.

1706-1714 A.D.-The Cherokee Indian replaced the Creeks and Yuchi (Children of the Sun), in the area of what is now Tennessee.

1797 A.D.-John Frere found a flint axe in association with a pleistonce elephant tooth near Hoxie, England.

1801 A.D.-Thomas Jefferson published a volume describing his investigations and excavations of a mound near his home, Monticello in Virginia. The first organized site work. Jefferson concluded that these mounds were the work of the ancestors of the Indians of his time, a view not generally accepted until 100 years later.

1838 A.D.-The removal of the Cherokees and other Indians from lands east of the Mississippi River was effected by the U.S. Army under command of General Winfeld Scott.

1891 A.D.-Eugene Dubois, a Dutchman, finds the skull of Java Man. The find was the result of extensive search and excavation on the banks of the Solo River inJava. Now called Homo Erectus, this was for many years the oldest evidence of early man.

1894 A.D.-Duck River cache found in Tennessee, dated to 1,500 A.D. This is the Finest assemblage of flaked artifacts ever found.

1911 A.D.-Hiram Bingham finds the timeless city of the Incas, Machu Picchu. The mountain-locked city is perched on a jungle crag of the Andes in Peru.

1929 A.D.-In China, in 1927, a young paleontologist named W.E. Pei found a skull cap embedded in deposits in a limestone cave at Zhoukoudian, near Beijing. Called Peking Man, it is a counterpart to Java Man.

1941 A.D.-A fluted point site was found near Enterline, Pennsylvania. The points were made from Onodago chert originating from a quarry about 200 MIles away. These points had multiple fluting which is now called the Enterline method of fluting, and considered to be an early form of fluting technique. the Williamson site in Dinwiddie County, Virginia and the Joffre Coe site in North Carolina also used the Enterline method of fluting.

1955 A.D.- The LeCroy site, seven miles north of Harrison Bay State Park in Hamilton County, Tennessee, was named after Archie LeCroy who had worked the site for ten years. This site produced points from Paleo to Mississippian. A large quantity of bifurcated stemmed points were found here and given his name.

1955 A.D.-Wheeler point named by James W. Cambron after the Wheeler Basin of North Alabama.

1959 A.D.-Mary D. Leakey makes a startling find-the skull of Zinjanthropus, or Australopihecus boisei, at the site of Tanzania's Olduvai Gorge.

1972 A.D.-Richard Leaky finds a skull similar to Zinjan at Lake Turkana in Africa.

TERMINOLOGY

Agate-A semi-precious chalcedony formed as quartz fossils of a previous geological age. The colors are cloudy, clear to banded.

Agatized Coral-Found in Florida and used to produce beautifully flaked points. All coral has small polyps visible under magnification.

Archaic-The archaeological period that falls between Paleo and Woodland.

Asymmetrical-A term used to describe points that are not of the same form on both sides.

Auriculate-Refers to rounded or pointed ears that project from the base or stem of certain points.

Barb-A protruding shoulder that forms a point. Also see *wing.*

Basal Edge-The bottom edge of a point.

Basal Grinding-When the edge around the hafting area of a point has been smoothed so that the lashing would not be cut.

Basal Notch-When the basal edge of a point is notched for hafting.

Basal Polish-A polishing of the faces of the hafting area that occurs on certain Paleo points.

Base-The bottom part of a point used for hafting.

Baton-A hand-held ceremonial object made of flinty material used in the eagle dances of the Mississippian peoples.

Beavertail-Refers to the point made by the Adena peoples that has a stem in the form of a beaver's

tail.
Bevel-The sloped edge of a blade or stem.
Bifurcated-Refers to the stem of points that have a central notch splitting the stem in two ears.
Bird Point-A term used to describe very small arrow points, believed by some to have been used for shooting birds. Actually, small triangular points have been found embedded in the bodies of deceased Indians during archaeological digs, suggesting they were used in war. Most of the Mississippi culture arrow points fall into this category.
Blade-The area of a point between the tip and stem of base.
Blank-See *preform.*
Blunt-Refers to a point which has a short, broad, rounded shape and is usually applied to point stems.
B.P.-Before present.
Buffalo River Chert-A colorful middle Tennessee chert with specks and bands of browns to reds to purples used in point production.
Bulbous-A term used to describe a circular or rounded shape and is usually applied to point stems.
Burin-A Lancet with one end fractured off at an angle, producing a sharp point.
Burlington Chert-A fossil bearing quartz found in Illinois and Missouri.
Cache-a group of points deposited in the same place, usually of the same type and origin.
Callche-Calcium deposited on points found in Texas and adjoining states.
Carter Cave Chert-Found in Northeastern Kentucky, a high quality, beautifully colored material of tans to orange to reds.
Ceremonial-Any object made for a specific use in a rite or ceremony denoting authority or power. i.e. *Duck River Cache.*
Chalcedony-A quartz-like material with a waxy luster.
Channel Flake-A longitudinal flake produced in the fluting process of Paleo points.
Chert-A flintlike quartz that often occurs in limestone.
Chisel Tip-A sharp, "squared" projectile tip produced by the removal of a burin flake from each face at opposite corners.
Classic Example-A term used to refer to a point that represents the truest form of a particular type.
Clipped Wing-A barbed shoulder that has been fractured off or clipped.
Collateral-Refers to a flaking style where parallel flakes are removed from each side of a blade and meet in the center, forming a median ridge.
Conchoidal Fracture-The breakage of rock in concentric circles or in a shell-like pattern.
Conglomerate-A Metamorphic rock that is geologically recombined and is composed of clay, sand, mud and pebbles.
Contracting-Refers to the width of a stem or point that is diminishing.
Concave-Slanting inward.
Convex-Slanting outward.
Core-A cone-shaped form of flint or chert produced from spalls. Long slivers are struck off the circular base used in point production.
Corner Notch-When the basal corners of a point are notched for hafting.
Corner Tang-When a single tang is located on one of the basal corners in a diagonal posture.
Coshocton Chert-From south central Ohio, a grey to blue to black chert used in point production.
Cross Section-A mid-section representation of the shape and thickness of a point.
Crystal Quartz-Clear, pure, hard silica from the quartz crystal, used in rare instances for points.
Distal End-The area of the tip of a point.
Dovetail-The other type name for *Plevna* , which refers to the shape of the base of this corner notched point.
Dover Chert-A high quality brownish to black material that comes from an ancient quarry located near Dover, Tennessee. This material is used in point production and has been popular with all cultures from Paleo to the current day.
Duck River Cache-The world's largest and best-known group of ceremonial flint objects ever found; from the Duck River in West Tennessee.
Duckbill Scraper A long, ovoid-shaped, uniface tool in the form of a duck's bill, steeply beveled on the broad end.
Eagle Claw-A Ceremonial object made of flinty material in the form of an eagle's claw, made by the Mississippian peoples and used in their ceremonial eagle dances.
Ears-Pointed or rounded projections from the base of certain points.
Edwards Plateau Chert-A Texas material found in limestone and ranging in color from browns, tans to greys.
Effigy Flints-Extremely rare flinty forms chipped into the shape of various animals such as human heads, turtles, snakes, eagles, etc.
E-Notch-The same as *Key notch.*
Enterline-Refers to an early method of fluting used by the Paleo Indians first recognized on a site near Enterline, Pennsylvania. Two parallel flutes are struck on each face before the final central flute.
Expanding-Refers to the width of a stem or point that is getting larger.
Fake-A modern reproduction that is sold as an authentic ancient artifact.
Fishhook-Authentic fishhooks made of flinty material are extremely rare. If they exist at all. Beware of recently made examples for sale.

Fishtail-A term used to describe auriculate or points with expanding ears.
Flaking-Refers to the chipping or shaping of the stone.
Flint-A greyish to black to brown quartz with a high silica content that produces a conchoidal fracture. It is usually found in association with chalk, limestone, and other rock deposits which contain lime. It commonly occurs in small and large ovoid nodules as well as in veins. Impure flint is known as chert, which varies widely as to texture, color, grain and knapping characteristics. Pure flint is so hard and even-grained that its use by early man was a vital necessity in producing arrowheads, spear-heads, knives, ceremonial objects, and other utility tools such as lancets, drills and other implements. Late Stone-Age man learned that when struck with high iron content rocks, the flint gave off sparks. Thus, it became Iron-Age man's method of producing fire.
Flint Ridge Chert-A high quality multi-colored material that is used in flint knapping from Paleo times to present day. The quarry is located near Columbus, Ohio.
Flute-A grooved channel on one or both faces of a point struck from the base. A technique used in Paleo times.
Fort Payne Chert-An Alabama material found in tans, greys, browns, and white mixed.
Fractured Base-See Snapped Base.
Gem Quality-When a point is made of semi-precious material such as agate, petrified wood, jade, etc.
Graver-A Paleo flint uniface tool with sharp projectins for puncturing or incising purposes.
Grinding-See *Basal grinding.*
Heat Treated-A process used by early Indians to improve the quality of the stone for easier flaking. The stone would be buried in sand under a fire and exposed to temperatures exceeding 400 degrees for several days. This would change the molecular structure as well as the color of the original material.
Hematite-(ironstone)-A reddish to purplish-brown iron oxide sometimes used in point manufacture.
Hinge Fracture-The termination point of a struck flake where it breaks off.
Historic-The archaeological period following Mississippian when the Indians came in contact with Europeans.
Horizontal Transverse-Refers to a flaking style where horizontal parallel flakes are removed that extend from one side of the blade, across the face to the other side.
Hornstone-A bluish to grey chert from Indiana and Kentucky.
Horse Creek Chert-A rare red, yellow and blue material from West Tennessee that is highly prized among collectors.
Impact Fracture-A grooved channel that begins at the tip of a point and runs towards the base, occurring during impact when the point is thrown or shot.
Jasper Chert-A reddish to yellow to brown variety of quartz used in point production.
Key Notch-A Blade notching technique that produces a spur or ridge at the base of the notch in the form of an E. See *Thebes* points.
Lanceolate-A term used to describe a stemless point.
Lancet-A thin, long, narrow flake of flinty material used for slicing.
Limestone-A sedimentary material formed primarily of calcium.
Lobbed-Refers to the base portion of a point that is eared. The ears are rounded and are formed by the meeting of two circles creating a lobbed effect.
Mace-A hand-held ceremonial object made of flinty material used in the eagle dances by the Mississippian peoples.
Median Ridge-Refers to a high ridge that forms in the center of a blade due to angle parallel flaking.
Mississippian-The Archaeological period that occurred after Woodland and before Historic, about 1000 to 1500 A.D.
Mottled-Any point material that contains spots of different colors or shades.
Nodule-A concretion of chert, flint and other substances that occurs in chalks and limestone. Nodules are broken into spalls which are chipped into cores.
Oblique Transverse-Refers to a flaking style where oblique parallel flakes are removed that extend from one side of the blade across the face to the other side.
Obsidian-A dark glassy volcanic rock.
Paleo-The earliest archaeological period.
Patina-A chemically created coating caused by oxidation due to long exposure to oxides.
Percussion Flaking-The first stage in the process of shaping a point or blade when flakes are removed by striking the edge with a blunt tool.
Perforator-Usually an arrowhead that has been rechipped with a sharp needle-like point for puncturing or incising purposes.
Petrified Wood-A colorful agatized chalcedony used in point production.
Polished See *Basal polish.*
Pre-Colombian-Occurring before Columbus 1492.
Preform-A roughly shaped elliptical blank prepared for later finishing into a point or blade.
Pressure Flaking-The final stage of shaping a point or blade when flakes are removed with the point of a tool through forced pressure rather than blows.
Projectile-A body impelled or projected through the air.
Pudding Stone-See *Conglomerate.*
Quartzite- See *Sugar quartz & Tallahata quratzite.*

Reproduction-A recent facsimile of an ancient artifact.
Sandstone-A metamorphic stone composed of layers of sand.
Scraper-A tool that is made either from scratch or from broken points used to scrape hides. See *Duckbill, Turtleback, Thumb & Side Scraper.*
Serrated Edge-A saw-toothed cutting edge pressure flaked on the blade edge.
Shoulder-The area of a point that divides the blade from the stem.
Side Notch-Refers to a notch in the side of a point for either hafting purposes or decoration.
Side Scraper-A lanceolate shaped uniface blade with a prepared edge on one or more sides for scraping.
Slate-A metamorphic sedimentary material that forms in thin layers and contains various amounts of organic material.
Snapped Base-A term used to describe points that have a part of the base intentionally fractured or snapped off. See *Decatur and Kirk.*
Spall-A chunk of flint or chert broken off a nodule from which long slivers can be fractured off for point production. Spalls are converted into cores.
Stem-The area of a point behind the shoulders that is used for hafting.
Striking Platform-A raised area prepared on the base of Paleo points from which a flute can be struck. See example under *Clovis.*
Stunner-A short blunt arrow point believed by some to have been used only to stun the animal for capture. These were probably used as knives or scrapers.
Sugar Quartz-Also known as quartzite, a granular low grade form of quartz used in the production of some point types.
Sun Disc-A circular ceremonial effigy form of the Sun made from flinty material.
Tallahatta Quartzite-A greyish fossiliferous stone used in point production. This material oxidizes easily, resulting in a pitted appearance and a reduction in mass.
Tang-A projection that extends from the base of a point (see Ears).
Thumb Scraper- An elliptical-shaped uniface scraper in the form of a turtle's back.
Thunderbird-A legendary bird-beast that the Indians believe had power over all. Flint effigies have occurred of this animal, but most are recently made.
Torque Blade-Refers to a blade that twists or turns in one direction from base to point. This occurs during the manufacturing process when a piece of flint is fractured off a round spall at an angle.
Transitional Period-The time between two cultural periods.
Turkeytail-A narrow point with a diamond shaped stem in the Adena family.
Turtleback Scraper-An elliptical shaped uniface scraper in the form of a turtles back.
Typology-The study of point types.
Umbrella Tangs-Shoulder projections that droop forward.
Unfluted-A term used to describe points that usually occur fluted but are not.
Uniface-A point or tool finished on only one face (see *Double Uniface*).
Upper Mercer Chert-A black chert from south central Ohio used in point production.
War Points-Small triangular points that were used by the Indians against each other in war.
Willow Leaf-A long slender ovate point in the form of willow leaf.
Wing-Same as barb.
Woodland-The archaeological period that is after the Archaic Period but before the Mississippian.

INDEX OF POINT TYPES

REGIONAL CODES

Desert Southwest - SW	Great Basin-Westward - GB	Northern Central - NC
Eastern Central - EC	Gulf Coastal - GC	Northern High Plains - NP
Eastern Seaboard - ES	Northeastern - NE	Southern Central - SC

Abbey (6,000) GC
Abasolo (7,000) SC
Addison Micro-Drill (2,000) EC
Adena (3,000) EC, ES, GC, NC, NE
Adena Blade (3,000) EC, NC, NE, SC
Adena-Dickson (2,500) EC, NC, SC
Adena-Narrow Stem (3,000) EC, NC
Adena-Notched Base (3,000) EC, NC
Adena-Robbins (3,000) EC, ES, NC, NE, SC
Adena-Waubesa (2,500) EC, NC
Afton (5,000) EC, NC
Agate Basin (10,500) EC, NC, NE, NP, SC, SW
Agee (1,200) NC, SC
Ahumada (1,250) SW
Alachua (4,000) GC
Alamance (10,000) EC,ES
Alba (2,000) NC, SC
Alberta (9,500) EC, GB, NP, SC
Alder Complex (9,500) NP
Alkali (1,500) GB
Allen (10,000) NC, NP, SC, SW
Almagre (6,000) SC
Amos (10,000) NE
Andice (8,000) SC
Angostura (10,000) EC, NC, NE, NP, SC, SW
Appalachian (6,000) EC, ES
Apple Creek (1,700) NC
Archaic Knife (6,000) NP
Archaic Side Notched (6,000) NP
Archaic Triangle (6,000) NP
Arden (9,000) NE
Arkabutla (10,000) SC
Armstrong (2450) ES
Arredondo (5,000) GC
Ashtabula (4,000) EC,NE
Augustin (7,000) SW
Autauga (9,000) EC
Avonlea-Carmichael (1,300) NP
Avonlea Classic (1,300) NP
Avonlea-Gull Lake (1,800) NP
Avonlea-Timber Ridge (1,300) NP
Badin (1,000) ES
Bajada (3,000) SW
Baker (8,000) SC
Bakers Creek (4,000) EC
Bandy (8,000) SC
Barber (10,000) SC
Bare Island (4,500) NE
Barnes Cumberland (see Cumberland)
Basal Double Tang (3,500) SW
Bascom (4,500) GC
Base Tang Knife (4,000) GB, NP, SC
Bassett (800) SC
Bat Cave (9,000) SW
Beacon Island (4,000)EC
Bear (300) GB
Bear River (1,300) GB
Beaver Lake (11,000) EC, GC, NC, NE
Bell (7,000) SC
Benjamin (3,000) EC
Benton (6,000) EC
Benton Blade (6,000) EC
Benton Bottle Neck (6,000) EC
Benton Double Notch (6,000) EC
Benton Narrow Blade (6,000) EC
Besant (1,600) NP
Besant Knife (1,600) NP
Big Creek (3,500) SC
Big Sandy (10,000) EC, ES, SC
Big Sandy Broad Base (10,000) EC
Big Sandy Contracted Base (10,000) EC
Big Sandy E-Notched (10,000) EC
Big Sandy Leighton (10,000) EC
Big Slough (7,000) EC
Billings (300) NP
Bitterroot (7,000) GB, NP
Black Rock Concave (11,000) GB
Blevins (1,200) SC
Blunt (12,000) EC
Boggy Branch Type I (9,000) GC
Boggy Branch Type II (9,000) GC
Bolen Bevel (10,000) ES,GC
Bolen Plain (9,000)ES,GC
Bone Pin (1,500) GB
Bone Pin (12,000) GC
Bonham (1,200) SC
Bradford (2,000) GC
Bradley Spike (4,000) EC
Brazos (see Darl Stemmed)
Brewerton Corner Notched (6,000) EC, NE
Brewerton Eared Triangular (6,000) EC, ES, NE, SC
Brewerton Side Notched (6,000) EC, ES, NE, SC
Broad River (3,000) GC
Brodhead Side Notched (9,000) NE
Broward (2,000) GC
Browns Valley (10,000) EC, NC, NP, SC
Buck Creek (6,000) EC
Buck Gulley (1,500) GB
Buffalo Gap (5,500) NP
Buffalo Stemmed (6,000) ES
Buggs Island (5,500) EC
Bull Creek (950) SW
Bulverde (5,000) SC
Burroughs (8,000) NC
Burwell (5,000) NE
Buzzard Roost Creek (6,000) EC
Cache River (10,000) EC, NC, SC
Caddoan Blade (800) SC
Cahokia (1,000) NC
Calapooya (1,000) GB
Calf Creek (8,000) NC,SC
Camp Creek (3,000) EC
Canalino (800) GB
Candy Creek (3,000) EC
Caracara (600) SC
Caraway (1,000) ES
Carrizo (7,000) SC
Carrolton (5,000) SC
Carter (2,500) NC
Cascade (8,000) GB
Castroville (4,000) SC
Catahoula (800) SC
Catan (4,000) SC, SW
Cave Spring (9,000) EC
Charcos (3,000) SC
Charleston Pine Tree (10,000) NE
Chillesquaque (6,000)NE
Chindadn (11,300) GB
Chipola (10,000) GC
Chiricahua (5,000) SW
Chopper (14,000) GB, SC
Chumash (9,000) GB
Chumash Knife (9,000) GB
Citrus (3,500) GC
Clarksville (1,000) ES
Clay County (5,000) GC
Cliffton (1,200) SC
Clovis (14,000) EC, ES, GB, GC, NC, NE, NP, SC, SW
Clovis-Colby (12,700) NP
Clovis-St. Louis (14,000) NC
Clovis Unfluted (14,000) EC, ES
Coahuila (4,000) SC
Cobbs Triangular (8,000) EC, NC
Cody Complex (9,500) GB
Cody Complex Knife (9,500) GB
Cody Knife (9,500) NP
Colbert (1,000) SC
Cold Springs (5,000) GB
Coldwater (10,000) EC
Colonial (1,200) SW
Columbia (2,000) GC
Columbia Mule Ear (700) GB
Columbia Plateau (500) GB
Conejo (4,000) SC, SW
Conerly (7,500) EC, GC
Conodoquinet/Canfield (4,000) NE
Coosa (2,000) EC
Copena Auriculate (5,000) EC
Copena Classic (4,000) EC, NC
Copena Round Base (4,000) EC
Copena Triangular (4,000) EC
Corner Tang Knife (4,000) EC, NP, SC
Cossatot River (8,000)NC
Cotaco Creek (2,500) EC

Cotaco Blade (2,500) EC
Cotaco Preform (2,500) EC
Cotaco-Wright (2,500)EC
Cottonbridge (6,000) GC
Cottonwood Leaf (700) GB, NP, SW
Cottonwood Triangle (700) GB, NP, SW
Cougar Mountain (10,000) GB
Covington (4,000) SC
Cowhouse Slough (10,000) GC
Crawford Creek (8,000) EC
Crooked Creek (9,000) NE
Crescent (11,000) GB
Crowfield (11,000) NE
Culbreath (5,000) GC
Cumberland (12,000) EC, NC
Cumberland Barnes (11,000) NE
Cumberland Unfluted (12,000) NC
Cuney (400) SC
Cupp (1,500) EC, NC, SC
Cut Bank (300) NP
Cut Bank Jaw Notched (300) NP
Cypress Creek (5,000)EC
Cypress Creek (7,000)GC
Dagger (arrow) (1,200) GB
Dagger (large) (4,000)EC
Dallas (4,000) SC
Dalton-Breckenridge (9,500) NC, SC
Dalton Classic (9,500) EC, GB, NC, NE, NP, SC
Dalton-Colbert (9,500) EC
Dalton-Greenbrier (9,500) EC, SC
Dalton-Hemphill (9,500) EC, NC, SC
Dalton-Nuckolls (9,500) EC, NC, NE
Dalton-Sloan (9,500) NC
Damron (8,000) EC
Dardanelle (600) SC
Darl (2,500) SC
Darl Blade (2,500) SC
Darl Stemmed (8,000)SC
Datil (7,000) SW
Dawson (7,000) SC
Deadman's (1,600) SW
Debert (11,000) EC, NE
Decatur (9,000) EC, ES, NC, NE
Decatur Blade (9,000) EC
Delhi (3,500) SC
Desert-Delta (700) GB, SW
Desert-General (700) GB, NP, SW
Desert-Redding (700) GB, SW
Desert-Sierra (2,500) GB, NP, SW
Desert-Stemmed (2,500) NP
Dewart Stemmed (5,000) NE
Dismal Swamp (3,500)ES
Double Tip (see Elko)
Dovetail (9,000) ES, NC, NE, SC
Drill (14,000) EC, ES, GB, GC, NC, NE, NP, SC, SW
Dry Prong (1,000) SW
Drybrook Fishtail (3,500) NE
Duck River Sword (1,000) EC
Duncan (4,500) NP, SW
Duncan's Island (6,000) NE
Duran (3,000) SW
Durant's Bend (1,600)EC
Durst (3,000) EC
Duval (2,000) EC, GC
Early Eared (8,000) GB
Early Leaf (8,000) GB
Early Side Notched (see Archaic --)
Early Stemmed (9,000) SC
Early Stemmed Lanceolate (9,000) GB, SC
Early Triangular (9,000) SC
Eastgate (1,400) GB, NP
Eastgate Split Stem (1,400) GB, SW
Ebenezer (2,000) EC
Eccentric (see Exotic)
Ecusta (8,000) EC, ES
Eden (9,500) NC, NE, NP, SW
Edgefield Scraper (9,000) ES, GC
Edgewood (3,000) SC
Edwards (2,000) NC, SC
Erie Triangle (1,500) NE
Elam (4,000) SC
Elk River (8,000) EC
Elko (3,500) GB, NP
Elko Corner Notched (3,500) GB, SW
Elko Eared (3,500)GB, SW
Elko Split Stem (3,500) GB
Ellis (4,000) SC
Elora (6,000) EC, GC
Emigrant (900) NP
Ensor (4,000) SC
Ensor Split Base (4,000) SC
Epps (3,500) SC
Erb Basal Notched (2,000) NE
Escobas (6,500) SW
Eshback (5,500) NE
Etley (4,000) EC, NC
Eva (8,000) EC
Evans (4,000) EC, NC, SC
Exotic (5,000) EC, ES, GB, NC, SC
Fairland (3,000) EC, SC
Ferry (5,500) NC
Figueroa (3,000) SC, SW
Firstview (8,700) GB, NP, SC, SW
Fishspear (9,000) EC, ES
Flint Creek (3,500) EC
Flint River (4,000) GC
Flint River Spike (4,000) EC
Folsom (11,000) EC, NC, NP, SC, SW
Forest Notched (3,000) NE
Fort Ancient (800) EC
Fort Ancient Blade (800) EC
Fountain Creek (9,000) EC, ES
Fox Creek (2,500) ES, NE
Fox Valley (9,000) EC, ES, NC
Frazier (7,000) EC
Frederick (9,000) EC
Fresno (1,200) SC
Friday (4,000) SC
Friley (1,500) SC
Frio (5,000) SC
Frost Island (3,200) NE
Gahagan (4,000) SC
Garth Slough (9,000) EC, ES
Garver's Ferry (1,800) NE
Gary (4,000) NC, SC
Garza (900) SC, SW
Gatecliff (5,000) GB, SW
Genesee (5,000) NE
Gibson (2,000) EC, NC,SC
Gila Butte (1,500) SW
Gilchrist (10,000) GC
Godar (4,500) NC, SC
Goddard (1,000) NE
Godley (2,500) SC
Gold Hill (800) GB
Golondrina (9,000) EC, SC
Goshen (11,500) NP, SC
Gower (8,000) SC
Graham Cave (9,000) NC, SC
Grand (1,800) NC
Graver (14,000) EC, GB, NE, NP, SC
Green River (11,500) NP
Greenbrier (9,500)EC, NC
Greeneville (3,000) EC,ES
Ground Slate (6,000) NE
Ground Stone (300) GB
Guerrero (300) SC
Guilford Round Base (6,500) ES, NE
Guilford Stemmed (6,500) ES
Guilford Straight Base (6,500) ES
Guilford Yuma (7,500)ES
Guntersville (700) EC
Gunther (1,000) GB
Gunther Triangular (1,000) GB
Gypsum Cave (5,000)SW
Gypsy (2,500) ES
Hafted Knife (2,300) GB
Hale (Bascom) (4,000)SC
Halifax (6,000) EC, ES
Hamilton (1,600) EC
Hamilton (8,000) GC
Hamilton Stemmed (3,000) EC
Hanna (4,500) NP, SW
Hanna Northern (4,500) NP
Harahey (700) EC, GC, NC, NP, SC
Hardaway (9,500) EC, ES, NE
Hardaway Blade (9,500) ES
Hardway Dalton (9,500) EC, ES
Hardaway Palmer (9,500) ES
Hardee Beveled (8,000) GC
Hardin (9,000) EC, GC, NC, SC
Hare Bi-Face (3,000) SC
Harpeth River(9,000) EC
Harrell (900) NC, SC
Haskell (800) SC
Haskett (10,000) GB
Haw River (11,000)EC,NE
Hawkens (7,000) NP
Hayes (1,200) NC, SC
Heavy Duty (7,000) EC, ES, NC
Hell Gap (10,900) NC, NP, SC, SW
Hellgramite (3,000) NE
Hell's Canyon Basal Notched (1,200) GB
Hell's Canyon Corner Notched (1,200) GB
Helton (4,000) NC
Hemphill (7,000) NC, SC
Hernando (4,000) GC
Hi-Lo (10,000) EC, NC
Hickory Ridge (7,000) NC, SC
Hidden Valley (8,000) SC
High River (1,300) NP
Hillsboro (300) ES
Hillsborough (7,000) GC
Hinds (10,000) EC
Hog Back (1,300) NP
Hohokam (1,200) SW
Holcomb (11,000) NE
Holland (9,500) EC, NC, NP, SC
Holmes (4,000) ES
Homan (1,000) NC, SC

Hoover's Island (6,000) NE
Hopewell (2,500) EC, NC
Horse Fly (1,500) NP
Howard (700) SC
Hoxie (8,000) SC
Huffaker (1,000) NC, NP, SC
Humboldt (7,000) SW
Humboldt Constricted Base (7,000) GB
Humboldt Expanded Base (8,000) GB
Humboldt Triangular (7,000) GB
Irvine (1,400) NP
Ishi (100) GB
Itcheetucknee (700) GC
Jack's Reef Corner Notched (1,500) EC, ES, NE
Jack's Reef Pentagonal (1,500) EC, NE
Jackson (2,000) GC
Jeff (10,000) EC
Jetta (8,000) SC
Johnson (9,000) EC, SC
Jude (9,000) EC, ES
Kanawha (9,000) EC, ES, NE
Kavik (300) GB
Kay Blade (1,000) NC
Kays (5,000) EC
Keithville (see San Patrice)
Keota (800) EC, SC
Kerrville Knife (5,000)SC
Kessel (10,000) NE
Kinney (5,000) SC
Kirk Corner Notched (9,000) EC, ES, GC, NC,NE
Kirk Serrated (9,000) EC, ES, GC, NE
Kirk Serrated-Bifurcated (9,000) EC, ES
Kirk Side Notched (9,000) ES
Kirk Snapped Base (9,000) EC
Kiski Notched (2,000) NE
Kittatiny (6,000) NE
Klickitat (300) GB
Kline (9,000) NE
Knight Island (1,500) EC, SC
Koens Crispin (4,000) NE
Kramer (3,000) NC
La Jita (7,000) SC
Lackawaxen (6,000) NE
Lafayette (5,000) GC
Lake Erie (9,000) EC, NC, NE
Lake Mohave (13,200) GB, SW
Lamoka (5,500) NE
Lancet (14,000)EC, NP,SW
Lange (6,000) SC
Langtry (5,000) SC
Langtry-Arenosa (5,000) SC
Lecroy (9,000) EC, ES,NE
Ledbetter (6,000) EC
Lehigh (2,500) NC
Lehigh (4,000) NE
Leighton (8,000) EC
Leon (1,500) GC
Lerma Pointed (10,000) SC
Lerma Rounded (10,000) EC, NC, NP, SC, SW
Levanna (1,300) EC, NE
Levy (5,000) GC
Lewis (1,400) NP
Limestone (5,000) EC
Limeton Bifurcate (9,000) EC
Lind Coulee (see Parman)
Little Bear Creek (4,000) EC
Livermore (1,200) SC
Logan Creek (7,000) NP
Lookingbill (7,000) NP
Lost Lake (9,000) EC, ES, NC, NE
Lott (500) SC, SW
Lovell (8,500) NP
Lozenge (1,000) EC
Lundy (800) NC
Lycoming Co. (6,000) NE
MacCorkle (8,000) EC,NE
Madison (1,100) EC, ES, NC, NE
Mahaffey (10,500) SC
Maljamar (3,500) SW
Mallory (4,000) NP
Mansion Inn (4,000) NE
Maples (4,500) EC
Marcos (3,500) SC
Marianna (10,000) EC,GC
Marion (7,000) GC
Marshall (6,000) SC
Martindale (8,000) SC
Martis (3,000) SW
Matamoros (3,000) SC, SW
Matanzas(4,000) NC, SC
Maud (800) SC
McIntire (6,000) EC
McKean (4,500) NP, SW
Meadowood (4,000) EC, NE
Mehlville (4,000) NC
Merom (4,000) EC
Mescal Knife (700) SW
Meserve (9,500) EC, NC, NP, SC, SW
Mid-Back Tang (4,000) NP, SC
Midland (10,700) NP, SC, SW
Milnesand (11,000) NP, SC, SW
Mineral Springs (1,300) SC
Molalla (see Gunther)
Montell (5,000) SC
Montgomery (2,500) EC
Moran (1,200) SC
Morhiss (4,000) SC
Morill (3,000) SC
Morris (1,200) SC
Morrow Mountain (7,000) EC, ES, GC, NE
Morrow Mountain Round (7,000) EC
Morrow Mountain Straight (7,000) EC, ES
Morse Knife (3,000) EC, NC
Motley (4,500) EC, SC
Mount Albion (5,800) NP, SW
Mountain Fork (6,000) EC
Mouse Creek (1,500) EC
Mud Creek (4,000) EC
Mulberry Creek (5,000) EC
Mule Ear (see Columbia Mule Ear)
Mummy Cave (7,500)NP
Muncy Bifurcate (8,500) NE
Nanton (1,400) NP
Nawthis (1,100) SW
Nebo Hill (7,500) NC
Neff (3,500) SW
Neuberger (9,000) EC
Neville (7,000) NE
New Market (3,000) EC
Newmanstown (7,000) NE
Newnan (7,000) GC
Newton Falls (7,000), EC
Nodena (600) EC, NC,SC
Nolan (6,000) SC
Nolichucky (3,000) EC
Normanskill (4,000) NE
North (2,200) EC, NC
Northern Side Notched (9,000) GB
Northumberland Fluted Knife (12,000) NE
Notchaway (5,000) GC
Nottoway (300) GB
Nova (1,600) EC
Oauchita (3,000) GC, SC
Ocala (see Lafayette)
Occaneechee Large Triangle (600) ES
Ohio Double Notched (3,000) EC
Ohio Lanceolate (10,500)EC, NE
O'leno (2,000) GC
Oley (2,200) NE
Orient (4,000) EC, NE
Osceola (7,000) NC
Osceola Greenbrier I (9,500) GC
Osceola Greenbrier II (9,500) GC
Otter Creek (5,000)ES,NE
Ovates (3,000) NE
Owl Cave (9,500) GB
Oxbow (5,500) NP
Paint Rock Valley (10,000) EC
Paisano (2,500) SC
Paleo Knife (10,000) GB, SC
Palmer (9,000) EC, ES,NE
Palmillas (6,000) SC
Pandale (6,000) SC
Pandora (4,000) SC
Panoche (1,500) GB
Papago (400) SW
Parman (10,500) GB
Parowan (1,300) SW
Paskapoo (1,000) NP
Patrick (5,000) EC
Patrick Henry (9,500) ES
Patticus (3,500) SW
Patuxent (4,000) NE
Pedernalis (6,000) SC
Pee Dee (1,500) ES
Peisker Diamond (2,500) NC, SC
Pekisko (800) NP
Pelican (10,000) NC, SC
Pelican Lake (3,500) NP
Pelican Lake "Harder" Variety (3,500) NP
Pelican Lake "Keaster" Variety (see Samantha) NP
Pelona (6,000) SW
Penn's Creek (9,000) NE
Penn's Creek Bifurcate (9,000) NE
Perdiz (1,000) SC
Perforator (9,000) EC,SC
Perkiomen (4,000) NE
Pickwick (6,000) EC, GC
Piedmont Northern Variety (6,000) NE
Piedmont Southern Variety (see Hoover's Island)
Pike County (8,000) NC, SC
Pine Tree (8,000) EC
Pine Tree Charleston Variety (8,000) NE
Pine Tree Corner-Notched (8,000) EC, NC
Pinellas (800) GC
Piney Island (6,000) NE
Pinto Basin (4,000)GB,NP
Piscataway (2,500) NE
Pismo (3,500) GB
Plains Knife (6,000) NP
Plains Side Notched (1,000) NP
Plains Triangular (1,000) NP
Plainview (10,000) EC, NC, NP, SC
Plateau Pentagonal

(700) GB
Pogo (2,000) SC
Pontchartrain Type I (4,000) EC, SC
Pontchartrain Type II (3,400) EC
Poplar Island (6,000) NE
Port Maitland (2,500) NE
Potts (3,000) ES
Prairie Side Notched (1,300) NP
Pryor Stemmed (8,000) GB
Putnam (5,000) GC
Quad (10,000) EC, ES, NC
Quillomene Bar (3,000) GB
Rabbit Island (4,000) GB
Raccoon Notched (1,500) NE
Raddatz (5,000) NC, SC
Ramey Knife (5,000) EC, NC
Randolph (2,000) ES, NE
Rankin (4,000) EC
Red Horn (700) SW
Red Ochre (3,000) EC,NC
Red River Knife (9,500) SC
Redstone (13,000) EC, ES, GC, NE
Reed (1,500) SC
Refugio (5,000) SC
Rheems Creek (4,000)EC
Rice Contracted Stem (see Hidden Valley)
Rice Lobbed (9,000) EC, NC, SC
Rice Shallow Side-Notched (9,000) SC
Rio Grande (7,500) NP, SC, SW
Robinson (4,000) NC
Rochester (8,000) NC
Rockwall (1,400) SC
Rodgers Side Hollowed (10,000) SC
Rogue River (see Gunther)
Rose Springs (1,600) GB ,SW
Rose Springs Corner Notched (1,600) NP, SW
Rose Springs Side Notched (1,600) SW
Ross (2,500) EC, NC
Ross County (see Clovis)
Rowan (9,500) ES
Russell Cave (9,000) EC
St. Albans (9,000) EC, ES, NE
St. Charles (9,500) EC, NC
Sabinal (1,000) SC
Sabine (4,000) SC
Sacaton (1,100) SW
Safety Harbor (800) GC
Salado (1,500) SW
Sallisaw (800) SC
Samantha Arrow (1,500) NP
Samantha Dart (2,200) NP
San Gabriel (2,000) SC
San Jose (6,000) SW
San Patrice-Hope (10,000) SC
San Patrice-Keithville (10,000) SC
San Patrice-St. Johns Var. (10,000) SC
San Pedro (2,500) SW
San Saba (3,000) SC
Sand Mountain (1,500) EC
Sandhill Stemmed (2,200) NE
Sandia (14,000) SW
Santa Cruz (1,400) SW
Santa Fe (9,500) GC
Sarasota (3,000) GC
Sattler (1,400) NP
Savage Cave (7,000) EC, SC
Savannah River (5,000) EC, ES, GC, NE
Scallorn (1,300) SC
Schild Spike (1,500) EC
Schuykill (4,000) NE
Scottsbluff I (9,500) NC, NE, NP, SC,
Scottsbluff II (9,500) NC, NE, NP, SC, SW
Scraper (14,000) EC, GB, NE, NP, SC
Searcy (7,000) EC, SC
Sedalia (5,000) EC, NC
Seminole (5,000) GC
Sequoyah (1,000) NC, SC
Shoals Creek (4,000) EC
Shumla (3,000) SC
Side Knife (2,300) NP
Sierra Stemmed (2,800) SW
Silver Lake (11,000) GB, SW
Simonsen (8,500) NP
Simpson (12,000) ES, GC
Simpson-Mustache (12,000) GC
Sinner (3,000) SC
Six Mile Creek (7,500)GC
Smith (7,000) EC, NC
Smithsonia (4,000) EC
Snake Creek (4,000) EC
Snake River (2,000) GB
Snaketown (1,200) SW
Snook Kill (4,000) NE
Snyders (2,500) EC, NC
Sonota (1,000) NP
Soto (1,000) SW
South Prong Creek (5,000) GC
Southhampton (8,000) ES
Spedis (10,000) GB
Square Knife (10,000) EC, GB, NC, NP, SC
Squaw Mountain (5,000) SW
Stanfield (10,000) EC,GC
Stanly (8,000) EC, ES, NE
Stanly Narrow Stem (8,000) ES
Starr (1,000) SC
Steiner (1,000) SC
Steuben (2,000) NC, SC
Steubenville (9,000) EC
Stilwell (9,000) EC, NC
Sting Ray Barb (2,500) GC
Stockton (400) GB
Stone Square Stem (6,000) NC
Stott (1,300) NP
Strike-a-Lite Type I (9,000) NE
Strike-a-Lite TYpe II (3,000) NE
Sublet Ferry (4,000) EC
Sub-Triangular (11,300) GB
Sumter (7,000) GC
Susquehanna Bifurcated (9,000) NE
Susquehanna Broad (3,500) NE
Susquehannock Triangle (1,500) NE
Suwannee (12,000) GC
Swan Lake (3,500) EC
Swatara-Long (5,000) NE
Swift Current (1,300) NP
Table Rock (4,000) EC, NC, SC
Talahassee (9,500) GC
Talco (800) SC
Tampa (800) GC
Taunton River Bifurcate (9,000) NE
Taylor (9,000) ES
Taylor Stemmed (3,000) GC
Tear Drop (2,000) EC
Temporal (1,000) SW
Tennessee River (9,000) EC
Tennessee Sword, (see Duck River Sword)
Texcoco (6,000) SW
Thebes (10,000)EC,ES,NC
Thonotosassa (8,000)GC
Tock's Island (1,700) NE
Tompkins (1,200) NP
Tortugas (6,000) EC, SC
Toyah (600) SC, SW
Trade Points (400) EC, ES, GB, NE, NP, SC,SW
Travis (5,500) SC
Trinity (4,000) SC
Triple T (5,500) GB, SW
Truxton (1,500) SW
Turkeytail-Fulton (4,000) EC, NC
Turkeytail-Harrison (4,000) EC, NC, SC
Turkeytail-Hebron (4,000) EC
Uinta (1,200) GB
Union Side Notched (10,000) GC
Uvalde (6,000) SC
Uwharrie (1,600) ES
Val Verde (5,000) SC, SW
Valina (2,500) EC
Ventana-Amorgosa (7,000) SW
Vernon (2,800) NE
Vestal Notched (4,500) NE
Victoria (8,000) SC
Virginsville (5,000) NE
Vosburg (5,000) NE
Wacissa (9,000) GC
Wade (4,500) EC
Wadlow (4,000) NC
Wahmuza (9,000) GB
Waller Knife (9,000) ES, GC
Wallula (1,000) GB
Wapanucket (6,000) NE
Waratan (3,000) ES, NE
Warrick (9,000) EC, NC
Wasco Knife (see Plateau Pentagonal)
Washington (3,000) EC
Washita (800) NC,NP, SC
Washita Northern (800) NP
Wateree (3,000) ES
Web Blade (1,500) NE
Weeden Island (2,500) GC
Wells (8,000) SC
Wendover (7,000) GB
Westo (7,500) GC
Wheeler Excurvate (10,000) EC, GC
Wheeler Expanded Base (10,000) EC, GC
Wheeler Recurvate (10,000) EC
Wheeler Triangular (10,000) EC
White River (6,000) SC
White Springs (8,000)EC
Will's Cove (3,000) ES
Williams (6,000) SC
Windust (10,200) GB
Windust Knife (10,200) GB
Wintu (1,000) GB
Yadkin (2,500) EC, ES,
Yadkin Eared (2,500) ES
Yarbrough (2,500) SC
Yavapai (3,300) SW
Yonkee (4,500) NP
Young (1,000) SC
Ytias (8,500) GB
Zella (4,000) SC
Zephyr (9,000) SC
Zorra (6,000) SC

Alabama Projectile Point Types, by A. B. Hooper, Ill. Albertville, AL, 1964.
Album of Prehistoric Man, by Tom McGowen, illustrated by Rod Ruth, Rand McNally and Co., Chicago-NewYork-San Francisco, 1975.
American Indlan Almanac, by John Upton Terrell, Thomas Y. Crowell Co., New York, N.Y., 1974.
American Indian Point Types of North Florida, South Alabama and South Georgia, by Son Anderson, 1987.
American Indian Ways of Life, by Thorne Deuel, Illinois State Museum, Springfield, IL, 1968.
Americans Before Columbus, by Elizabeth Chesley Baity. The Viking Press, New York, N.Y., 1951.
America's Beginnings-the Wild Shores, by Loften Snell, National Geographic Society, Washington, D.C., 1974.
America's Fascinating Indian Heritage, The Readers Digest Association, Inc., Pleasantville, N.Y., 1978.
Americans in Search of their Prehistoric Past, by Stuart Struever and Felicia Antonelli, Holter Anchor Press, Doubleday, New York, 1979.
The Arkansas Archeologist, Bulletin, Vol. 19, Univ. of Arkansas, Fayetteville, AR., 1978.
The Ancient Civilizations of Peru, by J. Alden Mason, Penguin Books, Ltd., Middlesex, England, 1968.
The Ancient Kingdoms of the Nile, by Walter A. Fairservis, Jr., N.A.L. Mentor Books, The North American Library, Thomas Y. Crowell Co., New York, N.Y., 1962.
Ancient Native Americans, by Jesse D. Jennings, editor, W.H. Freeman & Co., San Francisco, CA, 1978.
Antiquities of Tennessee, by Gates P. Thurston, The Robert Clarke Co., Cincinnati, OH, 1964.
An Archaeological Survey and Documentary Histroy of the Shattuck Farm, Andover, Mass., (Catherine G. Shattuck Memorial Trust), Mass. Historical Commission, March, 1981.
Archaeology, by Dr. Francis Celoria, Bantom Books, New York, N.Y., 1974.
Archaeology-Middle America (A science program) - U.S.A., Nelson Doubleday, Inc., 1971.
The Archaeology of Essex County, by Gwenn Wells, Essex Life, summer, 1983.
Arrowheads and Projectile Points, by Lar Hothem, Collector Books, Paducah, KY, 1983.
Arrowhead Collectors Handbook, produced by John L. Sydman, Charles Dodds (author), Danville, Iowa, 1963.
Artifacts of North America (Indian and Eskimo), by Charles Miles, Bonanza Books, Crown Publ., Inc., New York, N.Y., 1968.
Beginners Guide to Archaeology, by Louis A. Brennan, Dell Publishing Co., Inc., New York, N.Y., 1973.
The Bog People (Iron-Age Man Preserved), by P.V. Glob, Faber and Faber, London, 1965.
The Book of Indians, by Holling C. Holling, Platt and Munk Co., Inc., New York, N.Y., 1935.
The Chattanooga News-Free Press, Thursday, Nov. 14, 1989, page B5, U.P.I. dateline, Los Angeles, CA article by James Ryan.
Cherokee Indian Removal from the Lower Hiwassee Valley, by Robert C. White, A Resource intern Report, 1973.
The Cherokees, Past, and Present, by J. Ed Sharpe, Cherokee Publications, Cherokee, NC., 1970.
The Columbia Encyclopedia Edition, Clarke F. Ansley, Columbia University Press, New York, N.Y., 1938.
The Corner-Tang Flint Artifacts of Texas, University of Texas, Bulletin No. 3618, Anthropological Papers, Vol.1., No. 3618, 1936.
Cro-Magnon Man, Emergence of Man Series, by Tom Prideaux, Time-Life Books, New York, N.Y., 1973.
The Crystal Skull, by Richard Garvin, Pocket Books-Simon & Schuster, Inc., New York, N.Y. 1974.
Cypress Creek Villages, by William S. Webb and G. Haag, University of Kentucky, Lexington, KY., 1940.
Death on the Prairie, by Paul I. Wellman, Pyramid Books, Pyramid Publications, Doubleday and Co., Inc. New York, 1947.
Digging into History, by Paul S. Martin, Chicago National History Museum, Chicago, IL., 1963.
Duck River Cache, by Charles K. Peacock, published by T. B. Graham, Chattanooga, TN., 1954.
Early Man, by F. Clark Howell, Time-Life Books, New York, N.Y., 1965.
Early Man East of the Mississippi, by Olaf H. Prufer, Cleveland Museum of Natural History, Cleveland, Ohio, 1960.
Etowah Papers, by Warren K. Moorehead, Phillips Academy, Yale University Press, New Haven, CT. 1932.
Eva-An Archaic Site, by T.M.N. Lewis and Madelin Kneberg Lewis, University of Tennessee Press, Knoxville, TN., 1961.
Field Guide to Point Types of the State of Florida, by Son Anderson and Doug Puckett, 1984.
Field Guide to Point Types (The Tennessee River Basin), by Doug Puckett, Custom Productions (printer), Savannah, TN., 1987.
A Field Guide to Southeastern Point Types, by James W. Cambron, Decatur, AL.
A Field Guide to Stone Artifacts of Texas Indians, by Sue Turner and Thomas R. Hester, 1985, Texas Monthly Press.
Field Identification of Stone Artifacts of the Carolinas, by Russell Peithman and Otto Haas, The Identifacs Co., 1978.
The First American (Emergence of Man), by Robert Claiborne, Time-Life Books, New York, N.Y., 1973.
Flint Blades and Projectile Points of the North American Indian, by Lawrence N. Tully, Collectoir Books, Paducah, KY, 1986.
Flint Type Bulletin, by Lynn Mungen, curator, Potawatomi Museum, Angola, IN., 1958.
Flint Types of the Continental United States, by D.C. Waldorf and Valerie Waldorf, 1976.
Fluted Points in Lycoming County, Penn., by Gary L. Fogelman and Richard P. Johnston, Fogelman Publ. Co.,

Turbotville, Pennsylvania.
The Formative Cultures of the Carolina Piedmont, by Joffre Lanning Coe, New Series-Vol. 54, part 5, The American Philosophical Society, 1964.
Fossil Man, by Michael H. Day, Bantam Books, Grosset & Dunlap, Inc., New York, N.Y, 1971.
Frontiers in the Soil, (Archaeology of Georgia), by Roy S. Dickens and James L. McKinley, Frontiers Publ. Co., Atlanta, GA, 1979.
Geological Survey of Alabama, Walter B. Jones, Geologist, University of Alabama, 1948.
The Great Histories-The Conquest of Mexico, The Conquest of Peru, Prescott, edited by Roger Howell, Washington Square Press, Inc., New York, N.Y., 1966.
Guide to the Identification of Certain American Indian Projectile Points, by Robert E. Bell, Oklahoma Anthropological Society, Norman, OK., 1958, 1960, and 1968.
A Guide to the Identification Of Florida Projectile Points, by Ripley P. Bullen, Kendall Books, 1975.
A Guide to the Identification of Virginia Projectile Points, by Wm. Jack Hranicky and Floyd Painter, Special Publ. No. 17, Archaeological Society of Virginia, 1989.
Handbook of Alabama Archaeology, by Cambron and Hulse, edited by David L. DeJarnette, Universtiy of Alabama, 1986.
A Handbook of Indian Artifacts from Southern New England, drawings by William S. Fowler, Mass. Archaeological Society.
A History of American Archaeology, by Gorgen R. Willey and J.A. Sabloff, Thomas and Hudson, Great Britain, 1974.
Hiwassee Island, by T.M.N. Lewis and Madeline Kneberg, Universtiy of Tenn. Press, Knoxville, TN. 1946.
How to Find and Identify Arrowheads and Other Indian Artifacts (Southeastern United States), by Frank Kenan Barnard, 1983.
A Hypothetical Classification of some of The Flaked Stone Projectiles, Tools and Ceremonials From the Southeastern United States, by Winston H. Baker, Williams Printing Inc., 1225 Furnace Brook Parkway, Quincy, MA, 1995.
In Search of the Maya, by Robert L. Brunhouse, Ballentine Books-Random House, Inc., New York, N.Y., 1974.
The Incredible Incas, by Loren McIntyre, National Geographic Society, Washington, D.C., 1980.
Indian Artifacts, by Virgil U. Russell & Mrs. Russell, Johnson Publ. Co., Boulder, CO., 1962.
Indian Relics and Their Story, by Hugh C. Rogers, Yoes Printing and Lithographing Co., Fort Smith, AR., 1966.
Indian Relics and Their Values, by Allen Brown, Lightner Publishing Co., Chicago, IL., 1942.
Indian Relics Price Guide, by Lynn Munger, published by Potawatomi Museum, Angola, IN., 1961.
Indiana Archaeological Society Yearbook, The Indiana Archaeological Society, 1975-1986.
Indlanology, by John Baldwin, Messenger Pnnting Co., St. Louis, MO. 1974.
Indians and Artists In the Southeast, by Bert W. Bierer, published by the author, State Printing Co., Columbia, SC, 1979.
Indians of the Plains, by Harry L. Shapino, McGraw-Hill Book Co., Inc., New York, NY, 1963.
An Introduction to American Archaeology (Middle & North America), by Gordon R. Willey, Prentice-Hall, Inc. Englewood Cliffs, NJ, 1966.
Ishl-In Two Worlds (The Last Wild Indian in North America), by Theodora Kroeber, Univ. of Calif. Press, Berkely & Los Angeles 1965.
Journal of Alabama Archaeology, David L. DeJarnette, editor, University of Alabama, 1967.
Man's Rise to Clvilizatlon, by Peter Faro, Avon Books, The Hearst Corp., New York, N.Y., 1966.
Massachusetts Archaeological Society, Bulletin of the, by William S. Fowler, Vol. 25, No. 1, Bronson Museum, Attleboro, Mass, Oct., 1963.
The Mighty Aztecs, by Gene S. Stuart, National Geographic Society, Washington, D.C., 1981.
The Mississippian Culture, bv Robert Overstreet & Ross Bentley, Preston Pnntinq, Cleveland, TN, 1967.
The Mlssouri Archaeologist (The First Ten Years, 1935-1944), The Missouri Archaeological Society, Inc., Columbia, MO, 1975.
The Missouri Archaeologist Edition, Carl H. Chapman, University of Missouri, Columbia MO.
The Mound Budders, by Henry Clyde Shetrone, D. Appleton-Century Co., New York, N.Y., 1941.
Mysteries of the Past, by Lionel Casson, Robert Claibome, Brian Fagan and Walter Karp, American Heritage Publ., Co., Inc., New York, N.Y., 1977.
The Mysterious Maya, by George E. and Gene S. Stuart, National Geographic Society, Washington, D.C., 1983.
The Mystery of Sandia Cave, by Douglas Preston, The New Yorker, June 12, 1995.
National Geographic, National Geographic Society, Numerous issues, Washington, D.C.
The Neanderthals, The Emergence of Man Series, by George Constable, Time-Life Books, New York, N.Y., 1973.
New World Beginnings (Indian Cultures in the Americas), by Olivia Viahos, Fawcett Publ., Inc., Greenwich, CT, 1970.
North American Indian Artifacts, by Lar Hothem, Books Americana, Florence, Al, 1980.
North American Indian Arts, by Andrew Hunter Whiteford, Golden Press-Western Publ. Co. Inc., New York, N.Y., 1970.
North American Indlans-Before the Coming of the Europeans, by Phillip Kopper (The Smithsonian Book), Smithsonian Books, Washington, D.C.
Notes In Anthropology, by David L. Dejarnette & Asael T. Hansen, The Florida State University, Tallahassee, Fl, 1960.
Paleo Points, Illustrated Chronology of Projectile Points, by G. Bradford, published by the author, Ontario

Canada,1975.
The Papago Indians of Arizona, by Ruth Underhill, Ph. D., U.S. Dept. of the Interior, Bureau of Indian Affairs, Washington, D.C.
The Plants, (Life Nature Library), by Frits W. Went, Tme-Life Books, New York, N.Y, 1971.
Pocket Guide to Indian Points, Books Americana, Inc., Florence AL, 1978.
Points and Blades of the Coastal Plain, by John Powell, American Systems of the Carolinas, Inc., 1990.
Prehistoric Art, R.E. Grimm, editor, Greater St. Louis Archaeological Society, Wellington Print., St. Louis, MO, 1953.
Prehistoric Artifacts of North America, John F. Berner, editor, The Genuine Indian Relic Society, Inc., Rochester, IN, 1964.
Prehistoric Implements, by Warren K. Moorehead, Publisher, Charley G. Drake, Union City GA, 1968.
Prehistoric Implements, by Warren K. Moorehead, Publisher, Charley G. Drake, American Indian Books, Union City, GA, Amo Press, Inc., New York, NY, 1978.
Projectile Point Types In Virginia and Neighboring Areas, by Wm. Jack Hranicky and Floyd Painter, Special Publ. No. 16, Archaeological Society of Virginia, 1988.
Projectile Point Types of the American Indian, by Robert K. Moore published by Robert K. Moore, Athens AL.
A Projectile Point Typology for Pennsylvania and the Northeast, by Gary L. Fogelman, Fogelman Publ., Co., Turbotville, Pennsvivania, 1988.
Projectile Points of the Trl-Rlvers Basin, (Apolachicola, Flint and Chattahoochee), by John D. Sowell & Udo Volker Nowak, Generic Press, Dothan, Alabama, 1990.
The Redskin, Genuine Indian Relic Society, Inc., published by the Society, East St. Louis, IL, 1964.
Relics of Early Man Price Guide, by Philip D. Brewer, Athens, AL, 1988.
Secrlst's Slmpilfled Identlficatlon Guide (Stone Relics of the American Indian), by Clarence W. Secrist, pub lished by the author, Muscatine, Iowa.
Selected Preforms, Points and Knives of the North American Indian, by Gregory Perino, Vol. No. 1, Idabel, OK, 1985.
Selected Preforms, Points and Knives of the North American Indian, by Gregory Perino, Vol. No. 2, Idabel, OK, 1991.
Shoop Pennsylvanla's Famous Paleo Site, Fogelman Publ., Co., Turbotville, Pennsylvania.
Solving The Riddles of Wetherill Mesa, by Douglas Osborne, Ph. D., National Geographic, Feb. 1964, Washington, D.C.
Southern Indian Studies, by The Archaelogoical Society of N.C., University of North Carolina, Chapel Hill, NC, 1949.
Stone Artifacts of the Northwestern Plains, by Louis C. Steege, Northwestern Plains Publ., Co., Colorado Springs, CO.
Stone Implements of the Potomac Chesapeake Province, by J.W. Powell, 15th Annual Report, Bureau of Ethnology, Washington, DC, 1893-1894.
Story In Stone (Flint Types of Central & Southern U.S.), by Valene and D.C. Waldorf, Mound builder Books, Branson, MO, 1987.
Sun Circles and Human Hands, Emma Lila Fundaburk & Mary Douglas Foreman, editors. Published by the editors, Paragon Press, Montgomery, AL, 1957.
Ten Years of the Tennessee Archaeologist, Selected Subjects, J.B. Graham, Publisher, Chattanooga, TN.
Tennessee Anthropologist, Vol. XIV, No. 2, Fall, 1989, U.T., Knoxville, 1989.
Tennessee Archaeologist, T. M.N. Lewis and Madeline Kneburg, University of Tennessee, Knoxville, TN.
Tennessee Anthropologist, Vol. 14, No. 2, 1989, The Quad Site Revisted, by Charles Faulkner
A Topology and Nomenclature of New York Projectile Points, by William A. Ritchie, Bulletin No. 384, New York State Museum, NY, 1971.
U.S. News and World Report (Weekly News Magazine) article by William F. Amman and Joannie M. Schrof- "Last Empires of the Americas," April 2, 1990 issue, Washington, DC.
The Vail Site (A Paleo Indian Encampment in Maine), by Dr. Richard Michael Gramly, Bulletin of the Buffalo Society of Natural Science, Vol. No. 30, Buffalo, NY, 1982.
Walk with History, Joan L. Franks, editor, Chattanooga Area Historical Assn., Chattanooga, TN, 1976.
Who's Who In Indian Relics, by H.C. Wachtel, publisher, Charley G. Drake, American Indian Books, Union City, GA, 1980.
The World Atlas of Archaeology (The English Edition of "Le Grand Atlas de Parcheologie"), executive editor- James Hughes, U.S. & Canada, G.K. Hall & Co., Boston, Mass, 1985.
World Book Encyclopedia, Field Enterprises, Inc., W.F. Quarrie and Company, Chicago, Ill., 1953.
The World of the American Indian (A volume in the Story of Man Library), National Geographic Society, Jules B. Billard-Editor, Washington, DC, 1989.